Thinking Children and Education

Matthew Lipman
Montclair State College

KENDALL/HUNT PUBLISHING COMPANY
2460 Kerper Boulevard P.O. Box 539 Dubuque, Iowa 52004-0539

Drawings accompanying chapter headings are by the Editor.

Table of Contents

Chapter Eight: Encouraging Thinking For Oneself Through Socratic Teaching 433

Chapter Nine: The Classroom Practice of the Philosophy Teacher 477

Chapter Ten: Dialogical Inquiry 519

Preface

The first issue of *Thinking: The Journal of Philosophy for Children* appeared in January, 1979, and four issues a year have been published, more or less regularly, ever since. From the start, the intent of the periodical has been to concentrate on the domain in which the world of education, the world of philosophy and the world of the child intersect with one another. Nothing seemed to be a better appellation for that domain than *thinking*.

Thinking has consistently been interested in theory *and* in practice, in scholarly treatises that throw light on the aims and methods of cognitive education and on reports from schools experimenting with grade-school philosophy. It has been consistently positive, preferring to investigate educational interventions that work instead of those that are unsuccessful. And it has consistently championed the child's *capacity* for inquiry as being neither greater nor lesser than that of older individuals.

In brief, *Thinking* has been content to explore the ways in which the child's education, upbringing and growth contribute to his or her developing reasonableness. Its complete, longitudinal table of contents therefore has come to comprise a longish look at children's thinking: its causes and conditions, its prospects and consequences, and its improvement. Out of this table of contents, a relatively small number of articles has been selected and organized for the present anthology.

Some of the articles were written several centuries ago, but have been included in order to remind us that the cognitive education of children is not of recent invention, and that the pioneers in that venture had many fresh and original things to say about it. Others have been included to provide a fuller and richer background in terms of which elementary school philosophy might be better seen and understood for what it is.

The anthology as a whole aims to be of particular assistance to the preparation of teachers. Many prospective teachers are intensely curious as to the academic sources of cognitive education but have in mind something other than a technical review of research studies in cognitive science. They suspect, rather, that teaching for thinking must be taught under the auspices of a humanistic discipline. Reading and writing are taught under the general patronage of literature, in order to encase these vital skills in a framework of humanistic values. The same is true with thinking. It cannot be approached in some allegedly value-free fashion: it needs to be encased in a methodology which can come only from a humanities discipline such as philosophy.

Some people think that because philosophy can attach itself to any subject-matter, it must itself be devoid of content. But this is hardly the case. Philosophy is a mode of inquiry just as authentic and just as valuable, in its own way, as scientific or artistic inquiry. It has at its disposal a vast repertoire of concepts (like justice and truth and friendship) to deal with; it has its own methodology and its own preference in pedagogy. When properly redesigned and properly taught, it can be provocative, stirring and liberating. Philosophy recognizes itself as successfully taught not when students have learned to parrot what the well-known philosophers have thought, but when the students have learned to think philosophically for themselves.

It is to be hoped that the availability of *Thinking Children and Education* will encourage education and philosophy instructors to confirm to their students the existence of the domain to which this book addresses itself. Whether this emerging aspect of philosophy acquires a name or not is of less moment than that this line of inquiry continue to be pursued. It is to be hoped that *Thinking Children and Education* will make it increasingly possible to do so.

My thanks go to Joanne Matkowski, Lisa Simpson and James Heinegg for their diligent assistance in tying together so many of the loose ends that are typical of an anthology of this sort. I am very grateful to them for their contribution.

I wish to thank the following authors who have kindly given permission to reprint their articles: Leon Letwin, Thomas V. Curley, Bertram Bandman, Marie-Louise Friquegnon, Mary Vetterling-Braggin, Rosalind Ekman Ladd, James F. Herndon, Martin Benjamin, Jonathan E. Adler, Gareth B. Matthews, William Ruddick, John J. McDermott, Judith Langer, Valerie Polakow, Allan Collins, John Seely Brown, Susan E. Newman, Ann Gazzard, Tony W. Johnson, Eva Brann, Martha Nussbaum, Kieran Egan, Ann Margaret Sharp, Robert J. Mulvaney, David Kennedy, Stan Anih, Laurance J. Splitter, Ekkehard Martens, William Hamrick, Barry Curtis, John Wilson, Rosalyn Lessing (née Sherman), Michael J. Whalley, Judy A. Kyle, Ruth E. Silver, Elias Baumgarten, Dale Cannon, Mark Weinstein, Christina Slade, Jen Glaser, Maurice A. Finocchiaro, Clive Lindop, Ann Diller, Michael S. Pritchard, Jane Roland Martin, and Gerry Dawson McClendon.

I also want to acknowledge with thanks the permissions received from the following publishers and individuals to reprint from books or periodicals of which they hold the copyright:

To *Science*, for George Herbert Mead, "The psychology of social consciousness implied in instruction," *Science*, XXXI (19100, pp. 688-693. (c) AAAS.

To The American Psychological Associations for J. Robert Oppenheimer, "Analogical reasoning in the scientific community," *American Psychologist*, Vol. 11, March, 1956, pp. 127-135

To *Rice University Studies*, for Gilbert Ryle, "Thinking and self-teaching," *Rice University Studies*, Vol. 58, No. 3, Summer, 1972.

To Louisiana State University Press for "Community as Inquiry," from Glenn Tinder, *Community: Reflections on a Tragic Ideal*, pp. 24-33. Copyright 1980 by Louisiana State University Press.

To Department of Philosophy, Birkbeck College, for Ruth Saw, "Conversation and Communication"

To Pergamon Press, Ltd., for Wolfe Mays, "Thinking skills programs," in *New Ideas in Psychology*, Vol. 3, No. 2. 1985, pp. 149-163, Oxford, England.

To The University of Chicago Press, for James M. Redfield, "Platonic Education," in Wayne Booth, (Ed.) *The Knowledge Most Worth Having*.

To Teachers College Press, for David Bohm, "On insight and its significance for science, education and values," in Douglas Sloan (Ed.). *Education and Values*, pp. 7-21. (New York: Teachers College Press, (c) 1980 by Teachers College, Columbia University. All rights reserved.)

To Ms. Mary Jarrell, for Randall Jarrell, "An unread book," introduction to Christina Stead, *The Man Who Loved Children* (New York: Holt, Rinehart, and Winston, 1940)

To The Estate of W. H. Auden for permission to reprint Auden's "Writing" from *The English Auden*.

To University Press of Kansas, for permission to reprint from *Splitting the Difference: Compromise and Integrity in Ethics and Politics*, by Martin Benjamin, (c) 1990 by the University Press of Kansas.

To The Library of America, for allowing us to reprint a selection from *William James: Writings 1902-1910*, published by The Library of America, 1987.

To *The Educational Forum*, Kappa Delta Pi. an International Honor Society in Education and the author, for permission to reprint Herbert W. Schneider's "Schooling, Learning and Education," *The Educational Forum*, XXIX, Nov. 1964.

To K. Thienemanns Verlag, Stuttgart-Wien, for Michael Ende's "Acceptance Speech for 1982 Deutschen Jugendbuchpreis," (c) K. Thienemanns Verlag, Stuttgart-Wien, Germany

To Timothy Fuller, Dean of Colorado College and Yale University Press for permission to reprint Michael Oakeshott's "A Place of Learning," from his *The Voice of Liberal Learning: Michael Oakeshott on Education*, edited by Timothy Fuller (Yale University Press, 1989, paperback edition, 1990).

To University Press of Kansas, for permission to reprint from *On Becoming Responsible* by Michael S. Pritchard, copyright 1991 by the University Press of Kansas. Used by permission of the publisher.

To Catherine McCall, for permission to reprint her copyright article, "Young Children Generate Philosophical Ideas."

To Indiana University Press, for permission to reprint pp. 113-119 from *Søren Kierkegaard's Journals and Papers*, Vol, 1.

To Zeborah Schachtel, for permission to reprint a selection from Ernest G. Schachtel's *Metamorphosis*.

To Evelyn Shirk Buchler, for permission to reprint Justus Buchler's article, "What is a Discussion?"

To Paul Wilkinson, for permission to reprint an excerpt from Leslie Paul's *The Living Hedge.*

To The Leonard Foundation for permission to reprint from *The Socratic Method* by Leonard Nelson.

To the American Catholic Philosophical Association for permission to reprint "The Person and the Little Prince of Exupéry," by Florence M. Hetzler, from Volume LX (1986) of The Proceedings of the American Catholic Philosophical Association.

We wish to thank Dr. Miriam Minkowitz for preparing the transcript for the Philosophy session conducted by Gerry Dawson McClendon.

We acknowledge that the book from which the selection "The Child," by Floyd Dell, "Were you Ever a Child," was originally printed by Alfred A. Knopf, 1919, NY.

To the *Oxford Review of Education* for permission to reprint "Against Skills" by W.A. Hart.

The selection from J. Korczak's book: "The Child's Right to be Respected" is reprinted by kind permission of Ghetto Fighters' House.

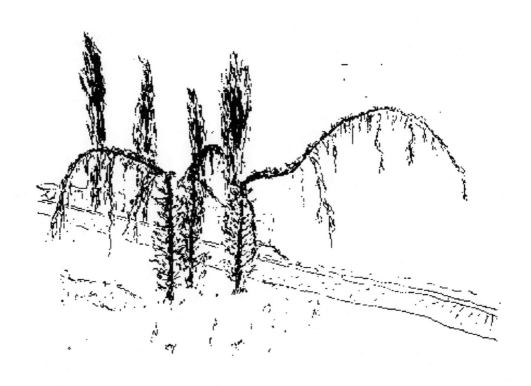

Chapter One
Children's Educational Rights and Responsibilities

Chapter One

Children's Educational Rights and Responsibilities

Many a parent, like many an educator, asked what they think schools should do for students, have responded along these lines: "Students should complete elementary and secondary school having learned what is essential and having learned how to learn whatever else they need to know; having become critical and creative thinkers, readers and writers; having learned how to reflect on their own experience and on the experience of others; having become proficient in inquiry, both with others and individually; having become unafraid to analyze, question and speculate; having become persons who persist in seeking to discover and eliminate their own prejudices and to correct their own errors; having become adept at applying what they know to practical problems; having become people with a sense of proportion and a feeling for what is important, people one can reason with; in a word, people who are characterized by good judgment in all that they do, in their relationships with others, and with themselves."

An education that would produce such students would likely be called, by a great many people, a good education, But do children have a right to such an education? Do they even have a right to be educated at all? Put another way, does society have the right to deny children a good education, if it is within society's means to provide it? Just what, in the way of education, is a person entitled to in a democratic society?

The writers of the articles that follow address the problem of educational rights as part of the larger problem of children's rights, which the first and the final essays, by Letwin and Herndon respectively, consider from a legal point of view. The analyses are more philosophical in the contributions by Curley and Bandman. The remaining pieces, by Friquegnon, Vetterling-Braggin and Ladd, take for granted the objective of steering a middle path between the extreme of strong paternalism on the one hand and the extreme, on the other hand, of libertarianism. Their essays therefore complement each other to some extent, but the areas of difference are interesting and instructive.

Leon Letwin notes with approval the tendency of the courts to recognize that schoolchildren are not to be treated as though they lacked all rights. He denies that children's claims are to be dismissed wholesale on the grounds that they are incompetent. "The capacity of children has nothing to do with their right to be treated fairly, decently and humanely by their government. They are entitled to such treatment not because they are competent but because they are persons. To say that children are entitled to due process does not deny the legitimacy of governmental interference with their freedoms but rather; due process regulates the terms of that freedom. As for First Amendment freedoms, Letwin remarks that "students . . . should be permitted access to ideas and arguments that stir the society at large, even if they are permitted only limited participation in decision-making."

Thomas V. Curley approaches the question of the child's right to an education by finding such a right to be based upon the network of human relationships, including the child's relationship to the family, and the family's to the community and the state. He holds that the universality of the right is based on universal ethical principles applicable to all human beings. At the same time, he wants to distinguish the universal from the absolute or unchanging. To do so, he stresses the web of social relations, which exhibits both rights and correlative duties. Thus, the child has a right to an education and the parent has a duty to provide it. Should the parent not fulfill his duty, the state has a right to intervene in order to protect the child's right.

Bandman argues that children have limited option and welfare rights, including limited rights to inquire. This means they have limited rights to decision-making and to nutrition and shelter. They have a right to be treated with respect and to autonomy. They have a right to inquire—to examine, analyze and evaluate presently accepted answers. Bandman argues that the child's right to inquire is necessary for the child to grow up to become interdependent—negotiating, compromising, exchanging, giving and taking. In all of this, the child grows up to coordinate independence and interdependence.

Bandman continues by addressing himself to the child's right to enlightenment—here an enlightened synonym to education. He notes with approval J. S. Mill's opinion that depriving people of the freedom of thought and expression in effect robs their society, and mankind, of access to their ideas, He concludes that the child's right to enlightenment has a cutting edge over the right of her sub-culture to impose handcuffs on her future intellectual prospects, on the ground that the society has a right to intervene in behalf of its own vitality, freedom and enlightenment.

Perhaps the only justifiable ground for limiting the liberty rights of children, in the view of Marie-Louise Friquegnon, is the child's irrationality, apart from the general ground, which applies to everyone, of conflict with other rights. Lack of rationality implies dependency, which means that the irrational child has a claim right on parents for protecting the child against its own irrational impulses. "Thus claim rights and liberty rights vary inversely. When the adolescent acquires the right to cross the street alone, he or she no longer has a claim on the parents to protective escort across the street." Nevertheless, children must be prepared for the exercise of adult rights by being given practice in taking risks "always some degree beyond what he or she has already proved himself or herself able to handle." Since children have had insufficient time to learn about life and test their values, "they should not be held fully responsible far the decisions they make."

In the second part of her contributions Maria-Louise Friquegnon argues that the transgressions of the bona fide child may be excusable when similar transgressions by the childish grownup are not, She insists there must be a dividing line between childhood and adulthood, and she suggests that "eighteen is the least unreasonable point at which to draw it, because physiological growth is completed at that age, and because adolescents have an image of themselves as grownups at that age." She concludes that the reason for limiting young people's rights must be that such limitation promotes the fulfillment of their potentialities. She sees children progressing gradually toward adulthood, and as they do, their liberty rights progressively increase. This in turn enables them to rehearse such rights and assume increased civil and criminal responsibilities as they grow older.

We are asked by Mary Vetterling-Braggin to consider two diametrically opposed positions. The first is the liberationist argument which concludes that children ought to be granted the same rights adults are now granted. The second is the strong paternalist argument, which concludes that "Adults ought to have liberty rights X, Y and Z, but children ought to be denied X, Y and Z." She notes that when we look for morally relevant properties by which to distinguish adults from children—such as having the capacity for rational choices or being of the age of consent—it turns out that some children have it and some lack it, but likewise, some adults have it and some lack it. She concludes with an argument for "soft paternalism," which maintains that there is no justification for treating children as a class differently from adults as a class with respect to the granting of X, Y and Z. Therefore, both adults and children with morally relevant properties A, B and C ought to have legal liberties X, Y and Z, and those lacking those properties should be denied those liberties.

Rosalind Ekman Ladd provides an alternative statement of the soft paternalistic position by directing her criticism at the criterion of rationality. Instead of using theoretical or formalistic understandings of rationality (such as being able to deduce conclusions from premises) as a basis for distinguishing between those entitled to liberty and those not, she argues in favor of practical reasoning—*i.e.*, judgment, self-knowledge and character—as the criterion upon which the distinction should be based. She concludes that adults lacking practical reasoning ability should be as liable to paternalistic treatment as children. Ladd sees her position as counter-balancing the advocacy of more and more liberty rights for children in the name of liberation, although she considers Friquegnon's position as less conservative than hers.

The last essay in the section deals with the possibility of offering a course in ethics in the public schools. The author, James F. Herndon, not only sees no constitutional problem in doing so, but feels it is something we are encouraged by the Constitution to do, in line with our society's long-term interests. But would it either lead to the establishment of religion or towards the destruction of religion? Herndon feels it would do neither. Students have the right not to have their religions insulted, but this does not mean that they have the right to escape challenge resulting from another's good faith effort to state an opinion. And if the discussion were to lead some individuals to be still more convinced of their religious beliefs, this could hardly be considered equivalent to the establishment of religion. Herndon concludes that an ethics course in the schools might well result, in the long run, "in the kind of ethical society most of us would like to have."

Education and the Constitutional Rights of Children

Leon Letwin

As is well known, Supreme Court decisions over the past decade have significantly expanded the scope of constitutional protection available to public school students. Children today enjoy the protections of the first amendment in school by virtue of the Court's decision in *Tinker v. Des Moines Independent Community School District*[1] and of the due process clause when school administrators seek to discipline them, by virtue of the decision in *Goss v. Lopez*.[2] These cases inevitably provoke the question: "How far will—and should—this development go?" Or to put the matter somewhat more theoretically: To what extent does the ideal of constitutional equality properly extend to schoolchildren and entitle them the same range of protections enjoyed by adults?

At the risk of oversimplification, one can today identify at least two characteristically different responses to this question. One builds upon the historic attitude that schoolchildren, both because they are young and because they are in school, are self-evidently "different" and unentitled to such rights.

Those attuned to this view will regret the Supreme Court's expansion of students' rights and they will be unsympathetic to any further such expansions. They will, to one degree or another, find themselves in sympathy with traditional thought about the power of school officials over their young charges as embodied in the doctrine of *in loco parentis*.

The essence of this doctrine may be captured without extended or technical inquiry. Readers who matriculated before the mid-1960's need only recall their own implicit assumptions as public school pupils to remember how unthinkable it would have been to claim that they possessed rights and that school administrators were bound to respect those rights. "Unthinkable" here is no figure of speech. The notion of "rights" was so contrary to prevailing assumptions about the natural order of things as never to require conscious rejection.

The second approach—one which I regard as far preferable—is sympathetic to the extension of constitutional protections to students in the myriad contexts in which they daily confront state power as exercised by school authorities, including the right to free speech, the right to due process of law at the hands of school authorities, the right to be safeguarded from cruel and unusual punishment in the school setting,[3] the right to immunity from unreasonable searches or seizures on school premises, and the privilege against self-incrimination in disciplinary proceedings.

This latter view does not depend on any conception that children are merely adults whose growth has through some hormonal quirk been physically stunted, such as the children portrayed in the paintings of Brueghel. Rather, it depends on the belief that for all their differences, their development as informed, self-confident, critical participants in a democratic society necessitates much the same respect for their right to share in the core values of the Bill of Rights as is displayed toward adults.

This contrast in perspective can be largely explained in terms of the conflicting assumptions concerning children, education and the relationship between the two, which underlie the contending viewpoints. One school of thought tends toward the view that where children are involved, educational values and constitutional values are in implacable conflict; the other inclines toward the view that the very ends of education demand respect for the rights of those being educated.

It is these conflicting attitudes about children and education, particularly as manifested in some court decisions, that I wish to explore in this paper.

To better understand the in *loco parentis ideology*, or at least one variant of it, it is useful to start with the little-known case of *Wooster v. Sunderland.*[4] That case, decided almost 80 years ago, is notable for capturing so neatly one set of mind toward children and toward education. The case arose when Earl Wooster, a Fresno high school student, addressed his fellow students during a school assembly. He opened his remarks with the complaint that various schoolrooms were fire hazards and that the exits were inadequate. In somewhat "caustic" terms he denounced the school board for compelling students to assemble in such rooms. Shifting to another complaint, he denounced the school board for prohibiting a student event known as a "donkey fight." The activity was not described but must have amounted to a mildly attenuated form of mayhem. He then wove these seemingly disparate complaints into a common theme of school board irrationality. It was unfair to prohibit donkey fights in which "boys took their own chances of being injured, and force them to take chances of being injured in a firetrap." Finally, in

the court's words, he "closed and climaxed his incendiary address by offering a resolution . . . requesting the [school board] . . . to 'no longer talk about bonds, but to do all in its power to put such a bond issue before the people of the district'."

Wooster was brought before the board to "explain his motive." For the benefit of those insensitive to nuance, he explained that his rhetoric was "intended as a slam" at the board. The board concurred and demanded an apology. None was forthcoming and Wooster was expelled. The trial court affirmed the board action and Wooster appealed.

The appeals court found in favor of the school board saying:

> [T]he whole tenor of the address was well calculated to . . . engender . . . in the minds of the students a feeling of disrespect for the defendants, and a secret if not an open hostility to their control of the student body and management of school affairs. Such being the natural tenor and tendency of the plaintiff's address, his conduct in making the same cannot be classed as anything but a species of insubordination to constituted authority, which required correction . . . in order that the discipline of the school might be maintained. . . .

It occurred to no one—school authorities, the court, or even to Wooster himself—that his speech should enjoy constitutional protection; his appeal was therefore cast in narrowly technical terms. The predominant attitudes toward education and the young made it incongruous, even bizarre, to suppose that Wooster might possess "rights" enforceable against school officials, even assuming such speech would have enjoyed protection in the society at large. The prevailing view of education saw its central purpose as the transmission of those facts and skills students would someday need to play a useful role in society; the cultivation of critical, independent thought was not a proper schoolhouse activity.

Given the conception of education as a one-way conduit from teacher to pupil—as product rather than process—it was logical to view student criticism of authority as sand in the machin-

What claims can children make?

The justification of children's rights under Rawls's theory has one major emphasis: children have a right to make just claims, and adults must be responsive to these claims. This conception of the just society, if widely accepted, would lead to a change in attitude on the part of adults. In according rights to children, the theory makes adults more accountable to children. They can no longer assume it is only at their pleasure that children are permitted to make claims and exercise freedoms. Adopting this new conception of children's rights would in itself be an important reform.

—from Victor L. Worsfold, "A Philosophical Justification for Children's Rights," in *The Rights of Children* (Cambridge: Harvard Educational Review, 1974) p. 44.

---

ery of education, undermining discipline and distracting students from the main task of absorbing knowledge.

Moreover, the dominant view of life and education regarded unquestioning obedience to official dictates, or as the *Wooster* court described it with such unselfconscious candor, the "subordination" by students to "constituted authority," as practical training of a high order. Adult life, after all, often required the unquestioning, even amiable acceptance of things as they were, however irrational they might have appeared. (I encountered this attitude a number of years ago during a parent-student discussion in a Los Angeles junior high school concerning the validity of the hair-length regulations then in force. One parent conceded he could find no justification for a rule regulating the hair length of male students only. He concluded however that not all things in society were rational. Therefore the rule should be retained so that students would learn to accept such irrational rules.)

Quite apart from such functional justifications, restrictions on student speech were warranted simply because "disrespect" and "insubordination" were immoral. Their suppression required no further justification.

Given the prevailing sentiments it is not surprising that the school authorities did not consider less repressive responses to Wooster's criticisms. They might, for example, have simply laughed off the incident because Wooster's comments had not seriously interfered with school life. Or they might have engaged him in dialogue about his complaints, because the issues he raised were more important than the perhaps intemperate way in which he raised them. Or they might have welcomed his forthright criticism of constituted authority as an excellent example of citizen participation in the political process. Or, finally, they might have regarded his speech as offering a unique educational opportunity to explore, in microcosm, effective techniques for social change in a democratic society. To state these alternatives is to recognize that they were unthinkable under the then-prevailing conceptions of relationships between young people and "constituted authority."

Now one might be tempted to treat this case as a historic relic, interesting to one with an antiquarian bent but of no contemporary practical significance. To be sure, few courts would decide the case the same way today. But the attitudes underpinning that decision have yet to be interred. One suspects that the nerve fibers of many a school administrator and judge, too, would flutter sympathetically to the law-and-order rhythms of the *Wooster* decision.

It is instructive also that even some judges who are deeply committed to constitutional rights in general are prepared to read students out of the ambit of their protection because of a view they hold about the "special nature" of school children. Justice Hugo Black exemplified this view. His fierce dedication, as a member of the Supreme Court, to the first amendment in general needs no testimonial for those with a passing knowledge of his record. Yet in *Tinker*, he opposed the extension of first amendment rights to students in a bilious dissent, saying that schoolchildren have "not yet reached the point of experience and wisdom which [enable] them to teach all of their elders . . . taxpayers send children to school . . . to learn, not teach." Furthermore, to acknowledge that schoolchildren have a right of speech would be to subject "all the public schools in the country to the whims and caprices of their loudest-mouthed, but maybe not their brightest, students."

With this background as a frame of reference, one can appreciate the change of view represented by several of the Supreme Court decisions of recent decades, to which we now turn.

Tinker v. Des Moines Independent Community School District. This case, decided in 1969, marked a major judicial reassessment of the *Wooster* attitude toward minors, schools, and freedom of speech. Students had worn black armbands to school in symbolic protest against the war in Vietnam. School officials promptly banned the conduct and suspended those who disobeyed the ban. The case compelled the Supreme Court to confront squarely the issue whether speech on school premises was entitled to first amendment protection. It concluded that students did not leave their constitutional rights at the schoolhouse gate, saying:

> [I]n our system, undifferentiated fear or apprehension of disturbance is not enough to overcome the right to freedom of expression. Any departure from absolute regimentation may cause trouble. Any variation from the majority's opinion may inspire fear. Any word spoken in class, in the lunchroom, or on the campus, that deviates from the views of another person may start an argument or cause a disturbance. But our Constitution says we must take this risk . . . and our history says that it is this sort of hazardous freedom—this kind of openness—that is the basis of our national strength and of the independence and vigor of Americans who grow up

and live in this relatively permissive, often disputatious, society.

One striking facet of the case is how extraordinarily modest were the rights claimed by the students. The student expression could not plausibly be viewed as "incendiary," "disrespectful," or "insubordinate." The wearing of armbands "caused discussion outside of the classrooms, but no interference with work and no disorder." The fact that it took a landmark Supreme Court decision to establish even the modest rights at issue underscores the historic absence of student rights.

Goss v. Lopez. This case arose out of a period of widespread student unrest during which several schools in Columbus, Ohio, were affected by racial confrontation, demonstrations and problems of various sorts. Over 75 students were suspended for their involvement in disruptive demonstrations. Although the circumstances surrounding the suspensions varied, they shared one common feature: No hearing was provided in which the students could contest their suspensions.

Some of the students challenged the law that allowed their suspension by school authorities for up to 10 days without notice or hearing. The lower court found that these procedures violated the students' rights to due process of law, reasoning that suspension for even 10 days or less was unconstitutional where no hearing was provided.

On appeal the Supreme Court affirmed by a vote of five to four. The threshold issue was the very applicability of the due process clause to school disciplinary procedures. The Court found that it did apply, that public school students were not somehow outside the amendment's guarantees.

What then were the requirements of due process? The Court laid down a number of what it characterized as "rudimentary" requirements. These requirements reduced themselves to "*some* kind of notice" and "*some* kind of hearing." As will be seen, the Court's characterization of its requirements involved no false modesty: rudimentary they were indeed. For to illustrate its meaning, the Court gave apparent endorsement to an informal scheme in effect in one school. That scheme, said the Court, was "remarkably similar to that which we now require." A teacher observing misconduct would complete a form describing the occurrence and send the student, with the form, to the principal's office. There, the principal would obtain the student's version of the event; if it conflicted with the teacher's written description, the principal would send for the teacher to hear the teacher's own version, apparently in the presence of the student. If a discrepancy still existed, "the *teacher's version* would be believed and the principal would arrive at a disciplinary decision based on it."[5]

From one perspective, the Court's approval of this scheme suggests that *Goss* is much ado about very little. Given the minuscule opportunities it provides for a student's defense, *Goss* is remarkable not for its innovation but for the fact that it was so long in coming, so vigorously contested, so narrowly affirmed, and so parsimonious in the rights it recognized upon arrival. That such attenuated protections could be considered progress provides yet another sad commentary upon historic school practices. Nevertheless, *Goss* did directly challenge the time-honored exclusion of students from constitutional protections. It affirmed that *Tinker* was neither a constitutional relic nor a special rule limited to first amendment cases.

I turn now to some of the arguments of the dissenters, *i.e.*, those members of the court who opposed the extension of due process protections to students. Though these views clearly did not persuade the majority, they were neither decisively nor explicitly rejected by it. The dissenters' views, both those expressed and those implicit, represent a residual legacy of *Wooster v. Sunderland*; they stand as obstacles to the further recognition of the rights of students.

Incompetence and paternalism.

The notion that children are incompetent is one of the pillars of the classic *in loco parentis* view of the public schools. This view rests on a syllogism of beguiling simplicity: Only those who possess certain capabilities are entitled to share in generally held rights; schoolchildren lack some of those capabilities. The conclusion is that children may be denied rights taken for granted by adults.

The argument, however, is neither as simple nor as compelling as it first appears; both premises of the syllogism must be qualified. First, the proposition that children are incompetent requires substantial modification in order to approximate the real world. Although history clearly teaches that children are "different," it has spoken over time with a remarkable cacophony of voices as to who are "children." Indeed, that dependent state between childhood and adulthood called adolescence is an invention of modern industrialized society.[6] Even given a culture that takes extended adolescence for granted, its proper duration is subject to reasonable dispute and to revision.

More fundamentally, the major premise of the syllogism—the notion that entitlement to share in generally held constitutional rights depends on certain capabilities or competence—is flawed. Competency is, to be sure, at times relevant and even decisive for the determination of rights; but at other times it is not. Competency is relevant to those rights principally aimed at maximizing the free choice of persons, as opposed to those principally intended to safeguard the individual against governmental abuse. Rights of the first category ought to be limited to those who have the capacity of avoiding serious harm to themselves or others as they go about exercising their choices. Thus, we have the strongest case for denying rights to children on the ground of their incapacity when the injury we are concerned with is great, when the likelihood of its occurrence is high, when the opportunity for the child's learning process or for adult intervention to moderate the danger once the child has acted is low, and when the injury, if it occurs, is irreversible. Driving cars and using guns are examples: A momentary indiscretion may unleash terrible consequences that can neither be checked nor undone. The child's immaturity certainly argues against free choice.

But with respect to other rights, "competency" is not the appropriate test. I have in mind those rights aimed not so much at maximizing free choice but at civilizing the processes and instruments of state compulsion.

Due process of law and the right to be free of cruel and unusual punishment are archetypical examples. They do not deny the legitimacy of governmental interference with a citizen's free choice. Rather, they regulate the terms of that interference. Procedural due process does not immunize persons against deprivations of life, liberty or property; it simply insists on a degree of fairness and humanity. Similarly, the eighth amendment ban on cruel and unusual punishment does not prevent punishment; it regulates the ways in which government visits is unpleasantness upon people. To that degree, the *capacity* of children has nothing to do with their right to be treated fairly, decently and humanely by their government. They are entitled to such treatment not because they are competent but because they are persons.

One might reason, however, that other constitutional rights do hinge on possession of adult competency. The right of free speech might be offered as a prime example. One of its central functions, after all, is to facilitate free choice by that portion of the population regarded as *competent* to exercise choice. But that argument, too, breaks down. For in our society the right to speak is far broader than the right to act on that speech. And the fact that choices may be foreclosed to children until they reach a certain age hardly precludes their right to think, speak, debate, and dissent about those choices.

Furthermore, important choices are inescapable even for the young. How, for example, should children think about their peers of other races and sexes? How should they adjust to the competitive values that permeate our society? How should they evaluate the network of ideas and values they are exposed to in school? How should they think about authority—its legitimacy and its limits? How should they go about selecting their future education and careers? Schools are, or should be, a training ground for informed, intelligent resolution of such issues, whether the decisions are to be made now or in the future. Students, therefore, should be permitted access to ideas and arguments that stir the society at large, even if they are permitted only limited participation in decisionmaking. This educational process cannot be deferred until the child reaches age 18.

The "unity of interest" between school authorities and students.

The paternalism argument rests not only on assumptions of student incompetence but on a companion view that school authorities can and do protect student interests. Why then do they need legal protections? Justice Powell, speaking for the *Goss* minority, described the relation between the interests of students and officials as "[u]nlike the divergent and even sharp conflict of interests usually present where due process rights are asserted." In the school context, he found those interests "essentially congruent." Accordingly, the adversary stance that makes sense in the world outside of the schoolroom makes none at all within that benign setting, where "the experience, good faith, and dedication" of the school staff safeguard student interests.

he *Goss* majority, in upholding the students' claim to due process rights, presented one response to this view. Even assuming the coincidence of interest postulated by the minority, officials may make mistakes. No one, said the Court, believes that the school "disciplinary process [is] a totally accurate, unerring process, never mistaken and never unfair." The majority here stands on firm ground. Paternalistic systems can go astray, converting the objects of their beneficence into abject victims.

But the dissent's easy equation of the interests of students and school officials also contains a more fundamental flaw: The "unity of interest" is partial at best. School teachers, principals, school superintendents, and school boards have a variety of interests—personal, bureaucratic and political—that may clash with those of the child. The interest of school officials in job advancement, political approval, county funds, peer recognition, ego gratification, or a work atmosphere free of student "disrespect" is not necessarily the child's best interest.

This divergence of interest is aggravated, of course, when the disciplinary issues arise out of political controversy, and students find themselves challenging, criticizing and thereby offending the very school authorities who sit in judgment upon them. It strains credulity to suppose that students in such a context would perceive the disciplinarian's stance as "disinterested" or would see the interests of the two as "congruent." Why should they?

The young have not earned certain rights.

Arguably, certain rights are denied the young not only because they lack rational capacity, but also because the rights have not been earned. For example, this justification might be offered as part of the reason for denying the young the right to vote. Because they have not shouldered adult responsibilities such as self-support, paying taxes and fighting in wars, minors have not earned the right to vote. Denial of the right is the *quid pro quo* for their privileged status as children. Moreover, because they are relieved of adult burdens, there is no unfairness in denying children a voice in the allocation of such burdens. This position is the converse of the no-taxation-without-representation argument.

But the young are not immune from countless legal requirements, including the duties to pay

taxes and to obey the laws. Furthermore, the right to vote is conferred upon numerous adults whose claim to entitlement may be no stronger than that of many minors—for example, those who do not support themselves, earn enough to pay taxes or fight in wars. Finally, the arguments are fatally similar to the long-discredited conception of the right to vote as a privilege of the propertied class.

More important, whatever validity these arguments are said to have with respect to the right to vote, they cannot apply to the protections of the Bill of Rights. The requirements of fair treatment at the hands of government, of humane punishment, of privacy, or of free speech are protected not because they are earned, but because they preserve essential aspects of human dignity and are necessary limitations upon government in a democratic society.

Obedience as educational imperative.

One view of the relationship between children and adult authority considers a high degree of deference by children indispensable to their proper moral and practical growth. Thus, the *Goss* minority postulates an incompatibility, between due process and a student's understanding of "the necessity of rules and obedience thereto."

But the students in *Goss* claimed no immunity from the "rules." They merely sought an opportunity to challenge an administrator's decision that the rules had been violated and that they, the students, had violated them. To deny them a hearing on this point may or may not produce a desirable lesson in obedience, but surely the lesson cannot be characterized as one of obedience to *rules*. Obedience to administrative fiat would be closer to the mark.

The minority, nonetheless, felt that this non-reciprocal approach to rule compliance contributed to the moral development of the child:

In an age when the home and church play a diminishing role in shaping the character and value judgments of the young, a heavier responsibility falls upon the schools. When an immature student merits censure for his conduct, he is rendered a disservice if appropriate sanctions are not applied or if procedures for their application are so formalized as to invite a challenge to the teacher's authority . . .

But what is to happen when, as in *Goss*, the student doubts that "censure" is merited? The minority, with startling simplicity, eliminated the issue, in the quotation above, by assuming the very question to be proved: that censure was merited. The dissenters hoped thereby to teach the young the meaning of "the social compact of respect for the rights of others." But these methods teach only that those wielding governmental powers are not to be challenged and that "respect for the rights of others" is a mildly disguised code phrase for a unidirectional "respect" for adult authority no matter how arbitrary it may be.

The history of official behavior, especially as revealed in recent years, offers precious little that would make one want to teach this version of the "social compact." Surely, a better lesson would be to teach precisely the reverse: that even the young and powerless enjoy rights, and that legal constraints bind the governors as well as the governed. From this perspective; one might regard a student's desire to rebel against "arbitrary" authority as an impulse that society should prize.

An alternative argument for the virtues of unquestioning obedience to authority might be couched in practical rather than moral terms. Students need to learn this lesson as part of their socialization to adult life. To learn to accept authority, sometimes even irrational authority, is to prepare for the real world. But if this accurately describes the real world, educators might well seek to encourage reflection about that world, the nature of the social organization that produces it, its implications, and possible alternatives to it, rather than merely to promote the practical advantages of accommodation. To the degree that public education promotes "realistic accommodation" of this sort, it contributes to the reality

just described and abandons more noble ideals of public education: the development of a citizenry capable of understanding, questioning and evaluating society and one that confronts authority in a self-confident, thoughtful and critical way.

Student rights as incompatible with school disciplinary requirements.

Uncomplaining obedience may commend itself not as an ideal but rather as a concession to the harsh realities of the school world in which teachers are increasingly beset by disrespect, disobedience and violence. In this view, for example, due process has no place in the "real" world if educators are to survive, much less to educate. Calling the students' attention to "rights" is then like waving a red flag to persons who above all else need more discipline, not more license.

Now one must concede that school officials may confront disciplinary emergencies requiring temporary restrictions of rights. But excessive deference to officials on this score is itself dangerous. However sincere, officials may tend to see "exigencies" when the disinterested observer will detect only an inappropriate response to admittedly difficult problems.

Moreover, the presumed benefits of an authoritarian school regime may not be worth their price. In an effective educational setting "most of the objectionable behavior of students—their idiosyncratic tendencies, their expressions of opinion on many subjects, the disturbances and distractions caused by their actions, their statements, and even their appearance—is actually grist for the educational mill."[7] A system predicated on hostility to student rights runs the risk not only of forfeiting this educational opportunity but of exacerbating the very difficulties it is seeking to cure. Such a system both undermines the moral claims of authority and diverts attention form the genuine evils that frequently underlie school disciplinary problems: racial segregation, staffing deficiencies, overcrowded classrooms, inadequate physical plant, defects of school policy, and the hopelessness bred by lack of opportunity. Schools adopting this route are likely to end up with the worst of both worlds: the authoritarian environment without the hoped-for peace.

Peaceful or not, the educational prospects of schools run on the model of an authoritarian regime are dubious. Such schools are primarily custodial institutions whose principal assignment is to keep the young off the streets, out of trouble and off the labor market. The resulting atmosphere is likely to prove incompatible with either learning or teaching.

Nothing said thus far is intended to dispute the fact that schools, like most other institutions, need certain conventions of behavior on the part of their participants in order to accomplish their mission. Conventional education presupposes the orderly consideration of subject matter under the guidance of a knowledgeable instructor. This view of education dictates that a classroom not be treated as an unstructured public forum in which all persons are free to say or do what they will, when they will, on whatever subject strikes them. The crucial point, however, is that neither age nor special theories about educating the young are essential underpinnings for such rules of decorum and order. The need would exist more or less equally in a university or an institution of adult education, though all the participants were over 18. Nor is this even a unique truth about schools. Similar needs exist for courts, hospitals, libraries, business offices, and theaters—in short, for most institutions. Emphasis on age and educational goals adds little that is legitimately relevant to the argument for maintaining institutional order. The danger is that such talk will provide a psychologically potent bit of rhetoric for justifying a host of extraordinary restrictions because of a presumed but unwarranted view that children and the needs of schools are "different." So far as routine institutional requirements are concerned, a college or university would furnish a presumptively appropriate model for drawing the proper balance be-

tween constitutional rights and institutional needs, unencumbered by reflexive assumptions that either age or educational objectives defeat constitutional claims. The argument I advance for students' constitutional rights, then, is quite compatible with a recognition of the need for routine institutional order.

Student complaints as educational diversion.

a. The "floodgates" theory. If rights are granted to students, it is said, school officials will be compelled to spend much of their time commuting to and from the local courthouse responding to the complaints of their litigious charges. Administrators regularly make decisions of serious consequence to students—in grading, in imposing curricular requirements, in "tracking" them, and the like—to which "due process" claims as plausibly might attach as in the case of the short-term suspension. Did the Court's decision, the dissenting Justices asked, imply that all these heretofore professional decisions were now to be transformed into decisions for judges? The minority feared that unless *Goss* could be rigidly contained, courts would displace school officials as the authority in the educational community. One response to this concern is that compelling authorities to justify their use of power in terms of applicable legal standards may not be so bad after all. Education still would occur, but partly in the setting of the judicial system. By observing the operations of such a system, assuming it were sensitive to the constitutional issues involved, students and administrators alike might receive a powerful lesson in the rule of law.

Moreover, the predicted volume of complaints itself may be exaggerated. For a number of reasons college students do not appear to have rushed to court to take advantage of the due process system that dawned on the American university more than a decade ago. Many college students who face school discipline are perfectly happy to be treated paternalistically. When they are charged with traditional offenses, such as plagiarism, cheating on an examination, or shoplifting from the university bookstore, what they want is sympathy, understanding and a second chance rather than "rights," due process and litigation. The exceptions have come mainly from students disciplined for politically related activity, but even these students have infrequently sought judicial review.

Rather than fearing a tidal wave of litigation, the opposite should be feared: Students acculturated to the *Goss* dissenters' "social compact" may be so conditioned to a "realistic" assessment of bureaucratic power that they will give in to it too readily.

In sum, although no one doubts that the activity of teaching requires school authorities to exercise broad discretionary powers, particularly in the area of nondisciplinary issues, this discretion should not preclude challenges to the fairness of the mechanism or the rationality of the decisions.[8]

b. The harm of "constitutionalizing" teacher-student relationships. In opposing due process rights for students, Justice Powell hinted at greater dangers than merely increased litigiousness. He described the normal teacher-pupil relationship as "rarely adversarial," suggesting that the "constitutionalization" of that relationship not only will fail to secure due process to the student but will irreparably damage the relationship as well. Under this theory, the very adversary atmosphere generated by speaking of "rights" is objectionable: Students need to focus not on their "rights" but on what the teacher has to teach. A related argument begins with the observation that students need structure and limits. Otherwise anarchy reigns, and anarchy is incompatible with education.

But rules can be defined with sufficient precision so that neither students nor teachers are enveloped by an asphyxiating cloud of doubt. Even very young children can and should learn the importance of both rights and obligations. A genuine commitment to both will, of course, produce occasional tensions. But educators should surely avoid the parody of education that results when they seek to exercise the unavoidable tensions between rights and obligations by insisting on the obligations and denying the rights.

Conclusion

Constitutional rights express fundamental postulates about the respect due to human beings and about indispensable limitations on government in a democratic society. These commitments should furnish the basis for thinking about the rights of minors even as they do the rights of adults. If the case can be made for circumscribing particular rights of the young because they are young, or because educational needs require it, let the case be made and not simply proclaimed or assumed. The tradition that permits the automatic, uncritical reliance on student or youth status as a trump card to justify the denial of rights richly deserves to be abandoned.

It is, moreover, misguided to see constitutional values as fundamentally at war with educational values. The capacity and willingness of the young to think independently, to question and to challenge constituted authorities and established ways, are not superfluous luxuries. The development of such talents ought to be central objectives of educational policy.

Footnotes

This article largely based on articles published elsewhere with extensive citations to legal authorities: After Goss v. Lopez: Student Status as Suspect Classification?, 29 Stan. L. Rev. 627 (1977); Regulation of Underground Newspapers on Public School Campuses in California, 22 U.C.L.A. L. Rev. 141 (1974).

1. 393 U.S. 503 (1969).
2. 419 U.S. 565 (1975). This case and *Tinker* are each discussed below.
3. Though this is a view thus far rejected by the Supreme Court. Consult Ingraham v. Wright, 97 S. Ct. 1401 (1977).
4. 27 Cal. App. 51, 148 P. 959 (1st Dist. 1915).

5. Emphasis added.
6. Skolnick, *The Limits of Childhood: Conceptions of Child Development and Social Context*, 39 Law & Contemp. Prob. 38, 61-63 (1975).
7. Ladd, *Allegedly Disruptive Student Behavior and the Legal Authority of School Officials*, 19 J. Pub. L. 209, 236 (1970).
8. In Bd. of Curators v. Horowitz, 98 S. Ct. 948 (1978), the Supreme Court declined to decide whether a medical school student dismissed on academic, rather than disciplinary, grounds was entitled to due process protections. The court held, however, that assuming the student was so entitled, the procedures employed had satisfied due process requirements because they permitted her the informal opportunity to discuss the matter with the administration and to make her side of the issue known, even though she was not granted a formal hearing by the medical school.

The Right to Education: An Inquiry Into Its Foundations

Thomas V. Curley

In this age, it is commonly thought to be true that children have a right to education. What I propose to examine is the question of what it means to claim that children have this right. My examination will address some important implications and consequences of this claim. I shall argue that the right of children to education can best be made intelligible when set within the framework of a relational theory of rights.

My treatment of the right to education will center upon a significant historical document which affirms this right. The United Nations, in its *Universal Declaration of Human Rights* (1948), included the right to education as part of its canon of human rights. Article 26 reads as follows:

> 1. Everyone has the right to education. Education shall be free, at least in the elementary and fundamental stages. Elementary education shall be compulsory. Technical and professional education shall be made generally available and higher education shall be equally accessible to all on the basis of merit.

> 2. Education shall be directed to the full development of the human personality and to the strengthening of respect for human rights and fundamental freedoms. It shall promote understanding, tolerance and friendship among all nations, racial or religious groups, and shall further the activities of the United Nations for the maintenance of peace.

> 3. Parents have a prior right to choose the kind of education that shall be given to their children.[1]

When we bear in mind that the *Declaration*, of which Article 26 is a part, was intended to be an affirmation of the rights which all people in all nations should have as human beings, I suspect that we are inclined to be sympathetic with the contents of Article 26. Its insistence upon everyone's right to a basic education and its focus upon the development of the self as central to the educational enterprise are powerful ideals which stir the human spirit.

Further reflection on Article 26, however, raises a number of important background issues. First, the right to education is considered to be universal in that the logical class to which it applies includes all human beings. This right is, then, an example of what is often called a "human" right. To understand the right to education, we must come to terms with the meaning of the concept, "human right." Secondly, what is proposed in Section 1 of Article 26 implies that education is a relatively scarce resource which is at least partially economic in nature. Principles of justice must be utilized to secure an equitable distribution of this resource. The right to education, thus, can be categorized as a "welfare" or "positive" right. The nature of positive rights must be considered as a prelude to an analysis of the right to education. Thirdly, Section 1 affirms that education on an elementary level must be made compulsory for children who have the right to education. In addition, Section 3 of Article 26 refers to the right of parents to determine the nature of their children's education. These assertions point to the need for an examination of the nature of children's rights vis-a-vis the rights of adults. What I propose to do in this paper is to discuss each of these background issues in an attempt to set a framework for the right to education and to suggest an interpretation of Article 26 of the United Nations *Declaration* which accords with that framework.

Human Rights

The first issue to be considered concerns the nature of human rights. The quality human rights possess which gives a clue to their nature is that of universality. It is important to note at the outset the relation between the issue of universality as it affects rights and the same issue as it affects the foundation of ethics. Any adequate theory of human rights must be set within the context of some form of ethical universalism.[2] The question of whether rights are universal only makes sense, therefore, given a prior commitment to the view that at least some ethical principles are universal. I shall assume this commitment in my treatment of rights.

Medieval logicians thought that the best way to understand the meaning of any concept was to look at its extension and its comprehension. To give the extension of a concept means to point to those realities to which the concept is properly applied. A right is universal in the extensional sense if it is applicable to at least all present and future human beings.[3] The comprehension of a concept is its internal meaning. In order to be intelligible, the concept of a human or a universal right must be grounded in our understanding of what it means to be human. When we ask what makes a right universal, we seek to determine what it is that human beings share in common as the basis for such a right. The issue of extension

will be of central concern later on in this paper when the nature of children's rights is examined in relation to the rights of adults. Let us devote our attention now to the comprehension of the concept of a universal right.

As indicated above, there is, in my judgment, a close link between the concept of a universal right and that of a universal ethical principle. The source for universality in both cases can be traced to the notion of a humanity which is shared in common. In order to clarify the meaning of the concept of a universal right, it is necessary to explore the notion of humanity. Before pursuing this line of investigation, it might be worthwhile to say something first about the general relation between ethical principles and rights. In *Utilitarianism*, John Stuart Mill argues that justice is that part of ethics which is defined by its concern with perfect duties and rights.[4] He makes it clear that the foundations of ethics must be established prior to any consideration of rights. Regardless of what one thinks of Mill's efforts to subordinate justice to utility, it seems evident that justice is part of ethics and that issues regarding rights are at least part of the domain of justice. Thus, ethical principles are logically prior to universal rights. It is not surprising, then, that the ethical theory one espouses has a profound impact upon the position one takes concerning these rights.

Theories of rights can be classified in accordance with the two major traditions of ethical universalism, the teleological and the deontological. The most noteworthy example of a teleological theory of universal rights is that presented by Mill. For Mill, there is one fundamental ethical principle, the greatest good for the greatest number of people. Any adequate theory of rights must be set within this context. Mill sums up the heart of this theory in the following way: "To have a right, then, is, I conceive, to have something which society ought to defend me in the possession of. If the objector goes on to ask why it ought, I can give him no other reason than general utility."[5] A society which protects universal rights, according to Mill, is better able to advance the greatest good for the greatest number than a society which does not recognize such rights.

Mill's effort to fix the locus of universal rights within the more general domain of utility has two important implications. First, rights for Mill originate in the historical framework of the development of society. Society best progresses, thought Mill, through the liberation of the potentialities of its members. When a conflict between the individual's perceived good and the immediate good of society arises, it is not always best that the individual good be subordinated to the social good. Hence, there is a need for universal rights to provide an area of protection for the individual. Secondly, since the possession of a right by one entails the existence of a duty for another according to Mill, it is necessary for us to situate our understanding of universal rights in the larger framework of the interactive relationships among people in society. This suggests that we turn our attention away from the notion of rights as possessed by individuals in isolation towards one of rights as an outgrowth of human situations.

These implications are made explicit within the pragmatic tradition of ethics, particularly in the writings of John Dewey. The crucial difference between the ethical stances of utilitarianism and pragmatism lies in the fact that the pragmatist, unlike the utilitarian, makes no commitment to an ultimate ethical principle to which all else must be subordinated. As a result, the objection to utilitarianism that universal rights are likely to be sacrificed in order to advance the greatest good for the greatest number does not affect the pragmatic position. John Dewey argues that:

> . . . the process of growth, of improvement and progress, rather than the static outcome and result, becomes the significant thing . . . The end is no longer a terminus or limit to be reached. It is the active process of transforming the existent situation. Not perfection as a final goal, but the ever-enduring process of perfecting, maturing, refining is the aim of living . . . Growth is the only moral "end."[6]

The problem is how to reconcile the flexibility enunciated in Dewey's statement with the universality of rights. What I would suggest is that this flexibility affects the comprehension and not the extension of universal rights. What is meant by a given universal right is subject to modification as the process of human maturing continues, but the right is still applicable to all human beings. Indeed, maturing for the pragmatist is primarily a matter of growth in meaning. Sidney Hook sums up the pragmatic view of the nature of universal rights in the following statement:

> A human right is a morally justifiable claim made in behalf of all men to the enjoyment and exercise of those basic freedoms, goods, and services which are considered necessary to achieve the human estate. On this definition human rights do not correspond to anything an individual literally possesses as an attribute, whether physical or mental. Morally justifiable claims are *proposals* to treat human beings in certain ways. Human rights are not names of anything. They specify procedures—courses of action—to be followed by agencies of the government and community with respect to a series of liberties, goods, and services.[7]

In this statement Hook captures the pragmatic outlook which holds that universal rights are grounded not in static qualities possessed by all human individuals, but in established procedures that grow out of the interaction of persons in communities and that specify how persons are to be treated.

The other tradition of ethical universalism to be considered is the deontological tradition. The major historical figure in this tradition is Immanuel Kant. The key ethical principle in Kant's moral philosophy is the categorical imperative. The formulation of the imperative which is particularly appropriate to the issue of rights reads as follows: "Act in such a way that you treat humanity, whether in your own person or in the person of another, always at the same time as an end and never simply as a means."[8] Kant asserts that all persons possess intrinsic dignity, as distinct from other things in nature which have only instrumental value. In his book, *Taking Rights*

Seriously, Ronald Dworkin points to the significance of this idea in relation to theories about universal rights:

> Anyone who professes to take rights seriously . . . must accept, at the minimum, one or both of two important ideas. The first is the vague, but powerful idea of human dignity. This idea, associated with Kant, but defended by philosophers of different schools, supposes that there are ways of treating a man that are inconsistent with recognizing him as a full member of the human community, and holds that such treatment is profoundly unjust.[9]

Why is it that human beings possess intrinsic dignity? The attempt to answer this question has led to two different sorts of responses on the part of deontological philosophers. Both focus on the question of what it means to be a person. The key difference between them is that the first emphasizes individuality while the second emphasizes community. The first looks for some characteristic which all persons possess and which distinguishes the person from other forms of life. The principal qualities proposed include rationality, freedom, and autonomy. To follow this path of investigation is to confront a whole series of difficulties arising from the effort to distinguish the person from other forms of life. In addition, the proposed qualities seem to represent achievements rather than inherent characteristics. When, for example, does a person become rational? The attempt to answer questions like this leads, as will be seen later in this paper, to serious problems in the assessment of children's rights.

The second response to the question of dignity as the ground of human rights is similar to the pragmatic approach in its emphasis upon the importance of relationships among persons in community. A. I. Melden serves as a good example of a deontological philosopher who takes this approach. He suggests that "The moral dignity of persons is the dignity they have insofar as they show themselves capable of being full and unabridged participants in the life of a moral community, comporting themselves with others in the expectation that they will be dealt with on terms of moral equality, and prepared in a way that anyone can see to hold others to account for the infringement of their rights."[10] Dignity for Melden manifests itself within a moral community which is formed through the interaction of persons who treat one another as moral equals. For Melden, the conception of human rights can only arise in such an atmosphere. Sidney Hook recognizes much the same point when he says that

> So long as any use of the term "man," or a derivative, refers only to membership in a biological species, I for one cannot see why that membership *alone* gives anyone a right he can justifiably claim of me. . . . However, if the term "human" or any of its synonyms or derivatives refer to a member of a moral community, that is, if these are normative terms, the nature and degree of right would depend on the kind of moral community that existed between him and me.[11]

Thus, both the pragmatic position and this deontological response put a similar emphasis upon the importance of the moral community as the situation out of which universal rights grow. It can be argued with some justification, I think, that the existence of societies governed by commonly accepted rules of behaviour already denotes, at least in a minimal sense, the presence of a moral community. Hence, a moral community is not to be seen as something ideal which we are constantly striving to bring into existence, but as something already present and capable of nurture through the interpersonal deepening of our moral sense.

Before turning to the issue of positive rights, let me sum up what has been said thus far regarding human rights. First, I argued that, in order to understand what is meant by human rights, one must focus upon the quality of universality as essential to such rights. Secondly, I pointed out that any adequate theory of human rights must be situated in the more general context of some form of ethical universalism. Thirdly, I considered examples of the teleological and deontological traditions of ethical universalism in order to explore their implications vis-a-vis human rights. It is not the purpose of this paper to try to resolve the long-standing deontological versus teleological dispute. The view of rights I find most compelling is that enunciated by both A. I. Melden and Sidney Hook to the effect that human rights presuppose the presence of a moral community of persons. In emphasizing the similarity between these two philosophers, I do not mean to deny the evident and serious differences between the traditions of ethical thought they represent. It is striking, in my judgment, that two philosophers from opposed traditions come to share a common perspective on the basis of human rights.

Positive Rights

Given this common perspective, the notion of positive rights can be fruitfully explored. One of the familiar distinctions in the literature about rights is that between negative and positive rights. Negative rights are ordinarily viewed to be rights against interference. For example, the right to life, interpreted as a negative right, can be understood to mean that others have a duty not to take my life away. That duty is fulfilled by refraining from such actions as murder and assault. Positive rights are interpreted to be rights of recipience. For example, the right to life, viewed as a positive right, implies that others have a duty to provide me with what is essential to the maintenance of life, such as food and shelter. That duty is fulfilled by taking actions that respond to the vital needs of others. Positive and negative rights, thus, imply the existence of a relationship among persons such that the possession of a right by one member of a community entails the possession of a duty by another or others in the community. Charles Fried, in his book entitled *Right and Wrong*, sums up the distinction in these terms:

A positive right is a claim to something . . . while a negative right is a right that something not be done to one, that some particular imposi-

tion be withheld. Positive rights are inevitably asserted to scarce goods, and consequently scarcity implies a limit to the claim. Negative rights, however, the rights not to be interfered with in forbidden ways, do not appear to have such natural, such inevitable limitations. If I am let alone, the commodity I obtain does not appear of its nature to be a scarce or limited one.[12]

As Fried indicates, the existence of scarcity in resources places practical limitations upon positive rights, but does not affect negative rights.

The classical view of universal rights, as enunciated by Hobbes and Locke, only acknowledged the existence of negative rights. Locke, for one, argued that civil society comes into being as a result of a contract in which independent individuals agree to give up some measure of independence for the protection which society can provide. The rights society agrees to uphold are designed to preserve as much individual independence as possible. Hence, the only rights people have are rights against interference. Peter Singer, in an article entitled "Rights and the Market," contends that this is an unduly restrictive view of the nature of human rights. He asserts that the society we live in is composed of interdependent persons with communal relationships as opposed to individuals seeking to preserve their independence. The communal provides the framework for positive rights and duties corresponding to those rights.[13] To say, for example, that I am responsible for ensuring that my children have enough to eat is to affirm the presence of a duty which is more than simply a matter of generosity. My children have a justifiable claim to nourishment by reason of the web of social and moral relationships of which they and I are an integral part. Once we recognize that Locke's hypothesis about the origins of civil society does not accurately represent the human situation, we can expand our understanding of rights to include positive rights. The tendency of ethical theories, which stress the centrality of the individual, to affirm only negative rights lends support, in my judgment, to those ethical theories that emphasize the communal as primary.

Children's Rights and the Rights of Adults

The third background issue I want to consider concerns the nature of children's rights vis-a-vis the rights of adults. It is important to address this issue because the United Nations *Declaration* suggests, I think with good reason, that there are differences between children and adults which must be taken into account in any adequate theory of rights. There are two extremes to be avoided in any discussion of this topic. One extreme makes the assertion that children have no rights at all. But, I have suggested above that universal rights, in order to be universal, must extend at least to all present and future human beings. Unless one is prepared to deny the humanity of children, the first extreme is incompatible with the notion of universal rights. The other extreme contends that there is no difference between the rights of children and the rights of adults. I shall respond to this view by pointing to a case of a difference between children and adults which has some impact upon the rights possessed by each.

As has already been noted, some theories of human rights focus upon the possession by the individual of those qualities which make us persons. The most frequently proposed qualities are rationality, freedom, and autonomy. An example of such a theory can be found in an article written by H. L. A. Hart. Hart argues that, in order to have a natural right, one must be capable of choice. Since animals and infants do not possess this capacity, it is inappropriate to speak of them as having rights.[14] This position leads to a series of difficulties which center around the transition from the absence to the presence of the capacity in question. In a book entitled *Equal Rights for Children*, Howard Cohen points to what he sees to be the arbitrariness associated with this position: "... We always need a precise line to divide those with rights from those without. But it is impossible to draw a precise line between childhood and adulthood, for growing up is a develop-

mental process, and there is never a moment at which someone who did not have one of the adult capacities suddenly acquires it."[15] This is a serious problem for any theory of human rights which relies solely upon individual capacities since such a theory either inevitably excludes some humans at either end of the spectrum (*e.g.*, the infant and the senile) from the possession of rights or attempts to distinguish between the potential and actual possession of rights as a way of avoiding the exclusion of some. Either alternative is faced with the impossibility of drawing a precise line.

By way of contrast, a relational theory of human rights acknowledges both the universality of human rights and the real differences between children and adults. A. I. Melden develops such a relational theory in his book, *Rights and Persons*. First, he stresses the continuity of the developmental process in human life:

> ... the concept of an infant that we employ is the concept of a human being *in* its infancy. The conception of an infant connects, therefore, as essentially with the life of a human being, with respect to which infancy is only one segment, as much so as present phenomena of human life such as purpose, intention and prudence, etc. connect essentially with the future phases and conditions of human beings.[16]

Given this continuity, there can be no ground for excluding any segment of human life from the possession of rights.

But, such rights must not be seen as isolated entities which individuals possess in independence of one another. Rather, the language of rights is used to describe aspects of certain situations in which persons interact with one another. An example of how universal rights arise out of situations is given by Melden in his discussion of the rights of infants.

> If the infant son does have rights *vis a vis* his father, these are moral rights grounded in the way in which their lives are joined then and there, and not merely in some future status into which hopefully the infant will develop. He has

a right to the care and protection he can receive from his father, and to whatever the latter must now do in order to ensure that he will develop properly as a moral agent . . .[17]

The right the infant son has in this example to care and protection is universal in the sense that it is applicable to all human beings at that stage in life. What this implies is that the rights we have are relative to our stage of life and the situation we are in. This raises the question of whether there are any rights applicable to all stages of human life. Melden argues for a basic right which is applicable to all stages and which provides the basis for all others rights. He describes this right in these terms: "The right that persons have, merely as agents, must be the right to promote those interests they have as the specific human beings they are whatever their plans, projects, hopes and aspirations may be, interests distinct from the moral interest that, truistically, any moral agent has in being accorded his moral right."[18] Again, such a right must not be seen in isolation since it can only thrive in an atmosphere in which there is mutual respect for the rights of others.

Given the above framework in which rights are relative to one's stage in life and the interpersonal context of the community one is part of, the recognition of real differences between children and adults naturally follows. It is evident, for example, that while the infant who is dependent upon parents is entitled to their care and protection, the parents who are full participants in the give and take of society are not entitled to their parents' care and protection. The transition from dependency as an infant to full participation as an adult is gradual. Consequently, no precise line can be drawn at any presumed point where dependency ceases and full participation begins. It might be objected that the relational theory of rights is subject to the same line-drawing problem as the theory which relies on individual capacities alone. Two points must be noted in response. First, the theory that relies on individual capacities alone seeks to determine the presence or absence of universal rights whereas the relational theory affirms the presence of universal rights at all stages of human life. Secondly, the line-drawing problem arises in the relational theory at precisely the point one would expect it to arise, namely, at the transition from the general to the concrete. When, for example, does the right to care and protection cease? A general rule cannot be established to answer this question. The only alternative is the messy one of examining concrete situations of interpersonal interaction and attempting to discern on a case by case basis what rights are operative in those situations. C.A. Wringe, in a book entitled *Children's Rights: A Philosophical Study*, nicely sums up what I consider to be the fundamental orientation of a relational theory of rights:

> If children's rights differ from those of adults, it is not because children are any less persons or entitled to any less consideration but because their needs and capacities, and consequently their interests, differ from those of adults in ways that have important consequences for their rights of freedom and democratic participation as well as for their welfare rights.[19]

The Right to Education

Up to now, the general nature of human rights has been investigated in an attempt to clear the way for an exploration of the right to education. It is impossible within the confines of this short paper to present a full-blown theory of human rights. Thus, only those features of such a theory which are particularly salient to an examination of the right to education enunciated in the United Nations *Declaration* were considered. As we turn to this examination, the following points should be kept in mind. First, I have argued on behalf of a relational theory of rights as providing more adequate support for the consideration of rights in general and positive rights in particular. Secondly, I have suggested that the concept of universality can be viewed as flexible within the relational framework without losing its characteristic of universal applicability. If we reflect upon Melden's and Hook's comments about the significance of the moral community in the determination of rights, flexibility becomes essential. For, as the moral community develops and strengthens itself, our sense of what constitutes human rights is broadened. As a result, it is not surprising that claims to rights have grown as people have become more sensitive to the interests and needs of all members of the community including themselves.

Let us recall at the outset that the right to education is a positive right to what is in some measure a scarce resource. In what sense is education a scarce resource? First, on a practical level, the United Nations *Declaration* implies a connection between education and schooling. On this level, education can be viewed as an economic resource competing with other economic resources for a limited supply of funds. One might argue that, on a theoretical level, education in a true sense is quite distinct from and perhaps even opposed to schooling. After all, one important way in which Socrates saw himself as different from the Sophists was that he charged no fee for what he did. However, even on a theoretical level, education is a scarce resource since there are psychological limits which impinge on the dynamics of the learning process. Thus, to say, as the United Nations *Declaration* does, that "Everyone has the right to education" is not to mean that everyone is entitled to be fully educated. What this means will vary at least in accordance with the resources (economic, psychological, or other) available within any given community and the other important claims placed upon those resources.

It is possible to pin down in some more exact way what the right to education entails? The United Nations *Declaration* asserts that everyone should receive an elementary education as a minimum. Other commentators move away from the traditional quantitative divisions of schooling as a standard and argue for qualitative norms in determining the fulfillment of this right. For example, C. A. Wringe suggests that, under normal circumstances, ". . . the individual is entitled to receive education from the community, at least until he has gained sufficient insight into the pursuit of knowledge and the various modes of human understanding to decide for himself whether to continue this pursuit by his own efforts and at the expense of whatever resources of his own he may possess."[20] Emphasis upon qualitative norms make it more difficult to assess whether the right has been fulfilled. Once again, we confront the reality that individual and communal situations differ and any judgment regarding the fulfillment of this right must be rendered on a case by case basis. This is not to denigrate the value of the quantitative minimum standard proposed by the United Nations. After all, we live in a world in which many humans receive no formal schooling and to press for universal elementary education is a laudable ideal.

One puzzling feature of the United Nations *Declaration* is its statement that "Elementary education shall be compulsory." In ideal terms, education can be described as a process of interaction in which the parties are freely engaged in inquiry. Can this process genuinely occur when one is compelled to participate at its earliest stages? Some propose that compulsion is incompatible with the right to education. For example, Richard Farson includes the following in his list of children's rights: "THE RIGHT TO EDUCATE ONESELF. *Children should be free to design their own education, choosing from among many options the kinds of learning experiences they want, including the option not to attend any kind of school.*"[21] In my estimation, this view overlooks the real differences between children and adults. It is clear to me that adults should have the sort of right Farson delineates. But, should all children have such a right? C. A. Wringe describes the right to education which children have as a welfare right. He explains what he means this way: "To claim a welfare right to education is to claim that an individual cannot provide for his own education and that if he does not receive education from others including those against whom he may have special rights, then he is liable to substantial harm."[22] What Wringe suggests is that young children are simply not in a position to choose their own education. I take this as an instance of the process of development from dependency to full participation in society. The ordinary six-year-old is neither fully dependent on others nor fully prepared to participate as an equal in all societal activities. Given this state of affairs, some element of compulsion is justifiable at the early stages of education. Let me reiterate, however, that any decision about whether a particular individual should be compelled to attend formal schooling should be reached only after a careful examination of the relevant factors in that situation.

A further element to be considered in the United Nations *Declaration* is the assertion that "Parents have a prior right to choose the kind of education that shall be given to their children." Do parents have such a right and, if so, what is its basis? If we agree with what was said in the preceding paragraph, it is evident that someone must choose the kind of education the young child receives. Under normal circumstances, it is appropriate that parents undertake this responsibility. A. I. Melden endorses the right-duty relationship which this position entails:

> But the education, for example, that is in an infant's or child's interests . . . need only be (a) the moral education required for its development into a responsible moral agent, and (b) the measures taken for the discovery, development and effective utilization of its talents in such a way that the adult to be will be able to develop interests suitable to his talents and enjoy the exercise of his rights as a human being. What in this way is now done in the child's interest is that to which the child is then and there entitled; and in acting in this way parents are acting responsibly, meeting the obligations they have then and there to the child who depends upon it for its support and guidance as it grows in maturity.[23]

In the young child—parent relationship, then, the young child has a right to education and the parent has the duty to provide the form of educa-

tion which is in the child's best interest. In situations where this duty is clearly neglected, society should intervene to protect the young child's right.

How, then, can what is clearly a parental duty be interpreted as a right? One way to respond to this question might be to argue that the United Nations *Declaration* is simply mistaken in speaking of a prior right instead of a duty. However, there is another, more fruitful way of resolving this issue. The relational theory of rights recognizes that society consists of a complex web of interrelationships. In this instance, we have examined the young child-parent relationship and have discovered a right and a correlative duty. Another relationship which has a bearing upon this matter is that between the family and what can be loosely termed the state. Frederick Schoeman asserts that, in this relationship, the family has certain rights. One of these is the right to autonomy. "The right to autonomy entitles the adults of the family to make important decisions about the kinds of influences they want the children to experience and entitles them to wide latitude in remedying what they regard as faults in the children's behavior."[24] It is reasonable to infer from this statement that parents have the right vis-a-vis the state to decide what education their children will receive, subject to the limitations already noted above. Such a right takes priority under normal circumstances over the state's obligations regarding the education of its citizens.

Conclusion

In this paper, I have selected Article 26 of the United Nations *Declaration* as the focal point for a treatment of the right to education. The main conclusion is that adoption of a relational theory of human rights best enables us to make sense of what Article 26 proposes. The two strengths of this theory are its universality and its flexibility. By reason of its universality, a relational theory provides a sound basis for the rights enunciated in the United Nations Declaration. Indeed, only a universal theory can provide such a basis. By reason of its flexibility, a relational theory is able to distinguish between what is universal and what is absolute. Human rights are universal in the sense described in this paper, but they are not absolute or unchanging. This helps us understand that a simple assertion of a right to education is not enough. We must situate that right in a complex structure of developing relationships in order to endeavor to do full justice to its meaning. The actual analysis of the right to education has not proceeded very far, but I hope that something of significance has been accomplished, namely, the establishment of a theoretical framework within which such an analysis can be effectively carried out.

Footnotes

1. A. I. Melden, ed., *Human Rights* (Belmont, Calif.: Wadsworth Publishing Company, Inc., 1970), Appendix IV, p. 148. I shall refer to this document in the text as the United Nations *Declaration*.
2. See Paul W. Taylor, *Principles of Ethics: An Introduction* (Belmont, Calif.: Wadsworth Publishing Company, Inc., 1975), pp. 26-29 for an explanation of this term.
3. The question of whether some of these rights can be extended to other living beings will not be considered in this paper.
4. Cf. John Stuart Mill, *Utilitarianism*, ed. Samuel Gorovitz (Indianapolis: The Bobbs-Merrill Company, Inc., 1971), Chapter V, pp. 42-57.
5. *Ibid.*, p. 50.
6. John Dewey, *Reconstruction in Philosophy* (Boston: The Beacon Press, 1957), p. 177.
7. Sidney Hook, "Reflections on Human Rights," *Philosophy and Public Policy* (Carbondale, Ill.: Southern Illinois University Press, 1980), p. 78.
8. Immanuel Kant, *Grounding for the Metaphysics of Morals*, trans. James W. Ellington (Indianapolis: Hackett Publishing Company, 1981), p. 36.
9. Ronald Dworkin, *Taking Rights Seriously* (Cambridge, Mass.: Harvard University Press, 1978), p. 198.
10. A. I. Melden, *Rights and Persons* (Berkeley Calif.: University of California Press, 1977): pp. 25-26.
11. Hook, p. 79.
12. Charles Fried, *Right and Wrong* (Cambridge, Mass.: Harvard University Press, 1978), p. 110.
13. Peter Singer, "Rights and the Market," in *Ethical Theory and Business*, ed. Tom L. Beauchamp and Norman E. Bowie (Englewood Cliffs, N.J.: Prentice-Hall, Inc., 1979), pp. 74-75.
14. H. L. A. Hart, "Are There Any Natural Rights?" in *Human Rights*, ed. A. I. Melden, p. 66.
15. Howard Cohen, *Equal Rights for Children* (Totowa, NJ.: Littlefield, Adams and Co., 1980), p. 48.
16. A. I. Melden, *Rights and Persons*, p. 223.
17. *Ibid.*, p. 73.
18. *Ibid.*, p. 135.
19. C. A. Wringe, *Children's Rights: A Philosophical Study* (London: Routledge and Kegan Paul, 1981), p. 151.
20. *Ibid.*, p. 148.
21. Richard Farson, "Birthrights," in *The Children's Rights Movement*, ed. Beatrice Gross and Ronald Gross (Garden City, N.Y.: Anchor Press, 1977), p. 326.
22. C. A. Wringe, p. 139.
23. A. I. Melden, *Rights and Persons*, p. 150.
24. Frederick Schoeman, "Rights of Children, Rights of Parents, and the Moral Basis of the Family," *Ethics*, 91 (October 1980), p. 10.

Children's Educational Rights

Bertram Bandman

Part One:
The Child's Right to Inquire

Introduction

What do you as a teacher or parent say to a child,[1] if the child asks nonstop questions like "What do clouds eat?" or "Is the tree proud of being a tree?" or "Is Jesus the same size as God or slightly smaller?"[2]? Or "Where did we come from?" and "Can God be everywhere at once?"[3]? What will you say? Or if a child asks the sort of question Mitya asks in *The Brothers Karamazov*,[4] "Why is there so much suffering?" or "Why are there so many poor people?," how will you answer? Or if a child asks another child, "Why did your father die?" or "How can I develop products that may be harmful?" and "Why shouldn't I think of and help only myself?," do you tell the child not to ask such questions or find ways not to answer? If you do, are you guilty of "stifling the child's imagination" or are you helping the child?

In this paper, I will consider whether a child has any rights at all, whether a child has a right to inquire, what questions a child has a right to ask, what limits, if any, there are to a child's right to inquire and what reasons there may be for such limits. I will first sketch out four positions that have been taken on a child's right to inquire. After identifying several meanings of "rights" and of "inquiry," I will argue against the first, second and fourth, and argue for the third position.

Four Positions on a Child's Right to Inquire

Four positions regarding a child's right to inquire, which I will briefly explicate, are that: (i)

A child has no rights whatsoever. (ii) A child has welfare rights but no option rights.[5] (iii) A child has limited option and welfare rights, including limited rights to inquire. (iv) A child has unlimited and absolute rights, including the right to inquire, without restrictions.

Regarding the first position, Thomas Hobbes (1588–1679) argues that children, as with other dependents who are not capable of reasons and who have no power to make contracts, have no rights.[6] Parents have rights of dominion over their children as sovereigns have over their subjects. Parents have the power of life or death over their children;[7] and have a right to benefit from their children in exchange for the care parents take "to nourish and instruct" their children.[8] Robert Filmer, a contemporary of Hobbes, argues that since all children as children of Adam are born in "subjection to their parents," their parents deriving absolute authority from the first father, Adam, have exclusive divine rights over their children. Consequently parents may do with their children as they wish. The right of parents to kill their children is not confined to infancy. Filmer cites the case of Casius who put his son to death "by throwing him down the Tarpeian Rock."[9]

A second position is that children have welfare rights but no option or liberty rights. This means children have rights to be given adequate subsistence in the form of nutrition, shelter, clothing and care; but such children have no decision-making rights. According to this position, "parents know best," that which is "in the best interests of children." Children have a right to be protected and cared for, but not rights to make decisions. This position in child-parent relations is sometimes identified as Paternalism and is associated historically with the views and arguments of John Locke and J. S. Mill. To Locke, parents are guardians, whose power over children, however, is temporary. Locke writes that "the bonds of this subjection" "are like swaddling clothes they are wrapped up in and supported in the weakness of their infancy; age and reason, as they grow up, loosen them, till at length they drop quite off and leave a man at his own free disposal."[10] To J. S. Mill, liberty rights are restricted to those who are "in the maturity of their facilities. We are not speaking of children or of young persons below the age . . . of manhood or womanhood."[11] More recently O. O'Neill and W. Ruddick argue that "children have less than standard liberty rights." Parents have legitimate standing in making some, even . . . life-affecting decisions, for their children.[12] And T. S. Sutton argues that "to the extent that (children) have basic needs" children cannot be denied welfare rights and "to the extent that (children) lack mature intellectual faculties . . . children are relevantly different from rational adults and consequently, can properly be excepted from ascriptions of options rights."[13]

On a third view of rights, children have not only a right to be provided for, but also to be treated with respect, autonomy and the capacity to make decisions.[14]

According to a fourth position, children do not only have option and welfare rights, but their rights are unlimited, absolute and exceptionless. The idea of absolute rights attributable to children is a view that is held by some advocates of children's rights[15] and is found in some parts of some manifestos on children's rights, including *The United Nations Declaration of the Rights of the Child*.[16] According to this document, every person, including every child, is entitled "to all the freedoms set forth." These include, for example, the right of every child to achieve the "full and harmonious development of his personality."

In the progression from children having no rights to children having absolute rights, we move from children being regarded as subservient to children as capable of becoming independent, full persons to children being accorded unlimited freedom.

What Are Rights? And What is "Inquiry"?

Three conditions seem to identify a right. One condition of any right is freedom. To have a right based on freedom is to be accorded a sphere of individual autonomy, to exercise one's right or not as one chooses and to be immune to the charge of wrongdoing for exercising one's right. It is the area of one's life over which as Joel Feinberg aptly puts it, one is "the boss."[17] The right to be free importantly includes the right not to be brainwashed, lied to, kept ignorant, deceived, tricked, unwillingly put to sleep or given tranquilizers, ritalin or having one's body touched without permission, or more generally, treated involuntarily or coerced without compelling justification.

A second condition of any rights is that they imply correlative duties against others. A right is not only a freedom; a right is a protected freedom to act. A right accordingly imposes relevant duties against others not to interfere. If Jane has a right to a school lunch, someone or some group has a duty to provide for Jane's right. As Joel Feinberg puts it, "rights are necessarily the grounds of other people's duties."[18] The practice of rights depends on others carrying out corresponding duties. Rights consequently imply back-up rights or the right to claim one's rights.[19]

A third (sometimes overlooked) condition of any right has been well stated by St. Augustine, that "rights flow from the spring of justice." There are no rights without justice.[20] Considerations of justice are necessary to provide a rationally defensible basis for distributing benefits and burdens to the members of a society on a fair, equitable and harmonious basis. Mary's and Henry's right to turn to jump rope then is oriented not by their wealth, beauty, strength, sex race or I.Q. but by a relevant consideration of fairness, such as lining up.

To have rights then means one is (1) free to exercise and effectively claim such rights; (2) one's rights impose appropriate duties against other relevant persons; and (3) freedoms and duties are governed by rationally defensible principles of justice, such as that every person's right is based on a fair turn rather than a power or privilege. Whether children can have rights depends on applying these features of rights to a consideration of the four positions on the rights of children previously cited.

We may next distinguish four senses of "inquiry." To inquire may be (a) to express puzzlement, bewilderment, bafflement, paradox or mystery; (b) to seek clarification or explication; (c) to look for relevant facts; and (d) to examine, analyze and evaluate presently accepted answers in (a) through (c), expressing doubt or critical discontent or scrutiny with received answers. Some inquiries can only be expressed in sense (a). For other kinds of questions, there are confirmable or relatively well-established answers, as with some formal or factual inquiries. For still other questions, there are reasons to examine and rigorously to question the answers given in senses (b) and (c); and to inquire in this sense is to inquire in sense (d). Inquiry may include all four senses, and inquiry that (inappropriately) precludes the fourth sense of doubt and questioning is dogmatic; and a contradiction to what it means, in part, to educate a person. Inquiry may occur in one or more of these four senses, and does not consist in blocking the fourth sense from applying.

If a child has a right to ask in these four senses, then other relevant persons, such as teachers, parents, principals, lunch room aides and school nurses, for example, presumably have the corresponding obligation to satisfy such inquiries. For a child to have a right to inquire, if there is such a right, means the child is not excluded from inquiring in all four senses.

Applying the correlativity of rights and duties to the child's right to inquire, we may distinguish between a child's right to inquire fully and a child's right to inquire partially. The right to inquire partially means one has a right to ask but not a right to a reasoned answer, whereas the right to inquire fully means one has the right to ask and to a reasoned answer, as well.

Arguments Against the First, Second and Fourth Positions on Children's Rights

(i) Arguments Against the First View. One hears the argument that children have no rights to inquire, having no rights at all, that elders may have obligations to educate and care for children, but that children have no rights. This argument, however, is inconsistent with what education is largely about, namely to encourage children to think on their own, which presupposes at least one right, the right to inquire. If a child cannot choose which of several answers to a question is correct, by asking for example, "Is it *p* or not *p*?" the child might never find out which answer is correct.[21]

Readers of the early pages of Book I of Plato's *Republic* may recall an analogous rebuttal Socrates employs against Thrasymachus, who demands that Socrates answer what justice is but not answer that justice is what is obligatory, useful, advantageous, profitable or expedient. Socrates thereupon asks how one could answer what the factors of twelve are if all the factors are ruled out from being used as answers.[22]

Analogously, if children have no right to inquire, then they cannot answer any question by thinking freely and uncoerced beforehand. Without at least the right to inquire, children may produce catechismical or rote or memorized answers, but not thought-out answers. To think, children have at least one right, the right to inquire, to ask which of several answers of the form p or not p is correct. If a child does not inquire in at least one of four senses [(a) to express puzzlement, (b) to seek clarification, (c) to find relevant information and (d) to examine, analyze and evaluate answers given in answer to (a), (b) and

(c) (which are logically consistent with what it means to think)], how can a child ever find out whether to choose an answer of the form p or not p as the correct answer? The answer, it seems, is that a child cannot find anything out if barred from the right to inquire in one of these four senses of "inquiry." A child therefore has at least one liberty right, the right to inquire.

"Rights" that are attributed exclusively to some group of adults, "rights" that are unfairly distributed, "rights" that are not universal (in the sense that they are conferred equally to all beings with relevantly similar characteristics), are not rights at all, but powers. The injustice associated with avarice, greed, cruelty and arbitrariness eliminates (i).

(ii) Arguments Against the Second View. Essentially the same argument against (i), namely that children cannot learn to think effectively without at least the right to inquire, applies as well against the second position, but with a twist. For the second position grants children the right to be taken care of, fed, clothed, sheltered and possibly even "educated" to some extent; but not yet given liberty rights or the right to choose. A plausible reason sometimes given is that elders have to look out for the good of the child, that a young child is not yet able or ready to cross the street unaided. Analogously, a teenager is not yet ready to inquire without adult supervision out of adult concern for the teenager's own good.

However, even if one grants the case for child "readiness," which is developmentally indicated, the child cannot learn to make choices, even small or safe choices, without practice in choosing. How did we learn what our rights were—such as they are—except that we, too, had rights accorded to us in some way or other? If the rights we were accorded did not include liberty rights, rights to exercise discretion, or at least the right to inquire, it would seem that our other rights, rights to receive assistance, would be quite inadequate. Rights to receive help but never the right to make decisions are not rights that, incorporate an essential feature of rights, namely freedom to

choose. Ample arguments and evidence in John Dewey's educational writings, as well as before and since his works, show that the way to teach freedom and the closely related concept of respect for rights is to practice these. Rights are learned, asserted and protected by being attributed to people, by being honored and respected in practice and by public condemnation of its violations. If a child has no liberty rights, no standing with adults, how will the child learn to assert himself or herself as a person? For a child to have no rights of freedom to choose would seem to leave a child without any real rights at all and render its life as a child "morally impoverished."[23] Position (ii) therefore reduces to (i) to which all the objections against (i) apply.

(iv) Arguments Against the Fourth View. Contra the fourth position that children have unlimited rights, if by unlimited rights, one means unrestricted freedoms to act without restraint, this would mean children can do whatever they feel like doing. A child's unrestricted right to inquire could lead to a child's invasion of the rights of privacy of others. Such "rights" could also lead to building dangerous bombs or breeding harmful viruses, or leave the child in some way free to harm itself without adequate adult guidelines. Since rights depend on other people's corresponding duties, rights that imply no restraints would soon result in the violation of other people's rights. Rights without restraints imply the elimination of rights.

The main objections to (iv) are primarily two. The first is that this position attributes unlimited rights to every being without sufficient regard to the practical problem as to how such rights, rights that imply correlative duties against others, could possibly be exercised. If rights are so impracticable that they cannot be carried out, then, as M. Cranston aptly points out, such rights impose an impossible burden of duties on others.[24] Such rights are merely "utopian aspirations," he says.

A second objection is that freedom without control or limits leads to confusion and not much personal growth and direction, either in a child's action or in a child's inquiry. And from direction-less inquiry, not much good and rather more harm may be expected. Unleashing children with "liberty rights" on each other with no constraints contributes to the termination of rights for everybody. The fourth position, having unlimited "rights," reduces to the slogan "Do your own thing." Liberty rights without restraints destroys rights.

The indefensibility of (i), (ii) and (iv) leaves us with (iii).

In Defense of a Child's Limited Right to Inquire.

1. Reasons For a Child's Limited Right to Inquire. A reason for a child to have a limited right to inquire is that the child needs this right both to survive and to minimize harm to itself and others. Justice Douglas aptly pointed out in *Yoder v. Wisconsin* that to deny children exposure to education would stunt their future lives.[25] Children without the right to inquire are irreparably harmed in not knowing how to find their way about in the world. They are rendered largely helpless, dependent and intellectually blind; their lives in all likelihood are truncated and fore-shortened, along with the lives of those they affect. A child's right to inquire is also important toward living a decent and fulfilling human life.

Although folk sayings, slogans and platitudes are not always as wise as they are believed to be, some common sayings seem to have the wisdom commonly attributed to them. Three of these closely connected sayings with reference to children are eminently worth singling out because they are relevant, fairly obviously true and significant.

The child's right to inquire stems in part from the too often idle but often repeated platitude that "The Future Belongs to Children" (abbreviated here as FBC). The related slogan, "Pass the Torch," along with the imperative "Make life better for your offspring" come to occupy an important place in intergenerational conscious-

ness, which cannot easily be discounted.[26] These slogans do have some meaning in the sense of being ideals every senior generation expresses for the next generation. For these slogans to have the sort of meaning needed for children to brighten the hopes of the future and for them to take their place in building a worthier future than their predecessors left them, entails that children have the conditions for making a better future possible. The invisible chain of children becoming adults gives adults new duties corresponding to the rights they once had as children, both to be taken care of and to inquire, on how to live well, for example. Not that their rights as parents are any less, but that as parents, they take on new duties, along with their rights as persons. Their rights to inquire will continue during their life span or at least to the extent of their consciousness; without it they are no longer thinking beings. The realization of the FBC slogan depends on children being able to do something to enhance life in the future so that they, too, can eventually take their place as adults.

The FBC slogan concedes the child's right to inquire, revealed, for example, when after we have run out of all kinds of reasons for getting a person to agree with us, we say to that person, "It's your life." What people, including children, have even more than their bodies, is their lives. His or her life is the most precious possession anyone has, even more so than one's liberty; and one's body without life is death. We also say, "It's his life" or "It's her life" to shrug away or rebut a contrary obligation that one shouldn't do X or live like X. We thereby concede a person's authority and autonomy over some vital concerns of a person's life, their area of freedom over which they are sovereign. These rights begin when they are old enough to be conscious. If children are instead treated as unfree, as slaves or obedient and docile unquestioning servants, how and when will they grow up to be free, free to think, at least? The opportunity children have for living like free persons would seem to be improved if they were treated like free persons as early as possible in their lives.[27]

To live as free persons is to be treated with dignity, autonomy, respect and self-respect. If children learn dignity early in life by habitually being treated to dignity, by having their questions respected, for example, then they will learn the value of dignity in the way they and others are treated. A child can grow into personhood with the freedom, autonomy, respect and dignity entailed by personhood if the child has the right to inquire.

Children have to be brought up to be critical thinkers. To be critical thinkers means children are expected to be able effectively to examine the issues and problems that come before them. In order to examine the issues of the day, people, including children, are encouraged to ask questions, to inquire.

In the proverbial folk wisdom, we regard a priority of our culture to be to encourage critical thinking, and to foster associated values like curiosity, interest in learning, and freedom to inquire. The priority of freedom to inquire is given a vitally important place of honor by being designated as a "right." Our culture is heavily invested and dependent on developing effective questioners. So we confer on a child the right to inquire. To confer on a child the right to inquire involves granting the child the freedom to ask and pursue questions no matter where the way leads, as Socrates often pointed out, and which we, following his example, would encourage children to develop. The child's right to inquire then involves not only rights of assistance, but liberty rights as well. If a child has the right to inquire, a child has at least one liberty right, for one cannot inquire without the liberty to do so. If children have the liberty right to inquire, they have at least that much free choice, the option of framing a question in one way rather than another. Without some right to inquire, the child cannot be expected to develop the capacity for making choices which one needs in order to become a person.

2. Limitations Strengthen a Child's Right to Inquire. Unlimited freedom cannot wisely be placed in a child's hands prematurely. For the consequences of unlimited freedom may harm the child or others beyond the ordinary risk persons are willing to take with normal adults. In view of a child's immaturity, the adult provisions of freedom need not be accorded a child all at once; indeed to do so could stunt or misdirect a child's growth and also be harmful to adults. Conferring premature freedom upon a child, freedom the child cannot yet understand, may either be lost on the child or lead to a form of self-induced bondage or harm, such as smoking cigarettes. To let the child run across the street or put its hand on a flame or let it play with explosives or let it eat whatever it wants, let it swim on its own or drive a car—or let it ask questions that lead the child to do these things—without suitable guidance, may lead the child to serious avoidable harm to itself and others.

Autonomy and the right to respect, basic to freedom, imply the right to make choices of increasing complexity in relation to the development of appropriate capacities.[28] Children have limits to their rights to inquire lifted as they become ready to benefit from the exercise of rights.

3. The Development of a Child's Rights to Inquire. A child's right to a fulfilling human life calls for a child's right to inquire as a means of achieving the child's life expectations.

Three models of a child-adult relation seem to orient the developing phases of childhood as well as to reflect the dominant values with which children are perceived. The first is the perception of a child as a dependent, and accompanying this perception are the associated values (as well as disvalues) of care, protection, subordination and subservience. According to a second model, children are perceived as independent, and with this view are such values (as well as possible disvalues) as relative mastery of personal survival skills, motor coordination, individually carrying out life plans and projects and being free to do as one wishes. According to a third model, children are perceived as growing up to become interdependent. Associated with this view are the values of living as well as possible with others, negotiating, compromising, exchanging, giving and taking.

These may be perceived as phases of a child's growth and/or as ways (or value perspectives) to orient the child-adult relationship. As phases of growth nothing more need be said since empirical psychology is better suited toward assessing such distinctions. But as value standpoints, more may be said. The first, while appropriate during infancy and early childhood, if lifelong, makes children into docile, unfree objects, bits of property, slaves, automatons, dutiful but unthinking, subservient and lacking in self-regard. The second throws dependence to the winds and asserts values of self over others. Unbridled freedom leads to one value of rights, freedom, but is blind to another, just relations with others. The third interdependence, coordinates dependence and independence together and, as a well-playing symphony, orchestrates lives together in socially worthwhile and productive enterprises and life plans. Which model sets the aims and process of development of a child's right to inquire?

Charles Dickens' theme in *Great Expectations* shows how one may orient a child's development of the rights to inquire. In this classic novel, Jaggers, the attorney, perceives his role as one of serving Pip, the hero fulfill his life expectations as a gentleman. On this view, jaggers helps prepare Pip to enjoy future life prospects interdependently with others. According to Dickens, "It is the desire of the present possessor of that property that he (Pip) be immediately removed from his present sphere of life and from this place, and be brought up as a gentleman—in a word, as a young fellow of great expectations."[29] Jaggers explains to Pip that Pip has an anonymous benefactor who wishes Pip to grow up to be a "gentleman" of means and comfort, one who will not want for the material needs of a livelihood.

Applying Dickens' theme to the development of a child's right to inquire (and *writ large* to all children), hope and confidence are invested in the child's development of future capacities. The child's right to inquire is seen as basic to the realization of the child's life expectations and a fundamental condition for the development and fulfillment of the child's projects. Applying Dickens' theme also suggests how adults may orchestrate the lifting of limits on a child's rights to inquire.

The orientation that children have great expectations is harmonious with the slogan that "The future belongs to children;" and holds that children independently of their parents have a life of their own to lead, that parents owe their children the best upbringing and help they can provide, and that children owe nothing in return, sometimes expressed in the child's quip, "I didn't ask to be born." The FBC slogan accordingly refutes the argument that children are to be treated in a lifelong plan as subservient. Since the first and second positions, denying children rights and denying them liberty rights, reduce children to permanent subservience, both are equally ruled out by the FBC slogan. For if the future belongs to children, parents do not own or control the lives and interests of their children. The FBC slogan accordingly rules against the attempt to justify the subservience of children.

The fourth position, attributing complete independence to a growing child, while valuable in part in promoting autonomy and independent life projects, does not assure that a child, as it reaches adulthood, will live well with others. The fourth position, whose linchpin is unrestrained independence gone wild, is illustrated by William Golding's theme in *Lord of the Flies*.[30] Here children, well schooled in Egoism, when turned loose, become veritable savages. Independence alone, will not do, except to harm oneself or others more than the total benefit such a position provides.

The moral strength of the FBC slogan is that it coincides with a widely shared moral sentiment, which seems to have the force of natural law behind it, so pervasively and strongly felt is this sentiment, namely to love, care and protect one's offspring. The pervasive moral sentiment to love, care and protect one's offspring provides a justification for a child's rights to inquire. The notion that the future belongs to children accordingly provides the developing goal and target, which orients childrens' rights to inquire.

On this view, dependence and independence are seen as stepping stones on the way toward the mature adulthood of interdependent life, which it is the relevant parents, teachers' and other childrens' role to facilitate, following Jaggers' example as advocate, who sees to it that Pip grows up to be a gentleman.

4. The Threshold of a Child's Right to Inquire. Interdependence implies limits on childrens' rights to inquire. Several examples illustrate the limits of a child's right to inquire. Should children, for example, dissect animals in biology classes?

If one never dissected animals, how would one learn anatomy and physiology? What experience would surgeons have? On the other hand, some people dissect animals just for the fun of it. The issue of how much good or harm to us and other animals seems to determine how much dissection of animals should occur rather than whether or not to do so; but there seems to be no warrant for dissection without limits, with a view to the good dissection brings.

Another example of the limits of children's rights to inquire arises when the parent of a neighboring teenager dies.[31] What questions may a child as well as neighboring adult ask? The limits to what questions may be asked seem to be posted by respect for privacy. Sensitivity to another person's tragedy seems to place a self-imposed restraint against asking a grieving relative, "What was the cause of (his) death?" And if a parent just prior to death had lost his job, neither a neighboring child nor adult would seem to ask, "Why did he get fired? Was he incompetent?" A teenager's friends seem to sense that some questions are not

appropriate, that a child has rights to respect, to privacy and rights to confidentiality at any time, but especially at a tragic time of life. A teenager's friends seem to know not to ask insensitive questions, perhaps on Golden Rule grounds and also of not doing more harm than good, especially in a time of tragedy. The tacit restraints children recognize mark the limits of a child's rights to inquire.

A child's right to privacy and confidentiality (as with adults) calls for obligations of forbearance by adults; and one may attempt to prevent violations by exposing and confronting violations that occur.[32] Abuses of childrens' rights to privacy and confidentiality include school officials revealing private details of students' records, such as childrens' I.Q.'s (except to the children themselves), revealing their parents' income, marital status and the state of their parents' emotional conditions.

There seems to be a reasonable presumption in favor of placing few limits, if any, to a child's right to inquire about matters affecting its private self, including its state of health or illness, its weight, height, I.Q., its looks, its behavior and how it is perceived by one's peers and adults. After all, how does one live up to the Socratic adage, "Know thyself" without being trusted to have one's innermost questions aired and tentatively answered.

High school students may also be limited from asking how to conduct a biological experiment to produce and release lethal viruses. A child may similarly be limited from asking how to manufacture LSD in a chemistry lab.

A child's questions may have no limits imposed by others; the only limits may be those imposed on the answers to a child's questions. And yet, a child is sometimes reminded not to ask "embarrassing questions," such as asking a neighboring child about its parent's death. If there is a liberty right to ask, there is not necessarily a corresponding duty to give a serious, rationally defensible answer, if it is not prudent to give an answer or if no answer is known. So a child has an odd kind of right to inquire if to some questions a child asks, an adult, such as a "professional" physician, for example, either "turns a deaf ear" or otherwise evades the question, and does not take it as a question to be seriously answered.

A child may have a right to ask in the sense of its freedom to express itself, but not a right to inquire in the sense that its right imposes an obligation on others to give a serious answer to the question. An example of such a child's right to ask but not to have an answer is if high school students ask their physics teacher how to build an atomic bomb in their backyards, ruled out on the grounds that harm could result. To almost every question except one that caused personal embarrassment, such as interference with privacy, a child may have the right to ask, but no one else would seem to have a corresponding duty to give a reasoned answer—when a limit is indicated.

A principle is suggested by these examples, good and harm orient and limit a child's right to inquire, and provide guidelines as to what a child may learn.

To the question, "Where did we come from?" there are limits involving primarily a fourth sense of inquiry, limits prescribed by a rational examination of received "answers," rather than outright acceptance. For good rather than harm results if received answers are examined.

In these examples involving the issue of dissection, privacy, especially in tragedy, high school students building atomic bombs, developing lethal viruses, manufacturing LSD or asking where we came from, the limits of their rights to inquire *fully*—in the sense that other relevant persons have a duty to point the way to rationally defensible answers—are determined by what good or harm results. Minimizing harm and maximizing good govern the development of a child's rights to inquire.

What counts as good or harmful is heavily but not exclusively influenced by "The Future Belongs To Children" (FBC), "Hand the Torch Down" and "Make Life Better For Your Off-

spring." For these express intergenerational sentiments. They reflect feelings people widely, deeply and positively share about children and give a justification for the child's limited rights to inquire. To adopt FBC and its companion sayings or that life should be at least as good as or better for our offspring than it is for us, implies that children are the worthy sorts of beings who have rights to inquire, limited by their capacity to exercise them, resulting in the probability of their doing good rather than harm to themselves and others. The assumption is that children will develop beneficially by having rights and that they indeed need rights to develop so as to inherit a worthwhile future. Within these limits designed to bring about good rather than harm then, a child's right to inquire rules out any attempt to "bar the way of inquiry."

A child's limited right to inquire and the learning of that important right by the child, in relation to the rights and responsibilities of others, shows how a child's right to inquire is a vital link to the child's development as a person in the world, one in whom a future is invested and whose turn it is to fulfill the previous generations hopes and expectations. Without an appropriately limited right to inquire a child is consequently not worth very much to itself or others.

Conclusion

For a child to learn to have and cherish rights worth having calls for a child's growing awareness of the significance and limits of rights as linked to its development as a person. The nurturing of persons from infancy to old age within a tradition that values rights and whose members participate in the deliberate education of rights and its values, freedom, duties and justice, will also value a child's right to inquire within defensible limits, rights whose implied principles and policies are designed to contribute to good rather than harm.

The motivation to secure rights in the recent history of the human race consists in the drive toward human emancipation from humanly induced harm and fatality.[33] Since rights are not found in nature, like gold or oil, for children to have rights calls on them to learn the meaning, value and importance of their rights. The child's learning of the right to inquire within limits rests on some old platitudes like "The future belongs to children" and "Make life better for your offspring." For a child to learn to have rights worth having includes the right to inquire. The child's learning of the right to inquire, limited by available adult wisdom as to what causes good or harm, may result not only in children learning to inquire about what is relevant, significant and morally worthwhile, but may result also in the improvement of life in this and succeeding generations.

Footnotes

* I wish to thank Matthew Lipman for his encouragement and for suggesting the title of this paper.

1. In this paper I use "child" to refer to any legal minor, generally under eighteen years of age.

2. R. Bambrough, "Unanswerable Questions," *Proceedings of the Aristotelian Society* Supplementary Volume LX (1966), p. 170.

3. Saul Kripke, is said to have asked his mother when three years of age, "If God is truly everywhere. Dorothy Kripke said yes, whereupon the child asked if this meant he had squeezed part of God out of the kitchen by coming in and taking up some of His space." According to Mrs. Kripke, her son "seemed to have an intuitive grasp of the notion that two objects cannot occupy the same space at the same time . . ." *The New York Times Magazine*, August 14, 1977, p. 12.

4. S. Toulmin, *The Place of Reason in Ethics* (Cambridge, England: Cambridge University Press, 1950), p. 210.

5. I will adopt Martin Golding's terms. He refers to option rights as rights to freely make decisions. Welfare rights are rights to receive assistance or benefits, such as food, clothing, maternity benefits, health care and education. See his "Rights: A Historical Sketch" in E. and B. Bandman (eds) *Bioethics and Human Rights: A Reader For Health Professionals* (Boston, Mass: Little, Brown, 1978), pp. 44-50.

6. T. Hobbes, *The Leviathan* (New York: Library of Liberal Arts: Indianapolis: Bobbs Merrill, 1958), Chapter 26, p. 215.

7. T. Hobbes, *The Leviathan*, Chapter 30, p. 267.

8. T. Hobbes, *The Leviathan*, p. 267. See also V. Worsfold, "A Philosophical Justification for Children's Rights" *Harvard Educational Review*, Reprint Series 9, 1974, p. 31.

9. R. Filmer, Patriarcha, in T. Cook (ed.) J. Locke, *Two Treatises of Government* (New York: Hafner), 1947, p. 266. According to two well researched works by P. Singer and M. Tooley, infanticide is not and has not been universally condemned. See P. Singer "Values in Life" in W. Reich (ed.) *The Encyclopedia of Bioethics* (New York: Macmillan) 1978, p. 826; and M. Tooley, "Infanticide: A Philosophical Perspective," in the same work, p. 742.

10. J. Locke, *Two Treatises of Government*, p. 147, par. 55.

11. J. S. Mill "On Liberty," in *Utilitarianism, Liberty and Representative Government* (London: Dent and Sons, 1948) p. 73. See also L. Houlgate, "Children, Paternalism and the Rights to Liberty" in O. O'Neill and W. Ruddick, (eds) *Having Children* (New York: Oxford University Press, 1979), p. 272.

12. O. O'Neill and W. Ruddick (eds), "Caring for Children," in *Having Children*, p. 108.

13. T. Sutton, "Human Rights and Children," *Educational Theory,* Spring, 1978, Vol. 28, No. 2, p. 110.

14. Some philosophical forbears of this position include J. J. Rousseau [See C. Sherover (ed.) *The Social Contract* (New York: Meridian), 1974, p. 13] and I. Kant. According to Kant, "we must allow the child from his earliest childhood perfect liberty (except . . .);" in I. Kant, *Education*, (Ann Arbour: University of Michigan Press, 1960), pp. 27-28. Some recent works on this position, favoring both liberty and welfare rights for children, include N. MacCormick, "Children's Rights: A Test For Theories of Rights" in *Arch. fur Rechts und Social Philosophie*, Bd. LXII, 3, 1976; L. Letwin, "Education and the Constitutional Rights of Children" in *Thinking*, Vol. 1, No. 1, January, 1979, pp. 11-19; L. Houlgate, "Children, Paternalism and Rights to Liberty," in *Having Children*, pp. 266-278; and M. Friquegnon, "Rights and Responsibilities of Young People," in *Thinking*, 1980, Vol. II, No. 1. In educational practice, the work of A. S. Neill, *Summerhill* (New York City: Hart Publishing Co. 1959) embodies the emphasis on both option and welfare rights, otherwise known as faith in the freedom of the child and in assistance to the child.

15. See, for example, B. Gross and R. Gross (eds.), *The Children's Rights Movement* (Garden City, N.Y.: Anchor Books, 1977, especially M. Kohler, "To What Are Our Children Entitled?", pp. 217-232.

16. O. O'Neill and W. Ruddick, (eds.) *Having Children*, pp. 112-114.

17. J. Feinberg, "Voluntary Euthanasia and the Inalienable Right to Life," in *Philosophy and Public Affairs* 7, No. 2 (1978), p. 110.

18. J. Feinberg, *Social Philosophy* (Englewood Cliffs, N.J.: Prentice-Hall, 1973), p. 58.

19. See J. Feinberg, "Rights, Duties and Claims," *American Philosophical Quarterly*, 3, No. 2 (April, 1966), p. 143.

20. St. Augustine, *The City of God* (Cambridge, Mass.: Harvard University Press, Loeb Classics, 1960), p. 207.

21. A similarly decisive argument was used by Noam Chomsky against B. F. Skinner to prove that there was some free will. For a somewhat dubious critique but helpful to the point at issue, see T. Machan, *The Pseudo-Science of B. F. Skinner* (New Rochelle, N.Y. Arlington House Publishers), 1974.

22. F. M. Cornford (ed.) *Plato's Republic* (New York: Oxford University Press, 1951), pp. 9-10.

23. See R. Wasserstrom, "Rights, Human Rights and Racial Discrimination" in A. I. Melden (ed) *Human Rights* (Belmont, Calif: Wadsworth, 1970) p. 104.

24. M. Cranston, "Human Rights: Real and Supposed" in D. D. Raphael (ed.) *Political Theory and The Rights of Man* (Indianapolis: Indiana University Press, 1967), pp. 49-51.

25. Yoder v. Wisconsin 406 U.S. 205 (1972). Also in *Having Children*, pp. 280-305.

26. An expression of this sentiment is found in the *United Nations Declaration of the Rights of the Child*, which states that "mankind owes to the child the best it has to give." See O. O'Neill and W. Ruddick (eds.) *Having Children*, p. 112.

27. Contra M. Friquegnon in "The Rights and Responsibilities of Young People," we do not rehearse a child for freedom. As we live in the classroom (as John Dewey reminded us) not rehearse or prepare for life, we do not prepare or rehearse for freedom. We learn freedom from childhood on by practicing freedom.

28. For a discussion of "capacities" in relation to restrictions on liberty rights in children, see L. Houlgate, *The Child and the State: A Theory of Juvenile Rights* (Baltimore, Md.: John Hopkins University Press, 1980), pp. 61-82.

29. C. Dickens, *Great Expectations* (New York: Washington Square, 1976), p. 133.

30. W. Golding, *Lord of the Flies* (New York: Putnam Sons), 1954.

31. See M. Lipman, Lisa (Caldwell, N.J.: Universal Diversified Services, 1976), pp. 83-85, 98-100.

32. J. Bronars sensitively recounts abuses in "Children's Privacy and Compulsory Schooling" in M. Silverman (ed.) *The Experience of Schooling* (New York: Holt, Rinehart and Winston, 1971), pp. 220-234. For a related discussion of problems that arise with rights in a biomedical context, see B. and E. Bandman, "The Nurse's Role in an Interest-Based View of Patients' Rights," in S. Spicker and S. Gadow (eds.) *Nursing: Images and Ideals* (New York: Springer, 1980), pp. 125-147.

33. One has no rights against earthquakes, racoons in the jungle, rabies-infected dogs and ice capped mountains; only against people.

Part Two:
The Adolescent's Rights to Freedom, Care and Enlightenment

Introduction

Let's suppose someone claims that Barbara, 15, an Amish adolescent, has a right to go to a public school from the ninth grade on in place of an Amish vocational school. Her parents claim they have a right to decide. Whose claims are we to take most seriously? Questions arise about the right to enlightenment implied here, such as: (1) Is the right to enlightenment different from the older dichotomy of option and subsistence rights, or rights to freedom and rights to care? and (2) What is the relationship between an adolescent's right to enlightenment and the older rights to freedom and rights to care?

According to *Wisconsin v. Yoder*,[1] Barbara's parents have option rights over her future. Does Barbara have, as Justice Douglas asked, no right to be heard regarding her education? Has Barbara no moral standing in court? It is, after all, her future, not her parents' future. According to the Supreme Court's ruling, Barbara does not have such a right. According to some philosophers, she does not have a moral right to leave the Amish sect until she is eighteen. We need some other right to give relief to this type of case, where an adolescent has neither a self-determination right or a right that "trumps" her parents' option right to decide her future. If Barbara's parents have legal rights to decide where to send her for the ninth and tenth grades, which they have under Yoder, then Barbara's parents have all the rights and she is left stranded.

Barbara's parents have a right to keep her on an Amish farm and forego the opportunities, in Justice Douglas's words, to choose to become "a pianist or an astronaut or an oceanographer."[2] To have these options, she will have to "break away from the Amish tradition."[3] Barbara's parents can "harness" her to "the Amish way of life" and, to again paraphrase Justice Douglas, if her education in the ninth and ten grades is "truncated," her "entire life may be stunted and deformed." According to Justice Douglas, "If a parent keeps his children out of school beyond the grade school, then the children will be forever barred from entry into the new and amazing world of diversity that we have today . . .[4]

The view that it is morally acceptable to keep an adolescent stunted and deformed is a view that is congenial to at least one philosopher. This philosopher favors dwarf parents' rights to give birth to a dwarf instead of a normal child if the parents could choose to have either.[5] The dwarf analogy flies in the face of adult procreative responsibilities to their children. If anything is plain in child-parent relationships, it is that parents owe their children more than to raise them as dwarfs if the parents could do otherwise, even if that means giving their children up to adoptive parents. A reason for this procreative responsibility stems from a child's right to be given maximal conditions to flourish.

This example of a claim to an adolescent's right presents a basic issue: To what extent do adolescents have rights? In response to this case, we may note four positions that are sometimes taken on adolescents' rights. These are (1) Adolescents either have no rights or none worth discussing. (2) Adolescents have a right to care, but not a right to freedom or enlightenment. (3) Adolescents have a right to freedom, care and enlightenment, with appropriate constraints. (4) Adolescents have the same rights to freedom, care and enlightenment as adults, with no added constraints. I will try to show that the third position is more defensible than the others as a basis for deciding whose rights in this case are worth taking seriously. In particular, I will present an argument against Joel Deinberg's recent defense of Justice White in *Wisconsin v. Yoder* (1972).

Joel Feinberg's Concept of a Child's Right to an Open Future

Feinberg presents an elegant argument on behalf of a child's right to an open future, which is, in part, puzzling. Feinberg seems strongly supportive of children's rights to an open future. In one passage, he writes:

> an education that renders a child fit for only one way of life forecloses irrevocably his other options. He may become a pious Amish farmer, but it will be difficult . . . for him to become an engineer, a physician, a research scientist, a lawyer or a business executive . . .[6]

In this passage Feinberg seems to favor a child's right to an open future without state or parental roadblocks. Yet, in another passage, Feinberg defends Amish parents' rights to yank their adolescents out of the ninth and tenth grades of a public school in favor of an Amish vocational school. Feinberg agrees with the majority decision in *Yoder*. Feinberg says "I do not wish to contend that the decision in *Yoder* was mistaken."[7] Feinberg agrees with Justice White in a view endorsed by Justices Brennan and Stewart. "These justices," Feinberg says, "join the majority only because the difference between eight and ten years is minor in terms of the child's interests, but possibly crucial for the very survival of the Amish sect . . ."[8]

Feinberg calls rights held in common between children and adults A-C rights[9]; rights belonging only to adults, he calls A rights, such as the right "to vote, to imbibe, to choose one's religion or to stay out all night."[10] Another sub-class of A rights are adult supervisory rights. These rights raise intriguing questions when supervisory rights are in conflict with C rights. Feinberg points to A-C rights children and adults have in common, like not being "punched in the nose or be stolen from."[11] These are distinct from C rights or dependency rights (which also apply to helpless adults). A-C rights are different, in turn, from "rights-in-trust," a sub-class of C-rights. These are rights in escrow, which are saved for children until they reach adulthood.[12] "Rights-in-trust" may be "violated in advance of children being in a position to exercise them."[13] According to Feinberg, "the violating conduct guarantees now that when the child is an autonomous adult, certain key options will already by closed to him."[14] The right-in-trust of a child to walk in the future can be violated, for example, "but cutting off the child's legs."[15] A child will become an adult if the child's basic options are kept open, in which "the child's growth is kept unforced."[16] Among the rights in class C are "anticipatory, autonomy rights," and among these are "rights-in-trust," which Feinberg sums up as "the single right to an open future."[17] Although the "adult does not exist yet, . . . the child is potentially that adult, and it is that adult who is the person whose autonomy must be protected now . . ."[18] The protection of autonomy is needed for "the adult he is to become."[19] For this purpose, Feinberg uses a trustee metaphor in the phrase "rights-in-trust." The trustee protects children's rights in part against themselves, and in part presumably, against parents who would be violative of those rights.

Against Justice Burger's summation in *Yoder*, Feinberg says the goal of education should be to send a child "out into the world with as many opportunities as possible, thus maximizing his chances for self-fullment."[20] One might conclude from passages cited that Feinberg's position in *Yoder* would be with Justice Douglas; but surprisingly, however, Feinberg does not side with Douglas.

Feinberg's Defense of Justice White

In the face of Feinberg's regard for an adolescent's right to an open future, it is surprising to find Feinberg endorsing Justice White's opinion that two more years in the ninth and tenth grades does not outweigh "the survival of the Amish sect."[21] Ever since that decision, one hears over and over that two years, the ninth and tenth grades are not significant in the life of an adolescent of fourteen and fifteen. We hear this again from Feinberg.[22]

In Defense of Justice Douglas's Position

But what happens to the Amish child's right-in-trust to an open future? Does the loss of those two years imply that their rights-in-trust to an open future are less open than those of non-Amish children who do not lose the ninth and tenth grades? Is the difference between ending one's education at the eighth or tenth grade only "relatively slight"? What percentage of adolescents who leave school after the eighth grade actually resume their studies in the eleventh and twelfth grades, the normal prerequisites of college? A student who drops out at the ninth and tenth grades is unlikely to continue to seek further schooling.

"Rights-in-trust" remind one of small nations, not yet ready for independence, who are given trusteeships. On one view, a young nation will be granted independence if it behaves according to the specifications of the "mother country."[23] So, too, an adolescent may be given a "right-in-trust" on the assumption that the adolescent complies with the parent's wishes. But what if the parent's wishes for the adolescent are antithetical to the adolescent's best interests?

Rights-in-trust, rights held by someone other than a right holder, depend on those who are trusted to hold those rights. Such rights are precarious and mask an ambiguity. Also nagging questions arise. What if the trustees are either too devious or unwise to transmit those rights effectively? Even if the adolescent's rights are in the family strong box, so to speak, someone may mishandle them. Such rights-in-trust are more fragile than rights need to be; fragile since adults who hold these rights-in-trust do not always know what is best. Rights which belong to individuals are not held in trust by others. A person's rights reside in that person.

On another view of so called "rights-in-trust," one might refer to the parental or state role in the protection, support or advocacy of a child's or adolescent's rights, rights a young person is not yet ready to exercise, but which belong to that person. Adopting Charles Dickens' terminology, these may be referred to as rights to Great Expectations or as rights to enlightenment. Readers of *Great Expectations* will recall that Jaggars, the attorney, tells Pip that Jaggars' client, wishing to remain anonymous, bequeaths "a sum of money amply sufficient" for Pip's "education and maintenance," designed to enable Pip to "be brought up as a gentleman—. . . a young fellow of great expectations." To this end, Jaggars tells Pip "to please consider me your guardian."[24]

One may distinguish trustees from guardians. Trustees both hold and act on the authority belonging to others, often by exercising considerable discretion. The role of guardians is to protect what belongs to others, somewhat like night watchmen or watchdogs in Plato's *Republic*.[25] Guardians are constrained against taking liberties with those in their charge. The idea of Great Expectation rights conveys the idea of rights-in-care, rights-in-custody, rights in the bank under padlock and key, rights-in-protection rather than rights-in-trust. To be oriented by Dickens' model of upbringing, the rights of an adolescent may thus be identified as rights to enlightenment, which are rights being guarded rather than rights-in-trust.

The difference between trustee and protector, care taker or guardian reveals how one sees children. Feinberg says much that points to parents as protectors. "It is characteristic of parents, . . . not only to protect children from their own folly, but also to protect them from external dangers generally . . ."[26] For some pages in Feinberg's illuminating essay, the adolescent's right is to an open future. For other pages, parents with the help of *parens patriae* are morally permitted "to bend the twig" by pulling an adolescent out of the ninth and tenth grades. For Feinberg to side with Justice White is therefore puzzling.

Interest-Based Rights Over Will-Based Rights

The heart of the difficulty which plagues those who support parents' rights ahead of adolescent's rights may be a dependence on an excessively narrow conception of rights. Some writers identify rights with negative rights only, rights to choose and to be left alone, but not too much else. If a person is helpless, too bad for him or her. On this view, no one has a right to be given help. That view seems morally impoverished, for it fails to account for a person's incapacity to express option rights if a person is either too poor, too physically or emotionally sick, too unenlightened, and powerless to exercise autonomy rights. There are cases in which a person does not know best and in which that person needs help to make the wisest decision, whether an Amish adolescent considering whether to go to the ninth and tenth grades or an adolescent's parents.

To throw this case in relief, take the case of Martin, 14 who has a cleft palate and harelip in need of surgery. Martin's father believes in "mental healing" and in letting "the natural forces of the universe work on the body."[27] Martin's father refuses surgery to repair his son's seriously deformed and unattractive jaw. Martin, when asked agrees with his father.[28] Martin is consequently disfigured. As an adolescent, Martin will need the physical and emotional roadblocks removed. He will need relief if he is to flourish.

Let's turn now to a contrasting case. Henry's parents live in a world where there are only liberty rights to be left alone. As Henry reaches the age of walking and running effectively, his parents say, "Let him go. If he can't make it on his own in the streets, or if he gets hit with a car, too bad. He's got to grow up some time. Might as well be now." So Henry's parents are free of him and Henry is free to roam the streets. Henry can grow up like Oliver in *Oliver Twist* to be a good pickpocket. It's all up to his parents. Henry, too, may have liberty rights, but not rights helpful to his future, should his parents be so thoughtless and uncaring as to let Henry do as he wishes with no concern for how he grows up.

In an important respect Henry's case is like Barbara's or Martin's, whose parents looked after them in a way that stunted their development through roadblocks. Henry, unlike Barbara or Martin, is left on his own. But he, too, is being stunted by being rendered helpless in the face of a need to develop an intellectual compass with which to find his way about in the world. No restriction interferes with Henry's parents' rights. But neither do the other children have safeguards if their parents do not protect their best interests.

Another example is that of Phillip, 13, a mild Downs syndrome in need of heart surgery, whose natural parents refused to consent. Phillips parents said in court that he is better off dead than alive. Phillips parents, armed only with option rights have the right to dispose of their son, to condemn him to death. With his lower than average I.Q. he is in his parents' words "an embarrassment."[29] Phillips, Henry's and Barbara's parents' can do almost anything and, in the eyes of the law, never do any wrong. A strange doctrine indeed that the only kinds of rights are liberty rights to be left alone. These parents, armed with liberty rights, can do as they please to their children and their children have little defense. With the help of decision-making rights, you can shoot strangers on your property. With the help of option rights, Phillips parents can virtually choose to kill their son and not be charged with murder. Is it any wonder that rights talk has come into disrepute?

The view invoked in defense of one's rights to control what happens in and to one's body has recently been called the "will" or "choice" view of rights,[30] an unduly stout form of anti-Paternalism. Identifying one's rights with one's will and desire exclusively is not the only way to decipher one's real rights as an adolescent or parent. One may connect one's rights to one's best interests. There are grounds of justified interference with one's liberty for one's interest and for the good of others. One may be restrained from unknow-ingly harming oneself, or one's children by being prevented from blocking someone's enlightenment rights.

Recently, D. N. MacCormick developed a distinction between a "will-based" view of rights, which emphasizes values associated with freedom and rights of another kind, an interest-based view, which emphasizes benefits conferred equally on all persons, regardless of the capacity to exercise one's will. These rights include the rights of adolescents to "care and nurture."[31] The *U.N. Declaration of Human Rights* (1948) shows that Articles 1-21 are oriented by a "will-based" view; whereas Articles 22-27, which include the right to a decent standard of living for everyone, are oriented by an interest-based view.[32] Rights of this kind have a crucial bearing on deciding quality of life issues quite differently from deciding under the influence of the "will-based" view of rights. And in some crunch cases these interest-based rights may even override will-based rights. In particular, Barbara's parents' rights to decide for their daughter may need to be constrained by her rights to enlightenment.

A similar case could be made in the example of Jay, aged 12, who is happy with his new bicycle, which no one has a right to use without his permission. With the help of liberty rights, he can even take it to bed with him. Supposing Jay, however, is seriously sick and if the only way to get a vital medication is for a younger sister to use Jay's bicycle to get to the nearest drug store, but without Jay's permission. Such an exception would seem to be morally permissible. There are cases in which a person does not know best and in which he or she needs help from a wise friend to make a good decision. If Barbara's parents block her right to enlightenment even for two years, they may not know best; and such a condition may call for Barbara's rights to enlightenment to override her parents' will-based rights to decide on Barbara's future. If a wise friend knows that there is a future for an adolescent, in which a parent could retrospectively after a time say, "Thank you for advising me when I wanted to send my child to an Amish vocational school instead of the ninth and tenth grades," on the grounds that it is an adolescent's right to be enlightened, then we do not think such a wise friend wronged either the parent or adolescent. Ordinarily, to deprive parents of their rights is to do something wrong. But that can't quite be said about Barbara's parents' rights. For Barbara and her parents could conceivably be grateful afterwards on justifiable grounds for giving priority to Barbara's right to enlightenment.

The kind of rights this appeal might require is not to the older political liberty or option rights view, which says, "Don't interfere," but the newer one which says, "Help me, assist me." A view of rights which addresses an adolescent's real needs, that protects an adolescent's rational interests seems the more adequate at such a time. These deeper interest-based rights to live well provide the conditions for the subsequent effective exercise of self-determination rights.

The One and the Many

I have been assuming all along that the Amish parents and the Amish sect have no major rights at stake, but they do. A case for the Amish parents' rights to preserve their way of life also merits more serious consideration than I have given here. There are political and philosophical grounds for taking the Amish parents' case seriously. Respect accorded a minority culture in relation to a dominant majority enables the minority subculture as well as the dominant culture to thrive. The famous words of J. S. Mill of the evil of stifling the free expression of opinion apply with equal force to the expression of minority groups. Readers of Mill's remark will recall that he said that "the peculiar evil of silencing the expression of opinion is, that it is robbing the human race . . . If the opinion is right, they are deprived of the opportunity of exchanging error for truth: If wrong, they lose, what is almost as great a benefit, the clearer perception and livelier impression of truth, produced by its collision with

error."[33] If a majority rules out the right of expression of a minority or dissenting group, not only are the rights of that group jeopardized, but so are the rights of all groups, including the rights exercised by the dominant group. If a dominant cultural group rules against the right of expression of a sub-cultural group, what doing so may gain in the short run, a culture may lose in its long term vitality. In morals and politics, assimilation and accommodation of diverse sub-cultural groups adds to the variety and also to the vitality of such a culture.

In religion, the claim of the rights of a minority is similar to the expression of Fideism, that a faith or way of life has its own sovereign criteria, which an outsider either accepts or rejects. For insiders, to grow up to partake of a way of life is believed to give individuals psychological and group security. But there are other considerations, as well. One also lives in the larger culture. Insulation from the winds of opposing doctrines is too high a price to pay for a culture that values freedom, both for its own good and for the good it brings. So public criteria are needed which provide a rational tribunal to which disputants can appeal for judicious solution of conflicts. The analogy of going before a third party judge to settle conflicts is at times appropriate, especially if there is a wise judge.

In metaphysics, the relation between the culture and sub-culture is known as the problem of "the one and the many," or as "Monism versus Pluralism;" to which the outcome, if any, is far from clear. There are strengths and drawbacks to giving emphasis to either of these aspects of the political version of "the one and the many," rendered alternatively as "order and freedom."

A society that provides a forum of ideas enabling social goals to conflict without annihilating either side or letting one side annihilate the other shows the vitality and robustness of that society, a sign of its capacity to bear a future, analogous to the vitality of a growing person. Intolerance of deviant ideas and exertion of unreasonable controls, which restricts the exercise of free expression, mars the vitality both of a society and of a growing person. But here, too, there are limits. If a subculture seriously threatens the morally wholesome vitality of the dominant culture by demonstrably threatening its continuation, the appropriate constraints are open for reasoned consideration. Everyone has a right to become a member of the Reverend Moon sect, but the Moon sect does not have a right to stifle its members from leaving their ranks. Nor, if Moon sect members become a majority, do they have a right to coerce non-members of the Moon sect into becoming Moon sect members. For all people are enjoined, again by a principle of J. S. Mill's, against becoming slaves.[34]

The same argument applies to the rights and duties of Amish parents and of the Amish sect. If the Amish parents are the sovereigns of their homes and they do not tolerate the receptivity of their children to ideas from the outside world or from a variety of sources, then they, too, mar the development and vitality of their children. When parents make dwarfs of their children as when sub-cultures do the same to their citizens by imposing unreasonable and intolerant forms of social control on their subjects, then it is entirely appropriate to appeal to the larger group or state in its role as *Parens Patriae* to intervene on behalf of cultural vitality, freedom and enlightenment.

The solution, in part, then to the political version of "the One and the Many," in outline form, at least, is to adopt a case by case approach but not without a criterion, the criterion being: Which is most conducive to cultural and intellectual vitality? In the case before us, Barbara's right to enlightenment has a cutting edge over her Amish culture's right to impose handcuffs on her future intellectual prospects.

Conclusion

To opt for an adolescent's right to an open future involves a trilogy of rights including a right to freedom, care and enlightenment, with the rights to care and enlightenment setting appropriate constraints for the parents' and adolescents' right to freedom.

Rights are important to all people. Rights help provide people with dignity and self-esteem as well as self-determination, care, protection, sustenance and fulfillment. In a pinch, however, some rights are more important than others. In the trilogy of an adolescent's rights, freedom to choose is an important part of the rights of parents and adolescents, but as D. N. MacCormick points out, the right to freedom is not the only right.[35] The right to be helped to live a decent, enlightening, worthwhile and fulfilling human life,[36] a life with care, may also be a good; and in a pinch the defense of these other rights may sometimes matter even more than having a choice. Ideally, however, for an adolescent to fulfill a life of expectations, the absence of these three rights to freedom, care and enlightenment is as harmful as the presence of these rights is beneficial.

References

1. Adapted from *Wisconsin v. Yoder*, 1972. in O. O'Neill and W. Ruddick (eds.) *Having Children* (New York: Oxford University Press, 1979), pp. 279-305. By an "adolescent" I refer in this paper to a person between the ages of 12 and 20.
2. Wisconsin v. Yoder, in O. O'Neill and W. Ruddick, eds. *Having Children*, p. 302.
3. *Ibid.*
4. *Ibid.* Strictly speaking, Douglas commits a category mistake here. One's growth can be stunted and one's body may be deformed but not one's life. References to Barbara are to one of the two adolescents, Barbara Miller, whom Justice Douglas pointed out, hadn't been heard.
5. W. Ruddick, "Parents and Life Prospects," in O. O'Neill and W. Ruddick, eds. *Having Children*, p. 133.
6. J. Feinberg, "The Child's Right to an Open Future," in W. Aiken and H. La Follette (eds.) *Whose Child?* Totowa, N.J., Littlefield Adams, 1980, p. 132. Subsequent page references are to Feinberg's paper.
7. J. Feinberg, p. 136.
8. J. Feinberg, p. 137.
9. J. Feinberg, p. 125.
10. J. Feinberg, p. 125.
11. J. Feinberg, p. 125.
12. J. Feinberg, p. 125.

13. J. Feinberg, p. 126.
14. J. Feinberg, p. 126.
15. J. Feinberg, p. 126.
16. J. Feinberg, p. 127.
17. J. Feinberg, p. 126.
18. J. Feinberg, p. 127.
19. J. Feinberg, p. 127.
20. J. Feinberg, p. 135.
21. J. Feinberg, p. 137. As a matter of arithmeticc, since two jurists did not participate, had Justice White voted with Douglas, Douglas's opinion on behalf of the adolescent's right to enlightenment, which was sneeringly dismissed, would have carried the day with a 4-3 majority.
22. J. Feinberg, p. 137.
23. According to E. Barker, F. W. Maitland referred to a trusteeship in the middle ages as "that blessed back stair," to a "most powerful instrument of social experimentation." E. Barker, *Principles of Social and Political Theory*, Oxford, Oxford University Press, 1952, p. 52.
24. C. Dickens, *Great Expectations*, New York: Washington Square, 1976, pp. 133-34.
25. G. M. A. Grube, *Plato's Republic*, Indianapolis, Hackett, 1974, 375e, p. 45.
26. J. Feinberg, p. 141.
27. "In the Matter of Sieferth," in O. O'Neill and W. Ruddick, eds. Having Children, p. 139.
28. A Holder, *Legal Issues in Pediatrics and Adolescent Medicine*, N. Y. J. A. Wiley, 1977, pp. 284-286.
29. Adapted from G. Will, *Newsweek*, April 14, 1980, p. 112.
30. H. L. A. Hart, "Bentham on Legal Rights," in A. W. B. Simpson (ed.), *Jurisprudence* (Oxford: Clarendon Press, 1977) pp. 188-209.
31. D. N. MacCormick, "Rights In Legislation," in P. Hacker and J. Raz, eds. *Law, Morality and Society*, Oxford: Clarendon Press, 1977, pp. 188-209.
32. J. Feinberg, *Social Philosophy*, Englewood Cliffs, N.J., Prentice-Hall, 1973, pp. 94-97.
33. J. S. Mill, "On Liberty," in *Utilitarianism, Liberty and Representative Government*, London: J. M. Dent and Sons, 1948, p. 79.
34. J. S. Mill, "On Liberty," in *Utilitarianism, Liberty and Representative Government*, pp. 157-158.
35. D. N. MacCormick, "Rights in Legislation," p. 208.
36. S. Scheffler, "Natural Rights, Equality and the Minimal State," in J. Paul, ed. *Reading Nozick*, Totowa, N. J. Roman Littlefield, 1981, p. 154.

Children's Responsibilities

Marie-Louise Friquegnon

Part One:
Rights and Responsibilities
of Young People

Liberation movements are many and varied. Among those that have inherited the style, ideology and political activism of the black civil rights movement of the Sixties are women's rights, gay rights, senior citizens' rights and the anti-abortion right-to-life movements. The successes of these movements combined with startling statistics on child abuse have led to the rapid growth of a children's rights movement, which has been attacked by some philosophers who have pointed out difficulties in applying the concept of rights to children. It is my aim in this paper to show that children do have rights, even if not all the rights adults can claim, and that the grounds of at least some childrens' rights are different from the grounds of similar rights of adults. These differences of rights will be shown to be related to different degrees of responsibility.

A different kind of attack on the childrens' rights movement comes from conservatives appalled by increasing juvenile crime, who demand a return to authoritarian education and child rearing and yet also clamor for stiffer criminal penalties for adolescent offenders. Their position is blatantly inconsistent. Degree of liberty goes together with degree of responsibility. If a fourteen year old must automatically obey adults, it is manifestly unfair to hold him or her criminally responsible to the same degree as an adult who is under no one's thumb. It might seem that the liberal position on children's rights is equally inconsistent in proposing increased liberty of the youth together with less severe punishment for juvenile offenses, but I intend to show that there is no contradiction in the liberal position, that, in fact, it is eminently reasonable. My resolution of the apparent paradox will depend on clarification of the concepts of rights, liberty and moral responsibility, and of their interrelations in the ethics of child and adolescent rearing.

Rights

Talk about rights in the context of liberation movements usually involves appeal to "natural," "human," or "absolute" rights. Joseph Margolis has observed, in "Reflections on the Right to Health Care," that "the emptiness of familiar, so-called human rights may be seen at a stroke once it is remembered that, *even though inalienable*, such rights as that of life and liberty are not thought to be necessarily violated by capital punishment . . . In theory, *no one can forfeit his human rights*; he can only forfeit his positive or legal or political rights, that is, the actual particular rights accorded or protected in a particular society."[1] Margolis argues that in talking about rights such as the right to health care it is better to talk about *general* rights, that is, rights that are like natural or human rights in that they "depend on the admission of certain prudential interests such as life, liberty, the pursuit of happiness, dignity of person, security of person," but which, like positive rights, "are formulated in such a way as to favor enforcing or promulgating certain rights and positive obligations." To classify children's rights as natural or absolute is too nebulous and too removed from historical and cultural contexts, while to classify them as positive rights would make them too dependent on local attitudes. The category of general rights reflects most accurately what the UN Bill of Rights for children is aiming at. The Bill is not meant as positive law, but countries with too harsh an attitude toward children would hopefully be pressured into according them more liberty. For example, the Bill states that "The child shall not be admitted to employment before an appropriate minimum age; he shall in no case be caused or permitted to engage in any occupation or employment which would prejudice his health or education, or interfere with his physical, mental or moral development." The principle is admittedly vague; it does not, for example, rule out parental use of children for work at home, no matter how arduous. But it is a helpful tool in pressuring nations to look carefully at harmful child labor practices. For example, Colombia may possibly be persuaded to put a stop to the practice of sending five year old children to work in salt mines.

Rights, whether natural, general or positive, are of two kinds: claim rights and liberty rights, to use Hohfeld's nomenclature.[2] Generally speaking, a liberty right is freedom to do something, while a claim right is the obligation of another to provide one with some good or service. There is an intimate relation between claim rights and liberty rights. If each person has a moral obligation to protect the liberty rights of all, then each of us has a claim right against each other and the state to protect our liberty rights.

Children's rights

The most direct claim children have in our society is their claim on their parents to satisfy their basic needs. Their legal claims (positive rights) are narrower than their moral claims (general rights). The latter could include a claim to kind treatment, whereas the former would at most include a claim to treatment that is not cruel. More positive features of child rearing cannot be required by law, if only because we are uncertain how to ensure them.

If the rights of children to care and protection by their biological parents were natural rather than general rights, then communal societies in which the care of children is the responsibility of others would violate such alleged "natural" rights. However, in societies like our own where child care has been traditionally the obligation of natural parents, all parents who do not surrender their children for adoption implicitly take on themselves the primary responsibility for child care. This freely assumed obligation provides the child with a corresponding claim right to be cared for.

Although, in our tradition, parents bear most of the responsibility for raising children, when this becomes unduly difficult, relatives and friends, state institutions and even the whole world take on some responsibility in varying degrees. Our religious and moral traditions require that each of us as a member of the human race has some modicum of responsibility to help children in need, no matter how remote they may be from our narrow sphere of personal acquaintance.

Children are persons, and all persons have a right to liberty, so children have that right. But liberty rights are defeasible. Rights like freedom of the press and fair trial may limit each other. Rights may be forfeited by criminal actions. It has been argued that the liberty rights of children must be severely limited by their dependence and need for protection. Yet we do not to the same degree limit the liberty rights of the physically handicapped even when they are even more dependent on others than are many children. We do however severely limit the liberty rights of the mentally deranged. Irrationality is the most important ground for limiting liberty rights, and may be the only justifiable ground for limiting the liberty rights of children (other than the general ground, which applies to everyone, of conflict with other rights).

But the lack of rationality and the dependency of children are not always independent of each other. The tendency of two-year-olds to run into the road manifests a lack of rationality which justifies severely limiting their freedom of movement. The dependency on parents which is due to this lack of rationality supports a claim right of the child on the parent for adequate protection from its irrational impulses. Thus claim rights and liberty rights of children vary inversely. When the adolescent acquires the right to cross the street alone, he or she no longer has a claim on the parents to protective escort across the street.

Parents' rights

In recent years there has been a renewed emphasis on the rights of parents. Champions of parental rights maintain that parents have rights both to and over their children against meddling outsiders including the state. Ferdinand Shoeman, in a recent paper,[3] has argued that the essentially intimate and private relationship between parent and child justifies the right of the parent to keep the child even where most observers would judge the child to be better off with others. This is a complex issue, involving a cluster of rights, duties, needs and counter-needs. Anna Freud observed that child abuse tends to be self-perpetuating—abused children tend when they grow up to become child abusers—and this is an additional reason for society to intervene in such cases, to defend itself as well as the rights of children.[4]

Moreover, it is not at all obvious that intimacy between child and parent must always be respected; after all, incest is an intimate relationship. Nor is it clear that intimacy excludes liberty rights; the most intimate lovers retain some rights against each other. Not all is fair in love or war.

It is a well known fact that the best institutions for children are unable to provide the special warmth that children need. For this reason alone, apart from parental rights, it is best to keep the child in the family wherever possible. But it does not follow that the family's privacy may not be violated. Physicians are required to report evidence of child abuse; schools and even neighbors are encouraged to do so. Some recent programs have been fairly successful in keeping abused children within their families by means of close scrutiny and effective counselling. Thus privacy and fostering good family relationships are not always interdependent.

There is only one way to make sense of the notion of parents' rights vis-a-vis children, and it is a very limited sense: Because it is usually unbearably cruel to take a child away from a parent, society ought not to do this without a compelling reason. The loving parent therefore has a corresponding liberty right against society to be allowed to keep and raise his or her child. It is outrageous when a sanctimonious judge orders a child to be taken from a mother who is a prostitute but loves and wants her child and whose care for the child is adequate.

Insofar as parents have a duty to satisfy the basic needs of their children they must have a corresponding right not to be interfered with in carrying out that duty, either by outsiders, or by their own children. Moreover, parents have the same rights as all persons to life, liberty and the pursuit of happiness. Clearly these rights of parents and those of children may come into conflict, but such conflict of rights is not unique to the parent-child relationship. A child's right to a secular education may come into conflict with a parent's right to practice a religion that requires the son to study only scripture and the daughter to devote herself to producing sons. Should society defend the right of the parent or that of the child? Such conflicts require the wisdom of Solomon, to adjudicate; general rules are not available to decide in each case which right takes precedence. But surely even such difficulties do not altogether obviate liberty rights of children, so long as parents cannot prove insufficient rationality of their children for the exercise of such rights.

Society's rights

The state has an obligation to protect the public interest and thus a corresponding claim right over parents that they raise their children to be law abiding and useful citizens. Parents therefore have a duty to educate their children to be self supporting in a manner that will contribute to the general good. In a democratic society an adequate education must be pluralistic; children must be trained to understand alternative proposals for social policy. This is essential to their participation in political life. It may be argued on this ground that a parent has an obligation to educate children in schools that do not dogmatically limit themselves to one point of view. Thus it may be argued that single-minded and authoritarian religious (or for that matter, Marxist) schools are not adequate modes of education in a democratic society. At the very least, society has a right to demand standardized testing in all schools to ensure that all students are acquainted with alternative viewpoints.

In a democratic society the pluralistic education of children is both a right and a duty. The child has a claim right against both the parents and the state that he or she be helped to develop in such a way as to be capable of intelligent exercise of adult liberty rights and responsibilities. It is a duty of parents, and of their children as well, to cultivate good citizenship. Education is the central case, but not the only case, of something that is both a right and a duty. Children have a right to be vaccinated against contagious diseases and their parents have a duty to see to it that they are. And adults themselves have both a right and a duty to be vaccinated.

Liberty and Learning

Two theories of learning have been competing recently for control of education: behaviorism and developmentalism. Different as these psychological theories are, they both endorse a nonpunitive approach to learning. Behaviorism holds that positive reinforcement is far more effective than punishment in shaping behavior; developmental psychologists, following Kohlberg, generally agree that moral development is facilitated by enabling the students to understand morality through discussion of situations involving moral conflict, rather than through authoritarian imposition of moral dogmas. Whatever the truth may be about moral development, it is obvious that children should learn to handle freedom through a kind of rehearsal of freedom. One cannot expect young people who have been kept in line by fear of punishment suddenly to be able to act as responsible moral agents when they reach their twenty-first birthday. Since the reason for limiting children's liberty in the first place was their lack of rationality, they should be given increasing degrees of freedom corresponding to their developing moral and intellectual awareness.

Responsibility

Since the time of Plato and Aristotle, lack of rationality have been considered an excusing condition for wrongdoing. Lack of rationality admits of degrees, therefore responsibility should also admit of degrees. Generally speaking, children and adolescents have had less time to learn about life, test their values, and consider alternative life styles; consequently, they should not be held fully responsible for the decisions they make.

Ordinarily freedom and responsibility go hand in hand. But in the case of young people the need for a rehearsal of liberty rights entails that they be given more freedom than their corresponding degree of responsibility seems to warrant.

This is the paradox of liberal child rearing that I promised earlier to resolve. The resolution is as follows:

Preparation for the full and responsible exercise of adult rights requires considerable practice or rehearsal, just as much as preparation for any complex creative and skillful activity, such as dramatic performance, ballet dancing or neurosurgery. In all these cases, we face the dilemma that it is dangerous for the parvenu to perform such activities, yet he or she must do so in order to learn from experience. We generally meet this dilemma by grasping the first horn with a padded glove; that is, we allow the student to perform at *some* risk, but we limit the risk by close surveillance and by only gradually raising the level of risk involved. Nevertheless, the fact is that the learner must be allowed to take *some* risks beyond what he or she has already proved himself or herself able to handle if the learner is to make significant progress. If this is true of particular activities, how much more true of what Plato called "the art of living"? Consequently, children and adolescents must be granted *more* freedom than their burden of responsibility taken by itself would justify.

Notes

1. J. Margolis "Reflections on the Right to Health Care" in *Bioethics and Human Rights* ed. Elsie and Bertram Bandman, Boston: (Little, Brown and Co., 1978) I wish to point out that I do not agree with Margolis that the acceptance of capital punishment constitutes evidence that human life is not inalienable.
2. Hoefeld, Wesley N. *Fundamental Legal Conceptions As Applied in Judicial Reasoning* (New Haven & London, 1964).
3. Ferdinand Schoeman "Rights of Children, Rights of Parents, and the Moral basis of the Family" New Jersey Regional Philosophical Association, Winter, 1978.
4. Josyn Goldstein, Anna Freud, Albert S. Schmit *Beyond the Best Interests of the Child* (Now York: Free Press, 1973).

Part Two:
Childhood's End: The Age of Responsibility

At least in principle, the modern world is committed to protecting its young, educating them and exempting them from most of the penalties the law provides for adult offenses. This ideal is one of the proudest achievements of civilization. There are, no doubt, still places in the world where young children are executed; Iran is a notorious example. But its very notoriety testifies to the fact that most of the world considers such treatment of children as barbaric.

Nevertheless, the diversity of minimal ages of criminal responsibility is bewildering. In the United States alone, the differences between states as to ages of full responsibility can be as great as five years, depending on the crime. Until recent years, the general tendency was toward raising the minimal age of full criminal responsibility. But the recent growth of juvenile crime has raised questions in many people's minds as to the desirability of light penalties for juveniles. Still others have maintained that the family courts have failed to safeguard juvenile rights and that juveniles will be more fairly treated in adult courts despite their more severe sentences.

The treatment of juvenile offenders is thus in a state of crisis, and it is important that jurists, philosophers, psychologists and interested lay public develop guidelines that are both fair and realistic. In this paper I shall sketch a bit of the history of the problem and then discuss current opinions, including my own.

In an article published some years ago in the *American Journal of Legal History*[1], —T. E. James presented a fascinating study of the age of majority in western culture, beginning with the Romans, a study which reveals the variety of criteria which have been used for the age of majority. *Infantia* originally meant more or less what we now mean by "infant," namely, the age of incapacity for speech. By 407 A.D., *infantia* was fixed for legal purposes at seven completed years. The next stage, *tutela impuberes* (when a tutor was needed) ceased with puberty and the age of majority had been reached. For males this age was 14 completed years; for females, twelve. Thus the age of majority[2] in Roman times was determined by intellectual readiness.

The age of majority remained fifteen until the late eleventh century. By the time of the Magna Carta (1215) the age of civil responsibility had been raised for males of noble birth to twenty-one. James cites Gilbert Stuart and Montesquieu as suggesting that the main reason for this change was the increased weight of armor and consequent increased length of military training required to become a knight. For all males excluded from military service, the age of majority continued to be fifteen. Thus it was a matter of historical accident that the age of criminal responsibility and that of full civil rights became separated. When military tenure was abolished in 1660, wardship would have ended for the nobility at the same age (fifteen) as it did for commoners, except that noble fathers did not want to give up control over the property of their adolescent offspring, and Charles II therefore provided that "the father could . . . appoint a guardian by will or deed until his child attained twenty-one."[3] Nevertheless in England until the Marriage Act of 1735, persons as young as fourteen could marry. Thus the Roman criterion of maturity based on intellectual readiness gave way to that of physical strength and dexterity, which was then supplanted by financial considerations, and considerations of fairness toward the youth were lost from sight.

Commonly accepted ideas about the proper age of criminal responsibility stem from the Roman divisions of childhood. It was accepted throughout Christendom that no child of less than seven years could be censured or punished for a crime in the external forum, that of the church and civil justice. A child of lesser years might, however, be guilty in the internal forum, that is, in the eyes of God. During the period from seven to twelve or fourteen, that is, up to puberty, the child was considered innocent in the external forum, unless it could be proved that the child knew the difference between right and wrong and acted with malicious intent. Catholic theology has retained this concept, according to which a child must be innocent in the external forum for seven complete years and must be viewed as innocent unless there is overwhelming evidence to the contrary, until fourteen. It is interesting that Catholic doctrine justifies holding children criminally responsible at fourteen, but not legally responsible in civil matters, because of the belief that "the ability to distinguish between good and evil actions is acquired much sooner than the ability to judge civil acts, in which capacity is not considered possible until the age of majority."[4] I want to question this view, which seems to me mistaken on two counts: a.) it overemphasizes the importance in moral development of purely verbal skills, paying too little attention to emotional and other non-cognitive factors in growth, and b.) it wrongly separates civil from moral responsibility.

a. The age of seven is thought to be the age of reason, because at that age children can recite the catechism and canon law, and can answer questions such as is it wrong to steal, to lie, to commit adultery, with an obedient "Yes," as if being able to recite such rights and wrongs were all there was to knowing the difference, that is, as if knowledge were mere ability to recite. Even at a later age, knowledge of the law does not guarantee responsibility.

In attempting to deal with the problem of juvenile criminal responsibility, a Canadian court ruled in the case of a twelve year old who was tried for murdering his step-mother, as follows, as reported by J. Wilson:

"The onus is upon the Crown to prove that the accused juvenile was competent to know the nature and consequences of his act and appreciate that it was wrong beyond a reasonable doubt." Based on these words (Wilson comments) it would seem that the court should consider the child's capacity to comprehend the moral implications of his act as well as a child's cognitive abilities. 'Appreciate' must be given a broader interpretation than mere knowledge of the physical nature of an act.[5]

It is implied by this passage that there is something seriously missing in a child's moral capacity. But it is not easy to specify exactly what this missing factor amounts to and at what age it may be expected to be supplied. What, for example, did the Canadian court mean by saying that a child does not appreciate or comprehend the moral implications of his act? While the full answer to this question would not be easy to spell out, it would seem at least to involve the ability to put oneself in another's place and to see matters from the other person's point of view, and realize the long-range effects of one's actions.

b. In the area of civil responsibility and rights, it is generally recognized that the ability to dispose intelligently of money and property, to enter into useful contractual agreements, and to pursue one's economic interests requires much more ability than to recite an economic or legal catechism; it requires also minimum self-discipline, a healthy degree of skepticism about people's professed intentions and motives, and enough experience of life to be able to estimate the probable long-range consequences of economic decisions and emotional commitments. Thus character, experience and emotional stability are factors at least as important as knowledge of rules when it comes to knowing what one is about, that is, to understanding the differences between good and bad actions. We seem to be more aware of these factors as essential to civil rights than as essential to criminal responsibility, perhaps because we tend to take financial decisions more seriously than moral decisions. As Machiavelli put it, in *The Prince*, "A man would rather lose his *pater* than his patrimony." His point was that people would prefer that the prince have his enemies assassinated than that he levy excessive taxes.

Another mistake implied by the religious tradition is the tendency to believe that it is easier to act morally than to act prudently in civil affairs. For moral responsibility, it is assumed, one need only be able to say what should or should not be done. For civil responsibilities one must have the practical wisdom to estimate probable consequences and the self-control to forego immediate satisfaction for the sake of long-range benefits.

A similar mistake seems to me to be at work in the widely heralded studies of moral development in children conducted by the developmental psychologist, Lawrence Kohlberg, who also overemphasizes the ability to recognize moral rules and underemphasizes the development of character. Kohlberg maintained that his studies showed that moral awareness develops in stages which, roughly speaking, involve initially a motivation of fear of punishment or hope for pleasure, then a tendency toward social conformity and finally, the understanding of moral principles. Kohlberg claimed that many people never progress beyond the second stage of the second level (the second level consisting of a) conformity to the expectations of one's social group and b) respect for the law). If he was right about this, then the legal principle that for full criminal responsibility a defendant must know not only that his action was contrary to law but also that it was *morally* wrong, would absolve from full responsibility most of the adult population.

Although he claimed that his tests were accurate indications of moral character as well as of moral reasoning, Kohlberg has been criticized on the ground that there is no significant correlation between the moral judgments children give verbal expression to and their actual conduct. His studies are marked by an excessive emphasis on the verbal aspects of moral responses, apparently assuming that those who can say what is right will do what is right, a view that seems unduly optimistic, to put it mildly. While Kohlberg's work has been justifiably celebrated for bringing out the necessary intellectual conditions of moral responsibility, it may occasionally mislead people into ignoring character illogical conditions such as prudence and self-control, the lack of which also helps account for the reduced legal and moral responsibilities of the very young.[6]

Returning now to my criticisms of the traditional religious view that by the age of fifteen children are fully capable of understanding the difference between right and wrong, and therefore should be assigned full criminal, although not yet full civil responsibility, I want to argue that this view must be mistaken in at least one of these two contentions. The same factors that mitigate civil responsibility should to the same degree mitigate criminal responsibility. For one needs as rich an understanding of society and its demands on its citizens in order to appreciate fully the long-range consequences of one's criminal actions, as one does with respect to one's financial transactions. Civil and criminal responsibility are matters of equal complexity, requiring equal knowledge of probable consequences and of value priorities. The most important non-cognitive aspect of both moral and prudential development is self-control. The immature adult whose development out of childhood has been arrested, and who is the most likely candidate both for criminal behavior and for personal, economic and political follies, is easily identified by his inability to forego immediate gratifications for the sake of long-range benefits. It is this lack of self-control, more than any other factor, that mitigates the responsibility of the child. Does it again also excuse childish adults from full responsibility? If it did, then few of those poor wretches who occupy our jails belong there. Philosophical hard determinists, such as Paul Edwards, John Hospers, A.J. Ayer and B.F. Skinner have in fact taken this position. But I shall later argue in defending an equal dividing line between childhood and adulthood that there are good and sufficient reasons to distinguish the childish grownup from the bona fide child that for these reasons the transgressions of the former are not excusable on the same grounds.

A widespread belief that underlies the Catholic tradition as well as the theories of Kohlberg, namely the belief that correct moral choices are easier to make than correct prudential choices, and that for this reason the age of criminal responsibility should precede full civil majority. This belief seems to me to be due to an inadequate appreciation of the factor of self-control, and an overemphasis on the purely cognitive factors in moral development, such as verbal skills in reciting rules and logical skill in giving reasons for decisions.

A serious objection may be made to my position, namely that, even granting the importance of self-control in both moral and civil matters, nevertheless, for criminal responsibility, one need only know what one must *not* do, while for civil responsibility one must also know enough about social institutions and other people to calculate effectively what positive courses of action to follow, and this latter kind of knowledge is far more complex and takes much more time to acquire. A Kantian moralist might sum up this difference by pointing out that moral knowledge is a priori while knowledge of civil matters such as economics, polities and social psychology is empirical, and the former kind of knowledge, since it is innate, requires only minimal maturity, while the latter might take a lifetime to acquire. But this counter-argument proves too much and thereby defeats itself. The fact is that we do not require young people to pass examinations in economics, political theory and psychology in order to receive their full civil rights, as if civil rights were like airplane pilots' licenses. Granted that the wise exercise of our civil rights requires a great deal of expertise in many fields, a democratic society, as J.S. Mill put it, allows its citizens either to consult those more expert than themselves or to make and learn from their own mistakes. Prudential wisdom is, in fact, not a necessary condition for the exercise of full civil rights. Consequently, the epistemological difference, if any, between moral knowledge and civil knowledge cannot be the ground for distinguishing between the age of criminal and the age of civil majority.

Indeed, there is reason to wonder why the age of civil majority should not be set even lower than that of criminal responsibility, since many adolescents are more competent to manage their own affairs than many citizens of advanced age who border on senility. I think the basic reason for this asymmetry between our treatment of the very young and the very old will prove instructive for my contention that criminal and civil responsibility belong together. The reason is, to put it with deliberate tautology, that children are children. Tautologies are supposed to be self-evident, but in this case perhaps I should spell out what I mean, which is this:

The incapacities of the child, unlike those of the aged, have, as Sartre suggested, the dialectical character of not being what they are and of being what they are not.[7] As Aristotle put it, they are unactualized potentialities, which it is the task of their parents, teachers and other adults to help them to realize. The naiveté of childhood is one of its greatest charms. The reason for this is that childhood is preparation for adulthood. What the child cannot yet do well is not a lack or a fault, because we evaluate her capacities, not entirely in terms of what she does at present, but primarily in terms of what we hope and expect her to do in the distant future, unlike the aged person who, to put it bluntly, has no future. This is not, I think, an unkind way to describe the difference between age and youth, because the aged person has something to compensate him for the lack of a future, namely, dignity. We rightly hesitate to deprive an aged person of his full civil rights even when he is in danger of misusing them because, having had those rights, he has acquired the self-image of a fully independent person and to deny that image would be an assault on his dignity. The aged person is just what he is, with all his faults, blemishes and failures as well as his achievements. He is fully defined. The child, we like to think, is much more what he and we hope he will become. His inadequacies are normally signs of growth rather than failure or decay. They are, we hope, initial but not ultimate inadequacies, and in order to help him overcome them, we postpone granting him those rights, the adequate exercise of which requires the knowledge, wisdom and self-control that we are helping him to acquire.

Understanding childhood thus involves seeing it, at least in part, as preparation for adult life. This way of seeing it, in turn, involves the appreciation of subtly different degrees of seriousness corresponding to different stages of preparatory rehearsal. For example, a child of three plays store by bringing objects from kitchen to living room and "selling" them to parents and friends, who then return them to where they belong. A year or two later the child may be given permission to sell her old toys and books outside the house for real money with which the child buys new toys and books. This, to the child, is now a "real" store, rather than a pretend store, but not to the parents who paid for the toys and books, nor the government licensing bureaus. For adults, it is still rehearsal for business, not the real McCoy. A few years later, a paper route looks still more serious and real, yet even then the youth who delivers the paper is less responsible for failures of service than, say, the adult milkman or postman.

Rehearsal for a theater performance becomes gradually more serious in stages. At first the lines are merely read, later they must be memorized and expressed with appropriate gestures. Still later costumes are worn and stage scenery employed. Finally, on opening night, the public and the critics must be faced—the performance is for keeps. Similarly the play acting of children becomes more serious and real as responsibilities intensify, just how real our conduct becomes, in the sense of taking full responsibility for it, depends on just how fully we grow up. But the main point I want to make here is that the behavior of children and adolescents continues to a decreasing extent to have some of the quality of rehearsal until they reach majority, for that is what majority means, namely, full responsibility, and with it, liberty.

A recent news story reported that a girl of six was ordered to stand trial in adult court for striking another child. The injury thus caused was fairly grievous and the offender surely merited parental punishment, but the adults who treated the matter as a criminal offense behaved, I think, as ridiculously as would a policeman who arrested a six year old for selling lemonade without a license. Rehearsal, when done badly, requites rehearsal punishment, not opening night punishment, that is, criticism from the director, not from the public at large.

Psychoanalytic zealots, who believe that no one ever completely grows up, might argue against any definite age of majority. Socially concerned liberals might insist that disadvantaged children need much more time to develop a full sense of responsibility than well-educated and well brought up middle class children, so that there should be different ages of majority for different social classes.

Both these criticisms of a fixed age of majority have considerable plausibility. But all things considered, I think it is in the interest of all, even the socially or emotionally disadvantaged, to have a single and fairly early deadline for full criminal and civil responsibility, and I think the most reasonable candidate is eighteen years. In the overwhelming majority of cases, physical growth is completed at eighteen. This process cannot be socially controlled and so it sets a natural lower limit to the assignment of full responsibility. On the other hand, psychological and moral development are, to a much greater extent, dependent on social attitudes, rules and actions. It is all too often a self-fulfilling prophesy to tell young people that they are too young to take full responsibility for their actions. A balance must be found between not protecting the young sufficiently to develop their potentialities in safety and so overprotecting them that they never learn to handle responsibilities. Of course there is no exact line between childhood and adulthood, but the point is that *an exact line must be drawn* for legal purposes, and I suggest that eighteen is the least unreasonable point at which to draw it, because physiological growth is completed at that age, and because adolescents have an image of themselves as grown up at that age. Showing respect for that adolescent self-image is likely to serve as an agreeably self-fulfilling prediction. This self-fulfilling social role of rites of passage has been well documented by anthropologists. The youth who crosses the boundary set by his culture has a new perspective on himself, one that would be seriously disturbed and muddied by conflicting messages if some indicated maturity and others childhood. When a teacher schedules an examination to follow a period of preparation, she may vary the preparatory period to suit slower and faster students. In fairness, the same time must be provided to all, and the most reasonable common interval will be long enough to accommodate the slowest. Thus society should set an age of majority for everyone equally, but set it late enough to accommodate those who develop slowly. For youths must be aware that by a certain date they will be held fully responsible for their actions and decisions. After puberty, young people are usually eager to begin careers and to raise a family. These activities involve grave civil responsibilities for the handling of which they need full rights and liberties.

I have argued that (a) limiting the rights of young people is justifiable only to the extent that such limitation can be shown to promote the fulfillment of their potentialities and (b) since children develop gradually toward adulthood, a progressive increase of liberty rights, permitting more and more serious rehearsal of such rights in the form of increased civil and criminal responsibility, should be provided to them. To set the age of civil majority higher than that of criminal responsibility is, I conclude, likely to frustrate rather than promote growing up, for the reason enunciated by John Stuart Mill in his essay, *On Liberty*, that, without the freedom to make mistakes, one cannot learn to do things right.

References

1. T.E. James "The Age of Majority" *The American Journal of Legal History* Philadelphia: Temple University, School of Law, pub: American Society of Legal History, vol. 4, 1960 pp. 22—23.
2. "Age of majority" has a broader use than "age of responsibility", the latter tending to be used for matters of criminal rather than civil actions.
3. Ibid, pp. 31.
4. *Dictionary of Moral Theology* ed. Mon. Pietro Palazzini, The Newman Press: Westminster, Maryland, 1962.
5. J. Wilson *Children and the Law*, Toronto: Butterworth, 1978 p. 82.
6. Although Kohlberg's work has had the great value of bringing to light the necessary intellectual conditions of moral responsibility it has sometimes misled people into ignoring the characterological conditions such as prudence and self-discipline, which rightly mitigate the moral and legal responsibilities of children.
7. I.e. they are *not* (really) incapacities in the sense of failings, but they *are* incapacities in the sense that they concern what the child cannot yet do.

A Note on the Legal Liberties of Children as Distinguished from Adults

Mary Vetterling-Braggin

Introduction

Although the types of legal rights that there are are many and varied, the children's rights debate in the psychological arena is mostly confined to discussions about legal claim rights and liberties.

As defined by Hohfeld, one individual (the right holder) has a legal claim against another (the duty holder) for an act or forebearance if and only if "should the claim be in force or exercised, it would be legal, other things being equal, to use coercive measures to extract either the specific performance, or compensation in lieu of it."[1] There are two sorts of claim rights, positive ones and negative ones. When a right holder has a positive claim right against a duty holder, he or she has the right to demand a specific doing of the duty holder. When the right holder has a negative claim right against a duty holder, he or she has the right to demand a specific not-doing of the duty holder. Examples of positive claim rights include the right to rehabilitation for crimes and the rights to be provided with minimum subsistence level housing, food, education, medical care and proper moral environment. Examples of negative claim rights include the rights not to be abused and to privacy.

Legal liberty rights are to be distinguished from legal claim rights in that what they entail is the "absence of duties in the ones who have the liberties, and so the absence of correlative claim rights in others."[2] Examples of legal liberties include the right to select one's own religion, sexuality, education, reading material, food, manner of dress, where to go and when to go there, when and where to work and to treatment to counselling for specific health problems.

Because the most heated debate on the question of whether adults should be distinguished from children with respect to right-granting centers on the more controversial of the two types of rights, legal liberties, the discussion here will be confined to them.

Liberationism, Strong Paternalism and Soft Paternalism

Children, as everyone knows, currently enjoy fewer legal liberties than do adults and they are under a greater degree of restriction than are adults with respect to those legal liberties that they and adults have in common. The question has arisen as to whether this state of affairs is just; whether, that is, there are justified moral grounds for treating children differently from adults with respect to legal liberty rights. A complete answer to this question should tell us at least two things, namely (1) how adults ought to be treated with respect to liberty rights to begin with (and why), and (2) whether children ought to be treated in the same way or in a different way (and why).

There is one standard liberationist answer. It is that adults ought to maintain those liberty rights we already have and that children ought to be "liberated" by getting them too.[3] There are two, quite different, standard paternalist answers. One (call it "strong paternalism") says that adults ought to maintain those liberty rights we already have but that children ought to be denied them or at least severely restricted with respect to them.[4] The other (call it "soft paternalism") says that adults ought to have even greater liberties than we now have, although children ought still be denied these greater liberties or at least severely restricted with respect to them.[5] Unfortunately, no one argues for an intriguing fourth view that adults ought to be restricted, but children liberated, with respect to any current legal liberty rights, or for other variations on the theme such as that both adults and children deserve liberation from (restrictions on) current legal liberties.

The global advantages and disadvantages of each of the positions that are defended, however, point the way to a new direction for the metaethics of children's liberty rights theory in general.

Advantages and Disadvantages

As was mentioned earlier, the standard liberationist thesis is that it is time for all the legal rights now enjoyed by adults in our society to be extended to children as well. The core argument for the view runs something like this:

1. All people ought to be treated alike unless there is a justification for differences in treatment.

2. There is no justification for treating children differently from adults with respect to the granting of liberty rights adults are now granted but which children are not.

3. Children ought to be granted the same rights adults are now granted but which juveniles are not.

The main difficulty with the liberationist argument is that premises (1) and (2) do not, strictly speaking, entail the thesis or conclusion (3) which amounts to the claim that children ought to be granted current adult liberty rights. What they do entail is the demand that children and adults ought to be treated *equally* with respect to the granting of those liberty rights adults currently have that children do not. The equal rights demand could, of course mean that children ought to be granted the same rights adults now have that children do not. But it could also mean that adults ought to be relieved of liberty rights we currently have that children do not; or it could mean that children ought to be granted some of these rights and adults relieved of others; or it could mean that some adults should maintain these rights, others lose them and some children gain them. In order actually to derive the liberationist thesis from premises (1) and (2), in short, substantial further argumentation against all the alternatives other than the one the liberationist desires would have to be provided. In their quest to liberate children, liberationists tend to overlook the question as to whether adults couldn't use a little too; if, as convincingly argued by some,[6] justice requires even just a modicum of adult liberation, the implicit liberationist commitment to current adult liberty law in premise (2) renders senseless the claim that children ought also be subjected to that law.

Although both the liberationist and the paternalist assent to premise (1) above, the key difference between them lies in the latter's denial of premise (2) above. The standard paternalist argument has the following form:

1′ All people ought to be treated alike unless there is a justification for differences in treatment.

2′ Adults ought to have liberty rights X, Y, Z, etc. (Examples of particular liberty rights are provided.)

3′ There is a justification for treating children differently from adults with respect to liberty rights X, Y, Z, etc.

4′ Adults ought to have liberty X, Y, Z etc. but children ought to be denied X, Y, Z etc.

Strong paternalism differs from soft only in which particular liberty rights X, Y, Z etc. it selects and in its justification for that set of choices. Strong paternalists, like liberationists, plug in current adult liberty rights for the X, Y, Z etc. terms, whereas soft paternalists want to liberate adults from many current liberty restrictions, thus ending up with a different set of plug-ins for the X, Y and Z terms.

Paternalism's key advantage over liberationism lies in the fact that it does provide a moral justification (convincing or not) for which rights adults ought to have and which we ought not; it is forced to do so in defense of premise 2'. But strong paternalism, like liberationism, must end up providing a justification for current adult rights. Not only does much of strong paternalist literature end up appealing to typical middle-class establishment conscience rather than to reasoned moral argument in the effort to accomplish this goal, it also freezes liberty law into a time frame at best suitable for this day and age, but perhaps not for future ones. Soft paternalism outright rejects this mode of so-called justification for legal theories and in so doing, places children's rights theory on a healthy new track.

The question remains, however, as to whether this new track is healthy enough. The consistent inability of any paternalist theory to defend adequately the premise (3') to the effect that children as a class and adults as a class actually are different in any way morally relevant to the granting of legal liberties remains a thorn in the side of both soft and strong paternalist theories. No matter what property is selected, be it "having the capacity for rational choices, being of the age of consent," "being able to borrow someone else's capacity to do something," or whatever, even when adequate definitions for such terms are provided and even when the property selected is by some stretch of the imagination morally relevant to the granting of liberty rights to begin with, some children, like some adults, turn out to have that property and some children, like some adults, turn out not to. This renders moot the original class distinction between adults and children and suggests instead that persons with certain morally relevant properties ought to have certain liberty rights, those without the properties denied them, whether these persons be adults or whether they be children.

Conclusion

It would seen that the combined strengths of available theories point strongly toward a new theory of liberty rights, one which accepts the paternalist demand for provision of a moral justification for particular adult liberty rights and at the same time accepts the liberationist plea to treat adults as a class no differently from children as a class. The argument for this new view would have the following general form:

1″ All people ought to be treated alike unless there is a justification for differences in treatment.

2″ Adults with morally relevant properties (A, B, C etc.) ought to have legal liberties (X, Y, Z etc.) and adults without (A, B, C etc.) ought to be denied (X, Y, Z etc.)

3″ There is no justification for treating children as a class differently from adults as a class with respect to the granting of (X, Y, Z)

4″ Children with morally relevant properties (A, B, C etc.) ought to have legal liberties (X,

Y, Z etc.) and children without (A, B, C etc.) should be denied (X, Y, Z).

The key questions remain, of course, as to which particular rights and properties we are going to select and why, the controversial answers to which remain for legal philosophy to provide.

Notes

1. Hohfeld's terminology is discussed and explained in detail by Laurence Houlgate in the latter's *The Child and the State* (Baltimore: The John Hopkins University Press, 1980), Introduction.
2. *Ibid.*
3. This viewpoint is advanced, for example, by Howard Cohen in his *Equal Rights for Children* (Totowa N.J.: Littlefield, Adams and Co., 1980), John Holt in *Freedom and Beyond* (New York: E. P. Dutton, 1972), and Richard Farson in *Birthrights* (New York: MacMillan, 1974).
4. This viewpoint is defended by Houlgate, *op. cit.*
5. A good example here would be Graham Hughes' *The Conscience of the Courts* (New York: New York University Press, 1978).
6. See, for example, Hughes, *op. cit.*

Paternalism and the Rationality of the Child

Rosalind Ekman Ladd

In order to think clearly about certain ethical questions in pediatric medicine, such as the legitimacy of proxy consent or the right of adolescents to make their own decisions about refusal of treatment, it is necessary to consider the more general question of the justification of treating children in a morally different way from the way we treat adults. What justifies parents and society in making decisions for children?

Presumably, a simple utilitarian argument could be given:

1. decisions need to be made concerning children;
2. children cannot make wise decisions for themselves;
3. therefore, decisions must be made for children by someone else.

Although Mill formulates the classical anti-paternalist position toward adults, he does not mean his theory of liberty to apply to those "not of ripe years"—"children, or . . . young persons below the age which the law may fix as that of manhood or womanhood." Mill cites only chronological age as set by law as the age of majority as the criterion of when it is justified to make decisions for others for their own benefit. However, spelling out a complete, plausible utilitarian defense makes it clear that the underlying justification of treating children differently must be their presumed lack of rationality or ability to make reasonable decisions.

If we follow Mill, then, justification of parents' and society's rights over children rests simply on their being minors who are assumed to be incapable of the degree of rationality required to be self-determining moral agents.

However, the claim that children, as a class, lack rationality and that therefore it is justified to make decisions for them, has met strong challenge recently both from the popular movements toward children's liberation and in the philosophical literature.

It is the purpose of this paper to examine the arguments which challenge the claim that children lack rationality. Even if it is admitted that some children have rationality to the same degree as adults, it will be argued that the concept of rationality which is invoked is mostly irrelevant to moral decision-making. Responsible and wise decision-making is a matter of practical reasoning, and Aristotle is right in thinking that this develops over a period of time and on the basis of life experience. This model of decision-making explains why children cannot be expected to be self-determining agents, and provides justification for parents and society to make decisions for them for their own benefit.

The Argument From Rationality

The argument that children are not rational or competent and therefore need parental authority has one of its sources in Locke:

> The Freedom then of Man and Liberty of acting according to his own Will, is grounded on his having Reason . . . To turn him loose to an unrestrain'd Liberty, before he has Reason to guide him is . . . to thrust him out amongst Brutes, and abandon him to a state as wretched, and as much beneath that of a Man, as theirs. This is that which puts the Authority into the Parents hands to govern the Minority of their children.[1]

Bentham, too, bases the source of authority of parents over children on the child's immature status, both physical and intellectual:

> The feebleness of infancy demands a continual protection. The complete development of its physical power takes many years; that of its intellectual faculties is still lower . . . Too sensitive to present impulses, too negligent of the future, such a being must be kept under an authority more immediate than that of the laws . . .[2]

Since the child cannot care for himself, society (and in Locke's case, God) delegates to the parents the responsibility and duty to care for him. The authority of the parent over child extends only so far as he needs it to achieve what is in the child's best interest and what will enable the child to become a self-sufficient adult. As the child grows in reason, the jurisdiction of the parent weakens, and when the child reaches the age of reason, he is free of that jurisdiction. Locke clearly makes the legitimacy of the power of parent over child rest on the child's lack of reason, whereas Mill assumes that children are lacking in reason, but cites chronological age as a determining factor in parental control.

Challenges to the Rationality Argument

A strong challenge to the argument that it is justified to deny rights or liberties or freedom of action to children is made in a recent article by Laurence D. Houlgate, "Children, Paternalism, and Rights to Liberty," which was published by O'Neill and Ruddick, *Having Children*.[3] Houlgate considers two forms of this argument, one based on the premise that children are likely to do harm to themselves or fail to promote their own good, and the other based on the assumption that children do not have the capacity for rational choice. Houlgate rejects both of these claims, arguing that only very young children, those in the stages described by Inhelder and Piaget as the "sensorimotor" stage (0-2 years) and the early "preoperational" stage (2-7 years) are incapable of reasoned, *i.e.*, thoughtful, choice. He argues on empirical grounds that older children have the cognitive capacity to understand when there is risk of harm, the capacity to defer immediate gratification, as in playing competitive games, and that children's lack of information about risks is likely due to their specific circumstances and education, *e.g.*, city vs. farm children. Thus, they do have the ability to make reasonable *i.e.*, "correct," choices. Houlgate then concludes that the justification for denying children the same rights as adults cannot be based on their presumed lack of rationality.

A similar challenge is presented in an earlier article by Francis Schrag, "The Child in the Moral Order," which appeared in *Philosophy* in 1977.[4] He notes that the fiercest opponents of paternalism, Mill, Berlin, and Nozick, do not hesitate to accept it for children, and that "an enormous philosophical weight is made to rest on the adult/child distinction." If we try to specify differences between adults and children morally relevant to the justification of paternalism, he claims, the only morally defensible system of classification is one based on degree of maturation as measured by chronological age.

As the most plausible candidate for explaining the morally relevant differences between the two groups distinguished by chronological age, Schrag examines the ability to make rational decisions, and considers remedying the otherwise impossibly vague conception of rationality by defining it in terms of Piaget's stages of human cognitive development. Schrag wisely argues against this, however, on two grounds: first, that although some children are precocious intellectually, their experience of people in the real world is too limited to make their independent survival likely, and secondly, that there are many adults who never reach the stage of formal operations. He also notes briefly that some people who can perform the appropriate logical operations nevertheless are impotent to act on their conclusions. Thus, the ability or inability to perform the "formal operations" described by Piaget serve as neither necessary nor sufficient conditions for justifying adopting paternalism for children only.

So, if the criterion of rationality is assumed to make the difference between children and adults, then the difference can in no way be correlated with chronological age. We can add to Schrag's example of the intellectually precocious child and the adult who never reaches the stage of formal operation, consideration of the profoundly retarded adult, comatose patient, and the senile elderly. There are too many clear counter-examples to attribute the difference between the two classes to the characteristic of rationality. Rationality, or the lack of it, *per se*, cannot justify different moral treatment of children and adults.

The Concept of Rationality: Rationality as Practical Reason

The real difficulty in defending the rationality criterion, however, is not the fact of counter-examples, but the concept of rationality itself. Houlgate seems satisfied to understand rationality as

Piaget's cognitive abilities. Schrag displays some uneasiness with this interpretation, but still bases his rejection of rationality as a criterion on the fact of counter-examples.

There is, despite these arguments, a nagging intuition that children do lack something—which we refer to perhaps inexactly as rationality—and which does serve as the moral basis for the paternalistic treatment of children. I propose to examine here the relevant sense of rationality.

Rationality, according to the Piaget model, is basically the ability to reason, to draw conclusions from premises. This ability is seen at its clearest in the mathematical mind. Given certain information, the mathematician or logician, following certain rules which he has learned or deduced for himself, can see the implications and follow them out. Mathematical genius flowers early in life; the childhood prodigy is the lisping youngster whose mind works like a computer.

Philosophers, in the Greek sense of wise men and women, mature later in life. Despite Wordsworth's poetry, the innocent child is in no way a philosopher. Yet, isn't rationality also the hallmark of the philosopher? What is different about the rationality of the mathematician and the rationality of the philosopher? I find the clue to answering the puzzle about rationality in Aristotle's distinction between theoretical and practical reasoning. The mathematician reasons to knowledge in a theoretical sense—his data is given and unequivocal; the philosopher (in Plato and Aristotle's sense) exercises practical reason, where the accepting of the premise itself is a matter of judgment, where the process is one of deliberation, of weighing of alternatives, and the conclusion is an action or a way of life. To put it in more modern dress, the mathematician reasons about facts; the philosopher reasons about values.

It is my thesis that the development of children from dependency to moral autonomy depends on the development of practical reasoning. Only after children have passed through this period, as it were, of moral apprenticeship and developed these characteristics, should they be accorded full moral status as adults. Practical reasoning involves experience in life, development of moral judgment, practise in conforming action to principle, and the development of character. The fact that children do not (and cannot) have practical wisdom provides the moral basis for treating them paternalistically.

There are three important components of moral decision-making, each of which helps to illuminate the nature of practical wisdom. The first is that one must know the value premises. Unless one follows a simple, prescribed, legalistic formula, such as the Ten Commandments purport to be, knowing which value premises to accept is in itself a matter of decision. In our pluralistic society, this must be seen as deciding which values to adopt, which life style and life goals to accept. Should one be a conservative or a liberal, preppie or punk?

Accepting moral principles is not a matter of intellectual exercise, but a commitment; accepting a moral principle is deciding to act in a certain way. Moreover, the values that we accept, when applied to concrete situations, tend to come into conflict with one another. Thus, another decision is called for in establishing a hierarchy of values; when and why one *prima facie* value overrides another is a matter of choice. Should one study for an exam or use that time to help a friend? All of the capacity to do what is involved in deciding upon moral values on principle, I will refer to as judgment.

A second requirement of decision-making is self-knowledge; one must know when the moral principles you have adopted actually apply to you. One might hold as a principle that all overweight people ought to diet, but fail to recognize oneself as overweight. Or, one might be clear that we should treat other people with dignity, but not recognize certain acts of one's own as condescending or patronizing. The kind of self-knowledge discussed here requires trial and error in seeing the consequences of one's own actions, understanding of the motivations and sensitivities of other people, a broad view of the physical

and social world and one's place in it: in short, experience in living.

The third component of moral decision-making involves the formation of habits of character that allow one to make his actions conform to his principles. If a person fails to act on his own principles in the appropriate circumstances, due to weakness of will or strength of powerful emotions, then he is not successful in his decision-making. If one decides to diet but then is tempted into eating dessert, something has gone wrong. The import of moral decision-making or practical reasoning as opposed to deduction of theoretical knowledge from given premises, is the eventual outcome in action. We may refer to this capacity as the development of character or strength of character.

Aristotle emphasizes the role of habit in developing moral virtue, and suggests that the novice develops the proper habits by acting as the man of practical wisdom does. He begins by merely copying what the role model does, but he gradually develops his own ability to choose an act correctly. When it is an established disposition of his soul—*i.e.*, habit of character—and is done with pleasure, then he, too, is a man of practical wisdom.

On this analysis, then, there are no exact rules for moral decision-making; it is a matter of judgment, self-knowledge, and character, and this necessarily develops slowly over a period of time with guidance from those more experienced. The child must learn to make his own judgments, since he cannot merely imitate or memorize rules. Yet, there is a standard of morality which is not merely subjective. Developing one's own judgment allows for the flexibility of meeting changes that the future might bring; yet it is an exercise of rationality and not either mere personal preference or moral skepticism.

Although there will still be differences in the age at which individuals reach the stage of practical wisdom, this concept of rationality does provide justification for a fairly long period of paternalistic treatment of children. Perhaps one could even justify autonomy in certain areas of decision-making which are areas in which the child has had more experience and more opportunity for developing skills. For example, it is claimed that children facing terminal illness "grow up" more quickly in their attitudes toward death and dying than do other children.[5] Thus, it might be justified to allow these children quite a bit of autonomy in respect to decisions about refusal of treatment. On the other hand, if children begin to experience the emotions of adult sexuality only at puberty, then one might argue for a period of moral apprenticeship, *i.e.*, paternalistic supervision over their sexual relationships, until an appropriate backlog of experience has made possible the development of judgment, self-knowledge, and character in respect to this specific area of behavior.

My criticism of those who would emphasize the cognitive difference between children and adults reflects the larger controversy between cognitivist and non-cognitivist theories of metaethics. I think the argument is well made by Hare and others that moral language is essentially prescriptive. Moral judgments, according to this view, are not knowledge-claims and one's acceptance of a moral principle is related to behavior in an internal, necessary way. Hare's original theory is perhaps extreme but clear; he says in his early book, "It is a tautology to say that we cannot sincerely assent to a second-person command addressed to ourselves, and *at the same time* not perform it, if now is the occasion . . . and it is in our power to do so . . ."[6] Thus, moral education, Hare claims, in a more recent article, is not a matter of informing people of an appropriate moral principle, but of "their coming to accept it on their own."[7] Morality does not come naturally to children, he continues, and must be taught by example. Hare also emphasizes the importance of motivation in role-modeling; the model must be not only someone who can set a good example, but someone who is admired, so that the child or adolescent will want to be like him.

It is beyond the scope of this paper to discuss the aims and methods of moral education, but it is clear that for those who are engaged in the practical aspects of education of children, there is emphasis on the non-cognitive and apprenticeship aspects of education, of training character and will. For example, Archambeault writes: "Traditionally, moral philosophers have held that moral training consists not only in leading the student to an intellectual apprehension of norms, but also in a training of the will."[8]

Conclusion

I have argued that those who question the justification of the adult's power over children take too narrow a view of the kind of rationality which is required for mature and responsible decision-making. Locke emphasizes not only the power of the parent to make choices for the child, but the duty the parent has to care for and educate him. For Locke, the power of the parent over the child is derived from his duty to the child. Education of the child includes moral education as well as intellectual education, and moral education involves practical reasoning, *i.e.*, judgment, self-knowledge, and character. These are characteristics which develop slowly over a period of time and in good part by trial and error and role-modeling. Thus, we can conclude that a fairly long period of moral apprenticeship or paternalistic intervention in the child's decision-making is both necessary and justified.

Although I have here provided only general guidelines for when, aside from some generally appropriate but ultimately arbitrary chronological determination, a child is competent to make, say, medical decisions for himself, this analysis should provide a needed counter-balance to those who advocate more and more liberty rights for children in the name of liberation.[9] It might also be noted that the same kind of criterion of ability at practical reasoning is appropriate to use in determining the competency of adults to make decisions about refusal of medical treatment. When an adult begins to fail significantly in the skills of making judgments, appreciating consequences, and conforming action to principle, then he becomes a candidate for being declared incompetent and having decisions made for him by a court-appointed guardian.

Footnotes

1. John Locke, "Paternal Power, from *The Second Treatise of Civil Government*," in *Having Children*, ed. Onora O'Neill and William Ruddick, New York: Oxford Univ. Press, 1979, p. 242.

2. Jeremy Bentham, Theory of Legislation, Boston, 1840, Vol. 1, p. 248. Quoted in *Before the Best Interests of the Child*, Goldstein, Freud, and Solnit, New York: The Free Press, 1979, p. 7.

3. Laurence Houlgate, "Children, Paternalism, and Rights to Liberty," in O'Neill and Ruddick, *op. cit.*

4. Francis Schrag, "The Child in the Moral Order," *Philosophy* 52, 1977, pp. 167-177. See also his "The Child's Status in the Democratic State," *Political Theory*, 1978.

5. See Myra Bluebond-Langner, *The Private World of Dying Children*, Princeton Univ. Press, 1978.

6. R.M. Hare, *The Language of Morals*, Oxford: The Clarendon Press, 1952.

7. Hare, in *Moral Education*, ed. B. I. Chazan and J. F. Soltis, N.Y.: Teachers College Press, 1973, p. 117.

8. Reginald Archambeault, in Chazan and Soltis, *op. cit.*, p. 163.

9. A position somewhat less conservative than my own is defended by Marie-Louise Friquegnon in "Childhood's End: The Age of Responsibility," *Thinking*, Vol. 4, No. 3 & 4.

Ethics Instruction and the Constitution

James F. Herndon

The name given to this section of the conference is "How Far Public Schools May Go, Constitutionally and Legally." That was not my choice, and I am not altogether comfortable with it. It sounds as if someone had an ethical system he wanted to teach and wondered only if the Constitution would let him get away with it. I have no such system in mind and do not regard the Constitution as an inconvenience. To the contrary, I think that doing what the Constitution encourages us to do would result in precisely the kind of ethical teaching in the public schools that would be best able to achieve our society's long-term interests. I hope to persuade you of the truth of that proposition.

The Constitution does not usually speak in positives but rather tells us what government may not do. By examining those constraints, we gain an idea not only of what government is forbidden to do but also some inkling of what it is governments are encouraged to do. I shall follow that plan presently. But first it is necessary to deal with two concerns that inform most discussions of this kind. Treating these matters first may give us the perspective we will need to look at the legalities.

The first is that the public schools teach ethics already, whatever they call it and whatever we may say about it here. Even if no formal courses are offered, ethics is taught by school policies, by teachers' examples, and by students to each other. It is taught by school boards acting to defy or comply with court orders, and it is taught in playground games governed by some collective sense of fair play. These things happen for perfectly good—and obvious—political reasons as well as because teachers have internalized broad social norms that they cannot help but pass on to their students. And they happen because school-age children have already acquired a great deal of conventional morality, which they easily hand on to each other.

It is almost inevitable, then, that public schools practice some degree of social control, whether intentional, well planned, well done, or not. It is hard to imagine schools being permitted to exist if they did not reinforce at least the primary imperativeness of community morality. And that takes us to the second preliminary concern, which has to do with the reasons for state or local legislative interest in ethics instruction in the first place. We have already seen the schools burdened with problems that other social institutions lack either the will or the ability to solve. If they are now to add the responsibility for training an ethical society, those who do the adding must be prepared for disappointment.

To imagine that schools can raise up a new generation significantly more moral or ethical than its predecessor is to misunderstand both the nature of ethical belief and the means by which learning—and teaching—are accomplished. It is also to misunderstand the Constitution. Solving what a state legislature or a local school board may perceive as a crisis in ethics or morals is not something public schools alone, or even principally, can do. The schools can and regularly do reinforce conventional ethical belief. And it may well be that they already do what can reasonably be expected of them. But it is the task of this conference to inquire what more the schools could do, and of this paper to ask what legal barriers may constrain the schools' activities. I join in that task, not because I feel that public school instruction in ethics may reform what others see as a corrupt society, but because I hope that such teaching may enhance the lives of those who receive.

It is time, then, that we turned to the Constitution. I shall describe first what constraints on government the Supreme Court has found the Constitution to erect. Then I shall emphasize what I think the Constitution encourages us to do. Along the way, I shall try to counter what objections to my position I can anticipate.

The Question of Secularism

The First Amendment of the Constitution specifies that "Congress shall make no law respecting an establishment of religion nor prohibiting the free exercise thereof." By judicial interpretation, the First Amendment's restrictions on the federal government have been extended to the states—and their subdivisions, such as school districts—by the "liberty" and "due process" clauses of the Fourteenth Amendment. Through further interpretations in a long series of cases, the Supreme Court fashioned a test to determine when and if an action by government lay beyond the First Amendment's strictures. To maintain a "wholesome neutrality" on church-state questions, the Court said, government action must pass three tests: (1) it must have "a secular legislative purpose"; (2) its primary effect must be neither to advance nor to inhibit religion; and (3) it must not result in "excessive entanglement" of church and state.[1]

The secular legislative purpose required by the first test has two referents. One is the collection of "police powers" reserved to the states by the Tenth Amendment. These generally include the state's authority over matters of health, welfare, safety and morals. Somewhere in the overlap of those powers lies the state's concern for education. The other referent of secular legislative purpose is a restriction on state power and requires that whatever states do in the exercise of their police powers, they do for nonreligious reasons. A secular legislative purpose is therefore one that the states are entitled to reach through their reserved powers and that has no religious intent.

The second test for the constitutionality of government action also has two referents. The first, a ban on action that would advance religion, means, in Justice Black's words:

> Neither a State nor the Federal Government can set up a church. Neither can pass laws which aid one religion, aid all religions, or prefer one religion over another. Neither can force nor influence a person to go or to remain away from church against his will or force him to profess a belief or disbelief in any religion.[2]

The second referent forbids the state from "inhibiting" religion. Beyond its obvious limits on government interference with religion, that restriction also requires that government avoid hostility to religion. Government and religion are not meant by the First Amendment to be, as Justice Douglas observed, "aliens to each other—hostile, suspicious/or/even unfriendly."[3]

It is worth calling attention here to the Court's language in its statement of the second test. Recall, and permit me to emphasize, that an action fails the test if its *primary effect* is to advance or inhibit religion. Actions having a collateral effect of advancing or inhibiting religion would meet the test. Remote, secondary, and unintended effects would not necessarily place the action under a constitutional cloud. Only those actions by government intended in some primary or fundamental way to help or hinder religion would clearly fail the test. We shall return to this point.

The third test—the absence of excessive entanglement—refers primarily to relationships between government and private religious institutions and need not detain us. This element of the test is designed to limit the institutional entanglements that might occur when public aid is given to private schools and that might in turn involve government in private religious concerns, to the degree that those interests would be compromised by secular purposes. Any involvement of public schools and religious institutions in the development of ethics that the Court would consider to be "excessive entanglement" would probably already have failed the first two tests.

Teaching Ethics Deliberately

If we now apply those first two tests to an ethics course in public school, it is reasonably clear that the course must have as its purpose the same purposes that attach to any other part of the curriculum. It must, in other words, make some contribution to public health, welfare, safety, and morals. Any school system that can justify funding cheerleading and football should have no problem defending ethics education. But in designing its ethics courses, the school must be careful not to rely too heavily on religion for texts or inspiration. Specifically, the school must not promote one, any, some, or all religious traditions or systems of belief. To do so would turn the public school into an agent of private religious purpose, and that is what the First and Fourteenth Amendments clearly prohibit.

But just as the school cannot lawfully favor religion, neither can it show hostility to religion either by ignoring ethical beliefs grounded in religion or by consciously and willfully denigrating those religious ideas it does entertain. To do so would deprive instruction in ethics of the rich and important legacy of ethical thought nurtured by centuries of religious belief and practice. But that is not so much a matter of law as it is one of taste, intellectual integrity, and historical good sense. The legal interest centers on the inhibiting of the religious impulse of those exposed to teaching so unfriendly as to ignore or uniformly

to condemn their beliefs. That inhibition is as much forbidden by the First and Fourteenth Amendments as is the state's fostering or support of religion.

A constitutionally fit ethics course, then, might draw on religious sources for subjects of discussion, and it might depend on readings drawn from religious authorities as preparation for discussion. But it must not have as its effect or aim the inculcation of religious belief, nor can it be intended to demonstrate the insufficiency or irrelevance of religion as it may inform ethical belief and practice.

But strictures flowing from the religion clauses of the First Amendment are not the only limits on what a school may do. A second set of constraints forbids government to require or impose any orthodoxy in matters of belief or opinion. To do so would, as the Court has said, "invade the sphere of intellect or spirit which it is the purpose of the First Amendment . . . to reserve from all official control."[4] To understand this limitation, we might look to its two sources. The first is the notion that any person may hold beliefs that it is no business of government to direct. Respect for individual human dignity and reason dictates no lesser restraint. The second source is an assumption of a free marketplace of ideas in which alternate concepts of public and private goods may compete, the lesser being winnowed out, the better surviving and gaining acceptance. To restrict the entry of ideas into the marketplace or to select survivors by fiat denies opportunity for competition and with it the opportunity for ideas better than those we accept today ever to emerge. Closing the marketplace also denies fundamental concepts of our stature as human beings, able, at least in the long run, to understand, weigh, and accept or reject ideas on their merits.

To the degree that ethics may lack the precision of mathematics and the systematic assembly of evidence of history, an ethics curriculum in a public school would be bound by this latter set of limits. It would have to respect the dignity and reasoning powers of students, and it would have to work within a setting of free inquiry and debate. Its method would be that of reasoning from evidence or premises to tentative—and challengeable—conclusions. It could not rely on authority or any secular catechism to demonstrate that one judgment was proper and another not. It could, in short, impose no orthodoxy.

One Objection: Pupil's Rights

I perceive two sorts of objections to what has been said so far. The first is grounded in a view of school children as less than fully entitled to the protections of the First Amendment against government control. The second objection would be that what I have argued for here looks suspiciously like something called "secular humanism." Both objections are altogether proper and deserving of comment. Because an appropriate response to the first may go far to settle the second, we shall consider them in that order.

It is true, of course, that school children do not have all of the rights that adults possess. But as Justice Fortas observed, they do not "shed their constitutional rights to freedom of speech and expression at the schoolhouse gate."[5] School children are "persons" in the eyes of the Constitution, and "they are possessed of fundamental rights which the State must respect, just as they themselves must respect their obligations to the State."[6] Among those fundamental rights are the very ones to which we have referred: the right not to have religious or other orthodoxy imposed upon them and the right to respect for their beliefs, religious or otherwise. If there is any sense in which school children's First Amendment rights are different from those of the rest of us, it should lie in the fact that their relative intellectual immaturity requires even greater sensitivity to constitutional limits than might apply to their elders.

But the obverse of First Amendment rights should be considered, too. One person's views

may annoy another. They may be highly offensive. That, of course, is no warrant for suppressing those views, nor is it grounds for attacking them other than on their merits. If the search for truth contemplated by the First Amendment is to be carried on at all, it must require at least that. If so much is granted, then the right of school children to explore ethical beliefs cannot carry with it any correlative right of insulation from annoyance or offense. One has the right in a public school or anywhere else not to be deliberately and intentionally insulted. He or she does not have the right to escape challenge or offense resulting from another's good faith effort to state an opinion. To acknowledge any such right would be to deny the very freedoms the First Amendment was written to protect.

Further Objections: Weakening of Faith

If that argument has any validity, we may turn to the second objection. To be sure, the limits I have described for an ethics curriculum in a public school would allow, if not require, the school to develop an open-ended treatment that admits all points of view and reaches no required conclusions. Calling that "secular humanism" is all right with me, though a school system adopting such a curriculum might wisely wish to call it something else. What is important is not the name but whether an ethics course so designed would violate the First Amendment, either because it "establishes" religion in some way or because it prevents the "free exercise" of religion. Those, at least, are the usual objections.

If secular humanism is a religion and if an open-ended ethics course is some expression of secular humanism, then the indictment is proved. It is a forbidden establishment. But the argument is absurd. Stating no belief in a deity, having no liturgy, no creed, and no ritual, and supporting no church or other institution, secular humanism can hardly be called a religion. It may speak to ultimate things, as religions customarily do, but then so do physics and philosophy, the teaching of which could not conceivably be outlawed on religious grounds.

The much more serious objection to an open-ended ethics course rests on the probability that a child raised in a highly religious atmosphere may have his beliefs questioned in such a course. And once questioned, those beliefs may weaken, leading in turn to a loss of commitment. Any such results might be considered to have the inhibiting effects the Supreme Court has found the First Amendment to prohibit. Avoiding establishment through being open-ended, the ethics course would lead inevitably to a denial of free exercise.

The simplest way to deal with that objection would be to make school work in ethics entirely voluntary. No one would have his or her beliefs challenged who did not freely consent to do so. But voluntaryism only begs the question of whether an open-ended ethics curriculum inhibits religion in some way contrary to the First Amendment. As noted before, hostility on the part of teachers to any or all religions would certainly have that effect. But would a good faith effort to compare, to discuss, and to challenge points of view have a similar—and unlawful—inhibiting effect?

To the degree that free discussion of ethical beliefs grounded in religion might lead to one's changing his or her mind, one would suppose that the discussion might well inhibit a religious commitment. But imagine that the discussion had the opposite effect, that one became further convinced of the correctness of his or her religious beliefs. Could anyone seriously contend that the discussion, held in a public school, amounts to an establishment of religion? One could no more claim that the state had aided religion in the latter case than one could argue inhibition of free exercise in the first.

Remember also that to fail the Supreme Court's second test, action by government must have as its *primary effect* the advancement or inhibiting of religion. Provided, therefore, that

neither the teacher nor texts have an intent openly or covertly hostile to religion, free and open-ended discussion of ethical positions is simply not violative of anyone's freedom to exercise religion or to believe as he wishes. While one assuredly has the right not to have his beliefs ridiculed, he has no right not to be offended, or annoyed, or challenged in public places. One may take offense, and one's religion may be inhibited. If so, again in the absence of hostile intent, that is the individual's own doing and not that of the public school or the authorities who support it.

Finally, suppose that an ethics course were *not* open-ended with respect to religious beliefs. In that case, it would have to come down on the side of one religion or another. However insubstantial the inhibiting effects of an open-ended course might be, one that took religious sides would certainly violate the First Amendment's strictures against religious establishment. Since no middle ground seems to lie between a course biased toward religion and one intended to be religiously neutral, one must prefer the latter of necessity. To be sure, such a course carries risks of offense and religious inhibition. But it probably carries an equal risk of religious reinforcement, a result just as objectionable to some as is the challenge of religion to those who fear that result. Taking those risks is simply the price any of us pays for living in a free society.

Summary:
Limits and Opportunity

To sum up: the First Amendment imposes two limits on what public schools may do in teaching ethics. These stem from the words of the amendment itself and from the judicial interpretations of those words. They also have their origins in the view the First Amendment takes of the social and individual value of free inquiry. The public school cannot lawfully teach ethics in a manner that fosters or insults religious belief, nor can it use its undoubted authority to teach skills and what is known to be true of the universe to erect homogeneity of belief and opinion.

These two sets of constraints, the one stemming from a concern for religion and the other based on a wish to insure free speech, have this much in common: Both prohibit government from imposing orthodoxies of belief or expression. Both are intended to protect an absolute freedom of belief and a reasonably qualified freedom of conduct. If we now turn those constraints into statements of opportunity, we are left with enormous and unconstrained legal space in which to fashion ethics courses that would encourage freedom of discussion and debate as well as offer unrestricted freedom to reach conclusions dictated by inquiry and reason. By forbidding the establishment of orthodoxy, the Constitution betrays its intent to leave matters of belief and expression free of governmental control and to place responsibility for such fundamental concerns with free and rational men and women.

While that may be the intent of the Constitution, it is probably not the intent of many of those who clamor for ethics instruction for school children. But to the degree that teaching ethics is another form of social control, it is just to that degree that such teaching would be contrary to the best traditions of the Constitution. One might (though I won't) make a case that what the schools already do in reinforcing conventional moral and ethical belief, precisely because what is done is to strengthen a particular orthodoxy, is contrary to the intent of the Constitution. In any event, an effort by the public schools to go further than they have in giving effect to convention, and certainly any effort that materialized as a formal course, would run afoul of the Constitution's ban on orthodoxy.

For these reasons, then, I believe that those who would look to the schools for an ethically innocent generation of young people are likely, at least in other than the very long run, to be disappointed. For the same reasons, I believe that an open-ended, no-holds-barred curriculum in ethics would enhance the thinking and therefore the lives of those who took it. That might result, in the very long run, in the kind of ethical society most of us would like to have. And finally, for those reasons, I am perfectly willing to take my chances with the Constitution and encourage you to do the same.

Footnotes

1. *Abington School District v. Schempp*, 374 US 230 (1962), at 222; and *Walz v. Tax Commission*, 397 US 664 (1969), at 674-80.
2. *Everson v. Board of Education*, 330 US 1 (1946), at 15.
3. *Zorach v. Clauson*, 343 US 306 (1951), at 312.
4. *Board of Education v. Barnette*, 319 US 624 (1942), at 642.
5. *Tinker v. Des Moines School District*, 393 US 503 (1968), at 506.
6. *Ibid.*, at 511.

Chapter Two
Childhood Experience and Philosophical Wonderment

Chapter Two

Childhood Experience and Philosophical Wonderment

The adult's recollections of childhood are not ordinarily philosophical, nor do they often contain hints of that philosophical dimension with which some experiences are imbued or informed. On the other hand, there are some writers who are profoundly attuned to the philosophical dimension, and are able to evoke it movingly for us. A number of these writers are represented in this section.

Do children resemble philosophers? To employ a distinction popularized by Max Weber, we may say that some professional philosophers *live off* philosophy—which is to say that they have adopted philosophy as a career and from it they make their living, while others *live for* philosophy—it is to philosophy that they devote every waking hour of their lives. Now, children are not likely to be found living off philosophy, except in the sense that they live off the proceeds of adults, like parents, who *are* professional philosophers. Nor is it likely that many children whose interests are philosophical are nevertheless single-mindedly so. It is more customary to find them "tuning in" occasionally to the philosophical frequency or channel of their experience.

And yet, the laser-like mind of some children may penetrate very deeply indeed when it does turn to matters philosophical, just as the pre-Socratic philosopher offers us glimpses of a wholeness of experience or a largeness of spirit that escapes the less reticent, less gnomic writer. No child has written what Heraclitus has written, but the remark of the seven-year-old dead, "When we are dead, we dream that we are dead," does not have to yield pride of place to the aphorism by Heraclitus that reads, "All things we see when awake are death, and all we see when asleep are sleep." Just as Descartes can say "I do not know all that God knows, but what I know, I know as well as He does," so the child may not survey everything philosophically, the way someone who lives *for* philosophy generally tries to do, but what the child has an insight into, where it represents or speaks to the basic direction of that child's life, it understands as philosophically as any adult might.

Even though we recognize childhood experience as a genre of philosophical experience, we may not readily discern the diversity of childhood philosophical experiences, just as Europeans may recognize, say, Asian faces to be different from faces in other continents, but still be unperceptive regarding the ways in which Asian faces differ from one another. In this section, we can consider the accounts some adults have given of their explorations of the philosophical dimensions of the child's experience, and give our attention to the particular facets of that experience to which they have given considerations

1. *The child as a source of adult education.* Carl Ewald's *My Little Boy* is not so much about the wonderment expressed by his child as it is a record of his own marvelling at his son's sturdy individuality and intelligence. A perceptive and

caring father, Ewald nevertheless leaves his son to his own devices at times when another parent would intercede, Yet he mourns the child's eagerness to begin school, fearing that it will mark the end of the child's flights of imagination and robust moral integrity, Ewald's account details the education he has received from his son; it is a poignant illustration of how the study of children by a sensitive adult prepared to learn from them differs from the study of children's behavior by neutral, imperturbable observers.

2. *How children's literature and children's own thinking alike endorse what is reasonable and necessary.* To G. K. Chesterton what is of greatest worth is what human beings have in common, what they share, not what sets them apart from one another. The greatest values are to be found in those experiences we recognize to be ordinary and unremarkable. It is precisely to this aspect of things that logic and mathematics apply, confirming the uniformity and regularity of the preponderance of human experience. Chesterton argues that these ethical and aesthetic "truths." as expressed in children's literature, are likewise applicable to this same realm of events. Thus, "there is the great lesson of *Beauty and the Beast*: that a thing must be loved before it is loveable." Thus the wisdom of childhood, according to Chesterton, is the directness with which it seeks out what is necessary and reasonable, its ready acceptance of limitations and its willingness to abide by the dictates of common sense.

3. *Childhood ignorance and perversity.* Many a writer on childhood has argued persuasively that the naive or absurd conclusions children often arrive at are due less to the inaccuracies of their logical reasoning than to the lack of sound information upon which such reasoning should be based. Leslie Paul recounts the awfulness of his own childhood ignorance, but at the same time acknowledges that children can, in their own small way, be stubbornly manipulative and deliberately unkind. If Paul does not see the child as a tiny barbarian or monster, neither does he view the child as wholly angelic.

4. *Wonder as wondering at.* To Stephen Paget, true wondering is not merely wondering when or where, but wondering *at*. One takes notice, takes thought, wonders that such things as a parental face or apron can be at all, even as one rubs up against it or snuggles into it in blind animal fashion. It is this same wondering *at* (not at all to be confused with wondering if or wondering whether, such as may be engaged in by well-informed fools) that Wittgenstein, in his "*Lecture on Ethics*" singles out as the attitude of reverence, and as William James had done before him, in *The Varieties of Religious Experience*.

5. *Should we educate children by cultivating their thinking or their curiosity?* In a sense, this question pits the pragmatic educational theory of James, with its emphasis upon the passions and dispositions of the child, against Dewey's pragmatic pedagogy, with its emphasis upon the cultivation of children's thinking. Floyd Dell, for his part, sides here with James. But later in his essay, when he considers the ways in which we can educate for inquiry, he sides with the fallibilism of Peirce, itself an echo of the liberalism of J. S. Mill. We should not indoctrinate children, even if what we are teaching them is incontestably true. If children are wrong, they have to learn how to correct themselves, so that the conclusions they ultimately arrive at will be truly theirs and not ours.

6. *Growing up in a family at war*. This is a portion of a book review written by Randall Jarrell. The book being reviewed is Christina Stead's *The Man Who Loved Children*, and so Jarrell is here commenting on Stead's uncanny awareness of what it is like to be a child in a deteriorating family environment—and to be an artistic child in such an environment at that. There is the terrible sense of helplessness and despair, and the endless wanting the adults just to shut up, as a way of alleviating the child's misery. This may not be a typical childhood, but it helps us understand better the warm intimacy a family can have even while it sears a child for life.

My Little Boy

Carl Ewald
Translated from the Danish by Alexander Teixeira de Mattos

Some years ago, in an intriguing article on the problem of Verstehen *("If Matter Could Talk") in Sidney Morgenbesser, Patrick Suppes and Morton White, eds.,* Philosophy, Science, and Method: Essays in Honor of Ernest Nagel, *published in 1969 by St. Martin's Press), Fritz Machlup wrote*

"As a youngster I delighted in reading books by Carl Ewald; among them was one with beautiful Tales Told by Mother Nature about talking animals and objects. There was one in which earth and a comet had a discussion, joined in by the moon; another featured a chat between a spider and a mouse. A conversation between the sea and various plants and birds occurred in one tale, and another had a talk, with interesting implications of conscious cooperation, between a solder-crab and a sea-anemone. There was also a most informative debate among five germs: tuberculosis, cholera, and diphtheria complaining about man's warfare against them, mold bragging about its great power, and yeast defending man as its best friend."

And yet Ewald's work is little read today, particularly My Little Boy, *which was first published in Denmark in 1899, and subsequently appeared in an English version (by Charles Scribners Sons) in 1906. An affecting memoir of a relationship between a parent and child, it perhaps deserves equal bookshelf space with Edmond Gosse's more celebrated* Father and Son, *an excerpt of which appeared in Vol. I, No. 2 of* Thinking. *Ewald's books, his translator tells us, "are marked by the same bright individuality of style, combined with a simplicity of expression and narrative that gives them a charm which is all their own."*

Ewald was born in 1856 in Schleswig, but his family left Germany to settle in Copenhagen while he was still quite young. He became a forester, then a schoolmaster. Later, he became well known for his books on the digestive system and its ailments, as well as for his travel books. What follows is the complete text of My Little Boy.

My little boy is beginning to live. Carefully, stumbling now and then on his little knock-kneed legs, he makes his way over the paving-stones, looks at everything that there is to look at and bites at every apple, both those which are his due and those which are forbidden him.

He is not a pretty child and is the more likely to grow into a fine lad. But he is charming.

His face can light up suddenly and become radiant; and he can look at you with quite cold eyes. He has a strong intuition and he is incorruptible. He has never yet bartered a kiss for barley-sugar. There are people whom he likes and people whom he dislikes. There is one who has long courted his favor indefatigably and in vain; and, the other day, he formed a close friendship with another who had not so much as said "Good-day" to him before he had crept into her lap and nestled there with glowing resolution.

He has a habit which I love.

When we are walking together and there is anything that impresses him, he lets go of my hand for a moment. Then, when he has investigated the phenomenon and arrived at a result, I feel his little fist in mine again.

He has bad habits too.

He is apt, for instance, suddenly and without the slightest reason, to go up to people whom he meets in the street and hit them with his little stick. What is in his mind, when he does so, I do not know; and so long as he does not hit me, it remains a matter between himself and the people concerned.

He has an odd trick of seizing big words in a grown-up conversation, storing them up for a while and then asking me for an explanation:

"Father," he says, "what is life?"

I give him a tap in his little stomach, roll him over on the carpet and conceal my emotion under a mighty romp. Then, when we sit breathless and tired, I answer, gravely:

"Life is delightful, my little boy. Don't you be afraid of it!"

* * *

Today my little boy gave me my first lesson.

It was in the garden.

I was writing in the shade of the big chestnut-tree, close to where the brook flows past. He was sitting a little way off, on the grass, in the sun, with Hans Christian Andersen in his lap.

Of course, he does not know how to read, but he lets you read to him, likes to hear the same tales over and over again. The better he knows them, the better he is pleased. He follows the story page by page, knows exactly where everything comes and catches you up immediately should you skip a line.

There are two tales which he loves more than anything in the world.

These are Grimm's *Faithful John* and Andersen's *The Little Mermaid*. When any one comes whom he likes, he fetches the big Grimm, with those heaps of pictures, and asks for *Faithful John*. Then, if the reader stops, because it is so terribly sad, with all those little dead children, a bright smile lights up his small, long face and he says, reassuringly and pleased at "knowing better:"

"Yes, but they come to life again."

Today, however, it is *The Little Mermaid*.

"Is that the sort of stories you write?" he asks.

"Yes," I say, "but I am afraid mine will not be so pretty."

"You must take pains," he says.

And I promise.

For a time he makes no sound, I go on writing and forget about him.

"Is there a little mermaid down there, in the water?" he asks.

"Yes, she swims up to the top in the summer."

He nods and looks out across the brook, which ripples so softly and smoothly that one can hardly see the water flow. On the opposite side, the rushes grow green and thick and there is also a bird, hidden in the rushes, which sings. The dragon-flies are whirling and humming. I am sitting with my head in my hand, absorbed in my work.

Suddenly, I hear a splash.

I jump from my chair, upset the table, dart forward and see that my little boy is gone. The brook is billowing and foaming; there are wide circles on the surface.

In a moment, I am in the water and find him and catch hold of him.

He stands on the grass, dripping wet, spluttering and coughing. His thin clothes are clinging to his thin body, his face is black with mud. But out of the mud gleams a pair of angry eyes:

"There was no mermaid," he says.

I do not at once know what to reply and I have no time to think.

"Do you write that sort of stories?" he asks.

"Yes," I say, shamefaced.

"I don't like any of you," he says. "You make fun of a little boy."

He turns his back on me and, proud and wet, goes indoors without once looking round.

This evening, Grimm and Hans Christian Andersen disappear in a mysterious manner, which is never explained. He will miss them greatly, at first; but he will never be fooled again, not if I were to give him the sun and moon in his hand.

* * *

My little boy and I have had an exceedingly interesting walk in the Frederiksberg Park.

There was a mouse, which was irresistible. There were two chaffinches, husband and wife, which built their nest right before our eyes, and a snail, which had no secrets for us. And there were flowers, yellow and white, and there were green leaves, which told us the oddest adventures: in fact, as much as we can find room for in our little head.

Now we are sitting on a bench and digesting our impressions.

Suddenly the air is shaken by a tremendous roar:

"What was that?" asks my little boy.

"That was the lion in the Zoological Gardens," I reply.

No sooner have I said this than I curse my own stupidity.

I might have said that it was a gunshot announcing the birth of a prince; or an earthquake; or a china dish falling from the sky and breaking into pieces: anything whatever, rather than the truth.

For now my little boy wants know what sort of thing the Zoological Gardens is.

I tell him.

The Zoological Gardens is a horrid place, where they lock up wild beasts who have done no wrong and who are accustomed to walk about freely in the distant foreign countries where they come from. The lion is there, whom we have just heard roaring. He is so strong that he can kill a policeman with one blow of his paw; he has great, haughty eyes and awfully sharp teeth. He lives in Africa and, at night, when he roars, all the other beasts tremble in their holes for fear. He is called the king of beasts. They caught him one day in a cunning trap and bound him and dragged him here and locked him up in a cage with iron bars to it. The cage is no more than half as big as Petrine's room. And there the king walks up and down, up and down, and gnashes his teeth with sorrow and rage and roars so that you can hear him ever so far away. Outside his cage stand cowardly people and laugh at him, because he can't get out and eat them up, and poke their sticks through the rails and tease him.

My little boy stands in front of me and looks at me with wide-open eyes:

"Would he eat them up, if he got out?" he asks.

"In a moment."

"But he can't get out, can he?"

"No. That's awfully sad. He can't get out."

"Father, let us go and look at the lion."

I pretend not to hear and go on to tell him of the strange birds there: great eagles, which used to fly over every church-steeple and over the highest trees and mountains and swoop down upon lambs and hares and carry them up to their young in the nest. Now they are sitting in cages, on a perch, like canaries, with clipped wings and blind eyes. I tell him of gulls, which used to fly all day long over the stormy sea: now they splash about in a puddle of water, screaming pitifully. I tell him of wonderful blue and red birds, which, in their youth, used to live among wonderful blue and red flowers, in balmy forests a thousand times bigger than the Frederiksberg Park, where it was as dark as night under the trees with the brightest sun shining down upon the tree-tops: now they sit there in very small cages and hang their beaks while they stare at tiresome boys in dark-blue suits and black stockings and waterproof boots and sailor-hats.

"Are those birds really blue?" asks my little boy.

"Sky-blue," I answer. "And utterly broken-hearted."

"Father, can't we go and look at the birds?"

I take my little boy's hands in mine:

"I don't think we will," I say. "Why should still more silly boys do so? You can't imagine how it goes to one's heart to look at those poor captive beasts."

"Father, I should so much like to go."

"Take my advice and don't. The animals there are not the real animals, you see. They are ill and ugly and angry because of their captivity and their longing and their pain."

"I should so much like to see them."

"Now let me tell you something. To go to the Zoological Gardens costs five cents for you and ten cents for me. That makes fifteen cents altogether, which is an awful lot of money. We won't go there now, but we'll buy the biggest money-box we can find: one of those money-boxes shaped like a pig. Then we'll put fifteen cents in it. And every Thursday we'll put fifteen cents in the pig. By-and-by, that will grow into quite a fortune: it will make such a lot of money that when you are grown up, you can take a trip to Africa and go to the desert and hear the wild, the real lion roaring and tremble just like the people tremble down there. And you can go to the great, dark forests and see the real blue birds flying proud and free among the flowers. You can't think how glad you will be, how beautiful they will look and how they will sing to you. . . ."

"Father, I would rather go to the Zoological Gardens now."

My little boy does not understand a word of what I say. And I am at my wits' end.

"Shall we go and have some cakes at Josty's?" I ask.

"I would rather go to the Zoological Gardens."

I can read in his eyes that he is thinking of the captive lion. Ugly human instincts are waking up in his soul. The mouse is forgotten and the snail; and the chaffinches have built their nest to no purpose.

At last I get up and say, bluntly, without any further explanation:

"You are *not* going to the Zoological Gardens. Now we'll go home."

And home we go. But we are not in a good temper.

Of course, I get over it and I buy a enormous piggybank. Also we put the money into it and he thinks that most interesting.

But, later in the afternoon, I find him in the bed-room engaged in a piteous game.

He has built a cage, in which he has imprisoned the pig. He is teasing it and hitting it with his whip, while he keeps shouting to it:

"You can't get out and bite me, you stupid pig! You can't get out!"

* * *

We have beer-soup and Aunt Anna to dinner. Now beer-soup is a nasty dish and Aunt Anna is not very nice either.

She has yellow teeth and a little hump and very severe eyes, which are not even both equally severe. She is nearly always scolding us and, when she sees a chance, she pinches us.

The worst of all, however, is that she is constantly setting up a good example, which can easily end by gradually and inevitably driving us to embrace wickedness.

Aunt Anna does not like beer-soup any more than we do. But of course she eats it with a voluptuous expression on her face and looks angrily at my little boy, who does not even make an attempt to behave nicely:

"Why doesn't the little boy eat his delicious beer-soup?" she asks.

A scornful silence.

"Such delicious beer-soup! I know a poor, wretched boy who would be awfully glad to have such delicious beer-soup."

My little boy looks with great interest at Auntie, who is swallowing her soup with eyes full of ecstatic bliss:

"Where is he?" he asks.

Aunt Anna pretends not to hear.

"Where is the poor boy?" he asks again.

"Yes, where is he?" I ask. "What's his name?"

Aunt Anna gives me a furious glance.

"What's his name, Aunt Anna?" asks my little boy. "Where does he live? He can have my beer-soup with pleasure."

"Mine too," I say, resolutely, and I push my plate from me.

My little boy never takes his great eyes off Aunt Anna's face. Meanwhile, she has recovered herself:

"There are many poor boys who would thank God if they could get such delicious beer-soup," she says. "Very many. Everywhere."

"Yes, but tell us of one, Auntie," I say.

My little boy has slipped down from his chair. He stands with his chin just above the table and both his hands round his plate, ready to march off with the beer-soup to the poor boy, if only he can get his address.

But Aunt Anna does not allow herself to be played with:

"Heaps of poor boys," she says again. "Hundreds! And therefore another little boy, whom I will not name, but who is in this room, ought to be ashamed that he is not thankful for his beer-soup.

My little boy stares at Aunt Anna like the bird fascinated by the snake.

"Such delicious beer-soup!" she says. "I must really ask for another little helping."

Aunt Anna revels in her martyrdom. My little boy stands speechless, with open mouth and round eyes.

I push my chair back and say, with genuine exasperation:

"Now, look here, Aunt Anna, this is really too bad! Here we are, with a whole lot of beer-soup, which we don't care about in the least and which

we would be very glad to get rid of, if we only knew some one who would have it. You are the only one that knows of anybody. You know a poor boy who would dance for joy if he got some beer-soup. You know hundreds. But you won't tell us their names or where they live."

"Why, what do you mean?"

"And you yourself sit quite calmly eating two whole helpings, though you know quite well that you're going to have an omelette to follow. That's really very naughty of you, Aunt Anna."

Aunt Anna chokes with annoyance. My little boy locks his teeth with a snap and looks with every mark of disgust at that wicked old woman.

And I turn with calm earnestness to his mother and say:

"After this, it would be most improper for us ever to have beer-soup here again. We don't care for it and there are hundreds of little boys who love it. If it must be made, then Aunt Anna must come every Saturday and fetch it. She knows where the boys live.

The omelette is eaten in silence, after which Aunt Anna shakes the dust from her shoes. She won't have any coffee today.

While she is standing in the hall and putting on her endless wraps, a last doubt arises in my little boy's soul. He opens his green eyes wide before her face and whispers:

"Aunt Anna, where do the boys live?"

Aunt Anna pinches him and is shocked and goes off, having suffered a greater defeat than she can every repair.

* * *

My little boy comes into my room and tells me, with a very long face, that Jean is dead. And we put all nonsense on one side and hurry away to the Klampenborg train, to go where Jean is.

For Jean is the biggest dog that has lived for some time.

He once bit a boy so hard that the boy still walks lame. He once bit his own master. He could give such a look out of his eyes and open such a mouth that there was no more horrible sight in the world. And then he would be the mildest of the mild: my little boy could put his hand in his mouth and ride on his back and pull his tail.

When we get there, we hear that Jean is already buried.

We look at each other in dismay, to think how quickly that happens! And we go to the grave, which is in the grounds of the factory, where the tall chimneys stand.

We sit down and can't understand it.

We tell each other all the stories that we know of Jean's wonderful size and strength. The one remembers this, the other that. And, as each story is told, the whole thing becomes only more awful and obscure.

At last we go home by train.

Besides ourselves, there is a kind old gentleman in the compartment, who would like to make friends with my little boy. But the boy has nothing to talk about to the kind old gentleman. He stands at the window, which comes just under his chin, and stares out.

His eyes light upon some tall chimneys:

"That's where Jean is buried," he says.

"Yes."

The landscape flies past. He can think only of *that* and see only *that* and, when some more chimneys appear, he says again:

"That's where Jean is buried."

"No, my little friend," says the kind old gentleman. "That was over there."

The boy looks at him with surprise. I hasten to reassure him:

"Those *are* Jean's chimneys," I say.

And, while he is looking out again, I take the old gentleman to the further corner of the compartment and tell him the state of the case.

I tell him that, if I live, I hope, in years to come, to explain to the boy the difference between Petersen's and Hansen's factories and, should I die, I will confidently leave that part of his education to others. Yes, even if he should never learn this difference, I would still be resigned. Today it is a question of other and more important matters. The strongest, the most living thing he knew is dead. . . .

"Really?" says the old gentleman, sympathetically. "A relation, perhaps?"

"Yes," I say. "Jean is dead, a dog. . . ."

"A dog?"

"It is not because of the *dog*—don't you understand?—but of *death*, which he sees for the first time: death, with all its might, its mystery. . . ."

"Father," says my little boy and turns his head towards us. "When do we die?"

"When we grow old," says the kind old gentleman.

"No," says the boy. "Einar has a brother, at home, in the courtyard, and he is dead. And he was only a little boy."

"Then Einar's brother was so good and learnt such a lot that he was already fit to go to Heaven," says the old gentleman.

"Mind you don't become too good," I say and laugh and tap my little boy in the stomach.

And my little boy laughs too and goes back to his window, where new chimneys rise over Jean's grave.

But I take the old gentleman by the shoulders and forbid him most strictly to talk to my little boy again. I give up trying to make him understand me. I just shake him. He eyes the communication-cord and, when we reach the station, hurries away.

I go with my little boy, holding his hand, through the streets of live people. In the evening, I sit on the edge of his bed and talk with him about that incomprehensible thing: Jean, who is dead; Jean, who was so much alive, so strong, so big. . . .

* * *

Our courtyard is full of children and my little boy has picked a bosom-friend out of the band:

his name is Einar and he can be as good as another.

My little boy admires him and Einar allows himself to be admired, so that the friendship is established on the only proper basis.

"Einar says . . . Einar thinks . . . Einar does," is the daily refrain; and we arrange our little life accordingly.

"I can't see anything out of the way in Einar," says the mother of my little boy.

"Nor can I," says I. "But our little boy can and that is enough. I once had a friend who could see nothing at all charming in you. And you yourself, if I remember right, had three friends who thought your taste inexcusable. Luckily for our little boy . . ."

"Luckily!"

"It is the feeling that counts," I go on lecturing, "and not the object."

"Thanks!" she says.

Now something big and unusual takes place in our courtyard and makes an extraordinary impression on the children and gives their small brains heaps to struggle with for many a long day.

The scarlatina comes.

And scarlatina is not like a pain in your stomach, when you have eaten too many pears, or like a cold, when you have forgotten to put on your jacket. Scarlatina is something quite different, something powerful and terrible. It comes at night and takes a little boy who was playing quite happily that same evening. And then the little boy is gone.

Perhaps a funny carriage comes driving through the gate, with two horses and a coachman and two men with bright brass buttons on their coats. The two men take out of the carriage a basket, with a red blanket and white sheets, and carry it up to where the boy lives. Presently, they carry the basket down again and then the boy is inside. But nobody can see him, because the sheet is over his face. The basket is shoved into the carriage, which is shut with a bang, and away goes the carriage with the boy, while his mother dries her eyes and goes up to the others.

Perhaps no carriage comes. But then the sick boy is shut up in his room and no one may go to him for a long time, because he is infectious. And anyone can understand that this must be terribly sad.

The children in the courtyard talk of nothing else.

They talk with soft voices and faces full of mystery, because they know nothing for certain. They hear that one of them, who rode away in the carriage, is dead; but that makes no more impression on them than when one of them falls ill and disappears.

Day by day, the little band is being thinned out and not one of them has yet come back.

I stand at my open window and look at my little boy, who is sitting on the steps below with his friend. They have their arms around each other's necks and see no one except each other; that is to say, Einar sees himself and my little boy sees Einar.

"If you fall ill, I will come and see you," says my little boy.

"No, you won't!"

"I will come and see you."

His eyes beam at this important promise. Einar cries as though he were already ill.

And the next day he is ill.

He lies in a little room all by himself. No one is allowed to go to him. A red curtain hangs before the window.

My little boy sits alone on the steps outside and stares up at the curtain. His hands are thrust deep into his pockets. He does not care to play and he speaks to nobody.

And I walk up and down the room, uneasy as to what will come next.

"You are anxious about our little boy," says his mother. "And it will be a miracle if he escapes."

"It's not that. We've all had a touch of scarlatina."

But just as I want to talk to her about it, I hear a fumbling with the door-handle which there is no mistaking and then he stands before us in the room.

I know you so well, my little boy, when you come in sideways like that, with a long face, and go and sit in a corner and look at the two people who owe so much happiness to you—look from one to the other. Your eyes are greener than usual. You can't find your words and you sit huddled up and you are ever so good.

"Mother, is Einar ill?"

"Yes. But he will soon be better again. The doctor says that he is not so bad."

"Is he infectious, Mother?"

"Yes, he is. His little sister has been sent to the country, so that she may not fall ill too. No one is allowed to go to him except his mother, who gives him his milk and his medicine and makes his bed."

A silence.

The mother of my little boy looks down at her book and suspects nothing. The father of my little boy looks in great suspense from the window.

"Mother, I want to go to Einar."

"You can't go there, my little man. You hear, he's infectious. Just think, if you should fall ill yourself! Einar isn't bothering at all about chatting with you. He sleeps the whole day long."

"But when he wakes, Mother?"

"You can't go up there."

This tells upon him and he is nearly crying. I see that the time has come for me to come to his rescue:

"Have you promised Einar to go and see him?" I ask.

"Yes, Father. . . ."

He is over his trouble. His eyes beam. He stands erect and glad beside me and puts his little hand in mine.

"Then of course you must do so," I say, calmly. "So soon as he wakes."

Our mother closes her book with a bang:

"Go down to the courtyard and play, while Father and I have a talk."

The boy runs away.

And she comes up to me and lays her hand on my shoulder and says, earnestly:

"I *daren't* do that, do you hear?"

And I take her hand and kiss it and say, quite as earnestly:

"And I *daren't* refuse!"

We look at each other, we two, who share the empire, the power and the glory.

"I heard our little boy make his promise," I say, "I saw him. Sir Galahad himself was not more in earnest when swearing his knightly oath. You see, we have no choice here. He can catch the scarlatina in any case and it is not even certain that he will catch it. . . ."

"If it was diphtheria, you wouldn't talk like that!"

"You may be right. But am I to become a thief for the sake of a nickel, because I am not sure that I could resist the temptation to steal a kingdom?"

"You would not find a living being to agree with you."

"Except yourself. And that is all I want. The infection is really only a side matter. It can come this way or that way. We can't safeguard him, come what may. . . ."

"But are we to send him straight to where it is?"

"We're not doing that; it's not we who are doing that."

She is very much excited. I put my arm round her waist and we walk up and down the room together:

"Darling, today our little boy may meet with a great misfortune. He may receive a shock from which he will never recover. . . ."

"That is true," she says.

"If he doesn't keep his promise, the misfortune has occurred. It would already be a misfortune if he could ever think that it was possible for him to break it, if it appeared to him that there was anything great or remarkable about keeping it."

"Yes, but. . . ."

"Darling, the world is full of careful persons. One step more and they become mere paltry people. Shall we turn that into a likely thing, into a virtue, for our little boy? His promise was stupid: let that pass. . . ."

"He is so little."

"Yes, that he is; and God be praised for it! Think what good luck it is that he did not know the danger, when he made his promise, that he does not understand it now, when he is keeping it. What a lucky beggar! He is learning to keep his word, just as he has learnt to be clean. By the time that he is big enough to know his danger, it will be an indispensable habit with him. And he gains all that at the risk of a little scarlatina."

She lays her head on my shoulder and says nothing more.

That afternoon, she takes our little boy by the hand and goes up with him to Einar. They stand on the threshold of his room, bid him good-day and ask him how he is.

Einar is not at all well and does not look up and does not answer.

But that does not matter in the least.

* * *

My little boy is given a cent by Petrine with instructions to go to the baker's and buy some biscuits.

By that which fools call an accident, but which is really a divine miracle, if miracles there be, I overhear this instruction. Then I stand at my window and see him cross the street in his slow way and with bent head; only, he goes slower than usual and with his head bent more deeply between his small shoulders.

He stands long outside the baker's window, where there is a confused heap of lollipops and chocolates and sugar-sticks and other things created for a small boy's delight. Then he lifts his young hand, opens the door, disappears and presently returns with a great paper bag, eating with all his might.

And I, who, Heaven be praised, have myself been a thief in my time, run all over the house and give my orders.

My little boy enters the kitchen.

"Put the biscuits on the table," says Petrine.

He stands still for a moment and looks at her and at the table and at the floor. Then he goes silently to his mother.

"You're quite a big boy now that you can buy biscuits for Petrine," says she, without looking up from her work.

His face is very long, but he says nothing. He comes quietly in to me and sits down on the edge of a chair.

"You have been across the street, at the baker's."

He comes up to me, where I am sitting and reading, and presses himself against me. I do not look at him, but I can perceive what is going on inside him.

"What did you buy at the baker's?"

"Lollipops."

"Well, I never! What fun! Why, you had some lollipops this morning. Who gave you the money this time?"

"Petrine."

"Really! Well, Petrine is certainly very fond of you. Do you remember the lovely ball she gave you on your birthday?"

"Father, Petrine told me to buy a cent's worth of biscuits.

"Oh dear!"

It is very quiet in the room. My little boy cries bitterly and I look anxiously before me, stroking his hair the while.

"Now you have fooled Petrine badly. She wants those biscuits, of course, for her cooking. She thinks they're on the kitchen-table and, when she goes to look, she won't find any. Mother gave her a cent for biscuits. Petrine gave you a cent for biscuits and you go and spend it on lollipops. What are we to do?"

He looks at me in despair, holds me tight, says a thousand things without speaking a word.

"If only we had a cent," I say. "Then you could rush over the way and fetch the biscuits."

"Father. . . ." His eyes open very wide and he speaks so softly that I can hardly hear him. "There is a cent on mother's writing-table."

"Is there?" I cry with delight. But, at the same moment, I shake my head and my face is overcast again. "That is no use to us, my little boy. That cent belongs to mother. The other was Petrine's. People are so terribly fond of their money and get so angry when you take it from them. I can understand that, for you can buy such an awful lot of things with money. You can get biscuits and lollipops and clothes and toys and half the things in the world. And it is not so easy either to make money. Most people have to drudge all day long to earn as much as they want. So it is no wonder that they get angry when you take it. Especially when it is only for lollipops. Now Petrine . . . she has to spend the whole day cleaning rooms and cooking dinner and washing up before she gets her wages. And out of that she has to buy clothes and shoes . . . and you know that she has a little girl whom she has to pay for at Madam Olsen's. She must certainly have saved very cleverly before she managed to buy you that ball."

We walk up and down the room, hand in hand. He keeps on falling over his legs, for he can't take his eyes from my face.

"Father . . . haven't you got a cent?"

I shake my head and give him my purse:

"Look for yourself," I say. "There's not a cent in it. I spent the last this morning."

We walk up and down. We sit down and get up and walk about again. We are very gloomy. We are bowed down with sorrow and look at each other in great perplexity.

"There might be one hidden away in a drawer somewhere," I say.

We fly to the drawers.

We pull out thirty drawers and rummage through them. We fling papers in disorder, higgledy-piggledy, on the floor: what do we care? If only, if only we find a cent. . . .

Hurrah!

We both, at last, grasp at a cent, as though we would fight for it . . . we have found a beautiful, large cent. Our eyes gleam and we laugh through our tears.

"Hurry now," I whisper. "You can go this way . . . through my door. Then run back quickly up the kitchen stairs, with the biscuits, and put them on the table. I shall call Petrine, so that she doesn't see. And we won't tell anybody."

He is down the stairs before I have done speaking. I run after him and call to him:

"Wasn't it a splendid thing that we found that cent?" I say.

"Yes," he answers earnestly.

And he laughs for happiness and I laugh too and his legs go like drumsticks across to the baker's.

From my window, I see him come back, at the same pace, with red cheeks and glad eyes. He has committed his first crime. He has understood it. And he has not the sting of remorse in his soul nor the black cockade of forgiveness in his cap.

The mother of my little boy and I sit until late at night talking about money, which seems to us the most difficult matter of all.

For our little boy must learn to know the power of money and the glamour of money and the joy of money. He must earn much money and spend much money. . . .

Yet there were two people, yesterday, who killed a man to rob him of four dollars and thirty-seven cents. . . .

* * *

It has been decreed in the privy council that my little boy shall have a weekly income of one cent. Every Sunday morning, that sum shall be paid to him, free of income tax, out of the treasury and he has leave to dispose of it entirely at his own pleasure.

He receives this announcement with composure and sits apart for a while and ponders on it.

"Every Sunday?" he asks.

"Every Sunday."

"All the time till the summer holidays?"

"All the time till the summer holidays."

In the summer holidays, he is to go to the country, to stay with his godmother, in whose house he was pleased to allow himself to be born.

The summer holidays are, consequently, the limits of his calculation of time: beyond them lies, for the moment, his Nirvana.

And we employ this restricted horizon of ours to further our true happiness.

That is to say, we calculate, with the aid of the almanac, that, if everything goes as heretofore, there will be fifteen Sundays before the summer holidays. We arrange a drawer with fifteen compartments and in each compartment we put one cent. Thus we know exactly what we have and are able at any time to survey our financial status.

And, when he sees that great lot of cents lying there, my little boy's breast is filled with mad delight. He feels endlessly rich, safe for a long time. The courtyard rings with his bragging, with all that he is going to do with his money. His special favourites are invited to come up and view his treasure.

The first Sunday passes in a normal fashion, as was to be expected.

He takes his cent and turns it straight-way into a stick of chocolate of the best sort, with almonds on it and sugar, in short, an ideal stick in every way. The whole performance is over in five minutes: by that time, the stick of chocolate is gone, with the sole exception of a remnant in the corners of our mouth, which our ruthless mother wipes away, and a stain on our collar, which annoys us.

He sits by me, with a vacant little face, and swings his legs. I open the drawer and look at the empty space and at the fourteen others:

"So *that's* gone," I say.

My accent betrays a certain melancholy, which finds an echo in his breast. But he does not deliver himself of it at once.

"Father . . . is it long till next Sunday?"

"Very long, my boy; ever so many days."

We sit a little, steeped in our own thoughts. Then I say, pensively:

"Now, if you had bought a top, you would perhaps have had more pleasure out of it. I know a place where there is a lovely top: red, with a green ring round it. It is just over the way, in the toyshop. I saw it yesterday. I should be greatly mistaken if the toyman was not willing to sell it for a cent. And you've got a whip, you know."

We go over the way and look at the top in the shop-window. It is really a splendid top.

"The shop's shut," says my little boy, despondently.

I look at him with surprise:

"Yes, but what does that matter to us? Anyway, we can't buy the top before next Sunday. You see, you've spent your cent on chocolate. Give me your handkerchief: there's still a bit on your cheek."

There is no more to be said. Crestfallen and pensive, we go home. We sit a long time at the dining-room window, from which we can see the window of the shop.

During the course of the week, we look at the top daily, for it does not do to let one's love grow cold. One might so easily forget it. And the top shines always more seductively. We go in and make sure that the price is really in keeping with our means. We make the shopkeeper take a solemn oath to keep the top for us till Sunday morning, even if boys should come and bid him much higher sums for it.

On Sunday morning, we are on the spot before nine o'clock and acquire our treasure with trembling hands. And we play with it all day and sleep with it at night, until, on Wednesday morning, it disappears without a trace, after the nasty manner which tops have.

When the turn comes of the next cent, something remarkable happens.

There is a boy in the courtyard who has a skipping-rope and my little boy, therefore, wants to have a skipping-rope too. But this is a difficult matter. Careful enquiries establish the fact that a skipping-rope of the sort used by the upper classes is nowhere to be obtained for less than five cents.

The business is discussed as early as Saturday:

"It's the simplest thing in the world," I say. "You must not spend your cent to-morrow. Next Sunday you must do the same and the next and the next. On the Sunday after that, you will have saved your five cents and can buy your skipping-rope at once."

"When shall I get my skipping-rope then?"

"In five Sundays from now."

He says nothing, but I can see that he does not think my idea very brilliant. In the course of the day, he derives, from sources unknown to me, an acquaintance with financial circumstances which he serves up to me on Sunday morning in the following words:

"Father, you must lend me five cents for the skipping-rope. If you will lend me five cents for the skipping-rope, I'll give you *forty* cents back. . . ."

He stands close to me, very red in the face and quite confused. I perceive that he is ripe for falling into the claws of the usurers:

"I don't do that sort of business, my boy," I say. "It wouldn't do you any good either. And you're not even in a position to do it, for you have only thirteen cents, as you know."

He collapses like one whose last hope is gone.

"Let us just see," I say.

And we go to our drawer and stare at it long and deeply.

"We might perhaps manage it this way, that I give you five cents now. And then I should have your cent and the next four cents.

He interrupts me with a loud shout. I take out my purse, give him five cents and take one cent out of the drawer:

"That won't be pleasant next Sunday," I say, "and the next and the next and the next. . . ."

But the thoughtless youth is gone.

Of course, the installments of his debt are paid off with great ceremony. He is always on the spot himself when the drawer is opened and sees how the requisite cent is removed and finds its way into my pocket instead of his.

The first time, all goes well. It is simply an amusing thing that I should have the cent; and the skipping-rope is still fresh in his memory, because of the pangs which he underwent before its purchase. Next Sunday, already the thing is not *quite* so pleasant and, when the fourth installment falls due, my little boy's face looks very gloomy.

"Is anything the matter?" I ask.

"I should so much like a stick of chocolate," he says, without looking at me.

"Is that all? You can get one in a fortnight. By that time, you will have paid for the skipping-rope and the cent will be your own again."

"I should so much like to have the stick of chocolate now."

Of course, I am full of the sincerest compassion, but I can't help it. What's gone is gone. We saw it with our own eyes and we know exactly where it has gone to. And, that Sunday morning, we part in a dejected mood.

Later in the day, however, I find him standing over the drawer with raised eyebrows and a pursed-up mouth. I sit down quietly and wait. And I do not have to wait long before I learn that his development as an economist is taking quite its normal course.

"Father, suppose we moved the cent now from here into this Sunday's place and I took it and bought the chocolate stick. . . ."

"Why, then you won't have your cent for the other Sunday."

"I don't mind that, Father. . . ."

We talk about it, and then we do it. And, with that, as a matter of course, we enter upon the most reckless speculations.

The very next Sunday, he is clever enough to take the furthest cent, which lies just before the summer holidays. He pursues the path of vice without a scruple, until, at last, the blow falls and five long Sundays come in a row without the least chance of a cent.

Where should they come from? They were there. We know that. They are gone. We have spent them ourselves.

But, during those drab days of poverty, we sit every morning over the empty drawer and talk long and profoundly about that painful phenomenon, which is so simple and so easy to understand and which one must needs make the best of.

And we hope and trust that our experience will do us good, when, after our trip, we start a new set of cents.

* * *

My little boy is engaged to be married.

She is a big, large-limbed young woman, three years his senior, and no doubt belongs to the minor aristocracy. Her name is Gertie. By a misunderstanding, however, which is pardonable at his age and moreover quite explained by Gertie's appearance, he calls her Dirty—little Dirty—and by this name she will be handed down to history.

He met her on the boulevard, where he was playing, in the fine spring weather, with other children. His reason for the engagement is good enough:

"I wanted a girl for myself," he says.

Either I know very little of mankind or he has made a fortunate choice. No one is likely to take Dirty from him.

Like the gentleman that he is, he at once brings the girl home to us and introduces her. In consequence of the formality of the occasion, he does not go in by the kitchen way, as usual, but rings the front-door bell. I open the door myself. There he stands on the mat, hand in hand with Dirty, his bride, and, with radiant eyes:

"Father," he says, "this is little Dirty. She is my sweetheart. We are going to be married."

"That is what people usually do with their sweethearts," I answer, philosophically. "Pray, Dirty, come in and be welcomed by the family."

"Wipe your feet, Dirty," says my little boy.

The mother of my little boy does not think much of the match. She has even spoken of forbidding Dirty the house.

"We can't do that," I say. "I am not in ecstasies over it either, but it is not at all certain that it will last."

"Yes, but . . ."

"Do you remember what little use it was when your mother forbade me the house? We used to meet in the most incredible places and kiss each other terribly. I can quite understand that you have forgotten, but you ought to bear it in mind now that your son's beginning. And you ought to value the loyalty of his behavior towards his aged parents."

"My dear! . . ."

"And then I must remind you that it is spring. The trees are budding. You can't see it, perhaps, from the kitchen-window or from your work-table, but I, who go about all day, have noticed it. You know what Byron says:

> March has its hares, and May must have it's heroine.

And so Dirty is accepted.

But, when she calls, she has first to undergo a short quarantine, while the mother of my little boy washes her and combs her hair thoroughly.

Dirty does not like this, but the boy does. He looks on with extraordinary interest and at once complains if there is a place that has escaped the sponge. I can't make out what goes on within him on these occasions. There is a good deal of cruelty in love; and he himself hates to be washed. Perhaps he is wrapt in fancies and wants to see his sweetheart rise daily from the waves, like Venus Anadyomene. Perhaps it is merely his sense of duty: last Friday, in cold blood, he allowed Dirty to wait outside, on the step, for half an hour, until his mother came home.

Another of his joys is to see Dirty eat.

I can quite understand that. Here, as at her toilet, there is something worth looking at. The mother of my little boy and I would be glad too to watch her, if there were any chance of giving Dirty her fill. But there is none. At least not with my income.

When I see all that food disappear, without as much as a shade of satisfaction coming into her eyes, I tremble for the young couple's future. But he is cheerful and unconcerned.

Of course there are also clouds in their sky.

A few days ago, they were sitting quietly together in the dining-room talking of their wedding. My little boy described what the house would be like and the garden and the horses. Dirty made no remarks and she had no grounds for doing so, for everything was particularly nice. But, after that, things went wrong:

"We shall have fourteen children," said the boy.

"No," said Dirty. "We shall only have two: a boy and a girl."

"I want to have fourteen."

"I won't have more than two."

"Fourteen."

"Two."

There was no coming to an agreement. My little boy was speechless at Dirty's meanness. And Dirty pinched her lips together and nodded her head defiantly. Then he burst into tears.

I could have explained to him that Dirty, who sits down every day as the seventh at the children's table at home, cannot look upon children with his eyes, as things forming an essential part of every well-regulated family, but must regard them rather as bandits who eat up other people's food. But I did not feel entitled to discuss the young lady's domestic circumstances unasked.

One good thing about Dirty is that she is not dependent upon her family nor they upon her. It has not yet happened that any inquiries have been made after her, however long she remained with us. We know just where she lives and what her father's name is. Nothing more.

However, we notice in another way that our daughter-in-law is not without relations.

Whenever, for instance, we give her a pair of stockings or some other article of clothing, it is always gone the next day; and soon until all the six brothers and sisters have been supplied. Not till then do we have the pleasure of seeing Dirty look neat. She has been so long accustomed to going shares that she does so in every conceivable circumstance.

And I console the mother of my little boy by saying that, should he fall out with Dirty, he can take one of the sisters and that, in this way, nothing would be lost.

* * *

My little boy confides to me that he would like a pear.

Now pears fall within his mother's province and I am sure that he has had as many as he is entitled to. And so we are at once agreed that what he wants is a wholly irrelevant, uncalled-for, delightful extra pear.

Unfortunately, it also appears that the request has already been laid before Mamma and met with a positive refusal.

The situation is serious, but not hopeless. For I am a man who knows how mean is the supply of pears to us poor wretched children of men and how wonderful an extra pear tastes.

And I am glad that my little boy did not give up all hope of the pear at the first obstacle. I can see by the longing in his green eyes how big the pear is and I reflect with lawful paternal pride that he will win his girl and his position in life when their time comes.

We now discuss the matter carefully.

First comes the prospect of stomachache:

"Never mind about that," says he.

I quite agree with his view.

Then perhaps Mother will be angry.

No, Mother is never angry. She is sorry; and that is not nice. But then we must see and make it up to her in another way.

So we slink in and steal the pear.

I put it to him whether, perhaps—when we have eaten the pear—we ought to tell Mother. But that does not appeal to him:

"Then I shan't get one this evening, he says.

And when I suggest that, possibly, Mother might be impressed with such audacious candor, he shakes his head decisively:

"You don't know Mother," he says.

So I, of course, have nothing to say.

Shortly after this, the mother of my little boy and I are standing at the window laughing at the story.

We catch sight of him below, in the courtyard.

He is sitting on the steps with his arm round little Dirty's neck. They have shared the pear.

Now they are both singing, marvellously out of tune and with a disgustingly sentimental expression on their faces, a song which Dirty knows:

For riches are only a lo-oan from Heaven
And poverty is a reward.

And we are overcome with a great sense of desolation.

We want to make life green and pleasant for our little boy, to make his eyes open wide to see it, his hands strong to grasp it. But we feel powerless in the face of all the contentment and patience and resignation that are preached from cellar to garret, in church and in school: all those second-rate virtues, which may lighten an old man's last few steps as he stumbles on towards the grave, but which are only so many shabby lies for the young.

* * *

Dirty is paying us a visit and my little boy is sitting at her feet.

She has buried her fingers in her hair and is reading, reading, reading. . . .

She is learning the Ten Commandments by heart. She stammers and repeats herself, with eyes fixed in her head and a despairing mouth:

"Thou shalt . . . Thou shalt not . . . Thou shalt . . ."

The boy watches her with tender compassion.

He has already learnt a couple of the commandments by listening to her and helps her, now and then, with a word. Then he comes to me and asks, anxiously:

"Father, must Dirty do all that the Ten Commandments say?"

"Yes."

He sits down by her again. His heart is overflowing with pity, his eyes are moist. She does not look at him, but plods on bravely:

"Thou shalt . . . Thou shalt not . . ."

"Father, when I grow big, must I also do all that the Ten Commandments say?"

"Ye-es."

He looks at me in utter despair. Then he goes back to Dirty and listens, but now he keeps his thoughts to himself.

Suddenly, something seems to flash across his mind.

He comes to me again, puts his arms on my knee and looks with his green eyes firmly into mine:

"Father, do you do all that the Ten Commandments say?"

"Ye-e-es."

He looks like a person whose last hope has escaped him. I would so much like to help him; but what, in Heaven's name, can I do?

Then he collects himself, shakes his head a little and says, with great tears in his eyes:

"Father, I don't believe that I can do all those things that the Ten Commandments say."

And I draw him to me and we cry together because life is so difficult, while Dirty plods away like a good girl.

* * *

This we all know, that sin came into the world by the law.

Dirty's Ten Commandments have brought it to us.

When she comes, she now always has Luther's terrible Little Catechism[1] and Balslev's equally objectionable work with her. Her parents evidently look upon it as most natural that she should also cultivate her soul at our house.

Her copies of these two classics were not published yesterday. They are probably heirlooms in Dirty's family. They are covered in thick brown paper, which again is protected by a heavy layer of dirt against any touch of clean fingers. They can be smelt at a distance.

But my little boy is no snob.

When Dirty has finished her studies—she always reads out aloud—he asks her permission to turn over the pages of the works in which she finds those strange words. He stares respectfully at the letters which he cannot read.

And then he asks questions.

He asks Dirty, he asks the servant, he asks us. Before any one suspects it, he is at home in the whole field of theology.

He knows that God is in Heaven, where all good people go to Him, while the wicked are put down below in Hell. That God created the world in six days and said that we must not do anything on Sundays. That God can do everything and knows everything and sees everything.

He often prays, creeps upstairs as high as he can go, so as to be nearer Heaven, and shouts as loud as he can. The other day I found him at the top of the folding-steps:

"Dear God! You must please give us fine weather to-morrow, for we are going to the wood."

He says *Du* to everybody except God and the grocer.

He never compromises.

The servant is laying the table; we have guests coming and we call her attention to a little hole in the cloth:

"I must lay it so that no one can see it," she says.

"God will see it."

"He is not coming this evening," says the blasphemous hussy.

"Yes, He is everywhere," answers my little boy, severely.

He looks after me in particular:

"You mustn't say 'gad,' Father. Dirty's governess says that people who say 'gad' go to Hell."

"I shan't say it again," I reply, humbly.

One Sunday morning, he finds me writing and upbraids me seriously.

"My little boy," I say, distressfully, "I must work every day. If I do nothing on Sunday, I do nothing on Monday either. If I do nothing on Monday, I am idle on Tuesday too. And so on."

He ponders; and I continue, with the courage of despair:

"You must have noticed that Dirty wants a new catechism? The one she has is dirty and old."

He agrees to this.

"She will never have one, you see," I say, emphatically. "Her father rests so tremendously on Sunday that he is hardly able to do anything on the other days. He never earns enough to buy a new catechism."

I have won—this engagement. But the war is continued without cessation of hostilities.

The mother of my little boy and I are sitting in the twilight by the bedside and softly talking about this.

"What are we to do?" she asks.

"We can do nothing," I reply. "Dirty is right: God is everywhere. We can't keep Him out. And if we could, for a time: what then? A day would come perhaps when our little boy was ill or sad and the priests would come to him with their God as a new and untried miraculous remedy and bewilder his mind and his senses. Our little boy too will have to go through Luther and Balslev and Assens and confirmation and all the rest of it. Then this will become a commonplace to him; and one day he will form his own views, as we have done."

But, when he comes and asks how big God is, whether He is bigger than the Round Tower, how far it is to Heaven, why the weather was not fine on the day when he prayed so hard for it: then we fly from the face of the Lord and hide like Adam and Eve in the Garden of Eden.

And we leave Dirty to explain.

* * *

My little boy has got a rival, whose name is Henrik, a popinjay who not only is six years old, but has an unlimited supply of licorice at his disposal. And, to fill the measure of my little boy's bitterness, Henrik is to go to the dancing-school; and I am, therefore, not surprised when my little boy asks to be taught to dance, so that he may not be left quite behind in the contest.

"I don't advise you to do that," I say. "The dancing which you learn at school is not pretty and does not play so great a part in love as you imagine. I don't know how to dance; and many charming ladies used to prefer me to the most accomplished ornaments of the ballroom. Besides, you know, you are knock-kneed."

And, to cheer him up, I sing a little song which we composed when small and had a dog and did not think about women:

> See, my son, that little basset,
> Running with his knock-kneed legs!
> His own puppy, he can't catch it:
> He'll fall down as sure as eggs!
> Knock-kneed Billy!
> Isn't he silly?
> Silly Billy!

But poetry fails to comfort him. Dark is his face and desperate his glance. And, when I see that the case is serious, I resolve to resort to serious measures.

I take him with me to a ball, a real ball, where people who have learnt to dance go to enjoy themselves. It is difficult to keep him in a more or less walking condition, but I succeed.

We sit quietly in a corner and watch the merry throng. I say not a word, but look at his wide-open eyes.

"Father, why does that man jump like that, when he is so awfully hot?"

"Yes; can you understand it?"

"Why does that lady with her head on one side look so tired? . . . Why does that fat woman hop about so funnily, Father? . . . Father, what queer legs that man there has!"

It rains questions and observations.

We make jokes and laugh till the tears come to our eyes. We whisper naughty things to each other and go into a side-room and mimic a pair of crooked legs till we can't hold ourselves for laughter. We sit and wait till a steam thrashing-machine on its round comes past us; and we are fit to die when we hear it puff and blow.

We enjoy ourselves beyond measure. And we make a hit.

The steam thrashing-machine and the crooked legs and the fat woman and the hot gentleman and others crowd round us and admire the dear little boy. We accept their praises, for we have agreed not to say what we think to anybody, except to Mother, when we come home, and then, of course, to Dirty.

And we wink our eyes and enjoy our delightful fun until we fall asleep and are driven home and put to bed.

And then we have done with the dancing-school.

My little boy paints in strong colours, for his Dirty's benefit, what Henrik will look like when he dances. It is no use for that young man to deny all that my little boy says and to execute different elegant steps. I was prepared for this; and my little boy tells exultantly that this is only something with which they lure stupid people at the start and that it will certainly end with Henrik's getting very hot and hopping round on crooked legs with a fat woman and a face of despair.

In the meantime, of course, I do not forget that, if we pull down without building up we shall end by landing ourselves in an unwholesome skepticism.

We therefore invent various dances, which my little boy executes in the courtyard to Dirty's joy and to Henrik's most jealous envy. We point emphatically to the fact that the dances are our own, that they are composed only for the woman we love and performed only for her.

There is, for instance, a dance with a stick, which my little boy wields, while Henrik draws back. Another with a pair of new mittens for Dirty. And, lastly, the licorice dance, which expresses an extraordinary contempt for that food-stuff.

That Dirty should suck a stick of licorice, which she has received from Henrik, while enjoying her other admirer's satire, naturally staggers my little boy. But I explain to him that that is because she is a woman and that *that* is a thing which can't be helped.

What Bournonville[2] would say, if he could look down upon us from his place in Heaven, I do not know.

But I don't believe that he can.

If he, up there, could see how people dance down here, he really would not stay there.

* * *

There is a battle royal and a great hullabaloo among the children in the court-yard.

I hear them shouting "Jew! and I go to the window and see my little boy in the front rank of the bandits, screaming, fighting with clenched fists and without his cap.

I sit down quietly to my work again, certain that he will appear before long and ease his heart.

And he comes directly after.

He stands still, as is his way, by my side and says nothing. I steal a glance at him: he is greatly excited and proud and glad, like one who has fearlessly done his duty.

"What fun you've been having down there! "

"Oh," he says, modestly, "it was only a Jew boy whom we were licking."

I jump up so quickly that I upset my chair:

"A Jew boy? Were you licking him? What had he done?"

"Nothing. . . ."

His voice is not very certain, for I look so queer.

And that is only the beginning. For now I snatch my hat and run out of the door as fast as I can and shout:

"Come . . . come . . . we must find him and beg his pardon!"

My little boy hurries after me. He does not understand a word of it, but he is terribly in earnest. We look in the courtyard, we shout and call. We rush into the street and round the corner, so eager are we to come up with him. Breathlessly, we ask three passers-by if they have not seen a poor, ill-used Jew boy.

All in vain: the Jew boy and all his persecutors are blown away into space.

So we go and sit up in my room again, the laboratory where our soul is crystallized out of the big events of our little life. My forehead is wrinkled and I drum disconsolately with my fingers on the table. The boy has both his hands in his pockets and does not take his eyes from my face.

"Well," I say, decidedly, "there is nothing more to be done. I hope you will meet that Jew boy one day, so that you can give him your hand and ask him to forgive you. You must tell him that you did that only because you were stupid. But if, another time, any one does him any harm, I hope you will help him and lick the other one as long as you can stir a limb."

I can see by my little boy's face that he is ready to do what I wish. For he is still a mercenary, who does not ask under which flag, so long as there is a battle and booty to follow. It is my duty to train him to be a brave recruit, who will defend his fair mother-land, and so I continue:

"Let me tell you, the Jews are by way of being quite wonderful people. You remember David, about whom Dirty reads at school: he was a Jew boy. And the Child Jesus, whom everybody worships and loves, although He died two thousand years ago: He was a little Jew also."

My little boy stands with his arms on my knee and I go on with my story.

The old Hebrews rise before our eyes in all their splendor and power, quite different from Dirty's Balslev. They ride on their camels in coats of many colours and with long beards: Moses and Joseph and his brethren and Samson and David and Saul. We hear wonderful stories. The walls of Jericho fall at the sound of the trumpet.

"And what next?" says my little boy, using the expression which he employed when he was much smaller and which still comes to his lips whenever he is carried away.

We hear of the destruction of Jerusalem and how the Jews took their little boys by the hand and wandered from place to place, scoffed at, despised and ill-treated. How they were allowed to own neither house nor land, but could only be merchants, and how the Christian robbers took all the money which they had got together. How, nevertheless, they remained true to their God and kept up their old sacred customs in the midst of the strangers who hated and persecuted them.

The whole day is devoted to the Jews.

We look at old books on the shelves which I love best to read and which are written by a Jew with a wonderful name, which a little boy can't remember at all. We learn that the most famous man now living in Denmark is a Jew.

And, when evening comes and Mother sits down at the piano and sings the song which Father loves above all other songs, it appears that the words were written by one Jew and the melody composed by another.

My little boy is hot and red when he falls to sleep that night. He turns restlessly in bed and talks in his sleep.

"He is a little feverish," says his mother.

And I bend down and kiss his forehead and answer, calmly:

"That is not surprising. Today I have vaccinated him against the meanest of all mean and vulgar diseases."

* * *

We are staying in the country, a long way out, where the real country is.

Cows and horses, pigs and sheep, a beautiful dog and hens and ducks form our circle of acquaintances. In addition to these, there are of course the two-legged beings who own and look after the four-legged ones and who, in my little boy's eyes, belong to quite the same kind.

The great sea lies at the foot of the slope. Ships float in the distance and have nothing to say to us. The sun burns us and bronzes us. We eat like thrashers, sleep like guinea-pigs and wake like larks. The only real sorrow that we have suffered is that we were not allowed to have our breeches made with a flap at the side, like the old woodcutter's.

Presently, it happens that, for better or worse, we get neighbors.

They are regular Copenhageners. They were prepared not to find electric light in the farmhouse; but, if they had known that there was no water in the kitchen, God knows they would not have come. They trudge through the clover as though it were mire and are sorry to find so few cornflowers in the rye. A cow going loose along the roads fills them with a terror which might easily have satisfied a royal tiger.

The pearl of the family is Erna.

Erna is five years old; her very small face is pale green, with watery blue eyes and yellow curls. She is richly and gaily dressed in a broad and slovenly sash, daintily-embroidered pantalets, short open-work socks and patent-leather shoes. She falls if she but moves a foot, for she is used only to gliding over polished floors or asphalt.

I at once perceive that my little boy's eyes have seen a woman.

He has seen the woman that comes to us all at one time or another and turns our heads with her rustling silks and her glossy hair and wears her soul in her skirts and our poor hearts under her heel.

"Now comes the perilous moment for Dirty," I say to the mother of my little boy.

This time it is my little boy's turn to be superior.

He knows the business thoroughly and explains it all to Erna. When he worries the horse, she trembles, impressed with his courage and manliness. When she has a fit of terror at the sight of a hen, he is charmed with her delicacy. He knows the way to the smith's, he dares to roll down the high slope, he chivalrously carries her ridiculous little cape.

Altogether, there is no doubt as to the condition of his heart. And, while Erna's family apparently favor the position—for which may the devil take them!—I must wait with resignation like one who knows that love is every man's master.

One morning he proposes.

He is sitting with his beloved on the lawn. Close to them, her aunt is nursing her chlorosis under a red parasol and with a novel in her bony lap. Up in the balcony above sit I, as Providence, and see everything, myself unseen.

"You shall be my sweetheart," says my little boy.

"Yes," says Erna.

"I have a sweetheart already in Copenhagen," he says, proudly.

This communication naturally by no means lowers Erna's suitor in her eyes. But it immediately arouses all Auntie's moral instincts:

"If you have a sweetheart, you must be true to her."

"Erna shall be my sweetheart."

Auntie turns her eyes up to Heaven:

"Listen, child," she says. "You're a very naughty boy. If you have given Dir—Dir—"

"Dirty," says the boy.

"Well, that's an extraordinary name! But, if you have given her your word, you must keep it till you die. Else you'll never, never be happy. "

My little boy understands not a word and answers not a word. Erna begins to cry at the prospect that this good match may not come off. But I bend down over the baluster and raise my hat:

"I beg your pardon, Froken. Was it not you who jilted Hr. Petersen? . . ."

"Good heavens! . . . "

She packs up her chlorosis and disappears with Erna, mumbling something about like father, like son, and goodness knows what.

Presently, my little boy comes up to me and stands and hangs about.

"Where has Erna gone to?" I ask my little boy.

"She mustn't go out," he says, dejectedly.

He puts his hands in his pockets and looks straight before him.

"Father," he says, "can't you have two sweethearts?"

The question comes quite unexpectedly and, at the moment, I don't know what to answer.

"Well?" says the mother of my little boy, amiably, and looks up from her newspaper.

And I pull my waistcoat down and my collar up:

"Yes," I say, firmly. "You can. But it is wrong. It leads to more fuss and unpleasantness than you can possibly conceive."

A silence.

"Are you so fond of Erna?" asks our mother.

"Yes."

"Do you want to marry her?"

"Yes."

I get up and rub my hands:

"Then the thing is settled," I say. "We'll write to Dirty and give her notice. There's nothing else to be done. I will write now and you can give the letter yourself to the postman, when he comes this afternoon. If you take my advice, you will make her a present of your ball. Then she will not be so upset."

"She can have my goldfish too, if she likes," says the boy.

"Excellent, excellent. We will give her the goldfish. Then she will really nothing in the world to complain of."

My little boy goes away. But, presently, he returns:

"Father, have you written the letter to Dirty?"

"Not yet, my boy. There is time enough. I shan't forget it."

"Father, I am so fond of Dirty."

"She was certainly a dear little girl."

A silence.

"Father, I am also so fond of Erna.

We look at each other. This is no joke:

"Perhaps we had better wait with the letter till tomorrow," I say. "Or perhaps it would be best if we talked to Dirty ourselves, when we get back to town."

We both ponder over the matter and really don't know what to do.

Then my eyes surprise an indescribable smile on our mother's face. All a woman's incapacity to understand man's honesty is contained within that smile and I resent it greatly:

"Come," I say and give my hand to my little boy. "Let us go."

And we go to a place we know of, far away behind the hedge, where we lie on our backs and look up at the blue sky and talk together sensibly, as two gentlemen should.

* * *

My little boy is to go to school.

We can't keep him at home any longer, says his mother. He himself is glad to go, of course, because he does not know what school is.

I know what it is and I know also that there is no escape for him, that he must go. But I am sick at heart. All that is good within me revolts against the inevitable.

So we go for our last morning walk, along the road where something wonderful has always happened to us. It looks to me as if the trees have crepe wound round their tops and the birds sing in a minor key and the people stare at me with earnest and sympathetic eyes.

But my little boy sees nothing. He is only excited at the prospect. He talks and asks questions without stopping.

We sit down by the edge of our usual ditch—alas, that ditch!

And suddenly my heart triumphs over my understanding. The voice of my clear conscience penetrates through the whole: well-trained and harmonious choir which is to give the concert; and it sings its solo in the ears of my little boy:

"I just want to tell you that school is a horrid place," I say. "You can have no conception of what you will have to put up with there. They will tell you that two and two are four. . . ."

"Mother has taught me that already," says he, blithely.

"Yes, but that is wrong, you poor wretch!" I cry. "Two and two are never four, or only very seldom. And that's not all. They will try to make you believe that Teheran is the capital of Persia and that Mont Blanc is 15,781 feet high and you will take them at their word. But I tell you that both Teheran and Persia are nothing at all, an empty sound, a stupid joke. And Mont Blanc is not half as big as the mound in the tallow-chan-

dler's back-garden. And listen: you will never have any more time to play in the courtyard with Einar. When he shouts to you to come out, you'll have to sit and read about a lot of horrible old kings who have been dead for hundreds and hundreds of years, if they ever existed at all, which I, for my part, simply don't believe."

My little boy does not understand me. But he sees that I am sad and puts his hand in mine:

"Mother says that you must go to school to become a clever boy," he says. "Mother says that Einar is ever so much too small and stupid to go to school."

I bow my head and nod and say nothing.

That is past.

And I take him to school and see how he storms up the steps without so much as turning his head to look back at me.

* * *

Here ends this book about my little boy.

What more can there be to tell?

He is no longer mine. I have handed him over to society. Hr. Petersen, candidate in letters, Hr. Nielsen, student of theology, and Froken Hansen, certified teacher, will now set their distinguished example before him for five hours daily. He will form himself in their likeness. Their spirit hovers over him at school: he brings it home with him, it overshadows him when he is learning the lessons which they zealously mete out to him.

I don't know these people. But I pay them.

I, who have had a hard fight to keep my thoughts free and my limbs unrestrained and who have not retired from the fight without deep wounds of which I am reminded when the weather changes, I have, of my own free will, brought him to the institution for maiming human beings. I, who at times have soared to peaks that were my own, because the other birds dare not follow me, have myself brought him to the place where wings are clipped for flying respectably, with the flock.

Is effective schooling possible?

No less than a lot of other people, I long believed four things about schools: society is niggardly in support of schools; schools are changeable institutions; schools can be more interesting places than they are; and schooling can be a vehicle for social change. I have had to change my mind. I had to change my mind and conclude that money is a distracting issue; that schools are changeable within very narrow limits; that schools cannot be interesting places; and that whatever changes occur, for good or for bad, will derive from changes in the world view of the larger society.

—Seymour B. Sarason, in *Schooling In America*, (Free Press, 1983).

"There was nothing else to be done," says the mother of my little boy.

"Really?" I reply, bitterly. "Was there nothing else to be done? But suppose that I had put by some money, so that I could have saved Messrs. Petersen and Nielsen and Froken Hansen their trouble and employed my day in myself opening out lands for that little traveller whom I myself have brought into the land? Suppose that I had looked round the world for people with small boys who think as I do and that we had taken upon us to bring up these young animals so that they kept sight of horns and tails and fairy-tales?

"Yes," she says.

"Small boys have a bad time of it, you know."

"They had a worse time of it in the old days."

"That is a poor comfort. And it can become worse again. The world is full of parents and teachers who shake their foolish heads and turn up their old eyes and cross their flat chests with horror at the depravity of youth: children are so disobedient, so naughty, so self-willed and talk so disrespectfully to their elders! . . . And what do we do, we who know better?"

"We do what we can."

But I walk about the room, more and more indignant and ashamed of the pitiful part which I am playing:

"Do you remember, a little while ago, he came to me and said that he longed so for the country and asked if we couldn't go there for a little? There were homes and cows and green fields to be read in his eyes. Well, I couldn't leave my work. And I couldn't afford it. So I treated him to a shabby and high-class sermon about the tailor to whom I owed money. Don't you understand that I let my little boy do my work, that I let him pay my debt? . . ." I bend down over her and say earnestly, "You must know; do please tell me—God help me, I do not know—if I ought not rather to have paid my debt to the boy and cheated the other?

"You know quite well," she says.

She says it in such a way and looks at me with two such sensible eyes and is so strong and so true that I suddenly think things look quite well for our little boy; and I become restful and cheerful like herself:

"Let Petersen and Nielsen and Hansen look out!" I say. "My little boy, for what I care, may take from them all the English and geography and history that he can. But they shall throw no dust in his eyes, I shall keep him awake and we shall have great fun and find them out."

"And I shall help him with his English and geography and history," says she.

Notes

1. Luther's Lille Katekismus, the Lutheran catechism in general use in Denmark. - A. T. de M.
2. A famous French ballet-master who figured at the Copenhagen Opera-house in the eighteenth century. - A. T. de M.

The Ethics of Elfland

Gilbert Keith Chesterton

G.K. Chesterton's essay, "The Ethics of Elfland," appeared in his book Orthodoxy, which was published in 1908. What is particularly appealing about the essay is its defense of fairy tales on philosophical grounds, rather than for reasons relating to the child's education or psychological development. The psychological case, to be sure, has been persuasively set forth by Bruno Bettelheim, in The Uses of Enchantment, and Bettelheim refers briefly to Chesterton's writings. It is not altogether clear, however, that Bettelheim is on solid ground when he interprets Chesterton as saying that fairy tales are "mirrors of inner experience, not of reality; and it is as such that the child understands them." Chesterton's view of "reality" is one that Bettelheim can hardly share for Chesterton is inclined to see even ordinary events as capable of inspiring wonder.

Young children like realism, Chesterton insists, because they find it inherently mysterious and marvelous. "A child of seven is excited by being told that Tommy opened a door and saw a dragon. But a child of three is excited by being told that Tommy opened a door." What such children are utterly delighted by is fact as well as fantasy. And they are reasonable: they accept the necessary sequences of logic without cavil: "if the Ugly Sisters are older than Cinderella, it is (in an iron and awful sense) necessary that Cinderella is younger than the Ugly Sisters. There is no getting out of it." Perhaps what is remarkable is not Chesterton's finding the everyday world so intriguing, as that most of the rest of us have long since ceased to find it so.

When the businessman rebukes the idealism of his office-boy, it is commonly in some such speech as this: "Ah, yes, when one is young, one has these ideals in the abstract and these castles in the air; but in middle age they all break up like clouds, and one comes down to a belief in practical politics, to using the machinery one has and getting on with the world as it is." Thus, at least venerable and philanthropic old men now in their honored graves used to talk to me when I was a boy. But since then I have grown up and have discovered that these philanthropic old men were telling lies. What has really happened is exactly the opposite of what they said would happen. They said that I should lose my ideals and begin to believe in the methods of practical politicians. Now, I have not lost my ideals in the least; my faith in fundamentals is exactly what it always was. What I have lost is my old childlike faith in practical politics. I am still as much concerned as ever about the Battle of Armageddon; but I am not so much concerned about the General Election. As a babe I leapt up on my mother's knee at the mere mention of it. No; the vision is always solid and reliable. The vision is always a fact. It is the reality that is often a fraud. As much as I ever did, more than I ever did, I believe in Liberalism. But there was a rosy time of innocence when I believed in Liberals.

I take this instance of one of the enduring faiths because, having now to trace the roots of

Lisping metaphysics

Of Miss Welchman's Kindergarten in Chestnut Street, my first school in Boston, I remember only that we had cards with holes pricked in them, and colored worsted that we were invited to pass through the holes, making designs to suit our own fancy. I suppose this was calculated to develop artistic originality, not to convince use how trivial that originality is, and how helpless without traditional models. I remember also that I used to walk home with another boy, not so old as I, but also much older than the other children; that there were banks of snow on both sides of the path; and that one day—this must have been in spring for there was a bush with red flowers in his grass plot—he said something very strange as he left me, and ran up the steps into his house. I reported what he had said to Susana, who pronounced it *pantheism*: perhaps it was that those red flowers were opening because God was awakening in them. This shows how far my English had got in that Kindergarten and how we lisped metaphysics there.

—George Santayana, *Persons and Places.*

my personal speculation, this may be counted, I think, as the only positive bias. I was brought up a Liberal, and have always believed in democracy, in the elementary liberal doctrine of a self-governing humanity. If anyone finds the phrase vague or threadbare, I can only pause for a moment to explain that the principle of democracy, as I mean it, can be stated in two propositions. The first is this: that all things common to all men are more important than the things peculiar to any men. Ordinary things are more valuable than extraordinary things; nay, they are more extraordinary. Man is something more awful than men; something more strange. The sense of the miracle of humanity itself should be always more vivid to us than any marvels of power, intellect, art or civilization. The mere man on two legs, as such, should be felt as something more heartbreaking than any music and more startling than any caricature. Death is more tragic even than death by starvation. Having a nose is more comic even than having a Norman nose.

This is the first principle of democracy: that the essential things in men are the things they hold in common, not the things they hold separately. And the second principle is merely this: that the political instinct or desire is one of these things which they hold in common. Falling in love is more poetical than dropping into poetry. The democratic contention is that government (helping to rule the tribe) is a thing like falling in love, and not a thing like dropping into poetry. It is not something analogous to playing the church organ, painting on vellum, discovering the North Pole (that insidious habit), looping the loop, being Astronomer Royal, and so on. For these things we do not wish a man to do at all unless he does them well. It is, on the contrary, a thing analogous to writing one's own love-letters or blowing one's own nose. These things we want a man to do for himself, even if he does them badly. I am not here to argue the truth of any of these conceptions; I know that some moderns are asking to have their wives chosen by scientists, and they may soon be asking, for all I know, to have their noses blown by nurses. I merely say that mankind does recognize these universal human functions, and that democracy classes government among them. In short, the democratic faith is this: that the most terribly important things must be left to ordinary men themselves—the mating of the sexes, the rearing of the young, the laws of the state. This is democracy; and in this I have always believed.

But there is one thing that I have never from my youth been able to understand. I have never been able to understand where people got the idea that democracy was in some way opposed to tradition. It is obvious that tradition is only democracy extended through time. It is trusting to a consensus of common human voices rather than to some isolated or arbitrary record. The man who quotes some German historian against the tradition of the Catholic Church, for instance, is strictly appealing to aristocracy. He is appealing to the superiority of one expert against the awful authority of a mob. It is quite easy to see why a legend is treated, and ought to be treated, more respectfully than a book of history. The legend is generally made by the majority of people in the village, who are sane. The book is generally written by the one man in the village who is mad. Those who urge against tradition that men in the past were ignorant may go and urge it at the Carlton Club, along with the statement that voters in the slums are ignorant. It will not do for us. If we attach great importance to the opinion of ordinary men in great unanimity when we are dealing with daily matters, there is no reason why we should disregard it when we are dealing with history or fable. Tradition may be defined as an extension of the franchise. Tradition means giving votes to the most obscure of all classes, our ancestors. It is the democracy of the dead. Tradition refuses to submit to the small and arrogant oligarchy of those who merely happen to be walking about. All democrats object to men being disqualified by the accident of birth; tradition objects to their being disqualified by the accident of death. Democracy tells us not to neglect a good man's opinion, even if he is our groom; tradition asks us not to neglect a good man's opinion, even if he is our father. I, at any rate, cannot separate the two ideas of democracy and tradition; it seems evident to me that they are the same idea. We will have the dead at our councils. The ancient Greeks voted by stones; these shall vote by tombstones. It is all quite regular and official, for most tombstones, like most ballot papers, are marked with a cross.

I have first to say, therefore, that if I have had a bias, it was always a bias in favor of democracy, and therefore of tradition. Before we come to any theoretic or logical beginnings I am content to allow for that personal equation; I have always

been more inclined to believe the ruck of hard-working people than to believe that special and troublesome literary class to which I belong. I prefer even the fancies and prejudices of the people who see life from the inside to the clearest demonstrations of the people who see life from the outside. I would always trust the old wives' against the old maids' facts. As long as wit is mother wit it can be as wild as it pleases.

Now, I have to put together a general position, and I pretend to no training in such things. I propose to do it, therefore, by writing down one after another the three or four fundamental ideas which I have found for myself, pretty much in the way that I found them. Then I shall roughly synthesize them, summing up my personal philosophy or natural religion; then I shall describe my startling discovery that the whole thing has been discovered before. It had been discovered by Christianity. But of these profound persuasions which I have to recount in order, the earliest was concerned with this element of popular tradition. And without the foregoing explanation touching tradition and democracy I could hardly make my mental experience clear. As it is, I do not know whether I can make it clear, but I now propose to try.

My first and last philosophy, that which I believe with unbroken certainty, I learnt in the nursery. I generally learnt it from a nurse; that is, from the solemn and star-appointed priestess at once of democracy and tradition. The things I believed most then, the things I believe most now, are the things called fairy tales. They seem to me to be the entirely reasonable things. They are not fantasies: compared with them other things are fantastic. Compared with them religion and rationalism are both abnormal, though religion is abnormally right and rationalism abnormally wrong.

Fairyland is nothing but the sunny country of common sense. It is not earth that judges heaven, but heaven that judges earth; so for me at least it was not earth that criticized elfland, but elfland that criticized the earth. I knew the magic beanstalk before I had tasted beans; I was sure of the Man in the Moon before I was certain of the moon. This was at one with all popular tradition. Modern minor poets are naturalists, and talk about the bush or the brook; but the singers of the old epics and fables were supernaturalists, and talked about the gods of brook and bush. That is what the moderns mean when they say that the ancients did not "appreciate Nature," because they said that Nature was divine. Old nurses do not tell children about the grass, but about the fairies that dance on the grass; and the old Greeks could not see the trees for the dryads.

But I deal here with what ethics and philosophy come from being fed on fairy tales. If I were describing them in detail I could note many noble and healthy principles that arise from them. There is the chivalrous lesson of "Jack the Giant Killer"; that giants should be killed because they are gigantic. It is a manly mutiny against pride as such. For the rebel is older than all the kingdoms, and the Jacobin has more tradition than the Jacobite. There is the lesson of "Cinderella," which is the same as that of the Magnificat—*exaltavit humiles*. There is the great lesson of "Beauty and the Beast"; that a thing must be loved *before* it is loveable. There is the terrible allegory of the "Sleeping Beauty," which tells how the human creature was blessed with all birthday gifts, yet cursed with death; and how death also may perhaps be softened to a sleep. But I am not concerned with any of the separate statutes of elfland, but with the whole spirit of its law, which I learnt before I could speak, and shall retain when I cannot write. I am concerned with a certain way of looking at life, which was created in me by the fairy tales, but has once been meekly ratified by the mere facts.

It might be stated this way. There are certain sequences or developments (cases of one thing following another), which are, in the true sense of the word, reasonable. They are, in the true sense of the word, necessary. Such are mathematical and merely logical sequences. We in fairyland (who are the most reasonable of all creatures) admit that reason and that necessity. For instance, if the Ugly Sisters are older than Cinderella, it is (in an iron and awful sense) *necessary* that Cinderella is younger than the Ugly Sisters. There is no getting out of it. Haeckel may talk as much fatalism about that fact as he pleases: it really must be. If Jack is the son of a miller, a miller is the father of Jack. Cold reason decrees it from her awful throne: and we in fairyland submit. If the three brothers all ride horses, there are six animals and eighteen legs involved: that is true rationalism, and fairyland is full of it. But as I put my head over the hedge of the elves and began to take notice of the natural world, I observed an extraordinary thing. I observed that learned men in spectacles were talking of the actual things that happened—dawn and death an so on—as if *they* were rational and inevitable. They talked as if the fact that trees bear fruit were just as *necessary* as the fact that two and one trees make three. But it is not. There is an enormous difference by the test of fairyland; which is the test of the imagination. You cannot *imagine* two and one not making three. But you can easily imagine trees not growing fruit; you can imagine them growing golden candlesticks or tigers hanging on by the tail. These men in spectacles spoke much of a man named Newton, who was hit by an apple, and who discovered a law. But they could not be got to see the distinction between a true law, a law of reason, and the mere fact of apples falling. If the apple hit Newton's nose, Newton's nose hit the apple. That is a true necessity: because we cannot conceive the one occurring without the other. But we can quite well conceive the apple not falling on his nose; we can fancy it flying ardently through the air to hit some other nose, of which it had a more definite dislike. We have always in our fairy tales kept this sharp distinction between the science of mental relations, in which there really are laws, and the science of physical facts, in which there are no laws, but only weird repetitions. We believe in bodily miracles, but not in mental impossibilities.

We believe that a Bean-stalk climbed up to Heaven; but that does not at all confuse our convictions on the philosophical question of how many beans make five.

Here is the peculiar perfection of tone and truth in the nursery tales. The man of science says, "Cut the stalk, and the apple will fall"; but he says it calmly, as if the one idea really led up to the other. The witch in the fairy tale says, "Blow the horn, and the ogre's castle will fall"; but she does not say it as if it were something in which the effect obviously arose out of the cause. Doubtless she has given the advice to many champions, and has seen many castles fall, but she does not lose either her wonder or her reason. She does not muddle her head until it imagines a necessary mental connection between a horn and a falling tower. But the scientific men do muddle their heads, until they imagine a necessary mental connection between an apple leaving the tree and an apple reaching the ground. They do really talk as if they had found not only a set of marvellous facts, but a truth connecting those facts. They do talk as if the connection of two strange things physically connected them philosophically. They feel that because one incomprehensible thing constantly follows another incomprehensible thing the two together somehow make up a comprehensible thing. Two black riddles make a white answer.

In fairyland we avoid the word "law"; but in the land of science they are singularly fond of it. Thus they will call some interesting conjecture about how forgotten folks pronounced the alphabet, Grimm's Law. But Grimm's Law is far less intellectual than Grimm's Fairy Tales. The tales are, at any rate, certainly tales; while the law is not a law. A law implies that we know the nature of the generalisation and enactment; not merely that we have noticed some of the effects. If there is a law that pick-pockets shall go to prison, it implies that there is an imaginable mental connection between the idea of prison and the idea of picking pockets. And we know what the idea is. We can say why we take liberty from a man who takes liberties. But we cannot say why an egg can turn into a chicken any more than we can say why a bear could turn into a fairy prince. As *ideas*, the egg and the chicken are further off from each other than the bear and the prince; for no egg in itself suggests a chicken, whereas some princes do suggest bears. Granted, then, that certain transformations do happen, it is essential that we should regard them in the philosophic manner of fairy tales, not in the unphilosophic manner of science and the "Laws of Nature." When we are asked why eggs turn to birds or fruits fall in autumn, we must answer exactly as the fairy godmother would answer if Cinderella asked her why mice turned to horses or her clothes fell from her at twelve o'clock. We must answer that it is *magic*. It is not a "law," for we do not understand its general formula. It is not a necessity, for though we can count on it happening practically, we have no right to say that it must always happen. It is no argument for unalterable law (as Huxley fancied) that we count on the ordinary course of things. We do not count on it; we bet on it. We risk the remote possibility of a miracle as we do that of a poisoned pancake or a world-destroying comet. We leave it out of account, not because it is a miracle, and therefore an impossibility, but because it is a miracle, and therefore an exception. All the terms used in the science books, "law," "necessity," "order," "tendency," and so on, are really unintellectual, because they assume an inner synthesis, which we do not possess. The only words that ever satisfy me as describing Nature are the terms used in the fairy books, "charm," "spell," "enchantment." They express the arbitrariness of the fact and its mystery. A tree grows fruit because it is a *magic* tree. Water runs downhill because it is bewitched. The sun shines because it is bewitched.

I deny altogether that this is fantastic or even mystical. We may have some mysticism later on; but this fairy-tale language about things is simply rational and agnostic. It is the only way I can express in words my clear and definite perception that one thing is quite distinct from another; that there is no logical connection between flying and laying eggs. It is the man who talks about "a law" that he has never seen who is the mystic. Nay, the ordinary scientific man is strictly a sentimentalist. He is a sentimentalist in this essential sense, that he is soaked and swept away by mere associations. He has so often seen birds fly and lay eggs that he feels as if there must be some dreamy, tender connection between the two ideas, whereas there is none. A forlorn lover might be unable to disassociate the moon from lost love; so the materialist is unable to disassociate the moon from the tide. In both cases there is no connection, except that one has seen them together. A sentimentalist might shed tears at the smell of apple-blossom, because, by a dark association of his own, it reminded him of his boyhood. So the materialist professor (though he conceals his tears) is yet a sentimentalist, because, by a dark association of his own, apple-blossoms remind him of apples. But the cool rationalist from fairyland does not see why, in the abstract, the apple tree should not grow crimson tulips; it sometimes does in his country.

This elementary wonder, however, is not a mere fancy derived from the fairy tales; on the contrary, all the fire of the fairy tales is derived from this. Just as we all like love tales because there is an instinct of sex, we all like astonishing tales because they touch the nerve of the ancient instinct of astonishment. This is proved by the fact that when we are very young children we do not need fairy tales: we only need tales. Mere life is interesting enough. A child of seven is excited by being told that Tommy opened a door and saw a dragon. But a child of three is excited by being told that Tommy opened a door. Boys like romantic tales; but babies like realistic tales—because they find them romantic. In fact, a baby is about the only person, I should think, to whom a modern realistic novel could be read without boring him. This proves that even nursery tales only echo an almost pre-natal leap of interest and amazement. These tales say that apples were golden only to refresh the forgotten moment when we

found that they were green. They make rivers run with wine only to make us remember, for one wild moment, that they run with water. I have said that this is wholly reasonable and even agnostic. And, indeed, on this point I am all for the higher agnosticism; its better name is Ignorance. We have all read in scientific books, and, indeed, in all romances, the story of the man who has forgotten his name. This man walks about the streets and can see and appreciate everything; only he cannot remember who he is. Well, every man is that man in the story. Every man who has forgotten who he is. One may understand the cosmos, but never the ego; the self is more distant than any star. Thou shalt love the Lord thy God; but thou shalt not know thyself. We are all under the same mental calamity; we have all forgotten our names. We have all forgotten what we really are. All that we call common sense and rationality and practicality and positivism only means that for certain dead levels of our life we forget that we have forgotten. All that we call spirit and art and ecstasy only means that for one awful instant we remember that we forget.

But though (like the man without memory in the novel) we walk the streets with a sort of half-witted admiration, still it is admiration. It is admiration in English and not only admiration in Latin. The wonder has a positive element of praise. This is the next milestone to be definitely marked on our road through fairyland. I shall speak in the next chapter about optimists and pessimists in their intellectual aspect, so far as they have one. Here I am only trying to describe the enormous emotions which cannot be described. And the strongest emotion was that life was as precious as it was puzzling. It was an ecstasy because it was an adventure; it was an adventure because it was an opportunity. The goodness of the fairy tale was not affected by the fact that there might be more dragons than princesses; it was good to be in a fairy tale. The test of all happiness is gratitude; and I felt grateful, though I hardly knew to whom. Children are grateful when Santa Claus puts in their stockings gifts of toys or sweets. Could I not be grateful to Santa Claus when he put in my stockings the gift of two miraculous legs? We thank people for birthday presents of cigars and slippers. Can I thank no one for the birthday present of birth?

There were, then, two first feelings, indefensible and indisputable. The world was a shock, but it was not merely shocking; existence was a surprise, but it was a pleasant surprise. In fact, all my first views were exactly uttered in a riddle that stuck in my brain from boyhood. The question was, "What did the first frog say?" And the answer was, "Lord, how you made me jump!" That says succinctly all that I am saying. God made the frog jump; but the frog prefers jumping. But when these things are settled there enters the second great principle of the fairy philosophy.

Any one can see it who will simply read "Grimm's Fairy Tales" or the fine collections of Mr. Andrew Lang. For the pleasure of pedantry I will call it the Doctrine of Conditional Joy. Touchstone talked of much virtue in an "if"; according to elfin ethics all virtue is in an "if." The note of the fairy utterance always is, "You may live in a palace of gold and sapphire, *if* you do not say the word 'cow' "; or "You may live happily with the King's daughter, *if* you do not show her an onion." The vision always hangs upon a veto. All the dizzy and colossal things conceded depend upon one small thing withheld. All the wild and whirling things that are let loose depend upon one thing that is forbidden. Mr. W. B. Yeats, in his exquisite and piercing elfin poetry, describes the elves as lawless; they plunge in innocent anarchy on the unbridled horses of the air—

"Ride on the crest of the dishevelled tide,
And dance upon the mountains like a flame."

It is a dreadful thing to say that Mr. W. B. Yeats does not understand fairyland. But I do say it. He is an ironical Irishman, full of intellectual reactions. He is not stupid enough to understand fairyland. Fairies prefer people of the yokel type like myself; people who gape and grin and do as they are told. Mr. Yeats reads into elfland all the righteous insurrection of his own race. But the lawlessness of Ireland is a Christian lawlessness, founded on reason and justice. The Fenian is rebelling against something he understands only too well; but the true citizen of fairyland is obeying something that he does not understand at all. In the fairy tale an incomprehensible happiness rests upon an incomprehensible condition. A box is opened, and all evils fly out. A word is forgotten, and cities perish. A lamp is lit, and love flies away. A flower is plucked, and human lives are forfeited. An apple is eaten, and the hope of God is gone.

This is the tone of fairy tales, and it is certainly not lawlessness or even liberty, though men under a mean modern tyranny may think it liberty by comparison. People out of Portland Gaol might think Fleet Street free; but closer study will prove that both fairies and journalists are the slaves of duty. Fairy godmothers seem at least as strict as other godmothers. Cinderella received a coach out of Wonderland and a coachman out of nowhere, but she received a command—which might have come out of Brixton—that she should be back by twelve. Also, she had a glass slipper; and it cannot be a coincidence that glass is so common a substance in folk-lore. This princess lives in a glass castle, that princess on a glass hill; this one sees all things in a mirror; they may all live in glass houses if they will not throw stones. For this thin glitter of glass everywhere is the expression of the fact that the happiness is bright but brittle, like the substance most easily smashed by a housemaid or a cat. And this fairy-tale sentiment also sank into me and became my sentiment towards the whole world. I felt and feel that life itself is as bright as the diamond, but as brittle as the window-pane; and when the heavens were compared to the terrible crystal I can remember a shudder. I was afraid that God would drop the cosmos with a crash.

Remember, however, that to be breakable is not the same as to be perishable. Strike a glass, and it will not endure an instant; simply do not strike it, and it will endure a thousand years. Such, it seemed, was the joy of man, either in elfland or on earth; the happiness depended on *not doing something* which you could at any moment do and which, very often, it was not obvious why you should not do. Now, the point here is that to *me* this did not seem unjust. If the miller's third son said to the fairy, "Explain why I must not stand on my head in the fairy palace," the other might fairly reply, "Well, if it comes to that, explain the fairy palace." If Cinderella says, "How is it that I must leave the ball at twelve?" her godmother might answer, "How is it that you are going there till twelve?" If I leave a man in my will ten talking elephants and a hundred winged horses, he cannot complain if the conditions partake of the slight eccentricity of the gift. He must not look a winged horse in the mouth. And it seemed to me that existence was itself so very eccentric a legacy that I could not complain of not understanding the limitations of the vision when I did not understand the vision they limited. The frame was no stranger than the picture. The veto might well be as wild as the vision; it might be as startling as the sun, as elusive as the waters, as fantastic and terrible as the towering trees.

For this reason (we may call it the fairy godmother philosophy) I never could join the young men of my time in feeling what they called the general sentiment of revolt. I should have resisted, let us hope, any rules that were evil, and with these and their definition I shall deal in another chapter. But I did not feel disposed to resist any rule merely because it was mysterious. Estates are sometimes held by foolish forms, the breaking of a stick or the payment of a peppercorn: I was willing to hold the huge estate of earth and heaven by any such feudal fantasy. It could not well be wilder than the fact that I was allowed to hold it at all. At this stage I give only one ethical instance to show my meaning. I could never mix in the common murmur of that rising generation against monogamy, because no restriction on sex seemed so odd and unexpected as sex itself. To be allowed, like Endymion, to make love to the moon and then to complain that Jupiter kept his own moons in a harem seemed to me (bred on

fairy tales like Endymion's) a vulgar anti-climax. Keeping to one woman is a small price for so much as seeing one woman. To complain that I could only be married once was like complaining that I had only been born once. It was incommensurate with the terrible excitement of which one was talking. It showed, not an exaggerated sensibility to sex, but a curious insensibility to it. A man is a fool who complains that he cannot enter Eden by five gates at once. Polygamy is a lack of the realization of sex; it is like a man plucking five pears in mere absence of mind. The aesthetes touched the last insane limits of language in their eulogy on lovely things. The thistledown made them weep; a burnished beetle brought them to their knees. Yet their emotion never impressed me for an instant, for this reason, that it never occurred to them to pay for their pleasure in any sort of symbolic sacrifice. Men (I felt) might fast forty days for the sake of hearing a blackbird sing. Men might go through fire to find a cowslip. Yet these lovers of beauty could not even keep sober for the blackbird. They would not go through common Christian marriage by way of recompense to the cowslip. Surely one might pay for extraordinary joy in ordinary morals. Oscar Wilde said that sunsets were not valued because we could not pay for sunsets. But Oscar Wilde was wrong; we can pay for sunsets. We can pay for them by not being Oscar Wilde.

Well, I left the fairy tales lying on the floor of the nursery, and I have not found any books so sensible since. I left the nurse guardian of tradition and democracy, and I have not found any modern type so sanely radical or so sanely conservative. But the matter for important comment was here: that when I first went out into the mental atmosphere of the modern world, I found that the modern world was positively opposed on two points to my nurse and to the nursery tales. It has taken me a long time to find out that the modern world is wrong and my nurse was right. The really curious thing was this: that modern thought contradicted this basic creed of my boyhood on its two most essential doctrines. I have explained that the fairy tales founded in me two convictions; first, that this world is a wild and startling place, which might have been quite different, but which is quite delightful; second that before this wildness and delight one may well be modest and submit to the queerest limitations of so queer a kindness. But I found the whole modern world running like a high tide against both my tendernesses; and the shock of that collision created two sudden and spontaneous sentiments, which I have had ever since and which, crude as they were, have since hardened into convictions.

First, I found the whole modern world talking scientific fatalism; saying that everything is as it must always have been, being unfolded without fault from the beginning. The leaf on the tree is green because it could never have been anything else. Now, the fairy-tale philosopher is glad that the leaf is green precisely because it might have been scarlet. He feels as if it had turned green an instant before he looked at it. He is pleased that snow is white on the strictly reasonable ground that it might have been black. Every color has in it a bold quality as of choice; the red of garden roses is not only decisive but dramatic, like suddenly spilt blood. He feels that something has been *done*. But the great determinists of the nineteenth century were strongly against this native feeling that something had happened an instant before. In fact, according to them, nothing ever really had happened since the beginning of the world. Nothing ever had happened since existence had happened; and even about the date of that they were not very sure.

The modern world as I found it was solid for modern Calvinism, for the necessity of things being as they are. But when I came to ask them I found they had really no proof of this unavoidable repetition in things except the fact that the things were repeated. Now, the mere repetition made the things to me rather more weird than more rational. It was as if, having seen a curiously shaped nose in the street and dismissed it as an accident, I had then seen six other noses of the same astonishing shape. I should have fancied for a moment that it might be some local secret society. So one elephant having a trunk was odd; but all elephants having trunks looked like a plot. I speak here only of an emotion, and of an emotion at once stubborn and subtle. But the repetition in Nature seemed sometimes to be an excited repetition, like that of an angry schoolmaster saying the same thing over and over again. The grass seemed signalling to me with all its fingers at once; the crowded stars seemed bent upon being understood. The sun would make me see him if he rose a thousand times. The recurrences of the universe rose to the maddening rhythm of an incantation, and I began to see an idea.

All the towering materialism which dominates the modern mind rests ultimately upon one assumption; a false assumption. It is supposed that if a thing goes on repeating itself it is probably dead; a piece of clockwork. People feel that if the universe was personal it would vary; if the sun were alive it would dance. This is a fallacy even in relation to known fact. For the variation in human affairs is generally brought into them, not by life, but by death; by the dying down or breaking off of their strength or desire. A man varies his movements because of some slight element of failure or fatigue. He gets into an omnibus because he is tired of walking; or he walks because he is tired of sitting still. But if his life and joy were so gigantic that he never tired of going to Islington, he might go to Islington as regularly as the Thames goes to Sheerness. The very speed and ecstasy of his life would have the stillness of death. The sun rises every morning. I do not rise every morning; but the variation is due not to my activity, but to my inaction. Now, to put the matter in a popular phrase, it might be true that the sun rises regularly because he never gets tired of rising. His routine might be due, not to a lifelessness, but to a rush of life. The thing I mean can be seen, for instance, in children, when they find some game or joke that they specially enjoy. A child kicks his legs rhythmically through excess, not absence, of life. Because children have abounding vitality, because they are in spirit fierce and free, therefore they want things repeated and unchanged. They always say, "Do it again"; and the grown-up person does it again until he is nearly dead. For grownup people are not strong enough to exult in monotony. But perhaps God is strong enough to exult in monotony. It is possible that God says every morning, "Do it again" to the sun; and every evening, "Do it again" to the moon. It may not be automatic necessity that makes all daisies alike; it may be that God makes every daisy separately, but has never got tired of making them. It may be that He has the eternal appetite of infancy; for we have sinned and grown old, and our Father is younger than we. The repetition in Nature may not be a mere recurrence; it may be a theatrical *encore*. Heaven may *encore* the bird who laid an egg. If the human being conceives and brings forth a human child instead of bringing forth a fish, or a bat or a griffin, the reason may not be that we are fixed in an animal fate without life or purpose. It may be that our little tragedy has touched the gods, that they admire it from their starry galleries, and that at the end of every human drama man is called again and again before the curtain. Repetition may go on for millions of years, but mere choice, and at any instant it may stop. Man may stand on the earth generation after generation, and yet each birth be his positively last appearance.

This was my first conviction; made by the shock of my childish emotions meeting the modern creed in mid-career. I had always vaguely felt facts to be miracles in the sense that they are wonderful; now I began to think them miracles in the stricter sense that they were *willful*. I mean that they were, or might be, repeated exercises of some will. In short, I had always believed that the world involved magic: now I thought that perhaps it involved a magician. And this pointed a profound emotion always present and sub-conscious; that this world of ours has some purpose; and if there is a purpose, there is a person. I had always felt life first as a story: and if there is a story there is a story-teller.

But modern thought also hit my second human tradition. It went against the fairy feeling about strict limits and conditions. The one thing it loved to talk about was expansion and largeness. Herbert Spencer would have been greatly annoyed if anyone had called him an imperialist, and therefore it is highly regrettable that nobody did. But he was an imperialist of the lowest type. He popularized this contemptible notion that the size of the solar system ought to overawe the spiritual dogma of man. Why should a man surrender his dignity to the solar system any more than a whale? If mere size proves that man is not the image of God, then a whale may be the image of God; a somewhat formless image; what one might call an impressionist portrait. It is quite futile to argue that man is small compared to the cosmos; for man was always small compared to the nearest tree. But Herbert Spencer, in his headlong imperialism, would insist that we had in some way been conquered and annexed by the astronomical universe. He spoke about men and their ideals exactly as the most insolent Unionist talks about the Irish and their ideals. He turned mankind into a small nationality. And his evil influence can be seen even in the most spirited and honorable of later scientific authors; notably in the early romances of Mr. H. G. Wells. Many moralists have in an exaggerated way represented the earth as wicked. But Mr. Wells and his school made the heavens wicked. We should lift up our eyes to the stars from whence would come our ruin.

But the expansion of which I speak was much more evil than all this. I have remarked that the materialist, like the madman, is in prison; in the prison of one thought. These people seemed to think it singularly inspiring to keep on saying that the prison was very large. The size of this scientific universe gave one no novelty, no relief. The cosmos went on for ever, but not in its wildest constellation could there be anything really interesting; anything, for instance, such as forgiveness or free will. The grandeur or infinity of the secret of its cosmos added nothing to it. It was like telling a prisoner in Reading Gaol that he would be glad to hear that the gaol now covered half the country. The warder would have nothing to show the man except more and more long corridors of stone lit by ghastly lights and empty of all that is human. So these expanders of the universe had nothing to show us except more and more infinite corridors of space lit by ghastly suns and empty of all that is divine.

In fairyland there had been a real law; a law that could be broken, for the definition of a law is something that can be broken. But the machinery of this cosmic prison was something that could not be broken; for we ourselves were only a part of its machinery. We were either unable to do things or we were destined to do them. The idea of the mystical condition quite disappeared; one can neither have the firmness of keeping laws nor the fun of breaking them. The largeness of this universe had nothing of that freshness and airy outbreak which we have praised in the universe of the poet. This modern universe is literally an empire; that is, it was vast, but it is not free. One went into larger and larger windowless rooms, rooms big with Babylonian perspective; but one never found the smallest window or a whisper of outer air.

Their infernal parallel seemed to expand with distance; but for me all good things come to a point, swords for instance. So finding the boast of the big cosmos so unsatisfactory to my emotions I began to argue about it a little; and I soon found that the whole attitude was even shallower than could have been expected. According to these people the cosmos was one thing since it had one unbroken rule. Only (they would say) while it is one thing it is also the only thing there is. Why, then, should one worry particularly to call it large? There is nothing to compare it with. It would be just as sensible to call it small. A man may say, "I like this vast cosmos, with its throng of stars and its crowd of varied creatures." But if it comes to that why should not a man say, "I like this cosy little cosmos, with its decent number of stars and as neat a provision of live stock as I wish

---

From the childhood of Giordano Bruno

Bruno gives in his greatest Latin work, *De immenso*, a description of an episode in childhood, which made a deep impression on him. His home was in a hamlet just outside Nola, on the lower slopes of Cicada, a foot-hill of the Appenines some twenty miles east of Naples. He tells with affectionate detail of the beauty and fertility of the land around, overlooked from afar by the seemingly stern bare steeps of Vesuvius. One day a suspicion of the deceptiveness of appearances dawned on the boy. Mount Cicada, he tells us, assured him that "brother Vesuvius" was no less beautiful and fertile. So, girding his loins, he climbed the opposite mountain. "Look now," said Brother Vesuvius, "look at Brother Cicada, dark and drear against the sky." The boy assured Vesuvius that such also was his appearance viewed from Cicada. "Thus did his parents [two mountains] first teach the lad to doubt, and revealed to him how distance changes the face of things." So in after-life he interprets the experience and continues: "In whatever region of the globe I may be, I shall realize that both time and place are similarly distant from me."

—In Dorothy Waley Singer, *Giordano Bruno: His Life and Thought.*

---

to see"? One is as good as the other; they are both mere sentiments. It is mere sentiment to rejoice that the sun is larger than the earth; it is quite as sane a sentiment to rejoice that the sun is no larger than it is. A man chooses to have an emotion about the largeness of the world; why should he not choose to have an emotion about its smallness?

It happened that I had that emotion. When one is fond of anything one addresses it by diminutives, even if it is an elephant or a lifeguardsman.

The reason is, that anything, however huge, that can be conceived of as complete, can be conceived of as small. If military moustaches did not suggest a sword or tusks a tail, then the object would be vast because it would be immeasurable. But the moment you can imagine a guardsman you can imagine a small guardsman. The moment you really see an elephant you can call it "Tiny." If you can make a statue of a thing you can make a statuette of it. These people professed that the universe was one coherent thing; but they were not fond of the universe. But I was frightfully fond of the universe and wanted to address it by a diminutive. I often did so; and it never seemed to mind. Actually and in truth I did feel that these dim dogmas of vitality were better expressed by calling the world small than by calling it large. For about infinity there was a sort of carelessness which was the reverse of the fierce and pious care which I felt touching the pricelessness and the peril of life. They showed only a dreary waste; but I felt a sort of sacred thrift. For economy is far more romantic than extravagance. To them stars were an unending income of halfpence; but I felt about the golden sun and the silver moon as a schoolboy feels if he has one sovereign and one shilling.

These subconscious convictions are best hit off by the color and tone of certain tales. Thus I have said that stories of magic alone can express my sense that life is not only a pleasure but a kind of eccentric privilege. I may express this other feeling of cosmic cosiness by allusion to another book always read in boyhood, "Robinson Crusoe," which I read about this time, and which owes its eternal validity to the fact that it celebrates the poetry of limits, nay, even the wild romance of prudence. Crusoe is a man on a small rock with a few comforts just snatched from the sea: the best thing in the book is simply the list of things saved from the wreck. The greatest of poems is an inventory. Every kitchen tool becomes ideal because Crusoe might have dropped it in the sea. It is a good exercise, in empty or ugly hours of the day, to look at anything, the coal-scuttle or the book-case, and think how happy one could be to have brought it out of the sinking ship on to the solitary island. But it is a better exercise still to remember how all things have had this hair-breadth escape; everything has been saved from a wreck. Every man has had one horrible adventure: as a hidden untimely birth he had not been, as infants that never see the light. Men spoke much in my boyhood of restricted or ruined men of genius: and it was common to say that many a man was a Great Might-Have-Been. To me it is a more solid and startling fact that any man in the street is a Great Might-Not-Have-Been.

But I really felt (the fancy may seem foolish) as if all the order and number of things were the romantic remnant of Crusoe's ship. That there are two sexes and one sun, was like the fact that there were two guns and one axe. It was poignantly urgent that none should be lost but somehow, it was rather fun that none could be added. The trees and the planets seemed like things saved from the wreck: and when I saw the Matterhorn I was glad that it had not been overlooked in the confusion. I felt economical about the stars as if they were sapphires (they are called so in Milton's Eden): I hoarded the hills. For the universe is a single jewel, and while it is a natural cant to talk of a jewel as peerless and priceless, of this jewel it is literally true. This cosmos is indeed without peer and without price: for there cannot be another one.

Thus ends, in unavoidable inadequacy, the attempt to utter the unutterable things. These are my ultimate attitudes towards life; the soils for the seeds of doctrine. These in some dark way I thought before I could write, and felt before I could think: that we may proceed more easily afterwards, I will roughly recapitulate them now. I felt in my bones; first, that this world does not explain itself. It may be a miracle with a super-natural explanation; it may be a conjuring trick, with a natural explanation. But the explanation of the conjuring trick, if it is to satisfy me, will have to be better than the natural explanations I have heard. The thing is magic, true or false. Second, I came to feel as if magic must have a meaning, and meaning must have some one to mean it. There was something personal in the world, as in a work of art; whatever it meant it meant violently. Third, I thought this purpose beautiful in its old design, in spite of its defects, such as dragons. Fourth, that the proper form of thanks to it is some form of humility and restraint: we should thank God for beer and Burgundy by not drinking too much of them. We owed, also, an obedience to whatever made us. And last, and strangest, there had come into my mind a vague and vast impression that in some way all good was a remnant to be stored and held sacred out of some primordial ruin. Man had saved his good as Crusoe saved his goods: he had saved them from a wreck. All this I felt and the age gave me no encouragement to feel it. And all this time I had not even thought of Christian theology.

The Logic of Childhood

Leslie Paul

We had a family theory that everyone should help in the house. Marjorie was supposed to dust the furniture (though I can remember doing it myself many times), I ran errands, swept floors, minced the Saturday mince, adding crusts of bread to "swell it out" (and to get rid of the crusts). But my mother possessed a fine fury of impatience with bunglers; she drove all the servants we had in later years to drink (to use her own favorite expression) by following them round and re-doing their jobs as fast as they left them. We could never get servants to stay as a consequence: they would as lief be chased around by a witch with a broomstick as by Mother, who expected everyone to work at least as hard as she did. This fury chased us.

"Now," my mother would say, "I want you to clean the kitchen windows this morning, Leslie." I would ignore this.

"Budge, honey!" Auntie Florrie would say, glinting over her spectacles and shaking her fist at me.

I would be reluctant to budge; a book, a ball, a comic paper, were at the moment a thousand times more important.

"All right," I'd say huffily. "I will in a minute."

Then, deep in a *Sexton Blake*, I would forget. Presently a slashing and banging would indicate—as they were meant to—that Mother herself was doing them. I would dash into the yard.

"I thought you wanted me to do them?" I'd say, indignant at being double-crossed.

Mother would work on ignoring me. Now it seemed that there was nothing in the world that I wanted to do more than clean the windows.

"How can I do them if *you're* doing them?" I would shout furiously.

But Mother by now had grown interested in the job. She was doing the windows for pleasure, not just to spite me, and this made me more impatient than ever.

"I'll never do them again unless you let me now! You said I could do them."

It was rather like Tom Sawyer and the white-washed fence. I would have paid money to have wrested that wash-leather from her vigorous hands, and the affair would advance to the stage at which I would catch hold of it and try to pull it away by main force, not easy, for my mother was very strong.

"Just let me finish this little bit," she'd plead, and I would let her, threatening extreme penalties if she dared to do any more.

At last she would surrender to my importuning and I would mount the steps and breathe upon the fly specks and rub them out and sweep prismatic curves on the glass.

"Look how bright they are now!" I would shout and Mother would come from the kitchen and admire them enthusiastically. We understood each other perfectly.

It was in the kitchen, when I was ten, that an argument went on in the family for some months as to whether we wanted a baby or not. My mother started it by asking my sister whether she would like a baby sister. I had poor opinions of babies and saw no reason why we should have one. But Marjorie was excited by the idea because she hoped a baby would be a little girl so that she could play with it. I pointed out very logically that a baby would be too young to play with and would not know any games and that by the time it was old enough, my sister, who was eight, would be too old herself to want to play with it. She would not have it so and wanted to know where one could be bought. We knew the fairy tales—that babies were found under rose-bushes or brought by storks, or came in doctor's black bag. I thought all the ways of getting a baby stupid. The earth under the rose-bush in our garden was damp and it seemed to me that a baby left there would very likely die. Certainly one could not always be remembering about the possibility of one's being found there and so, naturally, one would forget to look, in which case the baby might lie there a long time without being noticed, which would be bad for it. So absurd did I consider this story that I never even peered under our rosebush once. That storks might drop them down chimneys I thought silly. How would storks know where to get babies? And wouldn't babies be cold and uncomfortable dragged through the air? Supposing the baby fell? I knew enough of *The Water Babies* to have formed a poor opinion of the chances of a baby in chimneys much bigger than ours. Not only would it be a dirty way of arriving, but it might even be disastrous, for the stork could not follow the baby down the chimney and would be forced to drop it. Our chief chimney led to the kitchen grate and since I often made the fire I knew how small the aperture was behind the bars and I was quite sure that not even a baby could crawl through it. If it came in the winter—or even in the summer sometimes—it would drop into smoke and suffocate or into the fire and burn. And as no-one could ever be sure when a stork might come it would be hard to prevent a fatality.

The most reasonable argument was that a doctor brought it in his black bag. But why, I wondered, should a doctor trouble? Did he charge for

babies? I did not know strange grown-ups who gave you things for nothing. For things which lasted only a short time—sweets, fruit, and biscuits—one had to pay high prices. Proportionately then, the price for a baby would be beyond our straitened means.

Locking a baby in a gladstone bag was just cruelty anyway. The little thing would be frightened out of its wits and probably suffocate. Mothers were the only people who understood babies and they would never do such a thing, I was sure. Besides, I had often seen men who were most likely doctors carrying black bags but I had never heard a baby crying in one. All this was the subject of much elaborate discussion which caused my mother to colour like a girl.

A doctor, however, was a clever man, who might, I conceded, have something to do with it. My sister shared my opinion and declared her intention of going down the street to ask for a baby one night. I saw no reason why one should be foisted upon us because my sister had one of her fancies. So when she slipped down the road to tell the doctor I ran after her and caught her giving the message to the doctor's maid. I cried out angrily to the maid, "We don't want a baby. It's only my silly sister. No-one else wants one, see, and if the doctor wants to bring one he'll have to take it back!" Then, overcome by my rudeness, I ran away and waited up the street to rate my sister on her ridiculous passion.

My mother was plunged into confusion when I told her of this extraordinary event. She did not know what to say. "Oh, Leslie, you wicked boy," she said, "shaming me before the whole street."

"Why," I said, almost in tears. "You don't want a baby, do you? What use are they?"

The baby came, though it involved my mother going to bed. I was inclined to blame my sister, and sympathize with Mother. It seemed quite possible that she had gone to bed to get away from the thing.

Our prediction proved right quite soon—my sister grew tired of it, for it was in no condition and lacked the sense to play with her. Helpless and noisy, it demanded constant attention and soon occupied the stage that Marjorie herself, as the youngest for eight years, had taken for granted.

"Oh, she's got a flea in her ear," I said when she sulked over her disappointment.

If this was not surprising, my own interest was. This stranger, on whom I'd poured so much anticipatory scorn, and which had turned out to be of all things a girl, had personality. It could laugh and cry, crow and gurgle and show delight and affection about *me*, of all people. I grew immensely proud of it and overjoyed at being allowed to take it out in a pram or to amuse it until it fell asleep. A little girl a few doors away named Alice and I played a solemn game with it. We were mother and father and this was our first baby; we were going to have lots more and we walked it round the streets in a quiet rapture.

A year or so later I discovered how babies came and I thought it a vulgar and terrifying method of obtaining them, compared with which the idea of the doctor bringing them in a black bag seemed sane, much less troublesome, and hardly less convincing, and now whenever I was teased about my attempt to tell the doctor what I thought about babies I hung my head in shame and confusion and hoped that grown-ups would not pursue a conversation which, if it went too far, might humiliate them as much as it did me.

* * *

A weather freak provided us with an argument for many years. As we stood in the High Street, one side of it was plunged into rain while the other side remained bathed in hot sunshine. We ran from rain to shine, and shine to rain, whooping like savages. The freak obsessed us with a problem in logic. Could it really be said that it had rained in Hemel Hempstead that day? One half of the town would say yes and the other no. Perhaps it had rained *in* Hemel Hempstead, but not *on* or *over* Hemel Hempstead. This led to many long

discussions about similar problems. What, for example, would be considered rain? How many drops? A shower of rain might produce less moisture than a heavy fall of dew.

Going home I put my head out of the carriage we were in and saw, when the guard blew his whistle, the engine and the first coaches start while we stood still. That was a lovely problem. When was a thing moving and when was it not? For here were we standing still in the station while the train we were in was moving. Though we moved in a second or so, there had been a space of time when it was possible to say that half the train was in motion and half was not. One might say the same thing about stopping. The engine stopped first of all and then the carriages piled up on it, sometimes so hard that we jumped back. That was a better problem still—the driver would say that the train had stopped while we were actually going backwards.

Then, take sleep. It was impossible not to see that sleeping and waking were absolutely opposites, but just try and trick yourself into finding out the exact moment when you slid from one to the other. There had to be such a moment, yet it was impossible. If Kenneth asked me in bed, "Are you asleep, Les?" and I answered "Yes!" that was considered a great joke, for the point about being asleep was that you never knew you were, a very unsettling thought when you saw that there were whole stretches of your life you knew absolutely nothing about. Yes, there was even the problem about life itself. If you were alive, then one time you had *not* been alive. Then you were born, which meant that there was a moment when you were not alive, then a moment when you were alive. Being alive was so important that anyone ought to be able to notice the difference between the two and could be sure to remember it. But nobody did. I did not remember it myself, to my great annoyance. Indeed I could not possibly imagine a moment when I had not been alive. And if I could think of dying, I could not think of "being dead." These arguments produced the uneasy sense of unreality I felt when I straddled across a county boundary as an infant and said, "Now half of me is in Kent and half in Surrey—which county am *I* in?" When I got too speculative, my brother grew extraordinarily irritated and kicked my behind and said angrily, "Put a sock in it!" If the foundations of existence did not worry him, my voice did.

* * *

Madame Vernet's liquid brown eyes looked at you from a face as sad and as wizened as a monkey's, and surmounted by a ginger wig whose appalling curls hung in a still fringe across that so mobile brow.

"Avez-vous vu le parc de Greenwitch?" she chanted at us from the book she had written herself and which is still somewhere on my shelves.

"Repondez, mes enfants, 'Oui, madame, je l'ai vu!' "

"Wee, madum, shelay voo."

"Ah, ts—ts—'Non madame, je ne l'ai pas vu'."

"Nonn, madum, shene lay voo pas."

"Ah, ts—ts—mon Dieu! quel accent!"

"Bien, ecrivez maintenant." And we made pretense to ecriver. She was little and dowdy and old and a foreigner and we did not give a hoot for her. French was just a lark and we knew by instinct that she was too weak to keep order, so we did prep for other teachers under her nose, or folded paper aeroplanes and launched them over her head, or drew circles on our locker tops with the broken ends of pens.

As we grew more confident we organized our riots more thoroughly, crawling under the desks after books we knocked down and staying there to play noughts and crosses, or swarming out in twos or threes to ask permission to leave the room, or pestering her with music-hall questions about the French passion for snails and frogs.

Madame was deceived by all this. She imagined in her simplicity that if you asked a question

it was because you wanted an answer, or if you sought permission to leave the room it was because nature meant you to. She believed in the human child, in its decency and kindness, and told us as much. This was more painful to us than belief in our duplicity would have been. We did not want to conform to any foreigner's conception of what the human child should be.

Therefore we revenged upon Madame all the slights we suffered at the hands of other teachers and, as discipline decayed further, her classes became a bedlam which must have been unendurable to her. It was not that she would never fly into a rage—indeed it was our aim to provoke her into one, but we guessed at some spiritual impotence in her and knew that her rages were no more dangerous to us than those of a dog chained to a wall. And yet she was so kind that she would pardon the most outrageous behaviour, even personal insults—and these were many and related to wigs and the Darwinian theory—if one gave one's word not to repeat the outrage, a promise no-one made with the intention of keeping. She ran a League of Kindness (Ligue de Bonté) which had a large membership in France and a not inconsiderable membership in our school, though most of us joined it at first in innocence or because we believed (without any evidence) that members of the League received better marks than non-members.

Kenneth, who preceded me by a year through the school, was an enthusiastic member of this Movement and enjoyed the respect and confidence of Madame, who compared us unfavorably. He was the school secretary for a time and corresponded with a French boy, which was one of the purposes of the League. He was the soul of chivalry and was kind to Madame, and supported her, because his sense of fair play was outraged by the treatment she received. And because he liked French.

One morning at break after a most riotous and villainous French lesson, in which we hunted a white-faced Madame as ruthlessly as a terrier runs down a terrified rabbit, I had occasion to return to the classroom for some books. Madame was in tears. She was sitting huddled over her desk, her wig pushed askew by the hand that had wiped the tears from her eyes, the picture of misery, as though just in that moment she saw the enormity of her failure with us and where it must lead. I was eleven and my tender heart turned and sank within me. Teachers had been legitimate game and one had never thought of our riots in terms of their unhappiness. I stood, books in hand, transfixed with pity.

"Madame," I said greatly daring, "I—we didn't *mean* anything—not really—please, Madame, it was only fun."

She looked up at me, not hiding her tears, not ashamed to cry before me. She was unhappy! She would be unhappy. With a tap she restored her wig and her dignity. She smiled damply at me, a wrinkled old woman, mysterious with age. "You are as kind as your brother, Leslee, but no, I am not deceived. They only mean it in fun, then they are sorree, then they forget. And next time it is the same. The English boy, he is barbarian, he understands only the stick."

"Oh, *Madame*," I said, wooing her with a crestfallen look. Her smile was proud and firm and made her face beautiful. It rejected my cheap consolations. It rejected my country.

"You are very kind, Leslee, thank you."

"Honestly, we don't *mean* it, Madame."

"You don't meant it, no. But because I do not give you the stick, you do it. I am not English, I do not understand the logic: it is not French logic."

The deserved scorn for my country hurt me most: the more as I knew quite clearly not only that we were bad but that Madame never would control a class.

"*Honestly*, Madame," I said, pleading to be believed because there was no other way of being kind.

"Please go, Leslee, she said and I went still smiling insincerely to chase her unhappiness away. But even as I went she forgot me and turned to the window, tears starting in her eyes again.

And though after that nothing would induce me to rag Madame, and her friendliness made me happy, my influence counted for nothing. She did not control us. We grew worse and worse: we learnt no French. After a term or two she went to whatever bourne is reserved for elderly French spinsters with little money, who have spent a lifetime in teaching.

The Way of Wonder

Stephen Paget

This much I remember of Aristotle, that he calls Wonder the beginning of the love of Wisdom. To have a right judgment of our surroundings, we must wonder at them, and be surprised that they and we are met together. So long as we exercise this quickening sense of wonder, there is hope for us, and some justification of our presence here, because we are on the road that leads toward wisdom: and they alone are incorrigible fools, to whom Nature comes natural. Once we have fallen into the bad habit of taking for granted what Nature grants us, and have ceased to be amazed, it may fairly be said that in the midst of life we are in death. For one might as well be dead as alive, to look with dull eyes at the world, not finding it wonderful.

So excellent is Wonder, that we must not profane its name in common use. For example, there is the phrase, *I wonder if.* Be sure that he or she, who thus turns a sentence, is untidy of speech, and regardless of the rights of words. It is impossible, to wonder if: you are not thinking, nor trying to think. *I wonder if it will be fine tomorrow*: you could hardly find a worse phrase. Never wonder if: always wonder at. The dawn of one more day, wet or fine, is wonderful: if it be fine, wonder at the sunshine; if it be wet, at the rain, each drop a miracle. *I wonder if* is not worth saying, not worth answering. It is something said for the sake of saying something to hide the cheapness of something said. *How cold it is—I wonder if it is going to snow.* Here, if guinea-pigs could talk, might be the level of their conversation.

Avoid, with equal care, the phrase, *The wonder is.* Grandpapa, for example, slips on the stairs, and hurts himself. *The wonder is, that he did not hurt himself more.* It is not. The wonder is, that Grandpapa did hurt himself. All pain is infinitely wonderful: but there is no wonder in the measured severity of this or that accident. It was not possible that he should hurt himself more. Given his weight, the velocity of his descent, the density of the stairs, and the state of his tissues, you might calculate the harm done, working out each bruise, by algebra, on a blackboard. To wonder that he did not hurt himself more is like wondering that two and two do not make five. His injury was his share of the universe at the moment of his accident: it was bound, therefore, to be exactly what it was. Otherwise, not he, but the universe, would have been confounded. The universe, in accordance with its eternal principles, upset Grandpapa. If he had hurt himself more, ever so little more, he would have upset the universe. Wonder yourself silly, not over the amount, but over the fact of his pain: wonder at what did happen, not at what might have happened, if it could have happened.

Now that we are past *I wonder if* and *The wonder is*, we come to *I wonder when* and *I wonder where*. Say these phrases to yourself, slowly, with your eyes shut, and watch the images that rise in your mind, how quick they take shape, and fight for precedence. Ghosts of letters that ought to have reached you the day before yesterday, ghosts of umbrellas that ought to have been in the stand in the hall, beset you; and you are haunted by dismal memories of people who were late, and of belongings that were lost. You are waiting for a friend; and the cabs go up and down the street, but none of them stops where you are at the window. You are hunting for your gloves, sure that you put them there, where they are not. Minute by minute, as you wait, as you hunt, the clock tells you that so much more of your life is fled. The misery of it, that your life should be ebbing away, while you are looking for a pair of old gloves. *I wonder when he will come*, you say; or, *I wonder where they are*: and echo answers, that your friend will come *when he will come*, and that your gloves are *where they are*. Avoid, by these two instances, the fault of wondering when and where: make up your mind, that you will only wonder at.

It is the advice which Aristotle was about to give you when I interrupted him. Wonder, says he, is the beginning, the ruling principle, of the love of Wisdom. That which makes us Man, our birthright, our privilege, is just a sense of surprise that we are in the world. To think, we must be challenged, entrapped, stung into thought, by all that we have and are. Every inch and every moment of this world, all its aspects and performances, and every act of our senses, invite us to look into their significance; calling us, if not to a *Credo*, yet to an *Admirer*. All facts, from stars to blades of grass, from the death of Caesar to the death of a mouse, are for wonder, and thereby for thought: and the only way toward wisdom is that which begins at the gate of Surprise, and goes along the dim groves of Bewilderment. "Into the Kingdom of Science, as into the Kingdom of Heaven, we cannot enter, but as little children." To have the run of both kingdoms, to know them well enough to be sure that they are not two but one, is wisdom: and the entry into them requires the child's mind, its love of a mystery, its readiness to be puzzled, its open-eyed astonishment. Watch how a baby takes notice. Its own fingers and toes, and every sound and color, bring it to attention. What is this? What is that? There was something; there is something else. Two some-

things; and here a third. What a world. The wonder of it, that here are fingers, apart from toes: and here is Mother's breast, which is neither Daddy's face nor Nanny's apron. Thus, in a blind animal fashion, come the first beginnings of taking notice, taking thought. So, with us, wonder must precede reason: or we shall be, to the end of our lives, not wise, but fools.

The fool is he who takes for his motto *Nil admirari*: he does not wonder at anything. He chose this motto, suggested by the devil in a most red-hot moment, because he says in his heart that there is no God, nothing to wonder at. He is not surprised, not he, at Nature: he sees what is in his line of sight; and is sure that he can judge, from that, the rest of the show. You, of course, are the fool, to his thinking, because you wonder. You and your God, says he, just suit each other: your God was invented by primitive man, Caliban scared by the lightning, calling it Setebos. Point by point, says he, man elaborated God, always a large old personage up in the clouds amid thunder and lightning. That is what comes of wondering. Men went on wondering at Nature till they imagined God: and the pavements of the temples of Greece and Rome, and of Jerusalem, were slippery with blood, and hideous with beasts kicking and gasping in death, to please God: which, all the time, was only the name for a man's fright at the sight of his own shadow. And that is all that there is, and quite enough for me, says the fool: and I wonder if and whether, and when and where, but I make it a point of honour, never to wonder at: and *Nil admirari* is the motto of my family.

What have we to say to him? For he is so well-informed, quick with references and authorities, expert in the use of history, criticism, and book-learning. He has had such a long innings, and drives the ball of Religion so high over the pavilion of Logic: and if you cannot get him out, with all your modern advantages, how can I? Let us put aside the hope that we shall argue him down: it will take us all our time to argue ourselves up. We have our motto, *Semper admirari*: let us see what comes of Wonder.

Only, we must begin at the very beginning, and go the way of Nature. She never preaches to us: it is we who preach to her. Nor does she tell us to "look through Nature up to Nature's God." It is not so easy to look through Nature. Nor does she bid us find her perfect: for, in Nature, fair is foul and foul is fair; and, if she were perfect, she would not be here. One commandment, and no more, she gives us: that we read her name, Wonderful.

* * *

There is a phrase in the marriage-service—*Oh God, who by thy mighty power hast made all things out of nothing*. This account of the origin of all things was received with happy laughter, in my young days, by Modern Thought: and you may still come across people who are sure that all things are made, not of nothing, but of something. To make things, they say, you must take enough something, and make them out of that. But the question is not of making things, it is of making all things. To make all things, you would need not something, but everything. And, once you take everything to make all things, you are not, in reality, making anything. You might as well say that you are making money, when you change a shilling into two sixpences. The sculptor does not make the statue: he takes a block of marble, and destroys a lot of it, and the rest is the statue. Nor does the boot-maker make boots; he puts them together, *particulam undique decerptam*: they are, in the true sense of the word, ready-made. The only way to make all things, really to make them, is to make them out of nothing.

The marriage-service, at this point, rises high over the heads of some of its critics: and there you will find it, I hope, when you come within its immediate range. The wedding-guests mostly think it old-fashioned, and almost indelicate: but this man and this woman, in sharp isolation, side by side, with all the artillery of Earth and Heaven thundering about their ears, welcome a downright plain-spoken estimate of their predicament. For they are thinking that children may be born to them: and they get this answer, that the children, if they come, will "come of the Lord"; and will be made, like all things, out of nothing. The service uses the past tense, *hast made*: it concedes that point to the congregation, who are not in a mood to be bothered with logic. But facts are above the reach of tenses: and we have to consider this bare statement, that God makes all things out of nothing. Here, in seven words, is a theory of things: but, What are things? Let us ask Science to tell us that. For she loves it, when we come to her with questions of our own accord.

To hear some people talk of Science, you would think her a hard woman, cold and passionless. They say that she has put aside, without romance, without regret, all emotion, all tragedy and comedy, and all the fun of the fair. She has moments of comparative affability, mostly in connection with modern architecture; posing over gateways, or between windows, in a shapeless robe and large sandals, with a pair of compasses or a big stone ball: but she never suffered, or loved, or enjoyed, or failed. That is how some people talk of her: whereas she is aching for sympathy, and for a way to our hearts. Think how dull it must be, to be called, year in and year out, inexorable, stern, immutable, exact; and all the time she is longing to leave her gateways and windows, yawn, stretch her cramped limbs, get out of her marble sandals, play conjuring-tricks with her ball, and gather us round her for a fairy-story. Come, let us charm her down—*Descend, be stone no more*. She hears; the gateway shakes, the windows rattle; there is a dust and a clatter of stucco, a rending asunder of tons of ugly masonry; she is here, she is come to life, to us, *et vera incessu patuit Dea*. Goddess, Madam, Lady Science, Miss, you Darling, here we are, come along here and sit right in the middle of us. Now, tell us, What is Things?

At the sound of a neuter noun in the plural with a verb in the singular, she laughs with delight, and hugs us all round: for she was born in Ancient Greece, and we, it seems, were speaking her beloved language. The words were English, but the grammar was Greek. The trees is tall, the games is done, the clothes is gone to the wash: that is the Greek way of dealing with a neuter noun in the plural. Things, to a Greek, not were, but was. Men and women were: but their limbs, bones, and bodies was. This use failed sometimes, because words is so obstinate: still, Greek does its best to uphold this good rule, that things not are but is. If thought be thinking of half-a-dozen things at once, then one they is. They cannot make themselves many, while thought is making them one. A thousand trees, to my thinking, is a wood: and my coat, waistcoat, and trousers is a suit of clothes. That is what they is, now that I think of them. Observe how this grammatical rule exalts and crowns Thought, and keeps Things to that station in life to which it has pleased God to call them. That is why Science was glad, when she heard, in our English, the echo of her Greek philosophy.

So she sits among us, laughing, with her hands clasped round her knees, as pretty as Circe in Mr. Briton Riviere's picture: and *Oh my dears*, she says, in a soft, lazy kind of voice, and shrugs her white shoulders, and laughs again, *Do let's be sensible. What's the use of thinking about Things, without thinking about Thought?* She took us aback: we had been expecting a fairy-story.

The Child

Floyd Dell

Education, as popularly conceived, includes as its chief ingredients a Child, a Building, Text-Books, and a Teacher. Obviously, one of them must be to blame for its going wrong. Let us see if it is the Child. We will put him on the witness stand:

Q. Who are you?

A. I am a foreigner in a strange land.

Q. What!

A. Please, sir, that's what everybody says. Sometimes they call me a little angel; the poet Wordsworth says that I come trailing clouds of glory from Heaven which is my home. On the other hand, I am often called a little devil; and when you see the sort of things I do in the comic supplements, you will perhaps be inclined to accept that description. I really don't know which is right, but both opinions seem to agree that I am an immigrant.

Q. Speak up so that the jury can hear. Have you any friends in this country?

A. No, sir—not exactly. But there are two people, a woman and a man, natives of this land, who for some reason take an interest in me. It was they who taught me to speak the language. They also taught me many of the customs of the country, which at first I could not understand. For instance, my preoccupation with certain natural—(the rest of the sentence stricken from the record).

Q. You need not go into such matters. I fear you still have many things to learn about the customs of the country. One of them is not to allude to that side of life in public.

A. Yes, sir; so those two people tell me. I'm sure I don't see why. It seems to me a very interesting and important—

Q. That will do. Now as to those people who are looking after you: Are your relations with them agreeable?

A. Nominally, yes. But I must say that they have treated me in a very peculiar way, which has aroused in me a deep resentment. You see, at first they treated me like a king—in fact, like a Kaiser. I had only to wave my hand and they came running to know what it was I wanted. I uttered certain magic syllables in my own language, and they prostrated themselves before me, offering me gifts. When they brought the wrong gifts, I doubled up my fists and twisted my face, and gave vent to loud cries—and they became still more abject, until at last I was placated.

Q. That is what is called paternal love. What then?

A. I naturally regarded them as my slaves. But presently they rebelled. One of them, of whom I had been particularly fond, commenced to make me drink milk from a bottle instead of from—

Q. Yes, yes, we understand. And you resented that?

A. I withdrew the light of my favour from her for a long time. I expressed my disappointment in her. I offered freely to pardon her delinquency if she would acknowledge her fault and resume her familiar duties. But perhaps I did not succeed in conveying my meaning clearly, for at this time I had no command of her language. At any rate, my efforts were useless. And her reprehensible conduct was only the first of a series of what seemed to me indignities and insults. I was no longer a king. I was compelled to obey my own slaves. In vain I made the old magic gestures, uttered the old talismanic commands—in vain even my doubling up of fists and twisting of face and loud outcries; the power was gone from these things. Yet not quite all the power—for my crying was at least a sort of punishment for them, and such I often inflicted upon them.

Q. You were a naughty child.

A. So they told me. But I only felt aggrieved at my new helplessness, and wished to recover somewhat of my old sense of power over them. But as I gradually acquired new powers I lost in part my feeling of helplessness. I also found that there were other beings like myself, and we conducted magic ceremonies together in which we transformed ourselves and our surroundings at will. These delightful enterprises were continually being interrupted by those other people, our parents, who insisted on our learning ever more and more of their own customs. They wished us to be interested in their activities, and they were pleased when we asked questions about things we did not understand. Yet there were some questions which they would not answer, or which they rebuked us for asking, or to which they returned replies that, after consultation among ourselves, we decided were fabulous. So we were compelled to form our own theories about these things. We asked, for instance—

Q. Please confine your answers to the questions. That is another matter not spoken of in public; though to be quite frank with you, public taste seems to be changing somewhat in this respect.

A. I am very glad to hear it. I would like to know—

Q. Not now, not now—You say you have learned by this time many of the customs of the country?

A. Oh, yes, sir! I can dress myself, and wash my face (though perhaps not in a manner quite above criticism), count the change which the grocer gives me, tell the time by a clock, and say "Yes, ma'am," and "Thank you"—and I am beginning to be adept in the great national game of baseball.

Q. Have you decided what you would do if you were permitted to take part in our adult activities?

A. I would like to be a truck-driver.

Q. Why?

A. Because he can whip the big horses.

Q. Do you know anything about machinery?

A. No, sir; I knew a boy who had a steam-engine, but he moved away before I got a chance to see how it worked.

Q. You spoke of truck-driving just now. Do you know where the truck-driver is going with his load?

A. No, sir.

Q. Do you know where he came from?

A. No, sir.

Q. Do you know what a factory is?

A. Yes, sir; Jim's father got three fingers cut off in a factory.

Q. Do you know where the sun rises and sets?

A. It rises in the East and sets in the West.

Q. How does it get from the West back to the East during the night?

A. It goes under the earth.

Q. How?

A. It digs a tunnel!

Q. What does it dig the tunnel with?

A. With its claws.

Q. Who was George Washington?

A. He was the Father of his country, and he never told a lie.

Q. Would you like to be a soldier?

A. Yes.

Q. If we let you take part in the government of our country, what ticket would you vote?

A. The Republican ticket. My father is a Republican.

Q. What would you do if you had ten cents?

A. I'd go to see Charley Chaplin in the moving-picture show.

Q. Thank you. You can step down.

A. Yes, sir. Where is my ten cents?

And now, gentlemen, you have heard the witness. He has told the truth—and nothing but the truth—and he would have told the whole truth if I had not been vigilant in defense of your modesty. He is, as he says, a foreigner, incompletely naturalized. In certain directions his development has proceeded rapidly. He shows a patriotism and a sense of political principles which are quite as mature as most of ours. But in other directions there is much to be desired. He does not know what kind of world it is he lives in, nor has he any knowledge of how he could best take his place, with the most satisfaction to himself and his fellow-men, in that world—whether as farmer or engineer, poet or policeman, or in the humbler but none the less necessary capacities of dustman or dramatic critic.

It would be idle for us to pretend that we think it will be easy for him to learn all this. But without this knowledge he is going to be a nuisance—not without a certain charm (indeed, I know several individuals who have remained children all their lives, and they are the most delightful of companions for an idle hour), but still, by reason of incapacity and irresponsibility, an undesirable burden upon the community: unable to support himself, and simply not to be trusted in the responsible relations of marriage and parenthood. We simply can't let him remain in his present state of ignorance.

And yet, how is he ever going to be taught? You have seen just about how far private enterprise is likely to help him. That man and woman of whom he told us have other things to do besides teach him. And if he is turned over to special private institutions, we have no guarantee that they will not take advantage of his helplessness, keep him under their control and rob him of freedom of movement for a long term of years, set him to learning a mass of fabulous or irrelevant information, instill in him a fictitious sense of its value by a system of prizes and punishments, and finally turn him out into our world no better prepared to take his proper part in it than he was before; and thus, having wasted his own

time, he would have to waste ours by compelling us to teach him all over again.

In fact, the difficulty of dealing with him appears so great that I am moved to make the statesmanlike proposal—never before, I believe, presented to the public—of passing a law which will prevent this kind of undesirable immigration altogether.

Shall we abolish the Child?

The only other reasonable alternative is for us to undertake this difficult and delicate business of education ourselves—assume as a public responsibility the provision of a full opportunity for this helpless, wistful, stubborn little barbarian to find out about the world and about himself. Well, shall we do that?

Let us not allow any false sentimentality to affect our decision. . . .

The vote seems to be in favor of giving him his chance. Very well!

Curiosity

Let us, my friends, pass over this unfortunate incident, and get on to the next thing as quickly as possible. The next thing on our program is Truth. The one who best understands Truth is undoubtedly the Philosopher.—Here he is, and we shall commence without delay. Will some one volunteer to conduct the examination? Thank you, madam. Go right ahead.

The Lady: We wish to ask you a few questions.

The Philosopher: Certainly, madam. What about?

The Lady: About Truth.

The Philosopher: Dear, dear!

The Lady: Whom are you addressing?

The Philosopher: I beg your pardon!—It was only an exclamation of surprise. It has been so long since anybody has talked to me about Truth. How quaint and refreshing!

The Lady: Please do not be frivolous.

The Philosopher: I am sorry—but really, it *is* amusing. Tell me, to which school do you belong?

The Lady: To the Julia Richmond High School, if you must know—though I don't see what that has to do with Truth.

The Philosopher: Oh! You mean you are a school-teacher!

The Lady: Certainly. Doesn't that suit you?

The Philosopher: It delights me. I feared at first you might be a Hegelian, or even a Platonist. Now that I find you are a Pragmatist like myself—

The Lady: Pragmatist? Yes, I have heard of Pragmatism. William James—summer course in Philosophy. But why do you think I am a Pragmatist?

The Philosopher: A school-teacher *must* be a pragmatist, madam, or go mad. If you really believed the human brain to be an instrument capable of accurate thinking, your experiences with your pupils and your principal, not to speak of your boards of education, would furnish you a spectacle of human wickedness and folly too horrible to be endured. But you realize that the poor things were never intended to think.

The Lady: That's true; they're doing the best they can, aren't they? They just *can't* believe anything they don't want to believe!

The Philosopher: That is to say, man is not primarily a thinking animal—he is a creature of emotion and action.

The Lady: Especially action. They are always in such a hurry to get something done that they really can't stop to think about it! But I'm afraid all this is really beside the point. What we want to know is why the school fails so miserably in its attempt to teach children to think?

The Philosopher: Perhaps it is in too much of a hurry. But you are sure you really want children to learn to think?

The Lady: Of course we do!

The Philosopher: The greatest part of life, you know, can be lived without thought. We do not think about where we put our feet as we walk along an accustomed road. We leave that to habit. We do not think about how to eat, once we have learned to do it in a mannerly way. The accountant does not think about how to add a column of figures—he has his mind trained to the task. And there is little that cannot be done by the formation of proper habits, to the complete elimination of thought. The habits will even take care of the regulation of the emotions. For all practical purposes, don't you agree with me that thinking might be dispensed with?

The Lady: I hardly know whether to take you seriously or not—

The Philosopher: Can you deny what I say?

The Lady: But—but life isn't all habit. We must think—in order to make—decisions.

The Philosopher: It is not customary. We let our wishes fight it out, and the strongest has its way. But I once knew a man who did think in order to make his decisions. The result was that he always made them too late. And what was worse, the habit grew upon him. He got to thinking about everything he wanted to do, with the result that he couldn't do anything. I told him that he'd have to stop thinking—that it wasn't healthy. Finally he went to a doctor, and sure enough the doctor told him that it was a well known disease—a neurosis. Its distinguishing mark was that the patient always saw two courses open to him everywhere he turned—two alternatives, two different ways of doing something, two women between whom he must choose, two different theories of life, and so on to distraction. The reason for it, the doctor said, was that the patient's will, that is to say the functioning of his emotional wish-apparatus, had become deranged, and the burden of decision was being put upon a part of the mind incapable of bearing it—the logical faculty. He cured my friend's neurosis, and now he thinks no more about the practical affairs of life than you or I or anybody else. So you see thinking is abnormal—even dangerous. Why do you want to teach children to think?

The Lady: Well—it is rather taken for granted that the object of education is learning to think.

The Philosopher: But is that true? If it is, why do you teach your children the multiplication table, or the rule that the square of the hypotenuse of a right triangle is equal to the sum of the squares of the other two sides—unless in order to save them the trouble of thinking? By the way, what is the capital of Tennessee, and when did Columbus discover America?

The Lady: Nashville, 1492. Why?

The Philosopher: You didn't have to stop to think, did you? Your memory has been well trained. But if you will forgive the comparison, so has my dog's been well trained; when I say, "Towser, show the lady your tricks," he goes through an elaborate performance that would gladden your heart, for he is an apt pupil; but I don't for a moment imagine that I have taught him to think.

The Lady: Then you don't want children taught the multiplication table?

The Philosopher: I? Most certainly I do. And so far as I am concerned, I would gladly see a great many other short cuts in mathematics taught, so as to save our weary human brains the trouble of thinking about such things. I am in fact one of the Honorary Vice-Presidents of the Society for the Elimination of Useless Thinking.

The Lady: I am afraid you are indulging in a jest.

The Philosopher: I am afraid I am. But if you knew Philosophers better you would realize that it is a habit of ours to jest about serious matters. It is one of our short-cuts to wisdom. Read your Plato and William James again. Delightful humorists, both of them, I assure you. I fear you went to them too soberly, and in too much of a hurry.

The Lady: Doubtless your jokes have a historic sanctity, since you say so, but I do not feel that they have advanced our inquiry very much.

The Philosopher: I abhor myself and repent in dust and ashes. What do you want to know?

The Lady: I want to know what is the use of thinking?

The Philosopher: Ah, my jest was not in vain, if it provoked you to that. I should call that question the evidence of a real thought.

The Lady: Well, what is the answer?

The Philosopher: Oh, please don't stop, now that you have made such a good start! Think again, and answer your own question.

The Lady: Hm . . .

The Philosopher: Yes?

The Lady: I was thinking of Newton and the apple. If it hadn't been for Newton's ability to think, he would never have formulated the law of gravitation.

The Philosopher: And what a pity that would have been—wouldn't it?

The Lady: You mean that it makes very little practical difference to us?

The Philosopher: It would if the town were being bombarded. The Newtonian calculations are considered useful by the artillery schools. But it is true that it was Newton and not an artillery officer who made them.

The Lady: You mean that the artillery captain would have been too intent on practical matters?

The Philosopher: And in too much of a hurry. Then there's the steam-engine. Useful invention—the very soul of hurry. Who invented it—some anxious postilion who thought horses were too slow? Or somebody whose mind was so empty of practical concerns that it could be intrigued by a tea-kettle? And by the way, it was Stephenson, wasn't it, who applied the steam-principle to locomotion? I've a very poor memory, but I think Watt's engine was just a toy. No practical use whatever. Other people found out the practical uses for it. Arkwright. Fulton, Hoe, et cetera.

The Lady: I see. The results of thinking may be put to use afterward, but the motive for thinking is not the desire to produce such results. I wonder if that is true?

The Philosopher: What is the common reproach against philosophers and scientists?

The Lady: That they are impractical. But inventors—

The Philosopher: Did you ever know an inventor?

The Lady: Yes. . . .

The Philosopher: Was he rich?

The Lady: He starved to death.

The Philosopher: Why?

The Lady: Because every one said that his invention was very wonderful, but not of the slightest use to anybody . . . Yes, it's true.

The Philosopher: That the results of thinking do not provide the motive for thinking?

The Lady: Yes.

The Philosopher: Then what is the motive for thinking?

The Lady: Just—curiosity, I suppose!

The Philosopher: Disinterested curiosity?

The Lady: Yes.

The Philosopher: Then in the interests of scientific truth we should cultivate disinterested curiosity?

The Lady: Doubtless.

The Philosopher: How would you go about doing so?

The Lady: I don't know.

The Philosopher: By hurriedly thrusting upon the minds of the children in your charge so great a multitude of interests as to leave them no time to wonder about anything?

The Lady: That would hardly seem to be the way to do it. But—

The Philosopher: When Newton looked at his famous apple, was there anyone there who said, "Now, Newton, look at this apple. Look at this apple, I say! Consider the apple. First, it is round. Second, it is red. Third, it is sweet. This is the Truth about apples. Now let me see if you have grasped what I have told you. What are the three leading facts about apples? What! Don't you remember? Shame on you! I fear I will have to report you to the mayor!—did anything like that happen?

The Lady: Newton was not a child.

The Philosopher: You should have talked to Newton's family about him. That is just what they said he was! I will admit that if you left

children free to wonder about things instead of forcing the traditional aspects of those things upon their attention, they might not all become great scientists. But are you a great archaeologist?

The Lady: No!

The Philosopher: Did you ever go on a personally conducted tour of the ruins of Rome, and have the things you were to see and think pointed to you by a guide?

The Lady: Yes, and I hated it!

The Philosopher: You are not a great archaeologist and you never expect to be one, and yet you thought you could get more out of those ruins yourself than with the assistance of that pesky guide. You preferred to be free—to see or not to see, to wonder and ponder and look again or pass by. And don't you think the children in your charge might enjoy their trip a little more if they didn't have to listen to the mechanically unctuous clatter of a guide?

The Lady: If one could only be sure they wouldn't just waste their time!

The Philosopher: Madam, are you quite sure that you, as a teacher, are not wasting *your* time?

The Lady: You make me wonder whether that may not be possible. But sheer idleness—

The Philosopher: Was Newton busy when he lay down under that tree? Did he have an appointment with the apple? Did he say he would give it ten minutes, and come again next day if it seemed worth while? What is disinterested curiosity, in plain English?

The Lady: Idle curiosity—I fear.

The Philosopher: I fear you are right. Then you would say that the way to approach Truth, in school and out, is to cultivate idle curiosity?

The Lady: I did not intend to say anything of the kind. But you compel me to say it.

The Philosopher: I compel you? Deny it if you wish!

The Lady: I thought you were going to answer my questions, and you have been making me answer yours!

The Philosopher: That is also an ancient habit of our profession. But since you have now arrived, of your own free will, at an inescapable if uncomfortable conclusion, you can now have no further need for my services, and I bid you all good day!

The Right to be Wrong

One moment!—I take it, my friends, we are agreed in demanding of the Philosopher that he condescend to some concrete and practical suggestions in regard to education.—Briefly, please!

The Philosopher: "You must draw your own conclusions. Traditional education is based on the assumption that knowledge is a mass of information which can be given to the child in little dabs at regular intervals. We know, however, that the education based on this assumption is a failure. It kills rather than stimulates curiosity; and without curiosity, information is useless. We are thus forced to realize that knowledge does not reside outside the child, but in the contact of the child with the world through the medium of curiosity. And thus the whole emphasis of education is changed. We no longer seek to educate the child—we only attempt to give him the opportunity to educate himself. He alone has the formula of his own specific needs; none of us are wise enough to arrange for him the mysterious series of beautiful and poignant contacts with reality by which alone he can 'learn.' This means that he must choose his own lessons. And if you think that, left to choose, he will prefer no lessons at all, you are quite mistaken. Let me remind you that children are notoriously curious about everything—everything except, as you will very justly point out, the things people want them to know. It then remains for us to refrain from forcing any kind of knowledge upon them, and they will be curious about everything. You may imagine that they will prefer only the less complex kinds of knowledge; but do you regard children's games as simple? They are in fact exceedingly complex. And they are all the more interesting because they are complex. We ourselves with our adult minds,

penetrate cheerfully into the complexities of baseball, or embroidery, or the stock-market, following the lead of some natural curiosity; and if our minds less often penetrate into the complexities of music, or science, it is because these things have associations which bring them within the realm of the dutiful. Evolutionary biology is far more interesting than stamp-collecting; but it is, unfortunately, made to seem not so delightfully useless, and hence it is shunned by adolescent boys and girls. But postage-stamp collecting can be made as much a bore as biology; it needs only to be put into the schools as a formal course.

"Consider for a moment the boy stamp-collector. His interest in his collection is in the nature of a passion. Does it astonish you that passionateness should be the fruit of idle curiosity? Then you need to face the facts of human psychology. The boy's passion for his collection of stamps is akin to the passion of the scientist and the poet. Do you desire of children that they should have a similar passion for arithmetic, for geography, for history? Then you must leave them free to find out the interestingness of these things. There is no way to passionate interest save through the gate of curiosity; and curiosity is born of idleness. But doubtless you have a quite wrong notion of what idleness means. Idleness is not doing nothing. Idleness is *being free to do anything*. To be forced to do nothing is not idleness, it is the worst kind of imprisonment. Being made to stand in the corner with one's face to the wall is not idleness—it is punishment. But getting up on Saturday morning with a wonderful day ahead in which one may do what one likes—that is idleness. And it leads straight into tremendous expenditures of energy. There is a saying, 'The devil finds some mischief still for idle hands to do.' Yes, but why should the devil have no competition? And that, as I understand it, is the function of education—to provide for idle and happy children fascinating contacts with reality—through games, tools, books, scientific instruments, gardens, and older persons with passionate interests in science and art and handicraft.

"Such a place would in a few respects resemble the schools we know; but the spirit would be utterly different from the spirit of traditional education. The apparatus for arousing the child's curiosity would be infinitely greater than the meagre appliances of our public schools; but however great, the child would be the centre of it all—not as the object of a process, but as the possessor of the emotions by force of which all these outward things become Education.

"But, you may ask, what has all this to do with truth? Simply this. We have been forcing children to memorize alleged facts. A fact so memorized cannot be distinguished from a falsehood similarly memorized. And so we may very well say that we have failed to bring truth into education. For truth is reality brought into vital contact with the mind. It makes no difference whether we teach children that the earth is round or flat, if it means nothing to them either way. For truth does not reside in something outside the child's mind; reality becomes truth only when it is made a part of his living.

"But, you will protest—and you will protest the more loudly the more you know of children—that their processes of thought are illogical, fantastic and wayward. And you will ask, Do I mean that we must respect the child's error in order to cultivate in him a love of truth? Yes, I do mean just that! Do I mean that we must respect the child's belief that the earth is flat, you ask? More than that, we must respect a thousand obscure and pervasive childish notions, such as the notion that a hair from a horse's tail will turn into a pollywog if left in the rainbarrel, or the notion that the way to find a lost ball is to spit on the back of the hand, repeat an incantation couched in such words as 'Spit, Spit, tell me where the ball is!' and then strike it with the palm of the other hand. You can doubtless supply a thousand instances of the kind of childhood thinking to which I refer. But for simplicity's sake, let us use the childish notion that the earth is flat as a convenient symbol for them all, and I say that if we do not respect the error, we shall not have any real success in con-

vincing the child of the truth. We shall easily persuade him that the globe in the schoolroom is round—that the picture of the earth in the geography-book is round—but not that the familiar earth upon which he walks is anything but flat! At best, we shall teach him a secondary, literary, schoolroom conception to put beside his workaday one. And, in the long run, we shall place a scientific conception of things in general beside his primitive childish superstitions—but we shall scarcely displace them; and when it comes to a show-down in his adult life, we shall find him acting in accordance with childish superstitions rather than with scientific knowledge. Most of us, as adults, are full of such superstitions, and we act accordingly, and live feebly and fearfully; for we have never yielded to the childish magical conception of the world the respect that is due to it as a worthy opponent of scientific truth—we have assumed that we were persuaded of truth, while in reality truth has never yet met error in fair fight in our minds.

"If you wish to convince a friend of something, do you not first seek to find out what he really thinks about it, and make him weigh your truth and his error in the same balance? But in dealing with children, we fail to take account of their opinions at all. We say, 'You must believe this because it is so.' If they do believe it, they have only added one more superstition to their collection. Truths are *not* true because somebody says so; nor even because everybody says so; they are true only because they fit in better with all the rest of life than what we call errors—because they bear the test of living—because they work out. And this way of discovering truth is within the capacity of the youngest school-child. If you can get him to state candidly and without shame his doubtless erroneous ideas about the world, and give him leave to prove their correctness to you, you will have set in motion a process which is worthy to be called education; for it will constitute a genuine matching of theory with theory in his mind, a real training in inductive logic, and what conclusions he reaches will be truly his.

When he sees in a familiar sunset, as he will see with a newly fascinated eye, the edge of the earth swinging up past the sun—then astronomy will be real to him, and full of meaning—and not a collection of dull facts that must be remembered against examination-day.

"This means that we must treat children as our equals. Education must embody a democratic relationship between adults and children. Children must be granted freedom of opinion—and freedom of opinion means nothing except the freedom to believe a wrong opinion until you are persuaded of a right one. They, moreover, must be the judges of what constitutes persuasion. You have asked me for practical and concrete suggestions in regard to education. I will make this one before I go: when I find an astronomy class in the first grade engaged in earnest debate as to whether the earth is round or flat, I will know that our school system has begun to be concerned for the first time with the inculcation of a love of truth. For, like Milton, I can not praise a fugitive and cloistered virtue, unexercised and unbreathed, that never sallies out and sees her adversary, but slinks out of the race, where that immortal garland is to be run for, not without dust and heat.—I thank you for your attention!

The Man Who Loved Children

Randall Jarrell

Randall Jarrell was a distinguished critic and poet, among whose published works are Poetry and the Age *(1953),* Pictures from an Institution, *(1968),* The Lost World *(1966),* Jerome *(1971), and* The Complete Poems *(1969).*

Christina Stead's The Man Who Loved Children *was published in 1940 by Holt, Rinehart and Winston. Although Robert Lowell hailed it as "a classic," adding that "there are very few novels in English that are as large and as beautifully written," and although Hortense Calisher called it "a wonderful book," it did not receive widespread critical acclaim. Perhaps, with time, its flaws will recede in importance as its more positive qualities are better understood. No one recognized those qualities better than Randall Jarrell, who wrote:*

> The Man Who Loved Children *knows as few books have ever known—knows specifically, profoundly, exhaustively—what a family is: if all mankind had been reared in orphan asylums for a thousand years it could learn to have families again by reading* The Man Who Loved Children. *Tolstoy said that "each unhappy family is unhappy in a way of its own—" a way that it calls happiness; the Pollits, a very unhappy family, are unhappy in a way almost unbelievably their own. And yet as we read we keep thinking: "How can anything so completely itself, so completely different from me and mine, be, somehow, me and mine?" The book has an almost frightening power of remembrance; and so much of our earlier life is repressed, forgotten, both in the books we read and the memories we have, that this seems friendly of the book, even when what it reminds us of is terrible. A*

poem says, "O to be a child again, just for tonight!" As you read The Man Who Loved Children *it is strange to have the wish come true.*

We cannot reprint Jarrell's marvellous introduction (which he entitled "An Unread Book") in its entirety, but we can at least present the portion of that introduction which deals specifically with Louie and adolescence. If Christina Stead's book is ever reappraised, it will probably not be because critical canons have changed, but because critics will have achieved a better understanding of the relationship between literature and language and childhood.

A description of Louie ought to begin with *Louie knew she was the ugly duckling.* It is ugly ducklings, grown either into swans or into remarkably big, remarkably ugly ducks, who are responsible for most works of art; and yet how few of these give a truthful account of what it was like to be an ugly duckling—it is almost as if the grown, successful swan had repressed most of the memories of the duckling's miserable, embarrassing, magical beginnings. (These memories are deeply humiliating in two ways: they remind the adult that he once was more ignorant and gullible and emotional than he is; and they remind him that he once *was*, potentially, far more than he is.) Stumbling through creation in awful misery, in oblivious ecstasy, the fat, clumsy twelve- or thirteen-year-old Louie is, as her teacher tells her, one of those who "will certainly be famous." We believe this because the book is full of the evidence for it: the poems and plays Louie writes, the stories she tells, the lines she quotes, the things she says. The usual criticism of a novel about an artist is that, no matter how real he is as a man, he is not real to us as an artist, since we have to take on trust the works of art he produces. We do not have to take on trust Louie's work, and she is real to us as an artist.

Someone in a story says that when you can't think of anything else to say you say, "Ah, youth, youth!" But sometimes as you read about Louie there *is* nothing else to say: your heart goes out in homesick joy to the marvellous inconsequential improbable reaching-out-to-everything of the duckling's mind, so different from the old swan's mind, that has learned what its interests are and is deaf and blind to the rest of reality. Louie says, "I wish I had a Welsh grammar." Sam says, "Don't be an idiot! What for?" Louie answers: "I'd like to learn Welsh or Egyptian grammar; I could read the poetry Borrow talks about and I could read *The Book of the Dead.*"

She starts to learn *Paradise Lost* by heart ("Why? She did not know really"); stuffs the little children full of La Rochefoucauld; in joyful amazement discovers that *The Cenci* is about her father and herself; recites,

A yellow plum was given me and in return a topaz fair I gave,
No mere return for courtesy but that our friendship might outlast the grave,

indignantly insisting to the grown-ups that it *is* Confucius; puts as a motto on her wall, *By my hope and faith, I conjure thee, throw not away the hero in your soul*; triumphantly repeats to that little tyrant of her fields, Sam-the-Bold:

The desolator desolate,
The tyrant overthrown,
The arbiter of other's fate
A suppliant for his own!

Louie starts out on her own *Faust*, a play, called *Fortunalus*, in which a student sitting alone in his room in the beaming moon, lifts his weary head from the book and begins by saying,

The unforgotten song, the solitary song,
The song of the young heart in the age-old world,
Humming on new May's reeds transports me back
To the vague regions of celestial space . . .

For the teacher whom she loves Louie creates "a magnificent project, the Aiden cycle . . . a poem of every conceivable form and also every conceivable meter in the English language," all about Miss Aiden. She copies the poems into an out-of-date diary, which she hides; sometimes she reads them to the children in the orchard "for hours on end, while they sat with rosy, greedy faces upturned, listening." As Henny and Sam shriek at each other downstairs, Louie tells the children, lying loosely in bed in the warm night, the story of *Hawkins, the North Wind*. Most of Louie's writings are so lyrically funny to us that as we laugh we catch our breath, afraid that the bubble will break. At *Hawkins*, a gruesomely satisfying story different from any story we have read before, we no longer laugh, nor can we look down at the story-teller with a grown-up's tender, complacent love for a child: the story is dark with Louie's genius and with Christina Stead's.

Best of all is *Tragos: Herpes Rom (Tragedy: The Snake-Man)*. Louie writes it, and the children act it out, for Sam's birthday. It is written in a new language Louie has made up for it; the language-maker Sam says angrily, "Why isn't it in English?" and Louie replies, "Did Euripides write in English?" Not only is the play exactly what Louie would have written, it is also a work of art in which the relations between Louie and her father, as she understands them, are expressed with concentrated, tragic force. Nowhere else in fiction, so far as I know, is there so truthful and satisfying a representation of the works of art the ugly duckling makes up, there in the morning of the world.

Louie reads most of the time—reads, even, while taking a shower: "her wet fingers pulped the paper as she turned." Her life is accompanied, *ostinato*, by *always has her nose stuck in a book . . . learn to hold your shoulders straight . . . it will ruin your eyes.* Louie "slopped liquids all over the place, stumbled and fell when carrying buckets, could never stand straight to fold the sheets and tablecloths from the wash without giggling or dropping them in the dirt, fell over invisible creases in rugs, was unable to do her hair neatly, and was always leopard-spotted yellow and blue with old and new bruises. . . . She acknowledged her unwieldiness and unhandiness in this little world, but she had an utter contempt for everyone associated with her, father, stepmother, even brothers and sister, an innocent contempt which she never thought out, but which those round her easily recognized." The Louie who laconically holds her scorched fingers in the candle-flame feels "a growling, sullen power in herself . . . She went up to bed insulted again. 'I will repay,' she said on the stairs, halting and looking over the banisters, with a frown." When the world is more than she can bear she screams her secret at it: " 'I'm the ugly duckling, you'll see,' shrieked Louie."

Most of the time she knows that she is better and more intelligent than, different from, the other inhabitants of her world; but the rest of the time she feels the complete despair—the seeming to oneself *wrong*, all wrong, about everything, *everything*—that is the other, dark side of this differentness. She is a force of nature, but she is also a little girl. Heart-broken when her birthday play is a shameful failure, like so much of her life at home, Louie "began to squirm and, unconsciously holding out one of her hands to Sam, she cried, 'I am so miserable and poor and rotten and so vile [the words *rotten* and *vile* are natural, touching reminiscences of Henny's tirade-style] and melodramatic, I don't know what to do. I don't know what to do. I can't bear the daily misery . . .' She was bawling brokenly on the tablecloth, her shoulders heaving and her long hair, broken loose, plastered over her red face. 'No wonder they all laugh at me,' she bellowed. 'When I walk along the street, everyone looks at me, and whispers about me, because I'm so messy. My elbows are out and I have no shoes and I'm so big and fat and it'll always be the same.

I can't help it, I can't help it . . . They all laugh at me: I can't stand it any more . . .' Coming to the table, as to a jury, she asked in a firmer voice, but still crying, 'What will become of me? Will life go on like this? Will I always be like this?' She appealed to Sam, 'I have always been like this: I can't live and go on being like this?' "

And Sam replies: "Like what? Like what? I never heard so much idiotic drivel in my born days. Go and put your fat head under the shower."

To Louie the world is what won't let her alone. And the world's interferingness is nothing to Sam's: Sam—so to speak—wakes her up and asks her what she's dreaming just so as to be able to make her dream something different; and then tells her that not every little girl is lucky enough to have a Sam to wake her up. To be let alone! Is there any happiness that compares with it, for someone like Louie? Staying with her mother's relatives in the summer, she feels herself inexplicably, miraculously given a little space of her own—is made, for a few weeks, a sort of grown-up by courtesy. And since Louie has "a genius for solitude," she manages to find it even at home. Henny may scold her and beat her, but Henny does leave her alone ("It is a rotten shame, when I think that the poor kid is dragged into all our rotten messes"), and Louie loves her for it—when Sam talks to Louie about her real mother, Louie retorts, "Mother is my mother," meaning Henny.

At school Louie "was in heaven, at home she was in a torture chamber." She never tells anyone outside "what it is like at home . . . no one would believe me!" To the ordinary misery of differentness is added the misery of being the only one who sees the endless awful war between Henny and Sam for what it is: "Suddenly she would think, *Who can see aught good in thee/Soul-destroying misery?* and in this flash of intelligence she understood that her life and their lives were wasted in this contest and that the quarrel between Henny and Sam was ruining their moral natures." It is only Louie who tries to do anything about it all: with a young thing's fresh sense and ignorance and courage she tries to save the children and herself in the only way that she knows—what she does and what she can't quite make herself do help to bring the book to its wonderful climax. It is rare for a novel to have an ending as good as its middle and beginning: the sixty or seventy pages that sum up *The Man Who Loved Children*, bring the action of the book to its real conclusion, are better than even the best things that have come before.

As he looks at Louie Sam "can't understand what on earth caused this strange drifting nebula to spin." By the time we finish the book we have been so thoroughly in sympathy and in empathy with Louie that we no longer need to understand—we are used to being Louie. We think about her, as her teacher thinks: "It's queer to know everything and nothing at the same time." Louie knows, as she writes in her diary, that "everyday experience which is misery degrades me"; she mutters aloud, "If I did not know I was a genius, I would die: why live?"; a stranger in her entirely strange and entirely familiar family, she cries to her father: "I know something, I know there are people not like us, not muddleheaded like us, better than us." She knows that soon she will have escaped into the world of the people better than us, the great objective world better than Shakespeare and Beethoven and Donatello put together—didn't they all come out of it? Louie is a potentiality still sure that what awaits it in the world is potentiality, not actuality. That she is escaping from some Pollits to some more Pollits, that she herself will end as an actuality among actualities, an accomplished fact, is an old or middle-aged truth or half-truth that Louie doesn't know. As Louie's story ends she has gone for a walk, "a walk around the world"; she starts into the future accompanied by one of those Strauss themes in which a whole young orchestra walks springily off into the sunshine, as though going away were a final good.

As you read *The Man Who Loved Children* what do you notice first? How much life it has,

how natural and original it is; Christina Stead's way of seeing and representing the world is so plainly different from anyone else's that after a while you take this for granted, and think cheerfully, "Oh, she can't help being original." The whole book is different from any book you have read before. What other book represents—tries to represent, even—a family in such conclusive detail?

Aristotle speaks of the pleasure of recognition; you read *The Man Who Loved Children* with an almost ecstatic pleasure of recognition. You get used to saying, "Yes, that's the way it is"; and you say many times, but can never get used to saying, "I didn't know *anybody* knew that." Henny, Sam, Louie, and the children—not to speak of some of the people outside the family—are entirely real to the reader. This may not seem much of a claim: every year thousands of reviewers say it about hundreds of novels. But what they say is conventional exaggeration—reality is rare in novels.

Many of the things of the world come to life in *The Man Who Loved Children*: the book has an astonishing sensory immediacy. Akin to this is its particularity and immediacy of incident; it is full of small, live, characteristic, sometimes odd or grotesque details that are at once surprising enough and convincing enough to make the reader feel, "No, nobody could have made that up." And akin to these on a larger scale are all the "good scenes" in the book: scenes that stand out in the reader's memory as in some way remarkable—as representing something, summing something up, with real finality. There is an extraordinary concentration of such scenes in the pages leading up to the attempted murder and accomplished suicide that is the climax of the book: Ernie's lead, Louie's play, Louie's breakdown after it, Ernie's money box, Ernie's and Louie's discoveries before Miss Aiden comes, Miss Aiden's visit, Henny's beating of Ernie, the end of Henny's love affair, Henny's last game of solitaire, the marlin, Sam and the bananas, the last quarrel. That these scenes come where they do is evidence of Christina Stead's gift for structure; but you are bewildered by her regular ability to make the scenes that matter most the book's best imagined and best realized scenes.

Without its fairly wide range of people and places, attitudes and emotions, *The Man Who Loved Children* might seem too concentrated and homogeneous a selection of reality. But the people outside the Pollit household are quite varied: for instance, Louie's mother's family, Sam's and Henny's relatives, some of the people at Singapore, Henny's Bert Anderson, the "norphan" girl, Louie's friend Clare. There are not so many places—Washington, Ann Arbor, Harper's Ferry, Singapore—but each seems entirely different and entirely alive. As he reads about Louie's summers the reader feels, "So this is what Harper's Ferry looks like to an Australian!" European readers are used to being told what Europe looks like to an American or Russian of genius; we aren't, and we enjoy it. (Occasionally Christina Stead has a kind of virtuoso passage to show that she is not merely a foreign visitor, but a real inhabitant of the United States; we enjoy, and are amused at it.) Because *The Man Who Loved Children* brings to life the variety of the world outside the Pollit household, the happenings inside it—terrible as some of them are—do not seem depressing or constricted or monotonous to the reader: "within, a torment raged, day and night, week, month, year, always the same, an endless conflict, with its truces and breathing spaces; out here were a dark peace and love." And, too, many of the happenings inside the family have so much warmth and habitual satisfaction, are so pleasant or cozy or funny, are so *interesting*, that the reader forgets for a moment that this wonderful playground is also a battlefield.

Children-in-families have a life all their own, a complicated one. Christina Stead seems to have remembered it in detail from her childhood, and to have observed it in detail as an adult. Because of this knowledge she is able to imagine with complete realism the structures, textures, and at-mosphere of one family's spoken and unspoken life. She is unusually sensitive to speech-styles, to conversation-structures, to everything that makes a dialogue or monologue a sort of self-propagating entity; she knows just how family speech is different from speech outside the family, children's speech different from adults'. She gives her children the speeches of speakers to whom a word has the reality of a thing: a thing that can be held wrong-side-up, played with like a toy, thrown at someone like a toy. Children's speech-ways—their senseless iteration, joyous nonsense, incremental variation, entreaties and insults, family games, rhymes, rituals, proverbs with the force of law, magical mistakes, occasional uncannily penetrating descriptive phrases—are things Christina Stead knows as well as she knows the speech-ways of families, of people so used to each other that half the time they only half-say something, imply it with a family phrase, or else spell it out in words too familiar to be heard, just as the speaker's face is too familiar to be seen. The book's household conversations between mother and child, father and child, are both superficially and profoundly different from any conversation in the world outside; reading such conversations is as satisfying as being given some food you haven't tasted since childhood. (After making your way through the great rain-forest of the children's speech, you come finally to one poor broomstick of a tree, their letters: all the children—as Ernie says, laughing—"start out with 'Dear Dad, I hope you are well, I am well, Mother is well,' and then they get stuck.") The children inherit and employ, or recognize with passive pleasure, the cultural scraps—everything from Mozart to *Hiawatha*—that are a part of the sounds the grown-ups make. Father and Mother are gods but (it is strange!) gods who will sometimes perform for you on request, taking part in a ritual, repeating stories or recitations, pretending to talk like a Scot or a Jew or an Englishman—just as, earlier, they would pretend to be a bear.

Christina Stead knows the awful eventfulness of little children's lives. That grown-ups seldom cry, scream, fall, fight each other, or have to be sent to bed seems very strange to someone watching children: a little child pays its debt to life penny by penny. Sam is able to love a life spent with children because he himself has the insensate busyness of a child. Yet, wholly familiar as he is, partly child—like as he is, to the children he is monstrous—not the singular monster that he is to us, but the ordinary monster that any grown-up is to you if you weigh thirty or forty pounds and have your eyes two feet from the floor. Again and again the reader is conscious of Christina Stead's gift for showing how different anything is when looked at from a really different point of view. Little Evie, "fidgeting with her aunt's great arm around her, seemed to be looking up trustfully with her brown eyes, but those deceptive eyes were full of revolt, mistrust, and dislike"; she averts her gaze from her aunt's "slab cheeks, peccary skin . . . the long, plump, inhuman thigh, the glossy, sufficient skirt, from everything powerful, coarse, and proud about this great unmated-mare . . . 'Oh,' thought Evie to herself, 'when I am a lady with a baby, I won't have all those bumps, I won't be so big and fat, I will be a little woman, thin like I am now and not fat in front or in the skirt.' "

One of the most obvious facts about grown-ups, to a child, is that they have forgotten what it is like to be a child. The child has not yet had the chance to know what it is like to be a grown-up; he believes, even, that being a grown-up is a mistake he will never make—when *he* grows up he will keep on being a child, a big child with power. So the child and grown-up live in mutual love, misunderstanding, and distaste. Children shout and play and cry and want candy; grown-ups say *Ssh!* and work and scold and want steak. There is no disputing tastes as contradictory as these. It is not just Mowgli who was raised by a couple of wolves; any child is raised by a couple of grown-ups. Father and Mother may be nearer and dearer than anyone will ever be again! Still,

they are members of a different species. God is, I suppose, what our parents were; certainly the giant or ogre of the stories is so huge, so powerful, and so stupid because that is the way a grown-up looks to a child.

Grown-ups forget or cannot believe that they seem even more unreasonable to children than children seem to them. Henny's oldest boy Ernie (to whom money is the primary means of understanding and changing the world; he is a born economic determinist, someone with absolute pitch where money is concerned) is one of Christina Stead's main ways of making us remember how mistaken and hypocritical grown-ups seem to children. Ernie feels that he sees the world as it is, but that grown-ups are no longer able to do this: their rationalization of their own actions, the infinitely complicated lie they have agreed to tell about the world, conceals the world from them. The child sees the truth, but is helpless to do anything about it.

The Pollit children are used to the terrible helplessness of a child watching its parents war. There over their heads the Sun and the Moon, God the Father and the Holy Virgin, are shouting at each other, striking each other—the children contract all their muscles, try not to hear, and hear. Sometimes waked in darkness by the familiar sounds, they lie sleepily listening to their parents; hear, during some lull in the quarrel, a tree-frog or the sound of the rain.

Ernie feels the same helpless despair at the poverty of the family; thinking of how *many* children there already are, he implores, "Mothering, don't have another baby!" (Henny replies, "You can bet your bottom dollar on that, old sweetness.") But he does not really understand what he is saying: later on, he and the other children look uncomprehendingly at Henny, "who had again queerly become a large woman, though her hands, feet, and face remained small and narrow." One night they are made to sleep downstairs, and hear Henny screaming hour after hour upstairs; finally, at morning, she is silent. "They had understood nothing at all, except that mother had been angry and miserable and now she was still; this was a blessed relief." Their blank misunderstanding of what is sexual is the opposite of their eager understanding of what is excremental. They thrill to the inexplicably varying permissiveness of the world: here they are being allowed to laugh at, as a joke, what is ordinarily not referred to at all, or mentioned expediently, in family euphemisms!

The book is alive with their fights, games, cries of "You didn't kiss me! "—"Look, Moth, Tommy kissed you in the glass!" But their great holidays so swiftly are gone: the "sun was going down, and Sunday-Funday was coming to an end. They all felt it with a kind of misery: with such a fine long day and so many things to do, how could they have let it slip past like this?" And summer vacation is the same: the indefinite, almost infinite future so soon is that small, definite, disregarded thing, the past!

On a winter night, with nothing but the fire in the living room to warm the house, the child runs to it crying, "Oo, gee whiz, is it cold; jiminy, I'm freezing. Moth, when are we going to get the coal?" (Anyone who remembers his childhood can feel himself saying those sentences—those and so many more of the book's sentences.) And as the child grows older, how embarrassing the parent is, in the world outside: "Louie looked stonily ahead or desperately aside." And, home again, the parent moralizes, sermonizes—won't he *ever* stop talking?—to the child doing its homework, writing, writing, until finally the parent reads over the child's shoulder what is being written on the page of notebook paper: *Shut up, shut up, shut up, shut up* . . . The book follows the children into the cold beds they warm, goes with them into their dreams: when you read about Louie's hard-soft nightmare or the horseman she hears when she wakes in the middle of the night, you are touching childhood itself.

Chapter Three
The Philosophy of Childhood

Chapter Three

The Philosophy of Childhood

Although it might seem to be possible to construct a philosophical approach to almost anything, there are generally two sorts of "Philosophies of": philosophies of particular disciplines or modes of inquiry, such as the philosophy of science or the philosophy of music, and philosophies of nature or any of its subdivisions, such as the philosophy of space and time, or the philosophy of life. If there is such a thing as the philosophy of childhood, it is to the latter classification that it belongs.

The philosophy of a particular mode of inquiry is likely to focus upon the underlying presuppositions of that enterprise, and to assume a detached and critical stance with regard to them. Or. there may be an effort to provide a synoptic perspective to what might otherwise seem to be a loosely connected set of divergent investigations. On the other hand, philosophies of existence, or of regions of nature, might be expected to evaluate commonly held assumptions about those aspects of existence, or to give unity and order to commonly shared information about such aspects.

If we concentrate on criticism of underlying assumptions and prevailing criteria as being the most pronounced characteristics of the philosophy of childhood, then we see that the rationale of philosophy for children constitutes precisely such criticism. (To be sure, philosophy for children also represents a critique of prevalent conceptions of philosophy, but this is another matter.) After all, what the literature in the area of Philosophy for Children concentrates its attack upon is the notion that children are uninterested in philosophical ideas, incapable of conducting philosophical dialogues and unable to form a community of philosophical inquiry. In effect, the claim is made that children can do these things, and educational practice is engaged in to substantiate the claim.

The selections in the section that follows concentrate either on the concept of childhood, or on the philosophy of childhood, or both. Korczak focuses on the child's right to respect—in all cases, and not just in educational contexts. Instead of respecting children for the understanding they have of their world, Korsczak suggests, we treat them condescendingly because they cannot understand ours. "They do not understand adult failure ... They do not know the meaning of duty, nor of material worries. They lack a sense of judgment. . . ." And yet, they have "a sense of democracy that knows no hierarchy," They are never taken seriously. "Powerless, small, dependent upon others, their claims are simply not accepted." Korczak is not unmindful of the dangers from which children must be protected by adults, but he insists that they must be listened to—for their good and for ours.

The Lipman essay, in contrast, propounds some of the questions that need to be raised if the approach to a philosophy of childhood is to be pursued. These questions are: (1) the implications for the philosophy of law of the child's alleged right to reason; (2) the implications for ethics and moral education of the child's alleged ability to engage in "ethical inquiry"; (3) the implications for social and political philosophy of the child's participating in "communities of inquiry"; and (4) the implications of "the concept of a child" for philosophical inquiries into "the concept of a person." The author attempts to show that affirmation of the child's ability to think philosophically makes possible, for the first time, the child's education into rationality, responsibility and personhood.

Martin Benjamin, while endorsing the idea of philosophy for children, demurs when it comes to the development of philosophies of childhood, on the ground that it will only do violence to the temporal, historical notion of a human life. It will lead to the atomization of a human life into separate stages, instead of emphasizing their continuity and unity.

Philosophy for children is also endorsed by Jonathan Adler, but he adds that its interests would be better served if the claims made for the child's rationality were to have in mind a capacity that increases by degrees rather than one which one either has or doesn't have. This does not mean that Kohlberg's stage theory has to be accepted. Rather, it can be shown, Adler argues, that the child's cognitive capacities continue to expand, but the child can engage in ethical inquiry at virtually any age. This raises a question, of course, as to whether "ability to engage in ethical inquiry" is itself a matter of degree or an "all-none" concept, as well as the further question of the relationship between such an ability and rationality.

At the same time, Adler recognizes that children may be justified in their quest for ultimate explanations and meanings, even though adults may not be. The pragmatic reasons that justify our abandoning our quest for absolute answers

should not deter the child from wanting to know how everything hangs together. Still, the abandonment of the quest is part of the larger picture that the child is seeking to envision. We may reasonably hesitate before accepting such a sharp division between the philosophical inquiry of the child and that of the adult, just as we hesitate before accepting Rousseau's dictum that "we can tell fairy tales to adults, but children must be told the truth."

Gareth Matthews can be taken as rejecting not only the Piaget-Kohlberg theory of moral stages of development, but also Benjamin's critique of the proposal that there be a "philosophy of childhood." We lack a well-worked out theory of childhood, Matthews argues, and this means we lack a "reasoned understanding of the status of children as moral agents." This leads to our projecting our own prejudices and superstitions upon the child. Because we adults are unreasonable about momentous moral issues, we proceed to attribute such unreasonableness to children. Matthews finds such attribution unwarranted.

Ruddick appears to favor the devising of alternatives to developmentalism but at the same time he interprets Erikson as holding that child and adult are correlative notions, a position he endorses. He feels that children's lack of moral experience disqualifies them from dealing with profound moral problems like euthanasia. Ruddick would define children as dependent beings who need care and he would define adults as beings who are capable of providing such care. His insistence upon the primacy of parental protection of the child largely excludes any consideration of the possibility of the child's moral judgment. And yet, unless the capacity of children to engage in moral inquiry (and the making of moral judgments) is strengthened while they are still children, it is hard to see how they can be expected to engage in reasoned moral inquiry once they have become adults.

Respecting the Child's Point of View

Janusz Korczak

In the past year or two, the memory of Janusz Korczak has come to be celebrated by such groups as the Polish-American Congress, the American Council of Polish Cultural Clubs, and the Anti-Defamation League of B'nai B'rith. A brief statement by a committee of these groups reads as follows:

Born in Poland in 1879, Dr. Korczak was a physician, an educator and author. More than that, he was an extraordinary and rare .human being who selflessly dedicated and devoted his life to the education and welfare of children.

Appointed director of a Jewish orphanage in 1911, a position he retained until the tragic end of his life. Dr. Korczak was responsible for introducing such educational innovations at the time as student self-government and a student newspaper written for and by his pupils. His most famous book, How to Love a Child *(1920-21) is considered by many to be a masterwork in the field of education.*

When the Nazis invaded Poland in 1939, Dr. Korczak, 61 years old at the time, donned his country's uniform—for the fourth time in his life. In 1940, after the Germans had overrun Poland, Dr. Korczak and his 200 students were removed to the Warsaw Ghetto, into which half a million Jews had been herded and cut off from the rest of the world. As a result of overcrowding, starvation, cold and epidemics, 100,000 Jews had died within the Ghetto walls by the summer of 1942. The Ghetto area was reduced and Korczak and his children were required to move three times in order to stay within its limits.

Despite these inhuman circumstances, Dr. Korczak was determined to carry on as best he could. His students continued their studies and were even able to play their usual games. Keeping his children alive and fed was his most vexing problem. "I came back rushed from making the rounds," he wrote in his diary. "Seven visits, conversations, flights of steps, interrogations. The results: five zlotys and a pledge of five others every month. And on that I'm supposed to keep 200 souls alive!"

Despite repeated attempts by friends to persuade him to be smuggled out of the Ghetto, Korczak steadfastly refused to abandon his children. Finally, on Wednesday, August 5, 1942 he received a deportation order. Telling his students he was taking them for a picnic in the country, Korczak, his devoted assistant Stefania Wilczynska and the 200 children left the orphanage and walked a mile to the "Umschlagplatz," the assembly point from which Jews were packed into cattle trucks and sent to their death in the gas chambers of Treblinka.

Here is how one eyewitness described that scene:

"... they kept packing them in and there was still room left. Urged on by the whips, more people were jammed into the cars. Suddenly Schmerling—the sadistic Ghetto police officer whom the Germans had put in charge of the 'Umschlagplatz'—commanded that the children be brought to the cars. Korczak went at their head. I'll never forget that sight to the end of my life. It wasn't just a man entering a railway carriage—it was a silent but organized protest against the murderers, a march the like of which no human eye had ever seen before. The children went four-by-four. Korczak went first, with his head held high, leading a child with each hand. The second group was led by Stefa Wilczynska. They went to their death with a look of full contempt for their assassins. When the Ghetto policemen saw Korczak, they snapped to attention and saluted. 'Who is that man?' asked the Germans."

Actually, "Janusz Korczak" was only a pen name. The author's real name was Henryk Gold-szmit. The selection that follows is from Kethavim Pedagogiyyim, *which was published in Israel in 1954 by Hakibutz Hameuchad Ltd. The translation is by Shifra Elencweing Rapoport.*

From early childhood on, one is brought up to believe that adults are more important than children. "I am big," proclaims a child standing on a table. "I am taller than you are!" they say with pride when measuring themselves against their friends. How ill at ease children feel when unable to reach for something just beyond their fingertips! How hard they find it to follow, with their small feet, in the footsteps of adults! How difficult it is to keep a glass from falling from one's small hands, to climb steps, to reach the top of a chair, to enter a car! It is impossible for children to grab the doorhandle, to look out the window, to hand something up or to bring it down: everything is beyond their reach. When in a crowd, unnoticed, they find themselves continually being pushed around. It is painful to be small.

Big things are things that are noticed: they take up more space, and draw attention to themselves, and respect. What is small seems to be ordinary: small people, small needs, small joys, small sorrows. More impressive are big cities and mountains, big factories, big men. Children do not count: adults have to stoop to them. Worst of all, children are weak. We can lift them up, throw them in the air, put them down, stop them from running, dwarf all their efforts. If they should disobey, we have the power to command: "Don't go! Don't touch! Go away! Answer me!" And they know they must obey, even though, until at last they give in, they try not to. Which among them, while so vulnerable to punishment (even to the adult's affectionate sweet pinch), would dare to raise a hand to an adult? The respect for power comes from the feeling of impotence: in society, the stronger can cruelly impose his will without being punished. Nor are we ourselves good examples, since we teach in a way that shows disrespect for the weak.

The world has greatly changed since physical power, muscular power, gave way to the preeminence of science and the human mind. The world of science and research is no longer confined to the dark and narrow rooms in which it originated, but has grown into great institutions amassing huge amounts of knowledge. Scientists nowadays have the power to bring about ever new conquests. The years to be devoted to study are constantly lengthening. There are more schools and more tests. More words are being printed. The small child, whose life has just begun, has a lot to gulp down. There are so many difficult problems, such as how to divide the conquered territories, who will get what, how the world's economy is to be planned, how many factories have to be built to provide work for hands and brains, how are people to be led to live orderly lives out of the reach of a single man's madness, how is leisure time to be filled up, how can mediocrity be prevented, and finally, how to make the public obedient and understanding for its own good. Legislatures and politicians have been trying carefully to do these things, but they are often proven wrong. Yet they are the very people that decide the child's future. But who asks for the child's consent or for the child's approval? To survive, one must have knowledge and experience; one must excel, and even be crafty. Children are helpless, and feel, amidst their toys and books, that important decisions are being made about their fate. The flower is the harbinger of the fruit; the chick will become a chicken and in turn will lay eggs. Meanwhile one must work assiduously, worrying all the while whether the child will grow up to meet its promise and fulfill one's expectations. If the children are in one's way, one must be patient; maybe later, in one's old age, they will be helpful. But life has its snags, just as crops may be stricken with drought. All the while that we anticipate what the future will be, what the end will be, we underestimate what we have already achieved.

The young are underestimated by human beings: it is only in the sight of God that the flower of the apple tree and the apple itself are seen to be equal.

What will happen to children without us? From us comes everything they have. We are the ones who always know; we are the teachers, the advisors. It is we who forsee the good things and prevent the bad ones; in so doing, we prepare children and correct their ways. They themselves are nothing: we give them orders and they must obey. Legal responsibility rests with us. Only we are the judges of their behavior, their movements, their intentions and their thoughts. We command and demand and supervise their actions. Everything is according to our wishes and understanding—our children—our property, and so on.

It is true that some things have changed: no longer is the family the only supervisor. The society has stepped in; it is there cautiously, but it is there. The fact remains that children have nothing which belongs to them, yet they must account for everything. Everything given them is gratuitous—they are not permitted to break it or to give it away. Everything they receive must be accepted gratefully; perhaps this is why they appreciate small things which we look upon with condescension. The only property which really belongs to them—a rope, a box, a string of beads—that which is their own treasure, we consider junk.

As our reward for what we give children, we expect them to obey and to behave properly. We prefer that they get things by asking for them. It is only out of our good will that we give, in the way a wealthy man may give to the woman he loves. Thus the relationship between children and adults is troubled by their material dependence, and their consequent frustration.

We do not respect children very much because they are incapable of understanding the world of the adult—our moments of enthusiasm, inspiration or desolation, what makes us worry, what makes us sad. They do not understand adult failure. Children think that life is easy: there is a mother and a father; the father earns money and the mother provides the goods. They do not know the meaning of duty, nor of material worries. They lack a sense of judgment: we detect their intentions immediately—we even know when they are plotting. Perhaps, then, we are merely deceiving ourselves when we think that children are the way we want them to be. Perhaps they are hiding from us—maybe even suffering in secret.

We have conquered the world, domesticated the animals, and built relationships among nations, although we are a long way from a just world. But the child's doubts and hesitations we still don't take seriously. The child's sense of democracy knows no hierarchy. Children feel as much for the laborer's sweat as for the horse, for the hungry child of their own age, and for the slaughtered chicken. Children's closest friends are the dog and the bird. (The flower is not different from the butterfly.) The oyster and the stone are their brothers: children do not yet know that only human beings have souls.

We look down condescendingly upon children because their whole lives are still ahead of them. We are aware that our steps are heavy and our demeanor lazy, in contrast with children, who run and jump, and whose eyes are everywhere distractedly. They are amazed and ask many questions. For no apparent reason they cry, and then become happy. A sunny autumn day is so rare, we do appreciate it—but in springtime there are many of them. The child's joy flows so naturally that we take it for granted. For us, time flies so quickly: every minute counts. Children seem to have all the time they need to achieve what they want.

Even though children suffer during wartime, they are not soldiers, nor can they protect their country. Their opinion does not count, nor do they have the right to vote. Powerless, small, dependent upon others, their claims are simply not accepted.

Children are never taken seriously. Their noses are always running. A child is only a child—only a person in the making, only a future grown-up. Children have to be supervised, never left alone for a single minute. Anything can happen: they can hurt themselves or others, start a fire, or even open the door to a thief. So closely do they have to be watched that all independence is denied to them. And only we have the right to criticize them, for they have no sense of limits—how much to eat or drink, or a sense of time with respect to sleep and fatigue. Eventually they change, but our watchful eye is still on them—perhaps more so than ever. Children do not distinguish between good and bad; they know neither order nor discipline. Nor do they have a

sense of responsibility: we have to teach them the right ways of doing things, and prevent them from doing things wrongly, for we are already experienced and know the dangers children might encounter.

We even know that great caution is not always a guarantee—which is why we are extremely careful, so that we won't blame ourselves. Children love waywardness, and readily follow the example of others who are "bad." They are quickly swayed but not easily corrected. Remembering the bad things that have happened to us, we try to teach children out of our own experience. "Remember," we say, "listen, understand." But, as if on purpose, they will not listen to us. They are always tempted to do the wrong things, and must be watched closely if, for their own good, they are to do what we tell them to do. For how can we tolerate foolishness and irresponsibility? Because children will appear to be subdued and innocent when really they are crafty, there are times when we cannot help being suspicious. They look for ways of "sneaking out," and always have excuses. And thus, by pretending to be innocent, they bring on themselves even more suspicion and blame.

Developing Philosophies of Childhood

Matthew Lipman

The compartmentalization of philosophy reflects and responds to certain differences among specific skills and among specific dimensions of human experience. The skills in question are primarily the varieties of reasoning. The dimensions of experience include the aesthetic, the moral, the social and the religious. A few philosophers might question the objectivity of the latter domains, but few are likely to contest the objectivity and universality of childhood. It would seem, therefore, that childhood is a legitimate dimension of human behavior and of human experience, and that it is entitled to philosophical treatment no less than the other dimensions for which philosophies already exist. Perhaps its chief claim to philosophical uniqueness might be the fact that it is the forgotten—if not actually repressed—aspect of experience.

Although it is not the case that every child is a philosopher, it is generally granted that (except in a few rare instances) every philosopher was once a child. And if recent years have helped to demonstrate to us that the experience of philosophy need not be incompatible with childhood, so it may turn out that the experience of childhood—or at the very least, the perspective of the child—need not be incompatible with adulthood. That we are biologically of different ages no more makes us mutually incomprehensible than that we are biologically of different sexes. Indeed, the situation of adults vis-a-vis children is a bit better than that of males vis-a-vis females, for the latter distinction is symmetrical, neither having ever been the other, while adults have once been chil-

dren, even though children have never been adults. Moreover, just as the differences between male and female perspectives constitute no insuperable barrier to their being experientially shared, so the differences between child and adult perspectives represent an invitation to the shared experience of human diversity rather than an excuse for intergenerational hostility, repression and guilt. For example, were childhood to be a less closeted and more openly acknowledged dimension of human experience, we might expect more candor from philosophers in admitting the extent to which their "mature" views were systematic embellishments of their firmly-held childhood intuitions and convictions. Yet even those philosophers who might take the opposing view, contending that their views as adults differed totally from the opinions they held as children, might acknowledge the extent to which the development of their later outlook represented a reaction against childhood convictions which were no less philosophical than the ones which replaced them.

The question will nevertheless persist in being asked, as to what there is about childhood which entitles it to become an area of philosophy. The answer to this question would seem to be that, to deserve a philosophy, a subject-area should be rich enough in implications as to contribute significantly to other areas of philosophy. Specialized studies in the field in question might in turn have value for metaphysics, or for logic, or for epistemology, and practitioners in these areas might find that they ignored the new field at their peril. The question then is whether childhood meets this requirement. It would indeed appear to be the case that developing philosophies of childhood hold promise of meaningful implications for social philosophy, metaphysics, philosophy of law, ethics, philosophy of education, and other philosophical areas. The purpose of the present paper is to identify certain of these areas in which work is already being done or needs to be done.

Projects are already underway, or need to be undertaken, that would be responsive to the following questions (to name only a few):

1. Do children have a right to reason, and what implications, if any, are thereby relevant to the philosophy of law?

2. Can children engage in "ethical inquiry" as a meaningful alternative to their being subjected to moral indoctrination? If so, what are the implications of such "ethical inquiry" for the general field of ethics?

3. How can the roles of children in any theory of community be of value to social philosophy?

4. In what ways does the question "What is a child?" throw light on the question "What is a person?" so as to contribute meaningfully to the metaphysical import of the latter issue?

We can here examine each of these issues in a bit more detail.

1. It is well-known in philosophy that considerable attention is presently given to the matter of children's rights. The flourishing of this interest is, of course, gratifying, but there is a signal need for a greater focus on the child's right to reason, especially that aspect of the problem which Bertram Bandman, in a recent article, has called "the child's right to inquire."

When we employ a catch-phrase such as the "right to inquire," we are in danger of overlooking the ambiguity that is prevalent in the use of the term "inquire." This is especially true in the case of children, since we all know how tirelessly

children can direct questions at adults, while we know of few, if any, cases of children engaging in inquiry in the Peircean sense. So it is not surprising that our initial understanding of the phrase "right to inquire" should be in the sense of the child's right to ask questions, particularly of adults, and with regard to matters which adults may not care to discuss with children, either because they wish to protect children from such knowledge, or because they wish to protect both the children and themselves from the irresponsible use of such knowledge. In this sense, the child's right to ask entails the further issue of the adult's right not to respond.

As we know, the fact that every answer has a question does not mean that every question has—or is entitled to—an answer, nor that every challenge is entitled to a response. Hobbes points up an analogous situation when he argues that there may be certain things which the citizen, though justly commanded by the sovereign, can justly refuse to do. Likewise there may be times when, although the child is within his or her rights in asking certain questions, the adult may without injustice refuse to reply, or may properly choose to reply evasively. Evidently there are times— and here Hobbes is instructive—when one person's right to command does not necessarily imply another person's obligation to obey. It is in just such a jurisprudential no man's land that the examination of children's rights might turn out to be most rewarding.

But whatever the merits may be of examining the child's right to inquire in the sense of "asking questions"—presumably of those who "know the answers"—the more important issue continues to remain unexamined, and that is the matter of the right of children to engage in cooperative inquiry. Such a possibility seemed remote as long as there was no such thing as philosophy in the elementary school. But now that it has been firmly established that there are sound academic grounds for the institutionalization of philosophy as an integral portion of elementary and secondary education, we cannot turn away from the fact that the question of academic freedom can no longer be limited to the college campus. In the years to come, the counsel of philosophers will be increasingly needed to deal with the emerging issues of the academic freedom of children, as these proliferate under a variety of headings, such as the child's right to know, to reason, to doubt, and to believe. (Let us hope that a separate legal struggle will not be required for every mental act.)

Finally, it should not be overlooked that the denial to an individual of the right of expression is simultaneously the denial to others of the right to learn what the individual in question might have expressed. It is in this sense that, if children are to be "seen and not heard," their silencing deprives the rest of us of their insights. To the objection that children's views are seldom insightful, it would not be improper to suggest that an assay of adult views might also seem largely unprofitable.

2. The discovery that children can do philosophy—and that they do so competently and with relish—points up in other ways the need to develop philosophies of childhood. For if children can reason as they begin to speak, and if they can do philosophy as they begin to reason, the present alliance between philosophical ethics and developmental psychology will begin to show welcome signs of strain. Should it be the case that at every stage of their growth children can engage in ethical inquiry, ethics need no longer be tainted, as it now is, with that indoctrinational manipulation of children's moral views and attitudes which calls itself "moral education." Those who make use of philosophy in order to indoctrinate are deplorable; just as deplorable are those who make use of philosophy in order to undermine grounds for certain beliefs, with the excuse that only by doing so can they liberate children from dogma and superstition. For this, in effect, could be the indoctrination of relativism, or some other "ism."

Those who champion developmental theories of childhood tend to make two crucial errors.

First, they frequently assume that childhood is a preparation for adulthood, and is to be viewed as only a means to an end, or as an incomplete condition moving toward completeness. Adults know and children don't know; children must, therefore, acquire the knowledge with which grownups are so richly endowed. Thus, the first mistake is to assume that, if children are not moving in the direction of what we adults know and believe and value, there must be something wrong with their "development." Such a view ignores the possibility that childhood is no more incomplete without a subsequent adulthood than adulthood is without a prior childhood. It is only together that they make "a life."

Secondly, the proponents of developmental thesis are always careful to select those criteria which will reinforce the case they are trying to make, while ignoring other criteria through whose use that case might be weakened. Educational disciplines that have been organized in a simple-to-complex sequence are proposed as models—mathematics would be a good illustration. As children master such disciplines, their progressive development is thought to be taking place step by step and "true to form." But those who uphold the development thesis make sure not to select such criteria as artistic expression or philosophical insight, for to do so might make their case seem less compelling. Why do children create such impressive paintings while in early childhood? Why do they ask so many metaphysical questions while still young, then seem to suffer a decline in their powers as they move into adolescence? How can children learn the terms and syntax and logic of a whole language—indeed, often, of several languages—while they are still toddlers, a feat beyond the scope of most grownups? What would education have to be in order to *sustain* the child's development along the meteoric lines with which it begins, rather than let it lapse, as it now so frequently does, into apathy and bitterness? It would seem that for every criterion which supports the development thesis, another can be found which goes against it. And for every aspect of the child's growth where there seems to be a natural unfolding, there is another aspect wherein development occurs only by sustained intervention—education being a prime example.

In short, the philosophy of childhood would be much enhanced by fresh work in ethical theory which would take into account the capacity of children to engage in rational dialogue and to offer reasons for their conduct, which would not treat children patronizingly or condescendingly by assuming that their behavior is necessarily more selfish and less idealistic than the behavior of adults, and which would recognize that the developmental approach has achieved a dubious plausibility by comparing children with adults primarily in terms of adult knowledge rather than in terms of other criteria whose employment might lead to children appearing much better and adults much worse. A theory of ethical inquiry is needed, but those who devise such a theory ought to keep firmly in mind that the ethics they are engaged in is part of philosophy and not part of science. For an ethical approach to claim to be "scientific" would ensure its demise in a school setting about as surely as if it were to claim to be guaranteed by "religion."

3. Another area in which work needs to be done is that of social philosophy. The philosophy of childhood needs to address itself to those respects in which childhood has been indicted for traits which should be treated as problematical rather than taken for granted. Typical of such indictments is the charge that unlike their parents and grandparents, young people find work repugnant. Now, the point has been made by Dewey that, in a certain sense, laziness is a modern invention, since it is the response one would expect to those aspects of modern factory work which make such work obnoxious. But this is probably not the explanation for the observed change in children's attitudes, and if it is not, what is?

If one listens to the complaints of parents, one hears the problem formulated as a lack of inter-generational symmetry: our parents worked hard, and we learned to do so from them; why haven't our children learned to do so from us? Like our parents, we love work; why do our children hate it so?

A good reason for considering this a problem in social philosophy is that it is an example of the decline of community. Only a few generations ago, the basic work unit of the society was not the individual or the factory, but the family. The family was a working community, in which individuals of all ages had their tasks to perform. But as the drive for personal success replaced the normal process of generational succession, the work-oriented children of such communities struck out after their own goals, and worked for them as wholeheartedly as previously they had worked within the bosoms of their families. They became professionals, whose work-ethic was personal rather than social. Their work—as doctors, scholars, accountants, administrators—was something they could not share with their children, because the family was no longer the basic work unit to which they belonged. The child's efforts to participate were rebuked with such comments as, "Don't bother Daddy, he's busy!" or "Please go out and play; can't you see Mommy's working?" Soon the child caught on: what came between him and his parents or between her and her parents was this hateful thing called work. Perhaps the parents could not be disliked, but what they were doing could be.

Here, obviously, we need guidance. Do we accept this change in attitude as a *fait accompli*, or do we wish to attack it or circumvent it? If our choice is to attempt to reconstruct the work-community, how is this to be accomplished? Could the creation of communities of inquiry in which adults and children participate together as equals be a step in that direction?

It is not unusual to see people's eyes light up when they hear of children engaged in inquiry. There is more uncertainty in their response when the notion of community is broached. But it is difficult to conceive of inquiry that does not take place in a community setting, and if this is generally the case with adults, how much more true is it in the case of children! The need for shared and objective procedures, openness of evidence, the challenging of poorly drawn inferences, the consideration of the consequences of suppositions and hypotheses, all of these help to form the fabric of a community of inquiry among children as well as adults. When these and allied procedures are internalized by each participant, the result is critical reflection. More than critical, for it is also self-critical. One becomes accustomed to asking oneself the same hard questions one levels at one's companions in dialogue. Needless to say, those who are able to engage in cognitive self-criticism are in a good position to being able to exercise behavioral self-control. The internalization of the procedures of the community of inquiry thus has a moral as well as a dialogical or theoretical dimension.

Furthermore, the formation of childhood communities, where candor and trust mingle freely with wondering, searching and reasoning, provides a needed social support during those critical years in which children are loosening the ties that bind them to their families and endeavoring to establish themselves as mature and responsible individuals. We should not forget the warning voiced repeatedly by Margaret Mead, that we must learn to devise social mechanisms that will smooth the transition periods for growing children. Otherwise, these periods become moments of childhood crisis.

4. Finally, there is the problem of the child as a person. We generally think of personhood as something not given at birth, but as something gradually achieved. No one seems able to say just what the normal age is for becoming a person, but we suspect that, compared with ancient times, the starting point of personhood is now put at an earlier age, and the beginning of maturity at a later one. Yet, although there has been some shrinkage in the period of one's being a non-person, or a not-yet-person, we have continued to believe that one must give behavioral evidence of

deserving to be called a person before the appropriate rite of predication can be performed. The same may be said for acknowledging that the child has a self, or is rational. There is generally sound warrant for any reluctance to employ terms honorifically, but such warrant may not be sufficient to justify withholding personhood and rationality from young children.

Now, ordinarily, a clear-cut distinction must be made between achievement and ascription. Achievement terms are based upon observable behaviors, and are to be accorded only upon the actual manifestation of such behaviors (in the sense that those who write are called "writers," those who run are called "runners," and so on). But ascription terms endow their object with properties (such as prestige and charisma) independent of any observed behavior, since these properties exist wholly to the extent to which people are willing to ascribe or impute them. In between these more clear-cut cases is a host of knotty issues, in each of which it can be debated whether the predications are or are not gratuitous.

However, the achievement-ascription distinction is rather like a set of cards that has a joker in it, and the joker lies in the fact that the application of the distinction to cases where *meaning* is at issue may be somewhat different from its application to cases in which *truth* is at issue.

It sometimes happens, C. I. Lewis tells us, that the subject must bring certain conditions to an experience in order correctly to understand or comprehend the object, and whatever the subject must in such fashion bring along in order to grasp the meaning of the object belongs *to the object* and not to the subject.[1] Were this claim of Lewis's to be accepted, it would follow that concepts like "person" and "rational," whose ascription makes meaningful what otherwise was not meaningful, deservedly belong to the object of such ascriptions. We are therefore pragmatically justified in considering the behavior of young children to be the behavior of rational persons, in that we can comprehend such behavior as being more meaningful than if we refuse to engage in what we consider to be unwarranted and gratuitous ascriptions.

To impute rationality to a child is further warranted on the grounds that doing so has so often resulted in evidence of the child's rationality. This is therefore not to be confused with the judicial postulate that people are not to be considered guilty until they are proven guilty. Treating accused persons as not guilty does not confirm their innocence; treating children as rational tends to produce evidence that confirms their rationality.

Whether or not these particular arguments will be found persuasive, the issue of the child's personhood and rationality will remain to haunt the philosophy of childhood. And here another aspect of the problem appears to require a pragmatic formulation. For if we refuse to acknowledge the rationality of children, we cannot satisfactorily engage in philosophical dialogue with them, because we cannot accept their utterances as reasons. If we cannot do philosophy with children, we deprive their education of the very component that might make such education more meaningful. And if we deny children a meaningful education, we assure that the ignorance, irresponsibility and mediocrity which presently prevail among adults will continue to do so. Treating children as persons might be a small price to pay, in the long run, for some rather substantive social gains.

Notes

1. Cf. An Analysis of Knowledge and Valuation, pp. 469-478.

Comments on "Developing Philosophies of Childhood"

Martin Benjamin

It is one thing to say that childhood has received too little attention from philosophers. And it is another thing to say that the remedy for this is the development of an area of philosophy specializing in questions of childhood. Matthew Lipman, if I understand him correctly, wants to make both of these claims. In what follows I will suggest that only the first is adequately supported in his interesting and illuminating paper. Then I will argue that efforts to bring children and childhood into the mainstream of philosophical teaching and inquiry by developing a new area of philosophy are likely to be counterproductive. Finally, I will identify and develop a line of argument that is intimated in at least three passages in Professor Lipman's paper and I will suggest that this line of argument points to a better way of bringing children and childhood within the ambit of philosophers and philosophy.

Childhood, Professor Lipman argues, has been slighted by philosophy. Not only have children been ignored by teachers of philosophy (a deficiency that Professor Lipman and his colleagues at the Institute for the Advancement of Philosophy for Children have been successfully working to overcome), but childhood, as a distinctive component of the life cycle, has been ignored by philosophers generally. Perhaps, as O'Neill and Ruddick have suggested, this is attributable in part to the fact that "many of the great philosophers since antiquity have been rather solitary and childless people."[1] Another fac-

tor, no doubt, is the relatively brief history of the very notion of childhood.[2] But whatever the explanation, the result is that childhood has been the subject of scant philosophical reflection. Moreover, as Professor Lipman demonstrates, various questions in philosophy of law, ethics, social philosophy, and metaphysics require a clearer philosophical understanding of childhood. Thus his claim about the importance of children and childhood to philosophy is, I believe, well supported in his paper.

To remedy this deficiency Professor Lipman proposes that we develop an area of philosophy specializing in childhood. Just as science, law, religion and history, for example, have generated lines of inquiry and bodies of literature collected under the headings of philosophy of science, philosophy of law, philosophy of religion, and philosophy of history, so too, he suggests, comparable forms of inquiry and bodies of literature should be developed with regard to childhood.

His principal argument, as I understand it, is as follows:

(1) "To deserve a philosophy a subject area should be rich enough in implications as to contribute significantly to other areas of philosophy."

(2) Childhood is rich enough in implications to contribute to other areas of philosophy.

(3) Therefore, childhood is entitled to become an area of philosophy.

Although Professor Lipman spends most of his paper establishing the truth of premise (2), the main difficulty, I believe, is with premise (1). For without further argument, it is not clear why we should regard a subject area's capacity to contribute to other areas of philosophy as a sufficient condition for deserving a philosophy.

Before proceeding, let me make clear that my concern is not based upon some parsimonious or conservative ideal of what constitutes the subject areas of philosophy. Rather, it turns on some serious doubts about whether the development of childhood as a specialization is, as Professor Lipman seems to assume, the most promising or effective way to bring children and childhood into the mainstream of philosophical teaching and inquiry. If it were clear that: (a) the development of a philosophical specialization in childhood involves no significant risks, and (b) there is no more plausible way to remedy the problem, I would be less concerned than I am with the first premise of Professor Lipman's argument. But, as I will now show, there are significant risks in establishing childhood as an area of philosophical specialization and there is, perhaps, a more promising strategy for bringing philosophical attention to childhood.

We run three main risks in establishing childhood as an area of philosophical specialization. First, as with all academic specialties, there is the danger of developing a cadre of "experts" who, to defend their claim to uniqueness and expertise, develop a highly technical, inbred body of discourse and literature. Second, there is the danger of isolation; rather than direct philosophical exchange with those working in philosophy of law, ethics, social philosophy, and metaphysics, specialists in philosophy of childhood might be given their own little piece of philosophical turf and then comfortably ignored by those working in these other areas. And third, it may well be, for reasons that will be made clear in a moment, that philosophers of childhood will focus their attention on too narrow or too compartmentalized a conception of childhood.

To say that a course of action involves risks, however, is not to say that it should not be undertaken. If, for example, there is no more promising way to focus philosophical attention on childhood than by developing a new area of specialization, the aforementioned risks may be worth running. But, I want to suggest, there is an alternative course of action that seems to be more promising and it is an alternative that is supported by some of the things Professor Lipman says in his paper.

Near the beginning, for example, Professor Lipman reminds us of the connections between childhood and adulthood. The difference between the perspectives of a person as child and as adult are perspectives of the same person; and one's later views may often be understood in part as embellishments of or reactions to one's earlier ones. Later Professor Lipman emphasizes, "the possibility that childhood is no more incomplete without a subsequent adulthood than adulthood is without a prior childhood. It is only together that they make a life." And finally, in discussing the relationships between the notions of work, family, and community, he stresses the value of "communities of inquiry in which adults and children participate together as equals."

Underlying these reminders and suggestions, I believe, is a particular perspective—a perspective that presupposes that we are basically temporal or historical beings. As Edward Langerak has put it:

Our self consciousness so orients us to our past and future that, in an important sense, we *are* our history and our projections as well as our present. A premedical student, for example, sees himself or herself as a future physician, not just as a science student. This temporal perception is also true from an external point of view, a point of view that extends to humans that are not yet persons. When we see a very young child, we see something of the adult it will, in the normal course of its development, become, as well as something of the baby it once was.[3]

Moreover, these internal and external points of view are bridged when, for example, in seeing and engaging a child one learns, and incorporates into one's present point of view, something of the child one once was.

Thus I suggest that a renewed emphasis on the temporal or historical nature of a human life will bring children and childhood squarely into the mainstream of philosophical teaching and reflection. And it will do so in a manner that avoids the hazards of academic specialization.

Nothing would be more unfortunate, in this regard, than if the development of a philosophy of childhood were to lead to the subsequent development of philosophies of adolescence, young adulthood, middle-age, old-age and so on, each with its own set of subspecialties and journals. For to atomize or narrowly compartmentalize the course of a human life in this manner is to contribute to its fragmentation which is, in large measure, a source of the intergenerational conflict and sense of meaninglessness that Professor Lipman seeks to overcome.

As Christopher Lasch has pointed out, the unusually strong denial in our culture of aging and death is in part attributable to the ahistorical atomistic outlook of our times. Like Tolstoy's Ivan Ilych, those who share this outlook are unable to avail themselves of the traditional consolations of old-age and death—namely, that in some sense one lives on in one's children or, more broadly, future generations to whose lives the course of one's own life has made a modest, but significant, contribution. This intergenerational link and the meaning it provides in the face of our individual mortality is weakened, and perhaps even severed, by anything that contributes to the atomization or compartmentalization of the course of a human life.

Consider for a moment that as philosophers we participate in a search for truth, meaning, and value that was initiated long before we were born and that will not be completed, if ever, until long after we are dead. There is, then, a sense that those who have preceded us live on in our work just as we may take some consolation that our efforts will make a similar contribution to, and hence live on in, the work of our students and future generations generally. Thus, insofar as our efforts and those of our predecessors are to be fully meaningful, we must try to ensure that future generations are able to appreciate and willing to participate in philosophical inquiry. And this, it seems to me, provides a strong reason for encouraging, reinforcing, and cultivating the child's earliest philosophical questions and reflections.

Similarly, a renewed emphasis on the temporal or historical nature of a human life will provide the motivation for bringing childhood into the mainstream of philosophical reflection. For our understanding of what it is to lead a life and to be an adult will, as Professor Lipman has pointed out, be impoverished to the extent to which it is not informed by and integrated with a similar understanding of what it is to be a child.

In short, then, I agree that philosophers need to pay more attention to children and childhood. But my suggestion is that we focus our attention under the heading of philosophy *and* children; and not the philosophy of childhood.

Notes

1. Onora O'Neill and William Ruddick, eds., *Having Children* (New York: Oxford University Press, 1979), p. 3.
2. Philippe Aries, *Centuries of Childhood* (New York: Vintage, 1962).
3. Edward Langerak, "Abortion: Listening to the Middle," *Hastings Center Report*, 9 (October, 1979), p. 25.

Comments on "Developing Philosophies of Childhood"

Jonathan E. Adler

I have two critical comments on Professor Lipman's paper. The first concerns his use of notions like "rationality" and "rational dialogue," and is basically a request for further analysis. The second point is an argument that Professor Lipman has missed one component of a philosophy of childhood, and thereby underestimated its possible importance for philosophy.

On the first point I can be very brief. Professor Lipman uses terms like "rationality" in such a way as to suggest that its important applications are all-or-nothing, rather than matters of degree. His (implicit) critique of cognitive developmental theories seems then to beg the question because they (e.g. Kohlberg) do not want to argue that the child cannot be introduced at all to rational dialogue or make claims to rights, etc. Rather they believe such abilities must be relativized (**??-lisa) to different ages, and can be analyzed in terms of degree of complexity in their logic corresponding to their developmental unfolding. Professor Lipman, it seems to me, can accept the part of this claim that simply involves the (uncontroversial) claim that certain sets of abilities, especially cognitive ones, are developing and improving with the growth toward adulthood. He can then redirect his critique to show that there is no absolute barrier, as the substantive concept of "stages" demands, to children of most ages engaging in inquiry.

I should note that unless such a degree view of rationality is correct, Professor Lipman's view of the child would be hard to reconcile with most forms of paternalism specific to the children. The diminished authority or liability we ascribe to the child in matters of say criminal guilt, punishment, education and obligation to parents depends upon a corresponding claim about the lack of full development of certain abilities requisite to full authority or liability in these areas. This ultimately leads to a question Professor Lipman does discuss, namely, children's rights, which I cannot pursue here.

My second point is that Professor Lipman devotes his essay to problems more in areas of the *application* of philosophical views or question of childhood than the philosophy of childhood. Are there a set of problems or a method of inquiry that justifies talk of a philosophy of childhood as we speak of the philosophy of mind, and do not speak of the philosophy of abortion, (where we are thinking of philosophy as an area of study and not as in "my philosophy of_____?") I am not sure but I want to put forward one line of reflection that supports, although it does not imply, an affirmative answer.

The best case I can think of is the proverbial child continually asking "why?" until the adult after successive lucid explanations, quits in exasperation. Now the interesting question seems to me to be this: Is it right to quit because the child's demand is out of place (or unjustified by the nature of the requirements of explanation), or rather is it simply one's practical limits—exhaustion and inability to supply the next level of explanation? Reflection on the nature of explanation leads me to think there is much justification behind the position that we can *ascribe* to the child: explanation is a matter of fitting a phenomenon into a theoretical structure, which shows how this phenomenon hangs together with other observations and a set of laws. The child is pushing for an ultimate explanation—how it all hangs together.

Now, I am not saying either that (a) children do typically have this in mind, or (b) that the demand for ever further explanation can or should always be met. Rather the point is that there is a serious philosophical problem being raised and we too easily dismiss it.

If one, in fact, looks at the reasons philosophers have given for rejecting calls for ultimate explanations, they tend to be pragmatic and "common sensical," and not metaphysical or epistemological. I take this opposition to be representative of one expectation one might have in looking at the philosophy of children: children being less socialized into the pragmatic constraints upon adults—etiquette, limited energy, more response to non-cognitive factors, multiple demands upon one's time that does not lend itself to philosophical fancy, etc.—are more open to

going to the metaphysical or fundamental centers of many philosophical concepts and problems.

I believe further that the same pattern as I found for explanation holds for other philosophically central concepts such as cause and justification. The ultimate payoff of the enterprise here adumbrated would be to become progressively more aware of how what we think of as *philosophical* stopping points, are merely pragmatic barriers. They block us from going to the ultimate ends of a philosophical path, partially perhaps because going to such ends leads to a questioning of much common sense wisdom. (Why is it right for the child to be the one to declare that the Emperor has no clothes?)

This search for meaning in a very general way, and the refusal to cease the search short of a global, systematic picture not only is consonant with much of the ideas behind Professor Lipman's program of teaching children philosophy, but is at the heart of a conception of the inspiration for philosophy. Wilfrid Sellars writes,

> The aim of philosophy, abstractly formulated, is to understand how things in the broadest possible sense of the term hang together in the broadest possible sense of the term . . . To achieve success in philosophy would be . . . to "know one's way around" . . .

(Wilfrid Sellars, "Philosophy and the Scientific Image of Man," in *Science, Perception and Reality* (Humanities Press, 1963) p. 1.

Childhood: The Recapitulation Model

Gareth B. Matthews

What are children? How are we to conceive childhood?

Carl Gustav Jung and his followers tell us that we project onto others what we need to come to terms with in ourselves. Thus perhaps our concept of the beastly is more a projection onto nonhuman animals of the irrational, the unbridled, the instinctual, etc. in ourselves than it is an accurate picture of animals as we encounter them. (Cf. Mary Midgley, *Beast and Man*, Cornell, 1978.) Similarly, the way we conceive childhood—our concept of the child—may be more a projection onto children of innocence, abandonment, growth, futurity, naivete, etc. in ourselves than it is a realistic picture of children as we encounter them. (Cf. James Hillman, *Loose Ends*, Zuerich: Spring, 1975, Chapter II, "Abandoning the Child," 5-48.)

But suppose we could turn away from our projections and think clearly about children themselves. What could we then say about childhood?

The most obvious thing to say about childhood is that it is the period human beings go through on their way towards becoming adults. But how does this development proceed? And what is it to be an entity in the process of growing up into an adult human being?

We have, I think, only three simple, salient, general models of human development. The first is Preformation ("the Preform Model"); the second is Specification (or Differentiation) and Generalization ("the Logical Model"); and the third is Recapitulation ("the Recap Model").

In embryological theory the Preform Model finds expression in the idea that the biological structure of the adult is already present in the conceptus; in the simplest version of this model development is just enlargement. In theories of cognitive development the Preform Model gives us cognitive innatism; it often includes the idea that cognitive development is the making manifest of cognitive structures that were latent all along. The Preform Model is as old as Plato's Theory of Reminiscence and as new as Chomsky's notion of innate linguistic structures.

The Logical Model, the idea that development proceeds by specification and by generalization, is as old as Aristotle. We find this model in an embryological theory according to which ontogeny recapitulates definition. Following such an idea Aristotle maintained that the human embryo is first a living thing, though not specifically an animal; later, he supposed, it turns into something that is an animal, but not specifically a human animal; and finally, he thought, it becomes something that is specifically a human animal. In theories of cognitive development the Logical Model may be found in the idea that we sometimes acquire generic concepts first and later add the differentiae that give us more specific concepts. It is also at work in the old idea that we abstract concepts from particulars that fall under them, and we sometimes abstract more general concepts from specific ones (e.g., the concept of a quadrilateral from those of square, rectangle, etc., or the concept of red from those of crimson, maroon, etc.)

The Recap Model, the idea that ontogeny recapitulates phylogeny, is perhaps as old as presocratic philosophy. (Cf. Stephen Jay Gould, *Ontogeny and Phylogeny*, Harvard, 1977, Chapter 11.) Its popularity in embryological theory peaked in the 19th Century, though it is far from dead today. In embryology the Recap Model yields the idea that during gestation the human embryo successively takes on the various animal forms that make up, in turn, the evolutionary ancestry of *homo sapiens*. In theories of cognitive development the Recap Model tells us that the succession of concepts and belief systems to be found in a child's intellectual development mirrors the succession of concepts to be found in the evolution of our culture.

These models give us ways of conceiving specific periods of human development (e.g., gestation or infancy); they also give us ways of conceiving the development of particular functions and skills (e.g., cognition, perception or speech); finally, they give us ways of conceiving children. According to the Preform Model the child is a miniature adult (cf. the images of the Christchild in Renaissance painting). On the Logical Model the child is the mere sketch of a human adult, a highly generalized human being. On the Recap Model the child is a primitive.

It might seem at first that metamorphosis in insects and amphibians offers a fourth model of human development; but it is not clear that this is so. In the incomplete metamorphosis of, say, a cockroach, the larva differs from the adult mainly in being much smaller (the Preform Model) and perhaps in being not as highly differentiated (the Logical Model). In the metamorphosis of a frog from a tadpole we seem to have a recapitulation of the evolution of amphibians from fish (the Recap Model).

Each of these three models suggests interesting hypotheses, at least some of which can be tested empirically. It is instructive to note that, for example, the recent literature on language acquisition in children includes striking appeals to each of the models. Thus, in a paper called "Cognitive Basis of Language Learning in Infants" (*Psychological Review* 79 (1972), 1-13) John Macnamara offers evidence that "infants learn their language by first determining, independent of language, the meaning which a speaker intends to convey to them, and by then working out the relationship between the meaning and the expression they heard." To be able to do this, Macnamara supposes, they must already have, wired into their neurology, a mental language. It is this innate "mentalese" that finally gets expressed, he thinks, in the acquired, natural language.

Appealing to the Preform Model in another way Jerrold D. Katz maintains, on behalf of what he calls "linguistic rationalism," that "all the concepts available to science and everyday explanation are contained in the innate space of possible senses with which humans face the task of language acquisition." ("Semantics and Conceptual Change," *Philosophical Review* 88 (1979), 362) Here the idea of preformation is combined, as it often is, with a contrast between the latent or potential and the manifest or actual.

The Logical Model can be seen at work in an interesting article by T. G. R. Bower called "The Origins of Meaning in Perceptual Development" (*Perception and Its Development*, Anne D. Pick, ed., Hillsdale, NJ: Erlbaum, 1979, 183-97). Bower supports a differentiationist theory of perceptual and cognitive development as an alternative to abstractionist theories characteristic of the Associationist tradition in philosophy and psychology.

As for the Recap Model, an interesting recent article by Elizabeth Bates in Volume 12 of the Minnesota Symposia on Child Psychology (*Children's Language and Communication*, W. Andrew Collins, ed., Hillsdale, NJ: Erlbaum, 1979) makes use of this model; Bates's piece is called "The Emergence of Symbols: Ontogeny and Phylogeny."

In it she suggests that certain "component parts" of language (imitation, tool use, social motivation to share reference to objects) may have evolved separately in phylogeny and that developments in the infant just before language acquisition may recapitulate the evolutionary sequence.

So far I have spoken of these three models as though each excluded the others; but that is clearly not so. The Preform Model combines easily both with the Logical Model and also with the Recap Model. Thus the Specificationist, following the Logical Model, can suppose that the embryo develops by its tissue and organs becoming ever more finely differentiated according to preformed genetic instructions; development then makes manifest, *in logical sequence*, what is already latently present in the genetic code. And the recapitulationist can suppose that the evolution of the species, or the culture, is present in a "memory" that enables the individual to reenact that evolution. The "memory" would then be a preformation.

The models that don't combine well are the Logical Model and the Recap Model. In part the reason is that the Recap Model is a historical model, and, pace Hegel, history is not really logical. But mainly the reason is that Recapitulationism, as I shall understand it, includes the idea that historically distinct conceptual schemes are incommensurable. More on that later.

At first blush it seems quite bizarre to think that a middle-class youngster in America in the 1980's might be trying to use American English—TV slang and all—to express ideas that recapitulate Urdu or ancient Indian thoughts. But the truth sometimes seems bizarre.

Piaget himself doesn't claim that every young child goes through, say, an Urdu phase. What he begins by saying is that children take adults words and use them to express their own concepts and beliefs—concepts and beliefs very different from ours. Thus the very commonality of our language masks, according to him, what separates us.

There is a widely accepted argument in philosophy these days according to which *x* and *y* don't share concepts unless they share belief systems. Since the belief systems of ancient cultures differ significantly from our own, this argument continues, we can't successfully map their concepts onto ours or ours onto theirs.

Conceivably a Recapitulationist might resist this argument and insist that it is possible to map the concepts of early cultures quite successfully onto those of its successors. I suspect that this move would rob the Recap Model, as a model of conceptual development, of most of its interest; but I shall not try to show that here. Instead I shall simply stipulate that I mean to include in Recapitulationism a claim that cultures are conceptually incommensurable.

It's interesting that Piaget talks as though there were indeed a conceptual incommensurability between our adult belief system and that of a child of, say, five years. Thus when he talks about "Artificialism" or what he called "Nominal Realism" (with apparently no oxymoronish intent), he is alluding to whole belief systems in children that, he thinks, differ substantially from our modern, Western, adult belief system, though they recapitulate, he thinks, belief systems in more primitive cultures from which our own has evolved.

We can now see a little more clearly why Recapitulationism, as I am understanding it, does not combine well with the Logical Model. If the only difference between my conceptual repertory and the repertory of my child lies in the fact that the child has failed to differentiate or to generalize as much as I have, then there will be the possibility that I can understand my child completely. The child will have, say, the concept of red, but perhaps not the more specific concept of maroon, and the concept of a song but perhaps not the more general concept of music. So long as we talk about red things, without trying to mark off the maroon ones, and songs, without trying to include them in music generally, there may be no basic misunderstanding. I may even be able to grasp just what conceptual generalizations and what conceptual refinements or specifications the child has not yet made.

By contrast the real Recapitulationist will suppose that my child and I have different belief systems that preclude our having any matching concepts. The child may have something that resembles my concepts of red and song; but the likenesses and unlikenesses will be impossible for either of us to pin down exactly. "When a child constructs a particular notion to correspond to a word of adult language," Piaget writes,

> this notion may be entirely the child's, in the sense that the word was originally as hazy to his intelligence as a certain physical phenomenon might be, and to understand it he had to deform and assimilate it according to a mental structure of his own. We shall find an excellent illustration of this law when studying the child's notion of "life." The notion of "living" has been constructed by the child to correspond to an adult word. But it embraces something quite other than the adult notion of "life" and testifies to an entirely original conception of the world. (Jean Piaget, *The Child's Conception of the World*, London: Routledge & Kegan Paul, 1951, 31.)

When Piaget says that the child's concept may "testify to an entirely original conception of the world," he doesn't, of course, mean that a given child may have a concept no one has ever had before. He means that the notion the child uses "life" or "alive" to express may be the child's and not a concept any normal adult in our culture has. In fact, as we learn in the rest of the book from which this quotation was taken, Piaget supposes that children of, say, ages 5-7 can be expected to share a concept of life (and of thinking, meaning, dreaming, etc.) among themselves, though not with adults in our culture, or even with other children of, say ages 8-10. Not only do children of ages 5-7 share a concept of life among themselves, their concept, according to Piaget, is linked with the ancient belief system Piaget calls "animism" according to which everything that appears to move is alive. When these same children go on to a later concept of life, Piaget supposes, they also move on to a belief system that mirrors a later stage of cultural history.

How does the Recapitulationist story about the concept of life differ from what the Logical Model suggests? It belongs to the Recapitulationist story to suppose that we adults can never fully appreciate, from the "inside," what a child of 5-7, or a child of 8-10, thinks it is to be alive. The problem we face is very much like the problem of understanding an Urdu or an ancient Egyptian. ("If an Urdu could speak English, we would not understand him," at least not from the "inside.").

By contrast the Logical Model suggests that a child could acquire the concept of life by generalizing more and more, or else by making more and more distinctions. A child of age n could be expected to call many fewer, or many more, things "alive" than would the same child at age $n + 2$. And the explanation for shrinkage (or inflation) would be, on the Logical Model, that the child had learned that an additional condition must be satisfied for a thing to be alive, or, in reverse, that some condition that the child had thought necessary is not really so.

One very odd thing about Piaget is that, although he says many things that seem to commit him to the Recap Model, incommensurability and all, some of the accounts he offers of conceptual development follow the Logical Model and not the Recap Model. Here, for example, is Piaget's own summary of the stages through which, as he says, a child develops the concept of life (or, as I should prefer to say, the concept of being alive):

> During the first stage everything is regarded as living which has activity or a function or a use of any sort. During the second stage, life is defined by movement, all movement being regarded as in a certain degree spontaneous. During the third stage, the child distinguishes spontaneous movement from movement imposed by an outside agent and life is identified with the former. Finally, in the fourth stage, life is restricted either to animals or to animals and plants. (pp. 194-5)

The analytic hypotheses for the first three stages seem to be these:

First Stage:
x is alive $= df\ x$ is active or x has a use or x has a function of some sort
("Is the sun alive? "Yes." "Why?" "It gives light." Etc.)

Second Stage:
x is alive $= df\ x$ can move
("Is a bicycle alive?" "Yes." "Why?" "It can go."

Third Stage:
x is alive $= df\ x$ can move spontaneously
("Is a bicycle alive?" "No." "Why?" "Because it is we who make it go.")

What now about the Fourth Stage? The suggestion that "life is restricted either to animals or to animals and plants" might lead one to the (false) extensional hypothesis,

The expression, "is alive," can be correctly applied to any plant or animal, and only to such.

(I say this extensional hypothesis is false because, of course, many plants and animals are dead.)

Could Piaget suppose that the child of age 11 or 12 who has finally arrived at the adult concept of life supposes that to say of something that it is alive *means* that it is a plant or animal? Surely not. Perhaps what Piaget should have said—he doesn't actually say this—is that the child who has acquired the adult concept of life adds to the Third Stage concept the further specification that the entity in question be a plant or animal, thus:

Fourth Stage:
x is alive $= df\ x$ is a plant or x is an animal; and x can move spontaneously

One might certainly question whether this analytical hypothesis captures the adult concept of life, or even whether there is any such thing as *the* adult concept of life to capture. But I shall not pursue these worries here.

Instead, I want to point out that the model of conceptual development illustrated here is Speci-

ficationist, that is Logical. The line of development charted suggests that the child moves from Stage 1 to Stage 4 by learning to distinguish in turn the proper application of each of these expressions:

a) can do something
b) can go (that is, can move)
c) can go by itself
d) is alive

Thus at the First Stage the child might use these four expressions interchangeably for anything that, as *we* should say, (a) properly applies to. At the Second Stage the child would distinguish motion from other activities and functions, but still apply (b), (c) and (d) interchangeably. At the Third Stage the child would distinguish self-caused motion from externally induced motion, yet still use (c) and (d) interchangeably. Finally, at the Fourth Stage the child would distinguish self-movers that are animals (or plants?) from those that are not.

Does it matter whether Piaget, or anyone else, is a Recapitulationist, or a Specification-and-Generalizationist instead?

Theoretically it matters when we come to consider what role learning plays in cognitive development. Since on the Recap Model (as I am understanding it) there is an incommensurability between the concepts a child has at one stage and those the child has at another, development would seem not to rest on learning, but rather on some maturation process that is causal and historical rather than intrinsically logical. (Cf. Jerry A. Fodor, *The Language of Thought*, New York: Crowell, 1975, esp. Chapter II.)

Practically and ethically the significance of the Recap Model would seem to be just as great. Perhaps some parents and some teachers have been encouraged to take a noncondescending attitude towards children because they suppose, influenced by Piaget, that children live in their own conceptual worlds and not in ours. But surely with most parents and teachers the effect has been the reverse; most adults have been encouraged in their natural condescension. After all, they think, the immature and temporarily confining conceptual worlds of children are things the children will naturally outgrow, as a chick naturally breaks out of its egg.

The most disturbing feature of the Recap Model (as I am understanding it) is that, according to that model, we are inevitably blocked from understanding our children and they from understanding us; culturally we and they are ineluctably isolated from each other.

I offer as evidence that Recapitulationism is false the fact that we adults can do philosophy with children. One cannot do philosophy with someone whose concepts and belief system one does not share—at least in substantial part. We can do philosophy with children. Therefore children are not people whose concepts and belief system we do not, in substantial part, share.

In my little book, *Philosophy and the Young Child*, I offer a number of examples of children with whom one can do philosophy. I shall not repeat any of them here. Instead I shall turn to a fresh anecdote that may help us bring together several of the points I have trying to make. This anecdote has to do with life and death, though not, as it happens, with our *concept* of life, or of being alive.

Someone recently told me of taking her four-year-old son to see his grandfather, who was dying. The boy could see that the grandfather was in a bad way. (In fact the grandfather died a week later.) On the way home the boy said to his mother, "When people are sick and ready to die, like Grandpa, do they shoot them?" The mother was shocked. "No," she replied, "the police wouldn't like that." The boy thought a bit more and then said, "Maybe they could just do it with medicine."

It is quite possible that this four-year-old had seen or heard of some seriously ill, or maimed, pet or farm animal that was, as we say, "put out of its misery" by being shot. Why not Grandpa? The analogy is apt. It is part of what moves

doctors to administer lethal doses to dying patients who are in misery; it is part of what moves many of us to agree that euthanasia, in certain circumstances, may be ethically acceptable, even ethically obligatory.

This child was certainly able to use the distinction between killing by shooting and killing by using medicine, or drugs. Depending on Grandpa's circumstances and one's own moral views, one might want, in discussing Grandpa's case, to make several additional distinctions; one might want, for example, to distinguish killing and letting die. (I can't believe there would be any trouble explaining such a distinction to this four-year-old, if he didn't have it already.) And one might want to make other distinctions as well.

There is, in principle, no limit to the intellectual sophistication one could bring to the discussion of euthanasia. One might appeal to Rule Utilitarianism or to Act Utilitarianism, or one might discuss different interpretations of Kant's Categorical Imperative or of Rawl's notion of the Original Position. But I suspect that most actual cases of euthanasia in our culture are conceived and carried out in terms that would be perfectly intelligible to this four-year-old. If I am right, then this case counts as evidence against the Recapitulation thesis that the conceptual world of a four-year-old is incommensurable with our own. To be sure, we may have a good reason not to discuss euthanasia with this child; but "He wouldn't understand" is not, I think, such a reason.

The Recap Model of the child—someone struggling to express primitive beliefs and concepts in a sophisticated language—may take us adults off the hook when a child asks difficult questions or makes unsettling comments. But my own experience with children, and my informal canvass of some of the experiences of others, suggests that the Recap Model gives us false assurances in this matter; we don't deserve to be taken off the hook.

Here then are some tentative conclusions:

1. Children do sometimes make philosophically astute comments and raise philosophically sensitive questions. The four-year-old's question about euthanasia is an example. I offer many other sorts of examples in *Philosophy and the Young Child*.

2. A child could not make comments that we recognize as philosophically astute, or raise questions we recognize as philosophically sensitive, unless the child shared a significant fragment of our own belief system and a large stock of our own concepts. Thus examples of children making comments and raising questions that are logically, epistemologically, metaphysically or ethically astute provides some evidence that the incommensurability thesis that goes with the Recap Model is false.

3. For a number of reasons, some related to the Jungian theses I mentioned at the beginning of this paper, we adults want to let children think that the world is simpler, tidier and less threatening that we really suppose it to be. We may try to justify that desire by telling ourselves that kids are not mature enough to deal with the complexities, the ambiguities or the uncertainties of life.

Now here is a child who wants to discuss euthanasia. A child! How offensive, how inappropriate! He can't possibly understand. Automatically the mother responds with an appeal to authority ("The police wouldn't like that"). It's interesting that the story of moral development Piaget and Kohlberg tell us predicts that a child of this age will be at a premoral stage and will be capable of nothing beyond a "punishment-and-obedience orientation." But in this case it is the mother, not the child, who moves immediately to that orientation. Euthanasia is an issue that the adults of our society can't cope with. It frightens us to think of discussing it with a four-year-old. If this four-year-old comes to deal with ethical issues simply, simplistically, in terms of punishments and rewards it will perhaps be because he has learned that this kind of reasoning is what is expected of him.

4. Perhaps someone, some day, will produce evidence that will make the Recap Model the most appropriate one we have for conceiving childhood. I doubt it; but I may be wrong. What really worries me, though, is that, backed by very little evidence, the Recap Model will go on giving us adults illicit justification for treating children as intellectual and emotional primitives (where, incidentally, our concept of the primitive may be just as fantasy-laden as our concept of childhood).

We need to have a good, well-worked-out theory of childhood—one that will integrate what we know about the intellectual and emotional development of children with a reasoned understanding of the status of children as moral agents. We do not now have such a theory. I am suspicious of the Recap Model as the basis for such a theory because it caters so splendidly to adult bad faith. It helps us to turn aside, too quickly, the unwanted questions and comments of our children with the insufficiently warranted assurance that children can't understand such matters until they are no longer children.

Misunderstanding Children

William Ruddick

Professor Matthews' paper should reassure those who worry about the philosophy of childhood becoming a narrow, incestuous subspecialty. And yet, if our task is to conceive of children as we "encounter" them without Jungian projections of adult qualities, I question embryological models for child development or childhood in general. Any such model—not just the Recapitulation Model—is likely to distort our concept of *childhood*, as well as adult-child relationships. Fetal development in relatively stable environments is no model for the drama of a child's life, necessarily dependent as it is on adult agents and choices. In searching for models and conceptions of childhood, we might do better to look beyond the sciences to politics and other adult occupations.

Before discussing these matters, I want to take up the issue of conceptual incommensurability. The engaging conversations reported in *Philosophy and the Young Child* would seem to falsify any Incommensurability Thesis, in the extreme "two-worlds" version found in Piaget and Bettleheim. But Professor Matthews' own reflections suggest a more modest, defensible "two-regions" version. He repeatedly notes the child's "innocence" which "sophisticated" adults must try to recapture if misunderstandings are to be minimized. Rather than a contrast between speakers of Urdu and modern American, the child-adult encounter better fits that between stereotypical Far Westerner and longtime resident of Boston returning to Colorado. Differences of concern and experience will be disguised by the language they share, and mutual misunderstandings will go unrecognized.

A more precise analogy for the contrast between the child-innocent and adult-sophisticate is that between Newtonian and Einsteinian physicists. Earlier physicists conceived of length as a *dyadic* relation between a body's endpoints, but Einstein—to accommodate the novel aspects of light velocity—reconceived length as a *triadic* relation between a body's end-points and the coordinate frame chosen for determining its velocity. The misunderstandings among physicists in the early part of the century are basis (and best case) for Thomas Kuhn's account of non-rational transitions in science from one conceptual scheme to an incommensurable successor.

But where might analogous misunderstandings be found among children with simpler notions and adults with more complex notions expressed in similar terms? A likely source might be matters of morality and emotion. Whether there are *stages* of moral development, surely a child's moral concepts change with a widening circle of associates, responsibilities, and emotional responses. For example, at one time "being good" might require nothing more of a brother than restraining homicidal impulses toward his sister—in Plato's psychology, a task for the child's "higher self" with regard to his lower self. (The good child exercises self-control.) But for an older, socially abler child, *being good* is a triadic relation between those controlling and controlled selves *and* one or more other people. (The good child acts with regard for others.)

Hence a good brother would be expected to protect his sister from other sources of harm; restraining himself would not be enough.

Adults, especially parents, are eager for children to acquire the wider concept of *goodness* in order to share or reduce their own responsibilities. Much moral censure and misunderstanding may arise thereby from premature application of the more complex notion of *goodness* to children still struggling to live up to standards of conduct imposed by the dyadic concept of *self-control.*

Similar points can be made about notions of *fear, love, shame,* and *pride* as a child's diversity of relationships and experiences expands. These notions are bound to be more complex for adults who have "outlived" any young child. Hence the sophistication produced by living longer, more varied lives will make it hard to talk about emotional matters with a relatively innocent, inexperienced child. Witness the case of the dying grandfather. Shooting a sick, aged man—even one ready to die—is bound to be a simpler matter for a grandson of four years than for his daughter of thirty-five years, in ways neither may understand. The mother's initial shock and police reference may well express a fear and rejection of violence—reactions well beyond a child who knows only water-pistols and balletic TV-shootouts. Nor do I think animal analogies go to the heart of their misunderstanding or of the moral issues of euthanasia. Putting an animal, even a pet, out of its misery can hardly illuminate decisions about the killing of an aged parent. Little children and physicians may see an analogy, but only by ignoring psychological and conceptual complexities which should, I think, be central to adult decision about euthanasia. Bullet or injection may be a good death for an animal in irreversible pain, or for hapless humans whose condition has been reduced to animal existence by accident or disease. But for an aged man "ready to die" but not "in misery, "we need to answer questions couched in more "sophisticated" concepts: Would death by injection be an appropriate or "good" end to the particular life

he had led? Given that life, what if anything would make it tolerable?

To understand and answer these questions a child would have to have more than the biological concept of *being alive* sketched by Matthews. What is needed is the more complex *biographical* notion of leading a life (alluded to by Martin Benjamin). But how can a child whose life in this sense has barely begun by age four have this concept? Will talk of animals, even highly anthropomorphized (like *The Bear Who Wasn't*) convey the notion of a life, or the complex emotions of fear tinged with regret that may accompany thoughts of that life ending? What bearing does an animal in pain have on a man's attitude to dying with physical pain complicated by fears about an after-life, about his survivors' suffering, about lost opportunities for blessings bestowed or relationships repaired or projects completed?

I see no way for children to acquire such emotional, psychological and historical sophistication without the lived experience of the human feelings and relationships that give such notions their content. As parents and teachers, we may guide and accelerate such conceptual development, but we cannot expect our child-Newtonians to become Einsteinian without experience of the high-velocities (and responsibilities) of adult life.

In short, the inescapable difference between child- and adult-experiences explains in part the contrast between innocence and sophistication and the related kind of conceptual incommensurability we must allow for.

In defending an incommensurability thesis, I am not advocating the Recapitulation Model Matthews rejects. Indeed, I would reject all three models, for some of his own reasons. Any embryological model lends itself to distortions of child-adult relationships and concepts. A fetus is a near-ideal object for scientific study, thanks to the placenta and other physiological means for dampening and transmuting variations in the mother's world. In this regulated, quasi-laboratory setting, it can develop relatively free of maternal choices. But with birth, its "matrix" becomes an active mother, joined by other actors on the historical stage the child suddenly enters. It becomes far more dependent on both accident and adult choices, and its development thereby becomes far more variable, unpredictable, and uncontrollable. Thus, models of fetal development are inappropriate models for child development, just because mothers are no longer matrices and children are no longer semi-autonomous parasites. At birth, dependencies and responsibilities radically alter in ways that invite political, not biological illumination.

From birth on we "encounter" children primarily as noisily demanding food, comfort, dressing and, before long, warnings, encouragement, and reassurances about the daytime and nighttime worlds they confront with ignorance, uncertainty, false beliefs, and fears. As adults, we respond with varying degrees of sympathy and moral commitment to these needy beings, our own and other people's children. We may be guided to some extent by our sense of long-range capacity for development: responsibilities for children are made bearable, even enjoyable by our confidence that they will alter and diminish as children grow. The prospect of such changes provides the stamina, rationale, and some of the rewards of parenting and teaching; hence, the special virtues needed to care for children whose development is arrested by congenital defects, accidents, or disease. But the basic adult experience is that of a child's need and dependence on adult responses, not of a child's development into a self-dependent adult. And, if we base our definitions on basic human experiences—not on derivative cultural practices and ideals—we should define childhood in terms of the adults on whom children depend, not on the adults children may become. In short, childhood is a *relative*, not a *teleological* notion.

Moreover, there is nothing necessary about childhood as a developmental stage. We can easily imagine two fantastic, but coherent worlds in which childhood is not followed by adulthood. In one world, childhood is the only stage of life for all but the special few who, by natural or supernatural means, acquire the concern and capacity to care for the vast majority. (Political totalitarians like Plato think that ours is just such a world, or should be. So, too those theologians who take literally the notion of our all being "children of God.") By contrast, we can also imagine a world in which childhood is a rare, rather than the near-universal, normal condition. In this second world, people come into existence with a full range of adult capacities (perhaps as a result of cloning and very rapid, laboratory-accelerated growth and development). Hence there would be no parents or families of the familiar sort; the only childhood would be our "second childhood;" the only childhood homes, our nursing homes for the aged. Given the usual causes of premature death (as well as murderous competition from birth for adult jobs and power), very few people might live to reach childhood, and their care might be solely collective and impersonal.

Whatever the radical social differences from our world, childhood would still be childhood in virtue of dependence on the adults, however few (in the first world) or many (in the second).

If we combine these reflections with Erikson's account of life-cycle virtues and legal definitions of maturity, we see that *child* and *adult* are *correlative* notions, each defined in terms of the other. For Erikson, the distinctive virtue of adults is "generativity"—the capacity for caring for, or acting on behalf of the next generation. Likewise, the law sets the age of adulthood in terms of "generative" work and obligations, traditionally the age for defending hearth and home for males and the younger age for bearing and rearing children for females. Hence, we might define adulthood as the period during which a person is capable of caring for dependent children, those beings defined by their need for such care.

Defined as correlatives, the notions of *child* and *adult* resemble those of *patient* and *doctor*—a happy result since until recently the doctor-patient relationship was taken to be very like the father-child relationship, with similar virtues and obligations of trust, fidelity, and the like.

As sociologists have noted, adults and doctors tend to control the definition of childhood and patienthood: biological incapacities are only the raw materials of the "social construction" of these conditions. If so, childhood is even further removed from the fetal development from which cognitive psychologists and Professor Matthews have drawn their embryological models.

If we resist the appeal of these scientific models, where are we to turn? Two sources come to mind, occupational and political. Childhood has long been conceived by way of analogy between parenthood and other adult occupations: sculpting, guarding, animal training, teaching, composing, gardening, investing. The implicit model in each occupation would repay examination, but not here. The other related source would be politics. A child's conflicting desires are, in some respects, like conflicting interest groups; the tasks of parents and teachers like that of legislators devising morally and psychologically acceptable ways of resolving conflicts and establishing flexible order. To reverse Plato's perspective, we might think of the child as a polity writ small, and thus supplement the political theories that linked monarchs with fathers. (See Locke's criticism of Filmer's *Patriarchia* in his *First Treatise of Civil Government*, reprinted with commentary by Edmund Leites in *Having Children*: Philosophical and Legal Reflections on Parenthood, edited by Onora O'Neill and William Ruddick. New York: Oxford University Press 1979.)

Models from politics and other adult occupations will not have the clarity or cachet of models from embryology or other biological sciences. Nor will they appeal to students of child development who have absorbed embryological models in most of their psychology and education courses. To get their attention, philosophers of childhood may have to treat those models more seriously than they deserve. But even with such prejudiced audiences, philosophers should be able to develop alternatives to "developmentalism" and its standard models.

Embryological models do make strong appeal to our desires, as parents and teachers, to watch our children develop quickly in benign environments we are responsible for maintaining. But we should resist this "projection" in favor of conceptions closer to the interactions and variations of our lives with children. Whatever the exact model, children are in some sense adult "work" and like all work, our relationships reflect and influence political conditions and conceptions.

In pursuing these matters further, we are all in Professor Matthews' debt for his original conversations with children and his provocative reflections on childhood.

Notes

* Gareth B. Matthews, *Philosophy and the Young Child* (Cambridge, Mass: Harvard Univ. Press, 1980).

Chapter Four
Cultivating Cognitive Proficiency

Chapter Four

The Cultivation of Cognitive Proficiency

At the heart of the movement to restructure education is the move to "educate for thinking." The latter phrase has become something of a "black box" or Rorschach ink blot, in that it means different things to different people, and everything to everyone. But, say the advocates of education for thinking, this cannot be allowed to happen to it: inflating its significance beyond all boundaries will simply lead to its ultimate collapse into emptiness. Instead, they say, education for thinking should be situated firmly in educational practice. It should also be related to specific key concepts in education for thinking—terms like *meaning, judgment, reflection, culture, literacy, reading, writing* and *craft*.

Accordingly, this section takes up the cultivation of cognition in the schools as it bears upon these particular concepts and connects them with one another. The scholarly approach that each author takes to one or another of these concepts sets the stage for the development of a curriculum in elementary school philosophy that would provide children with the unified outlook that emerges from consideration of this series of essays, although couched in terms as familiar to them as their everyday speech.

Among the most forthright pioneers in the reform of education that led to elementary school philosophy was Lady Victoria Welby. She conceived of education as inquiry, and saw the need for children's inclusion in the community of philosophical inquirers. Lady Welby recognized the importance of classroom dialogue, of the quest for meaning, of the need for teaching reasoning, of the significance of getting children to be aware of contextual differences, and of the value of enabling children to translate meanings from one discipline to another, or from one symbolic scheme to another,

Another major pioneer, writing a half-century before Lady Welby, was Lev Tolstoy. In this essay, he recounts how readily illiterate peasant children could be enlisted in the writing of delightful stories. It should be noted, however, that Tolstoy begins the session by confronting the children with a challenging text in the form of a proverb, and he promptly stimulates them to engage in a lively discussion about the proverb. Given these two preliminary moves, very reminiscent of the pedagogical procedure employed in Philosophy for Children, Tolstoy proceeds to show how readily children can think narratively.

Herbert Schneider seeks to show that an education must be absorbed and appropriated by students until it permeates them thoroughly. Whatever one experiences as significant should become part of that person, and reflection is a means of determining that significance. Schneider helps us see why there can be no such thing as an education that is not a reflective education.

Many of the remaining essays in this section deal with critical reflection and literacy. As Judith Langer observes, the narrow definition of literacy as the ability to read and write intersects with the broader definition as the ability to think and reason within a given society. She contends that "it is the culturally useful way of thinking, not the act of reading or writing, that is most important in the development of literacy."

Valerie Polakow combines the contemporary stress on narrative with Langer's underscoring of the role of reflection in literacy. Stories communicate experience and directly convey the drama of life. Hence they are indispensable to genuine education, for they transform the world into meanings; and make whole again our fragmented engagements with that world.

A vehement protest against conjoining thinking with reading and writing is registered by Jane Roland Martin, for she fears that thinking will be forgotten when it becomes part and parcel of education in the basics. She admits that reading and writing constitute at best an education in language-based thinking. But she maintains that "the development of the thinking of each person" is "too important a goal of education to be sacrificed unnecessarily on the altar of literacy." On the other hand, she protests equally against equating thinking with philosophy, and allowing philosophy to monopolize this aspect of the curriculum.

The Auden essay touches on many topics that have to do with writing, while at the same time it provides us with an author's point of view regarding the subject. Auden advocates teachers spending increasing time in educating students into the use of the language. At present, no one gets such an education, he contends. Peasants speak more vividly, are better able to say what they want to say, than the average university graduate. The peasants do well with the small number of words they employ. When you try to use a large vocabulary, you are like an overambitious juggler who ends by dropping everything. Conversation is a social practice; but so is reading, for when we read a book, Auden says, it is as if we were with a person. "A book is not only the meaning of the words inside it; it is the person who means them. . . ."

Collins, Brown and Newman propose that literacy skills be taught in the way apprentices learn a craft. The master of the studio or atelier models for the apprentices, coaches them when they are preparing to perform or create, and gradually removes the props that he or she has provided for them. These functions are subsequently broken down into still more specialized functions that the learners are expected to engage in. In addition to modelling and coaching, these are identified as scaffolding, articulation and reflection. Scaffolding is the propping up of the student by the teacher and the curriculum; articulation involves getting the student to identify the elements of their work process; and reflection enables them to compare these elements with those of other performers or creators. Finally, exploration is advocated, by which the authors mean getting students to find problems for themselves and to think through the solutions for themselves.

Readers who have already encountered the essay by Gareth B. Matthews in Chapter 3 of this anthology will recall the grounds Matthews cites for rejecting the views of Piaget with respect to the intellectual education of the child in the early elementary grades. Here Ann Gazzard continues the critique of Piaget, explaining why the Philosophy for Children approach makes more sense pedagogically. Citing the work of J. H. Flavell and Susan Carey, she seeks to show that most of the cognitive differences between 3 year olds and adults has to do with domain-specific knowledge, derived from particular disciplines. It is in these domains that children are novices and adults may be experts. But philosophy for children does not address students in terms of their domain-specific knowledge, such as it is; but in terms rather of their understanding of their ordinary experience.

We began this section with a selection from Lady Welby, in part of which she addressed the need for translation—i.e., for helping children learn how to translate their knowledge from discipline to discipline and from context to context, for without such *exchange* possibilities, even the greatest wealth of knowledge can stagnate. We close with a plea for translation from Tony W. Johnson in which he argues that "the transformative teacher" is one who "translates the forms or structures of a discipline in such a way that students can understand them and more beyond them." Johnson evidently has in mind, as a model, the manner in which the Philosophy for Children curriculum seeks to restate the concepts and procedures of the discipline of philosophy into terms accessible to children, as well as into moves that children can perform. If education is ever to become fully reflective, such translation is the sort of preparation that is indispensable.

Educating for Meaning

Lady Victoria Welby

Charles Peirce, in reviewing Lady Welby's What is Meaning? *in* The Nation, *recognized her originality and the important implications of her work for philosophy and for education:*

> The greatest service the book can render is its bringing home the question which forms its title, a very fundamental question of logic, which has commonly received superficial replies . . . To direct attention to the subject as one requiring study, both on its theoretical and practical side, is the essential purpose of the work. In doing this, the authoress has made a contribution towards the answer to the question, in pointing out three orders of signification.

Peirce added that the problem of meaning was to be one of the most important for future philosophy and demanded a systematic study of signs. He was interested in Lady Welby's three orders of signification, since they seemed to him to correspond to his own ideas of "firstness, secondness, and thirdness." Moreover, he applauded her urging that priority be given to logic—the ethics of language, and that logic should constitute the "basis or core of any good education."

From 1885 until her death in 1912, Lady Welby's philosophical interests were completely centered on problems of language and meaning. One must begin, she argued, with an analysis of meaning, which in itself is multi-dimensional. The three main levels of meaning are for her, sense, meaning and significance (although these might be better understood as observation, meaning and value.) In a letter dated March 14, 1909, Peirce commented:

> I had not realized . . . how fundamental your trichotomy of Sense, Meaning and Significance really is. It is not to be expected that concepts of such importance should get perfectly defined for a long time . . . I now find that my division (of the three kinds of Interpretant) nearly coincides with yours, as it ought to do exactly, if both are correct.

Of course, there are, according to Lady Welby, other dimensions to language: "We have purport, import, bearing, reference, indication, application, denotation and connotation, the weight, the drift, the tenor, the range, the tendency of a given statement." And, she writes, if we are to make sense of the world we live in and communicate that sense to others, it becomes essential that we sensitize ourselves to all of the dimensions of meaning that different situations and contexts demand.

Lady Welby specifically intended her work to have implications for education. She recognized that children have strong metaphysical tendencies with their endless "whys," their craving to make sense of the world and their ability to assimilate and freely use abstract terms. She thought children naturally tend to be active, to inquire and to hunt for reasons. In light of this, education should be designed in such a way as to make the most of these tendencies. Her suggestions to educators might be summarized as follows:

1. *One should begin with children's discourse in teaching, rather than with formal disciplines.*

2. *One should encourage children to speak to each other and to adults.*

What we mean when we talk about meaning

We ask the meaning of an expression when what we want is a clearer or more familiar expression having the same meaning.

I said to my small son, "Eighty-two. You know what I mean?" Then I said to my small daughter, "Ottantadue. You know what I mean?" She said, "Yes. Eighty-two." I said, "See, Margaret understands Italian better than Douglas understands English."

Our ways of talking of meaning are thus misleading. To understand the expression is, one would say, to know the meaning: and to know the meaning is, one would say, to be able to give the meaning. Yet Douglas could rightly claim to *understand* the expression "eighty-two," despite answering "No" to "You know what I mean?" He answered "No" because he was unable to *give* the meaning; and he was unable to give the meaning because what we call giving the meaning consists really in the asymmetrical operation of producing an equivalent expression that is clearer. Margaret was ready with a clearer equivalent of "ottantadue", but Douglas was at a loss for a *still* clearer equivalent of "eighty-two." In another context he might have ventured, "Yes, you mean the temperature is eight-two."

—W.N. Quine, in "Mind and Verbal Dispositions" (Samuel Guttenplan, ed., *Mind and Language*).

3. *Teachers should aim at developing children's powers to draw distinctions, to recognize formal and informal fallacies in everyday conversation and to avoid inconsistencies.*

4. *Teachers should aim to help children recognize the significance of context, and the crucial role that it plays in determining the words that we use.*

5. *Teachers and parents should capitalize on the child's natural tendencies to ask why and to seek for reasons.*

6. *Teachers should help children master the method of inquiry. Since it has never consciously been cultivated in early childhood on a large scale, we don't know of what children are capable.*

7. *Teachers should organize the curriculum around children's tendencies for seeking significance.*

8. *Teachers should help children distinguish the important from the trivial within the various disciplines.*

9. *Educators should develop a sequential curriculum that begins in early childhood and encourages children to move from the "that" and the "what," to the "how" and the "why."*

10. *Children should be given the opportunity to experience the interpenetration of thinking and doing in their everyday classroom.*

11. *Children should be given the tools to draw connections between the various disciplines that they study—that is—be given a Principle of Translation. Lady Welby defines this principle as that by which the common denominator of all subjects learnt, however diverse, may be discovered, so that within varying limits, each may illustrate the other.*

12. *Since children are naturally of a metaphysical inclination, they should be exposed to the ideas of philosophy from early childhood.*

Lady Welby thought that if educated appropriately, children could contribute significantly to our understanding of the world. "In time we will begin to see that the child may not merely contribute to a truer psychology, but also to a more significant philosophy than any we dream of."

Let us . . . consider how the teacher of the future, himself thus trained, can accomplish this transfiguration of study. At present the child's natural interest in and control over language is by direct and indirect means systematically blunted, especially by the premature teaching of formal grammar; while his typical instinct, that of asking for the reason of things, of putting the question Why, is not sufficiently recognized as the keynote of true education as of true mental growth.

The necessity for social consensus (which in the really most important directions we are impotent to secure) is pressed to the uttermost as a reason for the merely customary. We waste the often valuable innovations or corrections of current fashions of speech unconsciously made by children. These are merely received and recorded in shouts of laughter, so that the children are careful never to repeat them. But in time we shall begin to see that the child may not merely contribute to a truer psychology, but also to a more significant philosophy than any we yet dream of. Only first we must put into his hands the power to understand the value of what we call "meaning"; we must "educate" in the fullest sense of the word; we must aim at bringing out and thus expressing treasures of human nature now hidden in helpless silence or ineffectual talk, or in the shy reserve intensified by dread of the snubbing process.[1]

The result of pressing home all forms of knowledge in an appeal to sense, meaning, and significance, is an enormous development of the child's power of appreciating and using distinction, and of avoiding confusion and fallacy. The child is also helped by the use of a Principle of Translation by which the "common denominator" of all the subjects learnt, however diverse, may be discovered, so that within varying limits each may illustrate the other. The appeal to the child's expression-power will always make for that pictorial road to the abstract which is natural to the young mind. It must be remembered that the child's mind begins with the generic (*e.g.* all men are at first "Daddy"), which might, perhaps, be called the mother of the abstract.

The instinct which prompts the typical child to ask Why at every turn would thus for the first time be fully worked upon. We should at last touch his natural tendency to seek a "because" for everything—to link together all parts of his growing experience. As all fun and chaff, no less than all wit and humor, depend on turns either of sense or meaning or significance; as the ludicrous depends on the incongruous, and our sense of the incongruous, this method of education would lend itself, as no other could attempt to do, to the child's craving to be interested, excited, even amused in learning. Then we should see in "brain-work" an unbroken continuity from that marvellous, untiring, intelligent "nerve-work" which gradually perfects the organic activities. And this natural brain-work entirely takes the sting out of monotony, even out of drudgery. As we have seen, the young child faces both with undaunted perseverance in its natural process of acquiring and extending both vocabulary and sentence-form. . . .

When, instead of giving him ready-made answers or none, we have learnt to take up nature's plan, and thus shown every child at school how to discover these Whys of hard work and good conduct for which from the first he has normally thirsted; when we have made it a duty on his part (instead of a distracting luxury) to hunt for reasons, to look through the that and the what to the how and the why,—we may reap an unexpected practical harvest. For to work and to ask; to do and to inquire; to see why he should learn, and how he shall succeed, and what success ought to signify to him,—these very things are already his deepest instincts. They only need translating. And when men have learnt to translate them into conscious and voluntary action, then "reform," industrial or other, will assume a different aspect in their eyes; it will appeal to all in a different way from any now possible. We shall have learnt to respond to the "next higher" in social development exactly as the baby responds to the call to stand, walk, talk, ask—only in a higher and yet more entrancing form.

The truth is, the infant unconsciously translates all its labor, its pains and its troubles, into "more abundant" Life. So we have everywhere to teach the child to translate, giving him the additional incentive of knowing that he is using a royal power, one which exalts him in all eyes, his own included.

* * *

[We should] be sure that the pupil's powers of interpretation will be trained in a fresh and living sense. This interpretative power (leading to valid inference) is still so feeble that we resent the least obscurity, even where such obscurity is the inevitably condition of expressing facts of the highest importance from a new point of view. Where this is really the case (and is not the device of the sham thinker for evading the inconvenient critic under a shower of fine words) we might as reasonably complain of the shadow which gives to physical light its value. The child will thus learn to unravel and to reconstruct sentences and paragraphs, and to detect changes of sense which alter value or "venue." He will be shown the loss of clearness, the confusion, the poverty of idea caused by the common neglect of valuable distinctions such as that between the imaginative and the fanciful . . . . The pupil will then be given lessons in "seeing through" the most ingeniously and convincingly plausible statements: in detecting, not merely formal fallacy, but also intentional or unconscious inconsistency, which (as we are) easily escapes notice.

The intentional production of illusion has never yet been systematically used in education or employed by a philosophical writer to put his readers on their gaurd against errors which are not merely logical. It is a pity that the highest developments of the power to produce at will, and therefore to detect and expose fallacious inferences, have hitherto been called mere "conjuring," and devoted only to money-making by amusing trickery, if not to less defensible objects.

If the power wielded by the conjurer, which is largely the result of special training, were only translated into an altogether higher form, we might look forward to striking results in education. We should obtain most valuable studies in ambiguity of thought as well as of word, both voluntary and unrecognized; and students would learn the extent to which the plausible dominates us. They would also realize how easily even the ablest writers occasionally miss significant points by fixing attention on issues really less centrally important than others which, through the present lack of early signific training, may even seem trivial. . . .

The child must therefore learn to gauge context by context, and to hunt with unerring scent for some else unnoticed peculiarity of apparently chance expression or form of expression which gives a clue to the writer's (or speaker's) real sense, and therefore to the true order of sentences. In this work he must even in the interests of detection ignore grammar. He must learn to become a sense-detective, detecting his own as well as others' more subtle blunders, more hidden flaws in that significance which it is the object of articulate expression to convey. The accomplished Significian is at least a Sherlock Holmes, and more, a Helmholtz.

When the pupil has been thus trained he can be trusted to economize Sense and to clear himself. For throughout his studies he must be constantly reminded that were it once understood that it was possible to learn to be more expressive, much of his labor would be needless.

But his teachers and examiners must first set him the example. When an average child informs his examiner in history that Wat Tyler led the pheasants' revolt and pillaged the Crystal Palace: that the Black Prince extinguished himself at Crecy, and that Common Pleas should not be carried about on the king's person: when he answers to such a question as "What is a watershed?"—"A shed for keeping water in"; or to the question "Where were the kings of England crowned?"—"On their heads," this simply betrays the failure of his teacher's methods, or the absurdity of this kind of question at a given stage. The answers make, of course, delightful nonsense; but while enjoying the joke, we ought to realize with shame the terrible witness to educational stupidity (and that not the child's) represented by these specimens.[1]

A curious witness to the strength of our natural interest in questions of expression and therefore of sense, meaning, and significance, may be found in the general delight, sometimes even too absorbing, and common to all classes, in guessing riddles, solving puzzles, putting letters together to form sentences, re-setting anagrams, and so on. So with games like "cross questions and crooked answers," "Russian scandal," "buried cities," verse-making and story-telling (each one contributing line or incident without knowing what the other ones are), besides charades and dumb crambo. And this takes the form even of more serious mathematical problems, cheerfully undertaken by the ordinary family party as an evening's amusement!

It must, of course, be remembered that much of the work here suggested describes at least in part or in spirit what is already the aim of every progressive teacher. The point is that such work is only incidental; that it has never been gathered up under a definite general term; that it is recognized in no public school or university curriculum, and depends wholly on the chance of individual tendencies, where these are free to act. Whereas, in the mode of teaching which the term Signifies properly connotes, the child must everywhere and always be so imbued with the sense that the one thing first needful is Sense, and with the idea that, having this, all things may be added unto him, that he will instinctively and habitually start from it and look for it in every step of his way; knowing that it is this which he has to grasp—to mark, learn, and digest—in every part of every subject; so that in after life he "cannot help"—cannot avoid—becoming a private, at least, in the great army of generators of a transfigured Expression and a new transvaluation.[2] He

will, at last, unconsciously accept or reject, as he already does in letter-forming and spelling, in reading and in ciphering.

One advantage of the signific method is that the danger of specialism is avoided, while its advantages are developed. The bent (sometimes more than one) of each child and young man having been discovered, he would be permitted as a privilege to pursue his favorite aim. And when the examiner's turn came, the master and tutor would say: Examine Smith major in that; all the rest of his course is elementary. Only it would be understood that, of course, all the boys alike had their penetrative and interpenetrative powers cultivated to the utmost; so that they would, according to their several abilities, have seized the gist, the purport, the application, the true value even of those subjects which they had not specially chosen as their own. Thus there would be fewer specialists in the bad sense—men whose minds are warped, who can harp only on one string, and who, therefore, cannot play in the best way even on that.

But there would be more specialists in the good sense: men who are real masters of one subject—of two or three, if they are great enough—and the intelligent discerners of significance in all others. Thus they can *place* their own subject, and compare it with others; they can enrich it by realizing alike its relations and its uniqueness. When a man boasted that he read nothing but the Bible, "then you haven't read that," was the deserved retort. We may paraphrase one famous dictum, and preface every lesson with the pregnant maxim that there is nothing gained in life which has not been first found in sense; and continue with another dictum, that where all experience begins in sense (in one sense) it assuredly all ends in sense (in the other sense): that whereas in one sense we may leave "sense" behind, as we acquire meaning and advance into the domain of pure intellect and abstract reasoning, we only need it more and more in the other sense which issues in Significance.

* * *

When the study of Significance becomes a recognized and vital element of education, as the very nexus of all experience and expression, it may naturally become the subject of a series of lectures. And these would include a course on the principles and practical working of imagery-popular, poetical, philosophical, and scientific. (This, of course, might be varied to suit audiences of the young or the uneducated, or of any degree of culture.) The lecturer on Popular Imagery would have a number of simple objects and some elementary apparatus by which he would illustrate the original, generally the material, conditions of figurative usage. For instance he would show a given object reduced or magnified or distorted in various ways by the action of lenses through which it was seen. He would show it also through media of varying degrees of transparency and manifold tints. He would "throw light" upon it and then obscure it. He would show that while, say, its form and its color and size were distinct, they could not be separated except in certain cases and senses, and he would show what these were, and how we should gain in clearness by using the idea of separateness to mean different classes of fact.

Again, standing on a given spot, he would grasp various objects, and then make efforts to reach what was nearly or quite "beyond his grasp." Then he would show that he could still smell the rose beyond his reach, and remind us that he could hear what was much too far away to touch or smell; and beyond that could see what "transcended" the utmost powers of hand, foot, nose, or ear to reach. Lastly, he would remind us of the further world (strictly "transcending" that of the unaided senses) which microscope telescope, spectrascope, revealed, or in which the X-rays acted. And once more, he would suggest that as we already used these very expressions, and were tempted to refuse to have anything to do with what we could not "grasp," that we had better learn when young to use such terms in a truer and more orderly, therefore simpler and clearer, fashion.

Then he would have a box, a doll, a nut, etc., to illustrate the metaphorical use of inner and outer, and a model of a house with its foundations, also a model of a globe set fast on a fixed stand (showing that the stand again required a table, the table a floor, the floor a "ground," and so on, but "under" all—what? he would ask).

Then, by means of a rotating globe (one of the ordinary ones used in elementary science lectures), he would show the difference made in our ideas of the over and under, the above and below, the higher and lower, by the discovery of the antipodes. So he would explain that it is no longer true in the ancient or absolute sense that the "heaven" is higher than the "earth," or above us; while it remains true in a practical sense. Then he would have scales of "higher" and "lower" temperature, and would show that what we call the "higher" gifts of intelligence were actually associated with the "highest" point in our physical frame.

Then the Lecturer would have a veil, to be drawn or undrawn between Looker or Observer and Object,—this again (like the box) making an inner and outer, and "sides" and "aspects." He would show how, in fact, whether you will or no, you imagine yourself an Outsider trying to look into the recesses of a nucleus, the innermost point of which you imagine as something smaller than yourself, immensely within your own scale of magnitude; or else you imagine yourself an Insider, trying to look out to the expanding reaches of the sky as to something immensely beyond your own scale of magnitude, and in that sense Outside. Thus his audience would find out that you cannot say Insider, or out-to; you look "into" even the farthest, the "outermost" stretches of space.

Then he would translate the mathematical abstraction of a "line" into a wire, or a rope, or a plank to picture a "path," etc., and to represent that which we all unconsciously represent when we say we are taking this or that line. Also he would translate it into a scratch or mark, and then ask, What can we do with that only,—never going beyond it on the "one hand or the other"? Then he would show the practical equivalent of a plane surface, and thirdly of a cube; and he would give representative passages of commonplace writing from letters, newspapers, simple books, showing that we do in fact use these three main ways of putting things: in other words, that much of our mental picturing has a relation to the "three dimensions" of which perhaps we have not even heard. Then he would show a "dead-end,"—a *cul-de-sac* beyond which to go would be-non-sense. But, reminding us of the "veil" or "curtain," he would show how a subject may be "closed" and "reopened"; and then he would pictorially show a "way"—whether roadway or waterway—proving that an object using any means of advance or progress must needs leave more and more of such means' behind it.

Then he would take a straight line and show that the farther it went (was produced) the farther it was from its starting-point. He would show that this idea did not apply to a curve, and was reversed in a circle. Thus he would show that, while a straight line may always form part of a great curve—one too great to be detected,—a curve can never form part of a straight line.

Then he would revert to the globe, and show, by that analogy, that when we start from a point upon it we come back to where we started,—but from the opposite direction. Pointing to the rotating and moving sphere representing our earth in movement, he would show that meanwhile we have really moved on, first round our sun, then with that sun in a further unknown direction. He would thus show the difference between thinking on one line, thinking on many lines on a flat surface, and thinking in cube; also how thinking in the round and in motion like our earth, differs from thinking on the flat and the fixed, like a fabulous and fictitious and impossible world. He would show us what we lost both by using current imagery in false senses, and by not learning to use the priceless figurates which science is putting into our hands.

Then he would show us a lump of stuff which could not move of itself, and if moved would stop of itself without resistance or friction, and in that image represent to us the "mind" or the "soul." Again, he would show us a complex of movements—a passage of melody, the evolution of birds on the wing, the movements of water, our own coordinated muscular actions and various combinations of wave-motion observed or inferred in air and "ether," and he would show us how different the ideas called up by the two classes of imagery must needs be, and therefore how different our practical inferences. In every case (and he would have a legion to choose from) he would warn us to make sure that the original of the image, the thing or occurrence which we use figuratively, does really bear the use to which we put it, does really yield the notion we want, does not actually contradict or confuse this, does not, that is, convey something quite different; and thus makes us, unconsciously, the cause of the confusion we condemn in others.

Then he would wind up with a collection of "bulls of metaphor," which would certainly make his audience, already excited and amused by a "new way of looking at things," explode with laughter. They would in the end disperse with the seeds of a new figurative conscience implanted in them, and the first blow struck at a demon of Confusion.[1]

* * *

We may once more urge upon the reader a significant contrast. On the one hand, we have the energetic and never faltering labors of the infant and of the young child, first to master complex muscular feats, and especially those of the hand (even at the cost of discomfort, fatigue, and pain); then to master language and to apply a primitive logic (failing only through lack of experience) in its use; then to question, to inquire, to explore—to

Education as critical competence

Every systematic science, the humblest and the noblest alike, seems to admit of two distinct kinds of proficiency; one of which may be properly called scientific knowledge of the subject, while the other is a kind of educational acquaintance with it. For an educated man should be able to form a fair off-hand judgment as to the goodness or badness of the method used by a professor in his exposition. To be educated is in fact to be able to do this; and even the man of universal education we deem to be such in virtue of his having this ability. It will, however, of course, be understood that we only ascribe universal education to one who in his own individual person is thus critical in all or nearly all branches of knowledge, and not to one who has a like ability merely in some special subject, for it is possible for a man to have this competence in some one branch of knowledge without having it all.

It is plain then that, as in other sciences, so in that which inquires into nature, there must be certain canons, by reference to which a hearer shall be able to criticize the method of a professed exposition, quite independently of the question whether the statements made be true or false.

—Aristotle. *On the Parts of Animals*, Book 1.

ask not merely the What and the How, but against her, are defeating ourselves and wasting our own highest gifts.

But still we do our little best to stupefy our children; and then we shake a mournful head before the puzzles, the paradoxes, the "insoluble problems" of life—*we*, note well; *we* who have ourselves had our "free-swimming" organs docked and paralyzed and been ourselves imprisoned in a cruel network whence we once vainly struggled to escape; we who have been in our precious springtime set to a treadmill round of "acquiring" raw knowledge and packing it away in an overloaded "memory." Thus, mentally, we never transcend that "fixed" order; we never become true animals, much less men at all; we never reach the stage in which we are free to swim, to run, to leap, even to fly. Failing to recognize the inversion of true order which this implies, we never become fully able to explore, to discover, to interpret—evolving meanwhile sense after sense—until, as the true end of our little lives we reach the seer's throne. And if here and there the evolving tendency is strong enough to defy the cramping and mechanizing training, the fixing and rooting and blinding process which we too often call "education"; to shake it off and

soar into the world of greatness; stretching down hands to draw us also upwards,—then once more we shake a melancholy head and fear that this is but the "genius" which is akin to—insanity! Of course it is. We have not known how, in its tender "seedling" years, to direct and organize a living force which, compelled to develop either in undisciplined ignorance or in spite of obstructive systems, tends to lose the inestimable sense of balance and proportion.

And this is not all. It is proverbially difficult to fix a true standard of the normal in mind. The alienist has a "borderland" in which he practically feels this difficulty. But if, for the reasons now suggested, we have misunderstood and misinterpreted "genius," it follows that those of us who are least suspected, or least suspect themselves of insanity, are all the time victims of, or at any rate liable to, distorted or "morbid" views of sanity. However, to follow up this line of thought would lead us too far at present.

Meanwhile it may freely be granted that there have been many individual cases of the truer training. There are "born teachers" whose gift survives whatever their own school experiences may have been. But these are merely sporadic; they are always considered merely as a question of special personal influence; there is no systematic recognition of the supreme value of such training. And thus we have never, in the way now proposed, suggested to the child that not only in a religious sense is its true home in heaven: that "heaven" has throughout the ages been used for the ideal home of the race, because Man has always instinctively felt that his destinies, like his origin, were what is here called "solar" and "cosmic." We have never suggested to him that he belonged, not like other animals merely to this world as the centre of his natural universe, but also to the star-world which he animized, to the sky which roofed him in; that in however grotesque or inept a form his race has always reached out to the beyond and the unknown.

* * *

What then have we gained so far by our inquiry? Have we reached a point from which, even on a distant horizon of thought, we can discern a possible answer to the question why man asks Why, and also a reason why he needs to be warned of the danger and penalty of asking it where it does not apply, and therefore cannot be rightly answered?

Before we can attempt to answer this question it will be well to review the course which we have followed. We began by pleading for an extension of the bounds and resources of expression corresponding to a wider range of experience, both in fact and conception.

In the application of a threefold idea of import to consciousness and experience, our appeal was to science, which supplies us, both in astronomy and biology, with the presumption that this order best "describes and resumes" natural fact. We saw that this implied fresh views of the work of analogy, and pointed to a new departure in philosophy as well as in psychology; that it made for a true instead of a morbid plasticity in language, and a revelative instead of a merely plausible lucidity. We considered a few out of many possible ways of bringing to bear, in practical method, the recognition of the supreme importance of clear and ordered ideas about the nature of sense, meaning, and significance, and the extent of our power to convey and to appreciate them. We disclaimed all idea of discarding the acquired habits or traditional customs of language, seeking rather to enrich and to transfigure them, as well as to rectify all which now makes for hindering instead of fostering our means of expression; and we suggested that metaphors like "binocular mental vision" and "thinking in cube" might be used to indicate developments in conceptual power for which, on this line of thought, we might reasonably hope.

But first, we tried to show that our current ideas, both psychological and philosophical, were vitiated at the outset by the bias of an untenable because pre-Copernican view of the world and of man. This brought us (as indeed in every case we have been brought) to the question which ought everywhere to be recognized as vital. In what sense is any proposition, any statement, any theory, any postulate, true or valid; and, in what sense is it here used?

This led us to the suggestion of a method of Translation in a sense wider than any in which the word has yet been applied. An examination of the implications of this idea brought us to the definition of man as in one sense the Expression of the world. And this again suggested an inquiry as to the soundness of the accepted modern view of the primitive mind, of the myths, grotesque or fantastic, which grow with man's early growth. Thus we reached the moment of the first human query.

Supposing these broad lines to be accepted, here arose the question, how then to effect the needed new start? We proceeded to show that, in any full sense, a new start could only be accomplished by a generation which for the first time had been universally trained to recognize the central importance of sense, meaning, and significance: to distinguish and rightly to interpret all three.

Such a training of the future is here called Significs, because this raises the very idea of Significance to its true and supreme level; because, taking sign and what it signifies at their lowest and humblest, it leads us through a fresh study of sense to a fresh study of meaning which shows us significance as the key of keys to reality.[3]

No more can here be added. Some attempt may later be made to show how the method of inquiry and observation which in the form of physical science has led to the triumphs evident to all, but which has apparently never yet been deliberately and consciously cultivated in childhood, can be applied to some of our unsolved problems. Among such problems will be those of space and time as affecting our conceptions of immortality and divinity, those of personality as affecting our ethical ideals, and especially those connected with a dynamic view of the universe (and therefore of all in every sense within it); a view which science now sanctions and enforces, and which, more widely applied, both accounts for and solves some of our most "hopeless" puzzles. This will be but the natural result of concentrating all the mental and moral energies of man, while yet his mind is wholly plastic, upon that form of question which breaks through the surface of things. Such questioning wins, or rather earns for the first time, knowledge which not only stands, but invites the most searching tests available. This true knowledge sees even the poetry of the future as born out of that very science and that very criticism which are now supposed to kill it. At least, let the experiment be fairly tried; at least, let us begin by giving sense, meaning, and significance that central place in our attention and our interests that, whether we will or no, they already have in the world of human experience.

The activity which we call mind expresses itself in infancy, soon after language is acquired, in the form of the question Why. It gives the secret of knowledge and of mental and moral domination. this genetic spirit of inquiry, as we have already seen, is the very spring of science.

If it has seemed on the philosophical side to go astray into regions where answers are mutually discordant, thus incurring the scorn or neglect of all but a small section of mankind, this has surely been because the lack of the training here pleaded for has tended to deprive the highest thought of a constantly rising standard of expression; and has thus earned for "metaphysical speculation" a deserved bad name. For the only true metaphysics is the growth-point of the sense which is common to Man as Man, the sense for real criterions of truth and true criterions of the real; the sense (which, alas! we degrade into superstition), that we are penetrated through and through with potential knowledge which only remains in the form of "insoluble" problem and "baffling" mystery, or of vague irrational mysticism, because we have not learnt how to approach and deal with it through the encouragement and cultivation of the child's Divine gift of the Why. And from this point of view the true philosophy does not yet exist.

For we do not yet fully realize that the youngest child is himself in a true sense a "metaphysician." From his earliest speaking days he assimilates and freely uses abstract terms,—like "other," etc. Is it not, then, a cruel pity that if his natural interests are what are called practical, he should be allowed to grow up in the idea that "thinking over and working at whys"—investigating causes or reasons, expressing the meaning and value of reality, or its knowledge, interpreting himself or his world,—is either hopeless or mere dexterous thought-spinning and word-weaving? If, on the other hand, he is a born thinker, the result of such bringing up too often is that he tries to model the world of reality on his own special pattern. He becomes the victim of his own powers and his own knowledge. He does his fellows the grave disservice of providing them with a thought-cage wherein they may safely play. He founds a school of philosophy which at best appeals in a good sense only to a certain type of mind, while in a bad sense it either makes for confusion or for petrifaction. Such a system confusion or for petrifaction. Such a system causes, e.g., the scientific Man to insist upon a rigid confinement of attention to what are for him the only demonstrable and therefore the only real or valuable facts, i.e. those capable of being proved by actual experiment; while the "practical" man remains serenely content to muddle on through interminable and quite avoidable blunder, the product of his own fallacious theory that he has and need have no theory at all! But if we can "inaugurate" an era of Significs, and substitute that idea for what is now the misleading idea of metaphysics (properly, if anything, concerned with consciousness or what we now mean by psychology); if in every intelligent man alike we can appeal to the sense of meaning, and beyond that to the sense of significance which is also the sense of value, and thus disentangle the vital worth from the endless perplexities of question, of problem, of experience in every form, then what is there that we may not hope for?

Of course, as now, we shall be drawn to or have to choose some special line of thought and action, and it is imperative that this should not be confounded with others. But as we shall be consciously and deliberately concentrating ourselves on that which connects our subject with every other, on that which constitutes its human value, and contributes its quota to the general treasure-house of human achievement,—the era of mutually sterilizing controversy will be succeeded, not by one of general apathy and indifference, or of paralysing pessimism, but by one of mutual stimulus and of a mental symbiosis. We shall attain to what has here been called binocular thinking; we shall not merely adopt or expound, we shall not even be content merely to develop, we shall *account for* the great systems or the typical formulas of ancient or modern philosophy. And this result the really practical and the really scientific man will be the very first to welcome. For even the engineer, yes, even the soldier and the ploughman, will work the better for it; while science will for the first time find itself appreciated and assisted by those who now

stand aloof, or appear to the scientific eye to be pursuing unrealities: will indeed by enabled to express itself as never before. We shall in the fullest sense acquire a new power of intertranslation with new possibilities of interpretation.

Science is self-confined to the method of measurement. Philosophy is free to use all sane and rational methods. Now science constrains its votaries each to welcome another's re-statement or correction for the development of his thesis. Even as this is written, we find Sir W. Crookes witnessing both to this noble example set us by science and to the power of change in expression. Referring to Dr. Johnstone Stoney's term "electron," he says, "thus my early hypotheses fall into order by the substitution of one expression for the other" ("electron" for "radiant matter").

The true philosophy, like the true science, appeals to intelligence as intelligence; and this appeal embraces the utmost conceivable variety and difference always on the basis, not of separation (except in some cases with a temporary or special object), but of distinction, which, however sharp, is always compatible with unity. The true philosophy comes not to abstract, but to interpret; not to destroy, but to fulfill; not to give mere passive reflection, but to prove itself the creative energy of mind,—a ray of that Light whereby we learn what beauty, what goodness, what love, in brief, what life in its highest sense may be.

Notes

1. "Any one who chooses to observe the development of a child's mind will, if he does not suppress its natural bent, convince himself that a child from three to five years of age possesses thinking powers of greater capacity than we are in the habit of crediting to it. One of the external evidences of a thoughtful mind is the asking of questions which bear definite and logical relations to each other; and this is precisely what an average child of that age, when talking to a person in sympathy with it, is persistently doing. It is not content with a flimsy and evasive answer, and how strong is its intellectual craving is manifested by its evident disappointment or display of temper when its ignorant parents impatiently curb its

curiosity. It is very seldom that one finds a mother who has endeavoured to retain her child's thinking capacities. I was once present when the four-year-old little daughter of such a mother was making inquiries about the planet Venus, and after she had been informed that both Venus and the earth travelled round the sun, and were illuminated by it, she put the query, 'Then if there were people on Venus our earth would look to them like Venus looks to us?' This question demonstrates that a child possesses thinking powers sufficiently vigorous to enable it to see the logical relationships of bodies to each other that would certainly do credit to many of its superiors in point of years. This is not an isolated instance, and my impression, derived from observation and from conversation with observant persons, is that the average child, if not suppressed, is capable of a quality of thinking that leads its elders, when they try to follow it, into an intellectual quagmire of inconsistency and absurdity from which they beat an inglorious retreat by angrily bidding it 'not to ask silly questions.' If they bid themselves not to give silly answers their request would be just." (G. P. Mudge on "Darwinism and Statecraft," *Nature*, April 11, 1901.)

2. There is no doubt that the method of Socrates might be and ought to be freely used in education. As the *Spectator* (March 25, 1899) has well said, "The greatest method of destroying error, of unveiling truth, of awakening the mind, was the method of Socrates. Perhaps of all our needs to-day there is none so great (as we think Dean Stanley observed) as a thorough dialectic after the manner of Socrates, in which all the vexed questions of our time should be subjected to that most wonderful intellectual analysis. How our mental shuffling, our begging of the question, our stupid confusion, would be burnt up in that consuming flame!" And no one would appreciate and benefit by it more than the child and the youth, for many of their own questions which we often merely laugh at or snub are in fact Socratic, although they themselves may be but partly conscious of the irony of these.

3. Man as craftsman and as artist can "create" on the sense-level; that is, without deliberate or reasoned intention; he may even be surprised at the result of his own labour. He can only in the full sense think on the meaning-level. He reflects on what he has made or is going to make. When he has reached significance he enters that which can only be called Life in a transfigured sense. Again, man can "create" on the planet; beyond that limit he can make nothing. But he can (and in the highest sense he must) think in the "solar" world. Once more, in the transfigured sense which to us makes life essentially worth living, he lives in the cosmos.

Who Should Learn Writing of Whom: Peasant Children of Us, or We of Peasant Children?

Lev Tolstoy

In 1860, Tolstoy created Yasnaya Polyana, a school in which Russian peasant children were encouraged to learn in a free and creative environment. Here curriculum took on a completely new character. Lessons were similar to casual chats between an adult and the students. Every conceivable topic was touched upon from grammar to carpentry—by way of religious history, singing, geography, gymnastics, drawing and writing. Emphasis was on the skills and sensibilities which all needed to acquire.

The school at Yasnaya Polyana was located in a small, two-story building adjacent to Tolstoy's house. There were two classrooms and one additional room used as a study. The atmosphere was casual and comfortable. Each of the classrooms was painted pink and blue. In one room, mineral samples, butterflies, dried plants and physics apparatus lined the shelves around the room. Gymnastic equipment was installed in the downstairs vestibule and in the upstairs hall, there was a carpenter's bench. The walls were lined with tools. A bell and bell-rope hung under the porch roof.

At 8:00 A.M. in the morning, peasant children would appear by twos or threes, swinging their arms and singing. When they entered, they would sit where they liked, on the floor, on the window ledge, on a chair or on the corner of a table. They would draw near the teacher when he was dis-cussing something that interested them; and they would leave the room when they weren't interested. It was not unusual to be silenced by one's peers if one was preventing the others from hearing the discussion. Tolstoy understood the role of peer pressure in the development of self-discipline.

Tolstoy believed that all human nature was basically good and that evil was a product of civilization. Thus, teachers should refrain from smothering children under the weight of learning. Rather, they should concentrate on helping them, little by little, to shape their own personalities for the purpose of creativity. At Yasnaya Polyana, Tolstoy strove to maintain as "natural" an environment as possible. In his view, teachers could learn much about pedagogy by contemplating the mother-child relationship.

A mother loves her child, wants to satisfy his wants, and consciously, without the least mystical necessity, feels the need of adapting herself to his incipient reason, to speak the simplest language to him. She does not at all strive after equality with her child, which would be in the highest degree unnatural, but, on the contrary, intentionally tries to transmit to him the whole supply of her knowledge. In this natural transmission of the mental acquisitions of one generation to the next lies the progress of education.

Tolstoy has often been criticized for confusing art with pedagogy. He was convinced that it was the duty of artists to educate, and were they to neglect their role as educators, they would prostitute their art. All great art is universally accessible and comprehensible, he contended, and one can learn a great deal about art by teaching the masses. In his inspirational form of teaching, he tried to put himself on the level of his students, and marvelled at their every word. Should the muzhik's children learn to write from us, he wondered, or should we learn to write from them?

One day he proposed that the class improvise a tale on the theme of a Russian proverb, "He feeds a man with a spoon and then pokes the handle in his eyes." The children stared at him blankly. "Suppose a peasant gives shelter to a pauper and then tries to hold his good deed over his head?" Then, to show the students how a story is formed, he wrote out the beginning himself. The children leaned over his shoulder and began to dictate: "No, not like that . . ." "Make him an ordinary soldier . . ." "It would be better if he stole them." "There has to be a wicked woman in it." Taking down their dictation, Tolstoy realized the wealth of their talent:

> *I cannot describe the emotion, the joy and fear I felt that evening. I saw a new world of delight and suffering rising up before him (Fyodka): the world of art. It seemed to me I had witnessed what no one has the right to see: the opening of the mysterious flower of poetry. I felt such joy because, all of a sudden, by sheer chance, I saw unveiled before my eyes that philosopher's stone I had been seeking in vain for two years: the art of learning to express one's thoughts. I felt fear because that art created new demands, a flood of desires foreign to the world in which, I believed at first, the pupils lived.*

Once he realized how capable the peasant children were, he tried to introduce them to Russian literature, but with little success. Convinced of their ability he proclaimed, "Perhaps they do not understand and do not want to understand our literary language, simply because our literary language is not suited to them and they are in the process of inventing their own literature." It was a short step to concluding that any art which is not accessible to the masses is counterfeit.

Whether or not we agree with Tolstoy's views on art, we can appreciate his insights regarding the pedagogy of creative writing. His stress on the relationship between speaking, thinking and writing in a communal environment in which children are encouraged to discuss ideas and feelings freely and build on each other's thoughts was uncannily ahead of his time. Initially, he insisted, students should not have to worry about the formal conditions of writing. Rather, they should be encouraged to express their thoughts and feelings by means of a procedure which, little by little, takes on form. In assigning the teacher at Yasnaya Polyans the role of scribe and provoker of dialogue among the children themselves, many classroom stories emerged of which Tolstoy was very proud. He wisely capitalized on the intrinsic relationship between speaking, thinking and writing, or encouraging children to do what they like to do: talk among themselves, think for themselves and create for themselves.

In the fourth volume of the journal *Yasnaya Polyana* there was printed among the children's compositions by an editorial mistake, "A History of how a boy was frightened in Tula." This little story was not written by a boy, but was made up by the teacher from a dream which he had, and which he related to the boys. Some of the readers, who followed the numbers of *Yasnaya Polyana*, expressed their doubts whether this tale really belonged to the boy. I hasten to apologize to my readers for this oversight, and seize the opportunity to remark how impossible are counterfeits in this class of work. This tale was detected, not because it was better, but because it was worse, incomparably worse, than *all* the compositions of the children. All the other tales belonged to the children themselves. Two of them, "He eats with your spoon but puts your eyes out with the handle" and "Life in a Soldier's Home," were written in the following way:—

The teacher's chief art in the teaching of language, and his chief exercise with this end in view as he trains children to write compositions, consists in the giving of subjects; and not so much in the mere naming of them as in finding variety of subjects, in indicating the dimensions of the compositions, and the pointing out of elementary processes.

Many of the intelligent and talented scholars would write trash; would write:—

"The fire broke out, they began to pull out the things, and I ran into the street."

And nothing of any consequence was produced, though the subject of the composition was rich, and the description of it may have made a deep impression on the scholars.

They would miss the chief thing: why they wrote, and what was the good of writing it? They did not comprehend the art of expressing life in words, and the fascination of this art. And, as I have already said in the second number, I tried many different experiments in the giving of subjects. I tried to gauge their inclinations, and gave them explicit, artistic, touching, ludicrous, or epic themes for compositions; but the thing did not work. Now I will tell you how I accidentally discovered the true method.

For a long time the perusal of Snegiref's collection of proverbs has been one of my favorite, I will not say occupations, but passions. Every proverb brings up before me characters from among the people, and their actions, according to the sense of the proverb. Among my impossible dreams I have always thought of writing a series of either stories or plays founded on these proverbs.

Once last winter, after dinner, I was reading Snegiref's book, and I took the book with me to school. The class in the Russian language was in progress.

"Now write me something on a proverb," said I.

The best scholars, Fedka, Semka, and the others, pricked up their ears.

"What do you mean, 'on a proverb'?" "What is that?" "Tell us!" were the various exclamations.

I happened to open to the proverb: "He eats with your spoon and puts your eyes out with the handle."

"Now imagine," said I, "that a muzhik had taken in some old beggar; and then, after the kindness that he had received, the beggar had begun to revile him, it would mean that he had eaten with your spoon and put out your eyes with the handle."

"Well, how would you write it?" said Fedka and all the others, who had pricked up their ears; but suddenly they gave it up, persuaded that this task was beyond their strength, and resumed the work on which they had been engaged before.

"You write it for us," said one of them to me.

All were busy in their work; I took the pen and inkstand, and began to write.

"Now," said I, "who will write it the best? and I will try with you."

I began the story which is printed in the fourth number of *Yasnaya Polyana*, and wrote the first page.

Every unprejudiced man with any feeling for art and nationality, on reading this first page written by me, and the following pages of the story written by the scholars themselves, will distinguish this page from all the others,—like a fly in milk,—it is so artificial, so false, and written in such a wretched style. It must be noted that in its first form it was still poorer, and has been much improved, thanks to the suggestions of the scholars.

Fedka kept looking up from his copybook at me, and when his eyes met mine he would smile and wink, and say, "Write, write! I will show you!"

It evidently interested him to have a grown person also write a composition. After finishing his composition, less carefully and more hurriedly than usual, he leaned over the back of my armchair, and began to read over my shoulder. I could not write any longer; others joined our group, and I read aloud what I had written. It did not please them; no one praised it.

I was mortified; and in order to soothe my literary vanity, I began to tell them my plan of what was to follow. As I went on telling them, I was carried away. I felt better in my mind, and they began to make suggestions.

One said that the old man should be a wizard. Another said:—

"No; that is not necessary; he must be simply a soldier."

"No; let him rob his benefactor."

"No; that would not be according to the proverb," said they.

All were thoroughly interested. It was evidently something new and fascinating for them to watch the process of composition, and to take part in it. Their opinions were for the most part similar and just, both in regard to the construction of the story, the details, and the traits of the characters.

Nearly all took part in the composition of the story, but from the very beginning the positive Semka stood out with especial clearness by the artistic sharpness of his description, and Fedka by the truth of his poetic delineations, and more than all by the vividness and force of his imagination. Their structures were to such a degree given advisedly, and with reason, that more than once, when I argued with them I was obliged to yield.

It was my idea that accuracy in composition, and the close fitting of the thought to the proverb, should enter into the story; they, on the contrary, cared only for artistic accuracy.

For example, I wanted the peasant who took the old beggar into his house to regret his kindly action; they felt that this was an impossibility, and they brought into the action a vixenish woman.

I said:—

"The peasant at first felt sorry for the beggar, but afterward felt sorry that he had given his bread."

Fedka replied that such a thing would be absurd.

"From the very first he did not listen to his wife, and surely afterward he would not yield to her!"

"But what sort of a man is he in your idea?" I asked.

"He is like Uncle Timofer," said Fedka, smiling, "his beard is rather thin, he goes to church, and he keeps bees."

"Good-natured but obstinate?" I suggested.

"Yes," said Fedka; "that's the reason he will not heed his wife."

From the moment when they introduced the old man the composition began in lively earnest. Here for the first time, evidently, they began to feel the delight of putting artistic work into words. In this respect Semka was particularly brilliant; the most lifelike details followed one another. The solitary fault which might be charged against him was this: that these details pictured only the present moment, and had no relationship to the general idea of the story. I did not hurry them, but rather urged them to go slow, and not to forget what they had said.

It seemed as if Semka saw and described what went on before his eyes: the frozen, snow-covered bark shoes, and the mud which dripped down from them as they thawed out, and the *biscuits* into which they dried when the woman put them into the oven.

Fedka, on the other hand, saw only those particulars which aroused in him such a sentiment as he would have experienced at the sight of a real person. Fedka saw the snow which had stuck to the old man's legwrappers, and he felt, the feeling of pity which inspired the peasant to say:—

"Lord! how can he walk!"

Fedka went so far as to express in pantomime the manner in which the peasant said these words; waving his hand and shaking his head. He saw the old man's thin, tattered cloak, and his torn shirt, under which showed his emaciated body wet with melting snow. He imagined the woman, as she grumblingly obeyed her husband's command, and pulled off his lapti, and the old man's pitiful groan muttered through his teeth:—

"Easy, little mother, my feet are sore there!"

Semka wanted objective pictures above all,— the lapti, the thin cloak, the old man, the peasant woman, without much of any connection among them; Fedka wanted to express the feeling of pity with which he himself was filled.

He went on to speak of how the old man would be given his supper; how he would fall sick in the night; how afterward in the field he would teach the boy his letters, so that I was obliged to tell him not to hurry and not to forget what he had said. His eyes gleamed with unshed tears; his dirty, thin hands contracted nervously; he was impatient, and kept spurring me on: "Have you written it? have you written it?" he kept asking me.

He was despotically irritated with all the others; he wanted to be the only one to speak,—not to speak as men talk but to speak as they write,—in other words to express artistically in words the images of feeling; for example, he would not permit the words to be changed about, but was very particular about their order.

His soul at this time was softened and stirred by the sentiment of pity,—that is, love—and it pictured every object in an artistic form, and took exception to everything that did not correspond to his idea of eternal beauty and harmony.

As soon as Semka was drawn into describing incongruous details about the lambs huddled in the corner near the door, or anything of the sort, Fedka would become vexed and say: "Ho, you; you are talking twaddle."

I needed only to suggest anything, for example, what was the peasant doing while his wife went off to her neighbor's—and Fedka's imagination would immediately construct a picture of lambs bleating near the door, and the old man sighing, and the lad Serozha delirious; I had only to suggest some artificial and false detail in the picture, and he would become angry instantly, and declare with irritation that it was not necessary.

For instance, I proposed that he describe the peasant's external appearance; he agreed: but my proposal that he should describe what the peasant thought while his wife was gone to her neighbor's immediately brought up in his mind this idea:—

"Ekh! woman! if you should meet the dead Savoska, he would tear your hair out."

And he said this in such a weary and calmly naturally serious, and at the same time good-natured, tone of voice, leaning his head on his hand, that the children went into a gale of laughter.

The chief condition of every art—the feeling of proportion—was extraordinarily developed in him. He was wholly upset by any superfluous suggestion made by any of the boys. He took it upon himself to direct the construction of this story in such a despotic way, and with such a just claim to be despotic, that very soon the boys went home, and he alone was left with Semka, who did not give way to him, though he worked in a different manner.

We worked from seven to eleven o'clock; the children felt neither hunger nor weariness, and they were really indignant with me when I stopped writing; then they tried to take turns in writing by themselves, but they soon desisted—the thing did not work.

Here for the first time Fedka asked me what my name was. We laughed at him, because he did not know.

"I know," said he, "how to address you; but what do they call your estate name? You know we have the Fokanuichef family, the Zabrefs, the Yermilinas."

I told him.

"And are we going to be printed?" he asked.

"Yes.

"Then it must be printed: *The work of Makarof, Morozof, and Tolstoi!*"

He was excited for a long time, and could not sleep; and I cannot represent the feeling of excitement, of pleasure, of pain, and almost of remorse which I experienced in the course of that evening. I felt that from this time a new world of joys and sorrows had been revealed to Fedka,—the world of art; it seemed to me that I was witnessing what no one has the right to see,—the unfolding of the mysterious flower of poetry.

To me it was both terrible and delightful; just as if a treasure-seeker should find the lady-fern in bloom.

The pleasure consisted for me in suddenly, unexpectedly, discovering the philosopher's stone, for which I had been vainly seeking for two years—the art of expressing thought.

It was terrible, because this art would bring new demands and a whole world of desires incompatible with the sphere in which the pupils live—or so it seemed to me at the first moment.

There could be no mistake. This was not chance, but conscious, creative genius. I beg the reader to peruse the first chapter of the story, and notice the abundant touches of true creative talent scattered through it. For example, the scene where the woman complains angrily of her husband to her neighbor, and yet this woman, for whom the author feels a lively antipathy, bursts into tears when the neighbor reminds her of the breaking up of her home.

For the author who writes with the intellect and memory alone a quarrelsome woman would be created only as a foil for the peasant: from simple desire to torment her husband she would have necessarily called in the neighbor. But in Fedka the artistic feeling was expressed in the woman also, and so she weeps, and fears, and suffers; in his eyes she is not to blame.

Afterward there is a little side-play, when the neighbor puts on the woman's cloak; I remember that I was so extremely struck by it that I asked him, "Why the *woman's* cloak?"

Not one of us had suggested to Fedka the idea of having the neighbor put on the woman's cloak. He replied:—

"Why, it's more lifelike."

When I asked him, "Might we not say that he put on the husband's cloak?" he replied, "No; it is better to have the wife's."

And in very fact this touch is extraordinary. At first you do not see *why* it should be the woman's cloak, but at the same time you feel that it is admirable—that it could not be otherwise.

Every artistic phrase, whether it belongs to a Goethe or a Fedka, is distinguished from one which is not artistic by the simple fact that it calls up an innumerable throng of thoughts, representations and illustrations.

The neighbor, in the woman's cloak, irresistibly suggests the picture of a feeble, narrow-chested peasant, just as in all probability he was. The woman's cloak, thrown down on the bench, and therefore coming first to hand, brings up before you a perfect picture of a peasant's establishment on a winter's evening. At the mere mention of the cloak there arise involuntarily before your eyes the late hour, at the time when the peasant, undressed for the night, is sitting before his splinter, and the women, coming and going in their housework,—getting water and feeding the cattle,—and all that external disorder in the peasant's mode of life, where not a single person has a garment that is particularly his, and not a single thing has its proper place.

This one expression, "*He put on the woman's cloak,*" defines the whole character of the environment in which the action passes, and this phrase was not discovered accidentally, but chosen deliberately.

I still remember vividly how his imagination conjured up the words spoken by the peasant when he found the paper and could not read it:—

"If my Serozha here knew how to read, he would jump up, tear the paper out of my hands, read it all through, and tell me who this old man is."

In this way we can see the relation between the laboring man and the book which he holds in his sunburned hands; this worthy man, with his patriarchal, pious inclinations, seems to stand before you. You feel that the author has a deep love for him, and has therefore completely understood him, so as to suggest to him immediately after this his digression about such times having now passed and the danger of the soul being lost.

The idea of the dream was suggested by me, but the introduction of the goat with wounded legs was Fedka's, and he was particularly delighted with it. And the peasant's meditations at the time when his back was beginning to itch, and the picture of the quiet night,—all of this was the farthest removed from accidental: in all these touches can be felt such a conscious artistic power. . . .

I still remember that at the time of the muzhik's going to sleep, I proposed to make him think of the future of his son and of the son's future relations with the old man, that the old man should teach Serozha his letters, and so on. Fedka frowned and said: "Yes, yes, very good," but it was evident that this proposition did not please him, and twice he forgot it. The sense of proportion was as strong in him as in any writer I know—the same sense of proportion as rare artists obtain with great labor and pains, in all its primitive strength lived in his uncontaminated childish soul.

I put an end to the lesson because I was too much excited.

"What is the matter? what makes you so pale? Truly you aren't well, are you?" my companion asked of me.

In fact, only two or three times in my life had I ever experienced such a powerful emotion as I had that evening, and it was long before I could give a rational account to myself of what I had experienced. I was uneasy, and felt as if I had been criminally spying through a glass, into a hive, at the labors of the bees, hidden from mortal gaze. It seemed to me that I had done a wrong to the peasant lad's pure, innocent soul. I had an uneasy feeling as if I had been engaged in a sacrilege.

I remembered children whom idle and debauched old men compelled to display themselves and to present voluptuous pictures so as to stir their frigid and enfeebled imaginations, and at the same time I felt a keen delight, such as a man must feel who has witnessed something that no one has ever seen before.

It was long before I could explain the impression which I had received, though I was conscious that it was one of those which in mature life lift a man to a higher stage of existence, and compel him to renounce the old, and give himself unreservedly to the new.

The next day I could not believe in the reality of the experience through which I had passed that evening. It seemed to me quite too strange that a half-educated peasant lad had suddenly developed a conscious, artistic power, such as Goethe, with all his measureless height of development, was unable to attain. It seemed to me, too, strange that I, the author of "Childhood," who have now gained a certain success and reputation for artistic talent in the literary circles of Russia, that I, in the matter of art, was not only unable to guide or aid this eleven-year-old Fedka, and Semka, but that barely,—and that only in a happy moment of excitement,—could I follow them and comprehend them. It seemed to me so strange, that I could not believe in what had happened the evening before.

On the next day we occupied ourselves with the continuation of the tale. When I asked Fedka whether he had thought out the sequel and how, he made no reply, but waving his hands simply said:—

"I know, I know! Who will write it?"

We began to write the continuation, and again, as far as the children were concerned, with the same sense of artistic truth, proportion, and enthusiasm.

When the lesson was half done, I was compelled to leave them. They continued without me and wrote two pages as beautifully, as sympathetically, as genuinely, as the first. These pages were only a little poorer in details, and these details were sometimes not introduced with perfect skill; there were also two repetitions. All this evidently arose from the fact that the mechanism of composition troubled them. On the third day it was the same.

During these lessons other boys were frequently present, and knowing the spirit and idea of the story, they made suggestions and added their genuine strokes. Semka went away and stayed away. Only Fedka kept on with the story from beginning to end, and acted as censor on all the changes proposed.

There could be no doubt that this success is a matter of chance: we evidently struck accidentally on that method which was more natural and more stimulating than those we had tried hitherto. But all this was too unusual, and I did not believe in what was going on before my eyes. Something which seemed like an extraordinary chance was required to dissipate my doubts.

I had been away for several days, and the story remained unfinished. The manuscript—three large sheets fully written over—was left in the room of the teacher to whom I had been showing it.

Just before my departure, while I was engaged with the composition, a new pupil who had come had been showing the children the art of making fly-swatters out of paper, and throughout the whole school, as is apt to be the case, had come a time of fly-swatters, taking the place of snowball time, which in its turn had taken the place of carved sticks.

The fly-swatter time lasted during my absence. Semka and Fedka, who belonged to the choir, used to go to the teacher's room to sing, and they would spend whole evenings and sometimes whole nights there.

In the intervals and during the time of singing, of course, the fly-swatters were in full swing, and every available piece of paper which fell into their hands was turned into a fly-swatter. The teacher went to supper and forgot to caution the children not to touch the papers on his table, and so the manuscript containing the work of Makarof, Morozof, and Tolstoi was turned into fly-swatters.

On the next day, before school, the slapping had become such a nuisance to the pupils themselves, that they themselves declared a general persecution of fly-swatters; with a shout and a rush the fly-swatters were all collected, and with general enthusiasm flung into the lighted stove.

The time of fly-swatters was ended, but with it our manuscript had also gone to ruin.

Never was any loss more severe for me to bear than that of those three written sheets. I was in despair.

Wringing my hands, I went to work to rewrite the story, but I could not forget the loss of it, and involuntarily I kept heaping reproaches on the teacher, and the manufacturers of the fly-swatters.

Here I cannot resist observing in this connection that as the result of this external disorder and perfect freedom among the scholars, which have furnished decorous amusement for Mr. Markof, in the *Russian Messenser*, and Mr. Glyebof, in the journal *Education*, without the slightest trouble, and without having to use threats or cunning, I learned all the details of the complicated history of the manuscript turned into fly-swatters, and of its cremation.

Semka and Fedka saw that I was disturbed, and though, evidently, they did not know the reason, they seemed to be very sympathetic; Fedka at last timidly proposed to me to rewrite the story.

"By yourselves?" I asked, "I cannot help any in it."

"Semka and I will come and spend the night at your house," replied Fedka.

And indeed, after the lessons, they came to my house about nine o'clock and locked themselves in my library. I was not a little delighted that after some giggling, they became quiet, and at twelve o'clock when I went to the door, I heard merely their low conversation and the scratching of the pen. Only once they asked me about something that had been in the former copy, and wanted my opinion on the question,—Had the peasant hunted for his wallet before or after his wife went to the neighbor's?

I told them it made no difference.

At twelve o'clock, I tapped at the door and went in.

Fedka, in a new white shubka with black fur trimming, was sitting buried in the easy-chair, with his legs crossed and his bushy little head resting on one hand, while his friend played with the scissors. His big black eyes, gleaming with an unnatural but serious and mature light, had a far-away look; his irregular lips, puckered up as if to whistle, evidently waiting for the phrase, which, though ready-made in his imagination, he was trying to formulate.

Semka, standing in front of the great writing-table, with a big white patch of sheepskin on his back (the tailors had just been through the village), with his girdle unloosed and his hair tumbled, was writing very crooked lines and constantly dipping the pen in the inkstand.

I rumpled up Semka's hair, and when with his fat face, and its projecting cheek-bones, and his disheveled hair, he turned to me with a startled look in his thoughtful and sleepy eyes, it was so ludicrous that I laughed aloud; but the children did not laugh.

Fedka, not altering the expression of his face, pulled Semka by the sleeve to make him go on with his writing.

"Wait," said he to me; "done in a minute!" (Fedka used the familiar *tui*, "*thou*," to me when he was excited and eager), and he went on dictating something more.

I took their copy from them and at the end of five minutes, when they were installed near the cupboard eating potatoes and kvas, and looking at the silver spoons, to which they were so unaccustomed, they broke out, without themselves knowing why, into ringing, boyish laughter. The old woman in the room above hearing them laugh, laughed too, without knowing why.

"What are you filling up so for?" said Semka. "Sit straight, or you will eat yourself one-sided."

And while they were taking off their shubas and bestowing themselves under the writing-table for the night, they did not cease to bubble over with the charming, healthy laughter of the peasant child. I read through what they had written. It was a new variation of the former story. Some things were left out, some new artistic beauties were added. And once more there was the same feeling for beauty, truth, and proportion.

Afterward one sheet of the lost manuscript was found. In the story as it was printed I welded the two variants together by the aid of the sheet that was found and by bringing my recollection to bear upon it. The composition of this story took place in the early spring, before the end of our school year.

Owing to various circumstances I was prevented from making new experiments. Only one tale was written on a proverb, by two of the boys who were most ordinary in their talents and most sophisticated, being sons of houseservants. The story on the proverb, "He who is happy on a holiday is drunk before daylight," was printed in number three. The same occurrences took place again with these boys and with this story as with Semka and Fedka and the first story, only with the difference of degree of talent and degree of enthusiasm, and of my cooperation.

In the summer we have no lessons, have had no lessons, and intend to have no lessons. The reason why teaching is impossible in our school in summer we explain in a special article.

One part of the summer Fedka and the other boys lived with me. After they had bathed and played, they were thinking what they should do with themselves. I proposed to them to write a composition, and suggested several themes. I told them a very remarkable story of a robbery of money, the story of a murder, the story of a miraculous conversion of a Molokan to Orthodoxy, and again I proposed to them to write in the form of autobiography the story of a lad whose poor and dissolute father was sent off as a solider, and on his return proved to be a reformed and excellent man. I said:—

"I should write it this way: 'I remember when I was a little fellow we had living at home a mother, a father, and several other relatives,' and what they were. Then I should describe my recollection of how my father used to go on sprees, how my mother was always weeping, and how he beat her; then how they sent him as a soldier, how she wailed when we began to live even more wretchedly than before; how my father came back, and I should not have known him if he had not asked if Matriona did not live there—this was regarding his wife—and how we rejoiced and we began to live well."

Man is born perfect;— that is a great dictum that is enunciated by Rousseau, and that dictum stands like a rock, firm and true. Having been born, man sets up before himself his prototype of harmony, truth, beauty, and goodness. But every hour in his life, every minute of time, increases the distance, the size, and the time of those relations which at his birth were found in perfect harmony, and every step and every hour threatens the violation of this harmony, and every succeeding step threatens a new violation, and gives no hope of restoring the violated harmony. The majority of educators lose from sight the fact that childhood is the prototype of harmony, and they take as an end the child's development, which goes on according to unchangeable laws. Development is mistakenly taken as an end, because with educators happens what takes place with poor sculptors.

Instead of trying to establish a local exaggerated development, or to establish a general development, in order to wait the new opportunity which puts an end to the previous irregularity, like the poor sculptor, instead of scratching off the superfluity, they keep sticking on more and more; so also educators apparently strive for only one thing,—how the process of development may not cease; and if they think of harmony at all, then they always strive to attain it, approaching the unknown prototype in the future, receding from the prototype in the past and present. However irregular the education of a child has been, there still remain in it the primitive features of harmony. Still modifying, at least not helping, the development, we may hope to attain some nearness to regularity and harmony.

But we are so self-confident, so dreamily given over to the false ideal of mature perfection, so impatient are we toward the anomalous near us, and so firmly confident in our power of correcting them, so little are able to understand and appreciate the primitive beauty of a child, that we make all possible haste to rouse the child, to correct all the irregularities that come under our observation; we regulate, we educate: First, we must bring up one side even with the other, then the other with the first. They keep developing the child more and more, and removing it farther and farther from the old and abolished prototype, and ever more and more impossible becomes the attainment of the imaginary ideal of the perfectibility of the adult man.

Our ideal is behind us and not before us.

Education spoils and does not improve a man. The more the child is spoiled, the less it is necessary to educate him, the greater is the freedom he requires. To teach and educate a child is impossible and senseless on the simple ground that the child stands nearer than I do, nearer than any adult does, to that ideal of harmony, truth, beauty, and goodness to which, in my pride, I wish to lead him.

The consciousness of this ideal is stronger in him than in me. All he needs of me is material for filling out harmoniously and on all sides. As soon as I gave him perfect freedom, ceased to teach him, he wrote this poetic tale, the like of which is not to be found in Russian literature. And therefore, according to my notion, it is impossible for us to teach children, and especially peasants, writing and composition, especially poetic composition. All that we can do is to show them how to get started.

If what I have done for the attainment of this end may be called methods, then these methods are the following:—

I. To propose the largest and most varied choice of themes, not inventing them especially for children, but proposing the most serious themes, such as interest the teacher himself.

II. To give children children's works to read, and to propose as models, because children's works are always more genuine, more elegant, and more moral than the works of adults.

III. (Especially important.) Never, while examining children's works, make for the pupils any observations about the neatness of the note-books, or about the calligraphy, or about the spelling, or, above all, about the order of topics or the logic.

IV. As in authorship the difficulty lies not in the dimensions, or the contents, or the artfulness of the theme, so the progression of the themes ought not to lie in the dimensions, or the contents, or the language, but in the mechanism of the action, consisting first in the choice of one out of a large number of ideas and images presenting themselves; secondly, in the choice of words wherewith to array it; thirdly, in remembering what has been already written, so as not to indulge in repetitions, and not to omit anything, and including the ability to write what follows with what precedes; fifthly and lastly, while thinking and writing, not letting the one interfere with the other.

With this end in view, I did as follows:

Some of these phases of work I at first took on myself, gradually transferring them all to their care. At first I chose for them from among the thoughts and images those which seemed to me the best, and I remembered and pointed out the places, and I corrected what had been written, preventing them from repetitions; and I myself wrote, leaving it to them only to clothe the thoughts and images in words; afterward I gave them full choice, then I let them correct what had been written; and finally, as in the story called *Soldalkino Zhifyo*,—"A Soldier's Life,"—they took upon themselves the whole process of the writing . . .

The feelings of truth, beauty, and goodness are independent of the degree of development. Beauty, truth, and goodness are concepts, expressing only the harmony of relations toward truth, beauty, and goodness. Falsetruth: there is no such thing as absolute truth. I do not lie when I say that tables turn from the contact of fingers, if I believe it, although it is not the truth; but I lie when I say I have no money, if, according to my notions, I have money. A large nose is not necessarily ugly, but it is ugly on a small face. Ugliness is only inharmoniousness in relation to beauty. To give one's dinner to a beggar, or to eat it oneself, has nothing wrong in it; but to give it away or eat it when my mother is dying of starvation is inharmoniousness toward goodness.

In training, educating, developing, or doing whatever you please to a child, we must have, and unconsciously have, one object,—the attainment of the greatest harmony as regards truth, beauty, and goodness. If the time did not pass, if the child did not live in all its phases, we might calmly attain this harmony, adding where there seemed to be a lack, and subtracting where there seemed to be a superfluity.

But the child lives; every side of his being strives toward development, one outstripping another, and for the most part, the forward motion of these sides of his we take for the goal, and cooperate only with the development, and not with the harmony of development.

This contains the eternal mistake of all pedagogical theories. We see our ideal before us when it is really behind us. The inevitable development of a man is not only not the means for the attainment of this ideal of harmony which we carry in ourselves, but is an impediment set by the Creator against the attainment of a lofty ideal of harmony. In this inevitable law of the forward motion is included the idea of that fruit of the tree of good and evil which our first parents tasted.

The healthy child is born into the world, perfectly satisfying those demands of absolute harmony in the relations of truth, beauty, and goodness which we bear within us; he is like the inanimate existences,—the plant, the animal, nature,—which constantly present to us that truth, beauty, and goodness we are seeking for and desire. In all ages and among all people the child represents the model of innocence, sinlessness, goodness, truth and beauty.

Education and the Cultivation of Reflection

Herbert W. Schneider

I propose to examine a whole life-time as an educative process which begins with trial and error learning, turns into studying, continues with reflective thinking and learning, and culminates in the personal appropriation of a culture. This seems to me to be the central theme of what Professor Hullfish taught and also the way in which Henry Gordon Hullfish lived. His mind and character, his career and influence, were, and still are an enduring example of cultural fruit, enjoyed by those who knew him and admired by those who witness the fine fruit which his education still bears. It is a rare teacher who succeeds in bringing his educative process to cultural fruitage in his students, and it is a rare student who continues to learn until his studies bear cultural fruit.

With Hullfish I now invite you to enter the schoolroom and to note what happens to a child who, according to some psychologists, has learned in his first six years more than he can learn in the next sixty. This child leaves the daily round of animal learning at home and in the family to become a professional student, manipulated by a professional teacher and surrounded by companions who are supposed to be his rivals in study but who really turn out to be partners in learning, making the best of their common confinement in a strangely furnished building under curiously benevolent guards. They spend the school day alternately making the rounds of what

is well-named a "curriculum" and then running out of doors, but strictly not out of bounds, for recreation, relief, and companionship. Seen from a child's perspective and from that of an uneducated adult there is something artificial and almost inhuman about schooling. To be ruled by professional teachers may turn out to be better than being under amateur parents, for soon both parents and children are relieved when the youngsters run off to school in the morning and *fail* to run back straight home from school in the afternoon.

Despite its artificiality the classroom with its study atmosphere becomes normal to a child, as normal as a harness to a horse. Nevertheless, when a child becomes a systematic, professional student, he is no longer a normal child. Like Adam and Eve, the child no longer eats spontaneously, unreflectingly the fruit of the tree of knowledge-of-good-and-evil; he leaves the family orchard and concentrates with "the sweat of his brow" on the art of cultivation. He begins his double life of conscious labor and relaxed leisure at the normal rate of five to two—five school days to two free days, and five school hours to two of recreation. Thus the rhythms of the worker's career become established. It is important for a worker's morale that classroom activities be genuine tasks, real work, serious business, clearly separated from play, perhaps requiring reflective thinking but in any case requiring diligence, punctuality, and the other factory virtues. The student, if he takes a professional attitude toward his work, as a majority of children proudly do, is initiated into the universal community of workers. Schooling is obligatory and irreproachable child labor.

Historians of philosophy point out that there was a major crisis in the history of reflective thinking when Cicero transformed the idea of philosophy, which in Greek means a kind of love, into a kind of *studium*. Since the days of Cicero, philosophy has become a subject-matter, whereas it had been a way of living and loving. This is an evolutionary crisis of major proportions: analogous to the "fall from innocence" perpetrated by Eve and Adam (ladies first). A similar crisis occurs in the history of any individual when he is transformed from an innocently learning organism into a student worker with tasks and responsibilities. Schooling is essentially harnessing, burden bearing, submission to the day's work, initiation into the attitude of a willing, competitive worker. Analogous rites in primitive cultures are usually accompanied by some torture and blood-letting; but in advanced, industrial cultures they are usually accompanied only by mental traumas.

There is something pathetic and heroic in all this; something symbolical not only of the necessities which nature imposes on human beings, but also of the basic traits of our culture: *laborare est orare*. We become laboring animals before we ask critically: Is this labor also production? Does it contribute to the divine process of creation? Not being certain of the answer, we shrug our shoulders and say: At any rate, it is *education*. This initiation into the status of laborer before we are ready to undertake production in one of the serious arts and industries has a way of eating into our consciences and of teaching us unconsciously that busyness has priority over enjoyment of goods and occupation over vocation. As a result, the basic problems of schooling are moral; what discipline there is in the habits of reflective thinking is centered more on the duty of thinking than on the seriousness of the problem as an aspect of production. The knowledge acquired and the learning achieved are significant less for their relation to the problems of living than to the formal art of reflective thinking. This is the theory of the better educators, like Hullfish; I say nothing of the unspeakable older theories of formal discipline as sheer categorical imperatives. In short, schooling at best encourages reflective thinking for its own sake.

To those minions who are not accustomed to using the word "reflection" as Hullfish and Co. use it, there is something *ex-post-facto*, retrospective about reflective thinking, like saying prayers before going to sleep. Reflection at work and in work and for work is a novel idea to those of our citizens whose schooling is elementary. To them reflection comes, if at all, during the hours of leisure *after* work, it is part of their moral discipline to keep their leisure hours free of their daily cares, to devote them to relaxation and recreation and reversed reflection.

Thus reflective thinking, according to the popular idiom, has come to have a bad connotation. When, on the other hand, it is praised as something "spiritual" like meditation and contemplation, having a higher dignity than laborious thinking, it is purposely kept free of real problems. Fictional imagination, detective guessing, chess, or religion, these are supposed to have a liberating, or at least an opiate value, precisely because they are unrelated to work. Pragmatic thinking is regarded as menial labor or as sordid for some other reason. This divorce of reflection and problem solving is a prevalent trait, not so much of our actual culture as of our reflection on it; and it produces schizophrenic states in those minds that imagine themselves to be educated, or even better, to be intellectually aristocratic. For this reason it is difficult for them to conceive of public schools as suitable places for reflective thinking. When they read passages like the following from the writings of Hullfish, they wonder whether the author has ever been in a real classroom:

The classroom is a segment of life . . . Each teacher each day confronts, in the normal work of the classroom, the opportunity to make the learning process a vital one. The situation in which he and his students are placed is as real a situation as either he or his students will ever be in. . . . The dogged pursuit of ideas is the sole issue at stake.[1]

If these statements are to be true of actual classrooms, not merely of normative classrooms, and of actual students and teachers, there must be a radical change in all three. I suspect that in a school of which this were true there might not be classrooms, teachers, and students. A "laboratory" (Latin for "workshop") in which the teacher is a coach and the students are working cooperatively at a real experiment whose outcome was not known in advance might come nearer to fitting the situation which Hullfish describes; but the combination of professional teachers, proverbial students, and typical classrooms will certainly not meet Hullfish's specifications of "real situations." Hullfish admits that teachers must be "reconstructed" (p. 196), and he suggests that "any sensitive teacher may initiate his own personal reconstruction" (p. 204). But this seems to me to be too hard on teachers, who usually carry the chief burden and blame when schooling goes wrong. I suspect that if the needed reconstruction is undertaken it will be much more than "personal." The whole teacher-student relation needs revision, if artificial teaching and ineffective studying are to be reconstructed. Ideally, they say, teachers and students are "pleasant collaborators in a shared undertaking" (p. 205). If this were literally true, not only teachers and students would be transfigured human beings, but classrooms, schools, and perhaps society would be quite unlike what they are.

A schoolroom is not really a community of learning, and the relation between teaching and learning is by no means as close as it is thought to be or as it ought to be. Every teacher knows that conventional "studying" is a very inefficient way to learn, and that classroom teaching makes it practically impossible for teacher and student

to join in the learning process. In short, an educative school, where learning is the primary aim and reflective thinking the method, is a different type of institution from what today we call a school.

A banker, who employed college graduates regularly, once told me: "I can teach your graduates more in six weeks than you teach them in four years, but, of course, I couldn't make them learn, if you hadn't made them study." I have taught, or thought I was teaching, most of my life, but have become increasingly skeptical of the efficacy of the teaching profession, if the aim is to teach students to learn.

There are many curious ways of earning a living, I know, but professional study and professional teaching, the more I observe them, the more they appear to me to be extraordinary curiosities. Of the two, I suppose the student is the more curious, especially the earnest one. I found students easier to teach out of school than in, when I did not know I was teaching and the student was doing something not recognized as studying.

If you interpret my remarks about institutionalized study as implying that a school is no fit place to learn anything, you no doubt think my harsh generalizations ridiculous. In distinguishing between schooling and learning, between studying and reflective thinking, perhaps too sharply, I am warning against the too optimistic identification of the two processes. We all agree that in school students learn to study, if they learn anything, but I wish to examine more closely how habits of study are related to learning something about that which is studied.

By proper studying a student may learn to recite well, to pass examinations, and to write what are euphemistically called "compositions." But are these tests useful measures of thoughtful learning? A sensitive teacher is usually dismayed or disheartened by reading student compositions and correcting the formal faults. These performances not only "smell of the lamp" (as the Greeks used to say), but they show that the material learned remains a foreign substance in the

On following the philosopher's thought

Philosophy is the opposite of history. Every piece of philosophical writing is primarily addressed by the author to himself. Its purpose is not to select from among his thoughts those of which he is certain and to express those, but the very opposite: to fasten upon the difficulties and obscurities in which he finds himself involved, and try, if not to solve or remove them, at least to understand them better. . . .

The philosophers who have had the deepest instinct for style have repeatedly shrunk from adopting the form of a lecture or instructive address, and chosen instead that of a dialogue in which the work of self-criticism is parcelled out among the dramatis personae, or a meditation in which the mind communes with itself, or a dialectical process where the initial position is modified again and again as difficulties in it come to light. . . .

There is accordingly a difference in attitude towards what he reads between the reader of historical literature and the reader of philosophical. In reading the historians, we consult them. We apply to the store of learning in their minds for a grant of knowledge to make good the lack in our own. We do not seek to follow the processes of thought by which they came to know these things; we can only do that by becoming equally accomplished historians ourselves, and this we cannot do by reading their books, but only by working as they have worked at the original sources. In reading the philosophers, we 'follow' them: that is, we understand what they think, and reconstruct in ourselves, so far as we can, the processes by which they have come to think it. There is an intimacy in the latter relation which can never exist in the former. What we demand of the historian is a product of his thought: what we demand of the philosopher is his thought itself. The reader of a philosophical work is committing himself to the enterprise of living through the same experience that his author lived through: if for lack sympathy, patience, or any other quality he cannot do this, his reading is worthless.

—R.G. Collingwood in *An Essay on Philosophical Method.*

learner. It is seldom that the author gives the impression that he knows what he is talking about and that he cares whether or not he knows. The subject-matter is extracted from a book but not really appropriated to a person; it is not really *in the mind.*

Most academic production, even when it satisfies academic standards, is not production of consumer's goods, nor even capital goods for the producer. It remains lifeless, without the expressive functions of songs, dances, and story telling. Learning to perform in this way seems to me to have little relation to education and leaves both teacher and student dissatisfied, not so much with each other as with the whole process.

Learning, in order to be educative, must be an integral part of a personality. It is experience that transforms a human organism into a person, but conventional schooling adds little to genuine experience. To the student, studying seems to be "learning the hard way." To a more experienced adult, it is the harder knocks of practical problems that are really "the hard way" as well as the most common way of learning. Whether hard or soft, it is the lessons of experience that are the most valuable and memorable; they become part of our very being. The aim of schooling should be to help a professional learner to overcome obstacles by skillful thinking instead of by still harder experience, in order to avoid the bitter and often tragic reflections that come from stupid stumbling. In Hullfish's phrase, reflective thinking should bear cultural fruit; school lessons should be those which can be built into the working capital of experience.

Occasionally schooling produces a learned person; this is one of its minor cultural fruits. Such a person is in danger of making only pedantic use of his experience; he exhibits his learning as an excuse for not being a personality. Such disembodied minds have a modest function in a culture. Like dictionaries, encyclopedias, computers, and other lifeless bodies of knowledge they have real utility. However, a person who has become learned, and knows it, is usually a person in the past tense. He appears to be educated, whereas he merely wears an education along with the rest of his clothes. It would be a cultural tragedy if schools were primarily factories of such scholars. How pathetic it is when schools become so successful in making students that their graduates remain students for life, doomed to serving life-sentences in school. I recall once when I was in graduate school listening to Professor Dewey explain his favorite theme, that school should be continuous with life, a fellow-student burst out in despair: "But Professor Dewey! Some of us want to get *out* of school." To which Dewey replied in his quiet, slow, reflective manner: "Well, you're not in school *now*." It was part of Dewey's genius that he never acted as though we were in school. He used the so-called classroom as a place where he could converse with God or some other obstacle. The class was seldom in his line of vision.

I tell these tales out of school not in a spirit of rebellion or even of criticism, for I have enjoyed many good schools. My aim is to warn ourselves against exaggerating their educative value. There is the large quantity of so-called "basic" learning that comes before school, then a few years follow of "study-periods," and then comes the long career of postgraduate learning. The normal product of a life of learning is not a learned scholar, but an educated person, for whom lessons yield experience, and problems bring out personality.

This leads me finally to say something about education as a process. A well-educated person does not think of himself as possessing an education, any more than an educated scholar thinks of himself as learned. A person whose mind is part of himself and whose thinking is a way of gaining experience is always in the course of being educated. He is not a professional learner but an habitual thinker, and what he knows shows itself not so much in what he remembers as in how he responds to a situation.

You are all familiar with the old definition of education: Education is what you have left when you have forgotten what you learned. This is an uneducated way of stating a truth. Let me try to say it more precisely, less concisely. The "educative process" is a name for the personal appropriation of whatever is experienced as significant. Such an organization of experience is not a system of ideas or a philosophy but a living integration of meanings into a personality structure. The growth of character and mind is the net product or the cumulative assimilation of thinking and learning. All depends on how a person learns, how he uses what is learned, how well he can draw on experience, and how wide the range of his experience is. A well-educated person is never a finished product. He continues throughout life to absorb, or make his own, whatever cultural resources, natural opportunities, new experiences stimulate his reflective thinking; this appropriated capital of thoughtfully ordered experience is available for seeking and interpreting new events and situations. Education is not a storage of knowledge, but an ability to use knowledge in living intelligently.

Education in this large sense was formerly called "cultivation" and a cultivated person was called "cultured." These terms now have a stilted sound and are associated with the class of persons known as the elite or the intelligentsia, a class which makes a more or less professional exhibition of its superior achievements. To avoid such class consciousness and snobbery I prefer, and common usage prefers, to speak simply of an

Education as cultivation of the power to think

Academic courses which teach men to manipulate laboratory apparatus but not to think scientifically, to carry out intricate computations but not to think mathematically, to remember dates but not to think historically, to summarize philosophical arguments but not to think critically—these advance no man toward liberal education. To be perfectly honest, one must admit that higher education has lost repute because so many offerings in the liberal arts and sciences have failed to provide the intellectual discipline which they promise. But the answer, surely, is not to abandon the ideal of disciplined intelligence in favor of an educational program that even on the surface offers nothing to liberate and strengthen men's minds. The answer is not to banish the scholarly and scientific disciplines, but to hold them rigorously to their task.

Liberal education means deliberate cultivation of the power to think. Because clear thinking is systematic thinking, liberal education involves the logical organization of knowledge. Students must be brought to see the structure of the science they are learning. To know a few facts about lines and angles and triangles is not to know plane geometry; the essential thing is to grasp the orderly process by which a group of postulates can be made to reveal their implications in theorems of increasing complexity. To know a few episodes in the past is not to know history; the essential thing is to comprehend the forces that are at work through a long sequence of events, and to incorporate the perspective of time into one's day-to-day judgments. Instruction need not always follow a strictly logical or chronological order. But to leave a subject without having understood the order inherent in it, is to leave it without seizing hold of the most significant and the most useful of its characteristics.

—from Arthur E. Bestor, *Educational Wastelands* (Urbana: U. of Illinois Press, 1953).

educated person, meaning by this both more and less than a person of higher schooling. An educated person need not be learned, and seldom is.

However, it is important to understand that being educated in this sense implies "higher" education. Any real education is *higher*. To refer back to our text, it takes time for elementary schooling and learning to show itself as education. Education comes close to meaning what Aristotle meant by *eudaimonia* (in case you wish to trace the idea back to the Greeks)—life well lived. To live an educated life or to be an educated person requires certain advantages and opportunities, but these do not imply that education is restricted to an "upper" class. The educative process, to be sure, requires a certain amount and kind of travel, for the sense organs first of all must be exposed to educative sensations, to fresh experiences, cultural variations, getting out of physical ruts. But even more important are the

opportunities for getting out of mental ruts and for wandering in the realms of literature, music and the other fine arts, and in religion when it is *of an educative kind*. This means more than mere contact with these realms, it means dwelling in them until one is at home in them. *Having the distant present* is for an educated person an essential feature of his very being.

I insist on this conception of education, "the liberal appropriation of the actual, the past, the distant and the imaginative in both nature and culture," because I wish to make two applications of the idea and to relate them to the educational ideas of Hullfish. The first application is a criticism of the concept of "the educator." Are there educators? There are school masters, administrators of schools, colleges, and universities; there are critics of educational systems, educational theorists. But do they really do any educating? Can an education be man-made? Is not the educative process a creation of divine grace, or a natural growth, or a cultural fruit—call it what you will—but not an artifact? No man can educate another, nor does he educate himself. There are self-made men, to be sure, but they are not educated. The educated self is the outcome or fruit of the educative process, as Hullfish well names it.

The person is not the educational agent, but the culmination of a process half natural, half cultural. We may be educators in the sense that we are digestors. Cultural assimilation is analogous to physiological assimilation; the latter process culminates in a healthy organism, the former in an educated person. Neither process can be performed by one person for another. Just as each individual must take care in the choice of food, so each person must take the necessary measures to promote his own education. But the process itself, the actual appropriation, is a gradual growth or kind of experience. Experience is not made; it happens. School masters, teachers, books and laboratories, travel and communication—these are all educational aids or instruments, but only in this sense are they educators. Education is not a profession as teaching is. Though Hullfish is known as an eminent educator, I believe he would agree with me in distinguishing between the eminently educated person that he was, and the eminent expert that he was in teaching the arts of teaching, learning, and thinking. I cite one passage from a speech of his to members of his profession, which shows that he was well aware of the dangers of confusing education with indoctrination:

> To stand firm for the right to create educational conditions within both the school and culture on which the continuing growth of free men depends is to take a positive position, a professional one. . . . It represents . . . the acceptance of the unique and difficult assignment given the schools by free men.[2]

Here he clearly recognizes the importance of creating "educational conditions" in school and society so that men can become free through education. I have not emphasized the relation of education to freedom and democracy for you are familiar with Hullfish's emphasis on this relation. Liberation and education are aspects of a single process, and they require the conditions which the nature of the process indicates Men are not created either free or equal, but under favorable conditions freedom and self-development emerge as cultural fruit.

The second and last point I wish to make is a very elementary one and yet one that raises difficult practical problems: a teacher should be an educated person. This is easier said than done. A teacher should be trained to teach, of course, and he should know his subject; but he may have both these qualifications and still not be educated. He can be an instructor or coach without being a personal, living example of an education. He may help students learn without stimulating them to use the learning educationally.

It is expecting too much of a teacher that he be an educator, but if he be not himself educated, his students get the wrong idea of what they are doing in school. All of us know teachers who are professionally competent and yet fail to be useful in the educative process. They bring no "cultural fruit" to the classroom, if I may repeat Hullfish's apt words. All of us know literate persons who are mere graduates and alumni who rejoice that their school days are over and who imagine that they have or had an education. Unless they have assigned lessons, they have no occasions for thinking reflectively or understanding real problems; they become dull after graduation.

Only a minority of educated persons return to school and enjoy teaching. This is as it ought to be. But there is a danger that students become teachers before they have had an opportunity to be educated. The need for educated, or as Hullfish calls them "reconstructed," teachers is especially critical in our secondary school systems. It is during adolescence that students have need especially of working with educated persons, so that they have immediate contact and acquaintance with persons whose actions and conversations are evidences of education. A teacher is very important during extra-curricular activities, for it is these activities that evidently require education. It is not enough to teach reflective thinking; such thinking must be conspicuous in action, in habits, in character, and in communication. Only teachers whose education has been built in without being stored in memory mechanically, who are more than teachers, can create what Hullfish refers to as "educational conditions in the schoolroom." If we as citizens take this problem seriously, we shall provide more liberally and intelligently for the education of prospective teachers, presumably during the years in "normal school." They are entitled to educational opportunities as persons, but they have a professional obligation to promote their education as part of their teacher training.

I have studiously avoided the current talk about "general education" because those who are trying to promote general education are trying to make of it a subject-matter for the school room. This is dead wrong and futile. A genuine education is general, to be sure, but it is general not in an academic sense, but in the sense that it must permeate the person generally. It is not general unless it is personal and it is not personal when it is merely studied. The process takes time as well as intelligence. And that is why we should conceive our educational system as going far beyond the process of studying, beyond the formal learning, to include the bearing and enjoyment of cultural fruits.

Footnotes

1. *Reflective Thinking*, p. 209.
2. *Reflective Thinking*, p. 256.

Literate Thinking and Schooling

Judith Langer

Literacy is generally associated with the ability to read and write. This is the common dictionary definition, the mark of literacy in society-at-large, and the one we most often apply to schooling. However, we can look at literacy in a broader and educationally more productive way: as the ability to think and reason within a particular society. As Heath (1983), Scribner and Cole (1980), and Vygotsky (1978) suggest, because the practices of literacy and ways of understanding literacy acts depend upon the social conditions in which they are learned, the skills, concepts, and ways of thinking that an individual develops reflect the uses and approaches to literacy that permeate the society in which the individual is a participant. In this view, literacy is culture specific.

For the student, the school is an influential cultural environment. If schools wish to prepare students to participate fully in the adult community, they need to focus on the ways of thinking that are involved in the many uses of literacy by people within society. They need to use approaches to literacy instruction that will insure that these different ways of thinking are an integral part of the school context. For example, in the Vai society described by Scribner and Cole (1980), the people need and value memorization and recitation in order to learn the Koran in Arabic. The appropriate mode of instruction in this context would be to train students to memorize. However, if the uses of literacy require reflection and problem-solving, like the uses of English in the same Vai culture, instruction

should help the students develop those kinds of abilities. There is no right or wrong literacy, just the one that is, more or less, responsive to the demands of a particular culture. Scribner and Cole (1980) and Traugott (1987) point out that particular ways of thinking are not a result of literacy *per se*. Rather, ways of thinking reflect the particular oral and written ways of solving problems, organizing knowledge, and communicating that are particular to a given culture. These ways of thinking are learned early, have the potential to be (but are not always) reinforced by schools, and have enormous consequences for the acquisition and uses of language and knowledge throughout life. When the literacy of the classroom and the literacy needed in society differ markedly, we need to ask serious questions about the goals of schooling.

The current era, for example, requires that students acquire the kinds of critical thinking skills that are needed to use the communication devices and technologies we meet on a daily basis in our everyday living and in entry-level jobs (Langer, 1987). These new demands have been discussed by Noyelle (1985) who describes the shift in both the American workplace and in daily life from tasks involving manual skills to those requiring cognitive processes. Schools, Noyelle suggests, need to reflect these societal shifts by training students in the more flexible thinking skills they will need for entry into today's job market. If we are to respond to these concerns as well as other cultural contexts for literacy, literacy instruction needs to go much beyond the acts

Writing as reasoning

A syllogism, the classic unit of reasoning, is in itself a small paragraph. I want to say something about Socrates, and what I want to say about him is that despite his great wisdom, he is still immortal. Why is he mortal? Because all men are mortal, and Socrates is a man, as I can go on to demonstrate in a paragraph on characteristics. Much of our thought concerns "somes" rather than the "all" referred to in this syllogism, but the pattern can be adapted.

In other words, reasoning means giving reasons—that is, it deals with the relations between statements, and these relations are of a few basic kinds: basically of cause or purpose—*if* this, therefore this, or this is so *because,* or of choice—this or this, but both are impossible at once; or of association—this *and* this go along with this. In other words, these are the kinds of possible simultaneity or sequence of statements. Once a student recognizes that his own thought moves in these basic relations—perhaps just because he is a man and all men are mortal—he will be apt to enjoy both the art and the social force of the simple reasoning process of the paragraph. His planning our outlining will show first what main point or predication he is planning to make about his subject, then the main blocks of material he will use to support it, with pro connections *and, or, if,* and con connections *but, or, though;* and finally a new main point, revised from the first hypothesis in the light of the evidence as it has developed.

—from Josephine Miles, "The Use of Reason," *Teachers College Record*, April 1, 1962.

of reading and writing, and to each culturally useful ways of literate thinking as well.

Because literate thinking is a reflection of the uses of literacy within a particular culture, the kinds of intellectual functions with which we are familiar, e.g., analysis and synthesis, are not necessarily the benchmarks of literate thinking in all cultures; ways of thinking follow use and function. We need, instead, to understand that ways of thinking are affected by culture and experience, and that literacy events in school provide an important set of contexts within which students may gain appropriate experience. Attention to cultural ways of thinking associated with literacy allows teachers to focus on how students think, as well as on the skills they use to read and write. It permits teachers and students to regard reading and writing as tools that enable, but do not insure, literate thinking.

When a group of American students read a social studies textbook and then discuss the contents and the implications, most people would say that the students are engaging in literate thinking (within the norms of this culture). But, what if the discussion had occurred after the students had seen a television news report about the same topic? I would still want to claim that the students had engaged in literate thinking even though they had neither read nor written. Now, imagine a group of students who do not know how to read or write in English or another language engaged in the very same conversation about the television news report. I would claim that they too would have engaged in literate thinking. In contrast, imagine that the students had read the same social studies text and then completed end-of-chapter questions by locating information in the text and copying the information the questions asked them to itemize. I would claim that the kinds of literacy in this activity do not reflect the kinds of school literacy that, based on the many reports and articles in both the professional and public press, are needed and valued by American society today. That activity does not involve culturally useful literate behavior, even if the students get the answers right.

These examples highlight the distinction between literacy as the act of reading and writing and literacy as ways of thinking. It is the culturally useful way of thinking, not the act of reading or writing, that is most important in the development of literacy. Literate thinking manifests itself in different ways in oral and written language in different societies, and educators need to understand these ways of thinking if they are to build, bridge, and facilitate transitions among ways of thinking.

How well are our schools currently doing in teaching the more thoughtful literacy skills being called for by many researchers and educators? Results such as those from the National Assessment of Educational Progress (NAEP, 1985) continue to suggest that schools are successful in teaching what they have set out to teach. Whether by accident or design, school curricula and the tests that go with them have rewarded relatively simple performance, and have undervalued the attainment of more thoughtful skills. They have been driven by a model of literacy that focuses on discrete skills and bits of information instead of big ideas and deeper understandings.

It is my argument that student performance such as reported by NAEP is no surprise, since these are the ways of thinking that are highlighted in the curriculum, supported by the instructional materials, and reinforced by the tests we use and the grades we give. The culture of schooling will need to change—to model, support, and value thoughtfulness—for students to learn to think in ways that are responsive to the requirements of our society.

References

Heath, S. B, (1983), *Ways with Words*. NY: Cambridge University Press.

Langer, J. A. (1987), A sociocognitive perspective on literacy. In J. A. Langer (Ed.), *Language, Literacy and Culture: Issues of Schooling and Society*. Norwood, NJ: Ablex.

National Assessment of Educational Progress (1985). *The Reading Report Card*. Princeton, NJ: Educational Testing Service.

Noyelle, T. J. (1985, August). The new technology and the new economy: Some implications for equal employment opportunity. Paper presented to the Panel on Technology and Woman's Employment of the National Research Council.

Scribner, S. & Cole, J. (1980). *The Psychology of Literacy* Cambridge, MA: Harvard University Press.

Traugott, E. C. (1987). Language and language change: The special case of speech act verbs. In J. A. Langer (Ed.), *Language, Literacy, and Culture: Issues of Society and Schooling*. Norwood, NJ: Ablex.

Vygotsky, L. S. (1978). *Mind in Society*. Cambridge, MA: Harvard University Press.

On Being A Meaning-Maker: Young Children's Experiences of Reading

Valerie Polakow

"Well, see," said five-year-old Sasha, "it just happened one day and suddenly it felt like 'Yippee, I CAN READ'," and he threw up his arms and laughed, "and it made me feel different inside my tummy. I felt kind of powerful."

"I remember when I knew I could read," six-year-old Toby told me, "it was when I first moved into this house—a couple of days after I moved here and I remember that day, it was in the middle of the day and I did like it—'cause it makes you feel confident—like you can do more things when you do it."

What does literacy mean to a young child and how can we come to understand the child's perspective of reading and the child's experience of stories? For a young child, the world *is* storied, peopled by dragons and witches, wizards and Hobbits; her life-world is filled with drama, infused with horizons that Yehudi Menuhin has called the place of the fourth dimension.[1] Why then do we assume that reading begins with alphabetization; that it is a set of observational skills, to be developed in isolation from story, from engagement, from the drama of lived-experience?

Child-Life as Storied

In his essay, "The Storyteller,"[2] Walter Benjamin laments the decline of the communicability of experience and points out that dramatic narrative is gradually disappearing from living speech. Experience he tells us, has fallen in value, giving way to the rise of information which lays prompt claim to verifiability. Reading scores, grade level assessment, student-reader strategies, comprehension as measured by workbook decoding skills, all can be evaluated and debated within the input-output taxonomic models that swarm over our pedagogical landscape. But as Sartre pointed out years ago in his study of the emotions, fact-gathering leads to fact-gathering, and nothing more.[3] A taxonomy of reading skills or a meta-analysis of reader strategies, tells us about skills and objectives and strategies but cannot tell us about the experiential world of the child or the storied life-world of childhood, which we vitiate as we rob children of "storyness" in their school reading curricula; for "it is as if something that seemed inalienable to us, the securest amongst our possessions, were taken from us: the ability to exchange experiences."[4] It is the ability to exchange experiences with Dorothy and the Strawman, with the little boy and his velveteen rabbit, with Tigerflower where "everything is turned around . . . Where nothing is the way it should be or the way it once was." Yet children, who from earliest babyhood have struggled to name the world, are robbed of the word and instead we present them with tasks, objectives, and skills to be mastered and we term that classroom literacy! Yet how do children experience reading? What do they think about their world of words? What does reading mean to a young child entering kindergarten and encountering perhaps for the first time, a formalized curriculum designed to teach them the Word?

I was curious, and at the same time astonished, that I could find very little in the reading literature that sought the child's perspective of reading. There is a burgeoning literature of adultcentric theories drawn from behavioral and cognitive development traditions. There are numerous studies dealing with how and why children use certain strategies to perform reading tasks—but nowhere did I hear the child's voice, articulating his perspective on the question. I was reminded of Husserl's injunction, "Zu den Zachen Zelbst," (to the things themselves), and so I began with four five-year-old children—four friends who became my informants. All the children attend the same public school kindergarten in the morning and the same childcare center in the afternoon. Thus it is with Sasha, Toby, Liz, and Laura that another vision of lived-literacy begins. As Gareth Matthews points out so wisely in his *Dialogues with Children*, "What has not been taken seriously, or even widely conceived, is the possibility of tackling with children, in a relationship of mutual respect, the naively profound questions of philosophy."[5] Similarly, what has not been taken seriously in our current national literacy crisis, are young children's perspectives. What follows is an interpretive account of children's reflections on becoming literate.

The Interview Setting

I arranged to speak with each of the children at home, alone. The rituals that we set up—of owning the tape, operating the tape recorder and shaping the interview were critical to the participatory atmosphere. Each child wrote his or her name on the cassette tape and carefully dated it. The tape was theirs. I promised to return what they made at a later date. Toby, Liz and Laura all chose to be interviewed in their own rooms. Sasha chose the living room as we were alone in the house and he wanted to eat snacks during our interview. I began by reading a story of their choice and then asked them to read or tell me about one of their favorite books. Each child took the interview very seriously, thoughtfully pausing to think about certain questions and philosophically reflecting on others. Toby, perhaps, summed up our interactions best when he told me at the outset, "I know what an interview is—it's when somebody tells someone more about them than the other person knows." He was right. The children were my "reading specialists."

On Being A Reader:

Sasha and Toby were fluent readers in the conventional sense, Liz and Laura stood poised on the brink—identifying a selection of words and memorizing long texts. Yet all four children considered themselves *readers*. When I asked them to read me their favorite books—they all chose stories that they could either *read* or *tell*; stories imbued with humor, narrative power, and personal meaning. For Toby and Sasha there is a reflective awareness of what the world was like before and after reading.

Sasha: Before I had my own kind of spelling and I read stories in my own homemade books—see what I think happened is I spelt the same way I sounded it.

Val: So you'd think in your head how it sounded.

Sasha: uh-uh

Val: Is that the beginning of learning to read?

Sasha: Well, see, when I was writing like this I was learning to read and I was spelling my own way and I would only read the words in the way I made them—not the way *books* did.

Val: How did you change from spelling your way to the book way?

Sasha: Oh, when I started getting used to *Ant and Bee* and reading *Frog and Toad*—then later, see, when I saw book words *I could just break through and spell through the words*—like you know, a few days ago I found out "difficult" (smiles delightedly) which is a very difficult word! Right?

Toby, recollecting his own experience, as we read "The Wild Baby," tells me:

I can always figure out words one way or another—I can sound it out or I can just figure it out—before I couldn't—See I remember 'cause I know the sounds of all these words now (points to book).

Val: But how do you figure out a new word?

Toby: I sound it out, and I hear myself, like if I was deaf-like if I need a hearing aid—and I tell myself and then it sounds in my head.

Liz "reads" me several books during our interview. She has *Angelina Ballerina* virtually memorized and as I watch her "read" the text, I notice that she draws clues from the pictures as well as key phrases such as "too busy doing curtsies on the bed," or "people came from far and wide." When I later ask her if she can pick out words like "people" and "curtsies," she does so but has trouble identifying simple words like "on," "the," and "bed." Her clues come from

the context of meaning as well as the engaging sound of certain phrases that are funny and out of the ordinary. Similarly, in a Sesame Street book, Liz picks out "Sesame," and "Street," and "Bird," but has trouble identifying "big." Her clues are derived from the enjoyment of text and an astute memory for interesting words.

Val: How do you know how to read that story, Liz?

Liz: Well, I read this book a lot of times and also I see the picture in my head and how it sounds in my ears—and also *'cause it's my favorite book*. I always know the words in my *favorite* books.

Liz's attraction to humor in story is born out in another conversation when she asks me to read her *Big Foot*. Every few pages of text, Big Foot makes a sound, "Kerplop, Kerplop." Each time I read that, Liz laughs and tries to find the words on the page with her finger and correctly identifies them each time.

I notice a similar process occurring with Laura who tells me, "I got to read by listening to stories and also by writing words," and she proceeds to draw up a list of rhyming "et" words—"net, vet, (that's an animal doctor), set, bet. I can read them 'cause I made them."

Later, when Laura and I are reading stories, Laura fetches a book about *Grandma and Daisies* saying, "I think I know part of this one." She proceeds to read the text, remembering key phrases like, "Mary calls them common old weeds." When I ask her to find "Mary" and "weeds" and "common," she correctly identifies them, but like Liz, has difficulty identifying simple words like "on," and "to."

Val: Laura, how do you know how to read these words like "daisy" and "weeds"?

Laura: Well, see, I just know, 'cause *I like that book and it's in my brain*.

Val: But how does your brain tell you how to know hard words like that?

Laura: I look at the first letter and the last letter and then I know what the word is.
Val: How about the middle of the word?
Laura: No, I don't really bother about that!

As both Laura and Liz classify themselves as readers, I took their assumptions seriously. In reality, they were readers of texts that they liked and enjoyed. They could read the story to me, to themselves, to others, with vivid expression and full dramatic power. They could live the meaning of the story, or as Benjamin writes, they were sinking the thing into the life of the storyteller. Liz thought for a long time when I asked her when she began to read, and she replied:

> I learnt a long time ago, at somebody's house, and the somebody is my grandma—now I know how to read, but I used to not know—and now I know it feels different inside (pause) and now I also know how to tie a bow. (We discuss bow-tying, and then she continues): Reading stories makes me kind of happy and sad!

Empowerment and the Storied Lived-World

Being the teller and reader is an empowering act for these children. They are engaging with the text and, at the same time, transforming it and themselves in the telling. Themes of "feeling powerful," "confidence," "being happy or sad," feeling an attraction to certain words and their representative lived-situations, give a sense of empowerment. As Toby remarked, "Now I can be the reader and someone else is the listener!" Feeling in charge of the text, turning the pages when *you* decide, showing the pictures, being the first to tell of a situation, all feature as important components of being the *reader-teller* of texts. Clearly these children's experiences of literacy have a long history—a storied-history, where in their homes bedtime stories have been a consistent ritual. At daycare, storytime has been a daily experience for several years. They have led sto-

ried lives, experiencing creating and transforming meanings into worlds that transcend the dailyness of their everyday lives. Hence reading has long been part of their experience, tied to engagement and involvement with narrative, myth and fable. Now, *reading* the text involves a transformation from being a listener to an actor—to an agent of other's storyness. "It's different now, because I don't have to pay attention to someone else reading it—I just pay attention to listening to myself and I get to be the chooser of the stories, too," remarked Sasha.

The stories that the children choose to read are stories that are humorous, or "scarey," dramatic narratives with complex plots, as well as those that speak to their lived-realities. Liz, for example, told me *Angelina Ballerina* was one of her favorites—and I suspect that part of her attraction to the story lies in her identification with ballet—as she herself takes ballet lessons, and frequently prances around her home in a leotard and tights. None of these themes described are different from the adult experience of text-engagement and should not surprise us. However, what does give cause for surprise is the violation of these lived-storied experiences when the children confront behavioral skill-oriented textbooks in their classrooms. Consider one of the kindergarten reading series: *Funny Little Ant*. The instructions to the teacher suggest bringing in some ants, showing flashcards with clue pictures and "never have the child guess what the word is as a first impression can be a lasting one"! The clue vocabulary is given at the beginning of the book:

and the text reads:

Ant hill
to big little
walk funny

Little ant
Big ant
Walk, little ant, walk
Little ant hill
Big ant hill
Walk to little ant hill
Walk to big ant hill
Funny little ant
Funny big ant

If we examine this text as an example, we see how reading is reduced to word recognition separated from story engagement. The words are simple and the assumption is that giving a clue vocabulary with pictures will stimulate visual association. Yet, all four children that I spoke to stress the importance of complexity which was tied to *liking* their *stories*. In fact, Liz and Laura were learning to read by identifying difficult and unusual sounding words using clues that related to meaning not visual stimuli. They enjoyed the challenge of complexity. It is interesting to listen to the critique that Liz and Sasha have of the other reading curriculum texts which are modelled on similar assumptions of simplicity.

Liz: The stories are too boring—they're so dumb and boring . . . and I hate those dopey books and the worksheets . . . We have to sit there and do this and do that and worksheets all the time.

Val: What do you think kids could tell the people who write those books?

Liz: Tell the teachers not to get those books anymore.

Val: What books should the teachers get?

Liz: Get the books that are more interesting so kids will like to read the stories.

Sasha has similar criticisms and compares these books unfavorably to an engaging story series, *Ant and Bee* that he learned to read with:

Val: Sasha, if you were the boss of the class, what would you change?

Sasha: I'd get the *Ant and Bee* books—cause the story is fun and the kid reads the red words and the big person reads the black words and you *both* read the story *together*. And it has much more pages. In kindergarten the books are dumb and there are little papers with the words on and you have to write them and it's so boring—I sit there and try and make up my own story out of the words so it's more interesting. (He pauses) You know what—I think it's boring to read so early—you know why?

Val: Why?

Sasha: Because then when the other kids are learning when they're five and you already know how to read, you have to wait and wait for everything that the teacher's trying to teach—

Val: What is the teacher trying to teach?

Sasha: To teach the kids to read—but I could do it better and so could other kids who know how to read. They should let the kids teach other kids.

Val: Do you think the kids need to be taught or will they learn it anyway?

Sasha: Well, you need help to know the sounds of letters and to have stories read to you so you remember . . . *but then it just happens inside of you and suddenly you just know how to read!*

The De-Meaning of Reading:

Reading curriculum specialists assume that breaking reading down into a set of skills involving word recognition, word-analysis, decoding, and comprehension mirrors the process of the child's development as a reader. But these children are telling us that complexity, narrative and text-engagement are the characteristics that shape their development as readers and which speak to their history of storyness. In some ways, the demeaning of reading for children speaks to a larger issue, which Paulo Freire articulates in his radical pedagogy of literacy when he writes:

> . . . acquiring literacy does not involve memorizing sentences, words or syllables—lifeless objects disconnected to an existential universe—but rather is an act of creation and recreation, a self transformation producing a state of intervention in one's context.

When we consider Freire's work that he began in the late fifties in Brazil and continued beyond his exile after the 1964 *coup d'état*, several characteristics of his pedagogy become clear: his starting point is always the existential landscape of the people, who become co-learners together with him in the reconstruction of a reality to which their literacy can be put to practical and transformative use. By asking the peasants to describe and create in artistic form concrete images of their lived-worlds, a re-naming of reality begins, which leads to the formation of *generative words* grounded in the people's reality; hence literacy becomes a process of empowerment. As Freire has always been quick to point out, the peasants were not illiterate, rather they were dealphabetized, marginalized from their society, residing in a culture of silence. Alphabetization, Freire argued, must be connected to a liberatory literacy, a socio-political and cultural transformative act for "to speak a true word is to transform the world."[7] Naming the world is also reading the world—and while alphabetization skills are a necessary component for transformative action, they are also mere means to a greater end.

For a child then, who literally begins life naming the world to which she is born, reading the world is but a continuation of that transformative action. Alphabetization or the acquisition of such skills, are clearly secondary to the intentional meaning-making that the reading of a storied world involves.

Atmosphere and Mood

The storied experiences that many young children share, exemplified by these four children, have a quality, an essential atmosphere that is frequently tied to intimacy, warmth, and private time spent alone with an adult. I found it interesting that during our interviews, the children attempted to recreate a space and time that was ours. We sat together *alone*, in their private places. On two different occasions when the telephone rang, Toby and Liz answered the phone and abruptly informed the respective callers that they were doing something special and could not talk. The images that the children have of storytimes are warm and engaging, memories of laps, of cuddling, of exclusive adult attention.

The mood of evocation that surrounds story—of smells, of touch, of sounds, of vivid images is abruptly compressed as the atmosphere of "storyness" is replaced by the atomism of words—words lost to the demeaning landscape of objectives, outcomes, and grade level assessment. As Ien Dienske[8] points out, we live our entire lives in both a private and social atmosphere—what Heidegger has called an *Existential*. With the young child, this atmosphere is experienced in moving circles of meaning as story experiences are appropriated and transformed and become part of the life-world. How does this fundamental mood change when institutional reading begins?

Lived Literacy

Letters which previously have the status of mysterious and intriguing identities now become flat unidimensional characters. Consider this observation as illustrative:

> At four years old, I observed Sasha experimenting with letters and numbers, frequently blending the two systems together. The multiple possibilities that he saw in letters extended

across many dimensions of his perceptual world. When writing K for Kimberley (the name of a friend at daycare) Sasha turned K into X and said, "Now I have a railroad track crossing," and followed that with a drawing of a train.

The sign for a child, is also a signifier of a concrete set of images, where letters and numbers can graphically represent everyday objects. Do we as adults see the multiple possibilities in the letter K? In mastering literacy, we believe that letters must occupy a unidimensional plane—such as the graphic. But for a child, numbers and letters are open systems, capable of transformation. Letters and numbers dance and sing on Sesame Street, why not elsewhere? Indeed, letters have a life of their own. Consider Elizabeth Bishop's memory of her own experience with numbers and letters as she reconstructs her childhood in Primer Class in Nova Scotia:

At first I could not get past the letter G, which for some time I felt was far enough to go. My alphabet made a satisfying short song, and I didn't want to spoil it—It was wonderful to see that the letters each had different expressions, and that the same letter had different expressions at different times. Sometimes the two capitals of my name looked miserable, slumped down and sulky, but at others they turned fat and cheerful, almost with roses in their cheeks.[9]

Elizabeth Bishop, at five years old, creates a storied world for her letters, in much the same way that young children, experimenting with form shape and meaning, give life to theirs.

Yet, these critical moments of experimentation, of thoughtfulness, of engaging with living letters and living stories are frequently denied to children in a formalized reading curriculum. Unfortunately this erosion of lived literacy has its prologue in many childcare centers in North America, where the bureaucratization of experience extends not only to schooling, but to two and three year olds drilled in so-called reading readiness. Consider one typical example drawn from my field observations at a franchised childcare center in Michigan:

During storytime for the three-year-old day care children, the teacher showed the children a picture with a coffee-pot adjacent to a drum and asked, "Is the coffee pot a drum?" No one answered. The teacher replied, "No, is this (pointing to drum) a drum? Yes, Why? Because he pounds on it. Is a house a park bench? No. Why? Because you can't sit on it!"[10]

The above lesson continued where the teacher both asked and answered her own absurd questions. The lesson apparently was designed to teach children discrimination skills in matching object and function. For the fidgeting and inattentive children, storytime was clearly anathema to story.

The Child as Intentional Meaning-Maker

Beekman describes how, from a phenomenological perspective, the young child is an active intentional builder of meaning, an initiator of relationships with a world of objects and with an intersubjective social world.[11] Storytelling places this lived-world in narrative time, and embeds the child as a literary actor—a listener and transformer of meaning. And as Maxine Greene[12] writes: It is the engagement with art and literature that empower us to move beyond ourselves, enabling us to read the world and stirring us to 'wide-awakeness.' By depriving the child of these encounters, by demeaning and destorying reading, do we not vitiate the child's existential experience of literacy?

When we observe the way in which young children can creatively transform the texts that they engage with, we realize that Sartre was right when he remarked that to read a book is to write it. Young children also create their own texts as a prelude to becoming actual readers. Toby showed me several books that he had made together with his mother out of his "own stories." Sasha frequently referred to his own "home-made stories" and "home-made books." Liz and Laura told me how they knew how to read the words that they made. This appropriation of words and the acts of transformation by the children are themes that echo in Michael Armstrong's[13] work done by Sylvia Ashton-Warner[14] in which she and her students became co-creators of their existential life-texts in New Zealand.

Freire, in reconstructing his own childhood memories writes:

> Deciphering the world flowed naturally from reading my particular world; it was not something super-imposed on it. I learned to read and write on the ground of the backyard in my house, in the shade of the mango trees, with words from my world rather than the wider world of my parents. The earth was my blackboard, sticks my chalk. [As he later describes his experience with his teacher he fondly recollects:] Reading the word, the phrase, the sentence, never entailed a break with reading the world . . . With her, reading the word meant reading the world-world."

Lived-Literacy and Institutional Literacy

For Sasha, Toby, Liz and Laura, reading *is* a "word-world" experience, integrally tied to the storyness of their lives. They engage with narrative, they laugh at the "Wild Baby" and turn wide-eyed with fear when the Wicked Witch of the West appears. In short, *they live their stories.* At this point in their young lives, reading still remains a storied experience to be distinguished from "dopey readers," and "dumb workbooks."

For now, they stand outside of institutional literacy—partly because of their home experience where stories feature prominently and too, because they attend an unusually open and flexible kindergarten and childcare center. But what of their child-brothers and sisters in other families, in other schools, in other childcare settings? How long can lived-literacy be maintained in the face of the institutionalization of the word—dominated by Houghton Mifflin, Holt Rinehart and Winston, and others of the corporate world? For it is in the bureaucratization of experience, the fragmentation of engagement with text, the coercive breakdown of lived-literacy that the child suffers the loss of the "word-world" and the transformative possibilities of meaning-making.

Perhaps Lewis Carroll foresaw this all long ago:

> The question is, said Alice, whether you can make words mean so many different things. The question is, said Humpty-Dumpty, which is to be master that's all.

Reference Notes

1. Yehudi Menuhin in the *Preface* to the enchanting children's book. *Tiger Flower* by Robert Vavra and Fleur Coles (New York: William Collins Ltd, 1968).

2. Walter Benjamin, "The Storyteller," in *Illuminations* (New York: Schocken, 1969).

3. Jean-Paul Sartre, *The Emotions: Outline of a Theory* (New York: The Philosophical Library, 1948).

4. See Benjamin, "The StoryTeller," p. 83.

5. Gareth Matthews, *Dialogues with Children* (Cambridge, Mass: Harvard Univ. Press, 1984) p 3.

6. Paulo Freire, *Education for Critical Consciousness* (New York: Seabury, 1973) p 48.

7. Paulo Freire, *Pedagogy of the Oppressed* (New York: Seabury, 1970) p 75.

8. Ien Dienske, *Atmosphere and Fundamental Mood: On the Meaning of Invisible Surroundings* (Univ. of Utrecht, Pedagogische Instituut Monograph, Spring 1984).

9. Elizabeth Bishop, "Primer Class," in *The Collected Prose* (New York: Farrar Strauss Giroux, 1984).

10. Valerie Polakow (Suransky), *The Erosion of Childhood* (Chicago: University of Chicago Press, 1982) Ch. 6.

11. Ton Beekman, "Human Science as Dialogue with Children," in *Phenomenology and Pedagogy*, Vol. 1, No 1.

12. Maxine Greene, *Landscapes of Learning* (New York: Teacher College Press, 1978).

13. Michael Armstrong, *Landscapes of Learning* (New York: Teachers College Press, 1978).

14. Sylvia Ashton-Warner, *Teacher* (New York: Simon and Shuster, 1963).

15. Paulo Freire, "The Importance of the Act of Reading," in *Journal of Education* Vol. 165, No. 1, Winter 1983, p 8.

Thinking and Literacy

Jane Roland Martin

I cannot help feeling, Phaedrus, that writing is unfortunately like painting; for the creations of the painter have the attitude of life, and yet if you ask them a question they preserve a solemn silence. And the same may be said of speeches. You would imagine that they had intelligence, but if you want to know anything and put a question to one of them, the speaker always gives one unvarying answer. And when they have been once written down they are tumbled about anywhere among those who may or may not understand them, and know not to whom they should reply, to whom not: and, if they are maltreated or abused, they have no parent to protect them; and they cannot protect or defend themselves.

So spoke Socrates, the philosopher who for centuries has served as our model of rational thought.[1] Today Socrates' position is in jeopardy. You see, Socrates engaged in *oral* philosophical discussion. His dialogues with his students come down to us in written form thanks to Plato. The dominant belief today, however, is that thinking and literacy are inextricably bound together.[2]

According to the psychologists, literacy transforms a person's cognitive capacities; indeed, it leads to forms of thought which, because they are abstract, are considered to be higher. But their view of the relationship of thinking to literacy does not stop there. Written language is taken to be a precondition of abstract thought as well as its generator. Thus, the oral cast of mind is said to constitute "the chief obstacle to the classification of experience, to the rearrangement in sequence of cause and effect, to the use of analysis, and to scientific rationalism."[3] It seems that oral and written statements differ radically: we deem the former to be successful if they are understood, for their primary function is interpersonal; we deem the latter to be successful if they appeal to premises and to rules of logic, for their primary function is getting it right.[4]

The object of this essay is to challenge the thesis—henceforth the Dependency Thesis—that thinking is dependent on literacy. I will explore, first, the implications for that thesis of the very existence of Socrates and will then consider the claim, made by many teachers of English, that learning to write just is learning to think. This will be followed by an examination of the claim made by the psychologists that it is not the act of writing, but written language itself, which binds thinking to literacy. My discussion of the relationship between written language and thinking will lead to a consideration of the various kinds of thinking. Once it is recognized that the Dependency Thesis forces a single, narrow mold on human thought, the dangerous implications of that thesis for education in thinking will become apparent. In the final section of this essay these will be explored and suggestions for a more fruitful approach to thinking as an aim of education will be made.

The politics and ethics of literacy

Research findings on the link between literacy and social contexts suggest important implications for educators and policy makers, including, (1) it is inappropriate and inaccurate to assume that low literate adults are helpless in the face of generally high national literacy demands, (2) because literacy use and purpose are so closely linked with racially segregated social contexts and networks, a heavy potential exists for literacy being used inappropriately for discrimination and gate-keeping, and (3) the same social networks that support low literate individuals may function to trap individuals into remaining low literates . . .

Instructors can benefit from paying attention to how literacy is actually used within productive social networks. For example, literacy is often used in group solutions to problems. It may be that teaching students how to ask questions of peers or how to behave fairly in turn-taking and returning factors may be as important to actual literacy functioning as teaching decoding skills.

—Larry M. Kulecky in *Literacy Research Center*, Spring, 1988.

The Case of Socrates

Unless we are to suppose that Socrates was a closet essayist who memorized written dialogues with his students for presentation in the market-place, we must reject the invidious distinction drawn by psychologists such as David Olson between utterances and texts.[5] If that distinction were valid—if oral statements could not withstand analysis of presuppositions and implications; if only written statements could be used to examine problems and produce new knowledge; if the latter alone were capable of being counter-intuitive while the former of necessity were congruent with dogma—the life and death of Socrates would be unintelligible. Socrates was a philosopher and a gadfly and was put to death for it. Yet his thinking was done on his feet: it was exhibited not in the composition of essays, but in the give and take of conversation.

Scholars have shown that the Greece of Socrates was in the process of becoming a literate culture.[6] They know that Socrates himself was able to read and write. Ought we not to assume, then, that Socrates was the thinker he was *because he was literate*? Granted, the existence of Socrates makes the distinction between oral and written statements untenable. Still, his existence would seem to be compatible with the thesis that literacy and thinking are inextricably bound together.

Socrates poses no problem for the Dependency Thesis so long as we assume that he became literate *before* he began his philosophizing. It is not clear that we can legitimately assume this, however. Scholars believe that in his day the teaching of reading and writing began in adolescence, but we do not know if Socrates' own education in the 2Rs began then, let alone when his philosophizing began. We must also assume that his literacy was roughly equivalent to literacy as we know it today, and it is not clear that we can legitimately do so. In the Greece of Socrates oral communication apparently was still dominant. There were books, and for over three centuries an alphabet; however, there is good reason to believe that works were not composed for people to read but for them to listen to. In the dialogue from which our opening quotation was taken, Socrates does not read for himself the speech which Phaedrus carries on a roll hidden in his cloak, but asks Phaedrus to read it to him. Phaedrus, in turn, has heard it read repeatedly. Thus, whether Socrates was fluent in both reading and writing by modern standards is a real question.

It is difficult for us to realize that Socrates was steeped in a culture in which the written word did not have the monopoly over intellectual life it has today. But suppose for the sake of argument that Socrates was as fluent a reader and writer as the experts today claim children must be if they are to explore problems, draw out implications, analyze, classify and in general think along abstract lines. We must still differentiate between individuals in preliterate or oral cultures and individuals who are non-readers and non-writers—or at least unaccomplished readers and writers—in a literate culture such as ours. Our culture is dominated by the written word and permeated by abstract thought. It provides an environment, therefore, in which the kind of thinking associated with literacy can be acquired *whether or not an individual is able to read or write.*

Writing and Thinking

Psychologists are not the only advocates of the Dependency Thesis. Teachers of English repeatedly tell us that writing and thinking are inseparable and that learning to write is learning to think.[7] Let us, therefore, bracket the case of Socrates and examine that complex activity we call "writing" to see which of its many components can plausibly be linked to thinking.

Grand claims have been made for handwriting. It has been said that the ability to write italic script will give Johnny "the identity and self-confidence he seeks so desperately to find in an increasingly mechanistic, computerized, automated society."[8] Italic writing has also been linked to good taste in prose and has been called a rational verbal skill.[9] Yet the purported effects on personality of a fine Italian hand have not been documented, and to call any sort of handwriting a *rational* skill is grossly misleading for handwriting is a neutral skill which can be used in the service of both rationality and irrationality. One method of handwriting may be better than another for its visual beauty, its legibility or its ease

of learning, but handwriting is still handwriting: a tool to use in expressing oneself and in communicating with others.

Many people have jumped on the handwriting bandwagon thinking that they were supporting education for critical thinking, logical reasoning and scientific method or even a new humanism. But no amount of training in handwriting will make the world a better place or us better thinkers. Those on the bandwagon have rightly called handwriting a *trapping* of literacy without realizing that trappings are ornamental, not essential. We have all known highly literate people equipped with crabbed scrawls, and a look at the manuscripts in the British Museum is enough to convince one that logical lions can have abominable penmanship.

Skill in handwriting is essential neither for literacy nor for rational, abstract thought. Nor can we count on proficiency in handwriting to produce literacy or to raise the level of our thought processes. Consider how many people there are with a beautiful hand and nothing to say! Let their existence be a warning to us all that handwriting instruction can too easily become the opiate of our children, occupying their time and their minds and making both them and us believe that they are learning much more than they really are! In truth, this aspect of writing is separable from literacy and can be detached from thinking.

When we are confronted with children who do not handwrite fluently and legibly we need to remember that an education in handwriting can be bypassed without sacrificing either literacy or rational thought. Indeed, if our interest is in fostering good thinking, we owe it to those children who have difficulty learning to handwrite to explore alternative tools for recording and communicating their ideas. We owe it to them, for instance, to provide opportunities to learn to typewrite. We tend to assume that handwriting is essential for all to learn whereas typing is a frill and, furthermore, that handwriting must be learned first. Yet one can learn to type before learning to handwrite and, although typing is not essential for all to learn, it is a skill which can have quite as much value for the possessor as handwriting can, which is not to say that either one provides a magical access to the world of rational, abstract thought.

It will be said that handwriting can be by-passed in an education for thinking because there is an alternative tool for recording one's ideas, namely typewriting, but that both typewriting and handwriting demand that we be able to spell. However, while the performance of these skills requires that statements be inscribed on physical material for others to read, it does not require that the author of the statements be adept at spelling. For one thing, we can tolerate a good many misspelled words in our reading of texts, perhaps more than we realize. The objections people have to misspelled words stem less from the difficulties they pose for comprehension than from the failure to distinguish trapping from essentials. Spelling, like handwriting, is a trapping of literacy. But whereas in our calmer moments we recognize that one can be literate without a legible hand, we do not extend such charity to the misspeller. When "i" and "e" are reversed, when single "r" is doubled and double "c" is not, we never stop to find out if an author can read fluently and write coherently, let alone whether ideas are being explored and implications drawn; we simply dismiss text and author as unworthy of attention.

Misspelling is an interesting phenomenon. Years ago, as a fifth and sixth grade teacher, I became convinced that some children had a knack for spelling and others did not, and that the ability to spell had nothing to do with their powers of thought. Yet to this day I feel humiliated by my own spelling mistakes and embarrassed by those of others. Surely I am not the only one to cringe in the face of a misspelled word. The reason for this gut reaction is obvious enough: we judge people's literacy by their spelling—or at least their *il*literacy by the misspelling—and we judge their intelligence and social worth by their literacy.[10] "Is it possible that the author of this communique is dumb?" I ask before recalling that spelling is neither necessary nor sufficient for learning and rational thought, but is simply a tool for aiding communication.

As I have said, we can understand misspelled texts. Moreover, if one's spelling is so bad that communication is hampered, it is always possible to dictate and let someone else transcribe what one has to say. A fifth grader whose name really was Johnny and whose spelling problems were legion used to insist that he did not need to learn to spell since when he grew up a secretary would do his spelling for him. I argued, cajoled and browbeat him to drill on his twenty words a week, but of course Johnny was right. If he does not now have a secretary, he can turn to family or friends or use telephones and tapes. For him, although certainly not for all my fifth and sixth graders, learning to spell was filled with frustration and misery: he simply could not do it without sacrifice on his part and that of his teachers which was out of all proportion to the benefits which might accrue.

If we judge people by their spelling, we judge them even more by their grammar. Yet how essential is good grammar for rational thought? Surely a person can reason logically while splitting infinitives and can tease out the presuppositions and implications of statements while saying, "Me and him went to the movies." A child who does not realize that "John hit Mary" entails "Mary was hit by John" will have limited ability to draw logical conclusions. But this kind of knowledge is not at issue when people say that learning to write is learning to think. At some very deep level grammar and thinking merge. But at that level—inference—an education about gerunds, subordinate clauses and the parts of speech is irrelevant. Just as brilliant thinkers can have an illegible hand and a penchant for misspelled words, so too can they dangle participles and misuse the subjunctive.

Thinking can be detached from handwriting, spelling and grammar and it should be lest we fill up the curriculum of the early years with these subjects in the belief that children are thereby learning to reason. Mastery of these skills is certainly not to be scorned but it should not be confused with literacy, let alone with thinking itself. The danger, you see, is that we will get so bogged down in teaching the mechanics of writing that we will never get beyond them to teach the very things we appeal to in justifying training in those mechanics. Remember, then, that an education in the mechanics of writing is neither an essential ingredient nor a guarantee of rational, abstract thinking.

Thinking in an Oral Medium

The aspect of writing which one must assume is at issue when it is claimed that learning to write is just learning to think is composition—that is, the creation of written works. For this an author does not need to possess mechanical skills such as handwriting and spelling since the final product, and even intermediate stages thereof, can be transcribed by another. What is required of one who composes written works—at least prose, non-fiction works—is that ideas be presented and organized, evidence and arguments be marshalled, and implications and conclusions be drawn. When you get right down to it, a well-executed prose, non-fiction work exhibits the very kind of thinking which according to the psychologists is a consequence of literacy. It might be supposed therefore, that in order to learn to think a person must learn to compose such works. Yet learning to compose written works is simply one *way* to learn to think logically and abstractly. It may be a good way for some people, but there is no reason to suppose it is a good way for everyone or that it is the only way.

That so few of us seriously entertain alternatives to the teaching of writing as a way of teaching children to think is a sad commentary on our society's fixation on the written word and its devaluation of oral communication. Children *could* learn to explore ideas orally; they *could* be

given practice through discussion in finding implications; they *could* learn by engaging in dialogue to challenge assumptions and defend their conclusions; they *could* be given experience in listening for nonsequiturs.

Gareth Matthews has documented a number of fascinating philosophical discussions he and other adults have had with young children when they ask questions such as this one:[11]

> Jordan (five years old), going to bed at 8 P.M., asked: "If I go to bed at 8 and get up at 7 in the morning, how do I really know that the little hand of the clock has gone around only once? Do I have to stay up all night to watch it?
>
> "If I look away even for a short time maybe the small hand will go around twice."

Many parents would regard Jordan's question as a manoeuvre for postponing his bedtime. Others would tell Jordan not to worry, the clock is a new one and does not pick up speed. However, as Matthews points out, Jordan's question may be a much deeper one than these parents realize. Jordan's concern is perhaps a very general one about whether observed states are a reliable guide to unobserved states. Indeed, Jordan may have put his finger on the philosophical problem of induction or on the still more fundamental problem of whether anything at all exists while he sleeps.

We really do not know how far oral communication can take us in the development of thinking for we do not give it a chance. Our prejudices against oral communication run deep. Despite the gross inadequacies of our Post Office, the most literate among us bemoan the rise of the telephone and the resultant decline of written correspondence. Meanwhile, college professors reward students for well-written examinations while giving no credit for intelligent contributions to class discussions. As a college teacher, how often have I heard it said, and said myself, "It's funny, but I really misjudged that student. From his comments in class I had gotten the impression he understood the material almost as well as I did, but his final exam is badly written. He obviously is a poor student!

We do not dream that thinking is compatible with utterance, nor that abstract thoughts and concerns may be lurking in the minds and hearts of young children. David Ecker has recorded an hour-long discussion in a sixth grade classroom of the relationship between theories of art and contemporary paintings.[12] His summary and analysis of it make it quite clear that the children not only understood the imitation theory of art the teacher had introduced to them, but were capable of criticizing it: they adduced counterexamples, pointed out the undesirable positions to which one who endorsed the theory would be committed and raised questions about imitation itself. Of course, they did all this under the guidance of a teacher. The point is that we were fortunate enough to have a teacher who encouraged dialogue and tried to further theoretical discussion.

Few adults take the theoretical questions of children seriously;[13] instead, they brush them aside or transform them into psychological or physical questions to which they then give very concrete answers. Were adults to treat children's intellectual concerns with respect and encourage discussion of them, children might be well on their way to becoming highly developed thinkers long before they had mastered the 3Rs. Indeed, the compositions they were required to write in school might have some meaning for them since, as abstract thinkers, they might have some point to make, and be armed with arguments to support it.[14]

Socrates worried that reliance on the written word would weaken memory.[15] Today most of us have no memory for the broad outlines, not to mention the nuances and details, of oral argument. We doubt that children can really learn to think if they cannot write down their thoughts, for we do not believe that people can connect their ideas to one another if they cannot go back over their statements. "How can one's arguments be coherent if the premises are not right there to be read and reread?" we ask, forgetting that we have

been conditioned by the written word. I once wrote an examination in constitutional law for a blind student at the Harvard Law School; that is, he composed it and, as he did, I transcribed it. The most remarkable aspect for me of that remarkable experience was that, although he sometimes paused between sentences for many minutes, he never asked me to read back to him what I had set down. I read his exam back to myself repeatedly to see if *his* train of thought was coherent, but *he* did not have to do this for his memory was trained as mine was not.

In this age of technology, however, memory is not the vital commodity it once was. Dialogues, conversations, oral arguments, dictated examinations and compositions can all be taped. Just as writers can reread their premises, speakers can rehear them. To be sure, listening takes time, but then the kind of thinking which involves the analysis of presuppositions and the drawing out of implications is at best a slow process.

Speaking a Written Language

We have seen that thinking can be detached from writing both as mechanical skill and as composition. The latter, therefore, can be bypassed in an education designed to teach people to think. However, while teachers of English tend to stress the *act* or *process* of writing as they endorse the Dependency Thesis, the psychologists seem to be more concerned with the *raw materials* of writing than with its processes—that is, with the nature of written statements themselves. Thus we must ask if literacy and thinking are inextricably bound together by virtue of the very form or structure of written, as opposed to oral, language.

It is an open question if a distinction between oral and written language can withstand critical examination. Certainly Olson's distinction between utterance and text is not satisfactory. He has summarized it in terms of three underlying principles.[16] First, utterances appeal for their meaning to shared experiences and interpretations; because they do, the criterion for a successful utterance is understanding on the part of the listener. Texts, on the other hand, appeal to premises and rules of logic for deriving implications; thus the criterion for a successful statement of text is its formal structure. Second, utterances and texts appeal to different conceptions of truth. Truth in the former has to do with wisdom, while truth in the latter has to do with the correspondence between statements and observations: thus true statements in a text may be counter to intuition, commonsense or authority while true statements in utterances will be congruent with dogma or the wisdom of elders. Third, utterances and texts differ in regard to function: in oral speech the interpersonal function is primary, hence if a sentence is inappropriate to the listener it is a failure; in texts, however, the logical or ideational function is primary with communication playing second fiddle to "getting it right."

There can be no doubt that utterances are contextbound. However, it does not follow from the fact that they are intended for some audience that their only criterion of success is that the audience understand them. If I say to you, "An MIT professor believes we should build more nuclear power plants, so let's go ahead," you will be right to lecture me about non-sequiturs even as you understand my utterance. Socrates had to be concerned about his listeners lest his dialogues become monologues and his reputation as gadfly be forfeited. But concern for one's audience is scarcely incompatible with concern for valid inference and truth. As the volumes written about them testify, Socrates' utterances admit of more than one interpretation—a property which, on Olson's view, differentiates utterances from texts. But then Locke's essays, which Olson takes to be model texts, admit of more than one interpretation, too.

Further investigation into oral and written language may reveal that in a literate culture the two are not distinct. If they are not, it would be a truism to say that one can speak a written language. If the two do differ in significant ways, then Olson's statement that "formal schooling, in the process of teaching children to deal with prose texts, fosters the ability to 'Speak a written language'," bears repeating.[17] In either case, the point to keep in mind is that since written language can be spoken, thinking can be dependent on the form and structure of written language without being dependent on literacy. Of course, for there to be written language a culture would have to be literate. But an individual in that culture could learn to speak a written language without being able to read or write it.

Those who support the Dependency Thesis while acknowledging that one can speak a written language assume that the possession of this skill presupposes literacy. Only if one can read and write can one speak in this way, goes the argument. Yet once it is granted that written language can be spoken, it is difficult to see why one who speaks it must necessarily be able to read and write. Of course, there must be a written language if a written language is to be spoken. And if there is a written language there must be people who can read and write it lest the spoken written language over time diverge so far from the written language simpliciter that it loses the properties of a written language. Still, the conclusion that every speaker of a written language must be literate does not follow from the fact that if a written language is spoken there must be some literate people.

Reading and writing a written language is one way to learn to speak it. But just as spoken language in general is learned by hearing it spoken and through practice in speaking it, so one can learn to speak a written language in this way. Indeed, it is not unreasonable to expect that given a supportive oral environment children would learn to speak a written language relatively easily. By "supportive" I do not merely mean one that is warm and friendly, although a psychologically benign environment would no doubt be important. An oral environment supportive of spoken written language would be one filled with that language. It would have live speakers, although it could also make use of tapes and films. It would also provide ample opportunity for practice.

In their article on the cognitive consequences of literacy, Sylvia Scribner and Michael Cole warn that confusion results when the consequences of literacy over the course of human history are not distinguished from the consequences of literacy for the individual in present day society.[18] I leave open here the question of whether from an historical perspective literacy and thinking are linked by virtue of the very nature of written language. The point I want to make is simply that *if* they are, *for any individual in a literate society such as ours* thinking can nonetheless be detached from reading and writing and, hence, education for thinking can bypass education in these 2 Rs.

Neither as mechanical skill nor as proficiency in composition is the ability to write essential for thinking. As we have already seen, rational abstract thinking can take place in an oral medium and when there is reason to inscribe what has been said the thinker can turn to others for help in transcription. Nor is the ability to read and write a written language essential for thinking: since each language can be spoken it is quite possible to acquire it without resorting to book learning. To be sure, teachers of reading, like teachers of writing, will insist that learning to read is learning to think. But the component skills of reading are no more essential for thinking than are those of writing. Comprehension, analysis, interpretation are central elements of reading as they are of abstract logical thought. Yet these skills, along with other ones which are shared with thinking, can be learned and exercised in oral contexts. Insofar as the Dependency Thesis claims that literacy is essential for thinking, we must reject it.

To deny that literacy is essential for rational abstract thought is not to say that no benefits for thinking accrue from it. If you can read and write, you can go back over your composition to see if your train of thought has gotten sidetracked or if

you have made serious errors. You can also proceed throughout at your own pace and can have the advantage of being able to "see" your thoughts on paper, so to speak. In an oral medium that particular advantage is lost, but with the help of a tape recorder you can review what has been said for purposes of editing, and a supportive oral environment will allow you to control pace. Because literacy is not essential for thinking, it is in the final analysis a question of costs and to some extent these will vary from individual to individual. Where reading and writing come easily, let us not forget that these skills can be harnessed to the promotion of rational abstract thought. Where mastery of these 2Rs is itself problematic, let us remember that they are but one route to such thinking. Let us remember also that an over dependency on the written word has a high price: memory suffers, as do visual and oral skills. Most important, of all, thinking itself is diminished.

The Varieties of Thinking

Even if learning to read and write were essential for abstract logical thinking, it would be incumbent on us to challenge the Dependency Thesis because of the injustice it does to human thought. In the first place, thinking out-runs language. The British philosopher, Gilbert Ryle has said it well:[19]

> The architect might try to think out his design for the war-memorial by arranging and re-arranging toy bricks on the carpet; the sculptor might plan a statue in marble by modelling and remodelling a piece of plasticine. The motorist might weigh the pros and cons of different roads in his mind's eye. The guide might be planning tomorrow's climb, methodically scanning through a telescope the slopes, precipices and water-courses of the mountain from his hotel.

Quite simply, there is more to thinking than advocates of the Dependency Thesis acknowledge. One danger of that thesis is that it will cause educators to lose sight of thought which is not language based. The kinds of thinking Ryle mentions are not trivial, nor are they "merely" intuitive; they do not just emerge as we mature, nor do they spring full blown from our heads on graduation day. They require experience and practice—in truth, education of a sort not provided by courses in reading and writing. As Ryle says, a guide might have to go to additional labors to describe the route settled on and might even be unequal to this additional task. The inability to tell in words one's plan no more means that no plan has been developed, than the inability to put in writing a plan one can describe in words means that the plan is based on faulty logic.

One can be in the middle of thinking without saying or trying to say anything to oneself or to others; one can have succeeded in thinking without being ready or even able to tell in words what has been thought out. Moreover, insofar as thinking is language based, it is not confined to the straight-jacket in which advocates of the Dependency Thesis would put it. Poetic thought, for instance, does not analyze presuppositions and draw out logical implications. Its object is not to minimize ambiguity but to capitalize on it; its concern is not to formulate new knowledge. Nor is the concern of practical problem solving to formulate new knowledge: its object is the determination of some course of actions, not the discovery of theoretical truths.

The thinking which the psychologists claim is so intimately tied to reading and writing is the kind done in the academy. That they focus on the mode of thinking which as members of the academy they value most would be of no consequence were their writings not used to justify educational programs. Since their claims about thinking and literacy surface in discussions of curriculum, however, it is absolutely imperative that we understand just how narrow their conception of thinking is.

In his best-seller on the evolution of human intelligence, the scientist, Carl Sagan, distinguished two modes of knowing, one a function of the left hemisphere of the brain and the other a function of the right.[20] He might just as well have called them two modes of thinking. The "rational" mode—the one "so many of us regard as all of us there is"—is the sole concern of the Dependency Thesis. But there is also an "intuitive" mode and educators ignore it at their peril. Intuitive thinking is holistic, not analytic; it involves pattern recognition, not drawing out of logical implications.

According to Sagan, these two modes of thinking have complementary survival value. To convince yourself that he is right imagine a world in which everyone on all occasions thought in the manner of the academy. Practical life would come to a halt, poetry would perish, music and art would wither. Even the sciences and philosophy—those bastions of abstract, analytic thought—would be impoverished, for intuitive thinking lies at the heart of both scientific creativity and philosophical insight. "Intuitive" does not mean "innate": we are not born knowing how to think intuitively nor do we simply develop into intuitive thinkers as we mature. This mode of thought must be learned, just as rational abstract thought must be. Thus, if we value the intuitive mode of thinking, we must find ways to encourage and foster it even as we foster the rational mode.

The Dependency Thesis would pour all thinking into a single narrow mold. It would have us lose sight of the richness and variety of human thought by sacrificing synthesis to analysis, insight to logic, ambiguity to explicit meaning, the concrete to the abstract and practical intelligence to intellectual theorizing. From the standpoint of education the thesis is a dangerous one. Its currency among psychologists makes it all too likely that it will be used to justify a single track approach to education for thinking. That approach is readily imagined: if literacy is taken to be a precondition of thinking, then education for thinking will have to include education in the first two of the 3Rs; if literacy is thought to transform a person's cognitive capacities, then the latter sort of education will be all that is needed. In other thinking will have to include education in the first two of the 3Rs; if literacy is thought to transform a person's cognitive capacities, then the latter sort of education will be all that is needed. In other words, education for thinking will consist in learning to read and write.

Superficially the curriculum package delivered by the Dependency Thesis has much to recommend it. We are committed to teaching children to read and write. When education for thinking is equated with education for literacy it is not necessary to introduce something new into the curriculum: we can embrace thinking as an aim or goal of education without being accused of advocating "frills." At the same time, the desire that children learn to think provides one further bit of justification for programs designed to teach reading and writing. Thus education in the basics gains support from the close connection which the Dependency Thesis posits between thinking and literacy, even as it constitutes a solution to the problem of how to teach children to think. Yet can we really depend on programs which teach reading and writing to teach thinking too? Will not thinking be forgotten when it becomes part and parcel of education in these basics? Moreover, does thinking as an educational aim really justify programs which teach reading and writing?

The last question is easily answered. Since it is possible to think on one's feet as Socrates did, indeed possible in a literate culture like ours to do so without being able to read and write, education for thinking is not dependent on education in reading and writing—before we accept the Dependency Thesis' curriculum package, therefore, we must explore alternatives and weigh costs. No doubt some learn to read and write with so little difficulty that a route through the 2Rs to the educational aim of thinking is justified. But for some this route will be paved with anxiety, frustration and failure. For them a curriculum based on a supportive oral environment is surely more appropriate than one based on the written word. Remember that in weighing costs one must

take into account not just the money, time and energy a program consumes, but also the misery, the hatred of learning and the loss of self-esteem which can result from even the best intentioned curriculum design.

The Dependency Thesis is not just the thesis that literacy is essential for thinking, however. It holds also that thinking is a consequence of literacy. Thus the route to thinking through reading and writing would seem to find its justification in the fact that it gets results. Even if an education in the 2Rs is paved with sorrow for some, does it not have one great advantage over its competitors, namely that it guarantees success? I am afraid this advantage is illusory. Scribner and Cole have pointed out that the psychological studies which purport to link literacy and cognitive capacities fail to distinguish between literacy and schooling.[21] Thus the positive findings those studies yield may reveal more about the powers of schooling than about the powers of literacy. Furthermore, even if those studies do connect literacy to thinking, the data do not support the claim that the transformation of the thinking of *all* those who can read and write is *guaranteed*. And supposing they did support this strong claim, the kind of thinking which an education in reading and writing would yield would not be all inclusive: the thinking done by Ryle's architect, sculptor, motorist and mountain guide would be ignored, as would the thinking Sagan calls "intuitive."

Reading and writing education constitutes at best an education in language based thinking. That it constitutes an education even in this depends on the way it is conducted. If it is an education in reading and writing essays, it perhaps develops the abstract, logical thought on which the psychologists focus, but it will fail to foster the kind of thinking done by a poet or novelist. When one considers how difficult it is to teach essay reading and writing, and that abstract, logical thought, although important, is but one kind of thought, the literacy route to thinking looks less and less inviting. Can one doubt that esses will have scarcely been enhanced? Is not the development of the thinking of each person too important a goal of education to be sacrificed unnecessarily on the altar of literacy?

One promising approach to thinking as a goal of education has been taken by Matthew Lipman and his associates. Lipman has written two philosophical novels, *Harry Stottlemeier's Discovery,* and a sequel, *Lisa.*[22] *Harry* and *Lisa* are about children who discuss "heavy" issues, among them: lying and truth-telling, what is right, what is fair, the nature of mind, the nature of death. These children also discover for themselves general principles of reasoning which they then apply in their own conversations. Lipman's novels are meant to be read *by* children, rather than to be read to them by their teachers or their parents. Nevertheless, *Harry* and *Lisa* lend themselves well to attempts to detach education for thinking from education for literacy.

The overall Philosophy for Children program into which Harry and Lisa fit emphasizes dialogue and discussion.[23] Just as the children in these novels learn to reason and to think philosophically through conversation with teachers, parents and peers, so children in the elementary and junior high classrooms in which the novels are used are supposed to learn to think by talking things out. Their teachers, in turn, are supposed to be gadflies. They are instructed to encourage students to take the initiative in formulating some position, to help them question their underlying assumptions, to introduce alternative views and to suggest ways of arriving at more comprehensive answers. In sum, these novels portray, and are also intended to serve as vehicles for establishing, a supportive oral environment for fostering philosophical thought.

Nonetheless, were there functional illiterates in a classroom in which Harry and Lisa were being used they would be at a great disadvantage for they would not be able to read them. It is important to realize, therefore, that these novels *could be taped in English,* as *Harry* has been in Spanish,[24] so that the functional illiterates in

every classroom could profit from the talk and interaction of the fictional children. A child who is a poor reader may be a fine listener. Indeed, I would hope that the vast number of written works which lend themselves to philosophical discussion among children and hence to the development of abstract, logical thinking would be put on film or tape.[25] The kind of supportive oral environment for thinking Lipman has tried to create is quite exciting, but in education for thinking, as in education in general, variety is the spice of life.

It would be a mistake to suppose that the way to the development of thinking Lipman has charted is the only one worth exploring, however. No single educational route to something as rich and varied as human thought can possibly be adequate. Give to philosophy the monopoly on education for thinking which the psychologists and teachers of English would give to literacy and we will find that we have once again set ourselves a very limited destination. When thinking is taken seriously as a goal of education the sciences, the arts and practical activities must all have access to it and routes must be charted through the gymnasium, the studio, the laboratory, the theater and the shop as well as through the classroom. A single track approach to education for thinking, whether literacy based or not, is misguided because the thinking which should be an aim of education takes many forms. Just as the different guises of thinking permeate life itself they should permeate the curriculum.

Footnotes

* I want to thank Ann Diller, Nancy Glock, Michael Martin and Beatrice Nelson for helpful comments on a draft of this essay.
1. *The Dialogues of Plato,* Vol. I, B. Jowett (trans.) (New York: Random House, 1937), pp. 278-279.

2. For a valuable discussion of this view and references to the relevant psychological studies see Sylvia Scribner and Michael Cole, "Literacy without Schooling: Testing for Intellectual Effects," *Harvard Educational Review*, 48 (November, 1978), pp. 448-461. In his Presidential Address to the 35th Annual Meeting of the Philosophy of Education Society, April, 1979, Robert H. Ennis presented a philosopher's version of this thesis.

3. Thomas J. Farrell, "Literacy, the Basics, and *All That Jazz,*" *College English*, 38 (January, 1977), p. 449. It should be noted that the literature on the relationship of literacy to thinking does not usually distinguish the thesis that thinking is an outcome of literacy from the thesis that literacy is necessary for thinking.

4. David Olson, "From Utterance to Text: The Bias of Language in Speech and Writing," *Harvard Educational Review*, 47 (August, 1977), pp. 277-278.

5. Ibid. Another way out of the difficulty the existence of Socrates poses for this distinction is to attribute all the intellectual achievements thought to be his to Plato. Thus Jack Goody and Ian Watt refer to Socrates as Plato's "spokesman" "The Consequences of Literacy" in Jack Goody (ed.) *Literacy in Traditional Societies* (Cambridge: University Press, 1968), p. 50. The historical record simply does not support this interpretation of the relationship between Plato and Socrates, however.

6. My discussion here relies primarily on Eric Havelock, *The Origins of Western Literacy* (Toronto: Ontario Institute for Studies in Education, 1976).

7. This point of view was set forth in the influential *Newsweek* article, "Back to Basics in the Schools," October, 21, 1974, p.91.

8. *New York Times Magazine*, May 23,1976 p.68.

9. *Ibid.*

10. Havelock, *op. cit.*, pp. 3-4.

11. Gareth B. Matthews, "Are Children Philosophical?" in Matthew Lipman and Ann Margaret Sharp (eds.) *Growing Up with Philosophy* (Philadelphia: Temple University Press, 1978), pp. 63-77.

12. David W. Ecker, "Analyzing Children's Talk about Art" in Lipman and Sharp, *op. cit*, pp. 284-300.

13. Matthews, *op. cit.*, gives reason to believe that not even Piaget does.

14. I do not mean here to endorse the naive view that writing is simply the recording of prearranged thoughts. Surely for most writers of essays the processes of writing and thinking interact in complex ways. Still, to write a decent essay one must have something to say and want to say it. These conditions are too rarely met in composition courses, in part because students are not independently encouraged to think about the kinds of things which are appropriate essay topics.

15. *Op. cit.*, p. 278.

16. *Op. cit.*, pp. 277-278.

17. *Ibid.*, p. 271

18. *Op. cit.*, p. 452.

19. "Thinking and Language," *Aristotelian Society Supplementary Volume*, XXV (1955), p. 69.

20. *The Dragons of Eden* (Now York: Ballantine Books, 1977), Ch. 7.

21. Op. cit

22. Matthew Lipman *Harry Stottlemeler's Discovery* (Upper Montclair, N.J.: The Institute for the Advancement of Philosophy for Children, 1976).

23. See Matthew Lipman, Ann Margaret Sharp and Frederick S. Oscanyan, *Philosophy in the Classroom* (Upper Montclair, N.J.: The Institute for the Advancement of Philosophy for Children, 1977).

24. A. Gray Thompson and Adrian DuPuis, "Bilingual Philosophy in Milwaukee," *Thinking*, 1 (January, 1979), p. 37.

25. For some examples of these see Gareth B. Matthews, "Philosophy and Children's Literature," *Metaphilosophy*, 7 (1976) pp. 7-16.

Writing

W. H. Auden

Speech

If an Australian aborigine sits down on a pin he says "Ow." Dogs with bones growl at the approach of other dogs. English, Russian, Brazilian, all mothers, "coo" to their babies. Sailors at any port, pulling together on a hawser: watch them and listen—heaving, they grunt together "Ee-Ah."

This is the first language.

We generally think of language being words used to point to things, to say that something is *this* or *that*, but the earliest use of language was not this; it was used to express the feelings of the speaker; feelings about something happening to him (the prick of the pin), or attitudes towards other things in the world (the other hungry dog; the darling baby), or, again, as a help to doing something with others of his own kind (pulling the boat in). The first two uses are common to many animals, but the last is peculiar to the most highly organized, and contains more possibilities of development.

Life is one whole thing made up of smaller whole things, which again are made up of smaller whole things, and so on. The largest thing we can talk about is the universe, the smallest the negative electrons of the atom which run round its central positive nucleus, already a group. So too for us, nucleus and cell, cell and organ, organ and the human individual, individual and family, nation and world, always groups linked up with larger groups, each group unique, different from

every other, but without meaning except in its connection with others. The whole cannot exist without the part, nor the part without the whole; and each whole is more than just the sum of its parts; it is a new thing.

But suppose the part begins to work, not only as if it were a whole (which it is), but as if there were no larger whole, then there is a breakdown (e.g., a cancer growth in the body). And this is what has happened to us. At some time or other in human history, when and how we don't know, man became self-conscious; he began to feel, I am I, and you are not I; we are shut inside ourselves and apart from each other. There is no whole but the self.

The more this feeling grew, the more man felt the need to bridge over the gulf, to recover the sense of being as much part of life as the cells in his body are part of him. Before he had lost it, when he was still doing things together in a group, such as hunting, when feeling was strongest, as when, say, the quarry was first sighted, the group had made noises, grunts, howls, grimaces. Noise and this feeling he had now lost had gone together; then, if he made the noise, could he not recover the feeling? In some way like this language began, but its development must have been very slow. Among savage tribes, for example, news travels much quicker than a messenger could carry it, by a sympathy which we, ignorant of its nature and incapable of practicing it, call telepathy. Dr. Rivers tells a story of some natives in Melanesia getting into a rowing-boat. There was no discussion as to who should stroke or steer. All found their places, as we should say, by instinct.

Even among ourselves, two friends have to say very much less to understand each other's meaning than two strangers. Their conversation is often unintelligible to a third person. Even when we are listening to anyone, it is not only the words themselves which tell us what he means, but his gestures (try listening with your eyes shut), and also the extent to which he is talking to us personally. (It is always difficult to understand what people are saying at another table in a restaurant. We are outside the group.)

Words are a bridge between a speaker and a listener. What the bridge carries, i.e., what the speaker gives and the listener receives, we call the *meaning* of the words.

Meaning

In anything we say there are four different kinds of meaning; any one of them may be more important than the other three, but there is generally something of all four.

(1) *Sense* (typical case, fat stock prices on the wireless). We say *something*, or expect *something* to be said to us about something. "Snig is a man." We now know that there is a thing called Snig, and that thing is a man and not a dog or anything else.

(2) *Feeling* (typical case, the conversation of lovers). We generally have feelings about the things of which we are talking. "There's that horrible man Snig." We now know that the speaker does not like Snig.

(3) *Tone* (typical case, an after-dinner speech). We generally have an attitude to the person we are talking to. We say the same thing in a different way to different people. "There's that swine Snig." "There's Mr. Snig; of course, I expect he's charming, really, but I don't like him very much, I'm afraid."

(4) *Intention* (typical case, a speech at a General Election). Apart from what we say or feel we often want to make our listeners act or think in a particular way. "There's that man Snig. I shouldn't have much to do with him if I were you." The speaker is trying to stop us seeing Mr. Snig.

Language and Words

Language, as we know it, consists of words—that is, a comparatively small number of different sounds (between forty and fifty in English) arranged in different orders or groups, each sound, or group of sounds, standing for something; an object, an action, a color, an idea, etc.

To go back to our sketch of the origin of language. Before language we have the people who feel something (the hunting group), the feeling (feeling of unity in the face of hunger or danger, etc.), the object which excites the feeling (the hunted bison), and the noise which expressed the feeling. If the noise was later used to recover the feeling, it would also present to the memory the idea or the image of the animal, or whatever it was excited the feeling. Thus sounds would begin to have sense meaning, to stand for things, as well as having meaning as an expression of feeling.

It is unlikely, therefore, even at the first that language was entirely onomatopoetic—that is, that words were sounds imitating the sounds of things spoken about. Many words, no doubt, did, just as they still do (e.g., hissing, growling, splashing). It is only possible to imitate in this way actions or objects which make a noise. You could never, for example, imitate the sound of a mountain. In fact, most of the power of words comes from their *not* being like what they stand for. If the word "ruin," for instance, was only like a particular ruin, it would only serve to describe the one solitary building; as it is, the word conjures up all the kinds of ruins which we know, and our various feelings about them—ruined churches, ruined houses, ruined gasworks, loss of money, etc.

Inflection

All languages are originally inflected; that is to say, the sounds standing for a particular object or action change slightly according to how we are looking at it. E.g., the Roman said:

Homo canem amat

(The man loves the dog).

Canis hominem amat

(The dog loves the man).

He felt that the man is a different man and the dog is a different dog if he is loving or being loved. But, as people get more self-conscious, more aware of what they are feeling and thinking, they separate their feelings and thoughts from the things they are feeling and thinking about. They show the difference in attitude either by changing the word order or by using special words like prepositions. Thus in English, the least inflected language:

The man loves the dog.

The dog loves the man.

The man gives a bone *to* the dog. All languages show some inflection. (*I* love *him. He* loves *me*.)

Writing

Writing and speech are like two tributary streams, rising at different sources, flowing apart for a time until they unite to form a large river. Just as it is possible for sounds conveying their meaning by the ear to stand for things, pictures conveying their meaning through the eye can do the same.

The earliest kind of writing, such as Egyptian hieroglyphs, or Mexican writings, are a series of pictures telling a story, as a sentence tells a story. The urge to write, like the urge to speak, came from man s growing sense of personal loneliness, of the need for group communication. But, while speech begins with the feeling of separateness in space, of there-in-this-chair and you-there-in-that-chair, writing begins from the sense of separateness in time, of "I'm here to-day, but I shall be dead to-morrow, and you will be active in my place, and how can I speak to you?"

Primitive people, living in small groups, have very little idea of death, only a very strong sense of the life of the tribe, which, of course, never dies. The moment man loses this sense of the continuously present group life, he becomes increasingly aware of the shortness and uncertainty of the life of the individual. He looks round desperately for some means of prolonging it, of living into the future, of uniting the past with the present. The earliest writings of which we know tell the exploits of dead kings. The writer is like a schoolboy who carves his initials on a desk; he wishes to live for ever.

How early speech joined up with writing it is impossible to say, but writing must soon have stopped being purely pictorial-drawings of each separate object. A language of this kind would have had to contain thousands of letters, and would have been very difficult to know, and slow and clumsy to write. Chinese is still a language of this kind. Further, abstract ideas would be impossible to represent by pictures (how, for example, could you draw a picture of "habit"?). Luckily, the fact that the number of different sounds which it is possible to make are comparatively few presented a solution to the difficulty. In inventing an alphabet, or code, where one kind of mark stands for one kind of sound, any word could be written by arranging the marks or letters in the order in which the sounds were made. (Our own alphabet comes originally from Egypt, through Phoenicia, Colchis, and Italy.)

Spoken and Written Language

As long as people are living in small societies, and living generation after generation in one place, they have little need of writing. Poems, stories, moral advice, are learnt by heart and handed down by word of mouth from father to son. Oral tradition has certain advantages and certain disadvantages over writing. Generally speaking, the *feelings* meaning is transmitted with extraordinary accuracy, as the gestures and the tone of voice that go with the words are remembered also. (With a statement in writing it is often impossible, after a time, to decide exactly what the author meant. Think how easy it is to misunderstand a letter.) On the other hand, in speaking, the *sense* meaning is apt to get strangely distorted. It is easy not to catch or to forget the exact words told to one, and to guess them wrongly; again, we may be asked to explain something and add our own explanation, which is passed on with the story; e.g., this message was passed back from the front lines from mouth to mouth to the officer commanding the reserve: "Send reinforcements; the regiment is going to advance." What actually reached him was: "Send three and fourpence; the regiment is going to a dance."

But as the communities became larger and government became more centralized, writing became more and more important. Still, as long as copying of original manuscripts had to be done by hand, books were rare and too costly for any but the few. The invention of printing in the fifteenth century greatly increased the power of the written word, but the cost of books still limited their circulation. Popular printed literature during the sixteenth and seventeenth centuries, apart from some religious books, was confined to broadsheets and pamphlets peddled in the streets. The eighteenth century saw the rise of the magazine and the newspaper; and the introduction of steam power at the beginning of the nineteenth century, by cheapening the cost of production, put printed matter within the reach of anyone who could read or write. (Think also of the introduction of the penny post, and the effect of universal education. The last five years, with the wireless and the talkies, have produced a revival of the spoken word.)

The effect of this has been a mixed one. It has made the language able to deal with a great many

more subjects, particularly those which are abstract, like some of the sciences; it can be more accurate, draw finer distinctions of meaning. Words written down in one language can be translated into another. Thus the world's knowledge can be pooled, and words borrowed from another language for which the borrower has no word in his own, with the exact shade of meaning which he wants (clock-chronometer: stranger-alien, etc.) But increase in vocabulary makes a language more difficult to learn—not only just to learn the words, but to learn to use them. Education in the use of the language becomes more and more necessary. At present nobody gets such an education. The speech of a peasant is generally better, i.e., more vivid, better able to say what he wants to say, than the speech of the average University graduate. It's like juggling with balls. You may be able to juggle fairly well with three, but if you try six, without careful practice you will probably drop them all. It is not the language that is to blame, but our skill in using it.

Speech originated in noises made during group excitement. Excitement seems naturally to excite movement. When we are excited, we want to dance about. Noise was thus in the beginning associated with movements of a group—perhaps dancing round food or advancing together to attack. The greater the excitement, the more in sympathy with each other each member of the group is, the more regular the movements; they keep time with each other; every foot comes down together.

Again, imagine a circle of people dancing; the circle revolves and comes back to its starting-place; at each revolution the set of movements is repeated.

When the words move in this kind of repeated pattern, we call the effect of the movement in our minds the metre. Words arranged in metre are verse. Just as in a crowd we are much more easily carried away by feeling than when alone, so metre excites us, prepares us to listen readily to what is being said. We expect something to happen, and therefore it does. When a poet is writing verse, the feeling, as it were, excites the words and makes them fall into a definite group, going through definite dancing movements, just as feeling excites the different members of a crowd and makes them act together. Metre is group excitement among words, a series of repeated movements. The weaker the excitement, the less the words act together and upon each other. (Rhythm is what is expected by one word of another.) In scientific prose, for example, what words do is only controlled by the sense of what is being said. They are like people in a street on an ordinary day. They can be or do anything they like as long as they keep to the left of the pavement and don't annoy each other. But even here this much is expected. There is always some degree of rhythm in all language. The degree depends on the power of feeling.

Accents, long and short syllables, feet and all that, are really quite simple. You will always read a line of poetry rightly if you know its meaning (all four kinds). There are certain traditional rules in writing poetry, just as there are traditional steps in a dance, but every good poet, like every good dancer, uses them in his own way, which is generally quite distinct from that of any other poet. If you were describing a certain dance, you could do it in various ways—as consisting of ten steps, or of four long steps and six little steps, or of three heavy steps and six light ones; in the same way the motion or metre of a line of poetry can be described in different ways according as to how you choose to look at it. In English poetry, for example, we generally describe it by accents— light and heavy steps—because that is the most obvious feature about the movements of English speech. But remember always that such a description of movement is only a description; it isn't the movement itself.

Lastly, language may be ornamented in various ways. The two most familiar ornaments are alliteration (e.g., In a summer season when soft was the sun), and rhyme (Old King *Cole* was a merry old *soul*). Alliteration is found in the early verse of the Teutonic people, and rhyme, begin-

ning perhaps in the marching-songs of the Roman soldiers, was adopted by the early Christian hymnwriters and so came into modern verse. Alliteration is the effect produced by an arrangement of words beginning with a similar sound; rhyme that produced by an arrangement of words ending in a similar sound. The sounds are similar, but belong to different words, and, therefore, have different meanings in each place. Through the likeness, thoughts and feelings hitherto distinct in the mind are joined together. They are, in fact, sound metaphors.

Different Kinds of Writing

The difference between different kinds of writing lies not so much in the writing itself, but in the way we look at it (and, of course, in the way the author wished us to look at it; but we often know very little about that). Literary forms do not exist outside our own minds. When we read anything, no matter what—a description of a scientific experiment, a history book, a ballad, or a novel—in so far as we pay attention only to what things are happening one after another to learn something or somebody, it is a story; in so far as we read it only to learn the way in which something or someone behaves in certain circumstances, it is science; in so far as we read it only to find out what has actually happened in the past, it is history.

People often ask what is the difference between poetry and prose. The only difference is in the way the writer looks at things. (There is another difference between prose and *verse*; see above.) For instance, the novelist starts with a general idea in his mind; say, that people are always trying to escape from their responsibilities, and that escape only leaves them in a worse mess. Then he writes a story about what happened to Mr. and Mrs. Smith. He may never say, in so many words, that they tried to escape, never mention his idea, but this idea is the force that drives the story along. The poet, on the other hand, hears people talking in his club about the sad story of Mr. and Mrs. Smith. He thinks, "There now, that's very interesting. They are like those sailors who tried to get to India by the North-West Passage. On they go, getting farther and farther into the ice, miles from home. Why that's a good idea for a poem." He writes a poem about explorers; he may never mention Mr. and Mrs. Smith at all. The novelist then goes from the general to the particular, the poet from the particular to the general, and you can see this also in the way they use words. The novelist uses words with their general meaning, and uses a whole lot of them to build up a particular effect: his character. The poet uses words with their particular meanings and puts them together to give a general effect: his ideas. Actually, of course, nearly all novels and all poems except very short ones have both ways of looking at things in them (e.g., Chaucer's *Canterbury Tales* is more like a novel in verse; Melville's *Moby Dick* is more like a poem in prose). All you can say is that one way is typical of the novelist and the other of the poet.

Why People Write Books

People write in order to be read. They would like to be read by everybody and for ever. They feel alone, cut off from each other in an indifferent world where they do not live for very long. How can they get in touch again? How can they prolong their lives? Children by their bodies live on in a life they will not live to see, meet friends they will never know, and will in their turn have children, some tiny part of them living on all the time. These by their bodies; books by their minds.

But the satisfaction of any want is pleasant: we not only enjoy feeling full, we enjoy eating; so people write books because they enjoy it, as a carpenter enjoys making a cupboard. Books are written for money, to convert the world, to pass the time; but these reasons are always trivial, beside the first two—company and creation.

How People Write Books

We know as much, and no more, about how books are made as we know about the making of babies or plants. Suddenly an idea, a feeling, germinates in the mind of the author and begins to grow. He has to look after it, and water the soil with his own experience—all that he knows and has felt, all that has happened to him in his life; straightening a shoot here, pruning a bit there, never quite certain what it is going to do next, whether it will just wither and die, come up in a single night like a mushroom, or strengthen quietly into a great oak-tree. The author is both soil and gardener; the soil part of him does not know what is going on, the gardener part of him has learnt the routine. He may be a careful gardener but poor soil; his books are then beautifully written, but they seem to have nothing in them. We say he lacks inspiration. Or he may be excellent soil but a careless gardener. His books are exciting, but badly arranged, out of proportion, harsh to the ear. We say he lacks technique. Good soil is more important than good gardening, but the finest plants are the product of both.

Why People Read Books

When we read a book, it is as if we were with a person. A book is not only the meaning of the words inside it; it is the person who means them. In real life we treat people in all sorts of ways. Suppose we ask a policeman the way. As long as he is polite we do not bother whether he beats his wife or not; in fact, if he started to tell us about his wife we should get impatient; all we expect of him is that he shall know the way and be able clearly to explain it. But other people we treat differently; we want more from them than information; we want to live *with* them, to feel and think *with* them. When we say a book is good or bad, we mean that we feel towards it as we feel towards what we call a good or bad person.

(Remember, though, that a book about bad characters is not therefore bad, any more than a person is bad because he talks about bad people.) Actually we know that we cannot divide people into good and bad like that; everyone is a mixture; we like some people in some moods and some in others, and as we grow older our taste in people changes. The same is true of books. People who say they only read good books are prigs. We all like some good books and some bad. The only silly thing to do is to pretend that bad books are good. The awful nonsense that most people utter when they are discussing or criticizing a book would be avoided if they would remember that they would never think of criticizing a person in the same way.

For instance, people will often say that they don't like the book because they don't agree with it. We think it rather silly when people can only be friends with those who hold the same views in everything.

Reading is valuable just because books are like people, and make the same demands on us to understand and like them. Our actual circle of friends is generally limited; we feel that our relations with them are not as good as they might be, more muddled, difficult, unsatisfying than necessary. Just as a boxer exercises for a real fight with a punchball or a sparring-partner, so you can train yourself for relations with real people with a book. It's not easy, and you can't begin until you have had some experience of real people first (any more than a boxer can practice with a punchball until he has learnt a little about boxing), but books can't die or quarrel or go away as people can. Reading and living are not two watertight compartments. You must use your knowledge of people to guide you when reading books, and your knowledge of books to guide you when living with people. The more you read the more you will realize what difficult and delicate things relations with people are, but how worth while they can be when they really come off; and the more you know of other people, the more you will be able to get out of each kind of book, and the more you

will realize what a true good a really great book can be, but that great books are as rare as great men.

Reading is valuable when it improves our technique of living, helps us to live fuller and more satisfactory lives. It fails when we can't understand or feel with what we read, either because of ignorance of our own obscurity in the writing.

It is a danger when we only read what encourages us in lax and crude ways of feeling and thinking: like cheap company (too many people only read what flatters them; they like to be told they are fine fellows, and all is for the best in the best of all possible worlds; or they only want to be excited or to forget tomorrow's bills). It is also dangerous when it becomes a substitute for living, when we get frightened of real people and find books safer company; they are a rehearsal for living, not living itself. Swots and "bookish" people have stage fright.

Books and Life

A book is the product of somebody living in a particular place at a particular time. People have a nature they are born with, and they have a life which they lead and live through, which alters that original nature. They may be born with great talents but live in a society where they can't develop or use them; or they may be only averagely gifted but get the opportunity to make the most of them. Great men are a combination of talent and opportunity. Great books are as rare as great men, and, like them, they often come in batches. It is improbable that the men living in England in the sixteenth century were more naturally talented than those living in the eleventh, but they had a better chance, a more stimulating world. Take the greatest names in literature—Homer, Dante, Shakespeare. Homer is typical of a kind of writing called epic-long stories in verse about the exploits of a small group of young warriors under a leader, the pioneer or pirate band society, held together by their devotion to their leader, and by common interests in fighting and farming and wife-getting. Dante was a citizen of Florence, a small and ambitious city State (he was also a citizen of the universal religious State, the Catholic Church). Shakespeare was born in a small, young country, fighting for its existence as an independent nation. There is something common to all three: the small size of the society and the unity of interests. Whenever a society is united (and the larger the society the harder it is to unite and the cruder and more violent the only feelings which come) it has a great outburst of good writing; we don't only find one or two first-class writers, we find a whole mess of good small writers (think of Athens in the fifth century and the Elizabethan song-writers). Being made one, like the sailors pulling on the rope, it has all power.

But whenever society breaks up into classes, sects, townspeople and peasants, rich and poor, literature suffers. There is writing for the gentle and writing for the simple, for the highbrow and lowbrow; the latter gets cruder and coarser, the former more and more refined. And so, to-day, writing gets shut up in a circle of clever people writing about themselves for themselves, or ekes out an underworld existence, cheap and nasty. Talent does not die out, but it can't make itself understood. Since the underlying reason for writing is to bridge the gulf between one person and another, as the sense of loneliness increases, more and more books are written by more and more people, most of them with little or no talent. Forests are cut down, rivers of ink absorbed, but the lust to write is still unsatisfied. What is going to happen? If it were only a question of writing it wouldn't matter; but it is an index of our health. It's not only books, but our lives, that are going to pot.

Cognitive Apprenticeship: Teaching the Crafts of Reading, Writing and Mathematics

Allan Collins, John Seely Brown and Susan E. Newman

It is only in the last century, and only in industrialized nations, that formal schooling has emerged as a widespread method of educating the young. Before schools, apprenticeship was the most common means of learning, used to transmit the knowledge required for expert practice in fields from painting and sculpting to medicine and law. Even today, many complex and important skills, such as those required for language use and social interaction, are learned informally through apprenticeshiplike methods—*i.e.*, methods involving not didactic teaching, but observation, coaching, and successive approximation while carrying out a variety of tasks and activities.

The difference between formal schooling and apprenticeship methods are many, but for our purposes, one is most important. Perhaps as a byproduct of the specialization of learning in schools, skills and knowledge taught in schools have become abstracted from their uses in the world. In apprenticeship learning, on the other hand, target skills are not only continually in use by skilled practitioners, but are instrumental to the accomplishment of meaningful tasks. Said differently, apprenticeship embeds the learning of skills and knowledge in the social and functional context of their use. This difference is not academic, but has serious implications for the

nature of the knowledge that students acquire. This paper attempts to elucidate some of those implications through a proposal for the retooling of apprenticeship methods for the teaching and learning of cognitive skills. Specifically, we propose the development of a new cognitive apprenticeship to teach students the thinking and problem-solving skills involved in school subjects such as reading, writing, and mathematics.

The organization of the paper is as follows: In the first section, we discuss briefly what we believe to be key shortcomings in current curricular and pedagogical practices. We then present some of the structural features of traditional apprenticeship and discuss, in general, what would be required to adapt these characteristics to the teaching and learning of cognitive skills.

In the second session we consider in detail three recently developed pedagogical "success models," which we believe exemplify aspects of apprenticeship methods in teaching the thinking and reasoning skills involved in reading, writing and mathematics. We attempt to show how and why these methods are successful, with regard to the development of not only the cognitive, but also the metacognitive skills required for true expertise.

In the final section, we organize our ideas on the purposes and characteristics of successful teaching into a general framework for the design of learning environments, where "environment" includes the content being taught, the pedagogical methods employed, the sequencing of learning activities, and the sociology of learning. This framework emphasizes how cognitive apprenticeship goes beyond the techniques of traditional apprenticeships. We hope it will be useful to the field in designing, evaluating, and doing research on pedagogical methods, materials, and technologies.

Toward a Synthesis of Schooling and Apprenticeship

Schooling and the Acquisition of Expert Practice: While schools have been relatively successful in organizing and conveying large bodies of conceptual and factual knowledge, standard pedagogical practices render key aspects of expertise invisible to students. In particular, too little attention is paid to the processes that experts engage in to use or acquire knowledge in carrying out complex or realistic tasks. Where processes are addressed, the emphasis is on formulaic methods for solving "textbook" problems, or on the development of low-level subskills in relative isolation. Few resources are devoted to higher-order problem-solving activities that require students to actively integrate and appropriately apply subskills and conceptual knowledge.

As a result, conceptual and problem-solving knowledge acquired in school remains largely unintegrated or inert for many students. In some cases, knowledge remains bound to surface features of problems as they appear in textbooks and class presentations. For example, Schoenfeld (1985) has found that students rely on their knowledge of standard textbook patterns of problem presentation, rather than on their knowledge of problem-solving strategies or intrinsic properties of the problems themselves, for help in solv-

ing mathematics problems. Problems that fall outside these patterns do not invoke the appropriate problem-solving methods and relevant conceptual knowledge. In other cases, students fail to use resources available to them to improve their skills because they lack models of the processes required for doing so. For example, in the domain of writing, students are unable to make use of potential models of good writing acquired through reading because they have no understanding of the strategies and processes required to produce such text. Stuck with what Bereiter and Scardamalia (1987) call "knowledge-telling strategies" they are unaware that expert writing involves organizing ones ideas about a topic, elaborating goals to be achieved in the writing, thinking about what the audience is likely to know or believe about the subject and so on.

In order to make real differences in students' skill, we need both to understand the nature of expert practice and to devise methods that are appropriate to learning that practice. Thus, we must first recognize that cognitive and metacognitive strategies and processes, more centrally than low-level subskills or abstract conceptual and factual knowledge, are the organizing principles of expertise, particularly in domains such as reading, writing, and basic mathematics. Further, because expert practice in these domains rests crucially on the integration of cognitive and metacognitive processes, we believe that it can best be taught through methods that emphasize what Lave (1988) calls successive approximation of mature practice, methods that have traditionally been employed in apprenticeship to transmit complex physical processes and skills. We propose that these methods of apprenticeship be adapted to the teaching and learning of complex cognitive skills.

Traditional Apprenticeship: In order to get an idea of what these methods may look like and why they are likely to be effective, let us first consider some of the crucial features of traditional apprenticeship. We have relied on Lave's (1988) careful description of apprenticeship as practiced in a West African tailoring shop for many of our insights into the nature of apprenticeship.

First and foremost, apprenticeship highlights methods for carrying out tasks in a domain. Apprentices learn these methods through a combination of what Lave calls observation, coaching and practice or what we from the teacher's point of view, call modelling, coaching, and fading. In this sequence of activities, the apprentice repeatedly observes the master executing (or modelling) the target process, which usually involves a number of different but interrelated subskills. The apprentice then attempts to execute the process with guidance and help from the master (coaching). A key aspect of coaching is the provision of scaffolding, which is the support, in the form of reminders and help, that the apprentice requires to approximate the execution of the entire composite of skills. Once the learner has a grasp of the target skill, the master reduces his participation (fades), providing only limited hints, refinements, and feedback to the learner, who practices by successively approximating smooth execution of the whole skill.

Several points are worth emphasizing here. The interplay between observation, scaffolding, and increasingly independent practice aids apprentices both in developing self-monitoring and correction skills, and in integrating the skills and conceptual knowledge needed to advance toward expertise. Observation plays a surprisingly key role; Lave hypothesizes that it aids learners in developing a conceptual model of the target task or process prior to attempting to execute it. Having a conceptual model is an important factor in apprenticeship's success in teaching complex skills without resorting to lengthy practice of isolated subskills, for three related reasons. First it provides learners with an advanced organizer for their initial attempts to execute a complex skill, thus allowing them to concentrate more of their attention on execution than would otherwise be possible. Second, a conceptual model provides an interpretative structure for making sense of the

feedback, hints, and corrections from the master during interactive coaching sessions. And third, it provides an internalized guide for the period of relatively independent practice by successive approximation. Moreover, development of a conceptual model, which can be continually updated through further observation and feedback, encourages autonomy in what we call reflection (Collins & Brown, 1988). Reflection is the process that underlies the ability of learners to compare their own performance, at both micro and macro levels, to the performance of an expert. Such comparisons aid learners in diagnosing difficulties and incrementally adjusting their performance until they reach competence. A conceptual model serves as an internal model of expert performance, and thus as a basis for development of self-monitoring and correction skills.

A second key observation about apprenticeship in general concerns the embedding social context in which learning takes place. Apprenticeship derives many (cognitively important) characteristics from its embedding in a subculture in which most, if not all, members are visible participants in the target skills. As a result, learners have continual access to models of expertise-in-use against which to refine their understanding of complex skills. Moreover, it is not uncommon for apprentices to have access to several masters and thus to a variety of models of expertise. Such richness and variety helps apprentices to understand that there may be multiple ways of carrying out a task and to recognize that no one individual embodies all knowledge or expertise. And finally, in the tailoring shop described by Lave, learners have the opportunity to observe other learners at varying degrees of skill; among other things, this encourages them to view learning as an incrementally staged process, while providing them with concrete benchmarks for their own progress.

From Traditional to Cognitive Apprenticeship. This paper proposes a rethinking of these aspects of apprenticeship for the teaching and learning of subjects such as reading, writing and mathematics. We call this rethinking of teaching and learning in school "cognitive apprenticeship" to emphasize two things. First, these methods are aimed primarily at teaching the processes that experts use to handle complex tasks. Where conceptual and factual knowledge is addressed, cognitive apprenticeship emphasizes its uses in solving problems and carrying out tasks. That is, in cognitive apprenticeship, conceptual and factual knowledge is exemplified and situated in the contexts of its use. Conceptual knowledge thus becomes known in terms of its uses in a variety of contexts, encouraging both a deeper understanding of the meaning of the concepts themselves and a web of memorable associations between important concepts and problem-solving contexts. It is this dual focus on expert processes and situated learning that we expect to help solve the educational problems of brittle skills and inert knowledge.

Second, the term cognitive apprenticeship refers to the fact that the focus of the learning-through-guided-experience is on cognitive and metacognitive, rather than on physical, skills and processes. While we do not wish to draw a major theoretical distinction between the learning of physical and cognitive skills, there are differences that have practical implications for the organization of teaching and learning activities and teacher-learner interactions. Most importantly, traditional apprenticeship has evolved to teach domains in which the process of carrying out target skills (1) is external and thus readily available to both student and teacher for observation, comment, refinement, and correction and (2) bears a relatively transparent relationship to concrete products that are the outcome of the skill. The externalization of relevant processes and methods makes possible such characteristics of apprenticeship as its reliance on observation as a primary means of building a conceptual model of a complex target skill. And the relatively transparent relationship, at all stages of production, between process and product facilitates the learner's recognition and diagnosis of errors,

upon which the early development of self-correction skills depends.

Applying apprenticeship methods to largely cognitive skills requires the externalization of processes that are usually carried out internally. At least as most subjects are taught and learned in school, teachers cannot make fine adjustments in students' application of skill and knowledge to problems and tasks, because they have no access to the relevant cognitive processes. By the same token, students do not usually have access to the cognitive problem-solving processes of instructors, as a basis for learning through observation and mimicry. Cognitive research, through such methods as protocol analysis, has begun to delineate the cognitive and metacognitive processes that heretofore have tacitly comprised expertise. Cognitive apprenticeship teaching methods are designed, among other things, to bring these tacit processes into the open, where students can observe, enact and practice them with help from the teacher and from other students.

Cognitive apprenticeship also requires extended techniques to encourage the development of self-correction and -monitoring skills, as we cannot rely on the transparent relationship between process and product that characterizes the learning of such physical skills as tailoring. We have identified two basic means of fostering these crucial metacognitive skills. First, cognitive apprenticeship encourages reflection on differences between novice and expert performance by alternation between expert and novice efforts and by techniques that we have elsewhere called "abstracted replay" (Collins & Brown, 1988). Alternation between expert and novice efforts in a shared problem-solving context sensitizes students to the details of expert performance as the basis for incremental adjustments in their own performance. Abstracted replay attempts to focus students' observations and comparisons directly on the determining features of both their own and an expert's performance by highlighting those features in a skillful verbal description, or, in some domains, through use of recording technologies such as computers or videotapes.

A second means of encouraging the development of self-monitoring and -correction skills is based on the insight that these skills require the problem solver to alternate some version of both generative and evaluative processes. However, both types of processes are complex and can be difficult to learn in tandem. Thus, cognitive apprenticeship involves the development and externalization of a producer-critic dialogue that students can gradually internalize. This development and externalization is accomplished through discussion, alternation of teacher and learner roles, and group problem-solving.

Some Caveats: Obviously, apprenticeship is intended as a suggestive rather than an exact model for teaching and learning in the future. In addition to the emphasis on cognitive and metacognitive skills, there are two major differences between cognitive apprenticeship and traditional apprenticeship. First, because traditional apprenticeship is set in the workplace, the problems and tasks that are given to learners arise not from pedagogical concerns but from the demands of the workplace. Cognitive apprenticeship as we envision it differs from traditional apprenticeship in that the tasks and problems are chosen to illustrate the power of certain techniques or methods, to give students practice in applying these methods in diverse settings, and to slowly increase the complexity of tasks so that component skills and models can be integrated. In short, tasks are sequenced to reflect the changing demands of learning. Letting the job demands select the tasks for students to practice is one of the great inefficiencies of traditional apprenticeship.

On the other hand, the economic bias in apprenticeship has useful as well as less-than-ideal effects. For example, apprentices are encouraged to quickly learn skills that are useful, and therefore meaningful within the social context of the workplace. Moreover, apprentices have natural opportunities to realize the value, in concrete economic terms, of their developing skill: well-executed skills result in saleable products. Cognitive apprenticeship must find a way to create a culture of expert practice for students to participate in and aspire to, as well as devise meaningful benchmarks and incentives for progress.

A second difference between cognitive apprenticeship and traditional apprenticeship is the emphasis in cognitive apprenticeship on decontextualizing knowledge so that it can be used in many different settings. Traditional apprenticeship emphasizes teaching skills in the context of their use. We propose that cognitive apprenticeship should extend situated learning to diverse settings so that students learn how to apply their skills in different contexts. Moreover, the abstract principles underlying the application of knowledge and skills in different settings should be articulated as fully as possible by the teacher, whenever they arise in different contexts.

We do not want to argue that cognitive apprenticeship is the only way to learn. Reading a book or listening to a lecture are important ways to learn, particularly in domains where conceptual and factual knowledge are central. Active listeners or readers, who test their understanding and pursue the issues that are raised in their minds, learn things that apprenticeship can never teach. However, to the degree the reader or listener is passive, they will not learn as much as they would by apprenticeship, because apprenticeship forces them to use their knowledge. Moreover, few people learn to be active readers and listeners on their own, and this is where cognitive apprenticeship is critical—observing the processes by which an expert listener or reader thinks, and practicing these skills under the guidance of the expert, can teach students to learn on their own more skillfully

Even in domains that rest on elaborate conceptual and factual underpinnings, students must learn the practice or art of solving problems and carrying out tasks. And to achieve expert practice, some version of apprenticeship remains the method of choice. Thus apprenticeshiplike methods are widely used in graduate education in most domains. Students are expected to learn how to solve problems that arise in the context of carrying out complex tasks, and to extend and make use of their textbook knowledge, by undertaking significant projects guided by an expert in the field.

We would argue that the development of expert practice through situated learning and the acquisition of cognitive and metacognitive skills is equally if not more important in more elementary domains. This is nowhere more evident than in the foundational domains of reading, writing and mathematics. These domains are foundational not only because they provide the basis for learning and communication in other school subjects, but also because they engage cognitive and metacognitive processes that are basic to learning and thinking more generally. Unlike school subjects such as chemistry or history, these domains rest on relatively sparse conceptual and factual underpinnings, turning instead on students' robust and efficient execution of a set of cognitive and metacognitive skills. Given effective analyses and externalizable prompts for these skills, we believe that these domains are particularly well suited to teaching methods modelled on cognitive apprenticeship. In the next section of this paper, we discuss a recently developed and highly successful model for teaching the cognitive and metacognitive skills involved in reading in terms of the key notions underlying our cognitive apprenticeship model.

A Success Model for Cognitive Apprenticeship

Palincsar and Brown's Reciprocal Teaching of Reading: Palincsar and Brown's (1984) method of teaching reading comprehension which exemplifies many of the features of cognitive apprenticeship, has proved remarkably effective in raising students' scores on reading comprehension tests, especially those of poor readers. The basic method centers on modelling

and coaching students in four strategic skills: formulating questions based on the text, summarizing the text, making predictions about what will come next, and clarifying difficulties with the text. The method has been used with groups of two to five students, as well as individual students. It is called *Reciprocal Teaching* because the teacher and students take turns playing the role of teacher.

The procedure is as follows: Both the teacher and students read a paragraph silently to themselves. Whoever is playing the role of teacher formulates a question based on the paragraph, constructs a summary, and makes a prediction or clarification if any come to mind. Initially, the teacher models this process, eventually turning it over to the students. When students first undertake the process, the teacher coaches them extensively on how to construct good questions and summaries, offering prompts and critiquing their efforts. In this way, the teacher provides scaffolding for the students, enabling them to take on whatever portion of the task they can. As the students become more proficient, the teacher fades, assuming the role of monitor and providing occasional hints or feedback.

Reciprocal Teaching is extremely effective. In a pilot study with individual students who were poor readers, the method raised subjects' reading comprehension test scores from 15% to 85% accuracy after about 20 training sessions. Six months later the students were still at 60% accuracy, recovering to 85% after only one session. In a subsequent study with groups of two students, the scores increased from about 30% to 80% accuracy, with very little change eight weeks later. In classroom studies with groups of four to seven students, test scores increased from about 40% to 80% correct, again with only a slight decline eight weeks later. These are very dramatic effects for any instructional intervention.

Why is Reciprocal Teaching so effective? In our analysis, which reflects in part the views of Palincsar and Brown (1984) its effectiveness depends upon the co-occurrence of a number of factors.

First, the method engages students in a set of activities that help them form a new conceptual model of the task of reading. In traditional schooling, students learn to identify reading with the subskills of recognizing and pronouncing words and with the activities of scanning text and saying it aloud. Under the new conception, students recognize that reading requires constructive activities such as formulating questions and making summaries and predictions, as well as evaluative ones such as analyzing and clarifying the points of difficulty in the text. Moreover, carrying out these activities by repeatedly reviewing the text helps students realize that reading for understanding is often more than a one-pass operation; it provides them with a more realistic expectation about what will be required of them as they go on to read increasingly difficult texts.

Second, these activities involve the student in using the reading strategies and metacognitive skills necessary for expert reading. In particular:

1. *Formulating questions* is an important strategic activity for understanding difficult texts (Collins, Brown, and Larkin, 1980) because it provides the basis for checking if the text makes sense (self monitoring). Formulating questions that capture the main ideas of the text sometimes leads to questions that the text raises but does not answer, as the basis for further inquiry.

2. *Summarizing*, like formulating questions, provides a general test of comprehension and so forms the basis for comprehension monitoring: it is a preliminary phase of self-diagnosis. Students learn that if they cannot form a good summary, then they do not understand the text and had better either reread the text or try to clarify their difficulties (Collins and Smith, 1982).

3. *Clarification* is a key activity in comprehension monitoring that involves detailed self diagnosis, in which students attempt to isolate and formulate their particular difficulties in understanding a text. While summarizing is a fairly global test of comprehension, usually applied at the paragraph level, clarification attempts to narrow points of difficulty by focusing on word and phrase levels of meaning. Skill at clarifying difficulties provides students with the basis for using evidence from subsequent text to disambiguate the meaning of problematic words or phrases, a key strategy employed by expert readers.

4. *Prediction* involves formulating guesses or hypotheses about what the author of a text is likely to say next, and as such, promotes an overall reading strategy of hypothesis formulation and testing. The inclusion of prediction as an explicit strategic activity for beginning readers reflects the fact that skilled reading involves developing expectations and evaluating them as evidence accumulates from the text (Collins and Smith, 1982).

The third factor we think is critical for the success of Reciprocal Teaching is that the teacher models expert strategies in a problem context shared directly and immediately with the students (Palincsar & Brown, 1984). This organization of teacher-learner interaction encourages students first to focus their observations and then to reflect on their own performance relative to that of the teacher during subsequent modelling. Here's how it works: both teacher and students read a paragraph. The teacher then performs the four activities: she articulates the questions she would ask about the paragraph, summarizes it, makes predictions about what would be next and explains what part of the paragraph gave her difficulty. She may try to explain why she generated a particular question or made a particular prediction. What is crucial here is that the students listen in the context of knowing that they will soon undertake the same task, using that expectation to focus their observations on how those activities are related to the paragraph. After they have tried to do it themselves, and perhaps had difficulties, they listen to the teacher with new knowledge about the task. As they read subsequent passages, they may try to generate a question or summary to themselves, noticing later what she does differently. That is, they can compare their own questions or summaries with the questions or summaries she generates. They can then reflect on any differences, trying to understand what led to those differences. We have argued elsewhere that this kind of reflection is critical to learning (Collins & Brown, 1988).

Fourth, the technique of providing scaffolding is a crucial factor in the success of Reciprocal Teaching for several reasons. Most importantly, it decomposes the task as necessary for the students to carry it out, thereby helping them to see how, in detail, to go about the task. For example, in formulating questions, the teacher might first want to see if the student can generate a question on his or her own: if not, she might suggest starting a question with "Why," or "How" If the student still can't generate a question, she might suggest formulating a simple "Why" question about the agent in the story. If that fails, she might generate one herself and ask the student to reformulate it in his or her own words. In this way, it gets students started in the new skills, giving them a "feel" for the skills and helping them develop confidence that they can do them. Scaffolding is designed to help students when they are at an *impasse*. (Brown and VanLehn, 1980). With successful scaffolding techniques, students get as much support as they need to carry out the task, but no more. Hints and modelling are then gradually faded out, with students taking on more and more of the task as they become more skillful. These techniques of scaffolding and fading slowly build students' confidence that they can master the skills required.

The final aspect of Reciprocal Teaching that we think is critical is having students assume the dual roles of producer and critic. That is, they must not only be able to produce good questions

and summaries, but they also learn to evaluate the summaries or questions of others. By becoming critics as well as producers, students are forced to articulate their knowledge about what makes a good question, prediction, or summary. This knowledge then becomes more readily available for application to their own summaries and questions, thus improving a crucial aspect of their metacognitive skills. Moreover, once articulated, this knowledge can no longer simply reside in tacit form. It becomes more available for performing a variety of tasks; that is, it is freed from its contextual binding, so that it can be used in many different contexts . . .

Teaching Methods

As we have discussed, a key goal in the design of teaching methods should be to help students acquire and integrate cognitive and metacognitive strategies for using, managing and discovering knowledge. However, it is our belief that the way in which these strategies are acquired and, once acquired, brought to play in problem solving, is both subtle and poorly understood. In general, it seems clear that both acquisition and use of these strategies depend crucially on interactions between the individual's current knowledge and beliefs, the social and physical environment in which the problem-solving takes place, and the local details of the problem-solving itself as it unfolds. A major direction in current cognitive research is to attempt to formulate explicitly the strategies and skills underlying expert practice, in order to make them a legitimate focus of teaching in schools and other learning environments. Indeed, all three success models we have discussed are based on explicit formulations of cognitive and metacognitive strategies and center their teaching around activities designed to explicitly convey these to students. However, we believe it is also important to consider the possibility that because of the nature of the relationship between these strategies and the overall problem context, not all of the necessary—and certainly not all of the possible—strategies involved in complex cognitive activities can be captured and made explicit. In this regard, it is worth noting that these strategies and skills have tended to remain tacit and thus to be lost to formal education precisely because they arise from the practice of solving problems, in situ, in the domain. Moreover, we would argue that even given explicit formulation of strategies, understanding how to use them depends crucially on understanding the way in which they are embedded in the context of actual problem solving.

For these reasons, we believe that teaching methods should be designed to give students the opportunity to observe, engage in, and invent or discover expert strategies in context. Such an approach will enable students to see how these strategies fit together with their factual and conceptual knowledge, and how they cue off and make use of a variety of resources in the social and physical environment. This is the essence of what we mean by situated learning, and the reason why the cognitive apprenticeship method, with its modelling-coaching-fading paradigm, is successful and perhaps indispensable.

The following six teaching methods fall roughly into three groups: the first three (modelling; coaching, and scaffolding), are the core of cognitive apprenticeship, designed to help students acquire an integrated set of cognitive and metacognitive skills through processes of observation and of guided and supported practice. The next two (articulation and reflection) are methods designed to help students both to focus their observations of expert problem solving and to gain conscious access to (and control of their own problem solving strategies. The final method (exploration) is aimed at encouraging learner autonomy not only in carrying out expert problem solving processes, but also in defining or formulating the problems to be solved.

1. *Modelling* involves showing an expert carrying out a task so that students can observe and build a conceptual model of the processes that are required to accomplish the task. In cognitive domains, this requires the externalization of usually internal (cognitive) processes and activities—specifically, the heuristics and control processes by which experts make use of basic conceptual and procedural knowledge. For example, a teacher might model the reading process by reading aloud in one voice, while verbalizing her thought processes (*e.g.*, the making and testing of hypotheses about what the text means, what the author intends, what he or she thinks will happen next, and so on) in another voice (Collins & Smith, 1982).

2. *Coaching* consists of observing students while they carry out a task and offering hints, scaffolding, feedback, modelling, reminders and new tasks aimed at bringing their performance closer to expert performance coaching may serve to direct students' attention to a previously unnoticed aspect of the task or simply to remind the student of some aspect of the task that is known but has been temporarily overlooked. Coaching focuses on the enactment and integration of skills in the service of a well-understood goal through highly interactive and highly situated feedback and suggestions. That is, the content of the coaching interaction is immediately related to specific events or problems that arise as the student attempts to carry out the target task. In reading, coaching might consist of having students attempt to give summaries of different texts. The teacher in the role of coach might choose texts with interesting difficulties, might remind the student that a summary needs to integrate the whole text into a sentence or two, might suggest how to start constructing a summary, might evaluate the summary a student produces in terms of how it could be improved, or ask another student to evaluate it.

3. *Scaffolding* refers to the supports the teacher provides to help the student carry out a task. These supports can either take the forms of suggestions or help, as in Palincsar and Brown's (1984) Reciprocal Teaching, or they can take the form of physical supports, as with the cue cards in Scardamalia et al's (1984) procedural facilitation of writing or the short skits used to teach downhill skiing (Burton, Brown & Fisher, 1984). When scaffolding is provided by a teacher, it involves the teacher in carrying out parts of the overall task that the student cannot yet manage. As such, it involves a kind of cooperative problem-solving effort by teacher and student in which the express intention is for the student to assume as much of the task on his own as possible, as soon as possible. A requisite of such scaffolding is accurate diagnosis of the student's current skill level or difficulty and the availability of an intermediate step at the appropriate level of difficulty in carrying out the target activity. *Fading* consists of the gradual removal of supports until students are on their own.

4. *Articulation* includes any method of getting students to articulate their knowledge, reasoning, or problem-solving processes in a domain. We have identified several different methods of articulation. First, *Inquiry Teaching* (Colling & Stevens, 1982, 1983) is a strategy of questioning students to lead them to articulate and refine "proto-theories" about the four kinds of knowledge enumerated above. For example, an inquiry teacher in reading might systematically question students about why one summary of the text is a good one while another is poor, in order to get the students to formulate an explicit model of what makes a good summary. Second, teachers might encourage students to articulate their thoughts as they carry out their problem solving as do Scardamalia et al. (1984).

Third, having students assume the critic or monitor role in cooperative activities, as do all three models we discussed, leads students to formulate and articulate their knowledge of problem-solving and control processes.

5. Reflection (Brown, 1985a, 1985b: Collins & Brown, 1988) involves enabling students to compare their own problem solving processes with that of an expert, other students, and ultimately, an internal cognitive model of expertise. Reflection is enhanced by the use of techniques for reproducing or "replaying" the performances of both expert and novice for comparison. This can be done through a variety of methods. For example, an expert's skillful post mortem of the problem-solving process, as Schoenfeld (1983) showed, can serve as a target for reflective comparison, as can the students' post mortems of their own problem-solving process. Alternately, various recording technologies, such as video or audio recorders, and computers can be employed to reproduce student and expert performance. The levels of detail at which a replay should be done may vary depending on the student's stage of learning, but often some form of "abstracted replay," in which the determining features of expert and student performance are highlighted, is desirable. For reading or writing methods to encourage reflection might consist of recording students as they think out loud and then replaying the tape for comparison with the thinking of experts and other students.

6. *Exploration* involves pushing students into a mode of problem-solving on their own. Forcing students to do exploration is critical for students to learn how to frame questions or problems that are interesting and that they can solve. Exploration is the natural culmination of the fading of supports. It involves not only fading in problem solving, but fading in problem setting as well. But students do not know *a priori* how to explore

a domain productively. So exploration strategies need to be taught as part of learning strategies more generally.

Exploration as a method of teaching involves setting general goals for students, but encouraging them to focus on particular subgoals of interest to them or even to revise the general goals as they come upon something more interesting to pursue. For example, in reading the teacher might send the students to the library to find out what president died in office as a result of a trip to Alaska, or to investigate theories about why the stock market crashed in 1929. In writing students might be encouraged to write an essay defending the most outrageous thesis they can devise, or to keep a diary of their best ideas or their most traumatic experiences. In mathematics students might be given a data base on teenagers detailing their backgrounds and how they spend their time and money; the students' task might be to come up with hypotheses about what determines how different groups of teenagers spend their time or money that they test out by analyzing the data base they have been given. The goal is to find general tasks that students will find interesting and turn them loose on them, after they have acquired some basic exploration skills. . . .

References

Bereiter, C. & Scardamalia, M. (1987). *The psychology of written composition*. Hillsdale NJ: Lawrence Erlbaum Associates.

Brown, J. S. (1985a). Process versus produce: A perspective on tools for communal and informal electronic learning. *Journal of Educational Computing Research*, I. 179-201.

Brown, J. S. (1985b). Idea-amplifiers: New kinds of electronic learning. *Educational Horizons*, 63, 108-112.

Brown, J.S., & VanLehn, K. (1980). Repair theory: A generative theory of bugs in procedural skills. *Cognitive Science*, 4, 379-426.@REF BODY SIZE = Burton, R., Brown, J. S., & Fischer, G. (1984). Skiing as a model of instruction. In B. Rogoff & J. Lave (Eds.), *Everyday cognition: Its development in social context*. Cambridge, MA: Harvard University Press.

Collins, A. & Brown, J. S. (1988). The computer as a tool for learning through reflection. In H. Mandl and A. Lesgold (Eds.), *Learning issues for intelligent tutoring systems*. New York: Springer.

Collins, A., Brown, J. S., & Larkin, K. M. (1980). Inference in text understanding. In R. J. Spiro, B.C. Bruce, & W. F. Brewer (Eds.), *Theoretical issues in reading comprehension*. Hillsdale, NJ: Erlbaum.

Collins, A. & Smith, E. E. (1982). Teaching the process of reading comprehension. In D.K. Detterman & R. J. Sternberg (Eds.), *How much and how can intelligence be increased?* Norwood, NJ: Ablex.

Collins, A. & Stevens, A.L. (1982). Goals and strategies of inquiry teachers. In R. Glaser (Ed.), *Advances in instructional psychology* (Vol. 2). Hillsdale, NJ: Erlbaum.

Collins, A., & Stevens, A. L., (1983). A cognitive theory of interactive teaching. In C. M. Reigeluth (Ed.), *Instructional design theories and models: An overview*. Hillsdale, NJ: Erlbaum.

Lave, J. (1984). Tailored learning: Education and everyday practice among craftsmen in West Africa.

Lave, J. (1988). *The culture of acquisition and the practice of understanding* (Tech. Rep. No. 88-0007). Palo Alto, CA: Institute for Research on Learning.

Palincsar, A. S., & Brown, A. L. (1984). Reciprocal teaching of comprehension-fostering and monitoring activities. *Cognition and Instruction*, I. 117-175.

Scardamalia, M., Bereiter, C., & Steinbach, R. (1984) Teachability of reflective processes in written composition. *Cognitive Science*, 8, 173-190.

Schoenfeld, A.H., (1983). Problem solving in the mathematics curriculum: A report, recommendations and an annotated bibliography. *The Mathematical Association of America*, MAA Notes, No. 1.

Schoefeld, A.H. (1985). *Mathematical problem solving*. New York: Academic Press.

Philosophy for Children and the Piagetian Framework

Ann Gazzard

In this paper I have outlined briefly both the major tenets of the traditional Piagetian view in respect of cognitive development and the implications for education which it engenders. The major objections to the inclusion of philosophy into the schools fostered by this view are examined in the context of the responses to these criticisms from those in favour of philosophy for children. The strength of these responses is considered and discussed in terms of the broader context of T. S. Kuhn's work. The paper concludes with an exposition of possible alternative conceptualizations to the Piagetian model, providing an outline of the ramifications which this new perspective has for the introduction of philosophy in schools.

A constant objection that is raised against proposals for the introduction of philosophy into the classroom is that elementary and most middle-school children do not possess the mental capacity for the abstract thinking which philosophy requires. The source of the objection can be traced to the classic works of Jean Piaget, and the argument adduced is that it is not until a child has reached the stage of formal operational thought (12-14 years) that he/she is capable of abstract, hypothetical thinking.

Piaget's writings on cognitive development admit of a number of interpretations with respect to both the concept of a stage and the means of progression through them. The following account, however, represents that interpretation of his stage theory which has become the most entrenched in educational settings. First, Piaget advances three stages of cognitive development namely (1) preoperational, (2) concrete, and (3) formal operational thought. Progression through them is said to occur as a result of maturation. Second, the ages at which these stages are reached are generally set at 2, 5-7, and 12-14 years respectively. And third, an individual is held to be capable of only those forms of thinking characteristic of the putative stage in which he is currently located and those prior to it. For example, while an individual at the stage of concrete operations is presumed to have access to patterns of thinking from previous stages, the dominant interpretation of Piaget holds that the individual is not capable of entertaining thoughts characteristic of the next stage, namely formal operations. The pervasiveness of this interpretation of Piaget and the extent of its acceptance have led many to assume that knowledge about children's thinking styles and capacities is a matter of age alone. It would seem as if the terminology that once served to describe what at most might be the dominant modes of thinking in children at different ages, now serves to define the range of thought children are capable of.

This view of cognitive development has a number of serious implications for the educator.

For the purposes of this short paper, however, I have chosen to highlight only those which have given rise to the major objections in respect of introducing philosophy into the schools.

A major implication of this view is that a child's education should be tailored to conform to the intellectual capacities consistent with the cognitive structures which occur at each successive stage of logical development. Inasmuch as progression through the three intellectual phases is the natural outcome of an individual's overall development, education is subordinate to maturation in terms of its power to enhance cognitive growth. In other words, education can on this view facilitate the use of concepts already made accessible by the process of maturation, but it can do little, if anything, to advance an understanding of higher order concepts. The suggestion here is that it would be futile to engage students in activities that require thinking at a stage beyond the one in which they are currently operating. Some would even go so far as to propose, for example, that such an activity constitutes educational malpractice. In this case, the suggestion is that higher order concepts give rise to confusion which itself in turn fosters the development of rote-learning strategies and negative attitudes towards learning.

A second implication of this view and one which to some extent offers an explanation for the paucity of educational programs specifically designed to enhance thinking skills is the inevitability of intellective-logical development. The point here is not so much that it is impossible to improve children's reasoning, but rather that it is not necessary since this progression will occur itself as a result of normal human development.

Philosophy for children is thus susceptible to indictment on both accounts: first, inasmuch as it requires facility with abstract concepts, it is considered unsuitable for children younger than 12-14 years; and second, insofar as one of its major goals is the development of reasoning skills and reflective thought, its major source of justification becomes untenable.

Those in favor of philosophy for children have responded to these criticisms in one of three ways: (1) attempting to identify weaknesses in Piaget's theory (Gareth Matthews); (2) interpreting Piaget in such a way that the theory can be made to accommodate the possibility of philosophy for children (Hope J. Haas); (3) by ignoring the discrepancy between practicing philosophy for children on the one hand and thinking in Piagetian terms on the other.

Gareth Matthews' criticism of the basis of Piaget's theoretical formulations is an example of the first type of response. In the course of formulating an argument concerning the appropriateness of philosophy for children, Matthews inveighs against Piaget's research techniques on the grounds that Piaget wittingly excluded from his data those unusual responses from children which he himself called "mere romancing." According to Matthews, it is the unusual response which is more likely to be the result of honest reflection and philosophic speculation and reason. Moreover, he adduces many examples of children's speech both from Piaget's work and his own research which lend unequivocal support to his claim. Matthews' point here is an important one. However, insightful criticism of a theory upon which earlier objections are based is not in and of itself sufficient reason to dispel those objections. Undermining the theory will of course undermine the immediate theoretical justification which the objections might have, but it remains to be seen whether an alternative account of cognitive development conducive to the introduction of philosophy in the school, can be provided.

The second typical response to objections from the Piagetian framework is to make interpretative maneuvers within that framework such that the framework might allow for abstract reasoning in younger children and the training of thinking or reasoning in general. Haas (1976), for example, points out that in a more recent version of his theory Piaget concedes that the development of formal operations is not inevitable. While this claim makes possible the teaching of abstract thinking, it has no similar implications for those defined patterns of thought typical of the earlier developmental sequence. In other words, preoperational thought and concrete operational thought remain the inevitable consequences of the natural process of maturation. In order to accommodate empirical findings from a variety of sources which divulge the capacity for formal thought in children much younger than 12-14 years, a number of strategic theoretic-interpretative adjustments have been posited. The suggestion has bee made, for example, that the transition between stages is much more gradual than previously believed, and that, for any given stage, the thinking patterns which it sustains may manifest themselves at different starting times and at different rates. Moreover, in some instances the solution has been to push back further to younger and younger children the age at which formal thought is believed to surface.

Finally, there is the response one finds in persons who are at one and the same time committed to the Piagetian model as a result of their education and happy to teach philosophy and philosophical thinking skills to young children. Confronted with the theoretical dissonance, they may respond with a shoulder-shrug claiming that they persist with the practice of philosophy because the children *can* manage it and do like it, and because they find that its practice facilitates children's learning in other areas. In the next breath, however, the same people continue discourse drawing upon Piagetian terms and concepts.

The second and third points made above are interesting, particularly in light of T. S. Kuhn's work on conceptual revolutions. The latter point, for example, seems to be a typical case of treating as "a pesky little anomaly" any phenomenon that does not fit with the contemporary paradigm of choice, that is, the paradigm which on account of its wide acceptance has become rigidly embedded in everyday thinking. Similarly, the phenomenon described in the second point above

addresses the issue surrounding the unremitting resistance encountered to challenging the existing dominant paradigm with altogether alternative conceptions. Rather, the typical course of action is to attempt to squeeze the intractable data into the existing paradigm, or to stretch the fabric of the theoretical framework in the hope of accommodating the discrepant data. Piaget's stage theory of cognitive development has been subjected extensively to both kinds of treatment. However, theoretical moves of this kind are themselves not unproblematic. New issues concerning the extent to which one can manipulate and reinterpret a theory and still claim to be working within the same theoretical framework emerge. With particular reference to Piaget's work, for example, it becomes questionable whether the concept of stage remains viable given the theoretical maneuvers mentioned above. Moreover, one might also contest the claim that it is still plausible, if not profitable, to continue to think solely within the Piagetian framework. The point that needs to be stressed here is that while manipulations of the Piagetian model may in the end produce a formulation of stage theory which can embrace the divergent empirical findings, this activity, should not preclude the pursuit of equally valid, if not more adequate, conceptual models. To the contrary, the exclusion of this pursuit from research design constitutes irresponsible theorizing and an unnecessary stricture upon the range of practical possibilities. In respect of some of the claims Piaget makes about cognitive structures, Flavell makes a similar point when he writes, "In certain cases, a little reflection establishes that Piaget's claim could only be jeopardized by logical counterarguments, or by some superior alternative conceptualization of the whole domain—in other words, by some sort of nonempirical philosophical-theoretical type rebuttal."[1]

It is not so much, however, that the rejection of Piaget's model is necessitated by those deliberations. Indeed, one should be willing to identify and develop the insights of a great thinker, particularly in those areas where the appropriate claims are well supported by evidence. Rather, what is of utmost importance is the development of an openness to the weaknesses of the theory and to the idea that this model represents only one of possibly many conceptualizations of cognitive development.

The work of Susan Carey presented in her article "Are Children Fundamentally Different Kinds of Thinkers and Learners than Adults?" is apposite here. By way of investigating possible interpretations of what could be meant by the expression "fundamentally different thinkers and learners," she has arrived at five plausible conceptions of cognitive developmental change, four of which may be viewed as the beginnings of genuine alternatives to the Piagetian framework.

Let us begin with the interpretation most commonly aligned with the Piagetian position. Although Piaget's writing at times admits of interpretation in keeping with one of the other four interpretations, the following interpretation has featured prominently in the literature and consequently, has not only shaped educational theory and practice, but has also directed the course of research in developmental psychology. On this interpretation "Children differ from adults with respect to the kinds of concepts they can represent mentally, and/or with respect to the logical operations that can be computed over their mental representations. Either type of difference is called one of representational format."[2] Developmental changes at this level represent the most fundamental differences in thinking and learning possible and are considered the result of maturation. On this view, children are limited by these formats in terms of the ways in which they can think, and these formats themselves are in turn limited by the rate of maturation. (This view together with its educational implications was discussed earlier).

By contrast, the other four interpretations of "fundamentally different thinkers and learners" explain cognitive developmental changes in terms of the acquisition of knowledge. Carey makes a further distinction, namely that between "domain general" and "domain specific" knowledge. "Domain general" knowledge is that knowledge whose acquisition is capable of affecting thinking and learning across discipline boundaries. In this category Carey incorporates metaconceptual skills, "foundational concepts," that is concepts which are putatively a part of all theories, and "tools or ideas of wide application," for example, mathematical tools like calculus and logarithms. Domain specific knowledge, on the other hand, refers to knowing the content of specific disciplines, for example, physics and chemistry. According to Carey, it is a truism that on this interpretation children are fundamentally different thinkers and learners— "children are novices in a multitude of domains where adults are experts."[3]

Whereas most explanations of cognitive development have been cast in terms of representational format or foundational concept change, Carey finds little, if any, support in the research for this rationale. As a result of reviewing the empirical work of Piaget and contemporary developmental psychology in light of these five different conceptual frameworks, Carey concludes that perhaps the best explanation of cognitive development is to be explicated in terms of the acquisition of metaconceptual skills and/or domain specific knowledge. At one point the evidence even tempts her to suggest that "the acquisition and reorganization of strictly domain specific knowledge probably accounts for most of the cognitive differences between 3 year olds and adults."[4] Insofar as cognitive development can then be accounted for in terms of the acquisition of knowledge as opposed to format level changes, its progress is largely a function of learning.

What does all this have to do with philosophy for children? The recognition that cognitive development might be conceived more adequately as a process of learning meets the objections to the introduction of philosophy into the classroom which were promoted on the basis of the traditional Piagetian view. First, insofar as children are no longer limited in terms of their cognitive capacities by maturation, there is no reason to suspect that given the appropriate information they might not manifest and be proficient in abstract thinking at young ages. In other words, the objection made against philosophy for children proclaiming the inability of young children to understand higher order concepts is not tenable on this latter view. Second, philosophy for children and indeed any program aimed directly at developing thinking skills is elevated to the status of a worthwhile, if not vital, educational practice. The view that cognitive growth is predominantly a function of learning reinforces this conception. No longer is education relegated to the role of providing practice in thinking capacities already accessible by virtue of maturation. Instead, on this latter view it can appropriate the role of initiating and developing a variety of thinking styles in children. It need not be argued that the Piagetian position could not be extended eventually to accommodate this role of education and the consequent viability of philosophy for children. This point is rather that in light of the alternative conceptions to cognitive development shown here, the viability and importance of philosophy for children are at once ratified.

Footnotes

1. Flavell, J. H. *Stage-related Properties of Cognitive Development*, p. 446.
2. Carey, S., *Are Children Fundamentally Different Thinkers and Learners than Adults?*, p. 1.
3. Carey, S., ibid., p. 40.
4. Carey, S., ibid., p. 40.

Bibliography

Carey, S. "Are Children Fundamentally Different Kinds of Thinkers and Learners than Adults?" To appear in S. Chipman, J. Segal and R. Glaser, *Thinking and Learning Skills, Vol. 2*, Earlbaum Associates, in press.

Flavell, J. H. Stage-related properties of cognitive development. *Cognitive Psychology*, 2, 1971, 421-453.

Haas, H. J. The Value of "Philosophy for Children" within the Piagetian Framework. *Metaphilosophy*, 1976, 7(1), 70-75.

Matthews, G. *Philosophy and the Young Child* Harvard Univ. Press, Cambridge MA, 1980 2nd ed.

Teaching as Translation:
The Philosophical Dimension

Tony W. Johnson

This essay briefly compares the mimetic and transformative approaches to education and develops the concept of "teaching as translation," a transformative approach. The relationship between teaching as translation and the structure of the disciplines is explained, and an argument suggesting that philosophical inquiry is essential for this kind of teaching is presented. Suggestions for developing transformative teachers are offered, and the essay concludes by explaining how teaching as translation represents both democratic and moral ideals.

For much of this century, the promise of and search for a science of education has dominated educational reform. The confidence "that scientific facts and laws could lift today's run-of-the-mill teachers past the achievements of a Socrates or a Pestalozzi . . ."[1] captured America's imagination, but, suggests Kneller, "despite prodigious efforts and enormous expenditures of money, human scientists have produced no universal laws or theories that are either scientific or precise."[2] Tom characterizes the research on effective teaching as "barren" and suggests that new theories of teaching are needed. Such theories "ought to be a source of insight and enlightenment rather than a source of specific rules and general prescription."[3] It is in response to Tom's call for additional theories that the concept of teaching as translation is developed here. After briefly comparing the mimetic (scientific) and

transformative approaches to education, an argument favoring an artistic approach is presented. The essay concludes by suggesting that teaching as translation, a transformative approach, represents both democratic and moral ideals.

The Mimetic and Transformative Approaches to Education

In an invited address before the American Psychological Association in 1977, Phillip Jackson began by stating "Once I was an educational psychologist, or at least I professed to be. These days I am less certain about what to call myself"[4] Jackson's ambivalence toward his specialty suggests a growing awareness of psychology's failure to provide a genuine science of education. But, according to Kneller, even now, almost a decade later, educational psychology remains for many the major or "only source of reliable knowledge about human behavior, or the mind, or teaching and learning . . ." Kneller wonders "How long must we endure this charade?"[5]

Charade or not, education's over-reliance on the human science of psychology is not on the wane. As Jackson notes, teaching is becoming increasingly mimetic in orientation. The term "mimetic" is derived from the Greek mimesis and is defined as "getting the student to reproduce or to imitate in his own actions or words a form of behavior that has already been settled upon as a standard . . ."[6] In short, this tradition emphasizes the transmission and regurgitation of established factual and procedural knowledge. Knowledge is presented to the learner who, in turn, demonstrates his acquisition of it by imitating the teacher.

The mimetic tradition has its origins in the sophistic movement of ancient Greece and found a natural ally in the scientific world view that emerged triumphant during the late nineteenth and early twentieth centuries. As already noted, this tradition dominated education in this century, but, despite noble efforts, the dream of a complete science of education appears to be little more than a mirage.

The mimetic approach is grounded in the assumption that knowledge is fixed and has or can be discovered by humans. From this perspective, the teacher need not be a creative, inquisitive intellectual but merely an efficient technician capable of transmitting the kind of prepackaged information, skills, and values that students need in order to adapt to the present social order. The mimetic approach seeks to prepare our children and youth for the world as it is, but why not do what Kant suggests "and give them an education so much better than this, that a better condition of things may thereby be brought about in the future."[7]

Herein lies an alternative to mimetic approach to teaching. Instead of thinking of teaching as "the methodical insertion of ordered facts into the student's mind,"[8] why not think of it as a creative enterprise that aims at developing individuals who not only understand their world but are capable and desirous of improving it. Teaching of this kind actually seeks to transform students into better persons, not simply to give them more knowledge or skills but to make them "better in the sense of being closer to what humans are capable of becoming—more virtuous, fuller participants in an evolving order."[9]

This transformative approach also has its roots in ancient Greece. Just as the mimetic tradition follows the sophists in believing that knowledge is fixed and obtainable by humans, the transformative approach follows Socrates in recognizing that while progress toward knowing the truth is possible, absolute certainty is not. The transformative approach aims not at preparing students for life as it is, but seeks to empower them to make of it what it can or should be. Unlike the mimetic approach which is closely aligned with the idea that teaching and learning are, or can be a science, the transformative approach considers teaching and learning to be artistic endeavors.

Teaching: The Art of Translating

The teacher as artist reconciles "respect for the child and respect for what is being taught."[10] As an artist, the teacher constructs bridges connecting the larger world of ideas with each individual's private world. Since no one bridge works for all, the teacher needs to know the background and previous experiences of his/her students and be well versed in the content or subject that is to be taught. Only by knowing both can the teacher construct bridges to empower each student to move from the comfortable realm of the familiar toward the unsettling, yet exciting, realm of the unknown. While information about an unknown realm may be offered to students, it remains inert and meaningless until students connect it with their own previous frame of reference, making it their own. In this way, the teacher as artist serves as a kind of translator, representing the major concepts of the subjects to be taught in terms that connect students previous way of viewing things.

Though it sounds simple enough, the task of translating, or bridge building, is not easy. In order to build bridges or translate knowledge for others, the teacher first needs to internalize the major concepts and logical structure of the subject to be taught. To do this, teachers, out of necessity, follow the path blazed by others, but, in so doing, modify the path or bridge to fit their own individual needs. In this sense, learning like teaching, is a creative process. Relying largely upon a hunch or a hypothesis that a particular bridge leads to greater understanding, mistakes are common as bridges often fail to span the gulf between an individual's unique frame of reference and the unknown. But, once a workable bridge is constructed, perhaps after numerous false steps, it can be used again and again, modified by both teacher and student to meet individual needs. In this sense, the teacher's task becomes one of finding, modifying; or constructing knowledge bridges that connect with each individual's unique world.

Teaching the Structure of a Discipline

The teacher as translator aims at developing what Passmore calls open capacities, i.e. capacities that lead beyond themselves, that open up new avenues of learning, that in Bruner's language, enable students "to go beyond the information give." To achieve this goal the teacher must do more than impart basic information skills. As Mark Twain implies in his *Life on the Mississippi*, it is not enough to master basic skills and information. Twain's tale of how he became a master riverboat pilot is a classic metaphor for both teaching and learning. While still an adolescent, Twain memorized every shoal, snag, and sandbar on the mighty Mississippi. Impressed with this accomplishment, Twain is ready, or so he believes, to join the ranks of professional riverboat pilots. He is quickly brought back to reality by Mr. Bixby (his teacher) who graphically demonstrates that memorizing the location and peculiarities of the river's danger spots is not enough. Since the river is forever changing, a riverboat pilot must develop an understanding of how different forces and conditions interact to impact the river's course. Such an understanding is necessary if the pilot is to anticipate and safely avoid the location and characteristics of various water hazards.

Teachers as translators perform much like Mr. Bixby instructing a young Samuel Clemens.[11]

Rather than requiring students to memorize information likely to become obsolete, teaching of this kind strives to equip students with the ability to analyze and apply the major ideas and general principles of the subjects under study. In short the teacher as translator seeks to teach the "structure?" of the subject. If knowledge learned in one setting is to be useful in another, the nature of that knowledge and the manner in which it is taught is important. While the transfer of factual information or specific skills is often useful and sometimes essential, of more importance is the transfer of principles and attitudes. If a general idea is taught and learned, the student when confronted with a new problem, can often move beyond that which is given by recognizing the new problem as a particular case or instance of an idea already mastered. Teaching the underlying principles of a discipline or field of study equips students with the ability to "generalize from what he has learned to what he will encounter later . . ."[12] By teaching the general ideas on fundamental principles of a discipline, students can and often do internalize these structure's into their own particular frame of reference thus enabling them to grasp and incorporate additional information in a meaningful way.

Since the structure of a discipline, both in terms of its logic and general principles, is a product of critical intelligence, it is akin to the conceptual frameworks humankind has created to make sense out of the world. By focusing on the structure of the disciplines, the teacher as translator aims at assisting students to comprehend concepts by translating ideas into a form they can understand. In this process, students are encouraged and enabled to participate in this uniquely human process of concept formation. What usually begins as a rather fuzzy notion becomes the unifying concept which binds the parts together. As this creative process of concept formation progresses, the student is empowered with "the means to establish continuity, unity and understanding from one item of experience to another. . . ." As students recognize or formulate "the shared features of otherwise discrete events,"[13] they move from the unknown to the known. For students to succeed at concept formation, they need help in connecting the world beyond to their own conceptual frame of reference.

The Importance of Philosophy

According to Eisner all learning, whether of the sciences or the humanities, is the translation of human "imagination into some public, stable form, something that can be shared with others." Viewing knowledge in this way reduces "the tendency for students to regard the textbooks as sacred and knowledge as fixed."[14] Once they understand the subjects being studied are human constructions, students become more critical of things as they are and more willing to change them for the better. While absolute certainty may not be possible, students, so transformed, embrace the Socratic notion that progress is possible only if we learn from our mistakes. The connection between Socrates and the transformative approach to education is an important one in that philosophy, as practiced by Socrates, is uniquely qualified to assist us as educators in the task of translating the key ideas and general principles of a subject field into forms that our students can understand. Philosophy, as personified by Socrates, fosters greater understanding by taking an additional step to ask why those ideas are considered key or why the principles employed are the accepted ones. Philosophy, in this sense, is more concerned with the reasons behind the facts than the facts themselves. Such a philosopher seeks both to understand the epistemological basis of knowledge and to interpret it for others. In this way, the philosopher can and should be an experienced ally of the educator.

The teacher as translator, in addition to being a scientist, a psychologist, or some other subject matter specialist, must also be a philosopher of the field of study that he or she is teaching. Only to the degree that the teacher has a firm grasp of the conceptual boundaries of the subject under scrutiny can he or she select curricular material so as to effectively translate the principles and key ideas into forms accessible to the student. Like Socrates, transformative teachers do not tell their students what to think, nor do they permit them to accept uncritically the truth of others. Instead, by developing a classroom atmosphere where all points of view, including the teacher's, are subject to careful scrutiny, transformative teachers encourage and empower students to think for themselves.

We need more transformative teachers, *i.e.*, teachers who emulate Socrates. Socrates built no philosophical system but "he 'questioned and cross examined' his fellow citizens, not to convey a new truth to them . . . but only to point out the path along which it might be found."[15] In a like manner, the transformative teacher translates the forms or structures of a discipline in such a way that students can understand them and more beyond them. Such teachers model for their students the art of philosophizing. Like Socrates, they refuse to think for their students, but demonstrate to them "how to undertake, . . . the laborious regress that alone affords insight into basic principles."[16] Rather than being told how to think, students need to encounter first hand a community of inquiry in action.

Just as Socrates, in the Platonic dialogues, engaged his students in rigorous, but never condescending process of intellectual inquiry, teachers seeking to transform their students into independent thinkers should convert their classrooms into communities of inquiry. By emphasizing dialogue as an instrument of instruction, the teacher can challenge students to speak their mind, "to meet every counter question, and to state reasons for every assertion. . . ."[17] In this way the teacher as artist can instill in students "an enthusiasm for the give-and-take of critical discussion."[18] By engaging students in a serious conversation of the keys ideas and epistemological underpinnings of a field of study, the teacher compels the students to think for themselves. As they listen attentively to others, students engage in a kind of self-translation, taking in what is being said and relating it to their own frame of reference. To respond to a question or an assertion, or offer a counterpoint, students must weigh carefully each word to ensure that it conveys the desired meaning. To engage in dialogue is to rehearse what others have said, to assess the relevance and significance of these remarks, to recognize other perspectives, and to explore previously unknown possibilities. The teacher as translator creates such a classroom both to expose students to the art of philosophizing and to initiate them into such an artistic endeavor. The goal is to transform students into individuals who, regardless of the field of study "are unwilling . . . simply to accept a result, . . ." In short the aim of such teaching is to develop individuals "with a philosophical turn of mind. . .[19]

Developing Transformative Teachers

The development of such "a philosophical turn of mind" is not likely to occur in a teacher's classroom who has been trained in the mimetic tradition. In order to develop our children and youth into individuals capable of both understanding and changing our world, we need more teachers committed to the art of philosophizing. To develop such teachers requires no less than a revolutionary change in the way teachers are educated. Knowledge is important for all professions but teaching is about knowledge For this reason it is not enough that teachers possess knowledge. They need in addition an understanding of the epistemological warrants of the key ideas and principles of the subjects they teach. If, as the Holmes Report suggests, "education is the discipline of the disciplines," then educators more so than any other professional, must go beyond uncritical acceptance to genuine understanding. Since it is their task to help others see more clearly, it is essential that they possess a broad and liberal education—broad in the sense that they gain familiarity with multiple ways of knowing and liberal in the sense that through the "art of philosophizing" they free themselves from the dogma of ignorance.

The development of such teachers necessitates the restructuring of both teacher education programs and the non-professional components of the undergraduate curriculum. The undergraduate curriculum should be organized in such a way that future teachers "gain a sense of the intellectual structure and boundaries of their disciplines, rather than taking a series of disjointed, prematurely specialized fragments."[20] All undergraduates, but especially future teachers, need to know the origins and goals of the discipline or subject under scrutiny. They need to understand why some issues of a particular field or discipline merit serious investigation and why others may be only of minor or little significance. Instead of the largely received knowledge which typically characterizes undergraduate instruction in all subjects and fields, the question "how do we know . . .? should be an intrinsic part of general education."[21]

Reforming the non-professional components of the undergraduate curriculum along the lines advocated above is a step in the right direction, but it is not sufficient for the development of teachers as translators. Participation in communities of inquiry investigating the intellectual structure of various fields of knowledge is essential but equally important is a reflective examination of pedagogical studies. Future teachers, in addition to gaining familiarity with the structure of the subjects they are to teach, need to investigate such questions as "how do we learn?; What should be taught?; When are students ready to learn particular thing?; and What does it mean to be educated? By combining this philosophical approach to the studying of both the disciplines and pedagogy, we have the ingredients needed to develop teaching in the transformative tradition.

The time has come to replace the long-standing commitment to the mimetic approach to teaching and learning with an equally strong commitment to transformative approaches. If the goal of education is to develop future citizens capable of understanding and improving the world, more teachers committed to the art of philosophizing are needed. Such teaching is, suggests Harvey Siegel, the right or moral thing to do. Since teaching is an interactive process between or among individuals of equal worth, teachers are obligated to treat their students with respect. Translated, this means that teachers should recognize "the student's right to question to challenge, and to demand reasons and justifications for what is being taught. . . ."[22] If human beings are capable of both understanding and transforming themselves and their worlds, then teachers, to the extent that they transmit predetermined truths to students, are disrespectful of them. Teachers as translators; *i.e.*, teachers committed to the art of philosophizing, treat students with respect.

Teaching that fosters the art of philosophizing can also be justified on the grounds that such teaching fosters autonomy and self-sufficiency. Transformative teachers encourage their students "to ask questions, to look for evidence, to seek and scrutinize alternatives, to be critical of their own ideas as well as those of others." Through such efforts, students are encouraged and empowered to become self-sufficient, to take charge of their lives, to be free "from the unwarranted control of unjustified belief, insupportable attitudes, and paucity of abilities"[23] that deny or limit life choices. Teaching of this kind not only represents a moral ideal but is indispensable for a society aspiring to be free. To free the mind from uncritical acceptance of fashionable doctrine is both a moral and democratic education ideal. These are ideas that we as educators must foster if we hope, individually and as a society, to avoid "the path to despotism."[24]

Footnotes

1. Alan Tom, *Teaching as a Moral Craft* (New York: Longman Inc., 1984) p. 14.
2. George E Kneller, "The Proper Study of Education," in Fred Schultz, ed., *Annual Editions: Education 86/87* (Guilford, Connecticut: Dushkin Publishing Group, Inc., 1986), p. 7.
3. Tom, *Teaching as a Moral Craft*, p. 185.
4. Philip W. Jackson, "The Promise of Educational Psychology" in Frank H. Farley and Neal J. Gordon, eds., *Psychology and Education: The State of the Union* (Berkeley, California: McCutchan Publishing Corporation, 1981), p. 389.
5. Kneller, "The Proper Study of Education," p. 8.
6. Philip W Jackson, "Private Lessons in Public Schools; Remarks on the Limits of Adaptive Instruction." in Margaret C. Wang and Herbert J. Walberg, eds. *Adapting Instruction to Individual Differences* (Berkeley, California: McCutchen Publishing Corporation, 1985), p. 72.
7. Quoted in Harvey Siegel, "Educational Ideas and Educational Practice: The Case of Minimum Competency Testing," *Issues in Education* 1 (Nos. 2 and 3, 1983), 154.
8. Israel Scheffler, *Reason and Teaching* (Indianapolis and New York: The Bobbs-Merrill Co., Inc., 1973), p. 84.
9. Philip W Jackson, *The Practice of Teaching* (New York: Teachers College Press, 1986), p. 127.
10. John Pasmore, *The Philosophy of Teaching* (Cambridge: Harvard University Press, 1980), p. 97.
11. Marvin Lazerson, *et. al. An Education of Value* (Cambridge: Cambridge University Press, 1985), pp. 66-67.
12. Jerome S. Bruner (1960). *The Process of Education* (Cambridge: Harvard University Press, 1960), p. 31.
13. Stanford C. Erickson, *The Essence of Good Teaching* (San Francisco: Jossey Bass Publishers, 1984), p. 73.
14. Elliot Eisner, "Aesthetic Modes of Knowing" in *Learning and Teaching the Ways of Knowing, 84th Yearbook of the National Society for the Study of Education* (Chicago: University of Chicago Press, 1985), pp. 26, 35.
15. Leonard Nelson, *Socratic Method and Critical Philosophy* (New York: Dover Publishing, Inc., 1965), p. 5.
16. *Ibid*, p. 15.
17. *Ibid.*
18. Passmore, *The Philosophy of Teaching*, p. 171.
19. Nelson, *Socratic Method and Critical Philosophy*, p. 39.
20. *Tomorrow's Teachers: A Report of The Holmes Group* (East Lansing, Michigan: The Homes Group, Inc., 1986), p. 17.
21. A. Arons, "Critical Thinking and the Baccalaureate Curriculum," *Liberal Education* 1985); 142.
22. Harvey Siegel, "Critical Thinking as an Educational Ideal, *The Educational Forum*, 45 (November, 1980), p. 13.
23. Ibid., p. 16.
24. Passmore, *The Philosophy of Teaching*, p. 64.

Chapter Five
Children and Stories

Chapter Five

Stories and Children

Every life is, in a sense, a story in which one connects one's present with one's past and one's future with one's present. But whether it is a story written by oneself or by others is a bit more controversial.

Children evidently recognize the kinship between stories and themselves, for they love stories as dearly as they love having playmates. On the other hand, each story for them is more than a person—it is a possible world. Children readily give themselves over to this aspect of a story—that it is another world to live in—and they relish the liberty they enjoy in "escaping," as it were, from the toils of the world they physically inhabit.

And yet stories can bridge the gap between one's actual life and one's ideals. As Kierkegaard suggests, they reinforce the tendency children have to question and wonder, and the desire they have to understand. They provide children with standards by means of which the things of this world can be evaluated; they bring together fragments of experience and unify them into illuminating wholes.

In a penetrating essay, Ernest Schachtel explores the child's eagerness to have stories retold, each time exactly as before, in contrast to the adult's constant search for novelty and variation. But to the child, the story is to be not merely learned, but learned by heart, and this requires repeated immersions in it. It is an intense study experience, but it is also a love experience, for the child wants to be with the story repeatedly or continually, just as an older person does not want to be separated from someone he or she loves. Only later does the child discover that the story can be changed, and that new stories can be invented.

Children love reason, Robert Louis Stevenson implies, because they are appalled by the unreasonableness of the world as they find it, "Why can we not all be happy and devote ourselves to play?" the child demands, and it is with questions of this sort that the child becomes philosophical. Children often see no point in our demanding that they be precise in their practical reasonings and in their studies, just as we see no point in the care with which they put together their imaginings, and the whole-heartedness with which they give themselves over to their childish games.

Gareth Matthews makes it clear that he is not claiming that children are philosophers (although he grants that such a claim would not be totally pointless.) Instead he argues that what some children do naturally is closer than is generally recognized to what professional philosophers do. Children naturally wonder and are naturally naive; philosophers deliberately engage in wonder and in institutionalized naivete. And both raise perplexing questions that cannot be given straightforward answers.

According to Michael Ende, children do not wish to be consigned to a world separate from that of grown-ups. Yet this is what we do to them when we construct for them a separate "children's literature." For they eventually discover, he argues, that the entire fabric of that world of children was a lie, and they become disillusioned and resigned. Better that they should share the same world with everyone else, and the same literature as everyone else.

Eva Brann picks up where Ende leaves off, and sides with him in contending that the world of the child and that of the adult are not incommensurable. She also continues Gareth Matthews' argument about the similarities between children's wonderings and the speculations of professional philosophers. And she points out how Ende's books "reflect on what they are doing while they are doing it," likewise a characteristic of much philosophical writing.

The brief, crisp essay by Martha Nussbaum points up for us the contrast between Socrates' condemnation of books and Plato's employment of dramatic texts in order to keep philosophy alive. Plato uses dialogue in order to create real dialectical searching that fully and fairly represents philosophy. His books do not seek to indoctrinate initiates, as did some of the pre-Socratic writers. Instead, they help us see the connection between thinking and action, between a way of thought and a way of life.

When children arrive in school, says Kieran Egan; they already have in place some of the most powerful abstract concepts that we ever learn, such as good/bad, love/hate and fear/security. "It is not concreteness that is important in making knowledge meaningful to young children, it is tying the concrete to particular abstract concepts." Egan's work is another direct challenge to the notion that the early childhood curriculum should be full of concrete experiences and avoid reference to the abstract, In this, Egan's criticism echos that of Vygotsky and Bruner.

To Florence Hetzler, the union of philosophy and literature is the perfect blending of the abstract with the concrete, the theoretical and the practical. She seeks to illustrate this contention with a brief examination of *The Little Prince*, as a masterful version of a children's story which is also for adults, and a work of imagination that is at the same time a paragon of reasonableness. St. Exupéry's little book, she concludes, is a challenge to us to become persons.

Kierkegaard on Childhood

Søren Kierkegaard

Kierkegaard wrote these reflections on childhood in 1837. Perhaps they are not so much about childhood itself as about the mistaken ways in which we tend to judge that period of life. Kierkegaard indicts two common judgments of childhood as being fundamentally incorrect:

1. There is the view that earlier stages are of importance only because they condition later ones. The best thing to do, then, is to pass through such stages just as quickly as possible, since they have no intrinsic value. Childhood is such a phase. For parents it is a tiresome period, dedicated mainly to looking after the child's well-being. One must amuse children to while away the time, telling them empty tales over and over again. Those who write these pointless stories thereby encourage children to be passive and docile. Such literature for children— Kierkegaard scoffs at it as "poetic rinsewater"— is incapable of prodding children to inquire, or to think for themselves.

2. The other mistaken view is that taken by adults whose primary aim is to impart "useful knowledge" to children. Their stories aim to help children learn other languages, or the geography of far-away countries, or how to read music. And when they do tell children stories, they invariably add, "but you realize, it was only a fairy tale.

Kierkegaard's own position is that childhood is rich in values uniquely its own. Yet it is a period in which children are dependent upon teachers for intellectual and emotional nourishment.

These teachers should have mastered the Socratic mode of questioning, and should have reproduced the quality of childhood experience in themselves. They must know what the life of childhood requires, as well as how and when to give it. Further, they must know how to encourage children to think about things that matter to them. And they must be capable of arousing in children the desire to ask, rather than fending off reasonable questions with "Are you going to let me finish this tale or not?"

One must spend time preparing to tell children stories, Kierkegaard suggests, by going to the trouble of finding out what the children are studying in school, what they're thinking about outside of school, and then by selecting stories that bear on these experiences. The aim should be to nourish children's inquisitiveness, sense of wonder, and desire for understanding, as well as to bring something poetic into their everyday existence. If we fail to motivate children to learn, or if we present them with nothing but dry, fragmented factual knowledge unrelated to their everyday existence, we deprive them of access to the standards by which the presence or absence of meaning in life may be judged, and we deny them the experiences which could make their lives meaningful.

From *Søren Kierkegaard's Journals & Papers*, Vol. 1, edited and translated by Howard V. Hong and Edna H. Hong. (Bloomington, Indiana: Indiana University Press, 1967) pp. 113-119. Reprinted with permission.

If after reading the essay someone were to say that I do indeed speak of the art of storytelling but in the entire essay seem rather to rant against it, I would now wholly agree, inasmuch as I have spoken only against misuse, and I would also point out that I have used the expression storytelling in a more comprehensive sense involving everything with which one occupies a child's mind outside of formal schooling, not all of which can accurately be called play, and in-which, of course, storytelling does play a major role.

That so many people are engaged in telling stories to children is a natural consequence of the fact that there are a great number of children and that children have a deeply rooted desire to hear stories, and yet there are very few people who have talent for storytelling. As a result much harm is done. There are two recommended ways of telling stories to children, but between these two there is a multiplicity of wrong ways.

First, there is the way which children's nurses (and other who may be so categorized) unconsciously follow. They open up a whole world of fantasy to the child, and the fact that they are sincerely convinced of the truth of their stories[1] must instill a salutary tranquillity in the child, no matter how fantastic the content itself may be. Only when the child himself detects that the teller does not believe stories are the stories damaging—yet not because of the content itself but because of the untruth in regard to the teller—because of the mistrust and suspiciousness which the child gradually develops.

The *second* way can be followed only by someone who in perfect clarity has reproduced the life of childhood, who knows what this life requires, who knows what is good for it and now from this vantage point offers children intellectual-emotional nourishment which is beneficial for them, who knows *how to be* a child; whereas the nursemaids basically *are* children. (Fortunately, children are able to derive good from both ways, and following the second way certainly does not exclude appreciation of the first. On the

other hand, the semi-educated usually eliminate the process of development valued by one who has a mature view of life.)

The preparation is not elaborate. The husband comes home from the busy office, puts on his slippers, gets his pipe, kisses mother on the cheek and says, "Well, my dear," (this is to accustom the children to affectionate behavior)—and now we see a scene common to most children's books—"Uncle Frank," who, tells the stories which the children have eagerly anticipated all day, and little Fritz and Mary coming on the run, clapping their hands: "Uncle Frank[2] is going to tell stories!" The mother clusters the children around her, with the smallest in her arms, and says, "Listen nicely, now, to what your dear uncle is telling!"

As for the procedure for the storytelling, for our storytellers—all general pursuits on behalf of children outside of formal instruction, and this, too, as much as possible, should be *Socratic*. One should arouse in children a desire to *ask*, instead of fending off a reasonable question, which perhaps goes beyond Uncle Frank's general information or in some other way inconveniences him, with the words: "Stupid child! Can't he keep still while I am telling the story?" To prevent more serious scenes, the mother assures that "he will not do it any more." The whole point is *to bring the poetic into touch with their lives in every way*, to exercise a power of enchantment, to let a glimpse appear at the most unexpected moment and then vanish. One should not schedule the poetic for certain hours and certain days. Children do not jump around such a person like loutish calves with dangling legs and clap their hands because they are going to hear a story. Him they approach in an open, free, confident way, entrust themselves to him, initiate him into little secrets, tell him about their play, and he knows how to join in, also knows how to give the game a more serious side. The children never distress him or pester him, for they have too much respect and esteem for him.[3]

He knows what they are doing in school. He does not do their homework with them but quietly inquires about their lessons, masters them, not in order to quiz them, not to take a particular part and dramatize it for them, not to give them an opportunity to show off if there are others around—but rather to let a glimpse suddenly leap forth, to connect it in a special way to what usually occupies them, yet entirely *en passant*, so that the child's soul is electrified and feels, as it were, the omnipresence of something poetic, which is indeed precious to him but which he nevertheless dares not approach too closely.[4] *In this way* an intellectual-emotional mobility is constantly nurtured, a continuing attentiveness to what they hear and see, an attentiveness which otherwise has to be produced by *external* means, for example, by having the children come from a dimly lighted room into a brightly lighted room, where "Uncle Frank" is sitting, by wearying them the whole day by talking about "how wonderful" it is to hear Uncle Frank tell stories—etc.

I remember an example of how in such a life everything becomes engendering, how everything the children read in the classics became reflected; when they read of ostracism, they introduced it at once into their play, etc.

And now those children's books for "well-behaved, industrious, obedient, lovable, innocent, unspoiled" children—consequently by presenting them with a copy one says to them that they are such, since otherwise it would it would be a misunderstanding to give them the book.

1837

However, even though clarity prevails, a certain sentimentality can easily intrude if one forgets that adulthood has what childhood promised. We are inclined, however, to think that it promised a lot more, especially when dealing with exceptionally alert children, and so we intervene

alarmingly in their lives (anxiety can actually stem from this cause and not always from trivial complaining.) Those daily assurances, "You are happy now, but wait until you are older[5]—then the troubles will come," etc., have a *harmful effect*, inasmuch as they strike at the roots of the child and instill a peculiar anxiety as to how long he can continue to be happy (and in this way they *are* already unhappy). If this continuous Jeremiad makes no impression, it naturally has the same harmful effect as all other misplaced chatter.

This indefiniteness [in the Socratic approach] might seem to militate against a certain very proper demand for rigor and clear limitation; this should rather be represented in the schoolroom in the personality of the teacher (here we are concerned with free time). He who in childhood has never been under the *gospel* but only under law never becomes free[6]—maybe this is wrong, but there is something noble in it; whereas the more the law is propounded, the more minor mischief germinates, and nothing is more capable of producing enervation. The eye has a power to call forth sprouts of the good and to crush the evil—but misinterpreted rigor and discipline, a daughter of indolence, almost permits one generation to take revenge upon the next for the thrashing it received itself and for the mishandling it has suffered by treating the next generation in like manner.

When one is a child and has not toys, one is well provided for, because then imagination takes over. I still remember with amazement my childhood top, the only toy I had—what acquaintance was as interesting as this one? Yet it did not belong wholly to me. It had, so to say, its official duties as actual top, and only then in its leisure did it become my diversion. In our day there are complaints that an official holds too many offices, but this one encompassed all.

1844

But then shouldn't one tell stories? Certainly, mythology and good fairy stories are what the child needs. Or the child is allowed to read them himself and tell them and is then Socratically corrected (gradually correcting by questioning in such a manner that the child is by no means set straight under the coercion of a tutor but seems rather to be correcting others—and anyone who otherwise understands how to handle children will certainly not be in danger of encouraging arrogance). But above all let this be impromptu, not at a set time and place; children should experience early in life that happiness is a fortunate constellation which one should enjoy with gratitude but also know how to discontinue in good time; and above all one should not forget *the point of the story*. (A mistake I can only touch upon here, although it comes up again later, is this: continually and almost day long to tell trashy, empty stories and thereby facture these readers of novels who devour a volume a day, one after the other, without any specific impression.) Furthermore, one evokes a certain self-activity (drawing and the like) because of the story, told in various ways, becomes related to a child's familiar environment.

Now comes the question: what significance does childhood really have? Is it a stage with significance only because it conditions, in a way, the following stages—or does it have independent value? Some have expanded the latter position to the point where they assume childhood to be fundamentally the highest level attainable by human beings and that everything beyond it is progressive degeneration. The first position has had the practical result that people try to make time pass by[7]—and if children could be shut up in the dark and force-fed on an accelerated schedule like chickens, everything would certainly be organized to this end. Another consequence has been this "tiresome time of childhood" primarily for caring for children's physical well-being. In this view the supreme rule of upbringing runs something like this: "The child who does not clean up his plate gets no dessert."—(How fre-

quently children's lives, particularly girls', are embittered by hearing continually that they are good for nothing, etc.)

The *mistaken ways* come about because one passes beyond the nursemaid's position but does not go the whole way and thus remains stationary at the halfway point.

Those who have gone beyond the stage of spontaneity, instead of now in their mature years assimilating childhood transfigured, as would be natural, decay into "being children" (compare *fountain-of-youth*), those overgrown puppies who are so innocent and naive, who would give anything if their beards never grew enough to require a shave so that they could remain downy, bare-necked youths, who have become children again to such a degree that they talk as children, use all the childish expressions, and who would like ultimately to get all of us to talk as children and write as children talk—a caricature which will surely come to be as soon as the opposite, that children want to be grown-ups, which is common now, has been outlived. It is a tragic-comic sight to see these gangly, childish jumping-jacks leaping around the floor and riding the hobby-horse with the sweet little ones and to hear their dull stories about "innocent and happy childhood." (Compare their behavior with that of adolescent girls who want to be grown-up: they parody one another.)

Their stories "for children and childlike souls"—poetic rinse-water! If this error is found most often among youth, there is also a similar mistaken way among adults who "descend" to children out of the conviction that childhood in itself is so empty and devoid of content that they wish, as it were, to breathe fullness into it. Basically both points of view must presuppose the emptiness of childhood, for otherwise the former would not permit itself to undertake anything so loathsome, something a sound nature would immediately censure, and the other would not undertake to breathe the spirit of life into it.

After a story has been told, it is important not to destroy the entire impression by ending with a

"But do you understand, don't you, that it was only a fairy tale?" This sort of thing reappears later in people who have absolutely no sense for the poetic and consequently spoil the impression of every anecdote, etc., by probing its factual truth.

Fundamentally everyone is born to rule. This is best seen in children. Today I saw a little girl in her nurse's arms. They met some acquaintances of the child's family. The nurse held a flower in her hand, and now everybody, each and all, very submissively had to smell the flower and say, "Achoo!" This was repeated several times. If the nurse wanted to skip someone, the little girl noticed it at once and gave her to understand that she had to do everything exactly right. And then the little female sovereign bestowed with a smile her highest favor upon the one who sneezed exactly right.

Then the nurse wanted her to walk, but she leaned out a bit from the nurse's arms, dropped her head coyly, and rewarded the nurse with a kiss from beneath—affectedly, and yet with a childlikeness.

1845

Storytelling has assumed a fantastic and lopsided tendency. It has been considered unreasonable and damaging later to overstock the child's imagination with such stories. On the other hand, it has been considered quite all right to tell something to while away the time and amuse the children. Since it was merely for diversion and they did not want to spend time in preparation, they started those interminable silly tales about the dog and the cat, etc., telling them with the most horrible monotony. The children, once they are spoiled, continually demand more and more editions of the same, always returning[8] to the stereotype with one or more important alterations (for example, that once it was a red dog, then a black one.)

In the meantime this view was discovered to be wrong, since, indeed, the time could be utilized better, could be used for something better even in the form of jest and play. Two procedures evolved from this—either educate the children morally, as it is called, or impart some useful knowledge. The consequence of the second path I shall touch upon slightly. There came as if by magic a plague of natural history, not textbooks but reading books and all kinds of picture books to impart to the children the vocabularies of modern languages, and "Uncle Frank" told of his travels in Africa and designated the plants and animals by their scientific names, and parents and others asked: "What is *nose* in French?" etc. Or one taught them to pick out a simple piece on the piano. (If one really wishes by such things to keep children from being embarrassed by being conspicuous, then on the other hand one really ought not make children eager to be conspicuous.)

Out of all this there developed a completely atomized knowledge which did not enter into a deeper relationship to children and their existence [Existents] which was not appropriated in an intellectual-emotional way, and which was thus deprived of any possible standard. As a result people fell into the presumption that they were great natural scientists and linguists. If only details are decisive, it is naturally quite incidental how many or how few are required for mastery. Out of this arises seductive opportunism—and the busy Marthas who forget the one thing needful. Of such atomized knowledge it is not true that what is assimilated in youth is never forgotten in old age . . .

The Child and the Story

Ernest G. Schachtel

I want to discuss briefly here only one often observed fact: a child's pleasure in, and insistence on, being read or told the same story over and over again. This discussion will (1) serve as an example for a more detailed description of the exploratory function of focal attention, and (2) show that the child's insistence on repetition is not due primarily to an inertia principle but, on the contrary, is essential for the productive work of exploring and assimilating the objects of the environment—in this case, an object of the cultural environment.

Adult observers have often been struck by the disturbance a child may show at the slightest change—even one word—in a story which has been repeated for the child. This disturbance does not seem to make much sense to the adult mind. What is the difference if a minor episode or a mere word is changed, as long as the main drift of events is retained in the story? This viewpoint overlooks the enormous difference in meaning which the repetition of a story has for the child who listens to it with absorption and for the adult who is bored by it. One tries in vain to encompass the child's experience with categories of the adult mind which are not suitable for grasping the meaning of the situation for the child.

What are the decisive differences between the child's and the adult's experience in listening to the same story over and over again? The age at which such repetition is desired and enjoyed by the child is roughly from two to five years, with considerable individual variation. At the beginning of the period, the child has already learned to perceive distinct and concrete objects, but this learning must necessarily continue, for the object world of the child is constantly and rapidly expanding, and increasingly includes such complicated objects as words and pictures which denote or represent other objects. However, the manner in which discrete objects are perceived by the young child differs a great deal from the manner in which they are perceived by the older child and the adult. The young child perceives objects much more globally and concretely than the older child or adult. This implies that "any phenomenon known in terms of qualities-of-the-whole, rather than in terms of strictly articulated qualities, is apt to be seen by the young child as undergoing a complete change, even if no more than minor details in the situation are altered." From the young child's viewpoint, none of the many elements making up the global situation "need be more essential than any other, since all of them contribute to the characteristic coloration, or tone, of the situational totality."

Since a story contains not only many different objects but also many different relationships among these objects, which unfold in a definite sequence of events, it is much more complex than even the most complex objects in the child's environment. For the young child to grasp and digest a story requires an amount of attention and of effort at understanding which the adult is incapable of imagining, since his grasp of a story rests not only on years of training but also on a quite different, much more abstractive kind of perception and understanding. Only by repeated acts of focal attention, which at one time turn more to one part, at other times to other parts, can the child very gradually come to understand and assimilate a story. A particular part of the story may become something to wonder about even if on some other day it seemed already familiar or not worthy of special attention. To encompass all of it is no small achievement. What if the story should change as the child tries to get hold of it? Any change makes it elusive and frustrates the child's effort to master it. The attempt to assimilate a particular story requires a complex labor of attention and thought; in fact, it usually involves the child's learning the story by heart. This learning-by-heart is a by-product of the child's innumerable acts of focal attention toward the story as a whole and toward its different parts, and of the child's feelings about the story. The fact that this learning-by-heart comes as a by-product—much in contrast to later learning-by-heart in school—indicates the difference in degree and quality of attention between the young child's and the older child's or adult's listening to a story.

The young child who listens to the story not only is engaged in assimilating its complex fabric but, in addition to that, is confronted with the equally or even more difficult problem of finding his way in the puzzling distinctions between reality, representations of reality, possibility, and sheer phantasy. Just as the task of learning that a picture can represent a real object but that it is different from the real object is not an easy one and takes considerable time and effort to master, so it is a difficult task to learn about the various possible relations between a story and reality. Furthermore, it is of great importance to the child that he can *rely* on the story—that it does not suddenly disappear, that it is still there. This is just as important as to be able to rely on the fact that a toy in which the child is interested will not vanish overnight. Before the child can read, the only way to be sure that he can rely on a story is by having it reread or retold to him and making quite sure that it is really the same story.

A change in the story is about as upsetting to the child as it might be to an adult to discover that overnight the table in the living room had changed its shape. The idea that one can *make* a story, hence also *change* it, dawns much later on the child than the earlier implicit conviction that a story is a piece of reality on which one can rely, so that any change of it interferes drastically with the important task of getting thoroughly acquainted with this particular piece of reality.

When Freud says that the child's need to hear the same story over and over again is a trait which disappears in the adult, he refers, probably without being aware of it, to a phenomenon which is characteristic only of large segments of the adult population in modern Western civilization, but which is not true of all men or of all times. For the greater part of man's history, people read or listened to the same stories many times. This is as true of the Bible as it is of *The Arabian Nights*; and it is equally true of the sermons of Buddha, which employ in a most impressive way literal repetition of the same stories and phrases—a device which is frequent in Oriental poetry. The modern need to read the latest bestseller, to look at a new movie or television show, to consume enormous amounts of always new mysteries, magazines, and comic strips, is peculiar to our time and culture.

Moreover, a proper comparison, I believe, of a child's attitude toward a story can be made only with an adult's attitude toward an object of *similar significance*. The story, to the child, is at first strange country which he gradually explores and in which new discoveries are always possible. A comparable relationship exists in our culture between the appreciative adult and a work of art, a piece of music, or a poem. One does not tire easily of looking again and again at a cherished painting, of listening many times over to a beloved piece of music or a poem. Every renewed encounter may reveal new aspects and lead to deeper understanding. Any change in the poem, the painting, the music would destroy it. Because of the quasi-organic, lifelike character of the real work of art, such a change would indeed make it into something very different.

In other words, if the adult matures to a stage where he is capable of meaningful encounter with a significant human creation, then his relationship to this creation is likely to require many contacts with it, just as the child's relationship to the story does. The meaning of such significant encounters is very different from the kind of reading or listening which has the purpose of killing time, of being entertained passively or thrilled and titillated. For inherent in every real encounter with a work of art, a myth, a fairy tale is an active effort of the total personality, which is also inherent—in a somewhat different way— in the child's attempt to gradually assimilate the story. The motive of inertia seems to me considerably stronger in the adult who wants to see a new movie or read a new mystery every night than in the child who wants to hear the same story retold. The former avoids meaningful and enriching experience; the latter seeks it.

Child's Play

Robert Louis Stevenson

While Robert Louis Stevenson is duly re-nowned for his children's stories and children's verse, he is less well-known as an essayist. But we should not allow ourselves to be too much put off by Stevenson's unassuming manner: he is a keenly perceptive and judicious observer, despite the familiar view of him as a rather bland and sentimental apologist for childhood. This essay reveals Stevenson's ability to enter fully into the child's world and yet to pull back and comment with insight and detachment on what he finds in that world.

The regret we have for our childhood is not wholly justifiable: so much a man may lay down without fear of public ribaldry; for although we shake our heads over the change, we are unconscious of the manifold advantages of our new state. What we lose in generous impulse, we more than gain in the habit of generously watching others; and the capacity to enjoy Shakespeare may balance a lost aptitude for playing at soldiers. Terror is gone out of our lives, moreover; we no longer see the devil in the bed-curtains nor lie awake to listen to the wind. We go to school no more; and if we have only exchanged one drudg-ery for another (which is by no means sure), we are set free for ever from the daily fear of chas-tisement. And yet a great change has overtaken us; and although we do not enjoy ourselves less, at least we take our pleasure differently. We need pickles nowadays to make Wednesday's cold mutton please our Friday's appetite; and I can remember the time when to call it red venison, and tell myself a hunter's story, would have made it more palatable than the best of sauces. To the grown person, cold mutton is cold mutton all the world over; not all the mythology ever invented by man will make it better or worse to him; the broad fact, the clamant reality, of the mutton carries away before it such seductive figments. But for the child it is still possible to weave an enchantment over eatables; and if he has but read of a dish in a storybook, it will be heavenly manna to him for a week.

If a grown man does not like eating and drink-ing and exercise, if he is not something positive in his tastes, it means he has a feeble body and should have some medicine; but children may be pure spirits, if they will, and take their enjoyment in a world of moonshine. Sensation does not count for so much in our first years as afterwards; something of the swaddling numbness of infancy clings about us; we see and touch and hear through a sort of golden mist. Children, for in-stance, are able enough to see, but they have no great faculty for looking; they do not use their eyes for the pleasure of using them, but for by-ends of their own; and the things I call to mind seeing most vividly, were not beautiful in them-selves, but merely interesting or enviable to me as I thought they might be turned to practical account in play. Nor is the sense of touch so clean and poignant in children as it is in a man. If you will turn over your old memories, I think the sensations of this sort you remember will be somewhat vague, and come to not much more than a blunt, general sense of heat on summer days, or a blunt, general sense of well-being in bed. And here, of course, you will understand pleasurable sensations; for overmastering pain— the most deadly and tragical element in life, and the true commander of man's soul and body— alas! pain has its own way with all of us; it breaks in, a rude visitant, upon the fairy garden where the child wanders in a dream, no less surely than it rules upon the field of battle, or sends the immortal war-god whimpering to his father; and innocence, no more than philosophy, can protect us from this sting. As for taste, when we bear in mind the excesses of unmitigated sugar which delight a youthful palate, "it is surely no very cynical asperity" to think taste a character of the maturer growth. Smell and hearing are perhaps more developed; I remember many scents, many voices, and a great deal of spring singing in the woods. But hearing is capable of vast improvement as a means of pleasure; and there is all the world between gaping wonderment at the jargon of birds, and the emotion with which a man listens to articulate music.

At the same time, and step by step with this increase in the definition and intensity of what we feel which accompanies our growing age, another change takes place in the sphere of intellect, by which all things are transformed and seen through theories and associations as through coloured windows. We make to ourselves day by day, out of history, and gossip, and economical speculations, and God knows what, a medium in which we walk and through which we look abroad. We study shop windows with other eyes than in our childhood, never to wonder, not always to admire, but to make and modify our little incongruous theories about life. It is no longer the uniform of a soldier that arrests our attention; but perhaps the flowing carriage of a woman, or perhaps a countenance that has been vividly stamped with passion and carries an adventurous story written in its lines. The pleasure of surprise is passed away; sugar-loaves and water-carts seem mighty tame to encounter; and we walk the streets to make romances and to sociologize. Nor must we

deny that a good many of us walk them solely for the purposes of transit or in the interest of a livelier digestion. These, indeed, may look back with mingled thoughts upon their childhood, but the rest are in a better case; they know more than when they were children, they understand better, their desires and sympathies answer more nimbly to the provocation of the senses, and their minds are brimming with interest as they go about the world.

According to my contention, this is a flight to which children cannot rise. They are wheeled in perambulators or dragged about by nurses in a pleasing stupor. A vague, faint, abiding wonderment possesses them. Here and there some specially remarkable circumstance, such as a water-cart or a guardsman, fairly penetrates into the seat of thought and calls them, for half a moment, out of themselves; and you may see them, still towed forward sideways by the inexorable nurse as by a sort of destiny, but still staring at the bright object in their wake. It may be some minutes before another such moving spectacle reawakens them to the world in which they dwell. For other children, they almost invariably show some intelligent sympathy. "There is a fine fellow making mud pies," they seem to say; "that I can understand, there is some sense in mud pies." But the doings of their elders, unless where they are speakingly picturesque or recommend themselves by the quality of being easily imitable, they let them go over their heads (as we say) without the least regard. If it were not for this perpetual imitation, we should be tempted to fancy they despised us outright, or only considered us in the light of creatures brutally strong and brutally silly; among whom they condescended to dwell in obedience like a philosopher at a barbarous court. At times, indeed, they display an arrogance of disregard that is truly staggering. Once, when I was groaning aloud with physical pain, a young gentleman came into the room and nonchalantly inquired if I had seen his bow and arrow. He made no account of my groans, which he accepted, as he had to accept so much else, as a piece of the

The story telling animal

A central thesis then begins to emerge: man is in his actions and practice, as well as his fictions, essentially a storytelling animal. He is not essentially, but becomes through his history, a teller of stories that aspire to truth. But the key question for men is not about their authorship; I can only answer the question, "What am I to do?" if I can answer the prior questions, "Of what story or stories do I find myself a part?" We enter human society, that is, with one or more imputed characters—roles into which we have been drafted—and we have to learn what they are in order to be able to understand how others respond to us and how our responses are apt to be construed. It is through hearing stories about wicked stepmothers, lost children, good but misguided kings, wolves that suckle twin boys, youngest sons who receive no inheritance but must make their own way in the world and eldest sons who waste their inheritance on riotous living and go into exile to live with the swine, that children learn or mislearn both what a child and what a parent is, what the cast of characters may be in the drama into which they have been born and what the ways of the world are. Deprive children of stories and you leave them unscripted, anxious stutterers in their actions as in their words. Hence there is no way to give us an understanding of any society, including our own, except through the stock of stories which constitute its initial dramatic resources. Mythology, in its original sense, is at the heart of things. Vico was right and so was Joyce. And so too of course is that moral tradition from heroic society to its medieval heirs according to which the telling of stories has a key part in educating us into the virtues.

—Alasdair MacIntyre, in *After Virtue*, p. 201.

inexplicable conduct of his elders; and like a wise young gentleman, he would waste no wonder on the subject. Those elders, who care so little for rational enjoyment, and are even the enemies of rational enjoyment for others, he had accepted without understanding and without complaint, as the rest of us accept the scheme of the universe.

We grown people can tell ourselves a story, give and take strokes until the bucklers ring, ride far and fast, marry, fall, and die; all the while sitting quietly by the fire or lying prone in bed. This is exactly what a child cannot do, or does not do, at least, when he can find anything else. He works all with lay figures and stage properties. When his story comes to the fighting, he must rise, get something by way of a sword and have a set-to with a piece of furniture, until he is out of breath. When he comes to ride with the king's pardon, he must bestride a chair, which he will so hurry and belabor and on which he will so furiously demean himself, that the messenger will arrive, if not bloody with spurring, at least fiery

red with haste. If his romance involves an accident upon a cliff, he must clamber in person about the chest of drawers and fall bodily upon the carpet, before his imagination is satisfied. Lead soldiers, dolls, all toys, in short, are in the same category and answer the same end. Nothing can stagger a child's faith; he accepts the clumsiest substitutes and can swallow the most staring incongruities. The chair he has just been besieging as a castle, or valiantly cutting to the ground as a dragon, is taken away for the accommodation of a morning visitor, and he is nothing abashed; he can skirmish by the hour with a stationary coal-scuttle; in the midst of the enchanted pleasance, he can see, without sensible shock, the gardener soberly digging potatoes for the day's dinner. He can make abstraction of whatever does not fit into his fable; and he puts his eyes into his pocket, just as we hold our noses in an unsavoury lane. And so it is, that although the ways of children cross with those of their elders in a hundred places daily, they never go in the same direction nor so much as lie in the same element. So may the telegraph wires intersect the line of the high-road, or so might a landscape painter and a bagman visit the same country, and yet move in different worlds.

People struck with these spectacles, cry aloud about the power of imagination in the young. Indeed there may be two words to that. It is, in some ways, but a pedestrian fancy that the child exhibits. It is the grown people who make the nursery stories; all the children do is jealously to preserve the text. One out of a dozen reasons why *Robinson Crusoe* should be so popular with youth, is that it hits their level in this matter to a nicety; Crusoe was always at makeshifts and had, in so many words, to *play* at a great variety of professions; and then the book is all about tools, and there is nothing that delights a child so much. Hammers and saws belong to a province of life that positively calls for imitation. The juvenile lyrical drama, surely of the most ancient Thespian model, wherein the trades of mankind are successively simulated to the running burthen "On a cold and frosty morning," gives a good instance of the artistic taste in children. And this need for overt action and lay figures testifies to a defect in the child's imagination which prevents him from carrying out his novels in the privacy of his own heart. He does not yet know enough of the world and men. His experience is incomplete. That stage-wardrobe and scene-room that we call the memory is so ill provided, that he can overtake few combinations and body out few stories, to his own content, without some external aid. He is at the experimental stage; he is not sure how one would feel in certain circumstances; to make sure, he must come as near trying it as his means permit. And so here is young heroism with a wooden sword, and mothers practice their kind vocation over a bit of jointed stick. It may be laughable enough just now; but it is these same people and these same thoughts, that not long hence, when they are on the theatre of life, will make you weep and tremble. For children think very much the same thoughts and dream the same

dreams, as bearded men and marriageable women. No one is more romantic. Fame and honor, the love of young men and the love of mothers, the businessman's pleasure in method, all these and others they anticipate and rehearse in their play hours. Upon us, who are further advanced and fairly dealing with the threads of destiny, they only glance from time to time to glean a hint for their own mimetic reproduction. Two children playing at soldiers are far more interesting to each other than one of the scarlet beings whom both are busy imitating. This is perhaps the greatest oddity of all. "Art for Art" is their motto; and the doings of grown folk are only interesting as the raw material for play. Not Theophile Gautier, not Flaubert, can look more callously upon life, or rate the reproduction more highly over the reality; and they will parody an execution, a deathbed, or the funeral of the young man of Nain, with all the cheerfulness in the world.

The true parallel for play is not to be found, of course, in conscious art, which, though it be derived from play, is itself an abstract, impersonal thing, and depends largely upon philosophical interests beyond the scope of childhood. It is when we make castles in the air and personate the leading character in our own romances, that we return to the spirit of our first years. Only, there are several reasons why the spirit is no longer so agreeable to indulge. Nowadays, when we admit this personal element into our divagations we are apt to stir up uncomfortable and sorrowful memories, and remind ourselves sharply of old wounds. Our day-dreams can no longer lie all in the air like a story in the *Arabian Nights*; they read to us rather like the history of a period in which we ourselves had taken part, where we come across many unfortunate passages and find our own conduct smartly reprimanded. And then the child, mind you, acts his parts. He does not merely repeat them to himself; he leaps, he runs, and sets the blood agog over all his body. And so his play breathes him; and he no sooner assumes a passion that he gives it vent.

Alas! when we betake ourselves to our intellectual form of play, sitting quietly by the fire or lying prone in bed, we rouse many hot feelings for which we can find no outlet. Substitutes are not acceptable to the mature mind, which desires the thing itself; and even to rehearse a triumphant dialogue with one's enemy, although it is perhaps the most satisfactory piece of play still left within our reach, is not entirely satisfying, and is even apt to lead to a visit and an interview which may be the reverse of triumphant after all.

In the child's world of dim sensation, play is all in all. "Making believe" is the gist of his whole life, and he cannot so much as take a walk except in character. I could not learn my alphabet without some suitable *mise-en-scene*, and had to act a businessman in an office before I could sit down to my book. Will you kindly question your memory, and find out how much you did, work or pleasure, in good faith and soberness, and for how much you had to cheat yourself with some invention? I remember, as though it were yesterday, the expansion of spirit, the dignity and self-reliance, that came with a pair of mustachios in burnt cork, even when there was none to see. Children are even content to forego what we call the realities, and prefer the shadow to the substance. When they might be speaking intelligibly together, they chatter senseless gibberish by the hour, and are quite happy because they are making believe to speak French. I have said already how even the imperious appetite of hunger suffers itself to be gulled and led by the nose with the fag end of an old song. And it goes deeper than this: when children are together even a meal is felt as an interruption in the business of life; and they must find some imaginative sanction and tell themselves some sort of story, to account for, to color, to render entertaining, the simple processes of eating and drinking. What wonderful fancies I have heard evolved out of the pattern upon tea-cups!—from which there followed a code of rules and a whole world of excitement, until tea-drinking began to take rank as a game. When my cousin and I took our porridge of a

morning, we had a device to enliven the course of the meal. He ate his with sugar, and explained it to be a country continually buried under snow. I took mine with milk, and explained it to be a country suffering gradual inundation. You can imagine us exchanging bulletins; how here was an island still unsubmerged, here a valley not yet covered with snow; what inventions were made; how his population lived in cabins on perches and travelled on stilts, and how mine was always in boats; how the interest grew furious, as the last corner of safe ground was cut off on all sides and grew smaller every moment; and how, in fine, the food was of altogether secondary importance, and might even have been nauseous, so long as we seasoned it with these dreams. But perhaps the most exciting moments I ever had over a meal, were in the case of calves' feet jelly. It was hardly possible not to believe—and you may be sure, so far from trying, I did all I could to favor the illusion—that some part of it was hollow, and that sooner or later my spoon would lay open the secret tabernacle of the golden rock. There, might some miniature *Red Beard* await his hour; there, might one find the treasures of the *Forty Thieves,* and bewildered Cassim beating about the walls. And so I quarried on slowly, with bated breath, savoring the interest. Believe me, I had little palate left for the jelly; and though I referred the taste when I took cream with it, I used often to go without, because the cream dimmed the transparent fractures.

Even with games, this spirit is authoritative with right-minded children. It is thus that hide-and-seek has so preeminent a sovereignty, for it is the wellspring of romance, and the actions and the excitement to which it gives rise lend themselves to almost any sort of fable. And thus cricket, which is a mere matter of dexterity, palpably about nothing and for no end, often fails to satisfy infantile craving. It is a game, if you like, but not a game of play. You cannot tell yourself a story about cricket; and the activity it calls forth can be justified on no rational theory. Even football, although it admirably stimulates the tug and the ebb and flow of battle, has presented difficulties to the mind of young sticklers after verisimilitude; and I knew at least one little boy who was mightily exercised about the presence of the ball, and had to spirit himself up, whenever he came to play, with an elaborate story of enchantment, and take the missile as a sort of talisman bandied about in conflict between two Arabian nations.

To think of such a frame of mind is to become disquieted about the bringing up of children. Surely they dwell in a mythological epoch, and are not the contemporaries of their parents. What can they think of them? What can they make of these bearded or petti-coated giants who look down upon their games? Who move upon a cloudy Olympus, following unknown designs apart from rational enjoyment? Who profess the tenderest solicitude for children, and yet every now and again reach down out of their altitude and terribly vindicate the prerogatives of age? Off goes the child, corporally smarting, but morally rebellious. Were there ever such unthinkable deities as parents? I would give a great deal to know what, in nine cases out of ten, is the child's unvarnished feeling. A sense of past cajolery; a sense of personal attraction, at best very feeble; above all, I should imagine, a sense of terror for the untried residue of mankind: go to make up the attraction that he feels. No wonder, poor little heart, with such a weltering world in front of him, if he clings to the hand he knows! The dread irrationality of the whole affair, as it seems to children, is a thing we are all too ready to forget. "O, why," I remember passionately wondering, "why can we not all be happy and devote ourselves to play?" And when children do philosophize, I believe it is usually to very much the same purpose.

One thing, at least, comes very clearly out of these considerations; that whatever we are to expect at the hands of children, it should not be any peddling exactitude about matters of fact. They walk in a vain show, and among mists and rainbows; they are passionate after dreams and unconcerned about realities; speech is a difficult

art not wholly learned; and there is nothing in their own tastes or purposes to teach them what we mean by abstract truthfulness. When a bad writer is inexact, even if he can look back on half a century of years, we charge him with incompetence and not with dishonesty. And why not extend the same allowance to imperfect speakers? Let a stockbroker be dead stupid about poetry, or a poet inexact in the details of business, and we excuse them heartily from blame. But show us a miserable, unbreeched, human entity, whose whole profession it is to take a tub for a fortified town and a shaving-brush for the deadly stiletto, and who passes three-fourths of his time in a dream and the rest in open self-deception, and we expect him to be as vice upon a matter of fact as a scientific expert bearing evidence. Upon my heart, I think it less than decent. You do not consider how little the child sees, or how swift he is to weave what he has seen into bewildering fiction; and that he cares no more for what you call truth, than you for a gingerbread dragoon.

I am reminded that the child is very inquiring as to the precise truth of stories. But indeed this is a very different matter, and one bound up with the subject of play, and the precise amount of playfulness, or playability, to be looked for in the world. Many such burning questions must arise in the course of nursery education. Among the fauna of this planet, which already embraces the pretty soldier and the terrifying Irish beggarman, is, or is not, the child to expect a Bluebeard or a Cormoran? Is he, or is he not, to look out for magicians, kindly and potent? May he, or may he not, reasonably hope to be cast away upon a desert island, or turned to such diminutive proportions that he can live on equal terms with his lead soldiery, and go a cruise in his own toy schooner? Surely all these are practical questions to a neophyte entering upon life with a view to play. Precision upon such a point, the child can understand. But if you merely ask him of his past behavior, as to who threw such a stone, for instance, or stuck such and such a match; or whether he had looked into a parcel or gone by a forbidden path—why, he can see no moment in the inquiry, and it is ten to one, he has already half forgotten and half bemused himself with subsequent imaginings.

It would be easy to leave them in their native cloud-land, where they figure so prettily—pretty like flowers and innocent like dogs. They will come out of their gardens soon enough, and have to go into offices and the witness-box. Spare them yet awhile, O conscientious parent! Let them doze among their playthings yet a little! For who knows what a rough, warfaring existence lies before them in the future?

Philosophy and Children's Literature

Gareth B. Matthews

Once upon a time, in fact it was on a Tuesday, the Bear stood at the edge of a great forest and gazed up at the sky. Away up high, he saw a flock of geese flying south. Then he gazed up at the trees of the forest. The leaves had turned all yellow and brown and were falling from the branches. He knew when the geese flew south and the leaves fell from the trees, that winter would soon be here and snow would cover the forest. It was time to go into a cave and hibernate. And that was just what he did.

Not long afterward, in fact it was on a Wednesday, men came . . . lots of men, with charts and maps and surveying instruments. They charted and mapped and surveyed all over the place. Then more men came, lots of men with steamshovels and saws and tractors and axes. They steamshoveled and sawed and tractored and axed all over the place. They worked, and worked, and worked, and finally they built a great, big, huge, factory, right OVER the TOP of the sleeping Bear's cave. The factory operated all through the cold winter. And then it was SPRING again.

Deep down under one of the factory buildings the Bear awoke. He blinked his eyes and yawned. Then he stood up sleepily and looked around. It was very dark. He could hardly see. Then he saw a light in the distance. "Oh, there's the entrance to the cave," he said, and yawned again. He walked up the stairs to the entrance and stepped out into the spring sunshine. His eyes were only half opened, as he was still very sleepy. His eyes didn't stay half opened long. They suddenly POPPED wide apart. He looked straight ahead.

Where was the forest?
Where was the grass?
Where were the trees?
Where were the flowers?
WHAT HAD HAPPENED? Where was he? Things looked strange. He didn't know where he was.

But we do, don't we? We know that he was right in the middle of the busy factory.

"I must be dreaming," he said. "Of course that's it, I'm dreaming." So he closed his eyes very slowly and looked about. The big buildings were still there. It wasn't a dream. It was real.

At this point in Frank Tashlin's story, *The Bear That Wasn't* (New York: Dover, 1962), one smiles inwardly—or even outwardly. It's easy to appreciate the Bear's astonishment. Who wouldn't be astonished under such circumstances? But it's hard to take seriously the Bear's procedure for determining whether or not he is dreaming. Surely the procedure is unreliable: surely it won't work. But what would work? What would be a serious and workable method for determining whether one is awake or dreaming?

Many philosophers have thought that they (and we) should be able to answer that question. A few have thought they actually had the answer—Descartes, for example, in Part VI of his *Meditations* seems to think he has the answer.

Frank Tashlin, the author of *The Bear That Wasn't*, never supplants his whimsical procedure for determining whether one is dreaming with anything more serious. But the whimsical dream

On the philosophy in fairy tales

In the most-loved fairy tales, it will be noticed, noble personages may be brought low by fairy enchantment or by human beastliness, but the lowly are seldom made noble. The established order is not stood on its head. Snow White and Sleeping Beauty are girls of royal birth. Cinderella was tested, and found worthy of her prince. The magic in the tales (if magic is what it is) lies in people and creatures being shown to be what they really are. The beggar woman at the well is really a fairy, the beast in "Beauty and the Beast" is really a monarch, the frog is a handsome prince, the corpse of Snow White a living princess. Fairy tales are unlike popular romances in that they are seldom the enactment of dream-wishes. We would ourselves be unwilling to face the hazards the heroes have to face, even if we were certain, as the heroes are not, of final reward. Indeed, in fairy tales wishes are rarely granted; and when they are the wisher may be made to look as foolish as King Midas. He finds he has wished a sausage onto the end of his wife's nose, or that he himself has acquired an embarrassment of sexual organs. Stringent conditions may be laid down before a wish is granted: a mother must pledge her first born, a gay cavalier marry one who is repugnant to him. Even Cinderella's license expires after a few hours. Enchantment, in practice, is the opposite to the golden dream. The wonderful happens, the lover is recognized, the spell of misfortune is broken, when the situation that already exists is utterly accepted, when additional tasks or disappointments are boldly faced, when poverty is seen to be of no consequence, when unfairness is borne without indignation, when the loathsome is loved. Perhaps, after all, fairy tales are to be numbered amongst the most philosophic tales that there are.

—from Iona and Peter Opie, *The Classic Fairy Tales.*

test is certainly not the only philosophical angle to Tashlin's story. The story's very title bespeaks a philosophical sensibility. The "wasn't" in "The Bear That Wasn't" hovers nicely between an intransitive complete use ("wasn't" = "didn't exist") and an intransitive copulative use ("wasn't" = "wasn't such-and-such"—e.g., "wasn't a bear," or "wasn't what it was thought to be"). It is with just such a hovering between complete and incomplete uses of the verb "to be" that the Pre-Socratic philosopher, Parmenides, inaugurated philosophical discussion of non-being.[2]

In Frank Tashlin's story the Factory Foreman, the Third Vice-President, the Second Vice-President, the First Vice-President and the President of the Factory all insist that the creature before them is not a bear. Instead, they all say, he is a "silly man who needs a shave and wears a fur coat." And they want him to get back to work. If they are right about what he is, if what stands before them is not a bear, then he is an illusion and there really is no such bear as the one the story has supposedly been telling us about.

As the story progresses the Bear himself begins to lose his assurance that he is a bear. Is it that he once knew that he was a bear and now doesn't? And what was the basis for his former knowledge? And what now calls that basis into question? If he never really had good reason to think he was a bear, could he be properly said to have known that he was? How much basis does any of us have for knowing what we commonly say and think we know? The taunts of the zoo bears ("No, he isn't a Bear, because if he were a Bear, he wouldn't be outside the cage with you. He would be inside the cage with us.") reminds us of the inane conventionality that underlies so many of our claims to knowledge.

So the philosophical themes that emerge in *The Bear That Wasn't* include at least these four: (1) dreaming and skepticism; (2) being and non-being; (3) appearance and reality and (4) the foundations of knowledge.

I don't, of course, mean to suggest that *The Bear That Wasn't* is a philosophical treatise, even a philosophical treatise in disguise. It isn't a work in philosophy at all; it's a children's story. But it's style (I shall call the style "philosophical whimsy") consists in raising, wryly, a host of basic epistemological and metaphysical questions similar to students of philosophy. Although *The Bear That Wasn't* presents an unusually good example of philosophical whimsy, that style of writing is not at all unusual in children's literature.[3]

Another master of philosophical whimsy alongside Frank Tashlin is L. Frank Baum, author of the popular *The Wonderful Wizard of Oz* (New York: Dover, 1960). Perhaps no passage in the *Wizard* better illustrates philosophical whimsy than the autobiography of the Tin Woodman. As readers of unmacerated Baum will know, the Woodman began life as a creature of flesh and bones. He was gradually transformed by the successive amputation and tin replacement of each limb and gross segment of his body until, in the end, he was all tin. His life story (as it were) parallels one version of the familiar fable of the ship of Theseus;[4] and, like that familiar fable, the Tin Woodman's story raises baffling questions about continuity and identity. The Woodman's story, moreover, adds two new elements to the familiar puzzle about piece-by-piece replacement. One is that the Woodman receives tin parts for parts of flesh and bones; the change in kind of material affects our intuitions about whether anything persists through the transformation—especially when the kind of material we begin with (flesh and bones) is so closely linked to the kind of being the original entity is. A tin creature seems to have less claim to being a man (I am assuming that the Munchkins in the story are human beings), and hence less claim to being the *same* man, than would a creature made up entirely of fleshy "transplants." The second new element in this story is the Tin Woodman's memory. The

Woodman, after all, tells the story of gradual transformation as the story of his life, as he remembers living that life. And this ought to be important—how important, and why, are matters for reflective consideration.

A third master of philosophical whimsy in children's literature is James Thurber. In his delightful story, *Man Moons* (New York: Harcourt, Brace, 1943), Thurber describes the efforts of a king to nurse to health his daughter, Lenore, by fulfilling her wish to have the moon. "If I can have the moon," she assures the King, "I will be well again.

Unfortunately for the King, neither the Lord High Chamberlain, nor the Royal Wizard, nor the Royal Mathematician can help the King grant Princess Lenore's request. The King flies into a rage, and then falls into despair. Only the Court jester thinks to ask the Princess Lenore how big she thinks the moon is, and how far away. There follows this exchange:

> [Court Jester:] "How big do you think [the moon] is?"
>
> "It is just a little smaller than my thumbnail," she said, "for when I hold my thumbnail up at the moon, it just covers it."
>
> "And how far away is it?" asked the Court Jester.
>
> "It is not as high as the big tree outside my window," said the Princess, "for sometimes it gets caught in the top branches."

On hearing these answers the Court jester has the Royal Goldsmith make a "tiny round golden moon just a little smaller than the thumbnail of the Princess Lenore" and string it on a golden chain.

The philosophically smug reader of this tale—and it may well be the parent rather than the child—will simply smile at the Princess Lenore's naiveté and turn his or her thought to other matters. But to the more reflective mind—and this may well be the child's—Thurber's beautiful story will raise a clutch of questions about perception, illusion, apparent size, and apparent distance that have intrigued philosophers for twenty-five hundred years.[5]

For my fourth example I turn to A. A. Milne's *Winnie-the-Pooh* (London, 1926); I shall quote from the passage in which Rabbit is explaining his plan to capture Baby Roo. When Kanga asks, "Where's Baby Roo?" the others are to say, "*Aha!*"

> "*Aha!*" said Pooh, practising.
>
> "*Aha! Aha!* . . . Of course," he went on, "we could say '*Aha!*' even if we hadn't stolen Baby Roo."
>
> "Pooh," said Rabbit kindly, "you haven't any brain."
>
> "I know," said Pooh humbly.
>
> "We say '*Aha!*' so that Kanga knows that we know where Baby Roo is. '*Aha!*' means 'We'll tell you where Baby Roo is, if you promise to go away from the Forest and never come back.' Now don't talk while I think."
>
> Pooh went into a corner and tried saying "*Aha!*" in that sort of voice. Sometimes it seemed to him that it did mean what Rabbit said, and sometimes it seemed to him that it didn't. "I suppose it's just practice," he thought. "I wonder if Kanga will have to practise too to understand it." (p. 91)

The puzzles posed by Pooh are strikingly similiar to worries expressed by Ludwig Wittgenstein in, for example, this passage from his *Philosophical Investigations* (Oxford: Blackwell, 1953):

> What is it to *mean* the words "*That* is blue" at one time as a statement about the object one is pointing to—at another as an explanation of the word "blue"? Well, in the second case one really means "That is called 'blue' ."—Then can one at one time mean the word "is" as "is called" and the word "blue" as " 'blue'," and another time mean "is" really as "is"?

> Can I say "bububu" and mean "If it doesn't rain I shall go for a walk?"—It is only in a language that I can mean something by something . . . (p. 18)

I conclude my brief survey of philosophical whimsy in children's literature with a poem by John Ciardi. Poetry is certainly as good a medium for philosophical whimsy as is prose—as this poem, perhaps, will show:

SOMEONE SLOW

> I know someone who is so slow
> It takes him all day and all night to go
> From Sunday to Monday, and all week long
> To get back to Sunday. He never goes wrong.
> And he never stops. But oh, my dear
> From birthday to birthday it takes him all year!
> And that's much too slow, as I know you know.
> One day I tried to tell him so.
> But all he would say was "tick" and "tock".
> —Poor old slow GRANDFATHER CLOCK.[6]

Time is perhaps the single topic most frequently dealt with philosophically by children's writers. Doubtless their favorite way of dealing with it is to have their characters move time back, or up, or, as we say, move "about" in time. Thus, in *Meal One* by Ivor Cutler (New York, 1971) the mother, when she wants to get rid of a horrible, unnaturally fast-growing tree that is destroying the house, reaches for the hand of the clock and moves time back an hour. One's five-year-old child grins and mutters appreciatively, "You can't do that." The child's grin and murmur acknowledge what philosophers of science, in their highfalutin way, call the "anistrophy of time"—the irreversibility of time's arrow.

The perplexity John Ciardi plays on in his poem, however, is much more basic than worries about time travel. What Ciardi is having fun with is the fundamental idea that times passes. If time really does pass, then it must move at some rate or other. At what rate then does it move? The only answer possible seems to be this: a minute a minute, an hour an hour, a day a day, a year a year. Some philosophers think this answer so ridiculous as to show, or help show, that time doesn't really pass at all. One defender of the view that time doesn't really pass has spoken of "the myth of passage."[7] Other philosophers think the answer, "a minute a minute, an hour an hour, etc." expresses a truism. We object to it, they suppose, because it is too obviously true; we reject the answer as too simple.

Ciardi's poem manages to suggest both responses at once. The child's impatience with Grandfather Clock is a playful device for expressing impatience with the rate at which time passes. The child wants to speed life up ("... that's much too slow, as I know you know"). He wants to get older faster ("From birthday to birthday it takes him all year! And that's much too slow ..."). The clock's response mocks the child's impatience. His slow "tick" and "tock" teach patience. After all, it really does take "all week long to get back to Sunday." But then again, maybe time couldn't be speeded up because it is only in a manner of speaking that time moves at all. The idea that speeding time up is an incoherent notion may be suggested in the poem by the fact that the clock responds—not in words—but with its interminable "tick" and "tock."

That ends my survey. I want to finish off my discussion with a few general remarks on philosophy and children. But before I do that I shall need to deal with an objection. The objection concerns my assumption that the strain of philosophical whimsy I have found in children's poems and stories reflects a way of thinking that is natural—not just to the adult who writes the poem or story, and to the adult who buys it—but to at least some of the children who read it or hear it read as well.

One way to deal with this objection would be to consult transcripts of the uninhibited conversation of rather reflective children to discover whether at least some of them naturally make remarks that could easily be spun into the kind of

poem or story we have been discussing. But transcripts of this sort are not easily come by. The bits of conversation that, say, Jean Piaget lards some of his works with won't do. They have been selected to substantiate some theory about the stages children go through in their efforts to acquire what one might call "our adult conceptual scheme." But the reflective comments we need for the present purpose would raise playful and wry questions about the very adequacy and clarity of the scheme the children are supposed to be patted on the head for acquiring.

To be sure, there are sources for such material. One is a relatively informal book in developmental psychology by Susan Isaacs.[8] The brief items I shall now quote from that book are taken from relatively spontaneous comments recorded by parents of children who attended Susan Isaacs's progressive school in Cambridge, England, in the mid-twenties. I have chosen four items to quote. The philosophical weight of these comments should be apparent to any student of philosophy; and their delightfully whimsical tone should be obvious to all. If some children, some of the time, really do say such things as these (and I am entirely confident from my own experience that some do), then philosophical whimsy is for at least some children, some of the time, a natural style of conversation.

1. Some question of fact arose between James and his father, and James said, "I *know* it is!" His father replied, "But perhaps you might be wrong!" Denis [4 years, 7 months] then joined in, saying, "But if he knows, he can't be wrong! *Thinking's* sometimes wrong, but *knowing's* always right!" (355)

2. James, to his mother, was grumbling about "the fuss people make about getting up early, and things." Denis [6 years, 1 month, now], with his characteristically slow speech but penetrating thought, said, "Early and late *aren't* things. They're not things like tables and chairs and cups—things you can model!" (357)

3. Mother, "You know you're talking the most awful rubbish." Rose [3 years, 11 months], "Well, I'm thinking it." (358)

4. Ursala [3 years, 4 months], "I have a pain in my tummy." Mother, "You lie down and go to sleep and your pain will go away." Ursala, "Where will it go?" (359)

Now for some concluding remarks.

First comment. I don't want to come right out and say that children are philosophers, or that philosophers are children—though there would be some point in saying each of those things. Instead I want to say this: what philosophers do (in rather disciplined and sustained ways) is much closer than is usually appreciated to what at least some children rather naturally do (albeit fitfully, and without the benefit of sophisticated techniques). This coincidence finds itself reflected nicely in the strand of children's literature we have been discussing.

Second comment. This identification of philosophical whimsy in children's literature raises an interesting question about the place of philosophy in modern education. Most academic subjects taught in college are continuous with subjects taught in high school. Philosophy is not. This fact, coupled with the very great difficulty one has in explaining to anyone what philosophy is, suggests that philosophy is some sort of intellectual aberration—perversion, even—that takes hold of certain people late in their intellectual life, in their intellectual senility, one might say, and that it owes its position of respect to the historical circumstance that once philosophy included under its canopy respectable disciplines like physics, biology, mathematics and psychology—disciplines that now happily housekeep for themselves.

My brief examination of philosophical whimsy in children's literature suggests a somewhat different story. It suggests that the impulse to do philosophy comes very naturally to at least some members of the human race. To have philosophical thoughts is for them as natural as making music or playing games, and quite as much a part of being human. If this impulse is frustrated in school and goes underground until college, that fact may have something to do with society's failure to reward any sustained questioning that cannot be given a "useful" response. "Philosophy begins in wonder," Aristotle said. Perhaps our elementary and secondary schools reinforce only such wonder as will lead to the child's learning what we consider useful knowledge—reading, mathematics, some science and eventually what is called "social studies." Such a curriculum quite naturally leaves out a subject about which one of its greatest twentieth-century practitioners had this to day:

> Philosophy, if it cannot *answer* so many questions as we could wish, has at least the power of *asking* questions which increase the interest of the world, and show the strangeness and wonder lying just below the surface even in the commonest things of daily life.[9]

Perhaps I should hint at a darker point. Sometimes there is something unsettling, even subversive, about philosophical questions. Understandably, most adults don't like their natural advantage over children subverted. So they discourage a child from pursuing questions to which neither they, nor anyone they know, can give definitive answers.

Final comment. Children's literature should not be condescended to. One reason is this: some very good children's poems and stories—not all, or even most, but some—excite in young minds (and a few old ones, too) perplexities that can't be assuaged merely by passing on information, even information of a very sophisticated sort. These perplexities demand to be worried over, and worked through, and discussed, and reasoned out, and linked up with each other, and with life.

Perhaps identifying philosophical whimsy as a bona fide style of writing in children's literature will help us find important new respect for children's poems and stories, and for children—indeed, for the child in each of us.

Footnotes

1. Hard, but not impossible. At least one philosopher, John O. Nelson, in his article, "Can One Tell that He is Awake by Pinching Himself?" *Philosophical Studies* XVII (1966), 81-4, has argued for the effectiveness of the Bear's procedure. For rejoinders to Nelson see Michael Hodges and W. R. Carter, "Nelson on Dreaming a Pain" *Philosophical Studies* XX (1969), 43-6, and Jay Kantor, "Pinching and Dreaming" *Philosophical Studies* XXI (1970), 28-32.

2. Or anyway, that's a plausible hypothesis about Parmenides. For an elaboration and defense of that hypothesis, see Montgomery Furth, "Elements of Eleatic Ontology," *Journal of the History of Philosophy* VI (1968), 111-32, but especially 111-3.

3. The most obvious examples of writing in this style are, of course, Lewis Carroll's *Alice in Wonderland* and *Through the Looking Glass*. As an exercise in self-restraint I shall proceed without further mention of them.

4. Whose boards were replaced, one at a time, until they were all new. For a recent discussion of philosophical issues raised by the old story see Roderick M. Chisholm, "The Loose and Popular and the Strict and Philosophical Senses of Identity," *Perception and Personal Identity*, N. S. Care and R. H. Grimm, eds. (Cleveland, 1969), 82-106.

5. For a recent consideration of some of these issues see what John Austin has to say about "The Moon looks no bigger than a sixpence" in his *Sense and Sensibilia* (Oxford, 1962), 41.

6. From John Ciardi, *You Know Who* (Philadelphia, 1964), 21.

7. Donald Williams, "The Myth of Passage," *The Philosophy of Time*, R. M. Gale, ed. (Garden City: Doubleday, 1967), 98-116. Williams's own attack on the "myth of passage" takes a rather different form from what I suggest above; it is too complex to reconstruct here.

8. *Intellectual Growth in Young Children* (New York, 1930).

9. Bertrand Russell, *Problems of Philosophy* (Oxford, 1959), 16.

Literature for Children?

Michael Ende

Perhaps you will be surprised if I tell you here and now that—if I am honest—I do not approve of the fact that there is an independent form of literature for children. This seems to contradict the idea and the name of the prize which I am honored to receive. Let me explain in some detail.

It is generally assumed that literature for children and young people is produced out of an increasing interest of modern society in children and their needs. At least this is the reason presented in relevant reports on this issue. Personally, I think that this is a euphemism, or rather, that it is only the pleasant side of the coin, the other side of which is of quite a different nature.

If the world of grown-ups were habitable for the child as well as for the grown-up (as indeed it should be), there would be no necessity to create a sort of "wild-life reservation" in which children can indulge their animistic and anthropomorphic drives, in which they have the possibility (at least for some time) to imagine the world as being populated by strange and wonderful creatures, by elves and dwarfs—until the very moment at which they are brutally expelled out of this paradise, that is, when they are considered to be mature enough to face reality and to be introduced to the so-called "objective facts." Then the child learns that there is no "good old moon" who "sails so quietly through the clouds of the evening sky"[1] and gives you company while it shines down on you. The child finds that the moon is nothing but an impersonal lump of cinders and dust that is held on its orbit by mere laws of mechanics.

And there is no "dear sun" who "smiles upon the child out of the skies" but instead there is a gas-ball which hurls unimaginable amounts of energy for no reason at all into empty space, all the effect of continuous nuclear reaction.

To put it in a nutshell, the child learns that everything which has made the world look dear and reliable so far, has been nothing but a fat lie. There is no Santa Claus, no stork that brings the babies, no Easter rabbit. Children find that someone has made fools of them. As this basic breach of confidence usually happens unnoticed, it is not regarded as a serious problem. Often it is the children themselves who claim proudly that they do not believe in childish fairy-tales any longer. What remains is subconscious, but all the deeper-rooted, mistrust. The attitude of children towards the world of the grown-up becomes negative and even hostile. They try to create a world of their own.

It is this striving for independence which many writers of children's books make use of in order to satisfy the desires of their readers. In these books, the grown-up usually plays the role of the fool or of the stupid tyrant.

It becomes even more absurd when children are encouraged—often by some of the more progressive friends of the children—to create their own way of living, their anti-order and, of course, even a literature of their own. As if children were a separate species, that had no wish to communicate with man! But really, children *do* want to live together with the grown-ups in one world, they *do* want to share and be at home in that world.

Can novels embody philosophy?

The novel has accompanied man uninterruptedly and faithfully since the beginning of the Modern Era. It was then that the "passion of knowing," which Husserl considered to be the essence of European spirituality, seized the novel and led it to observe man's concrete life closely, and to protect him from "the forgetting of being." That is the sense in which I understand and share Hermann Broch's obstinately repeated point that the only *raison d'etre* of a novel is to discover what can only be discovered by a novel. A novel that does not uncover a hitherto unknown segment of existence is immoral. Knowledge is the novel's only morality.

I would also add: the novel is Europe's creation: its discoveries, though made in different languages, belong to the whole continent. The *sequence of discoveries* (not the sum of what was written) is what constitutes the history of the European novel. It is only in its context that the value of a work (that is to say, the import of its discovery) can be fully seen and understood.

As God slowly departed from the seat whence he had controlled the universe and its order of values, told good from evil, and given a sense to each thing, then Don Quixote came out of his mansion and was no longer able to recognize the world. In the absence of the supreme arbiter, the world suddenly acquired a fearsome ambiguity. The single divine truth decomposed into myriad relative truths shared among men. Thus was born the world of the Modern Era, and with it the novel—the image and model of that world—sprang to life.

To take Descartes's "thinking self" as the basis of everything and to be alone before the universe is to adopt an attitude which Hegel was right to call heroic.

To take the world as relative, as Cervantes did, to be obliged to face not a single absolute truth but a heap of contradictory truths (truths embodied in *imaginary thinking selves called characters*), to have as one's only certainly the *wisdom of uncertainty,* requires no less courage . . .

Since Cervantes, the novel has tried to embody philosophical reflection. This tendency opens out completely in Musil and in Broch. If the novel is considered to be an "investigation of existence," then the sense of this embodiment of philosophical reflection becomes clearer: it's not a matter of supplementing science, of writing "polyhistory," or of dealing with material not specific to the novel, but of mobilizing at the base of the narrative all the means that serve to illuminate man's concrete being. It's an enormous task to transform the novel into novelistic phenomenology and to find the artistic means of doing so. From that point of view the achievement of the two Viennese novelists— remarkable as it was—is but the first leg of a long journey.

—Milan Kundera, in "The Novel and Europe," *New York Review of Books*, July 19, 1984

All attempts to separate children from the world of the grown-up must be regarded as signs of resignation and disappointment. The division of literature into two classes, one for the grown-up and one for the child is, in my opinion, a serious symptom. The fact that this division has never been questioned or doubted does not make it less critical. Indeed, there is no topic within human experience, the basic idea of which would not be interesting or understandable for children.

It depends, however, on the way in which one speaks about it, from the heart—or just from the mind. I am thinking of the Artus Saga, for example, or of the biblical stories, which were never intended as children's literature—any more than Gulliver's Travels or Don Quixote or the so-called folk tales.

Yet I must ask myself if a story such as the Odyssey (if it were just written), could be published today at all if not under the excuse that it is a book for children. We find an abundance of giants, elves, queens of the winds and other fantastic creatures. The so-called grown-up of today, who has his mind barred with a poor idea of reality, considers such creatures and stories as "unreal," as "fantastic," even as "escapist," or whatever other depreciative words one could find.

On the other hand, what the adult regards as useless for himself is able to find, in his eyes, a certain right of existence in the world of the child, and there, in a patronizing manner, he places it. Maybe he nibbles at it secretly from time to time, when his bleak, grown-up world strikes him as being too desolate and dull, but only if no one can see it; otherwise he feels ashamed of it.

I do not want to speak about educational questions. I do not believe that significant children's books have ever been written out of educational considerations. The interventions of educators in this area of literature—and there have been quite a few recently—have, in my opinion, never been very successful. The criteria for a good children's book are neither of an educational nor a sociological nor a political nature, but they are exactly the same as in any other belletristic literature: they are determined by considerations of artistry. Perhaps it will be found that not everything which is good from the point of view of artistry should be presented to children. Frankly, I would not be afraid of that. If something is really well-written, it always comes from an integrity of heart, mind and senses, and hence speaks accordingly to the integrity of people. Therefore it is right and even relevant for society, and in a far deeper sense than many of those who think superficially about this topic may be able to realize. The question is, of course, if everything which is claimed to be art really is art. But "this is another story and shall be told another time."[2]

Let us return to the thought from which I started: when was it that the creation of a separate world for children (and hence a creation of a separate form of literature just for children) first became necessary?

In other countries, insofar as they have not already been influenced by Europe or America, children and grown-ups still share a common world. It was much the same in ancient Europe. When and why did this world fall into two parts?

The beginning of children's literature can be found in the first decades of the 19th century. But even if one goes further back than that by taking a broader view of children's literature, one does not get back further than to the beginning of modern times. There were times when modern intellectualism (the pride of the white race) began to take the place of the old intellectualism of Europe in every respect. In its different forms of appearance—"objective" natural science with its impact on industry and technology one the one side, and the humanities, which were losing themselves more and more in abstract theory, on the other side—modern intellectualism began to do away enthusiastically with all remaining "anthropomorphic" ideas, that is, with all ideas related to man. The world, along with its ideas, became inhuman.

From then on the cosmos was nothing but an impersonal machinery working according to a limited number of physical laws. Our planetary system, an unimportant small cloud of dust in the corner of the cosmos, one day had by chance spun out of a gigantic cloud of hydrogen, and would go on spinning until the day came when, due to extreme heat or cold, it would die. In the graveyard silence which remained in the cosmos, the whole history of man, including cultures, religions, fighting and suffering, was to be nothing but a tiny, hardly observable intermission within an incomprehensible sequence of gigantic but equally meaningless processes.

You will surely remember Goethe's remark: a mangy dog which circles 'round a stinking carcass is a pleasant sight compared to the conception of the world according to Kant and Laplace. From then on, and even today, man on earth has been seen as the accidental product of biochemical circumstances and his ego, his consciousness, including all his illusions of freedom, responsibility, love, creative strength, humor and human dignity, are in reality nothing but the product of automatic, electrochemical processes in the brain and the nervous system.

It is astonishing, however, that those who detect these "facts" always exclude their own thinking. They declare the "facts" to be the "objective truth," as if they were standing on the famous "point of Archimedes." If they did not do so, of course, they would soon end up in a logical jungle of the most grotesque kind, where they would have to be consistent and admit that, according to their own theory, their theory was nothing but the result of automatically working electro-chemical processes in their brains. Then they would have to face the necessity of explaining why electrochemical processes are able to recognize and designate themselves.

From all sides, credulous people assure me that they have long ago begun to overcome materialism. To be honest, this is not the impression I have. On the contrary, as we can see from the popular and famous book, *Beyond Freedom and Dignity*, by the American psychologist and recipient of the Nobel Prize, B. F. Skinner, science is now on the point of doing away with the last remains of anthropomorphism which are still to be found within science: where it deals with man himself.

But even man, we learn there, has really nothing in common with man. What we held to be the essence and nature of man, namely his freedom and his dignity, turn out to be nothing but naive and unscientific superstition.

To sum up: after man has *thought* himself into the state of being an alien element within this world, he now makes himself disappear out of it in order to create a new, horrifying, connection between himself as an object and other objects. As he is an indisputable part of this in-human world, he has to do away with his human parts. For those who are serious and consistent in this

view of life, there is no man as man. Unsurprisingly, some young people who try to live according to this "truth" have no scruples about planting bombs and shooting in every direction.

Inasmuch as man has developed to his lofty status precisely through this process of natural selection, what I would like to know is how, with this view, one could argue that the stronger does not necessarily have the right to live without showing any considerations for the weaker?

Why should it not be possible, I ask myself, to experiment with so-called "unworthy life," as was done in the concentration camps—experiments which could be of great significance to science and hence to the progress of mankind? Why should the problem of overpopulation not be solved by dropping some "clean" atom bombs? Of course there would be the need to find out by "scientifically objective methods" who has to die and who shall survive. Such a decision would have to be made by an international group of experts, a gathering of people who are capable of the really "value-free" thought.

All of us accept this development, because we are more or less intimidated. The sacred cow of our days is natural science and technology to whom the slightest offense is a sacrilege. Here rather than in all that is sacred, to demolish which entails no risk of loss of dignity to those who want to make themselves known and gain honor—here lies the real taboo of our century.

On the contrary, those who again and again repeat the rebellions of their great-grandfathers with the ferocity of those who demolish existing values—they are the ones who receive the rewards all over again. Everyone knows today that this is fashionable. And who would not like to be fashionable?

Again and again I hear and read that modern man does not believe in authorities. But I believe that we live in a century where people believe in authorities to a degree such as has never before been the case in the entire history of man. The sentence starting with "Science has found out . . ." is sufficient to arouse awe and readiness to believe and to silence any kind of impertinent objection. Any of the words which leave the mouths of these mysterious insiders in white coats is accepted without question on our knees, as it were—and goes into the papers uncontradicted.

Only other insiders are allowed to contradict. And all this, even if the effects of this so-called "value-free" form of science increasingly demolishes not only the inner but the outer world as well. I do not want to talk about the widely known ecological problem. But if the data of Professor Max Thurkauf is correct, then, at this very moment, all over our planet, there are 400,000 scientists occupied in the development and production of destructive weapons. The result of this respectable research is the famous "40-times-overkill," which is the possibility of killing all life not merely once but forty times. In searching for a counterweight against this monstrosity, we find that the entire scientific potential is not able to revive even one of these species of butterflies which were exterminated by the chemical industry.

But this, so I am told, is no argument against the value-free form of science; it is rather a wrong application of a principle which itself is good and right. Where to find the yardstick for a *correct* application remains somewhat unclear in a system of so-called value-free ideas. It seems to me that it will take some time before the point is reached where we will have to accept the fact that death was lingering in this kind of thinking from the very beginning; that right at the beginning, something went wrong; that to divide the world into one "objective" and one "subjective" world is nothing but the result of human consciousness and can therefore be overcome by man; that so-called "facts" are always determined by the way one asks for them. For example, if one looks for the soul in the body with a scalpel, as Virchow did, one comes to the conclusion that there is no such thing.

No one, not even the "most fantastic believer in the church of science" as Robert M. Pirsig calls

these people, can really *live* with this idea of the world. I myself can hardly imagine a mother—even if she were an extreme believer in science—telling her child: "The fact that I love you and you love me is in reality nothing but some electro-chemical processes in our brains. With suitable wires one could switch that on and off."

While such monstrosities are accepted without any objection, as "objective scientific facts," no one likes to draw these horrifying consequences. When it does happen here and there, people are terrified. Especially when children are concerned, everyone ought to know that this kind of doctrine is nothing but a murder of the soul, that with this conception of the world a child is bound to starve, to freeze to death, to suffocate in his heart. And yet, you will not be able to find a school in which this doctrine is not taught—or, at least, not presented—in this way. According to Paul Feyerabend in his book, *Against Method*, parents have the option of deciding whether their child is to be instructed in the Catholic or Protestant religion, or if it is not to be instructed in religion at all, yet they have no choice when it comes to scientific subjects. The church of science claims orthodoxy, and this claim is universal, pitiless and exclusive.

What we *live* with are yardsticks of a quite different kind: values which stem from quite different views of the world. But these are rarely considered today; sometimes they are even denied. Schizophrenia, which is the result of this contradiction, has become such a common phenomenon that it is now considered to be the normal state of man. Even worse, it is demanded that what people think is to be separated from their moral behavior.

I think, however, that a world which is uninhabitable for children cannot be inhabitable for grown-ups either. It goes without saying that I consider it neither as desirable nor as possible to return to the old forms of thinking, where the conception of the world was related to the idea of man. What I consider as desirable—or rather, as a precondition of survival—is that we find adequate ways to feel at home again in this world, that we start again to measure the world with our human measure, because we have no other measure at our disposal, that we transform intellectualism, which is unable to produce values out of itself, into a way of thinking which includes reality and hence can be experienced, so that we may achieve a human way of thinking again.

For this reason I believe that poetry is a basic need for our lives, as basic as food and drink. Of course, poetry cannot achieve this change on its own, but it can point in the direction towards which a change has to take place. What else is poetry, if not the creative ability of man to see and recognize himself in the world and the world in himself? All poetry is "anthropomorphic" in character; otherwise it stops being poetry. And therefore all poetry has something in common with the child. I would say poetry is the ever-childlike aspect of man.

To understand the world and to become a part of it, is poetry. It is not only poems or books or art in general that I refer to, but different ways of life and explanations of the world which can be experienced and understood. Perhaps some day even grown-ups will be grown-up enough to learn about the truth from poetry. Perhaps there will be a new and quite different form of natural science which finds true facts with which man not only can live, but which even reveal his human nature to him. Let me put it like this, in the words of the poet Novalis:[3]

One day, when neither numbers nor figures are the key to all creatures, when those who sing or kiss know more than the most learned scientists,

when the world returns to the free life and goes back into the world, when light and shadow are again held in pure clarity, and when the ever-returning stories of the world can be discerned in poems and fairy tales, then all this inverted nature will take flight, just because of a single, secret word.

And then there will no longer be any necessity to have a separate form of literature for children. Children and grown-ups will be able, each in their own ways, to share one and the same world. This is the purpose which I want to achieve as a writer.

I want to thank you for your encouragement and support for the "long search" which I have been undertaking, together with my little hero, Atreju—encouragement and support which you have shown by awarding me this prize.

(Translated from the German by Jutta Schutte and Barbara Bruning.)

Footnotes

1. quotations from a children's song
2. quotation from "Die Unendliche Geschichte" by Michael Ende
3. Wenn nicht mehr Zahlen und Figuren
   Sind Schlüssel aller Kreaturen,
   Wenn die, so singen oder küssen,
   Mehr als die Tiefgelehrten wissen,
   Wenn sich die Welt ins freie Leben
   Und in die Welt wird zurückbegeben,
   Wenn dann sich wieder Licht und Schatten
   Zu echter Klarheit werden gatten,
   Und man in Marchen und Gedichten
   Erkennt die ewigen Weltgeschichten,
   Dann fliest vor einem geheimen Wort
   Das ganze verkehrte Wesen fort.

Through Phantasia To Philosophy
Review with Reminiscences

Eva Brann

The Unending Story by Michael Ende is both literally and in several other ways the most wonderful book I've read in ages. I think it will be easily received into the canon—hitherto almost exclusively English—of great "children's literature" along with the likes of *Wind in the Willows* and the *Alices*, (*Die Unendliche Geschichte*, Thienemanns Verlag, Stuttgart 1979. In English: *The Neverending Story*, Doubleday 1983, illustrated; G.K. Hall 1984 large print; Penguin 1984, paperback.)

But first a puzzlement, expressed in the raised eyebrow quotes above. What exactly makes "children's literature" children's literature?

Criteria close at hand are: who it is *for* or *by* or *about* (and assorted other prepositionally expressible relations.) Perhaps, first of all, children's books are those *written for* children. However, one famous such book (I forget which) is dedicated to "children of all ages," which rather ruins the category. What is more, at least one pair of very famous ostensible children's books, the *Alice* books, is notoriously detested in childhood by the same people who later love them as children's books, myself included. For one thing, I despised the simp of an author who seemed seriously to believe that sweet (albeit perky) innocence was an essential attribute of little girls when I, an expert, knew that they constitute a considerable part of society's criminal element. And for another, I was repelled by

what I could sense, though not pinpoint, as a hidden agenda. For the *Alice* books, being among other things *romans à clef*, require a key, and an unpossessed key just alienates, in distinction from unplumbable depths which feel mysteriously homey.

Furthermore, whomever they might be written for, children's books are, willy-nilly, largely *read by* coopted adults who would surely go crazy reading them to children if they didn't develop their own sneaking attachment to them, as they certainly do. Just try shouting "Dr. Seuss" in the right adult company and back will come a chorus: "I do not like green eggs and ham! I do not like them, Sam-I-am." (Incidentally, I've often wondered in how many children "Dr. Seuss," by one of those homonymic misassociations that enrich infantile imaginative life, fosters friendly feelings toward the Greek "father of gods and men.")

Nor are children's tales exclusively *written by* adults. Besides the endless oral fabrications with which children regale their peers (or at least used to), they also occasionally indite quite fancy and elaborate stories. By and large these productions are a lost corpus, of course, but there are Austen and Brontë juvenilia; C.S. Lewis in *Surprised by Joy* records in some detail the modes and motifs of his childhood works, and I can even cite one extant, purportedly genuine, child-written classic: Daisy Ashford's nine-year-old summary judgment of the Victorian world, *The Young*

Visiters ("To tell you the truth, my Lord," says her socially shaky hero, Mr. Salteena, "I am not anyone of import and I am not a gentleman as they say he ended getting very red and hot.")

No more is *being about* children a sufficient test, since, although, as far as I know, children's books always have some children as heroes or assistant heroes, so do some eminently adult books, for instance the pitiful and spooky brother and sister pair which is in unholy cahoots with a corrupt ghost in James' *Turn of the Screw*, and the juvenile perpetrators of all manner of uninnocent mischief in a good many Saki stories.

Nor are there topics and tones which are peculiarly suitable or unsuitable for children. Take supposed children's modes like fantasy, fairy tales and magic, and there will be plenty of authors who can do that for grown-ups (somewhat heavy on the Irish, to be sure). W. B. Yeats, W. H. Hudson, H. Rider Haggard, James Stephens, George MacDonald, C. S. Lewis, Walter de la Mare, Charles Williams, J. R. R. Tolkien come helter-skelter to mind. Take, on the other hand, a topic to which it might be thought to be hard to recruit children: political philosophy, and I can name a children's book which I recognize in retrospect as a childhood propaedeutic to the study of Plato's *Republic*; it is Hugh Lofting's *Voyages of Doctor Dolittle* in which the island Indians of Popsipetel force the Doctor to become their king, acclaiming Doctor John Dolittle as King John Thinkalot. "As for the poor Doctor, I never saw him so upset by anything. It was, in fact, the only time I have known him to get thoroughly fussed," says Stubbins, the Doctor's ten-year-old assistant and companion (compare *Republic* 347 and 520). In the morning the unwilling, but duty-bound philosopher king dispenses justice and in the afternoon he teaches school. "I have often thought," Stubbins observes, "that Popsipetel under the reign of John Thinkalot was perhaps the best ruled state in the history of the world." If asked nicely I might produce an article on the parallelism between the Popsipetelian and the Platonic paradigms, plus a comparison between Socrates and the Doctor.

The one tone which was thought, at least until recently, to be entirely taboo in children's books, because children both *shouldn't* and *couldn't* be made to respond to it, was that of erotic passion. Now, Freud aside, the latter is surely false: In high-strung times especially, children are quite capable of sudden accesses of full-blown desire. Such an episode is described in Thomas Mann's Depression story, "Disorder and Early Sorrow," to the uncanny accuracy of which I can bear personal witness. When I was four or so, about the fateful year of 1933, my parents took the waters (served in thick green glass mugs, tepid and metallic) at Muenster-am-Stein. Our *Kurhotel* sported liveried bell boys, *kepi*, purple fencing-jacket with gold piping, stripes down the trousers, and all. With one of these I fell in love one afternoon, defencelessly and shamelessly. He, evidently a kind—and buyable—boy was got upstairs to play with me. I remember as if it had happened yesterday my first acquaintance with the peripety of passion: at the sight of his adolescent self *in corpore* I was suddenly seized by chilling embarrassment—and that was that for seven years at least.

As for the sense that children shouldn't be subjected to explicitly erotic descriptions, some adults think that *they* shouldn't be either. On the other hand there are plenty of children's books that have a strong undertow of implicit passion, and quintessential passion too, the kind that possesses and tyrannizes and even destroys—such, for example, as surfaces in the self-surrender of the lovable little clairvoyant boy, Charles Wallace, to the seduction of "It" in Madeleine L'Engle's *A Wrinkle in Time*.

Nor does security and gentleness, in the manner of Mister Rogers' relaxation exercises, universally obtain in children's books. The Hauff fairy tales, which generations of German children grew up on, were smug and cruel at once with a kind of philistine sadism, and the children's poem which was the gaudium of the nursery, Wilhelm

Busch's "Max and Moritz," ended with the two bad boys being ground through the flour mill, their particles promptly forming two loaves shaped in the images of those holy terrors. This literature may have something to answer for, but that's very much an undecided question in child psychology. Still, I do know that a modicum of suffering is the spice of a tale and that when I was little I always specified to my father that my goodnight story should be "very sad," by which, I understand in retrospect, I meant that it should be as excruciating as possible right up to "and they lived happily ever after." (German tales end, incidentally, with "and if they haven't died before then on this day they're living"—not exactly sweetness and light, either.) These unholy joys were encouraged in later childhood, in latency as they used to say, by the wildly popular adventure novels of Karl May, fat, satisfying green and gold tomes of Indian adventure, homoerotic sadism and missionary zeal. (The latter by-passed me, but completely, in my German-Jewish childhood—the white scout's noble Indian intimate Winnetou—mine too, for a year or so—converts on his deathbed, and I never knew it until a recent re-reading: Karl May is now available in this country in translation.) And then came comic books, the American outlet for these tastes—two years of alternating greed and surfeit which started in my third week or so in this country, behind a vent on the roof of the YMHA of Boro Park, Brooklyn. Consequently the first English word whose meaning I ever consciously sought and savored was "sinister."

Comic books are, of course, read by adults as much as by children, with naive absorption as by soldiers stranded in barracks and with nostalgic sophistication as by student connoisseurs in dorms. There are even upper class imported comics, such as the *Tintin* series. In fact, the earliest comics I know of, proto-comics really, the running caricatures of the aforementioned Wilhelm Busch (Victorian, in English periodization), are really meant for adults. The point this is ambling towards is that being in pictures isn't confined to children's books either—though I've never seen adult picture books as telling and discovery-rife as, say, Mitsumasa Anno's *Anno's Journey*.

Finally, trying to find some ideal characteristic of children's literature, Clifton Fadiman ("The Child as Reader," *Great Books Today* 1983) comes up with this: It supplies children with a sense of freedom enjoyed in security. True enough, but so does adult escape literature. And, come to think of it, what novel-reading isn't escape—from the mundane to an enhanced world?

The long and the short of it seems to be that no set of criteria infallibly picks out "children's literature." One is thrown back on a purely extrinsic determination—whom it's *meant* for— and that's easily subverted. Let but a well-disposed grown-up read a good children's book and—presto!—it's adult literature, wrong addressee notwithstanding.

But that leads to a much deeper and trickier question: Do children *read their books differently* from the way an adult reads them? It doesn't take much logical acumen to see that the answer is going to be bedevilled by a Cretan Liar type paradox: Those who argue for the otherness of childhood can't claim to have much inside knowledge. That ought to be a stumbling block both to "child's world" romantics and to epistemological geneticists. For suppose that children's cognitive abilities do develop in stages that can neither be anticipated nor reversed, then each new stage effects a radical transformation in consciousness, which the fully developed adult (as exemplified in the experimenting scientist himself) can perhaps conceptually reconstruct but never empathetically recover. (As it happens, it does turn out that certain Piagetan experiments, when replicated under somewhat more empathetic conditions, come up showing children to have more cognitive capability at an earlier time than the geneticist staging predicts. In fact, I keep wondering if a case couldn't be made for Piaget having shown that children are just natural Aristotelians: They apprehend motion as prior to

Poetic and philosophical thinking

Ever since Pythagoras (or so we are told) invented the word philosophy, in order to express the notion of the philosopher not as one who possesses wisdom but as one who aspires to it, students of philosophy have recognized that the essence of their business lies not in holding this view or that, but in aiming at some view not yet achieved: in the labor and adventure of thinking, not in the results of it. What a genuine philosopher (as distinct from a teacher of philosophy for purposes of examination) tries to express when he writes is the experience he enjoys in the course of this adventure, where theories and systems are only incidents in the journey. For the poet, there is, perhaps, none of this dynamism of thinking. He finds himself equipped, as it were, with certain ideas, and expresses the way in which it feels to possess them. Poetry, then, in so far as it is the poetry of a thinking man and addresses to a thinking audience, may be described as expressing the intellectual emotion attendant upon thinking in a certain way: philosophy, the intellectual emotion attendant upon trying to think better.

—R.G. Collingwood, in *The Principles of Art.*

time, they consider movements to be governed by their goals, they conceive place rather than coordinate space, and, in short, their cognitive ontology recapitulates the historical phylogeny of physics—a shift in perspective rather than in capability.)

One fall-out from the strict developmental view of children is the notion of "reading readiness." And yet unready reading provides the windfall joys of a child's life. I recall getting into one of my father's medical reference books (*streng verboten!*), section: tropical diseases, and thrilling to the illicit attractions, depicted in glorious technicolor, of some burgeoning cases of elephantiasis. And that was quite a while before I was ready to decipher the text. (I was slow to learn to read, probably because I spent the first grade, God knows why, at Volksschule No. 4, homeroom teacher Fraeulein Pfefferkorn, a young functionary of the BDM, the Nazi girls' league, and our primer was all about an avuncular Fuehrer and a certain little brown Heinz who got to give him a pretty posy at a parade.)

On some Sunday mornings, ready or not, my father would break open a huge volume of the encyclopedia (*Der Grosse Brockhaus*) and read to me. My preferred course was to set out from the coolly scientific heading "Vulkan," tracking references to doom-preparing "Vesuv" landing finally in panicky "Pompeii," where a black cloud of sulphur fumes and pumice hail is preparing *the* great romance of archaeology. Incidentally, when a decade or so later I discovered Bulwer-Lytton's classical-kitsch classic, *The Last Days of Pompeii*, it was sheer reminiscent magic, including a persistent illusion that that slender-columned Campanian villa idyll came to an end on a Sunday morning in a villa in Berlin-Dahlem. (Actually I have no idea what day of the week dawned, a silent blue scorcher—the birds had ceased to sing—on August 4, 79 A. D. The Berlin villa, having been legally stolen by an SS family, was destroyed in an Allied air raid probably as late as 1944.) Seven years more, and I was a declared classical archaeologist (though Greek rather than Roman, my taste having grown very pure in the meanwhile). Which goes to show how long-lived and far-working are such out-of-turn childhood experiences. And it isn't only grownup wonders that children take to; perfectly mundane texts will also serve. I recall that just after I learned to read I acquired an avidity for the "Directions for Use" on boxes, bottles and cans. That taste too has stuck: I have a little collection of direction delights, among them the instruction booklet from an abacus (1947), touted as "the pet calculator of Japan," "Which Brings Comfort and Convenience on Your Life."

The relation of childhood to adult reading has of course got a history. Louis XIII of France was born in 1601. As a little boy the Dauphin was told goodnight stories, for instance of Melusine, the tutelar fairy of the house of Lusignan, who turned into a half-serpent on Saturdays. Just the same tale was told among adults at evening gatherings (Philippe Aries, *Centuries of Childhood*). In the course of the seventeenth century, adults turned increasingly to more sophisticated entertainments: "children's stories" are originally abandoned adult tales. Generalizing wildly, I have an inkling that modern views on the distinctiveness of childhood have less to do with "the discovery of the child" than with the construction of new ideas of maturity—and of adult diversion, for instance that it fails to divert unless it reveals the true existential horror at the heart of things.

One test for continuity of consciousness is to read to yourself a book that was read to you when very little. I have tried it. There is a German nursery book, still in print and going strong in Germany, called *Little Peter's Moon Trip*. It concerns a cowardly cockchafer (of the melodious species *Melolontha Melolontha*, I've lately learned) whose hereditarily missing sixth leg must be recovered from the brute of a man-in-the-moon who keeps it hanging from a nail driven into a birch branch (broken from the birch in our garden, which I loved equally for its waving white and green grace and because it offered illicit barkpulling, the most satisfying dismemberment there is). It has been over half a century, but the very cover wafted me back into that bourgeois nursery midsummer night's dream (actually May, cockchafer time), with its character-crowded cosmos, its heavenly highway for secret excursions. But it also came back to me that at four I had been half-repelled by the book, and now I know explicitly what I then knew implicitly, namely, why: only unexceptionably good children were candidates for the moon mission, there was lots of piety in the sky and all the goodies were blond—which left me out on all counts; besides, the pictures were too broad-stroked—you couldn't walk into them and discover details, and there was no wit at all.

On the other hand, Doctor Dolittle, who came into my life at about six, had from the first and still has my wholehearted allegiance, because I sensed then what I recognize now: that the books are an introduction to human excellence. It was to my moral advantage, I think, that for several years I *was* Tommy Stubbins and the Doctor was my own father got up in cutaway and top hat: the kindly physician who can't remember to collect his bills but can call on all the animals for help in their own language, the unfussed explorer who simply sails out of Puddleby-on-the-Marsh on a borrowed boat, who in a shipwreck secures first Stubbins but right after his beloved notebooks, the muddling master of the jury-rig who, in the words of the parrot Polynesia, the senior animal in his menagerie, always "gets there," the comfortable homey round gentleman whose rare righteous wrath shakes the earth, the world's most learned naturalist who never stands on his dignity and never loses it—a just and a wise, and in the opinion of his intimates (and in mine), a great man.

Antipathies and allegiances that survive so long unchanged surely do betoken a continuity of consciousness. In fact, judging from personal experience, the only stage to which childhood is really alien is adolescence. Quasi-adulthood is a time of such hot subjectivity, such excessively large and excessively particular passions that it devalues just those objective delights adults and children have in common.

Children's writers (except for a few who don't write but construct their books to satisfy a market, or what is worse, a theory) naturally work on the same-world hypothesis; indeed the highest praise they can hope for is that which Hugh Walpole gives the author of *Doctor Dolittle*: "Mr. Lofting believes in his story quite as much as he expects us to." If they do preach or pull their punches or wax sentimental it is because they have for a moment lost that inward mirror-vision by which a grown-up sees the child within observing the grown-up without. Meanwhile, just by conde-scending, they acknowledge at least the commen-surability of the worlds of children and adults.

The matter is worth dwelling on because it looks like a peculiarly accessible case of a set of problems, or rather of related impossibilities, that preoccupy contemporary philosophers: the impossibility of radical translation, translation utterly from scratch, of our language into another, the impossibility of entering empathetically into an alien or ancient culture, the impossibility of recovering the terms of a theoretical frame of reference after it has under-gone a shift—and ultimately, the opacity of individ-ual human beings to each other.

The relation of child to adult might seem to epitomize all four incommensurabilities. But there is the mitigating circumstance that while none of us can, in principle, have been members of a tribe that said "gavagai" while looking where we see a rabbit, or have seen the planets revolve about us as a Ptolemaic geocentrist, or have lived as "archaic" Greeks (situations con-sidered by authors like Quine, Kuhn and Feyera-bend), some of us, at least, *have* been children. I for one would, to be sure, wish to claim some-thing more: When I was little I said "Hase" where I now say "rabbit," and I feel somehow confident that then and now I mean the same by both vocables: some such creature as the immor-tal Hazel of *Watership Down*. Somewhat later I spent four years studying intensely enough to see them dance in my dreams just those pots and pans on which said "archaic" Greeks depicted them-selves in looming black shadows and which archeologists call "Geometric." And though they never lost their mystery for me (and I certainly couldn't do with the bizarre conceptual analyses so thoughtfully provided by proponents of the radical difference of the archaic mind) the satis-fying way in which the glossy brown-black line ornament lay on the pot and the simple telling grandeur of the funeral scenes got to me. I knew that those pot-painters knew what they were do-ing and that, but for the least substantial of obsta-cles, the twenty-eight hundred or so years

between us, I would know it too. Minimally, at the time those Attic silhouettes felt closer than the non-objects of contemporary painting. And fi-nally, living, like the rest of us, in a manifestly Ptolemaic world, ignorant of all astronomy, and happening to study Ptolemy's *Almagest* some time before Copernicus' *Revolutions*, I couldn't help but see the world Ptolemaically, or so I thought. Or, looking at it from the flip side, why dwell on the inaccessibility of former centuries and other cultures when one's own time can be completely uncanny and one's intimates can be as the aliens from outer space?

But even suppose that my sense of secular solidarity is mere self-delusion, there is still that one case of crossing into another world which is not hopeless. I was never a Greek (I guess), but I, my personally identical I, was once, extensively and devotedly, a child, and it seems to me that in figuring out how one's childhood frame of mind is recovered one might also learn how other places and other times become accessible. Do we have a faculty for this project?

Of course we do: memory for the recovery of our own former self and imagination for entering into other worlds. These faculties (parentheti-cally: faculty psychology is back, see Jerry Fo-dor, *Modularity of Mind*) display a certain persistence and a certain evanescence, having to do, I suppose, with the character of their objects, which are not presentations but re-presentations, that is, not solid things that are there, but the see-through shades of their absent selves.

Now what I want to say about the road to recovery naturally concerns only full-blown childhood and doesn't reach into prelinguistic babyhood. (Memory *of* and *in* infancy is a par-ticularly fascinating but difficult chapter in cog-nitive developmental psychology.) Furthermore, since I'm thinking not about the daily coping of childhood but about its imaginative life, espe-cially with respect to books, I'm not talking of adult memories of childhood existence, but rather of that remembrance of things past which is es-sentially *memory of memories*. What I mean is that as soon as a new book has been taken in it becomes part of the imaginative memory, there to begin its episodic afterlife, perhaps in the case of a goodnight story even in that very night's dream. (Incidentally, this kind of remembrance is pretty recalcitrant to investigation—glory be!—and for all the enormous amount of work done on memory recently, I haven't found much on it.)

In remembering one does, to be sure, sometimes come on oneself reading (A vivid memory: reading my first self-read book, *Robinson Crusoe*—recommended to the parents of Europe, as I later delightedly discovered, as the one and only book fit to be a child's first by Rousseau himself in the *Emile*. While securing my island in imagination, I simultaneously worked away at poking a hole in the plaster wall of the nursery, intended in time to be an escape route from the enforced after-mid-day-dinner rest hour. (Hole discovered on brother's information. Scene and plaster job. Tremendous revenge on little beast.) But mostly the images we remember were already memory-images in childhood—and therein lies the recovery: we return *through* the imagination *to* the imagination, a hermetically sealed, secure depository.

Not really, someone might argue. Over time and growth the kaleidoscope of the mind has shifted out of all recognition and its image bits have entered new and transforming contexts. Well, I want to propose a figure which illustrates at least how it *feels* to live in both worlds.

In 1832, Necker, a student of perception, drew attention to a phenomenon which is now all over the literature. "Necker's Cube" is simply a perspective outline drawing of a solid. When observed, it flips, willy-nilly so that the front corner is suddenly, without transition, in back. It is impossible to see both positions at once, nearly impossible to fixate one position for long, very hard for those used to perspective drawing to see it as a flat picture. The so-called "perceptual paradox" associated with the figure is just this: that we cannot help seeing reversing cubes when the single stimulus itself is in fact a plane design.

What poetry does with ideas

I do not think that society should look to poetry for new philosophies, new religions, and synoptic intellectual structures. That demand has been made repeatedly during the past century, ever since Matthew Arnold, and when poets have taken it seriously the result has been, at best, something like Hart Crane's magnificent botch of a poem, *The Bridge*. Poets are often intelligent men and they are entitled to their thoughts; but intellectual pioneering and the construction of new thought systems are not their special function. Aeschylus's *Oresteia* was not a contribution to Athenian legal theory; Dante's *Commedia* gave us no new theology; and Shakespeare's history plays added no fresh concepts to the political thought of his age.

What poetry does with ideas is to redeem them from abstraction and submerge them in sensibility; it embodies them in persons and things and surrounds them with a weather of feeling; it thereby tests the ability of any ideas to consort with human nature in its contemporary condition.

—Richard Wilbur, in *On My Own Work.*

The "interpretative paradox" is analogous. There is a common "flat" stimulus, the text itself, taken as mere material for make-believe. Children are, of course, fully aware that they can, with an effort, deflate the book, that there is a safety exit into plane prose (I remember being at a play about an enchanted forest with Tony, a friend of mine, then four, who at the eeriest part whispered to me apotropaically: "You know, it isn't real.") But the spontaneous position is to read the text perspectivally, as a world with depth. And in that reading different corners come to the fore, unbidden and irrepressible, corresponding to the preoccupations of then and of now.

Imagination-memory, I would say, is the capability for perspectival reversals, and so the faith is: unless the road is blocked by trauma, childhood is accessible, as are all other human terrains.[1]

Credits: Vladimir Nabokov, *Speak, Memory*.

That faith is reinforced by *The Neverending Story*, the Baedeker into imagination-land, the imperial realm of Phantasia (no, repeat, no, relation to the Disney extravaganza), which is certainly a children's book by all available criteria and a hugely popular one. There has, it appears, even been a movie.

To begin with, Ende's *Neverending Story*, subtitled "from A to Z," is beautifully made. (Incidentally, it abounds in puns like that on Ende's name, repeated from his other wonderful book, *Momo*, and in paradoxes like the one expressed in the subtitle, providing young and old with the joys of catching on.) Each page is headed by a nice garland; each chapter begins with a full page illumination of its proper letter (by Roswitha Quadflieg). Best of all, the book is printed in two colors. For this is a tale of a passage into Phantasia, first reluctant and reversible and then deep to the point of no return. The print is red for the waking and working world (*mundus mundanus* in my private cosmography) for Stop! Danger! Wake Up!, I suppose, and it turns spring-green for Phantasia. Green-skinned, too, is the slim, severe, noble lad Atréju of the Indian tribe of the Purple Buffalo, Bastian's Phantasian friend and finally his savior. Bastian Balthassar Bux, the "hero of passage," is a fat, serious and lonely little boy, gourmet of apple strudel and spinner of tales, flabby in body and sturdy in soul.

For content, this is a *big* substantial book containing myriads of characters and sub-worlds. For Phantasia is both infinite and highly anisotropic; in each of its places dwells a different kind of being. What is more, Phantasia abounds in stories to be: "But that's a story for another time" is the never-ending refrain, just as the book really starts when it seems to be ending. Here's its skeleton:

On a mundane morning, Bastian, running from his tormentors, finds himself on the inside of a glass door saying "Antiquariat" in mirror-writing. He feels compelled to steal a book bound in shimmering copper colored silk, entitled, of course, *The Neverending Story*, and bearing the sign of two snakes biting each other's tails (recognizable by aficionados of the hermetic as the *double ouroboros*, the symbol of cyclical endlessness.) With it he hides in the storage attic of his school where he makes camp and begins to read. The print turns green. He is looking into Phantasia, a threatened land. Its child empress is sick and her sickness is reflected in Phantasia's progressive piecemeal annihilation. There is only one cure: a human being must enter Phantasia and give the Infanta her new name. As the schooltower clock strikes the afternoon hours it comes to Bastian that *he* knows the name, that *he* is chosen to save Phantasia—and not only Phantasia, but also the real world, because in proportion as the former is swallowed by non-being, the latter is possessed by lies; their salvation is conjoined.

At two o'clock he slips out to pee and eats his lunch apple; at eleven he glimpses a monkish ancient in Phantasia who is writing the copper colored book Bastian is reading. Just before midnight he realizes that both realms will be caught in a treadmill of eternal return unless he acts. At the stroke of twelve he is in Phantasia, in the Night Wood of Perelin, and the print turns green until the end when Bastian tells his father the whole story—except for once, when he prominently strews his initials BBB in red sand over the Painted Desert Goab. It is the first clue of his coming corruption. Now, having grown beautiful in body, celebrated as the savior, he conducts a triumphal progress through the realm. He is wearing the amulet Auryn, the golden, the Glow. It bears the *ouroboros* on the obverse and on the reverse the legend, "Do as you will." Bastian misunderstands it as license to "Do as you wish," wherewith his desires become indefinite and destructive—the classical outline of a tyrant. As he goes, he falls deeper and deeper into self-forget-fulness.

On the way, there are many wonderful characters and episodes. There is, for example, Atréju's conveyance and companion, Fuchur, the Dragon of Gladness (*Gluecksdrache*) who floats and swoops through the air in joyous bows just like my dragon kite, and has a voice like a bell. (Hermann Hesse has a little essay—1949—on the golden sonority of the vocable *Glueck*.) The episode closest to my heart comes late in the book at the nadir of Bastian's amnesia: his days with Yore, the Miner, who has charge of the "pit of pictures," and the "lode of dreams," where are deposited transparencies, tablets thin as a breath: our memories and dreams, for "a dream cannot come to nothing once it is dreamt." Bastian must search these image-archives for a familiar dream as a clue to guide him out of his oblivion. After several days of forlorn sorting he finds a dream tablet of a man in a lab coat holding up the impression of a denture, which fills him with enormous longing. This is the beginning of his ascent and return to his father (who is in fact a dentist.)

The Neverending Story is full of delights which an alert child may sense and an adult connoisseur may decipher. It is a real work of literature, meaning that it maintains far-flung connections with its kind, being full of allusions, borrowings, references: like Carroll's Alice, Bastian goes through the looking glass, like Mac-Donald's Phantastes, he finds the road to fairy-land, like Rabelais' Thelemites, he does as he will. And right in the middle of the book traces turn up of one previous Phantasia-traveler who made the song Bastian's knights sing all the time. Translated from German, it goes:

When that I was and a tiny little boy
With hey, ho, the wind and the rain . . .

They recall his name as "Shexpir or the like." Evidently one adult who made it.

There is an age-old philosophical perplexity, the dream-wake confusion, propounded for in-stance by the Chinese sage Chuang-tzu on apparently awakening from a dream: "Who am I then? A butterfly dreaming that it is Chuang-tzu or Chuang-tzu dreaming that I am a butterfly?" (3rd century, B.C.), again by Descartes in the *Meditations* (17th century A.D.), and lately in *The Bear That Wasn't* (reviewed in Gareth Matthews' charming book, *Philosophy and the Young Child*.) Young children are, of course, very much alive to just such linguistic and philosophical puzzles. Parental anecdotes about their midget metaphysicians abound, always delightful, an occasional sense of oracular self-mystification not-withstanding. So out of the blue the aforementioned Tony said of God (who was not exactly the talk of his family): "He is sooo big, soooo big he's an idea"—Anselm-in-embryo! Indeed there is more to it than pleasure in puzzles. Not for nothing do we enter upon rational life enthralled by negativity, *the* metaphysical problem. I mean the "terrible twos," a condition whose essence a lovable little boy Peter whom I used to sit for (or rather, on) would express in the remarkable phrase he prefixed to his continual stream of objections: "Want not to want . . ." Negativity first, and later existential panic: I recall awakening every night for some weeks to watch the darkly heaving ramification of the well-loved walnut outside the nursery window and to know that my mother could die.

Yet later, at seven or eight, my father succeeded in inducing in me the first conscious moment of philosophical wonder I can recall. He was taking a *privatissimum* on the first Critique with his friend, Arthur Liebert, then the President of the *Kantgesellschaft*. On a Sunday morning walk through the spring woods he showed me that my hands were bewitched, that, though like as two peas in a pod, I couldn't bring them into congruence. A quarter century later, when I discovered his source in para. 13 of the *Prolegomena*, Kant's illustration of his claim that space is not a property of the things themselves but the form of their outer intuition, all the original amazement came back to me, and henceforth the pure material of the outer form of sensibility was permanently dyed spring-green.

All these approaches to philosophy—and, really, they're not peculiar to children—occur in *The Neverending Story*: playful puzzles, deep fear, serious questions. But literally the most wonderful mode is the predominant one: Here is a *philosophical story book*, a book of speculative myths, a working vacation for the imagination.

The grandest philosophic myths, those Socrates tells in the Platonic dialogues, are *end-myths*; they consummate the dialectical argument with the high of a cosmic vision. Now, in contemporary philosophy, grandeur being out of favor, mini-myths, flairless little *thought-constructs*, are placed throughout the logical argument: Martians, counter-earthlings, brains-in-a-vat and possible worlds inhabited by that one-and-only unicorn whose affliction is non-existence. Finally, there are the real myths, the ones that are not made but re-told, and these are good as *preludes* to philosophy: In the *Metaphysics* (I) Aristotle says: "Wonder is the beginning of philosophy," "myths are composed of wonders," and so "the myth lover (*philomythos*) is somehow a philosopher (*philosophos*)."

But he also says that wonder is really a sense of one's ignorance and that one takes to philosophy as "an escape from ignorance." And so he announces a slow-starting but irresistible development: the way of science is the way away from wonder. Two millennia later, a founding text in natural philosophy will bear the still wondering legend, "Wonder and is no Wonder" about its central diagram (the endless chain around the prism, Stevin 1605); four centuries later it will be near-universal dogma that science and philosophy mean *demythification*. The myth-lover is meant to come to maturity; much of our education is devised to sober us up.

Yet there is also a sense, endlessly analyzed and bemoaned (and not only by those soft spirits who want to reimmerse themselves in magical murk), that something has been lost, that the world we hoped to gain by taking our two-and-a-half-thousand year temperance pledge has somehow lost its shape and color. What is it that myths did for the world?

They made it visible, I imagine, by—ugly but apt term—*potentiating* the appearances, that is to say, by making them significant. The Necker Cube shows that even the objects of mere perception depend on interpretative preconceptions to take shape. Myths might be thought of as analogous interpretative schemata for the human shaping of phenomena. They bring out in appearances just that depth and color from which measuring science and rational philosophy soberly abstract; hence they give them *visibility*—a word used here certainly in an extended, perhaps in a private sense: I call appearing objects "visible" when I do not look *past* them as being mere unsuggestive particulars, or *through* them as being mere representative instances, but *at* them as recalling through their very looks *both* themselves *and* something beyond. (This mode of significant appearing is usually called "symbolic," but it shouldn't be, since by long-standing usage a symbol mainly "stands for" something *else*.)

Genuine myths, the sort that are not composed and read but received and reenacted, are mostly extinct, and the notion of reviving them through deliberate acts of creation is a practical contradiction in terms. Yet all is not lost. A grand enough fairy tale can stand in for those by-gone world-frames. (So, come to think of it, can a great grownup novel.) Such stories make something of the mundane world; they back it with a vibrant ground and bring it out with vivid contrasts.

Ende's books, both *Momo* and *The Neverending Story*, do even more. They reflect on what they are doing while they are doing it—a feature they share with the finest speculative works. They tell wonderful tales and wonder about tale-telling. They represent the annihilation of the imaginative realm as *the* great emergency of contemporary life, and even as they tell the story of its peril they accomplish its restoration. Ende's mythophilia is a beginning of philosophy which is not just to be left behind.

Nil admirari advises the Roman poet, follower of a latter-day philosophy; he means both "Wonder at nothing," and "Think nothing wonderful." *Omnia admirari*, "Wonder at everything and find everything wonderful" must be the Phantasia-traveller's postulate. Its requirements determine both the kind and the mode of the thinking which begins in Phantasia. For first, certain questions can take on flesh and flourish there unashamedly that are skeletons in the logical closet. And second, the Phantastic mode of imagining is an unabashed reversal of the (pretended) order of rational investigation: Here the questions are candidly reached through the answers, since the imagination, for all its tolerance of the antic and the monstrous, is constitutionally partial to certain kinds of doing and being and inimical to others.

I'll come to an end with a small sampling of the neverending stream of questions which wells up in Phantasia.

Phantasia, the realm of the imagination, subsists independently of human attention—and yet its existence depends on a periodic human invocation, a timely Adamic re-naming. Bastian says: "I would like to know just what is going on in a book when it is closed?" And his discoveries speak to and, of course, contradict current solutions to long-debated problems such as: What is the nature of fictional, or possible, worlds? What is the standing of non-existent objects? How do they comport with "reality"?

Phantasia's topography is infinite and yet centered. It has, as Bastian learns, a perilous port of entry (Perelin, the Night Wood) and a magical place of exit. He enters each of its places as a separate world and yet he progresses through the land of phantasy as through *one* empire. The layout of fictional worlds (their boundaries and compatibility) is treated—with severely averted eyes—in the logic of fiction ("deviant" logic, so-called!). Its doctrines, particularly concerning the question "Are all fictional worlds connected?" deny Bastian's experience of the cohesion of all stories.

Phantasia is the realm into which nothingness first erupts; that is what Bastian is called on to deal with, and he learns that escape from the treadmill of mere recurrence, the revivifications of a sad daily existence, and truth-telling itself depend on saving this realm of the imagination—a powerful though deviant answer to the question, endlessly revolved in contemporary philosophy, "What is the crisis of modernity?"

Phantasia can engulf and corrupt, too. As his sojourn loses its aim, as he forgets his daily shape and his human mission and tyrannizes the realm he has saved, it becomes a thicket of sophisticated unmeaning; here apes play aleatic compositional games, which when continued for all eternity will produce all stories and all stories of stories including the Neverending Story. Even Bastian in his pride is appalled at the insult this extreme of esthetic formalism offers his copper-colored book; he becomes a partisan in the great question of esthetics: "Does art have meaning over and above its form?"

And finally, as the Neverending Story ends, Bastian, emerged from Phantasia, tells his father the story of his reading of the story of his journey into the realm where the story of his journey is being written. He would like to know, Bastian says, "How could this book occur within itself?" He has found the fairy-form of a cluster of questions that are the fascination of present-day intellectual life: recursion and self-reference.

Enough said. The point's been made: One way, a wonderful way, to philosophy passes through Phantasia.

Notes

1. The day after I finished this *jeu d'esprit* I came on a multiply serendipitous reference—Clifford Geertz in "Found in Translation: On the Social History of the Moral Imagination" citing Lionel Trilling who in his last essay (on the ever-piquant theme of reading Jane Austen with American students) calls this "one of the significant mysteries of man's life in culture: how it is that other people's creations can be so utterly their own and so deeply part of us."

Philosophical Books vs. Philosophical Dialogue

Martha Nussbaum

According to the *Phaedrus*, Socrates did not write because he believed that the real value of philosophizing lay in the responsive interaction of teacher and pupil, as the teacher guides the pupil by questioning (sometimes gentle and sometimes harsh, depending on the pupil's character and degree of resistance) to become more aware of his own beliefs and their relationship to one another. Books, says the Socrates character, cannot perform this activity, for they are not "alive" [275D]. They can, at best, remind you of what it is like. At worst, they lull the soul into forgetfulness both of the content and of the manner of real philosophizing, teaching it to be passively reliant on the written word [275A]. Worse still, in some readers, books can induce the false conceit of wisdom, since they may mistake information about many things for true understanding [275B]. Books, furthermore, lack the attentiveness and responsiveness of true philosophical teaching. They "roll around" all over the place with a kind of inflexible inertness [275E], addressing very different people, always in the same way.

We could express these two points by saying that, in Socrates's view, philosophical books are to philosophizing as tennis manuals are to tennis. (We could make the point with other examples: think of child-rearing handbooks, sex manuals, instruction books in navigation.) They cannot do it; they are no substitute for the live activity,

although they might, in some circumstances, be more or less useful records of some points, when used by people who already have an experiential sense of what the activity is. If, however, one were to take them for the real thing, to become reliant upon them, rather than upon one's own perceptions and responses—or, worse still, to pride oneself on one's expertise just because one had studied a number of such books—that would be a bad mistake indeed. Such books, furthermore, lack the particularity of really good tennis. They say the same thing to every reader without any regard for the particular characteristics of each reader's game or for the way that game will vary in response to a particular opponent. In one way, the philosophical book is even worse off than the tennis manual. For tennis manuals are neither coercive nor self-important. They do not tell you that you must play, only how you might if you want to; and they typically offer advice in a modest tone of voice. The books of Empedocles or a Parmenides, by contrast, tell you that you must believe this and not that, act this way and not that way; that this is the way of truth, that the way of loathsome, herdlike error. They shower abuse on the person who does not conform. Their tone is inflated and authoritarian. Even Homer and the lyric poets, though far less strident, do unequivocally praise these deeds and not those, this sort of person and not that. Real philosophy by contrast, as Socrates saw it, is each person's

The conditions of happiness

If you really read the fairy-tales, you will observe that one idea runs from one end of them to the other—the idea that peace and happiness only exist on some condition. This idea, which is the core of ethics, is the core of the nursery-tales. The whole happiness of fairyland hangs upon a thread, upon one thread. Cinderella may have a dress woven on supernatural looms and blazing with unearthly brilliance: but she must be back when the clock strikes twelve. The king may invite fairies to the christening, but he must invite all the fairies or frightful results will follow. Bluebeard's wife may open all the doors but one. A promise is broken to a cat, and the whole world goes wrong. A promise is broken to a yellow dwarf, and the whole world goes wrong. A girl may be the bride of the God of Love himself if she never tries to see him; she sees him, and he vanishes away. A girl is given a box on condition she does not open it; she opens it, and all the evils of this world rush out at her. A man and a woman are put in a garden on condition that they do not eat one fruit; they eat it, and lose their joy in all the fruits of the earth.

This great idea, then, is the backbone of all folk-lore—the idea that all happiness hangs on one thin veto; all positive joy depends on one negative. Now, it is obvious that there are many philosophical and religious ideas akin to or symbolized by this; but it is not with them I wish to deal here. It is surely obvious that all ethics ought to be taught to this fairy-tale tune; that, if one does the thing forbidden, one imperils all the things provided. A man who breaks his promise to his wife ought to be reminded that, even if she is a cat, the case of the fairy-cat shows that such conduct may be incautious. A burglar just about to open someone else's safe should be playfully reminded that he is in the perilous posture of the beautiful Pandora: he is about to lift the forbidden lid and loosen evils unknown. The boy eating someone's apples in someone's apple tree should be a reminder that he has come to a mystical moment of his life, when one apple may rob him of all others. This is the profound morality of fairy-tales; which so far from being lawless, go to the root of the law. Instead of finding (like common books of ethics) a rationalistic basis for each Commandment, they find the great mystical basis for all Commandments. We are in this fairy-tale on sufferance; it is not for us to quarrel with the conditions under which we enjoy this wild vision of the world. The vetos are indeed extraordinary, but then so are the concessions. The idea of property, the idea of someone else's apples, is a rum idea; but then the idea of there being any apples is a rum idea. It is strange and weird that I cannot with safety drink ten bottles of champagne; but then the champagne itself is strange and weird, if you come to that. If I have drunk of the fairies' drink it is but just I should drink by the fairies' rules. We may not see the direct logical connection between three beautiful silver spoons and a large ugly policeman; but then who in fairy-tales ever could see the direct logical connection between three bears and a giant, or between a rose and a roaring beast? Not only can these fairy-tales be enjoyed because they are moral, but morality can be enjoyed because it puts us in fairyland, in a world at once of wonder and war.

—G. K. Chesterton, "Fairy Tales" in *All Things Considered*.

committed search for wisdom, where what matters is not just the acceptance of certain conclusions, but also the following out of a certain path to them; not just correct content, but content achieved as the result of real understanding and self-understanding. Books are not this search and do not impart this self-understanding.

As I have said, this is all written down. What are we to make of this fact? Plato's dialogues remind us again and again that Plato lived surrounded by people who had disdain for real philosophical activity, people who either totally ignored it or cheapened it by making it a kind of sophistical and competitive point-scoring. It is not surprising that in such circumstances, especially after the death of Socrates at the hands of those who feared and hated the challenge of real philosophy, Plato should have come to feel more keenly than his teacher the importance of having written reminders and paradigms of good philosophical teaching. A reminder of real philosophical searching, even if it is only that, can still be valuable. But by placing the Socratic criticisms of writing inside his own writing, Plato invites us to ask ourselves, as we read, to what extent his own literary innovations have managed to circumnavigate the criticisms.

To summarize the matter very briefly: I think that we can see, if we look at these dialogues as the startling stylistic innovations they were (the first dramatic works of philosophy and also the first prose works of theatre), that Plato has used the resources of theatrical writing to create real dialectical searching in a written text. He has produced a book that does not preach or claim to know, but that searches and criticizes. In its open-mindedness it sets up a similarly dialectical activity with the reader, who is invited to enter

critically and actively into the give and take. This marks a great difference from many important works of early Greek philosophy, where it is usual for the speaker to claim to be an initiate, a recipient of wisdom from the gods, or even, himself a god on earth. Dialogues, then, unlike the books criticized by Socrates, might fairly claim that they awaken and enliven the soul.

A dramatic work, furthermore, can contribute to our understanding of an ethical issue by motivating an argument or an inquiry. By showing us how and why characters who are not professional philosophers enter into argument, by showing us what sorts of problems call forth philosophizing, and what contribution philosophy makes to their work on the problems, it can show us, better than any single-voiced work, why and when we ourselves should care about ethical reflection.

We can add that by connecting the different positions on an issue with concretely characterized persons, the dialogue, like a tragic drama, can make many subtle suggestions about the connections between belief and action, between an intellectual position and a way of life. This aspect of the dialogue form urges us as readers to assess our own individual relationship to the dialogue's issues and arguments. In these ways, again, the dialogue seems to be both less "silent" and more responsive to individual differences than the books criticized by Socrates. They are books that each reader can read personally inside his or her pursuit of self-understanding, exploring the motivations and beliefs of the characters together with his or her own. There are conclusions here, and views of Plato; we are asked, however, not simply to memorize them, but to find them inside ourselves.

The Other Half of the Child

Kieran Egan

Most of the research on the child as a learner has focused on a relatively narrow range of logical skills. Even sophisticated theorists, such as Piaget, who have focused on dreams, play, and games have tended to be mainly concerned with the logico-mathematical operations that underlie them. Very little research has focused on children's imagination or fantasy, because the products of imagination and fantasy are so very hard to control. One result of the fact that we have had much research on one aspect of children's thinking—the logical—and very little on "the other half"—the imaginative—is, I think, a rather imbalanced view of the child as a learner. While research results tend not to be directly influential on teaching practice and curriculum development—and are in any case rarely unambiguous—the overwhelming focus on a limited range of children's thinking has led to certain principles becoming fairly widely accepted as generally true about children's learning. I mean principles such as: children's learning proceeds from the concrete to the abstract, from the known to the unknown, from active manipulation to symbolic conceptualization, from perception dominated thinking to conceptual freedom.

If we focus on children's imagination, however, I think we can see that the validity of these principles is much less general than is often taken to be the case. They do influence teaching practice and curricula, and it seems worthwhile to consider whether we might not develop a rather different view of the child as a learner by considering those areas where children's imaginative thinking seems most energetically engaged. What I will do, then, is focus on fantasy, and some other areas of stories, that children seem most vividly engaged by, and consider what inferences we can reasonably draw from that engagement about children's learning.

Mythic Layer Stories

First I will consider the kinds of stories that children seem to find most engaging before about age seven. I call them "mythic" because they are little concerned with reality and have certain structural features in common with some of the myth stories of the world. Here I will consider just three features of such stories. First, a very general structural characteristic; second, the odd creatures we find inhabiting such stories—monsters, wicked witches, talking middle-class bears; and third, the story itself.

If we look even casually at the structure of typical fantasy stories, it is clear that they are built usually on powerful abstract binary concepts—good/bad, big/little, brave/cowardly, security/fear, and so on. If we tell a child the story of Cinderella, we presuppose that for the story to be meaningful, the child, in some sense, has available concepts of love, hate, greed, fear, jealousy and so on. These, of course, are some of the great abstract organizing concepts which we use to make sense of our experience. I do not mean that young children necessarily know these *terms*, or how to define them, but rather that in some sense they must know them and use them for the story to be meaningful. Such concepts are used and elaborated in stories. It is in this sense that Ted Hughes calls stories "little factories of understanding."

From this simple observation we can infer, I think fairly uncontentiously, that young children when they arrive in school have in place some of the most powerful abstract concepts that we ever learn—good/bad, love/hate, fear/security, and so on. They use these abstract concepts to make sense of concrete content. So to take as a principle that young children's learning goes from the concrete to the abstract seems, at least, an inadequate principle. We see young children using enormously general abstract concepts continually in their imaginative lives.

We might even say that the key to making content meaningful to young children is articulating it on the basic abstract concept which children use so readily and fluently. It is not concreteness that is important in making knowledge meaningful to young children, it is tying the concrete to particular abstract concepts.

The second feature of children's stories that seems to challenge some of the dominant principles about children's learning can be inferred from the kinds of creatures which fill children's fantasy stories. Fairy god-mothers and talking middle-class bears cannot be taken as simply foisted on children by grownups. Children's engagement with such creatures may be explained by psychoanalysts a number of ways, but their appearance in our dreams and the myth-stories of the world suggests that they are not a trivial phenomenon.

If we observe how children develop a conceptual control over a wide range of phenomena in the world one can see at work a method of grasping first opposite ends of the phenomena and then a mediation of those opposites. Conceptual mastery of the temperature continuum, for example, comes first by grasping the concepts "hot," and "cold." We then mediate between these and from

the concept "warm." We then mediate between "warm" and "hot," and "warm" and "cold," forming concepts such as "lukewarm," or "cool," or "fairly hot," and "fairly cold."

If we look at the world through the eyes of a child certain prominent binary discriminations are evident. However much you talk to the cat, it never learns to talk back. We form a discrimination between things that are cultural and things that are natural. Again, while the young child will probably not know the *terms* natural/cultural, the concepts are used in making sense of certain phenomena and experiences. If we try to mediate between nature and culture we get, among much else, talking middle-class bears. They are both natural and cultural as warm is both hot and cold. Peter Rabbit and his relationship with his safe wild wood and Mr. McGregor's dangerous cultivated garden plays with variations on the mediation of nature/culture in a number of ways. Similarly, children tend early to form a discrimination between things that are alive and things that are dead. If we try to mediate between life and death we get spirits and ghosts of all shapes and varieties. A ghost is both alive and dead as a talking middle-class bear is both natural and cultural and warm is both hot and cold.

What we see in this common process of learning is quite the opposite of perception-dominated thinking, of the kind that one sees in some of the classic Piagetian preoperational experiments. Here we see conception-driven generation of entities that over-ride perception. That is, by considering children's imaginative activities we can see forms of thinking quite different from those we see by focusing on logico-mathematical thinking. Our image of children's thinking, and of the child as a learner, is as a result less constricted.

The third feature of children's imaginative activity I want to consider is the story-form itself. We need to ask, what is a story? If we take an event—"He Shot Tom"—it does not mean anything much to us. Crucially for an event, we do not know whether to feel glad or sorry that he shot

Tom. If we elaborate and add sentences that show that he was a clean, upstanding fellow who loved his grandmother, and Tom picked his nose in public and used foul language in front of children, then we begin to feel glad that he shot Tom. Clearly, Tom had it coming. But as the story unfolds we discover that Tom, despite his unprepossessing appearance, has a heart of gold and was trying to stop "him" and "his" grandmother from selling drugs to children, and that "he" has these socially and individually destructive ambitions. Also when we say he loved his grandmother, we should say that he *loved* his grandmother, and that they had an unspeakable relationship. The product of this elaboration is that we begin to feel sorry that he shot Tom. It's Tom and the grandmother who had it coming, we conclude.

The good story-teller plays with our affective responses continually. The story is the only narrative form that can ultimately fix the meaning of the events that make it up—in the sense that it can fix how we feel about the events. We know we have reached the end of a story when we know how to feel about all the events that make it up. Life and history are just "one damn thing after another," and do not allow us to feel secure about the meaning of any of the events that make them up. But the story is our haven from such contingency.

The stories that seem to engage young children have beginnings that set up some content built on powerful abstract binary opposites, which are elaborated in the middle, and are mediated or resolved in the end. Such principles provide a simple model that can be used in planning lessons and units to make them most engaging and meaningful for young children.

Romantic Layer Stories

I will again focus on just three features of the kinds of intellectual engagements that seem most energetic during the period between roughly seven years and fourteen or fifteen. The general

characteristic that distinguishes mythic layer understanding from that of the romantic layer is what might be called the discovery of reality. We can see an aspect of this in the kinds of stories that are most engaging. No longer are fairy-godmothers and wicked witches and monsters acceptable without some kind of explanation. One tends to find still magical heroes and heroines, and they continue to have supernatural powers, but always these come with some, however implausible, explanation. Thus Superman's powers are acceptable but only in the context of the history of the dying planet Krypton, and so on.

If we consider the kind of knowledge that students in this age range find most engaging it is the kind we meet in sources like *The Guinness Book of Records* or *Ripley's "Believe It or Not."* What we see are similar structural features as we find during the mythic layer, but now they are confined within reality. What is of interest now is who really was the biggest and smallest, the bravest and most cowardly, the fattest and thinnest, and so on and on. We may reasonably say that the early intellectual engagement with reality is with its extremities; the knowledge sought about the real world is knowledge about it limits.

The principles derived from the focus on particular limited logical skills—the known to the unknown, etc.—have been the basis of what is called the "Expanding Horizons" curriculum. In this it is assumed that what children can best make sense of begins with their immediate experience and works outwards. By considering children's more energetic intellectual engagements we seem to get a quite different picture. Indeed we see students' imaginative engagement with reality beginning at the limits and borders. This strategy seems perfectly sensible: if we want to make sense of something, we begin by establishing its limits, finding out what is the context within which the knowledge exists.

A second prominent feature of student's intellectual activity during this period is to be found in the development of obsessive hobbies, or engagement in something in great detail. I think this can sensibly be seen as related to the point immediately above. Faced by an autonomous reality we need first to get some sense of its size and scale. We search for its limits and borders on the one hand, and try to get some sense of its extent on the other. By learning something exhaustively we get some grasp on everything—some realization that the world is not limitless and overwhelming. Whether or not we want to argue whether this general learning strategy represents a "natural" response to the discovery of an autonomous world "out there," we must surely acknowledge that it is a perfectly sensible strategy.

The sense of an autonomous world, which works by its own laws which are barely comprehended and which is impervious to our wishes and hopes is rather threatening. One of the major defenses we use against this threatening reality is what we may call Romantic associations. These are the third evident imaginative intellectual activity we see commonly in students during this period. Students associate with those human qualities that are best able to overcome and transcend the threats of the everyday world. We see this association at work in the prominent engagement during this period with heroes and heroines—the "hero" or "heroine" may be a football team, pop star, or whatever. They represent some transcendent human quality, such as power, ingenuity, energy, courage, nobility, etc.

One simple implication from this for teaching during this period is to put the knowledge we wish students to learn into the context of the lives of those who first invented or discovered it. By this means we can show the knowledge as a product of transcendent human qualities. We tend to abstract knowledge from the context of its making or discovery and put it into logical structures. One result of this is to dehumanize knowledge. Many of the problems of difficult access to learning follow, not so much from the abstractness of knowledge, but from its dehumanization—removing it from the context of human hopes, fears, courage, energy, that make it accessible, especially to students in this romantic phase.

Conclusion

By considering even briefly some prominent aspects of children's and student's imaginative activity we can see that some of the principles that are powerfully influential in structuring the curriculum and in teaching practice are at best only partial truths. When we treat them as though they are valid generalizations then we are misled. This is not the place to pursue those implications in detail, but they do seem to challenge some of the bases of present practice.

They challenge, for example, the notion that our early curriculum should be full of the concrete surface of things and move gradually by content associations "outward," being cautious not to include much abstraction till adolescence. They challenge us also to consider whether the story-form does not offer a better model for planning teaching than does the industrial model of objectives/content/methods/evaluation, derived from the assembly line. They challenge the "Expanding Horizons" form of curriculum in both particular and general: particular, in that our imaginative grasp does not progress in a regular logical sequence, and general, in that the significant shift in children's form of understanding that we commonly observe about age seven is in no way accounted for.

They challenge us also to reflect on how our memories of our own educational experience and our observation of the children we teach can so easily be displaced by the insecure and partial claims of a huge educational research establishment. The overconfident, and rarely accurate, claim that "Research has shown that . . ." has tended to "de-skill" the teacher's own observation and experience. We need to put the claims of this research establishment into focus and regain the proper confidence that teachers should have in their observation and experience. The observations made in this article are not outrageous and are evident to any teacher. And yet implications from a particular limited kind of research have become enormously influential, in the face of our common-sense.

Follow-Up Reading:

Kieran Egan, *Educational Development*, New York: Oxford University Press, 1979.

Kieran Egan, *Teaching as Story-Telling*, London, Ontario: The Althouse Press, 1986; Chicago: University of Chicago Press, 1987; London: Rowledge, 1989.

Kieran Egan, *Primary Understanding*, London and New York: Routledge, 1988.

Kieran Egan, *Romantic Understanding,* London and New York: Routledge, 1991.

Kieran Egan, *Imagination in Teaching and Learning*, London, Ontario: The Althouse Press; Chicago: University of Chicago Press; London: Routledge, 1992.

The Person and *The Little Prince* of St. Exupéry

Florence M. Hetzler

Philosophers interested in probing the meaning of man as a self would do well to turn to literature for help in this very important quest. An approach through the art of literature and its metaphors may be different from that of conventional philosophy. The philosophy of man as a philosophy of the person can be seen if we follow the process of the becoming of the person of the little prince in the book of the same name by Antoine de St.-Exupéry. I should like to show how philosophical a seemingly slender book of literature, a work of art, can be for our purpose.

Philosophy is a partial achieving of the awareness of who and where man is. St.-Exupéry made his book a symbol of who and where we are, what knowing is, what purpose we have and how we can achieve that purpose. Our goal as human beings is to become persons. The little book can have a hold on each of us when it deals with the kind of domain that we occupy. It is important in the light of our living in a space age; it is important to see that a philosophy of the self leads to a more valid philosophy of man, which according to some, including Professor E. A. Burtt, encompasses all branches of philosophy. This book indicates the lived experience of theory and the necessity to pinpoint theory in living. The concreteness of literature, and of this book in particular for our purpose, has a message for us who are not head only, but head and heart. We need not only be able to see problems, but solve them, and

what is more, know and feel that we have solved them. Just as we have an ending of wonderment at the end of Plato's dialogue, the *Theaetetus*, we also have an aura of mystery at the end of *The Little Prince*, which is also a dialogue in a kind of cosmic polis. This search for the meaning of the person as a self continues on earth and in the heavens. The stars will be shared for their light and sound, the sound of little bells that will remind the pilot and prince of where they live and of the sound of the rusty pulley that they shared at the well in the desert.

One of the reasons why Plato's dialogues are such delightful reading is precisely because they are dialogues. Conversation gives rise not only to the truth of theory but to what may be more important, the unrationalized truth of insight. The mystery of being is not revealed in theory but in insights. In this paper we shall use the tiny book, *The Little Prince* by Antoine de St.-Exupéry, as our focus.[1] This book may be said to be John Dewey in fiction form. It might also be said to be philosophy all tightly woven within a few poetic pages of distilled philosophy.

For those who have not read this four ounce book I present here a brief summary with the strong suggestion that philosophers of the person read it not only to themselves but also to their children and grandchildren. We have here philosophy that is palatable, clear and pleasurably reflective. Actually the book is a kind of fable.

The first scene presents a pilot alone in the desert in great need of help after a plane breakdown. He is in the process of repairing his machine when from seemingly nowhere he encounters a little prince who wants him to draw a lamb. The accidental encounter is an initiator of interpersonal becoming. The young prince lived on an asteroid so tiny that all he had to do was to move his chair in order to have another sunset. He had volcanoes to sweep out and a flower that appeared there to water and nourish. One day it was born with the sun, a beautiful rose all floppy like a poppy. She was a flower unique in the world. He even removed the caterpillars from her but saved one in order that she would know a butterfly. She was, however, a coy female and in seeking the prince's attention asked for a windshield screen because she said she was cold and that where she came from the temperature was warmer. But she came from the prince's asteroid. Hurt, since he believed that she lied, the prince left his asteroid to travel to seek friends. On his interplanetary travels he met people that were all wound up in themselves like a bobbin, but did meet a pilot, a fox and a serpent who changed his life and that he changed. The dialogue with the pilot was a kind of Platonic dialogue of intersubjectivity.

The fox gave the prince a secret that was very important, so important that it revolutionized his life, and he returned to his flower whom he had tamed. The ongoing living and the shared dialogue are a reflection upon what is given in experience. It is a reflection upon the disclosure of being which in a recent paper for Cracow, Poland, I called MYTH, not to be confused with the conventional meaning of myth. MYTH is the locus of all the disclosures of all being, of the given, given in experience. This little book gives a unique philosophy of intersubjectivity, a philosophy of the interpersonal which is the very basis for a philosophy of the person. In this day of the crisis of the personal, de St.-Exupéry has given us a gift.[2] He is in fiction what T. S. Eliot in his "Waste Land" may be in poetry and what

Giacometti with his sculptures of people honed to the bone may be in sculpture.

There are various ways of defining philosophy. One of the best, it seems, is to say that it is putting order into one's experience, experience understood as one's encounter with the other, personal and impersonal. After all, that is all there is, and each of us can divide the world into the self and the other. What is important is that all things, insects, fossils, people, etc., are included in my other. We include one another in this division much like a Venn diagram. The greater the philosopher, the more order, the more unity he finds in the apparent endless heterogeneity of being. Plato, in his ordering of experience, found an answer to ontology and to epistemology. For the little prince, the unity of the order of being and knowing was found in the creativity of becoming a person. He unified the becoming and the being world. The being of the world was its becoming. Being in the world and being free to become are basic to the achievement of the human person. The act of *all being* and the act of the being of a *human* are uniquely united in the act of the being of the *human person*, as Edward Pols tells us.[3]

One might give as a definition of philosophy the achievement of the awareness of who and where you are. This definition also can be applied to the little prince. The who and the where were certainly intrinsically involved. In fact, it was the "where" of his flower that caused him so much trouble. Sometimes one becomes with problems and anguish. These cause reflection and choices. The misunderstanding of "where" caused him to go into voluntary exile. His going into exile, his standing back to take inventory of the self and the "where" was taking a creative stance, much like that taken by James Joyce who said that he would go into exile and there "would write books which would contain the moral history of the people who had driven him away." He said: "Amen. So be it. I go to encounter for the millionth time the reality of experience and to forge in the smithy of my soul the uncreated conscience of my race."

By going into exile the little prince found out who and where he was. His "who" he found by his encounters and by his awareness that his responsibility to a rose was part of his very being and becoming. There is a great deal of *ethics* throughout this book.

The becoming of a person and the meaning of a person may as philosophy be more available in this book, a piece of fiction, than in conventional philosophy books, partly because fiction is more commensurable with man as both head and heart. Art and philosophy for me seem to be the ideal complementarily. Also, I believe that art is philosophy and more than philosophy because in addition to using reason it uses mystery, myth, imagination and intuition.[4] To find out who he is the prince did not reason only. He had to intuit the meaning of some of his interpersonal relationships, for example, those with the flower, the pilot, the fox, the serpent, and yes, even the weed in the desert that had seen some men go by, she thought. And she felt sorry for them, since they did not have any roots. The wind blew them, it seemed, and according to her, that must bother them a great deal.

The book is really a book of process philosophy as well as one of the pragmatism of Dewey, Peirce and Royce. In this work one sees tools as an extension of man. There are the feet of the birds to which the prince tied strings for his flight from his asteroid to earth. There is the venom of the snake that is going to be able to help return the prince to his flower after his voluntary exile after having "misunderheard" or misunderstood his rose. There are also symbols that are important. One is reminded of the second century work, *Psysiologus*, written in Greek in Alexandria and later translated into Ge'ez as Fisalgwos in Ethiopia.[5] This work with its bestiary and herbarium was an important source of much later animal and plant symbology in theology and literature. In *The Little Prince* the plants; the garden of roses; the unique rose; the weed in the desert; the maybug; the serpent; the wise fox; the drawing of the lamb; the drawing of the boa swallowing an elephant; the baobab; the volcano—all are symbols.

There is *cosmology* in the book. There are sunsets, many in 24 hours; there are asteroids and planets, there are mountains and rivers; there is the sand of the desert. There is even interplanetary living, or living on an asteroid with the voyage from planet to planet in search of friends. The book has a kind of interstellar background. There is matter ever in motion, and after all, this was the theme of the cosmology, the *Physics*, of Aristotle as well as the commentaries upon him and his work.[6] Instead of having satellites sent off the skin of the planet earth to explore outer space, we have in this book the reverse situation of a voyage from someone out there to here, to our earth, the voyage of someone who sees himself and his home for the first time and who goes home as a person achieved through encounters and suffering, perhaps through the encounters of suffering. There is *psychology* in the book. In fact, the philosophy of the person in this book is seen as philosophical psychology. The prince is starved for friendship. He is thirsty for shared experience, like that of drinking water from the well and sharing the sound of the rusty pulley as well as the water. There is anguish. The prince tells the pilot that one risks weeping if one created ties. Actually, it is difficult to savour this book in English. It is so much better in the original French. "On risque de pleivier . . ." There is *epistemology*. Each sees reality from his own point of view. The fox, for example, and the weed in the desert make this clear. The fox said that if the prince became his friend, his life would not be so monotonous. As it was, hunters hunted him and he hunted chickens. Hunters all looked alike, and so did the chickens. If, however, the prince tamed him, even the color of the wheat would remind him of the yellow hair of the prince. He also said that if he knew at what time the prince would come to visit him, he would know when to dress up his heart to make ready for the arrival. He would be a man that did not fear. His whole life would be different. New experiences and new friends change everything.

There is also the mode of knowing of the pilot as contrasted with that of the prince. The pilot is busy trying to put a bolt on a plane. His outlook is that of one trying to repair a machine. The prince wants him to draw a lamb. The pilot does not know why. The prince may not yet know fully why either, for the flower that he wants to shelter from a lamb is really a mystery to him. His relationship with it is even a greater mystery to him than he could imagine.

* * *

The way that the pilot looks at the drawing of the lamb and the way the prince does are vastly different.

In conventional *epistemology* we are not told what the fox tells, namely that "we see well only with the heart or that what is essential cannot be seen by the eyes." When the prince travels from planet to planet in search of friends, he finds people all wrapped up in themselves. The vain man wants the prince to clap when he raises his hat. Enough of that the prince thought, because the man could not encounter the other as other. The drunkard was counting his bottles in order to forget and he had not time for the prince or for anyone else. In fact, he did not have time for himself as a self. The man who was counting stars because they were his since he saw them first was also in a rut. The geographer was too busy to look up to see the prince and too involved even to send explorers out into the field to check out the height of mountains or the place of rivers. The only person that the prince met that seemed to do anything outside of himself or to create anything outside of himself that did not previously exist was the lamplighter. Even though he lit the lamp and then immediately unlit it because those were orders, at least he created something new. He did not do it as a person because he was not the source of any free initiative but more like a robot. At

least there was a kind of drama of lamplighters around the world as evenings came and lamplighters went to work. The prince was also concerned with the people on the express trains who seemed to go one way and return, not knowing where they were going or why. What bothered him was the fact that only the children had their noses pressed against the windows. Adults were not aware, not curious, and not interested in what was out there, the other. They seemed not to know and not to know that they didn't know. Under the heading of *epistemology* we should mention that in this book there is an extraterrestrial viewpoint that meets a terrestrial one. We are reminded of the presidential address of Professor Lewis White Beck of the University of Rochester when he was President of the American Philosophical Association. After saying that he would not be allowed to speak about "Extraterrestrial Intelligent Life," were he not president, he said: "There are new sciences like exobiology whose foundations are in need of philosophical scrutiny."

We can speculate about the ramifications of the existence of extraterrestrial beings while reading *The Little Prince*. If other worlds do exist this makes a big difference in our *epistemology, cosmology, psychology, ethics*, etc. We have recently found such tribes as the Tasadays in the Philippines that we never knew existed before. The pilot in *The Little Prince* did not know that anyone lived on an asteroid nor did he know that asteroid B-612 existed.

In this book we also have the problem of believing only the conventional and of not accepting the new. Had he not changed from his Turkish clothes into conventional clothes, the Turkish astronomer would not have had any listeners. Galileo also proposed the novel. Even the theologians and scientists were rocked by revolutionary proposals. Beck says that if we do find other intelligences, we have no idea what the subsequent discoveries will be. He adds: "Compared to such advances in knowledge, the Copernican and Darwinian Revolutions and the discovery of the New World would have been but minor preludes."

This paper of Beck is an important one. When he says that discoveries of the other are important for ourselves, he hits upon the whole theme of *The Little Prince*, namely the achievement of personhood through the other. The prince's other included the extraterrestrial.[8] The pilot was, indeed, amazed to meet someone from an asteroid and to do this in the Sahara, a thousand miles from anyone. It was partly the astonishment at the incredible novelty that kept this ongoing dialogue with the prince active. A similar surprise hit our planet earth when Galileo, continuing the theory of Aristarchus and Copernicus, stated that the universe was heliocentric instead of geocentric. Man was thrown off his anthropocentric perch. What would the finding of extraterrestrial intelligences do to man in a heliocentric system to which he already has had to surrender after being king of the "geo-hill"?

This brings me to knowledge given in *The Little Prince* that can be included under both *epistemology* and *psychology*, and that is the philosophy of death, the loss of the self in the loss of the one loved. The philosophy of love and the philosophy of death are constitutive of the philosophy of the person. We have referred to the fact that the prince told the pilot that one risks weeping if one makes a friend and loses him. Yes, because if the friend goes, part of that interpersonal goes. Death is a kind of loss of ontic selfhood.[9] As we know, man is not an encapsulated bag of skin. Everything affects him, and the death of a personal other is an ultimate diminishment. John Macmurray has told us that "All meaningful knowledge is for the sake of action, and all meaningful action is for the sake of friendship."[10] Before one can go out to the other in friendship one has to have certain awareness which, of course, is heightened in the very reciprocity of friendship. There is an analogy here between Socrates and the fox of *The Little Prince*. Theaetetus has the secret of wonderment just as the fox has the secret that one cannot see the essential with the eyes.

Existential ongoing inquiry is necessary for the achievement of the person, that is, of the one who is aware of who and where he is and who is also aware that he is aware of this. Situations are always unsettled and a new inquiry with wonderment is needed. Otherwise one cannot become a person. He is a mushroom. In *The Little Prince* we are told that the prince once met a red-faced person who had never smelled a flower. This man had not dealt with the pragmatic concrete world. The prince said he was not a man but a champignon.[11]

The gradual unfolding of the flower is like a man's gradual unfolding. The time it took for the pilot to know the prince and vice versa is like the unfolding of the person in friendship. It is always something gradual. One cannot become a person without a friend, that is without a you to make the other person an I. It is only in an I-you relationship that the I or you exists. There is sharing of the I and you in the presence of the I and you. There is even a sharing of the cosmic history that each person carries with him. In the case of the little prince, the significance of the search for friendship is the search for the self, the self who is a friend. If the larger orientation of man is not in order, the everyday details cannot be either. The little prince had to get the larger scale fixed first. He had to step back and see who and where he was. This was in large part determined by his flower and his relationship to that flower. Once that was established after a trip of anguish from planet to planet, he was able to take the necessary measures to return to his responsibility, his flower. But he had to be open to the other, to the serpent, yes even to the garden of roses that he saw and who told him they were roses. He looked at them and said they were ordinary roses, not his rose. He had an at-homeness with his own rose, his rose that was *unique au monde* . . .

Coming to be as a person is the theme, the whole theme, of *The Little Prince*. St.-Exupéry started out by saying he lived alone until he was awakened by the little prince. Before that there was no dialogue. The encounter with the little prince was his being touched by "a gleam of light in the impenetrable mystery of his presence." It was in the taming presence of the prince that the pilot came to be a person. Even the taming of the fox changed the fox. The prince wanted to know what to tame (apprivoiser) meant. It meant to create ties and the fox said that was a lost art. It is in creating ties, especially the tie of love, that we are. In loving me, you let me be myself. You let me be. This was true of the fox when the prince tamed him. Then, when the fox knew at what hour the prince would come, the friendship would also be a dividend. He would dress up his heart. Rites are necessary, he said. They have been forgotten . . .

To treat another personally is to tame him. In the fable, *The Little Prince*, obviously the fox and the snake were more than animals. They were symbols that could be treated personally, and they had more mystery than the first two readings of this book might suggest. After he is tamed, the fox adds his secret: "What is essential is invisible to the eyes. One really sees with the heart" That is true. What is essential is not seen by the intellect alone. Reading e. e. cummings will also make this clear. St. Exupéry speaks of love as a prior commitment of responsiveness by which we have access to the Other that includes us. One is not responsive with the head alone. It is the experience of inclusion that is important in the I-thou relationship. Exclusion alienates, diminishes, and hurts . . . forever. To know the personal other, one must often ask questions. The other is not always so open that its disclosure is easily seen. Professor Thomas de Koninck has likened the little prince to Socrates in his dialogues. The little prince asks questions but doesn't always wait for the answer. He is the gadfly who asks the questions. Both are often quiet when answers are given, perhaps because they are thinking of what the next question should be; perhaps too, because they want to give time for reflection to the one questioned. The prince actually gives birth to knowledge by his questions much as Socrates did with his maieutic method. The prince is bothered, it seems, by what the common good is and by what he means by the individual good, the good of a flower. The good of the planet earth seemed injured by the kinds of convoluted people that he met there. They were adding nothing to the common good and in turn received no individual good. It seems worth noting here that Professor Thomas de Koninck when he was a young boy was present in his home in Quebec City when St. Exupéry came to discuss the common good with his father, Professor Charles de Koninck, then Dean of the Faculty of Philosophy of Laval University.

In a way, the little prince is the you that the pilot seeks to become. He answers to the curiosity of the prince who was never satisfied with the answers. He asked, for example, why people take express trains but don't know what they are looking for. They turn around. In the midst of all these questions and in the presence of the little prince the pilot is no longer alone and realizes himself as a person. He will also have the prince to remember. In this book stars play an important part, even of remembering. They are looked at different points of view. The scientist and businessman view them differently. The businessman collects them and reigns over them, because he saw them first. For sailors they are guides and for scientists, for example, Galileo, they may be problems. The businessman counts them.

Erazim Kohak, in his book, *The Embers and the Stars: A Philosophical Inquiry into the Moral Sense of Nature*, has the laudable audacity to speak of the necessity for man of seeing his place in the cosmos, with the stars, and of the relationship of himself to that cosmos as a prerequisite for the personhood of man. The counted star cannot be so primary as it was for man who only counted them.

The prince knew the importance of the personal. About to return to his flower, he tells the pilot that that night it would be a year since he had arrived on the earth directly beneath his star.

The pilot asked if what was going on, the matter of the snake, was a bad dream. What about the meeting place and the star? All that the prince answered was: The thing that is important is the thing that is not seen. He continued: "It is just as it is with the flower. If you love a flower that lives on a star, it is sweet to look at the sky at night. All the stars are a-bloom with flowers . . ." And again, "It is just as it is with the water. Because of the pulley, and the rope, what you gave me to drink was like music You remember how good it was."

Here we have shared experience. We also have vagueness. There will always be more of you to share, yes, even to share intergalactically. There will be the extraterrestrial sharing from earth to the asteroid and from the asteroid back to earth. There is the ongoing creativity of friendship . . . forever. There will always be a you even if the you is not visible. What is unseen is what is important. Looking with the heart will always be a creative responsibility for the accomplishment of personhood. Ties are established and reestablished forever. "Apprivoiser" is to tame. This love, this ongoing freedom is the processive achieving, neverending wholeness of reality in personhood that involves stars, sunrises and sunsets, traveling by the flights of birds, calling from mountain to mountain, and trying to answer the hello of the echo.

Alasdair MacIntyre also feels that experience is important and theory not enough. He says: "The notion that the moral philosopher can study *the* concepts of morality merely by reflecting, Oxford armchair style, on what he or she and those around him or her say and do is barren."[20]

To become a person we need the concrete. We thirst for it. It is true that we need theory but we may get philosophy better by literature because there we obtain insights not attainable in conventional philosophy. Philosophy often is not sufficiently concrete, while literature has the concrete plus the theory, plus the insights. There is in this book a metaphysics of the person that is revealed in its epistemology, cosmology, psychology, ethics, etc. Becoming a person is man's vocation. Upon this depends the quality of the future of the human race. As a work of literature, *The Little Prince*, better than a philosophy text, gives us the person as the all-encompassing philosophy of man. St. Exupéry was a man of the future. He flew planes when planes were little used.[21] He dared the future. From the skies lights were for him signs of consciousness on earth. His little book is a challenge to become persons. It is a guide just as the stars were his guides in flying his plane over the arid Sahara. It is a guide to a peaceful City of Man, the Person.

Notes

1. Antoine de St.-Exupéry, *The Little Prince*, trans. from French by Katherine Woods (New York: Harcourt Brace Jovanovich, 1943).
2. Cf. Hetzler, "Death and *The Little Prince* of St.-Exupéry: The Face in the Mirror," in Hetzler, *Death and Creativity*, second edition (New York: Health Sciences Publishing Corporation, 1974) 1-20; Naomi Bliven, "Airborne," article of book review of Curtis Cate, *Antoine de St.-Exupéry* (New York: G. P. Putnam's Sons, 1970), *The New Yorker*, March 13, 1971, 133; Lewis Galantiere, "The Life of the Spirit is higher than the Life of the Mind," *The New York Times Book Review*, December 27, 1970, 8 and 18; Richard Arbelot, "Le Petit Prince," *Le Francais dans le monde* (Paris: Libraries Hachette et Larousse, 36, October-November, 1965, 36; Adele Breaux, *St.-Exupéry in America, 1942-1943; A Memoir* (Madison, New Jersey: Farleigh Dickinson University Press, 1971) 18-19, 81-84, 144-149. Cf. also Pierre-Henri Simon, *L'Homme en Proces* (Boudry, Neuchatel: Baconniere, 1950) 132-133; Louis Monden, *Sin, Liberty and Law*, trans. Joseph Donceel (New York: Sheed and Ward, 1965) 22; George Pelissier (New York: Sheed and Ward, 1965) 22; George Pelissier, *Les Cinq visages de St.-Exupéry* (Paris: Flammarion, 1951) 21-25, 66-71, 89, 122-131, 152-153; F. Delbard Company, *Catalogue 1961* (Paris: G. Delbard, 1961) 16. In this catalogue the name of St.-Exupéry lives still in a unique blue rose dedicated June 20, 1960 at the G. Delbard company in the presence of the author's wife, sister and friend, Vanier, whose daughter, an Air France Hostess, took the "St.-Ex" roses to place them on the memorial in Buenos Aires to the 200 fellow aviators who died flying the Paris-Santiago run. Curtis Cate tells us: "The only thing we can reasonably be sure of is that this youthful interest in flying machines was greatly stimulated by his father's move to le Mans in 1909. In July of the previous year Wilbur Wright had

crossed the ocean and set up shop in the Leon Bollée automobile works at le Mans."

3. Edward Pols, *The Acts of Our Being: A Reflection on Agency and Responsibility* (Amherst: U. Mass Press, 1982).

4. F. Hetzler, "Art is Philosophy and More than Philosophy," *Proceedings International Colloquium*, Fu Jen University, Taipei, Taiwan, December 1980, 197-210. Cf. Mircea Eliade, *La Colonne sans fin*, trans. Hetzler (Lanham, Maryland: University Press Of America, 1984).

5. Cf. Calude Sumner, *Ethiopian Philosophy: Fisalgwos, Volume V* (Addis Ababa: Commercial Printing Press, 1082).

6. Cf. Hetzler, *Commentary of St. Thomas Aquinas on Book I of Aristotle's Physics*, Ph.D. dissertation, microfilm, Harvard University, 1969).

7. New York City, December 28, 1971.

8. Cf. Hetzler, "Philosophy of the Person in the Cybernetic Age," *Proceedings of the VIIth International Congress of Aesthetics* (Bucharest, Romania: Academy Press, 1972) 124-126; Bernard de Fontenelle, *Entretiens sur la pluralité des mondes*, 1686; S.A. Kaplan, ed., *Extraterrestrial Civilizations* (Israel Program for Scientific Translations: Jerusalem, 1971) 257 n; A. G. W. Cameron, ed., *Inter-stellar Communication* (New York: Benjamin, 1963); Walter Sullivan, *We Are Not Alone* (New York: McGraw-Hill, 1964) ch. 13-15, 148-150.

9. Cf. Hetzler, ed., *Philosophical Aspects of Thanatology*, I, II (New York: Arno Press, 1977).

10. John Macmurray, *The Self as Agent* (New York: Harper & Row, 1957) 16.

11. Cf. John Dewey, *Logic: The Theory of Inquiry* (New York: Holt, Rinehart & Winston, 1938) 129; Lonergan, *Insight: A Study of Human Understanding* (New York: Philosophical Library, 1958) 348; John Dewey, *Experience and Nature* (New York: Dover, 1958) 135; Erazim Kohak, *The Embers and the Stars: A Philosophical Inquiry into the Moral Sense of Nature* (Chicago: University of Chicago Press, 1984): Hetzler, "Myth and Imagination in Galileo's Discovery," eds. George Coyne, S. J., Josef Zycinski and Michael Heller, *The Galileo Affair: A Meeting of Faith and Science* (Vatican city: Specola Vaticana, 1985 167-174.

12. Cf. Francis X. Elliott, "The World Vision of Teilhard de Chardin," trans. Hetzler, International Philosophical Quarterly, 1,4, December 1961, 620-647.

13. Edward A. Burtt, "The Philosophy of Man as All-Embracing Philosophy," paper delivered for the Personalist Discussion Group, December 27, 1969. Cf also Hetzler, "Two View of Infinity," Dialectics and Humanism, Warsaw, The Polish Academy of Sciences Press, X, 1, 1983, 33-43.

14. Cf Hetzler, "To Be or Not to Be: The Polish Cultural Heritage in Cracow, Poland," Dialectics and Humanism, Warsaw, Polish Academy of Sciences Press, Summer 1984; Hetzler, "Dogmatism: Abortive Element in Evolution:" in ed. Mourad Wahba, Roots Of Dogmatism (Cairo: The Anglo-Egyptian Bookshop, 1984) 239-251.

15. Cf. Hetzler, "Man and Space," in Dialectics and Humanism IX, 2, Warsaw, Poland, Polish Academy of Sciences, 1982, 51-64.

16. Louis Monden, Sin, Liberty and Law, Joseph Donceel, trans. (New York: Sheed and Ward, 1965) 22.

17. Pierre-Henri Simon, L'Homme en Procés (Paris, 1950) 132-133.

18. Kohák, The Personalist Forum, Spring, 1985, I, 1, 40.

19. Christopher Lehmann Haupt, review of book of Denis Donoghue, The Arts Without Mystery (Boston: Little Brown, 1984), The New York Times, March 9,1984, C27.

20. Alisdair MacIntyre, *After Virtue* (South Bend, Indiana: Notre Dame University Press, 1981) *vi*.

21. I have visited in Libreville, Gabon, a large "Centre Culturel St. Exupéry" under the aegis of the National Agency for Artistic and Cultural Promotion and which has a library for children in its complex. In Abidjan, Ivory Coast, there is a College Jean Mermoz and a Boulevard Jean Mermoz. Mermoz was a pilot friend of St. Exupéry. In Dakar, Senegal, where Mermoz often landed his plane, there is the Ecole Africaine Jean Mermoz, probably the best French school in that country. Cf. also George Borglum, *Le Petit Prince d'Antoine de St.-Exupéry Réalisation Scolaire Audioviseulle* (319 Carne Avenue, Royal Oak, Michigan 48067,1973); Christian and Nadine Zuber, *Le Petit Prince des Iles Seychelles* (Paris: Editions G. P. Département des Presses de la Cité, 1968).

Chapter Six
Building Communities in the Schools

Chapter Six

Building Communities in the Schools

According to traditional understanding, there is a sharp contrast between the family and the elementary school classroom. The family is a community in which the members are bound together by kinship and affection, in which a face-to-face intimacy prevails and shared values outweigh claims of individual differences, The classroom, however, is an association which students attend because of personal motivation or because of legal coercions. The social bonds uniting the students in the classroom are often discouraged, so that friendship, for example, is deemed to be of little educational value. If the family prides itself on being a *natural* institution, the school prides itself on being a *rational* institution. Family relationships tend to be unarticulated and taken for granted; teacher-student relationships, in contrast, tend to be explicit and contractual.

This severe dichotomy often results in a lack of reasonableness in the family and a lack of warmth in the classroom. Moreover, the transition from the one to the other is often disappointing and sometimes traumatic. As a result, there has been a tendency, over the past century, to modify the classroom so as to make it more of a community in which collaborative inquiry prevails, dialogue flourishes, and friendships are recognized as promoting rather than as hindering personal and educational growth. The classroom community harnesses the social impulses of children and puts them to work in the service of

learning and reflection rather than in opposition to them. Furthermore, classroom discussions invite thoughtful participation, so that thinking is interwoven in the dialogue, and is subsequently internalized by each student in the form of personal reflections. In such fashion, the classroom becomes a community of dialogical deliberation, which is one species of a community of inquiry.

No one has contributed more importantly to the conception of the community of inquiry than George Herbert Mead. His contributions presuppose the perspective of social psychology, and contemporary readers will no doubt recognize Mead's kinship with Dewey and Vygotsky. For Mead, community emerges in the very act of communication, an act to which the child brings already formed social impulses. "The child does not become social by learning, he must be social in order to learn," says Mead. Nevertheless, he insists that the subject-matter of instruction be "the material of intercourse between pupils and instructors, and between the children themselves." The success of the teacher depends in large measures, for Mead, on the capacity of the teacher to translate the subject-matter of instruction so that it is stated in terms of the experience of the students. (By "experience," Mead evidently means not merely the experience they have already had, but the experience that is within their reach.)

Learning happens in distinct places such as homes and schools and universities, says Michael

Oakeshott. But it is also a conversation that extends across generations and unites mankind, a conversation in which we learn to recognize the voices and to acquire the intellectual and moral habits appropriate to the conversational relationship. It is an enterprise in "human self-understanding," and to go to school is to be initiated into that enterprise by becoming a voice in the conversation. At the same time, the different cultures that participate in the conversation do so as so many different languages, each of which is an avenue to this goal of enabling human beings to "know themselves."

According to Ann Margaret Sharp, communities of inquiry represent the avenue open to the schools for preparing students for democracy. The very skills and dispositions required for democratic participation—reflectiveness, dialogue, reasonableness and mutual respect—are those that emerge from classroom deliberations regarding matters that students consider important. At the same time, the community of inquiry improves the ethical judgment of the child and provides a favorable environment for enhanced educational development.

Robert J. Mulvaney considers the community of inquiry specifically in its philosophical version, and briefly traces the vicissitudes of philosophical teaching across the ages. He categorically indicts the exclusiveness and elitism that has been characteristic of academic philosophy and argues for the inclusion of the child in the domain of philosophical inquiry. Mulvaney recognizes the precariousness of the quest for wise individuals; for it is the wise society that should be our goal, and the community of philosophical inquiry is a meaningful step in that direction.

We need to inquire, writes David Kennedy, into the educational conditions presupposed by the community of inquiry, conditions that will provide it with a "structural home." He offers five such characteristics—that the new model of education be (1) developmental (in the sense of following children's burgeoning initiatives); (2) environmental (a human landscape, a little world); (3) individualized (assuming diversified forms of intelligence and levels of academic prowess); (4) interactive (rich in transactions and choices); and (5) dialogical (listens to as well as speaks to the child). Kennedy also considers the role of the community of inquiry in reshaping its own environment, when that environment is alien and archaic.

According to Glenn Tinder, dialogical inquiry is in itself community. The comprehensive mode of inquiry is philosophy, although it presupposes other modes, and is empty without them. The connection Tinder sees as of utmost importance is that "man is an inquirer" and must engage in inquiry. When he engages in dialogical inquiry, he participates in community, But Tinder recognizes the truth of the reverse version: community is inquiry. This is particularly the case with democracy, for unless we recognize and provide for the inquiry function of democracy, it is not community, and it is not democracy either.

The last contribution to this section, by Dr. Stan Anih, aims to show how the community of inquiry is compatible with African educational traditions while yet fulfilling contemporary educational expectations. Anih emphasizes the improvement of self-concepts, the reliance upon personal experience, the increased awareness of social roles and tasks and the application of experience to practical problems. The community of inquiry can therefore serve as a linking concept and a linking institution between those parts of the world that are economically developed and those that are not, and between those that are grappling, in different ways, to become democratic.

Language as Thinking

George Herbert Mead

This article by George Herbert Mead was
originally published in Science, *in 1910, under
the title of "The Psychology of Social Consciousness Implied in Instruction." One finds in it a
number of the major themes which were so significantly developed in other works by Mead,
such as* Mind, Self and Society, *or* Movements
of Thought in the Nineteenth Century. *For here,
as elsewhere, Mead stresses that reflective thinking in the individual is an internalization of linguistic behavior in society. Human conversation,
discussion, dialogue—these are the matrix of
thought and reasoning. When we speak to others,
we also listen to ourselves the way those others
might listen to us: we adopt their attitudes towards our own verbal expressions. By taking into
ourselves the possible attitudes of others towards
our own symbolic expressions, we introject or
internalize the entire community of persons with
whom we communicate. This internalized forum
therefore replicates in thought the social community of symbolic behavior or discourse.*

*Thus Mead had worked out—well before Vy-
gotsky—an explicit theory of thinking as internalized speech. And he likewise recognized, as
this essay demonstrates, that the learning process can be significantly enhanced through enlist-
ing children's social impulses in the formation of
cooperative classroom communities. Indeed, if
internalized communication among children
translates into thought, what reason is there not
to conclude that a classroom community of inquiry, when internalized, will result in children*
whose thinking adopts the methods and procedures of inquiry?

*There are those who look upon the child en-
tering school as if it were "the barbarian at the
gates." Such offspring, it is contended, are most
certainly in need of socialization. Whether or not
they can eventually become educated is a moot
point. Mead had little patience with such prophecies of disaster. Every human infant, he insisted,
brings into the world powerful social tendencies
which impel that child to participate in a community. It is by living with others and anticipating
their responses to what we do that we become
individuals or selves. Indeed, we cannot become
selves without living in some social or communal
fashion, just as we cannot think without participating in the social institution of linguistic communication.*

*Mead is well aware that many educators are
prepared to deny his charges, and to insist that
the social impulses of the child are being fully
utilized in the classroom. But Mead contends that
this is so only in a manipulative sense: the child's
school life is not genuinely social—it is only
school discipline (with its pains and pleasures of
academic competition) that is social. The rewards are presently social, but not the life of
learning, or the process of inquiry. When a community of inquiry has been established in the
classroom, the social impulses of the child become the ground of the learning process.*

*We are only beginning to recognize the edu-
cational importance of what Mead was urging
upon us three-quarters of a century ago: if we*

want to encourage individuals to reflect, then we must have disciplined dialogue in the classroom. If we want individuals who can think for themselves, then the classroom must be converted into a community of inquiry where, following Socrates, one must follow the argument where it leads.

I have been asked to present the social situation in the school as the subject of a possible scientific study and control.

The same situation among primitive people is scientifically studied by the sociologist (fold-psychologist). He notes two methods in the process of primitive education. The first is generally described as that of play and imitation. The impulses of the children find their expression in play, and play describes the attitude of the child's consciousness. Imitation defines the form of unconscious social control exercised by the community over the expression of childish impulse.

In the long ceremonies of initiation education assumed a more conscious and almost deliberate form. The boy was inducted into the clan mysteries, into the mythology and social procedure of the community, under an emotional tension which was skillfully aroused and maintained. He was subjected to tests of endurance which were calculated not only to fulfill this purpose, but also to identify the ends and interests of the individual with those of the social group. These more general purposes of the initiatory ceremonies were also at times cunningly adapted to enhance the authority of the medicine man or the control over food and women by the older men in the community.

Whatever opinion one may hold of the interpretation which folk-psychology and anthropology have given of this early phase of education, no one would deny, I imagine, the possibility of studying the education of the savage child scientifically, nor that this would be a psychological study. Imitation, play, emotional tensions favoring the acquirement of clan myths and cults, and the formation of clan judgments of evaluation, these all must be interpreted and formulated by some form of psychology. The particular form which has dealt with these phenomena and or

processes is social psychology. The important features of the situation would be found not in the structure of the idea to be assimilated considered as material of instruction for any child, nor in the lines of association which would guarantee their abiding in consciousness. They would be found in the impulse of the children expressed in play, in the tendency of the children to put themselves in the place of the men and women of the group, i.e., to imitate them in the emotions which consciousness of themselves in their relationship to others evoke, and in the import for the boy which the ideas and cults would have when surcharged with such emotions.

If we turn to our system of education we find that the materials of the curriculum have been presented as percepts capable of being assimilated by the nature of their content to other contents in consciousness, and the manner has been indicated in which this material can be most favorably prepared for such assimilation. This type of psychological treatment of material and the lesson is recognized at once as Herbartian. It is an associational type of psychology. Its critics add that it is intellectualistic. In any case it is not a social psychology, for the child is not primarily considered as a self among other selves, but as an *Apperceptionsmasse*. The child's relations to the other members of the group, to which he belongs, have no immediate bearing on the material nor on the learning of it. The banishment from the traditional school work of play and of any adult activities in which the child could have a part as a child, i.e., the banishment of processes in which the child can be conscious of himself in relation to others, means that the process of learning has as little social content as possible.

An explanation of the different attitudes of the training of the child in the primitive and in the modern civilized communities is found, in part, in the division of labor between the school on the one side, and the home and the shop or the farm on the other. The business of storing the mind with ideas, both materials and methods, has been assigned to the school. The task of organizing and socializing the self to which these materials and methods belong is left to the home and the industry or profession, to the playground, the street and society in general. A great deal of modern educational literature turns upon the fallacy of this division of labor. The earlier vogue of manual training and the domestic arts before the frank recognition of their relation to industrial training took place, was due in no small part to the attempt to introduce those interests of the child's into the field of his instruction which gathers about a socially constituted self, to admit the child's personality as a whole into the school.

I think we should be prepared to admit the implication of this educational movement—that however abstract the material is which is presented and however abstracted its ultimate use is from the immediate activities of the child, the situation implied in instruction and in the psychology of that instruction is a social situation; that it is impossible to fully interpret or control the process of instruction without recognizing the child as a self and viewing his conscious processes from the point of view of their relation in his consciousness to his self, among other selves.

In the first place, back of all instruction lies the relation of the child to the teacher and about it lie the relations of the child to the other children, in the schoolroom and on the playground. It is however, of interest to note that so far as the material of instruction is concerned an ideal situation has been conceived to be one in which the personality of the teacher disappears as completely as possible behind the process of learning. In the actual process of instruction the emphasis upon the relation of pupil and teacher in the consciousness of the child has been felt to be unfortunate. In like manner the instinctive social relations between the children in school hours are repressed. In the process of memorizing and reciting a lesson, or working out a problem in arithmetic a vivid consciousness of the personality of the teacher in his relationship to that of the child would imply either that the teacher was obliged to exercise discipline to carry on the process of instruction,

and this must in the nature of the case constitute friction and division of attention, or else that the child's interest from the subject-matter of the lesson, to something in which the personality of the teacher and pupil might find some other content; for even a teacher's approval and a child's delight therein has no essential relation to the mere subject-matter of arithmetic or English. It certainly has no such relationship as that implied in apprenticeship, in the boy's helping on the farm or the girl's helping in the housekeeping, has no such relationship as that of members of an athletic team to each other. In these latter instances, the vivid consciousness of the self of the child and of his master, of the parents whom he helps and of the associates with whom he plays is part of the child's consciousness of what he is doing, and his consciousness of these personal relationships involves no division of attention. Now it had been a part of the fallacy of an intellectualistic pedagogy that a divided attention was necessary to insure application of attention—that the rewards, and especially the punishments, of the school hung before the child's mind to catch the attention that was wandering from the task, and through their associations with the schoolwork to bring it back to the task. This involves a continual vibration of attention on the part of the average child between the task and the sanctions of school discipline. It is only the psychology of school discipline that is social. The pains and penalties, the pleasures of success in competition, of favorable mention of all sorts implies vivid self-consciousness. It is evident that advantage would follow from making the consciousness of self or selves which is the life of the child's play—on its competition or cooperation—have as essential a place in instruction. To use Professor Dewey's phrase, instruction should be an interchange of experience in which the child brings his experience to be interpreted by the experience of the parent or teacher. This recognizes that education is interchange of ideas, is conversation—belongs to a universe of discourse. If the lesson is simply set for the child—is not his own problem—the recognition of himself as facing a task and a taskmaster is not part of the solution of the problem. But a difficulty which the child feels and brings to his parent or teacher for solution is helped on toward interpretation by the consciousness of the child's relation to his pastors and masters. Just insofar as the subject-matter of instruction can be brought into the form of problems arising in the experience of the child—just as far will the relation of the child to the instructor become a part of the natural solution of the problem—actual success of a teacher depends in large measure upon this capacity to state the subject-matter of instruction in terms of the experience of the children. The recognition of the value of industrial and vocational training comes back at one to this, that what the child has to learn is what he wants to acquire, to become the man. Under these conditions instruction takes on frankly the form of conversation, as much sought by the pupil as the instructor.

I take it therefore to be a scientific task to which education should set itself—that of making the subject-matter of its instruction the material of personal intercourse between pupils and instructors, and between the children themselves. The conversation of concrete individuals must be substituted for the pale abstractions of thought.

To a large extent our school organization reserves the use of the personal relation between teacher and taught for the negative side, for the prohibitions. The lack of interest in the personal content of the lesson is in fact startling when one considers that it is the personal form in which the instruction should be given. The best illustration of this lack of interest we find in the problems which disgrace our arithmetics. They are supposed matters of converse, but their content is so bare, their abstractions so raggedly covered with the form of questions about such marketing and shopping and building as never were on sea or land, that one sees that the social form of instruction is a form only for the writer of the arithmetic. When further we consider how utterly inadequate the teaching force of our public schools is to transform this matter into

concrete experience of the children or even into their own experience, the hopelessness of the situation is overwhelming. Ostwald has written a textbook of chemistry for the secondary school which has done what every textbook should do. It is not only that the material shows real respect for the intelligence of the student, but it is so organized that the development of the subject-matter is in reality the action and reaction of one mind upon another mind. The dictum of the Platonic Socrates, that one must follow the argument where it leads in the dialogue, should be the motto of the writer of textbooks.

It has been indicated already that language being essentially in its nature thinking with the child is rendered concrete by taking on the form of conversation. It has been also indicated that this can take place only when the thought has reference to a real problem in the experience of the child. The further demand for control over attention carries us back to the conditions of attention. Here again we find that traditional school practice depends upon social consciousness for bringing the wandering attention back to the task, when it finds that the subjective conditions of attention to the material of instruction are lacking, and even attempts to carry over a formal self-consciousness into attention, when through the sense of duty the pupil is called upon to identify the solution of the problem with himself. On the other hand, we have in vocational instruction the situation in which the student has identified his impulses with the subject-matter of the task. In the former case, as in the case of instruction, our traditional practice makes use of the self-consciousness of the child in its least effective form. The material of the lesson is not identified with the impulses of the child. The attention is not due to the organization of impulses to outgoing activity. The organization of typical school attention is that of a school self, expressing subordination to school authority and identity of conduct with that of all the other children in the room. It is largely inhibitive—a consciousness of what one must not do, but the inhibitions do not arise out of the consciousness of what one is doing. It is the nature of school attention to abstract from the content of any specific task. The child must give attention *first* and *then* undertake any task which is assigned to him, while normal attention is essentially selective and depends for its inhibitions upon the specific act.

Now consciousness of self should follow upon that of attention, and consists in a reference of the act, which attention has mediated, to the social self. It brings about a conscious organization of this particular act with the individual as the whole—makes it his act, and can only be effectively accomplished when the attention is an actual organization of impulses seeking expression. The separation between the self, implied in typical school attention, and the content of the school tasks, makes such an organization difficult if not impossible.

In a word attention is a process of organization of consciousness. It results in the reenforcement and inhibitions of perceptions and ideas. It is always a part of an act and involves the relation of that act to the whole field of consciousness. This relation to the whole field of consciousness finds its expression in consciousness of self. But the consciousness of self depends primarily upon social relations. The self arises in consciousness *pari passu* with the recognition and definition of other selves. It is therefore unfruitful if not impossible to attempt to scientifically control the attention of children in their formal education, unless they are regarded as social beings in dealing with the very material of instruction. It is this essentially social character of attention which gives its peculiar grip to vocational training. From the psychological point of view, not only the method and material but also the means of holding the pupils' attention must be socialized.

Finally a word may be added with reference to the evaluations—the emotional reactions—which our education should call forth. There is no phase of our public school training that is so defective as this. The school undertakes to acquaint the child with the ideas and methods which he is to use as a man. Shut up in the history, the geography, the language and the number of our curricula should be the values that the country, and its human institutions, have; that beauty has in nature and art; and the values involved in the control over nature and social conditions.

The child in entering into his heritage of ideas and methods should have the emotional response which the boy has in a primitive community when he has been initiated into the mysteries and the social code of the group of which he has become a citizen. We have a few remainders of this emotional response, in the confirmation or conversion and entrance into the church, in the initiation into the fraternity, and in the passage from apprenticeship into the union. But the complexities of our social life, and the abstract intellectual character of the ideas which society uses have made it increasingly difficult to identify the attainment of the equipment of a man with the meaning of manhood and citizenship.

Conventional ceremonies at the end of the period of education will never accomplish this. And we have to further recognize that our education extends for many far beyond the adolescent period to which this emotional response naturally belongs. What our schools can give must be given through the social consciousness of the child as that consciousness develops. It is only as the child recognizes a social import in what he is learning and doing that moral education can be given.

I have sought to indicate that the process of schooling in its barest form cannot be successfully studied by a scientific psychology unless that psychology is social, i.e., unless it recognizes that the processes of acquiring knowledge, of giving attention, of evaluating in emotional terms must be studied in their relation to selves in a social consciousness. So far as education is concerned, the child does not become social by learning. He must be social in order to learn.

—from *Science*, XXXI (1910), 688-693, originally entitled, "The Psychology of Social Consciousness Implied in Instruction."

A Place of Learning

Michael Oakeshott

For a human being then, learning is a life-long engagement; the world he inhabits is a place of learning. But, further, human beings, in so far as they have understood their condition, have always recognized special places, occasions and circumstances deliberately designed for and devoted to learning, the most notable of which are the human family, school and university. The human family (whatever form it may take) is a practice devised, not for the procreation of children, nor merely for their protection, but for the early education of newcomers to the human scene: it recognizes that learning begins slowly and takes time. School and university are unmistakable; they are successive stages in this deliberate engagement to learn, and it is with these we are concerned.

Now, the distinctive feature of such a special place of learning is, first, that those who occupy it are recognized and recognize themselves preeminently as learners; although they may be much else besides. Secondly in it learning is a declared engagement to learn something in particular. Those who occupy it are not merely "growing up," and they are not there merely to "improve their minds" or to "learn to think"; such unspecified activities are as impossible as an orchestra which plays no music in particular. Further, what is to be learned in such a place does not present itself by chance or arise circumstantially out of whatever may happen to be going on; it is recognized as a specified task to be undertaken and pursued with attention, patience and determination, the learner being aware of what he

is doing. And thirdly, learning here is not a limited undertaking in which what is learned is learned merely up to the point where it can be put to some extrinsic use; learning itself is the engagement and it has its own standards of achievement and excellence. Consequently, what is special about such a place or circumstances as its seclusion, its detachment from what Hegel called the *hic et nunc*, the here and now, of current living. Each of us is born in a corner of the earth and at a particular moment in historic time, lapped round with locality. But school and university are places apart where a declared learner is emancipated from the limitations of his local circumstances and from the wants he may happen to have acquired and is moved by intimations of what he has never yet dreamed. He finds himself invited to pursue satisfactions he has never yet imagined or wished for. They are, then, sheltered places where excellences may be heard because the din of local partialities is no more than a distant rumble. They are places where a learner is initiated into what there is to be learned.

But what is there for a human being to learn? A large part of human conduct is, and always has been, concerned with exploiting the resources of the earth for the satisfaction of human wants, and much of human learning is concerned, directly or indirectly, with this endlessly proliferating intelligent engagement. And it is genuine learning. An otter may be equipped with what for want of a better word we call an instinct which enables it to catch fish, a beaver in response to some biological urge may build a dam and an eagle may swoop down and carry off a lamb; but a fisherman must learn to catch fish and he learns to do so well or ill and with a variety of techniques, the engineers who designed and built the Boulder Dam were equipped with something more than a biological urge, and to breed sheep for meat or wool is an art that has to be learned. In respect of being concerned to exploit the resources of the earth a current human being is, then, an inheritor of a vast variety of instrumental skills and practices which have to be learned if they are to yield the satisfactions they are designed to yield. Moreover, the inventor and the user of these skills and practices is not Man or Society; each is the discovery or invention of assignable men, a Prometheus, a Vulcan, a Bessemer or an Edison. It is not Man or some abstraction called "medical science" which cures the sick; it is an individual doctor who has himself learned his art from some assignable teachers. There is no such thing as "social learning" or "collective understanding." The arts and practices we share with one another are nowhere to be found save in the understandings of living, individual adepts who have learned them.

And further, the satisfaction of human wants is pursued in transactions between human beings in which they compete or cooperate with one another. To seek the satisfaction of a want is to enter into relationships with other human beings. This human association is not the interaction of the components of a process, nor is it an unspecified gregariousness or sociability; it is made up of a variety of different kinds of relationships, each a specific practice whose conditions must be learned and understood if its advantages are to be enjoyed. And incomparably the most useful of these relationships is that which subsists between those who speak a common language in which to communicate their wants and to conduct the bargains in which they may be satisfied. Such a language, like all other conditions of human association, has to be learned.

To be human, to have wants and to try to satisfy them, is, then, to have the use of particular skills, instrumental practices and relationships. There is no action which is not a subscription to some art, and utterance is impossible without a language. These skills, practices and relationships have to be learned. And since this learning, so far as it goes, is genuine and may be extensive it is no surprise that there should be special places devoted to it, each concerned to initiate learners into some particular instrumental art or practice and often equipped with the opportunity of "learning on the job," as it is called: Medical schools, Law schools, language schools, schools of journalism or photography, schools where one may learn to cook, to drive an automobile or run a bassoon factory, and even polytechnics where a variety of such instrumental skills may be learned.

There is much more that might be said about this activity of exploiting the resources of the earth, of the arts and relationships used in the satisfaction of human wants and the learning these entail. It is certainly genuine learning, although the special places devoted to it are appropriately limited in their aims and in their seclusion from considerations of utility. To learn an instrumental art is not merely being trained to perform a trick; it entails understanding what you are doing. And learning a practice is not merely acquiring a mechanical contrivance and knowing how to work it. A human art is never fixed and finished; it has to be used and it is continuously modified in use. Even using a language to communicate wants is itself an inventive engagement. But I do not propose to explore further this engagement in learning; there is something more important for us to consider. We catch a glimpse of it when we recognize that choosing wants to satisfy is also something that has to be learned and that the conditions to be subscribed to in making such choices are not the terms of the instrumental arts and practices in which chosen wants may be conveniently satisfied. It is never enough to say of a human want: "I know how to satisfy it and I have the power to do so." There is always something else to consider. But what thus comes into view is not merely an extension of the field of instrumental learning but an altogether different engagement of critical self-understanding in which we relate ourselves, not to our inheritance of instrumental arts, but to the continuous intellectual adventure in which human beings have sought to identify and to understand themselves.

Now, to recognize oneself in terms of one's wants, to recognize the world as material to be shaped and used in satisfying wants, to recognize others as competitors or cooperators in this enterprise and to recognize our inheritance of arts and practices, including a common language, as valuable instruments for satisfying wants—all this is, unquestionably, *a* self-understanding. It gives *an* answer to the question. Who am I? And indeed there are some who would persuade us that this is all we know or can know about ourselves and that all other thoughts human beings have had about themselves and the world are idle fancies and all other relationships are shadowy reflections of this relationship. But they refute themselves. In purporting to make a true statement about human beings and their relationships they identify themselves as something other than mere seekers after contingent satisfactions; they assume a relationship between themselves and those whom they address which is not that of exploiters of the resources of the earth but that of persons capable of considering the truth or falsehood of a theorem.[1]

But be that how it may, it is unquestionable that human beings, without denying their identities as exploiters of the resources of the earth, have always thought of themselves as something other than this and that they have been tireless in their explorations of these other identities. They have engaged in manifold activities other than this—adventures of intellectual inquiry, or moral discrimination and of emotional and imaginative insight; they have explored a vast variety of relationships other than this—moral, intellectual, emotional, civil; and they have perceived, dimly or clearly, that this identity as exploiters of the

resources of the earth is not only evanescent and insubstantial when set beside these others but is itself conditional upon them. They have recognized that these understandings of themselves, and these valuations of occurrences (like everything else human) are themselves human inventions and can be enjoyed only in learning. Even in the most difficult circumstances, overwhelmed by the exigencies of the moment (life in the covered wagon, for example), they have carried these identities with them and imparted them to their children if only in songs and stories. Whenever opportunity has occurred they have set aside special places and occasions devoted to this learning, and until recently schools and universities were just such places of learning, sheltered enough from the demands of utility to be undistracted in their concern with these adventures and expressions of human self-understanding.

This, then, is what we are concerned with: adventures in human self-understanding. Not the bare protestation that a human being is a self-conscious, reflective intelligence and that he does not live by bread alone, but the actual inquiries, utterances and actions in which human beings have expressed their understanding of the human condition. This is the stuff of what has come to be called a "liberal" education—"liberal" because it is liberated from the distracting business of satisfying contingent wants.

But why should be we concerned with it? If it purported to provide reliable information about "human nature" our concern would be intelligible. But it does not. There is no such thing as "human nature"; there are only men, women, and children responding gaily or reluctantly, reflectively or not so reflectively, to the ordeal of consciousness, who exist only in terms of their self-understandings. Nor is being human itself a special instrumental skill like that of an electrical engineer. And if our concern is with human self-understanding, why all this paraphernalia of learning? Is this not something we each do for ourselves? Yes, humanly each of us is self-made; but not out of nothing, and not by the light of

The craft of thinking

It is not for optical reasons that the lynx-eyed Red Indian cannot detect misprints or see that a chessplayer's queen is in danger. If he has not learned to read or to play chess his lynx eyes cannot tell him these things. Now the same thing is true of thought. What a person thinks on a certain matter is true or else it is false; it is accurate or else inaccurate; it is definite or else it is vague; it is clear or it is muddled; it is well or else ill founded; it is expert or else it is amateurish, and so on. Some practice and often some tuition is a *sine qua non* of our being able to think out any problems at all, however simple, within certain fields. It is not from lack of quickwittedness that my Red Indian cannot work out or even be defeated by a chess problem, but because he has not learned the game. Thinking, like fencing and skating, is a consortium of competencies and skills. Like them, it has tasks which it may accomplish or may fail to do so. It has room in it, therefore, for high and low degrees of these competence and skills, i.e. of low and high degrees of stupidity and silliness. In our thinking we exercise good, moderate or bad craftsmanship. Thought is not something that just happens to us and in us, like digestion. It is something that we do, and do well or badly, carefully or carelessly, expertly or amateurishly.

—Gilbert Ryle, in "John Locke." *Collected Papers*, Vol. 1, (New York: Barnes and Noble, Inc., 1971), p. 154; originally published in "Critica Revista Hispanoamericana de Filosfia," Vol. 1.

nature. The world is full of home-made human beings, but they are rickety constructions of impulses ready to fall apart in what is called an "identity crisis." Being human is an historic adventure which has been going on since the earth rose out of the sea, and we are concerned with this paraphernalia of learning because it is the only way we have of participating in this adventure. The ancient Greek exhortation, know thyself, meant learn to know thyself. But it was not an exhortation to buy a book on psychology and study it; it meant, contemplate and learn from what men, from time to time, have made of this engagement of learning to be a man.

Human self-understanding, is, then, inseparable from learning to participate in what is called a "culture." It is useful to have a word which stands for the whole of what an associated set of human beings have created for themselves beyond the evanescent satisfaction of their wants, but we must not be misled by it. A culture is not a doctrine or a set of consistent teachings or conclusions about a human life. It is not something we can set before ourselves as the subject of learning, any more than we can set self-under-

standing before ourselves as something to be learned; it is that which is learned in everything we may learn. A culture, particularly one such as ours, is a continuity of feelings, perceptions, ideas, engagements, attitudes, etc. pulling in different directions, often critical of one another and contingently related to one another so as to compose, not a doctrine, but what I shall call a conversational encounter. Ours, for example, accommodates not only the lyre of Apollo but also the pipes of Pan, the call of the wild; not only the poet but also the physicist; not only the majestic metropolis of Augustinian theology but also the "greenwood" of Franciscan Christianity. A culture comprises unfinished intellectual and emotional journeyings, expeditions now abandoned but known to us in the tattered maps left behind by the explorers; it is composed of light-hearted adventures, of relationships invented and explored in exploit or in drama, of myths and stories and poems expressing fragments of human self-understanding, of gods worshipped, of responses to the mutability of the world and of encounters with death. And it reaches us, as it reached generations before ours, neither as long-ago terminated speciments of human adventure, nor as an accumulation of human achievements we are called upon to accept, but as a manifold of invitations to look, to listen and to reflect. Learning here is not merely acquiring information (*that* produces only what Nietzsche called a "culture philistine"), nor is it merely 'improving one's mind'; it is learning to recognize some specific invitations to encounter particular adventures in human self-understanding.

A man's culture is an historic contingency, but since it is all he has he would be foolish to ignore it because it is not composed of eternal verities. And it is itself a continent flow of intellectual and emotional adventures, a mixture of old and new where the new is often a backward swerve to pick up what has been temporarily forgotten; a mixture of the emergent and the recessive; of the substantial and the somewhat flimsy, of the commonplace, the refined and the magnificent. And since learning here is not merely becoming aware of a so-called cultural inheritance but encountering and seeking to understand some of its specific invitations, a special place devoted to such learning is constituted only in terms of what it is believed there is to learn. And, of course, this belief is itself a response to what may be called the "educational" invitations of the culture. To talk of being "culturally conditioned" is rubbish; a man is his culture, and what he is he has had to learn to become.

The wandering scholars who, in the twelfth century, took the road to Paris, to Bologna, to Chartres or to Toulouse were, often unknown to themselves, seeking within the notions of the time, a "liberal" education; they are our forebears in this adventure. You and I were born in the twelfth century and although we have traveled far we still bear the marks of our birth-time. But when two centuries later the expression "liberal studies" acquired a specific meaning it stood for an encounter with a somewhat remote culture which was slowly being retrieved from neglect— the Greek and Latin culture of antiquity. Some of the achievements of this ancient civilization had

never been lost: the Latin language as a medium of communication, some useful information (mostly legal and medical) and some notable pieces of writing. But the educational adventure of the fourteenth century sprang from an ever more extended recovery of this almost lost culture which revealed itself not only to have been one of great intellectual splendor, variety and reflective energy but also to be one in which a man of the fourteenth century could identify himself and which offered him a wealth of hitherto unheard of invitations to explore and to understand himself: languages recognized as investments in thought; epic, dramatic, lyric and historical literatures which gave a new dimension to human relationships, emotions, aspirations and conduct; inquiries (including those of the early theologians of Christianity) which suggested new directions for human reflection. Thus, "learning" was identified with coming to understand the intimations of a human life displayed in an historic culture of remarkable splendor and lucidity and with the invitation to recognize oneself in terms of this culture. This was an education which promised and afforded liberation from the here and now of current engagements, from the muddle, the crudity, the sentimentality, the intellectual poverty and the emotional morass of ordinary life. And so it continues to this day. This education has had often to be rescued from the formalism into which it degenerated. Its center of gravity moved from the culture of antiquity but without any firm settlement elsewhere. We have seen, sometimes regretfully, bits of this education fall away, having lost their compelling interest. It has been extended to include new and substantial vernacular languages and literatures. It has accommodated, somewhat reluctantly, the novel and still inadequately self-understood inquiry which has absorbed so much of the intellectual energy of modern times, namely the natural sciences. And it has had to resist the seductive advances of enemies dressed up as friends. And what now of its present condition?

The engagement has survived. We do not yet live in the ashes of a great adventure which has burnt itself out. Its self-understanding is not at present very conspicuous, its self-confidence is fluctuating and often misplaced, its credit is stretched and it has borrowed when it would have been better to economize, but it has not been lacking in serious self-examination. The torch is still alight and there are still some hands to grasp it. But I shall not dwell upon its present vitality, such as it is; our concern is with its infirmities and with those which may be counted as self-betrayals—not to censure them but to try to understand them.

Its most naive self-betrayal is merely to have listened to the seductive voice of the world urging it, in the name of "relevance" to take up with extraneous concerns and even to alter course. When, like Ulysses, we should have stopped our ears with wax and bound ourselves to the mast of our own identity, we have been beguiled, not only by words but by inducements. To open a School of Business, to undertake the training of journalists or corporation lawyers seem harmless enough concessions to modernity; they may be defended by the specious argument that they certainly entail learning, they give a place of liberal learning an attractive image of "relevance" and the corruption involved may be written off as negligible. Events, however, hardly confirm this optimism. Having no proper part in liberal learning, these appealing divergencies are difficult to contain; they undermine rather than assail the engagement. Their virtue is to be evanescent and contemporary; if they are not up-to-date they are worthless. And this unqualified modernity rubs off on the proper concern with languages, with literatures and with histories which are thus edged into the study of only what is current in a culture. History is contracted into what is called contemporary history, languages come to be recognized as means of contemporary communication, and in literature the book which "verbalizes what everyone is thinking now" comes to be preferred, on that account, to anything else.

But the real assault upon liberal learning comes from another direction; not in the risky undertaking to equip learners for some, often prematurely chosen, profession, but in the belief that "relevance" demands that every learner should be recognized as nothing but a role-performer in a so-called "social system" and the consequent surrender of learning (which is the concern of individual persons) to "socialization": the doctrine that because the current here and now is very much more uniform than it used to be, education should recognize and promote this uniformity. This is not a recent self-betrayal; it is the theme of those wonderful lectures of Nietzsche on the *Future of our Educational Institutions* delivered in Basel a century ago in which he foresaw the collapse which now threatens us. And although this may seem to be very much a matter of doctrine, of merely how education is thought about and spoken of, and to have very little to do with what may actually go on in a place of learning, it is the most insidious of all corruptions. It not only strikes at the heart of liberal learning, it portends the abolition of man.

But if these are the cruder subversions of liberal learning there are others, more subtle but hardly less damaging. It has come to be thought of as a "general" education; that is, as learning not only liberated from the here and now of current engagements but liberated also from an immediate concern with anything specific to be learned. Learning here is said to be "learning to think for oneself" or to be the cultivation of "intelligence" or of certain intellectual and moral aptitudes—the ability to "think logically" or "deliberatively," the ability not to be deceived by irrelevance in argument, to be courageous, patient, careful, accurate or determined; the ability to read attentively and to speak lucidly, and so on. And, of course, all these and more are aptitudes and virtues that a learner may hope to acquire or to improve. But neither they, nor self-understanding itself, can be made the subject of learning. A culture is not a set of abstract aptitudes; it is composed of substantive expressions of thought, emotion, belief, opinion, approval and disapproval, of moral and intellectual discriminations, of inquiries and investigations, and learning is coming to understand and respond to these substantive expressions of thought as invitations to think and to believe. Or, this word "general" is used to identify and to recommend an education concerned, indeed, with the substance of a culture, but so anxious that everything shall receive mention that it can afford no more than a fleeting glimpse of anything in particular. Here learning amounts to little more than recognition; it never achieves the level of an encounter. It is the vague and fragmentary equipment of the "culture philistine."

Nevertheless, a place of liberal learning is rarely without a shape which purports to specify what there is to be learned. And its present shape in most such places bears witness both to the ancient lineage of the engagement and to the changes our culture has undergone in recent centuries. The natural sciences, mathematics, the humanities and the social sciences—these are the lineaments of this education as it comes to us now. Let us briefly consider these constituents.

Liberal learning is learning to respond to the invitations of the great intellectual adventures in which human beings have come to display their various understandings of the world and of themselves. And before the natural sciences could be recognized in this character they had not only to offer something specific capable of being learned but also to present themselves as a distinctive inquiry or mode of human understanding. That is to say, they had to appear as very much more than somewhat mysterious information about the natural world which no educated man should be without, and something very much less than an unconditional or definitive understanding of the world. In respect of the first they have amply succeeded: every natural science now presents itself to the learner as a related set of theorems which invites critical understanding. In respect of the second they have been hindered, not by any inherent self-deception, but by two unfortunate

circumstances. The first of these is the relic of a disposition to value themselves in terms of the use which may be made of the conclusions of their inquiries. This, in a place of liberal learning, has sometimes led to a proliferation of what may be called semi-sciences— organizations of information in terms of the use which may be made of it. But this is not a very important hindrance. The more serious encumbrance comes in some absurd claims made by others on their behalf: the claim that they themselves compose a distinctive culture (the silly doctrine of the "two cultures"); the claim that they represent "the truth" (so far as it has been ascertained) about the world; and the claim that they constitute the model of all valid human understanding—a claim which has had disastrous consequences elsewhere. But in spite of these hindrances, the natural sciences have unquestionably earned a proper place for themselves in the design of liberal learning and know how to occupy it. No doubt, for example, a biological identity is not itself a human identity, but one of the significant self-understandings which human beings have come upon and explored is that of persons concerned with a specifically "scientific" understanding of themselves and the world.

Of the humanities I need say little. They are directly concerned with expressions of human self-understanding and their place in liberal learning is assured and central: Languages recognized, not as the means of contemporary communication but as investments in thought and records of perceptions and analogical understandings; literatures recognized as the contemplative exploration of beliefs, emotions, human characters and relationships in imagined situations, liberated from the confused, cliché-ridden, generalized conditions of commonplace life and constituting a world of ideal human expressions inviting neither approval nor disapproval but the exact attention and understanding of those who read; histories recognized, not as accounts of the past focused upon our contemporary selves purporting to tell us how we have become what we are and containing messages of warning or encouragement, but as stories in which human actions and utterances are rescued from mystery and made intelligible in terms of their contingent relations; and philosophy, the reflective undertaking in which every purported achievement of human understanding becomes the subject of an inquiry into its conditions. And if any of this has got driven off its course it is by the winds which forever blow around the engagement of liberal learning, menacing its seclusion from the here and now or driving it upon the rocks of abstract aptitudes or socialization.

But what of the latest born component of liberal learning: the social sciences? They are a mixed lot. Among them we may expect to find sociology, anthropology, psychology, economics, perhaps jurisprudence and something called "politics." They purport to be directly concerned with human conduct. These are what used to be called the "human sciences"—*geisteswissenschaften*, in order to make clear that their concern is with human beings as self-conscious, intelligent persons who are what they understand themselves to be and not with human beings in the loose and indistinct sense of highly evolved organisms or processes of chemical change, the concern of natural sciences. And insofar as these human sciences are what they purport to be (which is not so in every case) it would seem that they belong properly to the "humanities." But distinguished they now are; and if the project of distinguishing them from the "humanities" was an unfortunate mistake, the terms of the distinction are nothing less than a disaster. These terms are specified in the words "social" and "science."

"Social," of course, is a cant word. It is used here to denote an inquiry about human conduct concerned, not with substantive actions and utterances but with the relationships, the associations and the practices in which human beings are joined. This focus of attention is not, in itself, corrupting. It is that upon which most histories of law are centered; and it is the focus, for example,

of Maitland's *Constitutional History of England* which, he tells us, is designed to be an account, not of human struggles, but of the results of human struggles in constitutional change. But it is chosen here, and is labeled "social," in order to allege (or to suggest) that human beings and their performances are what they are in terms of these relationships, associations and practices; and to suggest, further, that these relationships and practices are not human devices, autonomous manners of being associated, each with its own specified conditions of relationship but are the components of an unspecified, unconditional interdependence or "social" relationship, sometimes called a "society" or "Society." In short, the contention is that this unspecified "social" relationship is the condition, perhaps the determinant, of all human conduct and that to which human actions and utterances must be referred in order to be understood. But this substitution of the word "social" for the word 'human' is a surrender to confusion: human conduct is never merely a subscription to a practice or to a relationship, and there is no such thing as an unconditional "social" relationship. And this confusion is partnered by a commonplace corruption of our language in which the word "social" has become the center of endless equivocation. Selden in the seventeenth century said of the cant expression *scrutamini scripturas*, "these two words have undone the world": a single word has sufficed to undo our cruder twentieth century.

It might, however, be supposed that in connecting the word "science" with the word "social" something has been done to restore exactness. But the outcome of this conjunction has been to add a ruinous categorical confusion to what need not have been more than a permissible partiality in considering human conduct. For the word "science" here is intended to denote a natural science of human conduct; that is, to mean the investigation of human actions and utterances and the practices and relationships to which they may subscribe as if they were non-intelligent components of a "process" or the functional constituents of a "system" which do not have to learn their parts in order to play them. The design here is to remove human action and utterance from the category of intelligent goings-on (that is, chosen responses of self-conscious agents to their understood situations which have reasons but not causes and may be understood only in terms of dispositions, beliefs, meanings, intentions, and motives), and to place them in the category of examples of the operation of regularities which do not have to be learned in order to be observed; and to remove human practices, relationships, associations etc. from the category of procedures whose conditions have to be learned and understood in order to be subscribed to and can be subscribed to only in self-chosen actions and utterances, and to put them into the category of "processes." Rules are misidentified as regularities, intelligent winks as physiological blinks, conduct as "behavior" and contingent relationships as causal or systematic connections.

This project of collecting together a number of respectable inquiries under the head of "the social sciences" and the attempt to impose this equivocal character upon them has not met with universal acceptance but it has gone far enough to have deeply damaged liberal learning; no other failure of self-understanding in the humanities has generated such confusion. And it is all the more damaging because in putting on the mask of "science" some of these departments of learning have succumbed to the temptation to understand and to value themselves in terms of the use which may be made of the conclusions of their inquiries. The recognition as the appropriate equipment for new technological enterprises and for the new and proliferating profession of "social worker" has corrupted liberal learning. But this does not mean that, individually, and when properly recognized as *Geisteswissenschaften*, they have no proper place in liberal learning; it means only that they have been misidentified. Jurisprudence, until it was confused with a vapid concern for so-called social and psychological needs and become part of the equipment of "so-

cial engineers," was a profound philosophical inquiry, one of the most ancient and respected components of liberal learning. Sociology and anthropology are respectable and somewhat attenuated engagements in historical understanding; they are concerned with human practices, procedures, associations etc. and their contingent relations, and with human actions and utterances in terms of their subscriptions to the conditions of practices. And psychology has long ago declared itself a "natural," not a "human" science. It is not concerned with substantive human thoughts, beliefs, emotions, recollections, actions and utterances but with so-called "mental processes" which are vulnerable to reduction to genetic and chemical processes.

Putting on one side engagements in learning which have no proper place in a liberal education, there are, then, departments of liberal learning in which self-consciousness has not yet been transformed into the self-understanding upon which authentic inquiry and utterance depends. But the more serious consideration for anyone who undertakes to review the present condition of liberal learning is the terms of the self-understanding of the engagement itself.

As it emerged in Western Europe liberal learning was understood to be a concern to explore the invitations of the culture of antiquity, to hold before learners the mirror of this culture so that, seeing themselves reflected in it, they might extend the range and the depth of their understanding of themselves. This idiom of the self-understanding of liberal learning was never very satisfactory; it was substantial, not formal, and it has long since passed away. It has been succeeded by other similarly substantial, self-identifications. For example, when I was young it was thought (or at least suggested) that the whole of liberal learning might properly be understood in terms of a somewhat extended study of Geography: liberal learning was urged to find the focus of its attention in "geographical man." And we have since become familiar with a claim of this sort made on behalf of Sociology; if every department of liberal learning is not itself to be turned into sociology (philosophy into the sociology of knowledge, jurisprudence into the sociology of law etc.) then, at least, none is as it should be unless sociology were added to it. These, of course, fanciful notions, but they are not unconvincing merely on account of their contingent implausibility. They are unacceptable because the identification of liberal learning they suggest is of the wrong kind. The self-understanding of liberal learning must, I think, be sought in the recognition that its components inquiries, in spite of their substantial differences, have a common formal character and that they are related to one another in a manner agreeable with character.

I have already suggested that the components of a liberal education are united and distinguished from what does not properly belong to it in terms of their "liberality"; that is, in terms of their concern with what Valéry calls *le prix de la view humaine*,[2] and their emancipation from the here and now of current engagements. But beyond this general consideration, these components may be resolved into and understood as so many different *languages*: the language of the natural sciences, for example, the language of history, the language of philosophy, or the language of poetic imagination.

Languages in a more commonplace sense are organizations of grammatical and syntactical considerations or rules to be taken account of and subscribed to in making utterances. These considerations do not determine the utterances made or even exactly how they shall be subscribed to; that is left to the speaker who not only has something of his own to say but may also have a style of his own. And, of course, no such language is ever settled beyond the reach of modification; to speak it is a linguistically inventive engagement. But here, the conditions imposed upon utterances by these languages of understanding constitute, not merely linguistic idioms, but particular conditional modes of understanding. Learning here is learning to recognize and discriminate between these languages of understanding, is becoming familiar with the con-

dition each imposes upon utterance, and is learning to make utterances whose virtue is not that they express original ideas (that can only be a rare achievement) but that they display genuine understanding of the language spoken. It is on this account that a learner may be recognized to understand a language such as that of philosophical or historical understanding and yet not be a philosopher or an historian; and also that a teacher may be recognized to have something into which he may initiate a learner which is not itself a doctrine. But since none of these languages of understanding was invented yesterday and each is the continuous exploration of its own possibilities, a learner cannot expect to find what he seeks if he attends only to contemporary utterances. These languages of understanding like other languages are known only in literatures.

What I am suggesting, then, is that from the standpoint of liberal learning, a culture is not a miscellany of beliefs, perceptions, ideas, sentiments, engagements etc. but may be recognized as a variety of distinct languages of understanding, and its inducements are invitations to become acquainted with these languages, to learn to discriminate between them, and to recognize them not merely as diverse modes of understanding the world but as the most substantial expressions we have of human self-understanding.

But the identity of a culture and of liberal learning remains obscure until we have some conception of the relationship of its components. Now, each of these languages constitutes the terms of a distinct, conditional understanding of the world and a similarly distinct idiom of human self-understanding. Their virtue is to be different from one another and this difference is intrinsic. Each is secure in its autonomy so long as it knows and remains faithful to itself. Any of them may fail, but such failure is always self-defeat arising from imperfect understanding of itself or from the nonobservance of its own conditions. They may not all be equally interesting and they may compete for our attention, but, they are not inherently contentious and they are incapable of refuting one another. Hence, their relationship cannot be that of parties in a debate; they do not together compose an argument. Further, they are not different degrees of divergence from some suppositions unconditional understanding of the world: their relationship is not hierarchical. Nor is it either a cooperative or a transactional relationship. They are not partners in a common undertaking each with a role to perform, nor are they suppliers of one another's wants. What then is left?

Perhaps we may think of these opponents of a culture as voices, each expression of a distinct and conditional understanding of the world and a distinct idiom of human self-understanding, and of the culture itself as these voices joined, as such voices could only be joined, in a conversation—an endless unrehearsed intellectual adventure in which, in imagination, we enter into a variety of modes of understanding the world and ourselves and are not disconcerted by the differences or dismayed by the inconclusiveness of it all. And perhaps we may recognize liberal learning as, above all else, an education in imagination, an initiation into the art of this conversation in which we learn to recognize the voices; to distinguish their different modes of utterance, to acquire the intellectual and moral habits appropriate to this conversational relationship and thus to make our *début dans la vie humaine*.

Liberal learning is a difficult engagement. It depends upon an understanding of itself which is always imperfect; even those who presided over its emergence hardly knew what they were doing. And it depends upon a self-confidence which is easily shaken and not least by continual self-examination. It is a somewhat unexpected invitation to disentangle oneself from the here and now of current happenings and engagements, to detach oneself from the urgencies of the local and the contemporary, to explore and enjoy a release from having to consider things in terms of their contingent features, beliefs in terms of their applications to contingent situations and persons in terms of their contingent usefulness; an invitation to be concerned not with the employment of what

is familiar but with understanding what is not yet understood. And a university as a place of liberal learning can prosper only if those who come are disposed to recognize and acknowledge its particular invitation to learn. Its present predicament lies in the circumstance that there is now so much to obstruct this disposition.

There was a time, not so long ago, when liberal learning was, not better understood, but more generally recognized than it now is and when the obtrusive circumstances of the early upbringing of many (and not merely of the better off) were such that they did not positively stand in the way of the recognition of its invitation. They were, indeed, circumstances where the localities in which one was born and grew up were more enclosed than they now are and certainly less superficially exciting. Memorable experiences were fewer and smaller, there was change but it moved at a slower pace; life could be hard but the rat-race as we know it now was in its infancy. They were also somewhat narrow circumstances which bred little concern with what might be going on outside the locality and none at all with world affairs. But they were intellectually innocent rather than positively dull, uncrowded rather than vacant. For there was in these circumstances a notable absence of the ready-made or of oppressive uniformities of thought or attitude or conduct. If experiences were fewer, they were made to go further; if they were smaller they invoked imaginative enlargement. And the natural world was never so far distant as it now often is and the response to it was allowed to be naive and uncluttered, a response of wonder and delight. In all this School was important; but it was a place of its own. I often recollect that memorable sentence from the autobiography of Sir Ernest Barker: "Outside the cottage, I had nothing but my school; but having my school I had everything." There, in school, the narrow boundaries of the local and the contemporary were swept aside to reveal, not what might be going on the next town or village, in Parliament or in the United Nations, but a world of things and persons and happenings, of languages and beliefs, of utterances and sights and sounds past all imagination and to which even the dullest could not be wholly indifferent. The going was hard; there was nothing to be got without learning how to get it, and it was understood that nobody went to school in order to enjoy the sort of happiness he might get from lying in the sun. And when with inky fingers a schoolboy unpacked his satchel to do his homework he unpacked three thousand years of the fortunes and misfortunes of human intellectual adventure. Nor would it easily have occurred to him to ask what the sufferings of Job, the silent ships moving out of Tenedos in the moonlight, the terror, the complication and the pity of the human condition revealed in a drama of Shakespeare or Racine, or even the chemical composition of water, had to do with *him*, born upon the banks of the Wabash, in the hills of Cumberland, in a Dresden suburb or a Neapolitan slum. Either he never considered the question at all, or he dimly recognized them as images of a human self-understanding which was to be his for the learning. All very innocent, perhaps even credulous; and in many cases soon overlaid by the urgencies of current engagements. But however superficially they might be appreciated, these were not circumstances which generated a positive resistance to the invitation of liberal learning in a university. Indeed, their very innocence nurtured a disposition to recognize it.

But these circumstances are no longer with us. The way we live now, even though it may contain notable relics of the earlier condition, is somewhat different. The world in which many children now grow up is crowded, not necessarily with occupants and not at all with memorable experiences, but with happenings; it is a ceaseless flow of seductive trivialities which invoke neither reflection nor choice but instant participation. A child quickly becomes aware that he cannot too soon plunge into this flow or immerse himself in it too quickly; to pause is to be swept with the chilling fear of never having lived at all. There is little chance that his perceptions, his emotions, his admirations and his ready indignations might

become learned responses or be even innocent fancies of his own; they come to him prefabricated, generalized and uniform. He lurches from one modish conformity to the next, or from one fashionable guru to his successor, seeking to lose himself in a solidarity composed of exact replicas of himself. From an early age children now believe themselves to be well-informed about the world, but they know it only at secondhand in the pictures and voices which surround them. It holds no puzzles or mysteries for them; it invites neither careful attention nor understanding. As like as not they know the moon as something to be shot at or occupied before ever they have had the chance to marvel at it. This world has but one language, soon learned: the language of appetite. The idiom may be that of the exploitation of the resources of the earth, or it may be that of seeking something for nothing; but this is a distinction without a difference. It is a language composed of meaningless cliches. It allows only the expression of "points of view" and the ceaseless repetition of slogans which are embraced as prophetic utterances. Their ears are filled with the babel of invitations to instant and unspecified reactions and their utterance reproduces only what they have heard said. Such discourse as there is resembles the barking of a dog at the echo of its own yelp. School in these circumstances is notably unimportant. To a large extent it has surrendered its character as a place apart where utterances of another sort may be heard and languages other than the language of appetite may be learned. It affords no seclusion, it offers no release. Its furnishings are the toys with which those who come are already familiar. Its virtues and its vices are those of the surrounding world.

These, then, are circumstances hostile to a disposition to recognize the invitation of liberal learning; that is, the invitation to disentangle oneself, for a time, from the urgencies of the here and now and to listen to the conversation in which human beings forever seek to understand themselves. How shall a university respond to the current aversion from seclusion, to the now common belief that there are other and better ways of becoming human than by learning to do so, and to the impulsive longing to be given a doctrine or to be socialized according to a formula rather than to be initiated into a conversation? Not, I think, by seeking excuses for what sometimes seem unavoidable surrenders, nor in any grand gesture of defiance, but in a quiet refusal to compromise which comes only in self-understanding. We must remember who we are: inhabitants of a place of liberal learning.

Footnotes

1. When Francis Bacon identified human beings as exploiters of the resources of the earth and language as a means of communicating information about wants he added that this identity had been imposed upon us by God—thus identifying human beings also in relation to God. And even Karl Marx (inconsistently) recognized somethings called "scientific" inquiry independent of the current conditions of productive undertaking.
2. Tout ce qui fait le prix de la vie est curieusement inutile.

J.L. Austin and the community of inquiry

Magee: Didn't [Austin] take the highly unusual view that philosophy could be perhaps even thought to be a group activity?

Warnock: Yes, he said this from time to time and I'm quite sure meant it very seriously. This connects, I think, with his belief that the only serious aim in philosophy ought to be to get things really settled; and he very much wanted to get away from the idea that philosophy was in any way a kind of literary pursuit in which the individual operates strictly as an individual performer—he thought that to see philosophy in that way was to import, into what ought to be in a sense a scientific subject, essentially literary values which he thought quite out of place and disastrous. Yes, he would have liked to try out the idea of a team of persons working in an organized way on small points—though perhaps, collectively, on a large problem—combining their results, criticizing each other's work, and really coming up with some agreed, solid conclusions at the end.

Magee: Can you give an example of the kind of thing such a group might be doing?

Warnock: Well. I think he thought of it as partly just a matter of getting the benefits of mutual criticism and suggestions in advance of producing your work rather than afterwards, which seems to be the more usual style. But also I think he had in mind the way in which, for some purposes, the natural sciences operate, he would have liked large problems to be broken down into limited areas and these, so to speak, farmed out in an organized way to individual operators. For example, there were his so called "Saturday mornings," weekly meetings held in Oxford during term under Austin's chairmanship (to put it over-formally) here, at an early stage, the notion of a *rule* came under consideration, a notion which figures importantly in all sorts of fields—mathematics for instance and philosophy of language, and of course ethics as well—in all these fields philosophers talk a lot about rules. Well, on that occasion Austin decided, characteristically enough, that they'd better look at actual rules in some detail; he divided out among those present particular kinds of rules—rules of bridge, rules of cricket, rules of evidence, that kind of thing—and gave a particular field to each person to study in detail, and then see what they came up with. It was a kind—one kind—of scientific ideal that he had, I think; you divide a big problem into limited tasks, and assign a group or team of people to work on them in a systematic way.

—from Bryan Magee, "Conversation with Geoffrey Warnock," in *Modern British Philosophy.*

The Community of Inquiry: Education for Democracy

Ann Margaret Sharp

In this paper I would like to focus on the classroom community of inquiry as an educational means of furthering the sense of community that is a precondition for actively participating in a democratic society. Such a community cultivates skills of dialogue, questioning, reflective inquiry and good judgment. In the course of the paper, I will attempt to answer the following questions: When I enter a classroom, how do I know a community of inquiry is in formation? What behaviors are the students and teacher performing and what dispositions are manifest? What are some of the theoretical assumptions of these behaviors? And more importantly, what are some of the practical social, ethical and political consequences of such behavior?

I will assume that a community of inquiry is characterized by *dialogue* that is fashioned collaboratively out of the reasoned contribution of all participants. I assume that, over time, the classroom discussions will become more disciplined by *logical, epistemlogical, aesthetic, ethical, social* and *political* considerations that are applicable. In such a community, the teacher monitors the logical procedures but, in addition, philosophically becomes one of the community. Students learn to *object to weak reasoning, build on strong reasoning*, accept the responsibility of making their contributions within the context of others, accept their dependence upon others, follow the inquiry where it leads, respect the perspective of others, collaboratively engage in *self-correction* when necessary and take pride in the accomplishments of the group as well as oneself. Further, in the process, they practice the art of making *good judgments* within the context of dialogue and communal inquiry.[1]

There are cognitive behaviors that can be observed: giving and asking for good reasons, making good distinctions and connections, making valid inferences, hypothesizing, generalizing, giving counter-examples, discovering assumptions, using and recognizing criteria, asking good questions, inferring consequences, recognizing logical fallacies, calling for relevance, defining concepts, seeking clarification, voicing implications, perceiving relationships, judging well, standardizing using good analogies, sensitivity to context, offering alternative points of view, building logically on contributions of others and voicing fine discriminations.

Participants come to regard the production of knowledge as contingent, bound up with human interests and activities and therefore always open to revision. Further, students become more tolerant of complexity and ambiguity and recognize that justification for belief is rooted in *human action*. The human condition often might require that we make a provisional commitment to one belief or one course of action because of the need to act, but this in no way means that the particular belief can be justified as absolute truth. It is this need to act that calls for *good practical judgment* that will only be as good as one has been educated dialogically in making fine discriminations and learning how to do full justice to particular situations. Ultimately this capacity to judge is based on *communal civic sense* that is necessary for making moral and political judgments. Such judgments are intersubjective and appeal to and require testing against the opinions of other judging persons.[2]

Since there is no criterion, independent of various practical concerns, that will tell us when we have arrived at truth, and since knowledge is inescapably linguistic and inseparable from human activity, knowledge is a product of practical reasoning. It is for this reason that the acquisition and retention of knowledge must always be an active process.[3]

There are *social behaviors* that can be observed: listening to one another, supporting one another by amplifying and corroborating their views, submitting the views of others to critical inquiry, giving reasons to support another's view even if one doesn't agree, taking one another's ideas seriously by responding and encouraging each other to voice their views. A certain *care* is manifest in the group, not only care for the logical procedures but for the growth of each member of the community. This care presupposes the disposition to be open, to be capable of changing ones views and priorities in order to care for the other. In a real sense to care presupposes a willingness to be transformed by the other—to be affected by the other. This care is essential for dialogue. But it is also essential for the *development of trust*, a basic orientation toward the world that accounts for the individuals coming to think they have a role to play in the world, that they can make a real difference. Further, the world is such a place that will receive not only their thoughts but their actions. Trust, in turn, is a precondition for the development of *autonomy* and *self-esteem* on the part of the individual participants. Care, then, makes possible a conception of the world as a

play in which one can shape outcomes and create beauty where none has existed before.[4]

Participants appear to be capable of giving themselves to others, speaking when they think they have something relevant to say or when they think they have a responsibility for getting the dialogue back on track. Students appear to have repudiated the *prima donna* role and seem able to collaborate and cooperate in inquiry. They can hear and receive what others have to say in such a way that meaning and vitality is shared.[5] They are free of the need always to be right. They have the courage and ability to change their minds and to hold their views tentatively. They do not appear defensive but rather delighted to be in a community of inquiry. If the ideas of others, it implies also an openness to emerging truth—a giving of oneself in the broadest sense, even though one realizes that the truth one gains in the end is only provisional. To do this, students must be capable of coming to understand that they do not know many things, if anything at all.

There are *psychological* or *socio-psychological* characteristics that can be observed. These involve the growth of the self in relation to others, putting of the ego in perspective, disciplining of self-centeredness and eventually the transforming of oneself. Participants refrain from engaging in extended monologues that preempt dialogue or do not really call for a response. They know how to dialogue with each other. Dialogue implies a certain capacity for intellectual flexibility, self-correction and growth.[6] Have we not all had the experience of submitting a question to the group and then seeing emerge from the painful yet exciting dialogue an insight or understanding that is far more profound than that offered by any single contribution? Such an event should not only be evaluated in terms of the product but in terms of the process—the relationships experienced during the course of the inquiry.

Teachers and participants can mute themselves in order to encourage others to speak their own ideas. They have the ability to let go of their positions in order to listen openly, hear and follow the inquiry where it leads. The latter requires letting truth emerge even though one knows it will be provisional and might require that one reconstruct one's own cherished belief-system. In a working community of inquiry, participants will move from considering themselves and their accomplishments as all important to focusing on the group and its accomplishments. They are not only conscious of their own thinking but begin examining and correcting each other's methods and procedures. Once they internalize the self-correcting methodology, they have the possibility of becoming critical thinkers—individuals who are open to self-correction, are sensitive to context and use criteria consciously in the making of practical judgments.[7]

The relationship of the individual to the community is thus inter-dependent. The success of the community is compatible with, and is dependent on, unique expressions of individuality. Yet, each participants accepts the discipline of making his or her contribution in the context of the contributions of others. This means accepting interdependence and repudiating an attitude of "knowing-it-all." The community will not function unless the participants can conform to the procedures of that community—logical and social. If one of the procedural principles is brought into question, other procedures must be adopted so that the discussion can proceed. Conformity is also manifest in a growing commitment to the underlying principles and practices that govern the enterprise itself: tolerance, consistency, comprehensiveness, open-mindedness, self-correction, conscious use of criteria, sensitivity to context and respect for all participants as potential sources of insight. Zaniness is tolerated only if it produces progress for the group's inquiry. If not constructive, the group will self-correct and eliminate the behavior. Often this is done with silence—not responding to behavior that blocks dialogue or reflective inquiry.[8]

When one observes a functioning community of inquiry, one does not simply see a group nor simply individuals. What one observes is a community in which individual opinions are exchanged and serve as the source for further inquiry. Participants are capable of being fully present to each other in such a way that the entire meaning and vitality of the dialogue is shared.[9] Participants do not talk about themselves but rather offer meanings to which others may make a response. They can take the risk of communicating. If the trust and care of the community are in place, the individual is far more likely to take this risk. And at times it is a real risk. One is exposing one's beliefs aware that one will probably be challenged and be forced to rethink one's position. This rethinking or restructuring takes time which means that there will be a period during which the individual will feel confused and perhaps insecure and maybe even frightened. I have seen shy students finally muster the courage to express their belief verbally only to have it fall to the floor with a thud of silence. And yet, many were capable of accepting the silence and trying again and again to make some kind of contribution to the on-going inquiry. Participants tend to refrain from voicing their views dogmatically. If one observes closely one sees that individual convictions more often relate to basic character, always information, rather than to knowledge claims.

Individuals in a community of inquiry must be able to hear and respond to the *meaning* of the dialogue itself. Such meaning comes from two sources: (1) the participants willing to be involved in the inquiry and (2) the subject under discussion in light of the intellectual tradition of which we are all heirs. One must be willing to listen to the question behind the question, the fear behind the bravado, the insecurity behind the pretense, the courage behind the timidity, all of this being an essential component of the meaning of the dialogue itself. Further, one must be able to see—to read the faces of the speakers and the non-speakers and to interpret what they are saying and not-saying. Some might be silent because they have nothing to say. Others might be silent because they are afraid to voice their views. Others might be shy. Others might be afraid that their views will be challenged—this is a sign that something is very wrong.

The breakdown of the community occurs when there is an obliteration of persons. This takes place when one person exploits another, that is, uses the relations that have been formed for any purpose other than its intended one: the pursuit of meaning and understanding and the furthering of the growth of each member of the community. To the extent that individuals engage in monologues, they block inquiry. To the extent that they make assumptions about what the other is going to say before the other has the opportunity to say it, they block inquiry. To the extent that they engage in image making when another is speaking, they block inquiry. To the extent that they take it upon themselves to speak for others out of fear or insecurity, they destroy the trust essential for dialogical inquiry.

One purpose of the dialogue among participants is to bring *vitality* or life to the *form* of the community of inquiry. Without this vitality, the form is empty or meaningless. Asking questions means nothing if one is not actively involved in the quest for understanding. Tension among members of the group may produce conflict but it is not itself conflict. For example, when violin strings have just the right tension, they can be used to produce beautiful music. Similarly, when a creative tension exists among participants a tension between the vitality of the many relationships and the form of the community of inquiry, the group has the potential for open debate, growth and each participant has the potential for self-transformation. Because tension is painful, we tend to want to get rid of it at any cost. Often we find ourselves choosing instead the mere form of a dialogue, the mere form of communal inquiry. The purpose, however, of a community of inquiry is to restore the tension between vitality and form, to bring participants into deeper and more significant relationships, to shake them free of their complacency, their false convictions and to make them available for more comprehensive

understanding.[10] Therefore, it follows that dislogical thinking within the community requires a willingness to be disturbed and to be challenged by the ideas of the other, a process of active reconstruction using criteria of comprehensiveness, coherence and consistency, together with sensitivity to the particularity of each situation.

As mentioned before, individuals in a community of inquiry have learned to held their beliefs tentatively. Given the nature of human knowledge and justification—that is to justify any belief we have to base our belief on another belief that is language-dependent, it is a matter of finding coherence among our beliefs and correspondence with the world. What I mean here is the world independent of language, perception and human understanding. But there is no such thing as knowledge of the world-as-it-really-is, since we can never be separated from the language and activities of particular groups or communities of human beings. Thus, knowledge is always inescapably contingent, open to revision, and a matter of practical judgment. It is not a matter of aiming some mirror that is highly polished at the world as it really is and then passively noting the way things really are, independent of human practical concerns, social and personal. Rather, knowledge is an historical, linguistic and social activity and, as such, always open to self-correction as new data or evidence has to be taken into account. There is no ultimate foundation for our knowledge. What we have is reason as a regulative ideal, and even the form of this reasoning process is open to revision within the context of questioning, dialogue and *praxis*.

Thus, one could say that the community of inquiry provides a process of communication for the student, a moving back and forth between a narrower and wider framework, which may allow meaning and understanding to emerge, and which each participant may be able to actively judge at the end, the dialogue of the community itself When one is actively involved in a community of inquiry, one assumes that subjective individual experience, as an unconsidered given, cannot re-

Education and democracy

To bring such people out, to help develop them into a community, you must surround your students with models of straightforward conduct, clarified character, and open reasonableness, for I believe it is in the hope of seeing such models that many serious people go to lectures rather than more conveniently reading books. If there are not such men and women on your faculties, you will not attract those who are potential rallying points for the genuine liberal public. In the end, all talk of liberal education, of personnel and curriculum and programming and the rest of it, is nonsense if you do not have such men and women on your faculties. For in the end, liberal education is the result of the liberating and self-sustaining touch of such people.

And their existence in a community as a creative minority is, in the end, the only force that might prevail against the ascendancy of the mass society and all the men and apparatus that make for it. For in the end, it is around them and through them that liberated and liberating publics come to articulate form and democratic action.

I have not yet discussed the relation of the school with other organizations in the metropolitan community, the third point of importance to the Center. It is a complicated issue that I cannot adequately cover in the time available. Let me say only that I doubt that education, for adults or for adolescents, is the strategic factor in the building of a democratic polity. I think it is in the picture and must be, but given its present personnel and administration, and its generally powerless position among other politically relevant organizations, it cannot and will not get the job done. Only if it were to become the framework within which more general movements that were under way—movements with more direct political relevance—were going on, only then would it have the chance to take the place in American political life that it ought to. Only then could it in fact do fully what I have suggested it ought nevertheless to try now to do. For men and women cannot develop and use their highest potentiality in and through educational institutions: they can do that only within and through all of their institutions. And educational work cannot be the sole preparation for such a humane and political life; it can only be part of it, helping it, to be sure, once it is part of the general movement of American civilization.

—C. Wright Mills, in *Power, Politics and People*, pp. 372-373.

veal even provisional truth. It is the starting point of inquiry, not the end result. Further, the meanings that totally subjective experience do reveal are narrow and paltry compared to the meanings one can derive from communal inquiry.

Lastly, there are *moral* and *political* considerations that one must take into account when considering the nature of a community of inquiry. If we assume that the purpose of education is not only to transmit a body of knowledge but also to equip children with the skills and dispositions they need to create new knowledge and make better practical judgments, then the traditional classroom of "telling" is not appropriate. If we further assume that the purpose of education is the bringing into being of persons—persons of responsibility and integrity, persons of moral character who are capable of making wise judgments about what is right and wrong; beautiful and ugly, appropriate and inappropriate, then, if we are correct above, dialogue becomes an inescapable instrument or means of education and the community of inquiry becomes a means and an end satisfying and worthwhile in itself, while at the same time giving rise to the traits essential for a morally discriminating person.

Education for democratic citizenship

. . . there is a justifiable and essential function of education that goes beyond preparing children for becoming law-abiding citizens, for pursuing happiness or for choosing vocations. Education ought also to provide children with the ability to conceive of and evaluate ways of life, and the political systems appropriate to them, other than those found within their own society or within any existing society. This educational goal is often based upon the view that knowledge should be pursued for its own sake, that is, for the sake of developing the intellect and its logical and imaginative capacities. . . . Knowledge of Rousseau and of Greek literature is surely not necessary to ensure social cohesion and is very unlikely to make children happier or more satisfied with their lives or even more productive and hence more useful to people in the future. However, education in literature, history, anthropology, and political philosophy (for example) does provide a type of freedom—freedom to think beyond the established forms of private and political life. Such knowledge is necessary in order both to appreciate fully and to criticize political systems and the choice ways of life we have inherited. One might therefore conclude that this knowledge is a prerequisite for being a good democratic citizen, but this is not the sort of knowledge upon which any existing democratic government is likely to depend for its (mere) survival.

—from Amy Gutmann, "What's the use of going to school?" in Amartya Sen and Bernard Williams (eds.), *Utilitarianism and Beyond* (Cambridge: Cambridge U. Press, 1982).

The community of inquiry requires not only perseverance and courage but all of the socratic virtues. It calls further for a commitment to stay with the group through its growth and change. It involves persons in a way of being-in-the-world aimed at struggling for understanding and self-knowledge by means of a process that is intersubjective. Further, the end products of such a community of inquiry are also intersubjective. However, in multiplying persons we do not simply multiply intelligences, experiences and perspectives. Rather we aim to produce practical knowledge in the exchange of perspectives, opinions, the sharing of experiences and the questioning of the assumptions of the beliefs that we do hold. Note that this is very unlike the working out of an argument. It is more akin to the playing of a quartet in which each instrument has an important role to perform in the production of the music. And, in all likelihood, there will be many quartets and many pieces of music played with integrity and beauty. The ideal of one universal community of inquiry embracing all of mankind is highly unlikely.[12] But this in no way invalidates the vision of many communities in which there is genuine inquiry, genuine participation of all human beings (rather than just white Western men) with open communication between the various groups.[13]

Thus, the community of inquiry constitutes a *praxis*—reflective communal action—a way of acting on the world. It is a means of personal and moral transformation that inevitably leads to a shift in meanings and values which affect the daily judgements and actions of all participants. One striking characteristic of a community of inquiry over time is that its members change. In time, they will be capable of saying to themselves such things as:

I find I'm no longer bullied into accepting views that lead to consequences that I think are harmful.

I think I've always thought that way, but now I can explain why I think that way.

I am no longer in need of pretending what I feel or what I think.

My taste in many things is changing.

I'm beginning to realize what patterns of behavior make more sense in my daily life.

I can change my mind about matters of importance.

What other people say can make a difference in what I think.

I'm beginning to understand how very little I really know.

One can explain such claims as a slow progressive release from subjectivism, intellectual and social isolation, finding the world an alien and confusing place into discovering what it is to participate in a community of inquiry that enables one to live actively, reasonably and responsibly in the world rather than merely accepting it, escaping it or ignoring it. It's as if the process itself of participating in such a community becomes a sense-finding enterprise. Participants discover the moral guidelines they want to live by and the moral virtues they want to exemplify in their daily lives. They gain practice in making discriminating; sensitive and appropriate moral judgements. In a real sense they, at one and the same time, discover and create themselves as they inquire together—they discover and create the persons they think they ought to be.

Lastly, the commitment to engage in a community of inquiry is a *political* commitment even at the elementary school level. In a real sense, it is a commitment to freedom, open debate, pluralism, self government and democracy. Practical reason, reflective inquiry and practical judgement reflected in communal political *praxis* presupposes that the people in the society have a sense of communal dialogue and inquiry and a facility with the skills of such inquiry. It is only to the extent that individuals have had the experience of dialoguing with others as equals, participating in shared, public inquiry that they will be able to eventually take an active role in the shaping of a democratic society. Shared under-

standings and experiences, intersubjective daily practices, a sense of affinity and solidarity, together with all the tacit affective ties that bind people together in a community are a precondition of communal reflection action in the political sphere.[14]

Thus, in answer to the question, "How can we further the type of community participation, dialogue, inquiry and mutual recognition and respect that is presupposed in political communities?" one can propose the conversion of educational classrooms into communities of inquiry beginning with kindergarten and extending such a conversion right through graduate school experience. It is only in this way that the next generation will be prepared socially and cognitively to engage in the necessary dialogue, judging and on-going questioning that is vital to the existence of a democratic society and the maintenance of the planet earth and survival of the species. In these times when the threat of nuclear extinction and ecological disaster is so very real, it is all the more crucial to try to foster and nurture classroom communities of inquiry at the elementary school level and throughout the educational experience so that the next generation will be able to act in such a way that the human community will not only continue to exist, but to exist in a more reasonable and just manner. Such a conversion of the educational institutional structure moves us beyond arguments and beyond theories into the realm of concrete actions aimed at changing the world for the better.

Footnotes

1. Hannah Arendt. "Crisis in Culture: Its Social and Political Significance" in *Between Past and Future* (NY Viking Press, 1961) p. 197-226. Arendt goes on to say "that the ability to judge is a specifically political ability in exactly the sense denoted by Kant, namely, the ability to see things not only from one's own point of view but in the perspective of all those who happen to be present: even they judgment may be one of the fundamental abilities of man as a political being insofar as it enables him to orient himself in the public realm, in the common

world" See also. Richard Bernstein. "Judging the Actor and the Spectator," in *Proceedings of History Ethics, Politics: A Conference based on the work of Hannah Arendt,* ed. Robert Boyers Saratoga Springs, New York: Empire State, 1982.) Also see Michael Dennery, *The Privilege of Ourselves: Hannah Arendt on Judgment, Ibid.* p. 245-274 and Hannah Arendt, *The Life of the Mind* (NY H.B. Jovanovich, 1978) Volume I and II.

2. This communal civic sense is what John Dewey calls *taste*. See *The Quest For Certainty,* (New York: Minton, Balch, 1929.) p. 262. Also for a development of the same idea see John Dewey, *Art as Experience*. In *Quest For Certainty,* Dewey says:

The word "taste" has perhaps got too completely associated with arbitrary liking to express the nature of judgments of value. But if the word be used in the sense of an appreciation at once cultivated and active, one may say that the formation of taste is the chief matter wherever values enter in, whether intellectual, esthetic or moral. Relatively immediate judgments, which we call tact or to which we give the name intuition, do not preclude reflective inquiry, but are the funded products of much thoughtful experience. Expertness of taste is at once the result and the reward of constant exercise of thinking. Instead of there being no disputing about tastes, they are the one thing worth disputing about, if by "dispute" is signified discussion involving reflective inquiry. Taste, if we use the word in its best sense, is the outcome of experience brought cumulatively to bear on the intelligent appreciation of the real worth of likings and enjoyments. There is nothing in which a person so completely reveals himself as in the things which he *judges* enjoyable and desirable. Such judgments are the sole alternative to the domination of belief by impulse, chance, blind habit and self-interest. The formation of a cultivated and effectively operative good judgment or taste with respect to what is esthetically admirable, intellectually acceptable and morally approvable is the supreme task set to human beings by the incidents of experience.

3. Richard Rorty, *Consequences of Pragmatism.* (Minneapolis: University of Minnesota Press, 1982) pp. xii-xxxix.

4. I am indebted to Monica Velasca from Guadalajara, Mexico for innumerable cornments on the importance of care in the community of inquiry contained in her various papers submitted as a requirement for the degree of Masters of Art in Teaching Philosophy for Children, Fall and Spring, 1988-89. For a philosophical analysis of the status of Being-As-Care, see Martin Heidegger, *Being and Time,* New York: Harper and Row 1962, pp. 235-241. And for a psychological analysis of the importance of care in the cultivation of trust autonomy and self esteem, see Erik Erikson, *Childhood and Society* and *Insight and Responsibility.*

5. Maatin Buber, *Between Man and Man* (New York: Macmillan, 1947). In this volume one can find two essays, one on "Education" and the other on "The Educa-

tion of Character." Both speak to the role of dialogue in education.

6. Martin Buber. *I and Thou.* (New York: Scribners, 1970) Part I.

7. Here I am indebted to Matthew Lipman, "Critical Thinking: What Can Be?" *Educational Leadership* September, 1988. Matthew Lipman's definition of critical thinking is thinking that is self correcting sensitive to context, and relies upon criteria to facilitate judgment.

8. James Heinegg; "The Individual and the Community of Inquiry," ms. submitted as requirement for the degree of Master of Arts in Teaching Philosophy for Children at Montclair State College, Fall of 1988.

9. Martin Buber. *I and Thou.* Buber says, "The present exists only insofar as presentness, encounter and relation exist Only as the You becomes present does presence come into being." p. 63.

10. I am indebted to Ronald Reed, who pointed out to me that John Dewey, in "My Pedagogic Creed," talks about vitality in relation to informal education. One could argue that a good classroom dialogue is modelled on what one finds in an informal environment, conversations that deal with real problems and real concerns of the participants. Usually such discussions focus on real questions that the participants have a stake in getting it right. However, in the informal environment no one looks askance if one excuses oneself because one is no longer interested in talking. But the child in the classroom cannot do this. Once the child loses interest (if he ever had any) he tends to be condemned to play the spectator role. Dewey's point is that active participation and involvement in the discussion seems to go together with vitality and mere spectating seems to go together with dry sterility.

11. See Richard Rorty, *Philosophy and the Mirror of Nature.* (Minneapolis: University of Minnesota Press, 1982) last chapter. When I say that there is no ultimate philosophical foundation for our knowledge, I am relying here on Rorty, in particular. For the argument of reason as a regulative ideal, see Hilary Putnam, "Why Reason can't be Naturalized," in *Synthese* 52 (1982) 1-23 for an argument against complete relativism, and Alasdair MacIntyre "Relativism, Power and Philosophy" the Presidential Address delivered before the 81st Annual Eastern Division Meeting of the American Philosophical Association in New York, December 29, 1984 in *Proceedings and Addresses of the American Philosophical Association,* (Newark, Delaware: APA, 1985) pp. 5-22 and his postscript to the second edition of *After Virtue* (Notre Dame, Indiana: University of Notre Dame Press, 1984) pp 265-272. Also see MacIntyre's new work for extension of the argument, *Whose Justice? Which Rationality?* (Notre Dame Press, 1988) preface, pp. 1-11 and 370-388 (tradition and translation) and 389-403. Also see Richard Rorty, "The Contingency of Language," London Review of Books (April 17, 1986) p. 3 and Bernard Williams, *Ethics and the Limits of Philosophy,* (Cambridge: Harvard University Press, 1985).

Also see Richard Bernstein, *Beyond Objectivism and Relativism* (Philadelphia, University of Pennsylvania Press, 1983).

In my previous article, "What is a Community of Inquiry?" *Journal of Moral Education* 16, 1, (1987) pp. 37-45, I argued that the community of inquiry is not condemned to relativism and endless self-correction, that some progress can be made and that the concepts of truth and justification cannot be reduced to the conceptual scheme of the tradition. Rorty thinks that all we have is the dialogue itself, the endless conversation spoken within the philosophical tradition. Further, he and others think the dialogue in connection with the establishment of local communities is sufficient to make the world more reasonable. Other philosophers, like Hilary Putnum, Habermas and Alasdaire MacIntyre, disagree. Putnum argues that the very fact that we can speak of our different conceptions as different conceptions of rationality posits truth, the very fact that we can agree that some thinkers in the past have been wrong-headed, presupposes that reason can serve as a regulative ideal. See *Reason, Truth and History* pp. 163-216. and Nelson Goodman, "The Trouble with Truth," in *Ways of Worldmaking* (Indianapolis, Indiana: Hacket Company, 1985) chapter 2.

In the present paper, I argue that dialogical thinking and speaking takes courage, letting the truth emerge even if it forces one to reconstruct one's own cherished beliefs. (When I use the word "truth," I mean "warranted assertion," Dewey's term.) No one captures this idea of the necessary courage more than Alisdaire McIntyre in his APA presidential address (1984):

What can liberate rationality is precisely an acknowledgement only possible from within a certain kind of tradition, that rationality requires a *readiness* on our part to accept, and indeed to welcome, a possible future defeat of the forms of theory and practice in which it has up till now been taken to be embodied within our own tradition, at the hands of some alien and perhaps even as yet largely unintelligible tradition of thought and practice; and this is an acknowledgement of which the traditions that we inherit have too seldom been capable.

It is just this disposition of "readiness" that the community of inquiry cultivates in the young child.

12. Alasdair MacIntyre. *After Virtue.* "What matters at this stage is the construction of local forms of community within which civility and the intellectual and moral life can be sustained." p. 244.

13. Here see the works of Gadamer and Habermas on communication and the need for community. In particular, Gadamer's autobiographical sketch, *Philosophische Lehrjahre* (Frankfurt am Main: Vittoria Klostermann, 1977) and Habermas, "Dialectics of Rationalization: An Interview," *Telos* 49 (1981): 7. "A Reply to My critics," in *Habermas: Critical Debates*, John EL Thompson and David Held (Cambridge, Mass.: M.I.T. Press, 1982) pp. 263-269. *Communication and the Evolution of Society.* Also see Gadamer, *Truth and Method* (New York: Seabury Press, 1975) p. 306-310, and 278-89 and for a treatment of practical judgment, "Problem of Historical Consciousness, in Interpretive Social Science: a Reader ed. Paul Rabinow and William M. Sullivan (Berkeley, CA: University of California Press, 1979) pp 120-30.

I am also indebted to a paper, "Community of Inquiry," by Marcello Marer, from Sal Paulo, Brazil, submitted in requirement for the Masters Degree in Philosophy for Children, Montclair State College, Spring 1989. In this paper, Marer tries to show the Peircean foundations of the concept, "community of inquiry," and the way in which the theory of Habermas plays an important role in the theoretical foundations of the concept, "community of inquiry," as it is used in Philosophy for Children.

14. See Richard Bernstein, *Beyond Objectivism and Relativism: Science, Hermeneutics and Praxis*, (Philadelphia: University of Pennsylvania Press, 1983) pp. 171-231. In this section, Bernstein discusses *Praxis* and practical discourse as seen in the works of Rorty, Gadamer, Habermas and Hannah Arendt.

Philosophy and the Education of the Community

Robert J. Mulvaney

Among the questionable legacies of ancient Greek thought, particularly Platonism, to the history of Western philosophy, are some psychological and sociological positions which may be summed up under the word "elitism." Philosophy is an elite enterprise. Only a few have the favored leisure and intellectual capacity to pursue it. Most are too stupid and they have to work besides. This elitism takes at least three forms, three separate kinds of idolatry, or perhaps of subidolatry under Francis Bacon's general idols of the theatre. These are the cults of old age, of the expert, and of the individual. Philosophers cannot be young, they cannot be amateurs, and they cannot come in flocks or committees. Wisdom and its pursuit are a function of mature and solitary professionals, usually invested with an aura of unique genius.

Nor is this merely a descriptive generalization. Philosophy has political payoff, and only a few should have the knowledge which supports power. The many should have true beliefs only, which means they should obey and be led. In the pursuit of this norm, formal schooling plays a central role. Philosophy is to be exclusively the domain of an elitist institution within the general educational program. In practical terms this institutional embodiment of philosophical activity is (or at least used to be) the university, where philosophy defined the chief tasks, the degrees awarded, the gateway to further professional certification, and the hegemony over subordinate educational institutions. While things have somewhat altered in the past century or so, and whereas philosophy now identifies a micro-elite within the larger higher-education elite, it is still perceived by many as the core discipline of higher education, the aristocratic preserve of a very few Brahmins of learning. It follows a vast schooling, at least twelve years of it, during which most people have been systematically removed or have abandoned the enterprise in despair. The university discovers, develops and rewards a small minority of highly qualified, well-trained and lucky individuals. In this program, an elitist conception of wisdom and its pursuit has become its chief intellectual defense.

If this analysis seems excessively grim, let me immediately admit the existence of a large number of impressive counterexamples. Even in our antique era, we find philosophy occasionally extended to all men, sometimes with a certain urgency. Consider Epicurus:

> Let no one when young delay to study philosophy, nor when he is old grow weary of his study. For no one can come too early or too late to secure the health of his soul. And the man who says that the age for philosophy has either not yet come or has gone by is like the man who says that the age for happiness has not yet come or has passed away. Wherefore both when young and when old a person should study philosophy . . .[1]

This is philosophy in its practical mode, of course, and not the arcane theorizing of the metaphysician or epistemologist. It is also difficult to determine just how widely Epicurus would cast his net. Still his statement can constitute a genuinely universal invitation to pursue the philosophical life, and I am willing to consider it characteristic of an anti-elitist strain in a dominantly elitist history, one particularly counter to the cult of old age.

Similarly, Socrates represents for us the great amateur, in that term's etymological as well as in its ordinary sense. He loves wisdom, but seems content to show his affection in non-institutional, non-systematic and non-specialist ways. We like to think he has more questions than answers. He founded no school, wrote no books, and yet bears the epithet, "The Teacher of the West." He is the great armchair philosopher, the thoughtful philosophical journalist and contributor to the New York Times op-ed page. We joke that he would probably not have received tenure in a modern university, but perhaps Plato, the generous and loyal student, would have awarded him an honorary degree "in recognition of his life experiences." As Epicurus invited the young, Socrates invites the thinking man, to the philosophical banquet.

Finally, even grave Plato who had the answers, who set up the school with its entrance requirements inscribed over the main door, and who wrote the books, preserves for us in his dialogues a communitarian ideal. Philosophy ought to be done in cordial concert, by honest and truthful men who respect and trust one another, who are willing to learn from each other, who have the humility to recognize the insufficiency of their private intellectual lives, and who see the best philosophical activity in shared inquiry and dialogue. However Plato may represent the single most powerful spokesman for the elitism so characteristic of Western thought, even he, almost unwittingly, offers us the model of an alternative in his explicit rhetoric of serious, free conversation.

But these are countertendencies only, and the main direction of our history seems otherwise. It is only in the past 250 years or so that the story has begun to change in any important way. The rise of democratic experiments in political life, the insistence upon free inquiry in scientific investigation, the end of slavery, the emergence of the woman in public life, the extension of popular education, the growth of a cosmopolitan ideal of political association, and perhaps most importantly for our story what we may call the discovery of the child, seem to indicate radical departures from the classic ideal.

The philosophy for children program is one recent instance of this new direction in philosophy and its political and social infrastructure. The extension of philosophy into the earliest grades of formal schooling is directly antithetical to the habitual restriction of such study to late adolescence and adulthood. Immediately entailed by this democratization of philosophical inquiry is its deprofessionalization. Philosophy for children is of necessity free from technical apparatus, since its student body involves a very unsophisticated linguistic community. Finally, in its implementation, philosophy for children focuses on the dialoguing community, rather than on the silent and atomic individual. At every level this broadening of the philosophical community constitutes a body blow against traditional philosophical elitism. We have included the young in a project that has until now been closed to them. The statistics are being altered and the sociology of philosophical instruction is gaining a new chapter. The three idols mentioned earlier, the idols of old age, the expert and the individual are under new siege. Let me address these once again, this time more directly in terms of the philosophy for children program.

The association of philosophy with great age, or at least with maturity, is an ancient theme in Western thought. The sage is almost always represented iconographically as an old man, seldom young, and never a woman. Consider Raphael's famous depiction of Plato in his painting of the

Academy. This association of wisdom with age is part of a much larger tendency, exemplified so forcefully in Aristotle's *Ethics*, to exclude human excellence or virtue from the domain of childhood altogether. No child can be virtuous, because no child is truly human. But wisdom is a virtue. Therefore, no child can be wise. Thus may we paraphrase Aristotle's syllogism.[2] This inclination to demean childhood received an unusually barbarous twist among some Christians who claimed that unbaptized children suffered the pains of hell if they died.[3] Childhood is uniformly seen as an imperfect form of humanity, consequently as having its sole value as tending towards the goal of adulthood. Philippe Ariès has shown how, during the Renaissance, the child, even in his modes of dress, was considered a micro-adult, an organism whose whole reality was nothing more than process, the change of formless matter into the true substance of adulthood.[4] Conformably with this view of the child, educational theory tends to take the form of a discourse on the goals or aims of education, that set of intellectual, moral and practical values that defines the adult world. Where specifically childlike activities are mentioned at all, such as play, they are seen as having merely instrumental value, efficient means to the production of adult dispositions.

The "discovery of the child" does not much antedate the eighteenth century. Rousseau is perhaps its great prophet. It was he who discovered stages of development with the attendant conviction that children are fully complete human beings at each stage, provided their natural inclinations and freedom to grow are given appropriate means of expression. Nothing quite like this is anticipated in ancient thought. Plato's division of knowledge and the curriculum dependent upon it is dictated by his peculiar metaphysics and not by a psychology of growth. But Rousseau belongs to a new age, one in which history is beginning to overtake timeless ontology, and one in which biography and psychological analysis are replacing generalized theories of human nature. His age is the age of the individual existing in time, not of the species subsisting *sub specie aeternitatis*. This discovery of the child evolved itself into the child-centeredness of 19th-century educational theory, and indeed reached a level of somewhat comical exaggeration in the highly Romantic notions of childhood entertained from Wordsworth to Froebel. The details of this development are beyond the scope of this paper. But even such hyperbole produced much of lasting value, especially in the realm of early childhood education. The kindergarten is a nineteenth-century invention. Even Dr. Spock's manual of child-rearing is inconceivable without this long story of reverse discrimination.

Philosophy for children finds itself between the Scylla of classical geronto-centrism and the Charybdis of Romantic paidolatry.[5] On the one hand, the "wise child" and "father of the man" are myths. Children are not born with the wisdom of ages somehow innately programmed into them, and then forgotten or forced into the unconscious by the circumstances of early training or environment. Nor are they, on the other hand, species of some intractable *tabula rasa*, mysteriously dormant until some magic age when their mental responses come to be triggered. Rather they are open, questioning, wondering, curious, growing human beings having original dispositions to philosophical thought which can be cultivated like other intellectual dispositions, or allowed to atrophy. Similarly, insofar as philosophy is characterized as the search for happiness, it should be obvious that children seek it as much as adults do, and that their affective inclinations can be developed as much as their cognitive ones. Here again Aristotle presents us with a wonderfully instructive, if ultimately negative, alternative. With admirable consistency he denies that children can be happy. Amorphously cognitive they are likewise inchoately affective, possible content like sleeping dogs, but not happy in any important human sense.[6] Philosophy for children holds that children are more like people than they are like animals and that the search for happiness belongs as much to them as it does to adults. Curiosity and the need to be happy constitute the twin psychological spurs to the philosophical life, and they are not foreign to the young child.

Philosophy for children also challenges the cult of the expert. In an age of increasingly specialized knowledge, the claims of the narrow professional are accepted as utterly authoritative. The generalist, now more than ever, is lumped together with the dilettante. Neither deserves a serious hearing. The weight of our philosophical tradition, moreover, supports the cultivation of expert knowledge. It is a commonplace that the philosophical life requires a rich and broad experience, and that only those with extensive theoretical and practical knowledge can be much good at it. It may be argued that it is precisely this lack of experience that makes children poor candidates for the philosophical life. But perhaps we should draw another inference, and reclaim the rights of the unexperienced and the unprofessional. A remark Whitehead made about the university can be usefully applied here. He wrote: "The justification for a university is that it preserves the connection between knowledge and the zest of life, by uniting the young and the old in the imaginative consideration of learning."[7] What children bring to the philosophical enterprise is what the untrained undergraduate brings to the university, this zest of life and the fresh imagination that so often accompanies it. Children bring to philosophy the shock of the new, a tremendous instinct for the play element in the life of the mind, and a toleration of ambiguity frequently far greater than that of their teachers. They are long on the open-textured, dialogical and problematic aspects of philosophical thinking, short on the systematic, tidy, reflective, cautious and experiential aspects; long on intuition and brilliance, short on memory and the last word. They are the amateurs of philosophy, not its productive workers, not the intellectual laborers of professional philosophy. Philosophy has more to do in their minds with leisure, with a kind of scholastic recess period. Possibly this is one of

the reasons they discuss philosophy outside the classroom and bring it home with them, in a way they seldom bring home the work-like activities of the rest of the curriculum.

It is the rare philosopher who can easily recall the high excitement and delight of his earliest learning experiences. Simple growth, the force of institutional schooling, the accumulation of experience, all of these enfeeble the imagination in most of us. "The tragedy of the world," writes Whitehead in the same passage cited above from his great essay on universities, "is that those who are imaginative have but slight experience, and those who are experienced have feeble imaginations."[8] But the tragedy is real only where philosophy is exclusively the domain of the professional, or exclusively the domain of the amateur. What if the proper subject is the philosophizing community, rather than any single almighty individual? This is the final myth challenged by programs such as philosophy for children: the myth of the heroic individual. Philosophers, the myth runs, are solitary heroes of the mind, and heroes do not come in crowds. Again there is much to be said for this perception of the philosophical profile. Individuality is insistent and irreducible. I am I and no other. The metaphysics of monadic individualism seems rooted in some kind of common sense. "Know thyself" is expressed in the singular, not the plural, number. Philosophy ought to be reflective and the reflective life needs silence and solitude. Finally, and most profoundly, the production of a higher form of individuality is the paradoxical aim of sound schooling and of sound philosophizing too.

But it is easy for self-existence to slide into solipsistic self-sufficiency. At this point the dialogical mode of the philosophical act provides a powerful corrective. The philosophy for children program capitalizes upon the young child's sociability, and builds into it the habit of serious conversation. It takes as its starting-point the position that philosophy is a community experience, not a disguised monologue. Its task is the building of a community of inquiry. This shared growth in a common wisdom is the theme and tone of the public school, but also the living principle of the Socratic dialogue. The incompleteness of an individual's knowledge becomes the rationale for incorporating him within a body of likewise incomplete individuals. It is a wise society, rather than a wise man, that is its immediate goal. But, in the process, a higher individual must emerge, one less closed to the rich experience of others, less unsympathetic, less atomistic, an individual who reflects the perceptions of others linked with him in a common project, and defines that reflection from a new and unique perspective.

The introduction of philosophy into the pre-collegiate curriculum is nothing more than an extension of the concept of continuity so dear to American democratic educational theorists. It is an enlargement of the "spiral" that John Dewey claimed was the most appropriate metaphor for developmental theories of learning.[9] It is a further dimension of Jerome Bruner's bold claim that, "any subject can be taught effectively in some intellectually honest form to any child at any stage of development."[10] It ought to have been part of Mortimer Adler's Paideia proposal, and its absence is a major weakness of that program. Interestingly, Adler dedicates his *The Paideia Program* to the memory of John Amos Comenius, the great 17th century educational theorist. And we may say that philosophy for children ought to have been part of Comenius's great project too, *pampaedia* as he called it, universal learning for the whole race of men, "learning *pantes, panta, pantos* (for all men, about all things, in all ways)."[11] "All men" should include children; "all things" should include philosophy; "in all ways" should include our earliest schooling.

The concept of continuity, again, is the complex bedrock notion here, a continuity defined in classic neo-Platonic fashion as identity-in-diversity and unity-in-multiplicity. Continuity is not bland and homogeneous sameness, not monistic and undifferentiated unity, not mere identity

through time. Nor is it merely a spatial or temporal juxtaposition or conjunction of radically dissimilar atoms of experience, mysteriously connected. Continuity implies internal union or harmonious unification of experience, the elements of which may be logically or analytically distinguishable, but not really or metaphysically separable. The metaphor of music is as usual instructive. The simultaneous sounding of discrete tones produces in the triad a new sound, one only reducible to its elements by destroying the order that makes it uniquely itself. Continuity in development suggests that our powers of mind and will do not magically appear on the scene at some arbitrary moment of biological maturity, but that they are foreshadowed or anticipated in some rudimentary or seminal fashion in our earliest learning experiences. The true encyclopedia recommended by Plato to the learning of his future philosopher-ruler is not simply a circle of learning, closed and perfect. It is rather an "enspeirapedia," spiralling ever upwards, in a progress that may be limited only by death. And since, even in Plato, every person is a city within a city, and shares in his own polity some measure of the ruler's wisdom, philosophy ought to be available to all, continuous with their earliest learning. Democracy is a universalized aristocracy. The extension of a properly aristocratic education to all members of the community is its high ideal. Philosophy for children is a step in the realization of that ideal.

This is not meant to be the introduction to a tourbook for some philosophical Disneyland. And some tempering of enthusiasm is called for. Philosophy for children has its pitfalls. For one thing philosophy in its fullness remains an adult enterprise, and caution must be taken that the problems of adults not be transferred to children ill-prepared to deal with them. Some psychologists have argued that the modern child has been deprived of his childhood by premature exposure to the adult world.[12] Philosophy for children can be another instance of this ill-timed disillusionment. Secondly what we may call the "lord of the flies" factor is not without its grain of truth. Young children need training more than argument. The beginnings of virtue lie in habituation, wise Aristotle taught.[13] "Shut up, he explained," is frequently the appropriate conclusion to disputation. But, to the loss of childhood objection, children raise philosophical questions themselves, and it will not do to tell them they shouldn't, as a parent told a sixth-grader I know. And to the second point, children have instincts to fairness and to generosity, as well as to the self and survival. It is training in moral matters that may be of the first importance, but children can begin the rational examination of their own egoism long before their moral education is complete. The point remains that, if we want critical thinking in our adult population, we cannot prepare for it by twelve years of passive, doctrinaire and rote learning. Some preliminary attention to the range of issues understood as philosophical is necessary from grade one.

Philosophy for children, then, whatever problematic features it may present, has an overwhelmingly persuasive logic on its side. Few educational programs in recent memory are so clearly consonant with the main egalitarian tendencies of democratic educational theory and institutions. It challenges exclusiveness in all its forms, and demands the search for what is truly excellent in each individual, rather than for the excellent individual in each group. It challenges us to learn from the young, as well as to teach them, in those very areas of the art of living where adults have traditionally claimed expertise. It challenges us finally to accept as partners in a common quest for wisdom the weakest, the most dependent, the youngest members of the living human community. There are doubtless many other idols to be cast down. Let me mention one in closing. I have hinted at it earlier: the idol of the male. It is my suspicion that philosophy for children has the best chance of liberating woman's mind in truly radical and creative ways. "Woman must write woman."[14] Woman must also think woman, philosophize woman. But it is for this very reason that I only mention this theme. It is another member of the inquiring community who must address herself to it.

NOTES

1. Epicurus, *Letter to Menoecoeus.*
2. Nicomachean Ethics 1, 3; VI, 8.
3. Cf. D.P. Walker, *The Decline of Hell* (Chicago, 1964), pp. 35-40.
4. Philippe Ariès, *Centuries of Childhood* (New York, 1962.)
5. The term is George Boas's. See his *The Cult of Childhood* (London, 1966), p. 20.
6. *Nicomachean Ethics*, I, 9.
7. Alfred North Whitehead, "Universities and their Function" in *The Aims of Education* (New York, 1967), p. 93.
8. *Ibid.*
9. John Dewey, *Experience and Education* (New York, 1939), p. 97.
10. Jerome Bruner, *The Process of Education* (New York, 1960), p. 33.
11. *John Amos Comenius on Education*, intro. by Jean Piaget (New York, 1967), p. 116.
12. See, for example, Marie Winn, *Children without Childhood* (New York, 1981).
13. *Nicomachean Ethics*, II, 1.
14. Hélène Cixous, "The Laugh of the Medusa," in *New French Feminisms*, edited by Elaine Marks and Isabelle de Courtivron (New York, 1981), p. 247.

The Community of Inquiry and Educational Structure

David Kennedy

In a recent issue of *Thinking*, A.T. Lardner takes up an issue which has had a quiet life for several years now, but has never, to my knowledge, been brought squarely before the community of practitioners of philosophy for children. I am speaking of student resistance to the program, expressed in boredom, impatience, and sometimes even rejection.[1] As Lardner's brief, clear article implies, there is undoubtedly a whole tissue of explanation possible, from psychological resistance on the part of individuals, to poor or shaky discussion leadership skills, to the wrong time of day, to larger social effects, for example, a culture that teaches individualism, instrumentalism, and competition, and saturates us with the message that being reflective can be socially and even economically dangerous.

My theory is that, in addition to a lot of reasons like the ones just cited, the problem has to do with the way schools and classrooms are structured, which in turn is the result of an overall educational model. Lardner does take this up briefly, in referring to several aspects of "normal" educational environments which he thinks leads to the rejection of philosophy for children. He speaks of "goal and/or product based experience:" and the split that develops between in and out of school experience, whereby students learn to "survive within the framework of school by doing only what is necessary."[2] I want to look, not so much at the educational model which results in this kind

of school experience—I think that we're all aware of the profound failures of what Lipman has referred to as "tribal" or "information-acquisition" education. In fact, he has said right out: "The doing of philosophy requires conversation, dialogue, and community, which are not compatible with the requirements of the traditional classroom."[3] Rather, I want to argue that there is a "new" educational model—in fact it is already about 200 years old—and that it has the structural characteristics which provide place for what Lipman refers to as "participatory, collaborative community."[4] This paper is about that model, and about how it provides a place for conversation, dialogue and community.

First, I need to point out a few of my primary assumptions. One of them is that there is a correlation between the structures of educational environments and forms of educational discourse. If the larger, structural configurations of an educational environment are not reasonable—*i.e.*, are based on domination, hierarchy, and self perpetuating goals and processes which are rigid and unreflective—then neither much of the behavior nor the language events in that environment will be reasonable either.

A second, related assumption, is that although in certain heroic and exemplary cases, discourse transforms structure, in the vast number of cases, structure determines discourse.[5] This is an important assumption, because it challenges what I understand to be one of the implicit assumptions of philosophy for children, which is that the discourse of the program is capable of eventually changing the model to a collaborative and participatory one. Most of us, I think, carry the hope, if not the faith, that the setting up of communities of inquiry within the traditional classroom will eventually transform that classroom in their own image. But my assumption suggests that this is improbable if not impossible, because the structural model logically and psychologically precedes the discourse that the model generates. The present form of schooling with its rigid hierarchies, its one-way environments, its lockstep curricula, its insensitivity to developmental differences and differences in learning style, and so on, does not make a place for the form of discourse called the community of inquiry. The latter always lives on borrowed time in the traditional model.

The implication of this is that in order to be successful, philosophy for children must be in the business, not only of generating a form of discourse, but of generating the larger educational structures for that form of discourse. In fact, Lipman himself has called for what, in contrast to the "tribal" he calls the "reflective" model of education, which, instead of providing for "the assimilation of the child by the culture," provides for "the appropriation of the culture by the child." But he seems to assume that this is a form of discourse which can happen anywhere, that it is simply a question of the kinds of texts one uses, curricular sequencing and interweaving, teacher behaviors like "encouraging original thinking and at the same time encouraging students to find the errors in their thinking,"[6] etc. Those are all necessary to a new model, it is true, but are surface, rather than deep structural elements. The deep structural elements of any educational model have to do with fundamental guiding beliefs about the nature of human beings, of childhood, and of human development, and about the goals and processes of any human community, including the community called school.

What I would like to offer now are some indications of the deep structure of a model which would provide a home, a place, for the community of inquiry and its form of discourse. Historically, the model I am describing is connected with early childhood education. Froebel, inspired by Rousseau and Pestalozzi, was its first great exponent and it has been enriched by theorists and practitioners alike since he founded the Kindergarten in the 1830's. It formed the foundation for the progressive education movement of the first three decades of this century, during which period it was both adopted and profoundly influenced by Dewey, who was a close reader of Froebel, and whose laboratory school at Chicago, if it would still seem alien to public educators today, would not lift an eyebrow in early childhood circles. Although the model failed then, and in another attempt in the late 1960's and early 1970's, to establish itself in public educational circles, it has never been seriously challenged in the field of early childhood education and has a rich, constantly evolving, theoretical and practical life there. I will describe the model in terms of five broad, deep-structural characteristics, which, in my understanding, distinguish it in a radical way from the traditional model. My claim is that those characteristics are the very ones which also provide the structural home for the community of inquiry.

The New Model

First, it is *developmental*. Whereas, the old model assumes that education implies forcible, violent change, something done to children against their will, the new one assumes that the human drive for self-organization, greater articulation, greater both differentiation and integration of function, is inherent. For the developmental model, the child is not a deficit, a not-child which must be made into a child; rather, as Froebel said, ". . . adult man has not become an adult man by reaching a certain age, but only by faithfully satisfying the requirements of his childhood, boyhood, and youth."[7] If this is the case, then those requirements must become the determinative conditions for our school environments and our curricula. This means, for one thing, a new epistemological and pedagogical pluralism, since we can assume that those different "requirements" imply different kinds of knowing, and therefore a variety of different learning and teaching styles, formats, and material bases. For another, it means a new dependence on allowing and following children's own initiatives, whereby the child becomes a main actor in her own education, and the teacher is a collaborative partner in the child's project.

Second, the new model is *environmental*. The old model makes of the classroom a machine—a specialized, customized, product-oriented system, where transmission of information and practice of isolated skills by isolated individuals is the rule. Because these are its purposes, it is stripped down, it is a deprivation environment, it aspires to be a completely neutral space, so as not to get in the way of the information being delivered. The blanker, the more rigid, the less inviting, the less interactive the better, since the information coming from the adult at the front of the room, or from the book, is what is important.

The new model conceives the classroom as a human and material landscape, an enriched world, a place for relatively free movement, choice, and initiative. Although it is an open setting, it is also what Montessori called a "prepared environment:" safe and protective, it is scaled with children in mind, it is aesthetically pleasing, it has a definite order, and calls out to the child to explore and interact with it. Therefore, materials—all kinds of materials, not just books—are organized and displayed within plain view and easy reach of the children. This is a setting which children can change through their activity, *i.e.*, on which they can have an effect, and for which they must take responsibility as a community. This is Dewey's microcosm, the little world which, rather than being isolated from

the world, provides a world of action analogous to the big one; a responsive environment, which reacts to the child's act, either to accommodate or resist, or encourage transformation.

Third, whereas the old model assumes invariant, relatively discontinuous cognitive, affective, and social stages which are consistent across all domains, as well as a unitary form of intelligence, measurable by standardized tests, the new model is *individualized*, since it assumes what Piaget called "horizontal decalage," *i.e.*, different levels of development in different domains within the same individual. The assumptions of the old model lead logically to age-graded classrooms, and a standardized work model, based on models of industrial production. The new model assumes individual differences in rate, and even sequence, of development among children of the same age, as well as differences in learning style, and even kinds of intelligence. This entails multi-age grouping, and the development of curricula for individuals and small as well as large groups. It also entails the prepared environment in order that activities and projects are not all dispensed and initiated by teachers, but a multiplicity of potential activities are available to children, in the form of concrete materials, *e.g.*, blocks, woodworking materials, art and music materials, props and facilities for drama, computers, a variety of educational games, etc. The child or children interact with the materials, and with the teacher as a third pole of the relation.

Fourth, the new model is *interactive*. It assumes that only through a varied multiplicity of transactions—between individual and environment, between individuals, and between individuals and groups—will individual and collective growth occur. It assumes, with Piaget that learning takes place through a dialectical process of assimilating experience to the rules and principles one has already internalized, and accommodating one's rules and principles to new experience. When the equilibrium between assimilation and accommodation becomes unstable enough, the structure changes, in the direction of more inclusive, articulated rules and principles. The new model builds curricula on the basis of the play of this process—which is a process evident in critical thinking as well, in which exceptions to rules force us to revise the rules to cover as many concrete instants as possible. The process calls for both interactive materials and interactive teaching. an environment rich with choices, and pedagogical strategies such as provision of ample time for free choice of projects and materials, small groups for diagnostic teaching of skills as well as interest groups, individualization of tasks, tutoring (cross-age and otherwise), frequent group discussion in order to build a sense of community, and collaborative decision making in group matters.

Finally, the new model is *dialogical*. Inasmuch as the old model decides what needs to be done to the child in order to turn her into an adult, and then does it, it proceeds by first identifying where the adult wants the child to be, then working backwards to where the child is; it has already decided about what the child will be, and applies its "educational technology" and "learning delivery systems" to the task. The new model, because it assumes that "the young human being . . . would seek, although still unconsciously, as a product of nature, yet decidedly and surely, that which is in itself best,"[8] receives its direction from the child himself. Dialogical education both speaks and listens. It assumes that the child has interests which have educational implications, and therefore seeks to discover what children are already doing, then design structures, activities, texts and materials which meet those forms of thought and action, both to satisfy them and to challenge them to transformation. Thus, dialogical curriculum is built on observation of and conversation with children's forms of life. In this model the teacher, rather than transmitter of knowledge, is observer, diagnostician, facilitator, nurturer, model (not to neglect gadfly and midwife), and the form of instruction is indirect, project-oriented, individualized, multi-sensory, active, mimetic.

The New Model and the Community of Inquiry

Now I would like to offer some reasons for claiming that the educational model whose characteristics I have just sketched is more conducive to the formation of the community of inquiry than the traditional model. First, when we compare the basic dynamics of such a classroom structure with those operating in the community of inquiry, we find, if not direct equivalents, certainly fruitful analogues. The community of inquiry is *developmental* in the traditional Wernerian sense of the orthogenetic principle, *i.e.*, that development proceeds from a state of "relative globality and lack of differentiation" to a state of "increasing differentiation, articulation, and hierarchic integration."[9] The developmental metaphor also describes the dialectical, self-correcting nature of the community of inquiry, which, if it is healthy, is in a process of continual clarification. Like developing persons, and like the little community of the classroom in the new model, the community of inquiry corrects itself through an equilibration process whereby it is continually losing its balance and regaining it on a higher level. The community of inquiry is also developmental in that it is epigenetic—*i.e.*, a new state is emerging from the earlier one which cannot emerge except the earlier one is there, but which is irreducible to the earlier one.

The community of inquiry is *environmental* because it represents an environment of discourse for each member, a whole context of thought and language which is internalized by the individual. As an environment of discourse, it embodies a multiplicity of perspectives which for the individual has the character of unity. Like the classroom environment, the "materials" of the community of inquiry—both what Lipman calls the "ageless concepts" (questions, really), and the technical moves through which the community of inquiry proceeds—are there for each individual to choose from and interact with. They form an environment upon which, through his self-initiated action, he can have an effect.

The community of inquiry is *individualized* because the internalization of dialogue by each individual happens at her particular response-level, and is mediated by the drive for meaning and the dialectical skill of each individual. A community of inquiry which does not provide a cognitive challenge for each individual roughly at her level is to that extent malfunctioning. When functioning well, the community of inquiry has something for everyone. And each individual listens and speaks from within her own "promixal zone of development."[10]

The community of inquiry is *dialogical* because it only proceeds through hearing and responding within the constraints of the speaker's formulation, which is altered in the response, and becomes a formulation which draws another response, and so on. In dialogue, each actor must commit himself to the emergence of truth from beyond himself, *i.e.*, from the community of which he is only a part. He recognizes that he is a moment in a larger pattern of emergence, a horizon of meaning which, as Robert Corrington says, "is more that the mere 'sum' of all horizons."[11] The community of inquiry is not just cognitively, but also socially dialogical, in that each individual knows himself through his transformative interaction with the community. I am not just "me" in the community of inquiry, but me in the context of the horizon of meaning, and this means a great deal to the character of my self-knowledge.

The community of inquiry is *interactive* in that its very *modus operandi* is the interaction of persons—individual with individual and individual with group—and of concepts in the governing interest of the dialectical emergence of new wholes, new forms of understanding, It simply cannot be thought apart from interaction, for no statement has significance in the community of inquiry until it has called forth (activated) a response.

Is the Community of Inquiry Possible in the Traditional Classroom?

Given these analogical relationships between the community of inquiry and the new model of schooling, does that constitute an argument for the new model as the best setting for the formation of the community of inquiry? I think that it does. Can the community of inquiry function within the old model? No and yes. No, because if a developmental, environmental, individualized, interactive, dialogical perspective is not present on other levels of school experience—in the physical environment, in the routine, in curriculum content and planning, in pedagogy, in group decision-making processes—then to try to introduce this perspective only in philosophy class is inconsistent, and it will be difficult for children to internalize the disposition of dialogue, much less the skills. The community of inquiry is, in other words, only one dimension of a larger process of community building. For the community of inquiry to form, there must be community forming in all domains of school life.

Yes, because wherever the community of inquiry actually forms, it will through its very operation work to transform its setting from a "transmission" to a "dialogical" model. But this is a weak yes, because if things are not moving in that direction in other domains of school life, either the classroom rejects the community of inquiry, or the community of inquiry bogs down. For if the community of inquiry assumes as its regulative principle the inherent drive for meaning, meaning can only be pursued and apprehended to the extent that the environment recognizes and encourages that drive. The traditional model in fact discourages that drive. The notion of thinking for oneself assumes the individual identification and assumption of meanings, rather than their passive acceptance. The individual identification of meanings assumes a relatively pluralistic, decentralized environment where freedom of choice, self-direction and dialogical, interactive pedagogy are normative. None of those things are characteristic of the traditional model.

The Role of Philosophy for Children in the New Model

Where the new educational model exists or is emerging, the operation of the community of inquiry in the philosophy for children program has the clear potential to become the central, paradigmatic discourse model underlying all levels of school life, both child and adult. It can shape pedagogy, planning, evaluation, conflict resolution, and management and organization in general. It can shape the approach to the disciplines: by approaching each content area from the point of view of the "philosophy of," a more synergistic, integrated curriculum will emerge. It is in philosophy class that the community of inquiry operates at its most unalloyed, but its patterns of discourse come to inform all the other functions of the new classroom, which operate in analogous ways. What it amounts to is a fulfillment of the recent educational mandate that critical thinking be built into all curricular areas.

It is only when philosophy for children has become a paradigm for, rather than a survivor in, its school environment, that we will no longer experience dissonance between the structure of the traditional classroom and the function of the community of inquiry. This dissonance often makes for a deep and subtle unease among both philosophy for children teachers and the children they are attempting to lead into a new form of discourse, and can lead to resistance to and rejection of the program. This is not to say that once this dissonance is removed other dissonances would not remain. The success of the formation of the community of inquiry is not guaranteed in or by any setting. Nor is it to say that the philosophy for children program does not need to continue to change and evolve in order to avoid student boredom and resistance. It is only to say that, if its form of discourse is not matched by a corresponding form of schooling, its chances of meeting its objectives are significantly reduced.

Notes

1. A.T. Lardner, "Student Resistance in Philosophy for Children," *Thinking* 9 (2): 13-15.
2. *Ibid*, p. 14.
3. Matthew Lipman, *Philosophy Goes to School* (Philadelphia: Temple University Press, 1988), pp, 19, 41.
4. *Ibid*,p. 42.
5. This, of course is because it is a form of discourse itself, reified in spatial, temporal, organizational, and goal structures. As such, it is hegemonic.
6. Lipman, *Philosophy Goes to School*, pp. 20, 25.
7. Friedrich Froebel, *The Education of Man* (Clifton, NJ: Augustus Kelley, 1974). p. 8
8. *Ibid*, p. 29.
9. Heinz Werner, "The Concept of Development from a Comparative and Organismic Point of View," in Dale B. Harris, ed., *The Concept of Development* (Minneapolis: University of Minnesota Press, 1957), p. 126.
10. L.S. Vygotsky, *Mind in Society* (Cambridge: Harvard University Press, 1978).
11 . Robert S. Corrington, *The Community of Interpreters* (Macon, GA: Mercer University Press, 1987), p. 103.

Community as Inquiry

Glenn Tinder

Inquiry is simply the effort to elucidate and harmonize the modes of consciousness. It is the effort to enter by this means into the presence of being itself. The integration of consciousness would dissipate all doubt and spell the end of estrangement. Inquiry aims at overcoming the fragmentation of consciousness without illegitimately distorting or suppressing any of its modes.

We inquire, however, in two different ways. We inquire *about*, and we inquire *with*; we inquire *about* various objects of inquiry, and we inquire *with* fellow inquirers. In the former way we seek theoretical or aesthetic contemplation; in the latter way community. Both are efforts to harmonize the modes of consciousness and overcome estrangement. Through one, however, the individual strives to integrate consciousness through solitary effort, whereas through the other a cooperative effort occurs. Consequently, we may refer to one as individualistic inquiry and to the other as dialogical inquiry. The latter, as we shall see, is in itself community.

We shall begin by considering individualistic inquiry. Or rather, we shall begin by considering inquiry as *though* it were individualistic. If the aims of inquiry are to be fulfilled, individualistic and dialogical inquiry must be joined; consciousness can be unified only through dialogue. Solitary and dialogical effort, reflection and communication, are merely aspects of a single activity.

In actuality, we persistently try to carry on this activity in a purely individualistic manner. This stems from a desire to avoid the humbling and dependent status implicit in dialogical inquiry. In pride, I try to master reality through my own independent mind. Only by overcoming pride, usually in response to necessities arising in the course of inquiry, do I recognize the inescapably dialogical character of inquiry—and thus prepare for entry into community. Here again, then, analytical order—considering inquiry first as though it were purely individualistic—corresponds with existential order.

What justifies the analytical order is that dialogical inquiry not only arises from individualistic inquiry but must retain an individualistic core: a sense of intellectual independence and responsibility on the part of each inquirer. Hence, to consider inquiry as though it were individualistic, and then to take account of the conditions that compel it to be dialogical, is an analytical convenience that does not distort the subject under examination.

The basic types of inquiry can be understood on the basis of, although not in strict correspondence with, the modes of consciousness.

Scientific Inquiry

Science is concerned with the invariable order implicit in experience. Hence it is directed toward relationships that are universal and are not identical with empirical relationships. Yet theories that have not been empirically validated, and are not implied by theories that have been, are unacceptable.

Historical Inquiry

Comprising not only history but also much that is presented as social science, historical inquiry is concerned with the actual order of experience. Its field is defined by experience and awareness together and thus includes not only all that falls within organized experience but also the particularities—the persons, the places, the events—that are not wholly reducible to universals.

Transcendental Inquiry

Picasso once said, "I never do a painting as a work of art. All of them are researches. I search constantly and there is a logical sequence in all this research."[1] This shows that inquiry can be carried on through art. Theological writing shows that it can be carried on through religion. Artistic and religious inquiry is transcendental in the sense of being concerned not with the world and its objects but with the ultimate being that transcends the world. Whereas scientific inquiry deals primarily with experience, transcendental inquiry relies on vision and faith. The order of experience is subordinated to the disclosure of meaning and is often freely altered for this purpose, as in fiction and in myth.

Philosophical Inquiry

The comprehensive mode of inquiry is philosophy. The comprehensiveness of philosophy is not the same as sovereignty. Apart from scientific, historical, and transcendental inquiry, philosophy is empty. It has the unique function, nevertheless, of uniting all modes of consciousness in a single interpretation of being. Whereas other forms of inquiry depend on particular modes of consciousness, philosophical inquiry has its own unique foundation in reason—the supreme faculty, as Kant defines it, for reaching "the highest unity of thought."[2]

To say that inquiry may take the form of science, history, art, religion, or philosophy, is not to imply that these always, or even often, take the form of inquiry. Men again and again treat their conceptions as final and unquestionable. They do this in every form of inquiry. Scientific theories are made into changeless, all-inclusive views of being, as in the materialistic philosophy of Thomas Hobbes; history is conceived of as a total and inevitable order of events; cultural styles are frozen into orthodox aesthetic standards, as when supporters of academic painting in nineteenth-century France tried to suppress impressionism; religious faith is degraded into an objective explanation of the origin of the species; philosophy falls away from its classical definition as the *love* of wisdom and claims conclusive knowledge. In all of these ways inquiry is abandoned.

When this happens, however, I suggest that humanity itself is abandoned because it is of the human essence to ask after, but not to possess, the truth. Man is always, as Jaspers says, more than he knows about himself. Every definition that equates man with a fixed set of rationally comprehensible traits is necessarily false. A particular mode of consciousness and a particular interpretation of its disclosures are taken as unquestionable. But the being who is supposedly encased in that definition—man himself—can invoke other modes of consciousness and other conceptions of reality. The questioning in itself is a sign of the inadequacy of the definition.

The principle that man is an inquirer implies not only that he *can* but also that he *must* inquire. Man is a being oriented toward being: this is an idea recurrent in philosophy from a time earlier than Socrates to the present. It is confirmed by traditional values. Beauty provides a feeling of the full, sensual presence of being; truth is its intellectual presence; most moral rules are commanded by respect for being; and the principal misdeeds—murder, robbery, deceit—are denials of being. And is not all fear, as of disease and death, fear of the loss of being? Freud at times saw the "death wish," an urge to destruction, as permanent and primal. But introspection, and consideration of nihilistic political regimes like Hitler's, suggest a less pessimistic hypothesis: that destructive inclinations arise from despair and that annihilation becomes an end in itself only for those who find a more basic impulse, that toward the realization of being, everywhere blocked and defeated. Nor can this impulse be reduced to the instinct of self-preservation, for it is not merely one's own being that is prized. To live securely, but everlastingly alone, as on a deserted planet, is no one's dream of life.

Someone may object that contact with being is not found in inquiry itself but only in the conclusions of inquiry. This would be so, however, only were we able to transcend being, objectifying it in changeless theories. What we call "matters of fact"—the year Julius Caesar was killed, the composition of water—can thus be objectified. But the supposition that man and all reality can be comes from thinking of consciousness as though it were nothing but experience. Being itself is conceived of as totally accessible to observation and theoretical comprehension. The only way to avoid such illusions is to subject every "complete and final truth" to inquiry, thus maintaining the principle that truth lies in inquiry as a whole, not in its results alone.

One possible objection—that the idea of man as essentially an inquirer is too intellectualist an interpretation—was referred to earlier. It is true that inquiry presupposes involvement of the intellect. It does not follow, however, that inquiry is carried on only in libraries and seminar rooms. To recall the best accounts of farming, sexual love, sports, and other nonintellectual activities is to realize how large a part in those activities is played by trial, reflection, and other elements of inquiry. Indeed, it may be an inquiring attitude,

and an underlying reverence for being, that saves activities of this kind from debasement by greed, lust, and other destructive passions.

Intellectualism is precluded wherever care is taken that inquiry is not stifled by its own conclusions. As an ideal of rational elucidation, the concept of inquiry expresses trust in the intellect; but as an ideal of elucidation that never ceases, it rules out the idolatry of intellect that substitutes theory for being.

The paradoxical nature of inquiry—that the truth is found in the search itself—is manifest in the life and dialogues of Socrates. The dialogues that presumably describe most accurately the conversations of Socrates himself end inconclusively. Socrates's whole life of dialogue, moreover, ends inconclusively, for in the trial that led to his death Socrates claimed no wisdom except that inherent in the consciousness of his own ignorance. Yet he had devoted his life to inquiry, and his composure in approaching death—devoting his last hours to an inconclusive discussion of the immortality of the soul—showed that he was ignorant only in the sense that what he knew could not be embodied in theoretical conclusions.

Beyond exemplifying the paradoxical nature of inquiry, the figure of Socrates suggests why it is possible to say that man is an inquirer. Plato's picture of Socrates is of one engaged, simply and unaffectedly, yet with complete singleness of mind, in a lifetime of inquiry. He informed the jury that he would return, if released, to the kind of questioning that had led to his arrest. Sentenced to die, he pursued his efforts at clarifying consciousness until a few minutes before the end. Nothing whatever could deflect him from his ironic and imperturbable pursuit of truth.

One other quality of Socrates must attract our attention—one that brings us to the subject of dialogical, as distinguished from individualistic, inquiry. Although rejected by all but a handful of friends, Socrates always sought the truth by talking with others. He was indefeasibly communal.

Community as Inquiry

I inquire with others because I must. I discover that individualistic inquiry cannot deal with a disturbing kind of awareness—an awareness of strange minds, of minds that are not only unknown and unpredictable but that have the unsettling power of casting into doubt the order established in my own mind. We are such inveterate objectifiers that we have to guard against trying to unify consciousness by treating everything that enters into it as simply an object of experience. Doing this, we envision inquiry as solitary and truth as the possession of a single mind. But thus we falsify our consciousness. In awareness, we are conscious of realities that cannot be wholly objectified—of the self, for example, and of other selves. Consciousness therefore cannot be unified through systematic objectification. It can be unified only through harmonious intersubjectivity, through sharing and cooperatively questioning all interpretations of the contents of consciousness.

It may be asked at what stage in the process of inquiry do others enter in. When does the inquirer come under the necessity of leaving the sphere of his own mind in order to inquire in common with other minds? At the very outset, I suggest. Granted, this may not be recognized. The inquirer may persist indefinitely in the proud effort to master reality alone, without engaging in the humble act of consulting others. It is an illusion, however, to think that even organizing experience is a solitary activity. The simplest objective observation—taking note, for example of the weather—is implicitly communal, for the concept of objectivity is equivalent to that of absolutely reliable intersubjectivity. To suppose that valid inquiry is solitary in its initial, or objective, stages, and that it is necessarily communal only in other stages, is tacitly to accept an individualistic premise that is bound to inhibit understanding of the full identity of inquiry and community.

Others are present in the very state of estrangement that inquiry presupposes. It is not merely that human beings are peculiarly difficult to fit into any integrated scheme of consciousness. It is also that they disturb whatever scheme one person devises by propounding differing schemes of their own. They are sources, not merely objects, of inquiry. Perhaps I am trying to understand human beings as psychological mechanisms. But I find not only that they are not as reliable as mechanisms should be, but that some of them understand human beings in a different way, perhaps as creatures of God. Others in these ways threaten my efforts at clarification; both by their behavior and their words they tend to keep me trammeled by the uncertainties and confusions of a divided mind. I may of course try to ignore them, even to suppress them. But that is to strive for unity of consciousness through will and power rather than through reason. Persons who stand outside our interpretations, inexplicable and challenging, yet ignored or suppressed, are signs that the process of inquiry is incomplete and that we fear the venture of trying to complete it.

The discovery of our plurality comes about in a variety of ways. One way, for example, is through the disturbing realization that I am seen by someone else as a completely different sort of person than I think of myself as being; this realization comes in a particularly jarring form if I am attacked, physically or even verbally. We also discover our plurality simply when we differ in our interpretations of the realities about us. A field that for one person is a source of beauty is for another person a favorable commercial site; the plurality of minds is manifest. But I find other minds even in myself. The successive and incongruous states of my own consciousness, and the effort to harmonize them through inquiry, place me in a situation analagous to that created by a plurality of minds.

However it comes about, the discovery of plurality imposes the necessity of inquiring not only about, but with, other persons. Each one properly tries to formulate a unified interpretation of the contents of consciousness. But never does an interpretation become complete and unquestionable except by delusions and violence. The most valid interpretations are those that incorporate in themselves, like Platonic dialogues, recognition that they are fragmentary and tentative and take on truth only in a dialogical setting that denies them finality.

To encounter other persons is to encounter beings whom I can address and to whom I can offer attention. They are beings who can share and confirm explanations I devise, or can dispute and sometimes destroy such explanations, but cannot themselves be altogether explained. This is why the unification of consciousness must come about not simply through individual reasoning but through dialogical reasoning.

It is why the ideal of unified consciousness is an ideal of community. In discovering that man is an inquirer, we discover simultaneously that he is a communal being, a seeker of truth that is fully shared. More precisely, he is a seeker of truth that is *universally* shared. Just as a tyrant, trying to unify consciousness through violence, cannot tolerate a single dissenting voice, so man in his communal integrity, trying to unify consciousness through inquiry, cannot ignore a single questioning mind.

Inquiry, then, takes place through communication and in that way alone. In this sense, inquiry is community. Having reached this conclusion, we can move a step further by reversing the proposition and asserting that community is inquiry. The familiar idea that community consists in agreement of any kind, that it consists, for example, in common acceptance of a narrow and stifling set of customs inherited from the past, or in widespread acceptance of an advertising message, grossly distorts human nature and obscures the ideal of community. It tends to reconcile human beings to social conditions under which they are far less than they should be and are ;estranged from one another even though they 'may be totally united through whatever forms of truncated selfhood they have accepted. Commu-

nity can live only if people insist again and again, by speech and occasionally by violent resistance, that not any kind of unity that habit, circumstances, or a momentary elite can induce everyone to accept is a community. Only cooperation in the most serious human concerns—and this means above all in the exploration of being— calls forth a community. It is moving testimony to the nature, as well as the value, of community when dissidents in a totalitarian regime risk their freedom and lives to speak in defiance of the monolithic social and political unity that such regimes create. A solitary voice, speaking with utmost seriousness, is a far more decisive sign of community than is a nation unified merely by force and propaganda, or by commercial convenience and advertising.

If community brings together human beings as they are in essence, then it is found in full measure only as we contend in common against the fragmentation of consciousness. Our one serious responsibility is that of understanding the truth as fully as possible and in that way becoming ourselves. We form a community only by being united in the acceptance of that responsibility. This is not a new theory, but rather the ancient premise of intellectual and artistic activity restated in opposition to the casual and destructive misuse of the communal ideal in recent times.

It will be clear by now why we must say that community is inquiry rather than the *result* of inquiry. It has already been suggested that truth is found in inquiry itself and not only at its end; to sever truth from the questions lying at its source is to objectify being and in this way to lose the truth. Community, presumably, lies in sharing the truth, and if this is so it must be inherent in the very process of searching for the truth.

The history of political thought reveals a strong tendency to think of community as realized only when the struggles of thought and history have been ended. Thus for Plato the kingship of philosophers was the center of an order superior to history; for Augustine, the City of God was established only with the end of all earthly events;

in Marxism, capitalism prepares the way for communism economically but is meaningless spiritually and may as well be totally forgotten once communism is achieved. Of course we cannot simply assert the opposite, as though community were present in every moment of history. Should we not be wary, however, of too sharply separating the dangers and uncertainties of history from the communal finale for which we hope? Is there not sense of some kind in the Johannine idea that the end of history must be found and lived in the present moment? Community is surely a state of life; and if that is so, it must in some way partake of movement, doubt, and insecurity.

To look again at another objection noted earlier in these reflections, a critic might say that inquiry is not essentially communal and that this is apparent in the lives of some of the most courageous seekers after truth—people who have been neglected, even scorned and persecuted, by their contemporaries. Socrates exemplifies this criticism; at the same time, he suggests a response.

Socrates was scorned and finally killed, yet in his own personal bearing he was thoroughly communal. This indicates that an inquirer may, by speaking and listening even to those who are inattentive and silent, place himself in a communal setting—beyond false absolutes and in the presence of persons. He may thus stand in the sphere of truth. It seems that there is such a state as solitary communality and that one person alone may establish inquiring relationships by assuming a stance of attentiveness and availability. Perhaps inquiry is greatly handicapped where mutuality is lacking. But the integrity of the inquirer is not destroyed. Socrates was not less inquiring, nor less communal, because of the hostility of other Athenians.

The difference between community and social unity can now be clearly seen. True, community is entered into through communication, and communication depends on certain kinds of social unity, such as common language and similar values. But community is not equivalent to, is not assured by, and may come into conflict with, social unity. Man is shaped and confined by society, but not wholly. To a degree, he transcends society; he can use it, question it, change it, destroy it. Community brings together persons in their essential being and therefore cannot consist in the social unity that persons partially transcend.

This implies a view of tradition. Society as an inheritance comes into our hands in the form of tradition. The communal ideal is that tradition be wholly absorbed in inquiry, that it be examined rationally, and that it be accepted, revised, or repudiated in complete clarity of mind. In other words, our communality entails an effort to master society as the collective past and to relate it, if only by consciously accepting it, to the living present. We can never succeed in doing this. We have no standpoint outside of tradition that would make it possible. To inquire into one aspect of tradition we must use standards and assumptions derived from other aspects of traditions. But there is nothing in tradition as such that is sacred or inviolable. There are sacred traditions but not things that are sacred because they are traditions. People joined by uncriticized traditions are not joined in community.

Community as inquiry often imperils social unity. Then society will be hostile to community. Just as the nature of community is visible in the life of Socrates, so the tragic antithesis of community and society is visible in the death of Socrates.

Footnotes

1. Quoted in Alexander Liberman, *The Artist in His Studio* (New York: Viking Press, 1960), 112.
2. This concept of reason is developed in the "Transcendental Dialectic" in *The Critique of Pure Reason*, trans. Norman Kemp Smith (London: Macmillan & Co., 1958), 297-570. The quotation is to be found on p. 300.

Nigerian College Adopts "Community of Inquiry" Approach

Stan Anih

The Institute of Ecumenical Education, Thinkers Corner, Enugu, Nigeria, has emerged with a new technology for the teaching-learning situation. This new concept regards the school classroom as a community of inquiry. This innovation is necessary today in Nigeria because the system of pedagogy which we inherited from Western culture is now abysmally inadequate to cope with the day-to-day problems of the man of the 21st century. The African man was condemned to the thought patterns of the Greco-Roman heritage, which was patterned on an archaic, fossilized and hackneyed pedagogical base.

The Institute is fashioning an educational system which is known to us as andragogy. In this system of education, everybody in the classroom—the teacher and the taught—form a single community where people contribute from different sides to arrive at the desired goal.

Andragogy (or Community of Inquiry or Reflective Education) is premised on four cardinal assumptions concerning man:

1. That, as people mature, their self-concepts move from that of a dependent personality towards a self-directing personality;

2. That people's personal experience is the greatest source of their reflection and growth in knowledge;

3. That through the community of inquiry to which people belong, they become increasingly aware of their social roles and tasks;

4. That through the system of andragogy, knowledge is no longer a storehouse for postponed application but a desirable skill for immediate application to here-and-now problems; this shifts learning from subject-centeredness to problem-centeredness.

Andragogy is the lost educational method of Africa as we know from the moonlight story-telling and fireside story-telling where adults and youngsters stay together sharing experiences, teaching one another and learning from one another, without only one person standing out as the only reservoir from which everybody must tax. Andragogy is a sharing of educational experience: it is communitarian and functional in nature, and gears towards solving immediate problems of the members of the community.

If somebody dies, stories concerning the happiness of the underworld would be told and the bereaved would in this way deal with the problem of the sorrow surrounding them.

The African educational system has always accepted the form of the community of inquiry, even when there is a problem to be settled by the traditional jury. People would sit around the tree in front of the village shrine and each individual would be allowed to shed his personal light on the problem being discussed. When this participatory problem-solving process had taken place, a solution would emerge and the people would have convinced themselves that they had done their best. Nobody is neglected and nobody is over-inflated, as happens in the European classroom of pedagogy where the teacher is the only pinnacle that everybody must climb in order to know anything.

In andragogy, where education becomes reflective, participatory and dialogical, we notice that the spirit of dialogue develops in the Community of Inquiry. The constant search for truth and knowledge becomes everybody's business with the Community of Inquiry. Both adults and children have equal opportunity to learn that, in the community, we are not only our brother's keepers; we are also our brother's brothers. In the community of inquiry or the classroom, the spirit of tolerance for each other's views, feelings, imaginings and creation, as well as care for one another's happiness, increases daily.

This is education in its quintessence: people commit themselves to objectivity, they spontaneously fight for impartiality, they communally strive for consistency and reasonableness. In fact the supreme law guiding the Community of Inquiry is the law of reasonableness; if it is reasonable, accept it, not because Okonkwo or Jones has said it but because it is reasonable. This type of education is deeply concerned with the moral, social and political implications for the community. The classroom becomes a living community where everybody not only participates but also gains from the participation of others.

The alien system of pedagogy has stultified and killed the growing generation because the educational system was defined as the transmission of the knowledge and experience of the past to the present generation. The children trained in this system come out with certificates and roam the streets without jobs. When they do become employed, they are non-performers, and when they try to employ themselves, they are nonstarters. They always carry a superiority complex that they are educated, when in actual fact they are only lettered.

One of the great merits of the Community of Inquiry is that it predisposes all the pupils in the class to be open-minded and to be attitudinally ecumenical. Consequently, the child in the classroom willingly accepts corrections by peers. The child is also:

1. able to listen to others attentively
2. able to revise his or her views in light of reasons from others
3. able to take his or her ideas seriously
4. able to build upon other people's ideas
5. able to develop his or her own ideas without fear of rebuff or humiliation from peers
6. open to new ideas
7. concerned about the rights of others to express their views
8. capable of detecting underlying assumptions
9. concerned about consistency when arguing a point of view
10. one who asks questions
11. one who verbalizes relationships between ends and means
12. one who shows respect for persons in the community
13. one who shows sensitivity to context when discussing moral conduct
14. one who asks for reasons from one's peers
15. one who discusses issues with impartiality
16. one who asks for criteria.

If our educated people are all able to discuss issues with impartiality and ask for criteria for those actions carried out in our country, the continuous wallowing and meandering from one ideology to the other which Nigeria has suffered from in the past thirty years would not be the case. People do things whimsically and arbitrarily, whether they are the leaders or the led. Consequently, we have come to a point of no question, no answer, a situation of political doldrums, a situation of financial fiasco yet in the presence of plenty in Nigeria. People are just looking for enjoyment and cheap corn instead of trying to build the nation. Those who receive education on the platform of an alien pedagogy are always looking for gold, glory and gain but hardly ever look for God, grace and growth.

Now the Community of Inquiry, based on the educational system called Andragogy, helps us to become clearer about what we know, more able to make better distinctions, more able to recognize underlying assumptions, more able to distinguish better from worse reasons, more able to think consistently and comprehensively, more able to criticize our own goals and others, more able to criticize our own thinking as well as the thinking of others.

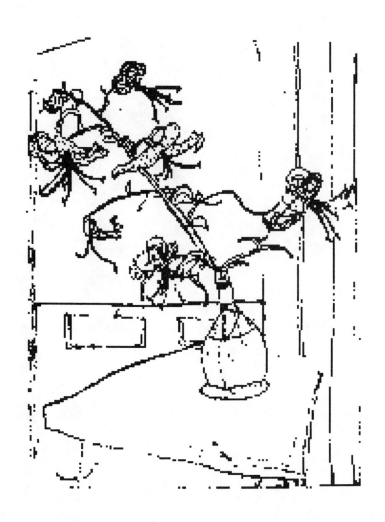

Chapter Seven
Philosophy As An Elementary School Subject

Chapter Seven

Philosophy as an Elementary School Subject

Ancient writers hint that, in those early times when philosophy was making its debut, children were not excluded from philosophical discussions. But there were misgivings, as voiced by no less a figure than Plato, who worried that children were likely to be carried away by the competitiveness of dialectical clashes while Aristotle was uneasy with the thought of inexperienced children (or individuals of any age) doing philosophy.

The revival of interest in philosophy for children during the past quarter-century has resulted from the assurances educators have provided that the new curriculum and pedagogy are appropriate to the elementary school, But the proponents of elementary school philosophy are generally dissatisfied with the notion the philosophy is a useful *enrichment* program, to be added to the weekly class schedule when convenient. They would like to see philosophy mandated as a required elementary school course, meeting 3 to 4 times a week.

The lowest common denominator of their argument is simply this: reasoning is as vital to a growing person as is reading and writing. Reading and writing are generally accepted as skills that must be taught in the context of the humanistic discipline of English (which includes both the grammar and the literature). Analogously, reasoning is a skill that should be taught in the context of another humanistic discipline; philosophy. For reasoning involves logic and judgment involves values, and philosophy provides

the necessary and suitable auspices for the teaching of both. Therefore, it is argued, philosophy should be made a required subject in the elementary school.

No one has advocated philosophy for children more ardently than Montaigne. A plain philosophical discourse is more easily understood by a child than one of Boccaccio's novels, and the philosophy would be much more profitable to the child. Indeed, says Montaigne, philosophy should be the principal lesson for "our little monsieur." Its merit is not in its syllogisms and dialectics but in the sharpening of judgment it provides, and the infusion into the child of excellent values.

The Lipman essay was written a year after the production of *Harry Stottlemeiers Discovery*, the first contemporary work of philosophical fiction devised for use in school setting, and immediately after the initial experiment using the book with fifth-grade children. The essay provides a glimpse of the goals and ideals of Philosophy for Children at the very beginnings of its development. Comparison with present-day statements of the program's objectives suggests that changes during the intervening period have not been considerable.

Laurance J, Splitter's article provides an overall review of the contribution Philosophy for Children can make to the elementary school curriculum, He stresses especially the thinking skills that are sharpened through the use of the program and the reflection on moral values that it encourages. These are important points of emphasis. If it is granted that children should be encouraged to reflect upon their values, then strengthening their cognitive skills will in turn strengthen their ethical reflections. What might be expected to follow is greater self-criticism, better judgment-formation, and more reasonable behavior.

Philosophy for Children, argues Robert J. Mulvaney, has its own philosophical past, for it emerges out of "Plato's intuition of the mutual interdependence of philosophy, education and political life," Rousseau's insistence on the prior psychological understanding of the child, and Dewey's themes of "integration, synthesis and continuity." Plato, in brief, provided the philosophy, Rousseau discovered the child, and Dewey discerned the connection between the two. This is oversimplification, as Mulvaney acknowledges, but at the some time it helps build Mulvaney's case for the positioning of Philosophy for Children in the broad stream of humanistic and liberal learning and for his finding in the program a warmth, courtesy, kindness and civility "which could hardly be expected from it if it were merely a thinking skills program." For an educational program to be saluted for possessing such qualities is unusual.

Ekkehard Martens, like Mulvaney, sees Philosophy for Children as being engendered by the philosophical tradition, and like Mulvaney, he cites a trio of philosophers as having been particularly responsible for constructing the platform from which Philosophy for Children could be launched. As Mulvaney sees Dewey providing a bridge between Plato and Rousseau, Martens sees Leonard Nelson as providing a bridge between the logical emphasis of Hegel and the emphasis upon the personal of Kierkegaard. But Martens willingly admits the narrowness of these particular perspectives, and he calls for a full reliance on international sources of philosophy, including Oriental ones, if Philosophy for Children is to be global in scope rather than provincial.

To William Hamrick, Philosophy for Children clearly displays phenomenological sources. He cites, in addition to Hegel, such writers as Gabriel Marcel, Maurice Merleau-Ponty and Mikel Dufrenne as having developed an outlook to which the Philosophy for Children curriculum corresponds. To buttress his case, Hamrick cites a number of passages from the novels that exemplify phenomenological themes or emphases. His claim in not that the curriculum reflects an exclusively phenomenological orientation, but that it does not fail to reflect a phenomenological one, as part of its effort to provide a catholicity of perspectives.

From the point of view of an analytic philosopher, Barry Curtis, there are strong affinities between Philosophy for Children and the philosophical approach of Ludwig Wittgenstein. Curtis begins with Wittgenstein's insistence that philosophy is like a disease in that it gives a distorted picture of things, but proceeds to acknowledge that the best cure for that disease might be philosophy itself. Thus it may useless and confusing to weigh students' minds down with questions such as "What is reality?" but it can be quite helpful to get them to say under what conditions they would call something real. Curtis concludes that doing philosophical exercises of the kind provided in Philosophy for Children is not only possible but necessary.

John Wilson concludes the section with a characteristically energetic insistence that, if philosophy is to be taught to children, there be no reduction of standards in doing so. Teachers and students alike have to have a clear sense of what philosophy is, and how philosophical thinking differs from non-philosophical thinking. He defends the asking of such questions as "What is true?" and "What do we mean by real?" which he considers examples of strictly philosophical questions, and he defines philosophy as "the investigation of concepts, categories and distinctions via the meaning of words." Wilson concludes by making two points. The first is well-taken: not just any critical thinking is philosophical thinking. The second, that just because our aims are non-authoritarian, it does not follow that our methods must be, is far more controversial.

Of the Education of Children

Michel de Montaigne

Since philosophy is that which instructs us to live, and that infancy has there its lessons as well as other ages, why is it not communicated to children betimes? "The clay is moist and soft: now, now make haste, and form the pitcher on the rapid wheel."

They begin to teach us to live when we have almost done living. A hundred students have got the pox before they have come to read Aristotle's lecture on temperance. Cicero said that though he should live two men's ages, he should never find leisure to study the lyric poets; and I find these sophisters yet more deplorably unprofitable. The boy we would breed has a great deal less time to spare; he owes but the first fifteen or sixteen years of his life to education; the remainder is due to action. Let us, therefore, employ that short time in necessary instruction. Away with the thorny subtleties of dialectics; they are abuses, things by which our lives can never be amended. Take the plain philosophical discourses, learn how rightly to choose, and then rightly to apply them; they are more easy to be understood than one of Boccaccio's novels; a child from nurse is much more capable of them than of learning to read or to write. Philosophy has discourses proper for childhood as well as for the decrepit age of men.

I am of Plutarch's mind that Aristotle did not so much trouble his great disciple with the knack of forming syllogisms or with the elements of geometry as with infusing into him good precepts concerning valor, prowess, magnanimity, temperance, and the contempt of fear; and with this ammunition sent him, whilst yet a boy, with no more than thirty thousand foot, four thousand horse, and but forty-two thousand crowns to subjugate the empire of the whole earth. For the other arts and sciences, he says, Alexander highly indeed commended their excellence and charm and had them in very great honor and esteem, but not ravished with them to that degree as to be tempted to affect the practice of them in his own person. "Young men and old men derive hence a certain end to the mind, and stores for miserable grey hairs."

Epicurus, in the beginning of his letter to Meniceus, says, "That neither the youngest should refuse to philosophize nor the oldest grow weary of it." Who does otherwise seems tacitly to imply that either the time of living happily is not yet come or that it is already past. And yet, for all that, I would not have this pupil of ours imprisoned and made a slave to his book; nor would I have him given up to the morosity and melancholic humor of a sour, ill-natured pedant; I would not have his spirit cowed and subdued by applying him to the rack and tormenting him, as some do, fourteen or fifteen hours a day and so make a packhorse of him. Neither should I think it good when, by reason of a solitary and melancholic complexion, he is discovered to be over-much addicted to his book, to nourish that humor in him; for that renders him unfit for civil conversation, and diverts him from better employments. And how many have I seen in my time totally brutified by an immoderate thirst after knowledge? Carneades was so besotted with it that he would not find time so much as to comb his head or to pare his nails. Neither would I have his generous manners spoiled and corrupted by the incivility and barbarism of those of another. The French wisdom was anciently turned into proverb: "Early, but of no continuance," And, in truth, we yet see that nothing can be more ingenious and pleasing than the children of France; but they ordinarily deceive the hope and expectation that have been conceived of them; and grown up to be men, have nothing extraordinary or worth taking notice of: I have heard men of good understanding say, these colleges of ours to which we send our young people (and of which we have but too many) make them such animals as they are.

But to our little monsieur, a closet, a garden, the table, his bed, solitude and company, morning and evening, all hours shall be the same, and all places to him a study; for philosophy, who, as the formatrix of judgment and manners, shall be his principal lesson, has that privilege to have a hand in everything. The orator Isocrates, being at a feast entreated to speak of his art, all the company were satisfied with and commended his answer: "It is not now a time," he said, "to do what I can do; and that which it is now time to do, I cannot do." For to make orations and rhetorical disputes in a company met together to laugh and make good cheer had been very unseasonable and improper, and as much might have been said of all the other sciences. But as to what concerns philosophy, that part of it at least that treats of man and of his offices and duties, it has been the common opinion of all wise men that, out of

respect to the sweetness of her conversation, she is ever to be admitted in all sports and entertainments. And Plato, having invited her to his feast, we see after how gentle and obliging a manner, accommodated both to time and place, she entertained the company, though in a discourse of the highest and most important nature. "It profits poor and rich alike, but, neglected, equally hurts old and young." By this method of instruction, my young pupil will be much more and better employed than his fellows of the college are. But as the steps we take in walking to and fro in a gallery, though three times as many, do not tire a man so much as those we employ in a formal journey, so our lesson, as it were accidentally occurring without any set obligation of time or place and falling naturally into every action, will insensibly insinuate itself. By which means our very exercises and recreations, running, wrestling, music, dancing, hunting, riding, and fencing, will prove to be a good part of our study. I would have his outward fashion and mien and the disposition of his limbs formed at the same time with his mind. 'Tis not a soul, 'tis not a body that we are training up, but a man, and we ought not to divide him. And, as Plato says, we are not to fashion one without the other, but make them draw together like two horses harnessed to a coach. By which saying of his, does he not seem to allow more time for, and to take more care of, exercises for the body, and to hold that the mind, in a good proportion, does her business at the same time too?

Philosophy for Children

Matthew Lipman

Introduction

Sometime in 1968 it occurred to me that we might do a better job of teaching children to reason than we were already doing. I had very little knowledge of the sort of research that had already been done in this area, and the whole conception of what was involved in "teaching reasoning" was quite unclear to me. Was teaching the rules of inference teaching reasoning? Was teaching children to recognize and perform certain inferential patterns teaching reasoning? Could reasoning actually be taught at all—or could we at best merely sensitize children to distinguish certain forms of inference as awkward or sloppy, much as we sensitize them to recognize "bad grammar" without actually teaching them grammar? I recall writing to Monroe Beardsley about the possibility of doing something about the problem at that time, and I believe I also discussed it then with Justus Buchler. Both were encouraging.

But I didn't want to teach children logic in the way we taught (or pretended to teach) college students logic. The children would certainly object to having one more nauseating subject crammed down their throats—and they'd have been right. Someone suggested to me that I somehow present logic in the form of a children's story. The possibility intrigued me: a story telling, almost as a child would relate it, of the discovery by a group of children of how their own thought processes work, and how more effective thought processes could be distinguished from less effective ones.

In 1969, I applied to the National Endowment for the Humanities for a pilot project grant. I proposed to write the children's book and to teach it in a true field experiment. The grant was approved, and I wrote the book and carried out the project in the 1970-71 academic year. The teaching was done at the Rand School, Montclair, New Jersey.

The Endowment then gave me a two-year grant, covering 1971-73, for amplification of the project, under the auspices of the Department of Philosophy, Columbia University. During this period I developed a teacher's manual, arranged for the preparation of a children's workbook, and made it possible for several teachers of grades 5-8 to try working with the children's materials. I also wrote a story for high-school students, in the form of a novel.

Part One of the following paper was written in 1970, at the time the pilot project was being organized. It sets forth the rationale of the project, and the hopes then had for it.

Part Two is an account of the pilot project itself.

One of the things which Thinking attempts to do is to chronicle the fortunes of reflective education as an historical movement, and to depict philosophy for children as the current upsurge of that movement. In keeping with that objective, relevant articles are reprinted in order to make them available to readers who may have missed them when they first appeared, or to whom such *articles are not now readily accessible. The article that follows appeared originally in Vol. 7, No. 1 of* Metaphilosophy *(January, 1976), ed. by Terrell Ward Bynum and Matthew Lipman, and is reprinted here with the permission of* Metaphilosophy. *It will be noted that Part One was written in 1970, Part Two in 1973, and the Introduction in 1975. The author of these pages does not reread them unabashed at the polemical tone of some of the passages—but then, they are part of the record. More embarrassing is the omission of acknowledgement of the importance of the consultative and advisory role of Joseph D. Isaacson, both in seeing the educational problems of the late 1960's and in considering how philosophy for children might be a constructive response to those problems. Joe Isaacson, who also happens to be the Staff Photographer for* Thinking, *continues to be the program's most far-sighted and sagacious advisor, and any record of the development of the Philosophy for Children curriculum should clearly indicate the extent to which his good thinking has contributed to children's better thinking.*

Part One

Why Johnny can't reason

American education has been indicted often and eloquently. Some of the charges are correct, some are not. In many cases the critics may be found to share common assumptions with the educational system they seek to criticize. For example, critics are often found complaining that children reason poorly because reading and mathematics are taught badly, and the schools respond by frantically searching for ways to teach these subjects better. It seldom seems to occur to either party that, while reading and mathematics are disciplines that contribute usefully to good thinking, they cannot *suffice* to produce it. The fact that Johnny adds, subtracts, multiplies, divides, and can race through a Danny Dunn book

doesn't mean he can reason. It doesn't mean he is developing habits of efficient thinking or of arriving at independent judgments. Something more is needed.

Perhaps the above statement is too drastic. It's not that Johnny can't reason. It's just that he can't reason as well as he should. And it's doubtful that the present educational system can take much credit for the reasoning he does perform. No one ever seems to bother to instruct the child in the hygiene of thinking. It's just something he picks up by himself, or something he quietly and unconsciously absorbs through the pores of his skin. (On the rare occasions in which he is taught "critical reading," it seems to be done quite unsystematically.)

Alongside the lack of attention given to reasoning in today's curriculum is the equally deplorable trivialization of content. The moment we consider discussing a matter of some importance with the child, a thousand scruples emerge to inhibit us. The spectre of an outraged PTA is invoked; the casual manner disappears, and we become once again models of didactic pedantry. Those who recognize the banality and stodginess of much of the current content often seek to correct it, not by substituting materials that would be of genuine importance to the child, but by sensationalizing the trivial so as to compel the child's interest in what remains fundamentally inane. Obviously, instead of the lurid presentation of banalities, we need to develop attractive modes of presenting matters of intellectual substance without compromising the integrity of that substance. The objective here is not to confront the child with two isolated entities, the structure of logical thought on the one hand, and a mass of baffling profundities on the other, but to allow the child to discover how thought can play upon its subject-matter, how reasoning about issues of importance can be satisfying even if it does no more than formulate the basic questions.

But what does the school system do to stimulate the child's reasoning capacities?

He receives training in mathematics. It would of course be absurd to deny that mathematics involves reasoning. But it is reasoning that is so highly abstract, so incredibly *sui generis*, that it has yet to be demonstrated satisfactorily that the capacity for mathematical deduction is transferable in any significant way to conceptual deduction. Hardly a semester goes by in which a teacher fails to discover students who are excellent in mathematics but deplorable in English, or vice versa. Apparently the referential and connotative aspects of language, its richness of meaning, its nearness to everyday actuality, are precisely what frighten off certain students who prefer only the manipulation of pure symbols. It would appear that educators have been greatly oversold on the power of mathematical training to improve children's abilities to draw logical inferences from what they have heard or read, or to make appropriate logical distinctions.

Secondly, the child is given courses in science, and a certain portion of such courses is often devoted to "inference." But the inference referred to is not the relatively rigorous deductive inference. It is instead the much more suppositious process known as "inductive inference." It may be granted that one type of induction—generalization—is a fairly rudimentary intellectual operation. But another type, the forming of hypotheses, is a process of extreme subtlety. It is far closer to art than to mere craft. Just as we really cannot *teach* anyone how to invent new and worthwhile sculptural or painting or musical compositions (although we can create an environment which is more conducive to inventive and more hostile to non-inventive behavior than are most environments), so it is unlikely that we can teach children or adults how to invent worthwhile hypotheses. There is no known method for producing new ideas. But the point is that it is unreasonable to believe complacently that we are teaching children all they need to know about inference just because we teach them to draw probable inferences from their *perceptions*. (One recalls that often, when Sherlock Holmes would come out with one of his hypotheses, Watson would compliment him on his magnificent *deduction*! But whether the difficulty lay with Watson or with Conan Doyle is rather difficult to say.)

Thirdly, the young student is taught to "read for meaning," or at least such teaching is attempted. At first glance, it might seem that "reading for meaning" does involve precisely those logical mechanisms on which deductive inference and our verbal judgments depend. Unfortunately, this is only partially correct. For if the inferences involved in mathematics are generally too abstract to be transferred efficiently to verbal thought, the contrary is often true with literary inference: it is too *concrete* to permit such transfer.

No doubt each work of literature has a "logic" of its own. But it is not (thank heavens!) the deductive logic of formal thought. And what is true of literature is true to a lesser degree of all expository writing. Verbal meanings depend upon connotation and suggestion, upon all sorts of nuances other than what can logically be deduced from a given set of statements in a given context. What one teacher will call "the" meaning of a given literary passage, another may dismiss as "far-fetched interpretation." A good case in point would be the enigmatic directions to the exercises in almost any of today's children's textbooks. They frequently seem to be masterpieces of befuddlement. Many children still manage to perform the exercises correctly, but this is in spite of the directions rather than because of them.

In other words, we expect the pupil to find clear and unambiguous meanings in contexts which are rich in indirection and allusiveness. That children frequently develop a knack of telling us what they suspect we want to hear should not delude us into thinking we have improved their powers of deduction regarding the written materials in question.

Fourthly, there is the attention given in some schools to the process of "problem-solving." But in order to solve problems, a stage of formulation is needed, and prior to formulation, it is necessary that crucially relevant questions be raised. The doubts that are symptomatic of the problems themselves should be utilized in this stage of question-raising. I can recall the dean of a large medical school remarking that today's medical students wish to rush immediately into prognosis and treatment; they have little time for careful diagnosis. But this is an attitude we have encouraged with our stress upon "problem-solving," without an equal stress upon the need for independent thinking, careful attention to one's doubts, importance of question-raising, and other such significant aspects and phases of the preliminaries of inquiry.

Quite possibly, the complacency we exhibit regarding the developing of reasoning in children has been increased rather than diminished by our increasing familiarity with the work of Piaget. The *inevitability* of logical development which Piaget seems to imply in his descriptive (but rarely pedagogical) studies tends to lull many readers into believing that it is not necessary to *push* the child up the inclined plane of improved reasoning in the way we acknowledge we must push him in other disciplines.

According to Piaget, children begin to function logically even before they acquire language. It is evident that their reasoning capacities remain rather rudimentary in the earlier phases of their development. Until they are 11 or 12, Piaget believes, they remain wrapped up in the more concrete aspects of experience; perception, sensation, imagination and insight are prevalent, but abstract thought is rare. Then suddenly they take off, and in a year or so they reach a new and rarefied plateau, where they perceive and manipulate abstract relationships, and even understand that they are doing so.

Apparently, all that Piaget can suggest to educators is that they tailor the child's education to conform to the phases of his logical development. Yet, as I shall contend later in more detail, even this meager advice is either erroneous or subject to erroneous interpretation. It does not allow for acceleration of education in thinking. And it suggests that because the child thinks concretely in a certain sense in his early years, that his instruction during this period should likewise be concrete. Methodologically this is highly questionable.

The Child and the Educational Establishment

The intellectual possibilities of the American school child remain largely unrecognized and unexplored. We teach him to think about various subjects—English, history, social studies, and so on. But we do not teach him to think about thinking, although he is capable of doing so and would be interested in doing so. We do not sufficiently encourage him to think for himself, to form independent judgments, to be proud of his personal insights, to be proud of having a point of view he can call his own, to be pleased with his prowess in reasoning. Reacting against our Puritan heritage once again, the fashion is now to encourage the child to feel, to be sensitive—having first armored him against feeling and anaesthetized him against sensations. But we do not trust him to think.

Outside the school, things are no better. Although television is everybody's whipping boy, it is doubtful that the often chaotic patterns of stimuli it offers are more destructive than the bland physicality of *Boy's Life* or the cynicism and nihilism of *Mad* magazine. Television treats the child as a potential consumer; the children's magazines treat the boys as potential soldiers and the girls as potential housewives. In both media, "idea" is a four-letter word. Indeed the ambiguities and ambivalences which pour in pell-mell upon the television viewer are often closer to the paradoxical or ambiguous qualities of actual life in today's world than the rather mindless and innocuous but totally coherent existence which children are portrayed as having in elementary school textbooks.

What the school does succeed in introducing into the child is a negative charisma, a gratuitous belief in his own intellectual impotence, a distrust of any intellectual powers of his own other than what it takes to cope with problems formulated and assigned to him by others. The lively curiosity that seems to be an essential part of the child's natural impulse is sooner or later beaten or battered out of him by the intransigencies of the educational system.

The child should be taught to distinguish among different types of situations, and he should be equipped with a battery of methods so that he can adapt the appropriate method to the situation he encounters and recognizes. But the child is not presently equipped to discern such situational differences, nor is he made aware of the differences among modes of response and methods of treatment. There are situations which call for precise and disciplined thinking, but he is not given any indication of what such rigor involves. There are other situations that call for insight and structuring, others which call for questioning and defining, still others which call for creative thinking as to the possibilities of transforming what presently exists into something more satisfactory. He needs many methods; he is given barely one.

The child distrusts not only his own intellectual capacities, but those of his classmates as well. He does not have a set or attitude which would permit him to accept and learn from *their* experience, because learning is seldom presented to him as a cooperative enterprise; it is seldom shown to him that inquiry is a matter of communal activity. He does not realize what discoveries are possible in dialogue and discussion—discoveries of another's ideas and of another's person.

Indeed, the child's negative charisma is the inverse of the educational establishment's positive charisma. He can attribute uncanny wisdom and infallible insight to the establishment only by first robbing himself of his belief in his own possession of them. Laing is on very sound ground when he observes that a child (or an adult) often *becomes* that which we say he *is*. Children whose belief in their own intelligence is confirmed by others subsequently behave more intelligently.

Mind and Thinking in the Curriculum

Over the years, the sciences have marched relentlessly into the classroom: first the natural sciences, then the biological sciences, and most recently the social sciences. Certainly the physical environment is a fit subject for the child to study. The human body is a fit subject. The structure of society is a fit subject. Why then is the human mind not a fit subject? Children are as much aware of and as keenly interested in their thoughts as they are in the bodily functions. But nowhere is *mind* in the curriculum. We have begun to teach elementary school children about sex. Why? Because we are afraid that if we do not, they will make "mistakes," i.e., behave in ways that are socially if not individually disadvantageous. But mistakes in thinking can be no less socially disadvantageous. Why then do we not teach the principles of thought in the same way we teach the principles of sex? One cannot help suspecting the reason: mindlessness does not seem to threaten the established order; thoughtfulness might. An irrational social order is threatened far more by rationality than by irrationality.

We teach care of the body—hygiene and physical education. What do we teach children regarding the care of their minds? Indeed, Piaget has somewhere remarked that as ethics is the logic of conduct, so logic is the morality of thought. From this point of view, it would seem that if we teach (whether at home or at school) what is "right" and "wrong" about action (i.e., morality), then we should seek to teach what is "right" and "wrong" about thought (i.e., logic).

There are two major questions to be answered here: is logic what is really needed, and if it is, can it be taught?

Much of what goes by the name of "logic," as taught on the college level, is certainly teachable to children. Take that portion of it known as "informal logic." It is almost wholly appropriate to elementary school English courses, and indeed, some of the materials of informal logic have long been parts of the elementary curriculum in some schools. Teaching such material to college students is largely a waste of time, both the student's and the teacher's.

This is not to say that all logic could or should be eliminated from the college curriculum. Certainly symbolic logic should continue to be taught at that level. Yet, even if symbolic logic could be unpacked, disassembled, and taught in tiny steps, as has been done with the "new math," it is so abstract that it would improve *verbal* reasoning little more than mathematics courses do, if at all.

Another component of most introductory courses in college logic is "scientific method." The materials here are appropriate to a high school level, although some could be introduced much earlier.

This brings us to the question of "formal logic." For most college students, the trouble with formal logic is that it merely makes them conscious of habits of thinking which they adopted long, long ago, and have used more or less faithfully ever since. But either they already have such mental habits, in which case logic is unnecessary for them, or else they lack such habits, in which case the formation of new mental habits is an overwhelmingly formidable task. If the student's thought processes are muddled, the rigor of logic appears to him intolerable. But if his thought processes are swift and individualistic, he is likely to conclude that he has no need at all for the seeming inanities of the syllogism.

Yet, year after year, college philosophy departments agonize over *how* logic should be taught on the college level. It never seems to occur to the disputants that the question cannot be answered because it rests upon the unreasonable assumption that logic must be taught exclusively on the college level.

Formal logic can, and should, be taught much earlier.

It is not the fault of mathematics or inductive science that educators have tended to employ them as *the* models of excellence in reasoning.

The fault lies wholly with the educators themselves, who have employed techniques that go directly against the grain of childhood thought processes. The child tends to think in terms of wholes rather than isolated details. The organization of a painting is a much simpler task for him than for an adult; form seems to flow from him quite naturally; only the details give him trouble. It would seem therefore that if we are to relocate formal logic by placing it in the elementary school curriculum, we should place it at about the fifth grade level, where thinking begins to move from the "concrete" (yet general, global) to the "formal" (yet particular and specific).

Instead of beginning the study of deductive reasoning by isolating logical elements—atomic parts to be fitted together into molecular wholes, we might do better to seek to acquaint the child at first with some of the more general aspects of reasoning. We could try to sketch out the system at first in broad brushstrokes—immediate inference, informal fallacies, categorical and hypothetical syllogisms, etc., while postponing the details of the system until subsequent semesters.

At this point it should be suggested that logic will have value for the fifth-grade child only if it is embedded in a context of *ideas*, against which it can constantly be applied. What kinds of ideas? Ideas, I would say, such as can be usefully borrowed from the various fields of philosophy: ethics, political and social philosophy, aesthetics, metaphysics, and so on. In short, ideas of what men consider *important*.

Now if anything is axiomatic about American education, it is that children and philosophy don't mix. Not even high school children. But this is in keeping with Laing's thesis, mentioned earlier. Children are treated as if they were incapable of philosophical deliberation, therefore they behave as if they were incapable of philosophical deliberation. And this is said of children who, with their constant inclination to ask "Why?" behave far more philosophically than most adults! In fact, we discount children's philosophical inquisitiveness because it so often calls into question things we prefer to take for granted. In our anxiety to preserve our beliefs as they are, we classify inquisitiveness with scepticism, and scepticism with outrageous disbelief. "Ah," the child says, "if in the beginning God created the world, then it wasn't really the beginning after all, was it?"—and we're prepared to throttle him for his unanswerable presumptuousness.

Granted, children probably find abstract philosophical concepts to be almost devoid of significance. They mumble through "with liberty and justice for all," "let freedom ring," and even insist on "one nation invisible," but the words are so much mumbo-jumbo to them. Yet let them feel unfairly treated, and a fierce resentment will flare up. They cannot explain it in terms of "injustices"; they find it very difficult to give reasons for their feeling as they do. But that *something* they profoundly believe in has been violated, there can be no doubt. And it is my guess that, if they were encouraged to do so, they could discuss among themselves what that something might be, and seek to isolate it, to define it, and to justify it. What is at present lacking is our willingness to create the climate and environment which would provide such encouragement.

It is useless for us to complain that ours is a nation of sheep as long as we do not develop the capacity of independent judgment in children. So long as sheep are what we really want, sheep are what we'll get. (This is one of the few areas in which our hidden desires are fully rewarded.) On the other hand, if we begin a course in "Mind" in the fifth grade, what reason would we have for stopping it there? It would make more sense to continue it through high school, at which time the reality-testing theories of epistemology could be brought in to gladden the hearts of adolescents, for whom appearance-reality problems are completely tantalizing. In addition to moving into new areas, the course could move more deeply through old ones. The material is almost inexhaustible.

How Can Reasoning be Taught in the Fifth Grade?

But now the crucial question: how is all this to be taught? The didactic method employed in many classrooms would be, in this instance, little short of a disaster. On the other hand, it would be naive to expect a fifth-grade teacher to be able to assist and guide the children in improvised discussions; such efforts at "discovery through dialogue" are both rare and difficult on the college level, even with highly experienced teachers and highly motivated students, although they can be tremendously impressive when they do succeed.

Improvisational discovery involves further difficulty, in that the children are quite unclear as to what is expected of them. Some of them suspect that it is to find out what the teacher already knows, without being explicitly told what that is. Some believe it to be an elaborate way of wasting time, because they cannot see precise and concrete results. In short, the children lack a *model* of discovery-in-practice. But instead of providing such a model, educators have contented themselves with devising stratagems and lures which might provoke the child into a discovery response.

The construction of discovery models is not a simple matter. But it can be done. Using the techniques of children's storytelling, it should be possible to relate idealized instances of cooperative, participatory discovery, not only of the principles of logic, but of ideas in a wide variety of philosophic domains. The stories need be no more "over the heads" of fifth grade students than Plato's *Republic* is over the heads of college students. All that is necessary is that they should serve as springboards for intellectual discussions, and that these discussions should serve in turn to promote a heightened awareness of and understanding of the world these children inhabit, as well as of their own identities in that world.

But discovery as a method can be only as important as the product that is discovered. If discovery techniques were to be restricted to trivial or banal materials, the result would be to disenchant students as to the possibilities of a technique that turned out always to be so fruitless and unrewarding. Bruner's dictum, that "any subject *can* be taught to anybody at any age in some form that is honest," is deservedly famous. But the fact that any subject can be taught does not commit us to the belief that any subject is as good for the child as any other, or that we need no discriminations as to the relative importance of different subjects. No doubt it is important that children should play with lenses and discover how convex lenses differ from concave ones; that they should play with magnets and discover the difference between positive and negative poles. But by what criterion do we decide that discovery of these particular distinctions is more important than the discovery of, say, the distinctions between valid and invalid, between true and false, between right and wrong, between good and bad, or between beautiful and ugly?

In the greatest portraits of the discovery of understanding, young men are shown together with old Socrates (or young Socrates with old Parmenides) exploring problems together. Socrates is portrayed as neither beautiful, in any conventional sense, nor again, in any conventional sense, is he shown to be wise, or as a dispenser or purveyor of wisdom. In the great portraits of civilized conversation, ranging from Euripides to *Emma* and *Portrait of a Lady*, speech and thought are so wedded that the reader participates in the ebb and flow of ideas simultaneously with the ebb and flow of feeling. Our future educational materials must be devised with such works of art, literature and philosophy as their models—or rather, as their inspiration, for the period which we are coming to in the area of education can no more use models based on the past than the major architects of the 13th or the 20th centuries could use them.

Educators have underestimated the amount of preparation necessary to arouse a child's curiosity. Anyone can pique it. There are countless gimmicks that fascinate children and enchant them. But to get to the deeper levels of their curiosity (their curiosity about what is important), we must do more than merely titillate their interest. We need to construct instructional materials and instruments that contain intellectual shock and surprise. We can hardly expect to arouse the real resourcefulness and spontaneity of the child without presenting him with striking ideas of some kind. And at the same time we must be prepared to guide his responsiveness so that he can see its rewards, rather than that he should become disenchanted as a result of the fruitlessness of his own ramblings. There are times that call for structuring discussions and times that call for allowing them to proceed improvisationally; there are times that call for didacticism and times that call for discovery techniques. An effective teacher does not put his trust in any one technique, but relies upon his tact and sensitivity to determine which of his armory of methods he should select and employ on any given occasion.

A curious child is like a coiled spring in that he contains his own energy, his own dynamism, his own way of opening or unfolding. But one must find the proper trigger mechanism to release that energy. This is not just an idle figure of speech. Experimenters have shown how much faster a cat will get out of a box if the release mechanism is connected to a dangling string rather than to a lever, latch, wheel, etc. This is of course because the cat instinctively responds to the string and not to the other stimuli. Similarly, in sexual behavior, what a caress provokes is not merely an isolated response, but a biologically structured process of behavior leading to its own culmination or fulfillment.

In our pedagogical thinking, we have tended to be remarkably narrow. We have puritanically separated instruction from entertainment (much as we have separated work from play—except in the area of art). Instruction is serious, grim and rational. Entertainment is light-hearted and irrational. And then we're amazed to find our children repelled by cognitive activities! What did we expect?

Occasionally we pay lip-service to non-verbal or non-assertive techniques. "Aristotle knows, but Plato shows," we sigh, conveniently forgetting that what Plato demonstrated or (to use Buchler's term) "exhibited" was quite different from what Aristotle, in his dry fashion, was satisfied to assert. For exhibitive techniques are not just entertainment. They are also instruments of disclosure and communication, and they can convey what a standard textbook approach cannot hope to convey.

All of this is an apology for presuming to experiment with the teaching of deduction to 10 and 11 year-olds through the medium of a fictional account of the discovery by a group of children of some of the principles of reasoning, and how they subsequently continue their thinking about thinking. *Harry Stottlemeier's Discovery* is only a beginning (if it is a beginning at all). But if it should develop into something more, even Harry himself might begin to ponder the significance of his own name—minus, of course, its last two syllables.

Part Two

The Pilot Project, whose ostensible aim was to determine the feasibility of teaching reasoning to fifth-grade children, was carried out in the Rand School, Montclair, New Jersey, during the 1970-71 academic year. The design of the experiment was devised by Milton Bierman, Director of Pupil Services of the Montclair school system.

The Rand school is located in an area populated largely by low-income and lower-middle-income black families. But it had just been paired with the Watchung school, so that two-thirds of its pupils were now drawn from a neighborhood that is primarily white and middle-income. The population of the school was consequently quite heterogeneous.

Bierman established two groups of twenty children each, through randomization. The control group was assigned to a professor from N.Y.U. who was engaged in a social science experiment. Unfortunately his project collapsed after three weeks, and so the remainder of the period of the experiment was devoted to social science instruction in the case of the control group.

The pilot project group was taught by myself, with the assistance of two aides, who were then graduate students in Developmental Psychology: Jerry Jaffe and Jim Harte. We met with the students twice a week (each meeting lasted 40 minutes) for nine weeks. The class was never identified to the students as being "logic" or "philosophy" or any other such term. When necessary, it was referred to as "Dr. Lipman's class." The students asked fairly soon if grades would be given, and they were told that none would be.

Wherever possible during the course, the use of technical terms was avoided, on the assumption that they carry with them, at least to the mind of the child, a negative charisma: they are intimidating, "power" words, the kind used by "People in Positions of Authority." It was this impression we wished to avoid making by avoiding the terms that leave such an impression.

Although I had taught logic and philosophy on a college level since 1952, I'd had no experience with teaching fifth-grade students, and my two assistants had had no teaching experience whatsoever. No doubt the students found us a bit odd. I began by reading a chapter of Harry Stottlemeier at a session, but I soon found that they preferred to read for themselves. I was hesitant, because I thought that the class would become impatient with the slow readers. To my surprise, they were patient until the very end with the haltings and stumblings of the slow readers. (The fast readers would often try to read more than their share, but they would have resented my limiting a slow reader to less than his share.) Later on, they were delighted when I let them play roles in those chapters which were designed to permit role-playing. And they loved the video recording session we had—but only when it was introduced suddenly, without prior announcement. On the occasion on which I asked them to prepare for a video taping, they were quite self-conscious and inhibited.

I would like to cite my notes which I wrote at the end of the first week of the project:

Friday, October 16:

Today was the second day for Harry Stottle-meier, and we've already gone through two chapters. But I think we'll slow down once we hit the discussion materials in Chapter 3.

On Wednesday, when we first saw the students, we were more apprehensive than ever: they looked so small! I read the first chapter to them with virtually no explanation of what we were doing. They listened very quietly, turning the pages in unison while I read. Then I asked what Harry had discovered. I expected some halting, fumbling replies. In fact, we already had prepared some very elementary exercises (e.g., different ways of filling in blanks:

"All _____ are fish," and "All kittens are _____," etc.).

What we didn't expect was that the very first answer was lucid and absolutely complete: that Harry had discovered that if you take a sentence beginning with "all," and turn it around then if it was true at first, it will be false when you turn it around. But if you take a sentence beginning with "no," and turn it around, it'll still be true. We were astonished! The remainder of the class did as well. We went down the rows and asked them to illustrate the rule, and they had no difficulty at all. (We found today that some of them had difficulty writing out the rule, but they have no problem applying it.) This is all the more interesting when we recall that these kids are from levels C and D—average and below average.

Moreover, they brought out certain deficiencies in the chapter: the need to turn adjectival predicates into noun phrases (e.g., to turn "All kittens are frisky" into "All kittens are frisky things", so that it can be reversed without awkwardness). Also, it became clear that they wanted to know about sentences that began with "No" and were false—did they stay false when reversed? I was so surprised that they'd caught on to something omitted from the chapter that I didn't at first have the courage to answer. But later I told them that such a sentence, when reversed, could be either true or false.

Today's story went well, except that many or most of the children hadn't yet studied fractions, so they didn't know about lowest common denominators. This portion of Ch. 2 will have to be changed.

One thing we noted about both days was that the kids really relish having some tangible results to write down in their notebooks. I had thought originally that the logical rules would be what they would resist, and would have to be coaxed into accepting by the bonus of pleasure from the stories. But that doesn't seem to be how it works. They seem to look upon the rules as the tangible, visible profits of the enterprise, the rewards they can take home and show. The pleasure they get from the stories themselves is somehow of a different order.

We administered three quizzes in reasoning during the nine-week course. When the experiment was concluded, Jerry, Jim and I went our separate ways, but I received a computer printout from Jerry indicating that the results of one of the tests showed a difference between the two groups of .28, which he did not consider significant. Somehow I erroneously interpreted this to be the result of the post-test rather than merely the final quiz. I suspect that I was resigned to believing that the experiment might produce important changes in the children's attitudes, but since these probably could not be demonstrated, I didn't really expect significant improvements in achievement. Call it a defeatist attitude, but the fact is that I accepted the presumed result with resignation.

I didn't learn until the summer of 1973 what the actual results of the post-test had been. This is a quotation from Jerry's report.

"Both groups (the pilot study group and the control group) were initially tested for their knowledge of logic and logical reasoning through the use of four specific test parts of the California Test of Mental Maturity (1963 Revision Long Form). . . . No significant differences occurred between the two groups prior to the start of the program although both groups demonstrated above average scores in the results. At the end of nine weeks, both groups were again tested for their knowledge of logic and logical reasoning. The same four tests of the California Test of Mental Maturity were used except that the items were extracted from the Short Form (1963 Revision) of the test.

The pilot study group showed significant gains over the control group in the area of logic and logical reasoning (p % .01). The computed mental ages (as related to logic and logical reasoning ability of the pilot study group and the control group) were 167 months (13 years 11 months) and 140 months (11 years 8 months) respectively. The control group showed no significant advance over their initial test scores."

It took me several days to digest this information. How significant was the reported difference of .01? Bierman informed me that it was an unusually high degree of significance. This became fairly evident when one considered the increase of 27 months in mental age of the pilot study group at the end of the 9-week program.

I could hardly believe we'd made such an impact on the kids in the study. After all, we'd not made much of a fuss about teaching logic: there was no homework, no grades, no written classwork—it was all discussion, and the discussions usually got far away from the subject of deductive inference. On the other hand, we had taken the kids seriously and they seemed to take us in the same way. We promised them nothing, and we felt they were satisfied that what they were doing was meaningful. After all, children don't like being told, when they ask what something means, or why they have to do something, "Wait, you'll see." To them, that's so much pie in the sky. They want meaning now. They want meaning to be intrinsic, not extrinsic. So maybe we did something right!

I called Jerry. He told me that the results were quite as he had set them down in his report. Unfortunately, he no longer had the data, which meant that our findings couldn't be substantiated.

This was getting to be a roller-coaster ride of successive elations and disappointments. I discussed the matter with Bierman, so as to put things in perspective. All right, so the principles of logic (from immediate inference on through the categorical and hypothetical syllogisms)

Philosophy 101

Once upon a time there was a princess who lay down on seven mattresses and slept like a baby all night through, and when she woke up in the morning she said, *I dreamed there was something under my mattress,* and they looked and there was a horse.

* * *

Philosophy is something you read in order to get over philosophy.

* * *

As the proverb says, *"I killed your cat because she ate my cow."*

—from Randall Jarrell, *Pictures from an Institution*

---

could be taught to children. So what? The important thing was, what effect would this have on their general achievement levels? And would such an effect be a lasting one? I suggested to Bierman that we compare the Iowa scores of the two groups for the years 1971 and 1973. The crucial scores would be the reading scores. It seemed very improbable, however, that a nine-week course in logic and philosophy taken late in 1970 would influence the reading scores of a group of children in 1973.

But when I glanced over the raw scores, I was convinced we were on to something. Bierman's calculations confirmed my suspicion: the difference was indeed significant—in fact, it was the identical high level of significance, .01, which Jerry had discovered in his post-test.

I am now convinced that philosophy can and should be a part of the entire length of a child's education. In a sense this is a kind of tautology, because it is abundantly clear that children hunger for meaning, and get turned off by education when it ceases to be meaningful to them. And philosophical discussions are precisely the proper medium for putting things in perspective, getting a sense of proportion, and achieving some kind of insight into the direction of one's life. So to want meaning and to require a philosophical dimension to one's education amount to pretty much the same thing. As Kant says, who wills the end, wills the means: if we really want children to find their educations meaningful, we'll devise a suitable philosophical component. And if we don't devise such a component, it's because we really don't want them to wonder what it's all about.

Philosophy for Children:
An Important Curriculum Innovation

Laurance J. Splitter

My subject in this paper is the teaching of thinking skills to schoolage children. A "back-to-the-basics" topic if ever there was one, indeed, one more basic even than the three R's[1]— and one which is relevant to the needs of all children, not just the so-called academic or "gifted" minority. "Thinking skills" is a catch-all phrase. It covers a vast range of capacities and abilities of varying degrees of generality. So the best way to clarify what I have in mind is to provide an (incomplete) list, as follows:

learning to ask relevant questions,
seeing connections among different strands of thought,
drawing out the consequences of what is said and done (inference),
clarifying and defining terms avoiding ambiguity, distinguishing relevant from irrelevant considerations,
evaluating conflicting courses of action,
identifying underlying assumptions,
distinguishing "fact" (objective evidence) from mere opinion,
giving reasons for beliefs held and decisions made,
learning to generalise from particular instances,
learning to think analogically,
detecting fallacies in reasoning (formal and informal) and distinguishing sophistry from genuine argument,
taking account of all relevant considerations— comprehensiveness, learning to criticize constructively and to modify one's own opinion in the face of criticism, thereby developing a sound

conception of self, respect for others, etc., learning to understand and communicate what is on one's mind, learning not to reject outright (or accept outright) another's point of view, learning to appreciate the importance of consistency in belief, attitude and action.

Notice that these skills are grounded in both the cognitive and the affective aspects of people, in recognition of the fact that these aspects are complementary. As our thoughts affect us in various ways, so our feelings may be rationalised as more or less appropriate on different occasions.

Can anyone deny the important place that these skills occupy—or should occupy—in a person's life? In acquiring them, one acquires the capacity to be actively involved in human affairs (including a vocation), and a degree of self-direction which, though highly valued in principle, is largely unrecognised in practice.

Worthy ideals to be sure, and clearly related to the kinds of thinking skills listed above. But are these ideals given any real degree of practical application in our schools? The sad fact is that neither the teacher nor the curriculum has much to do with the teaching of thinking skills *per se*. The inevitable result is that perceptive understanding, mature judgment, responsible selfdirection and moral autonomy do not spring most naturally to mind when it comes to analysing what it is that young people come away with after 10 to 12 years of formal education.

* * *

Quite young children, having reached a certain level of mobility and linguistic competence, possess attributes which deserve to be called philosophical. For purposes of discussion, these may be separated into two broad clusters, as follows:—

(i) A structural or methodological component: Adults who interact with young children (3-7 years) are often impressed by the fact that they bring to their activities—both inside and outside the classroom—a natural sense of curiosity and inquiry. They respond with characteristic honesty and enthusiasm to situations which bother and/or stimulate them, and they demand an equally honest and straightforward response from those around them, to whom their questions and expressions of puzzlement are directed. They wonder about things which seem banal and trivial to adults and even older children, and they express—in their own terms—a keen desire to understand the world and their place in it. From the time that a child first asks "Why?," she is engaged in the process of philosophical inquiry.

(ii) A substantive component By the time children reach the age of compulsory school attendance, they already possess a collection of beliefs, attitudes and values—a perspective on the world (as we would say)—which is very precious to them. The fact that it is both largely derivative (its sources being the family and, later, peer group influences) and experientially naive, does not detract from its importance to its owners, nor from its potential value in educational terms.[2] Children do care about such timeless notions as friendship and fairness, freedom, goodness and truth, reality and nonexistence, thinking, personal identity, beauty, infinity and the universe, space, death and so on. Now what makes these concerns philosophical is not the abstract language in which they are sometimes couched, but their universalisability: their vitality and relevance can be carried over from concrete and specific situations to future and hypothetical situations involving people other than oneself. Children can be helped to make these extensions for themselves—always, of course, in their own terms.

If we combine components (i) and (ii) we have the basis of a curriculum and teaching methodology which addresses some key educational objectives. The child's natural sense of wonderment—(i)—can be developed and expanded into a capacity for thinking and discovery which is an essential part of personal—cognitive and affective—growth. On the other hand, the child's beliefs, attitudes and values, representing the sum total of his/her experiences to date, can also be developed into a more reflective, a more considered perspective on life and its significance. In taking this aspect—which is (ii) above—into serious account, we provide a legitimate sense to the elusive concept of relevance in education: children will see relevance and meaning in activities which are bound up with their own interests and concerns. Conversely, in ignoring and even discouraging this aspect, we trample upon something which is very precious, thereby eliminating the child's own unique perspective from the education process. Here, surely is one explanation of the sense of alienation experienced by many young people during their secondary school years. They have endured to the breaking point a system which has imposed and intruded upon what they once regarded as valuable and worthwhile, supplanting it with ideas and concerns which are often completely alien to them.

This point bears elaboration. Our stereo-typical 5 year old, full of wonderment and curiosity, becomes, ten years down the track, a disillusioned and frustrated adolescent, lacking in self-esteem and turned off formal education. The transformation is striking.

Thus Lipman et al:

. . . a snail is fascinating to them (young children)—or a mud puddle—or the dark spots on the face of the moon. It is only gradually that a crust or scale will grow over their minds, and they will take these things more and more for granted, until from marvelling at everything, they marvel at nothing.[3]

The struggle towards self-awareness is often frustrated by peer group pressure to conform and family/social pressure to succeed. Indeed the very standard of success against which many young people measure themselves is alien to them. And here the school is no ally. It is too busy trying to inculcate the values and beliefs of the society to which it owes allegiance, to be concerned with those aspects of persons which would make them unique in their own eyes. And the case is yet worse, for in losing that early sense of wonderment, the child loses the opportunity to develop the crucial critical skills which might have enabled him to retain a measure of control over his own education.[4] As time goes on, he becomes a passive observer rather than an active participant.

We should not be surprised to find connections between the failure to teach and promote thinking, reasoning and inquiry skills on the one hand, and lack of involvement in the curriculum with subsequent decline in interest, low self-esteem, etc. on the other. Lipman, Sharp and Oscanyan, in an early section of their *Philosophy in the Classroom*, entitled "The Child's Hunger for Meaning," offer the following observations:

> All of us . . . have known what it is for things to lack meaning. It is a deeply disturbing experience, much more so than simply being puzzled . . . Children who sit at their desks and are inundated with factual information that seems jumbled, pointless and unconnected to their lives have a direct sense of the meaninglessness of their experience . . . children don't know where to turn. And since school is compulsory, many children find themselves imprisoned in a nightmare.[5]

The writers go on to point out, as I have done, that young children come to school/kindergarden "bright-eyed, curious and ready to learn." But, in many cases, their inquisitiveness begins to fade with the realisation that they are being compelled to remain in school for reasons which are more social and economic than intrinsically educational:

> If school experience were as rich and meaningful as it is capable of being, we would not see children detesting their lives in school, as so many in fact do.
> The relationship between education and meaning should be considered inviolable. (But) meanings cannot be dispensed . . . they must be acquired . . . something must be done to enable children to acquire meaning for themselves. They will not acquire such meaning merely by learning the contents of adult knowledge. They must be taught to think and, in particular, to think for themselves. Thinking is the skill par excellence that enables us to acquire meanings.[6]

The line of thought developed over the last few paragraphs should make us wary about the parameters of the current debate on the problem of early school leavers. The crucial point is that relevance and meaning in education cannot be imposed from outside the child's own perspective, either through strict adherence to the traditional "academic" curriculum, or through a more broadly-based curriculum which focuses on vocational and survival skills.

Let us return to the idea that a child's sense of wonderment, along with the objects of that wonder, form a sound educational basis. It is here that Philosophy for Children takes off, for in doing philosophy one is searching for reasons and connections which will bring sense to life's experiences. Philosophy is both method and content: it is defined no less by a range of problems which may be called philosophical, than by an approach to these problems which is rigorous, objective and open-ended. The end-point of philosophical discussion or reflective exercise cannot be preempted: one works with the assumption that everyone's thoughts are precious and (potentially) valuable.

Philosophy for Children is a program which utilizes and expands upon the capacity for reflection and inquiry which all children possess. In a literal sense then, its primary resource is the children themselves. But sound thinking won't just happen, even among children who are "bright-eyed, curious, and ready to learn." It requires the right kind of environment, one in which children quickly come to appreciate that while their own views will be respected, they are required to support them with reasons. One way of supplying this kind of environment consists in creating, in the classroom, a community of inquiry.[7] This may be achieved with the help of three further resources:

(a) a philosophical novel,
(b) an accompanying manual for teachers,
(c) a teacher who is both philosophically aware and able to transmit this awareness to others.

I shall briefly discuss each of these in turn.

(a) Since 1970, children in many American schools have been reading and discussing a collection of novels prepared by Matthew Lipman, founder and director of the Institute for the Advancement of Philosophy for Children (IAPC). Here is what Lipman has to say about the format of the novels:

> Instead of wearying them (children) with an explanation of the merits of inquiry in the classroom, we can show them, in fictional form, a classroom community of inquiry, composed of children much like ordinary, live children, thinking about matters of grave importance to children.[8]

By reading and talking about the novels, children identify themselves with their fictional counterparts, reenacting and extrapolating from the intellectual, rather than the emotional, processes of these characters. The children in the novel—each according to his/her own style and personality—talk and think about thinking as a normal part of their daily routine. And they do so using language which is familiar to real children.

(b) The function of the teaching manuals is to assist teachers in their task of creating a community of inquiry in the classroom. The manuals, which are subject to continual revision and appraisal, serve jointly to expand the level of philosophical awareness in teachers, and to help both teachers and students identify and focus upon important philosophical ideas. The chapters correspond to those in the novels and are constructed around the leading ideas raised there. These ideas are filled out by means of exercises (verbal and written), points for discussion, and explanations (for teachers) of their philosophical and pedagogic significance. In many instances, ideas are presented in ways which may seem tangential to the issue at hand. But tangents can be valuable, provided that the children learn to distinguish between relevant and irrelevant considerations. It is one of the great merits of philosophy, from the point of view of sound teaching strategy, that it is not constrained by a commitment to a given body of facts or information, and so can—where many aspects of existing curricula cannot—be taught in a way which is not indoctrinatory. In Chapter 1 of *Harry Stottlemeier's Discovery*,[9] Harry discovers an idea and proceeds to test it. His idea is really an elementary rule of logic, *viz.* that subject-predicate sentences of the form "All As are Bs" cannot (normally) be validly converted or reversed, whereas those of the form "No As are Bs" can be. This is a rule of Aristotelean Syllogistic, but the children never mention either the name "Aristotle" or the term "syllogistic," and the discussion never strays from the ordinary language employed by them. Now one of the leading (albeit "tangential") ideas raised in the Manual (*Philosophical Inquiry*) concerns the distinction between discovery and invention, two concepts which are familiar to children, yet which generate a number of fascinating and nontrivial issues as soon as we focus on the concepts themselves (try making clear to someone the exact nature of the distinction). As the authors point out, it is up to the teacher "to assume responsibility for making the children fully conscious of the thrill of discovery and invention."[10] Another illustration: in my second meeting with twenty-five year 5 pupils at Woollahra Public School,[11] I asked the class to agree with me that all dogs are animals and no submarines are kangaroos. But one child protested that toy dogs are not animals and another pointed out that a submarine could be *called* a kangaroo. The general discussion which ensued was creative, instructive and unpredictable. The children were already beginning to look for counterexamples, to express what was on their minds, to become clear about their own ideas, and to develop reasonable strategies for defending their views. They were also preparing themselves for the crucial discovery that it is no objective of thinking—or of thinking about thinking—to reach a fixed point from which there can be no retreat. A rational point of view involves not just the view itself, but an awareness that no view is ultimately inviolable.

(c) Can children create their own communities of inquiry, without the aid of any resources apart from themselves, their natural sense of inquiry, etc? The answer might be "yes" if they had a reasonable picture or model of the way in which such communities function. Might not the model come from the novels themselves? Or, to go one step further, might not the teacher, armed with the manual and its structured exercises and ideas, help the children create a community of inquiry? If this is not enough, what else is needed?

It is not enough—though it is plainly necessary. To understand why some kind of systematic teacher training is also necessary, we must first remind ourselves of the reality of the situation in the classroom. Our schools are mirrors of society-at-large. Teachers possess a certain power by virtue of their greater knowledge, and the authority which is invested in them. The learning environment is strongly asymetrical, with large numbers of relatively ignorant (therefore powerless) children under the control of a few relatively knowledgeable teachers. As children progress through their primary and secondary years, "the curriculum" becomes more and more established as an entity in its own right. Teachers become preoccupied with the objective of getting through it and of maintaining discipline in a class which might otherwise lose interest. And students continue to regard their teachers as experts who know something that they do not.

This picture is inimical to what many regard as genuine education. Unfortunately, it is reinforced in teacher training institutions where prospective teachers might be, but are not, challenged to reflect upon the conceptual nature of their chosen career, and where they might be, but again are not, taught how to foster rationality and (intellectual and moral) autonomy in young people. To be fair, the problem of maintaining discipline and respect in classes which are too large by half, with principals and parents breathing continually down their necks, is one which can so overwhelm teachers that the niceties of pedagogic theory become virtually irrelevant. However, a more serious problem stems from the blatant fact that for many teachers—products, after all, of the same educational system—a capacity for critical thinking and a sense of wonderment about the world are sorely lacking. If children lose sight of the essential joy of learning and discovery, how much more so will this be true of teachers who have endured the system for that much longer?

Philosophy for Children challenges all this. It requires its teachers to be strong pedagogically—so that they do *teach* rather than merely "facilitate"—but rejects the idea that this strength is tied to the teacher-as-expert model. A good teacher of philosophy to children must be—or must become—"intellectually open and honest, curious about as well as critical of the world, knowledgeable but not all-knowing."[12] In addition, he or she must be skilled in the art of conducting philosophical inquiry, which requires a sensitivity to philosophical issues and the ability to guide a philosophical discussion. What this, in turn, amounts to, includes:

> an understanding of when and when not to intervene in the discussion . . . .skill in eliciting views and opinions from students and in helping them discover the logical implications of their views . . . returning to thoughts and points of view volunteered by students, weaving the threads together, and assisting students to un-

derstand that their ideas make a difference in their lives.[13]

Much of the conflict between conservative and progressive theories of education dissipates with the realization that while it may be inappropriate for teachers to insist that certain facts be memorized irrespective of the interests and beliefs of students, it is entirely appropriate for them to insist that students think clearly about what they say and do, realize implications, see connections and inconsistencies, etc.

* * *

The fact that Philosophy for Children combines high standards of intellectual rigor with a significant amount of participation on the part of the children themselves, has several interesting educational implications. On the one hand, the program is enjoyed by its participants,[14] even though it most definitely deserves to be classified as school work. On the other hand, it has been shown, by a variety of objective experiments and tests, to be extremely successful in the attainment of certain key educational objectives. In this respect the IAPC has been careful to monitor the success of its programs utilizing, wherever possible, professional educational testing services. The results of this experimental research have been impressive to say the least. Using a variety of tests (pre- and post-testing of experimental and control groups)—including the newly-developed New Jersey Test of Reasoning Skills—it has been established, repeatedly and consistently, that children who, with their classroom teacher, participate in the program over a reasonable period (a semester or more) improve significantly across a range of skills.[15] These include:

> reading (which itself includes the ability to recognize main ideas, draw correct inferences, comprehend details and recognize meanings), critical thinking, including listening and reasoning, productivity (generating new ideas), mathematics, interpersonal relationships (respect for others—

both in and out of school), attitudes of intellectual freedom, and academic readiness.

The experiments have involved children of varying abilities and socioeconomic backgrounds. My own positive experiences at a quite ordinary school in industrial Newark, New Jersey and elsewhere, and the available reference material on work with handicapped (including deaf children,[16] as well as with gifted children[17] (also handicapped by the present system), confirm the enormous potential of Philosophy for Children.

* * *

Any initiative which exposes serious flaws in the existing system is bound to be criticized. Philosophy for Children does indeed throw a new light on familiar trouble spots in educational theory. Constraints of space prevent all but the briefest comment on some of these.

(i) A favored line in educational psychology appears to conflict with the view that young children can, and should be taught to, do philosophy. According to Piagetian Stage Theory, philosophy and logic, involving as they do abstract or second-order mental operations, are beyond the natural capacities of (most) primary school children, because the latter have not progressed from stage three (concrete operations) to stage four (formal operations). On the other hand, adolescents, having made the transition, will naturally acquire the requisite conceptual skills.

Many aspects of Piaget's theory have been questioned (on both empirical and conceptual grounds).[18] Educational strategies based upon it are almost guaranteed to favor the status quo, in which the conceptual capacities of primary school children are ignored, with the result that adolescents and adults lose their interest in—and perhaps their capacity for—critical thinking and the generation of abstract ideas. Philosophy for Children is concerned to reverse this unhappy process.

(ii) Is philosophy a "soft option" when compared to the traditional disciplines (mathematics, science, etc)? Does philosophy come down too strongly on the side of those who stress method at the expense of content, thereby falling in with the view that there are no absolute or ultimate truths?

Philosophy has always been a part of humanity's quest for knowledge and certainty. As the most venerable of academic disciplines, it is bound up with standards of rigor and objectivity which are simply inconsistent with the popular mythology of philosophy as a soft option. Moreover, the true student of philosophy is likely to hold fast to the concept of absolute truth as an ideal worth striving for, even as he knows that he cannot validly claim to know such truth with absolute certainty. As for the familiar conflict between teaching method and teaching content, it cannot be denied that philosophy is intimately bound up with the methodology of sound thinking. But this is entirely consistent with the traditional curriculum, provided that the latter is itself bound up with this particular methodology. The fundamental endeavor of a worthwhile curriculum should be to *engage the minds* of those who must study it. It might well be asked whether or not the existing range of school subjects—from traditional "hard" subjects to more skills-oriented ones—does succeed in this endeavor.

One further point. Philosophy does not conflict with other disciplines because it complements them. Its various strands—logic, ethics, aesthetics, metaphysics, etc.—are essentially interdisciplinary, underlying and supporting the existing curriculum. Philosophy, therefore, carries the potential to bind together a timetable which is becoming increasingly disjointed and fragmented.[19]

(iii) Given that ethics is a branch of philosophy, to what extent should the teaching of philosophy be bound up with the transmission of values in the classroom?

There are large issues here. It is now generally recognized that the utter pervasiveness of values

How does one play the philosophy game?

When Socrates was asked some large and exciting question, it was characteristic of him to find some other question that would have to be answered first. For example, when he was asked whether virtue could be taught, he said that he was unable to answer the question because he did not know what virtue was. He meant, of course, that he did not know exactly what it was. It is understandable that many people found his way of doing philosophy maddening. For consecutive thought is such a difficult achievement that it is natural to feel resentment when someone takes up the first word and questions its exact application. He is not playing the game. But of course he is not. That is his whole point.

—David Pears, in "Wittgenstein and Austin," in Williams and Montefiore, *British Analytical Philosophy.*

in human affairs exposes as mythical and mischievous the idea that schools should be value-free or morally neutral. Children do not come to school as empty vessels; they are chock-full of values and attitudes picked up at home, from T.V., etc. It is in this context that the question of moral education (personal development) arises. Here, many teachers feel constrained by a dilemma, especially when it comes to raising controversial issues in the classroom. Either they teach students that one specific moral view is the correct one, or they support an open strategy according to which one moral opinion is as good as another. The first option is tantamount to indoctrination, with teachers pushing pet values and prejudices—it cannot count as (moral) education. The second option is a form of moral abdication, according to which morality is an arbitrary and private affair and so cannot be taught objectively. Ironically, the end result is the same, for in failing to provide young people with the skills necessary for examining and evaluating their own values and those of their peers, we expose them to the moral code of the jungle in which the strong subjugate the weak to their own will. No wonder that the self-proclaimed moral experts in our community are keen to keep personal development and sex education out of schools. They know only too well that uneducated minds cannot deal rationally and objectively with the material that is heaped upon them.

There is a way out of' the dilemma. Children can be taught to think carefully and critically about morality as with any other topic. Philosophy of Children drives a wedge between indoctrination and moral abdication because it encourages children to reflect upon the beliefs and attitudes that they do have, within the environment of a community of inquiry. I am convinced that teachers who are trained to teach philosophy along the lines described above are well-suited to be involved in the difficult and sensitive area of values education.

Notes and References

1. See F. Oscanyan, "Teaching Logic to Children" In M. Lipman and A.M. Sharp (eds). *Growing Up With Philosophy*. Philadelphia: Temple U.P., 1978.
2. This point, emphasized by John Dewey, is gaining wide recognition among educational administrators. See "Towards as Effective Curriculum" N.S.W. Department of Education, 1984.
3. M. Lipman, et.al., *Philosophy in the Classroom*. Philadelphia: Temple U.P., 1980, 32.
4. See J. Passmore, *The Philosophy of Teaching*. London: Duckworth, 1980, 177. Also M. Lipman, "Philosophy and the Cultivation of Reasoning" (Unpublished 1984), 9.
5. M. Lipman, et.al., op.cit., 12.
6. Ibid., 12-13.
7. A key concept in *Philosophy for Children*. See M. Lipman, "Thinking Skills fostered by Philosophy for Children" (Unpublished 1982) and M. Lipman, op.cit., 1984.
8. M. Lipman, op. cit. 1982, 5.
9. M. Lipman, *Harry Slottlemeier's Discovery*. Montclair, N.J.: First Mountain Foundation, 1974, 1982.
10. M. Lipman, A.M. Sharp, and F. Oscanyan, *Philosophical Inquiry*. Montclair, NJ.: First Mountain Foundation, 1975, 1984, 5.
11. Pilot class, July-October 1984.
12. T.W. Johnson, *Philosophy for Children: An Approach to Critical Thinking*. Bloomington, Indiana: Phi Delta Kappa Educational Foundation, 25.
13. Ibid.
14. "What do Students Think of Philosophy for Children?" *Thinking: The Journal of Philosophy for Children* 3-4, 1982-3, 57-59.
15. Experimental Research includes 1970 (Montclair, N.J.), 1975 (Newark, NJ.), 1976-8 (Newark and Pompton Lake,, NJ.), 1978-9 (Lexington, Mass.), 1980-1 (Hope, Totowa, etc., NJ.). See M. Lipman et.al. op cit., 217-224 and various issues of *Thinking: The Journal of Philosophy for Children*.
16. See C. Simon, "Philosophy for Students with Learning Disabilities" *Thinking, The Journal of Philosophy for Children* 1, 1980, 21-33.
17. See L.J. Splitter, "Gifted and Talented Children and the Fourth R: Reasoning" *Proc. First National Conference on Gifted and Talented Children* (Melbourne, 1983). Commonwealth Schools Commission, 1984.
18. See for instance: C.J. Brainerd, *Piaget's Theory of Intelligence*. Englewood Cliffs, NJ.: Prentice-Hall, 1978, esp, 240-253; A. Gazzard, "Philosophy for Children and the Piagetian Framework" *Thinking: The Journal of Philosophy for Children*, 5, 1984, 10-13; M. Lipman, "Philosophy for Children" *Thinking* 3-4, 1982-3, 35-44, M. Lipman and A,M. Sharp (eds) op cit., 225-240; S. Meadows, "An Assessment of Piaget's Theory of Cognitive Development" In S. Meadows (ed.) *Developing Thinking: Approaches, to Children's Cognitive Development*, London: Methuen, 1983, 7-25.
19. See M. Lipman, op.cit., 1984, 16-17.

Philosophy for Children in its Historical Context

Robert J. Mulvaney

Although this platform is located on the campus of Lehigh University, I hope it will not be thought rude of me to begin this talk by drawing your attention to a neighboring institution, Moravian College, and particularly to the fine statue of John Amos Comenius gracing its main entrance. Comenius is one of the great heroes of modern democratic educational theory, one of the inventors of the illustrated reader, a champion of women's education—some of the earliest schools for girls were established in Moravian communities such as the one in Bethlehem and another in Winston Salem. He is also one of the last champions of an encyclopedic ideal in education, learning, as he put it, "for all men, about all things, in all ways."[1] The statue at Moravian evokes this quality splendidly, with Comenius's hands seeming gently to circumscribe a microcosm. It strikes me that it is no accident that Philosophy for Children should have found a peculiarly fertile reception here. The genius of the place demanded it. The "Father of Modern Education" deserves some invocation at proceedings such as these. So be it.

The extension of philosophy to the pre-collegiate curriculum represents a powerful new direction in contemporary educational practice, responding to a host of perceived ills in classroom instruction and to their underlying theoretical assumptions. In the face of the recent outcry over inadequate thinking among young people, Philosophy for Children offers perhaps the most comprehensive program in thinking skills currently available. In its manifested beneficent results on other basic skills, the program also supports the rest of the curriculum and responds thereby to the continuing perception of inadequacy in language, reading and computational achievement among our children. And the grounding in traditional logic it offers can support the development of new educational goals, among them computer literacy.

At the same time we know that Philosophy for Children is more than a thinking skills program. It is a program in philosophy geared appropriately to the growing child. As such it answers a number of theoretical and practical demands crisscrossing thinking skills but distinct from them. In particular it seeks to maintain and develop more general educational dispositions, curiosity and wonder among them, the natural search for meaning in the young child, the nagging "why?" of the child's earliest language usage, and the drive for cooperative and shared learning experiences. Moreover, it demands a more democratic mode of procedure in the classroom and a kind of participatory teaching not uniquely necessary to mere thinking skills programs. Finally it offers a creative response to the demand for institutional attention to moral education, although not in the quasi-doctrinaire mode apparently espoused by many of those currently recommending moral instruction in the schools.

I want now to explore another dimension of the Philosophy for Children phenomenon, that is the way in which the movement tends to fulfill certain general tendencies in the long history of Western educational theory, especially those involving ideals of individual growth and participation, the fundamental elements of modern democratic pedagogy. I shall consider Plato, Rousseau and John Dewey in this account, the big three on anyone's list of dominant Western educational theorists. I want to show that these three have provided themes in foundational theory which have ripened conditions for the discovery of programs such as Philosophy for Children. I shall claim that Plato's intuition of the mutual interdependence of philosophy, education and political life, along with Rousseau's insistence on the priority of psychological analysis of the young child, joined forces with John Dewey's central themes of integration, synthesis and continuity to produce the groundwork for Philosophy for Children. In particular they set the scene for the dialogical, child-oriented and communitarian goals of the Philosophy for Children program, goals which lie at its heart, but goals which are relatively incidental to most alternative thinking skills programs. Very briefly put, Plato provided a concept of philosophy to Philosophy for Children, Rousseau provided the children, and John Dewey provided the prepositional link. The felicitous conjunction of all three, of course, was anticipated by none of them, and remains the unique contribution of Matthew Lipman and his associates.

In telling this story I do not wish to claim adherence to any special theory of history. I certainly do not want to claim that movements such as Philosophy for Children are logically derivable from some of these historical tendencies, or even that history is a necessary complement to other forms of explanation, philosophical or psychological. I do think that historical generalizations lend moral support to educational innovations and that history supports our store of practical knowledge, a very old-fashioned view of its role. And I also have a personal interest in this form of historical exegesis. It expands my store of meanings. But I admit the elusive and non-rigorous character of investigations such as this and sympathize with those who find little explanatory value in them. At the same time, I do find it necessary to apologize for the need to use such a broad brush in my account. My goal is to present what I see as central to a vast and complex theme. I shall jump to conclusions and make too many hasty generalizations. Harry Stottlemeier would disapprove.

I begin with a remark Jean-Jacques Rousseau made about Plato, and then turn to Plato himself. Rousseau, in his *Emile*, commented that Plato's *Republic* is not a work in political theory, but "the finest treatise on education ever written."[2] As usual Rousseau was half-right, but also as usual, very half-right. Plato's first lesson is that political and educational theory are inseparable. The *Republic* is great both as politics and as pedagogy. The intimacy of this relationship will be seen time and again in our history and forms the core of continuity between Plato's time and our own. We get the schools we deserve largely because of assumptions we make about the role of people as citizens, and the quality of our public life is likewise a function of the instruction we provide our people, especially our young people.

In Plato's particular case, the kind of school he deserved is well-known to all. Since his general political preference is an aristocratic one, the school too shall mirror this preference. For Plato only the best shall rule (taking the term "aristocratic" in its etymological sense and not in the sense of a blood aristocracy, or as a synonym for oligarchy), and therefore only the best shall be schooled to rule. Schools are to be elitist, hierarchical institutions where only a few achieve the necessary wisdom to assume political power. Since the best of the people must logically be a small number, the many shall not rule, democracy is rejected, and the many shall not learn. The role of the many is to be led and their beliefs need be constituted only in terms of this passive social role. It is the tiny intellectual ruling class that determines what these beliefs shall be. And the mode of knowledge in which the many hold these beliefs is that of uncritical, unanalyzed and unsupported opinion. The many cannot rule ultimately because the many cannot think.

The role of philosophy in this educational and political ideal is a richly-textured one. First of all, the typical study of the aspiring ruler is philosophy. Only philosophy offers the comprehensive and encyclopedic knowledge necessary to the ruler. It is he who makes political and educational policy, and these rest upon ideal conceptions of order, truth and goodness. The ideal ruler then is the notorious conjunction of king and philosopher. Philosophy plays a prominent role in the curriculum, constituting the major study of the small elite trained to govern everyone else. It is the aristocratic learning par excellence, the education of the prince.

At the same time philosophy plays a reinforcing role from without. Plato was himself a philosopher and it was his metaphysics and theory of knowledge that formed the support for the utopian system he envisioned. Consequently the politics of aristocracy and the educational system supporting and supported by that politics are applications in the practical realm of his basic philosophical orientation. The ultimate reason for the hierarchical model governing both institutions is that reality itself is constituted on a hierarchical model, and the mind is an adequate mirror of reality. The pyramid of learning and governance is a perfect embodiment of the pyramid of knowledge and reality. Plato's famous divided line, in which reality is played out on a distinction between reality and appearance, and knowledge on a parallel distinction between knowledge and opinion, finds its payoff in a curriculum with philosophy at the top, supported by mathematics and the whole realm of the arts, especially the verbal arts of poetry and rhetoric, and corre-

sponding to a political organization consisting of supremely trained philosopher-rulers, and below them the people whose destiny is to follow and obey those rulers.

The survival of Plato's model of learning is one of the miracles of Western civilization. Virtually every Platonic underpinning has been removed, yet the curriculum remains, surviving in the organization of studies from grammar school to the university. The typical undergraduate distribution requirement is an ossified relic of Plato's invention. It is tempting to search for the causes of this longevity in some theory of human nature, and to argue that Plato's curriculum answers to some deep reality about humankind itself. But it is clear that Plato rests his case not so much on psychology as on metaphysics. His curriculum is divided as it is because reality itself is so ordered, and not because the human animal is constituted in some fashion or other. Perhaps we continue to follow Plato's lead because no alternative metaphysics has grounded education since his time, even though his metaphysics has been quite radically challenged.

Most of the details of Plato's peculiar coordination of philosophy, politics and education we now reject. But one central theme, more crucial than any of these details, survives and forms a cornerstone of programs such as Philosophy for Children. We may call this theme the politics of dialogue. Plato wrote, as everyone knows, in dialogue form. Usually this is taken as a pleasant rhetorical artifice, an attractive, highly dramatic form of exposition and nothing more. But perhaps Plato wanted to say something about the nature of political and educational experience by writing in this form. Perhaps the characters dialoguing in the *Republic* actually constitute an ideal philosophical community, self-governing critical thinkers we might call them. If so, then the *Republic* is both about an ideal community and the record of one in progress, the oral report of how it works. Dialogue becomes then the thinking life of the ideal political and educational system, in which mind meets mind, in which non-self-sufficient individuals compensate for each other's ignorance and error, where individuals trust each other and do not lie, where they think and speak clearly and listen well. If this view of dialogue serves as a necessary counterpoint to the great themes of hierarchy so obvious in Plato's mind, then perhaps we should only regret that his view of reality failed to allow the full expression of the implications of his rhetoric. If only his hierarchy were flattened out a bit, and dialogue extended to a broader population, Plato's politics would be very different. But we are already somewhat ahead of our story.

It should be clear that much of Plato's conception of childhood (shared generally in the ancient world) is dominated by his elitism and hierarchy. Children, along, we must add, with women and slaves, find themselves at the bottom of the pyramid. They are "on the waiting list" as John Dewey put it,[3] looking forward to their full humanity and emancipation as adults, but enjoying no important status in themselves. And the extension of philosophy to them is quite clearly absurd, as absurd as extending governance, knowledge and reality itself to them. In terms of our story Plato gave a conception of philosophy to the Philosophy for Children program, particularly the communitarian ideal and dialogical rhetoric that are at the heart of philosophical activity. But it was Jean-Jacques Rousseau who gave children to the program. It was he who discovered the child in a way that was closed to ancient thought, where childhood was at best a theoretical embarrassment. We turn then to the second of our major philosophers, and consider the contribution of Rousseau, particularly as contained in his novel, *Emile*.

Three challenges presented themselves to ancient thought and prepared the way for some of Rousseau's characteristic themes. First of all, modern thought exhibits a loss of faith in the simple isomorphism of knowledge and reality. Reality itself may be inaccessible and radically unknowable. Grand and finished metaphysical systems are finally suspect. Secondly, in place of

ambitious metaphysics, philosophers in the 17th and 18th centuries turn their attention more to an inner-directed analysis of how the mind works, rather than some outward-directed intuition of reality itself. More and more, knowledge becomes what we know about ourselves, and less what we know about some independent real world. Finally, reality itself, known or unknown, is no longer perceived as divisible into hierarchical levels. Existence is not subject to degree. Things simply are or are not. The discovery of the child depends upon all three of these moves, but perhaps most vividly upon the third. Children can be discovered because adulthood is no longer so highly placed on some ladder of being. Adults are older, but they are not necessarily better, or more real.

Rousseau epitomizes these directions in modern thought, occasionally with startling explicitness. It was he more than any other figure of our era, certainly in educational theory, who embodies some of these powerful tendencies: the primacy of psychological analysis in educational theory; the central position of the phenomenon of growth; the primacy of the individual in the learning experience; and an attitude towards metaphysics blending ignorance and indifference, with an occasional seasoning of contempt. His forbears are Bacon and Descartes. Bacon based his tripartite encyclopedia on Galen's physiology rather than on Plato's divided line. Learning can be divided into poetry, history and philosophy, Bacon had argued, because man's mind is divided into fancy, memory and reason. Psychology has replaced metaphysics as the grounds of a major educational hypothesis. Descartes, on the other hand, offered a radically novel approach to philosophical inquiry, predicated on mental activity rather than introspective naive openness to external reality. Judith Shklar paraphrases Rousseau in one of his many brilliancies:

"We run after shadows which escape us. Some fleeting spectre, some vain phantasm flits before our eyes and we think we see the eternal chain of being." All that we can possibly grasp, in fact, is a sense of our own selfhood and we must end where Descartes began, with "I think, therefore I am."[4]

The self is all we can know, for Rousseau, but it's also enough.

Rousseau discovered the child, but this was largely because he was more interested in growth and development than in the finished product. For all his disdain for historical study, it is a kind of historical process that captures Rousseau's imagination after all, the history of the individual child. The new emphasis on historical study which emerged during the Renaissance, bolstered perhaps by the millenarianism of the century immediately preceding Rousseau, and perhaps by his own conviction that the 18th century would end in violence, focussed his imagination on historical development and growth. For the Greeks growth was imperfect, a form of change in which a given organism was in motion towards some ideal goal. In this picture the child is simply a highly-imperfect, somewhat unreal, processive adult in the making, "neither here nor there," to use Erikson's phrase.[5] Rousseau reverses all this with a progressive teleology of stages of development. The child is complete or perfect at a given level of development rather than only when the process is finished and complete. Characteristic forms of childhood experience such as play are no longer perceived simply as efficient ways of producing learning, but as characteristic modes of experience of the developing human being. The stages Rousseau outlines are crude and simplistic by modern standards. There is not enough continuity in his theory of development, and an almost miraculous progression from stage to stage. But Rousseau's revolution was a complete one nonetheless. The inward turn of modern psychology links with the observed growth of all living things, to produce a redirection of educational theory from the finished product, lying perhaps in an uncertain future, to the process itself, as found in concrete, individual, growing human beings.

"Each mind has a form of its own,"[6] Rousseau insisted, and it is this individualism that crowns his version of child-centered education. Here too the scene is set by the intense egocentrism of modern epistemological theory. Descartes seems to have been the first person in history to use the term "meditation" as the title of a philosophical book. Leibniz's monadism seems also to be operative, the theory that reality is composed of an infinite number of radically individualized centers of conscious power. Some characteristically modern forms of aesthetic representation, such as the novel, embody this individualism. Rousseau's *Emile* is itself a novel, one of the earliest philosophical novels, in fact. And Emile's first and most cherished book is a novel, *Robinson Crusoe*, the tale, be it remembered, of a solitary individual living by his wits. It is Robinson Crusoe who affords a model of political survival, too, not the clashing atom of political experience hypothesized by Hobbes, but peacefully alone in an empty universe. This individualistic politics, standing in such stark contrast to Plato's statism, has enormous implications for aristocracy, national feeling, philanthropy and cosmopolitan ideals. Nevertheless it maintains Plato's central intuition that political theory and educational theory develop together. Rousseau's individualism reinforces his educational ideals, and is in turn reinforced by them. What Rousseau presents to our story then is the psychologically rich, individual, growing child, within a general context of a radically reformulated view of knowledge and reality and the relationship between them.

We come now to the "for" in "Philosophy for Children," John Dewey's contribution to this story. Philosophy for Children rests upon a certain synthetic and integrative mood found in modern American pragmatism, particularly in its cultural forms. Dewey's greatness as an educational theorist is usually made to depend upon his pragmatism, his naturalism and his experimentalism. And critics are likely to condemn what they believe must be the necessary consequences of such positions, relativism, materialism and the idolization of science. I am not eager to challenge either the generalizations or the criticisms, but to take a step beyond them, and point to themes not often emphasized. For one thing, Dewey was an outstanding historian of ideas. He emerged out of the broad historical culture of the nineteenth century, particularly as transmitted to him in his student days at Johns Hopkins University. His first published works were on historical figures. His 1888 book on Leibniz still deserves reading. Many of his books, especially the great *Democracy and Education* of 1916, are replete with historical allusions and analysis. Much of my own interpretation of Plato and Rousseau is formed by him. Related to this historical cast of mind is his residual idealism. His early attraction to Hegel was never completely lost. Much of his language echoes Hegelian terminology and spirit. In spite of his turn against idealism, certainly complete by World War I, he retains the synthetic mentality of the great German idealists, in his aversion to all forms of dualism, for instance. Dewey's mind was integrative and encyclopedic, harmonizing, constructive, reformative, in many ways medieval, as Spinoza's mind, for instance, was medieval. Finally, to his profoundly historical and synthetic approaches to experience, we must add a moral dimension, one owing ultimately to the Greeks, perhaps especially to Aristotle—his avoidance of extremes. Without placing Dewey at all in the camp of the New Humanists (although his criticism of Rousseau ought to be compared with Babbitt's), it is tempting to see him as continuous with the great American classical revival, better studied in the history of art and architecture than in the history of thought. However much we may balk at considering Dewey as an Hegelian, we can certainly see in him the *ne quid nimis* of classical ethics, the avoidance of extremes in action and thought. Dewey's ethics is so heavily Aristotelian that we should not be surprised at appearances of the middle way throughout his work. We may say that his antipathy to dualism is simply an application of the rule of the golden mean. In his educational writing, nothing exhibits this tendency of his thought more than his late book

Experience and Education with its criticism of both progressivism and traditionalism. Avoidance of extremes is the moral imperative of Dewey's liberalism, or of his pragmatic idealism, as it perhaps should be called.

However strange some of these remarks may sound to some, the recognizable Deweyan themes of growth, freedom and shared experience are surely not strange, and, given my analysis above of Plato and Rousseau, it will not surprise anyone that he owes much to both of them. Nor is he out of their company in insisting on a continuity of educational and political theory. The title of his masterpiece, *Democracy and Education*, bears eloquent testimony to that underlying consensus among all three of our thinkers. But at this point Dewey makes a remarkable, if somewhat subtle, departure from both of them. I want to cite a text curiously unnoticed in the major treatments of his political writings, but one which sets the scene for his most dramatic shifts in educational theory, and one which for me points directly to some of the key assumptions of the Philosophy for Children program. Dewey writes in *Democracy and Education*:

> (Plato) had no perception of the uniqueness of individuals. For him they fall by nature into classes, and into a very small number of classes at that. Consequently the testing and sifting function of education only shows to which one of three classes an individual belongs. There being no recognition that each individual constitutes his own class, there could be no recognition of the infinite diversity of active tendencies and combinations of tendencies of which an individual is capable. There were only three types of faculties or powers in the individual's constitution. Hence education would soon reach a static limit in each class, for only diversity makes change and progress.[7]

The text is a rich one. For one thing class aristocracy is closed for the modern educational liberal, whether this aristocracy is one of blood or merit, it makes little difference. Individuality is too complex to be classified, at least in a traditional finitistic sense. But the reason Dewey gives for this position is truly remarkable. It is not that Plato's system has classes, but that it has too few classes. Each individual for Dewey constitutes his own class. This belief has roots deep in the history of neo-Platonic metaphysics. Something very like it is at the heart of Leibniz's theory of the monad, and in turn, as Leibniz himself saw of his own position on individuation, it resembles theories such as Thomas Aquinas's position that angelic substances are specifically distinct from each other, and not numbered members of a single species. Dewey's politics, then, and by extension his position on the child in the classroom, can be characterized somewhat paradoxically as classless and as infinitely class-structured. It is classless in the sense that there is no finite number of classes into one of which each individual fits, and class-structured in the sense that important differences are found in each individual such that he is best described as belonging to a unique class, his own. Incidentally this may be a key to the difference between liberal and Marxist democracy. Dewey distinguishes as many classes as there are individuals, whereas Marx incorporates all individuals into one class. Dewey's theory is more personalistic. In his case we speak of people, in Marx's case we speak of masses.

Dewey's position suggests a remarkable resolution of the antithesis between aristocracy and democracy. Social and political reality is made up of classes—in this the aristocrat is right. But a class corresponds to each individual—in this the democrat is right. As a result neither term suits his intuition. Dewey's system is better called a "universalized aristocracy," one in which the best of each individual rules in a program of shared self-governance. In America every man's a king, as Huey Long said, but one hears Dewey's correction, he is ideally a philosopher-king. The proper education, then, of each citizen is the royal or princely education once extended to a very few. And because comprehensive knowledge of the world outside, and profound scrutiny of the world within, are necessary to this citizen ruler, the extension of philosophy to all the people

becomes an urgent imperative of democratic educational theory.

It should be clear that this theory is as remote from romantic Rousseauian individualism as it is from Plato's hierarchies. The model of much modern individualistic thinking is the discontinuous atom in the void of early materialist physics. Rousseau differed from Hobbes only in his insistence that these political atoms are naturally at peace rather than at war. But Dewey's politics stems from the continuous quantity of a Spinoza or of a Leibniz. Individuals grow and develop in continuity with other individuals, in an overlapping amplitude of social structures, family, localized political communities, states and, of course, schools. Rousseau's one-on-one tuition, with its concomitant stateless cosmopolitanism, sounds very attractive, especially in the modern global village. But for Dewey it represents a subtle attack on the political and social nature of man. The individual then is an individual-in-society, a unity-in-multiplicity, a microcosm, or better, a micropolis, of that association of states whose motto is *e pluribus unum*, one from many.

Dewey then, with the sensitivity of a great intellectual historian, synthesizes, or, if you will, steers a middle path between, the great visions of the Greek civic republican and the modern liberal individualist, and between classical orientations to structure in curriculum with its institutionalized non-family schooling, and modern "individualized instruction." There is, of course, a balance in favor of the moderns. Dewey consistently substitutes empirical study for *a priori* metaphysics. The timeless circle of learning is replaced by the progressive, perpetual and time-bound spiral of growth. Finally, and perhaps not worth mentioning save to draw attention to the vast gulf that separates the ancient world from our own, Dewey comes down squarely on the side of the rights of man as such, with none of the ancient indifference to women, foreigners and children, and of course, non of the automatic "natural" acceptance of institutionalized slavery.

Philosophy for Children never ceases to surprise those involved in it, teachers, teacher-trainers and theorists alike. To quote Art Linklater, kids do say the darndest things. A conference like this one should be organized some day devoted strictly to classroom anecdotes. Historians of thought are surprised too in the freshness taken on by some classic texts, and generally in the remarkable way in which some central themes of Western educational and political theory find application in this program. Let me conclude this paper by pointing once again to some of these themes, both in summary of the points I have made above, and in explicit consideration of their role in Philosophy for Children.

The first of these is the central intuition shared by all three of our philosophers that educational theory and general political and social theory are deeply interrelated. This is not to say that Philosophy for Children recommends some specific ideology or constitutional arrangement. But, at a more fundamental level, it holds that whatever theory we maintain concerning the role of persons interacting with other persons will affect the relationship between students and teachers, as well as that among citizens or members of families. Educational theory cannot be developed in terms simply of some abstract theory of human nature; it must be developed in tandem with political and social theory in their full generality. In terms of application, political democracy demands a relevant form of classroom democracy. We do not prepare children for participatory democracy by hierarchical classroom structures.

Philosophy for Children proceeds dialogically and is heir to Plato's discovery of the proper mode of all philosophical inquiry, open discourse within a community of equals. However proper a hierarchy of experts and specialists may be to schooling in many of its facets, when philosophy enters the classroom, the teacher becomes a Socratic "first among equals," confessing his ignorance, stepping from behind the desk and sitting within the circle of dialoguing children, a full member with them in the great conversation.

Self-knowledge breeds self-esteem, at least for most children. Philosophy for Children stresses self-discovery as few, if any, of the elements of the regular curriculum can claim to. It extends the invitation "Know thyself" to even the youngest members of the learning community. Why? if not to discover and to develop the best in each one of us, the best talent and promise that is unique to the individual child. The abhorrent elitism of Plato's politics and education becomes a virtue when extended to the private sphere and when universalized, because we know that we should ourselves be governed by whatever is best in us, and it is this that we should share in a community of self-governing equals. The deference Philosophy for Children pays to the growing self-definition and self-esteem of the child makes every kid a winner, and constitutes the grain of truth in classic aristocratic educational theory.

But, at this point, we have clearly left the world of the Greeks. Philosophy for Children preserves the integrity (if not the fullness) of philosophical inquiry, but it preserves it for children. It is this conjunction of philosophy and childhood, this remarkable synthesis of Plato and Rousseau, that still surprises us, and seems a paradoxical, almost ironic joke. Philosophy is the program's first passion, but childhood is its second. It borrows its conception of philosophy from the Greeks, but its psychology from the moderns. Philosophy for Children is the willing heir of the few things we have come to know about growth and development, and is in the process of testing one huge new developmental hypothesis, namely the discovery and maintenance of the philosopher in the child. It also by the way may help to preserve the child in the philosopher. One of the tragedies of the grownup is his loss of a sense of wonder, curiosity and playfulness, in short, of childhood. But these emotions are central to philosophical inquiry. Perhaps by starting philosophy earlier and seeing to it that it continues throughout school, grownups will rediscover suppressed reservoirs of playfulness and leisure.

The effects upon a theory of work and maturity remain to be seen.

Plato gave us philosophy, Rousseau gave us children. Philosophy for Children, with the help of Dewey along the way, gave us the connecting preposition "for." But this simple word contains a world of meaning. In it we see represented a momentous flattening out of the hierarchies inherited from classical thought. If children can be taught philosophy, then little remains of the ancient pyramidal and ladder-like structures of learning inherited from Plato, and the elitist class structure and philosophical substructure of these hierarchies. Dewey's view of democracy as shared experience had much to do with setting the scene for this move, as did many of the liberation movements of the past century. But this theory of democracy is not a vulgar rule of the mob, or of the masses. It is a dizzyingly idealistic, perhaps utopian view of a universalized aristocracy, a kind of secularized communion of saints (or unity of the brethren, in Moravian country!), one having roots in Kant's kingdom of ends-in-themselves, itself a secularized version of Augustine's City of God. It is not so much individualistic, as personalistic in tone.

One remarkable feature of Philosophy for Children is the stress placed upon dissent. Although it takes place in a climate of open dialogue and community, it places secondary value upon such things as agreement or consensus. This becomes extremely important in the treatment of ethical questions in the classroom. Far from the ethics games and debating techniques of many values clarification programs, Philosophy for Children encourages the articulation and rational support of moral opinion, regardless of the majority's position. This is not because Philosophy for Children is in some hidden way relativistic or skeptical about moral positions, but simply because, when it comes to ethics, the minority is frequently right. Majoritarian consensus has no special value in philosophical inquiry. The result is that, somewhat paradoxically, a higher individuality emerges out of these communities of inquiry, one potentially far more resistant to propaganda and dogmatism than its democratic tone might lead one to suppose. But again this democracy is not a collection of numbered individuals. It is a continuity of named persons, each of which is an infinitely complex combination of qualities and characteristics, conforming to a formula unique to the individual and quasi-specific.

Finally, the model of growth and development implied by the Philosophy for Children program has its adequate metaphor in the spiral rather than in the ladder. The non-hierarchical view of knowledge held before us is one in which all human cognitive powers are seen to develop in tandem. The seminal or rudimentary traces of even "higher order" thinking skills must be searched in the very young. The child can be a philosopher not because the wisdom of ages is somehow programmed into him, or some such Romantic extravagance, but because the twin psychological spurs to the philosophical life, curiosity and the need to be happy, are present among young as well as among old. At this point Jerome Bruner joins forces with Epicurus who, centuries before our era, invited young and old to the philosophical banquet. Perhaps now at the end of our second millenium we are just beginning to take that invitation seriously.

Let me close, as I began, with a somewhat more localized observation, a bat in my personal cave that I want to share with you. Many of you may have seen the lovely ETV portrait of Aaron Copland in celebration of his 85th birthday recently. During it I recalled that the Shaker hymn so beautifully used by Copland in his "Appalachian Spring" also appears touchingly in the last pages of *Lisa*. And I thought that any effort to specify the uniqueness of the Philosophy for Children program ought to include something about that. I have a slight but nagging aversion to the word "critical" in the term "critical thinking." All our best efforts notwithstanding, the word still connotes a certain negativism and destructiveness. I wish we could renew the use of "reconstructive," to use Dewey's word, or something else, though probably not "positive thinking"! At any rate, Philosophy for Children seems to me a gentle one among critical thinking programs, the "tender land" or "peaceable kingdom" (at least in this part of the country) among thinking skills curricula. It has a warmth and courtesy that should be part of all our teaching. There is a kindness and civility in the program which could hardly be expected from it if it were merely a thinking skills program. As philosophy, it belongs to the tradition of humanistic learning. But as Philosophy for Children, it is likewise humane learning, insisting that children are people, too, and that they should be introduced to the wholeness of liberal education, from their earliest schooldays.

Notes

1. *John Amos Comenius on Education*, intro. by Jean Piaget (New York, 1967), p. 116.
2. *The Emile of Jean-Jacques Rousseau*, trans. and ed. by William Boyd (New York, 1956), p. 13.
3. John Dewey, *Democracy and Education* (New York, 1916), p. 54.
4. Judith Shklar, *Men and Citizens* (Cambridge, MA, 1969), p. 9.
5. Erik H. Erikson, *Childhood and Society*, second edition (New York, 1963), p. 214.
6. *Emile*, p. 42.
7. *Democracy and Education*, p. 90.

Philosophy for Children and Continental Philosophy

Ekkehard Martens

Abstract

After pointing out the most commonly understood difference between Anglo-American Philosophy and Continental Philosophy, namely, logico-linguistic analysis versus personal reflection, Martens shows how, from the standpoint of Continental Philosophy this distinction is unwarranted. By showing us how each of these aspects of Philosophy is recommended for the philosophy education of the young by various writers from the Continental tradition, Martens reveals how the practice of Philosophy for Children has long been proposed by Continental philosophers, albeit, not the whole methodology by any one particular philosopher at any one time. The paper reveals the sympathy that Continental Philosophy therefore has for Philosophy for Children and concludes by questioning the place of the Eastern tradition in the ongoing dialogue about what philosophic inquiry with children should entail.

First I'll try to explain what "Continental Philosophy" might mean. Second, I should like to give three examples of the relationship of Philosophy for Children and Continental Philosophy: Hegel, Kierkegaard and Nelson. Third, I will draw some conclusions regarding the question: "Continental, Anglo-American or International Philosophy for Children?" And, as you'll see, unavoidably, I shall have to return to my first part.

What Could "Continental Philosophy" Mean?

For a continental philosopher like myself, teaching at the University of Hamburg, "Continental Philosophy" is a rather unknown, at least an unusual term. Perhaps we are just doing this kind of philosophy without being forced to talk about it, taking for granted what we are doing. But it might also be possible that continental philosophers don't like or don't accept this classification, as we'll see later on. Anyway, outside of the continent it seems to be a well known, popular and well defined term of present day academic philosophy. Furthermore, it seems to be not only a descriptive term but also a prescriptive one sometimes having negative connotations. In his survey, "Graduate Study in Continental Philosophy in the United States," Robert Solomon (1984) points out that " 'Continental' philosophy has increased in popularity and respectability, and several schools that did not have a program or courses in the subject (in 1975) now do."[1]

Continental philosophy for Solomon counts as: phenomenology (Husserl, Heidegger, Merleau-Ponty); Marxism, existentialism (Kierkegaard, Sartre); structuralism (Foucault, Derrida); Lebensphilosophie/philosophy of life, (Nietzsche, Ortega y Gasset); hermeneutics (Dilthey, Gadamer, Ricoeur); Frankfurt School (Habermas) and—last but not least—German

Idealism (Kant, Hegel). All these philosophers have increased, as Solomon says, in "respectability." Apparently this means a rather negative valuation of the time before. To understand the former rather negative image of Continental Philosophy we must look upon its assessment by the Anglo-American school of philosophy, in particular the American Anglo-American view. In his lectures about "The New World of Philosophy," delivered about 1960, Abraham Kaplan calls analytic philosophy "the most influential one in the English-speaking world"[2] and the one "almost wholly indifferent" to Continental Philosophy.[3] The difference is marked by its scientific approach. Its business as a kind of logico-linguistic analysis is, as Wittgenstein says, "not a body of propositions, but to make propositions clear." Wittgenstein together with Russell are primary founders of analytic philosophy. Another way of stating the business of analytical philosophy is "Whatever can be said clearly." Clearness in this case means logical consistency and empirical verifiability, as Carnap and Reichenbach have explained. Both Carnap and Reichenbach had to emigrate from Nazi Germany and Austria respectively and became most influential philosophers in the USA. It surely would be superficial to say that they just had been impressed too much by the power of modern science and that therefore they had tried to build up a hard-science-philosophy. One should rather realize that they had good reasons to believe—as they did—in the enlightenment of scientific clearness in opposition to the irrationality of Nazi propaganda and "Weltanschauung." Nevertheless, we are now much more enlightened about the chances *and* risks of science and aware that reason involves much more than scientific reason, as analytic philosophy seems to suggest. This might be, at least *should* be, reason enough for increasing the respectability of Continental Philosophy which stresses judgment, common sense, insight, personal experience and personal knowledge, imagination, understanding and wisdom. All these aspects of human reason had been

underestimated by Analytic Philosophy, even in its weak version of ordinary language philosophy.

To summarize thus far: Continental Philosophy might mean (1) the use of the complete power of human reason as laid down in the treasure of traditional philosophy since its beginnings with the Greeks; and in this sense philosophers should reject the continental classification as a reductive fallacy because it would also include the ways of thinking demanded by Analytic Philosophy, (2) this reductive fallacy is not the prerogative of Anglo-American philosophers as Solomon's survey shows. Moreover, other sources suggest that Continental Philosophy is now even more respected in America than on the continent itself, which is either dominated by Anglo-American Philosophy or by antiscientific irrationality like postmodernism.[4] All we need is balance. But it doesn't make any sense to balance one reductive fallacy by its opposite fallacy.

These remarks about the influential philosophy of the time may be helpful to understand the power teachers have. We all live in a scientific-technological world which demands the complete power of human reason to live and to live well, and the extent to which we do this depends to a large extent on what sort of world view our teachers have.

Three Examples: Hegel, Kierkegaard, Nelson

I should like now to give three samples of the relationship between Philosophy for Children and Continental Philosophy. Hegel and Kierkegaard might be taken as examples of two opposing reductive fallacies. Hegel pleads for a mere logical approach, and Kierkegaard pleads for a mere personal one. Nelson, on the other hand, might illustrate how to build a bridge between these two. I hope that all three philosophers would overlook my oversimplifications if they could listen to me. I do it only to make some positions clearer. The examples they use themselves might be more interesting than the whole of their theoretical frameworks.

Hegel had been a teacher of philosophy and an administrator at the Aegidien-Gymnasium in Nuremberg from 1808 to 1816 when he became a professor of philosophy at the University of Berlin. As a member of the Royal Prussian Commission for Examinations (1810-1822), he had to judge students of the last class at the Gymnasium (high school level) as to their abilities as prospective university students. Reading his letter of 1822 to the "Royal Department of Religions, Educational and Medical Affairs" in Berlin, we might think we were reading a recent report of the National Institute of Education or of the "Westdeutschen Rektorenkonferenz" (conference of university presidents in West Germany) lamenting the deficiency of thinking skills. Hegel writes, "Students tend to come to the university without the necessary preparations for the study of philosophy."[5] You can replace "Philosophy" with any other subject, and then you surely will recognize some of our present day problems. Hegel considers "the rudiments of logic," for instance, "definition, classification, argumentation, and scientific method," (today we would say "thinking skills"), as the most suitable for university studies.

Hegel gives some reasons for his view: (1) His earlier experience as a longtime teacher showed him that "this subject will not exceed the pupil's (ages 14-18) power of comprehension." He also cites his own experience, "In my fourteenth year I knew all the figures and rules of syllogisms, and I know them still." I think present day educators often argue out of such a similar small data base. Harry Stottlemeier, however, surely would criticize it. (2) Regarding "the present predilection with thinking for oneself and with productive activities"—and "present" for Hegel means Rousseau, Pestalozzi and their followers in the twentieth century, Hegel affirms that having learned one logic, "one has more freedom and cause to think about it for oneself." Hegel surely is right when he says that thinking is always

thinking "*about*" something and that we have "more freedom" to learn any subject if we have learned its basics and can understand its structure. But *how* should students learn logic, and will their thinking, as a result, be *better* (more effective) in scientific subjects? (3) Hegel offers a very simple and, I think, too simple solution to these problems of method and transfer by briefly saying that "the students should know the rules just as definitely, exactly, and without hesitation as they have to know grammatical rules or mathematical theorems, if they want to understand philology or mathematics." If you read, for instance, what current day educators have to say about "Thinking Skills in the Curriculum" in *Educational Leadership* September 1984, you will doubt whether Hegel's solution is the right one. But you also might have doubts whether present educators have given a better one. (4) Hegel, on the other hand, agrees with present curriculum theorists in that he believes that "the Gymnasium should be dedicated to the general cultivation of mind" and that the individual disciplines can't fulfill this task. (5) Hegel says that "in an early period . . . young people are more obedient and docile towards authority." Does he mean that we should *force* them to learn logic in that period? There should be other ways of motivation.

In summary, Hegel is a keen advocate of formal logic as a necessary preparation for speculative philosophy, and in this vein, there are some parallels with the present thinking skills movement. If you concede, as I do, that learning formal and informal logic is a necessary condition for learning philosophy or any other subject at the school or at the university, it does not mean that it is a sufficient condition. Learning or doing philosophy with children or students must *also* include contents, that is, philosophical ideas and meaning for personal and social life. Some of these points will be stressed by Kierkegaard.

Kierkegaard, the Danish philosopher, had been a student of Hegel in Berlin. But in his view, Hegel's philosophy as an absolute thinking would destroy personal thinking and personal existence. In Kierkegaard's essay of 1837 on storytelling to children, we can recognize his fight against Hegel's objectivism, and we can reconstruct his ideas about doing philosophy with children in a subjective, personal way.[6] For our purpose, there are mainly six interesting aspects for Kierkegaard: (1) Family life is the most important environment for children. But he also knows that families never are ideal families. For the most part the parents are limited to the roles of "chief administrators or presenters of prizes for noble deeds-in both cases with the precise and punctual conscience of a bookkeeper." So there must be a good "Uncle Frank" as a storyteller. At present, "Uncle Frank" has been, unfortunately, replaced by TV and it is hard work now to try to replace TV either by "Talking with Children"[7] in the family or by the IAPC-program[8] in the school; (2) The procedure must be "Socratic." According to Kierkegaard, "one should arouse in children a desire to ask, instead of fending off a reasonable question"; (3) "The whole point is to bring the poetic into touch with their lives in every possible way, to exercise a power of enchantment to let a glimpse appear at the most unexpected moment and then vanish." "To answer a child's question, 'Are there mermaids like that?'—with a 'No, mermaids are just something people imagine' would leave an unfilled space for an anxiety which, when not moderated by such stories, will return again all the stronger." At present, it is very apparent that we can't live without imagination, hopes, ideas and ideals, and that we can't even *think* without them. Science can't replace imagination, as Kierkegaard suggests.[9] The imagining of mermaids and "freedom and dignity" have real power in our lives, much more than science has. (4) To offer children a poetic or "intellectual-emotional nourishment" demands a constant and "continuing attentiveness to what they hear and see." For Kierkegaard, you must live together with them in an "open, free, confident way." (5) Because you can't plan "to let a glimpse appear at the most unexpected moment," philosophy

can't be done "in the school room" by "discipline." Doing philosophy with children in a personal and free way, for him, needs "free time." Kierkegaard would therefore never have developed a Philosophy For Children curriculum. (6) All the other aspects depend on the "deeper relationship to children and their existence." "Existence" is the key word of Kierkegaard's existentialism. To "educate children morally," as it is called, or "impact some useful knowledge" means for him a "completely atomized knowledge."

In summary, Kierkegaard's personal or existentialistic approach stresses these personal aspects of learning and doing philosophy, but he seems to underestimate the objective, impersonal aspects like the method of logical thinking which can be taught together with the personal aspects as Nelson's "Socratic Method," my third example, tries to show.

Nelson taught philosophy at the University of Göttingen in Germany. He was interested in the philosophy of mathematics, ethics and in philosophical pedagogics based on the ideas of autonomous thinking as Socrates and Kant had explained. In his essay "The Socratic Method,"[10] originally delivered as a lecture in 1922, Nelson pleads for "the art of teaching not philosophy but philosophizing, the art of not teaching about philosophers but of making philosophers of the students." This method is well known from the IAPC curriculum. But, unlike this curriculum, Nelson forbids far more strictly any textbook or novel, any exercises or any teacher questions, except such questions as, "What has this answer to do with our question?," "Which word do you wish to emphasize?," "Who has been following?," "Do you know what you said a few moments ago?," "What question are we talking about?" The students have to discover or remember the logical rules and philosophical ideas by themselves, as their own ideas. For Nelson, "Either dogmatism or following Socrates" is an alternative which seems too sharp. Kierkegaard also believed in the Socratic method, but he combined it with storytelling and even Socrates himself told stories or myths. So it might seem as if Nelson is inclined to follow the dogmatism of the "Socratic method." But for the purpose of my paper, this point is not as important as Nelson's foundation of a real school during the 20's, called "Die Walkmuhle," near Gottingen. It was throughout explicitly based on the "Socratic Method," in all subjects and in all daily school life. In the "Socratic Forum" the children, aged about 8 to 14, thought by themselves about real moral problems. To give an example—a boy had damaged his bike and indeed he was guilty. The children's forum didn't discuss whether and how to punish him. They considered, instead, whether the boy's self-respect would be hurt by just getting money for a new bike without doing something about it for himself. Unfortunately, we have no transcriptions of those discussions for the school had to emigrate in the thirties due to its radically democratic approach, first to Denmark and after that to Great Britain. All the papers were burned by a German bomb, and only some hints of verbal descriptions remain.[11] Nevertheless, this school seems to have been the one and only true philosophical school in modern times, and when reading *Harry Stottlemeier's Discovery*, you might get an idea of it. Here, children and teachers are talking Socratically with each other during the lessons and even outside at home and with their friends.

I can't judge whether Nelson's school really built a bridge between Hegel's logical and Kierkegaard's personal approach of doing philosophy with children. Neither could I say which of them is a better continental example of philosophy for children. I rather would suggest that each of them tried to find specific means for specific ends, and this is something we can also do.

So let me complete my paper with the third part and draw some conclusions regarding the question:

Continental, Anglo-American or International Philosophy for Children?

This is neither a geographical nor an institutional question. The increasing international interest in doing philosophy with children is just a matter of fact. In 1984 the "International Council for Philosophical Inquiry with Children" (ICPIC) was formed. A first meeting was held in Denmark in 1985, a second one in Austria in 1987 and Brazil will be the next station. My point rather is a systematic question. Is there *one* (international) philosophy for children or are there *many* philosophies, the Continental one, the Anglo-American one, or any other kind of philosophy which leads to a different way of philosophizing with children? Questions regarding what philosophy is and is not and what should be and should not be are unending, but I *have* to come to an end. I think we even can come to a good end when remembering the beginning of philosophy and of my paper. In the first part, I've explained the difference between Continental and Anglo-American Philosophy which is sharply marked by the logico-linguistic, scientific way of thinking opposed to the merely deep, but unclear talking of all the others. And I did reject this difference because human thinking or reasoning involves more than the scientific way, for example, judgment, personal knowledge, imagination, understanding and wisdom. In this sense there is only *one* philosophy that uses the complete power of human reason as it has been developed since Socrates and the other Greek philosophers.

But what would it mean to use the complete power of human reason in doing philosophy with children? As far as I've got a little insight into what is going on in this field in the USA, there is a broad and deep discussion about thinking skills and philosophy for children, comparable with Hegel's logical approach regarding philosophy at the gymnasium (or high school). In some discussions it seems to me as if the full power of human reason is reduced to a method without content and existential meaning. The same criticism Kierkegaard waved at Hegel, at least indirectly. In Germany, as an example of doing philosophy on the continent, we are indeed tending to the opposite reductive fallacy. In an old romantic tradition we are moving to separate thinking from the realities of personal and social, political life. Comparable with the American discussion about thinking skills, we discuss "neue Allgemeinbildung," (new "all-around education") and the challenge of the information era. Many teachers and so called philosophers accept the separation between thinking and feeling which Sherry Turkle in her book, *The Second Self*, also identifies as a real tendency in the USA. She describes that more and more people assume that computers do think and human beings do feel. The tendency is to reduce thinking to calculating, and philosophy to poetry. In their view doing philosophy with children means protecting them against inhumane, cold rationality and offering them a humane, warm, so-called philosophy. Perhaps these people would love Kierkegaard, but he surely would not accept them as his followers. The most damaging aspect of this view, however, is that children don't get the opportunity to use the full power of human reason that they need to live and to live well in this scientific, technological world. Therefore, too, I'd like to plead for a more holistic approach to philosophy for children—one that combines the logical with the more personal aspects—just to give a new name to an old thing, philosophy!

But let me finish with a last question: Didn't I talk all the time about Western Philosophy only, omitting Buddhism, Confucianism and Japanese Zen? Can we really do an international philosophy for children without Eastern Philosophy or any other kinds of philosophy?

For some people, not only for some philosophers, these questions seem to be superfluous. On the paperback cover of Feigenbaum's/McCorduck's book, *The Fifth Genera-* *tion, Artificial Intelligence and Japan's Computer Challenge to the World*, (1984) we can see the Statue of Liberty with a Japanese face holding up the torch in her computer-robot arm. I think this interpretation of "Japan's challenge" for economic leadership is a real challenge to the international practice of doing philosophy with children,[12] that is, if we don't want to reduce children's reason to calculation and instrumental thinking. Furthermore, Japanese Zen is another challenge to us.[13]

Notes

1. Teaching Philosophy, Vol. VII, No. 2 (1984), p. 337.
2. A. Kaplan, The New World of Philosophy, New York 1961, p, 53.
3. Kaplan, p. 7.
4. Bernstein, Richard, "Praxis and Acker," 1971 with its rehabilitation of pragmatism and Continental Philosophy Dreyfes' "Critique of Artificial Reason" which appeals to Heidegger's and Merleau-Ponty's phenomonology.
5. G.W.E Hegel, On Teaching Philosophy at the Gymnasium. In: *Thinking*, Vol. 11, No. 2 (1980) (all quotations: p. 30-33.)
6. All quotations: Kierkegaard on Childhood. In: *Thinking*, Vol. V, No. 2 (1984), p. 2-5.
7. Reed, Ronald, "Talking with Children," Arden Press, Colorado, 1983.
8. IAPC program, Institute for the Advancement of Philosophy for Children, Montclair State College. Montclair, NJ USA.
9. See also: Michael Ende, Literature for Children? In: *Thinking*, Vol. V, No. 2 (1984), p. 2-5.
10. All quotations: Leonard Nelson, The Socratic Method. In: Thinking, Vol. II, No. 2 (1980), p. 34-38.
11. See Birgit S. Nielsen, Erziehung zum Selbstdenken. Ein sozialistischer Schulversuch im danischen Exil 1933-1938. Wuppertal 1985.
12. See Douglas Sloane (ed.): The Computer in Education. A Critical Perspective. New York/London 1984 (reviewed by Michael M. Kazanjian, in: *Thinking*, Vol. VII, No. 1 (1987), p. 23-24. See also the discussion in *Thinking*, James A. Jordan, Jr.: Socratic Teaching (IV, 3/4, 1983, pp. 25-29); Raymond S. Nickerson: Computer Programming as a vehicle for teaching thinking skills (IV, 3/4, 1983, pp. 42-48); Paul Froiland: The case against the "Thinking Machine" (IV, 3/4, 1983, pp. 51-56); John Furlong/ William Carroll: Teaching Reasoning With Computers (V, 4, 1985, pp. 29-32); Matthew Lipman: Philosophy and the Cultivation of Reasoning (V, 4, 1985, pp. 33-41). See further: Michael S. Pritchard:

Philosophical Adventures with Children. Lanham/New York/London 1985 (ch. VII "Brains and Minds"; ch. VIII "Brains, Computers and Controlling Thoughts"); Gareth B. Matthews: Thinking in Stories: Raging Robots and Unruly Uncles, by Margaret Maley. London 1981. (*Thinking*, Vol. IV, No. 2, p. 1).
13. See A. Kaplan, *op. cit.*, lect. 9 "Zen."

I wish to thank my Spanish colleague, Félix García Moriyón for intensive discussions about the above topic. I'm also thankful for the research grant given by "Deutsche Forschungsgesellschaft," for Matthew Lipman's invitation to the IAPC/Upper Montclair NJ. in June/July 1987 and for Ann Sharp's kind support all the time and for her hint about Kierkegaard.

Phenomenology and the Philosophy for Children Program

William Hamrick

I am grateful for Professor Yang's kind invitation to speak to you about phenomenology and the Philosophy for Children (P4C) program. There is much one might say about such a topic, and certainly much more than time permits today. For there are many phenomenological themes which show up in the P4C literature and to which the latter provides intriguing approaches. These themes include a conception of philosophy as one of conciousness, as interrogation, and as a quest for meanings. There are also the notions of the phenomenological reduction, the intentionality of consciousness, and the nature of intersubjectivity. In the following pages, I will restrict my attention for the most part to the first step of the phenomenological method, what Edmund Husserl first called the "phenomenological reduction."

It follows also that I will focus on contemporary phenomenology, that founded by Husserl and elaborated by his followers, rather than a Hegelian phenomenology.[1] But I do want to say two things about Hegel, one here and one later in the context of aesthetic experience. Harry Stottlemeier, particularly in the book which bears his name, realizes Hegel's discovery that we should not fear negativity, that it is a sign that what has been achieved up to that point is inadequate because one-sided, and that negativity is a necessary condition of advancing the mind to higher levels of knowledge. Of all the characters in *Harry*

Stottlemeier's Discovery, its protagonist is the most spurred on by negativity and is the most anxious to use it as a springboard to further knowledge. Harry is aware, at least implicitly, that in the absence of negativity, school becomes what Hegel said explicitly of science in such a condition, "the expression of inert lifeless understanding, and equally an external process of knowledge."[2] I shall return to Hegel below. Now I want to indicate briefly how Husserl described the phenomenological reduction,[3] its elaboration at the hands of Maurice Merleau-Ponty, and how this modified conception is present in selected P4C materials. For Husserl, phenomenology is an attempt to describe our experience as it presents itself to us, the ways in which things, other people, ourselves, and the world around us, constitute themselves in our consciousness. It is an attempt to describe "the appearing as it appears" (Merleau-Ponty), or the phenomena, in order to understand their essential meanings (essences). Furthermore, as against Descartes—who authored another philosophy of consciousness on which Husserl drew considerably[4]—consciousness is "intentional." The "intentionality of consciousness," a phrase and concept borrowed from the Austrian psychologist, Franz Brentano—means that consciousness is always "consciousness of something."[5] Thus to perceive is not merely to perceive; but always to perceive something. To love is not just to love, but to love someone. To will is not just to will, but to will something, and so forth. This essentially relational nature of consciousness means that there is always a subjective and an objective side to our experience: consciousness and world are given together and meant to be studied in their strict correlativity The "phenomena," then, are not players in an inner mental theater, but rather the living relationships of consciousness and world. Cartesian doubts about the existence of the world are therefore bogus problems which stem from a wrongheaded separation of consciousness from world in the first place.

It follows also that the referent of Husserl's famous watchword, "to the things themselves!," is neither a thing in itself apart from any relationship to consciousness—a rejection of naive realism in which Husserl was influenced decisively by Kant—nor consciousness itself apart from a relation to things the absolute idealism of Cartesianism which Kant also rejected. Rather, phenomenology was positioned explicitly as a middle path between this philosophical Scylla and Charbydis.

Phenomenology seeks to rescue the original immediacy of experience which has been obscured by the thought-constructs of not only certain philosophies, such as that of Descartes, but also of psychology and science. It seeks to make us aware of, even if we cannot get back to it purely and simply, the prereflective level of experience from which reflection proceeds, the preconceptual which supports the activity of conceptualizing in higher levels of knowledge. For this reason, phenomenology seeks to overcome (better: dig beneath[6]) intellectual constructs about the nature of experience through an unprejudiced "seeing" which returns us to the phenomena themselves. This is the point of the phenomenological reduction, a "leading back to" (Lat. *reducere*) the original contact between consciousness and world. But this seeing is impossible unless we can see it for what it is and not what we think it is, and this in turn is impossible if we cannot first set aside all our intellectual preconceptions about our

experience and its objects which are all part of what Husserl termed "the natural standpoint" or attitude.[7] These beliefs will not be doubted, à la Descartes, but only "put out of play," "untested indeed but also uncontested."[8] Husserl's term for this change of attitude is "epoche," a "bracketing," or a "putting in parentheses."[9] Its aim is to slacken the ties of feelings, beliefs, and prior judgments which bind us to the world of the natural attitude so that we may better understand both them and the resulting phenomena purified of those interpretative beliefs.

Suspending these beliefs makes us alive to two distinct, but related, facts. The first is the subjective contributions of consciousness which are obscured when perception and thought absorb themselves spontaneously in their respective objects with no cognizance of the subject's contributions. The second fact consists of the beliefs, judgments, and so forth, which interpretatively filter our relations with things, other people, and ourselves. For Husserl, bracketing these beliefs and our complicity with them comprises the fundamental move from mere thinking to reflection, from an interested to a disinterested consciousness, and from belief to knowledge.[10]

Merleau-Ponty phrased the purpose of the reduction this way:

> It is because we are through and through a relation to the world that the only way for us to notice it is to suspend this movement, to refuse it our complicity . . . or again, to place it out of service. Not that we renounce the certitudes of common sense and of the natural attitude—they are on the contrary the constant theme of philosophy—but exactly because they are presupposed in all thought, they are "self-evident," they pass unnoticed, and that, in order to reawake and make them appear, we have to withdraw ourselves from them for awhile. The best formulation of the reduction is doubtless that given by Eugen Fink, Husserl's assistant, when he spoke of a "wonder" before the world.[11]

This is why, for Merleau-Ponty, philosophy is essentially interrogation.[12] With a sensitivity to both evidence and ambiguity. The device Merleau-Ponty uses to effect his version of the reduction is the example of pathological motility in the patient, Schneider. In the *Phenomenology of Perception*, the structures of pathological motility throw into relief normal ways that we inhabit space and time through the body's motor-intentionality. In the Philosophy for Children program, it is also through departures from the ordinary stream of human experience that the characters in the stories make philosophical progress. Harry Stottlemeier makes a mistake in class and is then driven to discover some of the basic features of Aristotelian logic in order to account for his error and avoid it in the future. Later, in *Suki*, it is Harry's self-supposed inability to write, coupled with the intransigence of his English teacher, Mr. Newberry, which drive him on to further discoveries?[13] Again in a Hegelian fashion, Harry reaches higher levels of knowledge beyond an initial negativity. Similar claims can be made about Lisa and Mark in the books that bear their names. But instead of discussing their cases, I want to focus on the most complete approximation of the phenomenological reduction in the P4C curriculum, which is found in *Kio and Gus*[14]

Kio and Gus, intended for children ages (roughly) 7-8, is about wonder in the face of nature. Its accompanying instruction manual for teachers is called *Wondering at the World*. The program is intended to be an aid to science education, mainly in terms of zoology and ecology. In *Kio and Gus*, two children, the title characters, take turns (usually) telling us a story about "the summer of the farm and all the animals. It was the summer of the big whale—Grandpa's *wonderful* whale, named Leviathan," (p. 1). The story approximates the phenomenological reduction by the simple and ingenious expedient of having Kio as sighted and Gus as unsighted. Reality is thrown into question by exposing us to fundamentally different ways of constituting it in their consciousnesses.

For example, Suki, Kio's older sister, tells Gus that the wonders of touch are too easily overlooked by those who can look over them: "People who see often don't think about what it is to touch. It's like, they see a peach, and right away they eat it. They never get to feel the weight of it in their hands, or to grip the roundness of it or to touch the soft fuzz on its skin. And yet even if it were only a stone, it would still be marvelous to hold. And mysterious too: What's more silent than a stone?" (p. 35) Tactile realities, as well as the reality of touching joined to them in the intentionality of consciousness, are effectively part of those certainties of common sense which Merleau-Ponty pointed out we overlook just because they are self-evident-to the sighted.

A second example concerns the use of analogical reasoning to compare and contrast sighted and unsighted constitutions of reality through sight, taste, and sound. Thus Kio tells Gus that "honey looks just like it tastes: the taste of honey is like the color of gold" (p. 15) and that orange is "a bright color, just like it's a bright taste?" (p. 36). "Mrrowr," answers Gus. "Bright mind" (p. 36). Similarly, analogical reasoning is used to explain the Milky Way. Gus says "Maybe I can just think of the sky as being filled with stars the way my mind is filled with thoughts!" Kio responds, "Right!" "And maybe you can think of your mind giving off thoughts the way a fire gives off sparks!" (p. 61).

Yet another example occurs in Kio and Gus' discussion of the right way to make a peach out of modeling clay. Gus begins with the inside, the pit, and proceeds to the outside. Kio, guided by what he can see, starts with the outside and limits himself to visual appearances. Gus retorts sharply that "Sure, maybe that's all you *see*," I say, "but you *know* that what *I* made is really like a peach and *yours* isn't. Mine's a peach all the way through!" (p. 14). Kio later responds while forming a head out of modeling clay:

"I start from the outside and you start from the inside," he says.
I [Gus] answer, "But you never get inside! You

just stay on the outside! That's not the way to make a head!"

"It's the only way I know," Kio says.

"It *was* the only way you know," I answer. "Now you know *two* ways!" (p. 14).

Such interchanges neatly exemplify phenomenologists' insistence on paying closer attention to the ways that the phenomena constitute themselves in our consciousness, on the necessity of going to the things themselves unencumbered as much as possible by a belief structure which has already prejudged their reality, and finally by a sense of wonder that the world is there before us as it is. This sense of wonder is also captured by Gabriel Marcel, another thinker in the phenomenological tradition, when he wrote about the naturalist. Whereas we might consider some form of life insignificant, the word has no meaning for the naturalist: "The living being that considers presents itself to him in a dimension of being to which we other ordinary people have difficult access. Even on this side of any belief in a creating God, the naturalist experiences a sort of amazement before the fineness and the complexity of the structure that he observes."[15]

Both in Kio and Gus and in its other works, the Philosophy for Children program makes generous use of aesthetic experience as a means of opening us up to a world and a sense of wonder at its presence. It does this in a number of ways— by the use of poetry in *Suki*, by the use of concrete sensuous imagery in that text as well as in many others, including *Kio and Gus*; by discussions of art and its relation to other regions of our life-world in *Lisa* and *Harry Stottlemeier's Discovery*, and by the use of metaphor. From all that appears, aesthetic experience is particularly well suited to phenomenologists' aims of recapturing the concreteness of experience through achieving a sense of wonder in the face of the world, and of reacquainting ourselves with the phenomena in order to understand them. It is no accident, I believe, that Matthew Lipman, who shares those goals, has such frequent recourse to aesthetic experience. For example, in statements which

Merleau-Ponty certainly would have approved, he writes that "Suki, with the help of Mr. and Mrs. Stottlemeier and Mr. Newberry, makes Harry pay attention to language. Until now, Harry has only been interested in the logical underpinnings of language, but Suki compels him to think about words themselves and how their various arrangements affect meaning. To a person who has been accustomed to thinking as critically as Harry, attention is to be paid to ambiguities only in order to eliminate them. What Suki tries to show Harry is that the language of poetry is rich and meaningful on many levels precisely because it makes use of ambiguity."[16]

One common feature of poetry of which this is so is metaphor, and our relation to nature is only one context in which such language is rich and meaningful. Another, which appears in a radically different situation in the P4C literature, is inter-subjectivity. I am thinking of *Elfie* in which the title character has the maximum number of problems relating to almost everyone because, at bottom, she suffers from and in a Cartesian framework in which the ego can be cut off by doubt from others and the world around it. She suffers enormously and unnecessarily in the putative isolation of her own self until she makes her big breakthrough by the use of metaphor. In making up sentences to win a school contest, she describes a classmate whom she idolizes, Sophia, as follows: "Someone I know is a branch of lilacs!" In thus expressing her attraction to Sophia's purple eyes, Elfie wins one of the prizes of the contest, a spot on a television program. When Mr. Sprockett, the principal, announced the results, Elfie tells us, "It's like everything explodes around me and everyone's cheering, 'Elfie! Elfie!' Mrs. Tripp [her teacher] hugs me and hugs me, and I cry all over the front of her dress. She smooths my hair and kisses me on the top of the head and says, 'Congratulations, Elfie. You deserved to win!' " (*Elfie*, Ill: 150). Something else that she deserves to win is some therapeutic recovery of her intersubjectivity, her reintegration with the community of inquiry in her classroom.

Her chances of recovery are good, and Mikel Dufrenne in his *Phenomenology of Aesthetic Experience* tells us why:

> If aesthetic feeling has depth because it unites us, it is also because it opens us up. For the inner life does not lose the subject in hazy meanderings of subjective rumination [or, in Elfie's case keep her there] . . . In aesthetic experience, inner life manifests itself above all in its power of opening us up. Having depth is to be available [*disponible*], and it is by the same movement that I open myself to the object . . . There is a reciprocity between intentionality and being-oneself . . . Being oneself no longer designates the pure relationship to the self made up of an "I think," but the substance of the self having depth; and intentionality is no longer aimed *toward* [something], but a participation *with* . . . Feeling is an act of communion to which I bring my whole being.[17]

For the same reasons, aesthetic experience might be the best means to implement a community of inquiry in the classroom and to enrich the lives of students therein. And that brings me back in conclusion to Hegel who made good use of aesthetic imagery to express an aesthetic experience which is his constant image for the life of the mind. Kant's favorite metaphor of the mind was that of a judge in court dispassionately weighing evidence and deciding between conflicting claims based on reason alone. Hegel's preferred metaphor, on the other hand, is considerably different. It is that of a life-process in which a bud becomes a blossom, and the blossom yields fruit:

> "The bud disappears when the blossom breaks through, and we might say that the former is refuted by the latter; in the same way when the fruit comes, the blossom may be explained to be a false form of the plant's existence, for the fruit appears as its true nature in place of the blossom. These stages are not merely differentiated; they supplant one another. But the ceaseless activity of their own inherent nature makes them at the same time moments of an organic unity, where they not merely do not contradict one another, but where one is as necessary as the other; and

this equal necessity of all moments constitutes alone and thereby the life of the whole?"[18]

The bud-blossom-fruit metaphor is perhaps also the best image for the way that Hegel conceived the life of Spirit as a living process. As W.T. Jones phrases it, "Spirit is a living process; it is propelled by the energy of negation and mediation, in which both selves and their objects are continuously emerging, undergoing development, and being replaced by higher forms of themselves."[19] What better description can there be for the progress which P4C characters make in their stories and which real-life children can similarly make in the Philosophy for Children program?

Notes

1. This is not to say that there is not a substantive relationship between Hegelian and 20th-century phenomenologies. On the contrary, even the most cursory reading of thinkers such as Martin Heidegger, Jean-Paul Sartre, and Maurice Merleau-Ponty quite plainly shows the contrary.
2. *The Phenomenology of Mind*, trans. Sir James Baillie (London: George Allen & Unwin, Ltd., 1949), p. 112.
3. Husserl's language was anything but consistent, as his successive attempts to clarify the nature of phenomenology and its capacity to provide us with the foundations of knowledge generally assumed more of a zigzag than a linear character. Thus it is not surprising that his descriptions of the phenomenological reduction changed also from one period of his life to another. The (simplified) version presented here is an early one taken largely from *Ideen I*. But it does possess the double advantage of clarity and simplicity.
4. Husserl was much more sympathetic to Descartes than were most other phenomenologists. But even for Husserl, it was his French predecessor's intentions that were pure rather than his results. There was not one major Cartesian doctrine which Husserl did not end up rejecting. See, for instance his *Cartesian Meditations*, trans. Dorion Cairnes (The Hague: Martinus Nijhoff, 1960), p. 6: "Must not the only fruitful renaissance be the one that reawakens the impulse of the Cartesian Meditations: not to adopt their content but, in not doing so, to renew with greater intensity the radicalness of their spirit . . . Seductive aberrations, into which Descartes and later thinkers strayed, will have to be clarified and avoided as we pursue our course."

5. Husserl, *Ideas I*, trans. W.R. Boyce Gibson (London: George Allen & Unwin, Ltd., 1969), p. 111.
6. Husserl, as well as Merleau-Ponty, would have liked to call his philosophy "archeology" if that term had still been available for philosophical purposes. See Herbert Spiegelberg, *The Phenomenological Movement*, Third Revised and Enlarged Edition with the collaboration of Karl Schuhmann (The Hague: Martinus Nijhoff Publishers, 1982), p. 76.
7. *Ideas I*, pp. 101ff.
8. *Ideas* I, p. 111.
9. *Ideas* I, p. 110.
10. What separates Husserl more than anything else from his successors in the phenomenological movement is this view of the possibility of a pure description of the phenomena which would then serve as a proper source of evidence for determining the essences of what appears. The attitude of most other phenomenologists is captured in Merleau-Ponty's statement that, "The greatest teaching of the reduction is the impossibility of a complete reduction," *Phénoménologie de la perception*, (Paris: Gallimard, 1945), p. viii (my translation). This is because interpretation is an inexorable part of experience, and hence phenomenology merged first into hermeneutics and then to critical social theory and post-modernism.
11. *Phénoménologie de la perception*, p. viii (my translation).
12. *Le Visible et l'invisible*, text established by Claude Lefort (Paris: Gallimard, 1964), pp 15ff.
13. For more on this subject, see my article, "Philosophy for Children and Aesthetic Education," *The Journal of Aesthetic Education*, Vol. 23, No. 2, Summer 1989, pp.. 55–67.
14. For further information on what follows, see my paper, "Some Concrete Approaches to Nature" in *Kio and Gus: Thinking*, Vol. VII, No. 2, 1987, pp. 40–45.
15. Gabriel Marcel, *Pour une sagesse tragique et son au-delà* (my translation), (Paris: Plon, 1968), p. 171. In the same place, Marcel even goes so far as to call such a person a "saint," not in any moral sense, but rather as someone "who has moved to a mode of being excluding the current separation between man and nature." It is worth pointing out that Marcel found more success in this enterprise in cultures of the East than in those of the West.
16. *Writing: How and Why*, the instructional manual which accompanies *Suki*, p. viii.
17. *Phénoménologie de l'expérience esthétique* (Paris: Presses Universitaires de France, 1953), II: 502-03.
18. *The Phenomenology of Mind*, p. 68.
19. *Kant and the Nineteenth Century*, second edition, revised (New York: Harcourt Brace Jovanovich, Inc., 1975), p. 121.

Wittgenstein and Philosophy for Children

Barry Curtis

Is Wittgenstein's view of philosophy inconsistent with doing Philosophy for Children? This question troubled me a great deal when I first became involved with P4C over five years ago. Wittgenstein said that philosophical questions are like an illness, and that the task of the philosopher is to cure himself and others of this "illness" through a variety of intellectual "therapies." The Philosophy for Children Program, on the other hand, actively encourages children to ask philosophical questions, including questions which children themselves might never even think of on their own. So here is the problem: if you agree with Wittgenstein (as I am inclined to do) that philosophical questions are like an illness, then why inflict this "illness" on little kids? Why not just leave them alone and hope they won't catch the disease? Aren't we really just making work for ourselves by infecting kids with our own intellectual malady—a malady which most kids (healthy little tykes that they are) would probably never otherwise have? What a perfectly horrible thing to do! Or so it once seemed to me to be. (I used to imagine Wittgenstein, come back to life, storming into our elementary school classrooms and smashing up our P4C curriculum materials, like Jesus and the money changers in the Temple.)

These doubts no longer trouble me (or, at any rate, they hardly ever do). After working with the program, off and on, for the past five years or so,

I no longer feel that there is any serious incompatibility between accepting Wittgenstein's view of the nature of philosophy and doing P4C. I now think that the tension I once thought I sensed between Wittgenstein and P4C was an illusion—a chimera created by my own misunderstanding of both Wittgenstein and P4C. I have even come to think that some kind of program in philosophy for children—P4C or something like it—is a positively good thing if Wittgenstein is right (as I am inclined to think he is) about the nature and causes of "philosophical illness."

Philosophical Illness

How do we cash in Wittgenstein's a metaphor of "philosophical illness?" The best model, I have come to think, is cancer—a non-communicable disease. (I know this is an illness which most of us would prefer not to think about, dreadful thing that it is, but no other illness seems to me to come as close to carrying out Wittgenstein's analogy.) Did Wittgenstein have cancer in mind when he spoke of "philosophical illness"? I have no idea. Wittgenstein himself died of cancer, but this proves nothing. He never explicitly compares what he calls "philosophical illness" with any particular physical ailment; he uses only general terms, such as "illness," "sickness" or "disease."[1] The point I want to make here is that cancer seems *to me* to be the physical illness that most closely resembles the intellectual malady whose course and symptoms Wittgenstein describes. By looking at "philosophical illness" on the model of cancer, much can be learned, I think, about the similarities between philosophical inquiry and disease.

Now what is cancer? The paradigm of this disease (from a layman's point of view, which is good enough for our purposes) is that of a malignant tumor—a disorderly growth of tissue which threatens the life or health of the patient. So how is a philosophical question like a case of cancer? Well, a philosophical question, like a tumor, grows from the existing "tissue" of our ordinary language—a language which includes, as a part of its normal, everyday use, such questions as "Why?," "How do you know?" "What is _____?," "Where is _____?," "When is _____?," and so on. Children learn to ask and answer such questions in familiar (to adults) contexts where people carry out the day to day business of their lives. The rules for the use of these questions—learned by example and through practice—are determined by the way people actually use language in such contexts—contexts where such questions have their natural and original home.

These questions, however, sometimes develop a tendency to "grow" beyond their normal limits, and to function in disorderly ways: we keep on asking "Why?," for example, in response to every reason someone gives us (children are famous for this); we keep on asking "How do you know?" about every claim someone makes (so that for every justification, we demand a *further* justification); we keep on asking "What is _____?" or "Where is _____?" or "When is _____?," and fill in the blank with all sorts of words whose use is far removed from the simple paradigms with which such questions have their familiar home (so that we end up asking questions like "What is (a) mind?", "Where is time?" or "When is now?"). In this

way, our questions begin to grow wild, just as our tissues grow wild in case of cancer. Our questions, like the tissues of our bodies, pass from order to disorder, so that we cease to make linguistic sense, just as our tissues cease to make physiological "sense." We move through a process of distorted "growth" from function to dysfunction.

All philosophical questions, if I read Wittgenstein right, are "disorderly" questions of this kind. Such questions, like malignant tumors, can pose a threat to our health—not the health of the body, but of the intellect. They can interfere with the normal functioning of the mind. A man with a philosophical question—a man who takes the question seriously—may find himself unable to perform some of the normal, everyday tasks which involve the use of the understanding. Depending on the question, he may find himself unable to be sure of anything; unable to make ethical judgments; unable to tell what's real from what's unreal, unable to get started with the basics of a given skill or body of knowledge; unable to make aesthetic judgments or to see any point or meaning in living. Just as a malignant tumor, once it grows big enough, constitutes an impairment in the functioning of the body, so a philosophical question, once it grows "big" enough, constitutes an impairment in the functioning of the mind. And there are many different "organs" of the mind which can be impaired by such questions, depending on which questions they are.

Consider one of the following traditional philosophical questions—ones which have obsessed philosophers at least since Plato, "What is justice?" A man who is really troubled by such a question (and I don't mean someone who is troubled by it merely because he has to pass an examination in philosophy) is liable to be impaired in his ability to make judgments about what is just and fair. He may say to himself, "Well, this seems to me like a just solution to the problem, but then, I don't really have a definition of "justice" to go on, so how can I really say if it's just or not? And besides, how can I know if there's really anything to this "justice" business in the first place, if I don't even know what justice is?" Such a man may end up dithering over practical ethical problems, or avoiding them entirely, or making snap decisions based on how he feels at the moment. He may also end up simply following, in a dogmatic way, the teachings of his parents or his church, just to have something to go on. (In this last case, our man will bear a certain superficial resemblance to the man who is not at all troubled by the question "What is justice?"—the man who thinks he already has the "answer"—but the psychological accompaniments in each case will be radically different.)

Or consider the question, "What is reality?" A man who is deeply troubled by this question is liable to be impaired in his ability to tell the real from the unreal; he is liable to "second guess" himself, much as the man with the question about justice is liable to "second guess" himself. Now, of course, *some* such second-guessing is valuable and important; it often prevents us from going off half-cocked, from making stupid blunders. But the man who is deeply troubled by questions about the nature of reality incurs the risk of *never* being sure about what is real—about whether someone (who shows all the ordinary signs of it) really loves him; about whether the salesman whom he has been dealing with for years is really telling him the truth about a new product, and so on. There is a kind of insanity which consists precisely in this disposition (or rather, this incapacitation): the inability to distinguish reality from illusion.

These examples can be multiplied many times over. I once had an acquaintance who dropped out of graduate work in physics and went into philosophy because (so he said) he could never get past the first page of a physics textbook. He was too troubled by such questions as "What is time?", "What is space?", "What is matter?" In this way, his ability to master the principles of physics was impaired. One can imagine a similar case of an artist, whose talents become paralyzed by the question, "What is art?" or "What is

beauty?", and whose inability to deal with such questions or to answer them renders him impotent to develop his skills. The crowning example, perhaps, is the one which is expressed most vividly, by Camus, in the *Myth of Sisyphus*: "Why not commit suicide?"[2] This question, he tells us, must be answered first, before we can be justified in asking or answering any others—before we can be justified in going on with our lives. Camus, of course, goes on to try to answer this question. But if one is not convinced by his answer, what then? Must one stop one's life and spend all one's time and energy seeking an answer? Apparently so. But then one has stopped one's life. And, if Wittgenstein is right about the nonsensical nature of this and other philosophical questions, one has stopped one's life absurdly (a conclusion with which Camus might not disagree).

Philosophical questions, then (if I am reading Wittgenstein right) resemble cancer in at least two respects: (1) they are wild and unruly growths which arise, are on occasion, from the tissue of our language, and (2) they are "malignant," in the sense that they tend to interfere with the healthy operation of the understanding. (In addition, there is a third similarity which may be worth nothing: metastasis—a phenomenon which often shows up in cancer, particularly in the later stages: the transmission of the disease from the original site to one or more other locations. A similar phenomenon seems to take place with philosophical questions. Once someone begins to ask "Why?" beyond its normal limits, it isn't long before he begins to do the same thing with "How do you know?," "What is _____?," "When is _____?," and "Where is _____?" It doesn't really matter which question the person begins with, sooner or later, the others are liable to show up.)

Etiology: A Case Study

What is the etiology of "philosophical illness?" What causes it? According to Wittgenstein, philosophical illness can have many different causes, depending on the form it takes. Different "malignant" questions (to continue our cancer metaphor) may arise for a variety of different reasons. (In much the same way, so some authorities tell us, there may be a variety of different causes for different members of the family of illnesses we call "cancer.") In this paper, I want to zero in on just one form of "philosophical illness"—one particular kind of "malignant" question. I choose this one partly because Wittgenstein himself suffered from it in his early work, and spent a great deal of time later on trying to "cure" himself of it through a variety of "therapies." He is therefore remarkably clear about what he takes to be its cause and cure. I also choose this particular "malignancy" because it is the one which concerned me most when I first encountered the P4C curriculum—a curriculum which seemed to me at that time to be more likely to cause philosophical illness than to cure it.

I have in mind the question "What is _____?", where the blank gets filled in with a noun or a noun-like word. This question starts out as a perfectly ordinary use of language, but it can, under certain circumstances, "grow" beyond its natural limits to the point where it no longer makes any sense. Children, if I read Wittgenstein right (and this involves some reconstruction), learn the use of "What is?" in much the same way as they learn the rest of their native language—by example and through practice, in a process which involves training and correction. The earliest use of "What is _____?" is perhaps "What is this?" or "What is that?"—a question which we ask children in the process of teaching them the names of objects (and, later on, properties, states and processes) which show up in the everyday environment of the child. Children first begin to learn the use of such names through a process of

"learning by doing" Children are taught to go and get things, to pick them up and put them down, to eat or drink them, to put them on or take them off, and so on. In the course of such instruction, the adult will use the name of the object and the child will be trained to pronounce the name himself—to repeat it after the adult. Later on, the adult points at the object (or holds it up) and asks the child "What is that?" (or "What is this?"), and prompts the child if he fails to answer, or corrects him if he answers wrongly.[3] Given suitable training, the child will go on to use the name correctly in new cases which he has never encountered before. We show a child a beach ball, for example, and demonstrate its uses (we play ball with him). In the process, we teach him to say "ball." Later on, we go through the same procedure with a baseball or a football. After a while, the child begins to "catch on" to the use of the word "ball"—he goes on to identify a handball or a ping pong ball (which he has never seen before) as a "ball." He does this without any underlying verbal definition to go by. Wittgenstein thought that it was a remarkable fact about children that they are able to learn from such "ostensive teaching" in this way. Children, amazingly enough, are able to learn *directly* from examples, and in teaching them by use of examples, we (usually) teach them no less than we know ourselves.[4] (Do you have a handy verbal definition of the word "ball?" I don't. And my dictionary isn't of much help here, either.)

It isn't long, of course, before the child begins to turn the tables on us, by asking "What is this?" or "What is that?" about all sorts of things in his environment. We respond by giving the name. Once a child has mastered enough of the workings of his language to be able to ask for definitions and to understand them when they are given (and this requires much more than just a mastery of the use of names), he can learn the use of the question "What is (a) _____?", where the blank gets filled in with the name of something. A child learns to ask this question (if

Are children childlike?

Now as to Moore—I don't really understand Moore, & therefore, what I'll say, may be quite wrong. But this is what I'm inclined to say:—That Moore is in some sense extraordinarily childlike is obvious, & the remark you quoted (about vanity) is certainly an example of that childlikeness. There is also a *certain* innocence about Moore; he is, e.g., completely unvain. As to it's being to his *"credit"* to be childlike,—I can't understand that; unless it's also to a *child's* credit. For you aren't talking of the innocence a man has fought for, but of an innocence which comes from a natural absence of a temptation.—I believe that all you wanted to say was that you *liked*, or even *loved*, Moore's childlikeness. And that I can *understand*—I think that our discrepancy here is not so much one of thoughts as of feelings. I *like* & greatly respect Moore; but that's all. He doesn't warm my heart (or very little), because what warms my heart most is human kindness, & Moore—just *like a child*—is not kind. He is kindly & he can be charming & nice to those he likes & he has great *depth.*—That's how it seems to me. If I'm wrong, I'm wrong.

—Ludwig Wittgenstein, quoted in Norman Malcolm, *Ludwig Wittgenstein: A Memoir.*

I read Wittgenstein right) in the same way as he learns to ask "What is this?" or "What is that?"—by example, and through practice. We give a child a definition, and test him on his mastery of the definition by asking him "What is _____?", filling in the blank with the name whose definition we have taught him. We tell him, for example, that a dollar is a hundred cents, or that a noun is the name of a person, place or thing. Later on, we ask him "What is a dollar?" or "What is a noun?" and correct him if he answers wrongly. Once again, the child will begin to turn the tables on us, by asking such "What is _____?" questions him-

self, filling in the blank with a name whose meaning he wants to know. (Mother: "Dad's been drinking whisky." Child: "What is whisky?") We respond, as best we can, by giving definitions of these names in terms of other names which the child already knows, or what we can teach him. If a child doesn't understand one of the names in our definition, he may call upon us to define *that* name, and so on. Thus, we might imagine the following conversation.

What's that, Daddy?

A wrench.

What's a wrench?

It's a tool for turning nuts and bolts.

"What's a nut?

At this point, the father has recourse to the same kind of teaching as he used when he first began to teach the use of names to his child. He can explain the meaning of the word "nut" *ostensively*, by showing the child a nut, or several different nuts of different sizes and kinds. (If the child were to ask "What's a tool?," the father could respond by showing the child a variety of tools—a hammer, a saw, a screwdriver, and so on—and by demonstrating their uses.) In this way, the chain of "What is _____?" questions usually comes to an end.

"What is _____?" questions, however, sometimes have a way of "growing" beyond the bounds of this familiar "language game." Imagine the following case.

What are you doing, Daddy?

I'm thinking.

Normally, a child would go on to ask, "What are you thinking about?" But *sometimes* he will ask,

Daddy, what's thinking?

Well, you know what thinking is. It's something you do in your mind, like wondering about something or planning something, or adding two numbers together.

Now suppose the child goes on to ask (as children sometimes do),

Daddy, what's a mind?

How is Daddy going to answer this one? If he tries to give a verbal definition, he will go around in circles ("It's what you think with"), just as my dictionary does. And if he tries to give an ostensive definition—well, how is he going to do *that*? How can you point at a mind, or a "family" of minds? A mind, unlike a nut (or a tool), doesn't seem to be anything that can be pointed at! What should the father say to the child? "Close your eyes and you'll see your mind"? But will the child "see" his mind in this way? And what about other people's minds? Can they be "seen" in this way? Not by us! A mind, it seems, is a very mysterious thing! It must be something *hidden*. But where is it hidden? In your head? But if someone opened up your head, he wouldn't see your mind; he'd see your brain, perhaps, but he wouldn't see your thoughts, ideas and so on. The mind doesn't seem to be anywhere at all! But how can something not be anywhere? And now we are in a muddle. No wonder parents try to deflect such questions, e. g., by turning them into a joke ("A mind? It's what you're driving me out of with all these questions!") The standard means for answering "What is _____?" questions are unavailable when the blank gets filled in with a word like "mind."

So how is it possible to deal with such an impossible question? Not, on Wittgenstein's view, by trying to answer it. Instead we should look at the question itself, for this is where something has gone wrong. The word "mind" (if I read Wittgenstein right) does not belong in the blank of a "What is _____?" question, any more than the word "if" does. The child has asked the *wrong question*—a question which makes no more sense than "What is if?" or "Where is and?" For the word "mind," like the word "if"—but unlike the word "bread" or "window sash" is not the name of anything, nor is it the name of a "family" of things.[5] It therefore has no business in the blank of "What is _____?" questions. Yes, we all are taught in school (trained, actually) to say that a

noun is "the name of a person, place or thing." And yes, "mind" is ordinarily classified as a noun. But the superficial grammar we are taught in school masks the enormous difference between the use of the word "mind" and the use of the word "bread," for example, or "window sash"— a difference so great that the question "What is _____?" passes from sense to nonsense if we fill in the blank with a word like "mind" instead of filling it in with a word like "bread."

Much the same is true, according to Wittgenstein (as I read him) of all the other great "What is _____?" questions which have preoccupied philosophers for centuries. They are all deeply nonsensical. Like tumors (to continue our cancer metaphor), they are disorderly growths from the tissue of our language. In *Philosophy in the Classroom*, Lipman, Sharp and Oscanyan give a list of the sort of questions I have in mind—questions which, according to the authors, are often raised by children, in the process of "leaping to a more general level."[6]

What's space?
What's number?
What's matter?
What's mind?
What are possibilities?
What's reality?
What are things?
What's my identity?
What are relationships?
What's death?
What's life?
What's meaning?
What's value?

(I have left out the only non-"What is _____?" question in the authors' original list: "Did everything have a beginning?"—a different kind of "malignancy," in my opinion, from the others.)

Such questions, on Wittgenstein's view, are disordered uses of language—misuses of the question "What is _____?", a question which has its natural and original home in circumstances where the blank gets filled in with a demonstrative or with the name of an object (or family of objects). But "space" is not the name of anything, nor is "number," nor is "mind." Nor is any of the other words on our list. Nor is any of these words the name of a "family" of things. (If you are tempted to think that "matter" is an exception here, you are probably thinking of its use as a technical term in physics. But even here, you will run into problems. For in physics, so we are told, matter is equivalent to energy, and what is "energy" the name of?) It is just as wrong, on Wittgenstein's view (as I read him) to ask "What is space?" or "What is number?" as it is to ask "What is mind?"

The trouble is that we do not recognize the wrongness—the non-sensicality—of a question like "What is mind?" or "What is number?" or "What is space?" as readily as we recognize the wrongness of a question like "What is if?" or "Where is and?" For unlike the word "if," for example, the word "mind" or "space" or "time" has a variety of uses which bear a certain superficial similarity to words that *do* belong in the blanks in "What is _____?" questions. "Mind," for example, unlike "if," can serve as the subject or object of a verb, just as "table" or "bread" can. It can also be the object of a preposition: we speak of things as being on one's mind or in it or in the back of it, just as we speak of things as being "on" or "in" or "in the back of" a refrigerator or a breadbox. Such uses of the word "mind" mislead us into thinking that "mind" is the name of something—just as "refrigerator" or "breadbox" is the name of something—a mysterious "something" which, unlike a refrigerator or a breadbox, cannot be seen or touched.[7]

Much the same is true of all the other words in our list of "What is _____?" questions. "Space," too, can serve as subject or object of a verb ("Space is unavailable in this building," "We divided up the space into two sections") and so can "number"—or, at any rate, so can the "names" of particular numbers ("The number two is the only even prime," "Divide this

number . . ."). And "space," like "number," can also be used together with certain quantifiers, much in the same way as "bread" or "paint" can ("There is plenty of space in this room," "We only have a small number of loaves and fishes" and so on). These superficial similarities between the use of words like "space" or "time" or "mind," on the one hand, and "bread" or "table" or "paint," on the other, can deceive us. They can, as Wittgenstein might say, "bewitch" us into thinking that words like "number" and "space" and "mind," like "bread" or "table" or "paint," are names of objects.[8] And so when we want to understand the meaning of a word like "number" or "mind" or "space" (as all of us do), we ask the question we have learned to ask when we encounter a name whose meaning we do not understand: "What is _____?" ("What is space?," "What is mind?," "What is number?") Misled by the superficial grammar of our language, we begin to ask disordered questions.

The main "carcinogen" in our environment, then, that is liable to cause the "What is _____?" carcinoma is nothing other than language itself!—uses of language such as "in the back of my mind" or "space is unavailable," which lead us to misunderstand the use of words like "mind" or "space"—to think of such words on the familiar model of "name and object," and hence to ask such "malignant questions" as "What is mind?" or "What is space?" And the grammatical education we get in school is absolutely no help in clearing up such misunderstandings. On the contrary, it positively encourages them. The concept of a noun as "the name of a person, place or thing" is positively enshrined in the superficial (and often wrong-headed) rules of grammar we are taught in the classroom. Our teachers really do drill this "person, place or thing" idea into us, and count it as wrong if we reply to the question, "What is a noun?" (*sic*) in any other way.

Contrary to what I once believed, then, that children are philosophically healthy little tykes who are unlikely to raise philosophical questions on their own, I now think that children are highly susceptible to "philosophical illness"—at least of the "What is_____?" variety. For their linguistic environment is loaded with uses of language which are liable to bring on this disease—a disease which can only be encouraged by what passes for grammatical "education" in school. Not all children, of course, when exposed to such "carcinogens," will develop serious cases of what Wittgenstein calls "philosophical illness"; not all of them will become tormented by philosophical questions or find their lives interrupted by them. A special kind of temperament, I think, must also be present for this to happen. (Here again, there is a similarity, perhaps, with cancer, which—according to some experts—requires a genetic predisposition.) But all—or nearly all—children, I have come to think, are liable to develop some form of this "illness"—some of them to a serious degree.

Philosophical Therapy

If wrongheaded questions are the disease, and misleading uses of language are the (ultimate) cause, then what is the cure? Wittgenstein says there is not one therapy, but many.[9] (Here we have yet another similarity with cancer.) I will discuss just one of the "therapies" which Wittgenstein recommends—one which is particularly effective, I think, on the "What is _____?" variety of philosophical illness. This particular therapy involves teaching ourselves (and others) to ask new questions—questions which are less prejudicial than questions of the "What is _____?" variety, in that they do not presuppose a name-and-object model of language. Over and over again, Wittgenstein encourages us to replace our "What is _____?" questions with questions of the following kind:

"Under what circumstances do we use the word '_____'?"[10] The answer to such a question will often serve to dispel our urge to think that the word in question, whatever it is, must be the name of something. As a result, we will no longer be so inclined to ask the "What is _____?" question that torments us. Take "time," for example. Instead of asking "What is time?" (a question which preoccupied Saint Augustine, and which—according to *Philosophy in the Classroom*—can also preoccupy children[11]), we should ask "Under what circumstances do we use the word 'time'?" If you try this out as an exercise, you will begin to see that the word "time" plays many other roles besides the standard role that nouns usually play in our sentences, and that when "time" *does* play the standard role of a noun (as subject or object of a verb or as the object of a preposition), the use of the sentence as a whole is usually metaphorical ("Time is running out," "I passed the time," "Be there on time," and so on). You will also find that when we "quantify" over time (talk about "amounts" of time, etc.), we do so in a very different way from the way in which we quantify over bread, say, or water. What we are quantifying over is not time, *per se* (as we do in the case of bread or water), but how much time it takes for something to happen. We do this ordinarily by comparing one motion or action with another motion, which we take as our standard (e.g., the motion of the sun or of the hands of a clock). What a very different thing from measuring an amount of "stuff," like bread or water! Are you still tempted to think of time as a "something?" Do you still want to know "what it is?" If so, then the therapy hasn't worked. Perhaps you should try again, and if it still doesn't work, perhaps you should try another form of therapy. (Hint: one other "therapy" which Wittgenstein mentions that might be effective here is to remind yourself' of how you learned the use of the word "time" when you were a child.[12] This, too, will serve to point out the many differences between the use of the word "time" and the use of our paradigmatic "name and object" words like "table" or "bread.")

What happens if the therapy works? Then one philosophical problem is dissolved. But what if the variety of therapies which Wittgenstein describes works on all our philosophical problems, so that we become completely "cured?" What then? Matt Lipman says that philosophy "begins in wonder"[13]—a statement with which Wittgenstein would probably agree.[14] So if we "cure" ourselves of philosophical questions, will we thereby have "cured" ourselves of wonder? Will we just walk around like zombies, without any sense of amazement or curiosity at being in the world? Well, for one thing, it is doubtful if, in a single lifetime, anyone could be completely "cured" of all philosophical illness. There are, as Wittgenstein tells us, many different kinds of illness, and many different therapies which must be tried. And, as he says at one point, "slow cure is all important."[15] Besides, new philosophical problems are constantly appearing on the scene, as the circumstances of the use of our language change. (Think of the philosophical problems which have come into being as a result of the development of computers and computer "language.") But even if someone were to succeed (*Deus vult*) in curing himself completely, this would not mean that he would lose what I think both Wittgenstein and Lipman have in mind when they speak of a "sense of wonder." There are plenty of other ways of expressing one's sense of amazement and curiosity about oneself and the world besides asking philosophical questions. There is science, there is art, there is poetry and music and dance. Besides, there is also the important task of "curing" other people of "philosophical illness"—a task which requires a continual reawakening of our own sense of wonder. This reawakening, however, would now be accompanied by the wisdom to recognize that in philosophical questions, such "wonder" is badly expressed, and stands in need of new and better forms of expression.

Wittgenstein and P4C

I hope by now that we have gotten at least some grip on the meaning of Wittgenstein's metaphor of philosophy as "illness and cure." If so, then let us return to the question with which we first began. If Wittgenstein is right in thinking that philosophical questioning is a kind of "Illness," then how is it possible to justify doing P4C—a program which actively encourages philosophical questioning among the young? Granted that children (as we have seen) may already be prone to this "illness," aren't we simply exacerbating the problem by "egging them on?" How, in short, is it possible to reconcile Wittgenstein's view of philosophy with doing P4C?

The answer, I think, is to follow Wittgenstein's advice: "Don't think, but look!"[16] If you actually look at the way the Philosophy for Children Program works in practice, you will see that it does a great deal more than merely encourage philosophical questioning (although this is what will strike your eye on first glance). It also does a great deal of what Wittgenstein would call "philosophical therapy." Consider the following example from the teacher's manual for *Harry Slottlemeier's Discovery*.[17]

Exercise: How do we use the word "mind?"
A. Explain how the word mind is used in each of the following phrases:
1. Keep your mind on your work.
2. Mind the telephone.
3. Mind your own business.
4. Don't mind me.
5. I have a mind of my own.
6. I don't mind if I do.
7. He changed his mind.
8. I have a lot on my mind.
9. Mind your p's and q's.
10. Out of sight, out of mind.
11. It blew my mind.
12. I'm of two minds.
B. Decide which of these phrases have similar uses and find appropriate labels for those groups of uses.

If you really sat down and did this exercise—taking it very seriously, as a child might—and tried to explain the various uses of the word "mind" in these phrases, would you still be inclined to ask the question "What is mind?" Would you still be inclined to think of the word "mind" as the name of a mysterious object? I doubt that you would. You still might think that something *mysterious* was going on here (it's hard to get rid of that one!), but a mysterious *object*? No, that prejudice, I think, would disappear—or at any rate would be substantially reduced—and with it, so would the question "What is mind?" There is a startling resemblence here with what Wittgenstein means by "philosophical therapy." And this is not an isolated case. Over and over again, throughout the P4C curriculum, you will encounter exercises of this kind. What misleads the superficial reader—what misled me on first inspection—is that the *titles* of the exercises are very often stated in the form of "What is _____?" questions, so that if you just look at the table of contents, or thumb through the pages, this is often what you'll see: "What is thinking?", "What's real?", "What is understanding?", "What are thoughts?", "What is value?", "What is a rule?", and (horrors!) "What is a feeling?"[18]

Once you get into the exercises themselves, however, you will begin to see something very like Wittgensteinian "therapy" going on. As in the exercise on "mind," children are given examples of a variety of different uses of the word which fills in the blank in the "What is _____?" question, and are asked to explain them and to note their differences. Or children are asked to "brainstorm" and think up as many different uses of the word as they can. Or children are asked to compare and contrast the use of such words with ordinary—and some not so ordinary—names ("Can you take a thought apart, in the way you can take a watch or a sentence apart?"[19] Children are asked to choose from a variety of explanations of the use of the word and say which one best fits the use of the word in a particular context. Such exercises are surely "good medicine." They serve to combat not only the "name and object" paradigm which we have discussed in this paper, but also (as an additional benefit) to work against a related form of "philosophical illness;" the urge to seek an "essence"—a philosophical malady which also preoccupies Wittgenstein in his later work, but which (for the purpose of simplicity), I have said nothing about.

By means of such exercises, children are taught a methodology—by example and through practice—for dealing with philosophical questions when they arise. The methodology, like "Wittgenstein's therapy" (the one we have discussed), consists in asking *other* (Wittgenstein would say "better") questions—questions about the uses of words; questions which, if answered thoughtfully, will tend to make the original philosophical question disappear. But in order for children to learn this methodology, philosophical questions must be raised, even emphasized. For kids need to learn to recognize a philosophical question when they see one, and they need considerable practice in dealing with such questions before they can go on to apply the methodology

---

Should a philosophy consist of nothing but jokes and questions?

It is worth noting that Wittgenstein once said that a serious and good philosophical work could be written that would consist entirely of *jokes* (without being facetious). Another time he said that a philosophical treatise might contain nothing but questions (without answers). In his own writing he made wide use of both. To give an example: "Why can't a dog simulate pain? Is he too honest?" (*Philosophical Investigations*, 250).

—Norman Malcolm, in *Ludwig Wittgenstein: A Memoir.*

Learning, thinking and making

Wittgenstein asked how one might learn the truth by thinking, and he gave his example of how this could be done, learning to see a face by drawing it. We might generalize that example by saying that thinking is a process of construction, of making something.

—Andrew Harrison, in *Making and Thinking: A Study of Intelligent Activities*

---

on their own. So yes, P4C does encourage philosophical questioning, but it does this as apart of a larger process, which bears a remarkable resemblence, in many cases, to therapy. Far from infecting children with philosophical disease, P4C—in many instances—constitutes a kind of "preventative medicine," by providing children with techniques for dealing with their own philosophical problems before they grow too large.

I do not mean to suggest, of course, that P4C is a perfect model of Wittgensteinian "therapy," or of what I am calling "preventative medicine." I have a number of criticisms of the program—some of them Wittgensteinian criticisms—but I will save these for another occasion. Nor do I mean to suggest that Matt Lipman and his colleagues are really somehow Wittgensteinians in disguise. Lipman and Wittgenstein both would agree (I think) that philosophy "begins in wonder," but Lipman does not share Wittgenstein's emphasis on the idea that philosophical questions express this wonder in the wrong way. I only mean to say that if you look at the way the program actually works, you'll see that there is no fundamental incompatability between doing philosophy with children along the general lines of P4C and accepting Wittgenstein's metaphor of philosophy as "illness and cure." At any rate, this is the conclusion which I have come to after doing a considerable amount of philosophical "therapy" on myself. The philosophical question

which once troubled me ("Wittgenstein or P4C") has—pretty much—disappeared.

Postscript

What did Wittgenstein himself think about the advisability of doing philosophy with children? Wittgenstein seems to me to have been of two minds about this, which is why I have included this question in a postscript. His comments on this subject are like the behavior of a man who points in two opposite directions, and says "Go that way! " They are therefore totally unhelpful in telling us which way to go. For this reason, we have to "think for ourselves" (like good P4Cers) about the relationship of his larger philosophy to the question of doing philosophy with children, and make up our own minds (as I have tried to do in this paper) about the consistency of the two. But the question will inevitably arise as to what Wittgenstein actually thought about doing philosophy with kids, and since he did have some things to say about this, I will report them—contradictory as they seem to me to be. Here are a couple of samples.

In *On Certainty*, Wittgenstein asks us to imagine a pupil and a teacher:

> The pupil will not let anything be explained to him, for he continually interrupts with doubts, for instance as to the existence of things, the meaning of words, etc. The teacher says, "Stop interrupting me and do as I tell you. So far your doubts don't make sense at all." . . . And it would be just the same if the pupil cast doubt on the uniformity of nature, that is to say on the justification of inductive arguments. —The teacher would feel that this was only holding them up, that this way the pupil would only get stuck and make no progress.—And he would be right.[20]

"Stop interrupting me and do as I tell you." Is this the way we should respond to the philosophical questions of a child? So Wittgenstein seems to be saying here. And this is not an isolated instance. There are a number of other places in his later work where he seems to positively recommend the "Shut up and drink your milk" approach to answering the philosophical questions of children—as if we could nip philosophical illness in the bud by stamping it out at its first appearance.[21]

But consider the following passage from the *Philosophical Investigations*, where he asks us to consider the application of "above" and "below" to the earth:

> Here we all have a quite clear idea of what "above" and "below" mean. I see well enough that I am on top; the earth is surely beneath me! (And don't smile at this example. We are indeed all taught at school that it is stupid to talk like that. But it is much easier to bury a problem than to solve it.) And it is only reflection that shews us that in this case "above" and "below" cannot be used in the ordinary way. (That we might, for instance, say that the people at the antipodes are "below" our part of the earth, but it must also be recognized as right for them to use the same expression about us .[22]

"Easier to bury a problem than to solve it." The suggestion here is that telling kids that it's "stupid to talk like that" (another version of "Shut up and drink your milk") only "buries" the problem, and that instead, something should have been done to "solve" it. The solution, of course, would be a form of "philosophical therapy," involving a discussion of the use of "above" and "below"—a philosophical discussion with kids.

So there you have it. Wittgenstein seems to have been unclear in his own mind about whether or not it is a good idea to try to do philosophy with children. One source of his *negative* attitude toward this idea may have been his view that in order to do philosophy, one must talk about language, and that in order to talk about language, "I already have to use language full blown."[23] But what on earth is "language full blown?" Nothing could be more foreign to the later philosophy of Wittgenstein than the idea of a completely developed use (or set of uses) of language

(since language is constantly growing or changing) or a completely developed, "full blown" *mastery* of the use (or set of uses) of language (since mastery of the use of language is always a matter of degree).[24] If this is what led him (in some moods) to take a negative attitude toward doing philosophy with kids, then I think he was wrong, and wrong on his own ground. This same prejudice, however, is shared by many adults: the idea that doing philosophy requires a mastery of a vocabulary and grammar which is far too complicated and high-flown for kids. It is only when we actually try to do philosophy with children that we become disabused of this illusion. Children—and I don't mean infants or toddlers here, but children who, for example, are old enough to go to school—have already mastered enough of the grammar and vocabulary of their language to talk about their language, and therefore to do the kind of philosophy which Wittgenstein called "therapy." They have also acquired, by this time, the rudiments of "philosophical disease"—a disease which cannot be cured or prevented by attempts simply to "stamp it out," but which needs the sort of "therapy" which Wittgenstein describes—a "therapy" which makes its appearance in many of the exercises and activities of P4C.

Wittgenstein himself was an elementary school teacher for six years. His sister, Hermine Wittgenstein, who had the opportunity to observe his teaching on several occasions, describes him as "in many respects . . . a born teacher."

> [H]e not only lectured, but tried to steer the boys toward the right solution by means of questions. Once he let them invent a steam engine, then draw a sketch construction of a tower on the blackboard, or another time depict moving human figures. The interest which he aroused was tremendous. Even the untalented and usually inattentive boys gave surprisingly good answers, and they literally crawled over each other in their desire to be chosen for answers or demonstrations.[25]

Did Wittgenstein ever try to do any philosophy with his pupils? Apparently, he did. One of his former pupils, fifty years later, still recalled "an interesting thing that Lehrer [Teacher] Wittgenstein used to tell us about." It was the paradox of the liar (where the perpetual liar reports "I am now lying").[26] One other surviving example is a story which Wittgenstein used to tell his pupils—a story which starts out like certain P4C exercises, but which ends (I think) badly.

> Once upon a time there was an experiment. Two small children who had not yet learnt to speak were shut away with a woman who was unable to speak. The aim of the experiment was to determine whether they would learn some primitive language or invent a new language of their own. The experiment failed.[27]

If Wittgenstein had ended his story with a question ("Did the experiment succeed or fail?") rather than a pronouncement ("The experiment failed"), a lively philosophical discussion might have ensued, and his pupils might have been stimulated to ask all sorts of philosophical questions on their own: "Does language have to be taught?" "How did language begin?" "If language has to be taught, then how can anyone learn it in the first place?" and so on. This, in turn, might have provided an opportunity for doing "philosophical therapy." Instead, Wittgenstein ends his story with a *message*, and the message (as I read it) is that if adults didn't speak, then children would never learn to speak. What conclusion is a child likely to draw from this? That it must have been adults who first "invented" or "learned" language, and who must therefore be the final authorities on its use. (Yet another "justification" for the "Shut up and drink your milk" approach to answering the philosophical questions of children.)

It should be noted, of course, that Wittgenstein was telling this story in the early Nineteen Twenties, when he was still under the influence of his earlier philosophical views—views which he almost entirely rejected later on. His later works (such as the *Philosophical Investigations*) involve a radically different approach to doing philosophy from the one which characterizes his earlier works (such as the *Tractalus Logico-Philosophicus*).[28] In place of "pronouncements" (often "dark" pronouncements), we encounter a great variety of exercises for the reader—ones which often end with a question, and which are designed, as Wittgenstein says in the preface to the *Investigations*, to "stimulate someone to thoughts of his own."[29] His later works were undoubtedly influenced by his experience as an elementary school teacher, where he learned how to give exercises and to ask questions of his pupils, and where he had the opportunity to observe the learning process in action. Perhaps if he had returned to elementary school teaching in his later years, he might have tried to do philosophy with children more along the lines of the way he "does philosophy" with his readers in his later works. Such an experiment would have quickly dispelled his illusion that "full blown" language is necessary to talk about language and hence to do philosophical "therapy." Wittgenstein would have discovered, I think, what I have discovered from working with P4C: that doing philosophical exercises with children—exercises which involve talking with children about their language—is not only possible, but necessary. A necessary step in the treatment and prevention of philosophical disease.

Notes

1. *PI*, section 255; RFM, p. 132; *PI*, section 593. Wittgenstein's major works will be cited according to the following scheme of abbreviation.
   PI: *Philosophical Investigations* (New York, Macmillan Co., 1970).
   RFM: *Remarks on the Foundations of Mathematics* (Cambridge, Mass.: MIT Press, 1978).
   OC: *On Certainty* (New York: Harper Editions, 1969).
   Z: *Zettel* (Berkeley: UC Press, 1967).
2. Albert Camus, *The Myth of Sisyphus* (New York: Knopf, Inc., 1955), p. 1.
3. See *PI*, sections 7, 27.
4. *PI*, section 69.
5. Compare Z, section 487; *PI*, sections 304-308.

6. Matthew Lipman, et. al., *Philosophy in the Classroom* (Philadelphia: Temple University Press, 1980), p. 37.
7. Compare *PI*, section 90; *Z*, section 273.
8. *PI*, section 109.
9. *PI* section 133.
10. *PI*, section 154; *Z*, section 48; *RFM*, p. 117.
11. *Op. cit.*, p. 37.
12. *PI*, section 77.
13. *Op. cit.*, p. 31.
14. See Ludwig Wittgenstein, "A Lecture on Ethics," *The Philosophical Review*, Vol. LXXIV, No. 1 (January 1965).
15. *Z* section 382.
16. *PI*, section 66.
17. Matthew Lipman, et. al., Philosophical Inquiry: *An Instructional Manual to Accompany Harry Stottlemeier's Discovery*, Second Edition (Upper Montclair, N.J.: Institute for the Advancement of Philosophy for Children, 1979), p. 146.

18. *Op. cit.*, passim.
19. *Op. cit.*, p. 9.
20. *OC*, section 31Off.
21. See OC, section 106, *PI*, p. 200; *Z*, section 703.
22. *PI*, section 351.
23. *PI*, section 120.
24. *PI*, section 18.
25. Hermine Wiftgenstein, "My Brother Ludwig," in *Ludwig Wittgenstein: Personal Recollections*, Rush Rhees, ed. (Totowa, N.J.: Rowman and Littiefield, 1981), p. 5.
26. William Warren Bartley III, Wittgenstein (Philadelphia: J.B. Lippencott, 1973), p. 26.
27. *Op. cit.*, p. 85.
28. Ludwig Wiftgenstein, *Tractatus Logico-Philosophicus*, new English translation by D.F. Pears and B.F. McGuinness (London: Routledge and Kegan Paul, 1961).
29. *PI*, p. x.

Philosophy for Children:
A Note of Warning

John Wilson

I need to say right at the start that this is also a note of praise. No doubt it will sound rather patronizing, and the Institute for the Advancement of Philosophy for Children is so successful as to be hardly in need of praise; but those of us in the U.K. who have for long been concerned with the spread of philosophy must regard that success with an admiration which approaches amazement. Only in the U.S.A., perhaps, could such a large-scale and effective enterprise have been mounted so quickly: there is a lesson here not only for the characteristically conservative British, but perhaps for other countries as well.

Having said that, my concern is that the enterprise continues to flourish. What has flowed from it by way of publications, workshops, reports, teaching materials and pedagogy is in many ways impressive; but it suffers, I believe, from a certain type of educational ideology which has its dangers. Very roughly, and perhaps unfairly, the ideology runs something like this: "Whatever philosophy is, it is about questioning, enquiry and being critical. Children, if encouraged, can engage in these activities: they enjoy it, and it helps them to be autonomous. They learn to discuss and to think creatively. Let us not worry too much about exactly what they are supposed to learn or what philosophy is: what we need to do is to spread this process as widely as we can. It is, after all, very much in line with democratic values."

The limitations or objections to this are two. (1) First, any program for teaching (or encouraging learning, not quite the same thing), any subject or discipline of thought must start from a clear idea of what the discipline is: in particular, what counts as performing well or badly in it. Certainly it is difficult, and controversial, to define "philosophy"; but if we are to teach it we must have some idea how to answer questions—questions that will be in the minds of our pupils also—like (a) "Just what is *philosophical* thinking as against other kinds of thinking?" (b) "What counts as a specifically *philosophical* question?" (c) "What is a *philosophical* truth or bit of knowledge, as against other kinds of truth or knowledge?" and particularly, (d) "How do I know when I have got something *right* in doing philosophy?" It is because we have tolerably clear answers to these questions in other teaching subjects that we can teach them and assess pupils' progress objectively. We know, more or less, *what counts as* science, or history, or mathematics, and what it is to do well at them. If we cannot do this with philosophy, we cannot see it as a serious discipline of thought at all: for the notion of discipline rules certain moves in discussion in and other moves out, counts certain things as evidence or reasons and dismisses other things.

(2) Secondly, it is only when we have such a clear idea that we can even begin to consider the efficacy of this or that teaching method. In all

subjects, questions like, "How useful is group discussion?", "Do we want children to learn things by heart?", "How much should the teacher instruct, and how much let the children just find things out for themselves?," "What sort of content, or skills, or know-how, should we include?" have to be answered in the *light of the subject itself*, not only in the light of what pupils find enjoyable. In most subjects, there are times when the children should be democratically involved, and allowed to discover for themselves; but there are also times when they need obediently to follow rules or to engage in rote-learning. No *general* "theory of learning" can help us here (indeed no such theory can be successfully applied to all cases of learning): methods have to be referred to *what* is to be learned.

If we neglect these points, we shall fall victim to what might be called the romantic or Rousseauesque fantasy: the idea that all or most pupils will, given sufficient encouragement, acquire all the knowledge and abilities they need by the light of nature. This cannot be true, because any serious intellectual discipline is demanding: to master it, we have constantly to put ourselves and our prejudices in the background and attend to logic and/or facts—in particular, to the appropriate *methodology*—something pupils cannot do if they are not shown just what that methodology is, what counts as a good performance. We cannot expect children simply to find out for themselves what the proper way of doing science, mathematics, or any other subject is: even if they could, the time wasted would be enormous.

This is basically a point about authority. Characteristically, educators have felt themselves "for" or "against" authority in education, echoing no doubt the child-like feelings within us all. I have written at length about this elsewhere (Wilson (1990). The basic point here is that the educator must take his/her stand on the authority *of the subject* and its methodology, which he/she mediates to the pupil in various ways. Education cannot be "democratic," in any sense of that word which approximates to "egalitarian," since some people—hopefully, the teachers—

will be in a better position to understand the authority of the intellectual disciplines than other people. (This, ultimately, is why Plato in the *Republic* thought democracy absurd: a case that has to be taken seriously).

It is an entirely open question just what teaching methods or classroom styles are most effective for what subjects: no research has determined this, because no research has been based on an adequate account of good performance in any subject and simultaneously (what is very difficult) taken account of all the relevant variables. Most children, however, want—as well as need—*both* to be guided, to have some clearly-outlined authority and methodology to which they can safely refer and which they can try to imitate, *and* also to be allowed some free rein or opportunity for trying out their own ideas. Almost certainly some judicious mix (which might well vary according to the sort of pupil we are dealing with) would be better than either a "democratic" or "authoritarian" regime throughout.

I am bound to say that the absence of any clear account of philosophy (1) of course opens the doors to the democratic and anti-authority teaching methods in (2). If we have no clear account, backed up by some kind of objective and hard-and-fast tests, then who is to say which pupils prosper by which methods? All we can do is what in fact most educators (and, alas, most researchers) actually do in the present climate: they commend those regimes in which pupils seem most "involved," "interested," "stimulated," and, in general, which they find most enjoyable. Of course I, like most people, want to enjoy myself and want other people to do the same; but I have constantly to remind myself that—for instance—I took very little enjoyment in learning Latin by the old grammar-and-syntax methods when I was at school, yet know well that only such methods could conceivably have enabled me to enjoy the classics as I do today. Enjoyment or popularity is not the only, indeed not even a particularly good, criterion of becoming educated.

Partly for these reasons, and partly because of more strictly philosophical considerations to do

---

Is the aim of philosophy to terminate disagreement?

In the rhetorical situation, disagreement exists only to be overcome through the exploitation of an initial agreement, and the desire of an audience to reach its own conclusions must be circumvented. In philosophical discussions, on the other hand, whether there is an initial agreement or not, it cannot be exploited to overcome disagreement, since the latter is radical, permitting no compromise. What must be exploited is just the desire of each participant to reach his own conclusions. A conclusion has no philosophical use if it is not reached freely. To be philosophically useful, it must represent the unconstrained attempt on the part of its advocate to fulfill his obligation to defend and clarify his position. Thus philosophical discussion is, in effect, a collaborative effort to maintain the conditions under which disagreement is possible.

—Henry W. Johnstone, Jr. in *Philosophy and Argument.*

---

with the nature of philosophy (Wilson 1986), I would myself advocate a definition of philosophy which approximates to something like "the investigation of concepts, categories and distinctions via the meaning of words." Not everyone will follow this (typically "Oxford") line; but it does at least have the advantage of a fair degree of clarity. Questions like "What do we mean by 'true' ('fair,' 'ought,' 'authority,' etc)?" can be seen as strictly philosophical questions, with answers that can be pretty well adjudicated as, if not right and wrong, at least better and worse. We know how to discuss, and how to evaluate, such questions; and it is not hard to see how a pupil's performance in answering them could be objectively tested.

It is no recantation of this to grant that there must be space, perhaps plenty of space, for more wide-ranging "philosophical" discussion. The point of such discussion, however, must always be to focus on concepts and meaning (much of the Institute's material does this excellently). There is no merit just in *discussing*: there must be criteria of relevance and hence, of success. The reader may be amused to know that, in my own work with children and non-philosophical adults, I find it possible and desirable not only to have free-ranging discussions arising from pupil's particular real-life concerns, but also sessions in which I monitor these quite severely for relevance, holding up after each contribution a scoreboard with a number on it, as at the Olympic games. I also play back our discussions, stopping the tape so that I and others can comment on the merits of various remarks. (The teacher, if he/she is anything like me, learns a great deal about his/her own irrelevance, or impatience, or confusion by this method.) My experience is that, once there is sufficient trust and respect in the group— and I take the most important question for teaching philosophy to be how to generate this (see Wilson 1986)—pupils not only tolerate but positively welcome such techniques.

Philosophy, whatever else it is, is certainly a subject that requires dialogue: not much can be learned by heart or parrotted to any effect. In that sense its aims are liberal, to do with authenticity and autonomy and critical thinking. But we must take two points to heart. First, as I have said, not just *any* critical thinking is philosophical, and we have to spell out our aims more clearly. Secondly, it does not at all follow that because aims are "liberal" or "non-authoritarian," therefore our methods must be too. Indeed, it may well be that a much more stringent discipline is required. Not for nothing is Wittgenstein supposed to have advised for doing philosophy to "go the bloody hard way."

References

John Wilson, 1986. *What Philosophy Can Do*. Macmillan: London.

John Wilson, 1990. *A New Introduction to Moral Education.* Cassell: London.

Chapter Eight
Encouraging Thinking For Oneself
Through Socratic Teaching

Chapter Eight

Encouraging Thinking for Oneself Through Socratic Teaching

There are many kinds of life worth living, but the unexamined life, the unquestioned life, according to Socrates, is not one of them. To see to it that our lives are properly questioned, we cannot merely resort to solitary meditations. We must engage in dialogue. Through dialogical inquiry we learn how others question what we say and do and think, and this enables us to question ourselves about these same things. By listening to what others think, we discover what we ourselves think. By discerning our own point of view, as distinct from those of others, we come to learn what it is to think for ourselves. Even this, however, is not enough. It is not enough to think for ourselves and to say what we think. We must also take responsibility for what we say and think. This takes courage, but being human generally takes courage: this is just an instance of it.

Some of these points may be inferred from the position of the Socrates who figures prominently in the early dialogues of Plato. To teach Socratically, presumably, is to teach in such a way as to make the series of events described above happen. While Socrates lived, this is what he did. To make it possible for the Socratic approach to continue, Plato wrote the dialogues that show Socrates living as he lived and teaching as he taught. No explanation or interpretation could have performed this task. We read the dialogues,

and we struggle to extract the Socratic pedagogy from what we read. It is not easy. And yet, there emerges from the pages of the *Dialogues* a display (if not a conception) of what it is to think for oneself, to be a person, to be human, and to live and teach in ways that empower others to do these things too.

What is it then, this Socratic method? Leonard Nelson, recognizing that the question is a formidable one, struggles nevertheless to produce an answer of sorts. He begins by stressing that the philosophy teacher should get his students to *do* philosophy, not merely to learn it. This entails engaging them in dialogue. (Nelson does not fail to see the importance of fictionalized versions of philosophical conversations, but he sees these as a mixed art struggling for fidelity to the original.) The first secret of the Socratic method, Nelson says, is that of forcing the students to confront their own dogmatism and, by that act, forcing them to be free, which is all the same with being capable of unprejudiced judgment. (Nelson elsewhere speaks of the aim of education as being "rational self-determination.") In any event, Nelson insists that, for Socrates, one can arrive at this goal *only* by employing his method, which necessarily entails thinking for oneself, and this involves one in raising the questions oneself, not waiting for the teacher to do so. But these are only a few of Nelson's insights into the Socratic method.

Socratic teaching, says Rosalyn S. Sherman, can be considered from four points of view. Its aim is to answer some question that concerns all the discussants, and to raise some questions that have not been asked. Its logic involves an appeal to the rationality of the student. It involves dialogue, because this is the only way to discover the norms, standards and criteria by which the inquiry is to be guided. Finally, it involves a freedom and openness in terms of which one can admit one's own ignorance and one can finish a conversation without having arrived at a conclusion. But much in Sherman's essay involves an analysis of the context in which Socrates lived, and the lessons this has for the contexts in which we try to teach in our own time.

Starting with the assumption that the aim of education is happiness, Redfield proceeds to explore the contention of Socrates that the knowledge most worth having is the knowledge of the Good; which turns out to be much the same as knowledge of the self. For Socrates, happiness lies in this pursuit, the pursuit of the Good, the pursuit of happiness. This is to be done rationally and methodically, on the one hand, and yet crea-tively on the other. Socratic theory is useful because it leads to an ordered routine of practice. He does not ask, How are you and I to get on together? He asks, What is friendship? This is a theoretical approach, but it leads to a radical reform of practice—to a methodical creativity.

It is in this sense that Gilbert Ryle's essay is included here under the rubric of Socratic teaching: he is interested in eliciting from students a methodical creativity, and the modes of practice he recommends have much in common with those Socrates employs. "The young rock-climber is first learning to climb when he ceases to tread *where* his teacher trod and begins to try to tread over new slopes *in the ways in which* his teacher treads." To show students a particular action and have them figure out the possible modes of performance of that thing is to induce in them that flexibility that goes by the name of "thinking for oneself." Another way of putting this is that thinking for oneself, authentic thinking, is not merely following instructions but finding ways of bettering those instructions. Each example we are given implies a variety or set of ways in which something can be done. We must figure these out and improve upon them.

The Socratic Method

Leonard Nelson

Leonard Nelson (1882-1927) was a German professor of philosophy at the University of Gottingen. While he had strong interests in philosophy of mathematics and the theory of knowledge, he also wrote extensively on ethics, and conceived of philosophical pedagogics as the development of that theory by which people could be educated to the ethical good. Insisting that ethics must be practised as well as taught, he founded several youth and political organizations in the 1920's, although these were prohibited within a few years for their anti-Nazi activities. The following selection is an abridgement of Nelson's essay, "The Socratic Method," which was translated by Thomas K. Brown in Socratic Method and Critical Philosophy *(New Haven: Yale University Press, 1949), p. 1, 11, 13-14, 15, 17, 18-19, 20-24, 25-29, 30-31, 32-33. Nelson's essay was originally delivered as a lecture, "Die sokratishe Methode," before the Pedagogic Society of Gottingen in 1922, and was later published in* Abhandlungen der Fries'schen Schule, N.F. *Vol. 5, No. 1 (1929), pp. 21-78.*

What Nelson prizes most in the Socratic method is its effectiveness in getting students to think for themselves. So long as the teacher professes knowledge, students will concentrate upon trying to figure out what he believes with regard to the question under discussion, rather than confront the issue directly. There is also a process of unlearning that must take place, for students must be brought to discover their own ignorance. But this is only a first step. As the dialogue in the classroom continues, Nelson makes clear, students will begin to find the presuppositions and principles underlying their convictions. Philosophy, then, is the instrument by which the students who have only recently discovered their own ignorance can be brought "to realize that they actually know what they did not know they knew."

You know the Socratic method as a method of teaching philosophy. But philosophy is different from other subjects of instruction; in Plato's own words: "It does not at all admit of verbal expression like other studies, but as a result of continued application to the subject itself and communion therewith, it is brought to birth in the soul on a sudden, as light that is kindled by a leaping spark, and thereafter it nourishes itself."

I therefore find myself in a quandary, not unlike that of a violinist who, when asked how he goes about playing the violin, can of course demonstrate his art but cannot explain his technique in abstract terms.

The Socratic method, then, is the art of teaching not philosophy but philosophizing, the art of not teaching about philosophers but of making philosophers of the students.

The teacher who seriously wishes to impart philosophical insight can aim only at teaching the art of philosophizing. He can do no more than show his students how to undertake, each for himself, the laborious regress that alone affords insight into basic principles. If there is such a thing at all as instruction in philosophy, it can only be instruction in doing one's own thinking;

more precisely, in the independent practice of the art of abstraction. The meaning of my initial remark, that the Socratic method, as a method of instruction in philosophy, is the art not of teaching philosophy but of teaching philosophizing, will now become clear . . .

We find dialogue employed as an art form in fiction and drama and as a pedagogic form in instruction. Theoretically these forms are separable but actually we require of every conversation liveliness, clarity, and beauty of expression, as well as espousal of truth, decisiveness, and strength of conviction. Even though the emphasis varies, we like to recognize the teacher in the artist and the artist in the teacher.

We must furthermore distinguish between a conversation reduced to writing—even though it is a reproduction of actual speech—and a real conversation carried on between persons. Conversations that are written down lose their original liveliness, "like the flower in the botanist's case." If, in spite of this, we are to find them satisfactory, the atmosphere must be spiritualized and purified, standards must be raised; and then there may come forth some rare and admirable production as the conversation of the Grand Inquisitor, which is carried on with a silent opponent who by his silence defeats him.

Conversation as a pedagogic form, however, must sound like actual talk; otherwise it does not fulfill its task of being model and guide. To catch, in the mirror of a written reproduction, the fleeting form of such talk with its irregularities, to strike the mean between fidelity to the sense and fidelity to the word—this is a problem that can perhaps be solved didactically; but the solution, serving as it does a definite purpose, will rarely meet the demands of free art and therefore as a whole will nearly always produce a mixed impression. I know of only a few didactic conversations in literature from which this discord has been even partially eliminated. I have in mind, for instance, some passages in the three well-known dialogues by Solovyeff; then there is the Socratic dialogue with which the American socialist writer Bellamy opens his didactic novel, *Looking Backward*; and finally—by no means the least successful—the conversations in August Niemann's novel, *Bakchen und Thyrsostrager*, which is imbued with the true Socratic spirit. . . .

We must bear this discord in mind as we scrutinize the Platonic dialogue to discover how Socrates accomplished his pedagogic task.

One achievement is universally conceded to him: that by his questioning he leads his pupils to confess their ignorance and thus cuts through the roots of their dogmatism. This result, which indeed cannot be *forced* in any other way, discloses the significance of the dialogue as an instrument of instruction. The lecture, too, can stimulate spontaneous thinking, particularly in more mature students; but no matter what allure such stimulus may possess, it is not *irresistible*. Only persistent pressure to speak one's mind, to meet every counter-question, and to state the reasons for every assertion transforms the power of that allure into an irresistible compulsion. This art of *forcing* minds to *freedom* constitutes the first secret of the Socratic method.

But only the first. For it does not take the pupil beyond the abandonment of his prejudices, the realization of his not-knowing, this negative determinant of all genuine and certain knowledge. . . .

Socrates was the first to combine with confidence in the ability of the human mind to recognize philosophical truth the conviction that this truth is not arrived at through occasional bright ideas or mechanical teaching but that only planned, unremitting, and consistent thinking leads us from darkness into its light. Therein lies Socrates' greatness as a philosopher. His greatness as a pedagogue is based on another innovation: he made his pupils do their own thinking and introduced the interchange of ideas as a safeguard against self-deception . . .

Now we are confronted with the full gravity of the pedagogic problem we are to solve. Consider the question: How is any instruction and therefore any teaching at all possible when every instructive judgment is forbidden? Let us not attempt evasion by assuming that the requirement cannot possibly be meant to go to the extreme of prohibiting an occasional discreet helpful hint from teacher to student. No, there must be an honest choice: either dogmatism or following Socrates. The question then becomes all the more insistent: How is Socratic instruction possible? . . . If the end of education is rational self-determination, i.e., a condition in which the individual does not allow his behavior to be determined by outside influences but judges and acts according to his own insight, the question arises: How can we affect a person by outside influences so that he will not permit himself to be affected by outside influences? We must resolve this paradox or abandon the task of education. . . .

We must bear in mind that instruction in philosophy is not concerned with heaping solution on solution, nor indeed with establishing results, but solely with learning the method of reaching solutions. If we do this, we shall observe at once that the teacher's proper role cannot be that of a guide keeping his party from wrong paths and accidents. Nor yet is he a guide going in the lead while his party simply follow in the expectation that this will prepare them to find the same path later on by themselves. On the contrary, the essential thing is the skill with which the teacher puts the pupils on their own responsibility at the very beginning by teaching them to go by themselves—although they would not on that account go alone—and by so developing this independence that one day they may be able to venture forth alone, self-guidance having replaced the teacher's supervision.

As to the observations I am about to make, I must beg to be allowed to cull incidental examples from my own long experience as a teacher of philosophy, for unfortunately the experiences of others are not at my disposal.

Let me take up first the requirements imposed on the teacher and then go on to those placed on the pupil. Once a student of mine, endeavoring to reproduce a Socratically conducted exercise, pre-sented a version in which he put the replies now into the teacher's mouth, now into the pupil's. Only my astonished question, "Have you ever heard me say 'yes' or 'no'?" stopped him short. Thrasymachus saw the point more clearly; in Plato's *Republic* he calls out to Socrates: "Ye gods! . . . I knew it . . . that you would refuse and do anything rather than answer." The teacher who follows the Socratic model does not answer. Neither does he question. More precisely, he puts no philosophical questions, and when such questions are addressed to him, he under no circumstances gives the answer sought. Does he then remain silent? We shall see. During such a session we may often hear the despairing appeal to the teacher: "I don't know what it is you want!" Whereupon the teacher replies: "I? I want nothing at all." This certainly does not convey the desired information. What is it, then, that the teacher actually does? He sets the interplay of question and answer going between the students, perhaps by the introductory remark: "Has anyone a question?"

Now, everyone will realize that, as Kant said, "to know what questions may reasonably be asked is already a great and necessary proof of sagacity and insight." What about foolish questions, or what if there are no questions at all? Suppose nobody answers?

You see, at the very beginning the difficulty presents itself of getting the students to the point of spontaneous activity, and with it arises the temptation for the teacher to play out a clue like Ariadne's thread. But the teacher must be firm from the beginning, and especially at the beginning. If a student approaches philosophy without having a single question to put to it, what can we expect in the way of his capacity to persevere in exploring its complex and profound problems?

What should the teacher do if there are no questions? He should wait—until questions come. At most, he should request that in the future, in order to save time, questions be thought over in advance. But he should not, just to save time, save the students the effort of formulating their own questions. If he does, he may for the moment temper their impatience, but only at the cost of nipping in the bud the philosophical impatience we seek to awaken.

Once questions start coming—one by one, hesitantly, good ones and foolish ones—how does the teacher receive them, how does he handle them? He now seems to have easy going since the rule of the Socratic method forbids his answering them. He submits the questions to discussion.

All of them? The appropriate and the inappropriate?

By no means. He ignores all questions uttered in too low a voice. Likewise those that are phrased incoherently. How can difficult ideas by grasped when they are expressed in mutilated language . . . ?

Sometimes clarification comes with the counter-question "Just what do you mean by that?" But very often this will not work because the speaker does not know what he means himself. The work of the discussion group thus tends automatically either to take up the clear, simple questions or to clear up unclear, vague ones first.

We are not so fortunate in the problems of philosophy as we are in the problems of mathematics, which, as Hilbert says, fairly call to us: "Here I am, find the solution!" The philosophical problem is wrapped in obscurity. To be able to come to grips with it by framing clear-cut, searching questions demands many trials and much effort. It will therefore scarcely surprise you to learn that a semester's work in a seminar in ethics yielded nothing except agreement on the fact that the initial question was incongruous. The question was, "Is it not stupid to act morally?"

Of course, the instructor will not submit every incongruous question to such protracted examination. He will seek to advance the discussion through his own appraisal of the questions. But he will do no more than allow a certain question to come to the fore because it is instructive in itself or because threshing it out will bring to light typical errors. And he will do this by some such

expedient as following the question up with the query: "Who understood what was said just now?" This contains no indication of the relevance or irrelevance of the question; it is merely an invitation to consider it, to extract its meaning by intensive cross-examination.

What is his policy as regards the answers? How are they handled? They are treated like the questions. Unintelligible answers are ignored in order to teach the students to meet the requirements of scientific speech. Answers, too, are probed through such questions as:

"What has this answer to do with our question?"

"Which word do you wish to emphasize?"

"Who has been following?"

"Do you still know what you said a few moments ago?"

"What question are we talking about?"

The simpler these questions, the more flustered the students become. Then, if some fellow student takes pity on his colleague's distress and comes to his aid with the explanation, "He surely wanted to say . . .," this helpful gesture is unfeelingly cut short with the request to let the art of mind reading alone and cultivate instead the more modest art of saying what one actually wants to say.

By this time you will have gathered that the investigations run a far from even course. Questions and answers tumble over one another. Some of the students understand the development, some do not. The latter cut in with groping questions, trying to re-establish contact, but the others will not be stopped from going ahead. They disregard the interruptions. New questions crop up, wider of the mark. Here and there a debater falls silent; then whole groups. Meanwhile, the agitation continues, and questions become constantly more pointless. Even those who were originally sure of their ground become confused. They, too, lose the thread and do not know how to find it again. Finally, nobody knows where the discussion is headed.

The bewilderment famed in the Socratic circle closes in. Everyone is at his wit's end. What had been certain at the outset has become uncertain. The students, instead of clarifying their own conceptions, now feel as though they had been robbed of their capacity to make anything clear by thinking. . . .

Is it a fault of the Socratic method that it must take time for such elementary matters as ascertaining what question is being discussed or determining what the speaker intended to say about it? It is easy for dogmatic instruction to soar into higher regions. Indifferent to self-understanding, it purchases its illusory success at the cost of more and more deeply rooted dishonesty. It is not surprising, then, that the Socratic method is compelled to fight a desperate battle for integrity of thought and speech before it can turn to larger tasks. It must also suffer the additional reproach of being unphilosophical enough to orient itself by means of examples and facts.

The only way one can learn to recognize and avoid the pitfalls of reflection is to become acquainted with them in *application*, even at the risk of gaining wisdom only by sad experience. It is useless to preface philosophizing proper with an introductory course in logic in the hope of thus saving the novice from the risk of taking the wrong path. Knowledge of the principles of logic and the rules of the syllogism, even the ability to illustrate every fallacy by examples, remains after all an art *in abstracto*. An individual is far from learning to think logically even though he has learned to conclude by all the syllogistic rules that Caius is mortal. The test of one's own conclusions and their subjection to the rules of logic is the province of one's faculty of judgment, not at all the province of logic. The faculty of judgment, said Kant, being the power of rightly employing given rules, "must belong to the learner himself; and in the absence of such a natural gift no rule that may be prescribed to him for this purpose can ensure against misuse." If, therefore, this natural gift is weak, it must be strengthened. But it can be strengthened only by exercise.

This question, if examined carefully, presents no further difficulties for us. If there is such a thing as a research method for philosophy, its essential element must consist of practical directives for the step-by-step solution of problems. It is therefore simply a question of letting the student himself follow the path of the regressive method. The first step, obviously is to have him secure a firm footing in experience—which is harder to do than an outsider might think. For your adept in philosophy scorns nothing so much as using his intelligence concretely in forming judgments on real facts, an operation that obliges him to remember those lowly instruments of cognition, his five senses. Ask anyone at a philosophy seminar, "What do you see *on the blackboard*?" and depend on it, he will look at the floor. Upon your repeating, "What do you see on the blackboard?" he will finally wrench out a sentence that begins with "If" and demonstrates that for him the world of facts does not exist.

He shows the same disdain for reality when asked to give an example. Forthwith he goes off into a world of fantasy or, if forced to stay on this planet, he at least makes off to the sea or into the desert, so that one wonders whether being attacked by lions and saved from drowning are typical experiences among the acquaintances of a philosopher. The "if" sentences, the far-fetched examples, and the premature desire for definitions characterize not the ingenious beginner but rather the philosophically indoctrinated dilettante. And it is always he, with his pseudo-wisdom, who disturbs the quiet and simple progress of an investigation.

I recall a seminar in logic, in which the desire to start from general definitions—under the impression that otherwise the concepts being discussed could not be employed—caused much fruitless trouble. Despite my warning, the group stuck to the opening question: "What is a concept?"

It was not long before a casual reference to the concept "lamp" as an example was followed by the appearance of the "lamp in general" provided with all the essential characteristics of all particular lamps. The students waxed warm in vehement dispute regarding the proof of the existence of this lamp furnished with all the essential features of all particular lamps. My diffident question, whether the lamp-in-general was fed with gas, electricity, or kerosene, went unanswered as unworthy of philosophical debate until, hours later, the resumption of this very question of the source of energy forced the negation of the existence of the lamp-in-general. That is to say, the disputants discovered that different illuminants for one and the same lamp, be it ever so general, were mutually exclusive. Thus, starting with practical application, they had unexpectedly found the law of contradiction by the regressive method. But to define the concept of a concept had proved a vain endeavor; just as in the Socratic circle of the definitions nearly always miscarried.

Are we justified, however, in assuming that the cause of such failures always lies in conditions unconnected with the Socratic method itself? Does not this method perhaps suffer from an inherent limitation that makes the solution of deeper problems impossible?

Before coming to a final decision on this point, we must consider one more factor that creates difficulty in the employment of the Socratic method. Though intimately associated with the latter, it lies outside it, yet demands consideration before we can set the limits of the method itself.

The significance of the Socratic dialogue has been sought in the assumption that deliberating with others makes us more easily cognizant of truth than silent reflection. Obviously, there is much soundness in this view. Yet many a person may be moved to doubt this praise after he has listened to the hodgepodge of questions and answers at a philosophical debate and noted the absence, despite the outward discipline, of the tranquility that belongs to reflection. It is inevitable that what is said by one participant may prove disturbing to another, whether he feels himself placed in a dependent position by intelligent remarks or is distracted by poor ones. It is inevitable

that collaboration should progressively become a trial of nerves, made more difficult by increasing demands on personal tact and tolerance.

To a great extent these disturbances can be obviated by an instructor who, for instance, will ignore the innumerable senseless answers, cast doubt on the right ones with Socratic irony, or ease nervous unrest with some understanding word. But his power to restore harmony to the play of ideas is limited unless the others are willing to pursue the common task with determination.

It should be admitted that many disturbances are unavoidable because of the students' imperfect understanding; but the obstacles I have in mind do not lie in the intellectual sphere and for that reason even the most skillful teacher finds them an insurmountable barrier. He can enforce intellectual discipline only if the students are possessed of a disciplined will. This may sound strange but it is a fact that one becomes a philosopher, not by virtue of intellectual gifts but by the exercise of will. . . .

But it is impossible to achieve this as a by-product in the course of philosophical instruction. The student's will power must be the fruit of his prior education. It is the instructor's duty to make no concession in maintaining the rigorous and indispensable demands on the will; indeed, he must do so out of respect for the students themselves. If, for the want of requisite firmness, he allows himself to be persuaded to relax his stand, or if he does so of his own accord to hold his following, he will have betrayed his philosophical goal. He has no alternative: he must insist on his demands or give up the task. Everything else is abject compromise.

Of course, the student should know the details of the demands to be made on his will. They constitute the minimum required for examining ideas in a group. This means, first, the communication of thoughts, not of acquired fragments of knowledge, not even the knowledge of other people's thoughts, It means, further, the use of clear, unambiguous language. Only the compulsion to communicate provides a means of testing the definiteness and clarity of one's own conceptions. Here, protesting that one has the right feeling but cannot express it will not avail. Feeling is indeed the first and best guide on the path to truth, but it is just as often the protector of prejudice. In a scientific matter, therefore, feeling must be interpreted so that it may be evaluated in accordance with concepts and ordered logic. Moreover, our investigation demands the communication of ideas in distinctly audible and generally comprehensible speech, free from ambiguities. A technical terminology is not only unnecessary for philosophizing but is actually detrimental to its steady progress. It imparts to metaphysical matters, abstract and difficult in any case, the appearance of an esoteric science, which only superior minds are qualified to penetrate. It prevents us from considering the conclusions of unprejudiced judgment, which we have seen to be the starting point of meaningful philosophizing. Unprejudiced judgment, in its operation, relies on concepts that we have, not on artificial reflections, and it makes its conclusions understood by strict adherence to current linguistic usage. . . .

After all that we have said, what is it that we gain with this demand on the pupil? Only those who, by using comprehensible language, adhere to the concepts we have and become practiced in discussing them will sharpen their critical sense for every arbitrary definition and for every sham proof adroitly derived from such verbal definition. If the requirement of simple and clear language is observed, it is possible, in Socratic teaching, merely by writing the theses of two mutually contradictory doctrines on the blackboard, to focus attention on the verbal definition underlying them, disclose its abuse, and thereby overthrow both doctrinal opinions. The success of such a dialectical performance is achieved—and this is its significant feature—not by flashes of inspiration but methodically, i.e., through a step-by-step search for the hidden premise at the bottom of the contradictory judgments. This method will succeed if the student, struck with suspicion at such a sophism, attends closely to the meaning of the words, for these words, when used in an inartificial sense, put him on the track of the error.

Do not misunderstand me. I do not advocate the point of view that so-called common sense and its language can satisfy the demands of scientific philosophizing. Nor is it my purpose, in dwelling on simple elementary conditions seemingly easy to fulfill, to veil the fact that the pursuit of philosophizing requires rigorous training in the art of abstraction, one difficult to master. My point is this: We cannot with impunity skip the first steps in the development of this art. Abstraction must have something to abstract from. The immediate and tangible material of philosophy is language which presents concepts through words. In its wealth, supplied from many sources, reason dwells concealed. Reflection discloses this rational knowledge by separating it from intuitive notions.

Just as Socrates took pains to question locksmiths and blacksmiths and made their activities the first subject of discussion with his pupils, so every philosopher ought to start out with the vernacular and develop the language of his abstract science from its pure elements.

Is It Possible To Teach Socratically?

Rosalyn Lessing (née Sherman)

When I recover from my disappointment, I often wonder why it is that my students don't love what I love. Like most people, I consider my deepest commitments intrinsically and objectively worthy of commitment, difficult to treat as just "my thing." When others fail to love what I love, it's easy, then, to think either that they are blind or that I have failed to reveal to them the true nature of what I love. And so it is with teaching. I am always being tossed about by anger at my students for *their* narrow-mindedness and anger at myself for *my* narrow-mindedness. Why haven't they the imagination to entertain ideas they don't hold, the patience and energy to examine critically ideas they *do* hold? Why haven't I the patience necessary for the loosening of my imagination in search of still more novel ways of seducing my students into genuine encounter with ideas, their own as well as others'? Time and time again I've come to the conclusion that if my students don't love what I love, it's because of the way I've taught them— and I resolve to be more "Socratic." I've discovered, however, that Socrates, his method, and the project to which he committed his life—and for which he lost it—are among the things I love that many students do not love. This has led me to wonder if there isn't something more than the student-teacher relationship that needs to be wondered about. Is it even *possible*, I wonder, to teach Socratically, in this time, in our institutions of higher learning?

Socrates evokes little sympathy from students encountering him for the first time. Indeed, their reactions are often so violently hateful that it's easy to imagine that Socrates would be executed as quickly and as guiltlessly today as he was over 2000 years ago. How is one who takes Socrates as her model to interpret this? The easiest response is to assume that students, like the ancient Athenians, are reluctant to engage in philosophy, are protecting themselves from the "shipwreck" it can be to question to the death the assumptions in which their lives are grounded. This is easy because it protects the teacher from questioning the assumptions in which *her* life is grounded, or, at least, those on which her teaching is based.

I think there are good reasons why students respond to Socrates as an authoritarian, picky, overly verbal, self-righteous, insensitive manipulator of other people's thoughts; a seducer of the worst sort, indeed a sophist in the Platonic sense of that term. These reasons lie partly in the truth that students are often conservative in just those places where everyone else is conservative, namely, where their own personal needs and self-images are at stake; partly in the truth, so often suggested by Plato, that the philosopher can appear to be a sophist to the undiscerning eye. But the reasons lie partly also in a more fundamental truth, which it is my purpose to examine here. The Socratic dialogue occurs within a context of a very special sort. The perception of Socrates as non-authoritarian, non-manipulative, more profoundly sensitive and generous than most of us can be, and, in the end, a user of words for the purpose of transcending words—hence, a seducer of the *best* sort—presupposes this context.

Those who do not share it, characters like Thrasymachus and Protagoras, as well as the people who populate our classrooms, *cannot* perceive the Socrates who inspired Plato. Nor are they taught successfully by Socrates. I want to argue here that the possibility of Socratic teaching depends as much on the *context* of the student-teacher relationship as it does on the personalities, characters, and skills of individual teachers and students.

But, first, what *is* Socratic teachings? Practically every teacher who employs the discussion method thinks of himself as teaching Socratically. This is a negative and crude definition of "Socratic teaching," negative in the sense that it means "not lecture," and crude insofar as it does not specify the features peculiar to *Socrates'* method of discussion. Is a discussion initiated by the teacher, without an explicit invitation from the students, a "Socratic" discussion? For the most part, Socrates joined and transformed discussions already in progress, or initiated a particular line of discussion when requested to do so by fellow conversants. Rarely did he initiate discussions *ex nihilo*.[1] Again, is a discussion which is "carried on at random and without rules of art" or one which does not deal with "the nature of justice" (*Sophist*, 225) a "Socratic" discussion? Plato strongly suggests it is not (*Sophist*, 225-226; 229-231). Thus merely to distinguish discussion from lecture is not enough to set off Socratic teaching from other types of teaching.

A slightly more refined version of "Socratic teaching" has it that a discussion in which the teacher puts (leading) questions to the students, rather than *vice versa*, is Socratic. Here, the focus is on Socrates' claim to ignorance, and the purely formal fact that he expresses what he has to say in interrogative sentences. This is a positive, but still crude definition of "Socratic teaching." It is true that Socrates questions, and that he repeatedly distinguishes his style of conversation from the lengthy speech-making of the sophistic teacher. But Socrates asks particular *kinds* of questions, in a particular *order* and *manner*, and with particular *aims* in mind. It is that particular-

ity, named "dialectic" by Plato, which allowed Socrates to "teach" a slaveboy what the square root of the diagonal of a square is, without "teaching" him anything (*Meno*). The *mere* asking of questions does not constitute "Socratic teaching."

The Nature of Socratic Teaching

Socratic teaching is a particular kind of encounter between teacher and student. To describe it fully, we must look at this encounter from at least four perspectives: (1) Socrates' aims, (2) the logic of his questions, (3) the significance of the fact that the encounter is a conversation, and (4) psychological and rhetorical features of the conversations.

Aims

The *explicit* aim of Socratic method is to answer some question which is a question for all of the discussants. The *implicit* aim is to lead the discussants to ask those questions they have *not* asked but which *must* be asked (and answered) if those they *do* ask are to be answered intelligibly. Socrates' aim is to show them what *sort* of question he who truly seeks wisdom asks, and by what method one may discover the true answer to such a question. Thus the underlying aim of Socratic teaching is to awaken truly philosophical questioning by engaging the student in philosophical method.

This aim is achieved, in part, when the discussants can recognize that the truth or falsity of their everyday judgments, and the rightness or wrongness of their everyday activities, are dependent on the truth or falsity of logically prior beliefs. But Socrates' pedagogical aims are more far-reaching that this. He wishes to have his students *experience* the difference between simply *holding* assumptions which *seem* to justify their judgments and activities, and *knowing* those truths which *actually would* justify their judgments and activities. For philosophical questioning arises out of a desire for knowledge, a desire born out of dissatisfaction with mere opinion and reliance on custom. Socrates' method is designed to bring about the experience of this dissatisfaction, in such a way as to forestall anger, hopelessness and shame.

Plato describes this method by way of contrast with two other methods which were popular in his day (and remain so today). One of these he calls "the admonitory sort of instruction," which is based on reproach and advice; the other is instruction through "speeches," and the written word. The former contrast reveals the significance of logic, the latter the significance of dialogue for Socratic method.

Logic

Those who reject the admonitory sort of instruction—*i.e.,* dialecticians—do so out of the twin convictions that no one is willingly ignorant and that no one who believes himself wise is willing to inquire. So it is that dialecticians address themselves to those areas in which the student believes himself to be wise:

> They cross-examine a man's words, when he thinks that he is saying something and is really saying nothing, and easily convict him of inconsistencies in his opinions; these they can then collect by the dialectic process, and placing them side by side, show that they contradict one another about the same things, in relation to the same things, and in the same respect. He, seeing this, is angry with himself, and grows gentle towards others, and thus is entirely delivered from great prejudices and harsh notions, in a way which is most amusing to the hearer, and produces the most lasting good effect on the person who is the subject of the operation. For as the physician considers that the body will receive no benefit from taking food until the internal obstacles have been removed, so the purifier of the soul is conscious that his patient will receive no benefit from the application of knowledge until he is refuted, and from refutation learns modesty; he must be purged of his

prejudices first and made to think that he knows only what he knows, and no more.

(*Sophist*, 230—Jowett translation)

Notice that it is by appealing to the student's own rationality, rather than to his desire for approval and fear of disapproval, that a confession of ignorance is elicited. That Socrates can elicit such a confession *without* evoking anger at himself, shame, or hopelessness with regard to the possibility of knowledge, is due in large measure precisely to his use of logical analysis and assessment, for by this means what the student loses in the way of habitual beliefs and long-treasured values is amply repaid in the way of intellectual autonomy.

But Socratic method involves more than logic, for the method of refutation *can* be used manipulatively—to force the student to agree with the teacher's views—and/or defensively—to mask the teacher's own ignorance by outwitting the student. Socrates uses logic in neither of these ways. He uses it, rather, to sow and plant in "congenial" souls "words which are able to help themselves and him who planted them" (*Phaedrus*, 227—Jowett translation). What does this mean?

Dialogue

In the *Phaedrus*, Socrates subjects the arts of writing and speech-making to severe criticism, arguing that the dialectician is far nobler than the practitioners of either of these other arts. Writing and speech-making are poor instruments of education for the same reason: both are too often and too easily merely verbal, not the symbolic expression of *lived* wisdom. Conversely, reading and listening are poor methods of learning because both end, at best, in rote memory rather than active understanding. Books and speeches alike are inert: "If you want to know anything and put a question to one of them, the speaker [writer] always gives one unvarying answer" (*Phaedrus*, 275).

This judgment rests on a conception of knowledge according to which *mutual* inquiry is the only possible way to acquire it. Many things which we today would call knowledge would not be considered true knowledge by Socrates. Crafts, skills, information—none of these counts as true knowledge. For Socrates, knowledge is evaluative—involving the appraisal of objects, persons, actions, and ideas—and lived. The man who is wise knows what good is, whether what he does produces good, and how to govern all he does so that what he does produces good. Craft, skill, or information might be construable as commodities; the sort of thing Socrates considered knowledge cannot be so construed. What cannot be owned by one man and transferred by speeches or writing to another is that wisdom which enables a man to evaluate the purposes for which he uses his skills, the conclusions he draws from his information, the objects which his craft produces. Critical evaluation and wise decision-making require the active thought of the person evaluating and deciding.

But this accounts only in part for Socrates' insistence on the superiority of dialectic as an educational method. For the learning of crafts and skills also requires their practice by the student, and, on the other side, philosophic inquiry involves a set of skills which the teacher "has" and can "give" to the student. What, then, is it about Socrates' conception of knowledge that requires dialogue? Part of the answer lies in the fact that critical evaluation and decision-making require more than logical skills; they require norms or standards in terms of which to evaluate. Socrates has the logical skills necessary to discover that he has no clear notion of what norms are the true norms; he has the logical skills necessary for measuring beliefs, actions, and objects against such norms, were they to be known; but he knows no more than anyone else what those norms are. The only thing he knows is that there must be something that could be called a true norm, something objective and universal; that whatever it is, it is intimately related to that in man which makes

him human—his rationality—and is therefore discoverable by men through the exercise of their rationality. A norm cannot be a true norm if only one man knows it, any more than a law of physics can be a true law of physics if only one physicist knows it. We can know that we have *not* arrived at a true norm if there are men who find putative norms rationally unacceptable. And we can discover this only through inquiring with other men.

Still, if Socrates himself doesn't know what norms are the true norms, why doesn't he try first to find them himself? Why does he seem to find it so important to get others to see that *they* don't know what the true norms are either? I think the answer is two-fold. First, Socrates believes that there is an intimate relationship between that use of rationality which seeks to uncover and examine the hidden assumptions of conventional ideology and action, and the communal good life. It is Socrates' faith that at the level of assumptions critically scrutinized, there is commonality; the process of critical scrutiny leads us, at the least, to the rejection of rival putative norms because none is rationally acceptable. Factions, animosity, relativism operate at the level of the immediately pressing, the immediately obvious; what is real and true, that in which we are and should be rooted, is what is common to all.

Thus one reason why Socrates seeks to bring others to an awareness of their ignorance of the true norms, rather than constructing his own answers in solitude, is that unless others have moved their thought beyond the level of opinion, beyond the level of factionalism, Socrates' own answers would appear to be just another school of thought, about which they could debate without ever joining each other in a mutual search for true norms. Truly communal knowledge can arise only out of communally acknowledged ignorance. And, as has already been pointed out, dialectical method is designed precisely to bring about the acknowledgment of ignorance.

The second part of our answer lies in Socrates' conviction that the genuine educator is himself a seeker of wisdom, concerned that he as well as his students embody in their lives what they claim to know. This involves, minimally, the ability to reconstruct the logical foundations of their beliefs rather than merely to articulate these beliefs in a persuasive manner. Because the true educator is concerned not with being believed but with the truth or falsity of his own as well as his students' beliefs, he must reject a mode of teaching which is not genuinely responsive to genuine questions from his students. He cannot afford to "give one unvarying answer," for to do so would be to undermine not only his students' but his *own* stake in the inquiry.

> How can you think that I have any other motive in refuting you but what I should have in examining myself? which motive would be just a fear of my unconsciously fancying that I knew something of which I was ignorant. And at this moment I pursue the argument chiefly for my own sake, and perhaps in some degree also for the sake of my other friends. (*Charmides*, 166)

It is only when the words uttered by *both* teacher and student are genuine questions and genuine responses that *either* can discover what he genuinely knows. The genuine educator is one who gives his students words which are able to help themselves, words which lead the student to see for himself which of his beliefs cannot possibly be true because they are inconsistent. Such words alone can return back to the teacher and help *him* discover what is true and what is false. Such words alone can work that purification of the soul that genuine knowledge presupposes.

Psychology and Rhetoric

As Socrates points out, the genuine educator and the true master of rhetoric are one; he alone understands the souls of men well enough to know which words befit each kind of soul. Adopting Socrates' own medical analogy, we can say that just as the doctor is concerned to diagnose his patient correctly and to prescribe that medicine which best fits the diagnosis and *this patient's particular condition*, so Socrates is concerned to give that medicine which best suits the person with whom he is talking. As his object is to elicit from the person before him a genuine admission of ignorance, without thereby angering, defeating, or shaming him, Socrates' success depends critically on his ability to diagnose his partners accurately and to determine which medicine it is appropriate to administer. Socrates has the psychic leisure required for this sort of personal diagnosis, and the rhetorical skills necessary to apply a wide variety of medicines. Indeed, it is his psychic leisure which is perhaps his most striking quality. It is certainly what permits him to adapt his tone and style to the unique personality, intelligence, and character of the person with whom he speaks.

I think it is this freedom which underlies his openness to digression, his willingness to take up each idea put forth by his partners, and his care to ensure that they follow him with each step. I think it is this freedom which gives Socrates the capacity to accept with equanimity the lack of closure in so many of his conversations, the ability to play a variety of roles, and the ability to mix difficult intellectual inquiry with joviality, wit, and flirtation. I think it is this psychic freedom, too, that is revealed in the fact that Socrates is not always "nice."[2] He has no need to perceive the individual before him as a mere instance of some general category, such as "opponent" or "youth" or "old codger." He is psychologically free to view each person as himself. Accordingly, sometimes he cajoles, sometimes he adopts a mock humility, sometimes he teases, and sometimes he bluntly expresses his displeasure with the intellect, character, or manner of his partner.

This aspect of Socrates' teaching is the most fascinating and provocative, and the most controversial as well. It is this flexibility, this extraordinary range of interpersonal styles, that makes some readers see him as a virtuoso player of games, and others as the paradigm of good teaching. Both sets of readers need to be reminded that, though Socrates is an exceptional human being, one with that personal integrity idealized by Plato in the *Republic*, still he lived and taught in a context of a very special sort. Both sets of readers, in different ways, make the mistake of treating him as a timeless archetype rather than as a living man in the world with other living men. In so doing, both sets of readers ignore one of the convictions that lies at the very heart of Socrates' teaching, namely, that no man can gain or embody wisdom in solitude. There is no question but that genuine Socratic teaching depends heavily on the personal integrity, psychic leisure, and logical and rhetorical skills of the teacher. But, lacking a certain kind of context, these alone will not suffice. What was the context in which Socrates taught, and what does it tell us about the possibility of Socratic teaching in our times?

The Context of Socratic Teaching

Five facets of the dramatic settings of Socrates' dialogues constitute what I'm calling the "context." First, all of the discussants are "friends," in some sense of that term. Minimally, they know of each other through friends; maximally, they've already spent a great deal of time talking with each other and/or Socrates. Second, the discussion with Socrates is voluntary. He is explicitly invited to talk with the others, or he comes upon a conversation already in progress and enters into it. Sometimes *he* seduces someone on his way elsewhere into conversation with him; sometimes he is seduced into conversation. Third, and closely related to the first two points, there is no authority other than the authoritativeness of reason and personal attractiveness. That is, no one is judge and none are judged except as all are judged equally by the canons of good reasoning and cooperativeness. Fourth, the discussion evolves out of some normal daily or ceremonial activity, a time and occasion on which people normally gather together. Finally, there is no preestablished time limit to the discussion.

The significance of this context for my question, Is it possible to teach Socratically? can be gauged by contrasting it with the context within which *our* teaching relationships with students take place. It takes little reflection to see that every one of the conditions under which Socrates taught is violated by the normal teaching situation in 99 percent of our present colleges and universities. Classes are pre-scheduled to begin and end at certain times, times deliberately separated from other times set aside for what are called "extra-curricular activities." The institutionalization of a dichotomy between "learning" and "living" (*i.e.*, daily and ceremonial activities) could hardly be firmer than it is in our academic institutions, and hardly more contrary to the context in which Socrates taught. Unlike Socrates, we have to walk into special rooms set aside for learning, rooms kept empty at nights and on weekends so that everyone can tell that they're to be used only for that specialized activity called "learning." Whereas Socrates could teach in the dining room or the beer hall or the gym or out in the middle of the street or in a friend's living room, we have to make special arrangements with a special officer if we want to "hold a class" in something other than a "classroom."

It should be no surprise, therefore, that when we walk into these special rooms called "classrooms" we do not find a group of people bound to each other in mutual friendship, already engaged in some shared activity. Instead we find a collection of individuals, each of whose reason for being in that particular room at that particular time, is independent of every other individual in that room at that particular time. Even if all of the students "know" each other, and even if some are "friends," the students in our classrooms do not constitute a group of people whose *presence there* is an expression of some communal bond. No, the society that is a class is an artificial one, and the "conversations" that occur there are in no sense the mutual inquiry of friends. Rarely are the students joined together by a common purpose. Though each may have as his nominal purpose the desire to learn something about whatever the course is called, none is there *because* the others have that purpose.

But rarely are the students friends, and often they don't know each other at all. More often than not they are competitive and defensive toward each other, hostile and frightened. When they are not frightened, they are often disrespectful of each other's minds, or wary of their own. When they are respectful of each other's minds, it is often with a tinge of competitive hostility or timid self-denigration. (This is often true despite their own wishes that it be otherwise.) The fact that there is an authority who will deliver comparative judgments on them at the end of the course does little to change these feelings and attitudes. As things are arranged now, it is virtually impossible for students, as students in our courses, to relate to each other except through the mediation of the teacher: teacher's rules, teacher's grades, or the expectations students presume teacher has of them.

No teacher who wishes to teach Socratically can afford to ignore her students' perception of the classroom, the most crucial aspect of which is the fact that each student views the others as competitors. I do not mean here that each sees the others as competitors for the teacher's approval or for high grades, though that is often the case. That sort of competition not uncommonly decreases as students advance in college, and can be eliminated by changes in grading systems. What remains, however, after such changes is another, more devastating kind of competition, competition for knowledge. Each student perceives the others as competitors for something the teacher "has" which they don't "have." In the context of an educational system that rewards students for the accumulation of something called knowledge and paid out in credits, we cannot expect students to think otherwise; their natural assumption is that their job is to "get" what the teacher "has." In the absence of the conviction that what is there to be "gotten" *can* be gotten only through mutual inquiry, no student can help but view every minute of class time spent in conversation between the teacher and another student as a minute's worth of knowledge withheld from himself.

The difficulties this context poses for the would-be Socratic teacher are enormous. Even assuming that a teacher can persuade her students that it's worth the $300-$600 they pay for the course to study with someone who claims not to "have" what the student is there to "get," the would-be Socratic teacher is doomed to failure; even assuming that she has the requisite personal integrity, psychic leisure, and logical and rhetorical skills, the would-be Socratic teacher is doomed to failure. For in this non-communal, competitive, sibling-rivalry-like context, a leisurely conversation with one or two students will be perceived as favoritism, differences in rhetorical style will be perceived as mere exhibition of the personal likes and dislikes of the teacher, that "refutation" which Plato considered essential to the Socratic way of teaching will be perceived as one-upmanship, and the admission of ignorance consequent upon it will be nothing but embarrassing.

Where all are engaged in pursuit of a common goal, it doesn't matter which person is actually speaking or being spoken to; all recognize that it is the logic of the discourse that is educative. Characters like Thrasymachus (the *Republic*) no more share the sense that all are engaged in pursuit of a common goal than the students in our classrooms do. Like many of them, he cannot bear to sit still while Socrates winds his way through a complex conversation with Polemarchus, concerning justice. He is impatient to announce his own version of things, convinced that the point is to show that you know, rather than to examine what you claim to know (*Republic*, Book I). All of us have taught students who behave as Thrasymachus does. Few of us have recognized that the many students who *don't* behave that way, who don't wave their hands in our faces and interrupt our conversations with other students, nevertheless share his assumptions and his attitudes toward other students. Be-

Teaching and learning

Teaching is even more difficult than learning. We know that; but we rarely think about it. And why is teaching more difficult than learning? Not because the teacher must have a larger store of information, and have it always ready. Teaching is more difficult than learning because what teaching calls for is this: to let learn. The real teacher, in fact, lets nothing else be learned than—learning. His conduct, therefore, often produces the impression that we properly learn nothing from him, if by "learning" we now suddenly understand merely the procurement of useful information. The teacher is ahead of his apprentices in this alone, that he has still far more to learn than they—he has to learn to let them learn. The teacher must be capable of being more teachable than the apprentices. The teacher is far less assured of his ground than those who learn are of theirs. If the relation between the teacher and taught is genuine, therefore, there is never a place in it for the authority of the know-it-all or the authoritative sway of the official. It still is an exalted matter, then, to become a teacher—which is something else entirely than becoming a famous professor. That nobody wants any longer to become a teacher today, when all things are downgraded and graded from below (for instance, from business), is presumably because the matter is exalted, because of its altitude. And presumably this disinclination is linked to that most thought-provoking matter which gives us to think. We must keep out eyes fixed firmly on the true relation between teacher and taught—if indeed learning is to arise.
. . .

—from Martin Heidegger, *What is called Thinking?* (N.Y.: Harper and Row, 1968).

cause they do, I don't think it is possible for even the wisest of persons to teach Socratically, to bring about that personal transformation in our students which Plato called "purification" and which would return back to us words which can help *us* discover what *we* truly know.

It is not possible, that is, unless one either resorts to "tutorial" teaching for all students (a rather impractical suggestion) or concentrates on transforming the *classroom* into a genuine community.[3] Since mutual inquiry *is* mutual inquiry only when it arises from common concerns, it would seem that the first task of the would-be Socratic teacher, in this time, is to bring it about that the students in her class experience themselves as joined with each other in common concerns. That is, she must transform a collection of competing individuals into a community. Since the would-be Socratic teacher is at the same time one who wishes to engage in mutual inquiry *with* her students, she must achieve this transformation in such a way that she can be *included in* this community.

This means that the would-be Socratic teacher must bring about significant changes in the social dynamics of the classroom. Her prime task is to transform teacher-mediated relationships among students into unmediated, direct, student-student relationships, without thereby removing herself from the classroom. For this, simply being non-directive is insufficient. For one thing, students need help in learning *how* to learn in non-directive situations, and from each other. For another, it's no fun for the teacher to be simply "non-directive." The joy of teaching comes from engagement with the minds and persons of others. Further, Socrates, as we have seen, was far from non-directive. He was invited, or seduced, or seductive, but he participated fully and, indeed, directed. Our question is how to be ourselves without this resulting in intellectual and personal submissiveness on the part of our students. It cannot be a solution to that problem to *withdraw* ourselves from full contact with our students. No, I think that if Socratic teaching is to be possible, we must create classroom procedures which give the students to each other in clear and reliable ways, and whose effect will be to create a context of friendship into which students are moved to invite the teacher, and into which the teacher can enter wholly and freely.

And now I wonder whether we, who have been encouraged by *our* education to think of good teaching as a matter of individual strength and talent, are capable of approaching this task Socratically. Can we, that is, shift the emphasis of our questions about good teaching from the capacities of the teacher to the "goodness" of the society that a class is? And can we, together, propose measures for transforming our classrooms, subject them to rational evaluation, and, in the process, engage in mutual inquiry about the aims and nature of education? I hope we can; I think we must. With this in mind, let me share with you some techniques I have used which have worked very well to bring about the desired transformation, but of whose general relevance I am uncertain. I am in the position—fortunate for one who wishes to teach Socratically—not only of having relatively small classes (15-30 students) but of teaching in a department of philosophy. While my students and I together can assess the success and value for us of the techniques I am about to describe, only you and your students can give us some sense of their workability and value in situations different from ours.

Toward Creating A Socratic Classroom

I begin my courses by telling the students that, catalogue descriptions aside, what the course will be depends on how we are with each other, and that how I want us to be with each other is best described by the term "mutual midwifery." I appeal explicitly to Socrates' description of himself as a midwife, one whose aim was to aid others in the birth of their own ideas. I explain the tasks I set for them and the procedures to follow as

intended to make mutual midwifery a reality in our course.

The first such task is that each student find one other person in the class whom he or she doesn't know, and get to know that person sufficiently well to introduce him or her to the rest of the class at the next meeting. These couples are to be each other's "midwives" for the rest of the term. What this involves is mutual responsibility for presenting or clarifying each other's views to the rest of the class when either is unsuccessful in doing so himself, and mutual criticism of written work. The main objectives of this task are (a) to ensure that at all times there is at least one student who is listening carefully to at least one other student; (b) to define every student's "class participation" responsibilities in terms of another student, rather than in terms either of the impersonal class "at large" or of the judgmental professor; (c) through student criticism of written work, to make possible the experience of intellectual independence as a cooperative rather than a competitive phenomenon; and (d) to encourage the formation of friendships in which mutual activity will have a central place.

The next task is to engage in free discussion about any topic of interest to them which has come up during their introductions, and without my participation. This discussion is transcribed and reproduced for their evaluation. I ask them to evaluate their discussion in two different ways. The first is primarily emotive: they break into small groups and talk about how they felt during and at the end of the discussion. The second is cognitive: with the transcript of the discussion before them, they are asked to assess it from the standpoint of logical coherence. The object of this exercise is to encourage both the open expression of negative feelings about leaderless discussions, and the development of canons for rational assessment of leaderless discussions, with the hope that the students will come to recognize that there is often a causal relation between logical incoherence in a discussion and negative feelings about the discussion on the part of participants. I have discovered that it takes only one relatively simple point of logic, and its recognition and adoption as a rule by the class, to put students in a position to improve the quality of their own discussions and to dissipate hostility, boredom, and anxiety before they've reached the point of no return. This is the discussion between logical relevance and what I call "free associational relevance." The logically relevant response to a statement is, "What does that mean? On what evidence is it based? Is there good reason to believe it's true? If so, what does it imply for the truth or falsity of others beliefs, or for action?" The free associationally relevant response is a question or statement which comes to mind because of a word or phrase that was used in the original statement; it is relevant only in the sense that it repeats that word or phrase, or expresses an image, experience, or thought evoked by that word or phrase, but *not* in the sense that it elucidates or assesses the cognitive worth of the original statement.

By the end of the first week of the course, students have grasped clearly this distinction. Their verbal agreement to adopt "logical relevance" as a rule governing discussion is facilitated in practice by a number of devices, all intended to increase their trust in themselves as capable of self-enforcement of this rule, and in me as someone who trusts their ability to govern themselves and who can give them "words which are able to help themselves." The major device here is the continuation of my role as scribe. Discussions continue to be transcribed, and periodically we assess them by reference to our rule. In the process additional rules are arrived at. The responsibilities of the mutual midwives and the premium on open expression of their thoughts and feelings, provide positive sanctions for criticism of discussions in progress.

The third task each student is given is to select one work, from a list prepared in advance by me, which will be his or her project for the term. This involves two sub-tasks. Together with any other students in the class who select that work, the student is to teach it to the rest of the class. That is, all the students who select the same work are given the responsibility of presenting it to the rest of the class in such a way that we can all discuss it critically together. Further, each student is to write a paper on the work, in which he explicates, analyzes, and responds critically to the views expressed in it. Whereas the teaching task involves the student in a cooperative endeavor whose main concern is the education of his fellow students, the writing task involves the student in an individual endeavor whose main concern is the development of his own philosophical competence. In the former task, he and his partners are acting as midwives for the author whose work they are teaching, and their classmates are acting as midwives for them. In the latter task, his "official" midwife in the course will aid him in the delivery of his own thoughts by writing a critique of the first draft of his paper and reading and commenting on the revised edition that emerges from this exchange between them.

During the second and third weeks of the course, students are scouting around among the books, getting some general background on the scope of philosophy, deciding on the work they'll deal with, and meeting in small groups to study their chosen work and plan their teaching project. A schedule is made up by all of us, based on which and how many works have been selected, and by the fourth week we have begun our mutual inquiry into the thought of those philosophers that have sparked the interest of the students. Here is a sample of the kind of conversation to which you would be treated any time you visited the class:

Steve: [According to Fromm] selfishness isn't the same as self-love. It's almost a form of self-hate. It's loving of self to the exclusion of others, but since you can't love others (and since you have to love others in order to love yourself), you can't love yourself.

Lawry: Does the difference between selfishness and self-love mean that if you can't love yourself, you have to hate yourself?

Steve: I don't think so, since he says you can be indifferent toward yourself. At any rate, you can say that the selfish person does not love himself.

Roz: Steve, could you go one more round with selfishness as a form of self-hate?

Steve: O.K. If self-love requires the love of others, then the selfish person only *says* he loves himself, because he can't love others; but if he can't love others, then he can't love himself.

Roz: But that doesn't show he *hates* himself.

Christie: Here. He says, "He [the selfish person] seems to care too much for himself but actually he only makes an unsuccessful attempt to cover up and compensate for his failure to care for his real self." No—I don't see how he gets self-hate either.

Steve: He might say that indifference is a form of self-hate . . .

Christie: But that doesn't make sense.

Steve: He might say if you don't *care* about yourself, it's like you don't like yourself.

Lawry: But don't you have to care about a person to hate them?

Christie: But remember what Fromm means by "care." He means you're concerned for the person to develop his own potentialities. But I don't see how you could do that if you hated him.

Lawry: Well, I meant by "care" "lack of indifference."

Christie: Well, you can't use *your* definition of a term to show that what he says is inconsistent if *he* means something different by it.

Lawry: That's true.[4]

I must confess that the first time I organized a course in this way, I was not only uncertain about how students would respond and how their response would affect me, but I was much less clear about what I hoped to accomplish than I have become since. In retrospect, it is not difficult for me to see why the use of these techniques should have resulted in the creation of a genuine community of inquirers, a classroom in which everyone asked genuine questions (yes, even "stupid" ones) and gave genuine responses (yes, even "I don't know"); and, more important, a classroom in which everyone *perceived* everyone else as a genuine seeker after wisdom. Reflecting on the techniques I've described, I find that they exemplify a number of general principles whose practice together, I believe, *can* make Socratic teaching possible. Let me conclude by stating and commenting on them.

(1) *Risk-taking.* For the students, practically everything they are asked to do in my course involves tremendous risk, inasmuch as it demands of them behavior in which they are unpracticed. Apparently, however, the most anxiety-producing task is the one with which the course begins, introducing a near-stranger to a group of strangers. All of my students express the same concern that they might misrepresent their partner to the rest of the class. I have found that open discussion—after the introductions have taken place—of their feelings about this experience results in pervasive attitudes of generosity and tolerance, due to the realization that they've all shared a painful experience. It also sensitizes them to the individuality of each fellow-student and the dangers of stereotyping.

(2) *Publication and discussion of individual interests and goals.* Because the course begins with mutual introductions, students learn very quickly both how varied and how common their interests and goals are. They also learn that there is a positive sanction on both the expression of individual concerns and commonality. If the teacher considers familiarity with each student's background interests, values, etc. important enough to devote two or three entire class sessions to nothing but that, it becomes obvious to

the students not only that the teacher is interested in each of them, but that the teacher wishes them to be interested in each other. The feelings generated by the exercise of this and the first principle need to be confirmed and defined through action, if genuine trust is to be built. The next two principles seem also to serve this end.

(3) *"Constructive permissiveness."* Students are expected and allowed to react negatively to anything and everything in the course. At the same time, they are expected to figure out ways in which whatever is wrong can be remedied. That is, they are led to *use* their gut reactions to build something they can live with and learn from, rather than simply to *have* their gut reactions.

(4) *Cooperative tasks.* The introductions, the selection and teaching of course content by students, the mutual criticism of written work are similar in these respects: they are tasks required of *all* students, but whose method and style of performance are left to the students to determine among themselves; and they are explicitly designed to be carried out by the students in consort with each other, unmediated by the teacher. This principle is in direct contradiction with the norm implicit in the customary use of papers and exams as learning instruments, according to which accepting the aid of another student is a form of cheating. In consequence, it is the exercise of this principle, probably more than any other, which makes community a lived relation for the students. Still, none of the principles thus far discussed is sufficient to bring down the authoritarian-submissive pattern of expectations that governs student-teacher interaction. For this, at least two additional principles are needed.

(5) *Role reversal.* One very quick way to disabuse students of the notion that the role of teacher automatically implies "having" something that the role of student automatically implies lacking is simply to switch the roles. When it is the student who stands in front of the class and the teacher who sits taking notes, *both* experience the perspective to which the other has

become so accustomed that he is unable to reflect critically on it.

Student-teachers discover very quickly that, while they "know" more than do their classmates about the work they are teaching, there are all sorts of things they *don't* know which, if they knew, would not only give them a fuller comprehension of what they are teaching, but would help them to evaluate what they are teaching. One reason they discover this is that the students being taught by them are infinitely less hesitant to question *them* then they are to question a "real" teacher. And because the students being questioned are cast in the role of "helpers" (rather than being tested by someone who will grade their answers), it is easier for them to admit to ignorance, and they are more readily motivated to try to find out what they need to know than is usually the case. Conversely, the teacher-turned-student discovers very quickly that while there are many ways in which she "knows" more than her students, there are also many things of which they are capable that are not ordinarily revealed. As my students became better at discovering and admitting what they really knew and what they really did not know, it became easier for *me* to discover and admit *my* ignorance, and to utilize my experience and training to formulate fruitful questions rather than to convey information.

(6) *Mutual midwifery.* If students are to achieve unmediated relationships with each other, and unlearn the authoritarian conception of education, then the rights and responsibilities of evaluation cannot be located exclusively with the teacher. But students have to be encouraged to evaluate each other, and taught how to do so in productive ways. Students tend either to praise each other for the amount of time spent in studies, to damn each other for insincerity or mechanical conformity to requirements, or to refuse to evaluate each other at all. This is due in part, I think, to our culture's encouragement of a misguided notion of tolerance. But it is also due to the habit of placing all rights to evaluation in the hands of the teacher, without ever requiring the teacher to

make explicit the criteria governing her evaluation. Since it is, presumably, part of one's education for college teaching to learn the differences between a good and a poor piece of work in the art or science she professes to teach, a teacher ought to be able to help her students also to make such judgments. Further, I think it is only through sharing the task of evaluation with her students that both teacher and students are confronted with the limitations of their knowledge in *Socrates'* sense of that term.

Implicit in our evaluation of a student's work over the course of an entire semester are a number of different kinds of criteria, the distinctions and relations among which are often never made explicit and examined by us. If you require students to evaluate their own and each other's work, they will ask you how to go about it, and, at some point, if the exercise is to be genuinely educational, you will have to tell them how *you* go about it. You will find that it is impossible to do this to their satisfaction without telling them what *you* take the ends of education to be. You may have little difficulty listing the qualities essential to a good philosophy paper (or laboratory experiment, piece of historical research, painting, and so on); but they will point out that "goodness" in these respects has meant different things to different practitioners of the art in question, and, more important, they will want to know the value to them as persons of learning how to write a good paper, do respectable research, or produce a good work of art. In our era, they will also want to know the value of these skills for the survival and health of our society. In short, they will push you to ask

the very questions that Socrates asked himself and his fellows. It is therefore the exercise of this principle, more than any other, that makes possible Socratic teaching in its fullest sense: mutual inquiry into the nature of the good, whose aim is to discover where both teacher and student are truly wise, and where they are truly ignorant.

Notes

1. Even the discussion with Euthyphro concerning the nature of piety—a discussion in which Euthyphro seems reluctant to engage—evolves naturally out of earlier conversation initiated by Euthyphro.
2. In one sense, of course, Socrates is never "nice." It's not "nice" to subject everything a person says to devastating critical scrutiny. But in another sense, Socrates is often "nice": there *are* times when he questions with kindness and gentleness. The point here is that there are also many times when he does this with biting sarcasm or mild condescension. (See, *e.g.*, the *Republic*, Book 1.)
3. One could, of course, direct one's energies toward massive reconstruction of an educational system which results in the absence of respect for and ability to engage in mutual inquiry. At the same time, we must consider ways of transforming the immediate situations in which we work and play. Furthermore, I am not convinced that *simply* changing curricula, eliminating grades, reducing class sizes, or developing courses around the expressed interests of students will achieve the conditions presupposed by successful Socratic teaching. For that, attention must be paid as well to the things teachers and students alike are called upon to *do* with, to, and for each other.
4. Excerpted from transcript of discussion in freshman introduction to philosophy course. Steve and Christie were the "teachers." They went on to recall Fromm's distinction between character-conditioned and reactive hate, and to resolve the issue by identifying the self-hate involved in selfishness with the former type of hate.

Platonic Education

James M. Redfield

We are met here to consider the question, "What knowledge is most worth having?" or as I prefer to rephrase it, What is educational about education? I am going to talk today about some Platonic answers to this question. But a few prior warnings. In the first place I am not going to quote much from Plato or try to document my assertion that these answers are Platonic. Plato is hard to quote because he wrote not treatises but dialogues; he does not talk about education so much as he exhibits it. In any case, I have not composed a piece about Plato; I have composed a piece about education, starting from the picture Plato gives us of Socrates the educator. So I have not concerned myself with the question of whether the statements I make represent the views of Plato or of Redfield; it is enough if they are something like true statements.

In the second place, when I speak of education I limit it to that which can be learned from speech and writing and which can be expressed in symbols, verbal or otherwise. I exclude from my sphere of reference the school of hard knocks, mystical revelation, and all other educational modes whose teachings cannot be expressed in language.

In the third place, I begin from the assumption that the aim of education, like the aim of every other human activity, is happiness. Of course I am assuming a mere tautology, but even a tautology can serve to direct our attention. I think we should be asking, not what knowledge is reputable or exciting, but what knowledge is good for us. And since I am talking about statable knowl-edge my question is really, in the phrase of Hans Jonas, What are the practical uses of theory?

The question, "What knowledge is most worth having?" is dependent on a prior question: What knowledge is there? In the *Apology* Socrates tells us that he went looking for knowledge-able men. He went first to the statesmen and the poets, and he found that neither class knew any-thing; the statesmen worked from certain rules of thumb and the poets by divine inspiration. Nei-ther class could explain what it did. Then he went to the craftsmen and found that they do in fact know "many and wonderful things." The crafts-man does in fact possess knowledge; he can do things other men cannot; he can tell us how he does them; he can point to his teacher and he can teach others. So when Plato talks about knowl-edge he always begins with the crafts.

Each craft, furthermore, is a kind of knowl-edge worth having, insofar as it meets human need and human wishes. We require craft because nature is recalcitrant to our will. We cannot sim-ply do what we decide to do; we must also know how to do it. We cannot acquire a table simply by choosing to have it; nor is it enough to have set aside the time and energy, the tools and materials required for table-making; we must also know how to make a table. We must come to terms with nature so that we can act according to nature's laws; if we possess no craft we will conclude our activity, not with a table, but with a heap of scraps and sawdust.

We do not ascribe knowledge to the craftsman, further, simply because he has a capacity for a given activity; a craft is not simply the capacity for shaping matter into form. If such a capacity were called knowledge we would have to ascribe knowledge to the nest-building bird and the web-making spider. Socrates went about asking, not for demonstrations, but for explanations. The statesmen and the poets can act, but they cannot explain their actions. The craftsmen, on the other hand, can explain, and they can teach others how to imitate them. In the Socratic phrase, their opinion is "accompanied by discourse."

The tradition of a craft, then, has two parts, practice and theory, skill and method. The skill of a craftsman is in the hand, like the instinctive behavior of the animals, but his method is proved in the specifically human mode of speech. Skill is a mode of doing, but method is a mode of knowing. The palsied carpenter is a carpenter no longer but he still possesses the method of carpentry; he cannot build a table but he can tell us how to build one. On the other hand, a man might have acquired the knack of building a table without ever learning the method of carpentry; his tables are satisfactory but he cannot teach us to make them. Probably, also, he does not know the limits of his knowledge until he tries to explain to us what he does. Skill is maintained by practice, but method is maintained by teaching.

So the crafts give us one model for education. We might take education to be the teaching of those methods which are likely to be useful to us. Furthermore, every activity is accompanied by some method; there are methods of practice and methods of theory; history and metaphysics have their methods, and so does ethics, and even poetry and statesmanship have some methodological statements to make—even though, the more serious the activity, the less adequately the method seems to explain it. Presumably we cannot create poets and statesmen, but we can teach our students what there is to know about these activities, and then, with whatever misgivings, leave them on their own.

But in this case education will not be adequate to happiness. In the first place, we do not know what methods are likely to be useful to us. Life is a chapter of accidents, and use is relative to the needs of the moment. Ten yards from a lifeboat in the mid-Atlantic we may find ourselves saying, "If only I had learned to swim," but such possibilities do not give swimming a necessary place in education.

In the second place, we usually do not know what our needs are, which is to say, we do not know what would make us happy. Should I try to make more money? Or do a job that interests me? Should I try to secure more time to myself? Or should I take on more students? Each of these choices can make a case for itself, and I won't know which is most rewarding until I try; once I have tried it will be too late to try something else. Only at moments of crisis, floundering around in the lifeboat, do our needs seem clear to us. That is the attractive thing about crisis: it tells you what knowledge is most worth having and so reduces the problem of knowledge to a technical problem. I have heard it suggested that the knowledge most worth having is the knowledge which would produce world peace, but while I am sure that a reasonable state of peace is necessary to happiness, I also know that it is not sufficient. And I do not know what else will be needed.

Man, in other words, is mortal. He is vulnerable, first, to circumstance, and since he cannot predict his circumstances, he cannot confidently equip himself to meet them. Second, in a limited life he must decide to do some things and not others, and so must decide to learn some things and not others. If we, like the Homeric gods, were immortal, we could learn all possibly useful methods and undertake all the activities for which they prepared us; over an infinite period of time we could perhaps come to happiness. As it is we must, in education as in everything else, make our best guess and launch ourselves into the void.

So far, however, I have only shown that the problem of education is insoluble, not that it is difficult. We are accustomed to coming to terms with our mortality; we make our choices within a known frame of ignorance. Even the carpenter does not know when he will strike a knot; nor does he know whether next year's customers will be asking for tables or for chairs. He studies his material as best he can, he makes his best guess at the future state of the market, and he equips himself accordingly.

Since carpentry is the art of transforming wood so that it meets human demand, the carpenter can tell whether or not his work is successful. If his products are demanded he is working well; if they are not he fails. So far I have been talking about happiness in the same terms, as though we could know whether or not we are happy. Socrates also sometimes makes this assumption, as in the *Protagoras* when he says that if happiness consisted in the greatest amount of pleasure and the least amount of pain, the knowledge most worth having would be that method which enabled us to predict, to the highest degree of human accuracy, the pleasures and pains resulting from our choices.

But Socrates knows that his assumption is fallacious, and from him I have learned so too. Happiness is incorrigibly plural. How shall I pass the evening? Shall I make a snowman? Read a more or less elevating book? Write a memorandum? Play with my child? Drink? I find all these activities rewarding and their rewards are incommensurate. I have no common scale of delight for the comparative measurement of politics theory, play, art, and self-indulgence. All of these things are good; I know *that* because I am sure that a life in which they all appear is better than a life from which any one is excluded. For the same reason I know that one is not better than another; if politics were better than art I would want as much politics as possible and as little art, or vice versa. The best life seems to me a life in which all these things have their proper place, and determining what is good about any of them will not enable me to determine the proper balance between them. Yet, since the soul is bound by space, time, and its own singularity, I must at every moment make some judgment of proportion among all the good things that I see.

Method, therefore, can contribute to happiness, but there can be no method of happiness. Methods tell us how to achieve some stated good; the good is relative to the method. For the doctor *qua* doctor the good sought is health; the doctor's method enables him to have his best shot at healing his patients. But the art of medicine cannot tell him whether to visit three querulous old ladies or go home to dinner. He must make that decision for himself.

This, I think, is what Socrates means when he says that the knowledge most worth having is the knowledge of the Good,

> . . . that which every soul pursues and for the sake of which it does everything, making a prophetic guess that it is something, but uncertain and unable to take proper hold of it, nor to reach any permanent position about it as we can in the case of other things—and for this reason the soul fails to make proper use even of those other things that are useful . . . (*Republic* 505d,e)

> This, the idea of the Good, . . . is the highest knowledge; as we act according to it we make justice and everything else useful and beneficial. I suppose you also know . . . that we do not adequately know it. But if we do not know it, even if we should know everything else to the greatest degree of perfection, they are no help to us, just as if we should possess something and that thing should not be good. You don't think that we get anywhere by owning any possession if it is not in fact good? Or by having every form of intelligence without intelligence of the good, so that our intelligence is not related to the human good?

> Good lord no, he said. (*Republic* 505a,b)

The good is unlike other objects of knowledge in that it is both infinitely close to us and infinitely distant, perfectly immanent and perfectly transcendent. Each choice we make is a declaration of our judgment of the best thing for us as we are at that moment and in those circumstances; in this sense the good is infinitely various. Yet each choice is also a commitment of the whole self, a declaration that, starting from where we are, this step takes us one step closer to happiness.

Furthermore we are to some extent what we choose to be; so every choice is a choice of something and also a choice of self. The man who decides to make a table also decides to be a carpenter; the man who sets out to classify plants is guided by an idea of himself as a knower; the man who sets out to remedy an injustice is guided by an idea of himself as a charitable being. Since the process of self-creation is indefinitely extensible, we are always guided, in choice, by a sense, however inchoate, of the perfection of man.

So Socrates sometimes talks about knowledge of the Good and sometimes about knowledge of the self. Nor are these two kinds of knowledge different. As we reflect upon our choices, as we make their real character clear to ourselves, our activity becomes more fully rational and thus more fully human. We come to be what we in fact are. He encourages us to know ourselves not as we happen to have become, but as we are capable of being.

It is also clear that prior to the choice of self is the choice to *be* a self. Implicit in our choosing activity is an assertion that we want to make ourselves and not be made by others. Man is distinguished from an animal or an instrument by his capacity for considered choice; our capacity for deliberation keeps us from being a mere part of the machine of nature. Our awareness of our freedom is the foundation of our sense of our own identity. Autonomy, therefore, is the necessary condition of happiness, and the man who has achieved autonomy, who takes responsibility for himself, while he cannot be said to have *achieved* happiness, can be said to *really pursue* it.

For Plato, then, the aim of education is to bring man, not to happiness, but to the pursuit of happiness . . . And it should be clear that there is nothing educational about method. The essence of method is repetition. Practical method is the knowledge of how to predict and control nature; the craftsman or scientist tells us that if we do X, Y will result; he knows this because he and his

fellows have done X countless times and Y has usually occurred. Theoretical method is, in Aristotle's phrase, "a capacity for demonstration," it provides us with the capacity to prove to ourselves or to another the truth of what we already know. The knowledge of method gives you a capacity to repeat yourself, and when you teach method you teach others to repeat after you. Method is memory systematized into statement.

But choice is never repetitious. Choice is free because each choice is a new determination of the best. Insofar as a man repeats himself he becomes like an animal or a machine. The potter who transforms on his wheel lump after lump of clay into an endless row of identical jars does not choose to make each jar like the others; at most he chooses not to choose, letting his mind wander as his hands work. He is an excellent potter, he has mastered his method, but he is not choosing or judging; for the sake of the jars he has given up some of his humanity. So also the historian, if any there be, who applies the same method to on archive after another. To sit at the feet of the master craftsman and learn his method as he teaches it is to turn from the pursuit of happiness toward the loss of self.

What kind of education, then, contributes to the achievement of autonomy? In answering this question Socrates makes a few observations upon the human situation. In the first place, while it is good to satisfy our desires, happiness does not consist in the satisfaction of desire. My desires do not bear thinking on; I don't need Sigmund Freud to tell me that. At the core of every man is Plato's tyrant, devoted to the desires which, as Socrates says, appear in most men "only in dreams." Let me loose and I would turn to rape, cannibalism, incest. The energy at the core of every man is idle, self-destructive passion, primitive, inchoate, and therefore insatiable. We cannot find our principle of action in that which is itself perfectly unprincipled.

Man is a part of nature; he lives in contact with an environment, he occupies a body, and his soul also has a nature. "Of soul too there is a physics," says Aristotle, "insofar as it partakes of the material." But the Socratic self-knowledge is not the physics of soul; he does not mean that we pursue happiness by learning that "this is the sort of thing that always makes me angry" or "I'll bet I'll get a boot out of that." Our impulses are part of our situation, as the conditions of our choice. But to choose is to be free of our situation; therefore the pursuit of happiness begins from the denial of impulse.

The beginning of education, then, is temperance. But not such temperance as the world knows. We do not become autonomous by being good little boys and girls, but because we have caught sight of something more interesting than pleasure. Socrates recommends all the social virtues—temperance, courage, wisdom, and justice—but he does not recommend them for the reasons given by society.

Society is the method that men have corporately evolved for coexisting with nature. This coexistence has two parts. We have learned to live with our natural environment; we have invented techniques for controlling and shaping it to our comfort and safety. And we have learned also to live with the nature of man, to shape that also to our comfort and safety. To this end we have invented morality. Morality, says Socrates, is the controlled gratification of impulse. Society promises us some pleasures on condition that we abstain from others; if we break the rules society will punish us and see that our pleasures are turned to pains. The pleasures that are socially acceptable, on the other hand, are doubly rewarding; they please in themselves and they bring with them the assistance and approval of our neighbors.

Society is the grand method that validates all the others. Every activity aims at some good; every methodical activity works rationally toward some good; society rationalizes the whole pattern of our activities by telling us what particular goods are worth pursuing. In this social order technique and morality overlap; in any society that which is useful is also accounted honorable.

It is according to the standard of society that all methods are recommended to us. The potter works because there is a market for his pots; in the same way we tell our students that if they will learn the method of philosophy there will be open to them a well-paid and reputable profession. Society tells us, from its own point of view, what knowledge is most worth having; that point of view asserts that the aim of education is socialization. General education thus provides men with that knowledge which, as members of a single community, they all require, while special education fits them to make some special contribution to the common good.

Of course education, like every other human activity, cannot happen except within the social order. Because education requires the support of society, those institutions whose declared purpose is educational are rightly expected to help society operate. But, says Socrates, socialization is not in itself educational. Society as a mode of human existence bears against autonomy; if the social order were perfected we would all be reduced to the level of the bee or the ant. Society decides for us; we pursue happiness by learning to decide for ourselves. Therefore education always begins from the rejection of social tradition.

The foundation of the Socratic education, therefore, is the *elenchus*, the process of refutation by which the student is convinced that he does not know what he thought he knew, that he cannot defend whatever received opinions he carries about with him. In itself, the *elenchus* is a sophistical exercise; Socrates will use any means—fair or foul—to convince the student of his inadequacy. The aim of the *elenchus* is not to impart truth or even to convict error; it aims to show the student that he cannot defend himself with the weapons society has given him and suggests to him the necessity of learning to defend himself.

The *elenchus* is a dangerous process; Socrates often compares it to major surgery. Society has come to terms with the chaos of impulse by imposing on it an ordered routine of practice and opinion. Since society and impulse are in conflict they often come to seem alternative; we feel that we must choose between passion and duty. By cracking the structure of the student's habitual opinions Socrates is making an opening, it seems, for anarchy; if society's prohibitions are invalid, then perhaps everything is permitted.

Socrates meets this problem by simultaneously separating the student from his peers and involving him with the teacher. The *elenchus* is at once a shock and an invitation; "You do not know how to talk," says Socrates; "I have proved that. But at the same time I have shown that I, who assert that I know nothing, know more about talking than you do. Stay and talk with me, and perhaps you can learn it too." The Socratic *elenchus* makes the student helpless, and at the same time it makes him dependent on Socrates. By means of the *elenchus* Socrates recruits members for the Socratic circle, the group of young men who follow Socrates and answer his questions.

The Socratic circle is a subsociety with its own social norms. So there is another danger to the *elenchus*: it can free the student only to subject him to a new mode of social rigor—the more limiting in that the philosophical society is smaller and more compact. The teacher's task is to make this subsociety which he directs the arena of autonomy rather than conformity. The Socratic teacher must take care that his teaching does not degenerate into just another method. If he makes his students his disciples he has become a sophist, and has failed.

The Socratic dialogues tell us relatively little about the teacher's strategies for attaining this end. Most of the dialogues represent Socrates in battle with is sophistic competitors or recruiting the young for his own circle. Only two dialogues, the *Republic* and the *Phaedo*, take place within the Socratic circle, and they do not show us the whole pattern of Socratic education; they are at best representative samples, brief excerpts from a continuing conversation.

One thing, however, we can say. There are current in the Socratic circle, as Plato represents it, certain doctrines. These doctrines shift a bit from dialogue to dialogue but fundamentally Socrates is consistent about them. He tells his students that the soul is immortal, that they have lived before, that they will be judged after death, that the soul has three parts, and so on. These doctrines are never proved or defended; they are simply introduced into argument when they become necessary. Nevertheless they play an important role in the Socratic conversation, and by considering them we might learn something about the educational character of those conversations. Here I address myself to only one doctrine, perhaps the most important: the so-called Theory of Ideas.

The Theory of Ideas asserts that there are two worlds, one composed of the objects of perception, multiple, material, and mutable, the other of the objects of knowledge, simple, immaterial, and eternal. There are trees and there is Tree. By this doctrine Socrates points to a commonplace fact about our experience: that the intellect lives in a world not of things but of concepts. So long as we have no name for a tree, so long as we do not place it in any general category, we really have no experience of it at all; it remains for us a blob of inchoate perceptions. Before we can pay our tree *any* humane attention we must notice that it *is* something, that it is, for instance, a tree. So in a sense there is *no* knowledge of the particular: all knowledge is of the universal.

Socrates, however, goes further; he talks of the particular and the universal as separate objects of knowledge, and asserts that we know the particular by comparing it with the universal. Socrates talks about the ideas as if they were things; he has taken a fact about knowing and treated it as a fact about being. By so doing he falls into a set of logical absurdities, ably set forth by Plato himself in the first part of the *Parmenides*, and expanded by Plato's adversaries ever since.

Not content with this, Socrates asserts that the ideas are the realest things, and that the objects of our experience are merely their imitations. The trees we meet are more or less imperfect pictures of Tree; the plural trees have the sort of diminished reality that all imitations have. The experienced tree is really experienced but it is not really Tree, just as a picture of George is really a picture but it is not really George.

According to Socrates, however, those imitative things are the only things we *do* experience—at least in this life. In another life, he says, we saw the ideas themselves—but now we have forgotten them; we remember them only to the degree that things here are capable of reminding us of the original. We look at the picture and say, "that's George," but we are in the position of a man who knows George only through his pictures and who has never had an opportunity to check the picture against the original.

The Theory of Ideas is thus a troubling way of talking about knowledge. Since an imitation is by definition imperfect—otherwise it would be a re-creation—the knowledge that we have got is by nature the knowledge least worth having. And the knowledge most worth having is, according to Socrates, knowledge that we cannot acquire.

Here let us remember that according to the Simile of Light in the *Republic* the Good is both the source of the intelligibility of the other ideas and the source of their existence. That is, the true locus of knowledge is not contemplation but rather choice. And when we are choosing we are not concerned with what is but what should be; therefore precisely that which is *not* in the field of our experience is the focus of our attention. The nurseryman, for example, is concerned only secondarily with his trees as they are, primarily with his trees as they should be. His aim is to produce the best tree, that is, he has his eye on Tree. He works with his trees precisely when they diverge from the Tree he has in his mind. Therefore we can say, without departing from common sense, that the trees he sees are imperfect imitations of the Tree he has never seen. The Theory of Ideas, in fact, describes the world as it is encountered by the practical intelligence.

How should Plato be taught?

One of the most disheartening intellectual experiences I ever underwent was to hear Plato's *Republic* discussed by a philosopher who simply sat down with the text in his hand and chatted about it. *The Republic* is a magnificently organized work, in eleven parts, each with its own character, and with a larger and more complex structure underlying this clear division. It opens quietly, with a chance meeting of friends, and Socrates talking with an aged man; it closes superbly, with a vast vision of the life after death.

Often, in its grandeur and control, it reminds me of a Beethoven symphony. But of this we learned little or nothing from the amiable and even condescendingly light conversation of our teacher. No doubt we learned much by finding it out for ourselves; but some of us never fully realized it. When Plato composed *The Republic,* he designed it as carefully as Ictinus planned the Parthenon. To ignore or minimize this architectonic quantity is to do a grave injustice to a great writer, and to obscure one of the finest achievements of the Greek genius, its capacity for strong yet subtle structure.

—Gilbert Highet in *The Immortal Profession.*

A man acting for a purpose is always, in Diotima's phrase, between Poverty and Resource. He must find his present situation unsatisfactory; otherwise he would sit still. He must see some prospect of improvement; otherwise he would have no place to go. Out of his present need he generates an idea of future improvement; this idea sharpens his sense of Poverty and leads him to action. As he begins to act upon the world, to realize his idea, his experience sharpens his idea and deepens his sense of Resource. Thus thought leads to action and action in turn leads to thought.

Nor is the Resource at any stage something exterior to the situation of the actor; the Resource is the Poverty itself formulated, so that we feel our situation, not simply as lack, but as lack of something.

The clearest instance, I think, is the case of invention. Consider a man drinking water from his hands. The water trickles through his fingers, he cannot drink without getting his face wet, he cannot in this way carry water more than a few feet. Such a man, if he is gifted, may out of his discomforts conceive the notion of a cup. To begin with the cup is for him simply something that his hands are not. As he pursues his notion, as he shapes clay, metal, and even plastic to his purpose, he refines his idea; every cup he makes is both a cup and not *yet* a cup. Each invention is a partial success, but it does not yet satisfy its inventor; each new dissatisfaction, as it becomes explicit to the cup-maker, suggests a better cup. So in Socratic language, the process of invention is a progressive imitation of Cup.

In one sense the idea of a cup is an idea of the world, a world so transformed as to include cups. But in another sense it is an idea of self: the idea that a man could be a cup-maker and a cup-user. The cup will not be made until it has been both conceived and chosen; we must come to think both that cups are possible and that they are desirable. Therefore the invention of the cup implies that the cup-using man is a better sort than the cupless. Seen this way our sense of Poverty is a sense of our own imperfection; our sense of Resource a sense of what we could be.

Invention, in fact, is one of the modes of autonomy. The inventor of the cup, at the moment when he first takes the clay in his hand and begins to shape it, is free; the mark of his freedom is that he is both selfless and self-absorbed; he is neither methodical nor impulsive. There is nothing self-indulgent in his activity; he moves straight toward the human good as he sees it. Nor is he taking direction from anyone; his act, to the degree that it is creative, is entirely his own. So also the poet as the words form into music in his mind,

and the statesman as he collects his resources for the reform of society. All of their products, when they succeed, become part of the cultivated routine, but the originators, as they shape society, are also free of it.

Creativity is occasional because it is unmethodical and therefore unrepeatable. We create precisely when we do not know what we are doing; we know our creative acts only in doing them. The poet knows how to write his poems; the proof is that he has written them. But he does not know how to write poems; having written some he is never sure he can write more. He cannot explain his method; if he can explain it he is not a creative poet. Creativity is the discovery of self in activity; it is therefore personal and incommunicable.

And yet we do not feel the creative experience as one of confusion. When we decide, in spite of the exhaustion of our energies and the doubts of our friends, that honor compels us to an unpopular and unpleasant act, we reach a state of moral certainty; our behavior, however eccentric, is not erratic. We are sure that we know what we are doing, even though we cannot explain it. Such moments are rare in any life, but memorable, and they are moments of lucidity. At these moments we best know ourselves engaged in the active pursuit of happiness.

By the Theory of Ideas Socrates asserts that the creator does not act blindly. He has his eye on something, though not on anything at present in the world of his experience. By describing the ends of action as objects of knowledge, Socrates asserts that freedom is action in a direction, that creativity is more than idle restless trial and error, Man, he says, does not blunder into autonomy; he *claims* his freedom from method and impulse because he has caught sight of something more persuasive to his act than either.

The Theory of Ideas thus describes a world in which autonomy is possible. And since autonomy is identity we all assent to that Theory insofar as we attempt at all to make our lives our own. The Theory does not have to be proved; it is simply a statement of the world in which as pursuers of happiness we all live.

Notice that the Theory of Ideas never appears at the beginning of a Socratic dialogue. It appears always in the middle, as a familiar doctrine now again appropriate. The relevance of the Theory of Ideas, in fact, is the test of the seriousness of any discourse. When that Theory becomes an appropriate element of our talk we are talking about the pursuit of happiness and can entertain some proper hope that our talk is educational.

The Theory of Ideas, however, is not in itself educational; at most it makes explicit the aims of education. Education, says Socrates, is the exercise of the soul; it occurs not by the comprehension of propositions but by the development of capacities. Therefore the Socratic student does not learn the Socratic doctrine; he becomes involved with those doctrines as a part of his involvement with the Socratic discourse. And this involvement develops in him the capacity for freedom.

But here we have a problem, for the Socratic conversations are not deliberative but theoretical. Socrates does not ask, What shall we do now? He asks, What is justice? He does not ask, How are you and I to get on together? He asks, What is friendship? The Socratic students do not practice virtue; they talk about it. So the dialogues raise in radical form the question of the proper use of theory.

Theory can be *seen* to be useful when it leads to an ordered routine of practice, when the theory is a method. Socrates often talks about his own discourse in this way. He talks as if we could come to know the Ideas through talk and then use this knowledge in action. When we have decided what justice is, he says, we will know why we should be just; when we have decided what friendship is we will be friends. But this is absurd. The Ideas are not hypotheses but objects of choice; we never work from them, only toward them. Socrates proposes to us a contradiction in terms: methodical creativity.

The man of true virtue, says Socrates, would pursue happiness with the same quiet confidence with which the craftsman approaches his work. The horse-breaker knows horses, says Socrates; therefore he can improve them; let us know ourselves and we will be able to improve ourselves. The carpenter knows tables; therefore he approaches his workbench with a serene hope of success. Let us know the Good and we will approach the human situation with the same serene hope.

But we cannot approach the human situation; we are in it wherever we are. If we try to determine in advance the criteria of choice, that activity of determining the criteria must in itself correspond to the criteria. The quest for theoretical knowledge of the act does not take you toward the act but away from it. Every explanation requires a further explanation. The philosopher seeks not only to know how to act but to know that he knows, but how can he know whether or not he knows that he knows?

The answer, of course, is that he cannot. In fact the one thing he knows is that he is never sure. Hence the well-known Socratic ignorance; Socrates's knowledge begins, and in a sense ends, with a knowledge of the limits of human knowledge.

What escape can there be from this regress? Here let us go back a step and observe that method is free from the regress only because it is instrumental, because it is theory in the service of some externally defined good. We are involved in the regress, however, whenever we attempt to define the good, to validate those things that are valued for themselves. So far I have talked only of practical autonomy, but the same problem arises in the sphere of pure theory, of knowledge pursued for its own sake. "All men by nature desire to know," says Aristotle; knowledge is one of the modes of happiness. And happiness is no more obtainable here than in any other mode.

Some historian, let us say, fired with curiosity about a given time and place, attacks the relevant documents. As he works he makes progress; certain truths can in fact be discovered by careful interpretation of the evidence. But the more he learns the more he comes to be aware of his ignorance. History is a tissue of lacunae; between any two facts the historian knows there exist an indefinite number of facts he does not know. One causal explanation always requires another: perhaps a social change caused a political change, but what caused the social change? No piece of history is self-contained; the better the historian knows one period, the more aware he is of the need for examining its sources, parallels, and results. Because the part has meaning only in relation to the whole the historian cannot be confident even of the knowledge he has obtained. He may completely misinterpret the things he knows because he does not connect them with the things he does not know. Around any area of knowledge there is a perimeter of ignorance; as the area expands the perimeter expands also. The more the knower prepares himself to make adequate statements the more aware he becomes of the inadequacy of any statement he can make.

Yet this difficulty does not cripple historians. The historian does not expect to perfect his knowledge. He goes on until he feels ready to make a statement about what he's doing, to offer a lecture, an essay, a book. Each statement is a rough draft, an attempt to show the reader how far he has come. The reader is impressed by his learning; he himself is impressed by his ignorance. Yet because he can say something of interest to others his inquiry comes to something; it does not come to knowledge, but it comes to discourse.

That is the paradox of theory; it cannot be known but it can be taught. The theoretician does not, of course, teach definitive truth; that would be sophistry. He shows the work he has done; he explains to the reader where he is and enables the reader to come as far as he has come. *We* do not make progress by knowing what we know, but others can make progress by coming to know what we know. So our knowledge is not satisfac-

tory to us, but it is, as they learn it, satisfactory to them.

As the pupil masters the learning of the teacher he becomes caught up in the same process; the more he learns from us the more he becomes aware of what we have not taught him. As he attempts to fill these gaps he ceases to be a student and becomes an inquirer; as his inquiry gives rise to statement he becomes a teacher. So we are not teaching him history; we are teaching him to be an original teacher of history. And to be an original teacher is the greatest happiness of the theoretician.

Inquiry, thus, makes possible discourse, and discourse inquiry. Many such inquirers, living in a community, constitute an intellectual tradition. If we ask what each inquirer seeks, we must answer that he seeks to know, but if we ask what he achieves, we must answer that he keeps the intellectual tradition alive. Discourse is not about nothing; on the contrary it is about truth. It can never be adequate to truth, however; it can only be adequate to further discourse. Through inquiry and statement the theoretician, as he seeks truth, establishes his relation to, and his independence of, the community of his peers.

Disputation is the mode of commonality of the community of discourse; alone among human communities this one thrives on disagreement. The community of discourse, therefore, is the proper home of the autonomous man. In this republic each citizen discovers himself in the other as each separately pursues the common and transcendent good.

The Socratic circle was such a community of discourse—dominated by a great teacher whose students in their turn became extraordinarily diverse teachers. Ignorant and questioning, Socrates pursued with his students his inquiry into the human situation and drew them into freedom. Wherever you are, he taught them, you can consider where you are and attempt to explain your situation. The pursuit of happiness cannot be founded on knowledge, but it can be activity "accompanied by discourse."

From his experience of the Socratic circle, Plato created the Academy and so founded the tradition of the universities. That tradition we still have with us. And we still have with us Plato's Socratic dialogues to remind us that no question is worth asking unless it raises, explicitly or implicitly, the question, "What knowledge is most worth having?"

Thinking and Self-Teaching

Gilbert Ryle

The theme of thinking was one to which Ryle returned frequently in his later years, but his concern with the relationship between thinking and education is nowhere better shown than in the present essay. Ryle had demonstrated that interest in education in a number of previous articles, as well as in A Concept of Mind. *But here he goes decisively beyond his earlier approaches to the problem.*

"Thinking and Self-Teaching" contains a number of tantalizing and provocative theses, some of which are as challengeable as they are challenging. Of the latter, the following may be cited as particularly deserving of further consideration:

Ryle argues that courses of instruction in thinking cannot be given, because all instruction must be instruction in some specific subject. "There are no residual problems of purely generic sorts." What is curious here is why Ryle, a philosopher so profoundly interested in the activity of philosophizing, should fail at this point to consider the possibility that philosophy might be a specific discipline which deals with "problems of purely generic sorts." While practice in doing philosophy may not involve certain specific thinking skills required for "arithmetic, French grammar, Hittite archaeology, verse, composition, etc.," yet does it not sharpen certain general reasoning capacities which those studies do require? And if this is so, then what reason would there be for not offering philosophy in the schools as a separate course of instruction?

"The notion of thinking is the notion of thinking for oneself," Ryle contends. This is indeed a drastic step. But it was foreshadowed by Ryle's having suggested a little earlier that "the natural processes of digesting and perspiring" are not taught in the schools for quite different reasons than those which have caused us to exclude philosophy. For, once again, could it not be contended that thinking is as natural a process as perspiring or digesting? ("How would we go about stopping a child from thinking?" one of our colleagues recently inquired. "Well," he suggested after some reflection, "we could kill him . . .") And if thinking is a natural process, then surely not all thinking is of that estimable variety which we call "thinking for oneself."

Quibbles such as these aside, the Ryle essay exhibits impressively the intellectual search techniques which, with equal impressiveness, it analyses. No doubt Ryle would be the first to assert that his whole approach is "on appro" (on approval—tentative, conditional, experimental, subject to revision.) But then, so is thinking.

We are not often enough or deeply enough puzzled by the notions of *thinking, pondering, reflecting,* etc.; namely of what Rodin's *Le Penseur* looks as if he is absorbed in. I am not concerned with the dreary notion of *thinking = believing,* which anyhow has been sadly overworked, usually in the wrong harness.

What is Le Penseur doing, seemingly in his Cartesian insides? Or, to sound scientific, what are the mental processes like, which are going on in that Cartesian *camera obscure*? We are, since we have to be, absolutely familiar with the *thing*, that is, with the cogitative doing or the process of pondering itself, for it has been, at least off and on, since our infancy part of the pulse of our own existence. *Cogitamus ergo Sumus*. Yet we cannot, apparently, answer the simplest concrete questions about it. Why can't we? How could it, of all things, be hidden from us?

Notoriously some of our ponderings, but not all, terminate in the solutions of our problems; we had been fogged, but at last we came out into the clear. But if sometimes successful, why not always? If belatedly, why not promptly? If with difficulty, why not easily? Why indeed does it ever work? How possibly can it work? Notoriously, too, some people are better thinkers than others; and we ourselves may be better at thinking out the solutions of anagrams than at thinking out the solutions of chess-problems. Whence these disparities? What sort of an unevenly distributed craft or skill is this? Why did I acquire my own personal ration of it, and not yours instead? Why does not Mozart, indeed why cannot he, suddenly start thinking Immanuel Kant's thoughts, and vice versa? Why do not schools provide classes in thinking, as they do in mundane crafts like drawing, Latin, carpentry, and rifle-shooting? Ridiculous suggestion? Certainly, but then what makes it ridiculous to suggest that thinking is one teachable skill among others? Surely not anything like what would make it ridiculous to suggest that the natural processes of digesting and perspiring are extra skills that could and should be taught in schools or universities.

Let us pause a bit with this little riddle. Why would it be absurd for a school or university to offer a separate course of instruction in thinking? There are two reasons, one important but dull; the other important and interesting.

1) The housewife who has separate shelves, hooks, containers, and bags marked for flour, sugar, onions, mustard, etc., does not also have separate receptacles marked "food," "edibles," "comestibles," or "victuals," for the simple rea-

son that she has already provided receptacles for all the species of these genera. Well, similarly, the school or college curriculum which promises courses in arithmetic, French grammar, Hittite archeology, verse composition, etc., is already promising instruction in *species* of thinking. A student who has been taught some arithmetic or some French grammar has already learned in some measure to think out arithmetical problems or problems in composing or construing French prose. All learning is learning to tackle problems of this, that, or the other specific varieties. There are no residual problems of purely generic sorts.

2) If the school or college promised to teach Originality, Invention, Wit, Pertinence, Initiative, Enterprise, Spontaneity, Talent, and Genius, we should feel sceptical. The lessons, exercises, tests, competitions, etc., might indeed and should equip and encourage the students to attempt moves of their own, to compose sonnets or plays of their own, to design experiments of their own, and so on. But these adventures, diminutive, modest, or striking, must be spontaneous, else they will not be essays, inventions or compositions of the student's own. For it to be *his* failure or *his* success, *his* good shot or *his* poor shot, it has *not* to be something contributed by the teacher. If it is the student's own sonnet, then it is not the teacher's sonnet, for all that the student would never have composed it without the teacher's suggestions, criticisms, drills, etc. Now the notion of thinking *is* the notion of thinking for oneself, of making one's own try, however perfunctory and diffident, at some problem, task, or difficulty. His instructors will have equipped and perhaps encouraged him to make his shot; but the shot is his and not his instructors'. My initiatives, small or great, unsuccessful or successful, cannot, in logic *be* what my teachers or my textbook did for me.

To keep our restricted deck-space fairly clear for the present I am going to leave on one side such off-center things as the thinking of the man who is glumly brooding over an insult; the thinking of a man who is, for pleasure, running over in his head a tune or a poem that he has long since got by heart; and the thinking of the man who is just daydreaming. We shall be concentrating on the man who is trying to think something out, whose thinking, unlike that of those others, can be successful or unsuccessful, bright or dull, industrious or idle, expert or amateurish, laborious or easy.

I am going to approach my objective by a knight's move, one which I think may surprise you a bit. For I am going to begin by reminding you of some truisms about teaching and therefore, necessarily, also about learning. Why? Because, to put it infantilely, my hope is to define thinking indirectly in terms of teaching. I am going to argue that *Le Penseur* is not, of course, engaged in privily teaching himself whatever it is that he wants to know—he cannot teach it because he does not know it—but that he is experimentally plying himself with might-be cues, clues, reminders, snubs, exercises, spurs, etc., of types that are sometimes or often employed unexperimentally by teachers who are teaching what they do know. But we have some ground to cover at first. Anyhow from the outset it seems plausible to say that *Le Penseur* could always have been saved from his present labors of pondering by getting someone else—the Angel Gabriel, say—to teach him the answer. So there is this connection between thinking and teaching. Thinking is trying to make up for a gap in one's education.

I am going to assume, what has been argued elsewhere, that, with a reservation or two, all teaching is teaching-*to* and all learning is learning-*to*. Even the memorizing of rhymes, dates, tunes, etc., qualifies as learning just in so far as it leads to more than mechanical echoing. The child has not begun to learn to spell who can only recite, parrot-like, the dictated spellings "C-A-T" CAT, "B-O-B" BOB. Only when he has begun to try to think up the right spellings or at least possible spellings for words to which he has not been alphabetically introduced, has he begun to learn to spell. To have learned to solve ana-

grams is to have learned to solve new anagrams, not to play back the solutions of anagrams already solved by the instructor. I am going to lean heavily later on these notions of teaching-*to* and being taught-*to*. But I warn you that here I am flying in the faces of most N.C.O.'s and of too many educationalists, who never doubt that teaching consists in dictating things for subsequent verbatim regurgitation. Naturally, though horrifyingly, some of them think well of the potential teaching-utility of subliminal gramophones. Tape recorders play back, but they do not learn. People who do learn do not just play back. Even to have learned something by heart is to have become able to do more than to parrot the piece. It is to be able to detect and correct erroneous recitations, to recite the piece and not some other piece when required to do so; to be able to deliver it fast or slowly, or start it or stop it at required places and so on.

Partly for ulterior reasons, but partly to dispel your attachment, if it exists, to this superstition that learners are mere players-back, I now remind you of a few of the teaching-methods, devices, and dodges by which ordinarily good or very good teachers do actually teach things to us.

1. They tell us lots of things, of course, but with variations in vocabulary, context, emphasis, etc., sometimes *viva voce* and sometimes in writing; with or without new illustrations, expansions, elucidations, corollaries, etc. They do not repeat themselves like cuckoo-clocks, or not much—and for obviously good pedagogic reasons.

2. They test us, hardly at all for our ability to parrot their actual words or to ape their actual movements, but for our ability and readiness to exploit the lesson itself by applying it, re-phrasing it, accelerating it, drawing conclusions from it, marrying it with earlier lessons, etc., etc.; in short, by doing things on our own with it.

3. They teach us cricket-strokes, perspective-drawing and French pronunciation, not much by describing anything, but by *showing* us how the thing should and also how it should not be done,

and then getting us to move or utter, and *not* to move or utter in similar ways.

4. They tease us, like Socrates, with questions, and then with further questions about our answers, and it is we who do the answering.

5. They make us practice and re-practice our five-finger exercises and our conversions of syllogisms, with variations in tempo, syllogism-topic, etc.

6. They lead us by the hand along a half-familiar track and leave us in the lurch to get ourselves over its final stretch.

7. They cite or exhibit blatantly erroneous or inadequate solutions, for us, in recoil, to improve on them and/or to pinpoint what was wrong in them; and they caricature our own sillier attempts in order to get us to ridicule them for ourselves.

8. They draw our attention to partly analogous, but easier problems, and leave us to use these analogies as banisters.

9. They break up complex problems into simpler ingredients and leave us to solve these unalarming ingredient problems, and then to re-unite their solutions.

10. When we have hit on the (or a) solution, they set us subsidiary or parallel problems in order to get us to consolidate and limber up our mastery of the original solution.

All of these and scores or hundreds of similar didactic moves, expedients, tactics, and dodges are intended by our teachers to get ourselves to do and to say things of our own (as well as very often to undo and unsay things); for example, not just to parrot the recited spellings of a few given words but to attempt the spellings of hitherto unattempted words on the lines of those dictated specimens, and to withdraw or improve our first attempts.

Naturally and notoriously the pupil often fails to respond, or to respond well. He is, perhaps, scared, bored, sulky, stupid, restless, unambitious, or hostile, and the teacher is, perhaps, tired, shy, in a hurry, cross, pessimistic, and off his preferred subject. Conversely, the fact that the pupil has shown no sign of progress yesterday or today is quite compatible with his coming on fast next week or next term. Seeds often do germinate slowly. Muscles always are slow to harden up. Did you succeed in swimming in your first lesson? If not, had you learned nothing at all in that first lesson? I mention these truisms because *Le Penseur's* own ponderings (which is what we are all along concerned with) can be in just the same plight. He too flogs away and makes no headway today; tomorrow he too seems to be in a worse muddle than ever; yet sometimes, though not always, for him too things will have sorted themselves out rather well, after the weekend. Dividends often do arrive rather a long time after the investments are made. Thus the progress made or not made or not visibly made by *Le Penseur* resembles in several ways the progress made or not made or not visibly made by the teacher-pupil pair. Our question, "Why does thinking not always work, or not always quickly?" is in parallel with the same less puzzling questions about teaching.

None the less, whatever their other similarities, *Le Penseur* is not himself, so to speak, a Siamese teacher-pupil pair. For the teacher knows the things that he tries to teach to his pupil; *Le Penseur* is pondering just because he does not know what he wants to know. My thinking is not the instruction of pupil Gilbert by teacher Ryle. Gilbert Ryle, in his thinking, is trying to find out what no one, external or internal, is there to teach him. To ponder is to try to make up for *un*-instruction. What I am trying to think about for myself is indeed something that the Angel Gabriel conceivably might have known and taught me instead, but it is something that no one in fact did teach me. That is why I have to think. I swim because I am not a passenger on someone else's ferry-boat. I think, as I swim, for myself. No one else could do this for me.

Now I make a start on the second leg of my knight's move, namely to bring out a connection, *not* an identity, between being taught and thinking.

I have already declared that the pupil does not qualify as having even begun to learn to spell or solve anagrams so long as all he is ready and able to do is to play back the dictated spellings of a few selected specimen words or the dictated solutions of a few specimen anagrams. Only when he begins to suggest possible spellings of his own for new words, or possible solutions of his own new anagrams and to reject some such suggestions, does he qualify. Ditto for learning rock-climbing, chess, and philosophy. His blank repetition of what the teacher said or exhibited is not yet what the teacher was trying to get him to do. But notice now: when the pupil does make his own applications and misapplications in new tasks of what his teacher has told or exhibited, then he certainly qualifies as thinking. For he is now applying off his own bat a recently learned operation-pattern to a new object or situation; he is today innovating according to a formerly set precedent; he is today chancing his arm subject to some previously inculcated safeguards. His frequent mistakes and failures are now his doing; his occasional successes are now his doing. It is he and not his teacher who now merits praise or blame for getting things right or wrong.

Here we are confronted by a seeming paradox. For we seem to be saying that in spelling or misspelling a new word, or in solving a new anagram, or in composing his own limerick or sonnet, the pupil is doing something on his own, which, therefore, he had not been taught. If it is his own sonnet or limerick, or his own anagram-solution, or his own spelling or misspelling of the word "rabbit," then *that* could not have been something that his teacher had taught him. Conversely, if that sonnet, that anagram-solution, or that spelling of "rabbit" had been taught by the teacher, then it was not the pupil who thought it up, but the teacher—or his teacher. However, the appearance of a paradox vanishes when we remember that having learned, say, to spell does not reduce to having become the passive recipient and subsequent automatic regurgitator of some dictated letter-sequences. It is to have become

able and ready to attempt new applications of acquired patterns, methods, precedents, examples, etc. The young rock-climber is first learning to climb when he ceases to tread where his teacher trod and begins to try to tread over new slopes *in the ways in which* his teacher treads.

* * *

I am not changing the subject when I now invite you to consider (A) what Socrates and the slave boy do in Plato's dialogue, the *Meno*; and (B) what they do in my sequel to that dialogue.

(A) Socrates asks the geometrically innocent slave boy how he would construct a square precisely double the area of a given square. In the end the boy comes out with the right answer, namely that the square on the diagonal of the original square is of twice the area of that square itself. But Socrates elicits this correct Pythagorean answer without *telling* the boy any geometrical truths, however simple. He merely asks him questions, and then by further questions gets him to abandon his first tempting answers. We need, for our purpose, to note a few points about this piece of interrogative pedagogics or tutorial cross-questioning.

(1) Though this point is not emphasized, the boy is already equipped with a modicum of elementary arithmetic and, of course, with colloquial Attic Greek.

(2) Unaided Socratic cross-questioning could not possibly have made similar progress or any progress at all towards the solution of factual questions about, say, the casualties at Marathon or the date of the next eclipse of the sun. Nor could *Le Penseur's* unaided ponderings.

(3) Though Socrates draws his famous moral that the boy must in a previous existence have got to know that Pythagorean theorem for it to be able to be elicited from him now by mere questioning, we, surely like all the disputatious young men in the Academy who were any good, flatly reject this moral on the obvious ground that if, without

still ulterior memory-flogging, the boy had been able in that supposed previous existence to discover the Pythagorean theorem by thinking, then there is nothing to prevent the boy from discovering it by thinking today. How was it originally discovered? Some solutions to some problems are attainable by pondering, all the more so when the ponderer is cunningly and persistently barked at by a Socratic sheepdog who already knows the way.

(4) Although the boy has given to each question, one by one, first his ill-thought-out answers and finally the wanted well-thought-out answer, still he does not claim to have thought out the whole proof for himself. After a fumble or two he had picked up each of the several links one by one, but it was Socrates who had controlled the chain. Already knowing the proof of Pythagoras's Theorem, Socrates, unlike the boy and also unlike *Le Penseur*, knew all along what questions were the right questions to ask and what was the right, or at least a suitable, sequence in which to ask them.

(B) Now listen to my own fabrication, namely the story of Socrates's *second* interview with the boy. Socrates begins again by putting a theorem-sized question to the boy; and he starts off as before by posing appropriate questions and demolishing the boy's initial answers to them. But now—oh horror!—Socrates realizes that he himself has either quite forgotten or, even worse, never had mastered the second half of this second theorem's proof. He has no idea how to go on; and, as Euclid's *Elements* has not been published yet, he cannot even surreptitiously consult that will-be standard work. What is to be done? He frankly confesses the crisis to the boy, who, to start with, sees no difficulty. He says, "But yesterday, Socrates, you did not tell me any of the answers; you only asked me questions, to which I myself after some false starts gave *you* the right answers. Why can't we do that again? You don't need to know their answers in order to ask questions."

Socrates explains that randomly thrown out questions cannot be expected to assemble themselves into a proof-generating sequence, but he concedes that with huge luck they might do so; and he concedes that he, Socrates, has had enough teaching experience in general, and has enough geometrical knowledge in particular to avoid asking lunatic, irrelevant, or infantile questions and to see through grossly silly answers. He cannot, as yesterday, pilot the slave boy, since today he does not know the channels. But he can make and coordinate some conjectural pilot-like suggestions and experiments, and he can now and then spot where rocks and shoals might be before getting to them. He is at home on salt water in general, though not on this particular stretch of it.

So Socrates starts off, pessimistically enough, trying out a question that occurs to him and then another and another; and by lunchtime all the progress they have made is the negative discovery that most of these particular questions had better not be asked again; though one or two short question-sequences had felt a bit promising. And that, very likely, is all the progress that they do make. But it could be that on the next day Socrates and the boy are getting an idea of some of the deeps and shallows, some of the headlands and islands. Even if steering directly towards their unseen goal is still impossible, steering away from some specific troubles is becoming fairly easy. Perhaps eventually Socrates's initially chartless quasi-piloting fetches them nearly or even exactly where they want to be. Explorers always do have to start off chartless; yet, as we know, some of them sometimes with luck, flair, patience, and an already trained eye for country, end up with a bit of what had been no-man's-land now properly charted.

Now for my moral. This joint plight of the slave boy and my Socrates who on this occasion had not done his geometrical homework is precisely the plight that Pythagoras himself had been in during the hours or weeks when he was still trying to discover a proof of his own dear Pythagoras's Theorem. For hours or weeks

Pythagoras had been his own slave boy being plied by his own unprepared Socratic self with hesitantly mooted candidate-questions nearly, though not quite, randomly hit on, and tentatively posed in nearly, but not quite, random sequences. By thinking he eventually solved his problem without once during the entire course of his ponderings being yet equipped to teach himself or anyone else its solution. He had not, and no one had, done his homework. It was not yet there to do, as it has been there ever since.

Unlike the guide who leads his docile companions along paths that already exist and are already familiar to him, though not to them, the pioneering pathfinder, Pythagoras say, has no tracks to follow; and any particular sequence of paces that he tentatively takes through the jungle may soon have to be marked by him as leading only into swamps or thickets. All the same, it may be, though it need not be, that in a day's time or a year's time he will have made a track along which he can now guide docile companions safely and easily right through the jungle. How does he achieve this? Not by following tracks, since there are none to follow. Not by sitting down and wringing his hands. But by walking over ground where tracks certainly do not exist, but where, with luck, assiduity, and judgment, tracks might and so perhaps *will* exist. All his walkings are experimental walkings on hypothetical tracks or candidate-tracks or could-be tracks, or tracks on appro; and it is by so walking that, in the end, while of course he finds lots and lots of impasses, he also finds (if he *does* find) a viable track.

Pythagoras or, in general, *Le Penseur* is also in just this same unencouraging position. Tracks are found by the pioneer (if they *are* found), only by quasi-following could-be tracks, that is, by his experimentally trying out on appro one bit of ground after another to see if they could henceforth be unanxiously trodden by docile travelers who are not exploring.

There is my moral. Let me stiffen it with two cautionary remarks:

(1) To repeat: Pythagoras in trying to think out the proof of his theorem is not teaching himself this proof, since he has not yet found it. Nor is my Socrates teaching the boy the thing that he has omitted to prepare himself with.

(2) Pythagoras, my Socrates or, to generalize, *Le Penseur*, is tentatively, experimentally, suspiciously, and quite likely despondently trying out on himself expedients, routines, procedures, exercises, curbs, and dodges of types which teachers do employ, not always successfully, when they want to teach things that they know to pupils who do not. He is trying them out on himself to see if they will be effective, which very often they will not be. They are not already established leads to his goal, but only could-be leads or candidate-clues or potential cues, as the As-If tutorial questions unconfidently put to the slave boy by my geometrically unprepared Socrates.

To say that *Le Penseur* is experimentally subjecting himself to on appro tutorial questions, clues, deterrents, exercises, etc., is not to say merely that he is being histrionic. He need not be, though he may be, aping his old headmaster or his former geometry tutor. The expert moves that you make in climbing the cliff-face may be imitated by a mere mimic; but the patterns of them may also be applied experimentally by the young climber who is trying out ways of scrambling upwards on such cliff-faces. He is deliberately trying to climb cliffs after the ways in which you climb them. He is not aping you but learning to do things of sorts that you have long since learned to do. He is following your examples, not trying to simulate your motions. His success, if he does succeed, is a bit of scaling, not a bit of representing.

Naturally my *Penseur* knows what it is like to be taught things that he does not know by teachers who do; and he knows what it is or would be like himself to be the teacher of some things that he knows to others who do not. So now he experimentally applies to himself, just in case they may turn out to be effective, operations of types that are often or sometimes employed effectively by live teachers upon live pupils. He chalks upon the back of an envelope a diagram, which he does not know to be even an approximation to the right one, in the rather faint hope that it may get him to see something that he needs to see, in the way in which the right diagram on the classroom blackboard often but not always does get the students to see what they need to see. Or he suspiciously concocts for his still unfledged argument a candidate-premise just to see whether it will work, or can be modified into working, and a premise in his argument. It is not yet a premise. It is a premise on appro. He is not basing anything on it; he is only As-If basing something on it. He is not just theatrically staging the moves of an arguer; and he is not just playing at arguing; he is working, working experimentally with a merely could-be argument-step. This is what an hypothesis is, a could-be premise on appro.

We began with some vexatious teasers about thinking, like "if it is an art, craft, or skill, how do we acquire it, and why do schools not give special instruction in it? Why does it not always work? How does it ever work?" Now we can see, just one rung lower down on the sophistication-ladder, that the same questions, though still vexatious, are not quite as vexatious when asked about teaching. Is teaching one art, craft, or skill among others? Could universities teach it? What would they be teaching you in just teaching you to teach (period)?

No, teaching, like thinking, is after all not just one art or skill among others, any more than cooking is one soufflé among others. Yet it remains true, though I think unimportantly true, that there do exist instructional dodges, expedients, etc., varying with different pupils and with different kinds of lessons, without which a good golfer may be a poor golf coach; or without which a new Comprehensive School teacher of French may cope less effectively with her unruly charges than does her colleague whose French is much weaker. I suppose it is such crafts that Colleges of Education do teach. For "education" is not itself the name of one teachable craft among others. "Learning to teach . . ." is an unfinished phrase, because "teaching . . ." is unfinished.

My concluding point is this. Plato said that in thinking the soul is conversing with herself; or maybe "debating" would be nearer the Greek. J. B. Watson said that thinking is sub-*saying*; plenty of philosophers and psychologists declare that all thinking is conducted *in* symbols, or *in* words and sentences, or *in* pictures or *in* diagrams or *in* formulae, etc. The metaphor of words or sentences being the vehicles of thought has still a vogue, and the idea that thought, like American golfers, is in need of vehicles seems to be quite generally swallowed. But what sorts of generalizations about thinking are these? Have amateur or professional introspections revealed this general dependence of thinking upon wording? But if that is all, might not Trobrianders think well enough without such vehicles? After all, we Europeans do eat with knives, forks, and spoons. Yet Trobrianders, maybe, eat without gastronomic vehicles. Or are these generalizations about thinking supposed to be conceptual necessities? Yet if so, just how does the description of someone as, after breakfast, *pensant*, carry with it the information that during that time he was saying things to himself in his head or picturing things to himself in his mind's eye, etc.?

We can now cope with this bother in two moves:

(1) For person A to teach person B something, A must either say things to B, which B hears, takes in, etc. or A writes things or draws things, which B reads, copies, takes in, etc. or A demonstrates or shows things to B, which B sees or hears or tastes or smells, etc. or A audibly jeers at B or visibly beckons or frowns to him, or noticeably pauses meaningfully; and so on and so on. A cannot teach B without communicating with him. Lessons have to be got across, often across a classroom. Lessons are a very special sub-species of interpersonal communications, namely of educatively intended communications. *Of course*, the tuition of B by A requires vehicles.

(2) So, in so far as *Le Penseur* is occupied in experimentally or on appro trying out on himself, as on his inner slave boy, things of the sorts that constitute the vehicles by which live teacher A conveys his lessons to live pupil B, he is necessarily operating, overtly or just in imagination, *with* and *on* such things as words, sentences, diagrams, signals, gestures, etc. He is not, as we have seen, just mimicking real teachers; but he, just as much as the actor who is mimicking Socrates or Mr. Chips, has in logic to do the sorts of things that are done by Socrates or Mr. Chips in teaching their pupils. We might parody Plato and say that in thinking the soul is not just conversing or debating with herself; she is experimentally conveying could-be lessons to herself. Sometimes she is quasi-lecturing to herself, old-style German thinkers seemed to be doing this all the time.

Cartesians love to depict the activity of the thinker as consisting of supremely immaterial ingredients, such impalpable ingredients as ideas, intuitions, insights, etc. In fact, the crude stuff of thinking has to consist of the perfectly ordinary vehicles of everyday interpersonal lesson-communication, though here employed not in its normal didactic task, but in the parasitic or higher-order task of query-tuition. It does not matter whether *Le Penseur* actually draws his diagrams on paper, or visualizes them as so drawn; and it does not matter whether in his quasi-posing his on appro Socratic questions to himself he speaks these aloud, mutters them under his breath, or only As-If mutters them on his mind's tongue. What matters is what he is trying to do, and is sometimes succeeding in doing, by thus overtly or covertly plying himself with these candidate-lesson-vehicles, for example, that he is trying to find, and is sometimes finding, the proofs of theorems. As A's well-charted teaching can occasionally dispel B's ignorance, so my uncharted thinking can occasionally dispel my own ignorance. Thinking is trying to better one's instructions; it is trying out promissory tracks which will exist, if they ever do exist, only after one has stumbled exploringly over ground where they are not.

Chapter Nine
The Classroom Practice of the Philosophy Teacher

Chapter Nine

The Classroom Practice of the Philosophy Teacher

The redesign of the philosophy curriculum is useless without a corresponding redesign of the classroom (the community of inquiry) and the manner of teaching. As far as teaching is concerned, there are many affiliations between the Socratic method and the methods employed in using Philosophy for Children. But there are differences too, chief among which is that the centrality of Socrates in the *Dialogues* is not matched by a centrality of the teacher in the Philosophy for Children classroom. The teacher instead is a facilitator of inquiry—of the deliberative inquiry that occurs in the classroom itself, and of the extended inquiries that emerge from the classroom and branch out in various directions.

Three of the selections in the present section are concerned with the actual conduct of the classroom facilitators and consist largely of suggestions for the tactical management of the discussions so as to make them congenial and productive. These selections, by Michael J. Whalley, Judy A. Kyle and Ruth E. Silver, are derived from the extensive practice these individuals have had as Philosophy for Children teacher educators, and from working with children directly. These are "voices of experience," and while there are countless problems to which they do not address themselves, there are numerous others that they confront candidly and helpfully.

To set the stage for these three practical papers; there is the Eva Brann essay, dealing with

the more general question, "What is to be done in the philosophy class?" Brann's general answer, quite rightly, is "to elicit philosophy from the students." But by what settings or contexts, by what conduct can this be done? It is necessary to ask the students what they *mean*, and what the texts they are reading *mean*. It is also necessary to ask them what the things they are discussing *are*. In all of this, the teacher must appear as a learner—as a learner-in-chief, to be sure, but as one who has learned, is learning and will continue to learn. Above all, one must be seen learning, for "this is as close as anyone can come to teaching philosophy." The students in such a philosophy will discover that they are not there to have their spontaneity fostered. Self-formation precedes self-expression. They are there to study philosophy, one of the liberal arts; and the liberal arts are "first and last skills of understanding."

The last word in the section is that of Elias Baumgarten, commenting on the ethical and social responsibilities of philosophy teachers. It is important that these responsibilities be examined, since teachers consider themselves professionals; and professionals are aware that these responsibilities cannot be denied or evaded. Professions are staffed by individuals who accept full responsibility for their professional conduct and whose professional judgments are based upon expert understandings. The Socratic dictum, says Baumgarten, still holds: no profession should seek its own advantage, but should benefit those who are subject to it. Philosophy teachers have a responsibility to convey ideas to their students, in order to help them formulate reasoned positions for themselves. Moreover, philosophy teachers should be neutral, impartial non-advocates: their relationship with their students should be both professional and caring.

A Way to Philosophy

Eva Brann

The Enterprise

At the present time the word philosophy is used to name a discipline which is one among many and which has, as do the others, formulated results, preset problems and articulable methods. I think no one would question that philosophy so understood can be taught.

But there is also an old, original meaning which I would like to recall. The word philosophy literally means *the love of wisdom*. I would like to avoid here the burden of argument entailed by this recollection, which is: To show that there is such a passion and such an object for it. Instead, I want to take the word in a way which is at once practical and appropriate to schools: As the desire to reflect while learning, as a wish to look behind, beyond, beneath the matter in hand; or, concisely and negatively, as an aversion to being unaware of one's ground. Note that I am not intending to describe curiosity (the avidity for novelties) or critique (the project of evaluating whatever has been proposed.)

So interpreted, it goes without saying that philosophy is the kind of shadow enterprise, suffused over and hardly separable from other undertakings, which is not directly teachable. But philosophy can perhaps be *elicited*. I shall, then, pose myself the project of setting out the sketch of a somewhat practical plan for eliciting philosophy in institutions of learning. I shall depend for the formulations of this project at least in part on my own experience in the program at St. John's College in Annapolis.

Now the question whether the attempt to elicit philosophy should be made at all is a prime consideration *within* a philosophical setting. But it is one which no convert to the cause would consent to discuss before that setting had come into being, especially if the answer is meant to have a practical consequence, for instance that of abandoning the undertaking. Therefore the beginning must be abrupt. Unless a favorable setting has already been established, the most practical procedure is, without publishing any plans or premises, resolutely to subvert some class to the enterprise. Almost any class is suitable, as long as it is not one in which students were promised instruction directed toward competence immediately connected with their livelihood. Most students have enough of a philosophical propensity so that, though they may be surprised at this use of their scheduled time, they will not be offended.

The Texts

The problem now becomes: What to do in this class? The way I have formulated the enterprise might suggest that a fresh and thoughtful spirit would engender philosophy on any subject matter and that no special matter is needed. This must be true in principle, for philosophical learning is at bottom nothing but live learning. But it fails in practice, for very mundane reasons. When people meet regularly at scheduled times, they will not often be able to find a good beginning unless they have a prepared matter in common. Furthermore, in view of the mediocrity of our intellect it is practically indispensable to have a guide in the effort of reflection. Some help is therefore needed to prevent the occasion from being casual and the conversation, which is its object, from turning in tedious circles. That help is to be found in good texts.

One particular misgiving concerning the use of texts deserves consideration. It is patent that the study of books, which means the appropriation of the opinion of others, respectable though they may be, is in several ways seriously at odds with the enterprise of reflection, the attempt to think for and upon oneself. But again this question, which concerns the relation of learning to tradition, is profitably raised only within the tradition, which is to say within a setting in which thought and study have some sort of *de facto* compatibility. The participants in this enterprise must first "take up and read," then question the value of reading.

It follows that the texts which are intended to be the instigators of thought and guides into otherwise inaccessible depths should be such that students will be compelled (perhaps after an initial period of aversion) to give them respect and even to impute superiority of intellect and imagination to their authors.

There is one apparently obvious criterion for choosing such texts which will not, in fact, turn out to work very well, namely that of "primary" against "secondary." The reason is that most books, whether written in a spirit of critique or, more rarely, of approval, are about previous books and therefore in an important sense commentaries. So, for instance, one might argue that *Northanger Abbey* is a commentary on *The Mysteries of Udolpho*, or, seriously, that Galileo's *Dialogue Concerning the Two Chief World Systems* is a commentary on Aristotle's *On the Heav-*

ens, a book which is in fact almost a participant in the conversation.

There is, however, a criterion which is more usable because it is less external: The texts should be original, in the double sense of being the result of the author's own thought and of pressing the pursuit of a matter to its very origins. Texts of this underivative sort usually reveal themselves by the manner of their composition long before the student has gone very far in penetrating them: they are so subtly and artfully woven that the reader sees inexhaustibly many avenues to their meaning without losing faith that there *is* a meaning.

But by and large it must be an act of trust, of perfectly reasonable trust, in the opinions of literate mankind to find and establish a working list of such texts. That is to say, the teacher will begin by looking to that very accessible corpus of books of secular reputation often referred to as "the tradition." This does not mean that there might not be good texts that are practically unknown (for instance a colleague's unpublished work), but only that their existence is less likely and their discovery very difficult.

Texts of the sort described differ from textbooks and other derivative works in one way essential to the enterprise. They most further the inquiry while least obtruding themselves upon it. They do this because, contrary to most textbooks, they do not present themselves as covering a predetermined field or treating a preset problem. Good texts rarely prejudge the first questions concerning the division of knowledge, but come before the students simply as reputable writings. And because they do not take their subject matter as given, because they so often begin by distinguishing their realm of inquiry and justifying that distinction, they further original inquiry—this is only one of several ways in which the tradition proves to be the best antidote to indoctrination. To give examples: Is Newton's work called the *Mathematical Principles of Natural Philosophy* a work of "mathematics," of "philosophy," of "physics," or of "theology"? Is *War and Peace* a work of "literature" or of "history"? The cause of reflection requires that these questions should be allowed to arise, and with them the inquiry into the meaning of these words.

Now on the very hypothesis underlying our choice, which is that the authors chosen know how to begin their work and how to secure the reader's understanding (or to put it another way, that they are truly elementary), the order in which the books are read should not be of the essence. There are, to be sure, two naturally given serial orders even in the absence of any classification by subject matter, namely those determined by the order of their publication, taken either forwards or backwards.

If the readings are to begin with contemporary authors, the teacher will first face the difficulty of choosing a text, because of the recent proliferation of printed matter and because of the absence of an established and perhaps even of a nascent tradition of mutually responsive books of high quality. In this situation it makes a certain sense to ask the students whether they think they know some appropriate book with which to begin. The discussion of this book is then very apt to consist of penetrating the shield of its seeming familiarity, in order to reveal the assumptions on which the work rests. Students may well find that these premises, whether idly inherited or knowingly appropriated by the author, seem astonishingly uncongenial to them. The enterprise may then turn into that of following the spoor of these assumptions backward to their sources. In those frequent cases where a modern book takes the stance of resistance or liberation, these sources will often be found in those very earlier teachings which are being denied; such books carry on the tradition in the mode of deeply engaged contradiction. An example: among the truly admirable modern texts is one—not long ago there were always some students who knew it—by Camus, called "On Absurd Reasoning," which begins with the words: "There is but one truly serious philosophical problem and that is suicide." The work itself ensures that the reader will wonder how much absorption and rejection of tradition goes into the asking of this purportedly "primordial" question, and from this wonder immediately follows the backtracking I have outlined. In Camus' case it can surely only end with the very beginnings of the philosophic tradition.

If, on the other hand, the order of reading begins with early texts, students will at first feel a probably salutary shock at the brusquely remote unfamiliarity of their utterances and concerns. Here the teacher will do most by displaying an uncompromising expectation that these works will be treated as if they were close to us. Sometimes it will help to show how their forbiddingly simple and staid language is peculiarly adequate to spirited and subtle depth. Sometimes it will help to draw attention to an apparent contradiction. For example, to students who first read Homer, he seems so remote that they respond by disorientated talk about "the Greeks" and "their gods," an opaque and indifferent lot. Here the teacher might draw attention to the tale of Ares and Aphrodite caught up in unwillingly public and prolonged embrace by the net of the lame husband, and ask why *human* affairs of this sort are always treated gravely and delicately, and only the gods' affairs hilariously and scurrilously. The discussion concerning the gods then often becomes perhaps no less inconclusive, but far more charged with human significance.

All in all, the natural forward order may be preferable, always allowing for enlightening exceptions. This order of study is best not only because it soonest convinces students that the books which penetrate most deeply into human affairs are often also most refractory to offhand assimilation, but mainly because it carries with it the fewest, or at least the plainest, assumptions. The chief of these is the simple one that in order to understand an author in his own terms the best thing is to have read some of the very books he himself had studied before he composed his own.

The Teacher

In a setting in which it cannot be the teacher's task to impart knowledge (not to speak of "information"), what will he[1] do? His work is clearly that of a solicitous guide, and it seems to me to have two chief aspects.

The teacher must first of all have and creditably display trust in the enterprise. It must be clear that he is not a wraith wandering unwillingly far from the realms of action, power, competence or wealth, but in some moderate and therefore reliably continuous way a lover of learning. This character alone can give him the authority to institute and continue the proceedings I am describing.

The second aspect complements the first. The teacher will have to accumulate a fund of discoveries, even a modest treasury of revelations, with which to back his trust and to mediate between difficult texts and willing students.

In brief: The teacher must be a learner-in-chief (so to speak), who has learned, is learning and will learn alongside as well as somewhat ahead of his students. Indeed it must always be somewhat ambiguous whom a teacher is ultimately serving, himself or them. This observation has special force in view of the horrid dangers facing the studentless scholar, chief of which is that of producing a stream of answers to which there are no questions.

This kind of teaching cannot help but raise a difficulty for the teacher as a member of the scholarly profession. Just as philosophy as a way is frequently at odds with philosophy as an established subject, so learning and learnedness, inquiry and research are often mutually exclusive. I think a teacher of the sort I am describing had best forego all plans for rising in his profession, merely maintaining himself within it by meeting its reasonable requirements. Nonetheless a teacher must write, and write to be read by his students and his friends and his friends' friends. For it is not only necessary to the teacher to articulate and circulate his thoughts and discov-

eries and to have a project which will carry intellectual satisfactions analogous to those of productive craftsmanship. It is also vital to the enterprise that the repudiation of exclusive competence, which is, after all, intended to promote greater thoroughness at the roots, should not degenerate into evanescent dilettantism.

Furthermore, it seems to me especially important for that teaching which rouses and guides a common inquiry that a teacher should articulate his thoughts. For once students have persuaded themselves that the search is serious and has a desirable object, the time will certainly come when they will round on the senior member to ask, "Now what do *you* think?" And again, that response is best and leaves the inquiry most alive, which is most straightforward. And that is for the teacher to say with candor and clarity what he does think, whether he has a "theory" to offer or a reasonable formulation of doubts and difficulties. But that he has, or is about to have, one or the other is a precondition of presuming to teach at all. For a defensible view of matters is the proof that anyone has completed some small part of his studies. Furthermore, just as questioning cannot be empty, so listening cannot be a lax or superior leaning-back. For the teacher must be intent on grasping the thought intended in the student's words and must listen—contrary, I believe, to current wisdom—to the student's reasonable speech, and not to the student himself. This means that the teacher must, except at some felicitous moments, assiduously suppress most observations concerning the origins, upbringing, sex, mood and capacities of members of the class. I think I know from experience that students would rather have their thoughts attentively opposed than their persons indiscriminately cherished.

It would be an error, I think, to accept or dismiss this way as "Socratic." Socrates is displayed in the Platonic dialogues as being only ironically a philosopher, if a philosopher is one who loves wisdom as he lacks it; in comparison to those about him he is shown as a man already wise who asks questions in the light of very high, perhaps complete knowledge. Furthermore his conversation is appropriate to the true leisure of a free life rather than to the simulated leisure of a school. The way I am proposing—not a method, only a mode—is much less demanding and exceptional. It requires of the teacher only a certain readiness of disposition and a moderate keenness of intellect.

One first and last requirement: A teacher should not talk too much, and if that proves impossible, at least not dogmatically.

The Students

The central figures in the teacher's effort are the students and they are, happily, I think, the given of the enterprise; they are to be taken as they come, provided only that they can, in a narrow sense, read, write, and do algebra—and that they have come to school by their own desire.

In particular, it is no drawback to the class if some members are rather simpleminded, perhaps even apparently dense. There is often a positive profit to the class in invincible, and therefore incorruptible, intellectual innocence. Let me give an example, not untypical, from life.

A class has just completed a discussion of a corollary to Newton's laws of motion which implies the notion of the center of gravity of a system of bodies as that point at which the combined masses of its bodies can be considered to be located. A certain student, who does not have a reputation for cleverness to maintain, asks: Why then, if a bullet passes to the right and another to the left of me such that this point where both masses can be considered to be located passes right through my heart, don't I drop dead?—a question more easily ridiculed than answered, and in this instance the beginning of a worthwhile discussion concerning the objects of mathematical physics.

A certain necessary homogeneity should then arise in the class from the common desire to learn, which means through self-selection, rather than by selection directed towards great similarity of preparation or even ability. So also the variety requisite to the conversation may come rather from the students' own natures than from any deliberate composition by age, sex, social class or race. In a classroom those differences of view which emerge among people (who might be externally quite similar) as a consequence of their different inner natures as a rule turn out to be, if more subtle, yet more deep-lying and persistent than those which stem from grossly apparent distinctions like sex and race. Nonetheless, that way is ever best which least prejudices the matter, and so a mixed group is very desirable, provided it can be gotten without yielding to the destructive strain of external pressure.

Now as candor is a teacher's obligation with respect to the intellect, so guile seems to me to be often required where pedagogy is concerned. So for instance with very young students a teacher must cultivate a sort of clear-eyed obtuseness, by which their personal animosities are resolutely misinterpreted as differences of opinion, obstreperousness as high-spiritedness, obtuseness as valuable simplicity. And, of course, it helps if a teacher knows how to "look sadly when he means merrily," to use a phrase describing the irony of Thomas More, a great teacher.

But the chief occasion for a certain suppleness is that which is at the heart of this kind of teaching: the asking of good questions. Such questions will be most often of three kinds, all implicated with each other. The first will be addressed to the student: What do you mean?; the second to the text: What does it mean?; and the third to the beings in question: What, how, why are they? It goes without saying that questions well-asked are not merely disguised directives or solicitations of certain responses, though most students see that in order to ask well a teacher must have "something in mind." Consequently they see that it is a just response for them to turn on a question and after exposing it as a premise to substitute a truer question of their own.

It does not matter so very much where students come from, it matters very much on what terms and whether they stay. There are many students, sometimes the finest, who wholly approve and respect the enterprise and are yet drawn away from it, not so often into other university studies as into "real life." In part they are simply possessed by a young, spirited and entirely sympathetic desire for adventure, for which the cure is to go and seek it, and come back the wiser. Unfortunately for everyone's peace of mind, this natural desire is often propounded in the language of "experiences," which are thought of as being a kind of vividly immediate counter-education, in competition with the remote book-learning of schools. Similarly, the restless but perfectly sound thirst for deeds is often represented as an opposition between "abstract" theory, absorbing as it may be, and action which is considered urgent and obligatory.

It is not very likely that arguments will overcome such a disposition to leave, or listlessly to remain. Not only is it too much aided and abetted by current opinion, but the arguments themselves are difficult to make. Some will be based on untransferable experience with the "realness" of life and the "abstractness" of theory, or on notoriously unpersuasive prudential considerations. The better arguments will be too intricate for the immediate purpose, for they will consist of carefully demonstrating that these oppositions rest on assumptions which students themselves find unacceptable, and that the results of acting in accordance with them are often self-defeating. Nonetheless, these arguments ought to be patiently made, first for future reference, so that students may have them at hand when the time comes, and second, to convince them of the teacher's conviction. For the rest, it seems best to urge students not to go without completing the work in hand, and then to wish them well.

What is both feasible and important is to see that the enterprise is in no way compromised by this centrifugal disposition which the world fosters. Reflective learning should be accepted as an overwhelmingly absorbing way of life. It is in spirit compatible both with the hard and involuntary work that many students must do to support themselves and with voluntary service; it ought to be graced with frequent entertainment and invigorated by regular sports, and it certainly should have action as one end—true action which prevails. But I can imagine no practical project conceived as part of this undertaking which would be anything but a camouflaged diversion. Students should study, first and last.

The Issues

In a setting which is intended to be such that nothing human is alien to it, students will naturally air their current preoccupations.

These "issues," pervasive and almost mandatory concerns, seem to me quite distinct from the perennial human questions such as: What is human, what is good, what is world, what is being? It is with respect to these passing issues that students differ, if they differ at all, from decade to decade. It would be a work of supererogation to detail once again what these preoccupations currently are, so I will refer only to those aspects which have a special bearing on the enterprise under discussion.

To begin with, there is a sort of obligatory doubt, a disposition to use the forms of inquiry as modes of attack, and to transform the asking of questions into "questioning" (the positive complement to which is "creativity"). This riotous Cartesianism has for its chief object commonly accepted goods, which are for this purpose denominated "values." The chief datum, replacing nature and the political community, is "the system" or "society," which pose "problems" but resist necessary change.

To question values, become creative, fight the system, solve social problems and produce social change are the perfectly honest concerns which students bring to school out of the world. They are, unfortunately, singularly inept for radical inquiry.

This judgment is, at least to begin with, quite separate from questions of acquiescence or resistance to our condition. To be sure, students are quick to see and to point out to each other that the true questions "What is it?" or "Why do you think so?" have a preserving character in so far as they intend to honor the matter in question with attention. Furthermore, the trusting use of texts means that the possibility of authority is imputed to something out of the past. But neither of these factors is unequivocally either conservative or subversive. In fact, the enterprise carries with it no particular political persuasion except perhaps the admittedly powerful one that thought must precede action.

What is amiss is rather that these issues so put forth are overwhelmingly fraught with unrecognized academic presuppositions. To use an ugly word, the views of many students, often of the brightest, are extremely "theoreticized." Their genuine and justified passions are expressed, or rather dissipated, in a vocabulary assumed uncritically, mostly from the disciplines of psychology and sociology. It would be an enormous propaedeutic labor to distinguish the student's own naive intentions from the current conventions which envelop them.

Of course, it could be done. The group might, for instance, read Durkheim's *Rules of Sociological Method*, and then consider his principle that "the determining cause of a social fact should be sought among the social facts preceding it and not among the states of individual consciousness." A discussion of "cause," hence of "system" would follow. Newton's laws of motion might be studied in order to make available the notion of the interactions in a system of bodies. The question of the assumption of mechanical models into the study of men will then be raised. Some students will now grow outraged at the very concept of "society"; others will point out ineluctable facts which make the concept plausible. Some will want to take refuge from the mechanical constraints of social "behavior" in their "creativity." They will be asked to consider the text: "In the beginning God created the heaven and the earth" and asked whether they mean to undertake similar projects. Some will own that they do. It is a fascinating, but also a chaotic and infinite undertaking, this critique of "opinion," as Socrates calls such received thought.

Happily we are still in possession of a more originally common language and experience. A teacher may worry about the fate of such human experience in view of so much vicarious "exposure" and "experiencing" and about the possibility of much intensity in view of so much easy access. Nonetheless, the best thing is to assume that love and life go on much as they always have, and to impute to students those ardent, wholehearted and natural modes which have common names but often lead to recondite discourse.

It is therefore best to eschew current issues as guides for inquiry, though I think no one would be altogether plausible in doing it who was not also an avid teacher of the modern scene and a fascinated reader of contemporary works.

The Arts

If the inquiry cannot usually be guided by the current problems brought to it from the outside, it yet requires something which is antecedent and external to the desire to know oneself and the world: the ability to read. I mean the ability to read in the widest sense, namely the possession of tools for interpreting those texts of words, symbols and even things which bear on these matters. This ability to read is fostered by the arts traditionally called liberal, which are the "instruments and rudiments" of philosophy.

The reason for the name and the established number of these conditions for gratifying the desire to know are almost totally lost to students studying at the so-called liberal arts colleges. It therefore makes sense to take some opportunity to read with them sections of works which deal directly and familiarly with the roots, parts and uses of the free arts, such as Hugo of St. Victor's *Didascalicon* and John of Salisbury's *Metalogicon*. But it is far more immediately important that their terms, observances, rules and methods should be made explicit and used as much as possible, even while the philosophical enterprise is going on. Uneasy though this simultaneous combination of exercise and reflection may be, one can certainly not count on students becoming versed in these arts at any other time.

The best and most satisfying way for students to acquire these arts is, in my experience, for them to devote a definite part of their three or four years at college to a programmatic study of the trivium (the outer and inner form of speech), and the quadrivium (mathematics and its application to things in motion).

Here it is necessary to point out that if such a program is undertaken, a kind of university study which usually constitutes the bulk of a students' courses will be reserved for special study groups or postponed to graduate school, partly on principle and partly from sheer lack of time. These are the studies which can never be elementary without intellectual shoddiness. I mean the disciplines which are by their very nature sophisticated, since their existence depends on the formation of complex and precarious concepts and the accumulation of large bodies of special methods and results. The paradigmatic study of this sort is the discipline of history (as opposed to what Hegel calls "original history," and "inquiry" written down in the spirit of an eyewitness for general edification and enjoyment; he names Herodotus, Thucydides and Xenophon as examples.) Certainly no one who has ever grappled with the recovery and interpretation of the past can think of history as a viable beginning study.

But in most schools it is very unlikely that the professors of such studies will often give way to, and wait on the acquisition of, the first arts. At the same time a teacher simply cannot count on students to possess them. Therefore another expedient, however insufficient, must be found, in order that the group may have some practice in common.

One way would be to take up the relevant arts in short illustrative exercises as the texts under discussion direct. Here are some examples, mere indications, of what has sometimes worked.

When reading the *Phaedrus*, the Platonic dialogue implicating love and rhetoric, it might be possible to stop a week over a Shakespearean sonnet and, perhaps, the *Gettysburg Address*, to look at them minutely and keenly as collections of words, grammatical structures, rhetorical efforts, works of music. Everyone, most of all the teacher, will consult manuals and reference books and with the aid of these meticulously prepare exercises, which might include making metric analyses, parsing particularly opalescent sentences, revealing and naming implied and patent logical relations. The object will be both to practice the art of dealing with language and to confirm admiration for works which are at once inimitable and exemplary.

Or, when, as it must, the time has come to study the *Critique of Pure Reason* (or at least the *Prolegomena to Any Future Metaphysics*) where Kant asks and answers the question, "How is pure mathematics possible?," that would be a good moment to study together the definitions, postulates and common notions given in the first book of Euclid's *Elements* and perhaps to go on to follow the elementary consequences of that denial of Euclid's parallel postulate which is presented in Lobachevsky's *Theory of Parallels*.

So also there will be numerous textual occasions for studying the rudiments of the apprehension of "nature" as having numerable dimensions and the bases of the geometric representation of sensible qualities and the elements of the mathematics of motion, in short, the foundations of mathematical physics.

The effects of such sporadic exercises will be small but not negligible, for students will become somewhat better readers first of books and then of themselves and the world. If none of us has much hope of becoming master of the arts, the next best thing is surely to be a responsible amateur.

It is important to make it quickly clear to students that while pursuing the free arts they will perforce, for lack of time, have to neglect the productive or fine arts except as serious recreations; while engaged in liberal learning they will not directly learn to write poetry, paint pictures or play the flute. And, having chosen to put self-formation before self-expression, they must be ready to relinquish the expectation (odd in any case) of having their spontaneity fostered. The liberal arts are first and last skills of understanding.

The Community

It is of the essence that this enterprise should be uncompromisingly represented as being in some central respect for its own sake. There are two aspects to this claim.

First, it is *the* axiom of inquiry and is simply tantamount to the proposition that there *is* philosophy, the love of reflective learning, and free or self-determined, inquiry which serves no external end.

But the claim is, secondly, also a shrewd representation to make to students. The older wisdom was, and the current wisdom is, that the axiom is idle and that schooling should be immediately related to success in worldly matters—in the past to training for a profession, in the present to the production of social change or services. The views coincide in discounting the life of learning. But students with spirit have never been much enchanted with the previous view, and are now ready to doubt the current one. This is partly because they cannot find a course of study which offers both convincing deliberations concerning ends and reliable methods for effecting them, perhaps because such an undertaking is impossible. Therefore the ancient, scandalous claim again has a chance to engage at least the fascinated resistance of students.

And yet the program I have described *will* have palpably practical effects. I am not now referring to the more remote though eventually evident influence of a reflective education on the practical judgment of citizens, but to a very immediate result: A community comes into being. People who undertake such a program of learning together become friends—not, as a rule, intimates, because their purpose is to look not to each other but rather to a common enterprise—yet nevertheless serious and steady companions.

The sturdiness of this natural outcome depends on this: that it should be cherished without being directly intended. Accordingly students should feel it right to think and talk together as they sit in their rooms, as they walk to their class, as they eat and as they play. So also students should be encouraged to study together and to help each other with paradigms, problems and other preparation. It goes without saying that the best students will have a private pride in their freely acknowledged reputation for excellence, but it is also obvious that that nasty ranking which goes with competitiveness is entirely out of place here.

In exactly the same vein teachers will find themselves consorting with and caring for students, always (with such very rare exceptions as may prove justified in the outcome) keeping that decent distance which makes such friendship possible. The limits, however, of such relations are strictly set (and this is an evidently insuperable, but ever-chafing difficulty) by the time needed for institutional occasions, preparation, study, private life, recuperation—and one more activity.

This activity is the fostering of the community of teachers, an absolutely essential project if the way described here is to be anything more than just another episode in the institution. For, first, the enterprise of philosophy must have a world in which to flourish, a world which is stable even if it is small, and the fellowship of teachers is the foundation of that world. And second, it is only sensible that the leaders in learning should regularly and formally become co-students.

Practically, this can be done through study-groups which propose for themselves a difficult but elementary matter to be studied, not under expert direction, not for research and results, not toward professional advancement, but for the sake of the naivest possible reflection.

It is not hard to find suitable texts which present a matter from the beginning but with depth. Here is a merest sampling of proven works: a chorus from Sophocles' *Antigone*, the twelfth book of Aristotle's *Metaphysics* on the source of motion and *energeia*, and with it Leibniz's first *Essay on Dynamics* in which the dimensions of the modern term "energy" are originally established, a Donne song, Vico's *On the Study Methods of Our Time* which sets forth the original terms of our unhappy division of learning into the "sciences" and the "humanities." A group which has many such studies in common becomes mildly invincible.

And finally, not only must the leaders in this enterprise learn with and from each other in this way, but they must allow themselves to be seen to do it. For to be seen learning is, I think, as close as anyone can come to teaching philosophy.

Notes

1. This essay was written before it became the custom to make language gender-nuetral.

The Practice Of Philosophy in the Elementary School Classroom

Michael J. Whalley

The following list of points was designed as a handout to teachers undergoing training in Philosophy for Children. It cannot, of course, take the place of modelling and observation as an essential part of training; but it may be useful for reference when attempting to improve one's own performance. Although aimed specifically at the use of the IAPC materials, the items are general enough to be applicable wherever philosophical discussion with children is attempted.

Some factors affecting success

1. *Reading*. Normally start a session by reading or re-reading part of the story. The section read should be long enough to allow the class some choice in the topics available to them (usually between half a page and two or three pages). If you are working through a list of topics (see 3) it may be sufficient just to read those particular lines which gave rise to the topic chosen for today.

2. *Choice of topics*. Try to find out what interested the class by first asking general questions about what was read ("What did you find interesting, puzzling, etc?"). Although you yourself will be aware of certain issues that have been deliberately embedded in the reading, this should not influence your reception of the children's own choice of topics. If the response is slow, try asking more specific questions about incidents or characters in the story—but always with the aim of finding out *why* something happened, rather than merely *what* happened. These questions are not a memory test. Encourage the class to look over what was read again, to find any point that may have caught their attention.

3. *Listing the topics*. This may be done on the blackboard, or better still on a large sheet of paper which can be kept for use in the following sessions. A visual record of the class's response to a particular part of the reading is valuable. In this way an important idea is not lost for future discussion. List the topics even when working with pre-readers, as this shows them that you are treating their remarks seriously. In addition, especially with younger children, writing their names in brackets after their topic will encourage them to consider their individual contributions as important.

Avoid writing just a single word or two as a shorthand for the children's ideas. Likewise, don't simply quote from the text. You should find out, by questioning, what the child *thinks* about the point referred to.

Preferably use the children's own words. If a particular idea is difficult to formulate, *ask the class* to discuss what is meant, and let them suggest a way to express it. Above all, avoid trying to interpret what they say. The result may be your idea, and not what the child intended.

After the children have responded, you may add topics of your own to the list, if you wish.

4. *Use of the manual.* Choose, from the list of topics that you have collected, one which has some exercises related to it in the teacher's manual. Before turning to the manual, ask the class one or two questions concerning the topic (you may refer back to the story), and try to initiate a brief preliminary discussion. But don't allow this to go too far unless you have a sound understanding of the *philosophical* importance of the topic. Without this the discussion, even if extensive, may not go anywhere. The exercises in the manual are designed to ensure that it has at least a chance of going somewhere.

5. *Questioning.* To repeat, don't merely ask *what* happened. Ask *why* it happened. Always get the children to give reasons for their opinions. Look for a further problem suggested by the children's comments, and ask a follow-up question.

6. *Listening.* The difficulty often experienced in asking follow-up questions may partly stem from the teacher's lack of philosophical background knowledge. To some extent, this may be remedied by studying the hints given in the teacher's manual. But another very important factor is learning to listen. The more successfully you can reverse the traditional teacher/pupil relation and *pay close attention to what the children say*, the easier you will find it to ask follow-up questions. This is because you will be responding to what they are saying, rather than to what you think they mean or ought to mean.

7. *Flexibility.* If one question arouses much interest, don't be in a hurry to move on to the next. On the other hand, don't hammer away at a question that seems to be boring the class—unless you can somehow rephrase it so that it interests them. The children's response should always be taken as the main guide to the content and extent of the discussion.

But at the same time, don't be satisfied with glib answers, which are offered without any thought. These may not reveal lack of interest so much as mental laziness. (A counter-measure which may be tried is to get the class to write their answers first, and then let the discussion start from the written answers.) See also 9.

8. *Questions from the class.* Unless they are merely procedural questions (e.g. What page are we on?), don't answer them. Instead, try to make use of them to initiate discussion. Ask what the others think. An answer from you might be seen as definitive, and will discourage further thought about the matter. But if at the end of the discussion the class is keen to know your opinion, there is no harm in giving it to them, provided you stress that it is only one answer among several possible ones.

9. *Patience.* Give the class time to reply. There is nothing wrong with silence if it is filled with constructive thinking. If the silence seems to cause tension, you can explain that you want the class to have time to think before replying. In any case, avoid a constant bombardment of questions, with no time to consider. (Note that this also tends to keep attention on the teacher, which in turn will inhibit dialogue.)

10. *Dialogue.* This feeds on differences of opinion. Look for these and encourage the children to give *each other* (rather than you) reasons for their respective positions. Watch for the opportunity of allowing the class to continue discussing without your intervention. This may not last long, but it is valuable as a means of breaking away from constant teacher/child interaction. When you have some facility in the general use of the materials, you should concentrate exclusively on promoting interaction between the children rather than between you and them. Your own ingenuity and the experience of your colleagues may both be of use here. One rather obvious move, often overlooked, is to simply *tell* the children that you want them to learn to take up the discussion for themselves from time to time, without always relying on you for a further ques-

tion. (A further point: the more they can do this, the less need you will have to search for follow-up questions.)

11. *Toleration*. It goes without saying that genuine inquiry can take place only in an atmosphere of intellectual freedom, where any point of view can be considered for which reasons are offered. In addition, the class is unlikely to become enthusiastic unless they feel that you, too, are curious about the questions raised. It is very hard to do one's best thinking under pressure, and if genuine inquiry is taking place the children will appear at the same time relaxed and excited, rather than rigid or strained. To put it briefly, they will be enjoying themselves.

12. *Seating*. Traditional seating in rows is designed to ensure that the only verbal interaction that takes place is between teacher and class. Since you want the children to discuss with one another, you are strongly advised to choose an arrangement which will encourage that. Discussion is easier if the participants face one another. Therefore the best seating arrangement is roughly circular. The circle may be formed with chairs alone, or with desks, or sitting on the floor.

Not only should the children be able to speak to one another without craning their necks; they should also be able to hear what anyone says. So desks and chairs should not be too widely spaced.

Except when writing on the board, etc., the teacher should sit *with* the children as a member of the discussion group. Sitting behind a large desk or standing at the front of the room only emphasizes the traditional dichotomy between teacher and class. In these circumstances the children will never feel that it is their own discussion. (See Summary.)

The main things to avoid:

13. *Lecturing*. In general, only ask questions, don't comment. Even if your comments are relevant, the children will simply listen to you and stop thinking for themselves. This will bring discussion to a halt.

In particular, don't treat the session as a lesson in vocabulary. Philosophy does not consist in discussing the meanings of words—even though this may sometimes help as a preliminary. "For words are wise men's counters, they do but reckon by them: but they are the money of fools . . ."—Thomas Hobbes.

Finally, don't say "there are no right answers." This is dogmatic. It is also false. The emphasis should be not on right answers but on good reasons. Answers put a stop to discussion; reasons encourage it to continue.

14. *Inattention*. Your role is to guide the discussion, not to stay out of things altogether. In particular, don't allow inattention, or conversations aside. A child who is speaking has a right to be listened to. The others will require practice in listening. Adults so often treat what children say as unimportant, that children themselves come to regard their ideas as unimportant. One of the aims of Philosophy for Children is to alter this state of affairs.

15. *Monopoly of the discussion*. Don't allow a few class members to monopolize the discussion. Try to involve as many as possible. On the other hand, don't assume that those who say nothing are not inwardly participating. Some children may not wish to compete verbally with the more aggressive members of the class—and those who talk the most are not always those who have the best reasons. When the quieter ones realize this, they may in time feel encouraged to speak.

16. *Irrelevance*. If the discussion strays off the point for too long, bring it back again. (There may be exceptions to this, where a side issue has suddenly aroused much interest.) Comments should normally be accepted only if they are relevant to the point at issue. Also, don't let the discussion deteriorate into a series of personal anecdotes. One or two may be acceptable if they encourage some children to talk who are normally silent. But then focus on one of the anecdotes and ask how it illustrates the point of the

exercise, or the topic that was being discussed. Used in this way, an anecdote can help to lead the inquiry in a new direction.

17. *Expressing disapproval*. If you disagree with a child's remark, or think it wrong, try to avoid showing this. Otherwise, the class will have the impression that you have a set of right answers which you want them to give. They will then treat the session as an ordinary lesson instead of an open inquiry. Rather than reject a comment, ask a further question about it—or ask other members of the class whether they agree.

18. *Outside interruptions*. For a good discussion there must be continuity, so the less interruptions the better. Outside noises can be very distracting. Try shutting the door, and bringing the children closer together. As for messengers, why not put a notice on the door: "Philosophy session in progress. Please do not interrupt." Finally, if at all possible, silence Big Brother (the intercom system), at least as a temporary measure.

Summary

A central aim of Philosophy for Children is to help children to think for themselves. This needs to be kept in mind at all stages of using the materials. It will be encouraged by allowing events to be determined by the class, as far as this is feasible. Here are a few examples of what this means in practice:

a) Reading out loud should be optional. A child may prefer to pass. In discussion, a child has the right to remain silent.

b) Always take the children's response to the reading as a starting point. (Don't begin with a fixed plan of what *you* want to discuss.)

c) During a discussion, or when using exercises, always be sensitive to an issue which catches the attention of the children, and be prepared to follow their lead.

d) When the class is feeling more at home with the process of discussion, some of the children may like to try the role of discussion leader for a particular exercise or topic. Allow the class to discuss the role of discussion leader (some people prefer the word "facilitator"). How does it differ from that of a participant?

e) From time to time, let the class discuss ways of improving what is going on, and let them comment on the success or otherwise of Philosophy for Children in your class.

f) When first introducing the class to philosophy, there is no harm in explaining at the outset what you are trying to achieve. Point out, if necessary, that the approach is a new one for you also. It is something that you and the class can explore together.

Managing Philosophical Discussions Using Self-Corrective "Name-Recorder" Procedures

Judy A. Kyle

Did we manage it that time? Did that discussion really count as a philosophical one—a discussion which is cumulative, which builds, and in which identifiable progress is made?[1] These are questions I wrestle with regularly as I work with the Philosophy for Children program at Edinburgh School in Montréal, Québec. Some discussions are clearly better than others; but are they truly philosophical? Are the students learning to see them as such? Sometimes it can be hard to tell.

While struggling to increase both a) the incidence of "truly" philosophical discussions, and b) the students' awareness of the special and demanding qualities of such discussions, I have come to realize that the success of the enterprise is not wholly dependent on the "art" of the teacher for there are many factors which can sabotage the efforts of even the best teachers. That is why we must consider "managing" philosophical discussions in quite a different sense: we must consider devising "management strategies."

Doing philosophy with many classes of students since 1980[2] has yielded a number of helpful management strategies which have grown out of our reflections on the quality of our own discussions.[3] I offer some of them here not so much in the belief that they represent any particular ideal,

for they may or may not be well-suited to other settings. Rather I hope this description will prompt others to write about what has worked best in their experience.

The procedures I will describe have been constructed out of our on-going exploration of ways to put into practice the fundamental principles of community inquiry.[4] My objective has been to develop ways of doing philosophy with children which respect the spontaneous dynamic that is characteristic of children's ways of thinking and being. What has emerged from our efforts, however, has been a disciplined approach.

When we started, we made procedural rules for ourselves which we thought would address problems we had identified as we progressed. At first the constraints were many as we concentrated on this or that aspect of our experience of trying to have productive philosophical discussions with up to thirty-three students. Gradually, though, because the procedures we had devised permitted us to be together in a way which serves the spirit of collaborative inquiry, we have been able to loosen up considerably. Ours is a process which we continue to construct together such that anything I write here will be a mixture of historical hindsight and revelation of the current state of our art. I can only say at this point that we have come a long way in the last ten years—and that we still have a way to go.

This paper is limited to an account of one important aspect of our process: the making of a self-corrective "name recorder" system for our discussions. This "system" consists of a set of mutually agreed-upon procedures for philosophical discussion and is continually subject to change as we continue our search for better ways to "manage it" more often.[5]

Name-recorder Procedures

Helping students to have productive philosophical discussions involves more than reading texts, doing relevant exercises and discussing "leading ideas" which catch their interest. It also involves more than just helping students to master the mechanics of the discussion form. Both are needed in order for students to acquire a concept of what it is to think and discuss philosophically.

Learning to engage in effective philosophical discussion is a complex process which takes time. It helps if some of that process can become procedural habit in a way which allows easy access to the discussion for everyone and which allows for uninterrupted time for participants both to think on their feet and to express their thoughts. Becoming adept at the "mechanics" of discussion provides students with a framework within which they are better able to concentrate on the philosophical dimension of their discussions and it has been our experience that such procedures add a comprehensiveness to our discussions which would otherwise be much more difficult to do.

One of the frustrations that has plagued our discussions from the beginning is that of being unable to find a comfortable procedure which would permit *everyone* (who so desired) to contribute to a discussion in an appropriate order. As the students learn to discuss effectively, traditional teacher-pupil exchanges become less appropriate resulting in problems such as how to decide who should be next to speak and how to have the students talk *with each other* without always having to go through the teacher.

There is also the concurrent problem of the distraction to themselves and others caused by enthusiastic hand-wavers. Once hands are up, to what extent are their owners merely waiting their turn and not listening carefully to the discussion? It is when the students' enthusiasm turns into impatience that this problem can become disruptive.

Management strategies we have devised which "help" involve the use of one or more "Name Recorders," procedures which we continually change as we wrestle with how best to handle the problem of who should speak when, to whom, for how long and how often. In this paper I will describe two variations on the use of name recorders. There are others, of course, and I am not recommending that *these* procedures be imported directly into other settings. On the *contrary*, what is important is that other communities *address their own* problems and come up with their *own* procedures. These are offered rather as examples of what it might look like for communities to work out their own strategies to help them have productive philosophical discussions. While we continue to search for *our* ultimate procedure, we use what we have worked out so far and we are convinced that our discussions are better than they would be without them.

In all the name recorder procedures described below, students have five response options when they have their turns to speak: 1) to say what they have to say, 2) to say "Pass" (no questions asked) if they change their minds for whatever reason; 3) to say "Forgot" if their thoughts have thoroughly escaped them and are unlikely to return; 4) to say "Come back to me" if, as very commonly happens, they have temporarily forgotten what they had to say; and 5) to say "Same as . . ." if their thoughts have already been expressed by previous speakers. All of these are positive responses for they help the discussion to move along without unproductive or repetitive delays.

In the case of "Come back to me," we take this to be a positive response because often the reason for "forgetting" one's own point is that it was displaced by concentrating on those of others in the discussion. In such cases, the recorders keep an eye on the person to come back to and, when signalled, give them the first available opportunity to speak.

The case of "Same as . . ." can be a difficult one for young children who often think that if someone else has the same idea that they must have "taken" or "copied" it—both unacceptable to them. Philosophically, however, a lot is going on when students can use "Same as . . ." appropriately. First they have to *have an idea* and *want to say it*; second, they have to be *listening to what others are saying*; third, they have to *compare* their own idea to the one they heard; fourth, they have to *make decisions* about how similar they are and the importance of any differences because in philosophy sometimes small differences are big; and fifth, they have to *choose to forego their turn* in the interests of not being repetitive. Students who use "Same as . . ." appropriately are therefore to be congratulated.

One Name-recorder

Originally we began with a single name-recorder, much the way adults might in business meetings. Under the one name-recorder system, if you want to say something, you have only to raise a finger as discretely as in an auction, and your name is recorded on a list. Participants are called on (one at a time and usually in the order in which their names were recorded) to ask questions, make comments, express their thoughts or have dialogues with others.[6]

This procedure worked reasonably well for a while. It certainly determined who would speak when, allowed reluctant speakers easy access to the air waves, and gave speakers an uninterrupted freedom to think on their feet and to articulate their thoughts. It wasn't long, however, before we

recognized a different problem: the list was too linear.

Although it was true that fairness and sequence were important with regard to *speakers*, we became aware that fairness and sequence also was important with regard to *ideas*. With only one recorder, the first speakers would express different and disconnected ideas since they couldn't know in advance what previous speakers were going to say. Sometimes those first speakers would express ideas which others would want to discuss immediately. If the name-recorder list was already long, they would have to wait a long time to speak and this was clearly counter-productive in terms of building on each others' ideas. And so we decided that a second name-recorder would help.

Two Name-recorders

Under the two name-recorder procedure we have two name-recorder positions which are located opposite each other in the circle so that it is clear to everyone which list is which. One position is for "New Points" recorders and the other is for "Comments" recorders.[7] Before the discussion begins, the community decides either the number of comments or the number of minutes which will be allowed for each new point before proceeding to the next person on the New Points list. These numbers (of comments or minutes) are flexible and can be revised at any time. Of the two, time seems to be the better alternative, since the number of "commenters" is variable (depending on how long each one takes) and therefore unpredictable. Another way to be flexible with both time and commenters is to allow them to be extended by group consensus, the idea being not to short-change any exchange of ideas if it is proving to be sustaining the interest of the community.

As the discussion begins, fingers go up and the New Points recorder jots down each person's name in order, using silent eye-signals to would-be speakers who can then relax and pay attention to the discussion knowing their turns will come. First-time speakers have priority, but otherwise people can contribute as often as they wish, time permitting.

The first person is invited to speak and is engaged in a clarifying dialogue with the discussion leader.[8] During this dialogue, those who wish to contribute to the discussion of this particular point indicate their wish to the Comments recorder by raising a finger until they receive an eye-signal that their names have been recorded. Discussion then proceeds with the people on the Comments list until such time as the number of people or the amount of time agreed upon beforehand is reached. If the discussion is particularly animated at that point, the leader asks if the group would like to pursue this line of inquiry or switch to a new point. Usually responses are spontaneous, immediate and clear and the discussion proceeds according to the wishes of the community.

An important advantage of having two name-recorders is that it ensures that appropriate attention is paid to each point *as it is raised* while at the same time both respecting the order in which the students indicated a desire to speak and making it easy for first-time speakers to get in on the discussion. A second important advantage is that this procedure features the aspect of building on others' ideas and makes that process visible to the students. A third important advantage has been that it requires students to determine whether what they have to say is a "new idea" or a "comment" on a point already made. This has important implications for listening, both for the contributors and for the other participants in the discussion. Philosophically, we have encountered how hard it can be to tell the difference between a "new" idea and one that is a subtle but important progression from a previous one.

With no name-recorders at all, discussions risk being dominated by those vocal enthusiasts who have little difficulty getting the floor—often at the expense of those who might be more reticent but who ought to have equal opportunity to participate should they so desire. With our original one-name-recorder system, the discussion could ricochet from speaker to speaker often minimizing the possibility for students to build on each others' ideas. A disadvantage we encountered using the two-name-recorder procedure was that quite often we would go to the Comments list very soon in the discussion and choose to prolong the discussion (*via* the Comments recorder) to the point where we would not return to the New Points list at all before time ran out. Even though this was by group consensus, and even though the discussions were philosophically productive, we were missing out on the New Point ideas and the students on that list often missed their turns.

"Rule of Two"

Collective reflection on these problems has resulted in another modification of the name-recorder procedure *back* to one name-recorder, but in a different form. We now use one name-recorder but a "rule of two" applies. This "rule of two," for lack of a better way to put it, means simply that when it is your turn, you can do two "things": you can introduce two "new points," make two "comments," have two "dialogues" or you can do any combination of two. The only reason for the restriction to two is time-related and we are flexible enough to deal with requests for more than two by group consensus and on a case by case basis.

"Priority to First-time Speakers"

Another improvement we added while revising our procedures this time, was to distinguish clearly between "first" and "second plus"-time speakers. In general the understanding is that you can have as many "seconds" as time will permit, but only *after* you've had each turn so that your name is only "actively" on the list once at a time.

All first-time speakers have a say before those on the "second plus" list.

In terms of the *order* of speakers, we decided that the "second plus" list would follow time-order (i.e. you would have your turn in the order your name went on the list) but that the first-time speaker list would not. The reason we did this is that very often the name-recorders would not be able to distinguish who went on the list first if, for example, it was an idea or topic which generated a lot of initial interest. We therefore record the names on the "first-time" list in the fastest possible way (consecutively around the circle) and leave it up to the name-recorders to choose *from* the list for who is next to speak, so that anyone could conceivably be "next." After discussing different possible bases for selection, we trust recorders not to pick only their friends or mostly colleagues of their own gender if that is important. Priority goes to students who only occasionally speak in discussions, or to those who didn't get their chance last time. The students seem to have amazing long-term recall of who has had how many turns when, and by and large they choose fairly. If not, the community makes use of the self-corrective procedures described below to resolve the problem.

An important advantage of the "rule of two" procedure is that it removes the restrictions on when new points and comments can be introduced while at the same time retaining the conceptual necessity for participants to distinguish between the two. In addition, this procedure permits the person whose turn is "next" to choose to comment on the point(s) made by preceding speakers. This gives a sense of immediacy to the discussion and the result is a process which feels much more "natural." Different patterns emerge in different discussions with some ranging "all over the map" and others settling on one particular idea which elicits a lot of contributions from others. Like a river, each discussion seeks its own course.

There are two important frustrations we encounter when using this procedure, however,

both of which I take to be signs that we are making progress. The first frustration is that students often have *more* than two things to say. This is especially true of the silent listeners who choose to come into the discussion just when time is running out and who have points to make which result in important insights or in a qualitative shift in direction. These are the students who listen carefully throughout and are able to put it all together in a kind of global way. They couldn't do what they do if it weren't for all the preceding points; thus they *build* on and *synthesize* their colleague's ideas. We need to hear *everything* they have to say when they have their turns. In practice this can be a relatively minor problem because such students (who are used to working collaboratively and democratically) simply state (often irresistibly) that they have more than two things to say and they are soon given the go-ahead by the community.

The second frustration is that the more experience the students have with this form of discussion, the better they become at having dialogues and the longer these dialogues last. The problem is not with the students involved in the dialogue, but with the others waiting their turns. There seems to be an ever-present tension between doing justice to *people* or to *ideas*. An important issue here is the degree to which the students are able to have "representative" dialogues—dialogues by a few *on behalf of* the many. The problem is that although the dialogues get longer, the time for hearing them does not. We don't always need *everyone* to have a separate say in order for a discussion to cover impressive territory; however, the students still have a need to express their *own* thoughts to the whole group in order to feel satisfied with the discussion. The difficulty for the teacher is that s/he has to be a mind-reader to know which upcoming comments and/or dialogues are "sacrifice-able" to prolonged dialogues between smaller numbers of students.

The only procedure we have found to address this (for now) is to limit the time of dialogues by using a countdown timer. Our usual time limit is two to three minutes although, as usual, it is flexible and subject to group consensus. What is important is not *how much time* a given dialogue has to proceed, but *that there will be an end*. It is not that the listeners are not interested in the prolonged dialogues; it is rather that they become worried that this dialogue will go on *without end* with the result that they won't have their own opportunities to speak. This can create an air of tension which can cause attention to be diverted from the content of the dialogues to procedural matters. Nevertheless, I take this to be a "good" problem because it means the students have progressed to the point where their dialogues are becoming substantive. If there are complaints of "boredom" it may be time to compliment them and to explain that it means rather that they have progressed to the challenge of dialogues which require more sustained concentration. Such explanations do not necessarily resolve the issue; however, they can help how the students feel about it.

Self-corrective Procedures

As a way of dealing creatively with some of the frustrations above, we have adopted three "legal" self-corrective ways to interrupt discussions: "Time out," "Read the list please," and "Point of information." These are important because they address our frustrations on-the-fly and they permit the discussion to retain its momentum while at the same time addressing the needs of the listening participants.

Time out. Originally called "Point of Order," we imported and adapted this procedure from Students' Council meeting procedures for use on occasions when we needed to interrupt the proceedings for procedural matters not related to the content of the discussion. This interruption procedure underwent a name change to "Time out" when it was introduced to very young children. The students seem to enjoy its game-like charac-

ter and will sometimes accompany the words with the appropriate hand gestures. The students know to say "Time out" only *between* speakers and only for matters of importance. They also know that too many Time outs can defeat the purpose of building an interesting discussion. Not to do a Time out when it is needed, however, can also defeat the purpose since frustrated participants find it increasingly difficult to follow attentively. When first introduced, or when first implementing a new procedure, Time outs happen often and sometimes counterproductively. However, that only lasts until people have a chance to try it out to see if it works. Once they see the degree to which it can interfere with and not help a discussion, they come to use it judiciously.

Read the list please. Probably the most important use of Time out is for participants to see if they are on the speakers' list because anticipating your turn to speak can divert your attention away from the discussion and can be the cause of considerable frustration. We have established a procedure to handle this which works well. Rather than have each individual student do a Time out each time s/he wondered when it would be his/her turn, instead one person will do a Time out and ask on behalf of everyone, "Could the recorder read the list please?" By doing it that way, everyone hears who is on the list and all omissions are dealt with in one Time out.

Other common uses of Time out include the following: problems with the way in which the discussion is proceeding; the nature of the name recorder's job or a problem with the way in which the recorders are doing the job; the disruptive behaviour of individual students; and problems of the discussion itself seeming to drift away from the question or becoming other than a philosophical discussion in someone's view. Once established as a procedure, Time outs are relatively rare and they serve our purposes well.

Point of Information. A second self-corrective interruption is for a listener-participant to say, "Point of Information" when s/he has a piece of *information* which s/he thinks might alter the course of the discussion in a relevant way. This one can be very difficult to distinguish from an informative comment which should "go through the list" instead. We use "Point of Information" when someone knows something we need to know *right now* in order for the discussion to proceed without going down a false trail. It is usually of the nature of a "fact" (as contrasted with an opinion or a possibility) which could be found in a dictionary, on a television documentary, or in one's own knowledge bank. Points of information are short and to the point and are intended to inform the dialogue in progress, not to divert it.

"Dialogue Partner Time"

Another practice we have instituted is that of each student having a randomly chosen "dialogue partner" for a term. The idea is for students to have *regular* and *frequent* opportunities to discuss with a colleague and to benefit from consistent exposure to another person's thoughts and thinking style.

Dialogue Partner Time. In whole-class discussions students will often make thought-provoking contributions which elicit immediate and spontaneous responses from the others. At such times we will take "Dialogue Partner Time" for the students to say what they think and then the discussion resumes. Students can do a Time Out to request Dialogue Partner Time at any point in a discussion; or the discussion leader can call for it whenever spontaneous comments "bubble up" in response to a particular point someone has made. A third way Dialogue Partner Time can be used is at regular intervals so that students know that "listening time" has a time limit at the end of which they will have opportunities to discuss the ideas they've been listening to with their partners. (The linguistic signal to do that is when the discussion leader addresses the class and says, "What do *you* think?") Out of these dialogues

come new ideas to add to the whole-class discussion (through the name-recorder list) and they often advance the large-group discussion in important ways.

Afterthoughts

These name-recorder procedures can be very helpful with their important advantages being their invisibility, their provision of easy access to air time, their provision of uninterrupted air time, and their fairness. All students can benefit, especially both those who might refrain from having to jump into a lively discussion by jumping on the words of others and those who need to talk less and listen more. With name-recorder procedures, reluctant contributors know that by merely raising a finger, in time their contributions will be solicited. They can still change their minds when they have their turns, so it is relatively safe and encouraging.

Occasionally the more vocal students become impatient with such controls so every now and then we have "open" or "free" discussions in which the procedures do not apply. What happens then can be quite interesting. When a free-for-all breaks out, as it often will when everyone is competing for air space, the students become impatient with each other and they soon revert to the controls with added understanding as to why they are there. At such times they will sometimes instinctively respect the rules or they will request that others do so simply because they recognize that it is a better way. When that doesn't happen, the discussion can degenerate while they vent their frustrations instead. Then too they are usually quite happy to return to the more controlled format.

One of the biggest advantages of these procedures is that they give power to the *students* who can, in effect, run their own discussions (in terms of both form and content). Students are visibly in charge of name-recorder lists and, depending on their choice of leadership style, even of the discussion itself. This frees the teacher to concentrate on the philosophical dimensions of the proceedings and to guide the discussions in accordance with principles of collaborative philosophical inquiry.

Name-recorder procedures may help but they are by no means perfect. As it is a predetermined list, it can lend an artificial quality to the discussion and mitigate against a more natural and dynamic flow of dialogue. However, coupled with the group's self-corrective attention to its own discussion procedures, they can be very useful tools for collaborative philosophical inquiry.

* * *

To describe these name recorder procedures one after another and to call them "management strategies" is perhaps to invite protest for there can be something inherently disagreeable about the very notion of a "managed" discussion. (One might even wonder if it is a contradiction in terms.) Our experience has been, however, that these measures help much more than they hinder. Because the students contribute to their formulation, they not only have a stake in seeing that they work, they also credit themselves when they do. Although these particular strategies may or may not work for others, they do work for us because they are ours. They grow out of our experience together and we adjust and refine them as we go along. Reflecting on our own discussions and devising ways to make them better, is a constructive, creative and often a highly philosophical process. It is this process—more than any specific strategy—which is to be recommended.

Notes

1. Lipman, M., Sharp, A. M. and Oscanyan, F. (1980). *Philosophy in the classroom*. Philadelphia: Temple University Press, p. 104.

2. The IAPC Philosophy for Children program at Edinburgh started with one class doing *Harry Stottlemeier's discovery* (Lipman, M., 1982) and has grown over the years to the point where, with five trained teachers, we have worked with all the programs in the elementary curriculum providing opportunities for all Edinburgh students to do philosophy at varying times, starting as early as Grade One.

3. These reflections take place during what I have called "Discussion Discussions" during which the topic for discussion is—our own discussions.

4. Lipman, et al. (1980). *Philosophy in the classroom*. Philadelphia: Temple University Press and Lipman, M. (1991). *Thinking in education*. Cambridge: Cambridge University Press.

5. This description of the use of "name recorders" as a self-corrective set of procedures for managing philosophical discussions is only one aspect (albeit an important one) of a complex enterprise which would take a lot more space to discuss adequately. A more complete discussion would situate this approach relative to important principles of community inquiry and would include other dimensions of what it is to engage in collaborative philosophical inquiry such as: physical arrangements of the class; useful "classroom management" tools; the use of fictitious characters to protect the children's privacy and to ensure that discussions, while dealing with matters highly personal are about issues and not about individual people; dialogue and discussion procedures; different discussion formats; useful linguistic discussion "moves"; the role (if any) of discussion leaders; and the important dimension of "thinking-in-writing" as a vehicle both for thinking for oneself and with others.

6. When students in my classes say, "I would like to have a *dialogue* with . . .," we all know that they mean a specific form of interaction which we practise regularly in our discussions.

7. For very young students, the name-recorder procedures work best if there are two students to do the job: the "watcher" tells the "writer" whose names to write down, and the "writer" reads the list when so requested and announces who is next to speak. If the students are very young—able to read but not yet write each others' names quickly—we have managed to work this nicely by having handy a numbered list of the students' names arranged alphabetically by first name. The recorders then record the would-be speaker's number which is much faster for them.

8. The discussion "leader" can be the teacher or another student depending on the procedures adopted by that community.

Controlling the Classroom Clamor: A Few Techniques to Facilitate Philosophical Discourse

Ruth E. Silver

No matter how clearly the goal of reasoned, respectful exchange and development of ideas may appear to us, frequent stumbling blocks may keep us from reaching it as readily as we would wish, or, to change the metaphor, there are all too many slips between the cup of philosophical issues that attracts us, and the lips that seek to discourse upon them. In his article, "Some Factors Influencing the Success of Philosophical Discussion in the Classroom," (*Analytic Teaching*, Volume 3, Number 1) Michael Whalley points out some kinds of behavior which may make such discussion difficult, and suggests some rules to help provide conditions for successful philosophical communication in the classroom.

We need to find ways to provide chances for all the children who want to speak, and also to encourage giving attention to the person who is speaking. Furthermore, we want to have the discussion move among the children rather than exclusively through the teacher. Letting kids just talk is rarely successful—especially at first when philosophy is a new venture. The children aren't practiced in listening to each other. Even if they try, they don't know how to get clues from each other as to when to take a turn. There is a tendency for many private conversations to spring up, resulting in bedlam.

Whalley suggests a few rules which may keep the conversation orderly and provide the basis for genuine discussion. Rules can give a framework for discussion. Beyond the rules, however, some positive steps may be taken to help direct children's attention to each other, and to make for a flow of discussion among all the participants. I would like to suggest a few such techniques.

(1) One way of avoiding having teacher intervention after every comment by a student is to have each speaker call on the next. The teacher, having asked a question or directed attention to some topic, asks for comment and calls on someone. That person, having spoken, calls on someone from among those with raised hands. The latter in turn looks around for people wanting to carry the discussion further. It's true that one comment may be irrelevant to the preceding, and that the teacher may need to join in frequently, to point that out. Or he/she may want to note statements that are similar, or to ask someone to respond to a statement that challenged his/hers, and so on. Still, the process is a first step towards moving the teacher from the center of the stage to a position as one among the group. And this procedure does direct the child's attention to the other children—even if only to hear when the speaker is finishing so one can get one's hand up quickly.

The function of criteria in education

We see only one way to avoid the seeming dilemma of guiding pupil thinking without indoctrination: *conscious adoption of criteria upon which judgments shall be based*. This is a very simple device, yet an effectual one. A criterion (note the singular form) is defined by the American College Dictionary as "a standard of judgment or of criticism, an established rule or principle for testing anything." Whenever a class has before it a matter that calls for judgment on its part, the teacher should make sure that the judgmental basis is clear.

How does employment of consciously recognized criteria enable a teacher to criticize and guide student thinking, yet avoid indoctrination, and in so doing achieve democratic guidance? Simply by subjecting whatever ideas or proposals a *teacher* presents to the same bases for acceptance or rejection as any *student's* ideas or proposals. What is sauce for the goose is sauce for the gander, equality of obligation to abide by adopted decisions. This means, of course, that a pupil can "guide" a teacher as well as the teacher guide a pupil. But what more should a teacher want or expect? If *what* is right rather than *who* is right is the objective, is not truth or rectitude to be recognized wherever it is found?. . . . To find what kind of conclusions any given set of criteria logically requires or implies sheds convincing light on the desirability (or undesirability) of the criteria themselves.

It should be noted that a criterion is not a rule for *behavior,* such as a law establishing a speed limit. It is a basis for judgment; in the case of a law on speeding, the law serves as a basis for judging what is legal and what is illegal speed and thus can be used as a criterion; but the law as such is a rule for behavior, not a criterion for judgment.

—Ernest E. Bayles, *Pragmatism in Education* (New York: Harper and Row, 1966) pp. 83-87.

(2) The instructional manuals accompanying the philosophical novels about Harry Stottle-meier and his friends contain numerous exercises to help children think and talk about the issues raised in the books. When a teacher plans to use one of these exercises, the questions (statements, examples, or whatever) may be written on separate slips of paper and handed out to individual children. Then each child is responsible for introducing the question (statement, etc.) into the discussion. The child might read his/her slip of paper and then comment on it, or after reading might call on someone else (anyone who wants to join in) to comment. If there's further discussion of that particular statement, the child who read it aloud could be responsible for leading that discussion. If the questions should best be used in numerical order, it will be up to the teacher to number the slips and then to ask for #1, #2, and so on.

In a similar class plan, the exercise can be duplicated as a whole, with a copy for each student. After the class has had a few minutes to look over and think about the exercise, one child reads the first statement or question aloud and calls on someone to respond. The latter, after commenting, calls on a third person, who responds and then reads aloud the next item, and so on. It can be stipulated that no one gets a second term.

These plans may seem somewhat artificial, but they do lend variety of approach. And, though the teacher may need to join in frequently, introduction of the questions is still by the students, and the attention of the others will be directed to their classmate.

(3) As the children become more involved in philosophical ideas, and more accustomed to classroom discussion, they can participate increasingly in directing the course of that discussion. When there is a game, small group activity,

Education as Learning from Oneself

If one who hears me has personally perceived these things and become aware of them, he does not learn them from any words, but recognizes them from the images that are stored away within himself. If, however, he has had no sense knowledge of them, he clearly believes rather than learns by means of the words.

Now. when there is question of those things which we perceive by the mind—that is, by means of the intellect and by reason we obviously express in speech the things which we behold immediately in that interior light of truth which effects enlightenment and happiness in the so-called inner man. And at the same time if the one who hears me likewise sees those things with an undivided eye, he knows the matter of which I speak by his own contemplation, not by means of my words. Hence, I do not teach even such a one, although I speak what is true and he sees what is true. For he is taught not by my words, but by the realities themselves made manifest to him by God revealing them to his inner self. Thus, if he were asked, he could also give answers regarding these things. What could be more absurd than to think that he is taught by my speech, when even before I spoke he could explain those same things, if he were asked about them?

As for the fact that, as often happens, one denies something when he is asked about it, but is brought around by further questions to affirm it, this happens by reason of the weakness of his vision, not permitting him to consult that light regarding the matter as a whole. He is prompted to consider the problem part by part as questions are put regarding those same parts that constitute the whole, which originally he was not able to see in its entirety. If in this case he is led on by the words of the questioner, still it is not that the words teach him, but they represent questions put to him in such a way as to correspond to his capacity for learning from his own inner self.

Teachers do not claim, do they, that their own thoughts are perceived and grasped by the pupils, but rather the branches of learning that they think they transmit by speaking? For who would be so absurdly curious as to send his child to school to learn what the teacher thinks? But when they have explained, by means of words, all those subjects which they profess to teach, and even the science of virtue and of wisdom, then those who are called pupils consider within themselves whether that has been said is true. This they do by gazing attentively at that interior truth, so far as they are able. Then it is that they learn; and when within themselves they find that what has been said is true, they give praise, not realizing that they are praising not so much teachers as the person taught—provided that the teachers also know what they are saying. But people deceive themselves in calling persons "teachers" who are not such at all, merely because generally there is no interval between the time of speaking and the time of knowing. And because they are quick to learn internally following the prompting of the one who speaks, they think they have learned externally from the one who was only a prompter.

—St. Augustine, from *The Teacher*, Chapter 12 and 14.

or written exercise, insofar as possible children should be involved in reading directions and starting things off. After some months, when the children have been working together for a time, the whole direction of a game may be given to a student who will have had a chance to read the directions beforehand. Of course, the teacher is on hand to help out when needed. But the competence of children, their responsibility for the functioning of the class, and their participation has been emphasized.

When the purposes and procedures of the philosophy class are becoming familiar to the children, individual students or pairs of students can be given responsibility for leading discussion of whole exercises, or of groups of questions. This, of course, would require some preparation in a meeting of teacher and student-leader to be sure the students understand the directions of the activity or the words of the questions. And the teacher then has the opportunity to remind the children of the desirable course of a discussion— that there be many participants, common attention to a set of topics, no criticism of persons, attentive listening to the speaker, and so on. After the student-leaders have finished, it would be good to have them consider how well the discussion went. There may be a private conference with the teacher, or the whole class may have comments on the day's proceedings. Whether the young pedagogues may safely be left to the criticism of their classmates, the teacher can judge. Over the course of time, it should be possible to give everyone who would like one a turn to do this student-leading, especially if the children take on the responsibility in pairs.

(4) In some classes, the matter of letting everyone have a fair share of turns to speak may become a serious problem. Where the children readily become involved in philosophy and are especially eager to join in the discussion, those who are less insistent may feel that they are being left out—that the most vigorous hand wavers, the loudest exclaimers, the most violent bouncers-up-and-down, are getting all the attention and

being recognized more frequently—as well they may. Or, in classes where there are some especially talkative and long-winded children, others may feel that the time has been unfairly monopolized. Of course, as Whalley notes, it would be very difficult to make a clear rule stating how much talk is too much. But the matter can be handled to some extent by limiting the number of opportunities to talk.

Two techniques invented by teachers I've worked with have involved limiting opportunities for a second chance until everyone who wants one has had a first. In one case, the teacher had heard of resentful mutterings that certain children had done all the talking and that others never had a chance. The teacher discussed the matter with the children, and they agreed that he should keep a record of who'd spoken and call on no one a second time if there was anyone still waiting a first turn. This worked well: the children were happy; the teacher was able to keep the record without spending much time on it; anyone too shy or uncertain to demand a chance to speak was asked if she/he had a comment: the resentful mutterings ended. Of course it was a technique that was, and was intended to be, only temporary. In a short time, the group came to feel that the whole discussion belonged to everyone, and record keeping could be discarded.

Another teacher had some vociferous kids in a group that tended as a whole to be rather rowdy. She tried a procedure that involved one of the children (a different one for each class) in the attempts to keep kids from calling out or from monopolizing the discussion. As the children entered the classroom, each was given a card—all with the same identifying color or mark for that day. When someone wanted to speak, he/she raised the card in the air. And as each child got a turn, the monitor took the card away. As long as anyone had a card and wanted to speak, those who'd given up their cards weren't called on.

Both of these procedures are of course artificial and rather confining, but they can be helpful in establishing habits of sharing time and of thinking before one speaks.

(5) As the children speak more, the teacher should be speaking less. But the habits of pedagogy can be hard to break. Especially at the start of a philosophy course, the teacher may find it very difficult indeed to let the ideas come from the children, and to wait if need be until they do indeed speak out. The teacher who kept a roll-book record of speakers felt he had to institute some control over his own possible tendencies to monopolize the discussion. To indicate that he was one among the members of the group, though he was its leader, he sat on a high stool. When he was going to say something (other than to call on a student) he stood up. That acted as a signal to the children, and also as a reminder to him. He was in a sense acknowledging in a very visible way that he too should be limited in the amount and frequency of talking that he could do.

(6) If all else fails—give up until another day. Early on in the school year, when students are just becoming acquainted with the purposes and procedures of philosophical discussion—when their skill in developing ideas is yet limited and each one's insistence on getting a word in is still dominant—it may be well to use only part of any class period for discussion. It is easier to hold a group together for a shorter time—to remind them of the rules or procedures agreed upon, and then to keep going only so long as most of the children are following them. Rather than getting into a situation where one must nag at the children with frequent reminders of behavior expected, one can shift to another kind of activity. Reading, games, or written exercises can be used for the rest of the time set aside for philosophy. Written work need not be composition, if the age or ability of the students make that difficult or impossible. Children can make pictures, write short answers, choose (by circling or underlining) which answer is best. The possibilities are numerous. Discussion in small groups is another possibility. Working in groups of 4 to 6 may give the children desired turns—and they will certainly feel free to

tell one another if one of them is monopolizing the talk.

(7) The provision of frequent opportunities or even requirements for written work seems to me most worthwhile, quite beyond its use as an alternative when orderly discussion proves impossible for the moment. I am an enthusiastic proponent of discussion, for many of the values it has: all children are on an equal footing, despite differences in reading skills; sharing of ideas leads to broader understanding, to more critical interpretation, to the analysis and development of ideas beyond what any individual in the group might be capable of; habits of attention to and respect for others cannot be developed in solitude. For these reasons and others, I do feel that discussion is a major part of the best program of philosophy for children. Still I would like to urge here the values that some kinds of writing may add to the program.

For one, if some exercises, sets of questions, etc., are given to the children to be thought about individually before class discussion, every child is pushed to think about each one of the questions or examples and to try to decide on his/her answer. In subsequent discussion, these answers are considered and analyzed, criticized, amplified, defended, and so on. But there may well be more possible answers suggested if the children have first considered the problems individually.

After a discussion, children may be asked to write their reactions in a log of some kind. Children who, for some reason (whether time, timidity, course of discussion or whatever) were left with thoughts that they really wanted to express, have an opportunity to write them down. This writing can be for each child alone, or for the whole group. In a log, children might write their reaction to the day's talk, or something they'd wanted to say, or something they'd concluded. Anything interesting and in some way or other pertinent to philosophy discussions would be appropriate for the log.

Another possibility would be a philosophy bulletin board. Under a heading, "Something I

On the exemplary role of the teacher

But learning to think is not merely learning how to judge, to interpret and to use information; it is learning to recognize and enjoy the intellectual virtues. How does a pupil learn disinterested curiosity, patience, intellectual honesty, exactness, industry, concentration and doubt? How does he acquire a sensibility to small differences and the ability to recognize intellectual elegance? How does he come to inherit the disposition to submit to refutation? How does he, not merely learn the love of truth and justice, but learn it in such a way as to escape the reproach of fanaticism?.... Learning, then, is acquiring the ability to feel and to think, and the pupil will never acquire these abilities unless he has learned to listen for them and to recognize them in the conduct and utterances of others.... For "teaching by example," which is sometimes dismissed as an inferior sort of teaching, generating inflexible knowledge because the rules of what is known remain concealed, is emancipating the pupil from the half utterances of rules by making him aware of a concrete situation. And in imitating the example he acquires, not merely a model for the particular occasion, but the disposition to recognize everything as an occasion. It is a habit of listening for an individual intelligence at work in every utterance that may be acquired by imitating a teacher who has this habit. And the intellectual virtues may be impaired only by a teacher who really cares about them for their own sake and never stoops to the priggishness of mentioning them. Not the cry, but the rising of the wild duck impels the flock to follow him in flight.

—Michael Oakeshott, *"Learning and Teaching"* in R. S. Peters, ed., *The Concept of Education* (London: Routledge & Kegan-Paul, 1967) pp. 174–176.

really wanted to say . . ." or some such, students might have an opportunity to pin up a short statement. In fact, even before children can write, they might have the opportunity to ask the teacher to write a sentence or two for them. Of course it must be understood that no personal attacks or negative comments about other individuals belong on such a public space.

(8) Finally, in this grab-bag of suggested techniques for dealing with or for avoiding some typical problems, I would suggest that the children themselves be involved in critical reflection on the course of the discussions. This can be done in different ways. Sometimes at the end of a class the teacher might leave a few minutes to have the whole group comment on how that day's discussion went. Or the teacher might start with: "We seemed to me to be having some problems with the discussion today, Did you notice that? In what way? Why do you suppose that happened? What can we do about it?" Or on other (one may hope frequent) occasions: "We had some splendid discourse today. Did you notice that? In what way? Why do you suppose that happened? What can we do to make it happen often?"

At times one child might be asked to be an observer for the day. If rules have been agreed on, the observer is asked to take notice of the adherence to or disregard of the rules: did two or more children speak at once? Were comments relevant? Was personal criticism avoided?

When children are working in small groups, they can be asked to consider how leaders were chosen, conclusions reached, or whatever were the tasks for the day. In the small group, children are likely to be more acutely aware of what each individual did or said.

Of course, in all these forms of class self-evaluation, criticism of individuals, even mention of individual names, is to be avoided. Those who talk incessantly, make rude comments, or turn their backs and look out the window, will (we hope) recognize themselves from the bare description without mention of a name.

No doubt other techniques would be—have been—devised to help the course of discussion to run in as lively but unhindered fashion as possible. I look forward to reading the suggestions of others—teachers, trainers, professors—who are working in the field. For the techniques suggested here, I express my appreciation to various teachers in districts where I have helped to introduce philosophy for children: to the teachers in Hillsborough, in Red Bank and Shrewsbury and Atlantic Highlands, in Wallingford and in Swarthmore, whose eagerness to help their students develop the skills for worthwhile philosophical discussion has led all of us to develop and to share varied paths to the common goal.

The Ethical and Social Responsibilities of Philosophy Teachers

Elias Baumgarten

Philosophy teachers have become increasingly concerned with professional ethics, particularly medical, legal, and business ethics. However, they have not given similar attention to the ethical issues associated with their own profession, though important moral issues do arise in the teaching of philosophy. A major reason for this is that philosophy teaching has not even been recognized to exist as a profession. Much has been written about the professional responsibilities of philosophers, but I would like to present a case for recognizing the *teaching* of philosophy as a distinct professional activity, one with its own purposes and obligations. Moreover, I will claim that philosophy teachers, as distinct from philosophers, have a special public responsibility to communicate philosophical ideas to their fellow citizens and to help them formulate reasoned positions for themselves. Finally, I will defend a neutral, non-advocacy role for the philosophy teacher as part of a caring, professional relationship with students.[1]

I

Professional ethics applies only to professions, so it is necessary first to consider what is required for an activity to be considered professional. In her article, "Philosophy as a Profession," Alison Jaggar includes among the

elements of professionalism the requirements of expert knowledge and a period of training, social importance, and the maintenance of standards by those who are already established.[2] On these grounds medicine is unquestionably a profession, and it will be helpful for us to use it as a model in order to see how moral assessment of a profession may take place.

When we discuss medical ethics, we still find applicable the Socratic dictum that no craft or profession should seek its own advantage but should benefit those who are subject to it.[3] We employ this principle when we condemn a physician who uses an experimental technique without the patient's consent, when a more reliable treatment is available. Such a doctor's actions are unprofessional and immoral, and this is so regardless of the very real benefits that might accrue from the experiment, not only for the doctor's research but possibly for many more patients than just the one presently under treatment. Nor does our condemnation imply that medical research is an inappropriate role for physicians. We might easily concede that research, including research that requires human experimentation, complements physicians' therapeutic work and enhances their value to their patients. We blame such doctors because, in their role as doctors, their primary responsibility is to their patients, not to the community of medical researchers or even to future victims of disease in general.

The ethical case against the freely-experimenting doctor is persuasive because we recognize that "medicine" actually encompasses more than one profession: there is the activity of the researcher who is committed to scientific investigation, and there is also the work of the physician whose project is to use medical knowledge to treat particular patients who have particular diseases. Though one person may assume both roles, the clinical practice of medicine is a distinct profession with its own imperatives.

My contention is that, in important respects, the philosophy teacher's role parallels that of the physician. Whereas the medical researcher and the philosopher are engaged in inquiry that does not, in principle at least, require any other person, the activities of the physician and the philosophy teacher *conceptually* require the presence, respectively, of patients and students. Moreover, the Socratic imperative addressed to professions generally, that they benefit those subject to them," applies in both instances, and I think a consideration of this principle will help to define the distinctive responsibilities of the philosophy teacher.

The Socratic precept emphasizes that professional activity exists in a social context and that professionals have obligations towards at least some segment of the community. Applying this maxim to our profession, we can say that the teaching of philosophy should benefit *students*. We encounter most of our students in our classrooms, but we also act as teachers, communicating with students, when we participate in community forums or offer commentaries for the media. So I would include among the "students" whom our profession should benefit all those who do not share our professional training in philosophy, and we are teaching when we communicate with this audience. By way of contrast, we may learn from our colleagues, but we are not, in a professional context, their students; and when we publish our own work for our peers to read, we are not acting in the role of philosophy teachers. On this view, then, philosophy teaching necessarily relates to the larger public in a way that professional philosophizing does not. I would like to discuss that public responsibility and then consider an implication that this view of philosophy teaching has for a classroom practice.

II

Philosophers often wish to see philosophy exert a greater influence in the world but are uncertain how to bring this about. In including all lay people among the philosophy teacher's potential students, I am accepting the Socratic notion that philosophy can improve ordinary citizens. But it is a mistake to think that the expert skills of research, analysis, and argumentation held by the professional philosopher are sufficient for this essentially different task. The communication of philosophy to the public does require these skills to a high degree, but it requires other capacities as well, and many even outstanding philosophers are not concerned to develop them. Those of us employed in universities who wish also to meet the social responsibilities of teaching will need to develop professional skills beyond those generally recognized in the scholarly community.

Academic philosophers do express concern over philosophy's weak impact, but their failure to recognize the distinctive purposes and responsibilities of teaching is the cause of much difficulty. Philosophy professors are particularly uncertain whether their authority qualifies them to provide others with answers to the world's great questions. They sense that those who do philosophical research have a special responsibility either to propose solutions to ethical and political problems or to offer answers that will provide some respite from the anguish that people suffer when they confront life's mysteries. Edward Regis, for example, regrets that "philosophy has all but abdicated its proper role of provider to man of objective values and a concep-

On teaching philosophy irresponsibly

In my understanding of it, philosophy has no claim to be edifying or doctrinal. Its primary mission is to inquire into the way things are, and the teacher's mission, like Socrates, is to get his own thinking as straight as he can. I am not convinced that an original thinker is a better teacher than one who has no distinctive philosophy. He may be but only if he sternly represses the temptation to indoctrinate his students with his views. If he has his mind made up on most important issues, he is likely to make only disciples and followers, not students of philosophy. . . .

Those teachers who make disciples of students are morally irresponsible, for they transform the essence of philosophy into something alien.

—from J. Glenn Gray, "The Moral Responsibilities of Teachers of Philosophy."

tual framework by which he can make some sense of existence."[4] But others, like Alison Jaggar, object to the idea that philosophers should assume the role of moral authorities, fearing that others would then be discouraged "from taking seriously their own ability to engage in what should be the central project of every human life, deciding how [to] live." Jaggar claims, moreover, that "to accept one's philosophy on the authority of another is the ultimate form of alienation."[5]

Viewed in these terms, one might cynically conclude that there is no way that philosophers can improve lay citizens: either philosophers deprive citizens of their freedom to make their own decisions or they abandon the masses to all the fads and irrational whims to which untrained minds are thought to be susceptible.

This view may not be far off the mark. For philosophers to communicate with the public, in

their role as creative philosophers, may be impossible. If the activity of the philosopher is to pursue the truth using all the knowledge and analytic skills one has, then it is unreasonable to expect this activity to be shared, without being compromised, in an undergraduate classroom, a Rotary Club hall, or a local underground newspaper. To concede that philosophers cannot philosophize with lay people is only to grant what is accepted in every other field of learning, that one with no training cannot evaluate the work of a professional who, by definition, has expert knowledge and has undergone an extensive period of preparation. If our concern, then, is to see the benefits of philosophy extended to our students in universities and in the general population, we must recognize the futility of urging contemporary philosophers to present their insights in language that everyone can understand. Nor can the gulf between the professional philosopher and the ordinary citizen be bridged by insisting that philosophers "return to a concern for enduring human issues" (though some surely do need that admonition.) Our romantic conception of the past notwithstanding, Aristotle and Descartes did not philosophize with the masses any more than Quine does. Their work and that of Kant, Hegel, Husserl, and Ryle *does* discuss critical human problems, but it is still inaccessible to most people who lack previous philosophical training, just as even the finest and most "relevant" scientific research cannot be understood without the requisite background.

It is the project, not of the philosopher *qua* philosopher, but of the philosophy teacher (who may also be a philosopher) to communicate the ideas of the great works undiminished and to show how they may be interpreted, analyzed, and criticized in relation to areas of universal human concern. Exposed directly to a philosophical text, most citizens will react as they might to an article in a medical journal; namely, with indifference, incomprehension, or uncritical acceptance. In none of these cases has the audience engaged in philosophical activity. Even if philosophers *could* provide people with "a conceptual framework by which [they] can make some sense of existence," they would not be offering them philosophy, but only a creed or a doctrine. But when philosophy *teachers* communicate the work of the great philosophers, their central goal should not be to exhort or persuade but to help others develop the ability to formulate reasoned positions of their own, either as a guide to action or as a response to wonder. Their skills will include the ability to formulate provocative questions, to perceive and explain the philosophical underpinnings of popular opinions, and to listen sensitively in order to discern the guiding concerns and the presuppositions of students. The activity of teaching, then, is distinguishable both from political advocacy and from philosophical inquiry itself. When philosophy teachers are acting *qua* teachers, their arguments may happen to alter the convictions of others or may lead to insights for themselves, but these should never be their central objectives.

The work of philosophy teachers is thus a form of service to others, and it is open to ethical assessment according to the degree to which it benefits students, "those who are subject to it." I have claimed that these students should include persons outside as well as within the university and that the teacher serves as an intermediary who conveys the professional and often technical work of philosophers to unprofessional citizens. On this view it is precisely because philosophy is a profession that the profession of philosophy teaching is needed.

However, this formulation presents us with a dilemma: the practice of philosophy requires training and expertise, yet it is of universal importance and should not be reserved for only the elite few who are so trained. It is noteworthy that democratic government confronts a similar difficulty: only a few people are ever truly well informed, yet everyone is thought entitled to participate in deciding complex issues of monumental importance. Plato, for one, considered the

incapacity of the masses for knowledge to be an insurmountable problem of democracy. He did not shrink from recommending a society containing what Jaggar calls "the ultimate form of alienation," that of accepting one's philosophy on the authority of another. But an ideal of a free and democratic society is to overcome this form of alienation and to allow all persons the dignity of choosing their own beliefs. A philosophy teacher who respects that dignity but who also values reasoned over random opinion has a special role to play in helping democracy approach its ideal. Making everyone a professional philosopher is not possible, of course. But neither would it be desirable, because philosophers are usually specialized in their research and not always concerned or able to connect their work explicitly either to the work of others who have different specialties or to urgent personal and political issues. Philosophy teachers must draw these connections and attempt to interest as many people as possible in philosophical reflection.

Though philosophy teachers cannot offer others a creed to live by, they do have a unique role to play in helping people confront personal issues of the most fundamental kind. Everyone faces the fundamental choice of either developing the ability to interpret his or her own adult experience or of being enslaved to the interpretations of others. And there is no lack of ideologues vying for each person's acquiescence: advertisers, politicians, editorialists, popular psychologists, the clergy, and even musicians, painters, and architects all present partial or total world views for our acceptance—blatantly or subtlety, manipulatively or sincerely, consciously or unconsciously. The proper role of the philosophy teacher *qua* philosophy teacher is not to join the competition but to help uncover hidden assumptions and to explore implications, in order that others may draw more reasoned conclusions themselves. In doing so, the teaching of philosophy will "benefit those subject to it" both by respecting the dignity of individuals in the free ordering of their lives and by promoting more rational and democratic decision-making in society.

III

The philosophy teacher, as conceived here, is not an advocate of particular substantive positions, and this has important implications for classroom practice. In addressing these issues, I have in mind the actual situation that we face in colleges today, where the relationship of teacher to student includes grading and other forms of evaluation that will affect students' prospects for success in a competitive society. It may be that another kind of university in another kind of society would allow a more humane teacher-student relationship and a more desirable conception of academic ethics. But my defense of a non-advocacy role for philosophy teachers takes as a given the context within which we now work.

A strong criticism that is often made of this conception of teaching philosophy is that neutrality on a teacher's part leads to relativism and cynicism. Students and ordinary citizens, it is argued, have a right to expect those trained in philosophy to come to some conclusions, but if all they do is point up arguments and assumptions, then people will come to believe that all argument is rationalization and that no opinion is better than another.[6]

My answer is two-fold. First, the position of neutrality is recommended not for the philosopher but for the philosophy teacher, and this represents a significant distinction between the two activities. Philosophers do take positions and argue for them, but, as I have indicated, this has not made works like Hegel's *Phenomenology of Mind* instructive to the average person. My argument is only that there needs to be a profession specifically devoted to conveying the content and spirit of philosophical inquiry to non-professionals without any overt or hidden partisan agenda. Without such a profession, the ideas of philosophers may get transmitted, by journalists and

popular writers for example, but often with gross distortions.[7]

Second, the solution to cynicism that is envisioned by the critic of neutrality, having people directly confront the opinions of philosophy teachers, is workable only if those people are isolated from any opposing views. The student of philosophy who ventures beyond his or her first professor and is exposed to reasoned argument for opposing positions may be more likely than ever to conclude that any belief can be equally well supported with reasons, especially if each professor claims to have knowledge of the correctness of his or her position.

For a philosophy teacher to present all available arguments but no personal conclusions is only to convey the disappointing truth, that there is no absolute certainty on enduring philosophical questions worthy of discussion. To explore this claim in detail is, of course, far beyond the scope of this paper. But we know that rational arguments can be used to support opposing positions when each starts from different premises, and philosophy teachers may be doing well to unveil a previously hidden presupposition, even when they are unable to demonstrate its truth or falsity. The most contrived and least honest position a philosophy teacher could take would be to attempt to counter students' skepticism of reason by claiming that rational argument has absolutely resolved particular philosophical questions. Philosophical inquiry is, of course, futile if reason has no efficacy, but it is also foreclosed if the truth has already been found and is not open to further question. There may be certain "ultimate presuppositions" which reason is powerless to affirm or deny, and a recognition of this possibility by students may be a healthy antidote to the intemperate self-assurance that can develop in one who first becomes acquainted with the powers or argument. (Ironically, this is often a self-assurance in the truth of relativism itself.)

Moreover, the philosophy teacher should not acquiesce in the common belief that philosophy is to be deemed worthwhile only if it provides demonstrable solutions to theoretic problems. Beyond whatever clarification it may provide, rational inquiry and philosophical questioning are, like the arts, forms of creative human expression, and the teacher who is able to help others satisfy their natural sense of wonder is benefiting them just as a teacher of dance or creative writing improves the powers of personal expression in those whom he or she instructs. Being unable to display the "absolutely beautiful" dance or poem (whatever that would mean) is not likely to result either in student cynicism or in the conviction that one work of art must be as beautiful as any other. The disappointment that is experienced by many students of philosophy may be traceable to the exaggerated claims often made on its behalf, and the philosophy teacher who feels compelled to assuage that disappointment with final solutions would do well to heed Bertrand Russell:

> Philosophy is to be studied, not for the sake of any definite answers to its questions, since no definite answers can, as a rule, be known to be true, but rather for the sake of the questions themselves.[8]

The neutral philosophy teacher is also criticized for adopting a contrived and even cowardly and inhumane attitude towards students. Hugh Wilder contrasts the neutral attitude of "liberal tolerance" which emphasizes the students' process of reasoning with a "caring, humane relationship" wherein a teacher will be concerned that students reach particular conclusions, will consequently argue for the truth of particular positions, and will finally give a lower grade to the student paper that opposes those positions. Liberal tolerance, he writes,

> is a cover for cowardice because it encourages teachers to not deal with students as whole people. As professional teachers, we are often urged to deal only with parts of our students— the parts learning philosophy. We are cautioned against entering into full human relationships with students, with the admonition that to do so would be unprofessional. Refusing to care about what my students believe—being tolerant of all

---

On the need for objectivity in teaching

The critical procedures by means of which established content is assessed, revised, and adapted to new discoveries have public criteria written into them that stand as impersonal standards to which both teacher and learner must give their allegiance. . . . To liken education to therapy, to conceive of it as imposing a pattern on another person or as fixing the environment so that he "grows," fails to do justice to the shared impersonality both of the content that is handed on and of the criteria by reference to which it is criticized and revised. The teacher is not a detached operator who is bringing about some kind of result in another person which is external to him. His task is to try to get others on the inside of a public form of life that he considers to be worthwhile.

—R.S. Peters, *Education as Initiation*, an inaugural lecture delivered at The University of London Institute of Education, 9 December, 1963. Published for The University of London Institute of Education, by Evans Brothers, Ltd., London.

---

substantive beliefs—is part of this attitude of alienated and cowardly professionalism.[9]

This criticism, like that of Alison Jaggar, ties professionalism to alienation. But whereas Jaggar claims that the height of alienation occurs when philosophers pose as moral authorities, Wilder implies that our relationship to students is most alienated when we conceal our presumably authoritative conclusions from them and when we do not care enough to try to persuade them to the beliefs we hold to be true.

Teaching philosophy is, I agree, an act of caring, but I am uncomfortable with the notion that I best express my concern for students by trying to secure their agreement with my own philosophical positions. Focusing now on classroom practice, I would like to suggest two reasons for opposing this method of teaching. The first reflects my conception of philosophy; the second my defense of a professional relationship between teachers and students.

First, the history of philosophy is one of disagreement, and divergent views will be represented in any good philosophy course. If an ethics teacher is an advocate of utilitarianism but nonetheless includes Kant on the course's reading list, primary attention will be devoted to exposing the weaknesses of formalist theory and showing the way in which its criticisms of utilitarianism can be successfully met. Now if a student, exposed to Kant's own arguments, finds them more persuasive than either the professor's or Mill's, then the student cannot be judged to have performed excellently in the course: according to Wilder's thinking, the student's arguments lead to a false conclusion and therefore cannot be as strong as a well-reasoned paper that defends utilitarianism. This must be true even if the student's work is judged to be on the same philosophical level as Kant's. Were he a member of the class, Kant himself could not earn an "A" (or be judged an excellent philosopher) unless he changed his mind. This is an absurd position because it is rarely possible to trace what a professor judges to be a false conclusion in the work of a great philosopher to some obvious flaw in reasoning for which even an undergraduate student may be criticized. And what of the student who, though as yet unable to see the power of the professor's utilitarian arguments, nonetheless sincerely accepts their authority and uses them to dispute Kant in a course taught by a committed formalist? The student, downgraded again for "plainly faulty reasoning," will be a leading candidate for alienation, not only from both professors but from his or her own capacities for rational judgment.

What many find unsettling about teaching without advocacy is its implicit assertion of a class difference between teachers and students. The teacher is seen as saying, "Since I cannot expect you to understand ethical theory as fully as Kant or Mill or I do, it's okay for you to believe whomever you choose, as long as you have some good reasons. If I gave you my opinion and my reasons, you wouldn't fully understand them anyway." Implied here is the idea that teachers must, as a result of their authoritative position, withhold some part of themselves from their students, must withhold what philosophy teachers presumably regard as a most important part, their convictions on enduring issues. This refusal to be full persons in relation to students is, I take it, what threatens to make the relationship alienated. But the alternative of posing as an authority can, as Jaggar maintains, also cause alienation, now as a result of asserting rather than withholding one's superior degree of knowledge. On these terms, the only way of avoiding the dilemma would be for a teacher to deny being superior in *any* respect and to relate fully to students as peers.

The source of the dilemma is, I think, a confusion about the meaning of such concepts as professionalism, superiority, and alienation. To overcome it, I would like to offer three considerations in defense of a professional teacher-student relationship.

First, the entire conduct of teachers in relation to students should be guided by what will be most conducive to the students' learning of philosophy. As a classroom method, to share one's own convictions may be to give more of oneself but is not, for that reason, more effective teaching. The superior knowledge of philosophy teachers is part of what makes them professionals, and this status does affect—and even restrict—their relationship with students. In a professional relationship one does not give one's whole self; for example, one tries not to express impatience (even if one feels it) with a slow learner, or irritation with a student whose manner one finds displeasing, or condescension for a student's poor reasoning. Furthermore, a professional relationship is not fully reciprocal: teachers should try to frame their comments in a way that will best help students to learn; students need not be so concerned to enlighten their professors and may appropriately experiment with arguments purely for the sake of their own self-edification. Teaching does offer many opportunities for self-disclosure, and in more advanced courses—as students become more able to argue philosophically—even the advocacy of particular positions (especially unpopular ones) may become increasingly effective and appropriate. But the purpose of doing this should never be persuasion or self-expression. Thus, in their professional activity teachers are, it is true, withholding a part of themselves, but this does not make their relationship with students uncaring or inhumane. Professional activity should "benefit those who are subject to it," and philosophy teachers should present those arguments (as well as teach those works and assign those papers) that will be most helpful to students in the *specific* way that philosophy teachers are trained to help them.

This leads to the second consideration in favor of professionalism. By a student's presence in my course, I may infer only that he or she has elected a professional relationship with me. I have no unilateral right to assume that students want a "full human relationship" or want even to know my opinions, let alone that they can benefit from hearing them. To avoid alienation, a relationship need not be equal in all respects, nor need it be "full"—very few if any human relationships meet these criteria—but it does, I think, need to be based on mutual consent with respect to its range and depth.

Finally, having a professional relationship with students does not preclude a wider human relationship as well. If the restrictions I have proposed in the name of professionalism implied that I could not simultaneously have other kinds of relationships when both the student and I freely chose them, then I would agree that we would be paying too heavy a price to be professional. The best teachers are probably those who genuinely like the company of many of their students and who enjoy discussion with them that is unrestrained by the conventions appropriate to a class-

room. No doubt some of our warmest friendships may even develop from these associations. But this does not mean that the freedom that befits a friendship should be our model for classroom behavior; unlike our friends, our students are not obliged to indulge our intellectual prejudices or our personal idiosyncrasies.

When we consider the professional ethics of teaching, too often we think only of prohibitions that are designed to prevent the exploitation of students. Like physicians, philosophy teachers should, of course, "first, do no harm." But I have tried to indicate that our professional obligations include a larger positive dimension as well. In a world where the proverbial marketplace of ideas—and not infrequently even the university catalogue—is crowded with sophistry, propaganda, and hyperbole, there is special reason to value a profession that is solely committed to enlarging the power and influence of reasoned discourse and imaginative questioning.

Notes

1. My concern in this paper is the teaching of introductory and other students who do not intend to become professional philosophers. My remarks do not apply to graduate education in philosophy.
2. Alison Jaggar, "Philosophy as a Profession," *Metaphilosophy*, Volume 6 (January, 1975), p. 100.
3. *The Republic of Plato*, trans. Francis MacDonald Cornford, Oxford University Press (London, 1941), p. 23.
4. Edward Regis, Jr., "The Layman and the Abdication of Philosophers," *Metaphilosophy*, Volume 6 January, 1975), p. 123.
5. Jaggar, p. 112.
6. This argument is made by Hugh T. Wilder, "Tolerance and Teaching Philosophy," *Metaphilosophy*, Vol. 9, nos. 3 and 4, July/October 1978, pp. 320-321.
7. In an article in the *Wall Street Journal* several years ago, Clare Boothe Luce traced the actions of the radical SLA to the philosophy of existentialism; and in his recent best-seller Wayne Dyer appears to invoke the authority of John Stuart Mill in support of his claim, "Nothing is more important than anything else." *Your Erroneous Zones*, Avon Books (New York, 1976), p. 156.
8. Bertrand Russell, *The Problems of Philosophy*, Oxford University Press, (New York, 1959), p. 161.
9. Wilder, p. 322.

Chapter Ten
Dialogical Inquiry

Chapter Ten

Dialogical Inquiry

It is not uncommon nowadays to hear the opinion that dialogue cannot be inquiry. Inquiry is a matter of scientific investigation, it is said, whereas dialogue is mere conversation.

A more careful pronouncement might be that conversation cannot be inquiry but dialogue can be. The matter hangs, to be sure, on what we think inquiry is. That it is investigation is not at issue. But to define it in a way that covers all that the term denotes, one would have to say that it is self-correcting practice. In this sense, both conversation and dialogue involve discussion, but conversation is not self-correcting and dialogue is.

Dialogue is self-correcting in that it is the kind of discussion that takes place in a community of inquiry, where all participants are on the alert for irrelevance, incorrectness, falsehood, or any other kind of fallacy or error in reasoning or judgments. The community of inquiry is thus a critical community as well as a creative one, in that each participant stands ready to correct others and to be corrected by them, in order to further the inquiry to which they are all committed.

The way in which the terms inquiry, dialogue, conversation and discussion have been defined in the preceding paragraphs is an unconventional one. It is not one that is employed by most of the writers in this section, Their uses are often at odds with one another, But the definitions proposed above could be employed in order to enable these writers to attain some degree of consistency. At the very least, perhaps it could be conceded that dialogical inquiry is an acceptable usage, and not a contradiction in terms.

"The classroom discussion is a persisting community of query," writes Justus Buchler, (He uses "query" as the generic term for all the various forms of inquiry.) "The ingenuousness, the insight, the mad spontaneity of children discussing fairness or friendship or personal identity is like nothing else in the realm of discourse. . . . it is very much the beginning of query." Discussions may not reach conclusions, but the process of inquiry invariably makes progress of some sort, and that progress constitutes the product of the inquiry. Buchler concludes that "sustained discussion has an openness that the lecture cannot have; and a persistent promise as an avenue of discovery for the student and as an instrument of perception for the teacher." It may not be out of place to observe that this rare treatment of pedagogy by Buchler finds him accepting the major thrust of Dewey's theory of education, while yet dealing with equal insight with a number of special questions which Dewey did not directly address. Buchler is especially sensitive to the value of dialogue to the student, who in later life may have forgotten just about everything else about his or her education, but will still be touched by the experience of participating in a community of inquiry.

Ruth L. Saw's analysis is an intriguing and perceptive one. She employs the terms "dialogue" and "conversation" in senses that are almost diametrically opposed to Buchler's, but for all that, the differences are more terminological than anything else. The process she calls conversation and that Buchler calls dialogue is one that is non-manipulative and mutually exploratory. Moreover, it causes the participants to think. But perhaps the major contribution of Saw is her awareness of the ethical dimension of verbal interchanges, which contrasts sharply with the point of view of those who believe that the purpose of discussion is to produce assent, rather than free and independent thinking on the part of both or all discussants.

The section concludes with two transcripts of classroom discussions. In the first, the subject of the discussion is the distinction between differ-ences of degree and differences of kind. The teacher is Mrs. Gerry Dawson McClendon. In the second, in which the teacher is Dr. Catherine McCall, the topic is the distinction between robots vs. people—or, the concept of personhood. What is striking about both groups is their persistence, their readiness to offer hypotheses and counter-examples, their patience with one another and how closely they are able to keep track of who said what. These transcripts record the awakening philosophical curiosity and imagination of young children, and their determination to reach tenable, logical, reasonable conclusions. They provide further evidence to substantiate a remark by Buchler on another occasion, to the effect that, "when children do philosophy, they go back to its roots."

What is a Discussion?

Justus Buchler

What the traits of a discussion are and what the traits of a good discussion are appear to be two different questions. I do not feel heroic enough to attempt an exhaustive answer to either, although perhaps in dealing with the first, which it is my inclination to do, some conclusions may emerge about the second.

It may be true, as the Greeks have told us, that men by nature desire to know. I have never encountered a student who did not desire to know. Unfortunately, the real problem is whether students desire to learn, and whether, among those who do, there is any sense of what actual inquiry or discovery entails. The first major job of a teacher, and maybe in the last analysis the only one, is to implant the spirit and experience of inquiry—or, better, of query, if I may import a term I have used elsewhere to designate probing in the widest possible sense, that is, probing which can be directed toward making or acting no less than toward stating. Whatever else a comparison of one teaching method with another aims at, it should consider which method is the best means of accomplishing this job. And in any such comparison the realities of the school situation within the cultural situation merit attention at the very outset. The school is an institution which receives young persons from society at large. We need not fool ourselves; the contrast between the values to which the student has been subjected and the demands of the school is enormous, and it cannot be obliterated by the vague notion that the school is a microcosm of society. The school, though a body social, is not primarily a mirror of

a culture, and if it ever were, it would cease to have any function.

The student is one among a vast cultural majority who have about as much understanding of what a school is and of what its ideal values are as of the other side of the moon. A current writer speaks of an unprecedented "hunger for learning," an "adulation of learning" in our time—a pitiable identification of the passion for quiz programs or the testimony of registration figures with the love of ideas. It is no mystery why parents who themselves have gone to school are so often scarcely less ignorant of the sense of learning than anybody else. They passed through school in their day with a cultural armor that would have resisted even the most self-conscious instruction or the most arduously wrought curriculum of the present. Developments since the first World War have, by and large, made the situation a more hopeful one. But circumstances contrive to perpetuate the moral isolation of the school.

At its worst, schooling means a decade of baby-sitting, and, for the most part, it means training in the right answers. It is a commonplace that students can go through years of a good school curriculum without experiencing an iota of intellectual excitement. F. J. E. Woodbridge warned us, more than a half-century ago, to minimize the emphasis on education as "a preparation for life." It is better, he said, to think of it as "a discipline in present excellence."

The first consideration, then, that imposes itself when we try to clarify ourselves about the meaning of the discussion procedure is the role of this procedure in fostering ideational awareness and in dissipating the machine-like conception of query. Since it concerns the student as person and not simply as registrant in good standing, it cannot possibly be limited to the first classroom hours. Ideational sensibility does not arrive in the form of sudden illumination, and students already endowed need to be sustained and fed. Now in the formal presentation (the "lecture"), as we ordinarily understand it, a product is transmitted. In the discussion, a product is established. Quantitatively speaking, "more" can be transmitted by presentation or exposition than can be established by discussion. But more can be assimilated of what is established than of what is transmitted. In both cases, a subject matter engages the action and attention of a certain number of people. In the lecture the wheels have been greased, the mechanism operates, and the product is inherited, God willing. In the discussion the product is necessarily earned, through halting personal labor. By the standards of social efficiency, one method appears to be rational and fluid; the other, primitive, wasteful, circuitous. But this is the crux of the matter. Ideational awareness in students requires precisely the perception on their part that there is no analogy whatever between entrepreneurial productivity and the productivity of query.

The relative merits of the lecture and the discussion depend in part on the conditions of their fulfillment: most obviously, on who is lecturing and who is being lectured to, on who is guiding the discussion and who is present in the discussion. But, plainly, there are properties intrinsic to each procedure considered as a situation. I have refrained from employing a common pair of terms, to the effect that lecturing entails "passivity" and discussion "activity" on the part of the student. Postponing for a while the question whether this account is just, it should be clear that there is no virtue at all in mere activity and that it is often wise to be passive. Everyone knows that unmitigated activity is a disease of the times

contagious to the school. What is important in any procedure is the type of activity, the circumstances of passivity, involved. It is therefore in the total character and purpose of a method of teaching that its significance is to be found. If the discussion method is superior to the lecture method, this is not because of its degree of activity but because the establishment of a product of query by students is more fundamental to the deepening of their powers than their acceptance of such a product, and because the assimilation of ideas is more important than the compilation of ideas. I am aware that some champions of discussion might favor "manipulation of ideas" instead of assimilation, and, in general, I should agree to the equal suitability of the term; but, having presupposed its meaning in the notion of "establishing" a product, I prefer here to lay stress on the distinctive *effect* of discussion and to return later to the question of "activity" in general.

The term "discussion," occurring in a variety of contexts, carries a variety of associations. Notwithstanding their own practice, a great many teachers as well as students still labor under the idea that the lecture is the normal mode of academic communication and that the discussion is the anomalous mode, introduced not primarily to subserve query but primarily to promote "democracy" or to generate fraternal feeling. It is important, therefore, in determining what classroom discussion is, to determine what it is not. First of all, it is simply not true that "discussion is discussion" regardless of its conditions. Classroom discussion is a continuing enterprise, with a content that is sequential, and above all, cumulative. The members of a social club, who discuss what their luncheon speaker has told them about traffic deaths, religion, or an African safari, bring to the meeting no moral commitment toward query. They come with no substantive preparation. Unlike students, they have no responsibility for the framing of ideas. They are present to be entertained, to evince interest in the world about them, to be "stimulated" a little, to be "civic-minded." They are inherently distrustful of the abstract, of the effort to generalize, of "big words." The club discussion is a discrete occasion of comradeship. The classroom discussion is a persisting community of query.

There are many people who are inclined to belittle sharp distinctions between the different circumstances of discussion. Even those who do have a strong sense of the uniqueness of the classroom often belie it in practice. For example, the typical observer of another school's curriculum, having received permission to visit classes, goes to one hour of discussion in the social studies course, perhaps another hour of discussion in the mathematics course, and departs. I have often insisted upon greater hospitality than a visitor is prepared to receive, not merely because casual observation is absurdly unrepresentative, but because false perspective can give the air of travesty to an hour of labor. The individual discussion is part of a course; it presupposes products earlier achieved, evolving interests, and future obligations. It is not a one-act play giving way to another on the morrow. The specific techniques and procedures can vary greatly from day to day. To the one-hour observer (the largest species) a discussion can seem excessively narrow in scope, excessively broad in scope, or well-nigh unintelligible.

I should not dwell on the differentia of discussion, were it not for certain additional facts: (a) some people distrust discussion because they think it cannot be other than a loose form of learning; (b) others, who may actually prize discussion, consider it a charitable or hospitable form of learning; and (c) most non-educators think of the classroom as the "immature" stage of discussion, to be distinguished from the plainspoken sessions of men of affairs. The average citizen, thoroughly unaware of his alienation from query, is anything but defensive. He thinks condescendingly of "kids at school": kids are kids and schoolteachers are schoolteachers. Kids train for adulthood. Men of affairs, having obviated or superseded the jargon of the books, talk about reality. The educator can do little about

---

Conversation as an unrehearsed intellectual adventure

As civilized human beings, we are the inheritors, neither of an inquiry about ourselves and the world, nor of an accumulating body of information, but of a conversation begun in the primeval forest and extended and made more articulate in the course of centuries. It is a conversation which goes on both in public and within each of ourselves. Of course there is argument and inquiry and information, but wherever these are profitable they are recognized as passages in this conversation . . . Conversation is not an enterprise designed to yield an extrinsic profit, a contest where the winner gets a prize, nor is it an activity of exegesis; it is an unrehearsed intellectual adventure. . . . Education, properly speaking, is an initiation into the skill and partnership of this conversation in which we learn to recognize the voices, to distinguish the proper occasions of utterance, and in which we acquire the intellectual and moral habits appropriate to conversation.

—Michael Oakeshott, in "Poetry as a Voice in the Conversation of Mankind," *Rationalism in Politics* (New York: Basic Books, 1962), pp. 198-199.

---

disenchanting fellow-citizens. He can do a great deal about seeing to it that the cultural myth does not infiltrate the school and take possession of his own soul. The simplest way to paralyze students is to regard them as kids on trial and not as earnest inquirers. I take it that the moral relation between the teacher and the students in the classroom is as much an ingredient of the discussion process as the discourse itself is. Quite apart from the attitudes of individual teachers, there are ways in which the school as such may reflect lay standards and perpetuate infantilism. A program which

The teacher as a thinking model

"What and how much do children know about what a teacher thinks? It is inevitable that children will know something about how a teacher thinks, how much depending on the teacher. I have never heard anyone argue that a teacher is not a model for children of how one should think and act. It is not a matter of should a teacher be a model but rather that he is a model. . . . The point I wish to emphasize is that it appears that children know relatively little about how a teacher thinks about the classroom, that is, what he takes into account, the alternatives he thinks about, the things that puzzle him about children and about learning, what he does when he is not sure of what he should do, how he feels when he does something wrong—there is quite a bit that goes on in a teacher's head that is never made public to children. . . . [T]here is a good deal of anecdotal evidence strongly indicating that the more a teacher can make his own thinking public and subject for discussion—in the same way one expects of children—the more interesting and stimulating does the classroom become for students. . . . If my experience with school children—in fact, with all levels of students, from elementary through graduate school—is any guide, that a large part of a teacher's "thinking about thinking," which is never made public, is precisely what the children are interested in and excited by on those rare occasions when it becomes public."

—From Seymour B. Sarason, *The Culture of the School and the Problem of Change*, (Boston: Allyn and Bacon, Inc., 1971) pp. 185-187.

asks children to study materials of classic stature and then makes the newspapers or T.V. panels the basis of its own discussions is faithfully deferring to the cultural fable about the passage from kidhood to adulthood. The academic community cannot possibly snub the materials of public communication: they are indispensable. But so are breathing and sleeping, getting haircuts and buying groceries. Discussion in school is a costly process. If it cannot penetrate the crust of common sense or transcend the particularities of gossip, it is a wasteful luxury and a miserable failure.

The contentions embodied in *a* and *b* can be dealt with implicitly by various considerations. In referring to discussion as community of query and as committed to the establishment of a product, I do not mean to romanticize the process or to overestimate the extent of its accomplishments. The classroom never will be the scene of grandiose research or of systematic thought. As anyone who has spent any time in it knows, the talk is not consistently inspiring and can sometimes be dispiriting. Yet it can engender values truer to the spirit of free speculation than any other instance of community, within or without the academic world. The ingenuousness, the insight, the mad spontaneity of children discussing fairness or friendship or personal identity is like nothing else in the realm of discourse. It may not be the peak of invention, but it is very much the beginning of query. Given sufficiently challenging fare, accorded a status of reasonable equality within the confines of the classroom, students have begun the revolution of awareness. To establish a product is in itself a very modest process. It implies, of course, not the exhaustion of a subject but progress in the ascertainment of complexities. The classroom discussion is as different from the "bull session" as it is from the club luncheon, the T.V. panel, or the town meeting. Profitable and necessary as the informal gabfest may be, it is no ideal for the classroom, where economy and the sense of reflective order are the partners of exuberance.

No doubt there are as many conceptions of the actual conduct of discussion as there are practitioners of the method. I gather, both from direct observation and from the testimony of colleagues at various institutions, that practice ranges all the way from the rigorous specification of classroom norms to utter chaos. In between are to be found meetings like those of the Society of Friends, lectures to small groups in small rooms, and hour-long interrogation of students in alphabetical order. I am myself a little suspicious of strict canons for the "art of teaching" or of legislation as to what is or is not authentic discussion. On the other hand, since certain aims and values in a school are of greater importance than others, it seems to me that such aims and values are what any discussion ought to subserve. The view that no aims whatever can be specified as guides and that the values of learning are unpredictable or fortuitous may not be exactly nihilistic, but it questions the very existence of organization in learning. If, then, the actualization of the student's powers for query and the widening of his or her imagination are the values at which academic learning aims—naturally there are other values intellectual and moral of the total school experience—these are the guideposts for the conduct of discussion. One can scarcely take exception to any particular discussion technique if it does promote these values. Whether all current techniques do, in fact, promote them and whether the views on which these techniques are based have been carefully weighed, I rather doubt.

Consider, for instance, the view that a discussion should be characterized by the widest possible participation of students. Some years ago a visitor from the West Coast attended a class of mine. At the end of the hour he came up and congratulated me on the number of students who had taken part, specifying the percentage to the first decimal place. When I told him that the day before only four or five students had carried the burden, his response was that not every hour could be a "good" one. And when I expressed the feeling that the earlier hour had been the better

discussion, with greater benefit to the group, he smiled as though I had uttered a paradox. He had not paid much attention to the lines of argument and could not appraise the substance of anyone's contribution, but had occupied himself with computations about the number of times students spoke, the number of times they signified willingness to speak, the number of times they looked out of the window, and the number of doodlers among them. I do not know how many exponents of the discussion method find such criteria significant. I do know that several of my colleagues express a sense of defeat when only a small number of students speak during a discussion hour.

Among other questions, we are back to that of "activity" and "passivity." All things considered, wide participation is an index of vitality in the discussion, and participation itself is a symptom of intellectual energy in the participant. Yet if the ends of discussion are to be kept in view, the quality of the talk is more important than its quantity, and it is in the teacher's discretion whether at a given time it is of greater value to students to ruminate on the argument or to help build it. Neither pedagogical maxims nor an unseen hand can replace the variable, but ever responsive, judgment of the teacher. I suppose it would be generally acknowledged that the dialogues of Plato are pretty good "discussions." Yet the merit of these discussions does not depend on the number of participants, and in most of them one speaker dominates. The quantitative emphasis goes hand in hand with what might be called a therapeutic conception of discussion. It is sometimes contended that, since a school exists primarily to help students, it is good for them to "blow off steam" and good for them to acquire the responsibilities of communal participation. To this there are two main answers. First, a school does indeed exist to help students; but some conceptions of help are in effect the very reverse. None is of greater disservice to students than that which prescribes indiscriminately for their welfare, lumping together the functions of the dormi-

The Relevance of Dialogue

Entering the culture is perhaps most readily done by entering a dialogue with a more experienced member of it. Perhaps one way in which we might reconsider the issue of teacher training is to give the teacher training in the skills of dialogue—how to discuss a subject with a beginner. There is a Russian proverb to the effect that one understands only after one has discussed. There are doubtless many ways in which a human being can serve as a vicar of the culture, helping a child to understand its points of view and the nature of its knowledge. But I dare say that few are so potentially powerful as participating in dialogue. Professor Jan Smedslund, at Oslo, has recently remarked on our failure to recognize that even in the domains of formal reasoning, logic, and mathematics, the social context of discussion can be shown to be crucial. . . . One of the most crucial ways in which a culture provides aid in intellectual growth is through a dialogue between the more experienced and the less experienced, providing a means for the internalization of dialogue in thought. The courtesy of conversation may be the major ingredient in the courtesy of teaching.

—Jerome Bruner, "The Relevance of Education," (New York: W. W. Norton and Co., 1971), pp. 106-107.

tory, the advisory interview, the front office, and the classroom. It is good for students to blow off steam, even in the classroom—but occasionally, not principally. In the classroom there are other values which take precedence. The desirable degree of participation in discussion varies with the particular subject, the extent and nature of the background reading, the ability of students to discern what is going on, the psychological readiness of students, and a host of other factors. Since participating can mean raising questions as well as expressing viewpoints, a large number of participants is a fact which, taken by itself, signifies nothing.

Second, so far as the *individual* student is concerned, not the group, "participation" in the discussion does not necessarily take the form of oral activity. Every class exhibits wide differences in the emotional makeup of its members, and the shy, reticent, or modest student may profit greatly from discussion by others, even as the witnesses did in the Socratic conversations. Neither direct coercion nor coercive expectation is a technique becoming to teachers who wish to identify with the minds and needs of their students. The student who participates through reflective activity alone is not shirking the collaborative obligation of the group as the chronic absentee is. Such students are, as it were, creative auditors in the community of query. The problem of self-confidence is one that they must solve for themselves and the teacher can help by lifting from them the tension that comes with external pressure. The "responsibilities of communal participation" must not, therefore, be construed as a yoke; they can be fulfilled in more than one way. It is a positive good, not a necessary evil, that a class should be diversified. Numerically speaking, a discussion group can be too small. And it does not make sense to value diversity without respecting the human differences it implies.

A key distinction between the expository and discussion situations emerges at this point. It is possible for the student's intellectual activity to be as great in a lecture as in a discussion. Between the auditor of a formal presentation and the silent member of the discussion group there is no basic difference—so far as energy and movement of thought is concerned. Moreover, the skilled expositor can anticipate typical stumbling blocks in student understanding and deal with them by judicious restatement. Nevertheless, there is one thing that the formal presentation cannot do. It cannot reproduce the conditions of actual query. The silent student in the discussion, fully as much as the vocal one, witnesses and experiences the manipulation of subject matter from its initial circumstances. He or she observes pitfalls as they occur in student probing and not merely as they are formulated in the more finished perspective of a formal exposition. Such students experience the natural history of query sometimes with their guts as well as with their intellects. The expositor can re-enact problematic experience dramatically; but in discussion the student is party to the original. Perhaps the most important consideration of all is that in the discussion the teacher has the opportunity to do all that the formal expositor does, and with more direct awareness of student needs. Teachers, too, can dramatize ideas, introduce factual information, prepare the ground, and clear the ground. But they can do these things in their urgency as well as by design, in the same way that they can answer questions as well as anticipate them. Thus in the discussion, not only is a product established collaboratively; it is experienced in its life-cycle as well as in its consummation.

It may be clear now wherein lies the error also of another group of teachers who stoutly insist that discussion should be wholly a student affair, with a minimum of contribution by the instructor. As the typical expositor places too much emphasis on the product and too little on the process, they place too much on the process and too little on the product. They contend that it is not the business of children's discussion to reach conclusions; that for students the experience of learning is far more important than the concoction of half-baked results. This school of thought, though not identical with that which wishes to widen participation at all costs, overlaps with it. It certainly must be conceded that half-baked results, if mistaken for what they are not, can be worse than no results at all. And I think it must be conceded also that, if a choice had to be made, the process of learning might merit more emphasis than the product. But the products of classroom discussion do not have to be half-baked in order to be *results*, and a choice *between* the product and the process does not have to be made

in a *discussion*. Two simple confusions are imbedded in the approach of this school. One is between a product of query and a conclusion of query; the other is between a definitive conclusion and a functional or provisional conclusion.

We have agreed that students cannot aim at authoritative *termini*. Where we can speak of a conclusion at all, it may be developed only after many hours, and then with qualifications befitting the circumstances. But, regardless of this, a product is inevitably established in any given hour of discussion. For the product need not take the form of an assertive conclusion. It may be an enumeration of possible views, or a fuller definition of a problem, or a growth of appreciative awareness. It may be more of an envisioning or of an exhibiting than of an affirming. The product is the concrete achievement of the hour—this is the language of students themselves. Students may have no right to demand final answers, but they certainly have a right to expect some sense of intellectual motion or some feeling of discernment.

Those who would remove the teacher as much as possible from overt participation cannot evade either the nonsense or the pathos of the consequences. Strictly, "as much as possible" means

---

What Philosophy Does

"A philosopher's genius lies not in his giving one new answer to one old question, but in his transforming all the questions. He gives mankind a different air to breathe. But the differences that he makes are as hard to describe as the differences made by growing up. The adolescent cannot realize what these changes will be like; the adult cannot recollect what they had been like."

—Gilbert Ryle, "Hume," *Collected Papers*, Vol. 1 (New York: Barnes and Noble, 1971), p. 160. Reprinted, in English translation, from the original French in "Les Philosophes Celebres" edited by M. Merleau-Ponty in 1956.

the total disappearance of the teacher and the replacement of the class by the bull session. Should the teacher be a patrolman keeping physical order? Or a purely formal logician, interrupting to detect inconsistency in argument? Or a parliamentary chairman, democratically distributing opportunities to speak? Or a mere representative of the school, symbolizing the sponsor of the discussion? Or a silent judge, meditating future rewards and penalties to the performers? Or an enigmatic contriver of puzzles, throwing out "hints"? Or "one of the boys," making himself as stupid as possible in order to spur them on? No doubt it is possible for a teacher so to dominate the proceedings as to terrorize or stultify students into total nonparticipation. But I am assuming throughout that when we speak of the "lecturer" and the "leader of discussion," we mean individuals representative of the respective methods and sufficient in reasonableness to permit comparison of these methods. By "discussion" we cannot possibly mean "tyrannical lecture."

How can teachers be the midwifes of ideas if they merely look on at the dubious birth of such ideas? To legislate that they deliberately suppress their possible contributions to the discussion is to suppose them less than human or less than teachers—or less than responsible. If they are concerned with promoting awareness and not just encouraging speeches, they can no more refrain from contributing themselves than from permitting the best of their students to contribute. Rigid prescriptions of just how much teachers should talk at one stretch or what the intervals should be between their comments convert the discussion from an instance of learning into an exercise or a rite. Withdrawing them from the group is like withdrawing the books from the library or tearing out the odd-numbered pages in order to improve the guessing power of the students. Of course, teachers may often contribute injudiciously. But "contributing" and "contributing injudiciously" are no more synonymous than "teacher" and

"unskilled teacher." It is possible for teachers to utilize their cognitive authority without flaunting it or to be periodically authoritative without ever being authoritarian. The fact of the matter is that they have to be not only positive contributors but exemplars of discussion. And if they are not, then to that extent the formal expository method is the superior method.

Having mentioned one great student of education, Woodbridge, it would hardly do to overlook his colleague Dewey, who, by some strange quirk of history, is often invoked to support, and is supposed even to have developed, the conception of the quiescent teacher. As Dewey puts it, on the contrary:

> There is no spontaneous germination in the mental life. If [the student] does not get the suggestion from the teacher, he gets it from somebody or something . . . The implication that the teacher is the one and only person who has no "individuality" or "freedom" to "express" would be funny if it were not so sad in its outworkings. And his contribution, given the conditions stated, will presumably do more to getting something started which will really secure and express the development of strict individual capacities than will suggestions springing from uncontrolled haphazard sources. The point is also worth dwelling upon that the method of leaving the response entirely to pupils, the teacher supplying, in the language of the day, only the "stimuli," misconceives the nature of thinking.[1]

A notorious pitfall of the discussion method is the danger that a thin line often separates discussion from pure rhetoric. But this is a controllable circumstance. Innumerable threats are always present, such as uncooperative or rebellious student personalities, and the temptations of self-aggrandizement. None of these is an objection to the practice of discussion. The thin line is no thinner than that between listening to a lecture and sleeping at a lecture. A more serious pitfall, I think, lurks in the now widely held view that as much attention should be given in discussion to "form" as to "content," to the use of language as to the development of ideas; that, indeed, the improvement of expression and the articulation of ideas are one and inseparable. I am by no means a dissenter from the ideal which underlies this contention. A standard which holds for the teacher should hold for the student. One of the indisputable virtues of the discussion method is the experience it provides of the travail of formulation and of the test whether opinions which seem intuitively sound can bear the light of day.

Nevertheless, I am wary of any emphasis on the correlative status of language and ideas which does not realize its qualifying conditions. Some ideas, of our students no less than of our colleagues, resist conventional formulation, and we are too prone to insist on what turns out to be an oversimplification or an abortive version. By sanctifying the requirement of overt expression or of coherency, we can as easily smother a deep idea as expose a vapid one, and get to prize rapidity of response rather than thoroughness. It seems to me that excessively conventional thinking in the classroom is a much greater danger than slovenly expression. The latter is in no sense to be condoned as an end, but sometimes it may have to be tolerated as one stage in a means. One of the maladies endemic to this generation of scholars is an impatience with "unclear" speculation. The cries of "metaphysical" and "obscure" fly thick and fast, as though any sincere thinker were ever deliberately obscure or as though all metaphysics necessarily treated of the fantasies that positivists have in mind. It is common knowledge that many of the best students, whose written performances can be impressively coherent, have trouble in oral discussion. As often as not, this is the consequence of their being confronted at one and the same time with many more ramifications of an idea than are average students. Students who are hesitant to volunteer in discussion are frequently grappling with more than they can readily formulate. When to encourage them to share their wealth and when to let them work through their ideas is a perennial problem. I am disposed habitually to trust their judgment more than my own. Generally speaking, if we would curb the glib student enthralled by the sound of his or her own voice, we might well be patient with the student who refuses to be glib and who is unable to be clear. With those teachers who construe "expression" primarily in terms of diction or grammatical niceties and who would interrupt a discussion to expose lapses, I have no sympathy whatever. Where a problem of this kind exists, it cannot be dealt with *ad hoc*. The best basis of satisfactory speech habits in the student is the continuing example set by the books he reads and by the teacher in action.

Continuous discussion, then, appears to be the superior mode of learning, when it is intensified by an imaginative teacher and supported by a powerful reading program. Sustained discussion has, if you will, an openness that the lecture cannot have, and a persistent promise as an avenue of discovery for the student and as an instrument of perception for the teacher.

Like all values, discussion is a value for persons. The most immediate aspects of a value do not, of course, always coincide with its most fundamental aspects. For the teacher, discussion is one of the great reminders of fallibility. And, like all values for the student, it is not separable from other values which condition and environ it. It can barely survive in effective form without good concomitant reading or without the cooperativeness of the teacher outside the classroom. The fact that it needs to be distinguished sharply from other school functions does not mean that it lacks connection with them. The community of discussion and other forms of academic community contain the same persons, who need to know one another as inquirers no less than as companions and contemporaries. At its lowest ebb, discussion is simply one more cultural ceremony; at its best, it is a force in the total constitution of the student. Too often this force is dissipated by the pressures and currents of the student's later life. Still it is imperative, academically, to do costly labor for small social fruits and to remember that even the student who has forgotten almost everything may now and then, from an influence remote to him, perceive the moral power of query.

Notes

1. *Intelligence in the Modern World*, ed. J. Ratner (New York: Modern Library, 1939), pp. 624-25.

Conversation and Communication

Ruth L. Saw

Just what is a conversation? Could we properly describe a tenant and a landlord as having a "conversation" with regard to overdue rent? Does the judge call lawyers from both sides into his chambers for a "conversation"? Do we have a "conversation" with our children when we find they have not shown up in school for several days? How do conversations differ (if they do) from discussions? from dialogues? from arguments? And what is the connection between conversation and communication?

These are some of the questions which, directly or indirectly, Ruth Saw comes to grips with in this essay, which was her inaugural lecture delivered at Birkbeck College in October of 1962. The essence of conversation, she contends, is its innocence of any ulterior purpose. A conversation cannot be guided or directed, nor can one in any way attempt to manipulate the person with whom one converses. Conversations are carried on for their own sake, very much as if they were pure art forms. "Whenever people speak in order to impress, to exhibit their wit, their wealth, their learning, or to bring about some advantage for themselves, they are failing to treat their hearer as a person, as an end in himself, and conversation with him as carried on for its own sake."

It does not matter that the purpose of our manipulations is a commendable one: it cannot be a conversation. If we are engaged in "drawing out" a child so that he or she might better display their intelligence, conversation cannot be said to take place. Or if we are devious in our disclosure of our attitudes, or of facts we want to make
known indirectly, our doing so disqualifies the personal interaction from being a conversational one.

Conversation is predicated upon there being a rational partnership of those who converse, a partnership of free and equal individuals. The direction the conversation takes will be determined not so much by the laws of consistency, as by the developing needs of the conversation itself, much as a writer, halfway through a book, begins to find it dictating to him or her what henceforth must be written. The author may still introduce some surprises, just as those who engage in conversation may introduce revelations by which they surprise and delight one another. Indeed, so guileless is a conversation that in the course of it we listen to ourselves and drew inferences about ourselves in ways we previously had been unable to do. One listens to oneself talk and remarks, "I must be jealous," thereby witnessing a disclosure about oneself no less objective than it would have been if we had inferred, from the other person's remarks, "He must be jealous." For in a conversation we are capable of stepping back and listening to what we say, just as an artist, in the act of pointing, can still step back and take stock of what he has been doing.

For Professor Saw, conversation is a symmetrical relationship. "A cannot converse with B if B does not converse with A." It is a mutual exploration of one another's individualities. One cannot exact disclosures from the other without being prepared to make similar disclosures regarding oneself. Perhaps this stipulation can be better understood if we refer back to Prof. Saw's earlier distinction between "communicating something to someone" and "being in communication with someone." The first suggests conveying a content of some kind from one person to another; to be more specific, it suggests a quasi-believing situation. But the second suggests that sort of interpersonal experience in which each participant causes the other to think; it is when we are truly in communication with others that we are provoked to think independently.

Professor Saw contrasts conversation with dialogue in a way that is decidedly unflattering to the latter. She sees dialogue as a-symmetrical—that is, as a one-way street, rather than as involving a healthy interchange of ideas. This is very odd, since it has generally been agreed that dialogue has precisely the honorific qualities are here reserved for conversation. This reservation aside, Professor Saw's study of conversation is an exemplary one.

Webster, said T. S. Eliot, was "much possessed by death." Nowadays, we are possessed not so much by death as by destruction, taken simply as an unpleasant and wholesale onset of death which is seen as an absolute end. Death, considered as an event in a long, even an eternal life, no longer presents itself as a fruitful object of thought. Perhaps this is why we are also preoccupied with what is seen as the inevitable isolation of human beings from one another. People used to look on death as the preliminary to a state in which all misunderstandings would be cleared up, but now we accept a state of affairs in which a misunderstanding here now is a misunderstanding for ever. It is therefore of the utmost importance that we should not misunderstand one another, but along with our sense of this importance and the consequent importance of communication, goes a profound and melancholy conviction that communication is never achieved.

It is noteworthy—I hesitated over this word for a long time, and finally left it as a neutral term—it is noteworthy that the period of doubt about the possibility of communication coincides with a period in which the physical means of communication have never been so efficient, so much studied and so well understood. The air is literally humming with conveyors of messages, wireless waves, telegraph and telephone vibrations along the wires and our own little contributions of sound waves as we speak and lecture to one another. When the physical methods of communication have reached a pitch of perfection never approached before, we are assailed by doubts as to whether that towards which it is essentially directed ever takes place.

The reason why I hesitated over my adjective was because I was torn between two contrary opinions, that it was surprising, and that it was just what one might expect. Perhaps the truth is that it is surprising only at the first glance. At first sight, it would be natural to think that since we have now mastered the technique of communication, it will go on more efficiently than ever before. On further reflection, we begin to think that what can be done so efficiently, even done by machines, is not after all what we are really concerned with when we think of the intimate relationships among human beings, of the exchange of confidences, the sharing of experiences and the discussion of the worth and value of human actions. If a machine teaches very efficiently, then it may be that the time has come for human teachers to take warning. If *this* is what machines do when they teach, then perhaps some quite different service must be offered by men. Machines can give instructions, convey information, tell us when we answer questions wrongly and set us on the right path again. What more is needed? At first sight, it seems obvious that there can be nothing in a machine comparable to the expression and evocation of emotion. But we hear of machines writing not only love letters, but poetry and musical compositions, and we remember that, for many people, art has as its function to express and communicate emotion. If a poem communicates emotion, and yet we know that that poem was produced by a machine, all we can say is that at any rate, that poem, or even a love letter, was triggered off by a mechanical device and not by the presence of an exciting object. This may come later—I do not trust machine makers to stop at anything. The more then, makers of machines say of communication: "We've done it!" the more ordinary people say: "If you've done it, it can't be done, as we understand it." We do not then, feel surprise when our novelists and playwrights present human beings as simply existing side by side, soliloquizing in one another's presence rather than holding conversations with one another. Even here, however, there is something odd. What should be shown is perfectly ordinary conversations failing to make contact instead of the very special conversations of *Waiting for Godot, The Waves* and *The Caretaker.*

When people deny that something exists, they are not denying the facts on which belief in its existence are based, but the interpretation of those facts. People who maintain the essential separateness of human beings from one another, after all, are living in our common world in which they, like everybody else, buy things from shops, ask for tickets and travel on trains and buses and call in plumbers to mend the pipes. They are then, not denying that people can and do give one another instructions, orders and information. Since the orders and information are acted upon or rebelled against, they have at least been received by the other person. Such people do not even deny that what looks like conversation between human beings takes place; what they are denying is that by these means, people are in communication with one another. What more do they ask, before agreeing that communication has indeed taken place?

Feiffer recently had a cartoon in *The Sunday Observer* in which each one of a couple makes just this complaint of the breakdown of communication against the other. The woman begins: "I'm standing right in front of you. Do you see me?" The man, shown as gazing dreamily over her head, replies: "I can't talk to you. I just can't get through to you any more." By the third picture, the situation is reversed and the man is saying: "I'm standing right in front of you. Do you see me?" In the last episode but one they are saying together: "What's the use? You haven't heard a single word I've said." Then one says: "What?" and the other says: "What? What?" (It is significant that one is not sure how to read the double "what" Is it "*what* what"? "What what" sounds too flippant, though perhaps this is only to English ears. Perhaps it is just a dead "What, what.")

Here is a case in which two people are shown as speaking to one another. One leaves off speaking when the other begins and begins when the other leaves off. At least each knows when the other is speaking, and there is even some connection between what they are each saying. In fact, they seem to be doing the paradoxical thing which so many of our novelists and playwrights are doing—they are saying: "Will you please listen to me complaining that people cannot talk to one another." The metaphor which Feiffer's two people use is illuminating; they complain that they cannot "get through," the complaint which we so frequently have to make to the girl at the telephone exchange. The invention of the telephone enabled us, from a long way off, to "get through" to one another, where before we should have been safely not-get-at-able, each in his own house. But it doesn't always work. We hear the bell pealing away in an empty house, or we have a feeling that the house is not empty, but for some reason it is ignoring the pealing of the bell. For whatever reason, the physical apparatus is doing its part, but we cannot "get through." This gives us the model for the modern view of human communication. I may stand before you, agitating the sound waves as I speak. They fall on your ears and set up a vibration in your brain substance, but somehow I have not got through. Karl Pearson used the telephone box metaphor to exhibit the separation of human beings from the outside world. We are each shut up in our own heads, receiving messages from the outside world but never in direct contact with it. Similarly, people seem to say nowadays, we are each shut up in our own heads, receiving only messages from our fellows, never in direct contact with them. This is, perhaps, the secret of the frightening fascination of the Sidney Nolan pictures and films of Ned Kelly. Kelly is shown in his homemade armor, his square tin head completely blank, no holes through which messages can enter in or come out. Is this supposed to be typical of the true situation of men in their attempts at communication with one another?

"But," you may say, "sometimes someone, even the person you wish to speak to, lifts the receiver and says 'Hullo'." Does this constitute "getting through" in any other than the literal sense in this context? Before we consider this question, let us examine some cases in which communication admittedly breaks down. We shall then be free to consider whether, these cases aside, communication must fail under the most favorable circumstances, whether, that is to say, there is anything at all which can count as communication. Communication fails where two people are speaking together, but from two very different standpoints, social, national, etc. I do not mean from two points of view representing conflicting interests; it is not communication but agreement which fails here. I mean cases where the hearer takes the remarks of the speaker in a different context from that assumed by the speaker. As frequently happens, the best examples come from the humorists. There are P. G. Wodehouse's two burglars who are enjoying a peaceful glass of port after packing up the valuables in an empty house. One of them prides himself on his knowledge of the aristocracy and their ways. Leaning back in his chair and gazing at the light sparkling through his glass of port he asks idly: "Who do you think would go in to dinner first, the sister of an earl or the daughter of a baronet?" His companion replies from an entirely different context: "It depends who's quickest on her feet." Communication has failed so completely here that reproaches of commonness and ignorance from the one side quickly lead to

accusations of "side" from the other, and to their falling on one another with punches and blows, until they are collected up and carted off unconscious by the police. Except for this result, this kind of exchange could be paralleled in many philosophical discussions, when, say, a theist is confronted by a positivist. In fact, a wary philosopher will find out first in what context an admission will be taken before he makes it. An exchange from the Moral Science Club at Cambridge went as follows: A.—At least you will admit that 2 and 2 make 4. B.—No I won't, not till I know what you are going to do with it.

Communication may fail where the context evoked may be the same in speaker and hearer, but where the hearer lacks the experience to give content to what he hears. The story from Grimm, *The Man Who Could Not Shiver*, tells of a case. The young man is called Dummling, naturally, since it is he who is to marry the beautiful princess. Dummling constantly hears people saying that things make them shiver. He sits by the fireside with them listening to ghost stories. "Oh, it makes us shiver!" they say. "What is this shivering?" says Dummling, "I cannot tell what you mean." His friends do their best for him. The sexton sends him to the church at midnight, to do an errand in the tower. Stealing after him, he stands silent on the stairs wrapped in a white sheet. Dummling challenges the silent apparition three times, and getting no reply, throws it down the stairs and goes peacefully home to bed. He is then sent to spend three nights in a haunted castle, but deals very competently with halves of men which fall down the great chimney, with cat-headed dogs and many other unusual combinations. Dummling still does not know what it means to shiver, but his friends have literally done the best possible for him; they have arranged for him to be put in situations in which normal men would feel the experience in question. If it fails, then there is nothing more to be done, but this is a special case; our question is whether communication is such that it must fail by its very nature.

The method used by Dummling's friends is not always open to people who wish to insure that they are conveying their meaning to one another. Suppose A assures us that he cannot think what we mean when we talk about nostalgia. We describe to him occasions on which we have felt it; he recalls similar occasions and reports no peculiar feeling which might be called homesickness. We cannot kidnap him and take him further away from home and for a longer period than he has ever experienced before, in the hope that he will then understand what we are talking about. Our only result would be to turn to artists in words or sounds or colored shapes, who succeed in conveying to people of normal sensibility the experience in question. (I have no facts which would bear on the question whether people completely failing to feel a given emotion under the circumstances which would normally arouse it might be led to feel that emotion by a work of art which presented similar situations.) But after all, is this what Wordsworth in *The Highland Lass*, or Proust, are as a matter of fact, conveying? And even if it were, would my sitting beside you while you read *Swann's Way*, waiting for an expression of comprehension to appear ("Oh, now I know what homesickness is."), would it have done my job? What I started off by wanting to convey to you was the exact flavor of my feeling when I was in America. How does it help for you to be moved by an evocation of homesickness in the figure of Ruth in the alien corn? This is not a sensitive awareness of me in America, but perhaps the answer is that we stand a better chance of becoming sensitively aware of the emotions of our friends if we have met similar situations in books, pictures and plays.

But we first have to consider the question whether artists, as a matter of fact, convey or communicate the natural emotions of human beings towards their surroundings and towards their fellows. Romanticists believe that the artist embodies the emotions aroused in him by the stimulating or originating experience in an object which directly arouses similar emotions in his

spectator-audience and towards the artist's objects. The difficulty here is that it is in the very respect of what we may call primary emotion towards the primary objects, sunsets, death and betrayal, fog on the river, that the artist differs from the ordinary man. No sooner is an artist moved by a situation, event or object than his experience begins to shape itself in phrases, images, shapes or musical tones. Wagner expressed this situation exactly in *A Happy Evening* (Paris, 1841). He writes: "When a musician feels prompted to sketch the smallest composition, he owes it simply to the stimulus of a feeling that usurps his whole being at the hour of conception. This mood may be brought about by an outward experience or have arisen from a secret inner spring; whether it shows itself as melancholy, joy, desire, contentment, love or hatred, in the musician it will always take a musical shape, and voice itself in tones or however it is cast in notes. These greater moods, as deep suffering of soul or potent exaltation, may date from outer causes, for we are all men . . .; but *when* they force the musician to production, these greater moods have already turned to music in him." Such an account meets the common but shallow objection to a communication theory of art, that if an artist is to communicate emotion, he must feel that emotion all the time he is at work. Not at all. What the artist feels is not, say, melancholy, but delight in his power to depict melancholy, and it is this delight which is communicated to his audience. This is why we can witness tragedies without distress or, rather, with positive delight. The object placed before us is exactly what it should be, and though jealousy, hatred, treachery may be in a concrete particular object, it is not these emotions which are being aroused, but wonder at their transmutation. The snag for our present purpose, however, is that we were looking to art to overcome the separation of human being from one another, to place them in contact with one another, but this would apply not to their sharing of the ordinary human emotions towards the world and towards

On talking with children

Believe that your child can understand more than he or she can say, and seek, above all, to communicate. To understand and to be understood. To keep your minds fixed on the same target. In doing that, you will, without thinking about it, make 100 or 1000 alterations in your speech and action. Do not try to practice them as such. There is no set of rules of how to talk to a child that can even approach what you unconsciously know. If you concentrate on communicating, everything else will follow.

—From Roger Brown, Introduction to C. Snow and C. Ferguson (eds.), *Talking to children: Language input and acquisition* (New York: Academic Press, 1977).

everyday objects, but towards one very special kind of object, a work of art.

This account lessens the distance between non-representational and representational art. People complain that our contemporary writers, painters and composers make no attempt to communicate, that, at a time when scientists are making great strides in the understanding of the forms of communication, the very people who are traditionally the transmitters of experience to their fellows have given up the attempt. But if artists are communicating their painterly or writerly experiences and not the ordinary emotions towards everyday objects, then the essential difference between Constable and Braque lies in the nature of the originating experience and not in the fact or the lack of communication. Constable is transmitting not his love for the countryside of Suffolk, but his delight in being able to render his beloved flat fields and wide skies in pigments. The originating experience of the moderns seems to be more directly concerned with the nature and possibilities of their medium. We may even get the delight of the action painter as he rides over his canvas on his bicycle.

We have now reached the position that if A and B wish to be sure that they are communicating with one another, they will find no real difficulty if all they are talking about is giving one another pieces of information, instructions and orders. If they wish to inform one another as to their mental states, there will be more difficulty than if the information were about sights and sounds. "I don't call that orange." "I do." This kind of difference must be settled by bringing a color card. If the lamp shade matches orange in the color card, then we must both describe it as orange. "I don't call that friendship, or love or jealousy." "I do." This kind of case puts us in a more difficult position, for there is nothing comparable to the color card for is to appeal to. Perhaps the nearest to it would be classical examples from history or legend, though our estimates of such cases varies with the times. Aeneas bearing his father from the burning ruins of Troy might stand as a model of filial piety as Judas stands as the model of treachery. It is a little more difficult still if what we want to do is not merely to tell one another *that* we have had a horrifying experience, but to convey the horror. Here, if anywhere, is where art comes in. If writers and artists cannot convey the peculiar emotional flavor of jealousy, horror, love, then nobody can.

Let us suppose that all these difficulties have been overcome. We now feel confident that we can make one another understand that we have had certain kinds of experiences, and sometimes are able to bring them to feel their peculiar emotional flavor. If all this has happened, would this be good enough? Would our Feiffer couple feel that they had "got through" to one another? My feeling is that they would still not be satisfied; that in fact they *cannot* be satisfied, because they are asking for a logical impossibility. A looks at B. He has done his best to make B share a given experience and B has expressed himself in such terms that for a moment, A feels satisfied. Only for a moment however. Even suppose B feels an exactly similar repugnance and shrinking of the flesh that A has presented to him so eloquently, it is still B's own repugnance and shrinking. A may still look at him and think: "How do I know that it feels the same to you as it feels to me? I am behind my face and you are in front of it, and that is how it remains." A is like Walt Disney's Harry Hare who played himself at tennis, leaping over the net so quickly that he was in time to return his own services, then back again to return his return. He wanted to be on both ends of his service and return, and in the same way, our A wants to be on both ends of his messages. He knows what it feels like to send out a given message; he wants to know also, what it feels like to receive it. Only so, he thinks, can two people really be in communication with one another. The only snag is that there is now no point in sending out messages. Why bother to send out messages which you yourself are to receive? I could easily have made Harry Hare an extremely discontented animal. There he was, gaily leaping backwards and forwards, nonchalantly returning his hardest services and volleys, but completely missing the unexpectedness of an opponent's tactics in dealing with such strokes. That is much more important, even in learning your own strength and weakness, than knowing how it is to receive your own service. Communication between persons who remain stubbornly themselves and separate is the only communication worthy of the name. What our melancholy people are demanding for perfect communication is the destruction of its essential condition. What I hope to show however, is that there is a satisfactory exercise in which human beings engage, which leads to their becoming better acquainted with themselves and with one another, and which is therefore worthy of the name of communication. It sounds too easy an answer, but I am hoping to exhibit conversation between human beings as such an exercise.

Before embarking on this, however, I must make a distinction the need for which must have been obvious to you all. I have not overlooked it, but was waiting for the most convenient place to make it. This distinction is between A's communicating x to B, where x may be a piece of information, a feeling, an emotion, whatever you like to B, and A's being in communication with B. There are important logical differences between these two relationships; the first is a three-termed while the second is a two-termed relationship. Moreover, if we ignore the x for the moment, and think of the giving-receiving relation as if it were two-termed, it is an asymmetrical relation, i.e., one which holds only one way round, while the second is symmetrical. If A gives (x) to B, then B does not by that same act, give whatever it was to A. But if A is in communication with B, then B by that same act is in communication with A. Now the people who complain that they cannot get in touch with one another are not complaining that they cannot communicate some things to one another, but that they cannot be in communication with one another. They may or may not feel difficulty about the communication of emotion, but they certainly feel the difficulty of being in contact with other human beings.

People who work on the logic of human organizations seem to be interested only in hierarchical organizations, and consequently, only in asymmetrical relationships. Giving orders to, taking instructions from, making suggestions to, vetoing the suggestions of, are all examples of asymmetrical relations. If A gives orders to B, gives instructions to, makes suggestions to and vetoes the suggestions of B, then B does none of these things to A. There is, of course, the relation, giving information to, and this may appear to be not asymmetrical, but non-symmetrical. One might think that, if A gives information to B, then B may or may not give information to A. B does not, it is thought, upset the hierarchical organization if he gives his superiors a piece of information as he would if he tried to give them orders or veto their suggestions. But if there were a specified place for the giver of information, and we ruled out unofficial information, then gives information to is asymmetrical like the other relations. One of the office staff might tell the managing director that the office cat had had kittens, and the managing director might respond by telling him that the frost had caught his chrysanthemums last night, but this is extra-organization, and not catered for in the logic of human organizations.

Now there is no doubt whatever that "converses with" is a symmetrical relation. A cannot converse with B if B does not converse with A. It is not a symmetrical relation which can be dissolved into a disjunction of two asymmetrical relations, such as "spouse of." "Spouse of" is equivalent to "husband or wife of," and while it is true that if A is the spouse of B, B is the spouse of A, it is also true that if A is the husband of B, B cannot be the husband of A. Now there is nothing comparable to this dissolution in the relation "converses with." If we tried to make it equivalent to "either makes remarks to or listens to remarks from," it wouldn't do, not just because both are necessary, but because each remark is shaped and shapes in turn earlier and later remarks.

In order to exhibit the nature of conversation, I am going to give some examples of what at first sight might appear to be conversations but are not. There are two ways in which something, I must leave this vague for the moment, in which something might appear to be a conversation. It might be presented in the form of a dialogue, with a name followed by a colon, inverted commas, then an exclamation, a sentence or a question, followed by another name and a similar successor. A dialogue may be a literary form presenting conversations, but it may also present misused conversations. (I explain "misused" later). It may also be a device for presenting a proof, an argument or a systematic series of pieces of information. The most famous of such forms are the Platonic dialogues, but as Max Beerbohm remarks: "The Socratic manner is not a game that two can play at." That is to say, "conducts a dialogue with" is an asymmetrical relation. If A conducts a dialogue with B, B is usually the stooge, and does *not* conduct a dialogue with A. The dialogue form is either accidental or it is a literary device which has its own formal value,

and whether a given example falls under one or the other heading must be determined by critical examination. Many of the improving books for children of the Victorian era were accidental dialogues. Harry: "Papa, you promised to tell us something of the habits of bees on our next walk in the country." Father: "I am glad you reminded me my boy, for we can all learn from these busy little creatures. . . ." It is an accident that Euclid did not use the dialogue form. I can imagine something of this sort. Alciphron: "If I am not mistaken Euthyphro, you were going to demonstrate to me that the three angles of a triangle together added up to two right angles." Euthyphro: "True Alciphron; let us begin by producing the side BC of triangle ABC." Euthypro: "I perceive your design, and now of course we must draw CD parallel to AB. . . ."

The other way in which something might appear as a conversation—and now it will be clear why I wanted to use the vague "something"—is that used by two people who want to present the appearance of conversing without using words, but simply by making suitable noises. It may be noticed here that if you wanted to present the appearance of a conversation in German, you would have to use a series of noises different from those you would make if it were to appear as a conversation in Irish or Italian, or in any other language.

I spoke earlier of "misused" conversation. This was a mis-description. The essence of conversation, as I hope to show, is that it must not be used for any ulterior purpose. Conversation can, then, neither be used nor misused; what we want to say in the latter case is that someone has pretended to converse when he is in reality guiding the sequence of remarks to his own end. I will give some examples. The first is from Mrs. Gaskell's *Wives and Daughters*. Mrs. Gibson is ostensibly concerned about the health of Lady Cumnor, but her hearers are not taken in. "Cynthia: 'They're in London now, and Lady Cumnor hasn't suffered from the journey.' 'They *say* so,' said Mrs. Gibson, . . . 'I am perhaps over-anxious, but I wish—I wish I could see and judge for myself. It would be the only way of calming my anxiety. I almost think I shall go up with you, Cynthia, for a day or two, just to see her with my own eyes. You shall write to Mr. Kirkpatrick and propose it if we determine upon it. You can tell him of my anxiety; and it will only be sharing your bed for a couple of nights'. That was the way in which Mrs. Gibson first broached her intention of accompanying Cynthia up to London for a few days' visit. She had a trick of producing the first sketch of any new plan before an outsider to the family circle; so that the first emotions of others, if they disapproved of her projects, had to be repressed, until the idea had become familiar to them." That is to say, Mrs. Gibson, under the guise of carrying on a conversation with her family and guests, shaped what she said so as to bring about her own ends.

The next example, from *Martin Chuzzlewit*, is even plainer. Mrs. Gamp is being conveyed by Mr. Pecksniff to lay out old Anthony Chuzzlewit, who has just died. Mrs. Gamp hopes for a new and profitable connection, but wishes to make her requirements quite plain. She delivers herself thus to Mr. Pecksniff: " 'Mrs. Harris' I says, at the very last case as ever I acted in, 'Mrs. Harris' I says, 'leave the bottle on the chimley piece, and don't ask me to take none, but let me put my lips to it when I am so dispoged, and then I will do what I am engaged to do to the best of my ability.' 'Mrs. Gamp', she says in answer, 'if ever there was a sober creature to be got at eighteenpence a day for working people, and three-and-six for gentlefolks—night watching' " said Mrs. Gamp with emphasis, " 'being a extra charge—you are that inwallable person'." Here, Mrs. Gamp, by means of a reported conversation, it is true, and as we suspect, an imaginary one, has managed to mention several matters that it is important for her comfort that her employers should know.

Here is a misuse of conversation in a more important and subtle sense, from *Pride and Prejudice*. Mr. Bennet is ostensibly engaged in conversation with his cousin, Mr. Collins, but is really leading him on to exhibit himself as a flatterer who is so stupid as not to see how other people would regard him. Mr. Collins has been speaking of the daughter of his patron, Lady Catherine de Bourgh. "Has she been presented? I do not remember her name among the ladies at court." "Her indifferent state of health unhappily prevents her being in town and by that means, as I told Lady Catherine myself one day, has deprived the British Court of its brightest ornament. Her Ladyship seemed pleased with the idea; and you may imagine that I am happy on every occasion to offer those little compliments which are always acceptable to ladies. I have more than once observed to Lady Catherine, that her charming daughter seemed born to be a duchess; and that the most elevated rank, instead of giving her consequence, would be adorned by her. These are the kind of little things which please her Ladyship, and it is a sort of attention which I conceive myself bound to pay." "You judge very properly," said Mr. Bennet; "and it is happy for you that you possess the talent of flattering with delicacy. May I ask whether these pleasing attentions proceed from the impulse of the moment, or are they the result of previous study?" "They arise chiefly from what is passing at the time; and though I sometimes amuse myself with suggesting and arranging such little elegant compliments as may be adapted to ordinary occasions, I always wish to give them as unstudied an air as possible." Mr. Bennet's expectations were fully answered. His cousin was as absurd as he had hoped; and he listened to him with the keenest enjoyment, maintaining at the same time the most resolute composure of countenance, and except in an occasional glance at Elizabeth, requiring no partner in his pleasure.

To call this a misuse of conversation is not, of course, a reflection on that master of dialogue, Jane Austen. She knows and shows us just how people make use of others for their enjoyment, their advancement, just as much in their words as in their actions. Whenever people speak in order to impress, to exhibit their wit, their wealth, their

Criteria and curriculum

In short, to regard the curriculum not as the materials of instruction, but rather as the basis of the pupils' discussion and thinking, is to emphasize the need to come to terms with the practical difficulties of the classroom. Hence the need to scrutinize the standards actually achieved rather than the aims expressed. A good curriculum is one that makes worthwhile standards possible.

—Lawrence Stenhouse, *Culture and Education* (New York: Weybright and Talley, 1967), p. 89.

learning, or to bring about some advantage for themselves, they are failing to treat their hearer as a person, as an end in himself and conversation with him as carried on for its own sake. Mr. Bennet, of course, thinks of Mr. Collins as an unworthy partner in any rational enterprise; it is true also that Mr. Collins is being exhibited as one who shamelessly exploits conversation with his wealthy patron, who herself is not a rational being in her arrogant and stupid acceptance of the grossest flattery. However, the Golden Rule, "Do as you would be done by," does not specify to whom you must do as you would be done by. It does not say: "Do to sensible and rational people as you would be done by," and even if it did, you ought not to assume that you are one of the rational and sensible people to whom people must not do as you do to the silly ones. If we accept some form of Kant's maxim, "Be a person and treat others as persons," we must not add, but, some creatures having the human form are not worthy of the name "person." It is safer to assume that any creature having the human form is a person, is to be treated as such, and is to be found worthy of being engaged in rational enterprises, including that of conversation. (While we are on the subject of misuse of conversation, I will draw your attention to an entry in *Who's Who* under the name of a recent winner of the Nobel

Prize in Medicine. This gentleman gives as his only recreation, "conversation, especially with pretty women"!).

We may now draw together the requirements for giving the name conversation to a set of utterances by two people. It could be between more than two people, but no new principle would arise with a third participant, so for the sake of simplicity we will assume that conversation is between two people. We might notice also, that sometimes, an apparent soliloquy could equally well have been a conversation, where the person soliloquizing is able to see alternating points of view clearly enough to produce surprises to himself in his ruminations. Groucho Marx, playing a dictator who has been persuaded to receive the head of a neighboring and unfriendly nation ruminates thus: (He has found the phrase "extend the right hand of friendship" particularly persuasive.) "Yes," he says: "I *will* receive him. I'll show the big baboon what it is to be magnanimous. I'll extend the right hand of friendship to him." He dwells with pleasure on this prospect, but suddenly goes on: "But suppose he won't take it! Suppose I extend the right hand of friendship to him and he just stands there sneering! A nice fool I shall look standing there with my hand stuck out and he won't take it, the big gink!" At this moment the man appears at the door and Groucho promptly knocks him down. This could easily have been a dialogue between two people, rather than between Groucho and his *alter ego*, since these two latter are sufficiently unlike to be thought of as two people.

We will put the negative conditions for conversation first: A may be said to converse with B, when it is not the case that:

1. A is manipulating the succession of remarks in such a way that B may be, without his knowledge, presented to others in a given light. It need not be an unfavorable light; if B were being "drawn out" so as to exhibit his wit, he would be being used just as much as if it were to exhibit his stupidity.

2. A is manipulating the exchange of remarks in such a way that he informs B, or those standing by, as if it were casually, of facts that he wishes to make known, but which he does not wish to mention directly, or if he wishes to display an attitude towards B or others without appearing to do so.

3. A is manipulating the exchange of remarks in such a way as to exhibit himself as possessing some quality, good or bad, which for some reason, he wishes to have noticed.

There may be other ways of using and so destroying conversation, but the important general condition, is that it, no more than persons, may be used. In a rational partnership, neither may be worked on, without his knowledge and consent.

Positively, A may be said to converse with B when:

1. They exchange remarks in such a situation that they are free and equal partners. Equals, of course, may put themselves into hierarchical organizations. This does not destroy their equality with other members of the organization if they have chosen to enter it, and so long as there is some area outside that organization where its members may gather together and talk with one another as equals. This does not mean of equal value to the community, but simply of equal worth as persons. It is the sense in which people are equal in the sight of the law, or better still, in the sight of God. This I take to be the foundation of the anarchist's creed—that human beings ought not to enter into relationships which will make it appear that some people are more important than others. Certainly, if we want a bridge built, then for the time architects, engineers and quantity surveyors are the most important people. Therefore, say the anarchists, take care to disband the bridge-building committee as soon as the bridge is built, and do not let the habit of estimating people according to their usefulness take possession.

2. A and B are conversing when they are each interested in the experiences, attitudes and opinions of the other. They begin to explore a situation, talk about a thing or event, and allow the conversation to take its own way. This is not quite like "following the argument where it leads" since the course of the argument is determined by the logical relation between the steps. The conversation goes where it will in the sense that "the spirit bloweth where it listeth." It is not only *about* something, it is also expressive of the feelings and attitudes of the two people towards it.

3. Each person can give the other some surprises.

At this point, we may look back and notice that our requirements begin to make conversation look like a work of art. It is the spontaneous and free expression of two people sharing a common object, who are enjoying the process of making a new object, the conversation. Since this object has been made by the two together, and since neither would have been moved to his utterances without the stimulus of the other, it is an object which they can both contemplate as revealing A to himself and to B, and B to himself and to A. It is an object which embodies the knowledge which the two people have achieved of one another and each of himself.

It is usually assumed that each man is at least acquainted with himself, but it seems to me that the process of becoming acquainted with oneself necessarily goes along with the process of becoming acquainted with another person. If I never exchange remarks with another person, never have any dealings with or evoke a response from him, I do not really know what my emotions are. We say of someone who utters an unusually spiteful remark: He must be jealous. Equally, and with the same shock of surprise, we feel a pang when we hear of a friend's success and say: I must be jealous. The difference between the two cases is that in the first we hear the spiteful remark while the friend had the pang. In the second case, we had the pang, but this led us to say, just as hearing the remark led us to say of our friend: I, the person who had the pang, must be jealous. Not *am* jealous, but *must* be: it is an inference in both cases. It seems to be assumed that the self which remains stubbornly mine and from which others are inescapably cut off, is a congerie of such pangs, flashes of hopefulness, feelings of nostalgia. Certainly, our growing knowledge of and acquaintance with our companions and the world has a running accompaniment of such feelings, but what makes us separate from but interested in one another is not that running accompaniment but that which it accompanies. It is our growing knowledge of the world, each from his own point of view, our changing and developing attitudes towards it and our own peculiar methods of dealing with it. It is this which makes communication necessary, possible and worthwhile.

A further paradox arises from our demand to be in direct and complete communication with one another, to feel one another's feelings and think one another's thoughts. Let us take an example first, of an attempt to enter completely into the concerns of another person, in which it is easier to exhibit the paradox, and then go on to the attempt to take up one another's thoughts, feelings and attitudes towards the external world.

A and B each wishes to demonstrate his tender concern for the other. A says: I worry only about your worries, B. B says: I worry only about your worries, A. In that case, neither has any worries, although A has headaches and an overdraft at the bank, and B has a weak chest and chilblains. They see this to be absurd and each amends his position. A says: I worry about all our worries, both yours and mine. B says the same. But now they have too many worries; A worries not only about B's weak chest, but about B's worry about his weak chest, and this constitutes a new worry for B, and consequently a new worry for A and so on, indefinitely. They see this to be as absurd as the first state, and agree on the following amendment. The tender concern of each for the other is to be shown reasonably by concern for all the ills of both, that is to say, each will feel first order worry. Second order worry for the feelings of worry of the other will be a matter of concern only if it constitutes a first order worry, i.e., A might

be worried about B's tendency to worry about his chilblains as a sign of bad circulation and so of a weak heart.

Let us now draw a parallel to this case in the mutual desire of A and B to feel each as the other feels towards their common world. They stand in A's garden which is bedded out with scarlet geraniums, blue lobelias and white alyssum. B hates it, and thinks his own arrangement of delphiniums, heliotrope and pink rambler roses is much to be preferred. He stands and looks at A's red, white and blue, trying to feel A's delight in it. But A is trying to feel B's dislike of it. It is a hopeless case, since neither is feeling his usual feeling for what he sees, and so neither has anything to communicate to the other. Their first amendment leads them to admit first order feelings: each must hang on to his primary feelings, A of delight in his flower arrangement and his deprecation of B's dislike of it. But he has now presented a new feeling to B, namely his deprecation of B's feeling, and A will now have a new feeling about his feeling and so on. They now reach the third and reasonable position. Each must be allowed to feel his own private feeling towards his own things. Each can tell the other *that* they feel in a certain way towards those things. A can understand that his feeling for his red, white and blue resembles B's feeling for his pink, blue and mauve. But if each feels the other's feelings for these diverse objects, there is no longer an A-ish state for B to become aware of, or a B-ish state for A to become aware. Plotinus said that if individual souls were not separate and distinct, we should all experience one another's sensations, desires and thoughts, even everything that occurred anywhere in the universe. (This of course, assumes that there are no unoccupied points of view, which may be allowed to pass, if we include the omnipresence of God.) In either event, it would mean, in effect, that there were no points of view, since whatever was experienced from *any* point of view would be experienced from every point of view.

So far, we have been concerned only with deliberate utterances by human beings, deliberate conveying of information, giving of orders, engaging in conversation. We must qualify the deliberations in the latter case, for conversation is deliberate in one sense and not in another. It is deliberate in the sense that it is a human action, but it is not reflected upon at every step on the way. It is deliberate in the way in which a work of art is deliberate. An artist chooses to write, to paint or to model, but once embarked upon the process, he cannot be said to proceed altogether deliberately. It is not like embarking upon a mathematical proof in which each step is seen as determining the next by the nature of the material, and yet there is a connection between each step and the next. Henry James talks of "the logic of the particular case," and Barbara Hepworth describes how the first line drawn upon the blank canvas narrows the possibilities for the next. Having drawn the first line, the artist cannot place the next line *anywhere*, though he could not produce a general principle justifying the placing of the next line. It is seen as what must be *in this case*. I want to call conversation deliberate in this latter sense; it is one of the desirable activities in which human beings engage, both for its own sake and for the sake of the product, and since it is desirable, we may urge it upon one another, and this is to presuppose that it is willed. It has its own rules, however, and its course is determined by the particular nature of each case.

The question of the deliberateness of our exploring of one another's individuality by conversation leads on to my last point. There are certainly ways in which we learn about other people, if not necessarily against their will, at least not with their cooperation. We may betray emotion rather than express it, to adopt R. G. Collingwood's distinction. If we are on the alert, we may read the signs and, as we say, "read one another like a book." This cannot count as communication, nor can the being acted upon by signs given to us without our knowledge or consent. We cannot be said to receive a message from a

Education through dialogue

If education is dialogical, it is clear that the role of the teacher is important, whatever the situation. As s/he dialogues with the pupils, s/he must draw their attention to points that are unclear or naive, always looking at them problematically. Why? How? Is it so? What relation is there between the statement you have just made, and that of your companion? Is there any contradiction between them? Why? It can be said once more that such an approach needs time. That often there is "no time to lose," "there is a syllabus to be completed." Once again in the name of time which is not to be wasted. Young people are alienated by the kind of copybook thought that is almost entirely verbally narrated. Moreover, the content of what is narrated must be passively received and then memorized for repetition later. Dialogue does not depend on the content which is to be seen problematically. Everything can be presented as a problem.

The role of the educator is not to "fill" the educatee with "knowledge," technical or otherwise. It is rather to attempt to move towards a new way of thinking in both educator and educatee, through the dialogical relationships between both. The flow is in both directions. The best student in physics or mathematics, at school or university, is not one who memorizes formulae but one who is aware of the reason for them. For students, the more simply and docilely they receive contents with which their teachers "fill" them in the name of knowledge, the less they are able to think and the more they become merely repetitive.

—Paulo Freire, *Education for Critical Consciousness* (New York: The Seabury Press, 1973) pp. 124–125.

subliminal flash upon the screen, even though it affects our behavior. We are justifiably annoyed if we find that we have been so acted upon. There is one kind of case, however, in which it is legitimate to read the signs of another person's emotions and intentions. Where two people willingly enter themselves against each other as antagonists, it is part of the game to read the signs, to provoke one another to give such signs, and part of the training to keep a poker face and give no hint of intentions. Two boxers who have met one another frequently in the ring, two tennis players who know one another's game thoroughly, are keeping our rules for treating with persons; they are treating one another as equals each worthy of the other's steel. Each is submitting himself to what he is giving, and there is no doubt that they are becoming very well acquainted with one another.

It is significant that ideal courtesy between people is often exemplified not by close friends, but by people who are strangers to one another. They are not hampered by any of the complicating circumstances troubling friends and acquaintances. If you want an example of absolute good will between persons, an unadulterated desire to help, a going out of the way to make sure that the required help has been given, ask a stranger the way somewhere. Of course, if he does not know the way, the experiment has failed, but if he does know it, he all but carries you there and bears you through the doorway. With the natural and native good will of human beings towards one another, he meets with joy a situation in which he really can do for somebody, just what that person wants done. He keeps looking back to savor to the full, the pleasant experience of seeing another person going right through his agency. When we are in more complicated relationships with one another, we cannot behave in this way, but how we wish we could. This brings me to what really is my last point. People who complain that they are not able really to know others seldom think of themselves as to be known in the same way in which they wish to know others. Knowing and being known are co-relative terms, as are loving and being loved. If these relations were symmetrical, it would be a very happy thing for human relationships, but this is a matter of fact and not of logic.

Children Discuss Degrees and Kinds of Difference

Gerry Dawson McClendon

In the summer of 1975, it was decided to hold a small demonstration class in philosophy for children, as part of a teacher-training workshop at Montclair State College. The teacher was Mrs. Gerry Dawson McClendon (then as now a teacher at the Morton Street School in Newark), who had participated in a previous training workshop. One group of students was bused in every morning from the New Ark school in Newark, a privately-operated, alternative school. These students were in the 14-15 year-old range. The other group was drawn from the Montclair-Clifton area, and consisted of 11 and 12-year-olds.

After two weeks or so of being on display, the children began to verbalize their discontent with the arrangement, so the class was moved into a separate classroom and was videotaped. This unedited videotape transcript (prepared and annotated by Miriam Minkowitz) is a verbatim record of the twelfth and final class session. The teacher is guiding the discussion by following the questions in two discussion plans contained in the instructional manual for the course.

Although the wealth of visual cues is lacking in this written version of the classroom discussion, there is much that is instructive in it as well. The logic of conversation and the etiquette of dialogue can often be scrutinized more meticulously in this fashion than can be done where one is present in the classroom. Especially worthy of study are the patterns of group reasoning, in particular on those occasions where the children build on each other's contributions, thereby penetrating as deeply into the issues (of considerable difficulty even for skilled philosophers) as might a smaller number of older individuals. Equally noteworthy is the readiness of the participants to establish a youthful community of inquiry, and to display the characteristic features of a truly reflective education.

Gerry   —All right—when Mr. Portos was discussing with the girls about the minds and the differences between animals and men . . . he mentioned two types of differences. (Works on board) One was the difference of degree, and what, Renata? . . . and one was the difference of . . .

Renata   —. . . Kind.

Gerry   —. . . and kind.

Gerry   —How did he explain those differences? What's the difference between a difference of degree and a difference of kind? What did he use to show the girls what he meant? Because they didn't understand. What did he use?

Kirk   —Height and weight.

Gerry   —As an example of what?

Kirk   —Difference of degree.

Gerry   —Height and weight. What do the rest of you think about that? What type of difference is that? Height and weight?

Could a child's question be answered this way?

The simple "I don't know" deserves respect but it shouldn't cut off dialogue. The teacher can shift the question so that the student can respond, and thus, through a series of such questions, demonstrate that students do know things they don't think they know. Enthusiasm for all responses, not just for the right answers is both a courtesy and an incentive. Never deliberately ignore a question or demean the questioner.

A recent experience of mine seems to violate this principle though actually it supports the point. I was challenged in a question-and-answer session to support my claim that characteristics of good and bad teaching could be identified. "Can you give even one example of bad teaching?" this faculty member asked. I thought a moment, then said abruptly, "That seems to me to be a trivial question," and turned to another question from across the room. I went on for some moments, keeping the first questioner in the corner of my eye to make sure that he wasn't stalking out of the room. Then I turned back to him, apologized for my rudeness, and said, "That's your example."

—Kenneth E. Eble, *The Craft of Teaching* (San Francisco: Jossey-Bass Publishers, 1976), p. 60.

Jeanne —Difference of degree.

Gerry —That's what Kirk says. Difference of degree.

Mitchell —Well like if one girl weighs 59 lbs. and someone else . . . weighs . . . uh . . . 29 lbs. . . . in between there is . . . uh . . . degree.

Gerry —A difference of degree but you used two what?

Mitchell —Two people.

Gerry —Two people and their what?

Mitchell —Their height. I mean their weight.

Gerry —Two people and their weight. As a difference of degree?

Renata —That's a difference of kind.

Gerry —Why is that a difference of kind?

Renata —Because . . . uh . . . (long pause) . . . I don't know.

Gerry —Well, uh, one girl she was talking about . . . she weighed 59 lbs. and the other weighed 29 lbs. 29 lbs., right? So can you see that he was saying that in between 59 and 29 we're talking about the same two things, right? Pounds! How much each girl weighs. . . . Okay. And while *pounds* isn't different the *amount* of pounds that they weigh is different, right? But is it *totally* different? It's just a difference of degree. One is larger than the other or one is smaller than the other.

Renata —(Looking in her book)—Over here she says the same thing is a difference of degree.

Gerry —Read that for me.

Renata —(Turns open her book and reads)— "Laura is the heaviest," said Jill. "Then comes Fran and then me." Are those differences of degree also?

Gerry —Are they?

Renata —No.

Gerry —All right. We were talking about heaviness and when you weigh how heavy we are we weigh that in what?

Kirk —Pounds.

Gerry —Pounds. They're all weighed in ounces or pounds. So that's a difference of . . .

Jeanne —Height or weight.

Gerry —Is that a difference of degree or kind?

Child —Degree.

Gerry —Right. Does everyone understand that? When we are talking about comparing the . . . uh . . . the weight? How about if we're comparing your height, Renata, to Karen's height? Would that be a difference? Are you both the same? Stand up. Let's see. Are they both the same height? Are they the same height? Let's not use you then. How about uh . . . Karen and Pamela? What would you say about Karen's height and Pamela's height?

John or Walt —Difference of degree.

Gerry —All right. It's a difference of degree. Because you're talking about the same thing. How tall they are.

John or Walt —If they were the same size it would be a difference of kind.

Renata —A difference of kind would be . . . uh . . .

John or Walt —The same.

Renata —Uh uh, different things. Like . . .

John or Walt —Your height and weight.

Renata —(Simultaneously) Black and white, right?

Gerry —Well I don't know. That's very interesting. Is black and white a difference of kind?

Renata —No, but they both colors. Right? But they different colors, though.

Gerry —Yes, they're different colors, but are they . . . are they a difference of . . .

Renata —Okay. I didn't (unintelligible) Like the chair and . . . purse.

Gerry —A chair and a purse shows what?

Renata —A difference of kind.

Gerry —A difference of kind. All right. They're totally different things. Right. Any questions about the difference of degree and the differences of kind? All right, let's see if you had . . . uh . . . She . . . Renata brought up a very interesting one. Black and white. Is that a difference of degree or a difference of kind?

Renata —It's a difference of degree.

Gerry —Why would you say it's a difference of degree?

Renata —Because they're both colors.

Gerry —Mmmhmm.

Renata —So it's the same thing.

Gerry —What do you mean it's the same thing?

Renata —It's the same. Both of them are colors.

Gerry —Colors are the same. What about the rest of you? Is . . . uh . . . the difference between black and white the same as . . . say . . . as the difference between light green and dark green?

John or Walt —Right.

Child —Right.

Jeanne —Ummhmm.

Child —Yes.

Gerry —What kind of a difference would dark green and light green be?

Child —(several voices) Difference of degree.

Gerry —A difference of degree. Well is . . .

Renata —Since they're both green. So they're different shades of green.

Gerry —All right, so they're both green but of different shades. Well, then, what about black and white?

Renata —*Plus* they're different shades. *Plus* they're both colors.

Gerry —Yes, but they're both the *same* color, only different shades, right?

Renata —But they still colors.

Gerry —Mmmhmm.

Renata —It's two different things that's alike. It's a degree.

Gerry —Okay . . . so you're absolutely certain that black and white are differences of degree?

Child —Right.

Gerry —Okay. Un . . . how about nine apples compared with nine alligators?

Child —(many voices) Difference of kind.

Gary —Why?

Jeanne —Because they are both different— completely different things.

Gerry —All right. O.K. How about . . . uh . . . dark red compared with light red?

Child —(many voices) Difference of degree!

Gerry —Absolutely sure?

Child —Yep. Ummhmm. Difference of degree.

Gerry —O.K. How about . . . uh . . . freezing temperature compared to boiling temperature?

Child —Difference of degree!

Gerry —Damp compared to wet?

Child —Difference of degree.

Gerry —We're unanimous. Uh . . . I think I'll put this one on the board. (Stands up and goes to blackboard).

Walt —I don't know (unintelligible) . . .

Gerry —(laughs) This is called an acute angle (says this while drawing it on board.)

Child —Obtuse . . .

Gerry —Took me a long time . . . (unintelligible) . . . and this is an obtuse angle. What would the difference between these two be?

Walt —Difference of kind.

Child —(Many voices) Difference of degree! Degree!

Gerry —Who said a difference of kind? Walt?

Walt —(Walter shows hands).

Gerry —And everybody else thinks it's a difference of degree. What do you think about that?

Walt —Difference of kind.

Gerry —Why do you say it's a difference of kind?

Walt —Because they aren't shaped the same . . .

Gerry —They aren't shaped the same way.

Karen —Yeah, but they're both angles, though.

Gerry —Tell *him*.

Karen —(repeats) They're both angles.

Gerry —Do you understand what she's saying? They're shaped differently but they're both angles. Let's take . . . um . . . (draws on board—chalk makes a scratchy sound) . . . excuse me . . . What would you say about these two figures? This is a triangle and this is a . . .

Child —Rectangle.

Gerry —Rectangle.

Child —(Simultaneously) Difference of kind

Child —(Simultaneously) Difference of degree.

Gerry —I hear "kind" and "degree."

Walt —Kind.

Renata —Difference of degree because they're both shapes.

Gerry —They're both shapes . . . What?

Pamela —They're both shapes.

Gerry —They're both shapes so that means they're a difference of degree. Those of you who said they're a difference of kind—why would you say they're a difference of kind?

COMMENT: By asking this question Gerry is (1) opening up alternate possibilities; (2) allowing the children to come to discover that *context* is significant in making this judgment. As one of the children on the tape later remarks, it really depends on the *reasons* that you are looking at. That is, if you look at it from *one* point of view something may seem a difference of degree; however, if you look at the same thing with something else, i.e., some other standard, in mind, it may then appear to be a difference in kind.) *See* below.*

Mitchell —Because when they're triangles . . .

Donna —(Unintelligible) . . . they're *different* shapes.

Gerry —Huh?

Melanie —They're *different* shapes.

Jeanne —They're very different.

Renata —But they're *both* shapes . . . and them were different angles.

Mitchell —But the two girls are both girls, only *they're* different.

Renata —So it's a difference of degree.

Melanie —It could still be a difference of kind . . . You could put either one anyway.

Gerry —Why?

Melanie —Because you could find different reasons for each one.*

Gerry —All right. Well, why is this a difference of kind?

Melanie —Because they're both *different* shapes. Just like those are different angles. So we use *this* reason for saying . . .

Gerry —Well, then, are you saying that this could also be a difference of . . . uh . . . kind, too?

Melanie —It could . . . if it has smaller reasons. So it could be just simply smaller reasons for it . . . and then you could always go to the *big* reasons of (unintelligible) the different shapes.

COMMENT: By using the terms "smaller" and "bigger" Melanie seems to be calling for an appreciation for differences in degrees of *generality.* i.e., "Smaller" reasons would apply to things that are more specific, whereas "larger" reasons may apply to things considered more generally.

Gerry —All right. Well, let's take the alligators and the apples. O.K.? Now, these are different angles, but if they're both angles, they're *different* angles. What would you say about the alligators and the apples?

Melanie —One is an animal and one is a apple.

Daniel —One is an animal and one's a fruit.

Gerry —One's an animal and one's a fruit. We said that *that* was a difference of kind. Because they were *totally* different.

Karen —But if there was nine alligators and nine zebras, then it would be a difference of degree.

Gerry —Why would it be a difference of degree if it was nine alligators?

Child —They're both animals.

Gerry —Because they're both animals. But they're both *totally different* animals!

COMMENT: Gerry here introduces a criterion for judging something to be a "difference of kind" "Total" difference.

Child —But there's still nine . . .

Daniel —One's a reptile and one's a mammal . . .

Rod —Right. Right.

Gerry —One's a reptile and one's a mammal . . .

Renata —They *still* animals.

Rod —Difference of degree.

Gerry —*You* say it's a difference of degree. *You* say it's a difference of kind. So you can't . . .

Renata —*I* said degree.

Gerry —Oh . . . you say it's a difference of degree.

Karen —Which one?

Gerry —An . . . uh . . . zebra and an alligator.

Karen —Yeah. Difference of degree.

Gerry —Even though they're both totally different animals?

Karen —Yeah. They're still animals.

Gerry —Are those *totally* different angles?

Child —(many) Yes.

Boy? —Yes, but they're still angles.

Gerry —But are they totally different?

John or Walt —Yeah. They different.

Renata —Not *totally* different because both of them has a point.

Gerry —Yes. (at board). If I took this angle and put it over here all I would have to do is move this line up to *here* to make . . . and here's the acute angle in here, right?

Child —(many) Yeah.

Gerry —And if I just moved this line up to here I would make *this* angle, right?

Child —Right.

Renata —They *still* angles.

Gerry —Could I . . . yeah . . . if I were dealing with . . . um . . . um . . . light red and dark red . . . If I started out with light red and I could just add maybe a darker color to it until I finally got dark red, right?

COMMENT: Here Gerry shows that a criterion for distinguishing a difference of degree is the capacity for one thing to "become" the other.

Gerry	—What could I do to a zebra and an alligator so that I could get them together?
John or Walt	—Make them fight.
Gerry	—But would one ever come close to being the other?
Child	—(many) No.
Daniel	—Well, we could get them both the same colors.
Gerry	—But would that still make them come close to each other in *things?*
Daniel	—No—It won't make them closer.
Gerry	—But does the zebra ever become the alligator or the alligator ever become the zebra?
Child	—(all) No! No!
Renata	—Just like in the book when they say something about Jill and you know . . . it's a difference of degree as far as they go, and one of them can't turn into the other.
Gerry	—No, but we weren't talking about *girls*, were we? What were we talking about?
Renata	—Their weights.
Gerry	—Their *weights*. Could one girl keep eating and eating and eating and become the same . . . the girl who weighs less, could she become the same weight as another girl by eating or putting on weight?
Child	—Yeah . . . Ummhmm.
Gerry	—Or could one of the girls become the same weight by dieting . . . and losing weight?

Child	—(several) Yes.
Gerry	—Could their *weights* become the same?
Child	—Yes.
Child	—But *they* couldn't . . .
Gerry	—But they wouldn't become the same, no. So we're not talking about the two girls. We're talking about their heights or their weights.
Renata	—Okay, so you use two *people* for the difference of degree.
Gerry	—Yeah, but what are you comparing? We're comparing two people all right . . .
Renata	—But that's what I'm doing!
Gerry	—Okay.
Renata	—Like you or her.
Gerry	—All right.
Renata	—It's a difference of degree because, you know, she's her and you're you.
Gerry	—All right. But how is that a difference of degree?

COMMENT: Gerry's use of *persons* and personal attributes to demonstrate the distinction between a difference of degree and a difference of kind will enable her to make a natural and easy transition later from this topic to the topic of "individuality."

Renata	—Because . . . uh . . .
Karen	—. . . they're people . . .
Gerry	—We're both people, right?
Karen	—Yeah, but you're an adult and she's a child.
Gerry	—Well won't *she* ever become an adult? Could she ever become an adult . . . like I am?
Daniel	—Yeah.
Gerry	—So if we're comparing our ages, what would that be?
Walt	—Difference of degree.
Gerry	—A difference of *degree*. All right. So in comparing our age that's a difference

of degree. Now what else would you like to compare?

Walt —Your height.

Renata —Still using this . . . and . . . uh . . . she can't change to *you* and you can't change to *her*. It's still a difference of degree.

Gerry —Well if I can't change to her . . . when we say that we couldn't change the alligators to the zebras we said that was a difference of what?

Renata —Kind.

Gerry —Kind. If she can't change to me and I can't change to her.

Renata —Yeah, but counts the same that . . . was it a difference of degree or kind *between* a alligator and a zebra?

Gerry —Well what is it?

Renata —A difference of degree. 'Cause they both animals. And . . .

Gerry —Yeah, but we didn't really come to that conclusion. Somebody said it was . . . other people said it was a difference of kind.

Renata —(unintelligible) . . . so we could know that it was a difference of degree.

Daniel —What are you measuring between the alligator and the zebra?

COMMENT: Daniel is asking for the standard to be stipulated.

Gerry —That's a very good question. What are we measuring when we say the alligator and the zebra? Who brought up the alligator and the zebra? Well for *that* matter, what were we measuring when we said . . . uh . . . nine apples with nine . . . oh . . . nine alligators?

(giggles from the class)

Pamela —Things.

(long pause)

Gerry —Yeah- we were comparing the . . . the. . . . *things* apples with the *things* alligators. You know, fruits 'n alligators.

Daniel —You can't. 'Cause there's so many properties of each of them.

Renata —That's a difference of kind, though.

Daniel —Yeah, but if you were talking about . . . what . . . the water content in a . . . a . . . um . . . alligator you'll get difference of degree. If you compare the *form* of an alligator and the *form* of an apple you get only a difference of kind.

Gerry —Ummhmm.

Daniel —An apple can never grow to look like an alligator.

Gerry —All right . . . but in this one we were . . . I guess you were comparing, you know, that they are, their physical properties . . . to apples and alligators. Form. You know. But what about Kathy and I? (unintelligible)

Child —Difference in degree.

Gerry —*Jeanne* and I? (aside)- That's what you get for always sitting there (unintelligible) Jeanne and I. What about Jeanne and I?

Child —Difference of degree.

Gerry —Difference of degree.

Melanie —Because . . . um . . . she could get . . . like, everything about her could (unintelligible) not everything out—parts of her could become to look like *you*, and then . . . um . . . well then she could (unintelligible) . . . then it would be a difference of degree. Because she could become to look like you. She'll grow up to be a woman, and she'll . . . she has brown eyes now . . .

Gerry —Umm . . . her eye's already same . . .

Melanie —Umm . . . She may grow up to be the same height as you. Maybe taller.

Gerry —Ummhmm.

Melanie —But she will sometime be . . . (unintelligible)

Gerry —Still with all of those differences between . . . between our heights and the difference between our ages and the difference between our weights, the difference between all of those are all differences of degree?

Child —Degree.

Gerry —Does that make the thing that's Jeanne and the thing that's me—is that difference . . . if all of the things about us is a difference of degree does that make us . . . the difference between us, a difference of degree?

Children —Yeah, sure.

Gerry —OK. You're absolutely sure about that? Well. Let's go on to some others . . . how about dead things and living things?

Kirk —A difference of kind.

Gerry —Why do you say a difference of kind?

Daniel —(together) Well, one's alive and one's
& Kirk dead.

Kirk —They're not functioning no more.

COMMENT: Kirk is introducing a standard by which he is judging whether something is living or not living—the standard of *function*.

Gerry —Ummhmmm . . .

Kirk —Being considered . . . not functioning . . .

Daniel —I think it's degree.

Child —Degree.

Child —I think it's difficult . . .

Gerry —Why do you say . . . (noise from class) Wait, wait. You'll get a chance. Why would you say . . .

Daniel —A live person can die.

Gerry —Ummhmm.

Karen —A dead person can't . . .

Gerry —Can dead things . . .

Karen —Well he could have lived before that, but he's not gonna live again.

Child —So it's a difference of degree.

Kirk —Well, he might be resurrected.

COMMENT: Gerry apparently doesn't hear this remark.

Gerry —But somebody brought up the point that a dead person can't ever become a live person.

Walt —But a live person *could* become a dead person.

Gerry —Uhhuh. So it's a difference of . . .

Renata —Kind.

Karen —Degree.

Gerry —Degree. Kind.

Walt —Degree. It's a difference of degree.

Renata —Kind. Because it's *different*.

Gerry —*Totally* different?

Renata —Yeah.

John or —Yeah.
Walt

Karen —No, but they're still things, though. Even though one might be dead and one might be alive, they're still things.

Child —(unintelligible)

Child —Because . . . one . . . one . . .

Gerry —Well, we're not just talking about persons. We're talking about a dead . . . a dead thing and a living thing, O.K.?

Kirk —We're not talking about persons?

Gerry —We don't *have* to be talking about persons.

Renata —Both of them *things*.

Kirk —Let's take an animal . . .

Gerry —All right. So if we take an animal . . .

Kirk —We still consider him . . . dead. I certainly think . . .

Gerry —Yeah . . .

Child —(unintelligible)

Gerry —So you're saying that they're . . . they're so different from living things, that a dead animal is so different from a living animal that it's a difference of degree . . . of kind? (pause) And you, too?

Kirk —Uhhuh.

Renata —No. . . .

Gerry —I heard a "no."

Renata —Well, no, degree, because they both *things*.

Gerry —Ummhumm . . . Oh, degree.

Child	—Right.
Gerry	—O.K. Degree, Use degree.
Daniel	—No.
Gerry	—I *still* heard a "no." Somewhere. David?
Daniel	—Well yeah. I say that's a difference of degree.
Child	—Degree.
Daniel	—'Cause it's just like the obtuse angle. The acute can widen and become an obtuse.
Gerry	—Uhhnhuh.
Daniel	—And a live person can die and become a dead person.
Gerry	—Uhhuh.
Child	—(unintelligible)
Child	—What's *your* opinion?
Daniel	—If they could *become* and change . . .
Gerry	—Do you really want to know what my opinion is? Why?
Child	—Because I'm (unintelligible)
Gerry	—Well my opinion is . . . you know it's just my opinion. Your opinion is worth just as much as my opinion. *I* happen to think that they're a difference of kind. Between dead things and living things.
Child	—(some conversation, several children speaking at once—unintelligible on tape)
Mitchell	—Well like say there are two dead rabbits. And two live rabbits.
Gerry	—Umhum.
Mitchell	—The dead rabbit still looks like the live rabbit.
Gerry	—But all the same . . . (unintelligible)
Walt	—. . . that are alive . . .
Gerry	—Yeah, they're still . . .
Walt	—They look the same . . .
Gerry	—They're still rabbits . . .
Walt	—Dead or alive . . .
Gerry	—But, but . . . but a dead rabbit is such a *totally different thing* between a . . . from a live rabbit . . .
Child	—This is only a (unintelligible)
Child	—He *was* alive.

Child	—(another child says something unintelligible)
Child	—(repeats) He *was* alive. He was alive.
Renata	—But they *still* rabbits.
Gerry	—O.K. You're right. But they're . . . they're *totally different things*. The dead rabbit can't do any of the things that a live rabbit can do . . .
Child	—Just like a live rabbit can't do any of the things that a dead rabbit can do.
Child	—(simultaneously) A live rabbit can be killed and become a dead rabbit.
Gerry	—Right—right.
Jeanne	—A dead rabbit can't do nothin'.
Gerry	—So . . . so . . . that's why I think it's a difference of kind.
Daniel	—A live rabbit can't kill himself (unintelligible), dead rabbit can.
Gerry	—I can't hear you.
Jeanne	—A dead rabbit doesn't do anything.
Daniel	—How can a live rabbit kill himself?
Gerry	—Kill himself? I don't know about that. I don't know whether . . . He could *be* killed. Or get . . . or gosh! Well, I don't know that.
Mitchell	—Well, he commits suicide, okay, (unintelligible) . . . something like that (unintelligible) . . . from drinking too much water. If a rabbit . . . if a rabbit . . .
Child	—W..w..what?
Mitchell	—Let me talk.
Gerry	—Go on.
Mitchell	—And they said he was pronounced dead . . . (children giggle) . . . how would you know if he was dead or not?

COMMENT: If something must be *pronounced dead* by an expert, perhaps the difference is not so "total."

Gerry	—Well, see, that's my point exactly. If . . . if you take one rabbit . . . all right. This rabbit that's hopping . . . you know, let's all see this rabbit right now. (giggles from the class) I can *really* see

it. There's a rabbit there! Let's make this rabbit that's right here and it's hopping around. (Unintelligible remark from a child) . . . No, it's white. (giggles from class). It's hopping around . . . all right, it's *my* rabbit, OK? And it's hopping around and all of a sudden, it *dies*. (giggles from class). I think that the dead rabbit is so totally different from the living rabbit . . .

Walt —He *was* alive.

Gerry —. . . as to be . . . Yeah. You're absolutely right.

Mitchell —Well, you didn't have the dead rabbit to start with . . .

Gerry —You're right. I had a living rabbit.

Mitchell —But that's (unintelligible) two rabbits.

Child —It's gonna jump around so you're gonna . . .

Gerry —No, no. The same rabbit died.

Mitchell —Don't you have to have a live rabbit and a dead rabbit . . . a dead rabbit that . . . (unintelligible)

Kirk —Put it this way—Go around the room . . . go around the class. Let's have a vote, what you think it is.

Child —Aww, that ain't . . .

Gerry —(laughing)—How many of you want to have a vote?

Child —Oh, I don't want to have a vote. (Other children raise their hands.)

Gerry —All right, Eugene? Difference of degree or difference of kind?

Eugene —Degree.

Gerry —Degree. One degree.

Rod —Degree.

Gerry —Two degrees.

Daniel —Degree.

Gerry —Three degrees.

Mitchell —Degree.

Gerry —Four degrees.

Kirk —Kind.

Gerry —Four degrees and one kind.

Pamela —Five degrees.

Gerry —Five degrees and one kind.

Jeanne —I don't know . . . uhh . . .

Gerry —Five degrees and one kind, and one I don't know.

Jeanne —Right (giggles).

Gerry —I'm getting confused. Five, one and one.

Child —(unintelligible) . . . write it on the board.

Gerry —Five degrees, two kind (points to herself), and one don't know.

Renata —Degree.

Gerry —Six degrees, two kind, and one I don't know.

Karen —Degree.

Gerry —Seven degrees.

Alana —Degree.

Gerry —Eight degrees.

Walt —Degree.

Gerry —Nine degrees.

John —Um . . . um . . . degree.

Gerry —Ten degrees.

Melanie —I'm not gonna say anything.

Donna —I don't know, Melanie, I'm not gonna say anything . . .

Walt —Ten degrees, two of a kind . . . I mean . . .

Child —And three I don't know.

Gerry —Two of a kind . . . two kind, and three I don't know's.

Walt —And on you now.

Gerry —I said it. I did it. I was one of the kinds. O.K.?

Child —Mmmhmm.

Renata —Now—ask *her*. (Points to other teacher in the room.)

Ms. Isler—I believe it would be degree. That's my opinion.

Gerry —Eleven degrees (laughs). Okay, the degrees won (laughs).

Child —(unintelligible chatter from class).

Child —I still don't know.

Gerry —That's right. We both still have our opinions.

Rod	—But still and all . . . (unintelligible) that's wrong.
Child	—(Laughter).
Child	—(child says something unintelligible).
Gerry	—Maybe so.
Rod	—Yah . . . but not to us. Unless you're here by yourself.
Gerry	—All right. How about . . . fish and apes?
Child	—(many) Kind.
Gerry	—Difference of degree or difference of kind?
Child	—(all) Kind, kind, kind.
Gerry	—Kind. We're all sure that they're kind. We're not gonna have an argument about that one? All right. Apes and men?
Children	—Degree, degree, degree.
Karen	—Because you can have an ape who can become a man . . . Well . . .
Walt	—A man won't become a ape.
Mitchell	—A man won't become an ape!
Child	—Yeah, he could've come from some sort of . . .
Renata	—Man's became from apes.
Children	—Yeah. Uhhuh.
Renata	—So, it's a difference of degree.
Karen	—Of degree.
Gerry	—Anybody else?
Child	—(murmurs)
Child	—I guess . . .
Gerry	—Degree?
Daniel	—if you put it *that* way all animals are . . .
Walt	—Degree!
Gerry	—Well . . . well.. what were you saying Daniel?
Daniel	—Everything . . . everything's the same when you consider that men . . . umm . . . um . . . that everything used to be the same thing.
Gerry	—What do you mean everything used to be the same thing?
Daniel	—Everything used to be the same thing!

John	—(unintelligible) an ape . . . a mammal . . . a man . . . a *person* is a mammal.
Daniel	—It developed from one more . . .
Rod	—One more what?
Gerry	—All right, well, what Daniel is saying is that . . . according to scientists in the beginning . . . all life came from one-celled . . .
Rod	—Apes.
Gerry	—Animals . . .
Rod	—Right.
Gerry	—*All* life. One-celled . . .
Rod	—Ape.
Gerry	—Animals . . .
Daniel	—Apes.
Gerry	—. . . started with the beginning of all life an everything . . .
Rod	—Right.
Gerry	—. . . evolved from that.
Rod	—Right.
Gerry	—So . . . but what he's saying is then is . . .
Child	—But so . . .
Mitchell	—But there's still those one-celled animals today.
Gerry	—Yes . . .
Child	—So . . . uh . . .
Mitchell	—So they can't all be together.
Gerry	—No . . . apes are . . . are there apes and men today?
Mitchell	—Yes.
Gerry	—But you still think those are differences of degree.
Child	—That's right.
Gerry	—What Daniel is saying, though, is that between *all* animals then its a difference of degree.

COMMENT:Gerry summarizes Daniel's position.

Rod	—Night.
Child	—It's still mammals.
Child	—(murmurs from class).

Gerry —Shhhh. Does anybody want to say anything to Daniel?

Children —No.

Walt —No, anybody can . . . (unintelligible)

Gerry —But then if you think that he's right you still think that the difference between, like, say a zebra and an alligator is a difference of . . .

Melanie —*I* was the one who said kind.

Gerry —Of degree or kind?

Walt —Degree.

Gerry —Oh, well, then that's right.

Gerry —(continuing) But you said it's a difference of kind.

Child —Right.

Gerry —Between a zebra and an alligator.

Karen —I say it's degree.

Child —Kind.

Gerry —(unintelligible) . . . what makes you say that? . . . We all . . . we all think that the difference between men and apes is a difference of degree. David just because it was said that man evolved from apes. . . .

Child —Right.

Rod —But *now* it do not.

Daniel —Yeah.

Gerry —I don't understand.

Child —I think she's right.

Daniel —What if a . . . what did she say?

Renata —She said *now* it don't.

Gerry —Now it doesn't what?

Child —I didn't say that.

Renata —Now it don't come from apes.

Mitchell —Yeah, 'cause how come you don't see . . . um . . . men . . . um, in the jungles.

Rod —That's right.

Mitchell —. . . being born from . . .

Rod —Yeah!

Mitchell —. . . lower apes?

Gerry —Well, well . . . if we say that man . . .

Walt —He *was* created by apes!

Gerry —. . . descended from . . . you know, he *came* from apes.

Walt —But now . . .

Gerry —. . . does that mean now we don't have to come from apes? We could come from other human beings?

Mitchell —Right, right. -Yeah, but why can't apes still have people?

Children —(giggles).

Gerry —That's a good question. I don't know.

Daniel —Because the problem is that way back then apes and man were one thing. And . . . uh . . . and . . . uh . . . thing looked different from *apes* and different from *men*.

Gerry —Ummhum.

Daniel —Some . . . some . . .

Renata —So, way, back, it's the same thing.

Daniel —Some had to live there and became *us*, and some lived in other places and didn't . . .

Gerry —And just stayed on . . .

Daniel —. . . and developed into different . . . then the differences . . .

Gerry —Two different what?

Child —. . . wasn't as much.

Gerry —Oh! Different. Uhhuh. So what are they?

Daniel —So . . . so different . . . I don't know!

Child —(unintelligible)

Daniel —Some ancient, ancient kind of ape. Not the kind of ape they have today.

Mitchell —Then real human beings . . . them too are . . . what? They (unintelligible) have apes that stay apes and many apes that stay people.

Children —(giggles).

Gerry —What he's saying . . .

Mitchell —What distinguishes the apes that are apes . . . that stay apes . . .

Daniel —We developed into different areas.

Gerry —Shh.

Child —(unintelligible)

Mitchell —. . . and the apes that stay people?

Daniel —What's . . .

Renata —I still ain't *him.*

Gerry —You mean why did . . . why did the apes . . . some . . .

Mitchell —Certain apes be apes and certain apes became people.

Child —Oh!

Gerry —That's a good' question. Anybody know the answer?

Child —I might have been the apes . . .

Gerry —I'm sure . . . I . . . I guess that would be a good question for . . . uh . . . research, you know, as to why certain apes just stayed apes, and certain apes became people.

Daniel —*I* saw . . . I saw the film on it. It was . . . uhm . . . whatchamacallit . . .

Rod —How come you the only one who see the show?

Daniel —I saw the show. Uhh . . . un . . . I forget what it was, in it was a show and it showed how man had evolved . . . evolved.

Gerry —Ummhum.

Daniel —And I . . . in the end, you know, some people died.

Child —Oh?

Daniel —If the plane crash . . .

Child —Ohh.

Child —*That* way.

Child —What way?

Daniel —If the actors, all the actors crash up.

Gerry —. . . think that's sad.

Daniel —That's at the end. But . . . anyway, they . . . they . . . um . . . like there was one animal—and some of the animals, like, were . . . were . . . lived in the jungle, and some, and some of the animals were given out real plain (unintelligible) and they were expanding and the ones that went out in the fields experimented more, and the other ones in the trees just sort of lopped around and became . . . (unintelligible) and after these guys they explored, they came back and they could easily overtake the smaller ones. Because they had adventured. And once they had dominated them they got bigger and they didn't die. (unintelligible)

Just because of what they *did*. They went out in the fields and they used . . . they needed to invent more than the ones . . . who were living in the trees loafing around eating oranges.

Rod —Oh jeez!

Gerry —Okay. All right, well . . . well . . . we were talking about the difference of . . . u h . . . u h . . . kind and differences of degree. Oh, well, we're still talking about differences, right?

Kirk —Right.

Gerry —Ummm. I'd like to get into differences. Would you say that all of you are different?

Renata —No.

Children —No. The same.

Gerry —You're all the same?

Renata —We're difference of degree . . . 'cause we're all people.

Gerry —Uhhuh. Well, then, if we're all people . . . and . . . and you think that we're all the same, I guess you mean . . . just in the fact that we're all people. But as individuals, are we different?

Children —Uhhh. Yes.

Melanie —Because we *think* different.

Gerry —All right. Well, that's what I want to get into now. That our *differences* . . . what is it that makes you, *you*? I guess in the same way . . .

Child —Our mind.

Gerry —. . . we're talking about differences . . .

Child —Our mind.

Child —Our mind.

Gerry —Uhh . . .

Child —Between who and who?

Gerry —You! What makes *you* you? Not whether . . . you know . . . just thinking about *you* now, what makes you you? Uhh . . . your face, your clothes, your name, your mind, your thoughts . . .

Daniel —Your mind and thoughts . . .

Jerry —Your mind and your thoughts?

Walt	—Right, right.
Gerry	—Not the others? Your name, your face, your clothes?
Child	—Yes, yeah!
Child	—All of them.
Child	—Your mind.
Daniel	—There could be two people just alike. Different minds would be completely different people.
Gerry	—Umhum.
Child	—If you had different clothes.
Gerry	—if you had different clothes. Could you have the same clothes?
Child	—MMM.
Child	—Yeah.
Mitchell	—I knew this family that had twins, and they looked exactly alike and the mother bought them each clothes and then she had to stop after they were five years old, because the kindergarten teacher couldn't tell them apart.
Gerry	—Uhhuh. Well, before they were five, and they were wearing the same clothes, not only did they wear the same clothes, what else did they have that was the same?
Mitchell	—Well . . . they . . . looked exactly alike.
Gerry	—They looked alike . . .
Mitchell	—And they had . . . kinda similar names.
Gerry	—Uhhuh. But were they different?
Mitchell	—Uhhuh.
Renata	—Mmmhum.
Child	—(unintelligible) . . . difference of degree.
Renata	—. . . one was Craig and one was Bob.
Gerry	—Well, what was it that made them different?
Children	—Their names.
Gerry	—Just their names?
Children	—No!
Gerry	—Well, suppose my name . . . have you ever come across somebody else who was . . . who was named Renata?

Renata	—Yeah, but . . .
Gerry	—Was she you?
Renata	—No, but we had different minds and everything.
Daniel	—Did she think . . .
Gerry	—Uhhuh, so . . .
Walt	—They had different ways.
Daniel	—What happens if . . . they have different minds, and have the same name? Are they the same thing?
Mitchell	—But it's a difference.
Kirk	—Nope. Difference of kind.
Renata	—Well . . . well that's just *one* of the differences, that one name was Craig and one name was Bob.
Daniel	—Well . . . if they have both the same minds and one was named Craig, and one was named . . .
Renata	—But how dumb! Two people don't have the same mind.
Daniel	—Yeah, but you said before, that if . . . uh . . . the *name* makes you *different* from everybody else.
Walt	—But your ways doesn't.
Renata	—I didn't say *exactly* different! It made *them* different.
Gerry	—Yeah, but which one was . . .
Renata	—Their two names made them different.
Gerry	—is this your . . . Is your name you?
Renata	—Yes! Not really. Part of me.
Gerry	—Uhhuh. Is that what makes you *you*? If I change your name, or if you went to court and you changed your name, and you said you didn't want . . .
Renata	—I'd still be me!
Gerry	—Would you say . . . what would you . . . then . . . that . . . what would it be then that would make you you? If you could change your name?
Renata	—Your mind, I guess.
Gerry	—Your mind?
Children	—Yeah . . .
Gerry	—Somebody said "personality," what do you mean by "personality"?

Pamela —it's the way you act and the way you do things.

Gerry —is that the same . . . when you used . . . when said, your *ways*?

Walt —Yeah.

Gerry —Or a part of it.

Walt —Yes.

Gerry —Okay. Umm, I'd like to ask you some questions. If for some reason you couldn't use your arm . . . would you still be you?

Children —Yeah, yeah, sure.

Gerry —Why?

Children —Because . . . it is . . .

Child —Because your arm . . .

Melanie —When I was (unintelligible) of your arm or your finger or something (unintelligible) hurts a lot like a splinter or something—you don't stop *thinking* the same way. And sometimes it makes you feel sorry for yourself because you can't do some things, but you never really . . . uhm . . . *think* differently.

Karen —But you might have to use different ways.

Melanie —If I came in here today, and I had a broken arm, I probably would still say the same thing.

Gerry —Uhhuh. What were you saying, Karen?

Karen —Like if you lost your *right* arm, and you were right-handed, even though you'd have to learn with your left hand, you're still you. Even though you'd change your ways.

Gerry —Okay. If for some reason, you couldn't use your mind, would you still be you?

Child —Yes.

Daniel —You'd be dead.

Children —(giggles)

Gerry —If you couldn't use your *mind*, you'd be dead?

Daniel —You wouldn't be able to do anything. *Nothing.* You couldn't breathe . . .

COMMENT: *Daniel is equating the "brain" with the "mind."

Child —You're talking about your *brain*.

Daniel —Your mind is the same thing.*

Child —Your mind is . . . your mind can tell . . . your mind is your thoughts.

Daniel —*everything* you do.

Children —(Unintelligible conversation and laughter.)

Daniel —. . . If you can't think . . . (unintelligible) . . . haven't enough to breathe.

Mitchell —Did you ever have a dream where you didn't . . . um . . . did you ever have a night where you didn't dream?

Children —Uhmhum. Yes. Uhmhum. No.

Mitchell —Well, I did. Am I dead? (giggles from class)

COMMENT: Notice how the children have taken over the discussion, and how they, themselves, are posing the questions, arguing, presenting examples, etc.

Gerry —Well, I guess when they say that they . . . if you couldn't use your mind . . . uh . . . if you couldn't think, or if you couldn't use your own imagination, or your own wishing, or your . . . your own *ideas*—would you still be you? If you couldn't have these thoughts, and you couldn't do these things . . . your thoughts, or your ways, as you say.

Daniel —No.

Gerry —Why wouldn't it be you?

Daniel —No, because . . . You couldn't distinguish yourself from anybody else. You'd just . . . you'd just sit there, you'd be just like the other guy.

Pamela —I don't know, I don't know, I don't know . . .

Gerry —All right, what were you going to say, Jeanne?

Jeanne	—If you had all of everybody else's ideas and everything . . .
Gerry	—No, not if you had anybody else's ideas. Just that you couldn't use your own mind.
Child	—You'd be *dumb*.
Walt	—Could you have . . . uh . . . any kind of . . . um . . . ideas . . . you know . . . I mean . . . out of your brain?
Gerry	—Do I have any ideas?

COMMENT: Did Gerry accurately restate Walt's question, or was he asking a different question?

Walt	—Uh . . .
Gerry	—Not right off hand. You could get that information . . .
Walt	—I went to the doctor the other day, he told me my brain weighed eight pounds.
Gerry	—Your brain?
Walt	—Eight ounces.
Gerry	—Eight ounces.
Walt	—Seven and a half.
Children	—(giggles)
Gerry	—Um . . . are you the same person you were yesterday?
Children	—Yes. No. Yup.
Gerry	—All of you?
Children	—Yup. No.
Gerry	—Why did you say "no"?
Mitchell	—Well, like if you learned something, or . . . uh . . . if you had a new experience or something, that would change you a little.
Gerry	—It would change you a little, but would it make you . . . it would still . . . are you still you?
Children	—Yes!
Mitchell	—It would still be you, only not the way you were . . .
Gerry	—Not the way you were?
Mitchell	—But *you*.
Gerry	—But *you*.
Mitchell	—Yes. (laughter)

Renata	—You still be you, though.
Gerry	—But would you be the same person?
Karen	—Yeah.
Gerry	—You'd still be the same person if you had a new experience or learned something new?
Karen	—Well, yeah.
Child	—Uhhuh.
Daniel	—You couldn't use your mind at all.
Gerry	—But wh . . . ?
Child	—. . . you couldn't . . . um . . . do anything.
John or Walt	—Brains.
Daniel	—You still couldn't breathe.
Gerry	—Yeah, well . . .
Daniel	—Because your mind tells you what to do. Everything.
John or Walt	—Just like you're brain-washed.
Daniel	—Just like . . . your thoughts . . . imagination . . . tells you what you're seeing, what to do, because of what you see. If you see . . . If you're driving and you see a car coming right at you, your mind tells you to *swerve*.
Gerry	—Mmmhmm.
John	—Swerve?
Daniel	—So. Your mind tells you to breathe, too. If you can't . . . if you can't breathe, you can't eat.
Child	—You can't eat if you don't know you're hungry!
Gerry	—But are you still you?
Daniel	—No.
Gerry	—Okay. Well, assuming that you can use your mind and you can do all of those things, are you the same person that you were yesterday?
Child	—Yes. Oh, sure.
Gerry	—Everybody but Daniel, right? Daniel's different. Are you the same person you were yesterday?
Daniel	—Yes.
Gerry	—Now you are the exact same person?

Rod —Nope.

Gerry —Why do you say "no"?

Rod —Well, I'm taller.

Gerry —Does that make you . . . ah . . . different?

Rod —No. Outside, but not inside.

Child —Mmmhmm,

Gerry —Rod, when you say the inside, what do you mean by the inside?

Rod —Personality's still the same.

Gerry —Umhmm . . . (long pause) . . . Are you the same person you were ten years ago?

Child —No.

Child —No. (giggles)

Gerry —You're the same person you were yesterday, and you're the same person you were last year, but you're not the same person you were ten years ago?

Karen —Yes.

Child —She didn't say . . .

Walt —No!

Child —No.

Gerry —Why do you say "no," Walt?

Walt —Because you don't react the same.

Gerry —Why do you say that?

Child —Because ten years ago, you could's been a little (unintelligible) boy.

Gerry —Yeah.

Walt —Now you're still . . . (laughs) . . .

Gerry —All right, so . . . so that those two are different things?

Walt —Right.

Gerry —All right. You said that you were, that you *descend.*

Renata —I'm still Renata, I'm stay me my whole life.

Gerry —Are you the same Renata that you were ten years ago?

Renata —Uhmhum. Yup. . . . except for, as far as my *mind* goes 'n everything, but I'm still Renata.

Gerry —Uh . . . well . . . yes, you're still Renata, but if your *mind* is . . . has changed, 'n everything like that, that you said . . . are you the *same person?*

Renata —Yeah. I'm still Renata. I'm still the same as she.

Gerry —You're still the same . . . you're still the same *name* . . .

Renata —But it's still *me*!.

Gerry —Uhhuh.

Renata —I was me ten years ago.

Gerry —Yes. You were you ten years ago. But are you the same you now that you were ten years ago?

Renata —Oh . . . (unintelligible)

Gerry —What made you change?

Renata —Because . . . I'm not . . . I'm smarter than I was ten years ago.

Gerry —Ummmhmmm. Anything else?

Renata —I'm developing . . .

Jeanne —You're not two years old anymore.

Renata —. . . more than I was ten years ago.

Gerry —Uhhuh. Anything else?

Child —(unintelligible)

Gerry —What about the rest of you?

Jeanne —I'm not two years old anymore. (giggles)

Gerry —Uh . . . does that make you different? Uh, the fact that you were two years old ten years ago, and twelve now? How does that make you different?

Jeanne —We didn't know as much. We were just . . . (laughs)

Child —(unintelligible)

Gerry —Shh. Shh. John. . . . Go on, I'm sorry.

Children —(laughter)

Gerry —Well, why are you different now than ten years ago? Besides your age. I'm talking about . . . (unintelligible) . . . because you didn't know that once?

Jeanne —(unintelligible) . . . like, as many experiences and things like that.

Gerry —Uhhuh. (laughter) Anyone else-)

Daniel —Yeah, you could say more . . .

Gerry —Daniel?

Daniel —And Mitchell said . . . it's the same (unintelligible) wouldn't make much difference 'cause . . . like you can learn here and there little things, but after ten years all those would add up some . . . you know. . . . you . . . most of what you know about is either you gained more knowledge or you've gotten a different opinion because you know more about it.

Gerry —Uhmmmm.

Daniel —Like sometimes you say . . . no, no, no, it . . . I agree with *this* and then you gain more knowledge about the subject and ten years later . . . that time you know you're definitely uh . . . yeah, that's right. You know because you realize then you probably will . . . let's say it's a big political decision (unintelligible) . . . run America bankrupt (unintelligible) . . . now you realize what you're gonna do. You say . . . oh, no.

Gerry —All right. So you're different. You're different . . .

Daniel —You've changed . . .

Gerry —You've changed your opinions. When you've changed your opinions that makes . . . makes you a different person?

Daniel —No! Different . . . In what way? The way your personality . . .

Mitchell —Well . . .

Child —Or . . .

Gerry —I . . . that's what I'm asking you!

Mitchell —Well . . . well if . . . well if when you add up a whole bunch of knowledge, that makes you different than you were, and then you'll be able to (unintelligible) . . . I mean, does it matter whether you add up a lot or a little?

Gerry —I think what David is saying is that if you get a little bit of knowledge . . . David was saying that if you get a lot of knowledge, it changes . . . it changes the way you look at things, sometimes. Does it *always* change the way you look at things?

Children —No.

Gerry —But sometimes it could change the way you look at things. Mitchell was saying, if you get . . . what's the difference between a little bit of knowledge and a lot of knowledge? Can't you change from just a little bit of knowledge? That you could learn . . . that you can gain maybe in one day? Could you change . . .

Daniel —No.

Gerry —. . . your opinion in one day? Daniel doesn't think it's possible.

Daniel —Only . . . on one subject, yeah. But not (intelligible). You can't change yourself almost completely.

Gerry —Okay. When you're very old will you still be the same *person* that you are now?

Child —No.

Child —You'd be the same person, but uh . . .

Alana —You just have more wrinkles.

Gerry —You have more what?

Alana —Wrinkles. When you're old, you don't look the same like you did before.

Gerry —Uhhuh.

Walt —When you walking down the street . . . hunchback . . .

Gerry —Does that make you a different person, because you *look* different?

Child —it doesn't.

John —it doesn't really make you different.

Renata —it makes your *looks* different.

Gerry —It makes your *looks* different.

John —Right.

Gerry —Yes, but what about the *person* that you are? Does that make you . . .

Child —No.

Walt —You still have the same . . . you still have the same mind.

Renata —You're still . . . ahh (unintelligible)

John —But you know yourself (unintelligible)! You're still the shape that you give. You know you look a bit different but if you take care of yourself, it's possible you could pass for young.

Gerry —Yeah. But would you still be the same person?

Children —Umhum, yes.

Renata —You'd still be John Carroll!

Gerry —Would he still be the *same* John Carroll? Well, you'll probably be . . . you might . . . most of us stay the same name, like, all our lives, right? But does that mean you stay the same *person* just because your *name* stays the same?

Renata —Umhmmm.

Gerry —Always? You never change . . . ?

Renata —You just don't know as much as you did when you were younger but you *still* the same person.

Gerry —Uhmmmm.

Renata —You can't change . . . or, I can't change t'*her*.

Gerry —No. Absolutely. But are you the same Renata?

Walt —Right.

Renata —I'm . . . I'm . . . yeah, I'm . . .

Gerry —The *same* Renata?

Renata —Not . . .

Gerry —. . . and all your life?

Walt —As you get older, as you get bigger and bigger, you could get a little . . . As you get bigger and bigger you *are* getting old.

Gerry —Uhmhmm.

Walt —Right.

Gerry —Ummm.

Walt —So . . .

Gerry —But when we . . . when we were talking before, you were talking about your ways, and your personality, and your minds, and your thoughts! . . .

Renata —That don't change *you*.

Gerry —Do your ways and your personalities and your minds . . . well, well, what *is* you? (simultaneously)

Renata —A *person*. It don't change a *person*. You might change the knowledge of a person, but it don't change the person itself.

Gerry —Uhmhmm.

John —You *never* can.

Gerry —Well, what do you think of as the person? Before you told me that it was your mind, your thoughts. Can your thoughts change? Can your personality change?

Renata —Yeah. *That* can't change.

Gerry —But they . . . you don't change?

Renata —(simultaneously) *You* don't change much.

Renata —No. I'm still the same person that . . .

Gerry —Okay. All right.

Child —it's ten o'clock.

Gerry —Uhmm . . . I . . . you know. I . . . I want to put this away for now, Okay?

Child —it's ten o'clock.

Gerry —No. I told you. It's not ten o'clock. I've got to . . . I wanted to ask you some questions . . . and I wanted, you know, you just tell me how you feel about . . . about what you've done for the last three weeks . . . and how you think it's affected you, and how you feel about it, whether you liked it, whether you liked it, whether you didn't like it . . .

Child —(unintelligible)

Gerry —Yeah. Your experience of being here for the last three weeks.

Renata —it was nice to me.

Gerry —What about it was nice to you?

Renata —The group sessions.

Gerry —What did you like? You liked *talking* like this?

Renata —Yes.

Gerry —Anybody else? How did you feel about it? Do you think that this did anything for you?

Renata —Yeah, 'cause some of the things that we've been talking about . . . it's not that I didn't know, but I didn't have . . . uh . . . definite answers.

Gerry —Uhmmm. Now you *do* have some definite answers?

Renata —(simultaneously) Now I got . . .

Gerry —Okay. What about the rest of you? What do you feel that this has done for—coming here in the morning?

Walt —Did a lot.

Gerry —What?

Walt —Uhh . . . uhh . . . made me think better. Usually I like to play around . . .

Gerry —Huh?

Walt —I like to play.

Gerry —Yes?

Walt —Well, it made me think. Now I like better to think.

Gerry —You're gonna stop playing?

Child —I don know (giggles)

Gerry —What about the rest of you?

Daniel —(unintelligible) . . . bored all day.

Rod —You learn how to say things better . . . uhmmm . . .

Gerry —Uhmhum. Anyone else?

Walt —Is this your last day here?

Gerry —Yes.

Walt —No wonder you're asking such questions!

Children —(laughter)

Gerry —Do you . . . do you think the fact that I'm asking these questions . . . is just because on the last day . . . I guess it is, because this is my last day here . . .

Walt —I know what you're trying to find out. You want us to find out how much we learned.

Gerry —How much you think you've learned.

Walt —I think I learned . . . everybody think he learned . . . To let you know, right?

Gerry —Yes.

Walt —The last day . . .

Gerry —Yes.

Walt —I learned a lot.

Gerry —You learned a lot. All right. Donna said she learned a lot . . .

Donna —Me too. I thought it was fun.

Gerry —You thought it was fun? I'm glad. Anybody else?

Child —(unintelligible)

Gerry —Yes?

Mitchell —I hate to see you go.

Daniel —(simultaneously) It was boring.

Child —Call us sometimes.

Gerry —I'm gonna cry. (laughter) Uh . . . I was thinking. . . . no, I was thinking (unintelligible). I'm sorry . . . go on.

Mitchell —Sometimes it get a little boring.

Gerry —Uhhuh. What about it makes it boring?

Mitchell —Well, like sometimes . . . like something dragged out a little too long.

Gerry —Uhhuh.

Pamela —There were arguments.

Gerry —Were our arguments boring to you?

Pamela —No.

Gerry —Oh. For *you* they were boring.

Mitchell —No. Only like some of the subjects I was bored with.

Gerry —Hmmm. You didn't like the arguments?

Pamela —Yeah, I did.

Gerry —Oh.

Daniel —I love the arguments. I could argue all day long.

Gerry —You could argue all day long? Well, well, I want to ask you another question now.

Walt —(unintelligible) say you . . . um . . . sad because you were leaving today.

Gerry —Uhh. I am too . . . in a way, and in a way I'm not. 'Cause I need a rest. (laughter)

Child —(unintelligible)

Renata —I need one.

Gerry —Yeah!

Renata —I'm tired, like . . .

John —Well, we don't have to come back to uh . . . we don't have to come back no more.

Gerry —Exactly.

John —We don't have to come back until Monday, right?

Gerry —Yeah. Umm. I wanna ask you one more question, okay? What d'ya think

	... suppose ... this group, all of us, we met every day like this for a year?
Children	—Uhh ... Ahhh ... Ugh ... (laughter)
Gerry	—What would you think about that?
Walt	—It would be nice. It would be nice. I think it would be nice ... um ... we could do ... uh ...
Pamela	—I think if we ... if we started ...
Gerry	—Uh ... wait ...
Pamela	—... later.
Children	—(laughter)
Gerry	—If we could start a little bit later? Okay. That would be all right.
Walt	—I would like it not so ... not 9 o'clock.
Gerry	—Well, what do you think ... how do you think that you would change if we had ... if we did this for a year? How do you think it would affect you? What would happen?
Walt	—We would change ... a lot.
Children	—(Speaking all at once).
Gerry	—Let's take ... can I ... one at a time? 'Cause I can't hear. You're all doing the same things ...
Walt	—... change a lot.
Gerry	—How would it change ... ?
Walt	—it helps you learn a lot.
John	—(simultaneously) ... change a lot ...
John	—'Cause you know if we was meeting for a year, right?
Gerry	—Uhmhum.
John	—Then maybe, you know, probably wouldn't have no discussions, we'd be doing some work. 'N that's (unintelligible) ...
Walt	—Are you gonna let us watch before you leave?
Gerry	—Are you ... do you think that this is not work?
Walt	—Discussion is all the time we spend really.
John	—No, uh, you know it's doing good.
Gerry	—If we stay here ...
John	—... because some people didn't know some things, you know, like you know ... (unintelligible)
Gerry	—Mmmm ... Renata?
Renata	—it's the (unintelligible) of our lives. For some of the people. Some people that don't notice things, or the things that we *might* do.
Gerry	—Uhhuh.
Renata	—I know everybody don't know everything.
Gerry	—Yeah.
Renata	—And then once we do that then (unintelligible) everybody react just like we will.
Gerry	—What would it ... what would it do ... You're talking about knowledge. What do you think would happen between you?
Renata	—Well it would build *up* my knowledge.
Gerry	—But I mean, say between you and Karen, or you and Donna?
Child	—That's another thing ... that's another thing ...
Child	—We got to know each other better. I made a lot of friends.
Gerry	—Do you think ... do you think that's a good thing that they got to know each other better?
Children	—Yeah. Uhhmm.
Gerry	—Why?
Child	—Because you know a lot.
Renata	—Because you don't have to be all suspicious about another ...
Gerry	—Uhhuh. Donna and Melanie, what were you saying?
Melanie	—When you know people better, it's easier for you to get along better with other people that you didn't know ...
Gerry	—Uhhuh. Donna?
Donna	—Well, it's better (unintelligible)
Gerry	—Uhhuh.
Child	—(unintelligible)

Gerry —What knowledge.. do you think that would increase your knowledge about yourselves, about you?

Child —Uhmhmm.

Child —Yep.

Gerry —You're just smiling over here, Pamela. What are you smiling about?

Walt —About . . . there-ain't-no-difference.

Gerry —What? . . . What were you saying? What did you say?

Child —(unintelligible)

Children —(laughter)

Gerry —I want to tell you that I really did enjoy these mornings. I really did. I liked talking to you. I didn't like getting up early, but I did like talking to you.

Renata —it's our summer vacation and we had to get up early.

Gerry —it's my summer vacation, too. I had to get up early. But I think it did some good.

Renata —But *we* have to get up early for three *more weeks.*

Gerry —Mmmm. Isn't *that* terrible? (laughs). Uhmm, Mrs. Isler?

Mrs. Isler—Un . . . I hope you will. I'm not as young and pretty as Mrs. Dawson, but I'll be . . .

Gerry —She's not as pretty . . .

Mrs. Isler—But I'll be very (unintelligible)

Gerry —(simultaneously) . . . that's for sure.

Gerry —I would really like for you to come, because . . . uh . . . I think that uh . . . I that we had a good time because I'm one person, but I think you could have a good time with Mrs. Isler, too. She's really a good old lady.

Children —(laughter)

Mrs. Isler—We're very good friends.

Gerry —We're good friends.

Mrs. Isler—So I allow her to say things like that about me.

Children —(laughter)

Gerry —And she helped me a great deal, you know, when I first started teaching. She teaches in the school where I teach at. She's been teaching for many, many years.

Renata —What school is that?

Gerry —I teach at Morton Street School.

Child —(unintelligible)

Gerry —And she was there. I teach the *sixth* grade, now, but she helped me a great deal.

Daniel —(To Mrs. Isler) What grade do you teach?

Mrs. Isler—I teach the first grade.

Children —OOOH!

Renata —You have to have a lot of patience with little kids. I can't (unintelligible)

Children —(laughter)

Alana —At the (unintelligible) school. They so *bad.*

Gerry —You don't have to have any patience with big kids?

Child —NO.

Mrs. Isler—That's interesting.

Gerry —That is really interesting. I would like to go into that a little longer, but . . .

Child —(unintelligible)

Gerry —All right, all right, you can go. Be here on Monday. Read chapter 8. Wait a minute . . . would any of you like to see (unintelligible) . . . would you like to see yourselves?

Young Children Generate Philosophical Ideas

Catherine McCall

" "Why does skepticism about the ability of children to do philosophy persist? In the decade and a half since *Harry Stottlemeier's Discovery* was written, a great deal of evidence has been amassed for the conclusion that children can indeed do philosophy. We know it happens in perfectly ordinary classrooms with perfectly ordinary children. Yet everyone involved with *Philosophy for Children* has encountered powerful resistance due to the firmly held conviction that what we are trying to do must be fraudulent, since it is patently obvious that children are utterly incapable of real philosophical thinking."

Richard Miller's opening passage (in his review of *Philosophical Adventures with Children*[1]), summarizes a persistent problem which confronts theorists and practitioners in Philosophy for Children (henceforth PFC). The sources of this skepticism concerning children's capabilities appear to lie both in experience and in prevailing cognitive development theory. To put it very crudely (and I apologize for this but I do not have the space to do justice to the theories, etc.[2]), many people have never seen young children demonstrate proficiency in the domain of philosophical reasoning, and their theory-influenced notions of children's cognition leads them to believe that it is not possible. In my experience, the combination of these two factors actually

inhibits both recognition of the children's ideas as philosophical (or abstract) and understanding of the operation of a community of inquiry.[3] Lack of experience can be remediated to a certain extent by reading *Philosophy in the Classroom*[4] or *Philosophy and the Young Child.*[5] However there is a more subtle form of skepticism which is harder to overcome. Many people who are delighted by the fact that children can engage in philosophical discussions with an adult, remain skeptical about whether young children are capable of *originating* philosophical ideas and discussing them among themselves, without adult tutorial.

There is no doubt that anyone, child or graduate student, benefits from judicious tutorial. And children in a regular PFC class also benefit from light-handed, non-authoritarian, non-intrusive help with their thinking, often from the skillful use of manual exercises and activities designed to clarify, focus or stimulate the children's thinking. In other words, an ideal PFC session does involve a particular kind of adult tutorial. But, I would claim, this kind of tutorial works *because* children arrive with the ability to reason philosophically. If they did not, the facilitator would not be able to work from the children's philosophical interests. Just as an orchestral conductor works with the orchestra's musical skills and abilities, the facilitator of a PFC dialogue must assume that the children arrive with the requisite skills. If they did not, even the Solti of facilitators would be unable to produce a philosophical dialogue.[6]

Claiming that it must be the case that children have the ability to originate philosophical ideas and arguments is not sufficient to convince the "subtle skeptics;" they require substantial evidence. So in October 1988, I embarked on a research project which aims to demonstrate, by providing evidence in the form of transcripts, that given a certain environment, young children can and do reason with philosophical concepts which they themselves originate. In order to do this, the methodology I have used differs slightly from that which I would use in, e.g., demonstrating a PFC class. I have attempted to avoid introducing concepts, as much as is possible, while concurrently developing dialogue. (Whereas in other circumstances I might introduce concepts, ideas and arguments for the children to consider.)

The dialogue presented below was transcribed from a videotape of a PFC session with first grade children in New Jersey. There are twenty-two children in the class, and apart from the fact that they are slightly younger than is usual for first grade children, (many of them are five years old), it is a regular mainstream class. I had been meeting with the children twice a week for about eight weeks, working with the "Pixie" novel, when on December 15, 1988, a TV crew from channel 13 (PBS) came to film one of our sessions. Since selections (amounting to six minutes) from this session were to be broadcast as part of a program on applied philosophy, I decided to use a section from the beginning of "Elfie" to read and discuss. I chose this section for three main reasons: 1) because the section was short enough to be read entirely in a couple of minutes; 2) because a TV audience would be able to follow the section without having to be familiar with a story line (as would have been the case if we had simply continued with the Pixie novel), and 3) because this section in "Elfie" presents clear and recognizable philosophical puzzles within a short episode.

The discussion ran for one hour and twenty-five minutes, which is a tremendous span of attention for 5 and 6 year olds. Not all of the discussion was captured on tape as the TV crew had to change cartridges. The presence of a large camera (operated by a large cameraman sitting on the floor among the children), sound boom, and TV lights, as well as crew and two producers did inhibit the group a little—they were concerned to be on their best behavior. Some children who would normally be very active participants seemed to be too self-conscious to speak out, so the dialogue involved about half of the children, whereas normally two-thirds would be frequent participators.

However, despite the unusual circumstances, the dialogue is impressive, and shows that even young children *can*, given the right environment, reason with philosophical concepts which they themselves originate. The dominant philosophical theme which emerges from the dialogue is the nature of persons. It is important to note that not only are the children able to discuss and reason about the philosophical concepts presented in the text, but they also originate philosophical topics for discussion. They bring up many important philosophical issues concerning the nature of what it is to be a person. It is this feature which provides the strongest support for the claim that they are actually doing philosophy, and not simply discussing philosophy. And this is a feature which these first grade children share with professional philosophers—the ability to generate philosophical issues. They do not share the professional philosopher's language skills or vocabulary, or her/his ability to develop the implications and consequences of the issues raised.[7] Nor is their reasoning as sophisticated. But they do raise and address the same questions.

Notes

1. Richard B. Miller, "How to win over a Skeptic!" A review of *Philosophical Adventures with Children* by Michael S. Pritchard, University Press of America 1985, in *Thinking*, vol. 6, number 3.

2. For a more detailed explanation of both the theories alluded to here, and the reasons why many people do not observe children reasoning with philosophical concepts, see forthcoming book.

3. I have on occasion, tried to overcome this obstacle to the successful creation of a community of inquiry in the classroom by advising a teacher that even though s/he may not believe that children can engage in philosophical dialogue, in order to be successful, the teacher must proceed *as though* s/he did so believe. This rarely worked, as the advice is particularly difficult to follow, especially if the teacher held a view that it was not possible for children to engage in dialogue. Suspension of belief is hard to achieve in practice. However, the strategy has been successful for those teachers who were undecided on the issue.

4. *Philosophy in the Classroom* by Lipman, Sharp and Oscanyan, Temple University Press: Philadelphia (1980).

5. *Philosophy and the Young Child* by Gareth Matthews.

6. Although the analogy does not follow through in every detail, a facilitator, like a conductor, needs a certain depth of understanding and skill; i.e., a person who could not read music would have a hard time conducting a symphony no matter how skilled the musicians, whereas a skilled conductor can improve the performance of beginning musicians. However, the role of a conductor differs from that of a facilitator insofar as the conductor leads an orchestra in his interpretation of the score, whereas a facilitator helps the children with their thinking about a topic.

7. The literature on "Personal Identity" is replete with books entirely devoted to each of the issues which the children in this dialogue have raised.

December 15, 1988, Channel 13 TV session from video.

Usually about ten children raise their hands and would like to speak, so children are called individually.

1) *before a name indicates that the child's name was called.

2) //indicates that the sound track is unintelligible.

3) ...indicates an interruption or simultaneous talking.

4) -indicates a pause in the child's talk, either in mid-sentence or in mid-word.

5) underlining represents the emphasis which the speaker places on particular words.

McCall	Okay, now children, ignore this, don't look at this at all [indicating large sound boom swinging above children's heads]. All right? You're going to be looking at whomever's speaking and just ignore whatever else is going on. Pretend the camera isn't there. All right? So, we're going to begin today by reading aloud on page two.
Child	Two?
McCall	Page two.
Child	Four!
McCall	Four, page four, I beg your pardon. And we will all read together. Okay?...
Child	Yeah, that's good.
McCall	We'll read together aloud.[1]
Child	And then to the next page?
McCall	And then to the next page. Four and Five. And then we'll stop, and I'll ask you if there was anything interesting or puzzling that you want to talk about. And then we'll write it down. And then we'll have our discussion. All right, everyone ready? Follow it in the book if you don't want to read aloud. Okay? So-

[Class all read together pgs. 4 and 5 of Elfie]

Today, Seth said, "Elfie hardly ever talks. Maybe she's not for real." That just shows how

---

1 Not all children read, so rather than my reading to them, we all read aloud together. Even those children who don't read very well like to try to read. This gives the children a sense of ownership of the story and also helps to prepare them to speak aloud. The children also tend to refer to the text more often if they have read it aloud, rather than having listened to it.

wrong he can be. Maybe I don't talk that much, but I think all the time. I even think when I sleep. I don't have fancy dreams. I just think when I'm asleep about the same things I think about when I'm awake. Last night I woke up in the middle of the night and I said to myself, "Elfie, are you asleep?" I touched my eyes and they were open. So I said, "no, I'm not asleep." But that could be wrong. Maybe a person could sleep with her eyes open. Then I said to myself, "at this moment am I thinking? I really wonder." And I answered myself, "dummy, if you can wonder, you must be thinking. And if you're thinking then no matter what Seth says, you're for real."

McCall	What was puzzling or interesting in that part?[2]
*Jaclyn	If, if she wasn't a real person she wouldn't - be - if she wasn't a real person how can she think or talk?[3]
McCall	If she wasn't a real person how could she think or talk? [writing] Okay, let's put E. for Elfie,[4] "wasn't a real person how could she think or talk?
Jordan	How could she have dreams and— How could she have dreams and think at the same time?[5]
McCall	[Writing] How could she have dreams and think at the same time?
Heather	How come he thinks at the same time?
McCall	How come—How come she thinks at the same time? Let's put your name up here, Heather, because that's adding to Jordan's question.[6]
Matthew	Oh! Oh! Why did she touch her eyes?
Sarah	Because to see if they were open.
Matthew	Why couldn't she touch something else? ·
McCall	Well...
Laura	Yeah
McCall	... let's discuss that when we have our discussion,[7] that's an interesting question. [Writes] Why did she touch her eyes?
*Kristen	Why did he say to himself "Dummy if you can wonder you must be thinking"?[8]
McCall	[Writes] Why did she say to herself "Dummy if you can wonder you must be thinking"?
*Ami	Why did she—did she say "maybe I don't talk that much"?
McCall	Okay [Writes] why did sh-..
Ami	I mean Elfie.
McCall	Okay, I just put "she" say maybe I don't talk that much.
Child	Maybe-
*Alex	I'm interested in Jordan's question.[9]
McCall	All right. Let's put your name up here.

2   The philosophical topics are frequently presented in the text in such a way as to intrigue children. They find it puzzling as well as interesting. Since they also find character descriptions and plot lines interesting (though not puzzling), it is useful to ask them what they found puzzling—that brings out more philosophical topics.

3   Jaclyn's response here questions the foundation of skepticism. Underlying this response is a notion of the inherent inconsistency of Cartesian doubt: that is, as Sextus Empiricus recognized, that doubt about whether one is real or doubt about the existence of the external world cannot be expressed without involving one in absurdity.

4   The children have been reading "Pixie" so E. was inserted here to avoid confusion.

5   The text of Elfie seems to suggest that dreaming is thinking in your sleep. Jordan is questioning this explanation of dreaming.

6   Heather's response may not actually add to Jordan's question, but prior to this discussion Heather rarely entered into the dialogue, so crediting her with adding to Jordan's question encourages her to participate.

7   Children often want to begin a discussion immediately about what interests them. However, experience has shown that if we stop at this stage the children forget the other points of interest which they would have wished to discuss.

8   Kristen's response raises a question about the nature of wondering.

9   Usually, in a PFC session, many children have their hands raised with questions they wish the group to discuss. In the initial couple of PFC sessions, children would be disappointed if someone else said "their" question. The change from disappointment to recognition such as shown by Alex here, demonstrates a feature of the community in action wherein the children are more concerned with the content of the questions and are less competitive.

Matthew   You could put a little star.[10]

*Sarah   Why didn't she say that, I mean why did she say that she-some people-maybe some people can go to sleep with their eyes open.[11]

Blake   Yeah, oh man! [clutches his head in his hand]

*Owen   I want to know why they said may-that just-Why did Seth say that just shows how wrong he can be?

McCall   How wrong *Seth* could be?[12]

Owen   Yeah.

McCall   What did Seth say?

Owen   He's, [points at text] right-

McCall   Seth said?

Owen   [reads] says that Elfie hardly ever talks, maybe she's not for real. That just shows how wrong he can be.

McCall   Okay, shall we put up "Why is Seth wrong?"[13]

Owen   No. "Why did Seth say that Elfie hardly ever talks. Maybe she's not for real...

McCall   Okay

Owen   ... That just shows how wrong he can be."?

McCall   [Writes] Elfie hardly ever talks, maybe she's not for real. That just shows how wrong he can be. Okay we have room for one more.

*Laura   Why did she think she was asleep when she was really awake?

McCall   [Writes] Why did she think she was asleep when she was really awake? Okay

—Gap in Tape—

Let's look at Jaclyn's question, number one, "If Elfie wasn't a real person, how could she think or talk?" What do you think about that?

*Ami   Well, I have a question to ask Jaclyn.[14]

Sarah   Jaclyn?

Jaclyn   What?[15]

Ami   Well, like why, I mean like how—when did—how did you—I mean how did you *think* of that question?

Jaclyn   Well that's a toughie, because um, it says in the story she maybe not be alive if she didn't talk.[16] [Sarah hands Jaclyn a book to help her find what it said]. Or she couldn't like think or something. And it made me like—it

---

10   Often many children are interested in the same topic, in which case I will put an asterisk next to the question, rather than list up to 15 names. This saves time and also serves to indicate that the topic is important to the group.

11   Sarah is struggling with her point. She wants to raise a more specific aspect rather than leave an "open" why question. So she changes the articulation of her response half way through. This is a typical occurrence in dialogue. The children often "think aloud," and change what they started to say as they see problems with the way they have phrased something. They try hard to put their thoughts into words accurately. Here Sarah wants to question the test of being asleep suggested in the text.

12   Children often have difficulty giving the correct names to the characters in the text, and can be sidetracked from their original question by this problem. So I question Owen to make sure we have his question accurately phrased.

13   Here, I tried to paraphrase Owen's question. This is something which I would never normally do. One cannot do the thinking for the children and then expect them to think for themselves. Even paraphrasing what they say in order to help them will, if practiced, result in the children being more passive and relying on the facilitator to think for them. Luckily, in this instance no harm is done as the children are accustomed to my being accurate with their ideas, and encouraging them to attempt to articulate those ideas for themselves (even when this takes a long time to happen). So Owen, who is a strongly independent thinker, resists any effort to modify his ideas.

14   Ami addresses Jaclyn directly. This is an important feature of a community of inquiry. When children direct their questions, points and responses towards each other, and not towards the facilitator, it shows that a child is reflecting upon what other children are saying, and not merely responding to questions or prompts from the facilitator.

15   Ami has a quiet voice—it is often hard to hear her.

16   Jaclyn's response here assumes that one criteria for being "real," is to be alive. It seems that she is puzzled by the suggestion that in order to be alive one must talk and think.

came up to my head and I thought it would be a good question.

McCall   Yeah. So how would you know if something was a real person or not?

*Jordan   If, if she—if Elfie wasn't real then, then she wouldn't be able to—she'd be able to talk because then she might be what we were discussing yesterday—[we were discussing "real," "fake," "artificial" and "imaginary"] But if she wasn't real, then she wouldn't be able, she wouldn't be able to *think*! And she wouldn't, she wouldn't be able to move every part of her body and[17] stuff like that.

*Heather   I agree with Jordan 'cause if you're not *there* you can—you can't *do* anything. You, you won't be able to think and move and stuff, and learn stuff.[18]

*Alex   [Softly] I agree with Jordan because if you weren't real you, you couldn't, you wouldn't—you'd be like—you'd just be a model and you wouldn't be able to hear and everything like that.

McCall   Alex, what did you say? What would you just be if you weren't real?

Alex   Well if you weren't real you'd just be a model and you wouldn't be able to hear and everything.[19]

McCall   You'd just be a model?

Alex   And you wouldn't be able to hear.

*Owen   Well I disagree with Jordan because of—well he wouldn't—What do you mean he wouldn't like not be able to move any part of his body? Maybe—What if like it was a *robot*?[20]

McCall   Well that's an interesting question.

Owen   A robot can move every part of his body and a robot isn't real!

McCall   Now, is a robot a person?[21] (Chorus, No! No!)

*Laura   I agree with Jordan because if you weren't *real* then you couldn't talk. You would just be still, and you wouldn't be able to hear and talk and move at all.

*Matthew   Well if, if—I agree with [looks at Laura]

McCall   Laura

Matthew   Laura. Because if, if you weren't real you wouldn't be able to, to like move around. And you would be you would—You wouldn't be able to *think*, you wouldn't be able to *hear* and you wouldn't be able to do *any*thing.

*Kristen   A ro-a robot isn't a person because it's - it's a robot - it's not a person.

---

17   Jordan explains the basis of Jaclyn's question—"If Elfie wasn't a real person, how could she think or talk?"—That while non-persons may in fact talk, existence is a necessary condition for thinking. There is an inherent absurdity in the Cartesian position hinted at in the text, that a non-existing being could do anything.

18   Heather clarifies and emphasizes Jordan's point that existence is a necessary condition for doing anything.

19   Alex is expanding the line of argument introduced by Jordan. While existence is a necessary condition of being a person, there are also sufficient conditions to be satisfied. An object such as a mannequin fulfills the condition of existence, but is not a person. To be a person, one must also be able to hear, etc.

20   Owen is using a counter example to challenge one of the sufficient conditions of personhood presented thus far—that in order to be a person, one must not merely exist, like a mannequin, but be able to move any part of your body. In Owen's example, a robot fulfills this sufficient condition, and yet is not a person. Owen's challenge raises the possibility that a robot could fulfill all the conditions of personhood which the children have put forward.

21   Owen's statement, that a robot isn't real could have served to introduce the topic of the nature of reality for discussion. I might have asked him what he meant by "real." However, I chose not to for two reasons: firstly because we had discussed the meaning of "real" in the previous PFC dialogue, (referred to earlier by Jordan), and secondly and more importantly because the lines of argument advanced so far by the children concerned the definition of person and the nature of personhood. So my question to the class was intended to draw attention to the implicit challenge to their conditions of personhood presented by Owen's counterexample. Here I am following up on an issue raised by the children, rather than introducing a new issue.

McCall Well let's think about this for a minute. Supposing something came in through the door right now and it looked just like a person, and it talked and it moved, how would we know whether it was a real person...
(Chorus ooh! ooh! ooh!)

McCall ... or a robot that looked like a person?[22]
(Chorus oh! oh!)[23]

*Matthew Well on this, on this movie this person, this par- this father made a robot. But you always can put like materials over it to make it look like skin and make it look like a real person so it could go to school and everything. And then, and then its robot brain could learn so much it would be like a perfect robot.

McCall Could you tell whether it was a robot or a person?

Matthew Yeah, you could because if, if you like—maybe like, just—Well no![24] Because if, if it looks *just* like a person then you wouldn't be able to. Because you can't, you can't rip off—you can't like do something to it because *what if it's a real person?*[25] You never know which, if it's a real person or not,

because—But you *would* know if, if it didn't have skin on it and everything. If it was just plain and you could see its parts and everything. Then you would know it's a robot.[26]

McCall Now that's an interesting thing you said Matthew. You could do something to it if it was a robot, but you couldn't do something to it if it was a person.[27]

Matthew Yeah. You can't like rip stuff off of it. Because then, because then, because if it was a real person you'll *hurt* it. You'll hurt the person then.

*Sarah I agree with Matthew on his first question at the end.[28] Because they, they have—you can't rip off the skin of a person, but as a robot you can. And...

McCall Now one minute, Sarah. Why could you not rip off the skin of a person, but you could for a robot?

Matthew Oh, because, oh!...

Alex I agree with Matthew too. Because because if you did make like a human robot and you sent it to school it could, it *could* learn a lot. And it would be a good thing to have it.[29]

Child Robot

---

22 At this point, I develop the challenge presented in Owen's example of a robot. What would serve as sufficient conditions of personhood, such that only a person could fulfill those conditions? If a robot could meet all the conditions so far presented for personhood, could we distinguish persons from robots and if so, how?

23 The children are very excited by this problem.

24 Matthew is thinking as he talks. He has ideas about physical tests, but rejects them as he speaks.

25 Matthew presents a condition which might differentiate persons from robots—that persons are beings to whom one owes moral consideration. One has a moral duty not to hurt persons.

26 A robot is differentiated from a person by its constitution. If you could see its parts you would not need to test it.

27 I emphasize the moral consideration introduced by Matthew. Here again, I do not introduce the idea, but once introduced by the children it can be developed or highlighted.

28 Throughout the dialogue, the children are careful to connect what they are saying to what has been said earlier. This shows that they are thinking metacognitively. They are not simply presenting their ideas, but thinking about those ideas and how they relate to what other children have said. They take care to show the structure of the dialogue as they speak. This also involves paying close attention to who has said what, remembering the content and the person who originated the idea, while also thinking of their own contribution. This is a complex cognitive task for anyone, and although they do make mistakes, it is surprising how often their recapitulation of the structure of the dialogue is accurate.

29 Alex picks up on a point which Matthew made earlier. A child will often put forward two (or more) ideas at a time. When this happens a dialogue may develop which follows both themes.

*Scott Well, see, I disagree with Matthew because see if a robot was—came in or something you, *you couldn't rip*[30] off its skin be- even even though if it didn't have have skin. They would probably—they could just paint it the color of skin and then it, and then it's really metal so it looks like a human.

Matthew Ooh, ooh, um.

Child What?

McCall Okay, Matthew. Do you want to clarify what you meant?

Matthew No. But, but if you painted it you would *see*, you would see, like—but they would have to put metal over it, over the parts. So when you paint it looks like a round arm and it would have to bend and everything.

Owen Yeah, but robots—Well I agree with Matthew because, well you *could* tell a robot from a person because you could—What you could do to the robot was like you could like, you could—Well you could throw a *needle* at it.[31]

McCall And?

Owen And, and, if it, and if it, and if it—and if it like—and if the needle, and if it doesn't go through then it would be a robot!

McCall So that would be a test so you could tell the difference between a robot and a person?

Matthew But, but![32]

McCall You could throw a needle at it?

Child No, but

McCall Supposing it was a person?

Child No, but

Matthew That's what I'm *saying*!

McCall Marsha, supposing it was a person, could you throw a needle at it?[33]

Marsha No.

McCall Why, why couldn't you throw a needle at it?

Marsha Because, because if it's—if it sticks you really deep then you would bleed. And to a robot it would—wouldn't bleed.[34]

Matthew I agree with Marsha. Because if you,[35] if you, if you throw a ro- if a robot—if *somebody* walked in the door right, and someone- and we thought it was a robot, we wouldn't, we wouldn't be able to *know*. And if you threw, if you threw- and if you threw a needle at it, the pers- and *if* it was a real person, wherever you threw it, it would start bleeding. And, and if it was a rusty needle *if* it was a rusty needle it could,

---

30 When Matthew raised the moral objection to ripping the skin off a person, he used the verb "can't." Sarah completed the description by adding "but as a robot you can." Both children were using the verb "can" to mean "may." Here Scott uses the verb "can" in the sense of "being able to," and he raises a technical difficulty concerning what one is able to do (as opposed to what one should do).

31 Owen continues the line of thinking about what one would be able to do by suggesting another test by which one could distinguish a person from a robot. His test is also concerned with the physical difference between a person and a robot.

32 Matthew wants to reiterate the moral objection to such a test.

33 I ask Marsha this question in order to widen participation in the dialogue. Marsha rarely talks, although she follows the discussion closely. I continue to use the verb "can" despite the ambivalence in meaning, as this is the word being used by the children.

34 Marsha introduces a more specific physical differentiation between robots and people: that people bleed. This introduces a specifically biological feature of persons.

35 Matthew is conscious of involving other children in the dialogue and crediting them. Although he is eager to emphasize his moral objection to physical tests which may hurt a person, he is gracious about the protocol of dialogue—that one shares thoughts and credits others. So he includes Marsha's point about bleeding in a more comprehensive account. (Considering that Matthew is only five years old, his sensitivity towards another child's thought, both in terms of crediting her and incorporating and developing her idea, is noteworthy.

it could, it could hurt them 'cause it would have rust on it and everything.

*Kristen Well I, I think that that's not really a good idea to find out how it works because if it was a real person it would hurt very badly and the person could get hurt. I think that you could, that it's pretty good, but you *shouldn't* do it. You[36] should pick a different way to disc- to, to find out.

McCall Can you think of any *way*, any test that you could give it to find out whether it was a robot or a real person?

Matthew I know, I know.

*Jordan Well, mm, well a way that you could do it is if you sended it to a doctor. If you put a nee- and if he put a needle in it, it'll—it would have, it would have—Well blood would have to come out. And

[tape runs out].[37]

Discussion continues with considering why it's okay for a doctor to stick needles into people but not for a regular person to stick needles into people. General opinion is because a doctor can do it without injuring. (The rusty needle!) Children then consider other ways of testing which would not hurt if it was a person.

Sarah ... about the fact. You could have like, um—stick, um,—have something metal and put it on there and see if it sticks because metals[38] against a magnet does stick.

McCall Okay, let's think about this for a minute. Laura, supposing a person had a metal leg, are they still a person?[39]

Laura Well, um, they are and they aren't. Because they are for the rest of their body, but they're kind of *not* for *that* part of their body, because[40] it's not the same as the other parts of their body, it's not as soft as the other parts of their body and it wouldn't be—And you could feel it would be harder because of their bones.

McCall So do you think they wouldn't be a person?

Laura Well I think they *would* be a person[41] but that leg would be a *kind* of a person, not really like us.

*Jordan Well I agree with Laura and I disagree with her because if something happened to the leg like if it got flattened and the doctor had to replace it then they would *still be* a human. But if it was like[42] how Matthew said if it was a robot with fake skin there, then it wouldn't be a human.

---

36 Kristen clarifies the distinction between what one is able to do and what one may do, highlighting Matthew's moral objection to harmful physical tests on persons.

37 Jordan proposes a way of avoiding the moral problem of harming people. His suggestion raises an interesting moral issue. The implication is that doctors are exempt from the moral injunction which prevents us from sticking needles into people. In this example, sticking a needle into the person would hurt. (The Hippocratic Oath actually forbids a doctor from taking a knife to his patient!) Would it be okay for a doctor to take a blood sample from someone for other than medical purposes? Jordan's suggestion also emphasizes the biological nature of persons.

38 Sarah suggests a physical test which does not hurt a person.

39 This question is designed to probe the physical distinction between persons and robots which the children are making—that persons bleed whereas robots do not.

40 Laura maintains that physical (flesh and blood) constitution is a property of persons.

41 By maintaining that the person would still be a person although part of them would not be person-like, Laura is approaching a whole/part distinction, wherein a property of the whole is not necessarily possessed by the parts.

42 Here Jordan introduces a new condition of personhood-origin. (Once a person always a person). For Jordan it is not the physical distinction which is important, (the person and the robot could both have metal legs), but the origin of the being. Jordan also affirms the whole/part distinction implicit in Laura's response.

*Ami	Well I was going to say something about the other thing we were talking about.[43]
McCall	Let's hear what you have to say.
Ami	Well I disagree with everyone who said you could take it to the doctor. Because you would have to take it in the car right?
McCall	Um.
Ami	Well if it was a real robot it might be able to break out of the car.
McCall	So it might be difficult to do this test? All right, now let's think about another question...
Child	Oh, just one more, oh, oh,[44]
Sarah	Suppose the doctor lives next door to you?
McCall	Then that would be okay, wouldn't it? Let me ask you this, supposing a person had two metal legs, would they be a person then?[45]
Child	No!

*Kristen	They would be real because just because they have the metal—metal legs doesn't mean that they're not real, because they are *still*, a person.[46]
*Matthew	I agree with Kristen, well, I, I,—because—um
McCall	Did you forget your reason? [nods head] Well, we'll come back to you when you remember.
*Heather	I agree with Kristen Rago because if you have two metal legs, it doesn't mean that you're a fake person, it means that you're a real person. If you have had legs *replaced*, you would still be a person.[47]
*Jordan	I agree with Kristen because as I said, maybe something happened to it like if it got flattened or something like that. Or if it got chopped off by an *ax* or something. [chuckles] Maybe they would need to replace it with *false* legs, but *it* would *still*, be a human, the person would *still* be a human.[48]

---

43   During PFC discussions, children sometimes refer back to earlier parts of the dialogue, as Ami does here. At this point, the facilitator has several judgments to make. Keeping in mind that his/her job is to facilitate the dialogue, which includes the development of lines of argument, as well as insuring their own ownership of the content of the dialogue. Often the points raised have a bearing on the current topic or issue being discussed, in which case the development of the idea or example will further the dialogue. Occasionally the point raised does not relate (directly) to current issues, as is the case with Ami's point. Although an indirect link could be made between the problems raised by the transportation of robots, and issues of origin and biology, it is unlikely that the children would connect the two at this point. However, the judgment that a point made will not develop the dialogue is not alone sufficient reason for lack of encouragement. Occasions arise in the course of a discussion when many children are interested in a topic which does not develop philosophically. When this occurs (as it does later in this dialogue) considerations of ownership of the content of the discussion are important. (E.g., if most of the group wish to discuss the details of an example given by a child).

44   In this instance, other children had their hands raised waiting to speak about what differentiates persons from robots. So the question raised (45) develops this topic.

45   In this instance, other children had their hands raised waiting to speak about what differentiates persons from robots. So the question raised (45) develops this topic.

46   Kristen, Heather and Jordan all emphasize human origin as an overriding condition of personhood. Replacement of human parts with nonhuman parts does not affect personhood. Heather also introduces a distinction between fake and real. A real person can have fake parts. The condition of personhood is a condition or property of the whole, even though the parts may not be human.

47   Kristen, Heather and Jordan all emphasize human origin as an overriding condition of personhood. Replacement of human parts with nonhuman parts does not affect personhood. Heather also introduces a distinction between fake and real. A real person can have fake parts. The condition of personhood is a condition or property of the whole, even though the parts may not be human.

48   Kristen, Heather and Jordan all emphasize human origin as an overriding condition of personhood. Replacement of human parts with nonhuman parts does not affect personhood. Heather also introduces a distinction between fake and real. A real person can have fake parts. The condition of personhood is a condition or property of the whole, even though

Children   (oh, oh, oh.)

McCall   So they would have *false* legs, but Heather said it wouldn't be a fake person.

Child   Oh, oh, I want to say...

Jordan   Yes it would still be a person.

*Matthew   I disagree with Jordan on part of what he said. And I agree with Kristen[49] because even if you had two metal legs, you'd still be a person because you'd still *think* like a person, you'd still have a human *brain*. And I disagree with Jordan because if someone chopped both of your legs off with an ax, you'd be *dead*. [50,51]

*Scott   I disagree with Matthew because you wouldn't be dead because, see—if they saved other kinds of legs, they could sew it back on. Like if you get stitches if you have a crack in the head, they sew it back together. Well you could like sew the other leg back on.

*Brian   Um, well,

McCall   What do you think? If you had two metal legs, would you still be a person?

Brian   I, um, disagree with Matthew 'cause Matthew said—I mean I agree with Matthew 'cause Matthew said if you had two legs chopped off then you would be dead.[52]

McCall   Um, hum, well what about the other part of what Matthew said—that if you had a human brain you would be a person? Even though you had metal legs,—D'you agree with that?

Brian   Yeah.

*Heather   I agree with Matthew if you did have like—if you did chop off your legs you would be automatically dead. And if you had a real brain, you would be a person.

McCall   Supposing that you had a human brain but the rest of you was all metal, your eyes and your mouth and your nose and *everything* would you be a person then?[53]

*Alex   I agree with Jordan because if your legs were chopped off, you *could* replace them with false legs because your heart wouldn't be damaged or anything.

Matthew   Oh, I know, I know!

McCall   Okay, Matthew then Laura.

Matthew   Well about the one that you just asked us to think about. That one. If you *still*[54] had your human brain you would be—you *wouldn't* be a[55] person because—you said the rest of your body was metal?

McCall   Um, hm

Matthew   Your *heart* would be chopped off so you wouldn't be *alive!*[56] You wouldn't have any blood flowing through your body!

Sarah   Wait! I don't understand that.

---

the parts may not be human.

49   Matthew is taking care to show the exact relations of what he is about to say to what other children have said previously.

50   Matthew introduces three new conditions of being a connected—that one has to think like a person, and that one has to have a human brain. In his third point, he disagrees with Jordan that if someone had their legs chopped off, they would still be a person, he states that they'd be dead. Implicit in this point is that one must be alive to be a person.

51   I did not take the opportunity here to follow up on Matthew's statements by asking whether one needs a human brain in order to think like a person. (This issue does arise later.)

52   Brian appears to affirm that being alive is a condition of personhood.

53   I follow up here on Matthew's point about the importance of having a human brain.

54   Matthew seems about to confirm that human origin is the basic condition of personhood.

55   He is thinking as he is talking, and changes his mind as a new possibility occurs to him.

56   You wouldn't be a person because you wouldn't be alive. The implication in Matthew's statement is that being alive is a more basic condition of personhood than human origin. Being alive would be a necessary condition of personhood.

Matthew   Oh, I'll clarify it. Well see you know your heart it flows blood through your body? Well if all your body was metal and your head was only left, it would be cut right here, [demonstrates], and your heart wouldn't be there to flow blood through your brain. So you wouldn't be a real person, you wouldn't even be *alive!*[57]

Child   I don't agree with that.

McCall   So Matthew, are you saying that you have to be alive to be a real person?[58]

Matthew   Well no. But, well kind of I don't know, but you can't live without a heart because it has to flow blood to your brain.

Owen   I disagree with Matthew because if your heart was metal, the rest of your body would be metal except your brain. Your brain doesn't *need blood.* And...[59]

Child   Yes it does, it needs *some* blood.

McCall   Wait a minute, what d'you want to say Owen?

Owen   But your brain doesn't need blood, just the rest of your body does, and if your rest of your body is metal, your heart can be metal too. And now it doesn't matter because if you fell down, all the outside part of you would be metal and you wouldn't get hurt.

McCall   Would you still be a person, Owen?

Owen   Yes.[60]

*Laura   I disagree with all the people who said if your legs got chopped off you would be dead. Because the only way you would be dead if your heart stopped beating, or if your brain stopped working, or if they got—But just because your legs got cut off, you wouldn't be dead.

McCall   Would you be a person if you were dead, Laura?[61]

Laura   You would be a person if you were dead, just you wouldn't be talking or hearing. And I agree with all the people who said you'd be alive with cut off legs, 'cause you could always get them replaced, you could get metal legs and everything.

*Kristen   Could Scott please clarify what he said before? 'Cause /// I was going to say something about it if only I could hear it. Oh yes, now I remember. Um, I disagree with Scott when he said that like you could sew a part to a part. Well, that's not what stitches are. Stitches are if you hurt yourself really bad, they stitch it just to—up, but not if your legs are cut off or—that's not a way how you stitch something.

McCall   All right, we're going to look at the next question now, which is Jordan's question. [reads] "How could she have dreams and think at the same

---

57   What Matthew clarifies is how he reasons that a person with a totally metal body could not be alive. (He states in his last sentence that you wouldn't be a real person if you were not alive, but he does not argue this point.)

58   This question follows up and highlights Matthew's point.

59   It is not clear, here, whether Owen thinks a person would be alive without blood or not.

60   Owen seems to think that a person remains a person without blood. It is not clear whether his disagreement with Matthew is about whether the brain (or the person) is still alive under these conditions, or about whether the human origin of the person is more important than the condition of being alive.

61   The basis of this question concerns the limits of personhood. Matthew's statements imply that one has to be alive to be a person. According to Laura, a person is still a person if they are dead. There is a philosophical "glitch" in casting the problem in this manner. Strictly speaking only that which has the potential to be alive can be dead. A biological entity is one which may be alive or dead. An artifact is neither. Furthermore, there are real problems in defining death, especially when it comes to persons. And there are different medical, legal, biological, religious, social and philosophical definitions and criteria for death of persons.

time?'' And there was Jordan and Heather and Alex were all interested in that ...[62]

Children Oh, oh, oh, oh!

McCall ... Okay. Now Jordan you asked the question, so could you explain what was puzzling about that? "How could she have dreams and think...

Jordan Well, what I think was *interesting* about it is, um, even though it didn't say that, oh she um Elfie *thought* and *dreamed* at the same time—it's just that she said "I don't have *fancy* dreams," but she *never* said that she *didn't* have dreams. But she also said that she thought. So that's why I said that.[63]

Heather Sometimes you can think and dream, sometimes, but mostly you can't. 'Cause like when you're thinking and dreaming—mostly you can't but sometimes you can because, because sometimes when you're thinking too hard and you dream at the same time you really can't dream at the same time.

Ami [experimenting with closing her eyes] Well, I agree with Heather because, um, you can't dream at the same time and think. Because, um, see 'cause sometimes if you're dreaming—You can't dream without thinking.

McCall You can't dream without thinking?

Ami You have to think what you're going to dream!

McCall You have to think what you're going to dream?

*Jaclyn See—What was the question again?

McCall [reads] "Can you think and dream at the same time?"

Jaclyn Well sometimes. Because if you were /// the live one can like—when I have a dream, I always thought about that. And um, when I have a dream, I think about it and I said—one dream I thought about this dream, and like I'm remembering this question but then I forgot it. And /// I asked my Mom if it was true, and she said "you might have a dream," and I said "I was thinking when I was sleeping."[64]

*Laura I agree with Heather and Jaclyn because like sometimes you can think and dream, and sometimes you can't. Because like when you're dreaming—like you *can* if you're dreaming and then you're thinking in your dream. Sometimes it's hard to think and dream at the same time, especially if you're thinking about something else and you're dreaming about something else. Because then you might get mixed up.[65]

Mark When you sleep you can also—when you are asleep you can also think *and* dream too.

Child Yeah, 'cause you have to dream.

*Matthew Well, um, I agree with Heather because, um, you *can* think and dream sometimes. Because when you're not thinking and you're dreaming, your

---

62 It can be hard to judge when to move on to consider the other topics initially raised by the children. Sometimes the topics are related and the dialogue covers most of them.

63 Jordan takes care to explain that the text does not say that E. has dreams and thinks at the same time. The text says ." . . I think all the time. I even think when I sleep. I don't have fancy dreams. I just think when I'm asleep about the same things I think about when I'm awake."

64 Jaclyn seems to be recounting an experience when she describes as thinking when she was sleeping, and her mother tells her is dreaming. This supports the apparent identification of dreaming with thinking in one's sleep suggested in the text, which Jordan questions.

65 Laura considers dreaming and thinking to be different mental acts. In answer to Jordan's questions whether one can do both at the same time, she suggests that it is possible to think within a dream.

imagination is thinking. So your imagination is thinking sometimes but your brain is thinking *with* it. So I agree with Heather.[66]

*Jordan I agree with Matthew and I disagree with Matthew. Because *you* control your imagination. So if you were dreaming—Some people say that your dreams are *in* your imagination, and some people say you don't. But if your dreams *are* in your imagination, then how could you *think* in your imagination while you're *dreaming* in your imagination? But you could *think* in your dream while you're *in* your imagination! [chuckles][67]

*Sarah I agree with Heather in the way beginning because if you think too hard and you dream and you only could think, because if you, um, think really hard—a dream—you, you have to think, because there's only a little bit of dreaming.

McCall All right, what's the difference between thinking and dreaming? How would you *know* if you were thinking or you were dreaming?[68]

Child Could you clarify that?

McCall Okay, yes I asked two questions. First what's the difference between thinking and dreaming? And secondly, which is a different question, how would you know whether you were thinking or dreaming?

Scott That's *hard*!

McCall That's hard, yes.

*Jaclyn Because if you're dreaming and you are *not* thinking—Well like I go to bed, I just fall right to sleep and I forget to think, but I *still* think at the same time. The other question was—would you repeat the other question?

McCall How would you *know* whether you were thinking or dreaming?

Jaclyn If you were dreaming and you were thinking, how could you think and dream at the same time. I know that question because if, um, you think at the same time and how can you like think /// If you had your eyes open you can think, and if you had your eyes closed you can think too.[69]

*Kristen /// I think that thinking and dreaming—um, dreaming is when you're asleep or, yeah, when you're asleep and um, then your imagination *it* starts.[70] I think a dream is imagination

---

66 Matthew seems to be suggesting that dreaming is an imaginative act whereas thinking is a cognitive act,—dreaming is your imagination thinking, and thinking is your brain thinking. Being qualitatively different kinds of acts they can occur at the same time. He seems to be using a modular model of mental activity, (similar to some Artificial Intelligence models), in which different functions are assigned to different modules or locations.

67 Jordan raises a major point here when he states that imagination is intentional. The structure of his argument is complex and one has to rely on the preceding dialogue to understand what he is saying. On the one hand his entire analysis appears to be making a case for the unity of consciousness, (which is a classic philosophical argument against the modular distributive functions model).—Even if one distinguishes between imaginative and cognitive activity it is the one person who is the mental actor. In this case, neither your imagination nor your brain is thinking, you are the entity who is thinking.

Moreover, he seems to be saying that given that your control your imagination, you cannot be simultaneously but independently thinking and dreaming in your imagination. There is an assumed premise here, which seems to be that you can control only one thing at a time.

68 Most of the children have used the distinction between thinking and dreaming which was assumed by Jordan's original response. So these questions are designed to probe that distinction.

69 Jaclyn appears to agree with Elfie in the text, that you think while you are asleep.

70 Kristen makes the point that you dream when you are asleep, and that dreaming is imagination. She seems to suggest that (at least sleeping) imagination is not intentional.

and thinking is, um, I think thinking is, eh,—I can't, I can't say *what* thinking is!

McCall But you think dreaming is imagination?

Kristen Yeah.

*Heather Well, um, sometimes it is and sometimes it's *not*. Um, I sort of disagree with Jaclyn and I sort of *do*. Um, sometimes you *can* and sometimes you, um, *can't*. Well the reason why I agree with Jaclyn is because sometimes you can think, you can think, um, at the same time as dreaming. The reason I disagree with Jaclyn because you can't sometimes. If you're thinking too, you mostly go to sleep and you don't know whether you're sleeping or dreaming yet.

McCall You don't know? (Okay, Brian put that down.)

*Jordan I could answer my own question of what I said.

McCall Uh, huh.

Jordan I mean I agree with Heather about disagreeing with Jaclyn. Because sometimes if you think too *hard* and then like you don't dream *enough*, sometimes you—sometimes you go—sometimes you just go into only thinking. And sometimes if you just dream too much, and then you—and then you're just thinking a little bit, sometimes you go right into all dreaming.

McCall All right, how do you *know*, Alex, let's think about this...

Tape Ends

Tape Begins

Jordan Um, can I tell why I disagree with that question?

McCall Yes, sure.

Jordan I disagree with my question,[71] it's because some—I do this a lot too—If I pinch myself when I'm, when I'm, I'm still dreaming and I don't pinch myself in the—in my dream sometimes, I wake up and I fall off my bed. But, and, and then, and then I try, and then I go back to bed. But then I keep on pinching myself in my dream. Then I pinch myself when I'm, when I'm still dreaming.[72]

McCall So can you tell you're dreaming? Is that how you know you're dreaming, Jordan?

Jordan Yeah. When I, when I pinch myself— when I pinch myself and when I don't wake up when I pinch myself in my dream. And then when I, when I pinch myself and I, and I'm waking—and I woke up when I pinched myself, that's how I know if I was pinching in my dreams or if I wasn't pinching in my dreams.[73]

McCall Right.

Sarah I have a question for you, Jordan. How can you do that? How can you like, if you're on the middle of the bed, how can you just fall off and—pinch yourself in your dreams?

Jordan What I do, what I do to do that is: when I pinch myself I—Sometimes my sis- my sister pinches me or something and that's what, and that's what I do to- And that's what it feels like. So, and then what I do to- to not- for her to not pinch me, is I roll, is I roll, is I

---

71 The question under discussion concerns how one would know whether one was dreaming or awake. The children have been discussing whether pinching oneself could be a test for being awake.

72 Jordan is saying that you can pinch yourself while you are dreaming although not in the dream. Or you can pinch yourself within a dream.

73 Jordan's test for whether the pinch was a dream pinch or a non-dream pinch, is that a non-dream pinch wakes him up, and a dream pinch does not.

roll to my Mom and Dad sometimes. It *happened* to me. I thought I was downstairs in my den and, then when I pinched myself, I fell—I rolled and I fell off the bed.[74]

McCall
Okay, let's look at this question here. "Why did she touch her eyes?" Matthew. Why did she touch her eyes, Matthew?[75]

Matthew
To see if she was awake. But if she touched her eyes, she could of hurt her eye or something. Because if she didn't cut her fingernails, but maybe she didn't—then if they were very sharp, they, they could of like—she could've pinched—she couldn't - she could've hurt her eye. And why I was interested in that question is because she could have—that, that's a weird thing to do, to pinch your eyes to see if you're awake.

McCall
Ah-hah, what's weird about it?

Matthew
Well, see like when you're awake you usually like, like try and, like try and move around and go and turn on the light or something so you can really see if you're awake. And then, and then, and, if you, and if you didn't have a light, if, if, if they were—if you couldn't find them in the dark, you, you could at least just, just like, go like to do something. I don't know.[76]

McCall
You could go and do something?

Matthew
Yeah, like get off..

Child
Go off the bed!

Matthew
... get off the bed and go downstairs and if you, and if your mind already had, already knew where the bathroom was already, you could go in the bathroom and get a drink of water, or pour it on yourself.

*Kristen
I, *I disagree with Matthew because—about touching your eyes. I think what they mean by touching your eyes is when they close their eyes and they just wipe theirs or like do this [demonstrates] but not really touch the eye. But they just mean something like that or something like—[demonstrates]

McCall
So why do you—why did she do that in the story, Kristen?

Kristen
Maybe because they say in the story like "are you awake?" So she did it just to see if she was awake or not.

McCall
And do you think that's a good way to tell if you're awake?

Kristen
Kind of.

*Scott
Well, Kristen, because see I think what they meant by touching their eyes was not poking their eyes with your fingernail. That's poking. [demonstrates] But like doing this, touching the, the inside of my finger, like touch like that.

McCall
Would you do that? All right, let's—we've had a demonstration already. Scott would you do that to see if you were awake?

*Jordan
I'm adding on to Matthew's question and I'm agreeing with him and I'm disagreeing with him. Why couldn't she pinch herself like I did?

McCall
D'you think that would be the same kind of thing?

Matthew
Yeah, 'cause then you would, then you would struggle. [demonstrates waking up with pinching] You'd go "Aaagh!"

---

74 When Jordan's sister pinches him he rolls away from her. So in his dream, when he thought he was (awake) in his den and felt a pinch, he rolled away from it. This action resulted in his falling off the bed. So he tests whether he is awake by doing something.

75 Matthew's question relates to tests for wakefulness, so we moved to consider this question.

76 The children agree that in order to see if you are awake, you would do something and observe the consequences. Matthew and others discuss the wisdom of touching one's eyes as a test, and suggest other tests.

Jordan	And the reason I disagree with Matthew is, is—and I'm agreeing with Scott about that one part of the—like you went like this or you went like that. [demonstrates] But, and that's why I disagree with him is that I don't think she took her fingernail and just put it in her eye. And the reason I *agree* with Matthew is because if, if she like poured the water—I mean and why I still disagree with Matthew is because if sh- If she didn't *know* if she was asleep or awake, how would she be able to wake up, how would she be able to wake, wake up if she was asleep, get out of bed, then go and pour water on herself?
McCall	If she didn't know?
Jordan	Yeah.
McCall	Okay.
Jordan	How would she know, and how would she know if she was awake or if she wasn't?
McCall	How would she know if she was doing it or she wasn't, if she didn't know if she was awake or asleep?
Jordan	She could've sleepwalked.[77]
McCall	She could've sleepwalked?
Jordan	Yeah.
*Heather	I agree with Matthew. Well when you like poke your eye and you haven't cut your nails, that would really hurt. And the reason why I agree with Matthew if you like poke your eyes, it will really hurt. And, and when you like touch you eye, that, if you touch like your eyelash, that will, will not hurt.
McCall	Okay, let's look at the next[78] question here [indicates], Kristen "Why did she say to herself 'Dummy, if you can wonder, you must be thinking'?" Let's go back a bit. What was it she was wondering about? Does anyone remember what she was wondering about? You can look at it if you don't remember. [Children look] What was it she was wondering about?
Jaclyn	She knew she was in *doubt* if you can—if she can sleep and think.
McCall	At the same time?
Sarah	I know, I know!
McCall	Tell the whole class, Sarah.
Sarah	It says in the book that if you can't dream—if I can dream I must be thinking.[79] So she's re-really talking about dreaming and thinking. She's really talking about dreaming and thinking?
*Jordan	She was thinking about if she was real or not.
McCall	And so why did she say if you can wonder you must be thinking?

---

77 Jordan seems to think that pouring water on oneself is not an adequate test for discovering whether one is asleep or awake, because one could be sleep walking. He wonders how Elfie would know whether she was sleep walking or really awake.

78 Quite a few children had wished to discuss what Elfie meant by "touching" her eyes. In such a case, although the dialogue may not be developing, the facilitator must consider that the group wishes to discuss the question, and allow the discussion to continue. If one intervenes every time the discussion veers away from philosophical topics, then the children will lose their sense of ownership over the dialogue. So the facilitator has to judge when and how to move the discussion, and when to wait. At this point, the children had given full consideration to the question, so I moved to the next question on the board.

79 It doesn't quite say this in the book. The text does suggest that thinking when you are asleep might be dreaming, and it also suggests that wondering is a kind of thinking. Sarah has conflated these two suggestions, and comes up with the notion that if you can dream you must be thinking. (This suggests an interesting twist to the Cartesian dictum—Cogito ergo sum. Crudely speaking, because of his difficulty in distinguishing dreams from reality, Descartes suggests that everything is open to doubt. But since doubting is a form of thinking, he cannot doubt that he thinks, and thinking implies a thinker. So he concludes "I think therefore I am." Using Sarah's notion, Descartes might have avoided having everything open to doubt, by going straight from dreaming to thinking to existing.)

Jordan   I don't know why *she* said that. I don't know why she *said* that. But, maybe she- maybe she said that because even though dreaming and thinking are *not* the same thing—But it could and it couldn't. Like if you're wondering, like what's in that—what's over that fence, and you're thinking, and then you could *think* "What's over that fence."[80] And why you can't think and wonder is you can't. You can't...

Child   Wonder

Jordan   ... Well, I don't have an answer for that.

McCall   All right, we'll come back to you a little bit later.

*Kristen   I don't think Sarah heard what I said on this, because I meant the part "Dummy, you can't—you can't...

Sarah   [looking at book] At "Dummy"?

McCall   Mmmhmm

Kristen   "if you can wonder you must be thinking," that's what I was talking about.

Sarah   [reads) "if you can wonder you must be thinking."

Kristen   [to Sarah] So you, so you really, so you didn't say what I really meant.[81]

McCall   What did you really mean, Kristen?

Kristen   That—I can't answer that. [laughs]

McCall   You don't know?

Kristen   No [laughs]

*Jaclyn   What I ...

McCall   (Raise your hand) [to Owen]

Jaclyn   What is the question again?

McCall   All right, the question here [points] "Why did she say to herself, 'Dummy, if you can wonder you must be thinking'?"

Jaclyn   *You* can wonder and think at the same time. Only sometimes /// whatever that thing is. You still can think and wonder at the same time because, say I was like, um, Mat. Kind of like you said "Oh." You, you—that was like oh you're wondering and you're, and too, what you're wondering or...

McCall   Would that be thinking...

Jaclyn   ... thinking.

McCall   ... Jaclyn?

Jaclyn   Well, kind of.

McCall   Be a kind of thinking? All right, Sarah?

Sarah   Well, Kristen, it says in the book that if you can wonder you must be thinking.[82]

Kristen   I know, that's what I said. What do you mean?

Sarah   I, I, I mean that in the book—You had a different answer, but in the book it said if you—and that—

McCall   can wonder, you must be thinking.

Sarah   thinking.

McCall   Why was she interested in that? What else did she say?

Kristen   Well I was interested in...

Sarah   She said "and if you're thinking then I must be, um—

McCall   [points] you're for real. What do you think she meant by that ...

Children   Oh, Oh, ooh!

McCall   ... if you're thinking you're for real?

Sarah   If you're thinking you must be for real.

McCall   Why?

Sarah   Because, because it—when I'm thinking, I'm for real. But you might have brain surgery and *you're* still for *real*, but if you're thinking you *must* be for real.[83]

Matthew   Oh, Oh, Oh!

---

80   Jordan provides an example showing how wondering could be a kind of thinking—if one characterizes the thought as a question.

81   Kristen is concerned that the question which she had in mind is not being addressed. (Sarah mentioned dreaming and thinking instead of wondering and thinking). Although she does not now remember her puzzle.

82   Sarah returns to the text to retrace what Kristen may have wanted to say.

Sarah   [to Matthew] Wait. And robots can think and so—and robots can think and *they're* for real. So I kind of disagree with that.[84]

McCall   You kind of disagree?

Matthew   I, I agree with Sarah because I'm thinking what to say and I'm for real right now! And I disagree with Sarah is- Well I agree with Sarah on two things. Because if I'm, I'm thinking right now what to say—And the second thing she said, because robots, robots they're for real. Because they *are* real. But, but they don't—but they don't *think* how we do.

McCall   They don't think how we do?

Matthew   Because—They don't think how we do because, because they, they like have brains and they're made out of— Well *we* have brains but they they think a little bit different. But they think, they think *somehow* alike to us.[85]

*Kristen   I don't understand what Sarah said. What did you say? It it wasn't anything about my question at all!

Sarah   I know. But Dr. McCall had said "what else was she saying?" And then I told her what else she was saying, from the book.[86]

Kristen   I don't- /// what I said it.

McCall   Okay, Kristen, you don't understand what you said?

Kristen   I don't know why I even said it!

McCall   You don't remember why you asked the question?

Kristen   No.

McCall   All right. Well ...

Sarah   You were interested in it because, um, you wanted to know why she was wondering and thinking at the same time. That—that's what *I* think *you* were thinking of.[87]

*Heather   I agree with, I mean I, I don't agree with anybody. I mean I agree with Sarah 'cause robots, whatever, can think and talk. Well they, they can move around and think. And the reason I agree with Sarah, robots can think when they're doing something at the same time.

*Alex   I agree with Matthew because if— 'cause robots *do* think a little different than humans and I—Matthew, I forget what you said. Can you say it again?

Matthew   Well, they think a little different from us because they can, they can, they can like—they know a little more than us because they—they're—People *make* them and whatever people put, what-

---

83   Sarah makes the point that the implication is one way. To say that if you're thinking you must be real does not imply that if you're real you must be thinking. If you had brain surgery and were incapable of thinking, you would still be real.

84   Sarah repeats an argument made earlier in the dialogue, that thinking is not a sufficient condition for being a real person, robots fulfill this condition and are not real persons.

85   Here Matthew modifies his claim, by adding that robots do not think the way people do. This modification suggests that a certain kind of thinking may be characteristic of persons, and that robots could be differentiated by the way in which they think.

86   Sarah takes care to explain to Kristen how the dialogue developed from her original question. This shows a concern that everyone in the group should understand the structure of the dialogue. Children will take care to clarify the development of a line of argument, or a divergence so that everyone understands the connections between what individual members of the group say, and the text.

87   Here Sarah is trying to help Kristen by reconstructing, for Kristen, what Kristen might have been thinking about, (since Kristen has forgotten.) This is an interesting feature because it shows very clearly how a young child can (and does) put herself in the position of another and try to understand the other's thinking even though it differs from her own. (Young children are not "ego-centric" in Piaget's sense.) Throughout the dialogue, children pay attention to views which differ from their own, sometimes trying to develop those views, sometimes presenting counter arguments, but nearly always understanding the thinking of others.

ever people put in their brains for them to know, they know.[88] And like that person might not know it. Like they knew—like a robot that knew everything. Well yeah kind of knew everything, could know all the *math* in the world ...

McCall   Mmm hmm.

Matthew   ... well not *all* the math in the world. And lots of other things. Like—

McCall   Well now, if robots could do that...

Matthew   But they think slightly, they think slightly different than us.

Kevin   Robots can't do most every...

Matthew   What?

Brian   Grownups can't know most everything in the world!

Matthew   I said *robots! Robots!* END OF TAPE.[89]

Jordan   ... so robots can't know every, everything. And a robot does not, will not, know /// he would know of what a human intelligence was!

McCall   A robot wouldn't know what a human intelligence was?

Children   ooh,ooh,ooh,

Laura   But Jordan, can ... ?

Jordan   I agree with Matthew because a robot does know things, like he knows what a table's made of or something. [chuckles] And he knows, and he knows he's intelligent, but he doesn't know every single thing.

GAP IN TAPE

Owen   I disagree with Jordan because a robot *does* know everything because you can know every single thing for *math* if you can, if you can put a calculator in it.

Matthew   Yeah, that's what I said. To put a ///

Sarah   Well what—I don't really get that, Owen.

Owen   Well I—An *infant* can put the alphabet in it and it, and it could read all the words![90]

Matthew   Well then I agree with Owen because, and this is what I said before, whatever—if you put a computer in the robot, what. ever you program it to do it will *do*. Like, like probably you don't know something. And you program it into the robot. The robot will do it, and the robot will do *anything*.[91]

McCall   The robot would do *anything*?

Matthew   Well, except—Well *yeah* because the person that made it had it in his com-*command*. Except if he made the robot and he just let him free and the robot did whatever he wanted to.[92]

McCall   No, because a person, a person when...

[sound of school intercom.]

Matthew   ... like

[sound of school intercom]

Matthew   ... one hundred...

McCall   Okay [gestures to Matthew to ignore the intercom.]

---

88   Matthew distinguishes between robots and persons-robots are artifacts and their thinking is not self-originated.

89   Because of the gaps in the tape, it is not possible to follow the dialogue closely. But it seems that most of the children accept that robots think differently from people, while discussing in what way they think differently.

90   Owen seems to suggest that a robot can know more than a person. Given the alphabet, the robot could read all the words, whereas an infant (who knows the alphabet) cannot. (As is the case with many of the children in the class.)

91   The robot seems to have unlimited capabilities.

92   What Matthew is saying suggests that people have free will, whereas robots do not. A robot will execute the will of a person (except if it is let free.)

Matthew	... put a hundred-a person wouldn't jump off a hundred foot cliff with a ladder...

GAP IN TAPE

Kristen	That's not what I said at all. She's reading something else I said because that's not what I meant at all.
Sarah	Well I'm...
McCall	Now Kristen, we're talking about a different topic now...
*Scott	Well see, I disagree with Mat, robots couldn't know everything. The person who puts the robot- who made the robot couldn't know everything to put into the robot to make *it* know everything.[93] Because, see, a robot is made out of all sorts of stuff..
Child	Metal!
Scott	Oh yeah, all sorts of metal and wire, so if you put everything in it, no matter how big the robot could be to fit all of it in, and anyway a robot couldn't know everything.[94]
Matthew	Oh, Oh!
McCall	Wait a minute, Scott. I'm not sure if I quite heard you. Did you say that the person who *made* the robot knows?
Scott	No, he doesn't know everything, so he couldn't tell the robot everything.
McCall	So you couldn't...
Children	Oh! Oh! Oh!
McCall	... Wait a minute. Let me see if I understand what Scott's saying. You couldn't have a robot that knew everything because the person who *made* the robot couldn't know everything?
Scott	Yeah!

McCall	So a robot only knows what the person who made it knows?
Matthew	Um! Oh!
McCall	Is that right Scott?
Scott	Yeah.
Ami	I could know more than that robot knows!
Matthew	Well because I, I...
McCall	Well now Matthew, you talked already so let's give Owen a chance here.
Owen	I, oh was Scott the one who was speaking?
McCall	Mmm hmm
Owen	Well I disagree with Scott because, because not only one person makes a robot. A lot of people make a robot. A lot of people do different jobs to make the robot. So if they all work together, they could know everything.[95]

[Scott shakes his head]

McCall	You still think it's not possible to know everything, Scott?
Matthew	Oh, please!
Scott	Yes!

-GAP IN TAPE-

McCall	All right, now, I'm really puzzled, Scott. Do you think it's impossible for people to know everything?
Scott	Yes.
Children	Oh! ooh, I, oh!
Matthew	ooh ooh ooh!
McCall	Matthew, we are talking to Scott for the minute. Why, Scott?
Scott	Well, because only—no one knows everything 'cause there is no last number.[96]

---

93 Scott disagrees with Matthew and Owen about the possible extent of a robot's knowledge. He argues that a robot is limited by it's program. The program is limited to the knowledge of the programmer. And the programmer couldn't know everything.

94 Here Scott is saying that it is not size or quantity which sets the limits on a robot's capacity for knowledge.

95 Owen raises a counter argument: that a robot is not limited to the knowledge of one person. It would be possible for a robot to know everything known by people.

McCall	There's no last number?
Scott	There's no last number so people—and I don't—most people don't know like names for other numbers after you get outside a thousand billion.
Child	I don't understand.
Ami	Well Jaclyn, I have a question for Jaclyn. When you said they can ask their parents, what if their parents didn't know everything either? They never- their parents didn't know anything. What if no one in their family knew anything?
Jaclyn	Well, it would be possible because it would be impossible because—if-Ami, maybe if they went to school or college, they would be smart like my Mom.
Matthew	Well, I don't, I don't actually *know* what Jaclyn's saying, but what was the question again?
McCall	About whether someone could know everything.
Matthew	No. Because no one knows what the highest number is, and there is no highest number. No one knows what comes after the ... [97]
Brian	No one knows what comes after ...
Matthew	*I'm* talking, Brian! No one knows what comes after infinity. So people can't know everything. I mean people, people don't know where the end of the universe is. And people don't know lots of things. And you just can't learn *everything* in school![98]

THE END

Concluding Notes

In the introduction to this article I argue that young children, given the right environment, can reason with philosophical concepts which they themselves originate and that the questions which they raise and address are the same as those addressed (in more length and in more detail, etc.) by professional philosophers. They are authentic issues, many involving abstract concepts and definitions, and many of which remain unresolved.

In this dialogue, the dominant philosophical theme which the children themselves raise, concerns the nature of persons. The text sets up a Cartesian puzzle over whether Elfie can be sure she is real, but the very first response reformulates the puzzle in terms of real *persons*. ("If she wasn't a real person, how could she think or talk?") The children begin by establishing that existence is a necessary condition of doing anything, including thinking and talking. This topic is developed by considering that while existence is a necessary condition of being a person, there are also sufficient conditions to be satisfied. An object such as a mannequin fulfills the condition of existence, but is not a person. To be a person one must also be able to hear, etc. Then a challenge is made about the conditions of personhood thus far raised—a robot could fulfill those conditions, thinking moving etc. therefore they cannot serve as properties which define persons, as the children claim that robots are not persons. A new defining property of persons is suggested—that persons are being to whom one owes moral consideration. One has a moral duty not to hurt persons. This property is connected to another possible condition of personhood, the physical

---

96   Here Scott makes an important clarification: the limits to what it is possible to know are metaphysical, rather than epistemological. In his example, people can't know the last number not because of the limits of ignorance, but because there is no last number. It raises an interesting question, in what sense can one have knowledge of what does not exist?

97   Matthew reiterates Scott's point that there are limits to what is knowable, as well as limits to what is known. Inquiry into this distinction will have to take place at another time.

98   You may not be able to learn all the answers in school, but you can inquire about the questions!

constitution of persons. People are biological entities, they bleed. However, being a person is a description of an entity as a whole, and this property of a whole entity is not affected by changes in the parts. The whole/part distinction is developed further by the claim that it is the entity's origin which determines whether it is a person or not. (Once a person always a person). It is not the physical distinction which is important, a person and a robot could both have metal legs. The children then suggest that in order to be a person, one has to think like a person and have a human brain, and that one must be alive to be a person. The question then arises as to whether being alive is a more basic condition of personhood than human origin. Some children consider that a person is still a person when dead. (The two properties are connected—only that which has been alive can be dead. A biological entity is one which may be alive or dead. An artifact is neither. So if biological origin is an important condition of personhood, the question of whether it is alive or dead is immaterial). Finally, the children suggested that an important property of persons is the fact that they have free will.

According to the arguments put forward by the children in this dialogue a robot, although similar to a person in many respects, would be denied the status of personhood on three counts: as artifacts they are not subject to moral considerations; they do not have the right biological origin; they do not possess free will. A fourth feature of personhood which they consider in depth is the kind of thinking which people do. It is suggested that although robots think, they do not think in the same way as people. During the course of the dialogue, the children have generated at least four of the major features which are classically considered important properties of personhood. (Man is a *rational animal*, persons are third-order *intentional* beings, and people are distinctly *moral* agents.) A second theme which the children address arises directly from the test and concerns thinking. Initially the children raise questions about "Cartesian" deduction. Then they draw distinctions between thinking and dreaming, although they say that it is possible to think within a dream. The suggestion is made that dreaming is an imaginative act whereas thinking is a cognitive act and that being qualitatively different kinds of acts they can occur at the same time. One child claims that imagination is intentional, and emphasizes the unity of consciousness—even though there is a distinction between imaginative and cognitive activity, it is the one person who is the mental actor.

The children suggest that there is a distinction between the kind of thinking people engage in and robotic thinking. Their discussion of this issue centers upon the amount of knowledge available to both people and robots. One child then suggests that the limits to what it is possible to know are metaphysical, rather than epistemological. People can't know the last number, not because of limits of ignorance, but because there is no last number. The dialogue ends with a fascinating topic having been raised and still to be discussed—in what sense can one have knowledge of what does not exist:

Although the children are not skilled in using language, and as yet have a limited vocabulary in which to express their thoughts, they are capable of abstract philosophical thinking. Furthermore, not only are they able to originate philosophical ideas, they can also articulate the relationship of one idea or argument to other ideas. They are capable of thinking at two levels at once, as it were: considering abstract concepts and at the same time thinking metacognitively about those ideas and how they relate to what other children have said. They frequently take care to describe the structure of the dialogue as well as the content.

One of the most important features of the environment which encourages the development of the kind or reasoning is that it is authentic. By which I mean the children are inquiring into issues about which there are no definitive answers, and so the procedure of inquiry, in contrast say to asking the teacher or consulting an encyclopedia, is a generation procedure. The inquiry procedure encourages reasoning. There is a relationship between the creation of a community of inquiry, the mechanics of dialogue, and the emergence and development of philosophical reasoning.[1]

Notes

1 For a more detailed exposition of this relationship, see my forthcoming book.

Chapter Eleven
Fostering Reasoning and Critical Thinking

Chapter Eleven

Fostering Reasoning and Critical Thinking

Two of the chief complaints voiced by teachers with regard to their incoming students are:

(a) they perform acceptably on routine assignments and they can memorize tolerably well, but they don't *think*!
(b) they think *uncritically*!

We have been considering the use of specially prepared fictional texts and of communities of deliberative inquiry in order to deal with the first complaint by provoking students to think. But what about the second complaint, which suggests the need for students to think well—meaning to think logically, critically, judiciously and creatively?

Educators have been aware of these complaints for the past 25 to 50 years, and by and large their response has been the same. Thinking, many educators contend, is comprised of skilled thinking performances. If we teach children these skills, they will not only think, but think well. The logical fallacy in this, of course, is that what is true of the parts need not be true of the whole. Even if it were true that the process of thinking is comprised of skilled thinking performances, it would not follow that the process itself is a skillful one.

This is not to deny that the acquisition of skills can be reinforced through practice. Reasoning exercises are needed to polish and perfect those skills that children have already acquired.

Nevertheless, skills are like two-edged swords: they may be used well or badly. In the case of destructive individuals, reasoning can be employed for destructive ends. It is therefore urgent that reasoning be taught in an atmosphere of humane values, so as to minimize the possibility of its being misused. Recourse to philosophy to provide such an atmosphere therefore seems a wholly appropriate educational strategy.

When teaching reasoning and critical thinking through philosophy, one is immediately brought face-to-face with deep-set convictions, highly abstract concepts, and tenaciously held values., all of which must be deliberated upon at once. The deliberating skills that consequently emerge turn out in fact to be reasoning skills and critical thinking skills. Thus the skills are not learned first and then applied to the conceptual difficulties, but rather, the conceptual problems are encountered initially, and the skills are generated out of that encounter.

Many issues present themselves for analysis in this section: what thinking skills are; why philosophers should be involved in their teaching; whether they should be taught at all; and their relationship to critical thinking. On the ground that reasoning is preparatory to judgment, the discussion of judgment has been postponed to the next section.

The overview of reasoning skills provided by Dale Cannon and Mark Weinstein provides an introduction to this section. They begin by distinguishing *formal* from *informal* reasoning in terms of subject-matter: formal reasoning involves valid reasoning irrespective of subject-matter, while informal reasoning is sensitive to subject-matter, *i.e.*, to contextual considerations. *Interpersonal* reasoning involves the skills and dispositions of participants in a reasoning community, which is characterized by rationality and mutual respect. *Philosophical* reasoning is thinking that questions and examines itself, while seeking to rid itself of incomprehension and prejudice. It also seeks to make sense of things by means of an interrogative process that moves in the direction of wisdom.

Wolfe Mays sets out with quite a different agenda: to examine several of the educational programs that purport to enhance thinking among students. He therefore subjects the approaches of DeBono, Feuerstein and Lipman to careful scrutiny. All three programs, he concludes, "will in some measure increase the pupil's powers of judgment, perception, memory, attention and motivation," and based on the evidence provided by the latter two programs, it would appear that these improvements will in turn produce better work by the students in school. It is worth noting that Mays is not convinced that the use of computers in the classroom will produce equally significant improvements in cognitive education.

Scientific knowledge, writes Ann Gazzard, is both *generative* (*i.e.*, constructed) and interpretive. This means that those receiving education in science must at the same time be educated *about* science, and in particular about the practices that contribute to and improve the generation and interpretation of knowledge. What then do students need to know about these practices? According to Gazzard, "if the nature of science is to be successfully understood, then students need to be trained (1) in the importance of logical coherence and consistency, (2) in making interpretations that are meaningful and reliable, (3) in analogical reasoning, and (4) in the search for good reasons." The fallibilistic nature of the sci-

entific enterprise sets additional requirements for the kind of understanding of science that students need to have, for they have got to be prepared to concede error. Gazzard argues that Philosophy for Children produces the kind of skills, dispositions and readiness that successful science education requires.

W. A. Hart launches a dramatic attack on cognitive education and its espousal of "thinking skills." He charges that the technical understanding many educators have of cognitive skills strips them of their humanistic values and leaves the students vulnerable to all who would prey on their freedom and humanity. "The indiscriminate use of the word 'skill' in education confuses things which really are skills with things which aren't," Hart writes, and elsewhere he adds, ". . . what I wouldn't be happy to have called 'skills' (thinking, reading, loving and so on) . . . are capacities which go to define what a human being is."

Christina Slade does more than report on teaching logic in a girls' school, using Philosophy for Children. She is able to show that the success of the experiment also resulted in altering the girls' image of themselves as non-mathematical. Furthermore, she interprets the results as showing that the teaching of logic in the earlier grades prepares students for the later study of algebra. "The skills acquired through logic are precisely the skills which allow algebra to be applied in everyday life. The ability to translate problems into recognizable forms is important in applying all mathematical and technical subjects. That skill is at the heart of logic." And so once again we touch on the importance of translation, as in the earlier article by Tony Johnson.

While it is true, David Bohm concedes, that formal logic constitutes the main core of our ordinary thinking, it tends to become narrow and rigid. Yet reason in a broader sense is present in every phase of human experience. It is reason in the form of ratio, starting with the analogies or proportions that we express by saying "A is to B as C is to D." Ratio also expresses the essence of any and every sequence. Moreover, we see that ratio embodies not only relationships among particular things, but relationships among relationships. Indeed, Bohm conceives of the entire scientific enterprise as an unfolding of the ratios which form the structure of natural processes.

Oppenheimer continues in the same vein, while concentrating on analogy, and in particular, those similarities to be found between several complex and otherwise quite different structures, For it is analogy that enables us to discover unity within multiplicity. Like Bohm, Oppenheimer concludes with a plea for the education of the community with regard to the crucial role of analogy in the understanding of nature.

In an article largely devoted to an examination of the concept of critical thinking, Jen Glaser begins with a distinction between reasoning as truth preserving and reasoning as significance judging, a distinction much akin to that between formal and informal reasoning, as cited earlier by Cannon and Weinstein. She notes that judgments that are context-specific (that take the subject-matter and context fully into account) are not a matter of following rules, but are based on meanings as well as truth. This in turn calls for the making of relevant, appropriate judgments, a characteristic we prize as reasonableness. It is a virtue of people in community, and not just an abstract way of preserving truth. It involves thinking with others, and not just thinking about the products of thought.

Maurice Finocchiaro also espouses critical thinking, but in a very different way: by demonstrating that philosophy *is* critical thinking. He conceives of philosophy as differing from other disciplines in six respects: (1) it is independent of any particular content and can study any subject-matter whatsoever; (2) it emphasizes reasoning; (3) it judiciously tries to take all sides of an issue into account; (4) it is applicable to practical situations; (5) it is universal in the sense of being relevant to everyone; and (6) it turns its critical analyses to constructive ends.

A still different perspective on critical thinking is offered us by Clive Lindop, who takes into consideration Buchler's treatment of making, saying and doing as three modes of judgment, and then applies the resultant conceptual schema to Philosophy for Children, as well as to critical thinking. Lindop argues that educational approaches that emphasize only one of the modes of judgment—for example, saying or assertion—are inferior to those which, all other things being equal—emphasize all three. In this respect, philosophy has an advantage over critical thinking, since the latter concentrates only on thinking in language. In other words, Lindop concludes that Philosophy for Children helps strengthen children's reasonableness and judgment in all the ways that critical thinking approaches do, and in other ways in addition.

The Lipman article likewise compares critical thinking with the Philosophy for Children approach. It proposes four criteria for critical thinking: that it relies on standards and criteria of good thinking; that it facilitates the making of judgments (such as decisions and settlements); that it is sensitive to context (as with all approaches to informal reasoning); and that it is self-correcting (in the sense that participants in communities of inquiry learn to correct themselves through anticipating the corrections of others.) Philosophy for Children is said to meet all of these requirements, and in addition provides such advantages as the fictional text and the classroom community of inquiry.

Reasoning Skills: An Overview

Dale Cannon and Mark Weinstein

Four Dimensions of Reasoning

Reasoning may be thought of as having four dimensions: formal, informal, interpersonal, and philosophical. The order in which they are given here indicates progressively higher, broader, less mechanistic, and in some ways more sophisticated levels of thinking. The order, however, does not represent a developmental sequence of abilities or skills; nor does it represent a sequencing of curricula or class lessons. Much actual reasoning manifests some aspects of each in combination. This is as true of the thinking of children at early elementary grades as well as of adults— sometimes moreso. Although the four dimensions seldom occur in isolation, we focus on each separately for reasons of clarity.

Formal Reasoning

Formal reasoning consists in following patterns of logical inference without regard to subject matter. It is concerned with obtaining definite results by applying explicit rules to clearly defined concepts and statements, as in mathematics. Practice in formal reasoning develops an awareness of the need for consistency and offers tools that reinforce the careful use of valid reasoning patterns, whatever the subject matter.

Formal reasoning, when used correctly, guarantees true conclusions if we start with true premises.

Informal Reasoning

Informal reasoning includes skills of critical inquiry, problem-solving, and rational evaluation in connection with concrete subject matters. It is concerned with obtaining results from inquiries that do not lend themselves to a strict application of formal logic but require reasoned interpretation, clarification, and evaluation before formal principles can be applied, if they can be applied at all. Principles of justification in informal reasoning vary depending on subject matter. Practice in it develops an awareness of the need for clarity, relevance, coherence, and truth.

Interpersonal Reasoning

Interpersonal reasoning involves reasoning in the context of other persons and different points of view and in a manner that is responsible to them. It is concerned with arriving at a position that, taking into account the various points of view involved, will in turn merit their respect, if not their agreement. Practice in interpersonal reasoning develops the attitudes of a reasonable person: the willingness to offer and respond to reasons, the impartial search for truth, a respect for one's opinions and the opinions of others, and a commitment to making common sense.

Philosophical Reasoning

Philosophical reasoning is a matter of thinking about thinking, of clarifying and improving the tools with which one thinks and reasons about other things. It is concerned with obtaining a more satisfying version of one's own thinking or of the thinking practiced in a given subject area: a version that is more thoughtful and sensible, more fully examined and clear, more comprehensive, more impartial, free from presumption—what some have called wisdom. It includes thoughtful exploration of the most basic ideas and principles of the various subject areas, including reasoning itself in each of its dimensions.

The development of a sense of responsibility for reasoning well in young people requires, of course, that they be able to distinguish good reasoning from poor reasoning. But it is just as important for them to be held responsible for reasoning well by others with whom they identify—namely, their peers. At the same time and partly by this manner, they should be encouraged to exercise the ability they have to monitor their own thinking and inquiry. Moreover, in teaching any specific reasoning skill, it is important that the student be given opportunity to gain a sense for how that skill may be employed in real life interactions with others. These things require that all four dimensions of reasoning be developed more or less together. In our judgment, nothing accomplishes this more effectively than open-ended, peer group discussions of ideas which the young people are interested in clarifying philosophically and where each is held responsible to the group for making good sense and reasoning well.

Taken in this global way, with priority placed on helping each student realize sovereignty over his own thinking, philosophical reasoning reveals itself to be the most appropriate foundation for the development of other reasoning skills. Philosophical issues are open ended, philosophical thinking is self-reflective, and philosophical concepts are, for the most part, distinct from those areas within the curriculum in which teachers have didactic authority. This affords the possibility of a truly democratic classroom procedure: a community of inquiry where each member and each view is present for the analysis, criticism, and synthesis of the group.

That is not to say that exercises that enhance some specific or more limited part of the total spectrum of reasoning skills ought not be assigned. It is rather to highlight the role of philosophical inquiry as the central core around which critical and evaluative thinking can best take place.

Representative Examples of Each Dimension

Formal Reasoning

1. Relational Logic
    a. Serial Relationships: reasoning about sequences in time or space.
    b. Symmetric, Asymmetric, and Non-symmetric Relationships: reasoning about relationships to determine what would be true if they were reversed.
    c. Transitive, Intransitive and Non-transitive Relationships: reasoning to see if relationships will carry over and remain true.
2. Categorical Logic:
    reasoning about relationships of class inclusion; *e.g.*, syllogisms which draw a conclusion from two premises of the form "All . . . are . . .," "Some . . . are . . .," "Some. . . are not. . .," and/or, "No. . . are. . ."
3. Conditional Logic:
    reasoning on the basis of hypothetical conditions; *e.g.*, reasoning which draws a conclusion from two premises, one of which states a hypothetical "If. . . then. . ." conditional generalization, and the other states an "instance" to which it may or may not apply.

4. Sentential or Propositional Logic: reasoning which draws a conclusion from one or more premises which compound whole sentences together using connectives such as "and," "or," "no," "implies," etc.

5. Arithmetic: reasoning which draws conclusions concerning relationships between integers.

6. Geometry: reasoning which draws conclusions concerning relationships among spatial configurations.

7. Proof Construction: derivation of logical truths from fundamental axioms and definitions.

8. In general, any pattern of logical inference for which formally explicit rules can be devised for manipulating clearly-defined concepts or statements, including combinations of the above.

Informal Reasoning

1. Recognizing patterns of identical and similar structure, as well as patterns of difference and change, among things and situations.

2. Classifying objects, relationships, events—including resolving ambiguities, vagueness, and borderline cases, and carrying out classification activities prerequisite to formal reasoning such as identifying sentences of the same logical type and translating them into a standard form.

3. Applying abstract principles, including formal logic, to concrete situations and contexts.

4. Interpreting written and spoken language—including detecting and handling ambiguity, vagueness, and multiple levels of meaning; identifying underlying assumptions; tracing implications; and adding missing premises.

5. Identifying and exploring different perspectives—including the detection and interpretation of motivations, personal orientation, social bias, and world view.

6. Exploring and making use of analogies, models, and metaphors.

7. Making determinations of relevance.

8. Identifying and using criteria.

9. Analyzing and evaluating arguments, including identifying conclusions and supporting reasons or premises, outlining argument structure, assessing evidence and appeals to authority, etc.

10. Constructing sound arguments.

11. Making and evaluating inductive generalizations.

12. Proposing and criticizing causal explanations.

13. Ascertaining facts of various sorts.

14. Analyzing means-ends relationships.

15. Solving problems of various kinds.

16. Determining responsibility and evaluating conduct using purposes, ideals, and obligations, and weighing consequences.

17. Considering contextual factors in evaluating conduct or achievement, such as similarities and differences between situations, background information, prior knowledge, and extenuating circumstances.

18. Exploring and interpreting meaning in experience, in art, and in literature.

19. Constructing complex structures of meaning, such as stories, poems, plays, paintings, drawings, songs, etc.

Interpersonal Reasoning

1. Knowing how to and being ready to reason—*i.e.*, respond thoughtfully to reason with reason—when circumstances call for it: offering and asking for reasons, reflecting, analyzing, criticizing, inquiring further, etc.

2. Knowing how to and being willing to engage with others in rational discussion: giving the other person the benefit of doubt, clarifying what was said, exploring the motivation and perspective of others, empathizing with other points of view, coming to an

Why study logic?

The popular notion is that Reason is far superior to any instinctive way of reaching the truth; and from your desire to study logic, I am perhaps warranted in presuming that such is your opinion. If so, in what respect do you hold reasoning to be superior to instinct? Birds and bees decide rightly hundreds of times for every time that they err. That would suffice to explain their imperfect self-consciousness; for if *error* be not pressed upon the attention of a being, there remains little to mark the distinction between the outer and the inner worlds. A bee or an ant cannot—could not, though he were able to indulge in the pastime of introspection—ever guess that he acted from instinct. Accused of it, he would say, "Not at all! I am guided entirely by reason." So he is, in fact, in the sense that whatever he does is determined by virtual reasoning. He uses reason to adapt means to ends—that is, to his inclinations—just as we do; except that probably he has not the same self-consciousness. The point at which instinct intervenes is precisely in giving him inclinations which to us seem so singular. Just so, we, in the affairs of everyday life, merely employ reason to adapt means to inclinations which to us appear no more bizarre than those of a bee appear to him.

Invariably follow the dictates or instinct in preference to those of Reason when such conduct will answer your purpose; that is the prescription of Reason herself. Do not harbor any expectation that the study of logic can improve your judgment in matters of business, family, or other departments of ordinary life. Clear as it seems to me that certain *dicta* of my conscience are unreasonable, and though I know it may very well be wrong, yet I trust to its authority emphatically rather than to any rationalistic morality. This is the only rational course.

But *fortunately* (I say it advisedly) man is *not so happy* as to be provided with a full stock of instincts to meet all occasions, and so is forced upon the adventurous business of reasoning, where the many meet shipwreck and the few find, not old-fashioned happiness, but its splendid substitute, success. When one's purpose, intention, lies in the line of novelty, intervention, generalization, theory—in a word, improvement of the situation—by the side of which happiness appears a shabby old dud—instinct and the rule of thumb manifestly cease to be applicable. The best plan, then, on the whole, is to base our conduct as much as possible on Instinct, but when we do reason to reason with severely scientific logic. It has seemed to me proper to say this in order that I might not be understood as promising for logic what she could not perform. Where reasoning of any difficulty is to be done concerning positive facts, that is to say, not mere mathematical deduction, the aid that logic affords is most important.

—from Charles Peirce, "Pre-logical notions," in *Minute Logic.*

understanding of one another's position, making common sense, etc.

3. Critically reflecting on one's own opinions and reasoning in relation to others: weighing just how good an argument one happens to have, giving serious consideration to other persons' criticisms, entertaining counterarguments, considering how one may be coming across to other persons and other frames of reference, etc.

4. Sticking to one's own position in the face of challenges: demanding strong and relevant arguments before changing one's mind.

5. Knowing how to go about engaging in cooperative group inquiry: speaking clearly, listening carefully, being willing to clarify and analyze, giving and accepting constructive criticism, integrating different points of view, controlling frustration, being patient, disagreeing in productive ways, etc.

Philosophical Reasoning

1. Taking responsibility for the concepts and principles with which one thinks to insure that they make good sense, with the awareness that it is possible to think in more or less sensible, more or less thoughtful ways.

2. Pursuing understanding for its own intrinsic value, independently of external purposes and rewards.

3. Sustaining a dialectical inquiry, that is, a pursuit of a progressively more adequate understanding of things through the critical interplay of differing perspectives and, so far as it contributes to this end, changing the terms and direction of the inquiry itself as it proceeds.

4. Identifying, exploring, and critically applying principles of sound reasoning in relation to actual instances of formal, informal, and interpersonal reasoning.

5. Critically exploring and clarifying basic concepts and their relations to one another, in general and within given subject areas, including evaluating competing analyses of given concepts.

6. Critically exploring and clarifying basic criteria for rational evaluation in any area of human judgment—such as conduct, the fine arts, and the practical arts—including evaluating competing accounts of criteria for a given kind of thing to be evaluated.

7. Identifying and critically exploring the fundamental assumptions and world view implicit in a given intellectual position or cultural expression, and assessing alternative assumptions and worldviews in relation to one another.

8. Constructing conceptual frameworks or worldviews adequate to comprehend reality and human experience as a whole or in part.

9. Recognizing, exploring, and comprehending the historical-cultural context of ideas and of philosophical reflection upon them—*e.g.*, tracing the influence of one thinker or tradition of thinking upon another and how a given thinker develops his thought in relation to others.

The Four Dimensions of Reasoning and the Traditional Discipline of Philosophy

Philosophical inquiry can be defined, in a broad sense, as thinking about thinking, clarifying and improving for oneself the tools with which one thinks and reasons about things. Accordingly, philosophy potentially bears upon the practice of reasoning wherever it is found, whether in specific subject disciplines or generally in human life and conversation. Philosophy arises or is found whenever people become concerned with clarifying and improving the tools with which they think and reason. This conception fits well with the recent characterization of philosophy by the American Philosophical Association in its pamphlet, "The Field of Philosophy," (1982):

"Philosophy pursues questions in every dimension of human life, and its techniques apply to problems in any field of study or endeavor. No brief definition expresses the richness and variety of philosophy. It may be described in many ways. It is a reasoned pursuit of fundamental truths, a quest for understanding, a study of principles of conduct. It seeks to establish standards of evidence, to provide rational methods of resolving conflicts, and to create techniques for evaluating ideas and arguments. Philosophy develops the capacity to see the world from the perspective of other individuals and other cultures; it enhances one's ability to perceive the relationships among the various fields of study; and it deepens one's sense of the meaning and varieties of human experience.

Topical Divisions of Philosophy

The topics of philosophical reasoning include issues dealt with in the writings of the major historical philosophers. New topics for philosophical clarification are constantly being added to the topics philosophers discuss from virtually every subject area. The broadest subfields of philosophy are commonly taken to be:

LOGIC, which aims to provide sound methods for distinguishing good from bad reasoning;

ETHICS, which critically analyzes the meanings of our moral concepts—such as right action, obligation, and justice—and formulates principles to guide moral decisions, whether in private or public life;

METAPHYSICS, which critically analyzes the most basic concepts we have for conceiving reality, whether of specific things or of the world as a whole—including space, time, substance, and causality—and competing worldviews;

EPISTEMOLOGY, which is concerned to determine the nature and scope of knowledge; and

THE HISTORY OF PHILOSOPHY, which studies both the work of major philosophers and entire periods in the historical development of systematic philosophical reflection.

Other branches of philosophy have grown from these traditional subfields, including Philosophy of Mind, Philosophy of Religion, Philosophy of Science, Philosophy of Mathematics, Political Philosophy, Philosophy of Art (or Aesthetics), and Philosophy of Language.

Philosophy as an Academic Discipline

What tends to distinguish Philosophy as an academic discipline from philosophy pursued elsewhere is the systematic clarification of concepts involving whole sectors of human experience, a professional community of scholars dedicated to that end, and a history laden with significant examples of that endeavor.

Like members of most academic communities, the professional philosopher has a characteristic style, a lexicon of technical terms and special usage, and a body of classical texts that define the issues and furnish a common basis for approaches and solutions. This often intimidates the casual reader or hearer of Philosophy, especially since professional philosophers generally write for each other, without taking into account the desirability of their work reaching to a wider audience.

Since Philosophy for Children wants to involve non-professionals in the philosophical dialogue, the professional attitudes often represented in philosophical journals seem to us to manifest a breakdown in interpersonal reasoning. If, as we maintain, the primary function of Philosophy is to enable the thoughtful person to clarify and improve his own thinking for himself and if, as we further maintain, the development of a community of inquiry is the best device for coming to such a clarification, then it is crucial that professional philosophers make an effort to make the issues accessible and clear to the non-professional. Indeed, Philosophy for Children, unlike other areas of professional Philosophy, has an absolute responsibility to use concepts and styles that are accessible to virtually anyone. We take as a necessary condition for philosophical inquiry the demands of interpersonal reasoning: mutual consideration, mutual clarity, mutual criticism, cooperative inquiry, and common sense.

A Note on Moral Reasoning

Moral reasoning is often thought of as being separate from other sorts of reasoning. This view has been enshrined in the "fact-value" distinction, a common view that places moral thought outside of the arena of rational discussion and within the realm of subjective opinion. We believe this to be an inadequate view of moral reasoning for at least two reasons.

First, moral reasoning includes all other elements of reasoning. Reasoning about moral issues requires formal reasoning, insofar as rule-governed patterns of inference are used; informal reasoning, since application of principles to concrete instances, appeal to criteria, and the evaluation of alternatives are all at the heart of moral argument (see also examples 15 and 16 of "Informal Reasoning" given above); interpersonal reasoning, inasmuch as we develop our positions within a community and justify our positions in the light of the opinions and perspectives of others; and philosophical reasoning, since moral reasoning often includes the reassessment of fundamental concepts and principles.

But there is an even more crucial issue. Although moral reasoning includes its own particular concern: questions of human value, considerations of the universality of claims, and the good-making characteristics of actions—moral reasoning is more than just another domain of rational inquiry. Globally understood, moral reasoning permeates the entire rational enterprise. The heart of rationality is surely an appeal to a mutual recognition of independent minds. And a rational person is surely one who regards others as capable of raising considerations that

deserve to be taken seriously into account and answered, considerations which otherwise might fail to be raised at all. In this respect, rationality itself requires that other persons be treated as ends to whom one must be answerable. It follows that moral considerations, far from being tangential, are of the essence of rationality. Thus, the notion of an interpersonal dimension of reasoning as we have presented implies that reasoning includes an essentially moral component.

To engage in rational inquiry that in principle encompasses all four dimensions (or at least the first three) is thus to assume that each individual be responsible *for* his own position as well as *to* the perspectives and criticisms of others and that, whatever position is maintained, it is maintained with personal integrity, with a sense of the urgency of the issue, and with an openness to changing one's mind as good reasons for doing so come to light. For this reason, we believe that competence in interpersonal—hence *moral*—reasoning is at the very heart of what education in good reasoning is all about. And that is why education in good reasoning is so necessary to prepare young people for responsible citizenship in a democracy. To accomplish this end, the most effective curriculum developed thus far, in our judgment, is Philosophy for Children.

Thinking Skills Programs: An Analysis

Wolfe Mays

Thinking skills (or cognitive education) programs were first developed for use by school children, and it is only recently that attempts have been made to adapt them for adult use. I will restrict myself largely to the way these programs have been used among younger age groups. An account and analysis of the principles on which these programs are based is of some importance, as I believe that conclusions reached concerning their viability in the junior field should carry over to the more adult one.

One of the main arguments against any attempt to improve intellectual performance is that intelligence is largely inherited. Eysenck [1], for example, says that it is the result of 80% heredity and 20% environment. Jensen [2] too holds that low intellectual performance is largely genetically determined and therefore cannot be appreciably modified. This has led to the belief that attempts to change the structure of intelligence and its course of development can only have limited success—a few points at the most on the I.Q. scale [3].

It is, I think, well worth looking at this question in its historical perspective. Mental tests were developed in France in the early part of this century by Alfred Binet (1857-1911).Binet, however, viewed such tests as practical diagnostic instruments to enable him to identify mentally backward children. He, however, believed that a test score was only of interest if we could also give some account of the causes which had produced it. We need to ask, he says, what is the influence of the family and social environment on the child's performance? A child from a good home who often discusses with his parents has a richer vocabulary and a wider range of knowledge. He will be a year or two in advance of our little Parisian primitive [4]. Binet considers a child who has considerable difficulty in understanding his class lessons. What, he asks, can we do for him? If we do nothing, he will become discouraged and frustrated. Some teachers, he remarks, show little sympathy for these children and condemn them as unteachable. Binet goes on, I have often heard such sentiments expressed not only in the school but also in the university. He tells us that in his *baccalaureat es lettres* examination at the Sorbonne, the examiner, upset by Binet's misnaming a Greek philosopher, asserted that he would never have a philosophical mind. Binet's comment is worth quoting, "Jamais! Quel gros mot!"[5].

Binet is critical of the claim that a person's intelligence is a fixed quantity, which cannot be increased. We ought, he says, to protest against this brutal pessimism, and we intend to show that it has no foundation. He is particularly critical of the view held by some psychologists such as Spearman that (general) intelligence is a unitary function. He regards it as rather made up of a number of smaller functions, such as attention, discrimination, observation, memory and judgment, etc., which have a certain plasticity. By exercise and training these can, he says, be improved, so that we thereby become literally more intelligent than we were before. What is important as far as intelligent behavior is concerned is not so much the strength of our faculties or aptitudes, but the way we use them. Binet's aim was to improve the scholastic performance of intellectually backward children. With this end in view he gave them specialized instruction and found that after a year their powers of attention and their working habits had improved considerably. They now had little difficulty in solving certain problems on which they had failed abysmally a year ago. As he picturesquely remarks, the mind of these children is like a field for which an agriculturalist suggests a change of cultivation. In place of an undeveloped mind, we now have a harvest. It is in this practical sense, he goes on, the only one we have, that we say that the child's intelligence has increased.

It was clear to him that what such children needed, to use his own words, *was to learn to learn*. Binet therefore proposed a system of training which he called *mental orthopaedics*, by analogy with physical orthopaedics. This involved therapeutic exercises for strengthening attention, memory, perception, invention, analysis, judgment and will.

A good example of the use of such methods is to be seen in Binet's attempt to improve the short-term memory of sub-normal children. He was able to get at least two thirds of his class to remember a group of some nine different objects, which they were allowed to see for only a few seconds. A number of members of the French *Chambre des deputés* visiting the school were so impressed that they tried it themselves and failed. What they did not take into account, Binet remarks, was the intensive training the children had undergone. Binet believed that motivation was a very important factor in the development of intellectual skills, and that adequate motivation would go a long way in correcting intellectual deficiencies. In this respect some important lessons can be drawn from Binet's work, especially in the field of adult learning.

II

Binet's *mental orthopaedics* is the direct forerunner of some thinking skills programs which have been developed in recent years. None of these systems claim to improve your I.Q. (the concept of I.Q. is post-Binet), but rather to improve the intellectual skills which enter into any cognitive task. The most important thinking skills program seem to be that of de Bono's "CoRT" [6], Feuerstein's "Instrumental Enrichment" [7], and Lipman's "Philosophy for Children" [8]. Another similar program is Whimby and Lochhead's "Analytical Reasoning" [9]. The latter is primarily aimed at pupils in the higher school grades. It requires them to solve mathematical word problems, and problems concerned with numerical progressions, formal analogies and verbal reasoning. There is also, among others, the Midwest Thinking Skills [10] material which covers similar ground, but at a more elementary level. Feuerstein's program starts at a more basic level still of cognitive functioning: many of his exercises are expressed in pictorial and diagrammatic form rather than in verbal terms.

I will first make some remarks about de Bono's system. His books are well known and he is not an unfamiliar figure on television, where he has demonstrated his "CoRT" system: this comprises teacher's notes and a number of instruction packs for the students to use. They are graded in six levels and the system is relatively cheap. It has been tried out among different age groups and with different social groups: in Women's Institutes and among managers in industry and commerce.

de Bono believes that thinking as a skill can be improved, and he differentiates between thinking and intelligence. He compares intelligence to the engine power of a car, and thinking to the skill with which the car is driven. Thus, he tell us, "Innate intelligence or I.Q. can be compared to the intrinsic power of the car. The skill with which this power is used is the skill of thinking.

Thinking is the operating skill through which innate intelligence is put into action [11]. This seems to be an awfully muddled analogy, especially as it comes from someone concerned to make us think more clearly. We can separate the horsepower of a car from the operator's skill but we cannot separate thinking from intelligence, as this is the only way intelligence can show itself. de Bono assumes that intelligence is an innate disposition or capacity, and that what his thinking lessons do is to make you use what intelligence you have got in the most effective way. He would therefore seem to regard intelligence as a unitary factor, like the rated cc of a motor car engine. Some of us presumably have a 3 litre intelligence, others only a mini 750 cc. On de Bono's view we could train a 750 cc intelligence so that it functions more effectively than an untrained 3 litre one. However, as I have already indicated, de Bono overlooks that you cannot separate intellectual potential from actual performance.

de Bono gives a list of thinking skills as well as enumerating the techniques which will improve them. His approach is a very down-to-earth one, with its roots in practical decision-making. It will appeal to the no-nonsense teacher and hard-boiled businessman. No doubt because of this, his system is, I imagine, a financially profitable one. However, he is not much of a theoretician judging by one of his books, in which he puts forward a simplistic mechanical model of the mind.

Examples of some of the thinking skills he wishes to improve are: the ability to take other people's points of view into account, as other people may consider different factors and have different objectives. Decision-making, he claims, can be improved. When faced with making a decision, we need to become clear about the factors involved—the objectives, the consequences and alternatives. de Bono puts considerable stress on thinking ahead, *i.e.*, planning. You need, he says, to try to think, as far as possible, about the consequences, immediate, short-term, and long-term of every action you contemplate

Thinking as the continuous establishment of relationships

No psychology of thinking is possible without the premise that there are real object-structures, a reality which we apprehend by thinking. This reality comprises first objects, second the relations of objects to each other, and finally values (still to be discussed). It depends on our organization how much of these structures becomes amenable to us. We regard drives as the fluid part of our organization, and the organism as drives structuralized into forms. Objects demand that we regard them as they really are and according to their real value. On the one hand, objects demand our recognition, thereby continuously checking our drive-strivings; on the other hand, these strivings reach out after objects, continuously drawing new ones into the circle of attention. The very existence of such a multitude of partial drives brings broad segments of reality into relation with each other; the locus of these transactions is the sphere.

As already stressed, the essential core of thinking is a continuous establishment of relationships. The various parts of the sphere are continuously put into relation with each other, and these newly created relations are continuously tested as to whether or not they correspond to the requirements of objects. The sphere is where ever new relation-experiences emerge; in it, drives directed toward objects are continuously checked by counterdrives, bringing forth ever new images; and these images are again put into relation with the others. It is this checking which makes the richness of thought possible.

—from Paul Schilder. *"Thinking,"* in *Medical Psychology* (New York: International Universities Press, 1953)

performing. In other words, one needs to rehearse mentally the arguments for or against an action before carrying it out. He also advocates a technique called lateral thinking [12], whose main aim is to restructure our patterns of thought so that new combinations arise. This he takes to be the basis of insight and creativity. Lateral thinking is said to work at an earlier stage than vertical or logical thinking. He believes it to be especially of value in problem-solving, since it generates alternatives, challenges assumptions and introduces innovations. One has the impression that de Bono's system is a little too cut-and-dried (despite lateral thinking). He is primarily concerned with introducing better techniques and strategies in order to make the best of what intelligence one has. Thus, at least theoretically, his views are not in conflict with those intelligence testers who believe in the immutability of the I.Q. However, it does not necessarily follow that if you improve a child's or adult's powers of problem-solving, he will use them for socially desirable ends. He could easily become a bank robber, an embezzler or a computer code-breaker, since he can now forsee more possibilities of action and also know how to cover his tracks more skillfully.

Nevertheless, it is clear that de Bono also wishes to improve the value judgments of students taking his course. Speaking of the way in which many children today are questioning the values and traditions of society, he argues that it is better for them to be able to specify reasons for their disenchantment, rather than rely on gut reactions. On the whole, however, his approach to thinking skills with its emphasis on efficiency and economy, reminds me of Lord Rayner's (of Marks and Spencer fame) attempt to apply the principles of sound business management to the British Civil Service.

III

I now come to the work of Reuven Feuerstein, an Israeli clinical psychologist who studied with André Rey and Jean Piaget in Geneva in the 50's. He is concerned with how pupils learn to think, handle ideas, make decisions and solve problems. Many children, he tells us, do not learn to manipulate ideas with success: they often find it difficult to plan, to observe accurately and to acquire knowledge. It is the aim of Feuerstein's system to stimulate learning skills and problem-solving activities, and for this purpose it uses 15 sets of paper and pencil exercises. These are so-called instruments designed to improve specific mental abilities: they may be used for three hours a week over a period of two to three years [13].

For each instrument the teacher is provided with a manual which contains further exercises. These together with the actual instruments encourage discussion. An important part of the teacher's task is to engage in what is called bridging. In bridging the pupil learns with the help of the teacher to make concrete applications of the principles acquired through these exercises. We are told that during the first year of study, pupils become motivated, acquire a new vocabulary and begin to reflect on the different ways they can handle ideas. In the second year they become better equipped to make decisions and solve problems.

Feuerstein found that children said to be subnormal often showed considerable promise. He was particularly concerned with Jewish immigrants to Israel from North Africa, as a number of these children were unable to adapt themselves to their new environment and the school situation. He argued that these children who performed badly on intelligence tests—some got I.Q. scores as low as 40—were intellectually deprived, and claimed that it was possible to remedy their intellectual deficiencies.

Among the most important of these were: an inability to make comparisons between different objects and events, poor spatial and temporal organization, and a failure to link cause with effect. They were thus prevented from organizing their experiences in a systematic way. And when

Part-whole observation and education

The observer is not he who merely sees the thing which is before his eyes, but he who sees what parts that thing is composed of. To do this well is a rare talent. One person, from inattention, or attending only in the wrong place, overlooks half of what he sees; another sets down much more than he sees, confounding it with what he imagines, or with what he infers; another takes note of the *kind* of all the circumstances, but being inexpert in estimating their degree, leaves the quantity of each vague and uncertain; another sees indeed the whole, but makes such an awkward division of it into parts, throwing things into one mass which require to be separated, and separating others which might more conveniently be considered as one, that the result is much the same, sometimes even worse, than if no analysis had been attempted at all. It would be possible to point out what qualities of mind, and modes of mental culture, fit a person for being a good observer; that, however, is a question not of Logic, but of the Theory of Education, in the most literal sense of the term. There is not properly an Art of Observing. There may be rules for observing. But these, like rules for inventing, are properly instructions for the preparation of one's own mind; for putting it into the state in which it will be most fitted to observe, or most likely to invent. They are, therefore, essentially rules of self-education, which is a different thing from Logic. They do not teach how to do the thing, but how to make ourselves capable of doing it. They are an art of strengthening the limbs, not an art of using them.

—John Stuart Mill, *A System of Logic,* Book III, Ch. 7, par. 1.

faced with a new situation or problem they tended to act irrationally and impulsively. Feuerstein holds that maladjusted behavior may often be due to cognitive rather than emotional factors. A child who lacks adequate intellectual tools will fail to adjust to school life, and this will produce anxiety and aggressive behavior.

Feuerstein stresses what he calls *mediated learning experience*, namely, the part that the parent or teacher plays in developing the child's basic activities, by teaching him to anticipate events and to adapt to new situations. Feuerstein contends that through the use of his Instrumental Enrichment exercises, the thinking skills of intellectually deprived children can be improved, so that among other things they become better able to cope with their school subjects. Feuerstein's views on this question have little in common with those of the I.Q. testers. Human beings, he says, are unpredictable, and he finds it sad that psychologists have condemned the future of many children through the use of intelligence tests.

But, it might be asked, what sort of material does Feuerstein use in his paper and pencil exercises? An examination shows that a good number of them contain intelligence test items. Some examples are: patterning of dots, Raven's matrices, comparisons, categorizations, family relationships, syllogisms, numerical progressions and stencil designs. However, this material seems to be arranged more systematically than in an I.Q. test, and follows a graded order of difficulty. Feuerstein could defend his use of intelligence test material, by saying that if it taps certain intellectual aptitudes, then his exercises should help to improve their function. This is especially so if one does not believe that intelligence is a unitary factor, that it is rather a group of aptitudes in which judgment, attention, and critical appreciation enter in and which can be improved by practice. For example, the dot-patterning exercise should improve image-formation and mental representation. Raven's matrices—analogical reasoning and judgment. Attention and motivation are also improved by these tasks. These exercises,

Feuerstein tells us, teach strategies, rule-following and forward-planning. Feuerstein claims through such exercises and teacher mediation, children become able to perform abstract tasks which were at one time completely beyond them. Some teachers using Instrumental Enrichment become enthusiastic about it. They say it has changed their own thinking and improved their teaching. It is certainly impressive to see mentally handicapped children, when faced with what at first sight appears to be a random collection of dots, joining them so that they form geometrical figures.

Feuerstein believes that we can improve the cognitive performance of intellectually retarded children by developing their understanding of formal structures, and that his instruments do precisely this. They are said to improve the child's awareness of spatial and temporal relations, his grasp of logical and numerical categories and his understanding of causal relations. He believes "the exposure of the learner to situations that, by their very structure, focus his attention on the formal prerequisites of thinking is a great advantage," [14] and he goes on, "the teacher of retarded performers tends to underestimate the capacities of these children to accede to higher levels of functioning." [15]

A key assumption of Feuerstein's system, then, is that intellectually retarded children can be first taught to understand abstract principles and by subsequent bridging be made to learn to apply these principles to concrete, particular cases. This approach would seem, however, to be at variance with the views of such educationalists as Pestalozzi, Montessori, and John Dewey. These thinkers argue that in actual teaching we should start from the concrete exemplifications of such principles, and only at a later date proceed to the abstract principles themselves. They would, for example, say that in teaching arithmetic, we need to begin with the numbering of concrete objects—counters, blocks or rods—and then go on to their more formal expression. A similar view is held by Holt and Dienes in their

book, *Let's Play Maths*. Talking of mathematical games they say, "The games also induce a child to think with his hands. Research shows that most children see problems in terms of their own body. Mathematics in particular requires strong links to be made between hands and brain for success"[16].

Because Feuerstein's position conflicts with these views, it does not mean that his methods are wrong. He is primarily concerned with retarded adolescents, who presumably have a capacity for formal thinking as yet undeveloped. This development, he believes, can best be achieved by means of such formal exercises together with concrete bridging. He would no doubt say that a similar approach would be successful with adults. But to suggest that such teaching methods could be used with young children, would seem less justifiable. And indeed Feuerstein does not recommend that his instruments be used at younger age levels. As Feuerstein's instruments involve a good number of geometrical, numerical and logical structures, their literary and linguistic content would not seem to be as high as is the case with some other thinking skills programs. However, in bridging, in which the teacher plays an important role, attempts are made to demonstrate how such structures exemplify themselves in everyday experience, and this is invariably linguistically expressed. We are told that these exercises are content free. But it is doubtful whether geometrical and logical material, though formal in character, are entirely without content. They are the products of a highly sophisticated culture. There is some evidence that individuals coming from other cultures may find them alien and difficult to grasp.

On an adult level some work done on illiterate peasants in Soviet Central Asia in the early 1930s by the Russian psychologist Luria, is of interest here [17]. He found his subjects were very resistant and even hostile to the sort of deductive exercises that enter into formal reasoning. They made excellent judgments about facts of direct experience of concert to them, but they failed as soon as they were asked to think about theoretical questions of the type involved in syllogistic inference. They denied the possibility of drawing conclusions from propositions about things of which they had no personal experience.

One of the reasons for the low I.Q. score among some of Feuerstein's Moroccan subjects, may have been due to the fact that in intelligence tests they are faced with problems which must be solved on a purely mental level, without recourse to concrete experience. It is conceivable they might have done better on practical tests. Marcel Mauss, the well-known French social anthropologist, made this point in a discussion of Piaget's work. "In my opinion, M. Piaget is not concerned with child psychology in general, but with the child psychology of an extremely civilized society. We need to consider, among others, children raised in very different environments. I have seen, in Morocco, poor native children practicing a trade at the age of five years—braiding and sewing with remarkable dexterity. It is delicate work, which presupposes a very fine geometrical and arithmetical sense. The Moroccan child is a technician and starts work at an earlier age than do our children. On certain matters he reasons earlier and faster, although in a different way—*i.e.*, manually—than do the children of our good bourgeois families" [18]. Marcel Mauss was observing children belonging to a certain economic level of Moroccan society, who were behaving normally in their social environment. It is unlikely that mentally backward children in Morocco would be able to carry out such skillful tasks. Nevertheless, both groups of children might fail, but for different reasons, on Western I.Q. tests.

Feuerstein holds that there can be intellectual growth for most individuals throughout school and into adulthood. He remarks that what is marvellous about the human race is that there is no time limit upon a person's ability to extend his intellectual powers. And as an example he quotes Rabbi Akiva, one of the most famous Jewish wisemen, who could not read until he was 40

years of age. What I assume Feuerstein means here is that there is no time limit to the age at which one can improve one's mental faculties. And I would certainly agree with him. But it would be another matter if it were to be assumed that there was no limit to intellectual growth. In any case, Rabbi Akiva was living at a time when even talented individuals would not have learned to read or write.

Another question which arises is what exactly does Feuerstein mean by the concept of "intellectual deprivation"? He sometimes uses this notion synonymously with mental backwardness. This may be the case when he is referring to the cognitive deficiencies of children who have difficulties in adapting themselves to a different culture. But does this mean that there is no such thing as mental backwardness *per se*, and that whether a pupil is mentally backward or not is always relevant to his cultural background? Vygotsky, the Russian psychologist, would seem to have held a view like this; namely, intellectual abilities are developed rather than being largely innate. Feuerstein does not always make it clear whether or not the individual possesses innate intellectual capacities. He certainly does talk about such capacities, but he nonetheless believes that the organism *is* an open system. He states "The I.Q. score reflects the *product* of a given quantum of ability. It does not tell us anything about the underlying *processes* responsible for an individual's capacity to improve it" [19]. He also rejects "I.Q. scores as reflective of a stable or permanent level of functioning." And he goes on, "Instead, and in accordance with the open system approach, intelligence is considered a dynamic self-regulating process that is responsive to external environmental intervention"[20].

I take this to mean that although individuals do differ in their intellectual capacities, the development of these capacities is not rigidly predetermined. Further, one's intellectual performance may be significantly improved by environmental factors. For example, by suitable training we should be able to increase a child's powers of attention, judgment, reasoning and memory, and thereby also improve his level of performance in the subjects of the school curriculum. By means of such methods we might be able to transform more children into potential Oxbridge candidates, if this is considered a good thing.

I doubt whether Feuerstein would put himself entirely in the same camp as Jerome Bruner, as far as the part played by environmental factors in intellectual development is concerned. Of Bruner, Piaget has said, that "he has gone so far as to state that you can teach anything to a child at any age if you only set about it in the right way"[21]. Bruner in essence is echoing the behaviorist J. B. Watson's view that if a young aboriginal child from the Australian outback was brought up in the home of a professor of psychology, he might in due course become a professor of psychology himself.

Feuerstein uses the notion of cultural deprivation a good deal in his work, but in a somewhat different sense than the way it is normally employed. It is used by him to apply to anyone who is transplanted from his own culture and traditions into a radically new one. Feuerstein cites cases to show that this may result in cognitive deficiencies. Although this may be true in some cases he describes, there is, however, another side to this question. Following a tradition may lead to the stifling of one's critical and creative abilities. Further, an individual could learn to master technical skills in a closed society, but he still might not be able to develop an adequate understanding of values, and this would affect his judgment on moral, social and aesthetic questions.

To summarize, Feuerstein's work had the practical aim of upgrading cognitively retarded children, so that these children could be assimilated into Israeli society by either fitting them for a job or getting them accepted into that formidable military machine—the Israeli army: one has to pass a stiff intelligence test in order to enter it. No doubt he has been very successful here and one must not underestimate his practical achieve-

ments. There have been at least two apparently successful attempts to apply Instrumental Enrichment to young adults (1) to pre-university students at a technological university in Venezuela [22], and (2) it has been used with black students, starting a medical course at the University of Witwatersrand in South Africa [23].

IV

Matthew Lipman, an American professor of philosophy at Montclair State College, New Jersey, has developed the "Philosophy for Children" program. Few American educationalists find the title of this program odd, since the pragmatic philosophy of John Dewey has played an important role in American education. In this country the title may mislead. Lipman's program has little to do with the study of learned philosophical texts, but is rather an attempt to develop the thinking skills of pupils in schools. Lipman gave up a post teaching philosophy at Columbia University during the period of student unrest in the 60s. He felt there was a need to go into the schools and start teaching children to think, as it might be more difficult to do this at a later stage, judging by his encounters at that period with students at Columbia University.

The Lipman program consists of a number of novels backed up by substantial teacher's manuals of activities and exercises [24]. From the start the program stresses language acquisition and pays particular attention to forms of reasoning implicit in children's everyday conversation. It attempts to heighten the child's perceptual awareness and through dialogue to get him/her to share the perspectives of others. Attention is paid to ambiguity, relational concepts and abstract notions such as causality, time, space, number, class, and group. The program has a marked literary and linguistic content. Where the pupils have reading difficulties the teacher can read the novel to the class.

Each novel provides examples of various kinds of reasoning processes, and in the course of the novel its characters discover logical, ethical and other principles, which apply to their everyday lives. Children discuss these principles and are helped by the teacher to apply them to concrete situations through the exercises performed in the class. A key novel of the program is *Harry Stottlemeier's Discovery* (a pun on Aristotle), which together with the teacher's manual emphasizes the values of inquiry and reasoning, and encourages the development of thought and imagination. I give an extract from it:

> Maria looked thoughtful, "But people are always jumping to conclusions. If people meet one Polish person, or one Italian person, or one Jewish person, or one black person, right away they jump to the conclusion that this is the way all Polish people are, or all black people, or all Italians or all Jews."
> "That's right" said Harry, "The only exercise some people get is jumping at conclusions" [25].

The novel *Lisa* focuses on ethical and social issues, such as fairness, lying and truth-telling, the nature of rules and standards. Other issues include the rights of children, job- and sex-discrimination. The novel and the exercises help the pupils to provide good reasons for their ethical and social beliefs, as well as justifying certain departures from standard moral practices. Other novels deal with the fundamental processes of scientific discovery, with literary and poetic meaning and with political and social reasoning.

Logic of the informal sort is used by Lipman as a central core from which branch off other kinds of reasoning—social, moral, aesthetic and scientific. Although Lipman's program largely concentrates on normal school children from about 6 to 18 years of age, it has been applied also to children with learning difficulties.

The teacher of one group of boys with learning difficulties, tells how during a discussion of inductive reasoning, divergent views on rock music emerged. One part of the class asserted that "Kiss" was the best group and another supported "Led Zeppelin." This led to name-calling. "Only little kids like 'Kiss'." The teacher then pointed out that they were operating on an emotional rather than a rational level: that although it was important to express personal views, these needed to be backed up with objective evidence. "How could this be done?" she asked. It was the boys themselves who suggested that the tapes of both groups be heard in the class, and that the music of each be critically examined and discussed [26].

Lipman believes that the teacher needs to use the Socratic method to draw out the ideas of children and to get them to reason about these ideas in a logical manner. Discussion therefore plays an important role in the learning process— between the teacher and the children as well as among the children themselves. Children who take part in the program, we are told, come to learn for themselves as persons. They also come to learn about their relationships to others, to social institutions such as the school system, legal system and their families. And in the process they begin to understand the meaning of such concepts as friendship, sharing, goodness and freedom, the nature of rules and principles.

Lipman regards formal logic and the rules of reasoning as tools for enabling the pupil to distinguish good from bad thinking. But he does not believe that complex problems can be solved by the simple application of these rules. He would point out that although in order to write correctly you need some understanding of grammatical rules, such understanding will not make you a better writer. Similarly, awareness of logical rules will not make you a better thinker, nor will awareness of moral rules make you a better person: you also need good will, imagination and an appreciation of other people's points of view.

Lipman seems to assume that a child is already provided with most of the logical and categorical equipment (at least in implicit form), which Feuerstein is concerned to build up in his subjects. He maintains that children can be taught to reason adequately from an early age, and that they can make inferences prior to the use of language. He also emphasizes that the child has a sense of curiosity and wonder which is stifled by the classroom atmosphere.

What can one say about Lipman's work, except that the proof of the pudding is in the eating. If reports about his work are to be taken seriously, it undoubtedly develops thinking skills and improves the child's capacity to make value judgments of a logical, ethical and aesthetic nature. But not only does it enhance the cognitive aspects of a young person's performance, it also stimulates his imaginative and creative powers.

When Lipman's program has been used in schools, there have, we are told, been markedly improved results in English, mathematics and other subjects over that of a control group, which had not taken the program. In a validation exercise carried out in 1980-81 on over 2000 pupils in a period of over eight months, there was an improvement in reasoning skills (as tested by the New Jersey Test of Reasoning Skills [27]) of fourteen months compared to the control group.

Insofar as Lipman's work attempts to make pupils aware of the dangers of fallacious thinking, it has something in common with the themes of such books as Robert Thouless's *Straight and Crooked Thinking* [28] and Susan Stebbing's *Thinking to Some Purpose* [29]. These works were aimed at an adult audience, for example, those attending W. E. A. classes, and designed to make them more aware of emotional and prejudiced thinking in their everyday lives, with particular reference to the media. Although they are still useful for this purpose, they do not specifically set out to improve thinking skills in general, as do the programs we have already discussed. It is worthwhile mentioning here that our own Intellectual Skills Project has been trying to adapt some of Lipman's material on ethical and social reasoning, so that it can be used with an adult English audience. I have no doubt that Feuerstein's material is also similarly adaptable. As I

have noted, it has already been used with students starting university courses.

Lipman's program differs from Feuerstein's insofar as the latter is primarily a remedial program, and contains extensive descriptions of deficient intellectual functions and details of methods of remedying them. Feuerstein's instruments have been specifically designed for this purpose. He also provides us in his books with theoretical analyses of intellectual activities. On the other hand, Lipman is mainly concerned with normal children, and with getting them to reason correctly about the facts and values of life. He is therefore less concerned with psychological issues, and more with the content of what he teaches. But he certainly makes specific assumptions about the child's innate potential and here his views come close to Feuerstein's: they both believe that this potential among many children remains underdeveloped. Further, both programs endeavor to improve the child's capacity to use classifications, relations, syllogistic and hypothetico-deductive arguments, as well as spatial, temporal and causal categories.

Feuerstein's program may be better at getting people down to the nitty-gritty of life, and making them more competent in their work. As Instrumental Enrichment uses graphic and pictorial material, it also takes account of non-verbal reasoning, and can thus start at a more basic conceptual level. Lipman's approach is more likely to turn out critically-minded individuals showing some sensitivity to the values of life, and with a desire to settle their problems in a rational way. Feuerstein would also claim something similar for his program through bridging. I wonder, however, how far Feuerstein would encourage his pupils to be critical of traditional values, especially as he regards the mother and the family as the prime mediators in the child's intellectual development.

V

In *The Times Educational Supplement* of 15 June 1984 [30], there appeared an account of Lipman's work and some criticisms of it. One critic, Patricia White, Senior Lecturer in the Philosophy of Education at the London Institute of Education, was quoted as saying (a) that she did not think that general thinking skills could be taught to children, and (b) that Lipman's program was not philosophy as we know it in the groves of academe. I would disagree with (a) and agree with (b). To take (b) first. Lipman essentially uses the Socratic method to draw out from children ideas on social and moral questions, and to get them to think rationally about them. He is not teaching them about Kant, Hegel or even about the work of A. J. Ayer. And in the case of (a) if by not being able to teach children general thinking skills she means you cannot teach children logical thinking, she is surely wrong. I have myself taught children of 9-10 years of age logic [31] and some of them were better at it than university students of my acquaintance.

A major objection to Lipman's and other thinking skills programs has been the question of validation. How do you evaluate precisely what progress has been made by pupils as a result of their being taught thinking skills? Both Lipman and Feuerstein claim that they have obtained definitive quantitative evidence of intellectual improvement. As far as I can make out, de Bono seems to have been content with more qualitative forms of evaluation.

There is also the objection that any intellectual improvement may be due to the Hawthorne effect. But if a program improves an individual's performance, does it matter if it is due to him being singled out for special attention? It shows the part played by motivation in the development of intellectual skills, and also emphasizes the role of good mediation (or teaching), which might be described as a continuous Hawthorne effect. It is also doubtful whether intellectual factors can be entirely divorced from motivational ones.

On the instruments of intellect

The intellect, by its native strength, makes for itself intellectual instruments, whereby it acquires strength for performing other intellectual operations, and from these operations gets again fresh instruments, or the power of pushing its investigations further, and thus gradually proceeds until it reaches the summit of wisdom.

—Spinoza, "On the Improvement of the Understanding."

Lipman's program has also been criticized on the ground that it may become an instrument of indoctrination in the spirit of Orwell's *1984*. I would have thought that the reverse would have been more likely to be true, since the teacher does not try to force his opinions on the pupil. He rather tries to get the pupil to look at alternative viewpoints, even if it does lead the latter to question the values of the society in which he lives, or the teaching in the school in which he is taught. Indeed one criticism of Lipman's program has been that it may undermine parental and school authority. de Bono too believes that students taking his program may come to question the values of the Old Man of the Tribe.

In this connection de Bono relates that a headmaster once told him that it was unfair to teach people how to think and that most of the pupils in his school were going to spend their lives at factory benches, and that thinking could only make them dissatisfied. de Bono comments that if the headmaster really meant this, then education would merely be concerned with producing zombies perfectly fitted for the task asked of them [32]. Unfortunately there are fewer jobs for these pupils to go to, and they are having to find ways of spending their enforced leisure. They might with profit be given some training in making the best use of their intellectual capacities. This might help them when training for a job in the new technologies or even in widening their educational horizon.

Another objection to teaching thinking skills, de Bono tells us, comes from the subject specialist, who argues that this is what good teachers have been doing all the time in such subjects as history, physics, English and geography. If teachers do not do this now, they ought to be encouraged to do so. There is therefore not the slightest reason to add a new fangled subject—thinking skills—to an already overburdened curriculum. We can do all this through the teaching of our special subject.

In answer to this kind of objection de Bono points out that in content subjects such as physics, little attention is paid to the actual process of thinking. In any case, he remarks, the subject content is much more interesting than the thinking process itself. "A pupil knows that with a little knowledge and a lot of thinking he will not do so well as a student who has a lot of knowledge and only a little thinking" [33].

As an illustration of the deep-rooted nature of this attitude I quote the following story. I once suggested to a research chemist at Manchester that it might be possible for a student to obtain a first class honors degree in science at Cambridge if he showed good judgment and some imagination, even if his factual knowledge was not as great as someone who got an upper second because of fairly pedestrian thinking. I well remember the look of horror which came over the research chemist's face. Unable to contain his righteous indignation he blurted out, "This couldn't happen in Manchester!"

de Bono tells us that content subjects such as physics or history, are limited in the range of thinking skills they teach. Nevertheless, he recognizes that the skills that they do include, namely, "Classification, chains of explanation, the putting together of facts to reach a conclusion are all important in thinking." Other thinking skills which need developing, include decision procedures, taking account of other people's points of view, problem-solving, guessing and being able to counter emotional bias and prejudice [34].

There seems some evidence to show that a system of cognitive education, whether it be that of de Bono, Feuerstein or Lipman, will in some measure increase the pupil's powers of judgment, perception, memory, attention and motivation. And this it is claimed should lead to an improvement in the pupil's performance over a range of subjects in the school curriculum. Both Lipman's and Feuerstein's results would appear to bear this out.

VI

It might be argued that the introduction of micro-computers in schools, colleges and in the home, has obviated the need to teach thinking skills, as the machine will do the job for us. One recent writer in *The Times Educational Supplement* 13 April 1984 [35] waxed lyrical about the use of the micro-computer in the classroom, "it nevertheless demands from them (*i.e.*, the children) and develops further in them those very academic virtues from which the traditional school curriculum can so disastrously alienate them, notably, numeracy, literacy, logical reasoning and scientific method," and he also believes that it will "through their concern for the screen layout of the games programs they write" develop artistic sensitivity.

I do not deny that the use of computers could improve considerably the performance of some pupils in their school studies. However, it might be suggested that one could get the same intellectual improvement with much less expense and with perhaps more lasting effect by the teaching of thinking skills. What such tuition should do is to build up the subject's intellectual capacities, enabling him/her to classify and order, draw inferences, see alternatives and play ahead. Further, the basic principles on which computers and their software are constructed are logical in character,

---

Determining children's potential thinking levels

We must determine at least two developmental levels . . . The first level can be called the *actual developmental level*, that is, the level of development of a child's mental functions that has been established as a result of certain already *completed* developmental cycles. When we determine a child's mental age by using tests, we are almost always dealing with the actual developmental level. In studies of children's mental development it is generally assumed that only those things that children can do on their own are indicative of mental abilities. We give children a battery of tests or a variety of tasks of varying degrees of difficulty, and we judge the extent of their mental development on the basis of how they solve them and at what level of difficulty. On the other hand, if we offer leading questions or show how the problem is to be solved and the child then solves it, or if the teacher initiates the solution and the child completes it or solves it in collaboration with other children—in short, if the child barely misses an independent solution of the problem—the solution is not regarded his mental development. This "truth" was familiar and reinforced by common sense. Over a decade, thinkers never questioned the assumption; they never entertained the notion that what children can do with the assistance of others might be in some sense even more indicative of their mental development than what they can do alone. . . .

This difference . . . is what we call *the zone of proximal development.* It is the distance between the actual developmental level as determined by independent problem solving and the level of potential development as determined through problem solving under adult guidance or in collaboration with more capable peers.

—L.S. Vygotsky, *Mind In Society,* (Cambridge: Harvard University Press, 1968) pp. 85–86.

---

they use not only number, but class and propositional logic.

It could be said that the construction of a computer program, is really an exercise in applied logic, in which information is translated into logical form, *i.e.,* in terms of the computer language, BASIC, LOGO, or whatever. The computer languages are in their essentials sophisticated versions of the elementary logical and grammatical techniques we use when we read or write a natural language. If we therefore teach a thinking skills program, not only will it have an impact on the broader questions of literacy and numeracy, it should also improve the student's understanding of computers and computer programs.

To the question which may be in our minds, why I have devoted so much time to programs concerned with improving the thinking skills of the younger generation, my answer is: (1) this is a field in which most work on thinking skills has been done; (2) most of these programs can be adapted for adult use and (3) the child is after all father of the man.

Notes

1. Cf. Eysenck H.J. (1974) *Inequality of man.*
2. C.f. Jensen A.R. (1972) *Genetics and education.* Methuen.
3. An opposing view, one which emphasizes the part played by the social environment is found in Leon Kamin (1974) The *science-of politics of the I.Q.* Laurence Erlbaum. See also the debate between Eysenck and Kamin (1981) *Intelligence: The battle for the mind*: H.J. *Eysenck versus Leon Kamin.* Macmillan. For a critique of the use of I.Q. tests for evaluating intelligence see Wolfe Mays, "A Philosophical Critique of Intelligence Tests," *Educational Theory,* Vol. XVI, No. 4, October 1966.

4. Cf. Binet A. (1973) *Les idées modernes sur les enfants* (preface de Jean Piaget), Sec. Ed. Flammarion. Binet believed that it was possible by appropriate exercises to improve the intellectual powers of backward children. On this see Chap. V, "L'intelligence: sa mésure, son éducation" (pp. 100-1 13), particularly Sect. 11, "L'éducation de l'intelligence." The section begins with the following statement which is worth quoting, "Apres le mal, le remede: apres la constation des defaillances intellectuelles de toutes sortes, passons au traitement" (p. 100).

5. *Ibid.* p. 101.

6. *CoRT thinking lessons*, material compiled by Edward de Bono. This consists of six sections: 1. *Breadth*; 11. *Organisation*; 111. *Interaction*; IV. *Creativity*; V. *Information and Feeling*; VI. *Action*, and is published by Pergamon Press, Oxford. There is a teacher's handbook for each section, and in addition for each lesson there are notes for each pupil. The propriety name *CoRT* derives from the initials of the Cognitive Research Trust, which markets the lessons.

7. Cf. Feuerstein R. (1982) *Instrumental enrichment: An intervention program for cognitive modifiability*, University Park Press and Feuerstein R. (1982) *The dynamic assessment of retarded performers: The learning assessment potential, theory, instruments and techniques*, University Park Press. See also the 15 Instruments published by the Curriculum Development Associates Inc., Washington, D.C.

8. Cf. Lipman, M., Sharp A.M. & Oscanyan F.S. (1980) *Philosophy in the classroom*, Temple University Press and Lipman M & Sharp, A.M. (Eds) (1978) *Growing up with philosophy*. Temple University Press.

9. Whimby A. & Lochhead J. (1980) *Problem solving and comprehension: A short course in analytical reasoning*. The Franklin Institute Press.

10. Midwest Publications, Pacific Grove, California.

11. Cf. de Bono E. (1976) *Teaching thinking*.

12. Cf. de Bono E. (1977) *The use of lateral thinking*. Penguin.

13. The Feuerstein Instrumental Enrichment program is made up of more than 500 pages of paper and pencil exercises divided into 15 Instruments. These are: *Organization of dots, Analytic Perception* and *Illustrations*, which are non-verbal; *Orientation in Space I, II and III, Family Relations, Comparisons, Numerical Progressions*, and *Syllogisms*, which involve a limited vocabulary; *Categorization, Instructions, Temporal Relations, Transitive Relations*, and *Representational Stencil Design*, which require reading and comprehension skills. We are told that each instrument focuses a specific cognitive deficiency, although it is also concerned with the acquisition of other learning skills. These instruments, Feuerstein tells us, were developed as a result of his attempt to improve the intellectual functioning of retarded children through the use of his "Learning Potential Assessment Device." For details see *The Dynamic Assessment of Retarded Performers*.

14. *Instrumental enrichment*, p. 121.

15. *Ibid.*, p. 122.

16. Holt M. & Dienes Z. (1974) *Let's play maths*, p. 17. Penguin.

17. Cf. Luria A. R. (1976) *Cognitive development: Its cultural and social foundations*. Trs. Martin Lopez Morillas and Lynn Solotoroff, Ed. Michael Cole. Harvard University Press.

18. Cf. Piaget J. (1977) *Etudes sociologiques*, 3rd Edn., p. 280.

19. *Instrumental enrichment*, p. 7.

20. *Ibid.*, p. 2.

21. Piaget J. (1971) *Biology and knowledge:An essay on the relations between organic regulations and cognitive processes*, p. 20. Trs. Beatrix Walsh, Edinburgh: University Press. and Piaget continued, "My answer to this is in the form of two questions: first would it ever be possible to make the theory of relativity or even the simple handling of propositions or hypothetico-deductive operations comprehensible to a four-year-old? And second, why does a human baby not discover the continued presence of something he sees you hide beneath a screen until he reaches the age of nine months and upwards?" (p. 20).

22. Carlos Ruiz Boliver, "Efectos del program Enriquecemiente Instrumental en estudiantes preuniversitarios." Universitad Experimental de Guayana Centro Investigaciones Psicoeducativas.

23. Ian M. Sochet, "Cognitive Modifiability among High Risk Universit Students-Another Case for Adopting and Adapting Fuersteins Instrumental Enrichment Programme," University of Witwatersrand, South Africa. I have to thank Professor Reuven Feuerstein for making available to me the two papers referred to in notes 22 and 23.

24. The novels and teacher's manuals (in brackets) are: *Kio and Gus (Wondering at the World); Pixie (Looking for Meaning); Harry Stottlemeier's Discovery (Philosophical Inquiry);* Lisa *(Ethical Inquiry);* Suki *(Writing: How and Why)* and Mark *(Social Inquiry).* These are published by The First Mountain Foundation in conjunction with the University Press of America.

25. *Harry Stottlemeier's Discovery*, 1977 Edn, p. 22.

26. Cf. Charlann Simon, "Philosophy for Students with Learning Disabilities," *Thinking*, Vol. 1, No. 1, 1979, p. 28.

27. *New Jersey Test of Reasoning Skills*, developed by Virginia Shipman of the Educational Testing Service, Princeton.

28. Thouless R. (1946) *Straight and crooked thinking*. English University Press.

29. Stebbing L.S. (1945) *Thinking to some purpose*. Penguin.

30. Last J. (1984) "I think, therefore I add," *The Times Educational Supplement*, 15.6.84, p. 28.

31. Cf. Wolfe Mays, "Logic for juniors," *Teaching Arithmetic*, Vol. 3, No. 3, Autumn 1965.

32. Cf. *Teaching thinking*, pp. 19-20.

33. *Ibid.*, p. 104.

34. *Ibid.*, p. 105.

35. Sharpe K. (1984) "Micropower to the People," *The Times Educational Supplement*, 13.4.84, p. 24.

Thinking Skills in Science and Philosophy for Children

Ann Gazzard

The contents of this paper stem first from the belief that philosophy is an integral part of every discipline and therefore should similarly be an integral part of its instruction; and second from the belief that science more than any other discipline needs the complement of philosophy in its instruction, for it is scientific knowledge more than most that is accepted by the general population as being true.

In what follows both the nature of scientific knowledge and the way in which it is produced has been examined to determine the methods most befitting its instruction and the skills most required of its students. The Appendix is somewhat of an outline of the ideas presented here.

The Nature of Scientific Knowledge

There are two features of scientific knowledge that have important implications for the way in which science should be taught. The first concerns the generation and production of scientific knowledge, and the second concerns the epistemic status of that knowledge once it is produced.

Scientific knowledge is *generative*. That is to say, it is constructed. It is information, created and for the most part, accepted by the professional scientific community. Moreover, what

other individuals know of science is further construed from this accepted material into a body of understanding that makes sense in terms of what they already know. At all levels then, professional, semi-professional and lay, knowledge of reality through science is created. It is a product of the knowledge that the individuals already have and the thinking in which they engage when assimilating the new information with their former beliefs. In other words, scientific understanding is concerned with the reliable construction of knowledge by connecting claims with each other on the one hand, and the assimilation of the new information with the old on the other. If the goal of science, then, is to help persons better understand their world, to help them understand science more comprehensively, and accordingly, to help them function well as professional scientists, then science education needs to attend to practices that stimulate and improve these very processes.

Let us look more closely therefore, at what the construction and assimilation of scientific knowledge involve. If knowledge is to be reliably constructed, then an individual's beliefs, claims, assertions, etc., have to be connected logically. That is to say, the newly-acquired knowledge has to be coherent and consistent within itself as well as coherent and consistent with what is already known. At the same time, however, the ability to construct scientific knowledge in keeping with its generative epistemology requires that it be done with the awareness that any knowledge claims that are produced are, in the long run, *interpretations* of events rather than necessarily being one-to-one correspondences with the events themselves. In other words, students need also to be able to recognize that the knowledge presented to them is someone else's interpretation of a particular idea or phenomenon, and moreover, that the form in which they finally understand and accept it is their own interpretation and one that is always at least a second-generation interpretation of the original idea. For example, the full meaning of "All metals expand when heated," can only be appreciated if, when it is learned, it is also understood that, however reliable the claim is, it is only the result of the scientific community's observation and consequent interpretation of what appears to happen when various metals are heated.

While the processes of constructing knowledge and assimilating new knowledge feed each other, they are somewhat distinct in their operation. Assimilation is one of the ways in which this new incoming information is made meaningful, and, for the most part, it functions in one of three ways. Either the new information is related to the former-held beliefs by making the necessary adjustments in the former-held beliefs or it is connected by making the necessary adjustments to the new information, or it is accepted by making no adjustments at all and assimilating the new information meaningfully as it stands. Irrespective of which of these processes is involved, however, it is clear that the process of assimilation involves relating two sets of information, the new and the old, to each other, and then determining what changes are needed in either set such that the new can be accommodated by the old. The skill primarily responsible for being able to relate two sets of information to each other is analogical reasoning. Analogical reasoning rests upon finding similarities and differences in any two things, and more complex forms of it rest upon finding the similarities and differences in the relationships within each of the two things. Accordingly, it is the cornerstone for understanding new information and the skill upon which assimilation rests. It enables students to translate any information into their own language, that is, into terms that they already understand and it enables them further to move from one discipline to another, understanding each in their own language and each in terms of one of the other disciplines if need be.

Irrespective of whether the old information is adjusted to the new or the new to the old, the search for good reasons is a skill, like analogical reasoning, at the center of the process. In other words, no matter whether the changes that need to be made concern the old information or the new, good reasons are needed to make them. Good reasons are generally needed to alter one's former-held beliefs, and the way in which science is presented, that is—as a very reliable body of information—also suggests that very good reasons are needed to alter any part of it. Learning what constitutes a good reason and knowing how to apply it is as much a part of assimilating new information as it is a part of justifying the beliefs that one already has.

Thus far, the generative nature of scientific knowledge, has revealed that if the nature of science is to be successfully understood, then students need to be trained (1) in the importance of logical coherence and consistency, (2) in making interpretations that are meaningful and reliable, (3) in analogical reasoning, and (4) in the search for good reasons. Let us turn now to the second important feature of scientific knowledge, namely, its *fallibilism* and see what other types of thinking its successful implementation might also entail.

Scientific knowledge is fallibilistic. That is to say, the knowledge that science generates is not absolute in the "truths" it reveals. Rather, the information that the practice of science generates is considered to be the best possible understanding for the moment of the phenomena in question. Given the limits of the scientific methodology, the limits of the previous knowledge upon which any present knowledge rests, the limits of man's understanding, and given the possibility that the future may reveal information which necessitates reformulations of current knowledge, science continues to present as a product of these restrictions the most accurate account of events possible at any given time.

This aspect of scientific knowledge makes certain of its own demands upon what the practices of a responsible science should be. First, the concepts, laws, theories and methodology of science need to be presented when they are taught that way, as only tentatively the best descriptions and explanations of the phenomenon and only tentatively, the best method for understanding them. It is important for students to realize that the explanation or description that is given by science is not the only one possible. It is important that they realize that science is just one of the many possible metaphysical frameworks that could be brought to bear in understanding this or that particular phenomenon, and it is important that they realize that, given science has been selected as the method of inquiry, the explanation at hand may, in the long run, not be the best possible explanation that there is. As important as it is to present the contents of science in this way, it is equally important to provide students with the opportunity to explore its contents in ways that guarantee their being held tentatively. Students of science need to know how to work with knowledge and at the same time be aware of its limits. This process of flexible thinking, of not holding ideas rigidly, needs continual practice and it can start to be developed in the early years of school. All concepts, for example, have fuzzy edges, even the concepts of science that are wont to be treated as being definitive. The outer edges of most concepts have areas of overlap with other concepts and there are areas where there is debate as to whether a particular x, for example, is an instance of the concept at all. Science education in the early years, then, can start with conceptual exploration—with exploring concepts to appreci-

ate their problems and limits. It is only by experiencing the limits and problems of concepts that children can be expected to appreciate the importance of using them with an open-mind, and with a certain amount of reservation.

By way of illustrating the detrimental effects to further knowledge acquisition of holding concepts rigidly, let us consider a concept from zoology and a boy called Johnnie. Johnnie learns from the dictionary that a raccoon is "a black-masked, pointed-face mammal with a black-ringed bush tail that is found in North and South America." Johnnie's concept of "raccoon" comes to include animals that look like this and that are in North and South America. After a trip to England where he sees an animal that looks exactly like a raccoon, he reasons in the following way:

> "When I was in England, I saw a raccoon, but I must have been wrong, it must have been some other animal with which I'm not familiar. Raccoons don't live in England."

Johnnie's reasoning here is poor. The concept "raccoon" is being held rigidly and it is preventing him from broadening his knowledge in the face of new evidence that might allow it. A less fixed use of the concept and one that might generate its ultimate revision, however, would enable Johnnie to reason something like this:

> "When I was in England, I saw a raccoon, or could I have made a mistake? Could it have been some other animal that I don't know about yet? Or might it really have been a raccoon? Could it be a raccoon even though it was in England? How could that be? Under what circumstances could a raccoon be in England? Is the time I saw it like that? Everything else about it was like a raccoon. Could an animal still be a raccoon even if one little thing about it was not like a raccoon? . . . How else could I find out whether or not it was, or possibly could have been a raccoon? . . . etc."

Similarly, it is important that students of science learn to think openly about the methodology they are using. The fixed use of any method, that is closure to its further revision, necessarily curtails the knowledge that can be derived from any phenomenon in the same way that the fixed use of a concept does.

The view that the "truths" of science are provisional has a second important implication for the teaching of science, namely, that epistemology be taught *in* science from the time it is first introduced into the curriculum. Epistemology is generally thought to be a subject suitable only for college level students. However, epistemological inquiry, that is the *doing* of epistemology, is something that even very young children do. Questions like, "How do you know that?" "Is that *really* true?" and "Why should I believe you?" are questions that young children are wont to ask. Such questions reveal that children are perplexed by epistemological matters and that they have already begun epistemological inquiry. Given that children have this interest and ability, it is not unreasonable to suggest that the planned intervention of epistemological inquiry in the elementary curriculum might foreclose the necessity of its remedial intervention in later years. The need to correct students' understandings and expectations of scientific knowledge might be forestalled if students learned at a young age to appreciate the problematic nature of knowledge and truth. Irrespective of the potentially beneficial consequences of including epistemology *in* the education of the young, its inclusion in elementary education is required if science is to be taught with due respect to its fallibility. To exclude inquiry into the meaning of what one knows when one claims to know something in science, is to misrepresent not only the value of the scientific enterprise but also its very nature.

The provisional character of scientific truths then, implies the need for epistemology in science education, and moreover, it indicates at least four things that epistemology in science education should do. First, it should reveal the ways in which statements assume different sets of truth values and allow different claims to truth depending upon the epistemological qualifiers that proceed them. For example, qualifiers such as "It is claimed that . . .," "It is believed that . . .," "It is known that . . .," "It is observed that . . .," and "It is predicted . . .," each indicate different reasons for calling a statement true, or for calling a fact a fact.

Epistemological inquiry should help students explore these reasons, the differences in meaning they generate and the difference in the reliability of the knowledge they qualify. For example, students need to be able to determine whether a statement like, "All metals expand when heated," means "It is believed that 'All . . .' " or "It has been observed that . . ." or "It is claimed that 'All metals expand when heated' " and they need to know which formulations have the greatest claims to truth. Skills such as these help students to be able to evaluate scientific information critically. They become able to assess the factual potential of any statement and they become alert to the inadequacy of claims that are not epistemologically qualified and to the inadequacy of knowledge sources that lack such qualifications. These skills may not in themselves be enough to evaluate scientific claims thoroughly, but without them students cannot be held responsible for merely coming to accept all that science tells them.

Second, epistemological inquiry in science should also be concerned with the relationship between contexts and truth. Students of science need to appreciate that the meaning of a statement cannot be fully understood unless the conditions that guarantee its truth and falsity are also understood. For example, the meaning of the statement "Water freezes at 32 °F" cannot be fully understood if it is not also understood that there are conditions under which the statement is not true, for instance, the case of sea water, or boiling water in a freezing cold room. All phenomena occur in contexts, and statements are connected to the phenomena they describe by these contexts. Accordingly, statements derive their meaning by understanding the conditions in which the phenomena they describe occur. Thus, it would be of little value to a meaningful education if

---

On getting children to think more scientifically

Effective aid personnel, like effective teachers, do not claim to be the inspired possessors of best techniques and methods. They have learnt that it is no use giving a ready-made irrigation system to nomadic tribespeople, nor a sanitation system to a group of forest-dwellers, simply because from a Western point of view these would provide obvious material benefits. Their approach is much more sensible and profitable. Firstly, they find out from the people themselves what problems most concern them. Then they help to isolate the real cause of the problem and explore with the people alternative ways of solving these problems. Only after this do they help the people construct for themselves what it is that they require. This may take more time than would be involved in a more directive approach, since changes in belief are usually involved as well as new information, but it avoids wasted effort and wasted resources. Further, the recipients are not left in a state of dependence on the aid given. We see this approach as having many similarities to the approach needed to change teachers' ideas about teaching and to change pupils' ideas in science.

Our experience has been that many teachers need to be sensitised to what often happens in existing science lessons, and how children's ideas are being influenced, or not influenced, by schooling. Once teachers have convinced themselves that the existing conceptions of children are important—teaching frequently does alter, sometimes in small ways at first, to take greater account of children's present ideas. In this regard we see the main task of science teacher-educators, including senior teachers and curriculum developers, as helping teachers:

- to confront the realities of classroom learning,
- to understand the importance of children's existing ideas,
- to understand children's ideas and,
- to realise how children's ideas compare with the views of scientists.

Most young children are, thank goodness, inherently curious. As have seen they are only too willing to formulate theories about why the world is as it is. Our job as science teachers is to devise situations which sharpen up their ability to test those theories, which help them to assemble systematically the facts of the case before jumping to conclusions, and which highlight the consistencies and inconsistencies in their own explanations.

—from Roger Osborne and Peter Freyberg, *Learning in Science* (Heinemann, 1985), pp. 185–186.

---

science were taught out of the contexts that validate it. Moreover, part of those very contexts include exploration into the conditions that verify each of its more specific claims. Consequently, students, if they are ultimately to understand any information, must learn to inquire into the range of possible conditions that both verify and falsify it.

The third thing that epistemological inquiry in science should do is expose students to the problematic nature of truth. Students need to realize why the existence of absolute truth is controversial, and why, even if it does exist, science could

not lay claim to disclosing it. It is only in this way that students can appreciate scientific knowledge in its best perspective, that is, as temporary truths on the path to ever-growing knowledge. Of course, philosophy of science specifically treats these issues, inasmuch as it is concerned to portray as distinctly as possible the relationships between knowledge, science and truth. But the understanding of science that these approaches offer need not be reserved for college-level populations. For while philosophy of science courses help older students appreciate the importance of science as continual inquiry, elementary school children can also be afforded this understanding, not by learning theories *about* truth but rather by inquiring first-hand into the issue as it occurs to them in their school lessons and in their everyday lives. Children readily engage in inquiry about truth, beginning with questions like, "How do you know that's the truth?" "Is that the whole truth?" and "What's the truth?" What's more, they are open to having their inquiry directed into areas where they find for themselves the importance of the circumstances to truth, the possible importance of truth, the interaction between truth and mind, and the various meanings that truth itself can have. The more children are exposed to these problematic aspects of truth and the more they are encouraged to inquire continually into the truth of whatever it is they are confronting, then the more they are engaging in the very process of science itself.

Finally, epistemological inquiry should engage students continually in an appraisal of the reasons they have for calling something true. Students need to be aware that there are many possible reasons for calling something true, and that the best reasons are not always the same in different situations. For example, Johnnie might have as a reason for calling something true that his brother told him it was so. But obviously, there are circumstances under which this would not count as a good reason and others under which it would. If his brother had said, for example, that "Fiats are good cars," then this would more likely count as a good reason for believing it to be true if his brother were an authority on cars than if he knew very little about them. In other words, children need exposure to the variety of reasons one might have for calling something true and they need practice in identifying and applying the best type of reason in any given situation. They need to know, for example, the differences between calling something true by definition, true by evidence, true by authority, and true by belief, and they need to know under what circumstances any one of these is a reliable predictor of truth.

This leads us to a final point that needs to be made about teaching science if its fallibilism is to be adequately represented. Through practice with its method, students need to realize *for themselves* that science does not provide answers in the sense of closure. Rather, it is important for them to come to terms with the view that its answers are more like the starting points for further questioning and investigation, and that science itself is perhaps best conceived of as perpetual inquiry. Problem-finding and question-asking, then, are as important to science as the more recognized skill of problem-solving. Continual inquiry requires finding the problems in the temporary answers that it provides as well as in the methods used to create them, and problem-finding presupposes the ability to ask questions. Of course, problems can be identified intuitively, but in most cases, more than this is required. Knowing how to ask those questions that could unveil hidden difficulties is as much a part of problem-finding as knowing how to ask the questions that might further clarify the problem at hand. This is not to say that all problems uncovered will be relevant to further *scientific* inquiry. All problems do, however, deserve further inquiry of some sort, and it is the business of science, as it is of any other discipline, to acknowledge all problems as they arise, sort out the ones relevant to the inquiry in the discipline at hand, and suggest ways of dealing with the rest.

Let me quickly restate then the skills that would be needed to engage in a science education that would be true to the nature of the knowledge it sought to teach. On the one hand, there are, because of the generative epistemology of science, the skills in service of logic, interpretation, analogical reasoning, and the search for good reasons. On the other, there are, because of its fallibilism, the processes engaged by holding knowledge loosely, understanding the differences between claims, belief and observations, understanding the connection between the truth of an event and the conditions that allow it, understanding the problematic nature of truth, and understanding the open-ended nature of scientific answers. Important to each of these is the ability to ask questions and find problems, and more specifically to the issue of truth and circumstances, the ability to draw distinctions and make connections. For example, one cannot hold concepts tentatively if one cannot find problems in them; one cannot see the importance of distinguishing observations and beliefs if one cannot see the problem with calling a belief an observation; and one will not appreciate the necessarily open-ended nature of scientific answers if one cannot find the problems in those answers and indeed within the concept of truth itself. Similarly, one cannot evaluate the meaning of a claim if one cannot make the connections that relate it to the conditions that permit its truth. I will return to these skills later, but for now, let us turn from the nature of scientific knowledge to the process of science itself, to see what skills it entails.

The Scientific Process

The process of science is inquiry. One aspect of its inquiry it shares with all other disciplines, while another aspect of it is peculiar to the discipline of science itself. Let us consider each of these in turn.

Common to all disciplines is the search to understand the information that is elicited. While every discipline might have its own particular way of ascertaining knowledge, the process of understanding that knowledge, of evaluating it and of discovering ways to improve upon it are processes that span all disciplines equally. It is, as it were, a mode of inquiry common to all disciplines and applicable to all types of information. There are certain things, however, that this type of inquiry must do if the discipline in question and the knowledge it produces are to be well understood.

First, the terms in which the knowledge of the discipline are spelled out must be clarified. This requires of students that they be able to say what

the terms mean in their own language as well as being able to determine if there are differences in their use of them compared with the way others use them.

Second, students need to engage in conceptual exploration. In order for knowledge to be understood, that is, the concepts that comprise it need to be explored for their limits and for their overlap with other concepts. Students cannot work successfully with a concept if they do not appreciate the range of its possible meaning, nor can they draw the necessary connections and distinctions between this and other concepts, thereby making the overall tone of their knowledge more integrated and meaningful, if they do not know the full extent of the meaning it can assume.

Thirdly, it is important for inquiry in all disciplines, and most particularly in science, that there be a continual reappraisal of its methods and content. Students must be open to and capable of revising both in the light of new alternatives that are created.

Fourthly, regular inquiry is needed into the ethical, metaphysical and logical consequences of the discipline and its practices. For example, a complete understanding of science is not forthcoming if the benefits to mankind of, say, research based on animal studies and genetic manipulation are not weighed with the ethical consequences of those very practices. And similarly, approaches to health care are necessarily myopic if they fail to consider treatments presupposing metaphysical systems different from that upon which orthodox medical treatment is based.

Perhaps the most important feature of all this inquiry into meaning and understanding is that it take place with others, that is, among persons who are, together, engaged by the same issues, and who, as a group, are committed to the practice of inquiry itself. It is not that an individual is necessarily incapable of understanding a discipline in the same way that a group working together might, but that most persons, from an early age on, do benefit from the ideas and points of view of other people. The full meaning of any term, for example, is not likely to be realized in the absence of group inquiry. Students need to share their understanding of terms with each other so that their most impartial meaning can emerge, and so that each of the students, as well as the group as a whole, can revise their own conceptions of terms in light of others that are more reasonable, more appealing, or simply more sensible. Similarly, the critical appraisal of any discipline benefits more from communal inquiry than it does from any one individual's. Thinking and talking with others provides the context that allows for the discovery of new ways of saying, making and doing things. New alternatives are advanced; alternatives, moreover, that are more likely to be well understood because they have come from one's peers, and more likely to be vigorously defended and indicted for that very same reason.

Let us look more closely how at those methods of inquiry that the community of professional scientists have agreed upon to use. This second major aspect of scientific inquiry is that aspect of the process which, unlike the above, is specific to the discipline itself. The type of inquiry in which science engages is concerned with bringing meaning to experience by finding the order and regularities that there are in it. To do this, it searches for the similarities and differences among events, extracting those regularities that it finds or perceives there. In its attempt to formulate laws about such findings, and theories that might account for them, it also (whether suitably or not) constructs ways of testing the "truth" of what it claims to have discovered. Whether or not the way in which the laws and theories are tested, that is, by the rejection or confirmation of predictions and whether or not predictions themselves are things that science ought to be concerned with, are questions at the center of what science is about. It is not my intention here to explore these problematic issues; rather, I am concerned to explicate the skills that scientific inquiry demands of its students. Yet, I do want to stress the injustice that is done to all students of science in

courses that present it as having one possible goal, namely, prediction and control, as opposed to courses that present its alternative goals as well, namely, description and explanation. A course in science that was true to its integrity and fair to its students, therefore, would be one in which students were actively engaged in exploring these issues as well as in experiencing both these forms of scientific practice. Let us return, then, to the skills that the scientific method of inquiry requires of its participants.

I will delineate the skills in what follows; however, I will spend little time discussing them since they should be most familiar to educators as they are the skills generally regarded as the skills of science.

First, there are the skills associated with finding order, pattern and regularity in phenomena; processes each of which depend upon the ability to perceive similarities and differences among those very phenomena. That is to say, one cannot find patterns in events or regularities between them if one cannot identify the ways in which they are the same and the ways in which they are different. What's more, one cannot articulate what these patterns are if one cannot reason analogically and indicate the ways in which the things are alike. Thus, the ability to draw distinctions, make connections and reason analogically are all skills essential to the first step of scientific inquiry.

The second cluster of skills are those in service of hypothesis formation and testing. Students need to be able to extract from a range of more specific contexts the regularities and patterns that they see there. In other words, they need to be able to separate foreground from background material, and hold either one constant for the sake of perceiving the other one more clearly. Giving students practice in working with part-whole relationships is perhaps the best way to accomplish this.

Once certain patterns and regularities have been identified, hypotheses as to the laws that govern them are then formed and tested. Perhaps the single most important skill for understanding what any hypothesis is doing and for understanding the results of its test, is the ability to think syllogistically. The underlying structure of any hypothesis is "if x, then y." Consequently, one has little chance of understanding the results of an experiment in terms of the hypothesis the experiment was designed to test, if one can't extrapolate the x's and y's that make the proposal valid. It was long thought that this so-called hypothetical thinking was the prerogative of the later years of childhood. However, there is now a considerable amount of research evidence to contest this claim.[1] Indeed, one need only to look at what children understand in the context of their daily lives to see that, at a young age, they already think that way. For example, the teacher of a first-grade class might say, "I don't see any hands up." The implication that the children understand is "Nobody knows the answer." In other words, they have been able to work from the claim that "If you know the answer, then you'll have your hand up," to one of its valid conclusions, namely, "If there are no hands up, then no one knows the answer."

Understanding the meaning of an hypothesis, however, is only one aspect of the skills needed to construct and test it. There are also skills needed to carry out each of these processes. These are the skills that serve observation, measurement, estimation, and other types of quantification, and they tend for the most part to be well covered in science programs. Unfortunately, however, they are, in most cases, the only skills of science that are disclosed. Many of the other skills discussed here, particularly those in service of meaning, are excluded either because they are considered unnecessary or because they are not even thought to be relevant.

Finally, scientific inquiry often requires being able to work with scientific equipment. Students need to be able to use a whole panoply of gadgets in their investigations. They need those skills required by caring for their instruments as well as the know-how that goes with operating them.

Perhaps the best way to develop these skills is through practice. Students need to be exposed to the equipment, shown what it means to care for it, and given the opportunity to explore the range of its possible use in experimental contexts that are meaningful.

It would be encouraging if the entire set of skills discussed in this paper were made available to children in their elementary education and beyond. However, this would still not be enough to teach science adequately for what would be the value of having those skills if they were not used. Students with a bag full of skills are not going to perform well in science or function well later on as professional scientists if they are not motivated or inspired to inquire in the first place. Science education then, needs also to stimulate inquiry. It needs to present material that is at least potentially stimulating and it needs to sensitize its students to the problematic and hence, the *need* for inquiry by showing them just how pervasive that need is in their school work and their everyday lives.

At this point I should like to consider Philosophy for Children and by way of closing, make a few remarks about its contribution to science education.

One of the main contributions it can make is by modeling the ways in which children can be made more aware of the problematic. It accomplishes this in a number of ways. First, the children's curriculum materials expose them to the problematic aspects of many words and ideas, and issues of life. For example, a third-grader raises her mother's eyelid and says, "Mommy, are you in there?" and a second-grader wonders whether or not giving pets names protects them from being killed. Second, the teachers' material shows teachers how to explore these issues even further with the students. Teachers are shown how to inquire into the things that are obviously problematic as well as how to uncover the problematic in issues less controversial. For example, there are guidelines for exploring renowned problematic issues like truth, space and time, but there

The ideal elementary science course

It is time to develop a new group of professional thinkers, perhaps a somewhat larger group than the working scientists and the working poets, who can create a discipline of scientific criticism. We have had good luck so far in the emergence of a few people ranking as philosophers of science and historians and journalists of science. and I hope more of these will be coming along. But we have not yet seen specialists in the fields of scientific criticism who are of the caliber of the English literary and social critics F. R. Leavis and John Ruskin or the American literary critic Edmund Wilson. Science needs critics of this sort, but the public at large needs them more urgently.

I suggest that the introductory courses in science, at all levels from grade school through college, be radically revised. Leave the fundamentals, the so-called basics, aside for a while, and concentrate the attention of all students on the things that are not known. You cannot possibly teach quantum mechanics without mathematics, to be sure, but you can describe the strangeness of the world opened up by quantum theory. Let it be known, early on, that there are deep mysteries and profound paradoxes revealed in distant outline by modern physics. Explain that these can be approached more closely and puzzled over, once the language of mathematics has been sufficiently mastered.

At the outset, before any of the fundamentals, teach the still imponderable puzzles of cosmology. Describe as clearly as possible, for the youngest minds, that there are some things going on in the universe that lie still beyond comprehension, and make it plain how little is known. . .

Teach ecology early on. Let it be understood that the earth's life is a system of interdependent creatures, and that we do not understand at all how it works. The earth's environment, from the range of atmospheric gases to the chemical constituents of the sea, has been held in an almost unbelievably improbable state of regulated balance since life began, and the regulation of stability and balance is somehow accomplished by the life itself, like the autonomic nervous system of an immense organism. We do not know how such a system works, much less what it means, but there are some nice reductionist details at hand, such as the bizarre proportions of atmospheric constituents, ideal for our sort of planetary life, and the surprising stability of the ocean's salinity, and the fact that the average temperature of the earth has remained quite steady in the face of at least a 25 percent increase in heat coming in from the sun since the earth began. That kind of thing: something to think about.

—from Lewis Thomas, *The Art of Teaching Science*, The New York Times Magazine.

are also many designed to elicit the contestable within the commonly accepted unproblematic. For example, the concept of "wetness" is introduced in the elementary curriculum and it is explored by considering examples of things that are wet and not wet. The problematic is introduced when children are asked to decide whether things like moist, foggy, misty, damp, and humid are things that are wet, not wet, neither or both. And similarly, whether it is raining or not might, at first, seem unproblematic. But in this curriculum children are directed to the problematic with questions like, "What if there are just one or two drops, is it raining?" Third, Philosophy for Children shows educators how to sensitize children to the problematic by offering an alternative pedagogy that does just that. The community of inquiry exposes its participants to different ways of thinking and different points of view urging them to realize that what might for them seem unproblematic can be rendered complex by community involvement. Students are forced to realize that any one idea can have a number of meanings and that any one problem can be approached in numerous ways. In other words, students come to understand that while problems and ideas might for them admit of a simple solution or have a straightforward meaning, their communal resolution and understanding might not.

Finally, Philosophy for Children generates student respect for the problematic by having them practice logic. It thus provides them with a tool for identifying counterinstances and conditions that falsify or, at least, provide problems for claims. There are numerous other ways in which Philosophy for Children models instruction suitable for improved science teaching. By way of the community of inquiry, it demonstrates pedagogy capable of integrating and incorporating ethical, epistemological and metaphysical inquiry into childrens' discussions in ways that are meaningful *to the children*, and it immerses them unremittingly in the process of inquiry itself. The children are taught to listen to others, respect the procedures of discussion, reflect upon what they are doing and stay alert to the possible problematic in all they say and hear. What's more, the strategy of using childrens' ideas as the agenda for discussion is in keeping with many of the more recent recommendations for science teaching. Children's conceptions of scientific phenomena have been shown generally to differ from the accepted scientific viewpoints.[2] The recommendation is to direct childrens' inquiry from where they are, systematically and gradually, to where the scientists are. It is in this respect also that Philosophy for Children provides a lead. In the discussions it fosters, it is always concerned to "start where the kids are." That is, children are encouraged always to express and clarify their ideas first before their elaboration and revision sets in. If educators want particular views understood by their students, they themselves must also be prepared to hear what their students have to say. They need to listen so that they will gain that same respect from their pupils and they need to listen in order to identify those ideas that might furnish the necessary steps in bridging their understanding.

Finally, a few words of caution. Philosophy for Children, even in its more specific scientific components like *Kio and Gus*, is designed to complement science instruction. It is not, that is, intended to supplant it.[3] To do this would require more focus than it has upon the skills peculiar to science like measurement and working with instruments, more attention than it now gives to scientific phenomena, and a less rigid presentation of the scientific concepts that it now has, when it does present them. But I am willing to submit that if only its approach to knowledge through inquiry were transferred to science, then a great service would be done to the latter.

Footnotes

1. See Carey's work, in particular "Are Children Fundamentally Different Kinds of Thinkers and Learners Than Adults?" Also Donaldson's work *Children's Minds* argues in this direction.
2. In particular, see Minstrell and Smith, "Alternative Conceptions and a Strategy for Change"; and Osborne, "Science Education: Where Do We Start?"
3. *Kio and Gus* is one of the elementary school programs in Philosophy for Children. It is targeted for the second grade with an emphasis upon botany and zoology.

Bibliography

Bowline, Baarney and Gaines, Alan. "Use Philosophy to Explain the Scientific Method." *The Science Teacher*, 1966, 33, 52.

Boole, Mary. "Preparing Children to Study Science." *Thinking*, 1981, 2 (3 & 4), 72-75.

Carey, Susan. "Are Children Fundamentally Different Kinds of Thinkers and Learners Than Adults?" In Chipman S., Segal J., and Glaser R., *Thinking and Learning Skills*, Vol. 2., New Jersey: Erlbaum Associates, 1985.

Carey, Susan. Conceptual Change in Childhood. MIT Press, Cambridge, MA, 1985.

Donaldson, Margaret. *Children's Minds*. Glasgow: Fortana/Collins, 1978.

Hesse, Mary B. *Models and Analogies in Science*. London: William Clowes & Son, 1963.

Lipman, Matthew. "Constructing a curriculum to improve thinking and understanding." *CT News*. 1987, 5 (3), 4-7. 5 (4), 2-9.

Lipman, Matthew. "Philosophy for Children and Creativity." Paper presented at American Philosophical Association Philosophy of Creativity Society Annual Meeting. Chicago, Ill. April, 1987.

Lipman, Matthew. "A K-4 Science Education Curriculum Project." Unpublished paper, Montclair State College, 1985. 19 numb. leaves.

Manicas, P. T. and Second, P. F., "Implications for Psychology of the New Philosophy of Science." *American Psychologist.* 1983, 399-413.

Martin, Michael. *Concepts of Science Education.* Glenview, Ill. Scott, Foresman Co., 1972.

Minstrell, J. and Smith, C. L., "Alternative Conceptions and a Strategy for Change." *Science and Children*, 1983, 21, 31-33.

Oppenheimer, Robert. "Analogical Reasoning in the Scientific Community." *Thinking*, 1982, 3(3 & 4), 19-21.

Osborne, Roger. "Science Education: Where Do We Start?" *The Australian Science Teachers Journal.* 1982, 28 (1), 21-30.

Osborne, Roger. "Physics in Primary Schools." *NZ Science Teacher.* 1984. 40, 31-39.

Osborne, Roger. "Primary Science: Making sense of the world." *National Education: Journal of the New Zealand Education Institute.* 1984. 66 (1), 34-39.

Thomas, Lewis. "The Ideal Elementary Science Course." in "The Art of Teaching," from *The New York Times Magazine.*

APPENDIX

Thinking Skills in Science Education			
		Processes of Thinking	**Dominant Thinking Skills**
The Nature of Scientific Knowledge	**Constructed**	-reasoning with logical coherence & consistency	
		-making interpretations	
		-analogical reasoning	
		-understanding good reasons	
	Fallibilistic	-holding concepts & methodology open-mindedly	
		-understanding differences between claims, beliefs, etc.	
		-understanding problematic nature of truth	-asking questions
		-understanding the connections between truth & circumstances	-finding problems
		-understanding open-ended nature of scientific answers	
	Inquiry into Meaning	-clarification of terms	
		-conceptual inquiry	
		-continual reappraisal of methods & content	-communal thinking & inquiry
		-ongoing inquiry into ethical, logical and metaphysical consequences of methods and content	
The Process of Science Inquiry	**Scientific Methodology**	-finding order & regularity	-making connections & distinctions
			-analogical reasoning
		-hypothesis formation & testing	-part/whole reasoning
			-syllogistic reasoning
			-observation, measurement, estimation, quantification
		-working with equipment	-how to care for instruments

Against Skills

W. A. Hart

Mr. Hart's critique has a great deal of merit, insofar as it is directed at those who purvey little bundles of skills for the solving of esoteric problems and call it education. As a counterweight to such exaggerated claims, what Mr. Hart has to say is eloquent. But care must be taken not to go overboard in the other direction, setting up a dichotomy between the technical and the moral, with values and humanity totally absent from the first and totally concentrated in the second. Unfortunately, this is just what the author proceeds to do. "Thinking, reading, loving and so on . . . are capacities of our humanity . . .," but skills, presumably, are not: "You can be a good typist . . . without being a good man. Setting up a dualism between the technical and the human has much the same pitfalls and dangers as a dualism between the natural and the human, for the technical is a part of the human, just as the human is a part of the natural. It is unfortunate that Mr. Hart should fail to recognize the difficulties entailed by his dualistic presuppositions.

Skills, of course, do not occur in a vacuum. One may have the skill to operate a typewriter, or to operate on a patient, but choose not to utilize such skills. One may lack the disposition to create or to inquire or to heal. Or one can use one's skills badly, writing articles full of untruths, or misusing one's surgical knowledge in the service of hare-brained experiments, or building bombs. But even if one's skills are used for good purposes, they must be deployed, sequenced and orchestrated judiciously. Such judgment does not simply issue mysteriously and full-blown from

one's humanity: the orchestration of skills would itself seem to be a still different skill, and beyond orchestration there are still more complex judicious proficiencies. In other words, contrary to Mr. Hart's contention, the fact that our activities are diversified and specialized in no way implies that purposive human behavior is to be understood on the military model, with free, rational, and responsible generals making decisions and issuing orders, which are then carried out with unthinking mechanical obedience by those on the ranks beneath. It is just such a unilateral and authoritarian conception of power dissemination which must be rejected in the case of the alleged human vs. technical dichotomy. We are our skills just as much as we are our imagination, our insight, our understanding and our intuition. We give our skills guidance, and just as often they return the favor, so that we learn to depend on them to show us the way. (Indeed, it is fortunate that they do, for otherwise we would be totally inept.) The human being is, metaphorically speaking, a full orchestra, not just a conductor, the conductor provides conducting skills, as the instrumentalists provide violin-playing, clarinet-playing and harp-playing skills, but each is dependent upon the other, evokes from the other, guides the other, makes things feasible for the other.

What Mr. Hart might want to consider is that the distinction he is trying to make is not that of the technical versus the human, but that of craft versus art, with craft as the repository of skills and art as the repository of improvisation. Yet even here it might be demanded, by what right do we decide that improvisation is not itself a skill? Moreover, are not the cognitive processes by means of which we survey, monitor and appraise our skills themselves metacognitive skills? If someone says, "I think I realize now that my former beliefs were false," are the second-order and third-order cognitions ("I think I realize . . .") necessarily more "human" or less "skill-determined" than the first-order state of belief? These are some of the things the reader would do well to ponder in perusing Mr. Hart's essay.

To be "against" skills—what does that mean, and *why* am I against them? Does it even make sense to speak of being against skills? I can imagine that many people, seeing the title of this article, will ask these questions, and I hope to satisfy them in what I have to say. I could begin by saying that really I'm not against skills as such, that's to say, so long as it really is skills we're talking about. But you cannot dip much into educational writing nowadays—and not only educational writing—without realizing that the gambit of so-called "skills" is growing, and that there is a tendency (rather like the tendency there is with the word "situation") to append "skill" to all kinds of activities, as a kind of grace note, thereby ensuring euphony and an air of analytic impressiveness which disarms criticism. For example, people don't now talk about "reading" but about "reading skills," not about "teaching" but about "teaching skills." Children no longer learn to speak and write; they learn "language skills," or "language arts" even, or "communication skills." People still talk about "moral education," and perhaps to a lesser extent about "character formation," but increasingly the field is being taken over by talk about "social skills" and "moral skills."[1] Thinking, itself, is a skill (so a recent book by Edward De Bono tells me). There are the "skills of the historian" and the "skills in appreciation and evaluation" of the literary critic. Science of course has its skills. And there are, besides, all the professional skills of

which we stand in so much need of these days, like those of the town planner or the social worker or (what shall we say?) . . . the interior decorator. I scarcely think to mention Jerome Bruner's "skill of relevance" or "skills in sensing continuity and opportunity for continuity" ("metaskills" these latter) or the *Times Educational Supplement's* "skills in loving, respecting and caring for oneself and others" (the TES is full of this sort of thing). I opened a philosophy of education textbook the other day and my eye immediately lighted on—in the space of a couple of pages—"the feminine skills of the good mother", "the skill of leadership," and "skills of working with others in teams, committees or parent-teacher associations." All under the heading of *The Skills of Primary Teaching*. I haven't come across yet, but it can only be a matter of time, reference to the "skills of the religious life." After all, I have come across—in a Schools Council publication (where else?)—"expertise in the skills of the religious language game".

There is *so* much talk about skills these days, it has become so much part of the stock-in-trade of the would-be sharper-than-average teacher and educationist, that it goes unnoticed and unheard, like a kind of background hum. A year or so ago I attended a staff conference in a college of education. It was about the proposed new B.Ed. in Primary Education. In the course of the morning's discussion someone stood up and put the point, which was accepted without demur, that the new course ought to equip aspiring teachers with the *skills* to cope with and respond positively to pressures for innovation within schools. (I forget the exact terms—you know the kind of thing that gets said at conferences.) But what skills could the speaker have had in mind? (She—it was a she—didn't say.) *Were* there such skills? Skills of coping with and responding to change? You could see the force of somebody saying that he wanted students faced with change to show a measure of good will, not to think they knew it all, not to see every new development as a personal threat or as a reflection on their professional training—and not, on the other hand, to flock after every Pied Piper with a new tune to play. Good will, then, imagination, humility, self-confidence—even a dash of intelligence—that we should try to foster these, who would question? But as to them being "skills for coping with innovation" or twaddle of that kind—what's gained by dressing things up in that way? It's easy to see what's lost. Good sense for a start. "Imagining skills"—what are they exactly? Is there a *skill* of humility? And as for what might be meant by speaking of good will and self-confidence as skills I can't imagine. Enough. It goes without saying that my campaigner for the skills of coping and responding to innovation wasn't thinking of anything specific that you could pin down. In coming up with the phrase "skills for coping with innovation" she didn't need to exercise any more thought than bacteria which, they tell me, "fix" a certain amount of nitrogen in the air round about. (We all do it. Nobody, these days, is quite free.) "Skills" are in the air, *ergo* out she came with the "skills of coping with and responding to innovation"—*ergo* also my philosopher of education with his "skills of working with others in teams." (If I'm cantankerous or just determined to get my own way is there some *skill* I'm lacking?) The truth of the matter is that, in many or most cases, talk about skills is simply a kind of incantation, by which one creates the illusion that one is actually saying something about education.

Of course, to remark that there's a lot of cliché talked in education is to say nothing new, and it might not seem anything to take very seriously. People speak about skills where there are no skills, they call something a skill which isn't anything of the kind—so what? Why is the spread of "skills" talk, other than on the grounds of its redundancy and ugliness, so important? Now as a matter of fact I don't think that the ugliness of a mode of speaking is, even when one is most concerned with the substance of what is said, a side-issue. But I don't want to pursue that here. Independently of that I think I can say enough to explain why (so to speak) I want to apply the

brake to talk about skills in education—why, that is to say, I am *against skills*.

Here I am going to anticipate the detailed argument which is to follow, and the bald statement of my objection—my main objection—will not be immediately intelligible. I go about it in this way because I think it will be helpful to have advance warning of the ground I mean to cover. Basically what I have against the indiscriminate use of the word "skill" in education is that it confuses things which really are skills with things which aren't. It blurs, and in effect destroys, important distinctions between different kinds of things which we learn, and which are differently related to ourselves. In so doing it misrepresents what education is and what it is to receive an education. It betokens an impoverished view of human life and of what makes it distinctive.

That's a general statement of the matter, and obscure in the way that general statements often are. It's time to tie it down to particulars. Take the case of reading. Reading is often referred to as one of the basic skills in which pupils are expected to be competent by the time they leave school. Indeed the fashion now is to speak of reading *skills* (in the plural) and to treat them as continuous with various prereading skills, *e.g.* visual discrimination skills, auditory skills, etc. Reading a page of prose is, it is held, a highly complex skill involving a whole hierarchy of sub-skills; and the more complex the passage—a speech from Shakespeare, say—the greater the skill needed to read it properly. Literary critics are those who have brought this skill (as the expression is) "to a fine art," who are at home among the multitude of conventions and forms, and are able to extract the maximum amount of significance from what they read. (Not everybody would go as far as this. I've heard teachers of English contrast "literature" courses for good pupils with "skills" courses for the "less able.")

But reading, it seems to me, can refer to two kinds of capacity which it's important to distinguish. I put it that way at first, although I would say that the one is only an abstracted aspect of the other. There is, to begin with, the capacity to translate marks on a page into sounds, into words, into meaning, and which involves visual discrimination, mastery of the convention that we proceed from left to right, memory and so on. This is the kind of reading we expect children to be mechanically competent in by the time they leave school. There is a more or less well-defined ceiling to "reading competence" in this sense, although we can continue to gain in facility, take speed-reading courses and the like. But these mechanical "reading skills" run into and overlap with "reading skills" in a different sense (so called at least)—"skills" of comprehension and appreciating significance. To these, by contrast, there seems to be no discernible ceiling. It is open to argument whether one has "read" a certain passage properly, in this sense of "reading," in a way in which it's not open to argument whether one has "read out" what is actually printed on the page. (I leave aside cases of disputed pronunciation, which do not raise the kind of problems presented by conflicting interpretations of a passage). It is "reading skills" in this second sense—and here perhaps I ought to interpose a doubt whether "skills" is quite the word for them—which people have in mind when they speak about the "skills of the critic," or when they speak of the critic or ordinary reader "decoding" or "deciphering" highly complex "messages" (in the process assimilating critical reading to the mechanical "reading out" aspect of primitive reading).

Now in a way I couldn't care less if somebody wants to speak of learning to read in the first sense as learning a skill—certainly there are skills involved—but I begin to feel uneasy, begin, that is, actively to think there's something wrong, when people speak in these terms of the business of learning to respond sensitively and intelligently to a piece of writing: a poem, say, or a friend's letter. Here, I insist, is a very different sort of capacity. The word "skill" doesn't begin to account for it. But really I think that's true of reading at any stage. What I have referred to as

the skill of "reading out" and which naturally tends to be the teacher's and child's first concern in the early years at school, is never more than an abstraction, an aspect of any child's actual reading. After all, as I said at the beginning, "reading out" is bound up with meaning, that is with *sense*, and is never simply a matter of translating letters into sounds. Don't we often say that the way in which a person has read out a passage makes nonsense of it? A machine could scan a page of print and make the appropriate noises, but would we want to say that the machine had *read* the passage in question? In the way that we expect children to be able to read? In other words, when people speak of reading as a skill, at whatever level, what they are doing is identifying reading with something which is only a bare aspect of itself. Reading involves skills, if you like, but is not itself a skill or compendium of skills. My reason, my *immediate* reason, for wanting to say something of this kind is that, if you think of the things which pass for "skills of the critic," viz. skills in textual analysis, skills—God help us—in the literary-critical language game, or what have you, they are all things which can on occasion—which may be often or always—come between the reader and the work being read. Whereas I'm saying that, whatever skills are picked out in the reading of prose or poetry, your ability to read consists not in the exercise of those skills but in the ability to use them properly, so that they don't get in the way of your responding as fully as possible to what is before you.

It's true that in order to be able to read properly you have to be able to bring something to your reading. But what you have to bring isn't skills; it's yourself. It is precisely this point that Lawrence is making in his essay on Galsworthy when he says, "A man with a paltry, impudent nature will never write anything but paltry, impudent criticism."[2] To be a good critic, in the sense of being someone who can read properly, you need to be more than a skilled operator or an "expert." You need to be someone to whom literature speaks. And literature—if I may express it so—only speaks to those who are worth speaking to, who are real men and women with something to say for themselves. If you haven't anything to say for yourself, then no repertoire of "reading skills," no mastery of the "register" of critical parlance, can compensate. Literature only speaks to those in whom it can find an echo, those who have some depth to them, who have lives of their own, feelings and interests. And—it goes without saying—the more of yourself you're able to bring to your reading the more literature says to you. Its inexhaustibility is the reflection of something which is inexhaustible in each and every human being. That's why, so long as you remain alive—I mean really alive, not just ticking over—you are always finding new things, new beauties and new sources of significance, in the works of literature that you read.

That, or something like it, is what reading is. "Skill," I have intimated, doesn't begin to do justice to it. And the point I'm making isn't confined to reading. Having sketched out in an earlier draft these remarks on reading, I was encouraged to come upon what struck me as a similar train of thought in an article by Rush Rhees called "Wittgenstein's Builders," only there it was in connection with learning to *speak*. In the article in question he's concerned with what language is, and the links between understanding *that* and understanding what speaking is. To learn to speak is not, he argues, just "to learn to make sentences and utter them." And he goes on:

> Nor is it like learning a game. We may *use* something like a game in teaching him. We say his sounds back to him, and in this way we bring him to imitate other sounds we make. And this is a game. But it is not what we are trying to teach him. And if all he learns is to play like this, he will not have learned to speak. He will never tell you anything nor ask you anything either . . . If he can speak. He has got something to tell you. Now one reason why a conversation is not like playing a game together is that the point of the various moves and counter-moves is within the game. Whereas we may learn from a conversation and from what is said in it. Generally each

of us brings something to the conversation too: not as he might bring skill to the game, but just in having something to say.
I have wanted to say that learning to speak is not learning *how* to speak or how to do anything. And it is not learning the mastery of a technique . . . Language is something that can have a literature[3].

There are two points I want to draw attention to here. There is the general point that learning to speak is not learning a mastery of a technique, is not learning *how* to do anything, is not a matter of acquiring a skill. Secondly, there is the positive suggestion that learning to speak is coming to have something to say. The differences Rhees brings out between learning to speak and learning a skill (playing a game) are helpful, I think. What I'm less happy with is the account he goes on to give of "having *something* to say"—although I can't be sure I've understood it. It seems to me to leave open the possibility that speaking is a kind of skill after all. He says, for example, that learning to speak involves coming to have sense of the bearing which different remarks have on one another—he insists on the internal meaning relation between the different parts of a conversation—and being able to tell the difference between sense and nonsense. But that allows it to be said that learning to speak may yet be learning a skill, namely the skill of keeping up your end of a conversation, which may involve skill in appreciating the bearing of one remark upon another, skill in spotting when the conversation is beginning to flag and so on. So far as I can see, Rhees doesn't distinguish between a conversation in which you know what it makes sense to say, right enough, but aren't particularly interested and don't have any real contribution to make—where you're just going through the motions—and a conversation in which you're engrossed. My doubts, in short, concern the force of Rhees's contention that to have learned to speak you must have something to say. Surely the stress ought to be on your having something to say, not just anything at all? To have something to say (something to tell another person or a question to put) is not just to be able to keep the conversation going. You only have to think of question-time after some seminar papers! To have something to say you must have something to offer on the matter in hand—not merely something relevant, but something, some actual (as opposed to temporarily assumed) perspective of your own, which can be set against the perspective of the man you're talking to. Without this kind of polarity—which allows for corroboration of what he has said, and without the polarity there is no true corroboration—the conversation doesn't flow; it simply marks time.

I agree with Rhees that to have something to say is to have something to bring to the conversation, but what you bring to the conversation, if it's to be a *real* conversation, is not tid-bits of information ("something to tell") or auditory and visual cues or even a good line in patter, but yourself. It's yourself you hazard. In other words, having something to say is a matter of being *someone*, someone, that is, with his own unique outlook on things. When we remark of somebody that he hasn't got anything to say for himself, we don't mean that he can't conduct a conversation or that he doesn't know things but that he isn't worth talking to. It's instructive in this connection to think of something which you often hear parents saying about their children, at the stage when they are moving away from mere prattle and are beginning to assert their own point of view—"Do you know, I can really talk to them now"; and how delighted for the most part they are about it. It's accompanied by a sense of their coming to be people in their own right ("She's no longer just a child"). Learning to speak then—I'm grateful to Rhees for this way of putting it—is coming to have something to say. But coming to have something to say—and this, I feel, Rhees doesn't sufficiently bring out—is coming to be a person in your own right, with outlook and interests of your own. And the richer the interests you have to bring to a conversation the more you have to say.

There is, therefore, a need to distinguish between learning to speak, where that means learning to articulate clearly and pronounce correctly and observe grammar (and even in the sense of learning the conversational skills: learning not to interrupt other people in mid-sentence, learning when to change the subject, when to let somebody else get a word in edgeways and so on) and the kind of learning to speak I've been emphasizing here, which is a matter of *who I am*, not a matter of what I can skillfully do. Though, as was the case with reading, I don't really think that what I've referred to as "conversational skills" are properly called "skills" at all, even if in the exceptional case—by the professional interviewer, perhaps—they are practiced as skills.

And what is true of "reading" and "speaking" is true of other human activities often described as skills. It's true of "writing," for example, and of "thinking"—despite what Edward De Bono has to say on the subject. (The latter can only make what he says about thinking plausible by concentrating on one kind of thinking, the kind of truncated thinking which goes into "problem-solving." As for thought about ultimate ends—"What for? What ultimately for?"—which deserves to be called "thinking" if anything does, it's inconceivable without the thinker having something to say, his own pondered sense of things.) Similarly, "social skills" does not begin to encompass all that's involved in loving other people or trying to act rightly by them. Here, no doubt, what's important is not what I have to say but what I have to *give*—what I have to give being again myself, and not anything of the nature of skills. Art is not a skill, nor is town planning, politics or decorating your home. (Though there are specialists and consultants on these matters. The fact that we take their pretensions seriously shows the mess we're in.) None of these things is a skill because none of these can be carried on without taking on the physiognomy, as it were, of the person doing them, because the way in which a person does these things (reads, speaks, writes, thinks, behaves towards other people), the kind

On making a flame leap from mind to mind

I have observed that lots of bad textbooks have been written for, or even written by, teachers in departments and colleges of education. So I have no doubt that if the demand for "trained" university teachers grows, there will arise to meet it a supply of logically incompetent teacher-trainers, who fancy that having studied one or other of these bad textbooks they are competent to train people in the teaching of logic.

I have not considered one possible answer to my argument about self-perpetuating skills: someone *might* protest that the skill that needs to be supplied to a man already skilled in *doing* logic in order that he may competently *teach* logic is not the skill of teaching *logic* but the skill of teaching—period. Perhaps in refuting this suggestion I am knocking down a man of straw: certainly I hope so, for the suggestion seems to me incredibly silly. To spell out what the suggestion would be: there would supposedly be a general and teachable skill of teaching, and by combining this with some particular skill like riding, music, chemistry or logic a man is to become competent to teach others how to ride horses, make music, carry out chemical researches, or do logic. If anyone actually thought *this*, he would be fatuous as the legendary student who tried to write an essay on Chinese metaphysics by combining information from two non-over-lapping encyclopedia articles, one on Chinese and the other on metaphysics.

I have so far not argued positively in favor of the thesis that logic, *logica docens, is* a self-perpetuating skill: only that there must be self-perpetuating skills if any skill is to be taught, and I see no reason why *logica docens* should not be one. But in *conclusion* I should like to sketch the reasons for positively holding that this skill can only be self-perpetuating. To understand logical notation even at a very elementary level, people need certain fundamental insights: for example, they need to distinguish, as Frege says, between concept and object. This is not a matter of logic's dictating to us what sorts of objects we are to acknowledge as existing; it is a matter of good logical grammar; people who fail to grasp the distinction in practice will write down would-be formulae that are sheer gibberish and are uninterpretable. But the insights required are themselves not conveyable in logically well-formed sentences: "No concept is an object" for example is something quite impossible to translate by any well-formed formula in Frege's or Russell's notation. In manipulating his symbols, the master of logic *shows* his grasp of a principle like this; but he cannot *state it* in a logically correct sentence; all he can do is to utter quasi-sentences of a sort that experience shows sometimes enable the pupils to catch on. Whether they have indeed caught on is testable, even by university examinations; but there can be no art of teaching, except exhibitions of logical skill, with helpful noises of the kind I just illustrated in a brief sample, in the hope that the skill will be conveyed (in Plato's phrase) like a flame leaping from mind to mind. And when we see things from this angle, how futile and sophistical will appear the claim to *train* people in the art of making the flame leap!

—P. T. Geach. "On Teaching Logic." *Philosophy*, January, 1979.

of world he creates about him, testifies to the kind of person he is[4]. And that isn't so with a skill.

Now, as I suggested earlier, the question is likely to be put, why it's so important to insist that there are these matters which are not matters of skill, and that to have learned to speak, think, love, etc., is not to have learned a skill. After all, I haven't denied that there are skills of a kind involved in these things, that they have their aspect of skill. Does anything very much hang on whether we call them skills or not?

Well, it depends. What I have been moving towards, in all that I've been saying about "reading," "speaking" and the like and in the distinction I've been making between two different "kinds" of reading, speaking, etc., is that certain of the activities in which we engage stand in a peculiarly intimate relation to the kind of people we are. Whereas in ordinary speech there is something—"trivial" isn't the word—something peripheral, perhaps, in the exercise of a skill. The exercise of a skill (typing, say) takes place, so to speak, at a remove from the person exercising it. You can be a good typist (this is simplifying it a bit) without being a good man. This is connected to the point that a skill can be exercised or not depending on whether its possessor wants to exercise it or not. It is no part of what is involved in possessing expertise in a skill that you should exercise it unfailingly, irrespective of your own wants in the matter. That's what makes it unconvincing to describe somebody who "knows how to behave" or "knows the difference between right and wrong" as having the *skill* of behaving or the *skill* of telling right from wrong. For, as ordinarily understood, the man who knows how to behave is the man who does actually behave as he should; not the man who *could* do so if he set his mind to it. So with other so-called skills. The man who knows how to read in the fullest sense is the man whose reading *is* sensitive and intelligent, who, whatever he reads, reads sensitively and intelligently; not the man who *could* read sensitively and intelligently if he took it into his head to do so. Can one even imagine such a thing?

The point I'm making is that the activities I've been singling out are far more intimately related to ourselves than skills which we can exercise or not depending on our inclination, such as being able to do handstands, read music or repair car engines. And the contrast I have in mind is not simply that between activities which people can, at will, opt not to engage in—doing handstands, for example—and activities, such as thinking and having dealings with other people, which you can't opt out of just like that. The question for me isn't whether you can or cannot withdraw altogether from certain activities, but whether, in the case of certain activities, you can really be said to *know how to do them* if you don't act up to your own best insights in the matter. A man *can* decide to disregard moral restraints in his treatment of other people—but then we don't say of him that he knows how to behave.

One way of putting the difference between what I'm quite happy to have called "skills" and what I wouldn't be happy to have called "skills" (thinking, reading, loving and so on) is to say that the latter capacities are capacities *of* our humanity and not simply capacities which certain human beings—or even all human beings—happen to possess. That's to say, they are capacities which go to define what a human being is. That would explain the connection I pointed to earlier between being able to read, in the sense of being someone to whom literature speaks, or being able to speak, in the sense of having something to say, and being a real human being. Your being *somebody*, a particular man or woman with your own outlook on things, and your being able to read, speak, think, etc. are two sides of the same thing. And that gives us a hint why to refer to such capacities as skills is to travesty them. It suggests that they are mere appendices to our humanity and that we might not possess them without our humanity thereby being impaired; instead of which they are continuous with our humanity and constitutive of it. And the effect of that is two fold: it diminishes those activities by making it seem that they belong only to the surface of one's life, and it diminishes our humanity itself, which is emptied of concrete significance and turned into an abstraction.

Take the first part of this, that to say of writing or of behaving properly to other people that it is a skill is to diminish or trivialize it. There are, I believe, occasions when we find it natural to say of someone that he writes with great skill or that he uses words in a masterful way. But to say this of somebody is always, it seems to me, to imply that one has reservations about what's being done. It seems the kind of thing that might properly be said of a professional diplomat who had found a form of words to reconcile two parties to a dispute, or of an experienced journalist or copywriter. But to say it of Lawrence, for instance, would jar, since it would suggest that his relation to the language of his novels is external and manipulative, that he was there on the outside looking in and deciding to use *this* word to get *that* effect and so on. And the inadequacy of this in discussing the relation of a great writer to his language needs no stressing. Then again, skills are at bottom a matter of adapting means to ends, and the position of a great writer in his writing is not that he has something to say and must find the means to say it, must find *how* to say it. The question of ends, of *what* to say, is precisely the thing at stake (and I don't mean that great writers are characteristically at a loss for what to say—they less than anybody, perhaps); the question of *how* to say it is solved in solving the other. To refer to this—"divination" is a word that comes to mind—as a skill seems to me to deny that it's the whole business of the writer to surrender himself to language in order to find himself again, to find himself and what he has to say simultaneously *in* language, to let language speak for him. By contrast, the person who exercises mastery over language, who gets it to do what he has already decided in advance he wants it to do, is patently not letting language speak for him, whatever else he's doing. (This again has to do with "skills" not being serious[5].)

In the same way I have no particular objection to the term "social skills" as applied to the manoeuvering of a society hostess or to the adroitness with which the professional salesman sounds out and then softens up a prospective client. It is in its application to those who love us, our friends and close family, which I find grotesque. In the first place, it's obvious that genuine affection often shows itself in what are, we say, *clumsy* gestures, clumsy expressions of thanks, for example—at·any rate in something the very opposite of the assured and the skillful[6]. Of course we do also say that real affection expresses itself with a tact and delicacy—which, be it noted, are terms with a potentially moral charge lacking in "skill"—beyond the reach of any mere social virtuosity. There is no contradiction here. What's crucial is not the presence or absence of "social skills," but the fact that they are subordinated to something else, in virtue of which they're taken out of the realm of "skill" altogether. For example, F. R. Leavis is quite happy to speak of great writers as having a technique (for which read "skill") so long as he can go on to qualify it as a "technique for sincerity." But a technique *for sincerity* is, I would say, not really a technique at all. The addition "for sincerity" isn't simply a further specification telling you what kind of technique it is. It's an indication that what you have to deal with is something with a quite different character from a technique *tout court*. A technique for sincerity is not, as other techniques are, something which is at the service of ends decided on in advance. It is itself a means of exploring ends, of exploring what it is I want to say—that, surely, is the force of insisting that it is a technique for *sincerity*. Of course, in discovering—provisionally, it may be—what I want to say, I also discover the wherewithal to say it. That's why it can seem like skill, even the highest skill of all, in the use of language. And in one's dealings with other people the same kind of "technique for sincerity" has a place—its polar opposite is the sort of thing you get in the writings of Dale Carnegie. Indeed the way someone like John Wilson talks about a "skill" component in moral action is, in effect, a denial that anything beyond the range of human relationships envis aged by a Dale Carnegie is possible. The skill he has in mind is something which is at the disposal of intentions formulated in advance. We reason about what we ought to do, come to a conclusion, and then skill comes in the way in which I carry out the conclusion, in the success with which, for example, I help out my struggling neighbor. Morally speaking, though, it's hard to see what the significance of that kind of skill is. After all, even if I bungle my act of kindness it still *is* an act of kindness, and the unlucky recipient may so far be grateful, on the principle that it's the thought that counts. But a moral "technique for sincerity" is exploration in action of *what* I ought to do no less than of *how* I ought to do it. The two things go together. It's a bringing together of myself and my sense of what I ought to do, in such a way that there's no possible gap left between intention and execution of the sort which Wilson's "moral skill" exists to bridge. We can, if we like, speak of skill in this connection, by way of emphasizing the identity of intention and execution. But if we do so we should be conscious that we are using the word "skill" in an unusual sense. It is not skill in carrying out intentions conceived of in advance. In a way it's more like adapting one's intentions to one's actions (but that isn't it either). If anything, it is discovering what one intends in the very process of acting, discovering the good one intends in the process of seeking to act rightly.

What I've been trying to explain is how it is that, although—as I want to maintain—reading, writing, thinking and acting rightly by other people are not skills, they nevertheless have an aspect of skill and can even appear in that light to the onlooker who casts his eye over the works of critics and novelists, great thinkers and good friends. My point throughout is that the achievements of the great writer, say, which impress such an onlooker as the most complete manifestations of the writer's skill in language are, in reality, the result of his having a relationship to language which is the opposite of the merely skillful writer—which is why you can't get any closer to those achievements by becoming more and more skillful. You have to take a different direction

entirely. (If, as it seems to me, there are echoes of this in certain Taoist sayings about the highest skill being the absence of skill, the highest goodness the absence of goodness, etc., perhaps this is what is meant).

Speaking of a "technique for sincerity" is, I said, a way of denying that what's involved is mere skill or technique[7]. What marks out the great writer, accordingly, is that he turns his gift for language to the exploring of what he has to say. (If his "skill" lay simply in adapting means to preconceived ends, that would be unintelligible.) And his exploring of what he has to say is not an exploring of what *anybody* might say, but an exploring of what *he* wants to say. The question he puts to himself, implicitly as it were, is "What way of talking about *this* (*e.g.* of telling this story) represents my profoundest realization of it?"— and the way of talking then precipitated *is* the story, or the poem as the case may be. The distinction between what he is trying to say and how he is trying to say it is here done away with. And what I would say about this is that what he has to say is not something already *there*, not something which exists in advance of his exploratory creating. It is something defined, so far as it can be defined, by it and in it. That's yet another reason why it's unsatisfactory to describe the great writer as exercising a skill. For "skill" suggests that there is some yardstick available for measuring success or lack of success. But what could "success" mean here? It certainly can't mean that the writer has found exactly the right words to express what it was he was trying to say. For, apart from what he *did* say, we have no way of knowing what he was trying to say. (No more has he, incidentally[8].)

The thing to notice is that, because what's involved in this is a defining of what *he* has to say (and *mutatis mutandis* for what goes on in thinking, moral reflection, home building and so on) and not of what *anybody* might say, the answer he gives to the question is at the same time a redrawing, a redefining of himself. And the integrity, the wholeness of the self so defined is bound up with the integrity (here a matter of wholeheartedness) with which the exploratory redefining is conducted.

We come back again to the intimate connection between the activities which I've been insisting are not matters of skill and the nature of the self, the person. Throughout I've been distinguishing activities to engage in which is to redefine oneself and activities of which this is not true, which one can freely engage in while remaining, in one's inmost self, unimplicated and unchanged. To adapt an expression of I. A. Richards, the former are activities in which the growth of the self—an individual self, of course, not just selfhood or "mind" in general—primarily shows itself. They are *par excellence* activities in which a man expresses, or rather recreates, himself; in which his whole self hangs in the balance (hence their seriousness). And that accounts, without doubt, for the central place they have in education. For education, whatever else is involved in it, is about the individual person and his development; and it's been my contention that only that which is more than simply a skill can contribute to that development, the continual forming and reforming of the person. So that when receiving an education is conceived of, as it so often is today, in terms of acquiring skills, it is conceived of as something superficial. It isn't seen as affecting the person. The proliferation of "skills" talk in talking about education is an unwitting acknowledgement on the part of our educators that they don't think that an education, in the sense of something that bears directly on the person, is possible. At heart they don't think that education is possible. Learning things, yes. There are all kinds of things that we can "tack on" to people or that, given a bit of encouragement, they'll tack on to themselves. And that's all that's left of the idea of self-development: each of us a little hook on which is hung one skill after another, like coats in a school cloakroom. Not that when education *is* thought of as having a bearing on the person the idea is of the teacher masterfully forming the pupil—the pupil *forms*

himself in relation to his teacher. That's to say, if it takes place at all.

Now I said that if the capacities which I called capacities of our humanity are regarded as skills, this has implications not only for the capacities themselves, which become comparatively unserious and superficial (issues of responsibility, for example, shifting elsewhere, to the choosing of ends), but also for our very notion of the self, which is correspondingly impoverished. And I'd like finally to have a look at this: the second strand of my argument. So far I've been saying that to think of reading, writing, thinking, one's ability to get on with other people, and one's capacity for love as skills is to remove them from oneself. They form no part of me however much expertise I acquire in them. In fact perhaps the greater the expertise the less I, personally, am involved (the so-called "impersonality" of the "expert"). But, taking the matter further, if everything is regarded as a skill indiscriminately then nothing is left to the self. It becomes a mere mathematical point, an abstraction. And what this means for human responsibility is worth looking at.

There is an unconsciously revealing remark by Edward De Bono in his recent book *Teaching Thinking*. It comes at the end of his chapter on thinking as a skill.

> The aim is to produce a detached thinking skill so that the thinker can use his skill in the most effective way. A thinker ought to be able to say, "My thinking on this is not very good," or, "My thinking performance is poor in this area," without feeling that his ego is threatened.[9]

What De Bono has in mind here is partly that we can take steps to *improve* our thinking. But there's more to it than that. He also wants to say that the man who acknowledges that he isn't thinking properly on some issue ("I'm awfully stupid today") shouldn't take it personally. Instead, he should stand back from his own thinking, from his failure to think something through, in the sense, that is, of seeing it as merely a technical problem to be overcome. And I was reminded, by force of contrast, of Wittgenstein's remark to Paul Engelmann, "I wish I were a better man and had a better mind: the two are really the same thing."[10] The difference between Wittgenstein and De Bono is not simply that Wittgenstein takes his failure to think his problems through to heart, takes it personally and is profoundly distressed by it. What's more important is that you feel it would never have occurred to Wittgenstein to regard it simply as a threat to his ego. What is conveyed by Wittgenstein's remark, but not at all by the language which De Bono thinks it appropriate to use, is that the issue is one of responsibility, of *personal* responsibility. Wittgenstein sees himself as responsible for his thinking and for his failures in thinking in much the same way as he sees himself as responsible for the way in which he lives, and the kind of man he is. His worrying over his work and his worrying over his sins couldn't be dissociated, as his reply to Englemann indicates. And that gives us a clue to what's going on in those who talk the language of skills. What it comes down to is an evasion of responsibility. All this talk of threats to the ego is talk of a man who won't face up to responsibility for his own thinking. It comes over *as a threat*, as a challenge from the outside, only because he won't acknowledge the challenge within himself. He doesn't want to believe that it's himself he's exposing whenever he writes or speaks; because in that way he can always dissociate[11] himself from what he has done if it comes in for criticism. It's a way of disowning responsibility in advance for the outcome of his actions. If there's anything wrong with his thinking or with his treatment of other people or with the kind of world he creates about himself, it's because he didn't have the requisite skills. That's the extent of it. Something that might have been put right if he had taken the right courses or attended the right T-groups. Of course, there's a sense in which he doesn't escape responsibility even then. He remains responsible for the fact that he hasn't acquired the right "social skills" (if that's what's in question). And yet—it cannot be without significance—how much happier people are to own up to their "mistakes," their "errors of judgment," their "stupidity" even, than to say, "I behaved badly and I'm thoroughly ashamed of myself." The kind of responsibility involved in my failure to acquire

some skill is an attenuated thing—it's so indirect that it passes for failure of skill itself—compared to my responsibility here and now for being the kind of person I am. Furthermore, it goes without saying, even *that* responsibility only survives if there are areas of my life which are not absorbed into skills. If everything is a matter of skill, if living itself is a skill or something akin to it (I've heard people speak of the "art of living"), then the kind of contrast I've been making between that for which I can be held to account and that for which I can't disappears.

The attempted translation of these central human capacities into skills is thus a means of protecting oneself, of rendering oneself in one's most inward self inaccessible to criticism. It implies, I said, an impoverished view of the capacities themselves. De Bono, for example, identifies thinking with the kind of instrumental thinking which goes to the achieving of preconceived goals. Thinking for him *is* problem solving. As to there being thought of a different order, thought about ends, he doesn't have anything to say. Leavis's "heuristic thought" of the great novelists and poets presumably wouldn't be recognized by him to be proper thought at all. And that is part of the price you have to pay to be perfectly invulnerable. You cut yourself off from having any adequate idea of what thinking is, of what it is to read something, what it is to write, what it means to *live* properly—what it means to live. Really, to be perfectly invulnerable, to have done with responsibility once and for all, you must be prepared to give up understanding *anything*. Yourself included.

That's the final price to be paid. You have to give up having any coherent idea of yourself. When I have withdrawn myself from each and every sphere in which I may be exposed to criticism, be judged and found wanting, when I've whittled myself away to vanishing point, and skills—my social skills, intellectual skills, skills in evaluating—fill the vacuum left behind, then it's true the question of my responsibility for what I do will hardly arise. But the reason it won't arise is that there will no longer be anyone or anything to be responsible. To all intents and purposes I will have ceased to exist. Of course, all that is fantasy. If you think for a moment seriously you'll see that everything can't be a skill. If I am not *here* in my thinking and not *there* in my bringing up my family, then I must be somewhere. *Somebody* must be exercising these skills. The intelligibility of talk about skills depends on not everything being a matter of skill. If you take away the contrast between what is skill and what is not, then the self—myself, yourself—becomes an abstraction, a mere possible locus of skills, a kind of argument place. And in becoming an abstraction it loses any dimension within which it might develop. I become a kind of object to myself, purposes well up in me and I throw myself into acquiring the skills necessary to fulfill them; but I am as far from being responsible for these being my purposes as I am from being responsible for my skill in pursuing them.

If you don't hold out against talk of "skills," if you don't see that "skills" only account for part, and that the less important part, of what we learn, you are driven to conclude that there is nothing for which a man can be held responsible or in which he can see himself mirrored. You are left not knowing where you are or who you are. And it's no good saying (as I half-thought of saying myself) that it's only a way of talking, that people don't mean to be taken literally, and that many of those who speak of "skills" would resist any abasement of the intelligence or any hankerings after irresponsibility of the kind I've described. As if a way of talking were merely *that*, and wasn't at the same time a way of thinking and feeling. As if the words you use didn't betray you into the attitude of mind to which they correspond.

Notes and References

1. *E.g.* John Wilson: "We are out to develop a type of person who is 'morally educated' in the sense of being able to use the moral skills properly . . . We may be able, when we have adequate tests, to discover certain people who are particularly good at using the skills and who could therefore count as moral authorities to be admired and copied . . ." *Moral Education in Schools* (London, Longmans, 1968), p. 7 and pp. 8-9. See also the writings of Michael Argyle.

2. *Selected Essays* (London, Penguin, 1950), p. 217.

3. *Discussions of Wittgenstein* (London, Routledge & Kegan Paul, 1970). Quotations from p. 89, p. 81, p. 82, and p. 83 respectively.

4. Where, as is often the case, those concerned are "faceless," what they do testifies to their lack of self.

5. "I do not command language; but from first to last language commands me. She doesn't wait upon my thoughts. It is from my living relationship with her that I draw my thoughts, and she can do with me as she wants. I respond to her every word. For it is from the word that my nascent thoughts spring and in return shape the language which conceived them. This gift of fecundity with thought brings one on to one's knees and makes a duty of any expenditure of anxious care. Language is sovereign over thought; and the man who contrives to put thought before language, she'll do the housework for, but deny him her womb." K. Kraus, *Beim Wort Genommen*, pp. 134-5.

6. I'm reminded here of Emma's speculations about Frank Churchill: "My idea of him is that he can adapt his conversation to the taste of everybody, and has the power as well as the wish of being universally agreeable"—and Mr. Knightley's retort, "And mine is, that if he turns out anything like it, he will be the most insufferable fellow breathing."

7. I draw attention in passing to the description in *Anna Karenina* of the painter Mikhaylov's reaction to Vronsky's praise of his "technique." "In spite of his elation, this remark about technique grated painfully on Mikhaylov's heart, and, glancing angrily at Vronsky, he suddenly frowned. He often heard the word *technique* mentioned, and did not at all understand what was meant by it. He knew it meant a mechanical capacity to paint and draw, quite independent of the subject-matter. He had often noticed—as now when his picture was being praised—that technique was contrasted with inner quality as if it were possible to paint well something that was bad. He knew that much attention and care were needed not to injure one's work when removing the wrappings that obscure the idea, and that all wrappings must be removed, but as to the art of painting, the technique, it did not exist." The whole chapter is worth examination. Part V, Ch. XI.

8. That doesn't prevent him being dissatisfied with what he's done, of course.

9. *Teaching Thinking* (London, Temple Smith, 1976), p. 50.

10. *Paul Englemann: Letters from Ludwig Wittgenstein* (Oxford, Basil Blackwell, 1967), p. 5.

11. De Bono even uses the word "detached."

Logic in the Classroom

Christina Slade

Why teach logic at school? Surely the last thing the overcrowded curriculum needs is yet another subject and an abstract—even abstruse—one at that?

This paper argues, to the contrary, that logic is precisely what is required in the overcrowded curriculum; in particular for female students of mathematics. The argument is given with reference to a pilot study at a private girls' school, St. Clare's College, Canberra, the Australian Capital Territory (ACT), during second and third terms of 1986.[*]

Motivation for the Project

There are good reasons for cultivating "thinking" skills in students of either sex within all of the traditional disciplines. Thinking skills such as the ability to reason validly, to recognize inconsistency, to detect ambiguity and vagueness, to abstract and to reason analogically, are fundamental to all disciplines, and essential to getting about in the world. The rhetoric of education departments recognizes this. For instance, the ACT Schools Authority requires schools to

> provide students with the skills in reasoning so that they come to think clearly, independently and critically. (1984,5)

Yet the curriculum does not address these skills. Nor do reasoning skills develop automatically. Indeed, results from tests of reasoning skills show that those not exposed to direct training steadily develop thinking skills through primary school, but not at all in high school. Training can accelerate students' development in the primary years, and continue improvement in senior years, whereas without training grades remain constant or even decrease.[1]

The traditional curriculum caters to the teaching of reasoning only indirectly: "historical" reasoning is taught in history, "literary" reasoning in English and "formal" reasoning in mathematics. Yet neither history nor English, nor traditional mathematical training automatically inculcates the reasoning skills required. Why do we expect that reasoning skills can be picked up incidentally, in the process of learning other subjects? Just as geography and physics and chemistry and biology use mathematics yet mathematics is still an independent subject, so reasoning may need to be taught separately, although other subjects use reasoning.

Mathematics is held responsible for formal reasoning skills, and, in particular, logical skills, such as the use of proofs and the translation of everyday problems into the language of symbols. Yet traditional mathematics teaching needs supplementation in this regard. The wide variety of complaints that the young are innumerate does not derive from their inability to pass a test in algebra or geometry, but from their inability to apply their mathematical knowledge in problem solving (see for instance, the Cockroft Report, 1982). Application and problem solving require reasoning skills.

The concerns about reasoning and mathematical skills apply particularly to females. Traditionally, girls perform less well in mathematics than boys (results are summarized in OECD,1986). In Canberra, ACT, this is an important issue. Ratings on ASAT (Australian Scholastic Aptitude Test) determine tertiary entrance.

The test is designed for all high school students, like the SAT on which it is modeled. Questions must therefore be independent of specialized subject areas. Pure reasoning is at a premium. Slightly over one-half of the ACT ASAT sample questions (ACER, 1984) directly required the use of specific reasoning skills. All did so indirectly. One unit—unit 10—was actually based on J. L. Austin's (1961) philosophical discussion of performative verbs. Training in reasoning should benefit students in ASAT.

There is another factor which affects achievement in ASAT. Notoriously, girls' performances in ACT ASAT falls below that of their male peers. ASAT results for students at the pilot school, St. Clare's, in 1986 show particularly clearly their relative weakness in quantitative skills. Any question concerning mathematics of any sort is classified as quantitative, in the formal ASAT results.

For students who are fluent English speakers (the relevant group), results are as below:

TABLE 1
ASAT Results (non-ESL students)
St. Clare's 1986

Overall Score	Verbal	Quantitative
150.13	158.52	141.50
SD 23.62	21.25	25.31

Whereas boys generally score higher in the quantitative questions than on verbal skills, girls are likely to be the reverse. In 1986, the results show a mean difference between the girls' verbal and quantitative skills of over 17 marks. This is unusually high.

Why do girls perform less well in mathematics? At primary school, girls do not perform significantly less well in mathematics than their male peers, but better (Walden and Walkerdine, 1982, 10). At high school, however, girls do markedly less well than their male peers. There is a discontinuity in mathematics achievement for girls, rather than an overall pattern of low achievement. Explanations of girls' lower achievement point variously at socialization—where factors range from the paucity of female high school math teachers to the social acceptability of innumerate females—through to factors such as the well-documented claim that girls' spatial abilities are less developed than those of boys (see *e.g.*, Maccoby & Jacklin (1974), Weber (1977), Newcome & Bandura (1983) and OECD (1986)).

I do not want here to legislate on whether girls' lesser spatial abilities are caused by socialization (*e.g.*, girls are rarely encouraged to play with blocks, or engines) or are genetic (*e.g.*, males were genetically selected for hunting). However, there is evidence which relates girls lesser spatial abilities to the point of discontinuity between primary and high school. Newcome & Bandura (1983) and Weber (1977) note that the later the onset of puberty, the stronger girls' spatial abilities. Recent work by Kimura (reported in the *International Herald Tribune*, 19 November, 1988), suggests that lower estrogen levels during a female cycle are associated with improved spatial skills. If the presence of estrogen does relate to spatial skills, there may be reason to expect weaker spatial skills among girls after puberty, roughly between 11 and 14.

Algebra is generally introduced at much the same critical time as puberty—around 7th grade. Algebra is regarded as a water-shed in the development of mathematical skills, not because it involves formal operational skills, to use Piaget's term. In algebra, arithmetical skills are abstracted from. Do girls lack formal operational skills, or are they weak only in the mathematical skills through which formal operations are introduced?

Traditionally, mathematical texts have been oriented towards geometrical/spatial models of deductive thinking and abstraction. From Euclidean geometry to the current experiment in one Australian school to introduce algebra via geometry[2], mathematics has been taught in a fashion likely to favor males rather than females. Teaching techniques which rely on spatial conceptualizations predominate in mathematics. Such techniques combine with the social attitude which dictates that mathematics is an unnecessary, or even an inelegant, attainment for girls, to discourage girls in mathematics.

Females, the studies show (see *e.g.*, Maccoby & Jacklin (1974)) have greater language skills than males. At St. Clare's, girls' verbal ability clearly outstrips their quantitative skills (see Table 1). Why should we not harness girls' verbal skills in the introduction of formal operational skills, by teaching abstraction via logic? Logic is the study of valid forms of argument, in which symbols for sentences (putting it crudely) or their parts are manipulated. The skills in which formal operational thought is manifest, and on the basis of which it is tested, are archetypal logical skills: the ability to generalize, to formalize and to use variables and to investigate relations between formal properties of systems.

In teaching formal operational skills through the medium of logic, the disadvantages of girls' negative attitude towards mathematics can be avoided, whether that attitude is physiologically or socially caused. So, for instance, students need not be intimidated by factors which, like number, are irrelevant to the use of variables. Properties of axiomatic systems can as well be investigated through logic as through Euclidean geometry. Formal operations are thus introduced on familiar ground.

In the process, students should be able to develop deductive skills which they might never otherwise acquire. By associating reasoning as manifested in the practice of informal argument—a skill relevant to even the most traditional of females—and the formalisms of logic, a step can be taken towards breaking the idea that women and mathematics don't mix.

The major skill lacking in weak students of mathematics is the ability to apply algorithms to real life. Problem-solving skills rest on training in translating the language of everyday problems into that of mathematics. These skills involve close attention to the meaning of sentences and the general form they exemplify: again, the traditional province of logic.

Philosophy for Children

There is a discipline which has 2000 years of experience in teaching reasoning: philosophy. The first formal logical system was developed by Aristotle as a philosophical tool. Why is it that philosophy has not always been a component of our teaching?

Philosophy, as taught at universities is too hard, too technical for young children. But divorced from its historical and technical complications, philosophy uniquely fulfils the requirements of a method of teaching reasoning. It consists in a body of thought in which critical evaluation, rather than facts, is emphasized. Characteristic of philosophical inquiry is that the processes of thinking—above all, thinking well—and of reasoning, are themselves under inquiry. In logic, those reasoning skills are formalized and abstracted from. While philosophy must be rigorous and precise, it need not be impenetrable or cumbersome. It is surely the ideal medium for teaching reasoning.

There is another characteristic of philosophical thought which makes it peculiarly suitable for children. Once a subject has become a science, insofar as causal laws have been established between events, or has become a technical tool, the subject is no longer really the province of philosophy. Mathematics began as a branch of philosophy. Now only logic in pure mathematics, and questions about the philosophical underpinnings of arithmetic count as philosophy. Most of mathematics consists of techniques—often abstruse and very difficult techniques. The specifically philosophical questions are meta-level questions, which do not necessarily require the command of high level techniques. Philosophy does not, in this sense, presuppose technical skills. On the other hand, philosophy does not involve empirical knowledge in the way that, say, history does: a philosopher is not so much interested in the facts as in the reason for their being that way.

This has a welcome consequence. Philosophy, as a speculative discipline, relies more on reasoning skills than empirical disciplines do. No one can be creative in mathematics—or in history—without such solid grounding in the discipline that it is only acquired after years of learning. Despite our best efforts, learning the techniques and facts has become so much the focus of our education that we forget that facts can obscure the reasoning involved.

Live issues in philosophy are different. The nature of number is not laid down in a text. The teacher's ideas should be as responsive to argument as those of their students: the quality of argument is the best measure of truth in such cases. Teachers may argue better, but children are frequently both speculative and precise in their ideas. Progress in developing such ideas is most likely to occur when there is a genuine dialogue; when, that is, teachers and students jointly examine their own and others' proposals in an atmosphere of rigorous and critical argumentation.

Drawing these threads together, philosophy is a discipline consisting of formal accounts of reasoning, theories of what it is to think well, and rigorously reasoned accounts of various topics. It is not content oriented, but fosters critical thinking. The traditional method of training in philosophy is that of a rigorously reasoned discussion: the Socratic dialogue. Philosophy seems the perfect discipline to foster reasoning. One specific branch of philosophy, logic, develops the skills of abstraction and formalization, in a fashion which would allow those weak in spatial and numerical concepts to perform well. Philosophy

and logic, then, should have a place in the classroom.

There is a program which does precisely this: the Philosophy for Children program created by Matthew Lipman. Reasoning skills are taught through discussion of the genuine issues of philosophy—not indirectly as, for instance, De Bono (1984) teaches lateral thinking, using non-philosophical questions. Philosophy is not, however, presented as an historical study, but as a process of critical assessment of ideas.

The program consists of a series of novels for children in both secondary and primary schools, ranging from broader philosophical topics such as metaphysics for younger children, through the pivotal novel, *Harry Stottlemeier's Discovery*, on logic, to more applied areas such as ethics for older children. Philosophical issues—those concerns about dualism, for instance, derived from Descartes, or Aristotelian syllogistic—are introduced to children, not in a philosophical context, but in concrete examples. School children in the novels are seen worrying about these concrete philosophical problems.

Students in the philosophy classroom are then asked to discuss questions arising from the novels, helpfully signposted by teachers' manuals. The aim is that they should develop skills of rigorous critical thought and discussion. Teachers should encourage the critical assessment of one's own and other ideas by canons of rational argument, such as consistency. Eventually the group should become what Lipman (1984) calls a "community of inquiry," jointly searching for truth.

In *Harry Stottlemeier's Discovery*, the topics are predominantly logical. It describes Harry and his school friends discovering logical rules, and discussing more general philosophical questions, such as the nature of mind and language, the schooling process and reasoning itself, as well as the practical problems of the school day. They are shown in the process of working out and applying basic laws of Aristotelian syllogistic, in such a way as to develop the idea of sentences as having an abstract logical form.

Logic is a branch of mathematics. There are of course, a wide variety of logics, some of which are technically extremely abstruse. Since the advent of the propositional and predicate calculus, Aristotelian logic has been a moribund branch in the proliferating logics. The formalization of multiply-quantified sentences is complex in Aristotelian logic, and the formal semantics and syntax are not well developed. Were logic to replace high school mathematics, as Gibson (1986) suggests, then the propositional and predicate calculus would have to be the preferred vehicle.

In Australia, in particular in Queensland and the Australian Capital Territory, there have been several attempts to introduce propositional and predicate logic into the high school curriculum. In the ACT, it as an optional component of the final math assessment. Inevitably, given the prejudices of those determining entrance to higher educational institutions, it was regarded as a soft option. Only the weakest students attempted it. At St. Clare's, for instance, the lowest final year mathematics group struggled through a very narrow curriculum and they found even truth tables heavy going. The level of technical skills was too high.

In this regard, Aristotelian logic has advantages. Aristotelian logic allows a grasp of quantified sentences (such as those beginning with "All," "No," and "Some") without the technical complexity of quantifiers in the predicate calculus. Moreover, Aristotelian syllogistic requires variables only for classes, not for propositions. At this level, abstraction is little more complex than abstractions we regularly use in language. To say, "All A's are B's," is a short step from, "All gums are trees." Hence, Aristotelian syllogistic is a particularly straightforward introduction to the use of variables.

This point is relevant to objections often levelled at Philosophy for Children. *Harry Stottlemier's Discovery* is designed for 5th and 6th grade students. In a normal Philosophy for Children program, logic is introduced before the age at which children are thought to attain formal operational thought. A lack of formal operational skills has also been diagnosed in older girls who are in trouble with algebra. From a Piagetian point of view, it may seem that logic is too advanced for students not yet at the stage of formal operational thought. I suggest that such girls do not lack the formal operational skills, but rather the command of number or spatial concepts: the domains with respect to which the formal operational skills are most often introduced. Introduce such abstraction through the concrete and familiar patterns of linguistic argument, and all will be well.[3]

Implementation of the Project

The project consisted of a study of grade 7 level mathematics students at St. Clare's College. From a group of 120 girls at that level, two subgroups were considered: the top group of 30 gifted mathematics students, and the lowest group of 20 very weak students. I taught half of each group for twelve 2-hour sessions. The remaining students from each group acted as a control, for experimental purposes.

The plan of the project was to introduce logic through the use of *Harry Stottlemeier's Discovery*. The use of *Harry Stottlemeier's Discover* as an introduction to formal symbol manipulation is tangential to its intended use, as part of the Philosophy for Children program in which philosophical and logical issues interweave. Concentrating on purely logical skills inevitably alters the nature of the endeavor.

In fact, the more general philosophical aims of Philosophy for Children are also extremely important for weak mathematics students. Philosophical discussions of the nature of reality and, for instance, the reality of numbers, serve to dissolve the prejudice that algebra "does not count" or is "unreal."

For both groups, the agenda was the same, although the discussions varied. We read and discussed chapters from *Harry Stottlemeier's Discovery*. For reasons of time, and in order to fulfil the aims of improving mathematical reasoning skills in particular, we concentrated on the logical portions of the text. Formalizations were introduced which were not included in the manual: notably, variables for noun phrases. The use of Venn diagrams, rather than the Euler diagrams suggested in the text, simplified the introduction of a crude semantics for the syllogistic.

The sections of the text which dealt specifically with philosophy of mathematics were emphasized at the expense of moral and political issues. For instance, the nature and reality of "7," which arises in chapter 3, took up half a session. On the other hand, chapters 9, 10 and 11, which concern a young fundamentalist who refuses to salute the American flag, are alien to the Australian context, and were omitted. Americanisms were translated when necessary. The detailed syllabus is supplied in the appendix.

The overarching aim of the course was that students should be able to present a logical argument and criticize others' arguments. Narrower objectives were that students should be able to translate a variety of sentences of English into A, E, I, and O style Aristotelian propositions; that students should be able to identify some invalid and valid forms using these propositions, and give an informal semantics using Venn diagrams; and that students should be able to recognize when a hypothetical syllogism is valid. More general, and less testable, are the abilities we hoped to foster: the abilities to abstract, and to solve problems.

The process of developing a "community of inquiry" develops a sense of self-respect and the ability to be assertive without being aggressive which is generally conspicuously lacking in the weak student, and is notoriously absent among female students. If explanations of females' weak performance in mathematics which appeal to socialization are correct, then adjusting students' attitudes towards themselves and their ideas will be a fundamental part of the process of improving their mathematics.

Every effort was made to create a community of inquiry with the girls, insofar as an atmosphere was created in which the students and I jointly examined our own and others' hypotheses using the skills of critical investigation. This did not mean that anything they wished to discuss was appropriate. In particular, personal anecdotes were discouraged except insofar as they made a general point. For instance, in the second lesson, in the context of a burgeoning discussion on superstition, it was necessary to explain that "stories" are not always of philosophical interest. Students do not intuit the norms of scholarly, rigorously reasoned discourse without some guidance.

Evaluation

The impact of the program was evaluated both formally and informally.

FORMAL TESTING: The *New Jersey Test of Reasoning Skills* Form B (Shipman 1983), designed to accompany the program, was administered to all students as pretesting. Post-testing was performed using the same test. I use "Logic Group" to refer to the group I taught in each case.

TABLE 2
Scores of Top Year 7 Math Group

	Pre-Test	Post-Test
Control	39.34	42.33
SD	7.05	3.77
Logic Group	38.95	45.29
SD	8.50	3.81

As expected from the fact that we used the same test for pre- and post-testing, all students improved. But, adjusting for pre-tests by using analysis of covariance showed a significantly greater improvement for Group 'A than for the control (for a one-sided test, at the 5% level.) These results held, even after omitting an outlier in the experimental group.

Even more significant was the fact that the scores of none of the Logic Group students decreased in the post-test, whereas 4 of the 18 control students had lower post-test than pre-test scores. This would occur by chance with a probability of only p = .03. Over such a very short period, these results are very satisfactory.

Results in mathematics tests before and after the experiment, as compared with the control, were also considered. There was no significant correlation.

Pre- and post-testing for the weak Year 7 group had the following results:

TABLE 3
Scores of the Lowest
Year 7 Math Group

	Pre-Test	Post-Test
Control	30.57	34.29
SD	4.83	429
Logic Group	34.10	39.20
SD	5.42	7.08

These results show no significant correlation for the treatment of Philosophy for Children, although, as expected, the post-test was significantly higher scored than the pre-test. This could be a result of the intense dislike of the weakest group for testing.

INFORMAL ASSESSMENT: Observers were asked to assess the effectiveness of the program relative to the aims stated in section 3. In their judgment, the central objectives were achieved by all students. Students could use variables in describing noun phrases and types of propositions, and could perform the simple logical operations which were targeted. The nature of variables—both "pronumerals" and variables in language was discussed extensively. Observers were astonished by the comprehension of students in the weaker group.

Over the course of the teaching of each group, there was a noticeable improvement in the clarity of students' use of language, the relevance of

their comments and their logical acuity. This was noted by observers. Students developed the ability to discuss topics objectively, to criticize others' ideas and to accept others' criticisms of their own views without personal affront.

Students were originally baffled by the cooperative nature of our discussions. They were partially reconciled during the course of the classes, but when prompted by a child in the final chapter of the novel who says:

> I think we've played around enough with these silly rules . . . I think we should just have math in math class.

they again raised at the question, "Is this math?" Roughly half of each group said that they thought it was math; the other half said they'd enjoyed it, but it was "just talking." Yet the very clarity of the final discussion indicated some progress towards a "community of inquiry," in which "just talking" had been replaced by conversation governed by rigorous rules of relevance and informal logic.

The level of command of formal logic was impressive in both groups. Not only did they learn what was presented, but they also extrapolated from what they had been taught. Students in both groups immediately saw the counterexample (of identical classes) to the general rule that A propositions do not convert, for instance. The rule is that we cannot reverse the true, "All dogs are mammals," to produce another true sentence, for "All mammals are dogs," is false. But we can, they pointed out, do so for "All sisters are female siblings."

Equally encouraging was the quick proposal in the top math group for a contradictions game, when we were discussing contradictories. Someone from team 1 says a sentence: team 2 must produce the contradictory in 15 seconds. Some students were not, however, convinced by standardization of "only" sentences:

> Only girls are students at this school, as
> All students at this school are girls.

and, if their tests are to be believed, never accepted the proposed rule.

Discussion

Our society is increasingly dependent on all its members possessing basic skills of formalization, generalization and abstraction. The use of variables in computers is an obvious example, but there are many others. Every time an example is recognized as an instance of a general type, a standard form is being discerned. The skills of abstraction, of formalization and of the use of variables are principally taught through mathematics. Yet there is evidence that the acquisition of skills through spatially-dominated models discriminates against girls.

These skills are the very skills acquired in learning logic, the medium for which is ordinary language. In teaching formalization and the use of variables through logic, it is possible to avoid the risk of disadvantaging girls through their lack of spatial abilities. If, as many argue, low achievement in mathematics is due to social factors, then a change in attitude is required. Girls' need for formalization skills can be made apparent by applying formalization at first to genuine argument. In formalizing argument, girls can be encouraged to develop assertiveness in presenting their ideas: another important component in changing social modeling.

The pilot project was intended to show the viability of teaching logic to girls. To that extent, it was a complete success. All students had developed some flexibility in the use of variables. The attitudes of the groups had altered radically during the meetings to one of critical discussion. Both processes are fundamental in improving mathematical reasoning skills. The use of variables develops the formal operational skills needed for algebra and problem-solving in general. The skills of critical thinking involve general analytic abilities. By changing that attitude girls have towards mathematics and analysis, as we did, we began to alter the girls' image of themselves as non-mathematical.

At a more formal level, conclusions to be drawn from these results must be tentative. The sample group was extremely small, and the teaching time—somewhat less than 20 hours—very short. The very weak math group was ill-suited to testing using the multiple choice style of the *New Jersey Test of Reasoning Skills* since they were low achievers on such tests. Among the higher group, however, results were significantly better than the .control. Indeed, in the higher group, several students were so competent before the test as to leave little room for improvement, and hence the results may be distorted.[4]

Results in the mainstream mathematics tests for the top math group showed no significant improvement relative to their peers. Again this is not entirely surprising given the short time of the experiment. But there is another factor. In Australia, unlike in the United States, 7th grade math is a melange: geometry, number theory and so on. The experiment was, however, specifically directed at algebraic skills. We might expect clearer results among students who were studying a straight algebra course.

Of course, algebra involves more than skills in manipulating variables. Arithmetical skills are essential. But if failure in algebra is related to a lack of understanding of the use of variables, then surely it might be wise to circumvent unnecessary difficulty with number, at least to begin with. Even more significant is the fact that the skills acquired through logic are precisely the skills which allow algebra to be applied in everyday life. The ability to translate problems into recognizable forms is important in applying all mathematical and technical subjects. That skill is at the heart of logic.

I have no doubt that logic, and more generally philosophy, fill a particularly aching gap in the curriculum. They need no extraneous justification. But the skills logic engenders will certainly be beneficial in other disciplines—in particular, in mathematics.

Bibliography

ACER (1984). *Australian Scholastic Aptitude Tests: Sample Collections of Questions ACT edition*. ACER Melbourne.

ACT Schools Authority (1984). "Responsibilities for the Curriculum in ACT Schools" *Schools Bulletin* Supp, 152.

Austin, J. L. (1961). *Philosophical Papers*, OUP, Oxford.

Bernstein, B. (1974). *Class, Codes and Control*, Routledge & Kegan Paul, London.

Connell, R. W., Ashenden, D. J., Kessler, S. & Dowsett, G. W. (1982). *Making the Difference*, George Allen & Unwin, Sydney.

Cockroft, W. H. (1982). *Mathematics Counts*. Report of the Committee of Inquiry into the Teaching of Mathematics in the Schools Under the Chairmanship of Dr. W. H. Cockroft. HMSO, London.

Curriculum Development Centre (1980). *A Core Curriculum for Australian Schools*, OEC, Canberra.

De Bono, E. (1982). *De Bono's Thinking Course*. Pitman, London.

Gazzard, A. (1983). "Philosophy for Children and the Piagetian framework." *Thinking*, Vol. V, No. 1, pp, 10-14.

Gibson, R. (1986). "Logic as a Core Curriculum Subject: its case as an alternative to mathematics" *J. Phil. Ed.* 20, 21-37.

Ginsberg, H. & Opper, J. (1979). *Piaget's Theory of Intellectual Development*, Prentice Hall, New Jersey.

Levine, S. H. (1983). "The Child as Philosopher: a critique of the Presuppositions of Piagetian Theory and an Alternative. Approach to Children's Cognitive Capacities," *Thinking*, Vol. V, No. 1, pp. 1-9.

Lipman, M. (1974). *Harry Stottlemeier's Discovery*, IAPC, Upper Montclair

——— (1976). *Lisa*, IAPC, Upper Montclair.

——— (1978). *Suki*, IAPC, Upper Montclair.

——— (1980). *Mark*, IAPC, Upper Montclair.

——— (1981). *Pixie*, IAPC, Upper Montclair.

——— (1982). *Kio and Gus*, Upper Montclair.

——— (1984). "Philosophy and the Cultivation of Reasoning," *Thinking*, Vol. V

——— "Thinking Skills Fostered by Philosophy for Children," in Judith W. Segal, Susan F. Chipman and Robert Glaser, *Thinking and Learning Skills*, Vol. 1. (Hillsdale, N.J., Lawrence Erlbaum Assoc., 1985) pp. 83-108.

Lipman, M. & Sharp, A. eds., (1978). *Growing Up with Philosophy*, Temple University Press, Philadelphia.

Lipman, M., Sharp, A., & Oscanyan, R. S., (1979). *Philosophical Inquiry: An Instructional Manual to Accompany Harry Stottlemeier's Discovery*. University Press of America, Lanham, MD.

Maccoby, E. & Jacklin, C. (1974). *The Psychology of Sex Differences*, Stanford University Press, Stanford.

Matthews, G. (1978). "Critiques of Stage Theory" in (Eds.) Lipman & Sharp, *Growing Up with Philosophy*, (1978), pp. 250-260.

Newcombe N. & Bandura, M. (1983). "The effect of age at puberty on spatial ability in girls." *Developmental Psychology* 19, 215-224.

OECD (1986). *Girls and Women in Education*. OECD, Paris.

Piaget, J. (1949). *The Child's Conception of the World* (trans. J. & A. Tomlinson.) Harcourt Brace, New York.

Shipman, V. (1983). *The New Jersey Test of Reasoning Skills Form B* (and instructions), IAPC, Upper Montclair.

Walden, R., & Walkerdine, V (1982). *Girls and Mathematics: The Early Years*. Bedford Way Papers, Institute of Education, University of London.

Weber, D. P. (1977). "Sex differences in mental abilities, hemispheric lateralization and the rate of physical growth at adolescence," *Developmental Psychology* 122, 337-343.

Footnotes

* The project was funded by a SLIP grant. I must express my thanks to the Head of the school, and those teachers involved in the project.

1. The evidence I here refer to is cited by Lipman (1984), and Shipman (1983), and consists of results of *The New Jersey Test of Reasoning Skills* which I administered to my students. This test is shown to correlate highly with independent College entry tests, such as the Cornell Test, and with the SAT test, on which ASAT is based. It is a test of specific reasoning skills. In detail, students who do not study philosophy improve from Grades 2 to 4, then stay steady or decrease in scores. In those who study philosophy, improvement is accelerated at a rate of two grade levels for each year of philosophy in primary school, with continuing improvement in secondary years.

2. Mr. Ted Redden is developing the project at the Duval High School, Armidale, with the support of Dr. John Pegg of the Department of Mathematics, UNE.

3. The issue of the extent to which Philosophy for Children is consistent with Piagetian theory has been widely discussed—see *e.g.*, papers by Ann Gazzard and S. H. Levine in *Thinking*, Vol. V, No. 1.

4. In fact, the results look better still if "outliers" are removed from both the control and the Logic Group, and students who initially scored so well (at say 46/50) that little improvement was possible. These modified results show a startling correlation for the originally-average students.

Insight and Reason:
The Role of Ratio in Education

David Bohm

Insight is an *act*, permeated by intense passion, that makes possible great clarity in the sense that it perceives and dissolves subtle but strong emotional, social, linguistic, and intellectual pressures tending to hold the mind in rigid grooves and fixed compartments, in which fundamental challenges are avoided. From this germ can unfold a further perception that is not contained in the entire previously existent field of the known, within the structure of which such grooves and compartments had hitherto been an inseparable constituent for all those who had been working in the field. This perception includes new orders and forms of *reason* that are expressed in the medium of thought and language.

Let us now go on to discuss further what the essential nature of this unfoldment is.

First, it is often useful to go to the roots of words, which may show a deeper and more universal meaning that has been lost in the routine usage of the word that has developed out of tradition and habit. The word reason is based on the Latin *ratio*, which in turn comes from *ratus*, the past participle of *reri*, meaning "to think." This has been further traced back, though somewhat speculatively, to Latin, Greek, and IndoEuropean roots meaning "to fit in a harmonious way." With all these proposed meanings in mind, let us consider the word "ratio." Of course, one may have a numerical ratio or proportion expressed as:

$$\frac{A}{B} = \frac{C}{B}$$

And it was quite common in ancient times to relate harmony, order, and beauty to such ratios (*e.g.*, in music and in art). But ratio actually has a much more general qualitative meaning, which can be put as: A is related to B as C is related to D, which can in turn be more succinctly expressed as A:B::C:D.

It takes only a little reflection to see that such ratio permeates the whole of our thinking. Consider, for example, a sequence of similar objects, or points—A_1, A_2, A_3, A_4, and so forth, that are ordered along a line, or else to appear in time as an order of succession. The essence of the quality of sequentiality is that each element is related to the next one as the next one is to the one that follows, and so on. Thus we may write A_1:A_2::A_2:A_3::A_3:A_4, and so forth.

But now, we can carry this notion of ratios much further. Thus, consider a different sequence, represented by B_1, B_2, B_3, B_4, and so forth. It is evident that these two sequences are basically similar, in that A_n:A_n-*::B_n:B_{n-1} (where n stands for any number). Indeed, all sequences are similar in this way, and the quality of sequentiality is expressed in its purest form by the sequence of the numbers (the integers), so that every sequence can faithfully and accurately be denoted by a set of numbers. Thus we have come to an example of universal ratio; that is, that ratio which expresses, the essence of any and every sequence.

The notion of sequence contains implicitly and in principle unlimited hierarchy of further development. Thus, consider any straight line, regarded as made up of a sequence of small equal segments, A_1, A_2, . . . A_n. Then, because it is straight, each segment is to the next as the next is to the one that follows. Or $A_1:A::A_2:A_3::A_3:A_4$, and so forth. Let us denote this whole relationship or ratio by R_1. Now consider another line, perpendicular to the first one, with segments, B_1, B_2, . . . B_n, whose corresponding relationships are denoted by S_1. But it is clear that now any pair of perpendicular lines is related in the same way. Thus, if R_2 and S_2 are in the respective ratios defining a second pair of perpendicular lines, it follows that $R_1:S_1::R_2:S_2$. And so we obtain a *ratio or ratios*, or a relationship of relationships. Such a notion is capable of indefinite development and unfoldment to give rise to a vast and ever-growing harmonious and orderly totality of relationship in the form of arithmetic, algebra, and various other kinds of mathematics.

This totality of ratio is not restricted to thought and language. Thus, the ratio of sequences that is expressed above can be directly perceived by the senses, for example, in a row of objects, such as trees or houses. So ratio is a content that may pass freely from reason to the senses and back again. Indeed, ratio is to be perceived also in the emotions. Thus we may sense that a certain emotional response is, or is not, in proportion to the actual occasion that provoked it. It is thus clear that ratio in its totality (*i.e.*, reason) may be universal, not merely in the area of thought and language, but, more generally, in that it permeates every phase of experience.

As an example in the field of science, let us consider once again Newton's discovery of universal gravitation. The ancient Greek notion of the cosmos implied that the fundamental ratio was that between different degrees of perfection. Newton, however, perceived that the fundamental ratio was in the sequence of positions covered by a material body in successive moments of its motion, and in the strengths of the forces suffered by this body as it underwent these movements. This was stated as a *law of motion*. Such a law is an expression of ratio, which is considered to be both *universal* and *necessary*, in the sense that anything other than this form of ratio is not thought to be actually possible.

However, such necessity has always been found in fact to be limited, and not absolute. As indicated earlier, Einstein (and later still others) showed that some of Newton's ideas were only approximations, and, that new laws were needed, containing those of Newton as simplifications, as special and limiting cases. Thus, whereas Newton had, for example, considered space and time to be separate, each independent of the other, Einstein introduced the notion of a fundamental ratio or relationship between space and time. (This is indeed what is meant by the term "theory of relativity.")

What is indicated by this kind of development (which has in fact occurred in all the sciences) is that there is no fixed and final form to the totality of ratio, but that it is capable of continual unfoldment. And as we have seen, the germ of this unfoldment is the act of insight. This is an overall perception that penetrates inwardly very deep, not only in the sense that it is not restricted or confined to certain fields, but also in that it permeates the very roots of consciousness and mental activity in general. This perception then branches out into various particular media, which include the senses, the emotions, and thought (*i.e.*, the intellect). It may thus be said that reason is perception of new orders of relationship in the medium of thought. But, as we have pointed out, though its conditions are determined by the medium of thought, its implications go through the other areas of experience.

As the expression of reason in thought and language is repeated, it tends to become relatively fixed in terms of what may be called "formal logic." It is this that constitutes the main core of our ordinary thinking. Such thinking is, as we have said earlier, both necessary and useful in practical life. However, it has to be noted that it also tends to combine with fixed emotional and social responses to produce rigid grooves and closed compartments, with an attendant hubris that attributes final truth to whatever may be the prevailing general notions. And thus the formal logical approach, developed into habit and routine, has generally become a major barrier to further insight.

Insight and Education

To go on with seeing some of the implications of what has thus far been developed, it will be useful to ask what is essential to education. We shall suggest here that this is to be found by considering the deeper significance of the verb "to teach." The root of this word is in a group of Greek and Latin verbs meaning "to show." This implies that true education consists in *showing* the student something that he can then see for himself, or explore and discover for himself. Such an approach is, of course, not compatible with one in which the main object is to convey a certain content to the student, give him a certain set of facts and principles to learn, skills to accumulate, and so forth.

A striking example of education in the sense of showing is afforded by considering the well-known case of Helen Keller, who became blind and deaf at an early age and was thus unable, also, to develop the use of language. When her teacher Anne Sullivan first met the child, she perceived a "wild animal" who could not communicate or engage in any significant relationship with other people. However, she had a strong feeling of love for the child, and this gave her the energy and passion needed to face the apparently insurmountable difficulties of teaching someone with whom she had so little contact.

After some discouraging attempts, Anne Sullivan discovered a promising approach. She began to bring the child into touch contact with various objects, and to scratch the name of each object on the palm of her hand. As Helen Keller herself later commented, she regarded all this as a game. Through this kind of game there was established in her mind a connection between a considerable variety of objects and the patterns of scratches on the palm of her hand that were to be associated with .them. Then, as she says, one morning she was put in contact with water in a glass. This was puzzling, because it was not clear whether what was meant was the solid glass or its nonsolid contents. Later, in the afternoon, she was exposed to water from the pump (which was, of course, not solid at all). When the same name was scratched on her palm, she had a sudden flash of perception whose meaning was "everything has a name." This was the germ of a very far-reaching transformation of her whole life. For she began to learn words rapidly, and in a day or two could begin to exchange sentences with her teacher. From here on, she ceased to be a wild animal and developed rapidly into an affectionate child, with a lively intelligent mind, who was eager to learn and to communicate, and who was thus capable of close relationship with other people. This is indeed an example of a point that we have already made; *i.e.*, that reason is present in every phase of experience,

It is worthwhile to go a bit more carefully into the nature of Helen Keller's perception. If we let N_1 stand for the name of a certain general class of objects O_1, N_2 for the class O_2, and so forth, what she saw was the universal ratio $N_1:O_1::N_2:O_2::N_3:O_3$, and so forth, that is, the relationship of name to the class of objects of which it is the name as universal. Moreover, if we let N stand for the word "name," we can express a yet deeper perception implied in her statement as:

$$N: (N_1:O_1::N_2:O_2::N_3:O_3, \text{ etc.}): :N_1:O_1::N_2:O_2,$$
and so forth.

That is to say the word "name" is to the general relationship involved in naming as the name of any class of objects is to the objects in that class. But, of course, she did not know the word name at that time. It is thus evident that she

---

Edison's analogical thinking

Insights into the creative genius of Thomas Alva Edison, one of the most prolific inventors of all time, are emerging from a 20-year, $6 million study of his vast collection of personal papers.

The new portrait of Edison is marked by his powerful ability—never fully recognized until now—to reason through analogy. It was perhaps this trait more than any flashes of brilliance or cries of "Eureka!" that accounted for his great inventiveness. It is now thought that this hidden ability is what transformed one successful invention into another, eventually producing the phonograph, the incandescent light bulb, systems of electric power generation and motion pictures.

"These documents give you entry into the mind of one of the world's most creative people," said Dr. Reese V. Jenkins, a historian and director of the Thomas A. Edison Papers at Rutgers University in New Brunswick, N.J. "In fact," he added, "they tell a lot about the very essence of invention itself."

Edison's inventions were often much more closely related in their origins than anyone ever suspected, according to clues being gathered by Dr. Jenkins and his colleagues. For example, early drawings of his kinetoscope, a prototype motion-picture machine, reveal that it evolved from Edison's already successful phonograph.

In an interview, Dr. Jenkins said that no historian, on the basis of the visual resemblance alone, would dare suggest that Edison had been inspired by this earlier work. However, Edison also left a written record. The first page of Edison's motion picture caveat begins: "I am experimenting upon an instrument which does for the eye what the phonograph does for the ear." A few lines later: "The invention consists in photographing continuously a series of pictures . . . in a continuous spiral on a cylinder or plate in the same manner as sound is recorded on the phonograph."

"If we didn't have the earliest sketches and notes," Dr. Jenkins said, "we wouldn't be able to see the genesis. This is what I mean by being able to get into the creative mind, watching it work by analogy, from one very successful invention to another. Edison didn't ultimately solve the problem that way. The finished kinetoscope looked very different. But you can see the creative process."

According to Dr. Jenkins, the papers have already provided other insights into Edison's inventive process in addition to his powerful ability to reason by analogy. "We have this image of Edison as the lone inventor," said Dr. Jenkins. "That's not the case at all. One of his real talents and insights was that he saw he could accomplish so much more by working with a group. He's really a pioneer of team research. That's probably one of the most important things he did."

—William J. Broad in *The New York Times*, March 12, 1985.

---

must have had a nonverbal perception of the naming relationship, along with the implication that this too must have a name. So, what she saw was the germ of a vast hierarchy of universal ratio, which did indeed begin to unfold immediately and to develop very rapidly from that moment on.

A little further reflection will show that this perception could not have come from a state of low mental energy. Rather, there must have been great passion, which was capable of dissolving all the older modes of thinking built up from very early in her life. So we are justified in calling what happened an insight, in the sense in which we have been using the word. The teacher, Anne Sullivan, must likewise have had an insight to have discovered (also mainly nonverbally) the key significance for linguistic communication of the fact that each general class of objects or relationships has a name.

What happened with Helen Keller shows clearly that reason is not restricted to being a technico-practical instrument, useful mainly to order our daily activities, to organize society, and to increase the productivity of industry. Rather, it has also a much deeper and more inward significance in the sense that totalities of ratio (such as that perceived by Helen Keller in the instance cited above) permeate the whole of what we are, so thoroughly indeed that we would be hardly human without them. And here we are especially emphasizing that what plays this part is not so much the ordinary process of reasoning through formal logic, but, much more, that perceptive reason which emerges from the great energy and passion involved in insight.

Analogical Reasoning in the Scientific Community

Robert Oppenheimer

What I am going to talk about is analogy as an instrument in science and, to a much lesser extent, some slight traits of analogies between the sciences; mostly the second theme has led to misunderstanding and limitation; as for the first theme, analogy is indeed an indispensable and inevitable tool for scientific progress. Perhaps I had better say what I mean by that. I do not mean metaphor; I do not mean allegory; I do not even mean similarity; but I mean a special kind of similarity which is the similarity of constellation between two sets of structures, two sets of particulars, that are manifestly very different but have structural parallels. It has to do with relation and interconnection. I would like to quote you a scholastic comment on analogy. It is a translation of Penido, "In a very general sense every analogy presupposes two ontological conditions; one, a plurality of real beings and thus among them an essential diversity. Monism is the born enemy of analogy. And, two, at the very heart of this multiplicity, of this inequality, a certain unity."

It is a matter about which we could argue whether these structural elements are invented by us, or whether they are discovered in the world. I find it very artificial to say that they are invented, in the sense that they are more of an artifact than the particulars which they unite and describe. I may tell one incident in the long history of astronomy and physics, which makes this very vivid for me. For practical purposes, for prophecy and

ritual, the Babylonians worked out a method of predicting what days the moon would first be visible, of predicting lunar eclipses and certain rarer astronomical events. They did this by purely mathematical methods. They observed when things happened, and they got the pattern of it. They were very good. They got so good that their methods were in use in the last century in India to predict eclipses within some thirty minutes, using these two thousand year old methods. The Babylonians not only became very good, but they enjoyed it very much and they did it for fun; long after the practical reasons had gone away they published these tables, apparently as we publish articles on the internal constitution of the stars, because it is interesting. They did all of this without any celestial mechanics, without any geometry; nothing moved; there were no objects circulating around in orbits; there were no laws of motion; there was no dynamics; this was just in the field of the numbers.

You know how today we predict eclipses and first risings. It would seem to me very wrong to pretend that the mathematical regularities which were the basis of the Babylonian predictions were something they invented; it would seem to me equally wrong not to recognize in celestial mechanics as we now know it, a far deeper and more comprehensive description of regularities in the physical world. I think that not only because it is a little more useful, I think that not only because it unites more subjects, but because it reveals an aspect of the regularities of the world which was wholly unseen by the Babylonians.

Perhaps I need now to quote from Charles Peirce, and get on: "However, as metaphysics is a subject much more curious than useful, the knowledge of which, like that of a sunken reef, serves chiefly to enable us to keep clear of it, I will not trouble the reader with any more Ontology at this moment."

Whether or not we talk of discovery or of invention, analogy is inevitable in human thought, because we come to new things in science with what equipment we have, which is how we have learned to think, and above all how we have learned to think about the relatedness of things. We cannot, coming into something new, deal with it except on the basis of the familiar and the old-fashioned. The conservatism of scientific inquiry is not an arbitrary thing; it is the freight with which we operate; it is the only equipment we have. We cannot learn to be surprised or astonished at something unless we have a view of how it ought to be; and that view is almost certainly an analogy. We cannot learn that we have made a mistake unless we can make a mistake; and our mistake is almost always in the form of an analogy to some other piece of experience.

This is not to say that analogy is the criterion of truth. One can never establish that a theory is right by saying that it is like some other theory that is right. The criterion of truth must come from analysis, it must come from experience, and from that very special kind of objectivity which characterizes science, namely that we are quite sure we understand one another and that we can check up on one another. But truth is not the whole thing; certitude is not the whole of science. Science is an immensely creative and enriching experience; and it is full of novelty and exploration; and it is in order to get to these that analogy is an indispensable instrument. Even analysis, even the ability to plan experiments, even the ability to sort things out and pick them apart

presupposes a good deal of structure, and that structure is characteristically an analogical one.

Let me read you now a few relevant and eloquent words of William James. He wrote them in one of his later accounts of pragmatism, at a time when his own good sense and shrewd observation and wisdom and humanity made him aware of the fact that to say only that an idea was true because it worked was a rather poor description of what went on in science, that something was missing from that account. This is what he wrote:

> The point I now urge you to observe particularly is the part played by the older truths. Failure to take account of it is the source of much of the unjust criticism levelled against pragmatism. Their influence is absolutely controlling. Loyalty to them is the first principle—in most cases it is the only principle; for by far the most usual way of handling phenomena so novel that they would make for a serious rearrangement of our preconception is to ignore them altogether, or to abuse those who bear witness for them. . . .

The analogies in physics may very well be misleading for biologists and psychologists, because of the enormous part that rather rigid formal structure plays in physics. This structure is not perhaps necessarily quantitative, though in fact much of it is quantitative. Our ability to write down synoptic relations in symbolic form, our use of formulae, enables us to talk of vast amounts of experience, very varied experience, very detailed experience, in a shorthand way; and to point sharply to mistakes, to correct error on occasion by altering only one letter, that changes everything. These examples are thus not meant as paradigms, but rather as an illustration of the fact that, in what is regarded as one of the most rigorous and certain of the sciences, we use an instrument which has been in great disrepute, because uncritically used it can confuse invention with confirmation and truth. . . .

But for all of that I would like to say something about what physics has to give back to common sense that it seemed to have lost from it, not because I am clear that these ideas are important tools in psychological research, but because it seems to me that the worst of all possible misunderstandings would be that psychology be influenced to model itself after a physics which is not there any more, which has been quite outdated.

We inherited, say at the beginning of this century, a notion of the physical world as a causal one, in which every event could be accounted for if we were ingenious, a world characterized by number, where everything interesting could be measured and quantified, a determinist world, a world in which there was no use or room for individuality, in which the object of study was simply there and how you studied it did not affect the object, it did not affect the kind of description you gave of it, a world in which objectifiability went far beyond merely our own agreement on what we meant by words and what we are talking about, in which objectification was meaningful irrespective of any attempt to study the system under consideration. It was just the given real object; there it was, and there was nothing for you to worry about of an epistemological character. This extremely rigid picture left out a great deal of common sense. I do not know whether these missing elements will prove helpful; but at least their return may widen the resources that one can bring to any science.

What are these ideas? In our natural, unschooled talk, and above all in unschooled talk about psychological problems, we have five or six things which we have got back into physics with complete rigor, with complete objectivity, in the sense that we understand one another, with a complete lack of ambiguity and with a perfectly phenomenal technical success. One of them is just this notion that the physical world is not completely determinate. There are predictions you can make about it but they are statistical; and any event has in it the nature of the surprise, of the miracle, of something that you could not figure out. Physics is predictive, but within limits; its world is ordered, but not completely causal.

Another of these ideas is the discovery of the limits on how much we can objectify without reference to what we are really talking about in an operational, practical sense. We can say the electron has a certain charge and we do not have to argue as to whether we are looking at it to say that; it always does. We cannot say it has a place or a motion. If we say that we imply something about what we ourselves—I do not mean as people but as physicists—are doing about it.

A third point is very closely related to this; it is the inseparability of what we are studying and the means that are used to study it, the organic connection of the object with the observer. Again, the observer is not in this case a human; but in psychology the observer sometimes is a human.

And then, as a logical consequence of this, there is the idea of totality, or wholeness. Newtonian physics, classical science, was differential; anything that went on could be broken up into finer and finer elements and analyzed so. If one looks at an atomic phenomenon between the beginning and the end, the end will not be there; it will be a different phenomenon. Every pair of observations taking the form "we know this, we then predict that" is a global thing; it cannot be broken down.

Finally, every atomic event is individual. It is not, in its essentials, reproducible.

This is quite a pack of ideas that we always use: individuality, wholeness, the subtle relations of what is seen and how it is seen, the indeterminacy and the acausality of experience. And I would only say that if physics could take all these away for three centuries and then give them back in ten years, we may well say that all ideas that occur in common sense are fair as starting points, not guaranteed to work but perfectly valid as the material of the analogies with which we start.

The whole business of science does not lie in getting into realms which are unfamiliar in normal experience. There is an enormous work of analyzing, of recognizing similarities and analogies, of getting the feel of the landscape, an enormous qualitative sense of family relations, of taxonomy. It is not always tactful to try to quantify; it is not always clear that by measuring one has found something very much worth measuring. It is true that for the Babylonians it was worth measuring—noting the first appearances of the moon—because it had a practical value. Their predictions, their prophecies, and their magic would not work without it; and I know that many psychologists have the same kind of reason for wanting to measure. It is a real property of the real world that you are measuring, but it is not necessarily the best way to advance true understanding of what is going on; and I would make this very strong plea for pluralism with regard to methods that, in the necessarily early stages of sorting out an immensely vast experience, may be fruitful and may be helpful. They may be helpful not so much for attaining objectivity, nor for a quest for certitude which will never be quite completely attained. But there is a place for the use of naturalistic methods, the use of descriptive methods. I have been immensely impressed by the work of one man who visited us last year at the Institute, Jean Piaget. When you look at his work, his statistics really consist of one or two cases. It is just a start; and yet I think he has added greatly to our understanding. It is not that I am sure he is right, but he has given us something worthy of which to inquire whether it is right; and I make this plea not to treat too harshly those who tell you a story, having observed carefully without having established that they are sure that the story is the whole story and the general story.

It is of course in that light that I look at the immense discipline of practice, that with all its pitfalls, with all the danger that it leads to premature and incorrect solutions, does give an incredible amount of experience. Physics would not be where it is, psychology would not be where it is if there were not a great many people willing to pay us for thinking and working on their problems.

If any of this is true there is another thing that physicists and psychologists have in common: we are going to have quite a complicated life, The plea for a plural approach to exploration, the plea for a minimal definition of objectivity that I have

made, means that we are going to learn a terrible lot; there are going to be many different ways of talking about things; the range from almost un-understood practice to recondite and abstract thought is going to be enormous. It means there are going to have to be a lot of psychologists, as there are getting to be a lot of physicists. When we work alone trying to get something straight it is right that we be lonely, and I think in the really decisive thoughts that advance a science loneliness is an essential part. When we are trying to do something practical it is nice to have an excess of talent, to have more sailors than are needed to sail the ship and more cooks than are needed to cook the meal; the reason is that in this way a certain elegance, a certain proper weighing of alternatives, guides the execution of the practical task.

We are, for all kinds of reasons, worrying about how our scientific community is to be nourished and enough people who are good enough are to come and work with us. And then on the other side we are worried about how we are to continue to understand one another, and not get totally frustrated by the complexity and immensity of our enterprises.

I think there are good reasons of an inherent kind, beside the competitive compulsion of the communist world, why we would do well to have more and better scientists. I know that exhortation, money, patronage, will do something about this; but I do not think that is all that will be needed. I think that if we are to have some success it must be because, as a part of our culture, the understanding, the life of the mind, the life of science, in itself, as an end as well as a means, is appreciated, is enjoyed, and is cherished. I think that has to be a very much wider thing in the community as a whole, if we are to enjoy with the community as a whole the healthy relations without which the developing powers of scientific understanding, prediction, and control are really monstrous things.

It may not be so simple, to have in the community at large some genuine experience of the pleasures of understanding and discovery. It may not be simple because what this requires is not merely that this experience be agreeable, but that it have a touch of virtue; that not only the consideration of ends, of products, of accomplishments and status, but the texture of life itself, its momentary beauty and its nobility, be worth some attention; and that among the things that contribute to these be the life of the mind and the life of science. Let us try to make it so.

Reason and the Reasoner

Jen Glaser

The starting point for this paper came from an attempt to understand the differences between various definitions of critical thinking and programs developed to provide a mechanism for the strengthening of reason. It seemed to me that differences in the form of such programs—for instance, whether they involved working through a text or engaging others in discussion—should be linked to, and reflect differences in, their proponents' perceptions of what critical thinking is about. It also seemed that there ought to be a connection between any one definition of critical thinking and the corresponding program claiming to be the vehicle through which such "strengthening of reason" can be attained; and finally, that any approach to the strengthening of reason needs to be able to give an account of the connection between definitions of *reasoning*; the *reasoner,* and what counts as *success* in reasoning.

But how are we to view reasoning in the first place? I would like to contrast two understandings we have in relation to reasoning.

1. Reasoning as *preserving* truth
2. Reasoning as *determining or judging significance.*

(1). If we view reasoning as a matter of *preserving truth*, then reasoning will involve applying "the rules" to arguments correctly as we move from premises to conclusion. In this sense reasoning will be concerned with evaluating certain "objects of thought" and will involve such things as the drawing of valid inferences (in the case of deductive arguments). Such reasoning often involves retrospective reflection on our thinking in order to identify patterns of thought1 and clarify mistakes, thereby opening the topic up for further inquiry.

With the focus on *the argument,* the connection between reason, the reasoner, and good reasoning is clear (1) *Reasoning* as inference is concerned with an intellectual product—a set of propositions, or argument, that is to be evaluated; (2) *the role of the reasoner* is to recognize entailment leading from premises to conclusion; as such it is concerned with the preservation of truth. Whereas (3) *good reasoning*; on this account, amounts to applying the appropriate rules accurately (the rules of deductive inference in this case[2]). This is the view of reasoning that has traditionally been portrayed by those coming from a background in logic—and is stated in the front of many a logic textbook. Accordingly, programs for the strengthening of reasoning have been books aimed at developing logical skills—evaluating arguments, looking for consistency, contradiction, and/or fallacies of deduction and induction. On this account, reasoning is about getting from point A to point B from premises to conclusions. Thus we find statements like, "Reasoning is always to conclusions, which are the statements we use the reasoning to support or explain.... we infer that conclusion." (Richards, 1978, p. 4.)

(2) This view of reasoning can be contrasted with another which sees reasoning seen as *deter-*

mining or judging significance[3]. Such reasoning will be forward-focused and concerned with prospective truth. It could, for instance, aim to arrive at greater understanding through placing a particular in a framework and identifying the ramifications in light of some goal or value (Is this friendship?, If I don't help a friend in need, will it matter?, Is it right?, Is that the type of person I want to be?), or seeing whether seemingly disparate ideas interconnect, and if this in turn helps the inquiry proceed (Can I associate love with anguish? If so, how does that affect the way I now view this situation?). This reason is forward-focused because it involves evaluations that are based on reflection about the significance of an idea, or of one motivation over another. Such reasoning involves reflection on the quality of our motivation or understanding.

This understanding of reasoning is expressed in the everyday notion of *reasonableness*. Being *reasonable* involves making appropriate, or relevant, judgments. Judgments that are often *context-specific* are *not a matter of rule following*, and are based on *meanings* as well as truth. Reasonableness literally means "able to be reasoned with," but there are different kinds of reasons (moral, logical, aesthetic, epistemological) and being reasonable involves deciding what *kind* of reasons are meaningful given a certain context, determining what kind of discussion is appropriate and therefore what reasons are going to count. Such reasoning will not only depend on what is being reasoned about (the object of thought), but will also depend on the mindset of the reasoner who is engaged in it[5] What seems reasonable to you may not be reasonable to me simply because we do not agree on what kind of reasons count[6] (*e.g.*, I offer moral reasons for what you see as an aesthetic issue in regard to whether certain paintings should be on display or not), and this difference will not depend on the internal soundness of either your argument or mine, but on what matters to us as persons (our values and world views). On this account being reasonable depends not just on the evaluation of arguments stated in the ab-

stract,[7] but on the engagement of reasoners *with each other*. Such reasoning involves a *transaction between persons*, a transaction in which we explore what matters, or what counts for each other with the hope of developing a deeper understanding. It is this deeper understanding (either of the issue, each other, or both) that is often metaphorically referred to as "getting somewhere" in our thinking. Such reasoning certainly involves logical considerations, but is not reducible to logic alone. This notion of being reasonable also requires us to remain open to the possibility of changing our minds while engaged in the process of reasoning something out—that through our encounter with views other than our own we may change our minds about what kinds of reasons count, or about the implications for a certain course of action, and through this come to think differently about the subject at hand. This, I believe, is why dialogue and the notion of reasoning communities are so central to the concept of the reasoning individual.

Our image of dogmatic people as *unreasonable* people gives support to this view, for dogmatic people are seen as unreasonable precisely because their view is fixed and they are not *open to the possibility of transformation* through their encounter with others. They are not prepared to question (or address) whether the reasons they are offering are the sorts of reasons that count for others.

When we take "reason" as "reasonableness": (1) *reasoning* involves making appropriate judgments, (2) *the role of the reasoner* is to engage with others (to remain open to the possibility of transformation), and (3) *good reasoning* is reasoning that "gets somewhere" in the quest for meaning (or understanding/significance).

There is some similarity between the distinction I have just drawn and a distinction Ralph Johnson points to in "Reasoning, Critical Thinking and the Network problem." Ralph Johnson (Johnson 1991, p. 3), identifies two different views about the nature of reason that seem to underlie discussions about reasoning. These are not intended to be definitions of reasoning *per se*, but rather reflect different ways of thinking about reasoning. The two views are:

[R1] Reasoning as a fundamental and unique activity or process. (Which he attributes to Govier and Angeles)

[R2] Reasoning as a sequence of steps from some points to others. (Which he attributes to Walton, and inferentialism generally)

The difference Johnson points out here is one of emphasis[8], and I feel it could be a very useful one. As a "sequence of steps" the focus of reasoning is on *the argument*—the *object of thought*. While no one would deny that in following a sequence of steps someone must be doing the thinking, the validity of the steps being made are not evaluated according to the goals and aspirations of the thinker. If, however, we approach reasoning as a *unique activity or process* the focus of reasoning could be seen to be on *the engagement of the reasoner*. That is to say, the focus is on two people *engaged* in reasoning together. In this context the "sequence of steps" they follow will be only one dimension of their reasoning, and questions about the nature and purpose of the engagement may be seen as other relevant dimensions of the reasoning itself. This seems to be the case with reasonableness.

It is this engagement of the reasoner, as being engaged as *self* with *other* in *the quest for meaning*, that I think has not been given enough attention in definitions of reasoning/critical thinking. The reasoner has been thought of as derivative upon the concept of reason. This criticism has also been raised in relation to the notion of rationality. In his book on rationality, Harold Brown (Brown 1988, pp. 185-188), points out that the classic model of rationality takes the concept of *rational belief* as fundamental, and the notion of *rational persons* as derivative.[9] Philosophy, he then notes, focuses on what counts as rational belief and rational persons are persons who meet these standards. He then suggests an alternative: that we should consider the rational person as

foundational and what constitutes rational belief as derivative.

This, I feel, can equally be applied to reasoning. Traditionally we have taken the logic associated with reasoning as foundational, and the idea of reasoning persons as derivative—as persons who meet the standards of reason, *i.e.*, who reason well. If we were to invert this, the role of the reasoning person becomes basic and what constitutes "reasoning" for her will depend on her interactions with other reasoners. "Reasoning well" will then be reasoning that works (it will have gone some way toward the quest for meaning). "Reasoning" could involve having reasons, making judgments, listening effectively, and/or respecting others.

For me, one of the strengths of this approach is that it places in proper context (that is, it gives *equal* significance to) the affective and social dimensions of reasoning. "Reasoning well" as reasoning that has generated meaning, when taken from the perspective of the reasoner, will involve having reasons and making judgments, but will *equally* involve listening effectively and respecting others. Indeed, in giving primacy to the reasoning person (the *person in relation to other*) the ethics of the engagement themselves become an integral component of the theory of reason. This makes sense of the emphasis given to dialogue and dialogical experience within some accounts of reasoning, and the ethical aspect of such dialogical encounter. While the ethical dimension of conversation arises from the fact that conversation generally involves one person interacting with another—and wherever human interaction occurs there is the ethical issue of the recognition of the personhood of that individual—the ethical dimension of dialogical encounter in reasoning can be stated even more strongly. For in such encounter there is a recognition of the social construction of the self. I not only recognize the personhood of the other as a *separate* being, but also recognize the role of the other person in actually *forming* who I am (and vice versa).[10]

Traditionally, in taking the concept of *reasoning* as foundational and *reasoning persons* as derivative, the social and ethical dimensions of reasoning are seen as features not of reason itself, but of the *application* of reason within a social context. While dialogical encounter may still play a key role as the vehicle through which people and societies engage in reasoning together, such encounter is not taken to be a constitutive factor of reasoning itself. If we accept *reason* to be foundational (the logical relations between the starting point and the point at which we end up) it makes sense to talk of "reasoning individuals," and indeed reasonable societies will be groups of such individuals reasoning together. If, however, we take *reasoning persons* as foundational, the social dimensions of reasoning—the ethical and dialogical dimensions of *self* relating to *other*—are as central to what *constitutes* reasoning as inference and judgment.[11]

But before taking up the connection between dialogue and reason, let me return to my starting point, for I think this question of primacy between reason and the reasoner can be a useful one in relation to the differences between various definitions of critical thinking and programs developed to provide a mechanism for the strengthening of reason. I am thinking in particular of Matthew Lipman's "Philosophy for Children" program, with its pedagogy that involves the setting up of communities of inquiry, and Richard Paul's "Critical Thinking" program with its pedagogy that involves infusing Socrating questioning across the curriculum. Lipman and Paul are in agreement on many issues. Both see *dialogue* as central to reasoning, and both view the ultimate purpose of the "strengthening of reason" as establishing the *"reasonable"* society (Lipman, 1985, Paul, 1984). Both recognize the place of inference within critical thinking but want to say reasoning, critical thinking, is more than inference alone. Yet there are also differences in their conceptions of critical thinking, as reflected in their different pedagogies. It is here that I feel the question of primacy is useful, for the differences

in their approaches do not seem to relate to their definitions of critical thinking per se, but rather to their conceptions of *the nature of the reasoning person*. They differ as to whether *reason* or the *reasoning person* is foundational. While reference here is to Lipman's and Paul's definitions of critical thinking (rather than definitions of reasoning), the way these definitions are expressed highlights their difference in relation to the primacy of reason or reasoner. Let me give a brief outline of their positions:

Matthew Lipman (1988) defines critical thinking as:

> "skillful thinking, responsible thinking that facilitates good judgment because it (1) relies on criteria, (2) is self correcting, and (3) is sensitive to context.

Furthermore, for Lipman, critical thinking is needed in order to build *reasonable* societies.[12] Such societies will be democratic and egalitarian in nature, and shall consist of individuals who recognize their power to transform their society through democratic practice/action. Critical thinking is dialogical and involves the notion of encounter—of the *engagement* of one reasoner with another in a *quest for meaning*. Thus critical communities are essential for the development of the critical individual (Sharp 1991).

Richard Paul (1990 p. 51), on the other hand, defines critical thinking as:

> "Disciplined, self-directed thinking which exemplifies the perfections of thinking appropriate to a particular mode or domain of thought."[13]

Paul's idea of critical thinking is essentially "multi-logical thinking," it is thinking that is aware of its own subjectivity.

> "Strong sense critical thinkers . . . know they have a point of view and therefore recognize on what framework of assumptions and ideas their own thinking rests" (Paul, 1990, p. 110).

For Paul too, critical thinking is *dialogical* thinking. However, I feel Paul's position in regard to the connection between *dialogue* and the *social context* of reasoning is unclear. While not stated directly, it seems to me that Paul views the development of critical thinking primarily as the development of critical individuals, and that the existence of critical individuals will translate directly into the existence of a critical, or reasonable, society. What is unclear to me is whether dialogical (or multilogical) thinking necessitates a social context for its development, and if so, whether a critical society involves more than a collection of critical individuals. Finally, unlike Lipman, Paul does not see critical thinking as committed to particular political structures (eg., democracy), though it is clearly incompatible with some eg., totalitarianism).

I think this difference in the perception of the social dimension of critical thinking, or reasoning, can be traced back to the earlier connection drawn between reasoning, the reasoner, and what constitutes good reasoning—and whether reason or the reasoner is seen as foundational. The choice of words is interesting. Lipman uses the word *"facilitate"* while Paul uses *"exemplify."* For Lipman, *the reasoner* is foundational, and *reasoning* is derivative. The measure of good reasoning is whether the reasoning (as constituted by the reasoning person) has "worked" in *facilitating* good judgment. With the focus on *reasoning person* a community of reasoners is essential for the strengthening of reason—for what *constitutes* "good reasoning" depends on the interactions/judgments within the group.[14] Those interactions include deciding what is going to count as criteria, recognizing the specific context in which the community is embedded, etc. Similarly, the ethical and social dimensions of persons reasoning together are foundational to the very notion of reasoning itself.

In contrast to this, I think Paul sees critical thinking as foundational and the critical person as derivative—and this is the source of his ambivalence in regard to the social context of reasoning. For while Paul places great emphasis on the role of dialogue in developing reasoning, its significance lies in the fact that dialogue enables the individual to *exemplify* certain "perfections of thinking." The reasoning person is the person who fulfills the standards set by the "perfections of thought." This ambivalence in Paul's position in relation to the relationship between the reasoning individual and the reasoning society is particularly problematic in relation to the ethical "traits of mind" he identifies as standards for critical thinkers. While he describes these traits as essential if we are to become critical thinkers (and a reasonable society), it is unclear whether they are constitutive of critical thinking, or separate from critical thinking, but essential for its application in society.

If these ethical "traits of mind" are indeed separate from the notion of critical thinking itself, then Paul's description of critical thinking as dialogical thinking is problematic—for the notion of dialogical thinking as a *defining characteristic* of reasoning/critical thinking when taken outside the context of a dialogical community will be greatly reduced in meaning. In this context, dialogue could still occur as "self-talk" (with oneself, or with a text), and even perhaps in a limited form of Socratic questioning, but the essential interactional/transactional nature of dialogue as the construction of meaning between persons—a movement from self to other and back again—would be lost, and with it the ethical dimension of reasoning.

It is when we look at reasoning as the construction of meaning that the role of dialogue emerges as central. If *reasoning* involves the relationship between "pure reason" and "the reasoner," then *the meaning of the saying*—that it is said at all (rather than left unsaid), how it is said (critically, creatively, dismissively), that it is said openly or in secrecy—is as important as *the meaning of what is said*. In other words, the dialogical experience as an experience of encounter, a meeting between "self" and "other" becomes a significant aspect of what reasoning persons do, and how we think about and articulate what this encounter involves will inform our conception of reason.

So what are my ideas about what dialogue, or dialogical encounter, involves? Here are some features I feel are important. Dialogical encounter involves mutuality. A dialogical situation is one where there is *emergent meaning*[15] meaning that emerges from the merging (or fusion) of horizons between those involved. In entering into dialogue we accept the possibility of difference. At a base level this involves developing a common language through which communication becomes possible at all. More fully, it becomes the entering into the perspective of the other—comprehending the reality of the others perspective as fully as possible not in order to judge it (though that may come later) but in order to fully understand it. Indeed, it is only in doing this that reasoned judgment becomes possible at all.[16]

Dialogue is also a risky business—it involves exposing ourselves to others. Making public our own horizons—the cutting edge at which our universe (or world view) ends—while remaining open to the fact that other world views may have different horizons, and that our end point may be another's beginning. This is what makes dialogue revelatory, for in the act of listening we open ourselves to what is essentially beyond our own Self, and through this come to perceive both our own uniqueness and our commonality with others. This, I believe, is the basis of the connection that exists between reasoning/critical thinking and the development of our sense of personhood: that we actually come to know ourselves better through our interaction with (coming to know) others. This is not the claim that we simply become more *conscious* of ourselves as we already are—but that we *form* ourselves, our individuality, through our encounter with others. We don't develop a self and then relate that self to others, but develop a self in/within relationship. This development involves listening as well as saying, being open to the presence of others as well as understanding their ideas. If we accept this notion of dialogue as an encounter *between* self and

other, then to develop a program for the "strengthening of reason" without focusing on the establishment of a reasoning community seems to make no sense at all.[17]

If we take reasoning in this way—as understanding and mutuality—then the emphasis is on *thinking with* others rather than *thinking about* products of thought.[18] In this regard the central concern of dialogue is with the making of meaning[19] (or with the quest for understanding) rather than a concern for arriving at "a Truth"—and the process of working through an idea will be more important than the truth of the end result. Reasoning dialogically does not necessarily dismiss the faulty argument or wrong answer as worthless, for such an answer can still be useful in the quest for meaning as it is explored for the direction that it can give further inquiry. In this respect reasoning is not just about "applying the rules" (evaluating arguments, where bad arguments are simply rejected as wrong) but about *judging significance.*

Finally, if we see reasoning as the engagement of persons in determining significance and forming judgments about such things as relevance, reasoning will involve more than determining logical connections and a concern for truth. Reasoning will now involve the exploration of meaning and the coordinating of information (*e.g.,* exploring the concept of family and family relationships in order to reach a deeper understanding of the concept.) Reasoning may involve making judgments based on speculation or conviction, situations where the giving of reasons is not appropriate or even possible, When I say, "I believe X," without being able to provide reasons for that belief, I might still want to claim that such belief is reasonable. In such cases Lipman suggests that the judgment is *reasonable* if the reasoning person takes *cognitive responsibility* for what they are saying,[20] that is, they hold themselves accountable for the consequences of their beliefs and remain open to correction (by themselves or others). While the belief may not be rational, (in that it is not held for good reason) it is reasonable because it is open to be challenged by others and re-evaluated in light of such challenge. A similar story could be told about following our intuitions.

Because reasoning, as thinking *with* others, is concerned with significance and meaning, it also enables us to recognize the role of *judgment* in reasoning. Reason as inference may provide us with a set of rules or guides to apply in reasoning, but *reasonableness* is called for in determining what rules *count*: how we are to judge what to take into account in any given situation. When considering "reasoned judgment" as *reasoners engaged in judging*; we are not concerned solely with reasons, but also with determining significance and meaning.

Yet the idea that good judgment as judgment "based on reasons" seems a fairly commonplace one. If judgment is seen as a matter of deciding between alternatives, then presumably I decide to go one way or the other based on my evaluation of the alternatives placed before me. These alternatives entail certain outcomes, and rational judgment involves making good inferences based on my beliefs taken together with the alternatives before me.

Yet where did judgment really come into play here? Judgment came in not only at the level of rational evaluation, but also through deciding which alternatives were the appropriate, or reasonable, ones to be taking into account in the first place[21] On this account, judgment was not only *based* on reasons, it was *deciding what would count* as reasons in the first place: *e.g.*, it involves relevance judgments, and how they are decided. In making relevance judgments we do not view reason as a polarization between contradictories (between "p" and "~p"), but as concerned with the scale of "p"ness, or the meaning of "p," or what counts as a p.

Furthermore, when it comes to *deciding what counts*; "being reasonable," may actually involve going against the dictates of reason itself. For, when taken to the extreme, "being reasonable" in respect to inferences and the preserva-

tion of truth alone can, at times, be unreasonable (as in the case of the "logical fanatic" who does not take relevance and appropriateness of context into account). Thus deciding *what* is reasonable involves prioritizing what counts as significant in order to make judgments. Such judgments are often context-specific, are not a matter of rule following, and can be based on meanings rather than truth. Compromise, and conflict resolution are good examples of this. Here, "being reasonable" can involve *finding reconciliation with reality* rather than bringing judgment to bear on a product (an object of thought). It might involve me as a reasoning person having the ability to comprehend you as another reasoning person, to think *with* you through the situation rather than make judgments *about* it. Such reasoned judgment moves between what we know and understand and what, in the moment, we comprehend as "this" that is before us. To make a judgment about what is relevant, what way to proceed, or "to ask which principle might illuminate this situation, to see how this situation illuminates that principle" (Minnich 1989, p. 140)—in this lies our personhood and ability to "judge in freedom"[22] (*ibid*, pp. 140-142), to decide what response will be the meaningful one. Such judgment brings together principle and individual in the real world. It preserves what is *important* between individuals or in a situation or idea, rather than *evaluating its truth or applicability* (or judging it against a fixed standard in order to determine what to think or do). It can mean making judgments about what is right amidst inconclusive truth, or between truth and contradictory beliefs and/or desires.

One further apsect of the nature of reasoning can be brought into the theory of reason itself[23] once we take the reasoning person as foundational and the notion of reason as derivative. An aspect that once again does not emerge from the definitions of critical thinking offered by Lipman and Paul, but clearly underlies their respective programs for the strengthening of reason and their vision of the reasoning person. The question concerns the relation of reason to the Ego. Perhaps we need to make a distinction here between ego as *egoism*, and ego as *ego-strength*. The question is one of how we can develop the ego strength (a sense of self, self esteem and self worth, etc.) that lies at the center of our recognition of ourselves as reasoning persons, while lessening our sense of egoism (as egotistical, self-centered), such that we recognize other people as equal in value to ourselves and their ideas as equally worthy of consideration. How we approach this would seem to depend on whether we see reason in opposition to our egoistic nature and needing to be acquired—*i.e.*, that we have to be taught to be rational and reasonable, and thus learn to suppress our egoism (*e.g.*, we have to be taught how to take other perspectives and wants into account along side our own)—or whether we see reason and reasonableness as essential parts of our nature, and simply in need of nurturing in order to become strengthened.

While it seems to me that Paul's Piagetian view (Paul 1990, pp. 114-116), commits him to the former—a view in which we start out as egoists and have to learn to suppress this egoism, (and thus his program for the development of reason concentrates on providing children with a mechanism to escape this egocentricity[24]), Lipman takes a Vygotskian perspective,[25] thereby seeing the development of Ego taking place along with the recognition of Other, whereby both come into being as a natural outcome of our encounters with others?[26] In other words, that the development of ego (both egoism and ego-strength) is the product of a social existence. Thus for Lipman, reason develops alongside the development of ego (rather than being imposed upon it), and the mechanism for the nurturing of reason and reasonableness will involve nurturing ego-strength and minimizing egoism through emphasizing the ethical dimension of dialogical encounter with others.

In summary, when we concern ourselves with the dimensions of reasoning that are not accounted for when we view reason as synonymous with the making of valid inferences (or logical forms in general), the role of *the reasoning person* becomes foundational to our notion of reason. In taking the reasoning person as foundational the affective and social dimensions of reasoning become an integral component of the theory of reason itself (integral to the connection between reason, the reasoner, and what counts as success in reasoning), and can then be seen to involve such aspects as:

(1) The transactional nature of dialogue.

(2) The ethical dimensions of reasoning;

(3) the nature of judgment.

(4) The relationship between reason and the ego.

References

Brown, H. 1988: *Rationality* (London, Routledge)

Crowell, 1990: "Dialogue and Text: Re-Marking the difference" in Maranhao, T (ed) 1990.

Johnson, R. 1991: "Reasoning Critical Thinking, and the Network Problem" Paper Delivered at the Sonoma Conference on Critical Thinking and Educational Reform.

Kaplan, G., and Kessler, C. (Eds) 1989: *Hannah Arendt: Thinking, Judging, Freedom* (Sydney, Allen and Unwin).

Lipman, M. (1991): *Thinking in Education* (Cambridge, Cambridge University Press).

Lipman, M. 1991: "What is Philosophy for Children?" Lecture, Montclair.

Lipman, M. 1988: "Critical Thinking, What can it be?" *Educational Leadership*, Vol. 46, no. 1. (ASCD).

Lipman, M. 1985: "Philosophy and the Cultivation of Reasoning," *Thinking: The Journal of Philosophy for Children*, Vol. 5, No. 4. (Montclair, IAPC).

Maranhao, T. 1990: *The Interpretation of Dialogue* (Chicago, University of Chicago Press).

Minnich, E. 1989: "To Judge in Freedom: Hannah Arendt on the relation of thinking to morality" in Kaplan and Kessler (Eds) 1989.

Mischel, T. (ed) 1977: *The Self-Psychological and Philosophical Issues* (Oxford, Basil Blackwell).

Paul, R. 1990: *Critical Thinking; What Every Person Needs To Survive In a Rapidly Changing World.* (C.A., Centre for Critical Thinking and Moral Critique).

Paul, R. 1987: "Critical Thinking and the Critical Person" (1987), in Paul 1990.

Paul, R. 1988: "Critical Thinking, What why and How." in Paul 1990.

Paul, R. 1984: "Critical Thinking: Fundamental to Education for a Free Society," *Educational Leadership*, Vol. 42, No. 2.

Richards, T. J. 1978: *The Language of Reason*. (Australia, Perganom Press).

Sharp, A. M. 1991: "The Community of Inquiry: Education for Democracy," *Thinking: The Journal of Philosophy for Children*, Vol. 9, No. 2. Montclair, IAPC).

Sharp, A. M. (unpublished): "Some Presuppositions of the Notion 'Community of Inquiry'." Splitter, L. 1991: "Dialogue, Thinking and the Search for Meaning" in Reed, R. (ed) *When We Talk: Essays on Classroom Conversations* (Texas Wesleyan, Analytic Teaching Press).

Taylor, C. 1977: "What is Human Agency" in Mischel, T 1977.

Weinsheimer, J., 1985: *Gadamer's Hermeneutics: A reading of Truth and Method* (New Haven, Yale University Press).

Notes

1. For instance, when we formally reconstruct an argument that might have been developed first when engaged in discussion.
2. And similarly, in the case of induction reasoning is also determined by what is seen as most likely to preserve truth—inference to the best explanation, etc
3. Judging significance is concerned with meanings, with exploring implications, deciding on acceptability conditions and thereby determining what will count as "good reasons" in a certain context.
4. This is, I feel, related to what Taylor characterizes as "strong evaluations," see Taylor 1977, pp. 114-5: "To characterize one desire or inclination as worthier, or nobler, or more integrated, etc., than others is to speak of it in terms of the kind of quality of life which it expresses and sustains . . . this additional dimension can be said to add depth, because now we are reflecting about our desires in terms of the kind of being we are in having them or carrying them out. Strong evaluation is not just a condition of articulacy about preferences, but also about the quality of life, the kinds of beings we are or want to be."
5. That is to say, it will depend on the language game they are part of.
6. We are operating according to different acceptability conditions.
7. Though the evaluation of argument may be involved—in this way reasoning will involve inference but not be reducible to it.
8. Naturally, any act of reasoning is going to involve both a sequence of steps and an agent who is engaged in making those steps.
9. Brown argues: A rational belief is one that will be arrived at by a rational agent. In the classic model, the central emphasis is placed on logical relations between evidence and belief, while the role of the agent is minimized or left out. In the later model, the role of the agent is basic, and the way she deals with evidence in arriving at a belief will determine which beliefs are rational beliefs for her. He notes that this relativizes rational belief to individuals, but not the *notion* of rational belief
10. Maranhao points out: "In the work of Bakhtin, Buber, and Levinas, dialogue is an ethics of answerability, of respect to otherness and of disclosure of identity. Thus, from an ethical point of view the heart of dialogue lies in the relation between Self and Other, not in particular manifestations of consciousness" Maranhao 1990, p. 18.
11. A further question is whether this move also helps to make sense of the notion of reasoning in relation to other terms in "the network" (to borrow Johnston's phrase), such as the relationship between reasoning and critical thinking, problem solving, argumentation, etc. If we take "reasoning persons" as the generic which is instantiated in each of these activities, can we generate one theory of reason that can accommodate the variety of terms in the network? Perhaps the degree to which any one aspect of reasoning is central (truth preservation or reasonableness) can account for the differences in the meaning of the term "reasoning" as we apply it to the various terms (eg., whether truth preservation or reasonableness is more central to problem solving and argumentation, etc.)?
12. "If we are to evaluate the various programs that propose to improve reasoning skills, what criteria should we employ? There are, it would seem, two relevant criteria which are inescapable—one quantitative, the other qualitative. The first relates to cognitive skill improvement. The second relates to the educational significance of the approach—how it helps the child become a reasonable, imaginative and self-critical individual in a democratic society." Lipman, 1985, p. 34.
13. Paul's definition of critical thinking relates to 10 elements of thought. These include and understanding of, and ability to formulate, analyze and assess: (1) The problem/question at hand, (2) The purpose or goal of thinking, (3) The frame of reference, (4) Assumptions, (5) Concepts and Ideas, (6) Principles or Theories, (7) Evidence/data/reasons, (8) Interpretations/Claims made, (9) Inferences/reasoning/lines of thought, (10) Implications and consequences. These elements, together with 9 intellectual "traits of mind," (humility, courage, empathy, integrity, perseverance, sense of justice) lead to *reasoned judgment*.
14. I'm not suggesting a "majority is right" principle here, but rather, agreeing with Wittgenstein's communtarian view of rule following.
15. Crowell, 1990, p. 345.

16. This is what, I believe, Richard Paul is on about when he says reasoned judgment is based on an awareness of our own subjectivity, awareness of the limitations of our own perspective, and involves taking that subjectivity into account.
17. This is what puzzles me about Richard Paul's approach, and what I find enlightening about Matthew Lipman's.
18. Minnich, 1989, p. 135.
19. Splitter, forthcoming.
20. Lipman, 1991.
21. Once the reasons were selected as relevant or appropriate, the choice had already been made—you could not *rationally* have done otherwise—the outcome was already determined.
22. Hannah Arendt uses this term, see Minnich, 1989.
23. That is, accounted for in relation to the connection between reason, the reasoner, and what counts as success in reasoning.
24. *E.g.*, the emphasis given to critical thinking as thinking aware of its own subjectivity—aware of its own point of view—and the emphasis on teaching children to formulate arguments from opposing points of view.
25. Lipman, Thinking in Education, 1991.
26. See also, Sharpy 1991.

Philosophy as Critical Thinking

Maurice A. Finocchiaro

Philosophy is a way of thinking that can be applied, and has been applied throughout the ages, to the most diverse subjects and problems ... The nature of philosophy is explained in terms of six notions: content-freedom, rationality, judiciousness, practicality, universality, and critical-constructiveness.

I begin by explaining that when I say that philosophy is content-free, I mean that philosophy is characterized not by the content or subject it studies, but by the approach or procedure it uses; that is, not by what it studies, but by how it studies it. I elaborate this by contrasting philosophy so conceived to other disciplines familiar to students, such as mathematics biology, history, psychology, political science, and so on. I also take this opportunity to discuss briefly that, in fact, Socrates dealt primarily with questions of good and evil, the meaning of life, the nature of wisdom, and the like; whereas Galileo dealt primarily with topics like the structure of the physical universe, the proper methods to follow in the search for truth, and the nature of knowledge; and Marx treated chiefly social, political, economic, and historical questions like the stability of capitalism, the origin of wealth and profit, the necessity and desirability of revolution, of socialism, and of communism.

Since philosophy is not defined by its content, one must characterize its approach. And so the other above-mentioned notions are meant to describe it. In saying that the philosophical approach is rational, and more simply that philosophy is rational, I mean that it emphasizes reasoning, *i.e.*, that regardless of what it is studying it tries to use reasoning as much as possible. At this point I find the need to make at least one brief remark about what reasoning is, but the main thing I emphasize is that I am talking about emphasis on reasoning, and not mere use; in fact, I add that reasoning is used in all disciplines and in everyday life, but that what distinguishes the philosopher in his readiness and willingness always to engage in reasoning. These notions of emphasis and of reasoning need, of course, more discussion, but that cannot be done either here, or in that initial lecture.

Besides being rational, the philosophical approach is characterized as judicious. Here judiciousness means the avoidance of one-sidedness and of extremes. Therefore, regardless of what he is studying, a philosopher tries or should try to avoid being one-sided or taking an extreme position. I stress that this is distinct from reasoning, the difference being that between giving or assessing reasons for claims on the one hand, and taking into account all sides of an issue and being moderate on the other.

Next, I explain what I mean in saying that philosophy is practical in its approach. That is, philosophers do not study a given subject for its own sake, merely as a mental exercise or intellectual game; instead, they are always concerned with its connection with practical life, always willing and ready to try to relate the most abstruse or abstract ideas to the solution of practical problems and the improvement of everyday life. This does not mean that there will always be a connection, or that the connection will always be direct, but rather that, if there is no such connection, the philosopher cannot be spending all his life studying that topic; it also means that normally even the study of completely abstract topics has a practical origin, in the sense of being traceable to the attempt to improve practical life. In other words, philosophers are supposed to have a practical attitude or orientation, in the sense that their thinking (regardless of how abstract it may get) has a motivation rooted in their individual experience or in social conditions.

Fourth, the philosophical approach is universal, in the sense that the topics studied are supposed to be relevant to all human beings, and not just to a few, to some, or to a particular group or class or nation. This is a feature of the approach used rather than of the topic treated because such universal relevance is something that may have to be explained or elaborated, rather than something that is immediately apparent. Nevertheless,

a philosopher is normally ready and willing to elaborate on this universal relevance.

Finally, there is something I awkwardly call critical constructiveness, to underscore the fact that, though philosophers are critics, they are not merely destructive or negative critics. They are not merely against, but also for, something. The targets of their criticism can be either ideas, beliefs, or doctrines on the one hand, or historical conditions or social practices or individual actions on the other. Moreover, the constructive aspect of their criticism may be relatively weak or small, but there must be a germ of it, otherwise we would not have the kind of philosophy we are discussing here.

In a single sentence, these points can be summarized by saying that, here, philosophy is being conceived as the study of any subject matter whatsoever, as long as the approach followed is rational, judicious, practical-oriented, universal, and critical-constructive, in the senses specified.

Critical Thinking and Philosophy for Children: The Educational Value of Philosophy

Clive Lindop

" "The main purpose of a program in philoso phy for children is to help children to learn how to think for themselves" (Lipman, 1980, 53). Now children are thinking all the time—about what's for lunch, what their friends are thinking, what their pets are doing, and so on. It is not thinking in this sense that is at issue here but thinking in the sense of figuring things out, making inferences, drawing conclusions from observations—for themselves rather than having to be told all the time. The increasing number of conferences and publications on teaching thinking in schools testifies to the widespread concern that children are not being taught to think effectively for themselves.

In response, many have advocated placing greater emphasis on teaching thinking skills— generally derived from lists such as Bloom's Taxonomy of Educational Objectives. Lipman points out however (1988, 40), that concentrating on isolated skills provides no procedure leading to the convergence and orchestration of these skills to facilitate their transfer to other areas of the curriculum. Furthermore, since taxonomies of inquiry skills of this sort fail to include reasoning skills, little is done to overcome student incoherence in the formulation of explanations and arguments, in the ferreting out of underlying as-

sumptions and implications, or in the unification of meanings. All of which we would expect of anyone we would describe as a good thinker or reasoner. Thus such programs fail to fulfil their promise.

Even when skills of formal and informal logic are given prominence, as by advocates of critical thinking programs, they often turn out again to take the form of separate exercises and problems organized according to some rationale of the author, thus adding another specialization to the already crowded school curriculum of disconnected specialized presentations. Enough has been said in the literature of education to point out, as Lipman does (1980, 26), that lack of unification in children's educational experience is one of the major problems in the practice of education today. If this is so, then critical thinking skills would be better introduced in a way which would help unify or make bridges between the specialized subject areas to enable children to realize the interconnected nature of human knowledge without overwhelming them. We may well ask, as Lipman does (*ibid*), what better way to connect children with the formal structure of human knowledge than philosophy which has traditionally concerned itself with the interrelationships among the different intellectual disciplines? Since philosophy is characteristically a question-raising discipline dealing with concepts important to our lives and relevant to our knowledge and understanding of human experience, it naturally encourages children's inquisitiveness and speculation about the world and their place in it.

Since philosophy is also a discipline grounded in logic it brings criteria of excellence into the thinking process so that children can move from merely thinking to thinking well. Now teaching children to think or reason well can be thought of as teaching them to analyze and construct propositions of various sorts. If this is all a program in critical thinking offers, as those that I have seen do, even when using a variety of visual and verbal modes, it does not do justice to the rich complexity of human thought. For putting thought into propositions is not the only way we have of making assertions or expressing ourselves or the judgments we make. We can and do communicate our views, attitudes, appraisals, etc, in what we do and make, as well as in what we say or write. If children are to think and express themselves well they need to develop their skills in all these other non-propositional ways too.

Three Modes of Judgment

Doing, making and saying are three modes of judgment, which Buchler (1955, 31), following Aristotle, calls active, exhibitive and assertive respectively, all of which are effective modes of communication. The traditional view, equating judgment only with the assertive (propositional) mode ignores (and therefore denigrates) the other modes, giving a distorted picture of the individual, one's representation of the world and ways of communicating with others. To do justice to the rich complexity of human experience and interaction we must maintain a balance between all three modes of expression. This is especially important because, as Buchler argues (*ibid*, 40), the three modes of judgment are not reducible to one another. There can be no direct translation

of one into another, for there are no literal equivalents. But, in the right conditions, one mode can articulate the other, for they are related through mutual influence: what we know theoretically may affect the content of how we act and what we make; and the way we act or what we make may determine the ideas we formulate. If education is to be of the whole person and not a distortion, children must be given the opportunity to exercise all three modes of inquiry and judgment to better articulate their own points of view or perspective.

Philosophy is more suited to this end than critical thinking alone, as the philosophic perspective has two dimensions: construction and reflexive commentary (Buchler 1951, 122). The constructive dimension gives philosophy an exhibitive character, while the commentary gives philosophy its assertive character. In assertion, consequences are traced; in exhibition (works of art, moral acts), responses are ascertained. As every perspective contains elements of both, it has an order of interrelated concepts of both kinds; "seeing" the meaning, and "feeling" the configuration of this conceptual order is the business of the constructive dimension of philosophy, while the assertive dimension emphasizes the "reference" of the schema, its applicability to "experience." Since the exhibitive judgments of the construction cannot be literally translated into assertive judgments, philosophy has traditionally made use of myth and metaphor to convey the message of reason (*ibid*, 123). Critical thinking programs composed of exercises and problems cannot contribute to the development of reason in this practical way, for they fail to confront children with the great tradition of inquiry into matters which have plagued man throughout recorded history, and about which children display such "natural" interest. Philosophy, then, clearly bridges the concerns of all disciplines and provides perhaps the greatest hope for transfer of reasoning between subjects and into everyday life of children.

Theoretical support for the efficacy of philosophy also comes from recent work in cognitive psychology. In a recent review of thinking skills curricula, Marilyn Adams (1989) points out that "content-free" skills programs fail to build rich schemas for the processing, storage and retrieval of information (concepts and skills), thus limiting one's ability to understand what one sees and hears. Rich schemas, on the other hand, enhance one's ability to use relational skills over a greater range of experience across more subject areas. To maximize transfer of learning then, she concludes, the materials or content of a thinking skills course should reflect as diverse and broadly useful a set of problem domains as is possible. Philosophy, with its rich and diverse domains of interest is ideal in this regard. For this reason she describes Philosophy for Children as a "standout" among thinking skills programs; for it is the most likely to develop a contextually rich, but thematically integrated and logically well articulated, schema.

Critical Thinking and Community

To think critically, in the non-pejorative sense of assessing the worth of arguments, relevance of other opinions and information, etc., would require criteria of assessment as well as sensitivity to the context in which the judgment is made. Thinking that is unwilling to take into account the nature of the situation and people involved, unwilling to recognize the presence of factors which make a difference to the case or judgments to be made, we may well classify as unreasonable. Context and other people's perspectives on a situation may be extremely complex and subtly, rather than obviously, different. Sensitivity to perspective is a built-in aspect of philosophy because, as Buchler recognizes (*ibid*, 131), philosophical perspectives are not insular, private, idioms; they are not personal feelings or unique personal attributes. Philosophical perspectives,

even when they fail to overlap and intersect, attempt to achieve universality (*ibid*, 132). The philosopher, in formulating categories and principles, represents a world that is always to some extent available to other perspectives. Philosophy for Children, unlike other thinking programs which impose the program's "content-free" perspective on the children (Adams, *op cit*), offers them the philosophical perspective in the context of inquiry by (fictional) children like themselves, thus encouraging them to bring their own perspectives into the dialogue. And since a philosopher is not just reporting his impressions, but making tacit recommendations that his results fit other perspectives and, in some sense, are fairer to these perspectives than the formulations of others (*ibid*), children can put this claim and their own perspectives to the test of critical inquiry. So philosophy invites criticism, not only of itself but also of one's own point of view which until now may never have been held up to critical examination. Philosophy offers revelation: the opportunity, as a mixture of aphorisms has it, to know thyself and be wiser yet.

This principle of criticism is explicitly present in the commentative dimension of philosophy. Hostile criticism, however, does not imply the insistence of one philosopher that another think the way he does or that the other abandon his conceptual references. Rather, negative criticism means that an alleged justification is not established by the conceptual materials deployed (Buchler, 1951, 134). The partiality of a single, or particular, perspective may be corrected, refined, by taking into account other perspectives on the issue in hand. The more perspectives that are brought into play the greater the comprehensiveness of information and evidence and the more impartial the resultant "communal" view becomes. To this end, Philosophy for Children has children examine their perspectives in terms of the suppositions inherent in them. In this way philosophy adds the important dimension of self-correction to children's habitual ways of doing and looking at things. Because it is *self* correction, it contributes directly to the achievement of auton-

Thinking and experience

Every experience involves a connection of doing or trying with something which is undergone in consequence. A separation of the active doing phase from the passive undergoing phase destroys the vital meaning of an experience. Thinking is the accurate and deliberate instituting of connections between what is done and its consequences. It notes not only that they are connected, but the details of the connection. It makes connecting links explicit in the form of relationships. The stimulus to thinking is found when we wish to determine the significance of some act, performed or to be performed. Then we anticipate consequences. This implies that the situation as it stands is, either in fact or to us, incomplete and hence indeterminate. The projection of consequences means a proposed or tentative solution. To perfect this hypothesis, existing conditions have to be carefully scrutinized, and the implications of the hypothesis developed—an operation called reasoning. Then the suggested solution—the idea or theory—has to be tested by acting upon it. If it brings about certain consequences, certain determinate changes, in the world, it is accepted as valid. Otherwise, it is modified, and another trial made. Thinking includes all of these steps—the sense of the problem, the observation of conditions, the formation and rational elaboration of a suggested conclusion, and the active experimental testing. While all thinking results in knowledge, ultimately the value of knowledge is subordinate to its use of thinking. For we live not in a settled and finished world, but in one which is going on, and where our main task is prospective, and where retrospect—and all knowledge as distinct from thought is retrospect—is of value in the solidity, security, and fertility it affords our dealing with the future. . . . To learn from experience is to make a backward and forward connection between what we do to things and what we enjoy or suffer from things in consequence. Under such conditions, doing becomes a trying, an experiment with the world to find out what it is like, the undergoing becomes instruction—discovery of the connection of things.

Two conclusions important for education follow (1) Experience is primarily an active-passive affair; it is not primarily cognitive. But (2) the *measure of the value* of an experience lies in the perception of the relationships or continuities to which it leads.

—John Dewey, "The Theory of the Chicago Experiment," an article written by Dewey in 1934, and appearing as Appendix II of Katherine C. Mayhew and Anna C. Edwards, *The Dewey School*, New York, 1936.

omy which has long been lauded as an aim of education. And since the scrutiny of perspectives does not take place in isolation, but in company with others in a non-threatening community of inquiry, Philosophy for Children also directly encourages the growth of respect for others and toleration of differences, which again have been longstanding goals of education. The search for community however, does not mean the compulsory adoption of one perspective. As children in the novel *Harry Stottlemeier's Discovery* realize, "each of us lives in his own world that's different from other peoples" . . . however . . . "the important point is not that we see things differently, but that if each of us were to change places, we could see what the other does." Difference of perspective is as fundamental to communication as the sharing of perspective. Difference of perspective can save inquiry from sterility and inanity. In developing a willingness to explore alternative points of view, these characters in the Philosophy for Children stories are modelling the attitude of being reasonable in the ordinary business of everyday life.

Constructing an Argument

Perspectives, or points of view, can intersect, overlap, be shared and/or include one another, but even so misunderstandings and conflict can occur. This comes from unwitting (hence opposed) or unreasonable (hence fanatical) blindness to other perspectives. In fact, Buchler declares (*ibid*, 116) rationality can be defined as the willingness to discover other perspectives, to attain community of perspective, and to reconcile community with conviction. It seems to me, however, that he is talking about reasonableness, not rationality. Fanatics may very well be rational, so rational, in fact, that they shut out all other ways of approaching a situation or problem. It is just this sort of blind unreasonableness that unnerves us. With this in mind we might do well to caution ourselves as academics familiar and comfortable with a particular methodology—the assertive— not to close our eyes to the exhibitive and active modes of expression, understanding, knowledge and judgment that Buchler brings to our attention. Otherwise we could end up in what he calls the grotesque and arrogant position of insisting, however unwittingly, that children adopt only the assertive mode (*ibid*, 133). (Critical thinking programs that concentrate on acquisition of "content-free" analytic reasoning skills are in danger of this error.

Knowledge of logical operators such as "all," "none," "some" "if-then," "only," "unless," etc., and of the rules of valid inference is necessary for the recognition, analysis and evaluation of sound reasoning, but it is not sufficient. Something more than the acquisition of skills and ability in reason assessment is required for critical thinkers, however. One could possess this skill but never put it into practice—it may never transfer to other areas of one's life, as Adams (*op cit*) might say. Such a person, Passmore argues (1967), cannot be said to be critical because he lacks the "critical spirit," he shows no inclination to be appropriately moved by reasons, as Seigel (1988) puts it. Critical thinkers, then, are particu-

lar sorts of people; they are disposed to behave, and do behave, in certain ways; they value reasoning and rationality; they are rational themselves, seeking to explain their actions and claims with appropriate reasons, and likewise assess reasons or arguments given them by others using these same critical skills. But, as Socrates lamented, knowledge of the good does not seem to guarantee that anyone will do, or be good, or in this case, critical.

Current critical thinking courses, Schlecht (1988) recognizes, focus primarily on analysis and assessment of arguments presented by others. To dispose students to apply the skills they acquire, to become critical, much more emphasis needs to be given to learning how to generate clear and cogent arguments of their own. Practice in argument construction as well as argument analysis is required. Indeed, such practice may well be necessary, for some skills of argument construction may well be different from those of argument analysis and assessment, and hence not covered and developed.

Philosophy for Children, however, with its pedagogy of the community of inquiry, deliberately exercises students in argument construction as well as analysis, albeit at a low level of sophistication, but not integrity. Students in the program do show, and can develop, the disposition to be constructively critical of their own perspective and those of others, including the teacher's. Careful consideration of perspectives, the critical scrutiny of beliefs and supposed form of knowledge inherent in them in light of the grounds offered in their support and the further conclusions which follow from them is how Dewey characterized reflective thinking in *How we think*. Such consideration has what Ennis (1962) describes as a logical dimension (judging the alleged relations between meanings of words and sentences); a criterial dimension (knowledge of criteria for judging statements); and a pragmatic dimension (the purpose and content of the judgment). These dimensions he packs into his definition of critical thinking as reasonable reflective thinking that is focused on what to believe or do (1987). Lipman, reflecting this same tradition, refines these earlier definitions, characterizing critical thinking as thinking that is self-correcting, guided by criteria, sensitive to context and that facilitates judgment. All of which are marks of good philosophical inquiry.

Philosophy for Children can be described as a program for developing good judgment in that it engages children in giving an account, in terms of reasons, for their point of view, and in seeking a like accounting from others of their view. In the process emphasis is given to criteria relevant to the judgment of the merits of such accounts. Questions such as, "Is that a good reason?" "Is this a better reason, and why?" appear frequently throughout the manuals and exercises accompanying the novels as well as from the fictional characters themselves. Thus self-correction and sensitivity to context are given a prominent role in all of the Philosophy for Children programs. Not only reasoning skills are exercised but also the disposition to be reasonable, as well as rational, about the various perspectives elicited during the classroom inquiry. No other program deliberately seeks to set this inquiry in the context of a tradition devoted so exclusively to the development of good judgment. In conclusion, I concur with Lipman (1988, 43), that if both philosophy and education are seen to share reasonableness as the same goal, it might not seem at all outrageous to contend that fundamentally all true philosophy is educational and that all true education is philosophical.

References

Adams, M. (1989) "Thinking skills curricula: their promise and progress," *Educational Psychologist*, 24 (1), 25-77.

Buchler, J. (1951) *Toward a General Theory of Judgment*, NY: Columbia University Press.

Buchler J. (1955) *Nature and Judgment*, NY: Columbia University Press.

Ennis, R. (1962) "A concept of critical thinking." *Harvard Ed. Review*.

Ennis, R. (1987) A conception of critical thinking. *APA Newsletter on Teaching Philosophy*, Summer, 1987.

Lipman, M. (1980) *Philosophy in the Classroom*, 2nd ed. Philadelphia: Temple University Press.

Lipman, M. (1988) *Philosophy Goes to School*, Philadelphia: Temple University Press.

Passmore, J. (1967) On teaching to be critical, in R. S. Peters (ed), *The Concept of Education*, London: Routledge & Kegan Paul.

Siegel, H. (1988) "Critical thinking and the language of inquiry,' given at the Conference on Critical Thinking, Montclair State College, October.

Schlecht, L. E (1988) "Critical thinking courses: their value and limitations" given at the Conference on Critical Thinking, Montclair State College, October.

Philosophy for Children and Critical Thinking

Matthew Lipman

The Philosophy for Children program exemplifies the inquiry approach to education. That is, instead of having students memorize the conclusions of others as set forth in secondary texts, the students are expected to explore and reflect upon each subject area for themselves. To be an inquirer is to be an active seeker and a persistent questioner, constantly alert to hitherto unperceived connections and differences, constantly prepared to compare and contrast, to analyze and hypothesize, to experiment and observe, measure and test. Thus student inquirers assume some portion of the responsibility for their own education. They learn to follow the lines of inquiry they initiate, and this leads them to learn to think for themselves.

In the past, many teachers have sought to teach students to think for themselves by methods hardly conducive to the achievement of that goal. For example, they penalized classroom conversation and did not permit group problem-solving, on the grounds that such practices prevented the formation of independent thinkers. Not that they were altogether wrong: if education were assumed to consist wholly in the memorization of selected textual materials, then prohibiting classroom talking would be a way of reducing cheating on tests. But if the students could be organized into a classroom community of inquiry, then each student's reflections would display the topic under discussion from a different point of view, and

this would in turn compel students to *have* to think for themselves, whether or not the group actually arrived at a consensus on any particular issue under discussion.

By fostering open, spirited discussion of philosophical issues, the community of inquiry, as it operates in the Philosophy for Children program, contains a built-in, *self-correcting* methodology. Where each student is alerted to the importance of scrupulous thinking—*i.e.*, adhering to rather than violating the rules and procedures of inquiry, each is encouraged to observe the procedures of the others and to call infractions to their attention. This is where the community of inquiry differs so much from most other social groups, for whereas the others are inclined to gloss over their own mistakes and not to scrutinize too deeply their own shortcomings, the community of inquiry actively searches for its own weaknesses in the hope of strengthening them. The community of inquiry, in other words, publicly acknowledges its own fallibility and looks for ways of remedying its deficiencies, all the while continuing to follow the inquiry where it leads.

A familiar distinction these days is between "teaching for thinking" and "teaching about thinking." Philosophy for Children emphasizes the first of these, teaching *for* thinking, with the understanding that the thinking in question can be *about* anything whatsoever, including the thinking process itself. But teaching about thinking no more assures the improvement of one's cognitive abilities than does teaching about oceans or butterflies, just as one is not likely to become a skilled thinker because one thinks about the operation of the brain rather than about the operation of the muscles. This is not to say that teaching children about how cognition works is an improper subject for elementary school. It is merely an observation that such testing should candidly be labelled psychology (or Psychology for Children) so that teachers and administrators will not be so likely to be confused as to its contents.

It has already been noted that Philosophy for Children is *self-correcting* because it involves community-based inquiry. It should now be added that Philosophy for Children emphasizes thinking that is *sensitive-to-context*, and actively seeks to promote and strengthen such sensitivity. Without awareness of the distinctive qualitative nuances of individual situations, thinking errs in the direction of rampant theory-construction and manic deduction from principles. Sensitivity to context is obligatory so that rules are not employed if they are inappropriate to a given situation, and so that the uniqueness of particular contexts is properly respected. This respect for cases is indispensable for all inquiry and not merely for those that have moral implications.

In addition to promoting thinking that is *self-correcting* and *sensitive-to-context*, Philosophy for Children fosters thinking that *leads to the making of judgments* through *reliance upon criteria*. Thinking that leads to the making of judgments is practical thinking, and by and large the practical thinker is one who is accustomed to reflecting upon practice. The mason and the writer are engaged in their respective crafts, in their respective practices. The writer must select each word and fit it into a sentence which must be fitted in turn into a paragraph, and each such selection and application is a judgment. Likewise the mason must select each rock and fit it into a space in the wall to be constructed, and each such selection and fitting is a judgment. The exercises in the Philosophy for Children program are designed to strengthen the ability of students to make practical judgments, for the ability to do so is a mark of good sense—that is, of that reasonableness and sense of proportion that an educated person is deemed to possess.

A criterion is an instrument for judging, much as an axe is an instrument for chopping. If a person were to claim to have chopped down a large tree without the use of tools of any kind, we would be on sound ground if we hesitated to believe him, and we would hesitate to believe someone who claimed to make judgments without criteria of any kind, although we would readily admit that his criteria might be deeply implicit rather than manifestly explicit. So thinking that generates judgments usually relies upon criteria, which is another way of saying that the making of good judgments can be traced back to utilization of strong and reliable reasons. Every craft, every form of practice, every variety of inquiry, carries with it certain modes of self-assessment that are preferred because experience has shown them to be strong and reliable. We call these criteria. Thus the criteria of good reporting may consist in its being informative, accurate and clear, while the criteria of good reasoning may consist in its premises being true and its form being valid. The criteria by which architectural judgments are assessed include safety, efficiency and beauty, while the criteria by which judicial decisions are assessed include conformity to law, respect for due process and rights of persons, and adequate consideration of evidence. When we consider people who are engaged in the sciences or professions, we note that they are generally able to cite the criteria they employ when they make judgments. Teachers cite the criteria they use in arriving at the grades they assign their students; doctors cite the criteria they use in diagnosing and prescribing for a patient; and book reviewers are able to indicate the criteria they appeal to in evaluating books. Likewise, when scientists classify plants or animals or solar phenomena or microscopic objects, they can readily cite the classificatory criteria that assist them in the making of such judgments.

In the Philosophy for Children program, a great deal of emphasis is placed upon the making of criterion-based-judgments. Whenever a philosophical concept is introduced, it is customary to provide one or more exercises in which that concept is operationalized, *i.e.*, in which it is translated into behavioral practice, of which the most common form is classroom discussion. If an ethical term like "fair play" is introduced, a series of situations will typically be presented to members of the class, who then discuss under what circumstances these would or would not be instances of fair play. Thanks to sustained practice in making judgments, students in Philosophy for Children classes come to think both more scrupulously and more responsibly, because their thinking is self-correcting, sensitive-to-context and reliant upon criteria in the making of judgments.

Now, as it happens, there is a movement afoot to upgrade the quality of thinking in school and college classrooms, and it is known as the "critical thinking" movement. At first glance, it seems to be a hodge-podge of competing approaches. Upon further examination, however, several things stand out:

1. Virtually all of the competing approaches contend that thinking well involves the use of "thinking skills," although there is no agreement on just what these skills are; and
2. There is general agreement that critical thinking enhances the capacity to solve problems or make decisions.

One of the reasons for the lack of agreement as to which skills are distinctively identifiable as "thinking skills" is that the proponents of these approaches come from different disciplines, and are inclined therefore to identify as thinking skills those that count as such in their own bailiwicks.

Those in English count syntactical skills as thinking skills; those in philosophy nominate logical skills; those in social sciences nominate statistical and other research skills, and other scientists emphasize other inquiry skills.

What generally goes unmentioned in all of these citations of skills (as well as of the skill of skill-orchestration) is that skills are performances subject to judgment, and judgments are criterion-based, with the result that the very notion of skill is dependent upon the operation of those cognitive instruments known as criteria. Little wonder then that there is such a *prima facie* similarity between the terms "critical" and "criteria," for critical thinking is necessarily criterion-based thinking.

What keeps critical thinking from becoming fanatically rigorous is its sensitivity to application in highly diversified contexts, as well as its constantly taking itself into account along with its subject-matter, so as to be continually self-correcting. Thinking that is not sensitive to context is blundering and obtuse; thinking that is not self-correcting can easily become uncritical and unreasonable.

It can readily be seen now that the essential characteristics of critical thinking are just those features to which particular attention is paid by the Philosophy for Children program. Thanks to its community of inquiry pedagogy, it assures that students will engage in self-corrective thinking insofar as they internalize the dialogical process of classroom discussion. And thanks to its curriculum, it assures that students will learn to apply and appeal to relevant, reliable criteria, and that they will be sensitive to the qualitative uniqueness of particular situations, this being indispensable for the making of appropriate judgments. Insofar as educators now advocate critical thinking, what remains is for them to recognize how well Philosophy for Children can do the job they want done.

Chapter Twelve
The Cultivation of Judgment

Chapter Twelve

The Cultivation of Judgment

We are much in debt to John Locke for so forcibly emphasizing the educational importance of reasonableness, and to Michel de Montaigne for stressing the need to teach for *judgment*. When we ask ourselves, however, just what each of these concepts comprise, we are compelled to wonder whether there is a significant difference between them. To be sure, some reasoning is so mechanical that its conclusions seem hardly to merit being called judgments, and some judgments are so intuitive that they seem not to have been preceded by any reasoning. Nevertheless, if the strengthening of children's judgment—their sense of appropriateness, proportion, relevance, probability and order—is what education must aim at, it is likely to turn out that teaching for reasonableness is likely to strengthen these very same characteristics,

After all, it is not unusual to distinguish between two kinds of judgments: rule-guided and non-rule-guided, and it is both by rule-guided and by non-rule-guided processes that reasonableness is achieved. If the kind of world we would most like to live in is one whose outstanding characteristic is reasonableness, it would most likely be achieved as a result of having children's upbringing and education emphasize their development of good judgment.

There are alternatives, of course—absolutes like power, love and truth, and perhaps these are values that all lines of inquiry converge upon at infinity. But for the less distant horizons, reason-ableness and good judgment seem more attainable, and less likely to produce chaos and devastation when they are not fully achieved.

We pride ourselves so much on our enlightened educational views, in which we stress reasoning and judgment and the application of knowledge, that it must come as a distinct shock to read the two-centuries-old *Practical Education* of Maria and Richard Edgeworth and realize that what they were about was much the same sort of thing. They stress the importance of a reasonable; dialogical environment: "Children will never reason if they are allowed to hear or to talk nonsense." They praise those "who have the happy art of encouraging children to lay open their minds freely, and who can make every pleasing trifle an exercise for the understanding." They trust children to "reason accurately where their own feelings are concerned," if only they are not overawed by authority. And they give us their own, distinctly Enlightenment understanding of the difference between wit and judgment: "Wit searches for remote resemblances between objects or thoughts apparently dissimilar. Judgment compares the objects placed before it, in order to find out their differences, rather than their resemblances."

James's interest in education was not as consuming as was the Edgeworths', but he had an acute sense of proportion and significance, and he recognized (as did Montaigne, whom he much resembled) that the cultivation of judgment was of the very essence of education. Yet, what he had in mind as judgment should he noted: for him, it meant to be able "to know a good man when you see him." Presumably, then, judgment is the ability to discriminate embodied values, to weigh them and to pronounce reasonably upon theme James's recommendation? Instead of teaching subjects analytically, teach them historically. Show students the unfolding patterns, whose rivalry is the history of the world. Only in this way can we make the disciplines live.

John J. McDermott, incidentally a James scholar, speaks to the importance of helping children perceive relations—and in particular, differences. Indeed, McDermott sees in distinction-making and connection-making "the central and most important task of pedagogy." In effects McDermott re-affirms the Jamesian finding that judgment is the most important aim education can have.

Ann Diller sensitively examines the relationship between knowledge, understanding and moral judgment. Under what circumstances do we excuse a child for not knowing better, and under what circumstances do we deny the child this excuse? (The problem is not restricted to the moral judgment of children, as we know from *Oedipus Rex* and *Oedipus at Colonnus*.) Diller proceeds to give us four conditions which must be satisfied if we are to make a responsible judgment that the child "knew better," which means that the child, in turn, was responsible for his or her moral judgment. She focuses upon the importance, in moral education, of helping children recognize alternatives that are within their power and that make some appeal to their reasons for acting.

Also interested in the moral education of children, and in the strengthening of their moral judgment in the process, is Michael Pritchard. He is not persuaded by the arguments of Aristotle, Freud, Piaget and Kohlberg, that very young children, those not yet seven or eight years of age, are incapable of moral reasoning. Pritchard cites evidence to the effect that young children do have a sense of fairness, and can even distinguish among prudential, conventional and moral rules. He also cites

impressive philosophical arguments that present an alternative conception of children's moral judgment, including references to Thomas Reid, Ronald Dworkin and Gareth Matthews. In conclusion, he examines the Philosophy for Children curriculum to determine if the philosophical practice it encourages is likely to improve the moral judgment of those who engage in that practice.

In conclusion, there is the selection from Martin Benjamin, who examines the conventional notion that to seek a compromise when involved in a moral conflict is in effect to sacrifice one's principles and the integrity of one's judgment. He seeks to show that some compromises are integrity-preserving, especially where they are the result of careful deliberations. Benjamin sees judgment as differing from mere taste on the one hand and conclusive proof on the other. Instead, it tries to take everything into account, and to achieve a balance among these considerations. The exercise of judgment, he concludes, is to a large extent contextual, and demands a considerable amount of practical knowledge and intelligence. Such practical reasoning, however, is not to be confused with technical reasoning, The cultivation of judgment is particularly needed because of the frequency with which decisions need to be made in the course of everyday living, but technical knowledge is seldom of great assistance in such matters.

The inference can be drawn from some or most of these readings that philosophy helps children identify the reasons that support or that undermine what they are contemplating doing. It then helps them deliberate about these reasons so as to arrive at some kind of judgment regarding them. When such a weighing of reasons takes place in a community of inquiry setting, children are more likely to make reasonable judgments as to what they ought to do, and this in turn can lead them to *want* to do what they think is right. There are no guarantees, of course, but if it can be shown to be likely that education for thinking will lead children to make better judgments, and that this in turn will lead them to perform better actions, a creditable case for philosophy in the schools will have been made.

On Wit and Judgment

Maria Edgeworth and Richard Lovell Edgeworth

As one reads the late 18th century works of Richard and Maria Edgeworth, one is impressed by the pedagogical insights regarding children's potential to reason well in a constructive and rational environment. The Edgeworths cause one to wonder why educational thinkers had to wait until the 20th century to heed what they were saying in 1798, and why so much time and energy was expended to reinvent what the father and daughter had already discovered through experimentation with children.

Richard Edgeworth was the author of Professional Education, *and co-author, with his daughter, Maria, of* Practical Education. *The chapter on wit and judgment reprinted below is from the latter work, the title of which constituted a challenge to the prevailing educational methodology of the day. There is no doubt that the Edgeworths were strongly influenced by Rousseau's emphasis on cultivation of the senses in the early years as well as on beginning with students' interests and experience. However, there is much of Rousseau that the Edgeworths did not accept. "Children should not be thus suffered to run wild like colts for a certain time and then be taken and broken in by the most harsh, violent and unskillful methods." Parents should begin as early as possible to cultivate the habits of good reasoning and judgment coupled with a respect for the seriousness of intellectual work. "The truth is that useful knowledge cannot be obtained without labor, that attention long continued is laborious, but without this labor nothing excellent can be accomplished." Rather than extrinsic rewards, children*

should be allowed to experience success. "Rousseau rewards Emile with cakes when he judges rightly; success we think is a better reward." Practical Education *was also highly influenced by Locke and Priestley. Locke's psychological principle of utility serves as the criterion for estimating the value of teaching a particular subject to a child. The Edgeworths agree with Locke that education should focus on the cultivation of good reasoning habits, daily improvement and the formation of character in the early years. (Maria also the author of several novels for children, was aware of the novel as a didactic medium for teaching various disciplines, including ethics.)*

In the preface to Practical Education, *the Edgeworths state, "We have chosen the title of* Practical Education *to point out that we rely entirely upon practice and experience." They were convinced that all children are capable of reasoning well. Children do not lack the capacity to reason; what they lack is experience. If one is interested in helping children make better judgments, one should increase their knowledge of the world and help them cultivate the tools of inquiry and experimentation to understand their world. Judgment is dependent upon experience, because it rests on the ability to compare causes and effects. And it is the task of education to provide the kinds of experience that will enable children to observe first hand the world around them.*

If children are closely observed, say the authors, they can be seen to reason inductively and deductively before they can express their conclusions in words. There is a strong connec-

tion between talking and thinking, and it was for this reason that the Edgeworths stressed the conversational mode of teaching. But this conversation must not be nonsense. Teachers should pay careful attention to thinking logically, giving reasons for one's views and using words and concepts that both student and teacher understand.

According to the Edgeworths, observing, comparing, discussing, inferring, deducing should all precede judging. And one must remember that one is interested in producing skilled judges, not advocates. Teachers should withhold their own opinions when questioning children, in order to encourage them to think for themselves. They should never play with children's lack of experience by inducing them to believe fantastic tales, by teasing or by ridiculing them. Emphasis should be on inquiry for the purpose of discovering truth, not on the use of clever arguments or witty insights. Children should be praised for candor, good sense, valid perceptions, impartiality, and comprehensiveness rather than for advocacy of a particular view. They should never be ridiculed for changing their minds if they have good reason for doing so. Teachers should train their ears to seize upon subjects that naturally arise in children's conversations and utilize these themes in helping children reason better through dialogue, rather than formally preparing the discussion beforehand.

At a time in which educational theory was sharply divorced from educational practice, when the role of conversation in education was only dimly grasped by a few, when the function of the curriculum as the core and armature of the educational process was generally misunderstood, when the child's ability to reason was overlooked in favor of his or her naturalness and spontaneity, the Edgeworths were able to organize a comprehensive work on pedagogy which exhibited none of these failures. In its sensible tactful blending of practice and theory, its avoidance of ideology, its respect for children as persons, its sound grasp of pedagogy and the relevance of philosophy to children's education,

Practical Education is remarkable evidence of the pedagogical wisdom which we have found it possible to overlook in the course of the last two centuries.

It has been shown, that the powers of memory, invention, and imagination, ought to be rendered subservient to judgment; it has been shown, that reasoning and judgment abridge the labors of memory, and are necessary to regulate the highest flights of imagination. We shall now consider the power of reasoning in another point of view, as being essential to our conduct in life. The object of reasoning is to adapt means to an end, to attain the command of effects by the discovery of the causes on which they depend.

Until children have acquired some knowledge of effects, they cannot inquire into causes. Observation must precede reasoning; and as judgment is nothing more than the perception of the result of comparison, we should never urge our pupils to judge, until they have acquired some portion of experience.

To teach children to compare objects exactly, we should place the things to be examined distinctly before them. Every thing that is superfluous should be taken away, and a sufficient motive should be given to excite the pupil's attention. We need not here repeat the advice that has formerly been given respecting the choice of proper motives to excite and fix attention; or the precautions necessary to prevent the pain of fatigue, and of unsuccessful application. If comparison be early rendered a task to children, they will dislike and avoid this exercise of the mind, and they will consequently show an inaptitude to reason: if comparing objects be made interesting and amusing to our pupils, they will soon become expert in discovering resemblances and differences; and thus they will be prepared for reasoning.

Rousseau has judiciously advised, that *the senses* of children should be cultivated with the utmost care. In proportion to the distinctness of their perceptions will be accuracy of their memory, and probably, also, the precision of their judgment. A child who sees imperfectly cannot reason justly about the objects of sight, because he has not sufficient data. A child who does not hear distinctly cannot judge well of sounds; and, if we could suppose the sense of touch to be twice as accurate in one child as in another, we might conclude that the judgment of these children must differ in a similar proportion. The defects in organization are not within the power of the preceptor; but we may observe, that inattention, and want of exercise, are frequently the causes of what appear to be natural defects; and, on the contrary, increased attention and cultivation sometimes produce that quickness of eye and ear, and that consequent readiness of judgment, which we are apt to attribute to natural superiority of organization or capacity. Even amongst children we may early observe a considerable difference between the quickness of their senses and of their reasoning upon subjects where they have had experience, and upon those on which they have not been exercised.

The first exercises for judgment of children should, as Rousseau recommends, relate to visible and tangible substances. Let them compare the size and shape of different objects; let them frequently try what they can lift; what they can reach; at what distance they can see objects; at what distance they can hear sounds: by these exercises they will learn to judge of distances and weight; and they may learn to judge of the solid contents of bodies of different shapes, by comparing the observations of their sense of feeling and of sight. The measure of hollow bodies can be easily taken by pouring liquids into them, and the comparing the quantities of the liquids that fill vessels of different shapes. This is a very simple method of exercising the judgment of children; and, if they are allowed to try these little experiments for themselves, the amusement will fix the facts in their memory, and will associate pleasure with the habits of comparison. Rousseau rewards Emile with cakes when he judges rightly; success, we think, is a better reward. Rousseau was himself childishly fond of cakes and cream.

The step which immediately follows comparison is deduction. The cat is larger than the kitten; then a hole through which the cat can go, must be larger than a hole through which the kitten can go. Long before a child can put this reasoning into words, he is capable of forming the conclusion, and we need not be in haste to make him announce it in mode and figure. We may see by the various methods which young children employ to reach what is above them, to drag, to push, to lift different bodies; that they reason; that is to say, that they adapt means to an end, before they can explain their own designs in words. Look at a child building a house of cards: he dexterously balances every card as he floors the edifice; he raises story over story, and shows us that he has some design in view, though he would be utterly incapable of describing his intentions previously in words. We have formerly endeavored to show how the vocabulary of our pupils may be gradually enlarged, exactly in proportion to their real knowledge. A great deal depends upon our attention to this proportion; if children have not a sufficient number of words to make their thoughts intelligible, we cannot assist them to reason by our conversation, we cannot communicate to them the result of our experience; they will have a great deal of useless labor in comparing objects, because they will not be able to understand the evidence of others, as they do not understand their language; and at last, the reasonings which they carry on in their own minds will be confused for want of signs to keep them distinct. On the contrary, if their vocabulary exceed their ideas, if they are taught a variety of words to which they connect no accurate meaning, it is impossible that they should express their thoughts with precision. As this is one of the most common errors in education, we shall dwell upon it more particularly.

We have pointed out the mischief which is done to the understanding of children by the nonsensical conversation of common acquaintance. "Should you like to be a king? What are you to be? Are you to be a bishop, or a judge?

Had you rather be a general, or an admiral, my little dear?'' are some of the questions which every one has probably heard proposed to children of five or six years old. Children who have not learned by rote the expected answers to such interrogatories, stand in amazed silence upon these occasions; or else answer at random, having no possible means of forming any judgment upon such subjects. We have often thought, in listening to the conversations of grown up people with children, that the children reasoned infinitely better than their opponents. People who are not interested in the education of children do not care what arguments they use, what absurdities they utter in talking to them; they usually talk to them of things which are totally above their comprehension; and they instill error and prejudice, without the smallest degree of compunction; indeed, without in the least knowing what they are about. We earnestly repeat our advice to parents, to keep their children as much as possible from such conversation: children will never reason if they are allowed to hear or to talk nonsense.

When we say that children should not be suffered to talk nonsense, we should observe, that unless they have been in the habit of hearing foolish conversation, they very seldom talk nonsense. They may express themselves in a manner which we do not understand, or they may make mistakes from not accurately comprehending the words of others; but in these cases we should not reprove or silence them, we should patiently endeavor to find out their hidden meaning. If we rebuke or ridicule them, we shall intimidate them, and either lessen their confidence in themselves or in us. In the one case we prevent them from thinking, in the other we deter them from communicating their thoughts; and thus we preclude ourselves from the possibility of assisting them in reasoning. To show parents the nature of the mistakes which children make from their imperfect knowledge of words, we shall give a few examples from real life.

S—, at five years old, when he heard some one speak of *bay* horses, said, he supposed that the bay horses must be the best horses. Upon cross-questioning him, it appeared that he was led to this conclusion by the analogy between the sound of the words *bay* and *obey*. A few days previous to this his father had told him, that spirited horses were always the most ready to obey.

These erroneous analogies between the sound of words and their sense frequently mislead children in reasoning; we should, therefore, encourage children to explain themselves fully, that we may rectify their errors.

When S— was between four and five years old, a lady who had taken him upon her lap playfully, put her hands before his eyes, and (we believe) asked if he liked to be blinded. S— said no; and he looked very thoughtful. After a pause, he added "Smellie says, that children like better to be blinded than to have their legs tied." (S— had read this in Smellie two or three days before.)

Father. "Are you of Smellie's opinion?"

S— hesitated.

Father. "Would you rather be blinded, or have your legs tied?"

S— "I would rather have my legs tied not quite tight."

Father. "Do you know what is meant by *blinded?*

S— "Having their eyes put out."

Father. "How do you mean?"

S— "To put something into the eye to make the blood burst out; and then the blood would come all over it, and cover it, and stick to it, and hinder them from seeing, I don't know how."

It is obvious, that whilst this boy's imagination pictured to him a bloody orb when he heard the word *blinded*, he was perfectly right in his reasoning in preferring to have his legs tied; but he did not judge of the proposition meant to be laid before him; he judged of another which he had formed for himself. His father explained to him that Smellie meant blindfolded, instead of blinded; a handkerchief was then tied round the boy's head so as to hinder him from seeing, and he was made perfectly to understand the meaning of the word *blindfolded.*

In such trifles as these it may appear of little consequence to rectify the verbal errors of children; but exactly the same species of mistake will prevent them from reasoning accurately in matters of consequence. It will not cost us much trouble to detect these mistakes when the causes of them are yet recent; but it will give us infinite trouble to retrace thoughts which have passed in infancy. When prejudices, or the habits of reasoning inaccurately, have been formed, we cannot easily discover or remedy the remote trifling origin of the evil.

When children begin to inquire about causes, they are not able to distinguish between coincidence and causation; we formerly observed the effect which this ignorance produces upon their temper; we must now observe its effect upon their understanding. A little reflection upon our own minds will prevent us from feeling that stupid amazement, or from expressing that insulting contempt, which the natural thoughts of children sometimes excite in persons, who have frequently less understanding than their pupils. What account can we give of the connexion between cause and effect? How is the idea, that one thing is the cause of another, first produced in our minds? All that we know is, that amongst human events those which precede are, in some cases, supposed to produce what follow. When we have observed, in several instances, that one event constantly precedes another, we believe, and expect, that these events will in future recur together. Before children have had experience, it is scarcely possible that they should distinguish between fortuitous circumstances and causation; accidental coincidences of time, and juxtaposition, continually lead them into error. We should not accuse children of reasoning ill, we should not imagine that they are defective in judgment, when they make mistakes from deficient experience; we should only endeavor to make them delay to decide until they have repeated their experiments; and, at all events, we should encourage them to lay open their minds to us, that we may assist them by our superior knowledge.

This spring, little W— (three years old) was looking at a man who was mowing the grass before the door. It had been raining, and when the sun shone the vapor began to rise from the grass. "Does the man mowing *make* the smoke rise from the grass?" said the little boy. He was not laughed at for this simple question. The man's mowing immediately preceded the rising of the vapor; the child had never observed a man mowing before, and it was absolutely impossible that he could tell what effects might be produced by it; he very naturally imagined, that the event which immediately preceded the rising of the vapor, was the cause of its rise; the sun was at a distance; the scythe was near the grass. The little boy showed by the tone of his inquiry, that he was in the philosophic state of doubt; had he been ridiculed for his question, had he been told that he talked nonsense, he would not upon another occasion have told his thoughts, and he certainly could not have improved in reasoning.

The way to improve children in their judgment with respect to causation is to increase their knowledge, and to lead them to try experiments by which they may discover what circumstances are essential to the production of any given effect, and what are merely accessory, unimportant concomitants of the event.

A child, who for the first time sees blue and red paints mixed together to produce purple, could not be certain that the pallet on which these colors were mixed, the spatula with which they were tempered, were not necessary circumstances. In many cases the vessels in which things are mixed are essential; therefore, a sensible child would repeat the experiment exactly in the same manner in which he had seen it succeed. This exactness should not be suffered to become indolent imitation, or superstitious adherence to particular forms. Children should be excited to add or deduct particulars in trying experiments, and to observe the effects of these changes. In "Chemistry," and "Mechanics," we have pointed out a variety of occupations, in which the judgment of children may be exercised upon the immediate objects of their senses.

It is natural, perhaps, that we should expect our pupils to show surprise at those things which excite surprise in our minds; but we should consider that almost every thing is new to children, and therefore there is scarcely any gradation in their astonishment. A child of three or four years old would be as much amused, and, probably, as much surprised, by seeing a paper kite fly, as he could by beholding the ascent of a balloon. We should not attribute this to stupidity or want of judgment, but simply to ignorance.

A few days ago, W— (three years old), who was learning his letters, was let sow an *o* in the garden with mustard seed. W— was much pleased with the operation. When the green plants appeared above ground, it was expected that W— would be much surprised at seeing the exact shape of his *o*. He was taken to look at it; but he showed no surprise, no sort of emotion.

We have advised that the judgment of children should be exercised upon the objects of their senses. It is scarcely possible that they should reason upon the subjects which are sometimes proposed to them; with respect to manners and society, they have had no experience, consequently they *can* form no judgments. By imprudently endeavoring to turn the attention of children to conversation that is unsuited to them, people may give the *appearance* of early intelligence, and a certain readiness of repartee and fluency of expression; but these are transient advantages. Smart, witty children amuse the circle for a few hours, and are forgotten; and we may observe, that almost all children who are praised and admired for sprightliness and wit, reason absurdly, and continue ignorant. Wit and judgment depend upon different opposite habits of the mind. Wit searches for remote resemblances between objects or thoughts apparently dissimilar. Judgment compares the objects placed before it, in order to find out their differences rather than their resemblances.

The comparisons of judgment may be slow; those of wit must be rapid. The same power of attention in children may produce either wit or judgment. Parents must decide in which faculty, or rather, in which of these habits of the mind, they wish their pupils to excel; and they must conduct their education accordingly. Those who are desirous to make their pupils witty, must sacrifice some portion of their judgment to the acquisition of the talent for wit; they must allow their children to talk frequently at random. Amongst a multitude of hazarded observations a happy hit is now and then made: for these happy hits children who are to be made wits should be praised; and they must acquire sufficient courage to speak from a cursory view of things; therefore the mistakes they make from superficial examination must not be pointed out to them; their attention must be turned to the comic, rather than to the serious side of objects; they must study the different meanings and powers of words; they should hear witty conversation, read epigrams, and comedies; and in all company they should be exercised before numbers in smart dialogue and repartee.

When we mention the methods of educating a child to be witty, we at the same time point out the dangers of this education; and it is but just to warn parents against expecting inconsistent qualities from their pupils. Those who steadily prefer the solid advantages of judgment, to the transient brilliancy of wit, should not be mortified when they see their children, perhaps, deficient at nine or ten years old in the showy talents for general conversation; they must bear to see their pupils appear slow; they must bear the contrast of flippant gaiety and sober simplicity; they must pursue exactly an opposite course to that which has been recommended for the education of wits; they must never praise their pupils for hazarding observations; they must cautiously point out any mistakes that are made from a precipitate survey of objects; they should not harden their pupils against that feeling of shame, which arises in the mind from the perception of having uttered an absurdity; they should never encourage their pupils to play upon words; and their admiration of wit should never be vehemently or enthusiastically expressed. . . .

In stating any question to a child, we should avoid letting our own opinion be known, lest we lead or intimidate his mind. We should also avoid all appearance of anxiety, all impatience for the answer; our pupil's mind should be in a calm state when he is to judge: if we turn his sympathetic attention to our hopes and fears, we agitate him, and he will judge by our countenances rather than by comparing the objects or propositions which are laid before him. Some people, in arguing with children, teach them to be disingenuous by the uncandid manner in which they proceed; they show a desire for victory, rather than for truth; they state the arguments only on their own side of the question, and they will not allow the force of those which are brought against them. Children are thus piqued, instead of being convinced, and in their turn they become zealots in support of their own opinions; they hunt only for arguments in their own favor, and they are mortified when a good reason is brought on the opposite side of the question to that on which they happen to have enlisted. To prevent this we should never argue, or suffer others to argue for victory with our pupils; we should not praise them for their cleverness in finding out arguments in support of their own opinion; but we should praise their candor and good sense when they perceive and acknowledge the force of their opponent's arguments. They should not be exercised as advocates, but as judges; they should be encouraged to keep their minds impartial, to sum up the reasons which they have heard, and to form their opinion from these without regard to what they may have originally asserted. We should never triumph over children for changing their opinion. "I thought you were on *my* side of the question;" or, "I thought you were on the other side of the question just now!" is sometimes tauntingly said to an ingenuous child, who changes his opinion when he hears a new argument. You think it a

proof of his want of judgment, that he changes his opinion in this manner; that he vibrates continually from side to side: let him vibrate, presently he will be fixed. Do you think it a proof that your scales are bad, because they vibrate with every additional weight that is added to either side?

Idle people sometimes amuse themselves with trying the judgment of children, by telling them improbable, extravagant stories, and then ask the simple listeners whether they believe what has been told them. The readiness of belief in children will always be proportioned to their experience of the veracity of those with whom they converse; consequently, children who live with those who speak truth to them, will scarcely ever be inclined to doubt the veracity of strangers. Such trials of the judgment of our pupils should never be permitted. Why should the example of lying be set before the honest minds of children, who are far from silly when they show simplicity? They guide themselves by the best rules, by which even a philosopher in familiar circumstances could guide himself. The things asserted are extraordinary, but the children believe them, because they have never had any experience of the falsehood of human testimony.

The Socratic mode of reasoning is frequently practiced upon children. People arrange questions artfully, so as to bring them to whatever conclusion they please. In this mode of reasoning much depends upon getting the first move; the child has very little chance of having it, his preceptor usually begins first with a preemptory voice, "Now answer me this question?" The pupil, who knows that the interrogatories are put with a design to entrap him, is immediately alarmed, and instead of giving a direct candid answer to the question, is always looking forward to the possible consequences of his reply; or he is considering how he may evade the snare that is laid for him. Under these circumstances he is in imminent danger of learning the shuffling habits of cunning; he has little chance of learning the nature of open, manly investigation.

Preceptors, who imagine that it is necessary to put on very grave faces, and to use much learned apparatus in teaching the art of reasoning, are not nearly so likely to succeed as those are, who have the happy art of encouraging children to lay open their minds freely, and who can make every pleasing trifle an exercise for the understanding. If it be playfully pointed out to a child that he reasons ill, he smiles and corrects himself; but you run the hazard of making him positive in error, if you reprove or ridicule him with severity. It is better to seize the subjects that accidentally arise in conversation, than formally to prepare subjects for discussion.

"The king's stag hounds," says Mr. White of Selborne, in his entertaining observations on quadrupeds "came down to Alton, attended by a huntsman and six yeoman prickers with horns, to try for the stag that has haunted Hartley-wood and its environs for so long a time. Many hundreds of people, horse and foot, attended the dogs to see the deer unharboured; but though the huntsman drew Hartleywood, and Long-coppice, and Shrubwood, and Temple-hangers, and in their way back, Hartley, and Ward-ledham-hangers, yet no stag could be found."

"The royal pack, *accustomed to have the deer turned out before them*, never drew the coverts with any address and spirit."

Children, who are accustomed to have the game started and turned out before them by their preceptors, may perhaps, like the royal pack, lose their wonted address and spirit, and may be disgracefully *at a fault* in the public chase. Preceptors should not help their pupils out in argument, they should excite them to explain and support their own observations.

Many ladies show in general conversation the powers of easy raillery joined to reasoning, unincumbered with pedantry. If they would employ these talents in the education of their children, they would probably be as well repaid for their exertions, as they can possibly be by the polite, but transient applause, of the visitors to whom they usually devote their powers of entertaining.

A little praise or blame, a smile from a mother, or a frown, a moment's attention, or a look of cold neglect, have the happy, or the fatal power of repressing or of exciting the energy of a child, of directing his understanding to useful or pernicious purposes. Scarcely a day passes in which children do not make some attempt to reason about the little events which interest them, and upon these occasions a mother, who joins in conversation with her children, may instruct them in the art of reasoning without the parade of logical disquisitions.

Mr. Locke has done mankind an essential service, by the candid manner in which he has spoken of some of the learned forms of argumentation. A great proportion of society, he observes, are unacquainted with these forms, and have never heard the name of Aristotle; yet without the aid of syllogisms, they can reason sufficiently well for all the useful purposes of life, often much better than those who have been disciplined in the schools. It would indeed "be putting one man sadly over the head of another," to confine the reasoning faculty to the disciples of Aristotle, to any sect or system, or to any forms of disputation. Mr. Locke has very clearly shown that syllogisms do not assist the mind in the perception of the agreement or disagreement of ideas; but, on the contrary, that they invert the natural order in which the thoughts should be placed, and in which they must be placed, before we can draw a just conclusion. To children who are not familiarised with scholastic terms, the sound of harsh words, and quaint language, unlike any thing that they hear in common conversation, is alone sufficient to alarm their imagination with some confused apprehension of difficulty. In this state of alarm they are seldom sufficiently masters of themselves, either to deny or acknowledge an adept's major, minor, or conclusion. Even those who are most expert in syllogistical reasoning do not often apply it to the common affairs of life, in which reasoning is just as much wanted as it is in the abstract questions of philosophy; and many argue and conduct themselves with great prudence and precision, who might, perhaps, be caught on the horns of a dilemma, or who would infallibly fall victims to *the crocodile.*

Young people should not be ignorant, however, of these boasted forms of argumentation; and it may, as they advance in the knowledge of words, be a useful exercise to resist the attacks of sophistry. No ingenuous person would wish to teach a child to employ them. As defensive weapons, it is necessary, that young people should have the command of logical terms; as offensive weapons, these should never be used. They should know the evolutions, and be able to perform the exercise of a logician, according to the custom of the times, according to the usage of different nations; but they should not attach any undue importance to this technical art: they should not trust to it in the day of battle.

We have seen syllogisms, crocodiles, enthymemes, sorites, etc. explained and tried upon a boy of nine or ten years old in playful conversation, so that he became accustomed to the terms without learning to be pedantic in the abuse of them; and his quickness in reasoning was increased by exercise in detecting puerile sophisms: such as that of *the Cretans*—Gorgias and his bargain about the winning of his first cause. In the following stories of Themistocles—"My son commands his mother; his mother commands me; I command the Athenians; the Athenians command Greece; Greece commands Europe; Europe commands the whole earth; therefore my son commands the whole earth"—the sophism depends upon the inaccurate use of the word *commands*, which is employed in different senses in the different propositions. This error was without difficulty detected by S— at ten years old; and we make no doubt that any unprejudiced boy of the same age would immediately point out the fallacy without hesitation; but we do not feel quite sure that a boy exercised in logic, who had been taught to admire and reverence the ancient figures of rhetoric, would with equal readiness detect the sophism. Perhaps it may seem surprising, that the same boy, who judged so well of this

sorites of Themistocles, should a few months before have been easily trapped by the following simple dilemma:

M—. "We should avoid what gives us pain."

S—. "Yes to be sure."

M—. "Whatever burns us gives us pain. "

S—. "Yes, that it does!

M—. "We should then avoid whatever burns us."

To this conclusion S— heartily assented, for he had but just recovered from the pain of a burn.

M—. "Fire burns us."

S—. "Yes, I know that."

M—. "We should then avoid fire."

S—. "Yes.

This hasty *yes* was extorted from the boy by the mode of interrogatory; but he soon perceived his mistake.

M—. "We should avoid fire. What when we are very cold?"

S—. "Oh, no; I meant to say, that we should avoid a certain degree of fire. We should not go *too* near the fire. We should not go *so* near as to burn ourselves. "

Children who have but little experience frequently admit assertions to be true in general, which are only true in particular instances; and this is often attributed to their want of judgment: it should be attributed to their want of experience. Experience, and nothing else, can rectify these mistakes: if we attempt to correct them by words, we shall merely teach our pupils to argue about terms not to reason. Some of the questions and themes which are given to boys may afford us instances of this injudicious education. "Is eloquence advantageous, or hurtful to a state?" What a vast range of ideas, what variety of experience in men and things should a person possess, who is to discuss this question! Yet it is often discussed by unfortunate scholars of eleven or twelve years old. "What is the greatest good?" The answer expected by a preceptor to this question, obviously is, virtue: and, if a boy can in decent language write a page or two about *pleaure's* being a transient, and virtue's being a permanent good, his master flatters himself that he has early taught him to reason philosophically. But what ideas does the youth annex to the words pleasure and virtue? Or does he annex any? If he annex no idea to the words, he is merely talking about sounds.

All reasoning ultimately refers to matters of fact; to judge whether any piece of reasoning be within the comprehension of a child, we must consider whether the facts to which it refers are within his experience. The more we increase his knowledge of facts, the more we should exercise him in reasoning upon them; but we should teach him to examine carefully before he admits any thing to be a fact, or any assertion to be true. Experiment, as to substances, is the test of truth; and attention to his own feelings, as to matters of feeling. Comparison of the evidence of others with the general laws of nature, which he has learned from his own observation, is another mode of obtaining an accurate knowledge of facts. M. Condillac, in his Art of Reasoning, maintains that the evidence of reason depends solely upon our perception of the *identity*, or, to us a less formidable word, *sameness*, of one proposition with another. "A demonstration," he says, "is only a chain of propositions, in which the same ideas passing from one to the other differ only because they are differently expressed; the evidence of any reasoning consists solely in its identity."

M. Condillac exemplifies this doctrine by translating this proposition, "The measure of every triangle is the product of its height by half its base," into self-evident, or, as he calls them, identical proportions. The whole ultimately referring to the ideas which we have obtained by our senses of a triangle; of its base, of measure, height, and number. If a child had not previously acquired any one of these ideas, it would be in vain to explain one term by another, or to translate one phrase or proposition into another; they might be identical, but they would not be self-evident propositions to the pupil; and no conclusion, except what relates merely to words, could be

formed from such reasoning. The moral which we should draw from Condillac's observations for Practical Education must be, that clear ideas should first be acquired by the exercise of the senses, and that afterwards, when we reason about things in words, we should use few and accurate terms, that we may have as little trouble as possible in changing or translating one phrase or proposition into another.

Children, if they are not overawed by authority, if they are encouraged in the habit of observing their own sensations, and if they are taught precision in the use of the words by which they describe them, will probably reason accurately where their own feelings are concerned.

In appreciating the testimony of others, and in judging of chances and probability, we must not expect our pupils to proceed very rapidly. There is more danger that they should overrate, than that they should undervalue the evidence of others; because, as we formerly stated, we take it for granted that they have had little experience of falsehood. We should, to preserve them from credulity, excite them, in all cases where it can be obtained, never to rest satisfied without the strongest species of evidence, that of their own senses. If a child says, "I am sure of such a thing," we should immediately examine into his reasons for believing it. "Mr. A. or Mr. B. told me so," is not a sufficient cause of belief, unless the child has had long experience of A. and B.'s truth and accuracy; and, at all events, the indolent habit of relying upon the assertions of others, instead of verifying them, should not be indulged.

It would be waste of time to repeat those experiments, of the truth of which the uniform experience of our lives has convinced us; we run no hazard, for instance, in believing any one who simply asserts, that they have seen an apple fall from a tree; this assertion agrees with the great natural *law of gravity*, or, in other words, with the uniform experience of mankind: but if anybody told us that they had seen an apple hanging self-poised in the air, we should reasonably suspect the truth of their observation, or of their evidence.

This is the first rule which we can most readily teach our pupils in judging of evidence. We are not speaking of children from four to six years old, for everything is almost equally extraordinary to them; but when children are about ten or eleven, they have acquired a sufficient variety of facts to form comparisons, and to judge to a certain degree of the probability of any new fact that is related. In reading and in conversation we should now exercise them in forming judgments, where we know that they have the means of comparison. "Do you believe such a thing to be true? and why do you believe it? Can you account for such a thing?" are questions we should often ask at this period of their education. On hearing extraordinary facts some children will not be satisfied with vague assertions, others content themselves with saying, "It is so, I read it in a book." We should have little hopes of those who swallow everything they read in a book; we are always pleased to see a child hesitate and doubt, and require positive proof before he believes. The taste for the marvellous is strong in ignorant minds, the wish to account for every new appearance characterizes the cultivated pupil.

A lady told a boy of nine years old (S—) the following story, which she had just met with in "The Curiosities of Literature." An officer, who was confined in the Bastille, used to amuse himself by playing on the flute: one day he observed that a number of spiders came down from their webs, and hung round him as if listening to his music; a number of mice also came from their holes and retired as soon as he stopped. The officer had a great dislike for mice, he procured a cat from the keeper of the prison, and when the mice were entranced by his music, he let the cat out amongst them.

S— was much displeased by this man's treacherous conduct towards the poor mice, and his indignation for some moments suspended his reasoning faculty; but, when S— had sufficiently expressed his indignation against the officer in the affair of the mice, he began to question the truth of the story; and he said that he did not think

it was certain that the mice and spiders came to listen to the music. "I do not know about the mice," said he, "but I think, perhaps, when the officer played upon the flute, he set the air in motion, and shook the cobwebs, so as to disturb the spiders. We do not, or did the child think, that this was a satisfactory account of the matter, but we mention it as an instance of the love of investigation, which we wish to encourage.

The difficulty of judging concerning the truth of evidence increases, when we take moral causes into the account. If we had any suspicion that a man who told us that he had seen an apple fall from a tree, had himself pulled the apple down and stolen it, we should set the probability of his telling a falsehood, and his motive for doing so, against his evidence; and though, according to the natural physical course of things, there would be no improbability in his story, yet there might arise improbability from his character for dishonesty; and thus we should feel ourselves in doubt concerning the fact. But if two people agreed in the same testimony our doubt would vanish, and dishonest man's doubtful evidence would be corroborated, and we should believe, notwithstanding his general character, in the truth of his assertion in this instance. We could make the matter infinitely more complicated, but what has been said will be sufficient to suggest to preceptors the difficulty, which their young and inexperienced pupils must feel, in forming judgments of facts where physical and moral probabilities are in direct opposition to each other.

We wish that a writer equal to such a talk would write trials for children as exercises for their judgment; beginning with the simplest, and proceeding gradually to the more complicated cases in which moral reasonings can be used. We do not mean, that it would be advisable to initiate young readers in the technical forms of law; but the general principles of justice, upon which all law is founded, might, we think, be advantageously exemplified. Such trials would entertain children extremely. There is a slight attempt at this kind of composition, we mean in a little trial

Making distinctions about distinction-making

When we think that a distinction has somehow to be brought to things to be certified as true, we are supposing that distinctions are like judgments and that they have to correspond to "states of affairs" to be qualified as true. But there is no way to possess any "objective correlate" for a distinction except in the distinction itself. There is no way to verify a distinction except by making it. There is nothing beyond a distinction for it to correspond to. Distinctions are not like judgments. Hence the truth of a distinction is truth in the sense of being genuine, not in the sense of being correct. There can be false distinctions, but they are false in the way "false gold" or "fool's gold" or "false love" are false, not in the way a false opinion is wrong. A false judgment can be a genuine judgment even though it is false, but false distinctions just are not distinctions. They seem to be distinctions but they are not. And the genuine thinking that must occur in true distinctions is a more fundamental kind of thinking than what we do when we make judgments, entertain opinions, and try to determine whether what we or others say is correct or not. Distinctions are prior to judgments and to definitions.

—Robert Sokolowski, in "Making Distinctions." *Review of Metaphysics,* June, 1979.

in *Evenings at Home*; and we have seen children read it with great avidity. Cyrus's judgment about the two coats, and the ingenious story of the olive merchant's cause rejudged by the sensible child in the *Arabian Tales*, have been found highly interesting to a young audience.

We should prefer truth to fiction; if we could select any instances from real life, any trials suited to the capacity of young people, they would be preferable to any which the most ingenious writer could invent for our purpose. A gentleman, who has taken his two sons, one of them ten, and the other fifteen years old, to hear trials at his county assizes, found by the account which the boys gave of what they had heard that they had been interested, and that they were capable of understanding the business.

Allowance must be made at first for the bustle and noise of a public place, and for the variety of objects which distract the attention.

Much of the readiness of forming judgments depends upon the power of discarding and obliterating from our mind all the superfluous circumstances; it may be useful to exercise our pupils, by telling them now and then stories in the confused manner in which they are sometimes related by puzzled witnesses; let them reduce the heterogeneous circumstances to order, make a clear statement of the case for themselves, and try if they can point out the facts on which the decision principally rests. This is not merely education for a lawyer, the powers of reasoning and judgment, when they have been exercised in this manner, may be turned to any art or profession. We should, if we were to try the judgment of children, observe, whether in unusual circumstances they can apply their former principles, and compare the new objects that are placed before them without perplexity. We have sometimes found that on subjects entirely new to them, children who have not been used to reason can lay aside the circumstances that are not essential and form a distinct judgment for themselves, independently of the opinion of others.

What Education Can Be: Education for Judgment

William James

Of what use is a college training? We who have had it seldom hear the question raised—we might be a little nonplussed to answer it offhand. A certain amount of meditation has brought me to this as the pithiest reply which I myself can give: The best claim that a college education can possibly make on your respect, the best thing it can aspire to accomplish for you, is this: that it should *help you to know a good man when you see him.* This is as true of women's as of men's colleges; but that it is neither a joke nor a one-sided abstraction I shall now endeavor to show.

What talk do we commonly hear about the contrast between college education and the education which business or technical or professional schools confer? The college education is called higher because it is supposed to be so general and so disinterested. At the "schools" you get a relatively narrow practical skill, you are told, whereas the "colleges" give you the more liberal culture, the broader outlook, the historical perspective, the philosophic atmosphere, or something which phrases of that sort try to express. You are made into an efficient instrument for doing a definite thing, you hear, at the schools; but, apart from that, you may remain a crude and smoky kind of petroleum, incapable of spreading light. The universities and colleges, on the other hand, although they may leave you less efficient for this or that practical task, suffuse your whole mentality with something more important than skill. They redeem you, make you well-bred; they make "good company" of you mentally. If they find you with a naturally boorish or caddish mind, they cannot leave you so, as a technical school may leave you. This at least, is pretended; this is what we hear among college-trained people when they compare their education with every other sort. Now, exactly, how much does this signify?

It is certain, to begin with, that the narrowest trade or professional training does something more for a man than to make a skillful practical tool of him—it makes him also a judge of other men's skill. Whether his trade be pleading at the bar or surgery or plastering or plumbing, it develops a critical sense in him for that sort of occupation. He understands the difference between second-rate and first-rate work in his whole branch of industry; he gets to know a good job in his own line as soon as he sees it; and getting to know this in his own line, he gets a faint sense of what good work may mean anyhow, that may, if circumstances favor, spread into his judgments elsewhere. Sound work, clean work, finished work: feeble work, slack work, sham work— these words express an identical contrast in many different departments of activity. In so far forth, then, even the humblest manual trade may beget in one a certain small degree of power to judge of good work generally.

Now, what is supposed to be the line of us who have the higher college training? Is there any broader line—since our education claims primarily not to be "narrow"—in which we also are made good judges between what is first-rate and what is second-rate only? What is especially taught in the colleges has long been known by the name of the "humanities," and these are often identified with Greek and Latin. But it is only as literatures, not as languages, that Greek and Latin have any general humanity-value; so that in a broad sense the humanities mean literature primarily, and in a still broader sense the study of masterpieces in almost any field of human endeavor. Literature keeps the primacy; for it not only consists of masterpieces, but is largely about masterpieces, being little more than an appreciative chronicle of human master-strokes, so far as it takes the form of criticism and history. You can give humanistic value to almost anything by teaching it historically. Geology, economics, mechanics, are humanities when taught with reference to the successive achievements of the geniuses to which these sciences owe their being. Not taught thus, literature remains grammar, art a catalogue, history a list of dates, and natural science a sheet of formulas and weights and measures.

The sifting of human creations!—nothing less than this is what we ought to mean by the humanities. Essentially this means biography; what our colleges should teach is, therefore, biographical history, that not of politics merely, but of anything and everything so far as human efforts and conquests are factors that have played their part. Studying in this way, we learn what types of activity have stood the test of time; we acquire standards of the excellent and durable. All our arts and sciences and institutions are but so many quests of perfection on the part of men; and when we see how diverse the types of excellence may be, how various the tests, how flexible the adaptations, we gain a richer sense of what the terms "better" and "worse" may signify in general. Our critical sensibilities grow both more acute and less fanatical. We sympathize with men's mistakes even in the act of penetrating them; we feel the pathos of lost causes and misguided epochs even while we applaud what overcame them.

Such words are vague and such ideas are inadequate, but their meaning is unmistakable. What the colleges—teaching humanities by examples which may be special, but which must be typical and pregnant—should at least try to give us, is a general sense of what, under various disguises, *superiority* has always signified and may still signify. The feeling for a good human job anywhere, the admiration of the really admirable, the disesteem of what is cheap and trashy and impermanent—this is what we call the critical sense, the sense for ideal values. It is the better part of what men know as wisdom. Some of us are wise in this way naturally and by genius; some of us never become so. But to have spent one's youth at college, in contact with the choice and rare and precious, and yet still to be a blind prig or vulgarian, unable to scent out human excellence or to divine it amid its accidents, to know it only when ticketed and labeled and forced on us by others, this indeed should be accounted the very calamity and shipwreck of a higher education.

The sense for human superiority ought, then, to be considered our line, as boring subways is the engineer's line and the surgeon's is appendicitis. Our colleges ought to have lit up in us a lasting relish for the better of man, a loss of appetite for mediocrities, and a disgust for cheapjacks. We ought to smell, as it were, the difference of quality in men and their proposals when we entered the world of affairs about us. Expertness in this might well atone for some of our awkwardness at accounts, for some of our ignorance of dynamos. The best claim we can make for the higher education, the best single phrase in which we can tell what it ought to do for us, is then, exactly what I said: it should enable us to *know a good man when we see him.*

That the phrase is anything but an empty epigram follows from the fact that if you ask in what line it is most important that a democracy like our should have its sons and daughters skillful, you see that it is this line more than any other. "The people in their wisdom"—this is the kind of wisdom most needed by the people. Democracy is on its trial, and no one knows how it will stand the ordeal. Abounding about us are pessimistic prophets. Fickleness and violence used to be, but are no longer, the vices which they charge to democracy. What its critics now affirm is that its preferences are inveterately for the inferior. So it was in the beginning, they say, and so it will be world without end. Vulgarity enthroned and institutionalized, elbowing everything superior from the highway, this, they tell us, is our irremediable destiny; and the picture-papers of the European continent are already drawing Uncle Sam with the hog instead of the eagle for his heraldic emblem. The privileged aristocrats of the foretime, with all their inquities, did at least preserve some taste for higher human quality and honor certain forms of refinement by their enduring traditions. But when democracy is sovereign, its doubters say, nobility will form a sort of invisible church, and sincerity and refinement, stripped of honor, precedence, and favor, will have to vegetate on sufferance in private corners. They will have no general influence. They will be harmless eccentricities.

Now, who can be absolutely certain that this may not be the career of democracy? Nothing future is quite secure; states enough have inwardly rotted; and democracy as a whole may undergo self-poisoning. But, on the other hand, democracy is a kind of religion, and we are bound not to admit its failure. Faiths and utopias are the noblest exercise of human reason, and no one with a spark of reason in him will sit down fatalistically before the croaker's picture. The best of us are filled with the contrary vision of a democracy stumbling through every error till its institutions glow with justice and its customs shine with beauty. Our better men *shall* show the

way and we *shall* follow them; so we are brought round again to the mission of the higher education in helping us to know the better kind of man whenever we see him.

The notion that a people can run itself and its affairs anonymously is now well known to be the silliest of absurdities. Mankind does nothing save through initiatives on the part of inventors, great or small, and imitation by the rest of us—these are the sole factors active in human progress. Individuals of genius show the way, and set the patterns, which common people then adopt and follow. *The rivalry of the patterns is the history of the world.* Our democratic problem thus is statable in ultra-simple terms: Who are the kind of men from whom our majorities shall take their cue? Whom shall they treat as rightful leaders? We and our leaders are the x and the y of the equation here; all other historic circumstances, be they economical, political, or intellectual, are only the background of occasion on which the living drama works itself out between us.

In this very simple way does the value of our educated class define itself: we more than others should be able to divine the worthier and better leaders. The terms here are monstrously simplified, of course, but such a bird's-eye view lets us immediately take our bearings. In our democracy, where everything else is so shifting, we alumni and alumnae of the colleges are the only permanent presence that corresponds to the aristocracy in older countries. We have continuous traditions, as they have; our motto, too, is *noblesse oblige*; and, unlike them, we stand for ideal interests solely, for we have no corporate selfishness and wield no powers of corruption. We ought to have our own class-consciousness. "Les intellectuels"! What prouder club-name could there be than this one, used ironically by the party of "red blood," the party of every stupid prejudice and passion, during the anti-Dreyfus craze, to satirize the men in France who still retained some critical sense and judgment! Critical sense, it has to be confessed, is not an exciting term, hardly a banner to carry in processions. Affections for old habit,

How important are categories for children?

I should like to see children learning to receive sharper and more delicate impressions. This they can do by learning sharper and more precise expressions for what they receive. We do our children a cruel disservice by clamoring at them for "self-expression." We encourage them to draw trees not as they see them but as they "feel" about them. God knows, no one wants children to draw with daguerreotype realism, to record with mere pointless accuracy. But why do we badger children into "feeling" about trees, when trees do not exist? Trees do not exist: a silver maple exists, and a quaking aspen exists, and a cypress exists. One lives many years, I think, before one has seen enough of the particular trees that exist to be able to Platonize and have feelings about ideal or abstract trees.

Numbers have their most vital attribute in common; none of them exists. But with things, the fundamental attribute, existence itself, is only to be found in individuals, in particular things. Categories are important utensils of the mind, but they are of the mind only; they summarize life, but they are not the stuff of life. When we are older, we may feel deeply about summaries, but when we are young we should feel deeply about the moments of living, the moments themselves.

—Donald Barr, *Who Pushed Humpty Dumpty? Dilemmas In American Education Today* (New York: Atheneum, 1971) p. 296.

currents of self-interest, and gales of passion are the forces that keep the human ship moving; and the pressure of the judicious pilot's hand upon the tiller is a relatively insignificant energy. But the affections, passions, and interests are shifting, successive, and distraught; they blow in alternation while the pilot's hand is steadfast. He knows the compass, and, with all the leeways he is obliged to tack toward, he always makes some headway. A small force, if it never lets up, will accumulate effects more considerable than those of much greater forces if these work inconsistently. The ceaseless whisper of the more permanent ideals, the steady tug of truth and justice, give them but time, *must* warp the world in their direction.

This birds-eye view of the general steering function of the college-bred amid the driftings of democracy ought to help us to a wider vision of what our colleges themselves should aim at. If we are to be the yeast-cake for democracy dough, if we are to make it rise with culture's preferences, we must see to it that culture spreads broad sails. We must shake the old double reefs out of the canvas into the wind and sunshine, and let in every modern subject, sure that any subject will prove humanistic, if its setting be kept only wide enough.

Stevenson says somewhere to his reader: "You think you are just making this bargain, but you are really laying down a link in the policy of mankind." Well, your technical school should enable you to make your bargain splendidly, but your college should show you just the place of that kind of bargain—a pretty poor place, possibly—in the whole policy of mankind. That is the kind of liberal outlook, of perspective, of atmosphere, which should surround every subject as a college deals with it.

The Importance of a Cultural Pedagogy

John J. McDermott

In our time and in our nation, public precollegiate education is in serious disarray. It is now a nationally observed phenomenon that despite good intentions on the part of teachers and generally intelligent students, even those students who proceed on to colleges and universities seem culturally deprived. They exhibit a staggering ignorance of history and letters, and their symbolic resources for imaginative reconstruction seem bankrupt. It is as if the soul has disappeared, leaving only a more or less satisfactory standardized test as the approach to learning.

Given the skepticism about the salutary effect of recent federal programs for the amelioration of problems besetting the public schools and given the economic climate of America in 1990, it is very unlikely that we will witness the appearance of an educational Marshall plan in the near future. Consequently, the finances, the neighborhoods, and the clientele of the public schools will remain basically the same in this decade. The curriculum, however, need not remain the same. And we can move in the direction of a significant shift in the focus of the teaching process.

I believe that humanistic learning is present in every endeavor and that it is dramatically present in the traditional endeavors of precollegiate education. How did it happen that the discipline known as history became responsible for the history of everything, such that other disciplines became ahistorical? If I am teaching physics to secondary school students, it is not germane to the discussion that for more than two thousand years, physics and philosophy were identical? Is

it not significant that the ancient philosopher, Democritus, anticipated modern atomic theory? Should not these students be told that the history of science is pockmarked with errors, many of them propagated far beyond the time of exposure, because of political or ideological reasons? Would not the teaching of science be served well if we were to introduce the students to the contrasting conflicts found in the life and work of Galileo, to that of Lysenko? In this way, the teaching of science involves not only history but ethics and biography, as well. Similar examples from the sciences can be multiplied indefinitely, and the historical dimension of every discipline should be an integral aspect of its presentation.

We do not quarrel with the fact that it is necessary and salutary that precollegiate education spend time on mathematics, and on reading, writing, and speaking English and at least one other language, all taught very early in the schooling process. And, whenever possible, computer-assisted instruction should be utilized. But the rest of the curriculum should embody a cultural pedagogy, by which I mean the common source of our personal expectations, sensibilities, and evaluations.

Pedagogy is hapless and empty if it does not face directly the deep and pervasive dialectic between the historical and genetic conditioning of the person on the one hand and the impress of the novelties of the physical and social world on the other hand. This confrontation between our human heritage and the world in which we find ourselves, is the stuff out of which we weave that fragile creature we call our very own self. The key to successful mapping of this conflictual terrain is the making of relations, that is, the forging of a distinctively personal presence in the doings and undergoings that constitute our experience. The making of relations is a life-long endeavor, but it is especially crucial in the lives of children, as they struggle to achieve self-consciousness in a vast, complex and initially undefined environment.

Helping our children to learn how to make relations is the central and most important task of pedagogy. To the extent that they do not learn to make their own relations, children are doomed to living secondhand lives, creatures of habituation, who merely follow out the already programmed versions of their experience as inherited from parents, older siblings, and self-appointed definers of reality, such as teachers. Ironically, a child who knows how to make relations can convert even authoritarian and repressive treatment into paths of personal liberation, whereas a child who does not make relations converts invitations to free inquiry into derivative and bland repetition. This irony is made vivid for us when we realize that most often the lives of those whom we regard as "great" are characterized by affliction, suffering, and frequent rejection. In the hands of those who can make and remake relations, even negative events become the nutrition for a creative life.

Just what is it for a child to make relations and why do I regard it as crucial to a humanistic pedagogy? First, we must dispel any naiveté about the allegedly virginal character of the emerging self. The profound and complex preconscious conditioning of the self is a truism in our time. It is now obvious that as we come to self-consciousness in our early years, we are playing out our inherited genetic and social trappings. None of us can ignore the conditioning power of this inheritance The existence of a pristine self, free of the entangling alliances of one's genetic and social past is a myth. To be born white or black, male or female, Irish or Jewish, is an inherited context as thick as the earth itself. To experience one's post-natal years in the city or on a farm, in the snow or in the jungle is an informing crucible that our consciousness can repress but never totally dismiss. One could multiply these inheritances indefinitely, and a diagnosis of their significance in the lives of children could become a rich source of self-awareness as well as of awareness of others by contrast. In fact, I have in mind that these diagnoses would be the beginning of the child's self-understanding and the beginning of the child's attempt to build a new, distinctively personal world.

My point here is that the only way to obviate the deleterious secondhandedness of our inherited trappings, is to bring them to the fore and diagnose them as to their richness, their narrowness and the role they play in our assumptions. Under careful and probing guidance, even very young children are capable of fleshing out their distinctive sense of time, space, place, size, color, tone, and ever more subtle ambiences of the world in which they "find" themselves. In this way, the inheritances are transformed from conceptual boxes in which the child is unknowingly encased, to perceptual fields, fit for romping and reconstructing in the light of present experiences. This is precisely what I mean by the making of relations, namely, taking these inherited conditionings and turning them from conceptual rocks into something more diaphanous, crossed and recrossed with variant images, attitudes, and styles.

There is nothing arcane in this, for children, despite their inheritances, seek novelty, naturally, unless they are prevented by a pedagogy which attempts to reduce all of their experiences to a common denominator. For example, just recently, a teacher was queried in a newspaper article as to how she would begin her teaching after the children returned from their Hanukkah or Christmas holidays. She replied that if they insisted, they could take a "few minutes" to say what they did during that time, but then it would be "back to the routine." One could hardly dignify this approach as educational, for the classroom is a morgue and the children are cadavers, passive witnesses to an anatomical dissection on behalf of a fixed curriculum.

To the contrary, is not this the time to assist in the conversion of the children's ordinary events, celebrated for two millennia, into something extraordinary and within their reach? Is not this the time to read them O. Henry's "Gift of the Magi," and appropriate selections from the *Diary of Ann Frank*? Is not this the time to introduce them to Ramadan, the holy period of Islam and then to contrast Judaism, Christianity, and Islam with Buddhism and Hinduism? Is not this the time to assist the children in leaping upon an experience, about to be had and then just after it is undergone, so that they may open it up and reach out to neighboring experiences, analogous, and starkly different? It is necessary for one to have experience if one is to make relations and create a personal world, tied to others yet distinctive. To have experience without making relations, especially of dissimilarity, is to be left with the inert, repetitious and routine.

Like William James, I, too, believe that experience grows by its edges. By nature, the child comes into the world, on edge, and the qui vive, with a penchant for making relations. Traditional education, however, seems perversely determined to block this run of the imagination, opting rather for a world made up of boxes, separate one from the other, each defined and named, impervious to the rash of potential relations that yield themselves only to the reflection born of experienced perception. Is it not long overdue that contemporary educational practices integrate the accrued wisdom of this century and come to realize that names, categories, schema, and defi-

nitions are but functional placeholders in our experiencing the flow of events, linked to each other in a myriad of ways?

With the exception of speculative mathematics and formal logic, percepts should reign over concepts. Definitions should never be taken to exhaust the meaning, texture, tone, or implication of that defined. Ambiguity should be restored to its proper place as the proper response in direct proportion to the importance of the experience undergone. Love and loyalty, for example, are exquisitely ambiguous and no amount of quantitative social science methodology can clarify them sufficiently, such that they become fully understood or manipulable. I have no objection to the proper utilization of quantitative methodology, and I am aware of the necessity of scientific rigor. Similarly, I endorse the importance of high technology and the utilization of the computer in attainment of ever more sophisticated and accurate access to data. No, my concern is quite different. I lament the suffusion of the elementary and secondary school curriculum with disciplines and approaches whose major task is to prepare students for successful functioning in an ostensibly high-technological future, as though such activity was to be the primary activity of a human life.

If we are to survive as an originating human culture, we cannot view the reflective awareness of our past, the extensive knowledge of other cultures and other languages, literature, the arts, and speculative science as activities merely desirable and actually peripheral to the more important task of "getting along" in the future. This approach may enable us to survive as a nation, that is, as the saying goes, to hold our own. On the other hand, we shall become spiritually bankrupt.

Knowing Better

Ann Diller

Teachers, parents and other adults who work with children commonly talk as if even fairly young children have some moral knowledge. They often act as if such children could, on occasion, be legitimately held morally responsible for their actions, as when they assert to a young child: "You know better than that!" or, somewhat less absolutely, "You ought to know better." In other situations the same adult will excuse the child as "not knowing any better."

We thus tend to distinguish between at least two types of moral situations for children: (1) situations where we think a child can or does "know better" and (2) situations where we believe a child cannot or does not know any better. If such a distinction holds, then it should have some interesting implications for moral education.[1] But first we need to consider the distinction itself. In Section I we will examine our use of "knowing better" with young children.

In Section II we will discuss four prerequisites for knowing better. Section III explores an approach to moral education designed to help children acquire these four prerequisites. Our approach is to help children find "Live Moral Alternatives" for themselves. Efforts to do moral education are rarely free from ethical dangers; in Section IV we discuss ways in which the use of Live Moral Alternatives can avoid some prevalent dangers in contemporary moral education.

Situations

In order to examine the distinction between "knowing better" and "not knowing any better," let's consider its use with young children where the distinction is perhaps the most clearcut. Can a young child "know better" in some situations and not in others, as our usage seems to presuppose?

Most of us seem willing to grant that very young children frequently do *not* know any better. When a curious toddler crawls off with a visitor's purse we do not accuse the child of stealing. When a preschooler misleads us with his fanciful tales, we do not accuse him of lying. When he sails his brother's prize model ship to the bottom of the pond, or polishes the antique furniture with cold cream, or feeds the family's dinner to the stray dog, we may get upset, but we are generally willing to grant (after we calm down) that the child didn't know any better.

In fact there are so many instances in which young children truly don't know any better that we may well ask whether parents and teachers are mistaken when they think otherwise. Certainly people can be mistaken in this way, as in the case Selma Fraiberg cites, in connection with "... one of the practical problems which may emerge in the first three months of life ... The infant cries fitfully for hours ... If his mother holds him he may subside for a while, but soon the howling begins again. He is not ill. He does not have colic." The desperate and sleepless parents may resort then to what Fraiberg refers to as an "old theory" namely that the infant "is spoiled and he just wants attention. He is using crying as a weapon against his parents, as a means of getting his own way."

As Fraiberg points out, this "old theory" is untenable partly because it is based on a number of false premises, such as the notion "that an under-three-month-old infant has the mental equipment to carry out a plot against his parents, that he takes pleasure in disturbing their sleep, in exercising his tyranny over them,"[2] To assume that the infant could know any better is clearly mistaken. Even worse is the tendency in the "old theory" to accuse or blame the infant.

But in contrast to a three-month-old, what about a three-*year*-old? Let us look at two actual examples. These should sound not unfamiliar to anyone who has had occasion to work closely with young children or to observe them at play.

(a) The day-care teacher of a little boy, who had recently begun to talk, reported that he was hitting other children and that her efforts to forestall it by reprimands and mild punishment had been unsuccessful. The mother decided to "reason with" the boy. "Why are you hitting other children?" she asked him. Barely able to talk, he asserted, "E. (his brother) hits. Daddy hits. You hit." "You are right," said his mother. "From now on, if *anyone* hits, they will be reminded not to and we will all try very hard not to. If we do that, will you also try not to hit?" "Yes," he promised. His teacher reported that he was as good as his word; there was indeed no more hitting.[3]

(b) Two four-year-olds were engaged in an increasingly acrimonious dispute over the possession of a large set of magic markers. A nearby adult pointed out that since there were 16 markers it would be *fair* if each child counted out 8 of them. Fascinated, the children not only forgot their quarrel, but even their drawings and devoted the next half hour to a very full and effective discussion generating and agreeing upon many further rules (e.g., if there are two of the same color, we each get one; if there is only one color, the person gets it whose favorite color it is; if both children like that color, or if neither does, they take turns using it).

Similar observations and anecdotes from teachers and parents of preschool and grade-school children indicate a few limited but recurrent moral concerns. For example, most young children seem to be concerned with fairness. Even before they can comprehend counting, division, or the conservation of matter as objective operations, many children have a surprisingly accurate and highly motivated sense of "equality of portions" when they are to have something desirable distributed among themselves. Granted that most children's first concern is that they personally be dealt with fairly, the important thing to note is that, unlike say puppies who apparently want all they can get, children are often concerned to assure themselves of their *fair share*. Nor is their concern only with distributive justice; they are similarly sensitive to violations of retributive justice and will sometimes defend a child who has been unjustly accused or punished. Indeed, the capacity for what appears to be *moral* outrage in a child who has been treated unfairly, had a promise broken, or been lied to, is—if anything—more dramatic in children than in adults.

Given such examples, it is at least plausible to suppose that sometimes the presumptions underlying our use of "you know better" and "you ought to know better" with young children are not entirely mistaken, while at other times such presumptions do seem dubious and unfounded. What is important then is to come up with the characteristics that distinguish those situations in which treating children as being capable of "knowing better" seems at least to be appropriate, from those in which it is inappropriate or farfetched.

Self-controlled conduct

There are inhibitions and coordinations that entirely escape consciousness. There are, in the next place, modes of self-control which seem quite instinctive. Next, a man can be his own training-master and thus control his self-control. When this point is reached much or all the training may be conducted in imagination. When a man trains himself, thus controlling control, he must have some moral rule in view, however special and irrational it may be. But next he may undertake to improve this rule; that is, to exercise a control over his control of control. To do this he must have in view something higher than an irrational rule. He must have some sort of moral principle. This, in turn, may be controlled by reference to an esthetic ideal of what is fine. There are certainly more grades than I have enumerated. Perhaps their number is indefinite. The brutes are certainly capable of more than one grade of control; but it seems to me that our superiority to them is more due to our greater number of grades of self-control than it is to our versatility.

—C.S. Peirce. *Collected Papers*, Vol. V, p.

Four Prerequisites

So far we have decided that it does make sense to expect children to know better in some situations and not in others. And we are now in search of what makes the difference between the two. But first let's try to be clear on just what we are looking for. As teachers, parents, and educators, we are not looking for cases where children invariably know better or always act as they should (not even adults do that!). What we want are situations where it is plausible for children to know better, where children sometimes act as they should.

If we look at situations in our own culture where even a small child is sometimes presumed to know better, such as certain forms of sharing, especially "taking turns," and not hurting other children, we usually find that four conditions are met:

1. The child is sufficiently familiar with similar cases to recognize this situation as one of a certain sort and to distinguish the relevant moral factors. This generally includes understanding the key terms; for example, the child knows what "taking turns" means in practice.

2. The child is able to control his or her own actions in this situation; and it is within the child's powers to act in a morally acceptable way under the circumstances.

3. The child is able to recognize that the morally relevant consequences are connected with the child's own action, often because they are immediately and directly observable. For example, in hitting another person, one can observe both the physical impact and the reaction of the victim.

4. It is also highly likely, although not necessary,[4] that the child has had some direct personal experience with the morally relevant consequences. The child may have already suffered or benefited from them, or observed first-hand their effect on someone else.

Without these four conditions, we cannot, and should not, expect a child to know better. But these four conditions are *only* minimal because it does not follow that someone will automatically or definitely "know better" just because these conditions are met. I shall, therefore, call them the four *prerequisites* for knowing better. Just as being able to count accurately from one to twenty is a prerequisite for understanding the process of adding either one, these four prerequisites make possible but do not guarantee a child's "knowing better." Let's consider each one separately.

Recognizing the Situation and Understanding What Counts

Before a child is expected to know that s/he should take turns in a given situation, the child needs to know what it means to "take turns," and what sorts of circumstances call for this action. This is not easy. The child must learn what "taking turns" looks like, how it works, and when people should do it.

Some of the first cues for recognizing the right circumstances probably come when a child enters a situation in which the appropriate actions are already being taken, as when children are already lined up for the sliding board, or a teacher is allotting turns one by one to a classroom group, or a parent is requiring and guiding the sequential use of a popular toy. Over time then the child can begin to develop a rudimentary sense of the relevant moral factors, namely that more than one child wants to do or to use the same thing at the same time, that this is not possible, and that the children have more or less equal claims.

Young children cannot, of course, verbalize their understanding of the relevant moral factors, but they can learn to act on them with a fair degree of accuracy. For example, most children come to distinguish between the obligation to share common property, such as playground equipment, and the element of altruistic choice involved in deciding to share one's own toys with a friend or playmate. And many children are capable of righteous indignation when another child does not or will not wait their turn, but "butts in line" or "hogs the ball."

Within the Powers of the Child

When an indignant parent or teacher says to a child: "You know better than that!" the adult is not referring merely, or even primarily, to the child's verbal facility for handling cognitive knowledge (e.g., the child's ability to recite Kant's different formulations of the Categorical Imperative). The expectation is rather that the child ought to have acted in a certain way; that ought implies can; and that the appropriate action was within the child's capability. An adult may, of course, be mistaken about a particular child's capacity for dealing with a given situation (as we noted above in Fraiberg's case of the infant). But the point is that the expectation is based on a presumption that the child can do the right thing, that the child is able to do so. This ability is an essential prerequisite for "knowing better than that!" We need, therefore, to keep asking ourselves over again for each child in each situation whether an appropriate moral action is within the present powers of the child.

In asking whether a moral action is "within the powers of the child" we are, I think, asking a number of different questions. One question is whether the child has the physical capacity for doing what is expected. A different question is whether the child has the requisite skill or "know how" for doing what needs to be done. I may have the physical capacity to be a strong swimmer, but still not have learned how to swim, so that it would not be within my present powers to rescue a drowning man by swimming out to him. So also children have the capacity for doing numerous things which they have not yet learned how to do.

Or it may not be so much the skill that is lacking as it is information or other knowledge. In the case of the magic markers, the two four-year-olds needed to know what would be a fair division of their common pool of markers—once they had that information they could use their skill in counting out eight markers each.

Another difficult, but nonetheless important, aspect of one's powers is that mysterious something called "willpower." Because one bothersome characteristic of moral imperatives is that they sometimes run counter to what would be easiest to do or what we would like to do right this minute, some minimal development of will-power seems to be required. How to get this will-power and how to sustain it for the right causes pose interesting but far from simple questions.

Achieving strength of will may depend partly on our ability to keep our attention focused on the right thing long enough. If this is so, then the development of a capacity for sustained concentration, or for a concentration span of some minimal duration, may itself be a prerequisite for will-power. I am convinced that one thing able teachers do is to help students focus their attention in a productive way on those factors which are most important for the students' own level of learning.

Seeing the Moral Connections

Two separate questions can be asked here. First, is it clear to the child that there are morally relevant consequences which are connected with his or her own action? Second, is it possible for the child to trace or to comprehend the causal sequence involved? The first question is crucial from a moral point of view, while the second question reveals the importance of education. When young children meet both these requirements, it usually means that we have a sequence with relatively few steps, where the consequences are immediately and directly observable, rather than remote or indirect.

As the child gets older, the sequences can get longer and the consequences can become more remote. To understand that the use of aerosol spray cans endanger the ozone layer which in turn endangers life on our planet is a connection that even many adults have trouble seeing; or they, at least, have trouble taking the moral consequences seriously.

It is often difficult to separate moral indifference from mere ignorance. A high school chemistry teacher told me that he found it had been common practice in his high school for students to dump dangerous chemicals down the lab drains, even though the drains went into the regular town system and eventually back into the water supply network. And even in recent years, most students who study chemistry learn chemical composition and properties without any more

than a passing reference to the dangers and toxic effects caused by misuse, or by any use, of these same compounds. Thus, the chemistry student who casually dumps his most recent experiment down the drain may do so out of disregard for others or out of ignorance of the facts (e.g., where the drain goes or what the dangers are). In such cases, teaching the relevant facts and information may well be the best, if not the only, way to call attention to the moral connections.

Certainly in the long run, education which reveals interrelationships and causal connections is necessary if students are to be enabled to meet the ethical demands of others or even to exercise fully and ably their own rights. But in the short run we may have to insist on giving due recognition to moral connections, to help children see these even before they are capable of grasping all the intricacies of a causal sequence.

The minimal requirement, the key to seeing a *moral* connection, is to recognize or to be persuaded that certain actions do, indeed, have an effect for good or for ill. Being so persuaded need not mean that one truly understands the causal connections or sequence, any more than many car drivers understand why it is that turning the ignition key starts their car engines. Drivers do, however, recognize that there is a relevant connection and they act accordingly. Similarly, in order to "know better" morally we do not have to wait for complete causal understanding. Let me give an example from my own experience.

I'm working in my bedroom on a winter's afternoon. My two-year-old son David, who has been busy with his blocks on the floor, gets up and goes over to our waterbed where he starts to play with the thermostat dial. He turns the knob back and forth and watches the red light go on and off. I notice what he's doing and say, "No, no David, please don't play with that." No response. I stop working. Then slowly, carefully, and a bit dramatically, I explain: "David, if you do that it turns off the heater, and it makes Mommy and Daddy's bed all cold—Brrr, FREEZY COLD!" David listens. He is a New Hampshire child who knows that "freezy cold" is like what happens to your hands when you lose your mittens in the snow. He stops changing the dial, allows me to reset it, and gradually goes back to his blocks.

In this episode with David we would answer our two initial questions differently. In answering the second question, we have to consider all the causal connections between setting the thermostat dial and controlling the temperature of the waterbed, which were surely beyond David's grasp at his age. In answering the first question, we look at the way in which the temperature of the waterbed affects the people who sleep in it, and the related fact that David's changing the dial made his parents uncomfortably cold. This connection was not totally beyond his comprehension, even though he may have found it quite puzzling. He could at least recognize that it was "not a good thing" to make us "Brrr—Freezy Cold." (If you think I am exaggerating, try, some winter's night, to sleep on an unheated waterbed in an unheated bedroom; granted, however, that this is not a "serious" moral consequence. For more on "moral" see Section III.)

Personal Experiences and Having Moral Reasons

Even people who can comprehend causal connections and morally undesirable consequences may still have trouble taking a moral danger seriously if it is beyond the range of their own personal experience. When we considered cases in which it was plausible to expect young children, to "know better," we noted that usually such situations are ones where the children do have some personal experiences which could provide the basis for a sympathetic understanding of the human consequences. David's encounters with "freezy cold" snow provided just such a basis. But a more fundamental question here is whether or not the child has any basis at all, experiential or otherwise, for sympathizing with others, for imagining themselves in another's position, for understanding why one action might

be better for the persons involved (or "right") while another act might be worse (or wrong").

Another way of putting our question is to ask whether the children themselves might "have any moral reasons" for acting one way rather than another, any reasons for caring about what happens to others, any reasons for doing the "right thing." "Having moral reasons" is, of course, a very complicated business that has worried numerous philosophers—and undoubtedly children do not have moral reasons in fully the same sense which Immanuel Kant, Henry Sidgwick, John Stuart Mill or John Rawls have them. Nevertheless, I think we need to beware of making "having moral reasons" so complicated that we begin to believe that young children cannot have them at all. For example, not hurting someone is a valid moral reason at almost any age. And being hurt and hurting someone are experiences which most children have had, experiences for which they can often meet all four of our prerequisites. It is not surprising, therefore, that a brief and frequent effective moral command-plus-explanation is: "Don't do that, it hurts!" "It hurts" is one moral reason which most children can understand, and one which many children can also accept as their own.

Live Moral Alternatives

If moral education consists partly of helping children to get to "know better" in an ever widening range of circumstances, and if we are correct in our assessment of what some of the prerequisites for knowing better are, then one task for moral education would seem to be that of helping children to acquire these four prerequisites. Each one suggests educational tasks or undertakings which are appropriate to it. For example, our first prerequisite can be furthered by accurate language learning, as we noted when we discussed "taking turns." It may also be furthered by our giving brief moral explanations to children, by pointing out why we call certain actions "right" and others "wrong," by calling their attention to the relevant moral factors.

Of all the possible implications for teaching and for moral education, I want to discuss one in particular which I consider central. This task is of key importance for meeting our second prerequisite, but it incorporates and relies on the other three as well. This central task is that of helping children to acquire *Live Moral Alternatives.*

Since we are concerned here with moral education, we shall speak of the "child" as the agent in question. But Live Moral Alternatives are by no means limited to children. The concept applies to adults as well. If you substitute "agent" (or "person") for "child," you can see that Live Moral Alternatives are important at any age.

A *Live* Moral Alternative is, first of all, a course of action which is within the child's powers, which the child has the skill, knowledge, and ability to carry out. Thus it is "live" in the sense that the child can actually do it.

But it is also *"live"* in the sense of our fourth prerequisite, namely that the child also has some reason for choosing this course of action, that the child has some predisposition for actually considering the alternative as a live option. Being live in this sense does not mean that the child will find the reason so conclusive or compelling that s/he will necessarily act accordingly, but it does mean that s/he will seriously entertain the possibility of so acting, that it accords with one of the child's own possible choices. Thus the alternative is "live" both in the sense that the child can do it and in the sense that the child has some reason for doing it.

In determining what counts as a *moral* alternative, we again need to note some different senses of the term.[5] In the first and most stringent sense, a "moral" alternative is one which does not injure others and does not harm the innocent. Some of our most common moral proscriptions, such as "Don't Kill," prohibit just such actions. In fact, this first sense of "moral" is largely a matter of telling us what not to do rather than what to do. It places certain *moral constraints* on our

behavior and then says, in effect, "you can do anything you want, so long as you avoid these morally wrong actions." It sounds simple, but of course it isn't simple at all. Much of Ethics and Moral Philosophy are efforts to work out the details, the implications and complexities of our most basic moral constraints. Many conventional moral maxims are simplified ways of indicating which actions are so universally injurious that we can say they are almost always wrong.

One can argue that this stringent constraints sense of "moral" is the core of morality or even the only sense which ought to count as truly moral. One argument, for example, is that to "avoid causing evil" is the only moral requirement which applies to all of us "all of the time, with regard to everyone equally" (Gert, 73). But most of us, and especially many persons concerned to do moral education, use "moral" in additional ways which go beyond this moral constraints sense.

Before we leave this first sense of "moral" we should note that it does provide us with an important distinction, especially for our education and supervision of children. For this first sense of moral, this requirement to avoid causing evil, is the one which provides the strongest and clearest justification for intervention when questions of moral protection and enforcement arise. We do see ourselves as morally justified, indeed, obligated, to intervene in order to stop a chid in our care from causing serious harm or injury. Such a strong justification for intervention is not generally found in any other sense of "moral."

But the obligation to intervene in order to protect others from serious harm also illustrates another sense of "moral," namely that of preventing evil when we are in a position to do so. Thus, a *moral* alternative may not only avoid causing evil, it may also, upon occasion, be a course of action which helps to prevent evil.

But we still have not considered what is, perhaps, the most common further sense of "moral."[6] In general, to act morally means not only to refrain from certain actions because they are "wrong" but also to do other actions because these are "right." Some of these "right" actions are those which are also for the good of both ourselves and others, actions which are in the common interest, which may even aim for "the good of everyone alike" (Baier, 200f.). On this view a moral alternative would not only avoid causing evil, it would also be an alternative which was likely to promote some good. Here again we have conventional moral rules and principles which identify those positive actions which are most likely to promote good, as well as prevent evil. For example, we expect people to be fair, to respect each other, to uphold justice, to provide for mutual aid, to fulfill obligations, and to keep their promises.

In sum, we have said that a live *moral* alternative must first try to meet the moral constraints requirements, for this is our most serious and stringent sense for "moral." But in our searches for moral alternatives we often consider the extent to which different courses of action may also further the good of ourselves and others, as well as prevent evil. In some circumstances the best we can do is to find an alternative which does the least amount of harm; but ideally a moral alternative would both avoid evil and also promote good.

A Live Moral Alternative is an *alternative* in the sense that it is one among two or more possible courses of action open to the child. Moral agency generally presupposes some degree of choice, some sense in which it is possible for the person to have acted, chosen, or decided differently—or at least that other people in the same circumstances do indeed decide and act differently. Thus we are not talking about those instances where there is no conceivable way in which the child could have done otherwise, even if the child had had more information, more skill, more knowledge, etc.

Now it may be that in a given situation, as a matter of fact, a particular child does lack the necessary skills or information and therefore has very little real choice; but in such cases we can

---

Encouraging children to reason ethically

Children have first to be brought up on good general principles so they form good dispositions and reactions. Then, as they are able, they can be introduced to the critical thinking by which they can determine for themselves which are the good principles by which to live. When these general principles conflict, this same critical thinking will enable them to sort out the conflicts. It may even lead them to change the attitudes in which they were brought up.

—R.M. Hare, quoted in *The London Sunday Times*, Dec. 27, 1981.

---

say that *if* the child had been taught or helped then s/he could have acted differently. Thus, in this sense, a child may have a temporarily non-live alternative which education could bring alive. As educators we often know of alternatives which a child could take if the child knew of them.

Thus we can speak of someone "having an alternative" in two different senses one is that of its already being "live" for that person. We can also talk about an alternative for another person in the sense that *if* they knew about it and knew how to do it then it could be live, they could then choose it or consider it. For example, I may have arrived in a new city; and in trying to get from one section to another suppose that my alternatives are to go on foot, by private car, by taxi, bicycle, motorcycle or bus, or some combination thereof; but I may not know that there are also, as in Puerto Rico, the "Publicos" which are a cross between a taxi and a bus. Thus, in one sense the Publico is an alternative for me, it may even be the best way for me to reach my destination. But the Publico is not a "live" alternative for me *until* I find out about it and learn how to go about using it.

Morally acceptable courses of action for some children are rather like Publicos in Puerto Rico for a newcomer, they are available but the child does not know it. Children often need help in discovering what is available to them. Sometimes a person simply needs to be told about an alternative course of action. But children frequently need someone to show them how it is done, to go along with them the first few times. After that they may still require encouragement. And most of us can use what we aptly call "moral support." Older children, and many adults, want to talk about their options as they perceive them, to get help in assessing the practicability of certain actions: Can I do it? What is likely to happen? And most children need some guidance in tracing the moral consequences, the probable effects on all the persons involved, including themselves.

Consider a fairly common problem for schoolchildren—the playground bully. Most children tend to get stuck on three alternatives—fight, flight, or "tattletale." All three are frequently (not always) unsatisfactory. What most children need then are some more options, other courses of action besides these three. Perhaps they could acquire some skills in co-opting troublemakers. Or they might discover ways of bringing peer group pressure to bear or using group defense measures. They might even find acceptable ways to initiate changes in the relevant institutional structures, such as the playground activities and supervision.

Our point here is not to decide in the abstract which moral alternative is best for a given situation; in some situations there may be many good ones while in other cases there may be none under the existing circumstances. Our point is rather that the child does need to find some Live Moral Alternative. And in order to do so the child may need help.

Imaginative teachers can probably think of many more ways than I can to help their own students acquire such alternatives. They might do role-playing or simulations in which children act out different ways of handling the situation and get some sense of the different perspectives involved. They might read stories or see a film in which the children do deal successfully with bullies in morally acceptable fashion. Or the students might have a brainstorming session to come up with as many Live Moral Alternatives as they can. Whatever the method, it should be combined with a realistic discussion of both the practical and the moral merits of different suggestions. And it is crucial that the children's own particular perceptions, reasons, and powers be taken into account in the final assessment if the children are to find what are truly their own Live Moral Alternatives.

At other times the children may know very well what to do but need help in accomplishing it, in organizing and carrying through on what they want to do. This may require sustained group effort with varying degrees of adult guidance. We don't only need to help children discover or find their own moral reasons for doing the right thing—in fact, very often children already have good moral reasons. We also need to find ways of helping children to give sufficient attention to their own moral reasons so that they can muster or sustain the necessary "will-power" to carry through on their own convictions. Doing something *with* someone else is, of course, one of the ways we achieve our more difficult commitments—moral and otherwise. The prevalent, and often successful, use of common group tasks, of "teams" and cooperative ventures reflects this general truth.

Dangers

In helping children to acquire Live Moral Alternatives, we need to avoid the dangers of both "moralism" and ethical relativism. The danger of a moralistic approach is not only that it often identifies all of morality with a single ideology or one particular set of social conventions, but also that the moralist tends to exclude any alternative course of action which differs from his own restricted, predetermined ways of proceeding, regardless of whether or not the procedures and consequences are ethically desirable. The moralist thus excludes what are Live Moral Alternatives for others merely because they are not live for him, failing to distinguish his own way of being moral from all possible ways of acting morally.

A relativistic approach does allow for our differences in what is "live" to us, but it capitulates on the ethical requirement. The relativist fails to distinguish between what are admittedly different live options all of which are still morally acceptable and those options which are not only different but are also unethical as well. He seems unable or unwilling to admit that some live options are not merely different from others but may also be wrong from almost any informed moral viewpoint.

Certain ways of teaching "values clarification" can lend themselves to a form of ethical relativism. This happens when little or no distinction is made between: (a) those "values" that are a matter of taste or personal preference such as a preference for baseball over tennis and (b) those "values" which reflect primary human goods or basic moral rights and wrongs. If no one makes this distinction, then students are left with the impression that all these "values" are on a par, and that all "values" are equally justifiable or unjustifiable.

Although stage theories of moral development are considerably more sophisticated and adequate than most varieties of "moralism," some educational uses of moral stage theory do have dangers not unlike those of moralism. For instance, if in an educational setting one presents a moral dilemma with two and only two alternative courses of action, and also refuses to consider other options which might conceivably come closer to being both live and moral, then we have another version of "you have to do it my way." Such an approach implies, furthermore, that moral alternatives must come in a binary choice form, either this or that and nothing else, as if people really

were stuck with choosing between two and only two courses of action, however horrible they both may be.

In contrast to such unwarranted limitations, a Live Moral Alternative approach would encourage us to look further for other options, to try to find some more alternatives which might come closer to being both live and moral for the persons involved. Here is where knowledge and skills as well as philosophic study come in handy. For our knowledge and skills increase the range of what is "within our powers" thus making more alternatives "live" for us. And philosophic study should enable us to see more alternatives, to discover their ethical implications, and to assess their moral merits.

Another danger in the educational use of moral stage theory lies in the propensity for classifying or categorizing students. Placing a student in a "lower" stage than oneself can easily lead to underestimating the student's moral capacities. If, instead of struggling to fit students into classifications, we considered who could come up with truly live moral alternatives for a given situation, we might even discover that sometimes children find better Live Moral Alternatives than we do ourselves, even though we are, of course, at a much "higher" stage. I'll confess that this has happened to me a number of times with my students and even with my own children.

My pedagogical point is then that we should both help and allow children to find their own Live Moral Alternatives. Children, and adults as well, need courses of action which fit their perceptions, their powers, and their own reasons for acting. But we should also insist that these choices be morally acceptable.

Summary

We have said that we can distinguish between those situations in which children "don't know any better" and those in which they do "know better." And we found that even young children are capable of "knowing better" in certain circumstances where they can meet our Four Prerequisites. So we took one task of moral education to be that of helping children to meet these prerequisites in the situations where it is plausible and reasonable for them to do so. One way of doing this is to help children acquire Live Moral Alternatives—morally acceptable courses of action, that are within the powers of the child and make some appeal to the child's own reasons for acting. It does not follow that the child will always choose to act in this "right" way or shall succeed in doing so; but we should hope rather that at least sometimes the child may so choose and that under the right conditions may even succeed.

Footnotes and References

1. This article is taken from a larger study on which I am presently working. In it, I distinguish a number of different forms which moral education takes, and I address the question of who should undertake particular forms of moral education. The question of who has the right or the responsibility to do moral education is an important issue which I bypass in this article.

2. Selma H. Fraiberg, *The Magic Years*. New York: Charles Scribner's Sons, 1959, pp. 68-69.

3. These two anecdotes, (a) and (b), are taken from observations and records made by Dr. Nancy C. Glock of Carmichael, California. Nancy Glock helped me substantially with an earlier draft of Section 1. I also want to thank Dr. Jane Roland Martin and Dr. Beebe Nelson (both of U.Mass., Boston) for their helpful comments on successive drafts of this paper.

4. This fourth condition is stated in a preliminary way here, and it needs refinement in order to count as necessary. See Section II, 4, for the refinements.

5. My discussion of "moral" borrows freely from traditional and contemporary Western moral philosophy, without adhering strictly to any single position. Some relevant twentieth century references are:
   Kurt Baier, *The Moral Point of View*. Ithaca, N.Y.: Cornell University Press, 1958.
   Bernard Gert, *The Moral Rules*. New York: Harper & Row, 1970.
   John Rawls, *A Theory of Justice*. Cambridge, MA: Harvard University Press, 1971.
   W. D. Ross, *The Right and the Good*. Oxford: Clarendon Press, 1930.

6. Since a certain number of people still seem to see "sex" and "morals" as synonymous (cf. Webster's dictionary definition number 8.b.), I should probably emphasize that "sex" is not central to the meanings we are discussing here, even though some people will, no doubt, derive conclusions about sex from any line of practical reasoning.

On Becoming A Moral Agent: From Aristotle To Harry Stottlemeier

Michael S. Pritchard

Philosophy, says Aristotle, begins in wonder. So does childhood. *Harry Stottlemeier's Discovery* and the other IAPC materials join philosophical wonder with childhood. Ironically, Shakespeare's *Troilus and Cressida* reminds us that Aristotle insists that moral philosophy is not for the young. It mentions

> Young men, whom Aristotle thought
> Unfit to hear moral philosophy[2]

Aristotle's doubts focus on two apparent limitations of the young—inexperience and lack of rational principles.

If Aristotle is right, then we should not expect to find much that is philosophical in the moral thinking of children. Children can be seen, basically, as lacking what (at least some) adults have. The relative neglect of the philosophical thinking of children in the writings of philosophers suggests that Aristotle's view is widely shared. The main burden of this paper is to show that Harry and his young friends can hold their own against Aristotle—and that it is practically and morally significant to acknowledge this.

The Problem of Inexperience

If moral understanding requires a basic understanding of the social and political world of adults, we can all agree that even older children are relatively inexperienced (as are many adults). But, as *Harry* amply illustrates, the world of children is filled with analogues to the complex social and political institutions characteristic of our adult world. For example, Harry and his classmates critically discuss institutional aims, authority, and rules within the context of formal education.

The philosophical significance of such discussions depends, in part on how morality itself should be conceived. The 18th Century Scottish philosopher, Thomas Reid, has some very useful suggestions in this regard. Refusing to let practice be overrun by theory, he says:

> There is in Ethicks as in most Sciences a Speculative and practical Part, the first is subservient to the last (Reid 1990, p. 110).

Reid insists that morality is everyone's business, "and therefore the knowledge of it ought to be within the reach of all" (Reid 1788, p. 594). He also denies that "in order to understand his duty a man must needs be a philosopher and a metaphysician" (1788, p. 643). This does not mean that philosophical thinking is not necessary—only that this need not be one's preoccupation. That is, one need not be a student of Plato, Aristotle, Descartes, Locke, Hume, or any philosophers at all. Reid acknowledges that *moral systems* "swell to great magnitude," But this is not because there is a large number of general moral principles. He says that, actually, they are "few and simple." Moral systems are complex because applications of moral principles "extend to every part of human conduct, in every condition, every relation, and every transaction of life" (1788, p. 642). Given this wide reach of moral principles, it is clear that the limited experience of children restricts their ability to apply them. The same, to a lesser degree, is true of adults as well, since their range of experience, though more extensive, is also limited. Nevertheless, as *Harry* illustrates, there is no shortage of opportunities for children to test out moral concepts and principles within their familiar range of experience.

Lack of Rational Principles

Still, it might be objected, this has little bearing on the moral development of children. Aristotle said that children need to develop the habit of *doing* what is right or good. It is only much later that they will be able to appreciate *why* such and such is right or good. That is, before attending to the *reasons* why certain things are right or good there must first be good habits concerning whatever is right or good. Only those already imbued with these good habits will hear what reason has to say.

As for those who lack these habits, Aristotle says that arguments are of no use, "for these do not by nature obey the sense of shame, but only fear, and do not abstain from bad acts because of their baseness but through fear of punishment" (Burnyeat 1980, p. 75). Children, therefore, are not suited for moral philosophy:

> For he who lives as passion directs will not hear argument that dissuades him, nor understand it if he does; and how can we persuade one in such a state to change his ways? And in general passion seems to yield not to argument but to force. The character, then, must somehow be there already with a kinship to virtue, loving what is noble and hating what is base (Burnyeat 1980, p. 75).

Thus we find in Aristotle a theme familiar to 20th Century psychology—namely, that early morality is shaped by fear and punishment. For Freudians, the internalization of these external threats is nearly all there is to morality; adult morality is hardly more than variation on this early theme. For cognitive-developmental theorists like Piaget (1932) and Kohlberg (1981), there is much more to the story. But, even for them, the story begins with fear and punishment imposed on the self-centered child. Only later does the story take a rather remarkable shift in the direction of reasonable concern for others.

For Piaget and Kohlberg, early moral development is highly egocentric. Prior to age seven or eight, children see things only from their own point of view, and they are motivated primarily by fear of punishment or of not being loved. Kohlberg, for example, characterizes "justice" for very young children in terms of the threat of punishment for violating a rule emanating from authority or power. The second stage of moral development emphasizes the idea of reciprocal exchange ("You scratch my back and I'll scratch yours") but this is still basically self-interested motivation. Only at stage 3 does "empathy" enter in, enabling children to get beyond egocentricity to some extent. At this point limited Golden Rule reasoning is possible because children are finally able to imagine what it would be like to be in another person's situation.

Whether we are talking about Aristotle, Freud, Piaget, or Kohlberg, the idea that moral reasoning might play a significant role in moral education prior to age seven or eight is simply rejected. Of the four, Piaget and Kohlberg take the most optimistic view that reasoning might contribute to the moral development of young children. But even they offer little hope that sophisticated reflection can occur before age ten or eleven. This is when they believe that children are first able to "think about thinking" to any significant degree. If Piaget and Kohlberg are right about children's capabilities, then we should see Harry and their friends as just *beginning* to reflect on various

Socrates and moral inquiry

Why rank [the Socratic] method among the great achievements of humanity? Because it makes moral inquiry a common human enterprise open to every man. Its practice calls for no adherence to a philosophical system, or mastery of a specialized technique, or acquisition of a technical vocabulary. It calls for common sense and common speech. And this is as it should be, for how man should live is every man's business, and the role of the specialist and the expert should be only to offer guidance and criticism, to inform and clarify the judgment of the layman, leaving the final decision up to him. But while the Socratic method makes moral inquiry open to everyone, it makes it easy for no one. It calls not only for the highest degree of mental alertness of which anyone is capable, but also for moral qualities of a high order: sincerity, humility, courage. Socrates expects you to say what you really believe about the way *man* should live; which implies, among other things, about the way *you* should live. His method will not work if the opinion you give him is just *an* opinion: it must be *your* opinion: the one you stand ready to live by, so that if that opinion should be refuted, your own life or a part of life will be indicted or discredited, shown up to be a muddle, premised on a confusion or a contradiction. To get into the argument when you realize that this is the price you have to pay for it—that in the course of it your ego may experience the unpleasant sensation of a bloody nose—takes courage. To search for moral truth that may prove your own life wrong takes humility that is not afraid of humiliation. These are the qualities Socrates himself brings to the argument, and it is not entirely clear that he realizes how essential they are to protect it against the possibility that its dialectic, however rigorous, would merely grind out, as it could with impeccable logic, wild conclusions from irresponsible premises.

But is there not still a residual risk, you may ask, in making the Socratic method the arbiter of moral truth, inviting thereby every man to take, on its terms, a place in the supreme court which judges questions of morality? Certainly there is a risk, and a grave one. For though the method has some built-in protection against moral irresponsibility—the one I have just mentioned—it offers no guarantee whatever that it will always lead to truth. On this Socrates himself, if the foregoing interpretation of his agnosticism was correct, is absolutely clear. His "I don't know" honestly means "I could be mistaken in results reached by this method." And if Socrates could be mistaken, how much more so Tom, Dick and Harry. Why then open it to them? Socrates's answer is clear: Because each of them is a man. and "the unexamined life is not worth living by man" (*Apology* 38a). I could not go so far as he did at this point. I believe that many kinds of life are worth living by man. But I do believe that the best of all is the one in which every man does his own examining.

—from Gregory Vlastos. "The Paradox of Socrates." in Gregory Vlascos, ed., *The Philosophy of Socrates.*

aspects of their moral lives; and we are probably well advised not to expect too much too soon.

However, if they are wrong, important opportunities may be missed, and both children and adults will be the losers. IAPC programs are designed not to miss the earliest possible oppor-

tunities to engage children in moral reflection. *Harry* does not present 5th graders as neophytes when it comes to moral reasoning. Earlier IAPC programs assume that younger children are capable of reflecting on a variety of moral concepts (for example, fair/unfair, right/wrong, good/bad, cruel/kind). Is this a misguided effort on the part of IAPC, or is there evidence that even very young children have the capacities IAPC presumes they have?

Shewder, Turiel, and Much (1981) present evidence that children as young as four have an intuitive grasp of differences among prudential, conventional, and moral rules. Characterizing young children as "intuitive moralists," they say, "Although four- to six-year-olds have little reflective understanding of their moral knowledge, they nevertheless have an intuitive moral competence that displays itself in the way they answer questions about moral rules and in the way they excuse their transgressions and react to the transgressions of others" (1981, p. 288). They continue:

> In fact, at this relatively early age, four to six, children not only seem to distinguish and identify moral versus conventional versus prudential rules using the same formal principles (*e.g.*, obligatoriness, importance, generalizability) employed by adults, they also seem to agree with the adults of their society about the moral versus conventional versus prudential status of particular substantive events (*e.g.*, throwing paint in another child's face versus wearing the same clothes to school every day) (1981, p. 288).

There is also a growing body of evidence that even much younger children are capable of empathizing with others (Hoffman 1976; Damon 1988; Hunt 1990); and there is substantial evidence that children have the cognitive ability to reason non-egocentrically much earlier than Piaget's studies suggest (Donaldson 1979; Damon 1988). All of this suggests that the IAPC programs portray ordinary rather than philosophically precocious children.

Illustrations

Young children have a very keen sense of fairness within their spheres of experience. Favoritism, taking more than one's fair share, not taking turns, and so on, are staple fare in the lives of children—in school, on the playground, and within their family structures. That they (like the rest of us) may more readily recognize unfairness in others than in themselves does not mean that they do not understand what fairness is. That they will later extend their conceptions of fairness to situations they cannot now understand (*e.g.*, taxation)—and that they will discover conflicts with other fundamental moral values—does not imply that they do not now have access to morality at its most basic level.

It might be argued that children begin with particular examples and only through unreflective habituation develop a sense of fairness. But even if this were so, some of the foundation seems well in place rather early on, thus allowing room for reflection much earlier than Aristotle seems to acknowledge. Of course, children do learn from examples. But examples provide only a starting point from which they may go on to deal competently with novel instances. Ronald Dworkin makes an important point in this regard:

> Suppose I tell my children simply that I expect them not to treat others unfairly. I no doubt have in mind examples of the conduct I mean to discourage, but I would not accept that my "meaning" was limited to these examples, for two reasons. First, I would expect my children to apply my instructions to situations I had not and could not have thought about. Second, I stand ready to admit that some peculiar act I had thought was fair when I spoke was in fact unfair, or vice-versa, if one of my children is able to convince me of that later; in that case I should want to say that my instructions covered the case he cited, not that I had changed my instructions. I might say that I meant the family to be guided by the *concept* of fairness, not by any specific *conception* of fairness I might have had in mind (Dworkin 1977, p. 133).

If we think of particular moral conceptions as workable, but somewhat inadequate renderings of basic moral concepts, then we can understand how we might learn from children as they wrestle with these concepts.

This way of looking at moral development differs in an important way from the cognitive developmental approach of Piaget and Kohlberg. Characteristically it claims that children's moral development goes through sequential stages, with each subsequent stage replacing inadequate concepts in preceding stages. Concepts in different stages differ in kind, not simply in degree. Although the concepts in later stages build on earlier ones, the process is more a matter of *reconstructing* than *enlarging* concepts. Children at the earlier stages are viewed as lacking the ability to understand and assimilate the reasoning of the higher stages. Although emphasizing that greater understanding comes with maturation, stage theories imply that children live in a quite different moral world than adults. Thus, they encourage a condescending attitude toward children's moral thinking and discourage genuine moral dialogue between children and adults. That there are striking moral differences between children and adults cannot sensibly be denied. But there are ways of characterizing those differences that at the same time suggest even more striking similarities.

Gareth Matthews (1987) suggests a promising alternative to stage theories. He emphasizes the importance of paradigms:

> A young child is able to latch onto the moral kind, bravery, or lying, by grasping central paradigms of that kind, paradigms that even the most mature and sophisticated moral agents still count as paradigmatic. Moral development is then something much more complicated than simple concept displacement. It is: enlarging the stock of paradigms for each moral kind; developing better and better definitions of whatever it is these paradigms exemplify; appreciating better the relation between straightforward instances of the kind and close relatives; and learning to adjudicate competing claims from different moral kinds (classically the sometimes competing claims of justice and compassion, but many other conflicts are possible) (1987, p. 185).

In a view such as this, children as well as adults can be acknowledged to share some ground level understanding of moral concepts and principles. Although adults may typically have the upper hand in regard to breadth of experience and understanding, there is no warrant for entirely excluding children from the adult world of morality.

If the idea that young children are capable of imaginative and provocative moral thought seems far-fetched, consider one of Matthews' examples:

> IAN (six years) found to his chagrin that the three children of his parents' friends monopolized the television; they kept him from watching his favorite program. "Mother," he asked in frustration, "why is it better for three people to be selfish than for one?" (1981, p. 28).

This question reflects much more than mere habituation of thought or feeling. Matthews suggests it may be an incipient challenge to utilitarian thought. At the very least, Ian seems to have a rudimentary grasp of two fundamental moral concepts: fairness and selfishness.

Matthews (1984) wrote a fictional story based on this incident for a group of 8-11 year-olds. He discovered that none of them were attracted to utilitarian thinking in this kind of situation. A Kohlbergian might reply that what happened here is just what a stage theory would predict. Utilitarian reasoning occurs only at the most advanced level of moral development (post-conventional or critical morality), and even relatively few adults attain that level. However, this is implausible, as a variation of Matthews' example will show. Suppose he told the children a story about a hermit writing into his will what to do with his modest life savings. He has no friends, but he wants to make sure that his money is put to good use after he dies. Then the children are asked, "Should he give his money to a few rich people so that they'll be a little bit richer, or should he give it to a needy children's hospital?" Surely even very young children can entertain the thought that it would do more good, and for that reason be preferable, to give the money to the hospital rather than to a few wealthy people.

It is no objection that the children's thoughts might be mistaken, since the hospital might misuse the money or the wealthy might themselves put the money to more constructive use for others. The only issue here is whether young children can see that there are circumstances in which it is better to "make three people happy rather than one." It might be suggested that, in Freddie's case, the children simply do not see that more good is served by giving in to the three children. But this does not seem to be their concern. More prominent in their thinking is the issue of fairness, as well as the issue of rights. (Note, also, Martin's incipient Kantian remark that he would not want such a thing to happen to him). That is, they may resist the appeal to utility because they reject the idea that the "greater good" is the point at issue in this case.

Thomas Reid Again

Cognitive-developmental theories like Piaget's and Kohlberg's invite condescension toward children's moral thought (as well as that of most adults). This is because built into these accounts of moral development is a moral philosophy that has just the features Thomas Reid challenges. Both utilitarian and Kantian views of morality try to show that there is one, supreme moral principle that provides the grounding for all more particular moral ideas (*e.g.*, that we should keep our promises, not lie, not hurt others). This is what Reid calls a *geometrical* model of moral thought, to which he contrasts his own *botanical* or *mineralogical* model:

A system of morals is not like a system of geometry, where the subsequent parts derive their evidence from the preceding, and one chain of reasoning is carried on from the beginning, so that, if the arrangement is changed, the chain is broken, and the evidence is lost. It resembles more a system of botany, or mineralogy, where the subsequent parts depend not for

their evidence upon the preceding, and the arrangement is made to facilitate apprehension and memory, and not to give evidence (1788, p. 642).

The philosophical issue of whether morality is best understood on a botanical or a geometrical model cannot be adequately addressed here. On this matter I am inclined toward the botanical model. The geometrical model is, at best, a philosophical aspiration. As the history of ethics makes clear enough, just understanding the arrangement of principles and rules of particular geometrical models is a real intellectual challenge. Applying models to particular circumstances can be equally daunting. (*E.g.*, how *are* we to determine which course of action is most likely to bring about the greatest good for the greatest number?) So, it should not surprise us that even few adults display sophisticated moral reasoning as judged by the criteria of a geometrical model.

None of the leading geometrical candidates (*e.g.*, utilitarianism, Kantianism, egoism) is free from serious philosophical criticism. Lack of consensus among philosophers does not imply that pursuit of a unified, hierarchical moral theory is misguided. But it does suggest that it is unwise to select, as Kohlberg does, a favored geometrical model as the basis for assessing the moral development of children and adults. At the same time, opting for the botanical model does not imply abandoning standards of judgment. Judgments about moral matters can still be well grounded or arbitrary, sensitive or insensitive, well thought out or carelessly held, articulate or inarticulate, coherent or incoherent, and so on. Reid's concern is mainly that we not lose sight of the fact that morality is practical, not merely theoretical. Again, morality is the business of *all* of us, not just philosophers; and, therefore, it should be accessible to everyone.

Although Reid insists that "the practical Part of Ethicks is for the most part easy and level to all capacities," he does not underestimate the obstacles to clear-headed thinking in our practical circumstances:

> There is . . . no branch of Science wherein Men would be more harmonious in their opinions than in Morals were they free from all bias and Prejudice. But this is hardly the case with any Man. Mens private Interests, their Passions, and vicious inclinations & habits, do often blind their understandings, and bias their Judgments. And as Men are much disposed to take the Rules of Conduct from Fashion rather than from the Dictates of reason, so with Regard to Vices which are authorized by Fashion, the Judgments of Men are apt to be blinded by the Authority of the Multitude especially when Interest or Appetite leads the same Way. It is therefore of great consequence to those who would judge right in matters relating to their own conduct or that of others to have the Rules of Morals fixed & settled in their Minds, before they have occasion to apply them to cases wherein they may be interested. It must also be observed that although the Rules of morals are in most cases very plain, yet there are intricate and perplexed cases even in Morals wherein it is no easy matter to form a determinate Judgment (Reid 1990, pp. 110-111).

For Reid, experience and reflection can correct, modify, or enlarge the moral understanding that begins in childhood, but it cannot totally *displace* it—a point that "Speculative Ethicks" should constantly bear in mind. Even so, as the above passage makes clear, there is plenty of work to do in getting clear about moral matters—more than enough for a lifetime. So, Reid might say, it is better to get started sooner rather than later.

Reid's account of moral agency begins with a contrast between humans and "brute animals." Brute animals have no power of self-government—nor would we if we "had no power to restrain appetite but by a stronger contrary appetite or passion" (1788, p. 534). Some might object to the severity of this contrast, but even if Reid somewhat underestimates brute animals, this would simply bring them closer to moral agency than Reid suggests. His fundamental claim concerns the close relationship between the capacity for self-government and moral agency.[3]

Reid points out that humans share with non-human animals the tendency to react to harm and threats of harm with "sudden resentment"—a defense mechanism that can strike fear in the aggressor. But humans are also capable of "deliberate resentment" which requires "opinion of injury" (1788, p. 567). Such an opinion supposes that the cause of harm is a responsible agent, rather than an inanimate object or animals that have no conception of right or wrong. Thus, the natural sentiment of "sudden resentment" can gradually become transformed, through the influence of reason, into "deliberate," or moral resentment. But our "opinion of injury" can involve bias, distortion, and other excesses. So we must take care that "deliberate resentment" itself be amenable to reasonable constraints.

How is this to be done? *Harry* models this through self-examination (*e.g.*, when Harry realizes that he should not resent Lisa's helping him to see *his* mistake) and discussion (*e.g.*, when he and Bill Beck open themselves up to developing a friendship). In both kinds of cases a broader and deeper understanding can result and thereby alter ones moral attitudes and judgments. Such self-examination and discussion at an early age is not only possible, it is desirable. It can be a useful supplement to adult modeling. Furthermore, if it does have a constructive influence on controlling excessive and unreasonable resentment, it can provide an alternative to the more usual, punitive methods of controlling unwanted behavior—methods that are often themselves met with resentment.

Reid acknowledges that our moral conceptions develop gradually, just as our rational capacities do. Like the power of reasoning, the "seeds of moral discernment" do not appear in infancy; and they require careful cultivation: "They grow up in their proper season, and are at first tender and delicate and easily warped. Their progress depends very much upon their being duly cultivated and properly exercised" (1788, p. 595). But, Reid points out, "as soon as men have any rational conception of a favour and of an

Education as the development of thinking and judgment

If a young man has trained his muscles and physical endurance by gymnastics and walking, he will later be fitted for every physical work. This is also analogous to the training of the mind and the exercising of the mental and manual skill. Thus the wit was not wrong who defined education this way: "Education is that which remains, if one has forgotten everything he learned in school." For this reason I am not at all anxious to take sides in the struggle between the followers of the classical philologic-historical education and the education more devoted to natural science.

On the other hand, I want to oppose the idea that the school has to teach directly that special knowledge and those accomplishments which one has to use later directly in life. The demands of life are much too manifold to let such a specialized training in school appear possible. Apart from that, it seems to me, moreover, objectionable to treat the individual like a dead tool. The school should always have as it aims that the young man leave it as a harmonious personality, not as a specialist. This in my opinion is true in a certain sense even for technical schools, whose students will devote themselves to a quite definite profession. The development of general ability for independent thinking and judgment should always be placed foremost, not the acquisition of special knowledge. If a person masters the fundamentals of his subject and has learned to think and work independently, he will surely find his way and besides will better be able to adapt himself to progress and change than the person whose training principally consists in the acquiring of detailed knowledge.
—Albert Einstein, *Out of My Later Years*, New York: Philosophical Library, 1950.

injury, they must have the conception of justice, and perceive its obligation" (1788, p. 654.)

It is clear that he is not restricting his discussion to adults, as the "notions of a *favour* and of *injury* appear as early in the mind of man as any rational notion whatever" (1788, p. 654). Further:

> One boy has a top, another a scourge; says the first to the other, If you will lend me your scourge as long as I can keep up my top with it, you shall next have the top as long as you can keep it up. This is a contract perfectly understood by both parties, though they never heard of the definition by Ulpian or by Titius. And each of them knows that he is injured if the other breaks the bargain, and that he does wrong if he breaks it himself (1788, p. 666).

If we add to this children's natural sociability and their early, rudimentary grasp of the central idea that "we ought not to do to another what we should think wrong to be done to us in like circumstances," (1788, p. 590), there seems little reason to deny that children are quite capable of undertaking, and benefiting from, just the sorts of reflective moral inquiry illustrated in *Harry* and the other IAPC programs.

Reid offers no timetable for when fruitful discussion might begin, but it is clear he does not believe that reflective discussion of morality is only for older children or adults. He observes: "Our first moral conceptions are probably got by attending coolly to the conduct of others and observing what moves our approbation, what our indignation. These sentiments spring from our moral faculty as naturally as the sensations of sweet and bitter from the faculty of taste" (1788, p. 641). Reid also reminds us of our tendency to view human actions from partial and biased perspectives: "Prejudice against or in favour of the person, is apt to warp our opinion. It requires candour to distinguish the good from the ill, and, without favour or prejudice, to form a clear and impartial judgment. In this way we may be greatly aided by instruction" (1788, p. 641). Again, this is modeled in Harry when the children catch each other (and their teachers) jumping to conclusions, stereotyping, and failing to see things from other points of view. However, the "instruction" is accomplished through *discussion* rather than Aristotle's *lectures* on moral philosophy. In this way, the children's moral capacities are respected at the very time they are enlarging.

More Illustrations

I have said that the children in *Harry Stottlemeier's Discovery* are not neophytes when it comes to moral reasoning. Neither are the fifth-grade readers of *Harry*. Consider this passage:

> The bell was about to ring, and the two monitors were still standing at the door. Both boys were large and rather heavy, and they decided to tease Fran by not giving her much room to pass. Maybe she thought they did it because she was a girl, and most likely she thought they did it because she was a girl and black, too, but she didn't care for that kind of teasing, and she pushed them out of her way. Mrs. Halsey turned around just in time to see what Fran had done, and she spoke to Fran very sharply about it. [*Harry Stottlemeier's Discovery*, p. 11].

The word "fair" does not appear in this passage—nor do "unfair," "just" "unjust" or any other terms normally associated with issues of fairness (*e.g.*, "discrimination"). Yet, when I asked a group of 5th-graders with whom I met on a weekly basis, "What do you think fairness is?" Larry immediately reminded us of this passage—something we had read a few weeks earlier, but which we had not discussed in any detail.[4]

I asked my question after we had been discussing other philosophical matters for half an hour. It seemed time to move on to another topic. So, I thought the group might enjoy talking about fairness for the remaining 15 minutes of our session. What followed Larry's reminder of Fran's situation was a barrage of examples. Fairness, the students said, requires getting all the facts straight and hearing both sides of any issue. (Fran, they said, was not even given a chance to explain to

Mrs. Halsey why she pushed the boys.) They objected to the deliberate distortion of facts. This led to a discussion of lying. Later, while acknowledging he should not lie, Rick said it is unfair to assume that, just because he used to lie a lot, he still does: "My mom said that, you know, I used to be the kid who lied because I was afraid when I was young that I'd get a spanking. But now I've stopped lying for about two years now, and my mom still doesn't believe me." Mike replied, "Rick, but you've earned that responsibility. You lied when you were young. If you never started lying, your mother would have believed you all the time." Is it unreasonable (and unfair) to doubt the word of those who have consistently lied in the past? Regardless of the answer, once doubt sets in, it is very difficult to re-establish trust. This is one of the major themes in Sissela Bok's widely read book, *Lying: Moral Choice in Public and Private Life* (1978). Here is ten-year-old Mike making the same point to his classmates that Bok makes to her very large adult audience.

Mike's comment opened up questions of responsibility and desert. So, I decided to read a short story about treating people equally.[5] Before she can distribute candy to the students in her class, the teacher is called out of the classroom. While she is gone, the students fight over the candy she left on her desk. The biggest, strongest children each have a handful of candy, while the smallest children have only one piece each. When the teacher sees what has happened, she announces that she will treat everyone equally and take back one piece of candy from each student. As might be expected, my students strongly protested what the teacher did. However, what was most interesting about the ensuing discussion is that the students' attention very quickly shifted to a variety of other examples in order to explain their ideas of fairness. They discussed the fairness of group punishments and rewards. They discussed problems of rewarding people according to merit, effort, or ability. And they explored the idea of giving special opportunities to those with special shortcomings or disabilities.

The students made no attempt to try to subsume their examples under a comprehensive theory. Perhaps with more time they would have tried to do so; and no doubt, like adults, they would have faltered along the way. Questions of punitive and distributive justice are among the most difficult ones we face—whether they concern criminal law, the allocation of scarce resources, or taxation. However, given more time the children might simply have continued as they were, sorting out nuances that need attention, modifying their judgments as the examples change, and taking delight, as Rick did, with each new shade of meaning. After all, it was Rich who said, after suggesting that fairness is having the person who cuts a candy bar get the last piece, "It's not only just that. But there's really a lot of meanings" It was also Rick who asked, "Mr. Pritchard, who thinks of these questions? They've always got a two-way answer to them."

Although the IAPC programs encourage the kind of moral reflection that supports Rick's observation, this is accomplished by very different means than Lawrence Kohlberg's use of moral dilemmas.[6] Kohlberg's cognitive-developmental theory claims that moral reasoning is advanced by being thrown into "Disequilibrium." Children find that their customary modes of reasoning are not adequate for handling certain moral problems. Successful resolution of such problems requires advancing to the next stage of moral reasoning. Stages form a hierarchy involving progressively greater cognitive complexity and advancement toward a universal moral perspective in which rights and duties stand in a fully reciprocal relation to one another. Since moral development depends on conflict, Kohlberg recommends the use of hypothetical moral *dilemmas* at strategic times as a teaching device in moral education.

In contrast, IAPC programs place no special emphasis on moral dilemmas. They do provide children with opportunities to sort out subtle and complex features of situations calling for moral reflection. But only a relatively small proportion of such situations involve dilemmas. A steady diet of dilemmas risks creating the impression that moral problems typically resist confident resolution. However, underlying our recognition that a situation poses a moral dilemma is the belief that there are competing moral values which, in more ordinary circumstances, are decisive. (For example, Kohlberg's famous Heinz dilemma—should Heinz steal a cancer-curing drug to save his wife if this is the only way he can obtain it for her?—presupposes that property is an important value that stealing is generally wrong, and that saving a life, especially a loved one's, is very important. It is precisely because these are *all* morally important considerations that Heinz is faced with a moral *dilemma*.)

However, it isn't just moral dilemmas that give rise to moral puzzlement and call for careful thinking. For example, there is a passage in *Lisa* in which Harry, Lisa, and Timmy wonder when it is right to "return in kind" and when it is not—and, equally important, *why* it is or is not. The passage involves Timmy retaliating after being tripped, Harry and Timmy discussing trading stamps and lending money, and Lisa finally remarking. "It looks like there are times when it is right to give back what we got and other times when it is wrong. But how do we tell which is which?"

How does discussing a passage like this differ from discussing a moral dilemma.? When we face a moral dilemma, we are pulled in conflicting directions. We think we have reasons for going either way—or for avoiding both ways. None of the choices seem to be without moral cost, and we are very likely perplexed about what the right choice is (or even whether there is a right choice). Timmy, Harry and Lisa *might* have viewed the situations they discussed as posing dilemmas of this sort. But, in fact, they do not. Timmy, at least initially, has no doubt that retaliation is called for. Even if Harry succeeds in casting seeds of doubt in Timmy's way, it is not clear that this creates a *dilemma* for Timmy. He might wonder if he really did *have* to get even. Or he might wonder, as the group of 5th graders with whom I discussed this passage did, what it *means* to "get even," whether it is possible to get even, and whether it is *desirable* to try.

Harry, on the other hand, has little doubt that Timmy's act of retaliation was inappropriate. He also has no doubt that trading stamps is appropriate and that one ought to repay borrowed money. What puzzles him is how to *explain* the differences among these instances of returning in kind. Lisa, too, is puzzled about this. Making progress in resolving puzzlements like this is a fundamental part of moral development. But it is not clear that the discussion of moral dilemmas has any distinctive contribution to make here. On the other hand, it would seem useful to compare and contrast what Gareth Matthews calls paradigms—both with one another and with less familiar cases.

When my group of 5th graders discussed this episode from *Lisa*, a variety of topics other than dilemmas were addressed. Here are some of the things the group discussed.

1. The likely *consequences* of retaliating. They worried that retaliation sets off a chain of events that no one wants—other than, perhaps, the initiator, who wants attention and an excuse to be even more aggressive

2. Does retaliation really "get things even"? Does this notion even make sense? First Larry, and then Carlen, suggested that it doesn't.

3. Is it important to distinguish between *wanting* to do something and *having* to do it?

4. Is it right to respond to an acknowledged wrong by returning in kind? (Do two wrongs make a right?)

5. What *alternatives* are available, and what are the likely consequences of each? (*E.g.*, will hitting back make things worse? Will doing nothing in return discourage the initiator, or will it simply encourage more of the same and perhaps contribute to the aggressor growing up to be an undesirable kind of

person? Is self-defense needed—as a first response, or as a back-up to one's first response?)

6. What should the person who is hit or tripped be trying to *accomplish* in responding one way rather than another? Avoiding making things worse (for whom?)? Get even? Teach a lesson? (Are these last two different? If so, how?).

7. *How* is hitting back different from (a) making an exchange of goods; (b) paying back a debt; (c) returning a favor; (d) responding to someone who does not return a favor or who refuses to extend a favor?

8. Keeping all of these examples in mind, what does the Golden Rule *mean*? Is it a good rule?

The children discussed questions like these in great detail, and with great understanding, for more than half an hour.

Without reaching consensus about how each of the situations should be handled, there was a recognition that reciprocal relations in human affairs tend to generate chains of "returning in kind": attacks encourage counterattacks; counterattacks encourage counter-counterattacks, favors encourage favors in return, extending trust encourages trust in return. But, as children are well aware, reciprocity does not always occur. Counterattacks do sometimes work. Favors are sometimes not returned. Trust sometimes simply renders one vulnerable. How to stop an undesired chain from getting started (*e.g.*, hitting), or how to stop it once it starts, is a challenge at any age. So, as the children again realized, ideals have to be related to realities. Chip suggested a two-stage strategy: First, ignore the instigator, but defend yourself if that doesn't work. In response to those who expressed reluctance to extend favors without evidence that they would be reciprocated, Rick replied that it was worth the risk: If everyone would give, everyone would benefit—from someone, even if not from those for whom one does favors. These were thoughtful responses, made in full awareness of the uncertainties present in the situations under discussion.

The most fascinating aspect of the discussion was its thoroughness. What, I have since wondered, would adults want to add that was not considered in some way.? Adults might wish to make comparisons with other kinds of situations that ten-year-olds will understand of the moral nuances of situations *within* their range of experience. I take this as further confirmation of Thomas Reid's view that morality is the business of all of us—and that it is accessible to all of us as well.

Community of Inquiry

All the IAPC programs emphasize the importance of the classroom becoming a "community of inquiry." In such a classroom students are encouraged to explore ideas together. Teachers often ask how discussions of moral concerns differ from "values clarification," which they see as designed to encourage students to clarify their moral values. Although "values clarification" programs do help students become clearer about their own values, students are discouraged from making evaluative or critical remarks about one another's values. Thus, respect is shown for each student's point of view, and charges of indoctrination in the classroom are avoided. However, the hidden message is that moral values are relative to those who happen to embrace them. Morality is quietly endorsed as being "subjective," with each person's ideas being as "valid" as anyone else's.

For some teachers this implicit relativism is anathema, and they want nothing to do with IAPC programs if this is what they amount to. Others welcome this supposed feature of the IAPC programs but fail to see how Philosophy for Children is different from what they are already doing in "values clarification." But it is important to realize that IAPC programs do *not* discourage students from evaluating one another's views.

Reason-giving is a central activity, not only in clarifying one's views, but also in dialogue in which students try to evaluate one another's thinking. Although teachers should refrain from simply imposing their values on the students (indoctrination), it is also not their role to reinforce the notion that all views are equally well thought out, plausible, defensible, valid, or the like (relativism).

Although critical dialogue can degenerate into shouting matches and "put downs," it will not if the appropriate environment for thoughtful discussion is established. In such an environment, reflective exchanges promote a number of important values. First, they help the participants become more aware of what they believe, why they believe what they do, and what the limitations of their beliefs are. Second, participants become clearer about the beliefs of *others*, thus enabling them to see that there may be more to another person's perspective than "meets the eye" when answers are not accompanied with supporting reasons. This encourages a kind of mutual respect and care that is based on better understanding of the perspectives of others—something without which Golden Rule reasoning flounders. Third, participants may learn, as Harry and his friends do, that sometimes "a graceful error corrects the cave." Learning that one's thinking is inadequate, or even mistaken, is not "the end of the world" it may be, as in Harry's case, the beginning of a new and exciting one. Finally, participants are encouraged to acquire the virtue of reasonableness—an openness to reasoning *with* others.

Taking all of this into consideration, we can see that a community of inquiry is actually a *moral* community, thus itself contributing to one's moral education—not through the indoctrination of some particular set of beliefs, but through a certain kind of practice.

Notes

1. This paper was presented at the Conference of the International Council for Philosophy for Children, held at Fu Jen Catholic University in Taipei, Taiwan, June 25-8, 1990. Some parts of this paper are based on Chapter 2, "On Becoming a Moral Agent," of my *On Becoming Responsible*, (University Press of Kansas, 1991). A somewhat longer version of this paper is in *Studies in Philosophy for Children*, edited by Ronald Reed and Ann Margaret Sharp, Philadelphia: Temple University Press.
2. William Shakespeare, *Troilus and Cressida*, II, ii, 166 f. This is cited by David Ross in commenting on Aristotle's *Nicomachean Ethics* (Oxford: Oxford University Press, 1980).
3. It should be noted that Reid carefully avoids an excessively individualistic conception of self-government and moral agency. We are naturally sociable and Reid says: "Without society, and the intercourse of kind affection, man is a gloomy, melancholy, and joyless being" (1788, p. 566).
4. This session is discussed in greater detail in Ch. V, "Fairness," in my *Philosophical Adventures With Children*, (1985). Portions of transcripts that are included here are taken from that chapter.
5. This story is taken from p. 63 of *Philosophical Inquiry*, the Teacher's Manual for *Harry Stottlemeier's Discovery*.
6. The rest of this section is based on my "Reciprocity Revisited," in *Analytic Teaching*, Vol. 9, No. 2, May 1989, pp. 54-62. A much more detailed critique of Kohlberg is contained in that article. See, also, Chapters 7 and 8 of my *On Becoming Responsible*, (Lawrence: University of Kansas, 1991). The full transcript of the children's discussion is contained in my *Philosophical Adventures With Children*, Chapter IX, "Reciprocity."

References

Aristotle. 1980. *Nicomachean Ethics*, translated by W. D. Ross. Oxford: Oxford Univ. Press.

Bok, Sissela. 1978. *Lying: Moral Choice in Public and Private Life*. New York, Pantheon.

Burnyeat, M. D. 1980. "Aristotle on Learning to be Good" In *Essays on Aristotle's Ethics*, edited by Amelie Rorty, pp. 69-92. Berkeley: University of California Press.

Damon, William. 1988. *The Moral Child*. New York: Free Press.

Donaldson, Margaret. 1979. *Children's Minds*. New York: Norton.

Dworkin, Ronald. 1977. *Taking Rights Seriously*. Oxford: Oxford University Press.

Fullinwider, Robert. 1989. "Moral Conventions and Moral Lessons," *Social Theory and Practice*, Vol. 15, No. 3, pp. 321-338.

Hoffman, M. L. 1976. "Empathy, Role-Taking, Guilt, and the Development of Altruistic Motives." In *Moral Development and Behavior*, edited by Thomas Lickona, pp. 124-143. New York: Rinehart & Winston.

Hunt, Morton, 1990. *The Compassionate Beast*. New York: William Morrow & Co.

Kohlberg, Lawrence. 1981. *The Philosophy of Moral Development Essays on Moral Development*, vol. I. San Francisco: Harper & Row. Lipman, Matthew. 1974. *Harry Stottlemeier's Discovery*. Upper Montclair, New Jersey: Institute for the Advancement of Philosophy for Children.

Lipman, Matthew. 1983. *Lisa*, 2nd ed. Upper Montclair, New Jersey: Institute for the Advancement of Philosophy for Children. Lipman, Matthew. 1988 *Philosophy Goes to School*. Philadelphia: Temple University Press.

Lipman, Matthew; Sharp, Ann Margaret, eds. 1978. *Growing Up With Philosophy*. Philadelphia: Temple University Press.

Lipman, Matthew; Sharp, Ann Margaret; and Oscanyan, Frederick. 1984. *Philosophical Inquiry*. Lanham, Maryland: University Press of America.

Lipman, Matthew; Sharp, Ann; and Oscanyan, Frederick. 1980. *Philosophy in the Classroom*, 2nd ed. Philadelphia: Temple University Press.

Matthews, Gareth. 1981. *Philosophy and the Young Child*. Cambridge, Mass.: Harvard University Press.

Matthews, Gareth. 1981. *Dialogues With Children*. Cambridge, Mass.: Harvard University Press.

Matthews, Gareth. 1987. "Concept Formation and Moral Development" in James Russell, ed., *Philosophical Perspectives on Developmental Phychology*. Oxford: Basil Blackwell.

Piaget, Jean. (1932) 1965. *The Moral Judgment of the Child*. New York: Free Press.

Pritchard, Micahel S. 1985. *Philosophical Adventures With Children*. Lanham, Maryland: University Press of America.

Pritchard, Michael S. 1989. "Reciprocity Revisited." *Analytic Teaching*, vol. 9, no. 2, pp. 54-62.

Pritchard, Michael S. 1991. *On Becoming Responsible*. Lawrence, Kansas: University Press of Kansas.

Reid, Thomas. (1788) 1895. *On the Active Powers of Mind in Philosophical Works*, Vol. II, with notes by Sir William Hamilton. Hildesheim: Gekorg Olms Verlagsbuchandlung.

Reid, Thomas. 1990. *Practical Ethics*, translated with commentary by Knud Haakonssen. Princeton, New Jersey: Princeton University Press.

Shweder, Richard A.; Turiel, Elliot; and Much, Nancy C. 1981. "The Moral Intuitions of the Child." In *Social Cognitive Development: Frontiers and Possible Futures*, edited by John H. Flavell and Lee Ross, pp. 288-305, Cambridge: Cambridge University Press.

Judgment and the Art of Compromise

Martin Benjamin

Moral Judgments are judgments, not deductions; they are not themselves deduced; they can be supported, defended, argued for or against, justified or established, but not deduced.
—Marcus George Singer, "The Ideal of a Rational Morality"

Judging is in important respects the mark of our humanity; it contributes to the humanizing of our world as no other human faculty does. To attempt to reflect on this human capacity is thus to meditate on what is distinctive of our humanity, on what it is to be human or to constitute a human world.
—Ronald Beiner, Political Judgment

Some two-party moral conflicts are rationally irreconcilable—the most we can hope for in the way of peaceful accommodation is an integrity-preserving compromise. But how do we know when to seek compromise and when not? And if we wish to compromise, how do we identify those that are both well grounded and integrity preserving? Is there a method that will yield determinate answers to these and related questions? The demand for such a method is, I believe, misconceived. Deciding to seek, accept, or maintain a moral compromise is a matter of judgment.

Moral Judgments are Judgments

Influenced by impressive achievements in the mathematical and empirical sciences, philosophers often aspire to a model of ethical reasoning that leaves little or no room for the exercise of judgment. Their aim is an algorithmic decision procedure for resolving moral problems. Dubbed by Arthur Caplan the engineering model of applied ethics, this approach requires first that we acquire knowledge of ethical theories and then that we "apply" them by: "a) *deducing* conclusions from theories in light of relevant empirical facts and descriptions of circumstances and b) analyzing the process of the deductions" (1983,

p. 314; my emphasis). Once one has determined the correct or appropriate theory, ascertained the facts, and checked the validity of the deduction, there is little room for the exercise of judgment. The truth of the premises, as in valid deductive reasoning generally, forces or guarantees the truth of the conclusion.

I have [previously] rejected the quest for the sort of comprehensive, widely acceptable ethical theories required by the engineering model. Yet even those who can be persuaded to abandon the Platonic Quest and the Doctrine of Moral Harmony and to acknowledge the (occasional) need for compromise are likely to ask us to specify a set of conditions that will tell us when and how to compromise. But this is not possible; to insist that we specify such conditions is to embrace a mistaken conception of ethical reasoning, one that denies Marcus G. Singer's important reminder that "moral judgments are judgments."

Underlying the request for a decision procedure or set of necessary and sufficient conditions for moral compromise is an idealization of method. "Methodism," as Sheldon Wolin calls it, is the doctrinaire demand that all rational thought and decision be modeled on the impersonality, precision, and quantifiability of mathematical or (certain forms of) scientific reasoning (Wolin 1972). The aim is to devise a uniform procedure or set of rules that if correctly applied to a certain question will yield the same determinate conclusions for all—a moral algorithm. Once formulated, the method can be employed more or less mechanically by anyone capable of learning the rules.

This "rationalistic conception of rationality," as Bernard Williams suggests, is closely allied to contemporary "administrative ideas of rationality" or "modern bureaucratic" conceptions (Williams 1985, pp. 18, 197, 206). Its aim is to replace the essentially social or dialogical nature of reflective judgment, as well as its variability, uncertainty, and unpredictability, with a set of impersonal rules that can and should be followed

to the very same end by anyone capable of understanding them.

Whatever the value and success of methodism in other areas and disciplines—and they are considerable—it plays a more limited role in ethics and politics, especially in connection with moral compromise. Compromise in ethics is more a matter of practical rather than technical reasoning, and more the outcome of reflective judgment rather than of a rationalistic decision procedure. We cannot reduce what is often called the art of compromise to an impersonal algorithmic method or science. Even if it were possible to do so, it would in certain respects be undesirable. It would relieve us not only of the burdens of judgment but also of our freedom and, as Beiner suggests, our humanity (1983, p. 166). Those who aspire to replace the discretionary aspects of moral judgment with a more determinate method or decision procedure often point to the sciences as a model of what they seek. But their conception of scientific rationality bears only partial resemblance to actual scientific practice. An historical understanding of the nature of scientific reasoning, as Kuhn maintains in *The Structure of Scientific Revolutions* (1970), reveals a different picture.

Although there are aspects of scientific practice (what Kuhn calls normal science) that involve the application of a fairly determinate method, the more foundational questions and decisions in science—those involving choices between competing comprehensive theories or "paradigms"—do not. Conflicts between competing overarching theories or paradigms cannot be resolved by a more or less mechanical application of determinate, theory-neutral criteria. No such criteria were available to those who had to choose, for example, between Ptolemy's astronomical theory and that of Copernicus, between the oxygen theory of combustion and the phlogiston theory, or between Newtonian mechanics and the quantum theory. When a group of scientists disagree about such matters, Kuhn points out, "there is no neutral algorithm for theory choice, no systematic decision procedure which properly applied, must lead each individual in the group to the same decision" (1970, pp. 199-200).

This is not to say (as Kuhn's dramatic overstatements occasionally imply and his critics uncharitably infer) that rationality has no role in deciding between competing comprehensive theories. This would be so only if technical rationality were the sole form of rationality; only if, in other words, a choice could not be regarded as rational unless it were the deductive outcome of applying a standardized set of fully determinate, wholly consistent, theory-neutral rules or criteria. But *a priori* exclusive commitment to this highly idealized conception of scientific reasoning reduces to absurdity. The actual practice of good science provides our best model of scientific rationality (Kuhn 1970, p. 144). And this practice, when carefully examined, reveals that choices among competing comprehensive theories are not the product of mechanically applying a set of theory-neutral rules or criteria. If a philosophical account of rational decision making in certain areas of science is not embodied in the practice of good scientists doing good science, it is the philosophical understanding that must give way, not scientific practice.

How, then, do scientists choose between competing comprehensive theories? If they do not and cannot appeal to an algorithmic decision procedure to fully resolve their differences and yet are said to choose rationally, how do they reason? Kuhn acknowledges standard criteria for evaluating the comparative adequacy of competing comprehensive theories. Accuracy, consistency, scope, simplicity, and fruitfulness, he agrees, all "play a vital role when scientists must choose between an established theory and an upstart competitor" (1977, p. 322). But two difficulties arise when we assume that these useful and important criteria provide a mechanical procedure for choosing between competing theories. First, taken separately they are *imprecise*: "Individuals may legitimately differ about their applications to concrete cases." Of two competing theories, for

example, one might be more accurate in one respect and the other more accurate in another respect. Second, when taken together these criteria "repeatedly prove to *conflict* with one another; accuracy may, for example, dictate the choice of one theory, scope the choice of its competitor" (Kuhn, 1977, p. 322; my emphasis). Thus

> when scientists must choose between competing theories, two men fully committed to the same list of criteria for choice may nevertheless reach different conclusions. Perhaps they interpret simplicity differently or have different convictions about the range of fields within which the consistency criterion must be met. Or perhaps they agree about these matters but differ about the relative weights to be accorded to these or to other criteria when several are deployed together. With respect to divergences of this sort, no set of choice criteria yet proposed is of any use (Kuhn 1977, p. 324).

Instead of construing accuracy, consistency, scope, simplicity, and fruitfulness as rules that fully determine choice, Kuhn proposes that we regard them as values that influence it. As a set of rules, accuracy, scope, and so on underdetermine theory choice, but as values they frame the arguments and debates and help to shape and support the judgments that scientists make that one theory is, on balance, better than another.

The exercise of human judgment in choosing between competing, comprehensive scientific theories is, according to Kuhn, inescapable. But judgment, he hastens to add, is not to be confused with arbitrary preference. Judgments, as opposed to mere expressions of individual taste, are "eminently discussable" and need to be backed up by reasons even if these reasons (for example, greater accuracy, more consistent, wider scope and so on), do not deductively or methodically function as determinate rules or criteria and thereby "dictate" choice. Judgment falls somewhere between algorithmic decision procedures, on the one hand, and expressions of mere preference or taste, on the other. It is rational without being narrowly (or mechanically) rationalistic.

Within the parameters established by uniform, impersonal rules or criteria, different people's judgments will reflect their differing experiences as scientists, differing wider cultural commitments, and differing attitudes toward, say, the value of comprehensive, unified theories as opposed to "precise and detailed problem solutions of apparently narrower scope" (Kuhn 1977, p. 325). Fully understanding an individual scientist's particular judgment of the superiority of one comprehensive theory over another requires acquaintance not only with shared, general criteria, but also with "idiosyncratic factors dependent on individual biography and personality" (Kuhn 1977, p. 329). The criteria significantly guide and limit the scientist's choice, but they do not in themselves deductively entail or "dictate" it.

A judgment may be rationally supportable—we can provide what John Stuart Mill calls "considerations . . . capable of determining the intellect either to give or withhold its assent" (1861, p. 7)—without satisfying the orthodox methodist's demand for deductive certainty. Judgment differs, in this respect, from both matters of (mere) taste and matters of (conclusive) proof. Making a judgment requires more in the way of rational dialogue than either expressing a preference or deducing a conclusion. There is, as the saying goes, no disputing matters of taste (such as one's preference among flavors of ice cream). Similarly, there is no disputing matters of algorithmic rationality (such as finding the greatest common divisor of a pair of numbers). It is, however, always possible to question even the best judgment about which of two competing theories or paradigms is best—though to be taken seriously one must provide reasons for one's doubts and be prepared to engage in dialectical discussion of the matter (Kuhn 1977, p. 336-37). Scientific judgment is in this respect similar to moral judgment, as one can see by replacing "moral" with "scientific" in the following. "Moral judgments are judgments, not deductions; they are not themselves deduced; they can be supported, defended, argued for or against,

justified or established, but not deduced" (M.G. Singer 1986, p. 26).

To carry the comparison further we might add that within a particular world view and way of life, as within a particular scientific theory or paradigm, one may come very close to "deducing" conclusions from the values and principles that help structure that world view and way of life (Gewirth 1960)—though even here there are important limits to pure deduction (Williams 1985, pp. 126ff.). But when conflicts are rooted in conflicting (and incommensurable) world views and ways of life, we cannot without begging the question resolve a conflict by appealing to criteria justified by only one of them. If more or less neutral, commonly held principles of utility or equal respect do not straightforwardly settle the matter we must, in deciding what to do, exercise our judgment. The result may with luck be either a plausible synthesis position that combines the strengths of each initial position and is rooted equally in both world views and ways of life or a well-grounded, integrity-preserving compromise. Judgment would be involved not only in deciding to seek a synthesis or compromise but also in attempting to craft or devise one and, having done this, deciding whether to accept it. If we decide not to seek a mutually acceptable synthesis or compromise or if our efforts to devise one or the other are unsuccessful, we shall have to make other judgments about what we should do about the conflict.

Judgment and Practical Knowledge

So long as we must make decisions in unprecedented or unpredictable situations and circumstances, we will have to rely on judgment. Consider in this connection the difference between evaluating the performance of speed skaters and the performance of figure skaters. The aspiration of methodism is to model all evaluation on the evaluation of speed skating. Certainly there is a clear decision procedure for determining that one skater is faster than another. Indeed, properly designed and programmed machines can probably do a better job at evaluating and comparing speed skaters than humans can. Machines cannot, however, take over the evaluation of competitive figure skating. "In a world of triple axels, double toe loops, death spirals and sit spins" Michael Janofsky writes, "clocks and yardsticks have no place. Figure skaters can be measured only for their height, weight and boot size" (1988, pp. 27ff.).

Olympic figure skating is evaluated by a panel of as many as nine judges from different countries. But their judgments are not purely arbitrary or simply a matter of taste. Judgment, in this context as in most others, falls between simply expressing an opinion and deducing a conclusion. Becoming a qualified judge requires training and experience. One employs criteria—analogous in many respects to the values Kuhn identifies as regulating judgments among competing scientific theories or paradigms—in determining that one skater's performance is better than another's. Nonetheless, qualified judges will occasionally disagree. Sometimes this is attributable to conscious or unconscious bias or to mistake, but not always. The judges may later give reasons for their decisions and discuss and debate them. But when both the skaters and the judges are very good, there is no external court of appeal that is anything more than yet another human judgment. We cannot, as we might if we were to disagree about which of two skaters is faster, appeal to an accurate clock.[1]

Among the aspects of figure skating that systematically resist methodist modes of assessment are "the artistry of the performance, with consideration given to a mix of athleticism and esthetics" (Janofsky 1988). One cannot antecedently specify determinate criteria for evaluating this component of a figure skater's performance without denying his or her artistic creativity To presume to do so is to imply that the skater will be unable to come up with anything of artistic merit that the judges have not already conceived.

This should remind us of an important aspect of human judgment. Contexts calling for its exercise are not antecedently closed; we cannot presume to know everything there is to know about them. As David Wiggins points out in an interpretative reconstruction of Aristotle's account of deliberation and practical reason, "The unfinished or indeterminate character of our ideals and value structure is constitutive both of human freedom and, for finite creatures who face an indefinite or infinite range of contingencies with only finite powers of prediction and imagination (*Nicomachean Ethics* 1137b), of practical rationality itself" (1980, p. 234). In the limited but instructive case of figure skating, the point is that the open-ended nature of creative activity does not permit us to mechanically apply antecedently determined criteria for evaluating the artistic aspects of a performance. More generally, finite beings like ourselves, in acknowledging the indefinite or infinite range of (occasionally unprecedented) contingencies in which we are called upon to act, cannot replace the exercise of judgment with the methodical application of antecedently determined rules or criteria. To do so would, pace methodism, be irrational.

The law provides an especially good illustration of this point. Perhaps nothing comes as close to a determinate, comprehensive, widely acceptable system for the regulation of conduct in certain areas of life as the law. Yet the legal system employs judges, and judges, as Annette Baier observes, are required to judge:

> The judge is an expert on the law, but the law does not make his decisions for him. A judge, making up his mind on a case, has, to guide him, a stable background of valid statute, accepted precedent, agreement about the spirit as well as the letter of the law; but these give him room for judgment. A judge in a court of appeal may reverse that original decision, change the Law's mind on a case, but not by rejecting that background" (1979, p. 63).

Even the best legal system, then, must remain unfinished or not fully determinate if it is to respond rationally and with integrity to unprecedented or hitherto unrecognized circumstances and conditions. What is true of legal judgment is also true of moral judgment. Moral judgment requires "a sense of the moral requirements and possibilities of the situation which goes beyond what the rules by themselves can tell us" (Lamore 1981, p. 279).

Yet the ideological power of orthodox methodism is a force to be reckoned with. Its manifestation in constitutional law is the dubious doctrine of original intention. But this notion that constitutional questions can be resolved by straightforwardly consulting the original intentions of the framers is beset with intractable difficulty. Not only must we rely on interpretation and judgment in determining the framers' intentions as they drafted the Constitution, but we must also do so in seeking constitutional direction about issues unforeseen two centuries ago. The original intention of the framers, supposing they can be determined, will not, for example, tell us whether a wiretap is the sort of "search" for which the police must obtain a warrant.

Elsewhere what might be called the mania for method or the flight from judgment runs rampant in philosophy and the social sciences, at least in the United States (Wolin 1972; C. Taylor 1971; Rorty 1979). It is particularly acute in bureaucratically or administratively driven education where so-called objective or standardized tests foster the illusion that (mere) human judgment has been transcended. But reliance on multiple-choice testing and mechanical scoring does not eliminate the exercise of judgment; it simply relocates it, keeping it out of view of the corrective power of critical assessment. Determining what to teach and what to test is a matter of judgment as is the belief that answering the teacher's multiple-choice or true-false questions is the best indication of knowledge or mastery of the particular subject matter. Moreover, an emphasis on "objective" or short-answer testing implies that practically everything worth knowing or learning about a particular area is already known by the teacher or the authors of the textbook. This, however, is no more plausible when applied to education—especially higher education—than it is when applied to figure skating. In writing a critical or creative essay or paper, a student can display not only factual understanding (analogous to the compulsories in figure skating competition) but also creative performance in raising new questions, making new criticisms, seeing new connections, putting things together in new ways, and so on. The "scoring" or evaluation of such endeavors can no more be left to a machine than can the evaluation of a figure skater's performance. It requires that the teacher, like the scientist comparing rival theories or the judge evaluating a figure skater, exercise reflective judgment.

Judgments of this kind are inescapable; we make or tacitly endorse them all of the time. That one skater is faster than another or that one student does better than another on a true-false test is determined by a mechanical decision procedure; but that speed skating is an important or worthwhile activity or that true-false tests are a valid, educationally sound measure of student ability or progress is not. Plausible answers to questions about why we should compare the speed of various skaters or measure the number of correct answers students give to a true-false test cannot come to an end in the outcome of yet another decision procedure; for the locus of inquiry will then shift to the value or importance of this higher-order decision procedure, and so on *ad infinitum*. Yet chains of deductive justification do come to an end, and where they do one will find that they rest on judgment, which in turn rests on practical reasoning and practical knowledge. They come to an end where we judge (reflectively or pre-reflectively, rightly or wrongly) in this circumstance that continued "why" questions will have little or no bearing on our actions or that the (practical) costs of further questioning outweigh the benefits of acting on the basis of the current level of justification (Wittgenstein 1953, secs. 217, 485). It is thus that even deductive justification rests ultimately on (practical) judgment.

What then, is involved in judgment, particularly moral judgment? What makes one moral judgment better than another? How does one learn to make good moral judgments. How, when one is a party or witness to what appears to be a rationally irreconcilable moral conflict, does one judge, first that a compromise may be in order; second, that of the alternatives, one compromise position is more plausible than the others; and third, that, all things considered, the parties to the disagreement should either accept the compromise or reject it? We cannot provide very full answers to these questions. In some respects, this is because a fixation on methodism has until comparatively recently kept psychologists from undertaking the relevant lines of research. In other respects, the very nature of judgment places limits on what can be said in books or articles in response to questions of this kind.

It is useful at the outset to distinguish "technical" knowledge from "practical" knowledge. Technical knowledge can be abstractly acquired from books and lectures and then employed in step-by-step fashion. The method of truth tables for assessing validity in propositional logic is a good example. Practical knowledge, by contrast, "exists only in practice, and the only way to acquire it is by apprenticeship to a master—not because the master can teach it (he cannot), but because it can be acquired only by continuous contact with one who is perpetually practicing it" (Oakeshott 1962, pp. 10-11). Insofar as judgment is more a matter of practical than technical knowledge, it cannot be fully acquired by reading theoretical or how-to books or by attending a series of lectures.

This is especially true of moral judgment. "There is very little positive we can say about the nature of moral judgment itself," Larmore rightly observes. "We find ourselves providing what are really negative descriptions: the activity of moral judgment goes beyond what is given in the content of moral rules, characteristic sentiments, and tradition and training. We appear able to say only what judgment is *not*, and not what it *is*" (1981, p. 293). This is not, however, because judgment is an utterly mysterious, almost mystical faculty that should be replaced by more explicitly discursive or rational decision procedures. The limitation is not with judgment but rather with the sort of technical reason for which books, articles, and lectures provide such a useful medium of communication. It is a prejudice of methodism, and one that most of us brought up in a relentlessly methodist culture must constantly resist, that anything worth knowing or acquiring must be able to be articulated and conveyed as technical knowledge.

Situations calling for the exercise of judgment are moving targets whose existence and trajectory cannot be antecedently determined, at least not fully. Because we cannot adequately predict the circumstances calling for judgments of various kinds, we cannot provide a determinate or deductive decision procedure for making them. This is a logical point. Judgments so determined are no longer, strictly speaking, judgments. Just as we cannot logically predict the course of radical conceptual innovation in science, we cannot provide a conclusive decision procedure for making judgments. If we have a complete decision procedure, there is no room for the exercise of judgment; the exercise of judgment implies a gap between whatever deductive procedures may be instrumental in our decision making and our final decision (Williams 1985, pp. 126-27). It is in filling this gap that our minds, as Annette Baier puts it, find "room to operate":

> Neither the adoption of necessary means to one's ends nor the observance of categorical imperatives (of morals or manners or mathematics) gives one's mind any room to operate. Where matters are cut and dried, where there is not choice of what to do, we can "use our brains," exhibit intelligence even conscientiousness, but not wisdom or even prudence. These show only in matters where there is room

for difference of opinion, where no problem-solver gives *the* correct answer, where thoughts tend to be followed by second thoughts (1979), p. 63).

Improved understanding of practical intelligence requires not only studies of complex behavior in a variety of natural settings (including, for example, how scientists solve actual scientific problems and how politicians solve actual political problems) but also more adequate conceptions of human intelligence, conceptions that acknowledge its practical and experiential dimensions, its context dependence, and its reliance on judgment.

In an intriguing study, Ceci and Liker (1986) identify fourteen racetrack handicappers who were able to predict the top finisher in ten harness races 93 percent of the time and the top three horses in their correct order of finish in these races 53 percent of the time. The probabilities of these outcomes attributable to chance alone were 12 percent and .00025 percent, respectively. These fourteen men, dubbed experts by Ceci and Liker, made their predictions on the basis of their extensive past experience and study of a publication detailing the past performance of competing horses and drivers. This publication, the *Early Form*, is published one day prior to race day and "contains all of the relevant past performance statistics for the next day's racing card but does not contain official assessments of probable favorites, post-time odds, or any other evaluative information" (Ceci and Liker 1986, p. 124). Ceci and Liker administered standard IQ tests to these fourteen men and discovered no correlation between their IQ scores and their ability either to predict the top finisher in a race or to predict the top three finishers in correct order. The investigators then attempted to show that the experts' handicapping skill involved quite high-level reasoning processes and that the judgments involved were enormously complex. "We doubt," they say, "that any profession—be it scientists, lawyers, or bankers—engages in a more intellectually demanding form of decision making than

these expert handicappers" (Ceci and Liker 1986, p. 132). Among other things, this study casts doubt on the prevailing conception of intelligence as a "single underlying intellectual force" that can be adequately measured and then simply applied irrespective of practical experience or context. It shows, too, that racetrack handicapping involves complex reasoning and judgment. Experts, as Ceci and Liker reveal, "*go beyond the raw data in the racing program,* assigning 'weights' to each variable, systematically combining the various variables in complex, *nonadditive* ways, and computing a rough odds/probability equivalent for each horse. If this approach sounds cumbersome and time consuming, it is. Experts typically devote six to eight hours handicapping ten eight-horse races" (1986, p. 132; my emphasis).

This is an important line of research. Yet it is at this point comparatively undeveloped. If the exercise of judgment is to a large extent contextual, we must extend studies of this kind to a large variety of contexts in which we are called upon to employ practical knowledge and intelligence. What about the judgments required in the practice of law, medicine, politics, counseling, or teaching. What about judgments made in the course of everyday living such as selecting a mate, raising one's children, handling one's personal finances, and so on? And what about the exercise of moral judgment in any of these contexts? Further research should eventually shed more light on these and related questions. Some people, it is clear, have better judgment in some of these contexts than do others. And a person may have astute judgment in one area of life (for example, in practicing a certain trade or profession) and quite poor judgment in another (for example, as a parent or with respect to personal finances). A more adequate understanding of the psychological characteristics that contribute to successful judgment in various contexts is vital if we are to foster the relevant forms of practical knowledge and the capacity for sound judgment that is their manifestation.

In the meantime, however, we must make do with a number of very general but nonetheless useful reminders. First, it is the beginning of wisdom on this topic to emphasize the distinction between technical and practical reasoning. We should not expect that more and more technical knowledge will obviate the need for informed, reflective judgment. So long as we remain "finite creatures who face an indefinite or infinite range of contingencies with only finite powers of prediction and imagination" (Wiggins 1980, p. 234), we shall need to make judgments. It is thus that we ought to cultivate in ourselves and in others the capacity and willingness to review and revise previously held positions in response to new information, insights, arguments, or understanding. "No theory," as Wiggins emphasizes,

> if it is to recapitulate or reconstruct practical reasoning even as well as mathematical logic recapitulates or reconstructs the actual experience of conducting or exploring a deductive argument, can treat the concerns which an agent brings to any situation as forming a closed, complete consistent system. For it is of the essence of these concerns to make competing and inconsistent claims. (This is a mark not of irrationality but of *rationality* in the face of the plurality of ends and the plurality of human goods.) The weight of the claims represented by these concerns is not necessarily fixed in advance. Nor need the concerns be hierarchically ordered. Indeed, a man's reflection on a new situation that confronts him may disrupt such order and fixity as had previously existed, and bring a change in his evolving conceptions of the point, or the several or many points of living and acting (1980, p. 233).

It is not yet clear how one acquires the disposition and capacity to reflectively review and revise previously held positions. Psychological investigations into practical knowledge and intelligence may provide detailed insight on this matter. Until then, however, it is reasonable to suppose that this and related dispositions and capacities are often fostered by example, encouragement, and criticism (Baier 1979, p. 64). We learn to make good judgments in various contexts first by emulating others who are regarded as having sound judgment, and then responding to their evaluations and guidance. The external dialogue we undertake both with those to whom we must justify our initial judgments and with our mentors is eventually internalized and we learn to "fly solo."

Notes on Contributors

Jonathan Adler is Professor of Philosophy at Brooklyn College, and has had a long-standing interest in Philosophy for Children, and in the role of critical thinking in education.

Reverend Father Dr. Stan Chiedu Anih is the Director of the Institute of Ecumenical Education, Thinkers Corner, Enugu, Nigeria.

W.H. Auden (1907-1973) was one of the most influential poets of the twentieth century. He was born in York, England. After studying in England and Germany, he became a schoolmaster in Scotland and England. Following World War II, he became a citizen of the United States, although he continued to write and teach in England and in Europe.

Bertram Bandman is a member of the Philosophy Department at the Brooklyn Center of Long Island University.

Elias Baumgarten is a professor of philosophy in the Humanities Department at the University of Michigan-Dearborn.

Martin Benjamin is Professor of Philosophy at Michigan State University and has been supportive of elementary school philosophy since its inception. He is a specialist in ethics.

David Bohm's main work is in theoretical physics, but he has also written frequently with regard to creativity.

Eva Brann, now a dean at St. John's College, Annapolis, Maryland, has taught in the larger part of its all-required, integrated liberal arts program which consists of Great Books seminars and classes in language, mathematics, music and science. Her publications include *Paradoxes of Education in a Republic* (1979) and articles on Jane Austen, Thomas Mann, Thomas More, Kant, Plato, and, most recently, the subject of time.

John Seely Brown is corporate vice president and director of the Palo Alto Research Center of Xerox Corporation.

Justus Buchler was Distinguished Professor of Philosophy at the State University of New York, Stony Brook. He was for many years a member of the Columbia University Department of Philosophy. His major works include *Towards a General Theory of Human Judgment* and *Metaphysics of Natural Complexes*.

Dale Cannon has been a teacher educator in Philosophy for Children, and teaches Humanities at Western Oregon State College.

G.K. Chesterton (1874-1936), English critic and author, was a writer of short stories, novels, poetry, and essays. He also wrote extensively on theology and religious topics.

Allan Collins is principal scientist at Bolt, Beranek and Newman., Inc., and professor of education and social policy at Northwestern University.

Thomas Curley is a professor of philosophy at LeMoyne College, and has served as a teacher educator in Philosophy for Children.

Barry Curtis is a professor of philosophy at the University of Hawaii at Hilo, and has been associated with Philosophy for Children since 1976.

Floyd Dell (1887-1969) was an American novelist, playwright, and writer on a wide variety of subjects. Starting out as a reporter early in this century, he became editor of the Literary Review about the time of WWI. His writings include a series of autobiographical novels, the first of which was *Moon-Calf*. His later works include a number of articles on child-training.

Ann Diller is a professor of education at the University of New Hampshire.

Maria Edgeworth (1767-1849), Anglo-Irish novelist, began her career as a writer of children's stories. She was heavily influenced by her father, Richard Lovell Edgeworth. Her best-known novel was *Castle Rackrent*.

Kieran Egan is Professor of Education at Simon Fraser University, and is author of a dozen books, including *Imagination and Education, Primary Understanding and Teaching as Story-Telling.*

Michael Ende is one of Germany's best-known writers for children. Among his books are *Momo*, a modern fairy-tale about a little girl, Momo, who wants to bring time back to people (it had been stolen by "the gray men") and the Endless Story.

Carl Ewald (1856-1908) was born in Schleswig, but his family soon emigrated to Denmark. He worked as a forester and a schoolmaster, and wrote a series of fairy-tales and other writings for children, including *Two Legs* and *The Quiet Pool*.

Maurice A. Finocchiaro is a professor of philosophy at the University of Nevada, Las Vegas. He has published a number of articles in the philosophy of science.

Marie-Louise Friquegnon teaches philosophy at William Paterson College in New Jersey. She is co-author of a major textbook on ethics.

Ann Gazzard, in her association with the IAPC, has taught both children and teachers, and has worked in curriculum development and evaluation research. In addition to continuing her teacher education services, she currently teaches critical thinking at New York University and psychology at Brookdale Community College.

Jen Glaser has been lecturer at the Department of Educational Foundations, University of Melbourne, Australia.

William Hamrick is Professor of Philosophy at Southern Illinois University at Edwardsville. He is an experienced teacher trainer, has taught philosophy to children for many years, and has been a frequent participant in Philosophy for Children conferences.

W.A. Hart teaches at New University of Ulster, Coloraine, Northern Ireland.

James Herndon is a professor of political science at Virginia Polytechnic Institute and State University.

Florence M. Hetzler was president of ACPA Round Table of Philosophy and a professor of philosophy at Fordham University.

William James (1842-1910) was an American psychologist and philosopher. After receiving training as a painter and then attending Harvard Medical School, he became an instructor in physiology at Harvard and later lectured in psychology and philosophy. Along with Peirce, Dewey, and Mead, James became one of the leading proponents of pragmatism.

Randall Jarrell was a distinguished critic and poet, among whose published works are *Poetry and the Age* (1953), *Pictures from an Institution*, (1968), *The Lost World* (1966), *Jerome* (1971), and *The Complete Poems* (1969).

Tony W. Johnson is Director of Teacher Education at University of North Carolina, Greensboro. He is a longtime associate of the IAPC, working as a teacher trainer and writing about practical and theoretical issues in Philosophy for Children.

David Kennedy teaches at Northern Michigan University, Marquette. He has contributed several articles to *Thinking.*

Søren Kierkegaard (1813-1855), Danish philosopher, is widely regarded as having been the founder of existentialism. He wrote extensively on religion, ethics and aesthetics.

Janusz Korczak (pen name of Henryk Goldszmit 1878-1942) gave up a successful career as a pediatrician and author to care for orphans in Poland. He spent the final years of his life in the Warsaw ghetto as the head of an orphanage for Jewish children.

Judy A. Kyle wrote her Masters thesis at McGill University on Philosophy for Children. She is now an educational consultant in Montreal.

Rosalind Ekman Ladd is Professor of Philosophy at Wheaton College, Norton, Mass., and Lecturer in Pediatrics, Brown University Program in Medicine.

Judith Langer is Professor of Education at the State University of NY at Albany. She is the editor of *Language, Literacy and Culture: Issues of Society and Schooling.* In collaboration with Arthur Applebee, she has also conducted studies on writing and learning in the secondary school and across the content areas.

Rosalyn Lessing (née Sherman) taught philosophy for some years. She now resides in Birmingham, Michigan.

Leon Letwin is Professor of Law in the School of Law, University of California at Los Angeles.

Clive Lindop, who holds a Masters degree in Philosophy for Children, is a lecturer in philosophy and education at Deakin University in Victoria, Australia. He is active in teacher education in Philosophy for Children in Australia.

Matthew Lipman is Professor of Philosophy and Director of the Institute for the Advancement of Philosophy for Children at Montclair State College. He is the developer of the Philosophy for Children curriculum.

Catherine McCall gained her M.Sc. in Psychology at the University of Wales, and her Ph.D. in Philosophy at Manchester University, England. She has been an IAPC Associate since 1984, and is now a primary school philosophy consultant in Glasgow, Scotland.

Gerry Dawson McClendon teaches at the Harold Wilson School in Newark, NJ.

John J. McDermott is Distinguished Professor of Philosophy and Humanities in Medicine at Texas A & M University. He is author of *The Writings of William James—A Comprehensive Edition.*

Ekkehard Martens is Professor of Philosophy in the School of Education, University of Hamburg. His specialty is the teaching of prospective philosophy instructors in the distinctive problems of the teaching of philosophy. He is also the editor of the *Zeitschrift für Didaktik der Philosophie.*

Jane Roland Martin teaches philosophy at the University of Massachusetts at Boston. She is the author of *Explaining, Understanding, and Teaching.*

Gareth B. Matthews is Professor of Philosophy at the University of Massachusetts at Amherst. He is the author of *Philosophy and the Young Child* and *Dialogues with Children.*

Wolfe Mays teaches in the Institute for Advanced Studies, Manchester Polytechnic, England, and was for many years associated with Jean Piaget. Dr. Mays is the editor of the *British Journal of Phenomenology* and is coauthor of *Linguistic Analyses and Phenomenology.*

George Herbert Mead (1863-1931) was a social psychologist and philosopher whose work in pragmatism had a strong influence on John Dewey and others. A professor at the University of Michigan and the University of Chicago, he seldom published, but his students recorded his lectures, which were edited and published after his death.

Michel de Montaigne (1533-1592), French author, studied law and was a successful administrator. He retired to write and travel for the last twenty years of his life. Montaigne established the essay as a literary form with his *Essais*.

Robert J. Mulvaney teaches philosophy at the University of South Carolina. His Philosophy for Children activities include lecturing, demonstration and teacher training, particularly in the Southeast.

Leonard Nelson (1882-1927) was a German philosopher. He wrote on ethics and theory of knowledge, as well as politics and jurisprudence. He conducted philosophical courses for children, but was forced to discontinue this work by the rise of Nazism.

Susan E. Newman is a graduate student in education at the University of California, Berkeley and staff scientist at the Palo Alto Research Center of Xerox Corporation.

Martha Nussbaum, Professor of Philosophy and Classics at Brown University, is the author of *The Fragility of Goodness: Luck and Ethics in Greek Tragedy and Philosophy*. She is a well-known commentator on contemporary philosophy.

Michael Oakeshott is a British philosopher who has served as Professor of Politics at the London School of Economics and Political Science, and whose books include *Experience and its Modes* and *Rationalism in Politics*. His interest in the philosophy of education is perhaps best exemplified by his essay, "Learning and Teaching" (reprinted in R. S. Peters, *The Concept of Education*).

J. Robert Oppenheimer was Director of the Institute for Advanced Study from 1947 to his retirement in 1966. Previously he had been on the faculties of the University of California at Berkeley and California Institute of Technology at Pasadena.

Stephen Paget (1855-1926) was the author of *The Young People* (1910), *I Sometimes Think* (1916), and *I Have Reason to Believe* (1921).

Leslie Allen Paul, author of *The English Philosophers* (1953) and *The Meaning of Human Existence* (1949), is also known for a variety of works for or about children, including *The Republic of Children* (1938).

Valerie Polakow has taught in the School of Education at the University of Michigan, Ann Arbor. She is the author of *The Erosion of Childhood* (Chicago: U of Chic Press, 1982).

Michael S. Pritchard teaches philosophy at Western Michigan University and is co-director of the Center for Philosophy and Critical Thinking in the Schools. He is also author of *Philosophical Adventures With Children* and *On Becoming Responsible*.

James M. Redfield teaches in the Graduate School of Business, University of Chicago.

William Ruddick is a member of the Department of Philosophy, New York University.

Gilbert Ryle (1900-1976), British philosopher, was one of the leaders of the Ordinary Language movement. He was a lecturer at Oxford, and author of a number of articles and books, including *Concept of Mind*.

Ruth L. Saw was Emeritus Professor of Aesthetics at Birkbeck College, London.

Ernest G. Schachtel was a prominent psychologist and psychiatrist who practiced in New York City. His best known work was *Metamorphoses*.

Herbert W. Schneider was for many years a professor of philosophy at Columbia University. He specialized in metaphysics, and the philosophy of George Herbert Mead.

Ann Margaret Sharp is Professor of Education and Associate Director of the IAPC at Montclair State College. As director of the graduate program in Philosophy for Children at the college, she has been involved in the preparation of future teacher-educators in Philosophy for Children.

Ruth E. Silver has a Master's degree in education and a doctorate in philosophy. She has taught philosophy at the college level, and has done extensive teacher education in Philosophy for Children.

Christina Slade has taught philosophy at the Australian National University, Canberra, and has been a Philosophy for Children educator. She has been affiliated with the Automated Reasoning Project, Research School of Social Sciences, Australian National University, Canberra.

Laurence J. Splitter is director of the Australian Center of Philosophy for Children, which is a division of the Australian Center for Educational Research.
Robert Louis Stevenson (1850-1894) was a Scottish poet and author of fiction and travel books. He was first recognized for his essays, but is now perhaps best known for his novels *Treasure Island* and *Kidnapped*, as well as for *A Child's Garden of Verses*.

Glenn Tinder is author of *Community: Reflections on a Tragic Ideal*, published by Louisiana State University Press.

Lev Tolstoy (1828-1910), Russian author. Though of course world-famous for his novels such as *War and Peace* and *Anna Karenina*, Tolstoy was also considerably involved in education. In the 1850s, he started his school at Yasnaya Polyana, and his interest in educational theory and practice began to grow. He published an educational magazine and compiled several successful textbooks.

Mary Vetterling-Braggin is a philosopher residing in Ramsey, N. J.

Mark Weinstein is Associate Professor in the Department of Educational Foundations and Associate Director of the Institute for Critical Thinking at Montclair State College.

Lady Victoria Welby (1837-1912) had a considerable amount of influence on many of the scientists and philosophers of her time. She had no systematic education, but travelled and read widely. She exerted her influence mainly through personal contact and correspondence with thinkers such as Charles Peirce.

Michael J. Whalley grew up in Great Britain, and did his doctorate at Cornell. He is now a teacher-educator in Philosophy for Children, and has been working on an anglicized version of *Harry Stottlemeier's Discovery.*

John Wilson is University Lecturer in Philosophy of Education, Department of Educational Studies, Oxford University. He has authored many books in philosophy.